ITALIAN WINES 1999

Gambero Rosso Editore

Slow Food Editore

italianwines

1999

ITALIAN WINES 1999

IS THE ENGLISH LANGUAGE EDITION OF THE ITALIAN JOINT PUBLICATION BY
GAMBERO ROSSO EDITORE AND SLOW FOOD EDITORE

GAMBERO ROSSO EDITORE
VIA ARENULA, 53 - 00186 ROMA
TEL. 39-6-68300741 - FAX 39-6-6877217
E-MAIL: gambero@gamberorosso.it

SLOW FOOD ARCIGOLA EDITORE
VIA MENDICITÀ ISTRUITA, 45 - 12042 BRA (CN)
TEL. 39-172-412519 - FAX 39-172-411218
E-MAIL: info@slowfood.it

EDITORIAL STAFF FOR THE ORIGINAL EDITION

CHIEF EDITORS
DANIELE CERNILLI AND CARLO PETRINI

SENIOR EDITORS
GIGI PIUMATTI AND MARCO SABELLICO

PRINCIPAL CONTRIBUTORS
ERNESTO GENTILI, VITTORIO MANGANELLI
FABIO RIZZARI AND SANDRO SANGIORGI

OTHER MEMBERS OF THE TASTING PANELS
GIULIO COLOMBA, GIANNI FABRIZIO, GIACOMO MOJOLI, MARCO OREGGIA,
NEREO PEDERZOLLI, PIERO SARDO, HERBERT TASCHLER, ALBERTO ZACCONE

CONTRIBUTORS
GILBERTO ARRU, ANTONIO ATTORRE, PAOLO BATTIMELLI, ALBERTO BETTINI,
BRUNO BEVILACQUA, WALTER BORDO, PIERLUIGI CALABRETTA, MARCO CASOLANETTI,
DANIELE CERNILLI, VALERIO CHIARINI, ANTONIO CIMINELLI, DARIO COLETTI,
GIULIO COLOMBA, MASSIMO DI CINTIO, GIANNI FABRIZIO, ERNESTO GENTILI, MARCO LISI,
VITTORIO MANGANELLI, GIACOMO MOJOLI, MARCO OREGGIA, STEFANO PASTOR,
MARIO PAPANI, NEREO PEDERZOLLI, CARLO PETRINI, GUIDO PIRAZZOLI, GIGI PIUMATTI,
MICHELE PIZZILLO, VITO PUGLIA, FABIO RIZZARI, LEONARDO ROMANELLI, GIOVANNI RUFFA,
MARCO SABELLICO, SANDRO SANGIORGI, PIERO SARDO, DIEGO SORACCO,
HERBERT TASCHLER, MASSIMO TOFFOLO, ANDREA VANNELLI, MASSIMO VOLPARI,
RICCARDO VISCARDI, ALBERTO ZACCONE

WITH SPECIAL THANKS TO
NINO AIELLO, ANTONELLA BAMPA, ENRICO BATTISTELLA, DANIELE BATTEGGIA,
MICHELE BRESSAN, ALESSANDRO BULZONI, DARIO CAPPELLONI, ROBERTO CASULLO, SERGIO
CECCARELLI, REMO CAMURANI, MARINO DEL CURTO, EGIDIO FEDELE DELL'OSTE, STEFANO
FERRARI, NICOLA FRASSON, DAVIDE GANDINO, BARBARA GARBARINO,
FABIO GIAVEDONI, VITO LACERENZA, GIANCARLO LO SICCO, PASQUINO MALENOTTI, ROBERTO
MINNETTI, ENZO MERZ, STEFANO MAURO, DANNY MURARO, FULVIO PIERANGELINI, NICOLA
PERULLO, MARIO PLAZIO, VALENTINO RAMELLI, CARLO RAVANELLO, ANGELO RICCI, GABRIELE
RICCI ALUNNI, LEONARDO ROMANELLI, MAURIZIO ROSSI, GAETANO ROTOLO, PAOLO TRIMANI,
PAOLO VALDASTRI, VALERIO ZORZI

EDITORIAL ASSISTANTS
MARCO OREGGIA AND UMBERTO TAMBURINI

EDITORIAL COORDINATOR
GIORGIO ACCASCINA

LAYOUT
FABIO CREMONESI

TRANSLATIONS COORDINATED AND EDITED BY
KAREN CHRISTENFELD

TRANSLATORS
M. ASHLEY, L. BAILHACHE, M. BENSON, A. COOK, A. L. MILLER, K. OLSON, B. WILLIAMS

PUBLISHER
GAMBERO ROSSO, INC.

USA OFFICE
636 BROADWAY - SUITE 1219 - NEW YORK, NY 10012
TEL. 212- 253-5653 FAX 212 253-8349 - E-MAIL: gamberousa@aol.com

DISTRIBUTED IN THE USA AND CANADA BY ANTIQUE COLLECTOR'S CLUB, MARKET STREET
INDUSTRIAL PARK, WAPPINGER FALLS, NY 12590, USA; IN THE UK AND AUSTRALIA
BY GRUB STREET, THE BASEMENT, 10 CHIVALRY ROAD, LONDON SW11 1HT, UK.

THE GUIDE WAS CLOSED SEPTEMBER 30, 1998

PRINTED IN ITALY BY CONTI TIPOCOLOR SRL - VIA G. GUINIZZELLI, 20 - CALENZANO (FI)

CONTENTS

INTRODUCTION

ITALIAN WINES 1999, published by Gambero Rosso and Slow Food Agricola, is the twelfth edition of this Guide. As has been the case with each edition, this is a completely new volume from beginning to end. The 10,120 wines from 1,536 producers, record numbers for a publication dealing with Italian wines, have all been tasted by panels of at least five experts from Gambero Rosso and Slow Food Agricola. The bottles are covered so that it is impossible to tell what they are or who produced them. The comparative tastings always cover wines from the same year and of the same category. The panels all worked in stages, the first stage taking place in the region where the wines were produced. Often they were guests in the tasting rooms of consortiums where the task of providing the wines and cloaking the identity of the bottles was left in the hands of their hosts. Hence we wish to thank the consortiums of the Marchio Storico of Chianti Classico, of Brunello and of Rosso di Montalcino, of Vino Nobile di Montepulciano, of Vernaccia di San Gimignano, of Morellino di Scansano, of Bolgheri, of the wines of Oltrepò Pavese, of the wines of Franciacorta, of Valpolicella, of Soave and, in addition, the Chamber of Commerce of Bolzano, the Enoteca Italiana of Siena, the Enoteca Regionale of Emilia Romagna in Dozza Imolese, the Chamber of Commerce of Nuoro, the Istituto Tecnico Agrario of Locorotondo, the AssiVip of Majolati Spontini, the Ersa of the Regione of Abruzzo and the Istituto Trentino del Vino. We should also like to thank all the producers who sent us samples of their wines, and who voluntarily submitted to our analyses. We ask the wine-makers to give us samples from their own cellars for two reasons. First, all producers are afforded the same treatment and there is no chance that the wines can have suffered from bad storage. Secondly, if we waited until we could get the bottles from wine shops, we would have to ignore all those wines that are not yet on the shelves during the months in which we are doing our tastings. And it would further result in our having judged wines already sold out by the time the Guide became available to the public. But let's go back to our way of working. The first phase of our tastings determines the cream of the crop. This year, of the more than 15,000 wines tasted, only about 600 made it to the final round. This was held in four different places, and the panel of tasters was expanded to more or less ten judges: publishers, assistant publishers, freelance and staff contributors from some of the regions contributing most wines to the final stage. The 154 wines which, this year, received our highest award, Three Glasses, were chosen at sessions held in Rome, in Bra at the headquarters of Slow Food Agricola, at Cassacco in Friuli and at Soave in the Veneto. This award was not based on the absolute value of the various wines, but rather on their fidelity to the best characteristics of their category, as well as the quality of the vinification technique employed in their production and the balance of their component parts as perceived by the examining eye, nose and palate. Our labors may be considered the fruit of a series of parallel stages, since it does not seem feasible to us to compare wines of different categories, from different places, grapes and vintages. This fundamental approach holds true as well in the cases of those wines that received Two Glasses, One Glass or just a mention. The perceived harmony of the wines, fidelity to the character of their "terroir" and grapes, competence in vinification and good judgment in aging in barrel and bottle are the standards by which the panels made their assessments. Naturally a certain flexibility in applying these criteria is necessary, given the great diversity of the wines under examination. But let's turn to what is strange and new in this year's edition of the Guide. The cry of alarm we raised last year about the increasing number of wines smelling and tasting of cork seems to be having an effect. Some important producers, principally from Friuli, a few even Three Glass winners, are experimenting with different ways of sealing their bottles. The effects are excellent, and consumer resistance seems to be minimal. This is especially true of synthetic corks made of colored silicone, which cause no problems if used for white wines intended for drinking in the first two or three years after bottling. It seems an excellent solution to us, inexpensive and practical. Next, a change. In addition to our Three Glasses and to the Stars assigned to those producers who have received that award more than ten times (Gaja has a double Star, with 21 Three Glasses to his credit, while 14 wineries shine with just one), we have also chosen a Wine of the Year, a Winery of the Year and an Oenologist of the Year. The wine is La Vigna di Alceo '96 (p. 437), from Castello dei Rampolla in Panzano, a cabernet sauvignon and petit verdot blend from Chianti which received a standing ovation from its judges. Luca and Maurizia di Napoli produce it together with the great oenologist Giacomo Tacchis. The winery of the year is Planeta in Sambuca, Sicily (p. 574), not only for a notable performance but above all for the promise it offers for the years to come. It is run by Alessio and Francesca Planeta, who total less than sixty years between them, with the expert technical assistance of Carlo Corino. The oenologist of the year is Guido Rivella, who directs operations at the Gaja estate (p. 26). He is a shy and enormously competent man, sometimes put in the shade by the fame and outgoing personality of Angelo Gaja, a great international wine star. But without his help Gaja would never have received the honors and awards that rain down on him wherever he goes. A final word about the number (154) of Three Glass awards this year, which brings the total for 12 years of the Guide to 872. We should like to point out to those who may consider this excessive that we began with more than 15 thousand samples, and that about one wine in a hundred has been chosen. As a percentage, this seems modest to us. In our first edition we gave 32 wines our highest accolade, but the wines considered were barely 1,500, thus there was one top award for every 50 wines. Hence we are now twice as severe as we were then (as the numbers show), even though the level of Italian wines has improved enormously in the last 12 years. So at this point we simply wish you a good read and many good tastings.

Daniele Cernilli and Carlo Petrini

THREE GLASS AWARDS 1999

PIEDMONT

Wine	Producer	Page
ASTI DE MIRANDA METODO CLASSICO '96	GIUSEPPE CONTRATTO	45
BARBARESCO COSTA RUSSI '95	GAJA	26
BARBARESCO SORÌ PAITIN '95	PAITIN	104
BARBARESCO SORÌ SAN LORENZO '95	GAJA	26
BARBARESCO VANOTU '95	PELISSERO	125
BARBARESCO VIGNA LORETO '95	ALBINO ROCCA	30
BARBERA D'ALBA CASCINA NUOVA '96	MAURO VEGLIO	83
BARBERA D'ALBA GIADA '96	ANDREA OBERTO	81
BARBERA D'ALBA MARUN '96	MATTEO CORREGGIA	41
BARBERA D'ALBA VIGNA GATTERE '96	MAURO MOLINO	80
BARBERA D'ALBA VIGNA POZZO '96	CORINO	77
BARBERA D'ALBA VIGNETO GALLINA '96	LA SPINETTA	47
BARBERA D'ALBA VITTORIA '96	GIANFRANCO ALESSANDRIA	90
BARBERA D'ASTI COSTAMIOLE '96	PRUNOTTO	23
BARBERA D'ASTI SUPERIORE LA VIGNA DELL'ANGELO '96	CASCINA LA BARBATELLA	106
BARBERA D'ASTI SUPERIORE MONTRUC '96	FRANCO M. MARTINETTI	123
BAROLO '94	E. PIRA & FIGLI	34
BAROLO ROCCHE DELL'ANNUNZIATA '93	PAOLO SCAVINO	54
DOLCETTO DELLE LANGHE MONREGALESI IL COLOMBO '97	IL COLOMBO - BARONE RICCATI	90
DOLCETTO DI DOGLIANI SAN FEREOLO '97	SAN FEREOLO	65
DOLCETTO DI DOGLIANI SIRI D'JERMU '97	F.LLI PECCHENINO	64
DOLCETTO DI DOGLIANI VIGNA DEL PILONE '97	SAN ROMANO	65
LA VIGNA DI SONVICO '96	CASCINA LA BARBATELLA	106
LANGHE ARBORINA'96	ELIO ALTARE	74
LANGHE ARTE '96	DOMENICO CLERICO	91
LANGHE ROSSO BRIC DU LUV '96	CA' VIOLA	100
LANGHE ROSSO BRICCO ROVELLA '96	ARMANDO PARUSSO DI TIZIANA E MARCO PARUSSO	96
LANGHE ROSSO QUATR NAS '96	ROCCHE DEI MANZONI	96
LANGHE ROSSO SEIFILE '95	FIORENZO NADA	125
LANGHE SAUVIGNON ALTENI DI BRASSICA '96	GAJA	26
LOAZZOLO PIASA RISCHEI '95	FORTETO DELLA LUJA	86
MONFERRATO ROSSO PIN '96	LA SPINETTA	47
NEBBIOLO D'ALBA LA VAL DEI PRETI '96	MATTEO CORREGGIA	41
ROERO AUDINAGGIO '96	CASCINA CA' ROSSA	40
VIGNASERRA '96	ROBERTO VOERZIO	85

LOMBARDY

Wine	Producer	Page
FRANCIACORTA BRUT CABOCHON '93	MONTE ROSSA	151
FRANCIACORTA COLLEZIONE '93	CAVALLERI	157
FRANCIACORTA CUVÉE ANNAMARIA CLEMENTI '91	CA' DEL BOSCO	157
FRANCIACORTA MAGNIFICENTIA S.A.	UBERTI	159
FRANCIACORTA VITTORIO MORETTI RIS. '91	BELLAVISTA	156
PRATTO '96	CÀ DEI FRATI	172
T. D. F. CHARDONNAY '96	CA' DEL BOSCO	157
VALTELLINA SFURSAT 5 STELLE '96	NINO NEGRI	152
VALTELLINA SFURSAT CA' RIZZIERI '95	ALDO RAINOLDI	153

TRENTINO

Wine	Producer	Page
GIULIO FERRARI '90	FERRARI	194
GRANATO '96	FORADORI	187
SAN LEONARDO '95	SAN LEONARDO	178

ALTO ADIGE

A. A. CABERNET FREIENFELD '95	CANT. PRODUTTORI DI CORTACCIA	211
A. A. CABERNET SAUVIGNON LAFOA '95	CANT. PROD. COLTERENZIO	209
A. A. CABERNET SAUVIGNON RIS. '95	CANT. VITICOLTORI DI CALDARO	206
A. A. CABERNET TERMINUM RIS. '95	CANT. PRODUTTORI DI TERMENO	219
A. A. GEWÜRZTRAMINER KASTELAZ '97	PODERI CASTEL RINGBERG E KASTELAZ DI ELENA WALCH	220
A. A. GEWÜRZTRAMINER PUNTAY '97	CANT. PROD. E&N	207
A. A. LAGREIN ABTEI RIS. '96	CANTINA CONVENTO MURI GRIES	200
A. A. PINOT NERO S. URBANO '95	HOFSTÄTTER	220
A. A. SAUVIGNON '97	CANTINA DELL'ABBAZIA DI NOVACELLA	221
A. A. SAUVIGNON ST. VALENTIN '97	CANT. PROD. S. MICHELE APPIANO	199

VENETO

AMARONE DELLA VALPOLICELLA CLASSICO '93	ALLEGRINI	229
AMARONE DELLA VALPOLICELLA CLASSICO AMBROSAN '93	ANGELO NICOLIS E FIGLI	253
AMARONE DELLA VALPOLICELLA CLASSICO CAMPOLONGO DI TORBE '93	MASI	248
AMARONE DELLA VALPOLICELLA CLASSICO CAPITEL MONTE OLMI '95	F.LLI TEDESCHI	254
AMARONE DELLA VALPOLICELLA CLASSICO VIGNETO MONTE SANT'URBANO '93	F.LLI SPERI	254
AMARONE DELLA VALPOLICELLA VIGNETO DI MONTE LODOLETTA '91	ROMANO DAL FORNO	231
CABERNET FRANC CAMPO BURI '95	LA CAPPUCCINA	241
COLLI EUGANEI ROSSO GEMOLA '95	VIGNALTA	224
IL ROSSO DELL'ABAZIA '96	SERAFINI & VIDOTTO	246
LA POJA '93	ALLEGRINI	229
PASSITO DELLA ROCCA '95	LEONILDO PIEROPAN	258
RECIOTO DELLA VALPOLICELLA '95	TOMMASO BUSSOLA	243
RECIOTO DI SOAVE I CAPITELLI '96	ROBERTO ANSELMI	239
SOAVE CLASSICO SUPERIORE LA FROSCÀ '97	SANDRO E CLAUDIO GINI	241
SOAVE CLASSICO SUPERIORE VIGNETO LA ROCCA '96	LEONILDO PIEROPAN	258
SOAVE VIGNA ALBARE DOPPIA MATURAZIONE RAGIONATA '97	UMBERTO PORTINARI	242

FRIULI VENEZIA GIULIA

BRAIDE ALTE '96	LIVON	324
COF BIANCO '97	MIANI	277
COF BIANCO ROSAZZO TERRE ALTE '96	LIVIO FELLUGA	288
COF MERLOT RONC DI SUBULE '96	RONCHI DI MANZANO	308
COF ROSSO '96	MIANI	277
COLLIO PINOT BIANCO '97	CASTELLO DI SPESSA	279
COLLIO PINOT BIANCO AMRITÀ '96	MARIO SCHIOPETTO	281
COLLIO ROSSO RISERVA DEGLI ORZONI '94	RUSSIZ SUPERIORE	280
COLLIO SAUVIGNON '97	MARIO SCHIOPETTO	281
COLLIO SAUVIGNON DE LA TOUR '97	VILLA RUSSIZ	282
COLLIO SAUVIGNON RONCO DELLE MELE '97	VENICA & VENICA	300
COLLIO TOCAI FRIULANO '97	EDI KEBER	288
FRIULI ISONZO BIANCO FLORS DI UIS '96	VIE DI ROMANS	311
FRIULI ISONZO SAUVIGNON DOM PICÒL '96	LIS NERIS - PECORARI	325
FRIULI ISONZO SAUVIGNON KOLÀUS '96	PIERPAOLO PECORARI	326

Wine	Producer	Page
FRIULI ISONZO TOCAI FRIULANO '97	BORGO SAN DANIELE	285
FRIULI ISONZO TOCAI FRIULANO '97	RONCO DEL GELSO	292
ROSSO NARCISO '94	RONCO DELLE BETULLE	309
VINTAGE TUNINA '96	VINNAIOLI JERMANN	303

EMILIA ROMAGNA

Wine	Producer	Page
CABERNET SAUVIGNON STOPPA '96	LA STOPPA	343
COLLI BOLOGNESI CABERNET SAUVIGNON BONZARONE '96	TENUTA BONZARA	340
COLLI D'IMOLA BOLDO '97	TRE MONTI	339
MAGNIFICAT CABERNET SAUVIGNON '94	DREI DONÀ TENUTA LA PALAZZA	338
MARZIENO '95	FATTORIA ZERBINA	337

TUSCANY

Wine	Producer	Page
ACCIAIOLO '95	CASTELLO D'ALBOLA	443
BOLGHERI ROSSO SUP. PALEO '95	LE MACCHIOLE	355
BOLGHERI SASSICAIA '95	TENUTA SAN GUIDO	356
BRUNELLO DI MONTALCINO LA CASA '93	TENUTA CAPARZO	398
BRUNELLO DI MONTALCINO VIGNA DEL LAGO '93	VAL DI SUGA	413
CABERNET SAUVIGNON '95	ISOLE E OLENA	352
CABREO IL BORGO '96	RUFFINO	441
CAMARTINA '94	AGRICOLA QUERCIABELLA	386
CASALFERRO '96	CASTELLO DI BROLIO - RICASOLI	377
CERVIOLO ROSSO '96	SAN FABIANO CALCINAIA	366
CHIANTI CLASSICO CAST. DI FONTERUTOLI RIS. '95	CASTELLO DI FONTERUTOLI	363
CHIANTI CLASSICO GIORGIO PRIMO '96	LA MASSA	435
CHIANTI CLASSICO MONNA LISA RIS. '95	FATTORIA DI VIGNAMAGGIO	389
CHIANTI CLASSICO POGGIO ROSSO RIS. '95	SAN FELICE	371
CHIANTI CLASSICO RIS. '95	AGRICOLA QUERCIABELLA	386
CHIANTI CLASSICO RIS. '95	CASA EMMA	352
CHIANTI RUFINA MONTESODI RIS. '96	MARCHESI DE' FRESCOBALDI	374
IL PRINCIPE '95	ANTICA FATTORIA MACHIAVELLI	451
LA GIOIA '95	RIECINE	378
LA VIGNA D'ALCEO '96	CASTELLO DEI RAMPOLLA	437
LUPICAIA '96	TENUTA DEL TERRICCIO	367
MAESTRO RARO '93	FATTORIA DI FELSINA	369
MASSETO '95	TENUTA DELL'ORNELLAIA	356
MONTECHIARI CABERNET '95	FATTORIA DI MONTECHIARI	415
OLMAIA '94	COL D'ORCIA	400
POGGIO GRANONI '93	CASTELLO DI FARNETELLA	461
REDIGAFFI '96	TUA RITA	464
ROMITORIO DI SANTEDAME '96	RUFFINO	441
SANGIOVETO '95	BADIA A COLTIBUONO	376
SIEPI '96	CASTELLO DI FONTERUTOLI	363
SOLAIA '95	MARCHESI ANTINORI	374
SUMMUS '95	CASTELLO BANFI	395
SYRAH CASE VIA '95	TENUTA FONTODI	434
VIN SANTO '88	AVIGNONESI	418
VINO NOBILE DI MONTEPULCIANO VIGNA DELL'ASINONE '95	POLIZIANO	430

MARCHE

Wine	Producer	Page
AKRONTE CABERNET '95	BOCCADIGABBIA	476
VERDICCHIO DEI CASTELLI DI JESI CLASSICO SUPERIORE GAIOSPINO '97	FATTORIA CORONCINO	489

THE STARS

Last year we decided to introduce a new symbol, joining our traditional wine Glasses, in recognition of the best Italian wineries. The star is conferred on those producers who have received our Three Glasses at least ten times and is, we feel, a clear indication of consistency of quality at the highest level. For example, the legendary Angelo Gaja adds a further testimony to the value of his wines by earning two Stars. Not far behind him is another historic winery, Maurizio Zanella's Ca' del Bosco. Fourteen highest awards have been given over the years to Elio Altare, one of the best producers not only in Piedmont but in all of Italy. The Fattoria di Felsina, by racking up 12, leads all the Tuscan wineries in this elite group. The distinction of having had 11 Three Glasses is shared by Allegrini, Aldo Conterno, Castello di Fonterutoli, Paolo Scavino and Vinnaioli Jermann. Hard on their heels is the platoon of producers with ten Three Glasses: Castello di Ama, Domenico Clerico, Giacomo Conterno, Tenuta Fontodi, Josko Gravner and Vie di Romans. But many famous names you would seek here in vain are not far from earning their first Star. In the vanguard are Marchesi Antinori (which would actually be quite close to two Stars if one were to consider their estates together), Ferrari in the Trentino, La Spinetta and the great Professor from the Abruzzo, Edoardo Valentini.

★★

21

ANGELO GAJA (Piedmont)

★

15

CA' DEL BOSCO (Lombardy)

14

ELIO ALTARE (Piedmont)

12

FATTORIA DI FELSINA (Tuscany)

11

ALLEGRINI (Veneto)
PODERI ALDO CONTERNO (Piedmont)
CASTELLO DI FONTERUTOLI (Tuscany)
PAOLO SCAVINO (Piedmont)
VINNAIOLI JERMANN (Friuli Venezia Giulia)

10

CASTELLO DI AMA (Tuscany)
DOMENICO CLERICO (Piedmont)
GIACOMO CONTERNO (Piedmont)
TENUTA FONTODI (Tuscany)
IOSKO GRAVNER (Friuli Venezia Giulia)
VIE DI ROMANS (Friuli Venezia Giulia)

A GUIDE TO VINTAGES, 1970-1995

	BARBARESCO	BRUNELLO DI MONTALCINO	BAROLO	CHIANTI CLASSICO	VINO NOBILE DI MONTEPULCIANO	AMARONE
1970	●●●●	●●●●	●●●●	●●●●●	●●●●	●●●●
1971	●●●●	●●●	●●●●●	●●●●●	●●●●	●●●●
1972	●	●	●	●●	●	●
1973	●●	●●●	●●	●●	●●●	●●
1974	●●●●	●●	●●●●	●●●	●●●	●●●●
1975	●●	●●●●●	●●	●●●●	●●●●	●●●
1976	●●	●	●●	●●	●●	●●●●
1977	●●	●●●●	●●	●●●●	●●●●	●●●
1978	●●●●●	●●●●	●●●●●	●●●●●	●●●●●	●●●
1979	●●●●	●●●●	●●●●	●●●●	●●●●	●●●●
1980	●●●●	●●●●	●●●●	●●●●	●●	●●●
1981	●●●	●●●	●●●	●●●	●●●	●●●
1982	●●●●●	●●●●●	●●●●●	●●●●	●●●●	●
1983	●●●●	●●●●	●●●●	●●●●	●●●●	●●●●●
1984	●	●●	●●	●	●	●●
1985	●●●●●	●●●●●	●●●●●	●●●●●	●●●●●	●●●●
1986	●●●	●●●	●●●	●●●●	●●●●	●●●
1987	●●	●●	●●	●●	●●	●●
1988	●●●●●	●●●●●	●●●●●	●●●●●	●●●●●	●●●●●
1989	●●●●●	●●	●●●●●	●	●	●●
1990	●●●●●	●●●●●	●●●●●	●●●●●	●●●●●	●●●●●
1991	●●●	●●●	●●●	●●●	●●●	●●
1992	●●	●●	●●	●	●	●
1993	●●●	●●●●	●●●	●●●●	●●●●●	●●●●
1994	●●	●●●	●●	●●	●●	●●
1995	●●●●●	●●●●●	●●●●●	●●●●●	●●●●●	●●●●●

HOW TO USE THE GUIDE

KEY

○ WHITE WINES
● RED WINES
⊙ ROSÉ WINES

RATINGS

LISTING WITHOUT A GLASS SYMBOL:
A WELL MADE WINE
REPRESENTATIVE OF ITS CATEGORY

ABOVE AVERAGE TO GOOD IN ITS CATEGORY, EQUIVALENT TO 70-79/100

🍷🍷

VERY GOOD TO EXCELLENT IN ITS CATEGORY, EQUIVALENT TO 80-89/100

🍷🍷🍷

OUTSTANDING WINE IN ITS CATEGORY, EQUIVALENT TO 90-99/100

(🍸, 🍸🍸, 🍸🍸🍸) THE WHITE GLASSES REFER TO RATINGS GIVEN IN PREVIOUS EDITIONS OF THE GUIDE, AND WHICH ARE CONFIRMED WHERE THE WINES IN QUESTION ARE STILL DRINKING AT THE LEVEL FOR WHICH THE ORIGINAL AWARD WAS MADE

STAR ★

GIVEN TO ALL THOSE ESTATES WHICH HAVE WON AT LEAST TEN THREE GLASS AWARDS

GUIDE TO PRICES [1]

1 UP TO $ 8 AND UP TO £6
2 FROM $ 8 TO $ 12 AND FROM £ 6 TO £ 8
3 FROM $ 12 TO $ 18 AND FROM £ 8 TO £ 11
4 FROM $ 18 TO $ 27 AND FROM £ 11 TO £ 15
5 FROM $ 27 TO $ 40 AND FROM £ 15 TO £ 20
6 MORE THAN $ 40 AND MORE THAN £ 20

[1] Approx. retail prices in USA and UK

ASTERISK *

INDICATES ESPECIALLY GOOD VALUE FOR MONEY

NOTE

PRICES REFER TO RETAIL AVERAGES. INDICATIONS OF PRICES FOR OLDER VINTAGES INCLUDE APPRECIATION WHERE APPROPRIATE

ABBREVIATIONS

A.A.	Alto Adige
Cl.	Classico
C.S.	Cantina Sociale
Cant.	Cantina
Cast.	Castello
C. Am.	Colli Amerini
COF	Colli Orientali del Friuli
Cons.	Consorzio
Coop.Agr.	Cooperativa Agricola
DOC:	initials standing for Denominazione di Origine Controllata. The term refers to classic quality wines made in traditional wine-making areas where production is regulated by law.
DOCG:	initials standing for Denominazione di Origine Controllata e Garantita. Like DOC, but subject to more rigorous governmental controls. The wines are tasted before bottling, and numbered official seals are applied to each bottle.
M.	Metodo
M.to	Monferrato
O. P.	Oltrepò Pavese
P.R.	Peduncolo Rosso
Prosecco di V.	Prosecco di Valdobbiadene
Rif. Agr.	Riforma Agraria
Spumante M.Cl.	Spumante Metodo Classico
Sup.	Superiore
T.	Terre
TdF	Terre di Franciacorta
Ten.	Tenute
Tenim.	Tenimenti
V.	Vigna
Vign.	Vigneto
V. T.	Vendemmia Tardiva

VALLE D'AOSTA

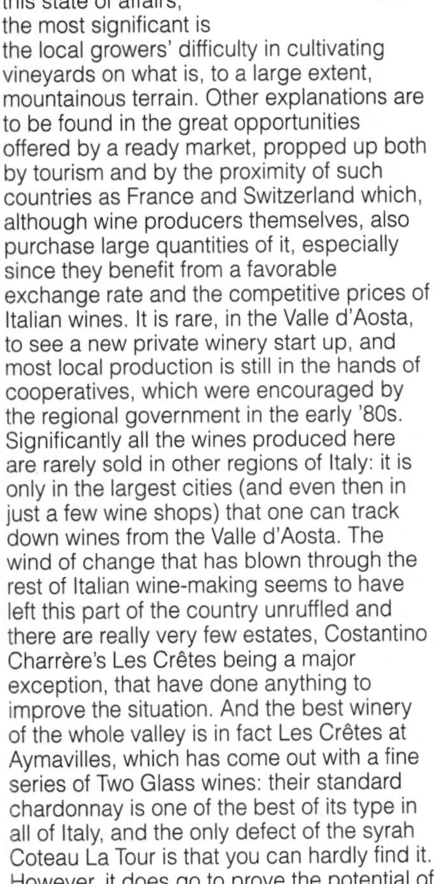

For some years now, the wine-making scene in the Valle d'Aosta has remained substantially unchanged. Among the many reasons for this state of affairs, the most significant is the local growers' difficulty in cultivating vineyards on what is, to a large extent, mountainous terrain. Other explanations are to be found in the great opportunities offered by a ready market, propped up both by tourism and by the proximity of such countries as France and Switzerland which, although wine producers themselves, also purchase large quantities of it, especially since they benefit from a favorable exchange rate and the competitive prices of Italian wines. It is rare, in the Valle d'Aosta, to see a new private winery start up, and most local production is still in the hands of cooperatives, which were encouraged by the regional government in the early '80s. Significantly all the wines produced here are rarely sold in other regions of Italy: it is only in the largest cities (and even then in just a few wine shops) that one can track down wines from the Valle d'Aosta. The wind of change that has blown through the rest of Italian wine-making seems to have left this part of the country unruffled and there are really very few estates, Costantino Charrère's Les Crêtes being a major exception, that have done anything to improve the situation. And the best winery of the whole valley is in fact Les Crêtes at Aymavilles, which has come out with a fine series of Two Glass wines: their standard chardonnay is one of the best of its type in all of Italy, and the only defect of the syrah Coteau La Tour is that you can hardly find it. However, it does go to prove the potential of the Valle d'Aosta's vineyards when they are cultivated with care and dedication. Among the other private producers, the most prominent is once again Costantino Charrère, who, at his family winery, produces four very unusual wines, obtained from old vines and indigenous grape varieties: we particularly draw your attention to the Prëmetta, made from a traditional varietal now grown exclusively by Charrère. The six cooperatives currently making wine cover the whole of the region's territory and its various sub-denominations: the best is still the one in Chambave, La Crotta. Apart from the classic Muscat Passito (which seems to have taken out a subscription to Two Glasses), it has also produced some other excellent wines. In addition to traditional methods of production, the winery has, for some years now, been experimenting with some new techniques. Among the wines in the new range, the Fumin is particularly worthy of mention: it is one of the best reds of the entire valley. The performance of the Institut Agricole Régional is also of great importance: after a slight slip in quality last year, the winery has returned in fine style to the upper echelons of wine-making in the region. The whites in the standard range are very good, with the Pinot Gris at the top of the tree; those in the barrique-aged line are excellent and even, in some cases, outstanding. The Chardonnay is as reliable as ever, as is the syrah- based red, Trésor du Caveau. The cabernet/merlot blend, Vin du Prévôt, is of equal quality. Finally, Ezio Voyat, with his wines from Chambave, and the Cave du Vin Blanc, with its Morgex, are doing laudable work.

AOSTA

Institut Agricole Régional
Reg. La Rochere, 1/A
11100 Aosta
tel. 0165/553304

The Institut Agricole's production is split up into two quite distinct lines, one consisting of wines of the current vintage, simpler and produced in great quantities, and the other more experimental, with just a few thousand bottles of each wine, some of which, vinified and aged in barriques, are on an international level. In the standard range, the whites are all very impressive, with their richness of extract and their high alcohol levels. The Pinot Gris (14° alcohol) in particular is full-bodied and aromatic, almost honeyed and fat. The very dry and savory Petite Arvine and the Müller Thurgau with its intensely floral and aromatic nose, are of similar style. The Müller Thurgau shows character, richness and a velvety texture on the palate, due mainly to the excellent ripeness of the grapes. The Blanc du Prieur and the Gamay and Pinot Noir reds are less interesting. Of the wines aged in barrique, the Chardonnay definitely stands out among the whites. It is a wine of great personality, with a fine, complex bouquet; on the palate, it is fat, rich and very long. Then comes La Comète, similar in style to the Chardonnay, whereas the Élite is more straightforward. The range of no fewer than five red wines begins with the fascinating Trésor du Caveau (100% syrah), which is impressive in the cleanness of its nose and its concentration on the palate. It is followed by the Vin du Prévôt (cabernet sauvignon and merlot), which is well-balanced and full-bodied; it has complex aromas of red fruit and a very characterful flavor. The very interesting Rouge du Prieur, made from grenache, is less complex than the preceding wines and reveals a slight imbalance. Closing the list are the '95 Petit Rouge (a little over-oaked) and the Sang des Salasses, a pinot noir, very typical in color, but without a particularly marked personality.

	Wine	Glasses	
●	Trésor du Caveau '96	🍷🍷	4
○	Vallée d'Aoste Chardonnay Barrique '96	🍷🍷	4
●	Vin du Prévôt '96	🍷🍷	4
○	La Comète '96	🍷	4
●	Rouge du Prieur '96	🍷	4
○	Vallée d'Aoste Müller Thurgau '97	🍷	3
●	Vallée d'Aoste Petit Rouge Barrique '95	🍷	4
○	Vallée d'Aoste Petite Arvine '97	🍷	3
○	Vallée d'Aoste Pinot Gris '97	🍷	3
○	Blanc du Prieur '97		3
○	Élite '96		4
●	Sang des Salasses '96		4
●	Trésor du Caveau '95	YY	4

AYMAVILLES (AO)

Costantino Charrère
Fraz. du Moulin, 28
11010 Aymavilles (AO)
tel. 0165/902135

Costantino Charrère, apart from being the moving force behind the Les Crêtes estate, also runs his family property with an equally sure hand. One way it differs from Les Crêtes is that only red wines are produced here, with a great regard for the Valle d'Aosta's indigenous varieties. The only concession to wines from across the Alps is provided by the Vin Les Fourches, a very interesting red made from grenache. In general the range of wines presented this year was very good, and really drew maximum benefit from the '97 vintage, a great one for the region. The winery's most fascinating wine is still the Vin de La Sabla, a red obtained from fumin and petit rouge grapes, which shows what can be done with the splendid '97 vintage. It has a very deep opaque color; its nose is still a bit dumb, but nevertheless reveals aromas of ripe red fruit. On the palate it is richly structured, mouth-filling and well-balanced and has a long, inviting finish. The Vin Les Fourches is no less enjoyable, but (as with the Prëmetta) only 1,300 bottles were produced. It is spicy on the nose, with evident black pepper notes, whereas on the richly-structured palate its tannins still need to integrate fully, showing good aging potential. The very attractive Torrette is less powerful than the two wines already described. The Prëmetta, on the other hand, merits space to itself. It is most definitely one of the products that deserve to be saved from extinction by the Slow Food Ark: it is the only example of this varietal to be found in the Valle d'Aosta and is defended by Costantino with great passion. This wine is a pale red (almost onion- skin) in color; its fragrances range from spicy scents (cloves) to the aromatic notes typical of the variety. It is particularly mouth-filling on the palate, and the bouquet is echoed on the savory and decidedly tannic finish.

	Wine	Glasses	
●	Vallée d'Aoste Prëmetta '97	🍷🍷	4
●	Vin de La Sabla '97	🍷🍷	4
●	Vin Les Fourches '97	🍷🍷	4
●	Vallée d'Aoste Torrette '97	🍷	3
●	Vin de La Sabla '96	YY	4

AYMAVILLES (AO)

LES CRÊTES
LOC. VILLETOS, 50
11010 AYMAVILLES (AO)
TEL. 0165/902274

Thanks to two vintages ('96 and '97) which were positive for Italian wines in general and for those of the Valle d'Aosta in particular, Les Crêtes submitted a very interesting range of wines this year. This estate, guided by the inimitable Costantino Charrère, has demonstrated in the few years since its establishment that one can produce great results even in a really problematic mountainous zone as long as one works with conscientiousness and passion. These results can be seen in the glass, and also in the Glasses, which rank this winery amongst the very best in Italy. We tasted eight wines, and five of them easily earned Two Glasses. We start with three excellently made white wines: the Petite Arvine Vigne Champorette, a typical product of the Valle d'Aosta, distinguished by floral aromas and savory flavor combined with good body and a notable alcohol level. The two versions of Chardonnay Cuvée Frissonnière Les Crêtes, one aged in stainless steel and the other in barrique ("Bois"), are very enjoyable. The former is a good example of what this vineyard can offer in a good year like '97: it is warm, well-balanced and almost honeyed, with delicate and elegant perfumes packing a rich bouquet. The latter, a '96, magnificently combines oaky notes with fruity sensations; on the palate it is complex, with a long, harmonious finish: an excellent wine of which, at the moment, unfortunately only 1,500 bottles are produced. Amongst the reds, the two wines that steal the show are oak-aged: the syrah-based Coteau La Tour (1,500 bottles) and the Vigne La Tour made from fumin (1,000 bottles). These are two world-class reds which from their impenetrable color onwards reveal their enormous power. The '97 reds, Torrette, Pinot Noir and Le Rouge, are enjoyable but certainly less full of character than these two star wines.

	Wine	Glasses	
●	Coteau La Tour '96	▼▼	5
○	Vallée d'Aoste Chardonnay Cuvée Frissonière Les Crêtes '97	▼▼	4
○	Vallée d'Aoste Chardonnay Cuvée Frissonière Les Crêtes Cuvée Bois '96	▼▼	5
●	Vallée d'Aoste Fumin Vigne La Tour Cuvée Bois '96	▼▼	5
○	Vallée d'Aoste Petite Arvine Vigne Champorette '97	▼▼	4
●	Vallée d'Aoste Pinot Noir Vigne La Tour '97	▼	3
●	Vallée d'Aoste Torrette Vigne Les Toules '97	▼	3
●	Coteau La Tour '95	▽▽	5

CHAMBAVE (AO)

LA CROTTA DI VEGNERON
P.ZZA RONCAS, 2
11023 CHAMBAVE (AO)
TEL. 0166/46670

La Crotta di Vegneron, in the center of Chambave, vinifies the grapes supplied by member growers from their neighboring vineyards in Nus, Verrayes, Saint Denis, Châtillon and Saint Vincent. A large array of wines is produced, equally divided between whites and reds, and the star of the whites is Moscato Passito, while Fumin shines brightest among the latter. Moreover, this year, thanks to the decidedly high quality of the '97 vintage which yielded wonderful grapes, all the dry white wines (with the exception of the pinot noir), are attractive and interesting. This is particularly true of the dry Muscat di Chambave, with its intense bouquet revealing musky notes and peach fragrance as well as the classic aroma of the grape from which it is made. On the palate it is rich and mouth-filling, with an excellent level of alcohol. The Müller Thurgau is also of a good standard, with its bright straw color and aromatic bouquet. The Malvasia is enjoyable and richly structured, if not altogether distinct on the nose. The Moscato Passito is as impressive as ever, and shows great depth even in its very bright golden-tinged color. Its perfumes are complex and intense, with hints of toasted hazelnut, dried fig and honey, while the palate is richly nuanced, full and persistent, with a satisfying vein of acidity underpinning the finish. The Malvoisie Flétri is also decent, but less rich and complex than the wine just described. The '97 Nus and Chambave reds merit no more than a mention, whereas the '97 Fumin is again very interesting. It has a garnet color and its wild berry aromas meld with those of the oak; it is soft, mouth-filling and characterful on the palate, but is less exciting than the '94.

	Wine	Glasses	
○	Vallée d'Aoste Chambave Moscato Passito '96	▼▼	4
○	Vallée d'Aoste Chambave Muscat '97	▼▼	3*
●	Vallée d'Aoste Fumin '96	▼	3
○	Vallée d'Aoste Müller Thurgau '97	▼	3*
○	Vallée d'Aoste Nus Malvoisie Flétri '96	▼	4
●	Vallée d'Aoste Chambave Rouge '97		2
○	Vallée d'Aoste Nus Malvoisie '97		3
●	Vallée d'Aoste Nus Rouge '97		2
○	Vallée d'Aoste Chambave Moscato Passito '95	▽▽	4
●	Vallée d'Aoste Fumin '95	▽	3

CHAMBAVE (AO)

Ezio Voyat
Via Arberaz, 13
11023 Chambave (AO)
tel. 0166/46139

For many years Ezio Voyat was, for anyone interested in wine, the touchstone for Valle d'Aosta viticulture. In fact one can admire, hung of the walls on the tasting room which forms an annex to his winery, the various awards and certificates of merit which Voyat has won around the world in his 30 years as a winegrower. To this day (even though their reputation has been somewhat tarnished, especially by detractors in the Valle d'Aosta itself) his wines are to be found on the wine lists of the world's most famous restaurants. Many experts, indeed, maintain that the only real Moscato di Chambave is Ezio Voyat's; indeed, apart from the one produced by the Crotta di Vegneron, the only example of this excellent "passito" available is that of this sprightly producer. The Passito Le Muraglie shows evidence, in both its color and its bouquet, of traditional techniques of production, including the oxidation process that makes this wine seem more like a sherry than a muscat. On the palate it lacks a little richness, though it does have an appealing and elegant honeyed aftertaste. The white La Gazzella, made from moscato grapes and dedicated to Voyat's daughter, an athletic star, is well made. Once again this year the Rosso le Muraglie is rather less interesting. This is a wine produced from a blend of several local grapes together with a small proportion of dolcetto.

○	La Gazzella Moscato '96	🍷	4
○	Vino Passito Le Muraglie '96	🍷	6
●	Rosso Le Muraglie '96		4

MORGEX (AO)

Cave du Vin Blanc de Morgex
et de La Salle
Chemin des Iles, 1
Fraz. La Ruine
11017 Morgex (AO)
tel. 0165/800331

As you make your way up the Valle d'Aosta along the Dora Baltea river, you come across the vineyards that produce the region's wines. Having passed Aosta itself, just when you think that vines have definitively given way to other crops, you suddenly see the last vineyards of the valley rise up ahead of you: the vineyards of Morgex. The landscape of this zone is breathtaking: just a bit further on is the glorious Mont Blanc, snow-capped throughout the year, and, to the right of the river, at altitudes varying between 900 and 1,200 meters above sea level, is the astonishing sight of the vineyards which produce the most famous wine of the region, the Blanc de Morgex et de La Salle. This is the domain of the Cave du Vin Blanc, which has, since 1983, vinified the grapes of the 95 member growers of the zone. The '97 Blanc de Morgex et de La Salle is a rather pale straw yellow in color; its bouquet is not particularly intense, but offers hints of flowers and freshly mown hay. On the palate it is tasty and quaffable, with crisp but not bothersome acidity. This white registers 11° of alcohol at most and makes a very good aperitif. The Blanc des Glaciers is obtained from the same grapes, but compared to the Blanc de Mogex et de La Salle is lacking in finesse and personality; it is simply a well-made wine whose principal merit is its low price. Using the same grape varieties, the Cave also produces a Metodo Classico sparkling wine, and we look forward to the release of the new vintage, the '96.

○	Vallée d'Aoste Blanc de Morgex et de La Salle '97	🍷	2
○	Blanc des Glaciers '97		2

PIEDMONT

The vineyards of Piedmont are in the best of health. This year, together with Tuscany, they have won the highest number of Three Glass awards, a staggering 35. The Langhe are in the lead: together with the adjacent zone of Roero, in the province of Cuneo, they boast 28 in all, while the Asti zone has gone back up to seven. But it is not only in the historic wine-growing areas of the region that wines have improved: the producers of Alessandria and Gavi first of all, but also those near Turin with their Erbaluce, and from northern Piedmont with their Gattinara and Ghemme have realized that quality pays, and have labored especially in the vineyard. Wine can lead the way for the whole agricultural economy of the region, and be particularly beneficial when linked to good restaurants and high-level tourism. This year Piedmont, though unable to present Barolo at its best, since '94 was one of the least satisfactory vintages of the decade for this venerable liquid, has confirmed that it has other strings to its bow. After last year's success, Dolcetto has continued its upward climb, going from three to four Three Glass winners. Dolcetto from the Dogliani zone seems to be pointing the way and is on the point of becoming a wine of international standing, and, according to the first results of scientific testing, would appear to be suitable for keeping for a number of years. The Pecchenino Brothers retain their place, and alongside them come the products of Nicoletta Bocca's San Fereolo and Bruno Chionetti's San Romano. A complete novelty in this category is the Dolcetto delle Langhe Monregalesi, which thanks to the skill of Carlo Riccati has given new prestige to a whole zone, mistakenly dismissed heretofore as better suited to everyday wines than to excellence in a bottle. For many years the Barbaresco explosion has been on the cards. Finally, thanks to a good year and to the determination of many young producers, five wines have made it to the top. For the first time Giorgio Pelissero and the Pasquero Elia brothers have won the coveted recognition with two extraordinary Barbarescos; Gaja and Albino Rocca are already classics in this category. Barolo has made no progress, with only two Three Glass winners: Scavino with his Rocche dell'Annunziata '93, and Chiara Boschis with her '94 Pira, surely the best of that mediocre vintage. But it is Barbera, in pure form or combination, which is the real protagonist of the 1999 Guide. Asti has for the first time received three top awards for Barberas: Prunotto, Martinetti and Sonvico have all made exceptional versions. There is no stopping Sonvico, who indeed has again bagged Three Glasses for his Vigna di Sonvico as well. Correggia (Barbera and Nebbiolo), La Spinetta (Pin and Barbera), Alessandria, Voerzio, Clerico, Ca' Viola, Altare, Nada, Rocche dei Manzoni and Forteto della Luja keep their position, while Veglio, Corino, Oberto, Molino, Ca' Rossa, Parusso and Contratto are very welcome newcomers. Gastaldi is out of this year's Guide (we had no wines to taste, as they were still maturing), and so are the giants of sparkling wine, Cinzano, Martini and Gancia, whose new company policies have led them to review their whole range of wines. We shall see more about it in future editions.

AGLIANO TERME (AT)

Agostino Pavia e Figli

Fraz. Bologna, 33
14041 Agliano Terme (AT)
tel. 0141/954125

In the last edition of the Guide we lauded the efforts being made to improve the quality of the wines from this winery: new vinification premises, no more wine sold in bulk, purchase of suitable terrain and experimentation with barriques. A year on, we can say with pleasure that our expectations have not been disappointed: Agostino, Giuseppe and Marco Pavia have produced a battery of quite convincing wines, with three worthy Barberas, among which the cru La Marescialla stands out. To begin with the Grignolino: very pleasing, with a pinkish color tending to ruby, showing a typically floral bouquet with a touch of pepper and spice; the taste is heady and satisfying. La Marescialla takes a strong lead among the three '96 Barberas and shows the expressive possibilities of this wine in the Agliano area. Of a deep ruby color, it has well-blended fruity aromas with vanilla and toasty touches from its year in the barrique; soft and elegant on the palate, it has an enduring aftertaste. The two "younger sisters" behave quite well: although simpler and more noticeably acidic, they are typical in their cherry nose, and lively, refreshing quaffability: One Glass apiece, with a slight preference for the Bricco Blina (softer and better-balanced).

Wine	Glasses	Price
● Barbera d'Asti La Marescialla '96	▼▼	4
● Barbera d'Asti Bricco Blina '96	▼	2*
● Barbera d'Asti Moliss '96	▼	2
● Grignolino d'Asti '97	▼	3
● Barbera d'Asti La Marescialla '95	▽	4

AGLIANO TERME (AT)

Trinchero

Via Noce, 56
14041 Agliano Terme (AT)
tel. 0141/954016

The Agliano zone is held by many to be choice for the production of Barbera d'Asti, a sort of "grand cru" capable of creating wines rich in color, aroma and extracts and made for keeping. There are not yet many producers here who have decided to stake their all on quality and get the best out of their "terroir". Among the few is the Trinchero family, with its selected vineyards situated on mainly clay soils. The seriousness of the winery can be seen from the decision to market their own wines after long bottle-aging. Thus, this year the Trincheros have offered us a Barbera Vigna del Noce from the 1994 vintage. The wine makes a good visual impression with its rich ruby hue tinged with violet, and then displays aromas of red fruit (cherry, blackberry, raspberry); it expands softly and persuasively on the palate, with a promise of greater things to come with age, but it is already pleasurable and satisfying. We re-tasted the '94 La Barslina, which earned Two Glasses last year, and it confirmed all its qualities, while pointing out the superior elegance of the Vigna del Noce. The last of the reds, Trabic '95, is a monovarietal table wine made from merlot; it's a bit lean, but it has a typical and pleasingly fruity and vegetal nose.

Wine	Glasses	Price
● Barbera d'Asti Vigna del Noce '94	▼▼	4
● Trabic '95	▼	4
● Barbera d'Asti La Barslina '94	▽▽	4
● Barbera d'Asti Vigna del Noce '93	▽▽	4
● Barbera d'Asti Vigna del Noce '90	▽	4
● Le Taragne '93	▽	4

AGLIÈ (TO)

CIECK
STRADA BARDESONO
FRAZ. S. GRATO
10011 AGLIÈ (TO)
TEL. 0124/32225 - 330522

The wines from this estate, which came into being in 1985 as the result of a merger of the properties of Remo Falconieri and Lodovico Bardesono, show an enviable consistency of quality. Among the six wines presented this year, there is not one that does not merit at least One Glass, confirming the talent and skill of these two winegrowers. The top of the line, the San Giorgio Brut vintage '91, earns its Two Glasses with a fascinating complexity of aromas and a harmonious full body. Of a limpid and intense gold-tinged straw color, it presents aromas of apple, apricot, yeasty dough and dried flowers; on the palate it is rich and soft, with a restrained effervescence and a long and persistent finish. The good basic San Giorgio Brut, richly straw-colored, displays fragrances of fruit and white flowers over marine hints of iodine and lemon. The effervescence seems a bit strong at first, but it is swiftly redeemed by a substantial body and a pleasingly crisp finish. The Erbaluce di Caluso, with its straw verging on gold hue, presents a not very intense but interesting nose, with traces of hazelnut, dried herbs, hay and flint. The palate (well-structured, silky and progressive) has a dry finish. Both the house reds are good: the Neretto di San Giorgio (hints of fruit and yeasts, balanced and inviting to drink), and the more mature Cieck Rosso, which has a complex nose and is rich and soft in the mouth. Finally, the Passito Alladium merits One full Glass, with its traces of fruit in syrup, dried fruit and high ripeness. On the palate it is fat, enticing and smooth, and not at all cloying.

	Wine	Glasses	Price
○	Erbaluce di Caluso Spumante Brut San Giorgio '91	🍷🍷	4
○	Caluso Passito Alladium Vigneto Runc '93	🍷	4
○	Erbaluce di Caluso Spumante Brut San Giorgio	🍷	4
○	Erbaluce di Caluso Vigna Misobolo '97	🍷	3*
●	Canavese Rosso Cieck '96	🍷	3
●	Canavese Rosso Neretto di San Giorgio '97	🍷	3
○	Erbaluce di Caluso Spumante Brut San Giorgio '90	🍷🍷 (white)	4

ALBA (CN)

BRICCO ROCCHE - BRICCO ASILI
LOC. S. CASSIANO, 34
12051 ALBA (CN)
TEL. 0173/282582

Bricco Rocche and Bricco Asili are the two "châteaux" of the Ceretto family. A visit to the Bricco Rocche winery gives you a panoramic view of the whole Barolo territory: you'll feel that you're at the center of this small privileged universe, and you are sure to sense its subtle magic. Here the Ceretti Barolos are produced, from the fruit of three different vineyards: Bricco Rocche (1.5 hectares) in Castiglione Falletto, Brunate (7 hectares) in La Morra, and Prapò (3.5 hectares) in Serralunga. The last of these particularly pleased us. Thanks to the characteristic vigor of wines from Serralunga, the Prapò '94 has unusual quality for this generally weak vintage. The color is a fairly intense garnet to ruby, and it displays an aristocratic nose with hints of red berries and spices ennobled by oak. The long-lasting palate (substantial but a little thin at the center because of the natural weakness of the grapes) reveals elegant tannins and licorice. The Brunate '94, less dense in color, offers a soft seductive bouquet; on the elegant palate it reveals a more marked acidity. From the Bricco Asili winery, in the heart of Barbaresco country, comes the Barbaresco Bricco Asili '95, one of their top wines, produced only in the best years. It has a fairly intense garnet to ruby hue and an extraordinarily elegant bouquet, intense and enticing, with violets in evidence, and a pleasing mineral note. Silky and lingering on the palate, it definitely seems a wine for keeping, and yet it's already perfectly drinkable, with elegant sensations of licorice and ripe plum. The Fasset '95 is a little less concentrated. As of next year the recently acquired Barbaresco vineyard, Bernadotti, will begin to bear fruit: it has one of the best positions in the Treiso zone.

	Wine	Glasses	Price
●	Barbaresco Bricco Asili Bricco Asili '95	🍷🍷	6
●	Barolo Brunate Bricco Rocche '94	🍷🍷	6
●	Barolo Prapò Bricco Rocche '94	🍷🍷	6
●	Barbaresco Faset Bricco Asili '95	🍷	6
●	Barbaresco Bricco Asili Bricco Asili '85	🍷🍷🍷 (white)	6
●	Barbaresco Bricco Asili Bricco Asili '86	🍷🍷🍷 (white)	6
●	Barbaresco Bricco Asili Bricco Asili '88	🍷🍷🍷 (white)	6
●	Barbaresco Bricco Asili Bricco Asili '89	🍷🍷🍷 (white)	6
●	Barolo Bricco Rocche Bricco Rocche '89	🍷🍷🍷 (white)	6
●	Barolo Brunate Bricco Rocche '90	🍷🍷🍷 (white)	6
●	Barolo Prapò Bricco Rocche '83	🍷🍷🍷 (white)	6

ALBA (CN)

CERETTO
LOC. S. CASSIANO, 34
12051 ALBA (CN)
TEL. 0173/282582

Marcello Ceretto was bemoaning the fact that his winery is considered a colossal producer, "whereas", he told us, "we produce only 700 thousand bottles, and in three different wineries". The number is large, but not so large as to make Ceretto a wine multinational. Each of the units, Bernardina, Bricco Asili and Bricco Rocche, is individually managed, and has its own style of vinification, in order to make the most of the different grape varieties in each of them. Bernardina makes the experimental wines for Ceretti, those made from the so-called international varietals, which next year will go to make up just two different blends, a Langhe Bianco and a Langhe Rosso. This year we tasted the individually fermented wines and noted a distinct improvement over previous years (of course the increased age of the vines plays its part, but so does a greater mastery of vinification techniques). The Pinot Nero '96 has a deep ruby hue, an extremely intense nose (with black currant and spice in evidence), and a substantial, elegant, rich palate with a long berry finish, especially blueberry. The Cabernet Sauvignon has gone beyond the strong grassy overtones of its predecessor: it has a bluish-violet color, a bouquet of undergrowth and bell pepper that doesn't cloy, and, in the mouth, ripe plum on the finish. The Blangé gets better and better. This fascinating wine has a greenish gold color, a distinct aroma of Golden Delicious apple and an open, clean and lingering flavor. The Dolcetto d'Alba Rossana '97 is very good, indeed one of the best ever produced. Intense ruby-red in appearance, it has a complex bouquet of violet, plum and orange peel; it's meaty on the palate, with a long finish and an elegant hint of licorice.

○	Langhe Arneis Blangé '97	🍷🍷	4
○	Langhe Chardonnay La Bernardina '96	🍷🍷	5
●	Dolcetto d'Alba Rossana '97	🍷🍷	4
●	Langhe Cabernet La Bernardina '95	🍷🍷	6
●	Langhe Pinot Nero La Bernardina '95	🍷🍷	6
●	Monsordo Syrah La Bernardina '95	🍷	6
●	Nebbiolo d'Alba Lantasco '96	🍷	4
●	Monsordo Rosso La Bernardina '93	YY	6
○	La Bernardina Brut '93	Y	5

ALBA (CN)

PIO CESARE
VIA CESARE BALBO, 6
12051 ALBA (CN)
TEL. 0173/440386

Pio Cesare is on the rise; this fact emerges from this year's tasting. We refer not only to the reliably good quality of all the wines they make, but also to a new dash and a delightful richness we found in some of the wines presented this year. While this is not a great surprise in a good year, we felt particularly grateful for the Barolo they managed to produce in '94, one of the most difficult vintages in recent years. First, the wine has a solid color indicative of excellent health. Ripe fruit and pleasing floral tones are evident in the wonderfully clean bouquet; the dense and persistent palate, rich in extract, maintains an excellent balance between tannins and acidity. The standard Barbaresco '95 is a model of modernity and finesse: it is intense and clear in the glass, and the fruity nose is lively and more and more interesting as one increasingly notices its elegant complexity. The taste has a smoothness that, far from compromising the concentration, makes it more pleasurable and distributes it on the tongue. The Nebbiolo d'Alba '96 is intended to be a substantial and persistent red; although it doesn't vaunt a very well-articulated structure, it still shows density and balance. The Dolcetto d'Alba is floral and graceful, while the Barbera d'Alba is too simple and peremptory. In the Chardonnay PiodiLei, which has returned to its former excellence, the oak has not prevented the wine's juicy ripe succulence from coming out in a typically Mediterranean manner.

○	Langhe Chardonnay PiodiLei '96	🍷🍷	5
●	Barbaresco '95	🍷🍷	5
●	Barolo '94	🍷🍷	5
●	Dolcetto d'Alba '97	🍷	3
●	Langhe Rosso Il Nebbio '97	🍷	3
●	Nebbiolo d'Alba '96	🍷	4
○	Piemonte Chardonnay L'Altro '97	🍷	4
●	Barbera d'Alba '96		3
●	Barolo Ornato '85	YYY	6
●	Barolo Ornato '89	YYY	6
●	Barbaresco '93	YY	5
●	Barbaresco Bricco '93	YY	6
●	Barolo Ornato '90	YY	6
●	Barolo Ornato '93	YY	6

ALBA (CN)

Poderi Colla

Loc. S. Rocco Seno d'Elvio, 82
12051 Alba (CN)
tel. 0173/290148

The style in which the main wines of this estate are produced is inspired by the established tradition of the great wines of the Langhe. This, however, has not prevented Tino and Federica Colla from gradually absorbing the changes taking place in the zone. The Barbaresco Tenuta Roncaglia significantly combines the two: the garnet color is quite lively; notes of red berries and violet together with delicately toasty nuances emerge on a nose of great finesse; this wine does not offer great structure, but with elegance, harmony and aromatic definition it fills the entire mouth. After the good performance of the '93, the Barolo Bussia '94 is somewhat on the defensive: it has less structure, but is not disjointed. The more decisive Bricco del Drago '95, with its inviting ruby color, shows in its bouquet that it is likely to open up considerably; this depth of sensation also characterizes the taste, in which the tannins are still the leading factor. The Dolcetto d'Alba, better than the '96, has greater concentration in the bouquet; meanwhile it is still supple, balanced and captivating. The Barbera and the Nebbiolo disappointed us somewhat; they lack the richness and expressive variety of the '96s. A wine which has, on the other hand, improved since last year is the Bianco Sanrocco (from pinot noir, riesling and chardonnay); it has a delicacy throughout. It is fragrant and light, but far from bland. The simple and sinewy Freisa is also worthy of mention. The Bonmé, a painstakingly made aromatized wine with a moscato base, recalls the great tradition of the Piedmontese vermouths of yore.

	Wine	Glasses	Price
●	Barbaresco Tenuta Roncaglia '95	▼▼	5
○	Bonmé	▼▼	4
○	Langhe Sanrocco '97	▼	3
●	Barolo Bussia Dardi Le Rose '94	▼	5
●	Langhe Bricco del Drago '95	▼	4
●	Dolcetto d'Alba '97	▼	3
●	Barbera d'Alba '96		4
●	Langhe Freisa '97		3
●	Nebbiolo d'Alba '96		4
●	Barbaresco Tenuta Roncaglia '93	▽▽	5
●	Barbaresco Tenuta Roncaglia '94	▽▽	5
●	Barolo Bussia Dardi Le Rose '93	▽▽	5
●	Bricco del Drago '94	▽	4

ALBA (CN)

Prunotto

Reg. S. Cassiano, 4/g
12051 Alba (CN)
tel. 0173/280017 - 281934

The Barbera d'Asti Costamiole '96 is the first Three Glass winner for the Antinori family at Prunotto; the success of the wine underlines the synergistic possibilities of a major Alba winery together with the rich and heretofore only rarely exploited vineyards of Asti. Aged in new barriques, this red perfectly expresses the potential of the barbera grape to produce deep and full-bodied wines that are nevertheless enjoyable and captivating. The cloudy ruby hue puts one on one's guard; then the Costamiole opens on the nose with a rush of fruit, spice and flowers, and continues its ample development on the palate, where one can sense the substance of a great vintage, and a notably well-composed harmony. But the whole line of Prunotto has been at an excellent level for years now. The Bussia Barolo '94 is surprisingly rich for that vintage, while the Barbera Pian Romualdo '96, lingering and densely aromatic, has the noble austerity of Alba together with a new mature elegance. The attractive Nebbiolo d'Alba Occhetti, also enlivened by the '96 vintage, has an intense ruby color; the bouquet displays a brilliantly evolving complexity. The palate slowly gathers considerable force, while revealing well-integrated tannins. The two Dolcettos, both delicate but not imposing, are attractive; the Barbera d'Asti Fiulot '97 and the Barbera d'Alba '96 are both very pleasing (and good examples of their type). The Barbaresco does not show particular vigor, but is fairly expressive and supported by good balance.

	Wine	Glasses	Price
●	Barbera d'Asti Costamiole '96	▼▼▼	6
●	Barbera d'Alba Pian Romualdo '96	▼▼	4
●	Barolo Bussia '94	▼▼	5
●	Nebbiolo d'Alba Occhetti '96	▼▼	4
●	Barbaresco '95	▼	5
●	Barbera d'Alba '96	▼	3
●	Barbera d'Asti Fiulot '97	▼	2
●	Dolcetto d'Alba '97	▼	3
●	Dolcetto d'Alba Mosesco '97	▼	4
●	Barbaresco Montestefano '85	▽▽▽	6
●	Barolo Bussia '85	▽▽▽	6
●	Barolo Cannubi '85	▽▽▽	6
●	Nebbiolo d'Alba Occhetti '89	▽▽▽	5
●	Barbaresco Montestefano '93	▽▽	5
●	Barolo Bussia '93	▽▽	6

ALFIANO NATTA (AL)

TENUTA CASTELLO DI RAZZANO
FRAZ. CASARELLO, 2
15021 ALFIANO NATTA (AL)
TEL. 0141/922124 - 922426

This fine and welcoming winery, (which has now changed its official name from "Fattorie Augustus, Castello di Razzano" to the simpler "Castello di Razzano") often hosts cultural and artistic events, in the hopes of attracting more people to the still comparatively unknown Monferrato, and of focusing more attention on its wines, which have been constantly improving. Augusto Olearo (the owner of the estate and promoter of these events) demonstrates the value of Monferrato wines with a series of very well-made ones of his own, among which a fine Barbera Campasso takes the lead this year. Aged in 20-hectoliter barrels, it has a dense, consistent ruby-garnet color and a complex nose with traces of black cherry, clove, coffee and resin. The palate confirms the rich visual promise; it is broad and meaty, with tonic acidity and a pleasant vein of tannin on the long fruity finish. The Barbera Vigna del Beneficio '96, slightly under par, has an intense dark ruby hue and a fascinating bouquet which offers hints of wild berries, spice and vanilla. Although concentrated, the palate is somewhat diminished by a slight excess of acidity. It is still a very good wine, and it won One Glass without any trouble. The typical, straightforward Grignolino Vigna di Ca' Delù displays aromas of spice and dried fruit, and is pleasingly dry and drinkable. The correctly executed Barbera Monte Ubaldo, of a purple-tinged ruby hue, offers aromas of cherry and yeasts, and a lively and pleasingly rustic palate.

	Wine	Glasses	Price
●	Barbera d'Asti Sup. Campasso Vigna di Ca' Farotto '96	🍷	3
●	Barbera d'Asti Sup. Vigna del Beneficio '96	🍷	4
●	Grignolino del M.to Casalese '97	🍷	3
●	Barbera del M.to Vivace Vigna Monte Ubaldo '97		2
●	Barbera d'Asti Sup. Vigna del Beneficio '93	🍷🍷 (open)	4

ASTI

F.LLI ROVERO
FRAZ. S. MARZANOTTO, 216
14050 ASTI
TEL. 0141/592460

The four Rovero brothers have divided up the roles in the management of their many-faceted estate, which is a comfortable country inn, an excellent grappa producer and an important Asti winery. Their fifteen hectares of vineyard are planted with grignolino, barbera, pinot noir, cabernet and sauvignon. The international varietals do quite well, but what Claudio Rovero is particularly keen on achieving is a really great Grignolino, and to that end he is experimenting with low-yield clones and untraditional wine-making techniques. And indeed we were quite interested by a sample of the Grignolino '97, which was still resting in the barrique. The Grignolino Vigneto La Casalina '97 is good too, with a peppery, dried flowery nose followed by a rich and slightly astringent palate. The Pinot Nero was surprisingly well executed: the characteristic aromas are well expressed and the taste is fruity and soft, with a slight hint of oak-derived vanilla. The convincing Sauvignon has clear vegetal aromas and a structure which, while not rich, is well-balanced. Between the two Barberas, each well made, we have a slight preference for the Rouvé, which is softer, more elegant and less aggressively acidic.

	Wine	Glasses	Price
●	Monferrato Rosso Pinot Nero '96	🍷🍷	3
●	Barbera d'Asti Rouvé '96	🍷	4
●	Barbera d'Asti Vigneto Gustin '96	🍷	3
●	Grignolino d'Asti Vigneto La Casalina '97	🍷	3
○	Monferrato Bianco Sauvignon '97	🍷	3
●	Barbera d'Asti Rouvé '95	🍷 (open)	4

BARBARESCO (CN)

CA' ROMÉ - ROMANO MARENGO

VIA RABAJÀ, 36
12050 BARBARESCO (CN)
TEL. 0173/635126

At Ca' Romé, Romano Marengo's children Paola and Giuseppe are becoming increasingly involved in the running of things. The latter, in particular, can often be found abroad on loan to important wineries where he adds to his knowledge of the wine-making process. The results of the dedication and enthusiasm of the new generation coupled with the experience of Romano are evident in the wines of Ca' Romé, which, while they are still in their way traditional, are now more elegant and balanced. We are further encouraged by their decision, soon to be put into practice, to make wine exclusively from their own grapes (today 20% comes from neighboring growers), and their refusal to produce a Barolo '94 because of the poor quality of the vintage. But let's get down to the wines we tasted this year. The Barbera La Gamberaja succeeds in drawing typical varietal notes out of the generous vintage '96, and what it lacks in balance and harmoniousness it makes up for in impact. The Da Pruvé, a classic blend of barbera and nebbiolo, is especially convincing on the fruity and sweet nose, that gives evidence of a knowing use of small oak barrels. However, the palate is a little disappointing in both concentration and length. The basic Barbaresco which presents typical aromatic hints of violet and lightly faded rose, is heady and enticing on the clearly tannic palate. The Maria di Brun special selection is more elegant and concentrated. It is produced only in major years, and dedicated to Romano's mother. A careful selection of the very best nebbiolo grapes has led to a Barbaresco which, in keeping with the house style, is a good marriage between tradition and innovation.

	Wine	Glasses	
●	Barbaresco Maria di Brun '95	🍷🍷	6
●	Barbaresco '95	🍷	5
●	Barbera d'Alba La Gamberaja '96	🍷	4
●	Da Pruvé '95	🍷	5
●	Barbaresco Maria di Brun '93	YY	5
●	Barbaresco '93	Y	5
●	Barbaresco Maria di Brun '90	Y	5
●	Barbera d'Alba La Gamberaja '95	Y	4
●	Barolo Rapet '93	Y	5
●	Barolo Rapet Ris. '90	Y	6

BARBARESCO (CN)

TENUTE CISA ASINARI DEI MARCHESI DI GRESY

VIA RABAJÀ, 43
12050 BARBARESCO (CN)
TEL. 0173/635222

Alberto Di Gresy means to keep his winery on its current path, involving an openness to innovation while maintaining an essential fidelity to a traditional idea of the wines of the Langhe. To tread this delicate tightrope may guarantee some pleasurable stimuli, but must also provide some disappointments: for example, the "modern" market that demands deep colors, massive concentration and woody aromas does not coincide with the style of this great house. His Barbaresco Gaiun '95 has a moderately intense ruby color; the nose, which evolves well, is a little dumb at first, with clear balsamic notes, opening then to very delicate hints of spice and coffee. On the palate the wine, if not extremely dense, has considerable sinew and substance and excellent length. The Dolcetto Monte Aribaldo '97, with its splendid violet ruby hue, made an excellent showing: an elegant nose with blackberry and cherry (and a faint hint of grass), followed by a rich, juicy and substantial palate with a ripe berry finish. The Langhe Chardonnay '96 is a fine example of the development of whites matured in small barrels: the nose still has hints of vanilla, but the fruit is on the point of getting the upper hand over the wood. On the characterful palate the wine is ample and heady, with notes of acacia blossom and honey well established in its full body. The Langhe Sauvignon '97, which has not seen wood at all, is simpler and quite quaffable. The Moscato d'Asti La Serra '97 is as good as ever. Finally we should mention the extraordinary range of Alsatian Rieslings from Michel Deiss marketed by this winery.

	Wine	Glasses	
●	Barbaresco Gaiun '95	🍷🍷	6
●	Barbaresco Martinenga '95	🍷🍷	6
●	Dolcetto d'Alba Monte Aribaldo '97	🍷🍷	3
○	Langhe Chardonnay Gresy '96	🍷🍷	5
○	Langhe Sauvignon '97	🍷	5
○	Moscato d'Asti La Serra '97	🍷	3
●	Langhe Rosso Villa Martis '95	🍷	4
●	Barbaresco Gaiun '85	YYY	6
●	Barbaresco Camp Gros '90	YY	6
●	Barbaresco Gaiun '90	YY	6
●	Barbaresco Camp Gros '93	Y	6
●	Barbaresco Martinenga '93	Y	5

GIUSEPPE CORTESE

VIA RABAJÀ, 35
12050 BARBARESCO (CN)
TEL. 0173/635131

Here is another family firm engaged in extending and modernizing its winery, and this will make it possible to tackle the work of production with greater confidence and efficiency. The Corteses are owners of about seven hectares of vineyards, planted primarily with nebbiolo (in the prestigious cru Rabajà), and in the remaining areas with dolcetto, barbera and chardonnay. The wines are made and matured in traditional fashion; steel for the whites and young reds, large and medium barrels of various types of wood for the more important reds. The Chardonnay '97 has a straw yellow color with a greenish tinge, the faintest aroma of banana, and evident acidity on the palate; the rather weak structure makes it just worthy of mention. The Dolcetto and the Barbera are a step up, and correspond to the typical characteristics of these two Langhe wines. The Barbera Morassina, matured for a year in 23-hectoliter barrels, offers attractive aromas of red fruit, and leaves a long aftertaste characterised by a contained acidity. The excellent Nebbiolo '96 opens on the nose with hints of dried rose petals, carrying through to the round, full-bodied, well-balanced and persistent palate. The top of the line is of course the Barbaresco: the Rabajà vineyards virtually guarantee wines of great structure and elegance. The Cortese offering is slightly rustic in character, but it won us over with its broad bouquet (red fruit, undergrowth and licorice), and with the well-judged tannins, which do not unbalance the taste.

●	Barbaresco Rabajà '95	🍷🍷	5
●	Barbera d'Alba '96	🍷	3
●	Barbera d'Alba Morassina '96	🍷	4
●	Dolcetto d'Alba Trifolera '97	🍷	3
●	Langhe Nebbiolo '96	🍷	4
○	Langhe Chardonnay '97		3
●	Barbaresco Rabajà '93	🍷 (outline)	4

BARBARESCO (CN)

★★ GAJA

VIA TORINO, 36/A
12050 BARBARESCO (CN)
TEL. 0173/635158

It's always hard to strike the right note when writing about a nonpareil. Either one goes overboard with encomium, or risks banalization with excessive understatement. Here we are in the presence of what is undoubtedly the best Italian winery, to judge from the quality of its wines; colleagues and wine critics from all over the world admit as much. For the tasters of this Guide, it's a desperate case. We accept the excellence of their wines with unruffled satisfaction; all, or very nearly all, score the highest points: the Costa Russi or the San Lorenzo, both '95s, for instance, bowled us over with their elegance, depth and richness. But really, to decide which Barbarescos should receive Three Glasses, we had to follow an almost cruel procedure of successive reclassification, with the gnawing impression all along that we were doing less than justice to some other wine. The most astonishing moment occurred during the tasting of the best Italian whites: we put a few Piedmontese samples up against the wines of the Alto Adige, Friuli and the Veneto, more or less as sparring partners, and it was one of these very outsiders, the Langhe Sauvignon Alteni di Brassica '96, that swept the board and emerged as one of the top Italian Sauvignons. The golden-green color is followed by a brilliant bouquet, all white flowers and exotic spices, not like those warm-up-act pyrotechnics frequent among Sauvignons. On the palate it is opulent, sweetly fruity, aromatic and dense; it succeeds in combining sinew and flesh. The Darmagi '95, the Sito Moresco '95 and the Barolo Sperss '94 are not far from Three Glasses. In short, when writing about Gaja a critic feels he has nothing to say.

●	Barbaresco Costa Russi '95	🍷🍷🍷	6
●	Barbaresco Sorì San Lorenzo '95	🍷🍷🍷	6
○	Langhe Sauvignon Alteni di Brassica '96	🍷🍷🍷	6
○	Langhe Chardonnay Gaia & Rey '96	🍷🍷	6
●	Barbaresco Sorì Tildìn '95	🍷🍷	6
●	Barolo Sperss '94	🍷🍷	6
●	Langhe Darmagi '95	🍷🍷	6
●	Langhe Sito Moresco '95	🍷🍷	6
●	Barbaresco '94	🍷🍷🍷 (outline)	6
●	Barbaresco San Lorenzo '90	🍷🍷🍷 (outline)	6
●	Barbaresco Sorì Tildìn '93	🍷🍷🍷 (outline)	6
●	Barolo Sperss '93	🍷🍷🍷 (outline)	6
●	Darmagi '90	🍷🍷🍷 (outline)	6
●	Langhe Darmagi '94	🍷🍷🍷 (outline)	6
○	Chardonnay Gaia & Rey '94	🍷🍷🍷 (outline)	6

BARBARESCO (CN)

I Paglieri

Via Rabajà, 8
12050 Barbaresco (CN)
tel. 0173/635109

About twenty years ago (though it seems as if more than a century had passed, so widespread has been the abandonment of stubbornly-held convictions and the acceptance of new ideas in Italian wine-making), when precious few people in the Langhe were experimenting with the use of barriques of French oak, Alfredo Roagna belonged to that pioneering vanguard. Thus he has had plenty of time to consider the advantages and disadvantages of this new technique, and to reach the conclusion, so dear to Gianni Brera, that wine should taste of wine. Hence I Paglieri, which a couple of decades ago was in the avant-garde, now seems a bit conservative; new wood is sparingly used, so as not to overpower the wine. Out of his wide range our favorites are the Solea '96, the Barbaresco Riserva '93 and the Barolo La Rocca e La Pira '93. The first, the result of a surprising blend of chardonnay and white-vinified nebbiolo, is more intensely fragrant than usual (tropical fruit and citrus), and more rounded and persistent thanks to the use of a small quantity of semi-dried chardonnay. The Barbaresco Riserva '93 already has an orange rim, but it offers a broad array of aromas (with licorice and clove in evidence), and a soft, warm palate, which makes it more complex and harmonious than the closed and austere '95. Of the '93 Barolos we prefer the Riserva, potent and long on the palate, and offering a delicate bouquet with aromas of licorice and leather mixed with hints of spice. The Opera Prima XII, a personal mixture of nebbiolo and barbera from various vintages, is less interesting because it has not yet achieved a balance between wood and fruit.

	Wine	Glasses	
●	Barbaresco Ris. '93	▼▼	6
●	Barolo La Rocca e La Pira Ris. '93	▼▼	6
○	Langhe Solea '96	▼▼	5
●	Barbaresco '95	▼	6
●	Barolo La Rocca e La Pira '93	▼	5
●	Opera Prima XII	▼	5
●	Barbaresco Ris. '89	▽▽	6
●	Barbaresco Ris. '90	▽▽	6
●	Barolo La Rocca e La Pira '91	▽▽	4
●	Crichet Pajé '88	▽▽	6
●	Crichet Pajé '89	▽▽	6
●	Barbaresco '93	▽	5

BARBARESCO (CN)

Cascina Luisin

Via Rabajà, 23
12050 Barbaresco (CN)
tel. 0173/635154

Young Roberto Minuto is already firmly in the saddle at Luisin, and is showing that he up to making very good use of some of the best vineyards in the zone. Their names are well known at home and abroad and include the illustrious Asili, Rabajà and Basarin crus. The Barbaresco Rabajà '95, which will certainly evolve for some time, is already laudable: the intense nose has some strong traditional tones, with reminders of licorice and leather; on the palate it reveals good structure, fair complexity and pronounced tannins. The Sorì Paolin, the other '95 Barbaresco, is correct but not particularly graceful: it does in fact suffer from some rather pronounced aromas, and a palate in which the acidity and tannins lord it over a not very imposing body. The wine, not for present drinking, will undoubtedly improve with more bottle age. The extremely successful Dolcetto '97 Bric Trifüla has very broad fruity aromas; though rounded and well-structured, it shows considerable tannin. The Barbera from the same vintage, which has quite a robust body with an acidic vein characteristic of this grape, is a little less elegant, especially on the nose.

	Wine	Glasses	
●	Barbaresco Rabajà '95	▼▼	5
●	Dolcetto d'Alba Trifüla '97	▼▼	3
●	Barbaresco Sorì Paolin '95	▼	5
●	Barbera d'Alba Asili '97	▼	3
●	Barbaresco '94	▽▽	4
●	Barbaresco Rabajà '92	▽▽	4
●	Barbaresco Rabajà '94	▽▽	4
●	Barbaresco Rabajà '91	▽	4
●	Barbaresco Rabajà '93	▽	4
●	Barbera d'Alba Asili '96	▽	3

BARBARESCO (CN)

MOCCAGATTA
VIA RABAJÀ, 24
12050 BARBARESCO (CN)
TEL. 0173/635152 - 635228

The best of the wines released in 1998 is the Barbaresco Bric Balin '95; still very fruity on the nose and yet distinctly toasty, it is a revelation on the enticing palate where it opens up with great length and fullness, and smooth and delightful tannins. The Cole is a little less impetuous: the traditional large barrels for aging have been abandoned in favor of the barrique. At the moment the oak is dominant because the structure is not equal to the spicy wood. There is a similar situation with the Barbera Basarin from the same vintage, characterized by mouth-puckering oak-derived tannins, and a nose under the control of vanilla. The Dolcetto, simpler and more direct, has a fruity nose and an undemanding palate. We round off the reds with the Freisa, not very fresh, and high in carbon dioxide. Their most important Chardonnay, the Buschet '96, has a lovely palate: alcohol, fat and wood divide the honors of creating a mouth-filling and lasting taste, never over the top or cloying; the nose is a little woody, but in three or four years it should be fine. The standard Chardonnay is by no means mediocre: it is glycerin-rich and mouth-filling, and on the nose displays traces of yeast in the oak-derived aromas. In the fine underground barrel-room there are now 400 barriques, which, together with the steel vats, give rise to about 60 thousand bottles a year.

	Wine	Rating	Price
●	Barbaresco Bric Balin '95	🍷🍷	5
●	Barbaresco Cole '95	🍷🍷	5
○	Langhe Chardonnay Buschet '96	🍷🍷	5
○	Langhe Chardonnay '97	🍷	3
●	Barbera d'Alba Basarin '95	🍷	4
●	Dolcetto d'Alba '97	🍷	3
●	Langhe Freisa '97		3
●	Barbaresco Bric Balin '90	🍸🍸🍸	5
●	Barbaresco Bric Balin '93	🍸🍸	5
●	Barbaresco Bric Balin '94	🍸🍸	5
●	Barbaresco Cole '93	🍸🍸	5
●	Barbaresco Cole '94	🍸🍸	5

BARBARESCO (CN)

CASCINA MORASSINO
VIA OVELLO, 32
12050 BARBARESCO (CN)
TEL. 0173/635149

The 1995 vintage brought about a great upsurge in the Barbaresco zone, which seems to have given up playing second fiddle to Barolo and is finally producing a long series of excellent wines. Despite these generally positive developments, the Barbaresco Ovello of Cascina Morassino has not taken full advantage of a good vintage: the aromas (correct, but not very elegant) are followed by a palate somewhat overwhelmed by bitterish tannins in a medium body. The Nebbiolo '96, with its sweetish, easy and satisfying aromas, does not have a corresponding palate because of rather raspy tannins and a slightly weak structure. The Barbera '97 stakes its all on fresh directness. The Dolcetto '97 has pleasing aromas but a rather understated and not altogether harmonious palate, with noticeable tannins and acidity. In general the wines released in 1998 puzzle us somewhat: they are correct but they lack the dash the Ovello vineyard is capable of offering. The winery, which is small, produces just under 25 thousand bottles a year, and the young and capable Roberto Bianco tends to make them elegant and graceful, not overly concentrated, and with contained tannins. Some of the vines surround the winery and the others are in the celebrated Ovello cru, from which the wines with the richest aromas and most structure come.

	Wine	Rating	Price
●	Barbaresco Ovello '95	🍷	5
●	Barbera d'Alba '96	🍷	4
●	Langhe Nebbiolo '96	🍷	3
●	Dolcetto d'Alba '97		3
●	Barbaresco '93	🍸🍸	5
●	Barbaresco '94	🍸🍸	4
●	Barbera d'Alba '95	🍸🍸	4

BARBARESCO (CN)

WALTER MUSSO
VIA D. CAVAZZA, 5
12050 BARBARESCO (CN)
TEL. 0173/635129

This year we tasted the Dolcetto and the two Barbaresco crus, which were creditable but failed to make a great impact on either nose or palate. The Dolcetto, ruby-colored with violet shading, is heady, fragrant and delicately fruity; on the palate it shows medium structure and persistence. Of the two Barbarescos, we preferred the Rio Sordo, which is more structured and complex. It is ruby with a garnet rim, and displays heady fruity aromas; on the palate it is structured, with red fruit joining the astringent tannins. The Barbaresco Pora is quite similar, but is not so structured and is less intense and lingering. From these two magnificent crus in a vintage like the '95 we would have expected two more impressive Barbarescos. They are both correct, but they lack the sinew and mouth-filling substance which make the wines of this area great. For some years now, in addition to the typical reds of the zone, Walter Musso has been making a simple and fragrant Chardonnay, which he sells at a very reasonable price, as well as a Spumante in need of further improvement.

●	Barbaresco Pora '95	🍷	4
●	Barbaresco Rio Sordo '95	🍷	4
●	Dolcetto d'Alba '97	🍷	3
○	Langhe Chardonnay '97		3
●	Barbaresco Bricco Rio Sordo '93	♀♀	4
●	Barbaresco Pora '93	♀	4

BARBARESCO (CN)

PRODUTTORI DEL BARBARESCO
VIA TORINO, 52
12050 BARBARESCO (CN)
TEL. 0173/635139

There are wine lovers all over the world who await with impatience the release of the special crus from the Produttori del Barbaresco: many of them have even been buying "en primeur", at very attractive prices. Unfortunately, for the second year running we are unable to review these gems: the '93 Rabajà, Ovello, Rio Sordo and Montestefano were not yet ready for tasting when we went to press. We are therefore limiting our comments to the other two wines produced by this historic winery, which vinifies the grapes of about sixty member growers: the Nebbiolo and the basic Barbaresco. The Nebbiolo Langhe is young, fresh and immediate, and the '97 is even better than its forebears, having taken full advantage of an excellent vintage. The not very intense color is followed by well-defined and attractive aromas; it has a good finish and is eminently drinkable. The Barbaresco '95 has a medium structure, and does not make a great impact, but it provides a small foretaste (and a positive one) of what the crus can do.

●	Barbaresco '95	🍷	4
●	Langhe Nebbiolo '97	🍷	4
●	Barbaresco Moccagatta Ris. '90	♀♀	5
●	Barbaresco Montestefano Ris. '90	♀♀	5
●	Barbaresco Paje Ris. '90	♀♀	5
●	Barbaresco Rabajà Ris. '90	♀♀	5
●	Barbaresco Rio Sordo Ris. '90	♀♀	5
●	Barbaresco '93	♀	4
●	Barbaresco Asili Ris. '90	♀	5

BARBARESCO (CN)

Albino Rocca

Via Rabajà, 15
12050 Barbaresco (CN)
tel. 0173/635145

Albino Rocca is not one to rest on his laurels, even though quite a number have come his way in recent years. So here he is, trying out ever more up-to-the-minute fermentation vats, comparing notes with the best oenologists he can find and dabbling, with success, in white wines. The extraordinary Barbaresco Vigna Loreto '95 is rich in fruity and licorice tones; on the palate it offers intense, soft tannins, an exquisite balance and excellent persistence. We should particularly point out the intelligent use of wood, carefully calibrated and absolutely not overbearing. In this fine vintage, then, Vigneto Loreto deservedly wins Three Glasses, overtaking the excellent Brich Ronchi '95, which is particularly warm and captivating, with good oak on the nose and a sweet succulence on the palate, where the tannins underpin the mouth-filling and elegant body. The Dolcetto Vignalunga '97 has very fresh and balsamic aromas, while on the palate the tannins are still a bit noticeable in a structure by no means devoid of character. The Barbera Gepin '96, which was splendid in '95, is a little disjointed and over-wooded on the palate. A very impressive performance, lastly, from the Bianco La Rocca '97, which is made from cortese and demonstrates that this grape, often dismissed as rather simple, can produce excellent results if handled with the proper care.

	Wine	Glasses	
●	Barbaresco Vigneto Loreto '95	▼▼▼	5
●	Barbaresco Vigneto Brich Ronchi '95	▼▼	5
●	Dolcetto d'Alba Vignalunga '97	▼▼	3
○	Langhe Bianco La Rocca '97	▼▼	4
●	Barbera d'Alba Gepin '96	▼	4
●	Barbaresco Vigneto Brich Ronchi '93	▽▽▽	5
●	Barbaresco Vigneto Brich Ronchi '91	▽▽	5
●	Barbaresco Vigneto Brich Ronchi '94	▽▽	5
●	Barbaresco Vigneto Loreto '94	▽▽	4
●	Barbaresco Vigneto Loreto '93	▽▽	4
●	Barbera d'Alba Gepin '95	▽▽	4
●	Barbaresco Vigneto Brich Ronchi '92	▽	5

BARBARESCO (CN)

Bruno Rocca

Via Rabajà, 29
12050 Barbaresco (CN)
tel. 0173/635112

The winery has been tastefully enlarged to make room for the vats, the new barrels and the aging cellar: this was necessitated in part by the purchase of new land and by the fact that the dynamic Bruno has no intention of slowing down a progress which has been regularly greeted by honors and awards. The Barbaresco Coparossa, in its debut appearance, seems very interesting: its bouquet is rich in fresh oak-derived hints of resin. The palate is intense and decided, almost austere, with a toastiness that contrasts well with the usual vanilla of the barrique. The complex aromas of the classic Rabajà are still more fascinating; however, it is less harmonious on the palate, and needs further bottle-aging: its lovely softness and sweetness are at the moment in the sway of bitter notes of Peruvian bark. The Dolcetto d'Alba lacks the impetus that many of its fellows have; the nose and palate are quite linear and simple, correct but not overwhelming. The Barbera '96 has good smooth wood underpinning the variegated fruit aromas; the clean palate has a woody, if not very long, finish. The Chardonnay Cadet '97, with its interesting bouquet, has made the best of a short time in the wood: it is fleshy and full-bodied on the palate, reinforced by a high alcohol level (13.5°), but it is still somewhat monotonous.

	Wine	Glasses	
●	Barbaresco Coparossa '95	▼▼	5
●	Barbaresco Rabajà '95	▼▼	5
●	Barbera d'Alba '96	▼	4
●	Dolcetto d'Alba Vigna Trifolé '97	▼	3
○	Langhe Chardonnay Cadet '97	▼	4
●	Barbaresco Rabajà '88	▽▽▽	5
●	Barbaresco Rabajà '89	▽▽▽	5
●	Barbaresco Rabajà '93	▽▽▽	5
●	Barbaresco Rabajà '90	▽▽	5
●	Barbaresco Rabajà '92	▽▽	5
●	Barbaresco Rabajà '94	▽▽	5
○	Langhe Chardonnay Cadet '96	▽▽	4

BARBARESCO (CN)

RINO VARALDO
VIA SECONDINE, 2
12050 BARBARESCO (CN)
TEL. 0173/635160

The first thing that strikes you at the Varaldo family's winery, which is making its debut appearance in the Guide, is the splendid view from the terrace at the front. You can see the land beyond the Tanaro and the lovely hills of Roero. When you reluctantly turn your back on the panorama, you notice that the winery is in the midst of being enlarged, and will soon greatly facilitate the work of Pier Mario and his sons (Rino and Michele, the latter with a degree in oenology from Alba). They produce 30 to 40 thousand bottles a year, produced from about five hectares of vineyards (both directly owned and leased). Among the wines presented, the Barbaresco La Gemma and the Barbera d'Alba are extremely good. The first, made with grapes from the Loreto vineyard in Barbaresco, and the Gallina e Bordini vineyard in Neive, has a ruby color with a garnet tinge and an orange rim. The nose is complex and distinctive (hints of blackberry, raspberry, spice and sweet pastry), enhanced by fascinating suggestions of overripeness. On the palate it seems substantial and soft, not very powerful (but harmonious and well-articulated), and it finishes with a corresponding and long finish. The Barbera, intense garnet-ruby in color, offers notes of cherry, red currant, menthol and coffee over complex undertones of damp earth. On the palate it shows broad, continuous substance with a long and richly aromatic finish. The good Nebbiolo, ruby-hued verging on garnet, has a bouquet of ripe red fruit with balsamic notes. On the palate it is robust and pleasingly dry. The agreeably rustic Freisa displays clean aromas of wild berries. Lastly, the Dolcetto d'Alba is properly made, simple and undemanding.

●	Barbaresco La Gemma '95	🍷🍷	5
●	Barbera d'Alba '96	🍷	4
●	Langhe Freisa '97	🍷	3
●	Langhe Nebbiolo '96	🍷	4
●	Dolcetto d'Alba '97		3

BAROLO (CN)

F.LLI BARALE
VIA ROMA, 6
12060 BAROLO (CN)
TEL. 0173/56127

Every year, the Bussia cru produces some pleasant surprises for this historic winery. Last year it was the Dolcetto that aroused particular interest, and this year the Nebbiolo comes to the fore. From the same propitious vintage, the '96, Barale has released its most recent and also best wines. The Nebbiolo Langhe, a red that combines the typical floral character of the great grape of the Langhe with an incisive elegance, has a clear and lively look; traces of rose and violet surround meatier notes of plum and cherry, giving the bouquet surprising richness. The entry on the palate is decisive, and if the development does not reveal great depth, the tannins are elegant and support a long finish. The Barbera Prede, while it doesn't have the same articulation, comes forward with great clarity; the color is deep ruby; the simple heady aromas are successfully matched by pleasing hints of red fruit; on the palate the acidity takes the lead, diminishing the force of the other sensations. The aftertaste is agreeably fresh. '94 was no friend to the Barolo but it keeps its head up amongst its peers: a garnet hue precedes ripe aromas and a lightly structured, moderately harmonious palate. The warm season of '97 did not help the Dolcetto, depriving it of its customary fragrance: the Barales' Costa delle Rose, although it has fair body, already seems mature.

●	Barbera d'Alba Preda '96	🍷	3
●	Barolo Castellero '94	🍷	5
●	Langhe Nebbiolo '96	🍷	3
●	Dolcetto d'Alba Costa delle Rose '97		3
○	Langhe Chardonnay '97		3
○	Roero Arneis '97		3
●	Barolo Castellero '91	YY	6
●	Barolo Castellero '93	YY	5
●	Dolcetto d'Alba Bussia '96	YY	3
●	Barbaresco Rabajà '90	Y	6
●	Barbaresco Rabajà '91	Y	6
●	Barbaresco Rabajà Ris. '93	Y	5
●	Barolo Castellero '90	Y	6

BAROLO (CN)

Giacomo Borgogno & Figli
Via Gioberti, 1
12060 Barolo (CN)
tel. 0173/56108

Although the '94 Barolo could hardly be a standard-bearer in this winery's renewed dedication to quality, even this wine from a poor vintage clearly indicates Borgogno's new policy. This is an impeccably made Barolo, the successful result of an attempt to modernize their production style without giving up an ounce of tradition. The fairly concentrated garnet color is followed by aromas which are already interestingly complex: they are not very profound, but they are clearly expressed; the palate reveals a lean, well-balanced body and is pleasingly clean, although not notably lingering. It's ready for drinking right now, and perhaps they would have done well to make an exception and release it a year early, given its delicate structure and all that implies about its probable future development. The Barbera is modern in style: an intense hue precedes a nose with clearly defined and pleasing fruity aromas. On the palate, the acidity is in the lead, but is well blended with a supple and fairly persistent body. The Dolcetto, an improvement over the '96, gives the same sensation of pleasurable immediacy, but it has more distinctive aromas and a greater presence on the palate, although still in the context of lighter wines. This year the Barolo Classico, selected from the best estate plots, was not produced, but a '95 is in preparation, and, happily, a '96, both very promising indeed.

	Wine	Rating	Price
●	Barbera d'Alba '97	🍷	3
●	Barolo '94	🍷	5
●	Dolcetto d'Alba '97	🍷	3
●	Barolo Classico '93	🍸🍸	5
●	Barolo '89	🍸	5
●	Barolo '91	🍸	4
●	Barolo '93	🍸	4
●	Barolo Classico '88	🍸	5
●	Barolo Classico '89	🍸	5
●	Barolo Classico Ris. '90	🍸	5
●	Barolo Liste '88	🍸	6
●	Barolo Liste '89	🍸	6

BAROLO (CN)

Giacomo Brezza & Figli
Via Lomondo, 4
12060 Barolo (CN)
tel. 0173/56354 - 56191

This winery has belonged since its establishment in 1885 to the Brezza family, but a while ago a restaurant and more recently a hotel were added. Thus while the rest of the family is engaged in these newer activities, the young and expert Enzo has been entrusted with running the winery, which vinifies grapes from their nearly 25 hectares of vineyards, all situated in the best crus of the district of Barolo. The strength of this historic winery lies in the size of its prestigious crus: they bear noble names (Cannubi, Sarmassa and Castellero), and they make it possible to produce an average of 90 thousand bottles a year, divided between Barolo (almost half the entire vintage), Barbera, Dolcetto, Freisa and Chardonnay. This year, apart from the standard '94 Barolo, Enzo has made and released only the Cannubi and the Sarmassa. The former, showing some signs of the poor vintage, was also suffering from its recent bottling when we tasted it; thus it still seemed closed and not perfectly harmonious on nose and palate. The latter has fair structure, and an already enviable balance; it is mouth-filling and satisfying, with a long and fruity finish. The Barbera d'Alba Cannubi '95 and the Dolcetto San Lorenzo '97 are also both good: the first has a powerful structure, good acidity and fresh, fruity aromas; the second, characteristically heady, fills the nose with aromas of raspberry. The Dolcetto Fossati '97 (a little less rich than last year's) and the Freisa Santa Rosalia '97 (semi-sparkling and slightly aromatic), and in particular the Chardonnay '97 (fat, powerful and distinctly redolent of almond) are still excellent buys.

	Wine	Rating	Price
●	Barbera d'Alba Cannubi '95	🍷🍷	4
●	Barolo Sarmassa '94	🍷🍷	5
●	Dolcetto d'Alba San Lorenzo '97	🍷🍷	3
●	Barolo Cannubi '94	🍷	5
●	Dolcetto d'Alba Fossati '97	🍷	3
●	Langhe Freisa Santa Rosalia '97	🍷	3
○	Langhe Chardonnay '97	🍷	3
●	Barolo Cannubi '90	🍸🍸	6
●	Barolo Cannubi '91	🍸🍸	5
●	Barolo Cannubi '93	🍸🍸	5
●	Barolo Castellero Ris. '90	🍸🍸	6
●	Barolo Sarmassa '91	🍸🍸	5
●	Barolo Sarmassa Ris. '90	🍸🍸	6
●	Barolo Bricco Sarmassa '93	🍸	5

BAROLO (CN)

MARCHESI DI BAROLO
VIA ALBA, 12
12060 BAROLO (CN)
TEL. 0173/564400

In each of the last five years, Marchesi di Barolo has presented a great Barolo of the 1990 vintage, almost as if they were offering a touchstone. This year it is the turn of the splendid Millenium, a Barolo which represents the cream of the best vineyards, and exemplifies the evolution of their philosophy of production (broader and more harmonious wines have been their aim for some time now). In color Millenium recalls Cannubi, and it also has the same profound richness of bouquet; the aromas are varied, complex and articulated, while a succulent vitality is well distributed on the palate, giving force to the finish and its recapitulation of the aromas. The eagerly awaited Barolo Estate '93 comes very close to Three Glasses: decisive, rich and mouth-filling, it does not have a particularly broad bouquet, but reveals a captivating crescendo on the palate. The Sarmassa, another showpiece of the '93 vintage, is characterized by a warm and mature physiognomy: this Barolo has a healthy air of the country, and a bouquet evocative of earth. The '94s we tasted were the Barolo Vintage, the standard Barolo and the Coste di Rose. The first, while it suffers slightly from a less than exciting vintage, is nevertheless among the best of that year, while the other two quite resembled each other (showing the usual impeccable execution), but without the "kick" of earlier versions. The Dolcetto Boschetti and the Barbera Ruvei are true to their different grapes, though we would have liked more personality. As always, the Gavi di Gavi gives a good performance.

	Wine	Glasses	Price
●	Barolo Estate Vineyard '93	▼▼	6
●	Barolo Millenium '90	▼▼	6
●	Barolo Sarmassa '93	▼▼	6
●	Barolo Vintage '94	▼▼	5
●	Dolcetto d'Alba Madonna di Como '97	▼▼	3
●	Barbera d'Alba Ruvei '96	▼	3
●	Barolo Coste di Rose '94	▼	5
●	Barolo Le Lune '94	▼	5
●	Dolcetto d'Alba Boschetti '97	▼	4
○	Gavi di Gavi '97	▼	4
●	Barolo Estate Vineyard '90	▽▽▽	6
●	Barolo Cannubi Ris. '90	▽▽	6
●	Barolo di Barolo Estate Vineyard '91	▽▽	6
●	Barolo Ris. '90	▽▽	6
●	Barbaresco Creja '93	▽	5

BAROLO (CN)

BARTOLO MASCARELLO
VIA ROMA, 15
12060 BAROLO (CN)
TEL. 0173/56125

Finally the eagerly awaited Barolo '93 of Bartolo Mascarello has made its appearance. The '91 and '92 had not been more exciting than those two vintages would lead one to suppose. But this time, since nature was willing, the wine has returned to its customary excellence. The style of the Barolo '93 to some extent reflects the changes taking place in the Langhe. We noticed it not so much in the aging, as in the vinification. Indeed, while the bouquet is heady and developed, in the traditional manner, the palate has achieved a greater balance between the characteristic tannins and the mouth-filling softness, an indication of more controlled maceration, aimed at extracting substances from the skin and seeds without excess. An intense garnet color is followed by a correspondingly expressive bouquet in which marked and lingering aromas of steeped oak, dried flowers and plum jam emerge. The palate is supported by an imposing, solid and unwavering structure: the well-diffused force of the alcohol is a match for the significant tannins. We have the impression that, with the '93, Mascarello's Barolo is on the point of recovering the distinct personality that characterized it not so very long ago. The Dolcetto, which was also released a year later, is again rustic and pleasing, with medium body.

	Wine	Glasses	Price
●	Barolo '93	▼▼	6
●	Dolcetto d'Alba '96	▼	4
●	Barolo '83	▽▽▽	6
●	Barolo '84	▽▽▽	6
●	Barolo '85	▽▽▽	6
●	Barolo '89	▽▽▽	6
●	Barolo '88	▽▽	6
●	Barolo '90	▽▽	6
●	Barbera d'Alba Vigna San Lorenzo '95	▽	4
●	Barolo '91	▽	6
●	Barolo '92	▽	5

BAROLO (CN)

E. Pira & Figli
Via Vittorio Veneto, 1
12060 Barolo (CN)
tel. 0173/56247

The success of Chiara Boschis' Barolo '94 should not be put down to chance; this would mean ignoring the commitment shown throughout the season, rigorous grape selection in a difficult vintage and the sensitivity of the wine technicians in charge of the various phases of vinification and maturation. And yet this preparatory work, which is, after all, common to many excellent wine-makers, is finally in the service of a process which (fortunately) cannot be entirely controlled. Hence the satisfaction one experiences when tasting this Barolo goes beyond its intrinsic qualities; there is also the surprise at an unexpected success; and then, one appreciates the way the wine has made the very best of all that the year had to offer. The intense and brilliant color perfectly expresses the polyphenols of a very successful nebbiolo in a lean year. The first signs of greatness appear on the nose: the development is gradual and one has to probe deeply to appreciate its richness; the initially floral and spicy aromas envelop juicier notes of sour cherry and raspberry, while hints of cocoa and vanilla make the bouquet more intriguing. The attack on the palate is unhesitating; the tannins are there from the start, preparing the way for the density of flavor. The finish is a triumph of length, as is its correspondence to the bouquet: a heady and powerful Barolo, made by someone who conceives of it as a modern wine, without forgetting its past. Hats off to Chiara Boschis, who has managed to win Three Glasses for her Barolo in a meager year for the Langhe!

Wine	Glasses	Price
● Barolo '94	🍷🍷🍷 (black)	5
● Barolo Ris. '90	🍷🍷🍷	6
● Barolo '93	🍷🍷	5
● Barolo '90	🍷	5

BAROLO (CN)

Giuseppe Rinaldi
Via Monforte, 3
12060 Barolo (CN)
tel. 0173/56156

It's always a pleasure to have a chat with that free spirit, Giuseppe Rinaldi. A good story-teller, he spices the discussion, and the account of his experiences with Barolo, with gentle irony: Giuseppe never lets himself get carried away by the controversy (tradition versus innovation) and is no dealer of deathblows, but just occasionally provokes an admiring "Touché!". His positive attitude and openness to discussion further communication and lead to an outpouring of ideas: he sets off from the value of place-names, sub-zones and crus in naming Barolos, and attacks the jungle of fantasy names which, in the end. devalue "a unique wine which should remain unique". He regards with favor the so-called defects (e.g. high tannin level) which contribute to its uniqueness, and ends up by expressing regret at seeing it adapted to international taste. Obviously, Rinaldi's wine-making methods involve lengthy maceration and long maturing in large oak barrels. On the ground, the estate includes such highly prized vineyards as Cannubi San Lorenzo, Le Coste and Brunate. The Barolo '94 which we tasted is in fact an asemblage from these two last crus (as stated on the label). The broad nose is preceded by a lovely deep and lively color. The bouquet opens with slight traces of spice, followed by plum, raspberry and violet. On the palate the best qualities are the full flavor, a certain softness and the balance: the tannins are perceptible but not rough. Although its progression on the palate is excellent, one misses the impact of great concentration.

Wine	Glasses	Price
● Barolo Brunate Le Coste '94	🍷🍷 (black)	5
● Barolo '90	🍷🍷	6
● Barolo '91	🍷🍷	5
● Barolo Brunate '90	🍷🍷	5
● Barolo Brunate '91	🍷🍷	5
● Barolo Brunate '92	🍷🍷	5
● Barolo Brunate Le Coste '93	🍷🍷	5
● Barolo Ravera San Lorenzo '93	🍷	5

BAROLO (CN)

LUCIANO SANDRONE
VIA ALBA, 57
12060 BAROLO (CN)
TEL. 0173/56239

This year once again the Nebbiolo d'Alba is the best of Sandrone's wines. Luciano purchased, a few years ago, a parcel of land near Vezza d'Alba, the Valmaggiore, and perhaps not even he expected that it could produce such an impressive red. The appearance is very like that of a new generation Roero Nebbiolo; it is not, however, surprising that a wine-maker from the Langhe should have sought to add a touch more austerity. Of a vivid garnet color, fairly intense, it displays a strikingly complex floral bouquet (a procession of notes on the border between freshness and maturity). On the palate softness is all, expanding confidently and only occasionally aroused by the graceful tone of the tannins. The Barolo suffers only mildly from the poor vintage of '94, and is in line with the delicacy characteristic of its older brothers. Sandrone's style for his Cannubi Boschis favors cleanness, without extreme concentration: this puts him less at the mercy of the vagaries of different vintages. The lively hue corresponds to the fragrance of the fruity bouquet, very slightly sweetened by a touch of vanilla. The structure on the palate is broad, subtle and fairly harmonious. The Barbera is admirably succulent; unfortunately a somewhat dominant wood diminishes the expressiveness of the aromas and, in part, the palate. The Dolcetto, with its fragrance of jam, is still one of the best in the Langhe.

Wine	Glasses	Price
● Dolcetto d'Alba '97	▼▼	4
● Nebbiolo d'Alba Valmaggiore '96	▼▼	4
● Barbera d'Alba '96	▼	4
● Barolo Cannubi Boschis '94	▼	5
● Barolo '83	▽▽▽	6
● Barolo '84	▽▽▽	6
● Barolo Cannubi Boschis '85	▽▽▽	6
● Barolo Cannubi Boschis '86	▽▽▽	6
● Barolo Cannubi Boschis '87	▽▽▽	6
● Barolo Cannubi Boschis '89	▽▽▽	6
● Barolo Cannubi Boschis '90	▽▽▽	6
● Nebbiolo d'Alba Valmaggiore '95	▽▽	4
● Barolo Cannubi Boschis '93	▽	5

BAROLO (CN)

GIORGIO SCARZELLO & FIGLI
VIA ALBA, 29
12060 BAROLO (CN)
TEL. 0173/56170

Giorgio and Gemma Scarzello are a well-matched couple: he, calm and even-tempered, has experience and knowledge of the life of the Langhe behind him, while she is dynamic and of an enterprising spirit. Their son Federico, who has almost completed his studies for a degree in oenology, is already active on the estate; perhaps his mother's urging will convince him to go and gain some experience in a winery abroad. On their five hectares under vine, the Scarzellos cultivate the traditional Piedmontese grapes, nebbiolo, barbera and dolcetto, producing some 20 thousand fine bottles a year from an average yield of about 7,000 kilos per hectare. Ciabot Merenda is the highly prized cru from which the family gathers the grapes for their Barolo: vinified with a quite extensive maceration (15-20 days), the wine remains faithful to a traditional concept of Barolo production. Certainly, when the year is not favorable (e.g. '94), there are unlikely to be miracles, but by working with care you can produce quite a respectable wine. The Barolo presented for tasting has a garnet color with a little orange showing. On the nose it is mild, by no means impetuous, but pleasing, with its floral notes and hints of walnut. It is fairly well-balanced on the palate and though it is light in structure, its nose and palate correspond and the clean and fairly long finish is good.

Wine	Glasses	Price
● Barolo '94	▼	5
● Barolo '93	▽▽	5
● Barolo Vigna Merenda '90	▽▽	5
● Dolcetto d'Alba '96	▽▽	3
● Barbera d'Alba '96	▽	3
● Barolo '91	▽	5

BAROLO (CN)

Sylla Sebaste
Loc. S. Pietro delle Viole
12060 Barolo (CN)
tel. 0173/56266

Starting this year we are including the two estates owned by the Limonci family, Colle Manora in Quargnento near Alessandria, and Sylla Sebaste at Barolo in the Langhe, in a single entry. The decision to unite under one heading two such different wineries was inspired by the limited number of wines presented. We consider this year a period of transition after the premature death of Signora Elena Limonci, the life and soul of the enterprise. In addition, the Langhe winery, which concentrates on producing wines for laying down, has had to deal with the dread vintage '94. Only two of these wines came our way: the Nebbiolo Passo delle Viole '97 and the Bricco Viole '94. The first is a red designed to be drunk fairly soon; it is garnet-hued; the aromas are delicate and heady, and on the palate there's an admirable balance between softness and tannins. The Bricco Viole '94 has suffered more than expected from its vintage; the wine, already perfectly mature, is fairly harmonious but not very long. We were pleased by a further taste of the Barolo Bussia '93 which we reviewed last year. From the Alessandria winery, dedicated to Barbera and white wines, we were able to taste only the Mimosa Collezione '97, a sauvignon. Of a fairly intense straw color, it offers notes of vanilla and apricot on the nose. It reveals good structure and balance in the mouth. The Palo Alto (pinot noir, cabernet sauvignon, merlot and barbera), Pais (a young Monferrato barbera) and La Barbera Collezione were not yet available so we shall write about them in next year's Guide.

●	Bricco Viole '94	🍷	4
●	Langhe Nebbiolo Passo delle Viole '97	🍷	3
○	Monferrato Bianco Mimosa Collezione '97	🍷	4
●	Barolo Bussia Ris. '84	YYY	6
●	Barolo Bussia '85	YYY	6
●	Barolo Bussia '93	YY	5
●	Barolo Bussia '90	YY	6
●	Monferrato Rosso Palo Alto '95	YY	5
●	Barbera del M.to Collezione '95	Y	4
●	Barbera del M.to Pais '96	Y	3

BAROLO (CN)

Tenuta La Volta - Cabutto
Via S. Pietro, 13
12060 Barolo (CN)
tel. 0173/56168

This is a winery rich in historical associations: the venerable Castello della Volta, for example, although now in decay, dominates the vineyards; the name they have chosen for their blend (nebbiolo with a little barbera), Vendemmiaio, recalls the name given to the month of September by the French Revolutionaries; and the time taken for maceration, as much as thirty days for the Barolo, in the age of rotomacerators seems almost to have archaeological value. The Cabutto brothers say this is not the case, and point out that one must always find exactly the right method for producing each wine, avoiding the sameness that results from the constant use of techniques which may well be fine in themselves but are not always the most suitable in a given situation. In the Langhe, '94 was certainly not a year to remember; thus the Barolo presented for tasting has a somewhat hard time of it. Its color is garnet, with traces of orange, and its fairly intense bouquet evokes undergrowth and violets. On the palate it shows a simple structure, and is neither intense nor persistent, though clean and reflective of the nose. The fair Vendemmiaio '95, brick-red in color, has rather evident acidity but reveals aromas of vanilla, sweet spice and fruit in spirit. The palate is warm and still tannic, but slightly lacking in structure. Both the Barbera '96 and the two Dolcettos have diminished bouquets: the Superiore version of Dolcetto is more agreeable, thanks to greater depth on the palate.

●	Barbera d'Alba Sup. Bricco delle Viole '96	🍷	4
●	Barolo Vigna La Volta '94	🍷	5
●	Dolcetto d'Alba Sup. '96	🍷	4
●	Langhe Rosso Vendemmiaio '95	🍷	5
●	Dolcetto d'Alba Vigna La Volta '97		3
●	Barolo Riserva del Fondatore '90	YY	6
●	Barbera d'Alba Sup. Bricco delle Viole '95	Y	3
●	Barolo '93	Y	5
●	Barolo Vigna La Volta '91	Y	4

BAROLO (CN)

G. D. Vajra
Via delle Viole, 25
Loc. Vergne
12060 Barolo (CN)
tel. 0173/56257

Aldo Vajra has come a long way since, way back in 1979, he took up the reins of the family estate, which included some of the best land near Vergne, halfway between Barolo and La Morra. Today the winery has excellent vineyards in this fairly high corner of the Barolo zone (Fossati and Bricco delle Viole), where wines of great finesse and aromatic complexity originate. Apart from Barolo and Barbera, Aldo has concentrated on Dolcetto, which is quite at home in this rather cool setting, a still Freisa and a Rhine riesling. Despite the difficult year, Aldo and Milena Vajra's Barolo Bricco delle Viole '94 did very well at our tastings. Although its nose is still reluctant to reveal its charms (for the moment the fruit is overshadowed by complex notes of herbs and dried flowers), the admirable balance on the palate makes it well-rounded and harmonious, quite doing away with any roughness. The basic Dolcetto '97 has a bouquet of strawberry with a vegetal hint, and is crisp and heady on the palate. The Langhe Nebbiolo '97 is rather better than last year's; the nose is redolent of a red fruit salad (strawberry, raspberry and cherry), while on the palate the sweet smooth tannins accompany delicious fruity flavors. The Dolcetto Coste e Fossati, and the Langhe Bianco, (Rhine riesling), do even better: the former, despite a still somewhat unsettled nose, offers the usual overwhelming power and sweetness. The latter, somewhat austere in style, has an amazingly aristocratic nose (enchanting floral aromas and faint mineral hints which with time will acquire the characteristic petroleum fragrance). The palate is distinctly structured.

●	Barolo Bricco delle Viole '94	🍷🍷	5
●	Dolcetto d'Alba Coste & Fossati '97	🍷🍷	4
○	Langhe Bianco '97	🍷🍷	4
●	Dolcetto d'Alba '97	🍷	3
○	Langhe Chardonnay '97	🍷	3
●	Langhe Nebbiolo '97	🍷	4
●	Langhe Rosso '97	🍷	3*
●	Barbera d'Alba Bricco delle Viole '93	🍷🍷 (outline)	5
●	Barolo '93	🍷🍷 (outline)	5
●	Barolo Bricco delle Viole '91	🍷🍷 (outline)	4
●	Dolcetto d'Alba Coste & Fossati '96	🍷🍷 (outline)	4
●	Langhe Freisa Kyè '96	🍷🍷 (outline)	5

BORGONE SUSA (TO)

Carlotta
Via Condove, 61
10050 Borgone Susa (TO)
tel. 011/9646150

The Valsusa denomination officially came into being in 1967, but it is generally acknowledged that it has existed for many centuries. The phylloxera blight (but even more the lack of manpower and the impossibility of mechanizing the vineyard work) had made this viticulture on the edge uneconomical. Before the complete disappearance of vines from the steeply sloping terraces, a few courageous and dedicated people have begun to restore the vineyards which have always been considered the best. Thus, almost as a hobby, Carla decided in 1990 to take up the activity her ancestors had practiced. The vineyards are Borgone, Costadoro (situated in the magnificent amphitheater which dominates the house) and Vignacombe, between Borgone and Condove. The winery also makes use of a parcel of land at Ramats di Chiomonte, almost 800 meters above sea level. Although she produces fewer than 10 thousand bottles in all, Carla vinifies (in stainless steel) and bottles the three crus separately. They differ not only in terrain and microclimate, but also in their blends. The Vignacombe '97, made from old native varietals, is light ruby in color and floral and vegetal in bouquet, which is reflected on the palate in the acidulous straightforward manner of the wine. The Rocca di Lupo, strongly characterized by the rare avanà grape, has an intense violet ruby color; on the nose, which requires further maturing, there are clear peppery tones. The acid and tannic structure is excellent. At present the Costadoro, a blend of neretta cuneese, ciliegiolo, barbera and freisa grapes, beats all the others for elegance and harmony. The wine combines a fine coloring with a delicate and complex fruity nose; on the palate it is enviably sweet and long-lasting. Finally, we should mention the pleasant and refreshing semi-sparkling Roceja.

●	Valsusa Costadoro '97	🍷🍷	4
●	Valsusa Rocca del Lupo '97	🍷	3
●	Valsusa Vignacombe '97	🍷	3
●	Roceja '97		2

BRA (CN)

CANTINE GIACOMO ASCHERI
VIA PIUMATI, 23
12042 BRA (CN)
TEL. 0172/412394

Matteo Ascheri has succeeded in a seemingly impossible task: producing wines of quality in the hinterland near Bra, the town where he has his winery and around which for decades no vineyards of any interest have existed. In order to achieve his goal, he chose a piece of land at Montelupa, about two and a half hectares in size, and, after extensive research, he decided to plant viognier and syrah, the grapes best adapted to the sandy soil of the selected zone. And so now the estate is for the first time releasing two Montelupa wines. The Bianco '97 has an attractive straw color tinged with green, and aromas of mint, green grass, citron and peach; on the palate it is ample, warm and redolent of green apple on a finish just slightly veiled by a touch of excess wood. The Rosso '96 has a fine ruby color with brown shading; typical syrah hints of iodine on the nose are followed by good concentration on the palate concluding with a slightly rough finish (with licorice and pepper to the fore). Among the classic wines of the estate we tasted the Barolo Vigneto Farina '94, a correct and well-balanced wine which, however, reflects the weakness of that vintage. The interesting Barbera d'Alba Fontanella '97, the name of its vineyard in La Morra, has an intense ruby hue; the nose is not very rich but presents delicate notes of plum and spice, and the palate is elegant, silky and long. The Dolcetto d'Alba Vigna Sant'Anna '97 is straightforward, heady and eminently quaffable; we would have expected more intense color from that vintage, and more alcohol too. However, it's an extremely well-balanced wine with excellent correspondence between eye, nose and palate.

	Wine	Rating	Price
○	Montelupa Bianco '97	🍷🍷	5
●	Montelupa Rosso '96	🍷🍷	5
●	Barbera d'Alba Fontanelle '97	🍷	3
●	Dolcetto d'Alba Vigna S. Anna '97	🍷	3
●	Barolo Vigna Farina '94		5
●	Barolo Vigna Farina '90	🍸	5
●	Barolo Vigna Farina '91	🍸	5
●	Barolo Vigna Farina '93	🍸	5
●	Bric Mileui '93	🍸	4
●	Rocca d'Auçabech '93	🍸	4
●	Verduno Pelaverga Costa dei Faggi '95	🍸	3

CALAMANDRANA (AT)

MICHELE CHIARLO
S.S. NIZZA-CANELLI
14042 CALAMANDRANA (AT)
TEL. 0141/769030

If we were to write a thorough profile of this Monferrato winery we would need quite a bit more than a page of the Guide. Every year (thanks to the inexhaustible efforts of the owner, Michele, and his children) we have new acquisitions to note, and the range of wines grows and grows. We rather think that sooner or later the Chiarlos will have to start limiting themselves, but for the moment they certainly have the market and critical opinion on their side. From their recent purchase of vineyards in Agliano we have two new Barbera crus. The Vespa '96, of a brilliant intense ruby color, presents a bouquet of red fruit, coffee and new wood. It is full-bodied, with a finish of plum and faintly noticeable alcohol. The other wine from Agliano, La Court '96, has a slightly less intense bouquet, but it shows structure, sinew and ripe fruit, with a long sweet finish. The Moscato Nivole, generally a little underrated, shows a notable aromatic intensity in the '97 version. The Monferrato Bianco Plenilunio '96, a blend of cortese and chardonnay, has sweet aromas of acacia blossom and yeasts and a very rich, almost unctuous palate. The Contacc! '95 is a little unbalanced (the wood may not be fully integrated yet), but the Fornaci di Tassarolo '95 is still one of the best Piedmontese whites: a bouquet of anice, sage and sweet pastries, followed by a rich and complex palate with honey and yellow plum flavors. The Barolo '94, though showing all the limitations of its year, offers a warm palate with tannins perhaps a bit overwhelming for the moderate fruit. The Barbaresco Asili '95 is excellent, perfectly in keeping with the nobillity of the cru in substance, balance and finesse.

	Wine	Rating	Price
●	Barbaresco Asili '95	🍷🍷	6
●	Barbera d'Asti Sup. La Court '96	🍷🍷	5
●	Barbera d'Asti Sup. Bricco Vespa '96	🍷🍷	5
○	Gavi Fornaci di Tassarolo '95	🍷🍷	5
○	Monferrato Plenilunio '96	🍷🍷	4
○	Moscato d'Asti Nivole '97	🍷🍷	3
●	Barolo '94	🍷	5
●	Barbera d'Asti Sup. '96	🍷	3
●	Langhe Barilot '95	🍷	5
●	Monferrato Countacc! '95	🍷	5
●	Barolo Cannubi '90	🍸🍸🍸	6
●	Barolo Cerequio '88	🍸🍸🍸	6
●	Barolo Cerequio '93	🍸🍸🍸	6
○	Gavi Fornaci di Tassarolo '90	🍸🍸🍸	5

CALOSSO (AT)

Scagliola

Fraz. S. Siro, 42
14052 Calosso (AT)
tel. 0141/853183

The winery is in the midst of the vineyards that surround the village of Calosso, almost all of which bear moscato grapes intended for the production of Moscato d'Asti and of Asti. The Scagliola brothers, successful producers of Moscato, also grow barbera, chardonnay, cortese, dolcetto, brachetto, freisa and nebbiolo on their fifteen hectares. Their special enthusiasm is for Barbera, which they seem to do very well. But turning first to the classic wine of the zone, Moscato d'Asti: the Volo di Farfalle is again at the top of its category, with a well-defined and persistent bouquet of fruit, musk and sage. On the palate the effervescence is not aggressive and the wine is properly sweet and not cloying. The Barbera SansSì is of a similar excellence; its dark ruby coloring is followed by a fruity bouquet with traces of vanilla. The wine reveals the exemplary use of small wooden barrels in its making; as a result the softness and balance typical of this grape are not covered by wood. The barriqued Chardonnay offers a bouquet in which fruit and wood have yet to be perfectly blended, and it also needs to develop greater balance on the palate. We shall be tasting it again in the course of the coming months to see how it is evolving. The Chardonnay Carsot dan Vian, simpler and more direct, reveals a fresh acidity and clear aromas of banana. The fragrant Barbera '97, vinified in stainless steel, has a ruby hue with traces of violet, and a full body, thanks to the vintage. We tasted the future Barbera SansSì '97 directly from the barrique: unless we're greatly mistaken, it should prove to be a very fine wine indeed. The basic Moscato d'Asti is good, and the price is moderate.

	Wine	Rating	Price
●	Barbera d'Asti SanSì '96	🍷🍷	4
○	Moscato d'Asti Volo di Farfalle '97	🍷🍷	3*
○	Moscato d'Asti '97	🍷	3
○	Piemonte Chardonnay '96	🍷	4
○	Piemonte Chardonnay Casot dan Vian '97	🍷	3
●	Barbera d'Asti '97	🍷	3
●	Barbera d'Asti SanSì '95	🍸	4

CALOSSO (AT)

Tenuta dei Fiori

Via Valcalosso, 3
Reg. Rodotiglia
14052 Calosso (AT)
tel. 0141/826938 - 966500

Walter Bosticardo is carefully organizing his coming retirement as a retailer of agricultural products, which will allow him to dedicate himself entirely to his wines. The renovation of the winery is proceeding apace, together with the construction of a farmhouse which will serve as a Bed and Breakfast inn, the first of its kind in the area. Everything should be in place two or three years from now. But meanwhile his wines have already taken a step forward, and made a very good impression on us this year. The Monferrato Rosso, from cabernet sauvignon, is excellent: the dark ruby color paves the way for an intense bouquet of red fruit accompanied by a light note of sweet pepper, well blended with the vanilla of the wood. On the palate the wine is warm, soft and highly concentrated. The Barbera Tulipano Nero is also successful: the intense, complex bouquet of red fruit with balsamic notes is followed by a palate revealing good structure and balance. Each year Walter presents very few wines; the vintage does not always permit him to produce the wines that have made this estate famous. So we re-tasted two unusual wines: the Gamba di Pernice '95 and the Pensiero '91. The former, made from a varietal not much used here, confirmed our positive impressions of last year. The color is pale ruby, and the spicy and vegetal aromas are reflected on the palate. The Pensiero '91, an original interpretation of moscato to produce a "méthode traditionelle" sparkling wine, has improved with maturing, and gives free range to its elegant aromas. On the palate it is rich, mouth-filling, elegant and creamy.

	Wine	Rating	Price
●	Monferrato Rosso '95	🍷🍷	4
●	Barbera d'Asti Vigneto del Tulipano Nero '96	🍷	4
●	Barbera d'Asti Vigneto del Tulipano Nero '95	🍸	3
●	Gamba di Pernice '95	🍸	4
○	Pensiero '91	🍸	5

CAMINO (AL)

Tenuta Gaiano
Via Trino, 8
15020 Camino (AL)
tel. 0142/469440

The Monferrato Casalese foothills rise a few kilometers from Trino Vercellese and Crescentino, villages of the plain noted for their rice crop. Pier Iviglia and Gigi Lavander have chosen these very hills to embark on their venture in the world of wine-making. After various occupations (Pier in the field of electronics and Gigi in agriculture), the two have leased the winery and the land of the Tenuta Gaiano. The vineyards, which have fine exposure, produce barbera and grignolino for the most part, with a few older freisa vines. Unfortunately the estate buildings, which have as their base the remains of an ancient French Cistercian abbey (the name Gaiano in fact comes from Gallia) long since deserted, are now unstable. The two friends, however, have managed to adapt both themselves and their wines, and by taking advantage of every nook and cranny in the cellars of the old monastery and of the scant equipment at their disposal they have made a brilliant debut in the Guide. The Grignolino del Monferrato Casalese '97 earns One Glass; it has a typical dense cherry color and a nose that, if not intense, is pleasingly redolent of spice (with white pepper in the lead), followed by a palate which, thanks to the particularly warm season, offers a soft succulence unusual for this grape. Their standard Barbera, (all of their Barberas are included in the Monferrato DOC denomination), is the Vivace '97, easy to drink, but not devoid of character. The two wood-aged special selections (large barrels and barriques for the Gallianum, and new barriques for the Vigna della Torretta) are the pride and joy of the Tenuta Gaiano. Both have a dark, almost impenetrable color, spicy and fruity aromas, and a powerful and harmonious structure (but the Vigna della Torretta is fleshier and has a more complex bouquet).

	Wine	Glasses	Price
●	Barbera del M.to Gallianum '96	🍷🍷	3*
●	Barbera del M.to Vigna della Torretta '96	🍷🍷	4
●	Barbera del M.to Vivace '97	🍷	1*
●	Grignolino del M.to Casalese '97	🍷	3

CANALE (CN)

Cascina Ca' Rossa
Loc. Case Sparse, 56
12043 Canale (CN)
tel. 0173/98348 - 98201

We had been eagerly awaiting Angelo Ferrio's debut on the red wine stage ever since tasting his various recent Arneis, and finally the moment of truth has come and we find with pleasure that the Roero Vigna Audinaggio, its first time out (the '96), is not merely a good wine but one coolly capable of walking off with Three Glasses. The grapes are grown in a fine, steeply sloping vineyard, cultivated perforce by hand, near Valmaggiore a Vezza. This Roero has a quite intense ruby-garnet color; the complex, rich nose shows an excellent balance between wood and fruit, with aromas of violet, wild berries, vanilla and menthol. The excellent palate is at first soft and full-bodied, becoming increasingly austere up to a harmonious, warm finish, balanced and pleasingly dry. The good basic Roero, ruby-hued verging on garnet, has a bouquet of violets and red fruit, simple but with some finesse. The palate is substantial and direct. The Merica, a special selection of Arneis offered for the first time this year, has a full straw color tinged with green and notes of apple, pear and ripe peach on the nose; the palate is substantial, crisply acidulous, and delicately bitter on the finish. They round off the range with two brachetto wines, the Bric Ciarot and the Birbét, both '97s. The former is a jovial, undemanding dry wine, just right with salami or fresh cheese. The latter is sweet and reveals, with some finesse, characteristic rose and wild strawberry notes on the nose; on the palate it is balanced, fresh and not at all cloying.

	Wine	Glasses	Price
●	Roero Vigna Audinaggio '96	🍷🍷🍷	5
●	Birbét Dolce '97	🍷	3
●	Bric Ciarot '97	🍷	3
●	Roero '97	🍷	3
○	Roero Arneis Merica '97	🍷	3*

CANALE (CN)

Cascina Chicco

Via Valentino, 144
12043 Canale (CN)
tel. 0173/979069

Roero is a wine-making zone on the rise. In the course of just a few years there has been a substantial increase in the number of wines that have earned high scores, as well as in the number of wineries that place quality first. And the Faccenda family (but it's hardly news to us) improves each year. Thus, partly because Enrico and Marco (both oenologists) accumulate more experience with every year that passes, and partly because having a couple of propitious vintages, after a run of difficult ones, certainly doesn't hurt, Cascina Chicco has carried off quite a respectable collection of Glasses this year. Their two Barberas, the Bric Loira '96 and the basic '97, are both excellent. The first, intensely ruby-hued with a purple rim, has a bouquet of wild berries, violets, licorice and vanilla. The well-structured palate is warm and broad, with an intense finish. The standard Barbera '97, impressive in its richness and concentration, has an opaque color and a clean nose with hints of cherry, red currant and coffee. On the palate it is succulent and broad, with a long and fruity finish. The Roero Valmaggiore, intense garnet in color, has a forward bouquet with notes of ripe cherry, menthol and clove. On the palate it is substantial and soft, with a vigorous tannic note on the finish. One full Glass goes to the Birbét Secco, which displays characteristic varietal aromas with elegance and balance. On the palate it is robust and decidedly tannic. The aromas of the Nebbiolo Mompissano are quite good, though slightly dominated by wood; hints of berries and pepper introduce a robust palate, with tannins evident on the finish.

	Wine	Glasses	Price
●	Barbera d'Alba '97	🍷🍷	3*
●	Barbera d'Alba Bric Loira '96	🍷🍷	4
●	Birbét Secco '97	🍷	3
●	Nebbiolo d'Alba Mompissano '96	🍷	4
○	Roero Arneis '97	🍷	3*
●	Roero Valmaggiore '96	🍷	4
○	Langhe Favorita '97		3
●	Barbera d'Alba Bric Loira '95	♈︎	4

CANALE (CN)

Matteo Correggia

Via S. Stefano Roero, 124
12043 Canale (CN)
tel. 0173/978009

With two favorable vintages at last (1996 and 1997), Matteo Correggia has taken that final step forward which places him among the top winegrowers of Italy. It's not just because of the two Three Glasses this time, or of those he has won for four consecutive years, but also (and above all) because of the many Two full Glass winners among his standard wines, a particular guarantee for the consumer. The style that typifies the crus finds echoes in the less costly wines, and this means that while the yield for the former is very low, that of the latter is at least reasonable. And Matteo has such a skilled steady hand in vinification and the use of wood that he doesn't miss a shot. His wife Ornella, who looks after administration, and his mother Severina, tireless and expert in the care of the vineyard, make up the rest of the staff. Let's turn to his wines, beginning with the Marun, which shows youthful traces of violet against an opaque garnet background. The sumptuousness of the nose is equalled by the definition of the aromas, which range from black cherry to custard, clove and coffee. The powerful broad and deep body leads to a warm, explosive finish. The more composed Nebbiolo, with a concentrated color verging on garnet, offers a choral bouquet of blackberry, raspberry, coffee custard and tobacco. The rich palate is supported by properly judged tannins, and has an articulated and complex finish. The impressively powerful Roero has a distinctly fruity nose, and a thoroughly satisfying palate. The Barbera shows ample substance and some sinew. Finally, the Arneis and the Brachetto Secco Anthos are both simple and pleasing.

	Wine	Glasses	Price
●	Barbera d'Alba Marun '96	🍷🍷🍷	5
●	Nebbiolo d'Alba La Val dei Preti '96	🍷🍷🍷	5
●	Barbera d'Alba '97	🍷🍷	3*
●	Roero '97	🍷🍷	3*
●	Anthos '97	🍷	3
○	Roero Arneis '97	🍷	3
●	Barbera d'Alba Bricco Marun '94	♈︎♈︎♈︎	5
●	Barbera d'Alba Bricco Marun '95	♈︎♈︎♈︎	5
●	Nebbiolo d'Alba La Val dei Preti '93	♈︎♈︎♈︎	5
●	Nebbiolo d'Alba La Val dei Preti '95	♈︎♈︎	5

CANALE (CN)

DELTETTO
C.SO ALBA, 33
12043 CANALE (CN)
TEL. 0173/979383

Antonio Deltetto's winery produces a wide range of wines, yet manages to guarantee a conspicuously high level of quality (not something to be taken for granted). The low yield of the vineyard and a very well-equipped cellar are Antonio's only secrets, apart from an indispensable and evident enthusiasm. Vintages like '96 and '97 play their part, saving him from wasting a year's work. And in fact there's a bumper crop of awards for his wines this year, starting with Roero Madonna dei Boschi, which is garnet-ruby in hue, with a slightly pale rim, and offers generous aromas with notes of violet, berries, vanilla and resin. On the palate it is substantial and harmonious, with a perceptible tannic tone and an intense, tasty finish. Two Glasses went to the Roero Arneis San Michele as well, lightly straw-colored, with fruity and vegetal aromas and hints of green peach, apple and a faint trace of vanilla. In the mouth it is crisp, silky and full, with an intense though not long-lasting finish. The Barbera d'Alba Bramè, with a ruby-to-garnet color of medium intensity, just missed Two Glasses. The Roero Braja, on its first appearance, gets One full Glass; it displays an intense garnet color, and a fascinating nose, still a little closed, with notes of red currant, blackberry and coffee. The chewy palate is caressed by a veiling of noble tannins. A newcomer, Arneis Daivej is of a light straw color with a green tinge. On the nose the secondary lemony tones lead to a simple, pleasurable drinkability. The basic Arneis, delicate and fruity, is simple and correctly made.

	Wine	Glasses	Price
○	Roero Arneis S. Michele '97	ŸŸ	3
●	Roero Madonna dei Boschi '96	ŸŸ	4
●	Barbera d'Alba Bramè '96	Ÿ	3
○	Roero Arneis Daivej '97	Ÿ	3
●	Roero Braja '96	Ÿ	4
○	Roero Arneis '97		3
●	Roero Madonna dei Boschi '95	♀	3

CANALE (CN)

FUNTANIN
VIA TORINO, 191
12043 CANALE (CN)
TEL. 0173/979488

Bruno and Piercarlo Sperone's winery is growing, and so is the number of Glasses their wines succeed in winning. The '96 vintage certainly played its part by endowing the reds with extract and body, but our impression is that the style of these two likeable producers is maturing with every vintage. So both the major reds of the house have won Two full Glasses for the first time. The Barbera d'Alba has a highly concentrated ruby-garnet color with a youthfully purple rim. The composite bouquet reveals dark and intriguing tones: traces of blackberry, black cherry and violet are firmly interwoven over complex undertones of cocoa, rosemary and clove. The same abundance of sensations can be found on the rich, soft and well-articulated palate with a long, nobly tannic finish. The Roero, of an intense ruby color richly flecked with garnet, offers variety on the nose, with notes of red currant, roasting coffee, menthol and spice. The palate offers concentration and grip, thanks to the substantial body and decided tannins, softened by the warm finish. The Arneis Pierin di Soc just misses Two Glasses; it has a crystal-clear straw color shot through with green and a nose redolent of banana, apricot and chlorophyll. The palate is crisp, and the finish fruity. La Favorita, clean and inviting, has a simple fragrance and a smooth quaffability. The basic Arneis is undoubtedly a sound wine, with a rather simple nose; it is delicate and goes down very easily.

	Wine	Glasses	Price
●	Barbera d'Alba '96	ŸŸ	3
●	Roero '96	ŸŸ	4
○	Langhe Favorita '97	Ÿ	3
○	Roero Arneis Pierin di Soc '97	Ÿ	3
○	Roero Arneis '97		2
●	Roero '95	♀	4

CANALE (CN)

Filippo Gallino
Fraz. Valle del Pozzo, 63
12043 Canale (CN)
tel. 0173/98112

The Gallino family winery has confirmed its excellence. After its debut in the Guide last year, it has now taken advantage of the fine '96 vintage to place its two important reds, the Roero Superiore and the Barbera d'Alba Superiore, in the realm of Two Glasses. This year, in fact, the Barbera is their most successful wine, thanks to its concentration and to the individual character of its bouquet. It is dense garnet-ruby in color, with a youthful, distinctly purple tinge; it offers heady and captivating aromas of blackberry, steeped cherry and coffee custard, shot through with fascinating mineral and leather notes. The entry on the palate immediately reveals all the richness of the fruit and the vitality of the grape, giving way then to an increasing breadth that grows to a very long finish which fully confirms the choral, seductive character of the bouquet. The Roero Superiore, only slightly inferior, is garnet-colored with a slightly faded rim, and a nose which has undoubted breadth but is slightly dominated by the wood. Strong notes of vanilla and sweet spice are countered by varietal aromas of violet and wild berries. It is full-bodied, robust and harmonious in the mouth, with a finish rendered pleasingly austere by the vigor of the tannins. The Arneis is straw-colored with a green tinge and presents fruited and lemony aromas; on the palate it is light and crisp, with a fruity aftertaste. Mention should also be made of the Birbét, with its rose and geranium fragrance, and its sweet and agreeably effervescent palate. When we went to press, the Roero and the basic Barbera '97 were not yet ready, but we had a taste and they seemed indubitably correctly executed.

	Wine	Glasses	Price
●	Barbera d'Alba Sup. '96	🍷🍷	3*
●	Roero Sup. '96	🍷🍷	4
○	Roero Arneis '97	🍷	3
●	Birbét Dolce '97		3
●	Roero Sup. '95	🍸🍸	4
●	Barbera d'Alba Sup. '95	🍸	3

CANALE (CN)

Malvirà
Via S. Stefano Roero, 144
Loc. Case Sparse
12043 Canale (CN)
tel. 0173/978057 - 978145

As usual, Massimo and Roberto Damonte's wines have walked off with a remarkable number of Glasses. The Roero '96, made from grapes from the Renesio vineyard, has a fine deep garnet color with a slightly orange rim. The nose is rich and broad, with notes of red currant, raspberry and violet against a delicate toasty background. On the palate it is rich and soft, well supported by the stylish and vigorous tannins, which give a dryness to the long, intense finish. Among the Arneis we especially admired the Renesio, with its intense green-tinged straw color; the fresh, well-blended aromas of banana, peach, pineapple and fresh greens are followed by a silky and consistent palate, splendidly concluded by an intensely fruited finish. The Roero Arneis Saglietto, on the other hand, is more structured, and enriched by its stay in the wood. The Tre Uve (arneis, sauvignon and chardonnay are the three grapes involved) also wins two Glasses. The wine, of an intense straw hue with golden highlights, has fruity and floral aromas slightly dominated by the wood. On the palate it is well-structured and nicely underpinned by a tonic acidity that gives freshness to the finish. The straw-colored Arneis Trinità has a slightly forward nose with notes of apple and chamomile, and a substantial and succulent palate, with fruit to the fore on the finish. The San Guglielmo (a blend of barbera, nebbiolo and bonarda), offers density throughout: in its opaque garnet color, its bouquet of red berries with hints of vanilla, and its palate which a host of pronounced tannins renders pleasantly rustic. Both the fruity and unusually rich La Favorita and the elegant, complex Birbét are good. The Roero Superiore '96, which is not yet bottled, will be reviewed next year.

	Wine	Glasses	Price
●	Roero '96	🍷🍷	4
●	Langhe Rosso S. Guglielmo '96	🍷🍷	4
○	Langhe Bianco Tre Uve '96	🍷🍷	4
○	Roero Arneis Renesio '97	🍷🍷	3
○	Roero Arneis Saglietto '97	🍷🍷	4
○	Langhe Favorita '97	🍷	3
○	Roero Arneis Trinità '97	🍷	3
●	Birbét Dolce '97	🍷	3
●	Roero Sup. '90	🍸🍸🍸	5
●	Roero Sup. '93	🍸🍸🍸	4
●	Roero Renesio '95	🍸🍸	4
●	Roero Sup. '95	🍸🍸	4
●	Langhe Rosso S. Guglielmo '95	🍸	4

CANALE (CN)

MONCHIERO CARBONE

VIA S. STEFANO ROERO, 2
12043 CANALE (CN)
TEL. 0173/95568

Marco Monchiero is a central figure in Roero, partly because, as mayor of Canale, he is a person of high standing, but even more because, as a successful oenologist (he is considered amont the best in Italy), he makes his own significant contribution to the improvement of wine-making locally. His wines, balanced and modern in style, have themselves improved this year, especially the reds. The very interesting Roero Srü, its first time out, is garnet-colored with a dense purple rim. It offers tempting notes of blackberry, raspberry, licorice, spice and tobacco on the nose; the palate is substantial and concentrated, and the varietal vein of tannin gives austerity to the long finish. The Barbera MonBirone also gets Two Glasses: ruby-colored, tinged with garnet, it is redolent of raspberry, cherry, vanilla and pepper; in the mouth it seems full-bodied and harmonious, with a many-faceted and savory finish. The Tamardì, a blend of chardonnay and arneis, earns One full Glass; its color, almost golden, is deep, and it has a bouquet of banana, acacia blossom, apple, vanilla and coffee, heralding a succulent and crisp palate. It is still in search of perfect balance between wood and fruit, but it has come a long way since the '95. The Arneis, the classic white wine of Roero, also wins One Glass; it offers a broad and pleasing palate, with lots of fruit underpinned by a pleasing lemony note on the finish.

●	Barbera d'Alba MonBirone '96	🍷🍷	4
●	Roero Srü '96	🍷🍷	4
○	Langhe Bianco Tamardì '96	🍷	3
○	Roero Arneis '97	🍷	3*
●	Barbera d'Alba MonBirone '95	☐☐	3
●	Roero Sup. '95	☐☐	4
○	Langhe Bianco Tamardì '95	☐	3

CANALE (CN)

MARCO E ETTORE PORELLO

C.SO ALBA, 71
12043 CANALE (CN)
TEL. 0173/978080 - 979324

Marco Porello manages the family estate with dedication and competence, guaranteeing it a productive standard of impeccable quality. This year again the wines are more than satisfactory, beginning with the two reds that deserve One brimful Glass apiece, the Barbera and the Roero Bric Torretta. The first, of a garnet-tinged ruby hue, undoubtedly has a fine nose, but perhaps the new wood could be in slightly better balance with the fruit. The bouquet suggests dark cherry, violet, vanilla and clove; the palate is quite robust, with distinctive acidity and a savory finish. The Roero, which is slightly better, has a garnet-ruby color of medium intensity, and a very interesting nose, with aromas of cherry, blackberry, mint and pepper and faint mineral undertones. The palate is not very profound, but it is well-constructed, soft and supported by fine tannins. The again delightful Arneis Camestrì, with flickering green highlights on a straw-colored background, has a straightforward nose revealing aromas of very ripe white- and yellow-fleshed fruit and dried herbs. On the palate it is easy and direct, with a delicate and balanced structure. Finally, there is the Birbét Secco, with a vivid clear ruby color distinctly tinged with purple. The nose reveals aromas of fresh rose and raspberry, and on the palate it is smooth and pleasingly soft, with tannins just barely suggested on the delicately aromatic finish.

●	Barbera d'Alba Bric Torretta '96	🍷	3
●	Birbét Secco '97	🍷	3
○	Roero Arneis Vigneto Camestrì '97	🍷	3
●	Roero Bric Torretta '96	🍷	3

CANELLI (AT)

Giuseppe Contratto
Via G. B. Giuliani, 56
14053 Canelli (AT)
tel. 0141/823349

With the presentation of this year's wines, the Bocchino siblings have completed the renovation of their winery. After a magnificent modernization of the cellar, the opening of elegant tasting premises and the remodeling of the aging rooms, they have at last released wines produced under the direct supervision of the oenologist Giancarlo Scaglione. And what a difference! The Asti De Miranda Metodo Classico '96 was a shoo-in for Three Glasses. The entire panel was captivated by the inebriating perfumes of this magnificent Asti, ranging from apricot to vanilla, fig and sage, and by the dense, throbbing creaminess of the palate. Although it is an atypical Asti, it also fully expresses all the varietal characteristics of this noble wine, which ought to be snatched up a lot faster than it is. We hope that an absolute gem like the De Miranda will give a boost to Asti in general. The very successful Solus Ad '96 makes a triumphal entry onto the stage of the great Barberas; a dense ruby color, a powerful nose where the wood does not overcome the aromas of red fruit and spice, and a sweet and ripely fruited palate with a long, tannic and licorice-tinged finish. Their very interesting top "spumante", the Brut Riserva Giuseppe Contratto '94, is richly effervescent: the bouquet offers very delicate notes of toasted bread and white flowers; the heady palate has a vigorous vein of acidity. The Piemonte Chardonnay La Sabauda '96, entirely fermented in small new barrels, is so extraordinarily concentrated that it may well need further aging to express its full potential.

○	Asti De Miranda Metodo Classico '96	🍷🍷🍷	5
●	Barbera d'Asti Solus Ad '96	🍷🍷	5
○	Spumante Metodo Classico Brut Ris. Giuseppe Contratto '94	🍷🍷	4
○	Piemonte Chardonnay La Sabauda '96	🍷	4
○	Spumante Metodo Classico Brut Ris. Giuseppe Contratto '90	🍸🍸	5
●	Barbera d'Asti Solus Ad '95	🍸🍸	5
●	Barolo Cerequio Tenuta Secolo '90	🍸🍸	6
●	Barolo Cerequio Tenuta Secolo '93	🍸🍸	6
●	Barbera d'Asti Solus Ad '93	🍸	4

CANELLI (AT)

Luigi Coppo & Figli
Via Alba, 66
14053 Canelli (AT)
tel. 0141/823146

The Coppos once told us that in their winery nearly a thousand barriques are in use, which is no small number. It involves substantial investment and a well-formulated wine-making policy. The use of French wood in the Coppa winery is not just a slavish adherence to current fashion; it has a long history here and arises from the idea that to make great wine, they must find a method of maturing that can express the potential of the wine without burying it under extraneous tastes and aromas. They have been experimenting for years and have perfected their technique. Their prize wine, the Pomorosso '95, is brilliant ruby in color, with a fine vein of orange. On the nose it offers notes of red berries and ripe cherry with a hint of eucalyptus. The palate corresponds beautifully and is equally elegant; the wine makes a heady and silky entry and builds to a long, spicy, mouth-filling finish. The Monteriolo '96, a chardonnay fermented in new wood, needs a few years to show what it can do; we recall some delicious samplings of Monteriolos 8-10 years old. This vintage has a straw color with greenish gold highlights, and a still somewhat closed bouquet with notes of peach and toasted bread and a faint mineral nuance. On the palate it is warm, rich, sinewy and remarkably long. The excellent Riserva Coppo '90, which shows what experts they are with sparkling wines, has a light mousse with a fine, long bead. Fruited aromas emerge on the nose, with undertones of yeasts and acacia blossom. On the palate it is at first lightly sweet, but then expands into a lively, persistent and concentrated structure.

●	Barbera d'Asti Camp du Rouss '96	🍷🍷	4
●	Barbera d'Asti Pomorosso '95	🍷🍷	6
●	Mondaccione '95	🍷🍷	5
○	Brut Riserva Coppo '90	🍷🍷	5
○	Piemonte Chardonnay Monteriolo '96	🍷🍷	5
○	Piemonte Chardonnay Costebianche '97	🍷	3
●	Barbera d'Asti Pomorosso '90	🍸🍸🍸	5
●	Barbera d'Asti Pomorosso '94	🍸🍸	5
○	Piemonte Chardonnay Monteriolo '95	🍸🍸	5
○	Piero Coppo Brut Riserva del Fondatore '86	🍸🍸	6
●	Barbera d'Asti Pomorosso '93	🍸	5

CANELLI (AT)

Villa Giada
Reg. Ceirole, 4
14053 Canelli (AT)
tel. 0141/831100

The Villa Giada property consists of three farms in three different zones near Asti, all particularly highly prized for winegrowing. Villa Giada, the headquarters, is at Ceirole, a few kilometers from Canelli; here, like their neighbors, they grow mostly moscato, cortese and chardonnay. At the Cascina del Parroco di Calosso, the grapes are barbera, freisa, brachetto and the unusual gamba di pernice, a local varietal which is in the process of being rediscovered. The Cascina Dani, near Agliano, where the Faccio family also runs an appealing country inn, is dedicated primarily to barbera. We tasted a well-made, very faintly fizzy Barbera del Monferrato '97 called Vezzosa which is a good example of its type. The Gamba di Pernice '96 has an intense and brilliant ruby color; spice (clove and cinnamon) and green pepper dominate the nose, flanked, not altogether agreeably, by a wild, almost foxy, note which returns on the palate. Here the wine reveals atypical impact and a medium body. The Barbera d'Asti Superiore Bricco Dani '95, their star wine, has a dense garnet color; a nose that is less than perfect is counterbalanced by the palate: the structure is admirable, and the finish, although showing some acidity, is quite long. From the hills of Canelli comes the Moscato d'Asti '97, a wine rich in fruit on both nose and palate, where it is full-bodied and fat. The Barbera d'Asti Arturo and the Cortese del Monferrato Aura complete the list; both are pleasingly drinkable and good value for money.

	Wine	Glasses	Price
●	Barbera d'Asti Sup. Bricco Dani '95	🍷🍷	4
●	Barbera d'Asti Arturo '97	🍷	2*
●	Gamba di Pernice '96	🍷	3
○	Cortese dell'Alto M.to l'Aura '97	🍷	2*
○	Moscato d'Asti Ceirole '97	🍷	3
●	Barbera del M.to Vezzosa '97		2

CAREMA (TO)

Cantina dei Produttori
Nebbiolo di Carema
Via Nazionale, 28
10010 Carema (TO)
tel. 0125/811160

In this viticultural area near the Alps, characterized by steep slopes that make the landscape a dream and the cultivation of the vine a nightmare, they grow nebbiolo ("picoutener" in the local dialect) by the sweat of their brows (and lots of it), using the traditional low pergolas supported by large stones, which also serve to reflect a little extra warmth to help ripen these red grapes at an altitude (400-600 meters) where any little variation in the weather can be enough to frustrate the hopes of the winegrower. These are the conditions under which the 30 member growers of the cooperative provide the raw material for producing 70 thousand bottles a year. The Carema Carema, with its characteristic white label, is made from a selection of the best grapes, and is produced only in very good years. The '93 has a garnet ruby hue with an orange rim and a complex and pleasingly developed nose redolent of dried flowers, raspberry jam, blueberry and dried fig, with fascinating undertones of leather. On the palate the structure is good, the acidity only just perceptible and the tannin distinct but graceful, giving dryness to the corresponding and long finish. The standard Carema '92, which we reviewed last year and have now re-tasted, confirms the good impression it made a year ago. Of a slightly pale ruby color, it offers aromas, still delightfully fresh, with notes of raspberry, strawberry and minerals; on the palate it manages to be both balanced and succulent, with a fruited finish. Their range is completed by a rustic red and a fresh, undemanding rosé.

	Wine	Glasses	Price
●	Carema Carema '93	🍷🍷	3
●	Carema Carema '90	🍷🍷 (outline)	3
●	Carema '91	🍷 (outline)	3
●	Carema '92	🍷 (outline)	2

CASTAGNOLE LANZE (AT)

La Spinetta

Via Annunziata, 17
14054 Castagnole Lanze (AT)
tel. 0141/877396

In the early 1800s the grandfather of "our" Giuseppe Rivetti, who was nicknamed Pin and founded the family winery, emigrated to Argentina from Neive. Pin, having returned to Piedmont, happily brought his children up in Castagnole Lanze to be dedicated and expert winegrowers. But for these children Neive has always retained a special meaning, hence the satisfaction of their acquisition there of the Gallina vineyard. And from the Vigneto di Gallina in Neive come an extraordinarily elegant Barbaresco and a Barbera of exceptional personality. Both wines reveal viticultural skill (thanks to Bruno and Giovanna) and great ability in the up-to-date vinification and maturation processes, for which Carlo and Giorgio are responsible. The Barbaresco, clearly a real nebbiolo, is garnet-colored; its salient features (which disclose an austere, deep-seated harmony) are the mature floral notes of the bouquet and the silkiness of the tannins which are extremely well-integrated into the structure on the palate. The splendid Barbera shows vigor, richness and a streak of severity that helps it to draw out the display of its mouth-filling qualities. The '96 vintage has given us the best Pin ever: its density is already evident to the eye, and it grants us the delicate mineral note of the cabernet in the midst of the irresistible fruity and spicy development of the bouquet. On the palate it is authoritative and graceful; the continuity of the aromas is inebriating, as is the incisive dynamism of the palate. The Moscato is satisfying and voluptuous, while the Barbera Ca' di Pian is robust, vivid and long-lasting. The Chardonnay Lidia is progressive, warm and creamy.

	Wine	Rating	Price
●	Barbera d'Alba Vigneto Gallina '96	▼▼▼	4
●	Monferrato Rosso Pin '96	▼▼▼	5
●	Barbaresco Vigneto Gallina Vürsù '95	▼▼	6
●	Barbera d'Asti Ca' di Pian '97	▼▼	3*
○	Moscato d'Asti Bricco Quaglia '97	▼▼	3
○	Piemonte Chardonnay Lidia '97	▼▼	5
●	Monferrato Rosso Pin '94	▽▽▽	5
●	Monferrato Rosso Pin '95	▽▽▽	5
●	Pin '90	▽▽▽	6
●	Pin '93	▽▽▽	5
○	Piemonte Chardonnay Lidia '96	▽▽	4

CASTAGNOLE M.TO (AT)

Marco Maria Crivelli

Via Vittorio Emanuele, 16
14030 Castagnole M.to (AT)
tel. 0141/292533 - 292357

"If someone at Castagnole Monferrato offers you Ruché, it's a sign that he likes you." This message can be found on a billboard at the entrance to the village, and it demonstrates the affection the inhabitants feel for this singular wine, little known outside the zone, which certainly should be further developed, perhaps with a change here and there in the denomination regulations. Marco Maria Crivelli is the leading local producer and the one who shows the greatest care in the vineyard and in the cellar, which he runs in the traditional manner. Marco owns about five hectares of vines, and he also works another which he leases, with 60-year-old vines: barbera, grignolino and ruché are the three varieties of grape cultivated. The wine which pleased us most this year was again the Ruché: ruby-red with a garnet rim, it vaunts inviting aromas of spice, flowers and fruit. The structure, backed up by fresh acidity, is good. The Barbera d'Asti '97, sampled shortly after bottling, showed good body and characteristic prune and cherry fragrances despite the unpropritious tasting time. The Grignolino and the Barbera Agiuiusa Vivace are both worthy of mention and especially suited to being drunk cool with a platter of good salami. The former has lovely floral aromas, and the latter a refreshing acidity.

	Wine	Rating	Price
●	Ruché di Castagnole Monferrato '97	▼▼	4
●	Barbera d'Asti '97	▼	3
●	Barbera del M.to Agiuiusa Vivace '97		2
●	Grignolino d'Asti '97		3
●	Ruché di Castagnole Monferrato '96	▽▽	4

CASTEL BOGLIONE (AT)

ARALDICA VINI PIEMONTESI
VIA ALBERA, 19
14040 CASTEL BOGLIONE (AT)
TEL. 0141/762354

Araldica is the result of the merger in 1990 of three cooperatives: the Antica Contea di Castelvero, the Cantina di Mombaruzzo and the Cantina di Ricaldone. The new label represents the best wine from these three wineries. The selection criteria are severe, beginning with the grapes brought by member growers; the three cellars and the headquarters at Castel Boglione, where the bottling takes place, have been the object of substantial investment. Daniela Pesce, Claudio Manera and Paolo Pronzato, under the supervision of the New Zealand oenologist Matt Thompson, direct operations in the cellars, while Luigi Bertini is in charge of the administration. All of the many wines presented are good. The Barbera Superiore Alasia (their top range) has a dense color, and aromas of coffee, vanilla and cherry; on the palate it shows good body, a robust character and a corresponding finish. The Moscato Alasia, which elegantly expresses its varietal characteristics, displays aromas of peach, lemon and sage, and a rich, almost fat, palate, balanced nicely by a decided effervescence. And now the two Chardonnays, both admirable: the Roleto has a good structure slightly dominated, however, by the wood, and the '97 is simpler but fully satisfying. The Muscat Sec would make a delightful aperitif, fresh and cheering. The Arneis Sorilaria offers aromas of ripe fruit and chamomile; the palate is fairly substantial and the finish intense. Finally, we were interested by the forward balsamic aromas of the Barbera Vigenti Croja, which displays a tonic and succulent palate.

●	Barbera d'Asti Sup. Alasia '95	🍷	2*
●	Barbera d'Asti Vigneti Croja '93	🍷	2*
○	Moscato d'Asti Alasia '97	🍷	2*
○	Muscat Sec '97	🍷	2*
○	Piemonte Chardonnay Alasia '97	🍷	1*
○	Piemonte Chardonnay Roleto Alasia '96	🍷	2
○	Roero Arneis Sorilaria '97	🍷	3

CASTEL BOGLIONE (AT)

CASCINA GARITINA
VIA GIANOLA, 20
14040 CASTEL BOGLIONE (AT)
TEL. 0141/762162

Cascina Garitina, in the Monferrato area between Nizza and Acqui, is a family estate built up over the years. Starting at the beginning of this century, generation after generation of Morinos have gradually assembled 13 hectares of vineyard, the core of which produces barbera. Circling it are dolcetto and brachetto, from which they will start to make wine next year, and two international varietals (cabernet sauvignon and pinot noir). Giovanni and Pasquale, grandfather and father, are still active, but it is now the young Gianluca, with a diploma in oenology from Alba, who is bringing a new energy to the estate. The modernization of the cellar (a brand new one will soon be ready), of the rooms for aging and the reception rooms for customers was followed by an improvement in the vinification techniques. Today the winery offers a range of good wines, clean, very drinkable and moderately priced. We begin with the Dolcetto d'Asti, a typical local red, of which the Vigneto Capasso '97 is an agreeable example; it has a distinctive spicy note on the nose and makes its presence felt in the mouth. The Barbera Bricco Garitta '96, produced in stainless steel, is a red to drink straight through a meal. Its color is a brilliant ruby of medium intensity; red berries emerge on the nose, and the palate is well balanced between the roundness of the fruit and the pleasing vein of acidity. The Morinaccio Barbera di Monferrato Vivace '97 is what one would hope for from a type of wine bred for freshness and a light sparkle. Lastly, their most important wine, the barrique-aged Barbera d'Asti Superiore Neuvsent '95, has a personality of its own, but if it is to advance significantly it will need more body and fruit.

●	Barbera d'Asti Sup. Neuvsent '95	🍷	4
●	Barbera d'Asti Bricco Garitta '96	🍷	3*
●	Dolcetto d'Asti Vigneto Campasso '97	🍷	3
●	Barbera del M.to Il Morinaccio '97		2

CASTELLINALDO (CN)

TEO COSTA

VIA SALVARIO, 1
12050 CASTELLINALDO (CN)
TEL. 0173/213066

Roberto Costa (one of the founders of a winegrowers' consortium called the Associazione dei Vinaioli di Castellinaldo, which, among other things, created the sub-zone of Castellinaldo for Barbera d'Alba), and his brother Marco have presented a range of very good wines this year. The Castellinaldo Barbera d'Alba stands out, of course, and has easily won Two Glasses. Of a concentrated ruby-to-garnet hue, it has a profound bouquet which gradually reveals notes of ripe cherry, coffee and toasty oak. On the palate it is full and broad, with tonic acidity and an intense finish, rendered dry by a decided vein of tannin. The excellent Arneis Ajnaldi Bianc, with a straw color of medium intensity, has subtle aromas of peach, vanilla and butter shot through with fascinating suggestions of overripeness; on the palate it is immediately rich and soft, generally well-articulated and intense and fruity on the finish. The other Arneis, the Serramiana, is less successful: its clear straw hue with lively green highlights precedes a fruity nose slightly unbalanced by imperfectly integrated vegetal tones. The situation improves on the palate, however, which is full-bodied and succulent. The Roero Batajot, of a fairly intense garnet-tinged ruby color, presents aromas of violet, vanilla and mint, and a moderately substantial palate, marked by lively but not unpleasant tannins that lend austerity to the finish.

	Wine	Glasses	Price
●	Castellinaldo Barbera d'Alba '96	🍷🍷	4
●	Roero Sup. Vigneto Batajot '96	🍷	3
○	Roero Arneis Ajnaldi Bianc '97	🍷	4
○	Roero Arneis Serramiana '97		3
●	Castellinaldo Barbera d'Alba '95	ϒϒ	4

CASTELLINALDO (CN)

EMILIO MARSAGLIA

VIA MUSSONE, 2
12050 CASTELLINALDO (CN)
TEL. 0173/213048

Among the wines presented this year by Marina and Emilio Marsaglia, the two versions of Barbera d'Alba struck us favorably, and easily won One Glass apiece. The Castellinaldo Barbera, a slightly pale ruby garnet in color, has a nose of generous breadth, with notes of violet, vanilla, red berries and licorice. The palate, of good substance, somewhat sinewy and dry, has a long finish a little dominated by the wood. The standard Barbera, of a fairly intense garnet ruby hue with a faintly faded rim, is redolent of cherry, red currant and mint. On the palate it is full-bodied, with energetic acidity and tannins which do not discompose a finish that is more harmonious and balanced than the Castellinaldo's. The good Arneis San Servasio has a light, clear straw hue and a nose in which delicacy and finesse prevail (traces of peach, flowers and exotic fruit). The palate offers crispness, body and a pleasantly fruity finish.

	Wine	Glasses	Price
○	Roero Arneis S. Servasio '97	🍷	3
●	Barbera d'Alba '96	🍷	3
●	Castellinaldo Barbera d'Alba '96	🍷	4
●	Roero Sup. '96	ϒϒ	3
●	Castellinaldo Barbera d'Alba '95	ϒ	4

CASTELLINALDO (CN)

STEFANINO MORRA
VIA CASTAGNITO, 22
12050 CASTELLINALDO (CN)
TEL. 0173/213489

This small Castellinaldo winery (some 55 thousand bottles a year, from just over six hectares under vine), well managed by its owner, Stefanino Morra, is making its first appearance in the Guide. Morra has the advantage of a spacious and well-equipped winery, and of excellent vineyards, as demonstrated, for example, by the very full Two Glasses won by the Castellinaldo Barbera d'Alba '96. The wine, a concentrated ruby to garnet in color with a dense purple rim, offers vivid aromas of violet, blackberry and red currant, with undertones of custard, toasty oak and resin. On the palate the concentration harmonizes well with the broad body. The less powerful Barbera d'Alba, with its dense, deep color, displays notes of black currant, sour cherry, menthol and clove on the nose, enhanced by fascinating hints of earth. The palate is rich and ample, with a touch of sinew characteristic of the grape. The Roero Superiore has an admirable structure; its bouquet offers notes of red fruit, pepper, violet and vanilla; the soft and broad palate is underpinned by mature tannins. The good Arneis San Pietro, aged in large casks, has an intense straw color, and aromas of flowers, honey, fruit and aromatic herbs; the palate, rich and confident, is silky and soft as it develops to a succulent and slightly bitter finish. Finally, the basic Arneis is perfectly satisfactory, fruitily fragrant and easy to drink.

	Wine	Glasses	Price
●	Castellinaldo Barbera d'Alba '96	🍷🍷	5
●	Roero Sup. '96	🍷🍷	4
●	Barbera d'Alba '96	🍷	3
○	Roero Arneis Vigneto S. Pietro '97	🍷	4
○	Roero Arneis '97	🍷	3

CASTELLO DI ANNONE (AT)

VIARENGO G. L. & FIGLIO
VIA ROMA, 88
14034 CASTELLO DI ANNONE (AT)
TEL. 0141/401131

Viarengo is reacquiring a distinctive character. The two years of transition between the Dania management and the present one of Giancarlo Massolo have served to prepare the way for a new policy of quality, backed up by the consultancy of Giancarlo Scaglione. The leasing of other vineyards to extend the selection of grapes, the technological improvement of the cellar (rebuilt after the floods of '94) and the use of barriques for maturing the most ambitious wines, are the main features of the general restructuring, which is also intended to place Barbera and Grignolino in the foreground. It is the latter that brings the first positive signs from '97. Don't let the pale color deceive you: the bouquet has a fascinating variety, and on the palate there is a light but by no means insignificant body. The Barbera Vivace, a fine example of its type, has a compellingly heady fragrance with a promising fruitiness; on the palate it is brilliant and impeccable in its straightforwardness. The real surprise is the basic '97 version: intense in color, this Barbera is rich, meaty and enticingly well-defined in bouquet; with its fine structure on the palate it seems to promise years of positive evolution, although you can drink it with pleasure right now. The energy of the Barbera Il Falé '96 has been kept within bounds by careful maturing in new barriques, which have taken the edge off its sharpness, giving it a well-articulated nose. The strength of the color is in line with the bouquet of ripe fruit; the palate opens up gradually, leading to a genuinely pleasing finish.

	Wine	Glasses	Price
●	Barbera d'Asti '97	🍷🍷	3*
●	Barbera d'Asti Il Falé '96	🍷🍷	4
●	Barbera del M.to Vivace '97	🍷	3
●	Grignolino d'Asti Della Tagliata '97	🍷	3
●	Barbera d'Asti Sup. Il Falé '93	🍷🍷 (white)	4
●	Barbera d'Asti Sup. Il Falé '95	🍷🍷 (white)	4
●	Barbera d'Asti Sup. Il Falé Ris. '90	🍷🍷 (white)	4
●	Barbera d'Asti Bricco Morra '96	🍷 (white)	3

CASTELLO DI ANNONE (AT)

VILLA FIORITA
VIA CASE SPARSE, 2
14034 CASTELLO DI ANNONE (AT)
TEL. 0141/401231

Villa Fiorita, which has benefited from huge investments by the Rondolino family, is a lovely estate near Castello di Annone. It consists of 18 hectares under vine, including such traditional grapes as barbera, grignolino, bracchetto and freisa, side by side with fashionable imported varieties like chardonnay, sauvignon, pinot noir and gamay. The up-to-the-minute cellar is in the hands of the highly esteemed oenologist Giancarlo Scaglione. Winery strategy is to produce a series of modern wines, concentrating on elegance and drinkability, in hopes of achieving that "international taste" which has now become the order of the day for many wine-makers. On the basis of this year's tastings, they seem to have accomplished their aim particularly with the Giorgione '94, a barrique-aged Barbera d'Asti Superiore which is notable for its quite intense color, fruity bouquet enhanced by the well-dosed wood, and good impact on the fairly persistent palate. The other wines are correctly executed and blameless, but never exciting. The Chardonnay Tavole di Villa Fiorita '97, of a not very intense straw color and a subtly varietal nose, does not offer much structure. The Pian delle Querce '97, a Grignolino d'Asti, has a fairly characteristic nose (notes of geranium and spice), an already over-evolved color tending to orange and good body. From the '96 vintage they have presented the Barbera d'Asti, of a faded ruby hue, faint in both aromas and structure, and the Maniero, a blend of barbera and pinot noir.

●	Barbera d'Asti Sup. Il Giorgione '94	🍷	4
●	Maniero '96	🍷	4
●	Grignolino d'Asti Pian delle Querce '97		3
●	Barbera d'Asti '96		3
○	Piemonte Chardonnay Le Tavole di Villa Fiorita '97		3

CASTELNUOVO DON BOSCO (AT)

CASCINA GILLI
VIA NEVISSANO, 36
14022 CASTELNUOVO DON BOSCO (AT)
TEL. 011/9876984

The wines presented by Gianni Vergnano are, as usual, very good, a proof of the attentive and efficacious care lavished on the substantial production of this winery (more than 100 thousand bottles a year) by Gianni and his colleagues (Carlo Feyles and Gianni Matteis). The Malvasia di Castelnuovo Don Bosco, the Gilli standard-bearer, is particularly admirable for the finesse of its varietal aromas, and the balance on the palate, which gives it grace and charm. It has a quite intense ruby hue with a hint of orange and a well-integrated and delicate nose redolent of rose, rhubarb and pear. On the palate it is silky, smooth and sweet with moderation, leading to a finish of rose petals on which a sober tannic vein emerges. The Freisa Vigna del Forno, of a ruby color lightly tinged with garnet, offers aromas of wild berries with a faint vegetal undertone. It displays substance and balance on the palate and a pleasingly dry finish. The less convincing Freisa Vivace lacks definition on the nose, but then provides an invitingly rustic and agreeable quaffability. The Barbera Vigna delle More (its first time out), garnet-ruby in color with a dense rim, has a bouquet of red and black berries, and a well-structured palate, characterized by energy and a lingering finish. The Chardonnay '97, smooth and silky in the mouth, has a clean fragrance with hints of quince, apricot and honey. To round off the list they offer a moderately stylish Bonarda with a distinct tannic presence.

●	Malvasia di Castelnuovo Don Bosco '97	🍷🍷	3
●	Barbera d'Asti Vigna delle More '97	🍷	3
●	Freisa d'Asti Vigna del Forno '97	🍷	3
●	Piemonte Bonarda '97	🍷	3
○	Piemonte Chardonnay '97	🍷	2
●	Freisa d'Asti Vivace '97		2

CASTIGLIONE FALLETTO (CN)

AZELIA
VIA ALBA-BAROLO, 53
12060 CASTIGLIONE FALLETTO (CN)
TEL. 0173/62859

Luigi and Lorella Scavino have good reason to be satisfied with the wines presented this year: their only defect is their vintage; in the cellar, certainly, everything that sensitive intelligence and painstaking care can do has been done for them. The year in question, 1994, was not at all bad in the summer, but during the harvest it seemed never to stop raining. This probably means that if the vines are well-cared for and not overloaded, the grapes gathered in for pressing remain in fairly good condition. In the cellar, rotary fermenters help to extract more substance in less time without having to resort to long maceration which certainly does not make for softness in the wine. This explains why the Barolo Bricco Fiasco '94 is among the best examples of this vintage that we have tasted: made from grapes selected during the harvest, and from a selection among barriques in the cellar, the wine has a fine deep ruby-red tone. The elegant bouquet is dominated by spicy aromas of vanilla and licorice. On the palate it is intense, warm and well-balanced. Its younger brother, on the other hand, has a distinctly garnet red color and a bouquet of dried herbs (mint). Less rich on the palate, it displays unintegrated tannins that stand out on the finish. The Barbera Bricco Punta '96, with admirably ripe fruit (cherry jam), spreads out beautifully on the palate thanks to the alcohol-derived softness, which prevails over the acidity, and also as a result of the worthwhile aging in new oak. The Dolcetto Oriolo '97 di Montelupo Albese, dark in color and young in fragrance, is most notable for its ready quaffability.

Wine	Rating	
● Barbera d'Alba Vigneto Punta '96	TT	4
● Barolo Bricco Fiasco '94	TT	5
● Barolo '94	T	5
● Dolcetto d'Alba Bricco Oriolo '97	T	3
● Barolo '91	YYY	5
● Barolo Bricco Fiasco '93	YYY	5
● Barbera d'Alba Vigneto Punta '93	YY	4
● Barolo '92	YY	5
● Barolo '93	YY*	5
● Barolo Bricco Fiasco Ris. '90	YY	6
● Barolo Bricco Fiasco '90	Y	5

CASTIGLIONE FALLETTO (CN)

CASCINA BONGIOVANNI
VIA ALBA-BAROLO, 4
12060 CASTIGLIONE FALLETTO (CN)
TEL. 0173/262184

In the cellar of one of the smallest wineries of the zone (barely 13 thousand bottles a year) there are wines laid down which are going to have people talking about David Mozzone in a few years. He got his diploma from the oenological institute in Alba and, after eight years of experience in two well-known wineries, and with the encouragement of several very good producers, he decided to look after his aunt's vineyards. The three hectares under vine are almost entirely located in Pernanno near Castiglione Falletto, a "sorì" (excellent vineyard site) with a southeastern exposure adjacent to Bricco Boschis. In its second year of production, Cascina Bongiovanni is releasing a new wine named Falletto (1,300 bottles from the '96 vintage), a blend of 50% barbera and equal parts of nebbiolo and cabernet sauvignon. It displays a good full ruby color tinged with purple and an elegant and delicate bouquet of red fruit (cherry) mixed with oak-derived vanilla. The palate reveals the strength of the nebbiolo grape in these parts, with distinctive and austere tannins, leading to a very long finish pervaded by toasty aromas. The Falletto has made a fine debut, although the name will have to be changed to avoid confusion with the celebrated vineyard in Serralunga. The Barolo '94, which is more or less average for this vintage, has a garnet hue; the aromas of raspberry and strawberry are already developed. On the palate the overwhelming force of the tannins really should have had the fruit of a better vintage to stand up to it.

Wine	Rating	
● Langhe Rosso Falletto '96	TT	5
● Barolo '94	T	5
● Barolo '93	YY	4

CASTIGLIONE FALLETTO (CN)

BROVIA

VIA ALBA-BAROLO, 54
12060 CASTIGLIONE FALLETTO (CN)
TEL. 0173/62852

Finally, after a six-year wait, the Solatìo makes its reappearance. Perhaps not everyone knows that this extraordinary wine is produced only when Mother Nature permits, which she graciously did with the vintages of '85, '88 and '90. The dolcetto grapes, which come from vineyards in Serralunga, are left to overripen on the vine until they reach a sugar content normally unthinkable for this variety. After careful selection of the bunches, the vinification proceeds with lengthy maceration (about 20 days), comparable only to those used with nebbiolo. After over a year of aging, half in barriques (from 1996 onward) and half in steel, and a further two years in the bottle, it is finally released, but there are not more than about 2,600 bottles of it. The Solatìo '96 has a very dark ruby color tinged with purple; the broad, heady nose offers aromas of fruit preserved in spirit and licorice as well as a hint of oak; on the palate it is powerful and velvety, with tightly knit, smooth tannins that lead to a long finish. The excellent Dolcetto '97 is simpler than the Solatìo, but equally well made. The color is an intense lively purple, and its fragrance is fresh and heady; on the palate it offers a satisfying balance, smooth tannins and a soft licorice finish. The Barbera '96, with its delicate aromas of violet, is full-bodied, and has acquired charm from an intelligent use of wood. The last in the series is the Freisa '96, characterized by attractive varietal aromas and a pleasing, slightly bitter finish, dry and firm. The Brovias did not bottle their '94 Barolo because it didn't meet their standards. The Nebbiolo d'Alba '96 and the Barbaresco '95 are not yet ready for tasting.

Wine	Glasses	Price
● Dolcetto d'Alba Ciabòt del Re '97	**YY**	3
● Dolcetto d'Alba Solatìo '96	**YY**	4
● Barbera d'Alba Sorì del Drago '96	**Y**	4
● Langhe Freisa La Villerina '96	**Y**	4
● Barolo Monprivato '90	YYY	6
● Barolo Garblèt Sué '91	YY	5
● Barolo Monprivato '89	YY	6
● Barolo Rocche dei Brovia '89	YY	6
● Barolo Rocche dei Brovia '90	YY	6
● Barolo Rocche dei Brovia '91	YY	6
● Barolo Rocche dei Brovia '93	YY	5
● Barolo Villero '93	YY	5

CASTIGLIONE FALLETTO (CN)

F.LLI CAVALLOTTO - BRICCO BOSCHIS

VIA ALBA-MONFORTE
12060 CASTIGLIONE FALLETTO (CN)
TEL. 0173/62814

The Bricco Boschis wine estate owned by the Cavallotto siblings extends for about 23 hectares, almost entirely within the vineyard of the same name; the remaining small part is in the Vignolo vineyard, a little further down towards Garbelletto. The vines are mostly nebbiolo, followed by dolcetto, grignolino, barbera and (in small quantities) freisa, pinot noir and chardonnay. These last two grapes go into the only whites in their vast range of wines. The Cavallottos' policy, based on respect for tradition, requires slow-maturing red wines, produced by slow maceration and long periods of aging in their fine large barrels of Slavonian oak. The wine that most impressed us was the Barolo Riserva Vigna San Giuseppe '93: of a moderately intense garnet color, it offers a broad, heady bouquet of hay, spice and leather. On the palate it is warm and powerful, with tannins that need to soften a little more. Two other successful wines are the Dolcetto Vigna Melera '96 (notable aromas of raspberry, rose and incense, which carry through onto the palate) and the Freisa '97, with an aromatic and fruity (cherry) fragrance, and well-balanced on the palate but not particularly long-lasting. On the other hand, even after repeated tastings over the year, the Barolo '94 seems a little under par, reflecting a far from successful vintage; it lacks the character that used to distinguish it. And another disappointment was the Barbera Vigna del Cuculo '96, with its excessively soft, nearly sweet palate, pervaded by an unusual toastiness which has not yet been properly integrated.

Wine	Glasses	Price
● Barolo Vigna S. Giuseppe Ris. '93	**YY**	5
● Barolo Bricco Boschis '94	**Y**	5
● Dolcetto d'Alba Vigna Melera '96	**Y**	3
● Langhe Freisa Bricco Boschis '97	**Y**	3
● Barbera d'Alba Vigna del Cuculo '96		4
● Barolo Vigna S. Giuseppe Ris. '89	YYY	6
● Barolo Colle Sud-Ovest Ris. '90	YY	6
● Barolo Colle Sud-Ovest Ris. '91	YY	5
● Barolo Vigna S. Giuseppe Ris. '90	YY	6
● Barolo Vigna Sud-Ovest Ris. '89	YY	6
● Barolo Vignolo Ris. '89	YY	6
● Barolo Vignolo Ris. '90	YY	6

CASTIGLIONE FALLETTO (CN)

★ Paolo Scavino

Via Alba-Barolo, 59
12060 Castiglione Falletto (CN)
tel. 0173/62850

Attention to details and diligent, almost excessive, care have made it possible for Enrico Scavino to develop into one of the best wine-makers in the whole area (and well beyond it). The splendid performance of the Barolo Rocche '93 has convinced us of his capacity to nurture a great wine, bringing out its potential over a period of time. And the '94 Barolos of Scavino have shown to the highest degree his qualities as a rigorous and fanatical observer of everything that concerns grapes and wine. The Cannubi draws an elegance and suppleness from the lesser vintages that make it an essential primer for those who are learning to love Barolo; the fruity sweetness of the bouquet and the grace of the flavor are the salient aspects of a harmony waiting to be enjoyed. In the Bric dël Fiasc, the tannins never play hooky, but the structure is so broad and meaty that it keeps them in their place. The wine, though not like the great vintages, is among the '94s with the best potential for development. Returning to the Rocche '93, a mature, vibrant garnet in color, its complex bouquet is at its peak at the moment; the youthful fruit is acquiring a voluptuous softness, while the floral and spicy elements in the bouquet are emerging with increasing broadness and charm. The palate, which opens out evenly, finishes its development and gives you the impression whenever you drink it that you have chosen just the right moment. The Barbera d'Alba gives its usual good performance, even though it is with the '96 that it will be able to show off its best qualities. The Dolcetto, on the other hand, has returned to the excellent level of several years ago, thanks to the density and depth which characterize both nose and palate.

Wine	Glasses	Price
● Barolo Rocche dell'Annunziata '93	▼▼▼	6
● Barolo Bric dël Fiasc '94	▼▼	6
● Barolo Cannubi '94	▼▼	6
● Dolcetto d'Alba Vigneto dël Fiasc '97	▼▼	3
● Barbera d'Alba Affinato in Carati '95	▼	5
● Barolo '94	▼	5
● Barolo Bric dël Fiasc '90	▽▽▽	6
● Barolo Bric dël Fiasc '93	▽▽▽	6
● Barolo Cannubi '91	▽▽▽	6
● Barolo Cannubi '92	▽▽▽	5
● Barolo Rocche dell'Annunziata Ris. '90	▽▽▽	6
● Barolo Cannubi '93	▽▽	6

CASTIGLIONE FALLETTO (CN)

Terre del Barolo

Via Alba-Barolo, 5
12060 Castiglione Falletto (CN)
tel. 0173/262053

The wines of a cooperative winery always offer valuable general information: they give us, for example, a very clear idea of the difference between vintages. In fact, in tasting the numerous Dolcettos of the Terre del Barolo, it is easy to understand how the hot summer of '97 influenced their bouquets, and their relative vitality, in contrast to the more balanced '96 vintage, which offered wines of greater freshness. This particular sensation of overripeness in the '97s (noticeable in both the Dolcetto d'Alba and the Dolcetto di Diano) is especially intense in the Castello and Cascinotto versions. Naturally, in addition to these "jammy" sensations there is a warmth on the palate, which brings out the rustic quality of this Langhe grape, which is increasingly viewed as a vehicle of youthful grapiness. Continuing with the subject of different vintages, '96 was definitely a more successful year for Barberas than the more difficult '95. The Sorì della Roncaglia is interestingly concentrated from the color onwards; the bouquet opens slowly, unlike the flavor, which has an immediate appeal. The Barbera Roere has complex aromas of toastiness, spice and black berries; the development on the palate is well-articulated and full-bodied. The very direct Nebbiolo d'Alba di Grinzane is an example of an easy wine with an added touch of zest. The well-made Pinot Nero is harmonious and full.

Wine	Glasses	Price
● Barbera d'Alba Sorì della Roncaglia '96	▼▼	3*
● Barbera d'Alba Vigneti Roere '96	▼	3
● Diano d'Alba Bricco del Ciabot '97	▼	3*
● Diano d'Alba Cascinotto '97	▼	3
● Dolcetto d'Alba '97	▼	3
● Langhe Rosso '96	▼	3
● Nebbiolo d'Alba Grinzane '96	▼	4
● Dolcetto d'Alba Castello '97		3
● Barolo Baudana Ris. '90	▽	5
● Barolo Castello Ris. '90	▽	5
● Barolo Castiglione Falletto '93	▽	4
● Barolo Codana Ris. '90	▽	5

CASTIGLIONE FALLETTO (CN)

VIETTI
P.ZZA VITTORIO VENETO, 5
12060 CASTIGLIONE FALLETTO (CN)
TEL. 0173/62825

Vietti belongs to the limited number of wineries dedicated to Barolo that have grappled successfully with the difficulties of the 1994 vintage. Both the wines presented this year are admirable, and clearly show the differences between the Lazzarito and Brunate vineyards. They were both produced in the traditional way, with medium-long maceration, and aging in large barrels. This has particularly affected the expression of their aromas: notes of licorice, cocoa and jam characterize a dry and profound development; however, while the Lazzarito expresses all this immediately, the Brunate takes its time. In the first, the palate is authoritative and solid; the granite-like density of the tannins is made supple by the warmth and softness, and the finish is long and pleasing. The Barolo delle Brunate is less direct; you perceive its richness only gradually, but the thorough development on the palate fully convinced us. The success of the nebbiolo-based wines is underlined by the Barbaresco Masseria '95, not a champion of intensity but an excellent model of balance and straightforwardness. The Dolcetto d'Alba Tre Vigne '97, which is their standard version, is correct, and pleasantly heady. The Dolcetto Lazzarito, which was excellent last year, is still fairly good, while the Barbera d'Alba Scarrone, which is better than ever, has acquired vigor and density from the '96 vintage, putting aside the overly rustic quality which diminished it in recent years. The Arneis '97 is stylish, concise and harmonious.

●	Barbaresco Masseria '95	🍷🍷	6
●	Barbera d'Alba Scarrone '96	🍷🍷	4
●	Barolo Brunate '94	🍷🍷	6
●	Barolo Lazzarito '94	🍷🍷	6
●	Dolcetto d'Alba Lazzarito '96	🍷	4
○	Roero Arneis '97	🍷	4
●	Dolcetto d'Alba Tre Vigne '97		3
●	Barolo Rocche di Castiglione '85	🍸🍸🍸	6
●	Barolo Rocche di Castiglione '88	🍸🍸🍸	6
●	Barolo Villero '82	🍸🍸🍸	6
●	Barolo Brunate '93	🍸🍸	6
●	Barolo Castiglione '93	🍸🍸	6
●	Barolo Lazzarito '93	🍸🍸	6
●	Barolo Villero Ris. '90	🍸🍸	6
●	Barbera d'Alba Scarrone '95	🍸	4

CASTIGLIONE TINELLA (CN)

CAUDRINA - ROMANO DOGLIOTTI
STRADA CAUDRINA, 20
12053 CASTIGLIONE TINELLA (CN)
TEL. 0141/855126

Some changes are taking place here. The first, essentially a bureaucratic matter, has modified the estate name (Caudrina di Romano Dogliotti); the second, far more important, involves the construction of a new cellar. The Dogliottis (Romano's son Alessandro is a young oenologist) concentrate their efforts on 16 hectares of property, all under vine, on steep, rugged hills that require great dedication and stamina. With an innate loyalty to tradition, Romano produces about 150 thousand bottles a year which, thanks to the abilities of this real poet of the vineyards, regularly adorn the best tables of the world. Three wines were presented, but only one grape: moscato. In our last tastings they all did very well. The Galeisa offers the intense and unmistakable aroma of its grape: you find it on the nose (enriched by balsamic notes and hints of citrus fruit and roses), and on the palate (soft, balanced and almost chewable); the wine is fresh, genuine and never cloying. The other cru, brilliantly limpid in its light straw color, and enlivened by its light perlage, offers delicate aromas of musk and rose; the satisfying taste is well-supported by the pleasing note of citrus. The Asti, with its tiny, long-lasting bubbles, is just below the other two; it has a good nose and corresponding taste, but is slightly diminished by a rather too noticeable bitterness.

○	Moscato d'Asti La Caudrina '97	🍷🍷	3*
○	Moscato d'Asti La Galeisa '97	🍷🍷	3*
○	Asti La Selvatica '97	🍷	4

CASTIGLIONE TINELLA (CN)

ICARDI

VIA BALBI, 30
LOC. S. LAZZARO
12053 CASTIGLIONE TINELLA (CN)
TEL. 0141/855159

Claudio Icardi certainly does not lack commitment and a will to achieve: he acts as consultant for various Italian wineries, keeps an eye on the major work of extension and remodeling of his cellars (together with various connected farm buildings) and, lest we forget, produces a wide range of wines in bottles decorated with unusual labels designed by his wife Ornella. It may be because of this variety of activities, however, that his range of wines is somewhat uneven in quality. Some are very good indeed, others satisfactory, and others again are in need of improvement. They are all aged in new barriques, which guarantee softness and introduces characteristic notes of vanilla. The Pafoj and the Barbera Surì di Mù are very good: the former is a nebbiolo with a broad nose and good structure, while the latter masters the exuberance of this variety, achieving elegance and softness. The Nebbiolo Surìsjvan, with its fruity and flowery bouquet, the Bricco del Sole (barbera and cabernet), which once again shows a happy marriage between these two grapes, the Chardonnay Surìssara, somewhat forward, with notes of overripe fruit, and the heady and fragrant Dolcetto are all only slightly inferior. On the other hand we did not find either the Moscato La Rosa Selvatica, sweet and slightly cloying, or the Pinot Nero Nej, too light on nose and palate, completely convincing.

	Wine	Glasses	Price
●	Barbera d'Alba Surì di Mù '96	🍷🍷	4
●	Langhe Rosso Pafoj '97	🍷🍷	6
●	Dolcetto d'Alba Rousori '97	🍷	3
●	Langhe Nebbiolo Surì sjvan '96	🍷	4
●	Monferrato Rosso Cascina Bricco del Sole '96	🍷	5
●	Langhe Rosso Nej '96		5
○	Piemonte Chardonnay Surì ssara '97	🍷	4
○	Moscato d'Asti La Rosa Selvatica '97		3

CASTIGLIONE TINELLA (CN)

LA MORANDINA

VIA MORANDINI, 11
12053 CASTIGLIONE TINELLA (CN)
TEL. 0141/855261

This estate, with its 15 stunningly situated hectares carpeted with vines, cultivates moscato, barbera and chardonnay. In recent years, experiments have been made with a little plot of land planted with viognier, and it is not impossible that this will produce a new wine next year. But, limiting ourselves to what currently exists, we admired a Moscato that confirms previous successes, offering an array of aromas with floral notes, hints of tomato leaf and suggestions of yellow-fleshed fruit. The full and convincing flavor reveals a sweetness perfectly integrated into the heady structure. The two Barberas are both excellent. The Zucchetto is a little reticent on the nose at first, but then opens up in aromas of raspberry and red currant; on the palate it shows a well-balanced structure. The Varmat, impressive for its warm charm, rich in color and extract, is full, uninterrupted and possessed of a well-balanced acidity, with a distinct but harmonious note of wood. The Chardonnay is also successful, with its yellow straw color and fresh, fruity aromas of pineapple and citrus. On the palate there are a refreshing acidity and a fair amount of fruit, which make it immediately pleasing.

	Wine	Glasses	Price
○	Moscato d'Asti '97	🍷🍷	3*
●	Barbera d'Asti Varmat '96	🍷🍷	4
●	Barbera d'Asti Zucchetto '96	🍷	3
○	Langhe Chardonnay '97	🍷	3
●	Barbera d'Asti Zucchetto '95	🍷🍷 (white glasses)	3

CASTIGLIONE TINELLA (CN)

ELIO PERRONE

STRADA S. MARTINO, 3
12053 CASTIGLIONE TINELLA (CN)
TEL. 0141/855132

Those who love the area between the Langhe of Alba and the Asti district, with its sun-warmed hills, its up and down paths that suddenly open up to breath-taking vistas, cannot fail to love the wine that expresses all the sweetness of this territory: the Moscato, offspring of a generous land and its open, good-natured inhabitants. This is the nature of the wine presented by the Perrones (Stefano and his parents, Elio and Anna), with the added grace of an airy, dream-like label designed by Giuliana, who is about to become a member of the family (the new house with a new cellar is almost ready). There are two Moscatos: for both, coarser filters are used so as not to remove too much from the wine, and no fining takes place. The Clarté has an elegant nose with intense aromas of citrus, musk and subtle aromatic herbs. The palate corresponds, showing good fresh fruit and an admirable balance between sweetness and acidity. The other Moscato, the Sourgal, displays fresh aromas with notes of chamomile and lemon balm. Although it is soft and mouth-filling, it is less enchanting than its brother. The range continues with a Dolcetto, a Barbera and a Chardonnay. This last doesn't disappoint either on the palate (where it is lively and invitingly broad in range) or on the nose, which displays well-integrated wood with suggestions of peach and grapefruit. The Dolcetto, long and pleasing in its fruity structure, is a soft, fresh, eminently drinkable wine. The good Barbera, with its well-judged wood, presents aromas of spice and black cherry as well as a hint of undergrowth and vanilla. This is all reflected on the palate, which has an enchanting crispness thanks to the acidity.

	Wine	Glasses	Price
○	Moscato d'Asti Clarté '97	🍷🍷	3*
●	Barbera d'Asti Grivò '96	🍷	3
○	Char-de S. '96	🍷	4
●	Dolcetto d'Alba Giulin '97	🍷	3
○	Moscato d'Asti Sourgal '97	🍷	3

CASTIGLIONE TINELLA (CN)

PAOLO SARACCO

VIA CIRCONVALLAZIONE, 6
12053 CASTIGLIONE TINELLA (CN)
TEL. 0141/855113

He's a curious type, this very able winegrower, firmly ensconced in the leading group of top producers of Moscato d'Asti: an individualist, reserved to a fault, he avoids publicity and confusion of any kind, going his own way without getting mixed up in all the hoopla of the market upsurge for Piedmontese wines. The first wines he released in the course of 1998 were his still whites, of which he presented three from the very successful vintage of '96. First the Graffagno, in its debut appearance, with only three thousand bottles. It is a barrique-aged blend of riesling, chardonnay and sauvignon. The nose is subtly persuasive and very varied, although the classic riesling fragrances are not yet fully expressed. The broad and rich palate, which avoids excessive opulence, stakes its all on finesse. The Chardonnay Bianch del Luv, one third of which is aged for a year in new French wood, is only slightly less varied and a little fuller-bodied; its remarkable structure guarantees that it will continue to develop for several years. The Chardonnay Prasuè '96, matured in steel and then at length in the bottle, is different in style but just as admirable. The ever enchanting Moscato d'Autunno is very rich in aromas and delectable softness, and should keep beautifully in the bottle for some years yet. As always, the basic Moscato '97 is good and reliable, characterized by greater immediacy and freshness, both in its aromas and on the pleasing palate.

	Wine	Glasses	Price
○	Moscato d'Asti Moscato d'Autunno '97	🍷🍷	3*
○	Langhe Bianco Graffagno '96	🍷🍷	3*
○	Langhe Chardonnay Bianch del Luv '96	🍷🍷	4
○	Langhe Chardonnay Prasuè '96	🍷	3
○	Moscato d'Asti '97	🍷	3

COCCONATO D'ASTI (AT)

BAVA
STRADA MONFERRATO, 2
14023 COCCONATO D'ASTI (AT)
TEL. 0141/907083

Each year the Bava family produces a notable and reliable range of wines, which can be counted on for quality. Unfortunately, this year the apple of their eye, the Barbera Stradivario, is slightly below par, but this does not affect the generally high level of the range. Let's have a look, then, at this Barbera: of a somewhat transparent ruby hue, it has a slightly forward nose (with notes of very ripe red fruit, crusty bread and roasted coffee). It is not very powerful in the mouth, but it saves the day with a balanced progression and a complex finish. The less demanding Barbera Arbest offers a fragrance of violet and red fruit; the fairly substantial palate leads into a corresponding finish. The Spumante Brut Giulio Cocchi '90 (of a full straw color, with aromas of apple, peach and yeasty dough) shows an admirable correspondence between nose and palate, although an exuberant effervescence somewhat disturbs its balance. The Monferrato Bianco Alteserre, of a rich straw color with gold highlights, offers fruity and floral aromas; in the mouth it is crisp and inviting. The Moscato Bass Tuba, whose hue is a fairly deep straw, has aromas of fruit in syrup and sage, and a pleasingly fresh taste. The correct Malvasia di Castelnuovo Don Bosco has an aromatic nose and a sweet but dry palate. Finally, we should mention that they make a Barolo Chinato, pleasingly distinctly aromatized.

	Wine	Glasses	Price
●	Barbera d'Asti Sup. Stradivario '95	🍷	5
●	Barbera d'Asti Sup. Arbest '95	🍷	4
●	Malvasia di Castelnuovo Don Bosco '97	🍷	3
○	Monferrato Bianco Alteserre '96	🍷	4
○	Moscato d'Asti Bass Tuba '97	🍷	4
○	Giulio Cocchi Brut '90	🍷	4
●	Barbera d'Asti Sup. Stradivario '93	🍷🍷 (white)	5
●	Barbera d'Asti Sup. Stradivario '94	🍷🍷 (white)	5

COSSOMBRATO (AT)

CARLO QUARELLO
VIA MARCONI, 3
14020 COSSOMBRATO (AT)
TEL. 0141/905204

Carlo Quarello, a recognized master of Grignolino, operates in the Cardona district, near Alfiano Natta. His Cré, a vineyard of three and a half hectares with excellent exposure, is in the Grignolino di Monferrato Casalese DOC zone, which has recently seemed to produce the best results with this traditional grape of Monferrato. With the help of his wife Bianca and his son Valerio, Carlo manages the vineyard in person, following a sound artisan tradition. Thanks to the selection of grapes during the harvest, two versions of a singular and intriguing red come from the winery of Cossombrato in the best years. The Cré Marcaleone '97 is a worthy successor to the Two Glass '96, with its admirable color and body, which is not what one might expect from a Grignolino, and its intense aromas, with an emerging spicy note that carries through onto the dry and lingering palate. The basic Cré, only slightly inferior, is a little paler in color, but like its elder brother it has a distinct and original personality. These are a pair of very interesting wines, not the run-of-the-mill pale red that you tend to find when you ask for a Grignolino. (In Monferrato, by the way, they seem finally to have decided that this characteristic local wine needs to be rediscovered and improved.) In recent years the winery has also been devoting some care to another product, the Crebarné. This is a blend (mostly barbera, but with a "correction" of nebbiolo), matured in barriques for the first time in 1996. The results are encouraging: a lovely garnet color in the glass precedes elegant and straightforward aromas, and a body which, while not exuberant, is well-balanced in its components and leads to a pleasing slightly bitter finish which invites you to continue.

	Wine	Glasses	Price
●	Grignolino del M.to Casalese Cré Marcaleone '97	🍷🍷	3*
●	Grignolino del M.to Casalese Cré '97	🍷	3
●	Crebarné '96	🍷	4

COSTIGLIOLE D'ASTI (AT)

PIETRO BENOTTO
FRAZ. S. CARLO, 52
14055 COSTIGLIOLE D'ASTI (AT)
TEL. 0141/966406

Since 1917 the Benotto family has been tending its vineyards in San Carlo, near Costigliole d'Asti. Today the Benotto brothers are in charge; they have 13 hectares under vine, mostly barbera, but other Piedmontese varieties keep it company, including freisa, grignolino, dolcetto, nebbiolo, cortese and the very rare gamba di pernice. The cellar is not very large, but is very well-equipped; temperature-controlled vats and numerous barriques make it possible for them to produce 40 thousand bottles a year; they still sell the rest of what they produce by volume. Among their many wines the Barberas stand out: the Rupestris, so called because the wine comes from vines on the not very productive Rupestris du Lot, and the Balau, from the vineyard of the same name, now 40 years old. The Rupestris '96, one third of which is matured for 14 months in new barriques, has an intense ruby color and a broad nose, where the oak-derived spice and vanilla are already well blended with the natural fruit of the grape (particularly cherry and plum). In the long, mouth-filling finish, the natural acidity of this grape is kept well in check by the balanced and full body. The Barbera Balau '96, aged in 15-hectoliter barrels acquired specifically for its first appearance on the scene, has a slightly brusquer temperament, both on the nose (balsamic and cherry aromas) and on the palate (austere and warm), but not a less interesting one. Among the other wines, we should mention the soft and fruity standard Barbera '97, the powerful and mineral Cortese '97, and a Monferrato (100% nebbiolo), which is spicy and lightly astringent.

●	Barbera d'Asti Sup. Rupestris '96	🍷🍷	4
●	Barbera d'Asti Sup. Balau '96	🍷	3
●	Barbera d'Asti '97	🍷	2*
●	Monferrato Rosso Nebieul '96		3
○	Piemonte Cortese Lacrime di Gioia '97		3

COSTIGLIOLE D'ASTI (AT)

CASCINA CASTLÈT
STRADA CASTELLETTO, 6
14055 COSTIGLIOLE D'ASTI (AT)
TEL. 0141/966651

Castlèt is short for Castelleto, a hamlet near Costigliola, where the Borio farmhouse lies, half hidden by vineyards. Here Mariuccia began her career as a winegrower by planting new vines and constructing her up-to-date cellar. The wines are the ones that command these hills: Barbera (in a variety of versions) and Moscato. With the oenological guidance of Armando Cordero (assisted by the young Giorgio Gozzellino, himself a promising producer in his own Cascina del Frate), Barbera plays a number of roles here. The Goj, for instance, is a pleasing faintly fizzy red, fresh, carefree and youthful, while the Barbera '97, a still dinner wine, has a color of medium intensity, followed by an intriguing heady and fruity fragrance. On the palate its attack is moderate, as is its meat. The Passum, their flagship, is made from slightly dried barbera grapes; this is the wine that has made Cascina Castlèt a name to conjure with. The '96 version has a dense ruby hue and a characteristic nose dominated by aromas of stewed fruit with delicate accents of spice and good wood, carrying through onto the palate, which has a rounded, almost sweet attack, balanced by a varietal acidity. The Policalpo, a Monferrato Rosso also made from barbera, has a deep, lively garnet color; the nose, still somewhat closed, offers an agreeable note of licorice. The wine, which will certainly benefit from a few months in the bottle, shows medium structure and finish. The winery is also presenting two versions of Moscato d'Asti: the semi-sparkling '97, with distinct varietal aromas, and the Avié '96, a Moscato Passito which never disappoints.

○	Piemonte Moscato Passito Avié '96	🍷	4
●	Barbera d'Asti Sup. Passum '96	🍷	4
●	Barbera del M.to Goj '97	🍷	3
●	Monferrato Rosso Policalpo '96	🍷	4
●	Barbera d'Asti '97		3
○	Moscato d'Asti '97		3
●	Passum '91	🍷🍷 (white)	4
●	Barbera d'Asti Policalpo '94	🍷 (white)	4
●	Passum '90	🍷 (white)	4
●	Policalpo '90	🍷 (white)	4

CUCCARO M.TO (AL)

LIEDHOLM
VILLA BOEMIA
15040 CUCCARO M.TO (AL)
TEL. 0131/771916

Carlo Liedholm's estate, situated in a very beautiful and lush green corner of Monferrato, produces a clean and rigorous interpretation of the traditional wines of the zone, as well as two house specialties, the Bianco and Rosso della Boemia, made from blends of several grapes planted at Villa Boemia by its previous owners. A careful tending of the vines and first-rate equipment in the cellar are the basis of the consistent quality we find in Carlo's wines, which also benefit from the assistance of the oenologist Donato Lanati. We were speaking of the rigor with which he makes his traditional wines, and the Grignolino '97 and Barbera '96 are good examples. The first, of a pale cherry color with a slightly orange rim, offers clear white pepper and roasted peanut aromas with a subtle floral undertone; on the palate it is balanced, though rather limited in scope, with a typical tannic note, introduced here with such delicacy that it does not overwhelm the finish. The Barbera has a ruby hue of medium intensity and a straightforward, appealing nose with notes of violet, raspberry and cherry; the palate shows grip and adequate substance. The Bianco della Boemia '97, made from pinot blanc and cortese, has a full clear straw color lightly tinged with gold. The inviting fragrance is characterized by notes of white-fleshed fruit and fresh undertones of lemon. On the palate the wine is fresh and approachable, with a finish which mirrors the fruity notes, enriched by light hints of custard.

Wine	Glasses	Price
○ Bianco della Boemia '97	▼	3
● Barbera d'Asti '96	▼	3
● Grignolino del M.to Casalese '97	▼	3
● Rosso della Boemia '90	▽▽	5
● Rosso della Boemia '91	▽▽	5
● Rosso della Boemia '94	▽	5

DIANO D'ALBA (CN)

CLAUDIO ALARIO
VIA S. CROCE, 23
12055 DIANO D'ALBA (CN)
TEL. 0173/231808

Matteo Alario, who has the admirable capacity to maintain an enviable consistency of quality in difficult years, is not put off by favorable vintages either: indeed he has made use of '96 and '97 to produce a series of excellent wines. Thus the Two Glasses awarded last year to both the '96 Dolcettos show up again with the '97s, and also adorn the Barbera '96. Not a bad total. The real star of this stellar season is undoubtedly the Dolcetto Costa Fiore: it has a dense dark garnet-ruby color, and a complex and fascinating nose, with notes of black cherry, red currant, licorice and pepper emerging from a harmonious bouquet. The wine is no less good on the palate: the sumptuous and concentrated attack heralds a broad, consistent progress, underpinned by a solid and elegant phenolic structure, leading into a composite, satisfying finish. The Montagrillo, only a little less good, has a concentrated garnet ruby color which has not yet lost its youthful violet rim. The nose displays hints of strawberry and ripe cherry, wild herbs, geranium and almond; the rich palate is supported by a slightly sinewy vein of acid, and a dry and fruity finish. The Barbera Valletta is dense in appearance and offers a captivating nose with notes of red currant, blackberry, pepper and vanilla. On the palate it is full, rounded and soft, enlivened by a decided tannic vein which plays its part in the fruity and spicy finish. The Nebbiolo Cascinotto deserves "only" One full Glass: it offers aromas of violet, vanilla and coffee, and a pleasing bite on the firm palate.

Wine	Glasses	Price
● Barbera d'Alba Valletta '96	▼▼	4
● Dolcetto di Diano d'Alba Costa Fiore '97	▼▼	3*
● Dolcetto di Diano d'Alba Montagrillo '97	▼▼	3*
● Nebbiolo d'Alba Cascinotto '96	▼	4
● Dolcetto di Diano d'Alba Costa Fiore '96	▽▽	3
● Dolcetto di Diano d'Alba Montagrillo '96	▽▽	3
● Barbera d'Alba Valletta '95	▽	4
● Nebbiolo d'Alba Cascinotto '95	▽	4

DIANO D'ALBA (CN)

BRICCO MAIOLICA

VIA BOLANGINO, 7
FRAZ. RICCA
12055 DIANO D'ALBA (CN)
TEL. 0173/612049

The Dolcetto Sörì Bricco Maiolica is certainly one of the best examples of a typical Diano d'Alba Dolcetto, with its grip and substance. The reliability we have come to depend on in this wine is by no means a negligible virtue in this winery, which is quite sizable for the Langhe (100 thousand bottles produced annually from about 17 hectares of vineyards). The '97 version is another Two Glass winner: it has an intense ruby-garnet color, with a compact and youthful purplish edge. On the nose it offers a fascinating weave of aromas from black cherry to vanilla and pepper, and on the palate it is full and vigorous, with well-judged tannins that add a dryness to the very long finish. The straightforward, easily drinkable standard Dolcetto, ruby verging on garnet in hue, has a nose of moderate finesse with fruity and spicy tones. In the mouth it is soft, smooth and well-ordered. The Langhe Rosso Lorié, a monovarietal pinot noir aged for 18 months in barriques, starts off life with One full Glass. The color is intense, while the interesting bouquet offers notes of red currant, blueberry, coffee, tobacco and mint. In the mouth it reveals a good, if not very powerful, structure and a lingering finish. The good Nebbiolo Cumot is redolent of blackberry and toasty oak and is robust and dry on the palate. The Langhe Bianco Rolando, a blend of arneis, chardonnay and favorita, has aromas of exotic fruit and hazelnut (with overripe notes), and is crisp and undemanding. A sound Moscato ends the list.

	Wine	Glasses	Price
●	Dolcetto di Diano d'Alba Sörì Bricco Maiolica '97	🍷🍷	3
●	Nebbiolo d'Alba Il Cumot '96	🍷🍷	4
●	Dolcetto di Diano d'Alba '97	🍷	2*
●	Langhe Rosso Lorié '95	🍷	5
○	Langhe Bianco Rolando '97	🍷	3
○	Moscato d'Asti Sorì Valdavì '97		3
●	Dolcetto di Diano d'Alba Sörì Bricco Maiolica '96	🍸🍸	3
●	Barbera d'Alba Vigna Vigia '95	🍸	3

DOGLIANI (CN)

CELSO ABBONA - CÀ NEUVA

REG. S. LUCIA, 36
12063 DOGLIANI (CN)
TEL. 0173/70668

Sergio Abbona has inherited from his father a grape indissolubly linked to the hills of Dogliani - the dolcetto. He has made it into captivating, reliable and affordable wine, joining the freshness and moderate structure of the variety to a bewitching softness. This style can be admired in two versions: the standard Dolcetto, 45 thousand bottles strong, is a blend of grapes from different parcels of his estate. Its ruby hue of medium intensity proclaims the simple and attractive character of the wine, which is also displayed by a heady but clean cherry fragrance. Further confirmation comes from the palate, with its succulent but balanced acidity. Although there is not enormous body, the finish does not vanish. The Dolcetto 'L Sambù, of which he produces 15 thousand bottles, has a more austere personality, and indeed it comes from a more clayey soil, and a longer maceration. The color is intense, the aromas are broad (fruit and grass), the palate is warm and the tannins are sound. The most successful wine is Il Bric, a nebbiolo of which 8 thousand bottles are made. The distinct ruby color invites one to sample the intense, direct aromas of peach and fresh grass; the encouraging warmth of the palate softens the tannins, giving a sense of satisfying fullness which wants only a greater aromatic and extractive richness. The Langhe Arneis is this year's novelty: it has a warm color, forward aromas and a very soft taste (intended for those who are fond of sweet sensations).

	Wine	Glasses	Price
●	Dolcetto di Dogliani 'L Sambù '97	🍷	3
●	Dolcetto di Dogliani Cà Neuva '97	🍷	2*
●	Il Bric '97	🍷	3
○	Langhe Arneis '97		3

DOGLIANI (CN)

MARZIANO ED ENRICO ABBONA
VIA TORINO, 242
12063 DOGLIANI (CN)
TEL. 0173/70484

The Abbona brothers are back in the Guide with their Dogliani estate after a few years' absence. Recently these two dynamic brothers, especially Marziano, have added to their already substantial property, and now own 40 hectares under vine. Most of the vineyards are near Dogliani (25 hectares), while the remaining 15 hectares include parcels of land purchased in some of the best zones of the Langhe. Hence their Barolo, from Novello (Ravera Terlo), and the Barbaresco, which comes from one of the historic crus of that zone, the Faset. Apart from the enormous investment in valuable land which allows them to grow first-class grapes, the Abbonas have secured the advice of one of the best oenologists of the Langhe, Beppe Caviola. But let's get down to the wines. The Dolcettos made an excellent impression. They appear this year in two versions (a third, Surì Montà, is missing): the Papà Celso and Bricco San Bernardo. The excellent Papà Celso is about as good an example of a Dolcetto di Dogliani as can be imagined: it has an impenetrable color and aromas ranging from dark cherry to spice, with clear hints of pepper and clove. It is mouth-filling and well-structured and offers a long, lingering finish. The Bricco San Bernardo is not far behind it: it is dark in color, and offers aromas of raspberry and a rich, satisfying palate. The finish, very slightly bitter, is characteristic. There is good news in the aristocratic wine department as well: the Barolo, though suffering somewhat from a not very good vintage, is clean and well-made, while the Barbaresco is more complex, fat and austere on the palate; hints of vanilla together with more developed aromas make up its rich bouquet.

●	Dolcetto di Dogliani Papà Celso '97	🍷🍷	3*
●	Barbaresco Vigna Faset '95	🍷	5
●	Barolo Vigneto Terlo Ravera '94	🍷	5
●	Dolcetto di Dogliani Bricco San Bernardo '97	🍷	3*

DOGLIANI (CN)

FRANCESCO BOSCHIS
FRAZ. SAN MARTINO DI PIANEZZO, 57
12063 DOGLIANI (CN)
TEL. 0173/70574

Despite a very hot summer, the Boschis family has produced some excellent Dolcettos. Dogliani is nestled among the closely packed hills which rise steeply to a height of more than 500 meters; it is land that puts up a certain amount of resistance to the farmer, and not all that many choose to fight it out. From the Vigna dei Prey (facing west, sharing a high plateau with the winery) comes a perfect expression of Francesco and Simona's idea of Dolcetto. It is a wine with a simple but lasting fragrance, and it presents the same pleasing qualities on the palate and holds them there too. The red fruit aroma of the Prey is varietal; the soft attack immediately gives way to the vivid acidity typical of high altitude grapes, but abundant alcohol smoothes all its rough edges. The tannins, youthful but not bitter, add a rustic note. The other cru of the Boschis estate (in which the younger members of the family, Marco and Paolo, are also employed) is the Sorì San Martino, which admirably gives rise to a Dolcetto that is poles apart from the Prey: fresh, fruity, full of verve but not aggressive, both vigorous and thirst-quenching. The finish has a warmth and astringency which might be out of place in another wine. The Pianezzo, a new name for their standard Dolcetto, has heady aromas of currant and strawberry; on the palate it is dense and long. The Freisa, with a faint aroma of nail polish and an acidic taste, is mentioned here because of the neatness of its execution.

●	Dolcetto di Dogliani Vigna dei Prey '97	🍷🍷	3*
●	Dolcetto di Dogliani Pianezzo '97	🍷	3
●	Dolcetto di Dogliani Vigna Sorì S. Martino '97	🍷	3
●	Langhe Freisa Bosco delle Cicale '97	🍷	3
●	Barbera d'Alba Vigna Le Masserie '95	🍷 (white)	3

DOGLIANI (CN)

Quinto Chionetti & Figlio

B.ta Valdiberti, 44
12063 Dogliani (CN)
tel. 0173/71179

It feels as if we were talking about a different geological era, and yet not very long ago, Quinto Chionetti was one of the very few in Dogliani who preached the gospel of quality, and believed that the Dolcetto of this zone could become a great Italian red wine. Now that many wineries have finally got the message, and Dogliani is a name that people in the most distant places are beginning to greet with interest and admiration, Quinto should feel a measure of satisfaction. Given his dry, ironic character, a real native of the Langhe in style, he will never admit to having been the inspirer of this extraordinary renaissance. And yet it was so, and those two now legendary crus of his, Briccolero and San Luigi, are emblematic of the whole "new wave" of Dogliano: two touchstones that hold an unchallenged place. This winegrower remains faithful to an idea and a style: he lets the "terroir" speak for itself. Chionetti uses only stainless steel, and takes the trouble to let his wine mature at length before putting it on the market - and the most recent research on Dolcetto di Dogliani seems to back him up. The Briccolero '96, with its lovely clear, dense ruby hue, offers intense, lingering aromas of black berries, pepper and earth. The palate, as usual, is denser than that of the San Luigi (indeed it comes from a robust terrain with a southern exposure) and offers hints of ripe plum and spice that carry through the long finish. The more graceful and rounded San Luigi offers light suggestions of pencil lead on the nose, accompanied by notes of ripe fruit; the palate is succulent and full-bodied; its strong vein of acidity is counterpoised by extraordinarily ripe fruit.

	Wine	Rating	Price
●	Dolcetto di Dogliani Briccolero '96	🍷🍷	3
●	Dolcetto di Dogliani San Luigi '96	🍷	3
●	Dolcetto di Dogliani Briccolero '95	♀♀	3

DOGLIANI (CN)

Poderi Luigi Einaudi

B.ta Gombe, 31/32
Cascina Tecc
12063 Dogliani (CN)
tel. 0173/70191

To celebrate its centenary in style, the Einaudi estate has carried off a coup which has astonished the wine world of the Langhe: the purchase of a sizable parcel of land in one of the most highly prized Barolo crus, Cannubi, and exactly where the Ca' dei Gancia used to be produced. But this does not mean that the winery has given up its historic role as the Dogliani trendsetter. The Dolcettos presented this year are of extraordinary quality, and they show how efforts do not cease in vineyard and cellar to keep improving Dolcetto di Dogliani. I Filari '96, with its fine ruby-violet hue, has intense aromas of spice, black berries and pencil lead. In the mouth it shows the substance and vigor of a great red, with a juicy finish of good ripe fruit and distinctive tannins. The Tecc '96 is on the same pattern, but slightly less elegant on the nose. Even the standard Dolcetto has the characteristics of a pedigree wine. The Rosso Einaudi '96 confirms last year's good impression; it's a blend of estate-grown barbera, merlot and cabernet aged for over a year in barriques. The intense ruby color tinged with garnet is followed by a rich nose, with hints of vanilla and pepper and a sinewy palate. The Barolo Cannubi '94, taken over from Gancia, shows all the contradictions of that vintage: rather obtrusive tannins, fruit somewhat lacking in concentration, but a mouth-filling, silky finish. The very interesting Vigna Meira '97, a barrique-fermented red tocai, is more complete than last year's: the heady nose displays notes of apple and minerals; the rich palate leads into an attractive finish redolent of exotic fruit.

	Wine	Rating	Price
○	Vigna Meira Bianco '97	🍷🍷	3
●	Dolcetto di Dogliani I Filari '96	🍷🍷	4
●	Dolcetto di Dogliani Vigna Tecc '96	🍷🍷	3*
●	Barolo Cannubi '94	🍷🍷	5
●	Dolcetto di Dogliani '97	🍷	3
●	Langhe Rosso Luigi Einaudi '96	🍷	5
●	Piemonte Barbera '96	🍷	3
●	Dolcetto di Dogliani I Filari '95	♀♀	4
●	Dolcetto di Dogliani Vigna Tecc '95	♀♀	3
●	Luigi Einaudi Rosso '95	♀♀	5
●	Barolo Costa Grimaldi '93	♀	5

F.LLI PECCHENINO
B.TA VALDIBÀ, 41
12063 DOGLIANI (CN)
TEL. 0173/70686

Attilio and Orlando Pecchenino are in that little pride of young lions who are revolutionizing Dolcetto di Dogliano. They have succeeded (by means of ruthless selection) in giving Dolcetto a complexity which would have been unthinkable until a few years ago. The Three Glasses awarded this year to three Dogliani Dolcettos are a public recognition of the collective effort, and should contribute to the definitive departure of this wine from the ranks of the simply quaffable. The Peccheninis reconfirm this trend by winning the prize once again for their Sirì d'Jermu '97, which is becoming a cult wine. It is pitch black in color and has a dazzling nose, in which a lightly overripe tone is splendidly harmonized by notes of ripe blackberry, spice and black currant; its entry on the palate is warm and mellow; it then acquires sinew and vigor and goes on to a long and vibrant note of ink and licorice on the finish. These characteristics are to be found in the Bricco Botti '96 also, but without the same balance; the nose offers a hint of vanilla and an almost resinous tone (in fact a little in excess); the final tannins are also a little intrusive. Some further time in the bottle should help smooth the rough edges and add grace to the muscularity. The Langhe La Castella '96 has a bluish ruby color and a still somewhat uncertain fragrance: mineral notes (pencil lead) are combined with hints of wood and menthol. On the palate it is impressive in the sweetness of its fruit and the extreme energy of the finish. The ever-fascinating Dolcetto di Dogliani Pizabò '97 has never seen wood. Its very lively, inky and peppery nose is followed by a sweet plum and blackberry fruitiness. There is an admirable correspondence between the nose and the palate.

Type	Wine	Glasses	Rating
●	Dolcetto di Dogliani Sirì d'Jermu '97	🍷🍷🍷	4
●	Dolcetto di Dogliani Bricco Botti '96	🍷🍷	4
●	Dolcetto di Dogliani Pizabò '97	🍷🍷	3*
●	Langhe La Castella '96	🍷🍷	4
○	Langhe Chardonnay Vigna Maestro '97	🍷	3
●	Dolcetto di Dogliani Sirì d'Jermu '96	YYY	3
●	Dolcetto di Dogliani Bricco Botti '95	YY	4
●	Langhe La Castella '95	YY	4

DOGLIANI (CN)

PIRA
B.TA VALDIBERTI, 69
12063 DOGLIANI (CN)
TEL. 0173/78538

The strength of the Piras consists not only in the production of noteworthy wines, but in their capacity to differentiate them, offering a varied range of consistent quality. The Dolcettos are a case in point, and actually come from different DOCs. The one from Dogliani is mature in its quite heady fruity aromas, which find a response in the warm and mouth-filling palate balanced by a keen acidity. The Dolcetto d'Alba, which is less fascinating this time, is very dense in color, but simpler in fragrance, although there is no lack of fruit, which is mirrored on the palate. The Barbera Vendemmia Tardiva has the potency of partially dried grapes, which does not, however, suffice to give it its customary fullness (either in the mature color or in the fruity aroma of strawberry). Mouth-filling and lingering on the palate, it shows there the acidic nature of its grape. The Barbera Vigna Fornaci, more discreet and direct, is again a versatile and thoroughly enjoyable wine, even more than the rougher and more traditional Bricco Botti.

Type	Wine	Glasses	Rating
●	Dolcetto di Dogliani Bricco dei Botti '97	🍷🍷	3*
●	Barbera d'Alba Vendemmia Tardiva '96	🍷	4
●	Barbera d'Alba Vigna Fornaci '96	🍷	3
●	Piemonte Barbera Bricco Botti '96	🍷	4
●	Dolcetto d'Alba Vigna Fornaci '97		3
●	Barbera d'Alba Vendemmia Tardiva '95	YY	4

DOGLIANI (CN)

San Fereolo
B.ta Valdibà, 59
12063 Dogliani (CN)
tel. 0173/742075

Nicoletta Bocca has succeeded in earning Three Glasses in a DOC (Dolcetto di Dogliani), which few people regarded as capable of offering such structure and complexity. It should also be mentioned that it was only in 1992 that she decided to leave the city and acquire the San Fereolo estate in Valdibà di Dogliani. So it really is quite astonishing. Furthermore, Nicoletta has managed to create a place for herself in the suspiciously watchful and closed environment of the Langhe. She clearly likes challenges: item, to go and live on a rocky, isolated precipice, or to make wine from 50-60-year-old vines, and to dream up a Dolcetto capable of overcoming the image of an easy drinking wine. The secret of her success is surely in her tenacious and determined character, but also in her ability to surround herself with excellent co-workers: Francesco Stralla, who knows those five and a half hectares inch by inch, Federico Curtaz who, after working for years with Angela Gaja, is now a freelance and Beppe Caviola, the rising star of Piedmontese oenology. The result: this San Fereolo '97, impressive in its richness of extract, density of fruit and aromatic personality. The opaque bluish ruby color is followed by a nose stilll developing, with a touch of new wood and a fine hint of pencil lead and ink. The entry on the palate is warm and silky, and is followed by a gradual opening to a long finish with notes of ripe plum and berry jam. This superb example of Dolcetto does not move far from its native soil; in fact there are still concentrated notes of the ferrous and mineral elements that characterize the wines of this zone. The interesting Langhe Rosso Brumaio '96, a red blend, has a superfluous note of coffee in the bouquet, but on the palate it is balanced, sinewy and structured.

●	Dolcetto di Dogliani San Fereolo '97	🍷🍷🍷	3*
●	Langhe Rosso Brumaio '96	🍷🍷	4
●	Dolcetto di Dogliani San Fereolo '96	🍸🍸	3
●	Il Brumaio '95	🍸🍸	4

DOGLIANI (CN)

San Romano
B.ta Giachelli, 8
12063 Dogliani (CN)
tel. 0173/76289

Dedicating his estate, which he has had for only a few years, to San Romano, the saint portrayed in the votive shrine which rises above these vineyards, has brought good luck to Bruno Chionetti. This young former adman who heeded the call of his Langhe genes and returned to the vineyards has, in only his third year of wine-making, managed to win Three Glasses. What's more, he has won them for a wine, Dolcetto, which until a few years ago was thought beneath the serious consideration of wine professionals. Bruno achieved this success thanks to his commitment, to intelligent efforts in both vineyard and cellar, and to his firm conviction that Dolcetto di Dogliani is capable of the concentration and complexity of a great red wine. His soil gives the grapes a significant aromatic component, which he is at pains to conserve. Bruno favors relatively brief maceration periods, and uses only stainless steel. Thus his Vigna del Pilone is fruity and soft, and offers the captivating density that only old (and ruthlessly pruned) vines can give. His Dogliani is reminiscent of the great Merlots; this '97, with its ruby-violet hue, has a superb nose, with aromas of red berries and ripe plum as well as a mineral note. The attack on the palate is vigorous and warm and the progression has the juiciness released by biting into a very sweet grape. The cru is extraordinary, but even the standard Dolcetto, which comes from the Romano vineyard, has a notable personality; its color is a little less dense, and it offers a lively, fragrant and simpler nose, which is, however, more intense than the Pilone's . On the palate it is meaty and sinewy, with a long and succulent finish.

●	Dolcetto di Dogliani Vigna del Pilone '97	🍷🍷🍷	3*
●	Dolcetto di Dogliani '97	🍷🍷	3*
●	Dolcetto di Dogliani Vigna del Pilone '96	🍸🍸	3

FARIGLIANO (CN)

GIOVANNI BATTISTA GILLARDI
CASCINA CORSALETTO, 69
12060 FARIGLIANO (CN)
TEL. 0173/76306

The secret of Giovanni and Pinuccia Gillardi's Dolcetto lies entirely in the selection of the grapes: in fact they use only the best bunches, less than half of what they harvest, for their 25 thousand bottles. Furthermore, for a few years now their son Giaculin has been making a wine based on syrah which gets better year by year. This is Harys, of which there are at the moment only one thousand bottles, but which should become more generally available starting with the 1997 vintage. When it's poured into the glass, the wine offers a distinct aroma of paprika from its violet density, conferring a spicy and piquant edge to a musky, earthy bouquet. These sensations are carried through into the mouth, which is filled with Mediterranean warmth by the substantial meatiness of the extracts and the tannins. The Cursalet, from a very high-density vineyard, emphatically elbows aside its brother Dolcetto; its broad, lingering and ripe fragrance skilfully combines the sweetness of fresh fruit (raspberry and cherry) with the maturity of hazelnut; on the palate it is warm and almost chewy, and has a lasting finish. The Vigneto Maestra is simpler and more direct, but it definitely has its points: an invitingly brilliant fuchsia hue is followed by a readier nose, which is fresh and herby. On the palate it is lively and light.

	Wine	Glasses	
●	Dolcetto di Dogliani Cursalet '97	🍷🍷	3
●	Harys '96	🍷🍷	5
●	Dolcetto di Dogliani Vigneto Maestra '97	🍷	3
●	Dolcetto di Dogliani Cursalet '96	🍸🍸	3
●	Harys '95	🍸🍸	5
●	Harys '93	🍸	5

FRASSINELLO M.TO (AL)

CASTELLO DI LIGNANO
REG. LIGNANO
15035 FRASSINELLO M.TO (AL)
TEL. 0142/334529 - 925326

Giuseppe Gaiero's lovely estate is making its debut in the Guide. He is a dynamic entrepreneur in the field of iron and steel and a dedicated wine producer. The imposing Lignano castle, built in the Middle Ages, is on the site of an important defensive settlement of the 7th century B.C.; the oldest part remaining today is the great tower in tufa and brick, dating from the 10th-11th centuries. The cultural events which the proprietor organizes here thus have a very evocative setting. Giuseppe has two invaluable co-workers in Ugo Bertana, who deals with marketing and advertising, and Francesco Ferrero, consultant oenologist. Among the wines presented, the Barbera Vigna Stramba won One full Glass. It is ruby-hued with garnet highlights, and has a fairly complex nose with aromas of raspberry, licorice, dark leaves and coffee. On the palate it is balanced and stylish, although it could perhaps do with a touch more concentration. The finish is dry and long-lasting. The Grignolino Vigna Tufara, light red with a pale rim, is gracefully varietal on the nose, with notes of dried rose petals, white pepper and peanut. The palate is substantial, with drying tannins and a corresponding finish. The good Freisa offers aromas of blackberry, raspberry and spice; the full-bodied palate has a properly tannic finish. The Cortese Grisello displays fresh fragrances (peach, citrus fruit and banana) and, in the mouth, softness and low but not inadequate acidity. At the end of our list come two simple and correctly made Barberas, one slightly fizzy (vivace) and the other still.

	Wine	Glasses	
○	Monferrato Casalese Cortese Grisello '97	🍷	3
●	Barbera d'Asti Vigna Stramba '96	🍷	3
●	Grignolino del M.to Casalese Vigna Tufara '97	🍷	3
●	Monferrato Freisa '97	🍷	3
●	Barbera del M.to '97		3
●	Barbera del M.to Vivace '97		3

GATTINARA (VC)

Antoniolo
C.so Valsesia, 277
13045 Gattinara (VC)
tel. 0163/833612

Rosanna Antoniolo and her children Lorella and Alberto run this historic Gattinara estate with dedication and competence. The measure of their skill can be seen from their standard wines: there is not one among them that does not merit at least One Glass. If you then consider the rich and generous Gattinara Osso San Grato '93, you get a full picture of a first-class winery. But let's see about this cru, a Two Glass winner: it is ruby-hued with a faintly orange rim; the bouquet opens with aromas of raspberry, red currant, almond and biscuit, with complex mineral undertones. On the palate it is full and austere, in the manner of local nebbiolos, continuous and substantial; on the long finish a well-judged tannic note adds an attractive dryness. The Gattinara '94, of an almost transparent ruby color lightly tinged with orange, offers distinctly animal aromas, with notes of dried flowers, wild berries and leather. The palate is full-bodied, succulent and appropriately tannic. The good Coste della Sesia Nebbiolo Juvenia is intensely ruby-colored and redolent of red fruit, and there's something there to get your teeth into. The Rosato Bricco Lorella, another nebbiolo, has a pale color and subtle secondary and fruity aromas, and is fresh and undemanding. The Erbaluce di Caluso is of a light, green-tinged hue; it's lemony and fruity on the nose and light and balanced on the palate.

●	Gattinara Vigneto Osso S. Grato '93	🍷🍷	5
●	Coste della Sesia Nebbiolo Juvenia '97	🍷	3
●	Gattinara '94	🍷	4
⊙	Coste della Sesia Bricco Lorella '97	🍷	3
○	Erbaluce di Caluso '97	🍷	3
●	Gattinara S. Francesco '90	YY	5
●	Gattinara Vigneto Castelle '90	YY	5
●	Gattinara Vigneto S. Francesco '89	YY	5
●	Gattinara Vigneto Osso S. Grato '90	Y	5
●	Gattinara Vigneto Osso S. Grato '91	Y	5

GATTINARA (VC)

Nervi
C.so Vercelli, 117
13045 Gattinara (VC)
tel. 0163/833228

The great 19th century palazzo in the center of Gattinara that houses the winery of the Bocciolone family is in the midst of being redone. When the work is finished it will be a lovely place to stay, if you happen to come this way. The estate consists of 32 hectares, of which 25 are currently producing (but some new vines will soon be joining in) Nervi's 80 to 90 thousand bottles a year, under the dedicated supervision of Giorgio Agliata and Carla Ferrero. Among the wines presented this year, which amply justify this debut in the Guide, the Gattinara Vigneto Molsino '93 is particularly impressive. It has a rather intense ruby hue with an orange rim. The rich and fascinating bouquet offers aromas of raspberry, violet and spice with complex undertones of minerals and overripeness; on the palate it is full-bodied, and shows a savory and somewhat austere progression to an intensely fruity finish. The Gattinara '91, only slightly less good, is of a ruby color tinged with garnet; the aromas of jam and dried flowers are shot through with hints of leather and tar. The structured, dry palate leads to an intense finish. The standard Gattinara '93, which is less rich than the wines just described, offers aromas of red fruit, sweet spice and leather, which carry through onto the well-balanced palate. The simpler Coste della Sesia Spanna, redolent of violet and raspberry, is medium-bodied and has a licorice finish. The last on the list is Amore, a nebbiolo, cabernet and merlot blend of medium body and slightly forward aromas.

●	Gattinara Vigneto Molsino '93	🍷🍷	4
●	Gattinara '91	🍷	4
●	Gattinara '93	🍷	4
●	Amore		3
●	Coste della Sesia Spanna '94		3

GATTINARA (VC)

GIANCARLO TRAVAGLINI
STRADA DELLE VIGNE, 36
13045 GATTINARA (VC)
TEL. 0163/833588

There is a kind of technological watershed between the two Gattinaras (the standard '94 and the Riserva Numerata '93) presented this year by Giancarlo Travaglini. In 1994 he began using rotary fermenters, which were really starting to catch on in the early '90s. These are machines for fermenting red wines (i.e. with maceration of the skins) which keep the skins and seeds in constant suspension, thus ensuring more rapid extraction (and hence a higher ratio of anthocyans and tannins), which produces greater softness. Giancarlo does not use these machines to excess, so the style of his wines has not changed radically; however, he was able to make a really good standard Gattinara even with the tricky '94 vintage. Rich ruby in hue, it has a various and fascinating nose with aromas of red fruit and dried flowers, and complex undertones of menthol, custard and leather. On the palate it is full-bodied and meaty, with an uninterrupted progression to a long dry finish. The excellent Riserva Numerata offers a more powerful structure. It is intensely ruby-garnet in color, and displays a broad and complex bouquet with fragrances of violet, blackberry and red currant as well as oak-derived balsamic and spicy undertones. The palate (rich, broad, continuous and substantial) vaunts a long and properly tannic finish.

● Gattinara '94	🍷🍷	4
● Gattinara Ris. '93	🍷🍷	5
● Gattinara '93	🍷🍷 (outline)	4
● Gattinara Ris. Numerata '88	🍷🍷 (outline)	5
● Gattinara Ris. Numerata '89	🍷🍷 (outline)	5
● Gattinara Ris. Numerata '90	🍷🍷 (outline)	5

GAVI (AL)

NICOLA BERGAGLIO
LOC. PEDAGGERI, 59
FRAZ. ROVERETO
15066 GAVI (AL)
TEL. 0143/682195

Gianluigi Bergaglio's wines have the traditional style, in which the varietal characteristics of the cortese grape dominate the straightforward nose. And there is good body in his wines, which are dry and make no concessions to opulence, but are always worthy of the excellent reputation this family enjoys among fans of Gavi. So, with the help of the fine '97 vintage, the top Bergaglio wine, Minaia, has won Two Glasses. This Gavi, of a quite light straw color, has a nose that opens out remarkably in the glass. The fresh initial notes of peach and banana give way to interesting hints of hay and dry flowers. On the palate it offers lots of substance, rendered light and silky by a well-judged vein of acidity; the finish is long and satisfying. This is a captivating, rather than an impetuous, wine. The standard Gavi (a sort of miniature version, but in the same style as the Minaia), has a clear straw color tinged with green. It offers aromas of wildflowers and herbs, white- and yellow-fleshed fruit, and sage. On the palate it reveals good body, with the softness conceded by relatively low acidity, and a finish of moderate length.

○ Gavi di Gavi Minaia '97	🍷🍷	3
○ Gavi di Gavi '97	🍷	3

GAVI (AL)

Gian Piero Broglia
Tenuta La Meirana
Loc. Lomellina, 14
15066 Gavi (AL)
tel. 0143/642998 - 743267

The first historical document that mentions the cultivation of the vine in the Gavi zone is from 972 and concerns the Bishop of Genoa's leasing, to two men from Gavi, of vineyards and chestnut groves at La Meirana, which is where the estate of that name lies today. While Gian Pietro Broglia's winery, with its 73 hectares, can rightly be considered the historic birthplace of Gavi, it is also true that the international renown La Meirana enjoys and the consistent excellence of its wines are the result of the modern style its owner has given it. A glance at the Glasses it has collected suffices to show that there are no weak points and that even the least important wines hardly ever go away Glassless. But this year there is also the outstanding Bruno Broglia, which is back in form and positively seizes Two Glasses. The wine, of a quite light straw color, has a fresh and distinct fragrance ranging from notes of grapefruit and citron to white-fleshed fruit and the green tones of aromatic herbs. On the palate it is soft and full, not overwhelmingly powerful, but remarkably elegant, thanks to an impeccable balance. One Glass goes to the Villa Broglia, with its green-tinged light straw color, aromas of banana, caramel and fruit with undertones of orange, and very well-balanced if somewhat restrained palate. Finally, the two standard products (Gavi La Meirana and the lightly fizzy Roverello), offer more than correct execution and receive One Glass each.

O	Gavi di Gavi Bruno Broglia '96	🍷🍷	4
O	Gavi di Gavi La Meirana '97	🍷	3
O	Gavi di Gavi Roverello '97	🍷	3
O	Gavi di Gavi Villa Broglia '97	🍷	3
O	Gavi di Gavi Bruno Broglia '95	🍷 (white)	4
O	Gavi Spumante Extra Brut '92	🍷 (white)	4

GAVI (AL)

Cascina S. Bartolomeo
Cascina S. Bartolomeo, 26
Loc. Valleggie
15066 Gavi (AL)
tel. 0143/643180

Three very convincing Gavis are responsible for this debut appearance in the Guide of the Cascina San Bartolomeo, which has belonged to the Bergaglio family since 1916. The estate, which was already a working vineyard back then, was sold to the Bergaglios by the Serra family, who played such an important role in the history of Gavi. The present-day protagonists of the Cascina San Bartolomeo are Quinto Bergaglio, his wife Teresa Carrea and their son Fulvio; they cultivate about ten hectares of vines and produce some 40 thousand bottles a year with the oenological assistance of Giuliano Noè. Their two more important wines, the Gavi Cappello del Diavolo and the Etichetta Nera, come from the same vineyard, which has a very high average vine age and a low yield per hectare. About 60% of the Cappello del Diavolo, which is made from a selection of the best bunches, spends some time in new wood. Not much of it is produced (about 3,000 bottles), but what there is is quite good enough to earn Two Glasses. It has a full and luminous straw color, and a broad, well-balanced nose with fresh aromas of citron, banana, apricot and anise. It displays a full body underpinned by a fresh vein of acidity and rounded off by a long finish punctuated by notes of fruit and custard. One full Glass goes to the Etichetta Nera: a quite intense hue is followed by aromas of peach, green banana, flowers and apple. The soft and succulent palate leads to a tasty, rich finish. The standard Gavi offers a faint straw color, fruity notes and a straightforward, well-balanced palate.

O	Gavi di Gavi Cappello del Diavolo '97	🍷🍷	3
O	Gavi di Gavi Etichetta Nera '97	🍷	3*
O	Gavi di Gavi '97		2

GAVI (AL)

Castellari Bergaglio

Fraz. Rovereto, 136
15066 Gavi (AL)
tel. 0143/644000

The Gavi Pilin, on its second appearance, has again decidedly earned Two Glasses. It is a special selection which spends some time in barriques, and has taken the place of the Gavi Barric, produced for the last time in '94. This '96 Gavi contains a small addition of slightly overripe grapes, whose function it is to confer more complexity and body. The wine has a rich and intense clear straw color; the broad and elegant bouquet, perhaps slightly dominated by the wood, offers aromas of apple, exotic fruit and vanilla, with smoky and balsamic overtones. The palate is better yet: a substantial, fat structure gives the sensation of breadth, while a well-judged vein of acidity provides a harmonic progression, ending in a very long finish with notes of fruit and fresh butter. The Gavi di Rovereto, produced in stainless steel vats, deserves One full Glass: a light straw color precedes aromas of sugared almond and banana, mingled with fresh notes of apricot and white flowers. On the palate it reveals good substance, with a softness not devoid of crispness. The finish is quite intense and reminiscent of almonds. The standard Gavi and the Brise are only slightly less good. The former, light straw-colored, offers subtle fruity and vegetal notes and an agreeable if not perfectly balanced palate; the latter makes a fresh and undemanding aperitif: it displays simple and delicately fruity aromas and a light effervescence.

O Gavi di Rovereto Pilin '96	🍷🍷	4
O Gavi '97	🍷	3
O Gavi di Rovereto '97	🍷	3
O Gavi Brise '97		3
O Gavi di Rovereto Pilin '95	♀♀	4

GAVI (AL)

La Chiara

Loc. Valleggie, 24/2
15066 Gavi (AL)
tel. 0143/642293

Roberto Bergaglio's passion for the grapevine has deep roots, going back to a childhood spent in the vineyards of La Scolca, where his father Ferdinando was the estate agent. For many years Roberto worked in a factory, while continuing, with great difficulty, to look after the roughly two hectares of family vineyard. Together with the vines he cherished a dream of becoming a full-time winegrower. In 1992 his efforts were rewarded, and with the purchase of additional vineyards he finally had an estate of a workable size. Today La Chiara produces some 60 thousand bottles a year. Roberto is assisted by his wife Silvana and their children Simona and Dario, and the oenologist in charge is Giancarlo Scaglione. The excellent Gavi Vigneto Groppella '96, a selection from the best vineyard which ferments and ages for ten months in barriques, would all by itself have earned an entry in the Guide. Of an intense straw color shot through with gold, it has a nose which immediately reveals great complexity and balance: aromas of apricot, apple and peach blossom create a delicate counterpoint with the hints of fresh butter and overripe fruit. It is immediately rich, fresh and silky on a palate quite without harshness that leads into a long finish redolent of citrus and caramel. The standard Gavi, quite correctly executed, has a light straw color with greenish highlights; the nose is fruity but a little faint. On the palate it is simple and undemanding.

O Gavi di Gavi Vigneto Groppella '96	🍷🍷	3*
O Gavi di Gavi '97		3

GAVI (AL)

LA GIUSTINIANA
FRAZ. ROVERETO, 5
15066 GAVI (AL)
TEL. 0143/682132

This important Rovereto winery, returning to the Guide after just a year's absence, has presented a convincing series of Gavis. The best of the lot is the Cru Centurionetta, which has earned itself Two Glasses, thanks to its delightful fragrance and full body. The wine, of a very pale straw color tinged with green, offers aromas of apricot, medlar, broom and peach blossom. On the palate it is substantial, decided, silky and harmonious, with an intense, long finish. The good Montessora, of a moderately intense straw color, is redolent of grapefruit, apple and peach. The palate is notably crisp and the finish is tasty. The Lugarara, their standard Gavi, is undoubtedly correct: the fragrance is composed mostly of secondary aromas of moderate finesse, and it is simple and light in the mouth. The lightly fizzy table wine, Roverì, notable for its clean execution, displays light aromas of apple, apricot and honey; the well-balanced palate is enlivened by a restrained effervescence. Passing to the Acqui side of the property (the Contero winery), we were favorably impressed by the finesse and balance of the Asti. It has a light color, aromas of elder flower, white- and yellow-fleshed fruit, and sage. In the mouth it is sweet, with a decided effervescence that makes it light and inviting. The good Bracchetto Spumante, which displays aromas of rose and pear, is undemanding on the palate. A Brachetto and a Moscato, both straightforward and easy drinking, end the list.

○	Gavi di Gavi Centurionetta '97	🍷🍷	4
○	Asti Contero '97	🍷	3
○	Gavi di Gavi Montessora '97	🍷	4
○	Roverì '97	🍷	3
●	Brachetto d'Acqui Spumante Contero '97	🍷	4
●	Brachetto d'Acqui Contero '97		4
○	Gavi di Gavi Lugarara '97		3
○	Moscato d'Asti Contero '97		3

GAVI (AL)

LA SCOLCA
FRAZ. ROVERETO
15066 GAVI (AL)
TEL. 0143/682176

The successful range of wines offered this year by La Scolca includes three particularly good sparkling wines, which have gathered up five Glasses between them. But we have long been admirers of the highly personal style of the spumante specialist Giorgio Soldati, and a taste of the Soldati La Scolca Brut Millesimato '87 reminds us of exactly why. The wine is delicately golden in color, with a tiny bead, and a nose which offers the usual warm, enticing aromas, but with an even lighter touch than in recent versions. Thus the pleasantly evolved hints of quince jam and fruit in syrup are joined by fresh suggestions of lily-of-the-valley and wild herbs. On the palate the wine is full-bodied, broad and well supported by a restrained effervescence that is not at all harsh. A long finish caps the pleasure. The excellent Gavi Brut La Scolca is richly straw-colored, with light golden highlights. Its broad array of aromas ranges from exotic fruit and crusty bread to notes of flint; on the palate it is rich and harmonious, with a densely fruity and flowery finish. The non-vintage Spumante Brut just misses Two Glasses: its vivid, intense straw color and fine-bubbled perlage are followed by a fruity nose (hints of damson, fig and exotic fruit), enriched by a faint mineral tone. It has good body and a decided but not aggressive effervescence. One Glass each goes to the two Gavis, the standard one and the Etichetta Nera, although we must say that we preferred the former, with its aromas of fruit, resin and hazelnut, and its well-balanced palate. Finally, the lively and refreshing Rugré is quite good.

○	Gavi Brut La Scolca	🍷🍷	4
○	Soldati La Scolca Spumante Brut '87	🍷🍷	5
○	Gavi '97	🍷	3
○	Gavi dei Gavi Etichetta Nera '97	🍷	5
○	Soldati La Scolca Spumante Brut	🍷	4
○	Gavi Rugré '97		3
○	Soldati La Scolca Spumante Brut '86	ΥΥ	5

GAVI (AL)

MORGASSI SUPERIORE
LOC. CASE SPARSE FERMORIA, 7
15066 GAVI (AL)
TEL. 0143/642007

The vines planted from 1990 onwards by the Piacitelli family are acquiring a respectable age, and with this age comes a notable improvement in the wines produced. After its debut in the Guide last year, this estate, with the oenological assistance of Giancarlo Scaglione, has presented a very successful range of wines. The Tamino '96, a syrah, stands out, as does the Cherubino '96, made from viognier. The Tamino, intensely ruby-garnet in color, offers impressively well-defined varietal spicy aromas: black pepper, resin and juniper berries form the background to warm tones of red fruit in alcohol. On the palate it is rich and full right from the start, with softness and breadth throughout its development, right up to a long finish, to which aristocratic tannins lend an attractive dryness. The Cherubino has a bright golden straw color and a broad and individual bouquet, with aromas of apricot, exotic fruit and tangerine and a light undertone of yeasty dough. On the palate it is continuous and silky, supported by a notable and refreshing succulence. The good Chardonnay Fiordiligi, with golden highlights on an intense straw-colored background, offers aromas of hazelnut, white flowers and fruit; the not very powerful palate is balanced and continuous. The Arbace, a blend of syrah and cabernet sauvignon with a little barbera, is slightly faded in color, and redolent of blackberry and raspberry, with mineral and balsamic nuances. The substantial progression on the palate leads into the warm, fruity tones of the finish. Last of all, the Gavi also earns its Glass, with its straw color with greenish highlights, fruity and floral nose and crisp, inviting palate.

	Wine	Glasses	Price
○	Cherubino '96	🍷🍷	5
●	Tamino '96	🍷🍷	5
●	Arbace '95	🍷	4
○	Gavi di Gavi '97	🍷	4
○	Piemonte Chardonnay Fiordiligi '95	🍷	4

GAVI (AL)

VILLA SPARINA
FRAZ. MONTEROTONDO, 56
15066 GAVI (AL)
TEL. 0143/633835

The wines from Villa Sparina just get better and better, but it could hardly be otherwise, given the care and attention that Mario, Stefano and Massimo Moccagatta devote to every detail of their production. The winery is increasingly oriented towards a reduction in quantity in the quest for the highest possible quality, even in their standard wines. They have chosen two eminent experts to assist them: the oenologist Beppe Caviola and the agronomist Federico Curtaz. Among the wines presented this year, three deserve Two very full Glasses indeed: the Barbera Rivalta, the Dolcetto d'Giusep, and the Gavi La Villa. The first has a dense ruby-garnet color with a compact violet rim and an ample and complex bouquet with notes of coffee custard, red currant, cherry and rosemary; on the palate it is broad and substantial, not extremely powerful, but harmonious and elegant, with a long fruity and balsamic finish. The d'Giusep confirms the excellent impressions that it made last year, with an added dash of elegance. The Gavi La Villa, richly straw-colored, offers a notably fresh and intense nose with fragrances of exotic fruit, peach, lily of the valley and flint. Then it's full-bodied, broad, soft and consistent, with a long fruity finish. The Cremant '91 and the Müller Thurgau '97 are also both excellent; the former is characterized by pleasantly evolved aromas and admirable balance in the mouth, while the latter shows full and succulent fruit, with notes of elderberry, sage and grapefruit. Finally, the Dolcetto Bric Maioli, easy drinking but quite meaty, and the standard Gavi, fresh and satisfying, are only a little less good, but still worthy of Two Glasses.

	Wine	Glasses	Price
○	Gavi Cremant Pas Dosé '91	🍷🍷	5
○	Gavi di Gavi '97	🍷🍷	3*
○	Gavi di Gavi La Villa '97	🍷🍷	4
○	Monferrato Müller Thurgau '97	🍷🍷	3*
●	Barbera del M.to Rivalta '96	🍷🍷	5
●	Dolcetto d'Acqui Bric Maioli '97	🍷🍷	3
●	Dolcetto d'Acqui Sup. d'Giusep '97	🍷🍷	4
●	Dolcetto d'Acqui Sup. d'Giusep '96	99	4
○	Gavi Cremant Pas Dosé '90	99	5
○	Gavi di Gavi La Villa '96	99	4
○	Gavi di Gavi La Villa '95	99	4

GHEMME (NO)

ANTICHI VIGNETI DI CANTALUPO
VIA MICHELANGELO BUONARROTI, 5
28074 GHEMME (NO)
TEL. 0163/840041

This year Alberto Arlunno again offers a series of excellent wines, with three Ghemmes (the Collis Breclemae '90, the Signore di Bayard '93 and the standard '93) that are particularly admirable for their structure and elegance. The first, released a full eight years after its vintage, wins Two very full Glasses. It has an intense ruby-garnet color with a faintly orange rim, and a complex and mature bouquet which offers aromas of wild berries, fig, plum and long-dried flowers. On the palate it is full and rich right from the start, and progresses, soft and well-articulated, to a long finish with a noble tannic presence. The Signore di Bayard, enriched by a well-judged period in barrique, shows an intense ruby hue with garnet highlights. There are aromas of raspberry, flowers, aromatic wood and clove, with an animal undertone. The full-bodied palate progresses evenly and without interruption. The standard Ghemme, somewhat less powerful than the others but just as captivating, comes very close to Two Glasses. Ruby-hued, it offers aromas that combine fresh tones and mature notes, with hints of red fruit, fig and biscuit; it is warm, mouth-filling and succulent on the palate, leading to a corresponding finish with a definite tannic.vein. The Carolus, a blend of greco and chardonnay with a little arneis, is a pleasingly crisp white wine with an intense fruity nose. The Agamium, an unpretentious red, is smooth and appealing. The clear and delicate Villa Horta, made from vespolina, has a straightforward, dry taste, while the rustic Primigenia has a decided character. Last in the list, Il Mimo, is a fruity and soft rosé.

	Wine	Glasses	Price
●	Ghemme Collis Breclemae '90	🍷🍷	5
●	Ghemme Signore di Bayard '93	🍷🍷	5
●	Colline Novaresi Agamium '96	🍷	3
●	Ghemme '93	🍷	4
○	Carolus '97	🍷	2
⊙	Il Mimo '97	🍷	2
●	Primigenia '97	🍷	2
●	Villa Horta '97	🍷	2
●	Ghemme Collis Breclemae '89	🍷🍷 (prev.)	5
●	Ghemme Collis Breclemae '91	🍷🍷 (prev.)	4
●	Ghemme Collis Carellae '89	🍷🍷 (prev.)	5
●	Ghemme Collis Carellae '90	🍷🍷 (prev.)	5
●	Ghemme Collis Carellae '91	🍷 (prev.)	4

INCISA SCAPACCINO (AT)

ERMANNO E ALESSANDRA BREMA
VIA POZZOMAGNA, 9
14045 INCISA SCAPACCINO (AT)
TEL. 0141/74019 - 74617

The vineyards belonging to this family include all the best sites of the Nizza zone: they own land in Fontanile, Castelnuovo Calcea, Vinchio, Incisa and Nizza. From this collection of locations, they produce the whole range of classic Monferrato wines, which are a real expression of their terroir, faithful to their categories, and are offered on the market without frills or furbelows. The sole exception is the Dolcetto d'Asti Vigna Impagnato, which is aged in barriques, some of which are new and some 2-3 years old. This wine, already a great rarity, succeeds, after its contact with oak, in expressing complexity without losing the character of a straightforward, generous and exuberant wine. The '96 has a reddish violet color, a touch of vanilla and red berries on the nose, and a broad, meaty palate with a not unpleasant roughness on the finish. The partially oak-aged Barbera d'Asti '96 is a little less convincing than it has been, especially on the somewhat closed nose. It has lots of body, however, and is broad, warm and remarkably lingering. We also liked the lively Monferrato Vigna Castagnei '97, sinewy and richly flavorful, with its clear strawberry and raspberry fragrance. The well-made Brachetto Carlotta '97 resembles previous vintages, but shows a strong personality this year: the deep rose color is followed by lively and distinct varietal aromas, with rose and peach to the fore. The body is quite rich for this category. The house Grignolino, Bric le Rocche '97, good as usual, is less unbalanced than many excessively tannic Grignolinos and has a peppery nose.

	Wine	Glasses	Price
●	Dolcetto d'Asti Vigna Impagnato '96	🍷🍷	3*
●	Barbera d'Asti Sup. Le Cascine '96	🍷	4
●	Barbera d'Asti Vigna Donato '96	🍷	3
●	Grignolino d'Asti Bric le Rocche '96	🍷	3
●	Piemonte Brachetto Carlotta '97	🍷	4
●	Barbera del M.to Vigna Castagnei '97		2

IVREA (TO)

FERRANDO E C.
C.SO CAVOUR, 9
10015 IVREA (TO)
TEL. 0125/641176

There are three Erbaluce wines presented by Ferrando this year, and they all got high scores, testifying to the undoubted capacity of this winegrower. We particularly liked the Cariola for the finesse of its fragrance and its full body; it has a straw color verging on gold, and aromas of hazelnut, apple and exotic fruit; on the palate it is soft and substantial, underpinned by a tonic acid vein, and concluding with a long, well-composed finish. The Erbaluce Ferrando, only slightly inferior, with an intense straw color, is redolent of banana, peach, dried fruit and citrus fruit; the well-structured palate has an intense finish. We were less impressed by the Cariola Etichetta Nera, which has a rich golden hue; the nose offers notes of vanilla, nutmeg and fruit; the substantial palate does not show a proper balance between wood and fruit. A series of decidedly admirable wines completes the list: the sparkling Cariola Brut, dark straw in color, has aromas of hazelnut and white-fleshed fruit, with undertones of custard, and a well-defined, straightforward palate. The Montodo Bianco has an intense straw color shot through with green; the fruity nose has a touch of vanilla and the palate is soft and restrained. Finally, the Canavese Rosso Montodo has a rich garnet-ruby color and aromas of dark cherry, blackberry and crusty bread; on the balanced and soft palate the tannins are only just perceptible. A few of the estate's traditional labels are missing: propitious vintages and the good quality of these wines have led Luigi to let them age a little longer. We shall see the results next year.

	Wine	Rating	Price
○	Erbaluce di Caluso Cariola '97	🍷🍷	3
○	Montodo Bianco '97	🍷	3
○	Cariola Brut	🍷	4
○	Erbaluce di Caluso Cariola Etichetta Nera '97	🍷	4
○	Erbaluce di Caluso Ferrando '97	🍷	3
●	Canavese Rosso Montodo '97	🍷	2*
●	Carema Etichetta Nera '90	🍷🍷 (white)	6
○	Solativo '96	🍷🍷 (white)	5
○	Caluso Passito Boratto '91	🍷 (white)	5
●	Carema Etichetta Bianca '90	🍷 (white)	5

LA MORRA (CN)

★ ELIO ALTARE
CASCINA NUOVA, 51
FRAZ. ANNUNZIATA
12064 LA MORRA (CN)
TEL. 0173/50835

Lucia Casetta, Elio Altare's wife, is a classic example of a great woman behind the success of a great man. The approach of these two has not changed: success has not confined them to their cellar but has really made them happier; though they may sometimes seem tired, they readily maintain that they feel blessed by fortune. In actual fact Elio and Lucia are allies of destiny, and always get the best out of hard times. This happened in the '94 vintage, when the Altare family was wise enough to reject part of their own production so as to create a Barolo way above the level of that year. The wine, from the Arborina vineyard as usual, has in its color, bouquet and flavor an overwhelming density, warmth and persistence which make it exquisitely harmonious, still capable of improving even further, but ready to be enjoyed immediately. Together with this small masterpiece, we note this year two great ones: the Arborina '96 has the intimate depth of the nebbiolo with a delicacy of bouquet as surprising as it is irresistible; the palate is articulated by the tannins, while the aromatic persistence is a virtue in itself. The Larigi '96 has acquired a completeness of expression which, while placing it in the ranks of the great international wines, has not robbed it of its qualities as a child of the Langhe. The deep color, the magnificent fusion of fruit and oak, and an inspiring progression on the palate are the salient points of a wine which is worth watching over time. Elio and Lucia have a stupendous red in preparation, a magical blend of nebbiolo, barbera and imported varieties.

	Wine	Rating	Price
●	Langhe Arborina '96	🍷🍷🍷	6
●	Barbera d'Alba '97	🍷🍷	4
●	Barolo '94	🍷🍷	5
●	Barolo Vigneto Arborina '94	🍷🍷	6
●	Dolcetto d'Alba '97	🍷🍷	4
●	Langhe La Villa '96	🍷🍷	6
●	Langhe Larigi '96	🍷🍷	6
●	Barolo Vigneto Arborina '89	🍷🍷🍷 (white)	6
●	Barolo Vigneto Arborina '90	🍷🍷🍷 (white)	6
●	Barolo Vigneto Arborina '93	🍷🍷🍷 (white)	6
●	Langhe Larigi '94	🍷🍷🍷 (white)	6
●	Langhe Larigi '95	🍷🍷🍷 (white)	6
●	Vigna Arborina '90	🍷🍷🍷 (white)	6
●	Vigna Arborina '93	🍷🍷🍷 (white)	6
●	Vigna Larigi '90	🍷🍷🍷 (white)	6

LA MORRA (CN)

Renato Ratti - Antiche Cantine dell'Abbazia dell'Annunziata

Fraz. Annunziata, 7
12064 La Morra (CN)
tel. 0173/50185

The Villa Pattono (a Monferrato made from barbera, freisa, uvalino and merlot) is undoubtedly the best wine presented this year by Pietro and Giovanni Ratti, together with Massimo Martinelli. The intense ruby color is enlivened by violet highlights; the bouquet (a mixture of varietal aromas and wood) is a concentration of cherry, blackberry and black pepper, and the harmony is not lost on the palate. Here softness debates with the lively acidity and smooth tannins, producing a lingering sensation of fullness. The Cabernet Sauvignon I Cedri, just a touch simpler but in the same style, has a deep ruby color; the distinct ripe cherry fragrance is followed by a medium body rich in alcohol. The Merlot (highly colored, sweetly fruity and rounded) is equally good The richest of the classic Langhe wines is the Barolo, which has the advantage of grapes from the Vigneto Rocche. On the nose prune and almond are blended with more pungent fragrances, while on the palate the wine is more convincing, despite the alcohol's being somewhat one-upped by the pleasing tannins and the dense extract. The quaffability of Nebbiolo is best expressed in the Ochetti, enlivened by ruby highlights, delicately fragrant and firm, thanks to the correct acidity and active tannins. The Barbera and the Dolcetto are not up to par: the first is somewhat disjointed and the second is simpler than usual.

●	Monferrato Villa Pattono '96	🍷🍷	4
●	Barbera d'Alba Torriglione '96	🍷	4
●	Barolo Marcenasco '94	🍷	5
●	Monferrato I Cedri '96	🍷	4
●	Dolcetto d'Alba Colombè '97	🍷	3
●	Monferrato Merlot '96	🍷	4
●	Nebbiolo d'Alba Ochetti '96	🍷	4
●	Barolo Rocche Marcenasco '83	🍷🍷🍷	6
●	Barolo Rocche Marcenasco '84	🍷🍷🍷	6
●	Barolo Conca Marcenasco '93	🍷🍷	6
●	Barolo Rocche Marcenasco '90	🍷🍷	5
●	Barolo Rocche Marcenasco '93	🍷🍷	6
●	Cabernet Sauvignon I Cedri '95	🍷🍷	4
●	Merlot '95	🍷🍷	4
●	Villa Pattono '95	🍷🍷	4

LA MORRA (CN)

Batasiolo

Fraz. Annunziata, 87
12064 La Morra (Cn)
tel. 0173/50130 - 50131

This year the Dogliani family's estate has not achieved the same results as in the past, in part because two of their most important wines, the Barolo Corda della Briccolina and the Moscato Passito, are missing from the list, and in part because of the objective decline of wines which on other occasions have shown more character. The Dolcetto Bricco Vergne may be taken as an example: it is pleasing on the nose, but rather short on the palate. The Barbera d'Alba Sovrana reveals more meatiness and breadth; the liveliness of the ruby color is equaled by the frank headiness of the bouquet; there is a warm impact on the palate, which progresses with youthful simplicity. The Chardonnay Serbato (juicy and satisfying, with a full, long finish) gives a sensation of immediacy and cleanness. On the other hand, the barrique-matured Chardonnay is under par; it has an encouraging golden color, but the nose does not open out very much, as if it were still caught in the grip of the oak. The same can be said for the palate, which only occasionally manages to show its quality. We had been eager to taste the Barolo Boscareto '93, remembering its illustrious predecessors; however, this wine from Serralunga left us a little baffled, not so much because of a lack of concentration, as because of a disjointedness on both nose and palate. For the Moscato Boscareto it would not have been easy to repeat the glories of the '96; it does, however, show its characteristic mature aromas, and a full sweetness of flavor.

●	Barbera d'Alba Sovrana '96	🍷	4
●	Barolo Boscareto '93	🍷	5
●	Dolcetto d'Alba Bricco Vergne '97	🍷	3
○	Langhe Chardonnay Morino '95	🍷	5
○	Langhe Chardonnay Serbato '97	🍷	3
○	Moscato d'Asti Boscareto '97	🍷	3
●	Barolo Corda della Briccolina '88	🍷🍷🍷	6
●	Barolo Corda della Briccolina '89	🍷🍷🍷	6
●	Barolo Corda della Briccolina '90	🍷🍷🍷	6
●	Barolo Corda della Briccolina '93	🍷🍷	6
○	Piemonte Moscato Passito Muscatel Tardì '96	🍷🍷	5
●	Barolo Bofani '93	🍷	5

LA MORRA (CN)

ENZO BOGLIETTI
VIA ROMA, 37
12064 LA MORRA (CN)
TEL. 0173/50330

Little Linda Boglietti, who is not yet one year old, will certainly know what to drink to celebrate her 18th birthday in far-off 2015: in fact her father Enzo has already laid up a stock of the Barolo '97, with special hand-written labels. The Case Nere, one of the two Vigneti di Barolo, is entirely barrique-aged. It offers a broad and spicy bouquet (licorice and fennel seed); on the well-structured palate, one senses the presence of important and long-lasting tannins. The Brunate, traditionally vinified, is readier, with a heady and somewhat one-toned nose with hints of raspberry and licorice; it is soft in the mouth and already quite drinkable. The small selection (2,000 bottles) of Barbera Vigna dei Romani '96 looks dark and dense in the glass: spicy aromas of leather are perfectly blended with the fruit and followed by a warm, powerful palate, with soft tannins lasting through a long finish. The excellent Barbera '97, heady and redolent of chocolate, has a generous and well-balanced body for one so young. As supplies of the Buio '95 have long been exhausted, we decided on an early review of the '96. A blend of nebbiolo and barbera, it has a real Langhe nose, all spice and undergrowth; on the palate it acts almost like a Barolo, so powerful are its tannins. We end with the Dolcetto Tigli Neri '97, an assemblage of the grapes from three old vineyards: the color is a dark violet, and the concentrated nose (with an almond fragrance) is followed by a well-structured palate and dense but fairly well-balanced tannins. The sound Dolcetto '97, with its fresh hints of raspberry and flowers, is simple and easy to drink.

	Wine	Rating	Price
●	Barbera d'Alba '97	🍷🍷	3
●	Barbera d'Alba Vigna dei Romani '96	🍷🍷	5
●	Barolo Vigna Case Nere '94	🍷🍷	5
●	Dolcetto d'Alba Tigli Neri '97	🍷🍷	3
●	Langhe Rosso Buio '96	🍷🍷	5
●	Barolo Brunate '94	🍷	5
●	Dolcetto d'Alba '97	🍷	3
●	Langhe Rosso Buio '95	🍷	5
●	Barbera d'Alba Vigna dei Romani '94	🍸🍸🍸	4
●	Barbera d'Alba Vigna dei Romani '95	🍸🍸	4
●	Barolo Vigna Case Nere '93	🍸🍸	5
●	Barolo Vigna delle Brunate '93	🍸🍸	5

LA MORRA (CN)

GIANFRANCO BOVIO
B.TA CIOTTO, 63
FRAZ. ANNUNZIATA
12064 LA MORRA (CN)
TEL. 0173/50190 - 50604

If you're a Barolo producer, the best approach to a dispiriting year like '94 must be Bovio's: bite the bullet and prepare the counter-attack. And indeed his most important wines have come out very well, scoring almost as high as the far richer '93s, while great changes in both vineyard and cellar promise excellent results for the fine subsequent vintages. Production has fallen by 20%, for the sake of a better concentration in the remaining bunches (now even the dolcetto is rigorously pruned); the fermentation room is nearing completion, with the most innovative vats in existence; the expert advice of oenological luminaries is being added to the precious viticultural experience of Walter and Carla Porasso, who are still in charge in the vineyards. In short, a revolution, proclaimed this year by the new graphic design of the labels. The Barolo Arborina, traditionally the fresher and more innovative one, has this year been nature's plaything: the aromas have evolved earlier than usual and the bouquet is already a fully enjoyable set of variations on the theme of cherries preserved in spirits, carried through onto the (perhaps even excessively) alcohol-rich palate. The traditional Barolo Gattera, though its color is more mature, shows a greener and headier energy in its aromas, which gives it charm if not complexity. The palate reveals fair fruit, lively acidity and well-behaved tannins, but you don't get a very long glimpse. This year's Dolcetto and Barbera are harmonious and agreeable, as is their wont.

	Wine	Rating	Price
●	Barbera d'Alba Il Ciotto '97	🍷	3
●	Barolo Vigneto Arborina dell'Annunziata '94	🍷	5
●	Barolo Vigneto Gattera dell'Annunziata '94	🍷	5
●	Dolcetto d'Alba Vigneto Dabbene dell'Annunziata '97	🍷	3
●	Barolo Vigneto Arborina dell'Annunziata '90	🍸🍸🍸	6
●	Barolo Vigneto Arborina dell'Annunziata '93	🍸🍸	5
●	Barolo Vigneto Gattera dell'Annunziata '93	🍸🍸	5

LA MORRA (CN)

Corino

Fraz. Annunziata, 24
12064 La Morra (CN)
tel. 0173/50219 - 509452

Hats off to the brothers Giuliano and Renato Corino for the excellence of this year's wines, all of which share intense color, fruit and concentration. This style (fashionable and international), when applied to different grape varieties, vintages and vineyards, ensures that the characteristics of each wine can emerge and be appreciated, even by the least sophisticated palate. The wines are so good that they have pushed the Corinos back up to the top ranks of Langhe producers, and have won them another Three Glasses. The Barbera d'Alba Pozzo '96 is first-class, characterized by aromas of ripe fruit (cherry) and licorice pervaded by toasty notes of oak; the admirable palate reveals silky tannins, a long finish and enormous body which counterpoises the acidulous nature of the barbera. Both Barolos easily win Two Glasses for their fine interpretation of one of the most difficult vintages in recent years. The Vigna Giachini '94, ruby verging on garnet, is redolent of leather and spice; on the palate the fruit (raspberry) is velvety but powerful. The Vigneto Rocche '94, on the other hand, is a little less deep in color, but definitely more elegant in bouquet, with fruity notes and chocolate nuances; on the palate it is even more elegant and soft, with a lovely sweet finish. The excellent Barbera '97 enchants with its generous body, ripe fruit and admirable balance. Finally, the Dolcetto '97, of a very dark ruby hue, has a heady fragrance with a blueberry note and a warm palate with tannins which are clearly present but smooth on the finish.

	Wine	Glasses	Price
●	Barbera d'Alba Vigna Pozzo '96	▼▼▼	4
●	Barbera d'Alba '97	▼▼	3*
●	Barolo Vigna Giachini '94	▼▼	5
●	Barolo Vigneto Rocche '94	▼▼	5
●	Dolcetto d'Alba '97	▼	3
●	Barolo Vigna Giachini '89	▽▽▽	5
●	Barolo Vigneto Rocche '90	▽▽▽	5
●	Barbera d'Alba Vigna Pozzo '94	▽▽	4
●	Barolo Vigna Giachini '90	▽▽	5
●	Barolo Vigna Giachini '93	▽▽	5
●	Barolo Vigneto Rocche '93	▽▽	5
●	Barbera d'Alba Vigna Pozzo '95	▽	4

LA MORRA (CN)

Dosio

Reg. Serradenari, 16
12064 La Morra (CN)
tel. 0173/50677

Dosio's wide range of wines requires a detailed review, and this leaves little space for a description of the lovely, well-ordered cellar from which Beppe (with the valuable assistance of Giorgio Vaira) annually turns out 60 thousand bottles. This year is a triumph for the classic Langhe wines over the creative blends, which are Dosio's other line. The star is the Barolo Fossati, which gave us more pleasure than it has for years; its garnet hue is encouragingly intense; the classic bouquet is heady and pruney; the restrained tannins underpin the softness of the palate, and the only sign of that tricky vintage is the rather short finish. The Barberas are not very convincing, especially on the nose, unlike the fresher reds. The Dolcetto Serradenari displays all the elegance of which its vineyard, next to the winery, is capable. It has a lively fuchsia color and the nose is cleanly redolent of cherry; the attack on the palate is good and the finish clean. The Freisa, of a deep, lively cherry red, offers fresh aromas of strawberry and pennyroyal, followed by a crisply acidic palate that makes for easy, enjoyable drinking. Among the barriqued wines, we particularly mention Eventi, a successful blend of barbera, dolcetto and nebbiolo. The wood has added a mineral tone to the fruity bouquet, and in the mouth the wine is fresh and direct, and not in a hurry. The Momenti, made from barbera and nebbiolo grapes, has tobacco tones on both nose and palate, and is also more mouth-puckering, while the Chardonnay Barilà should show more varietal richness.

	Wine	Glasses	Price
●	Barolo Fossati '94	▼▼	5
●	Dolcetto d'Alba Serradenari '97	▼	3
●	Eventi '96	▼	4
●	Langhe Freisa Serradenari '97	▼	3
●	Langhe Momenti '96	▼	4
●	Barbera d'Alba Sup. '96		3
●	Barbera d'Alba Sant'Anna '96		3
○	Langhe Chardonnay Barilà '97		4
●	Barolo Fossati '90	▽▽	5
●	Barolo Fossati '91	▽	5
●	Barolo Fossati '93	▽	5

LA MORRA (CN)

Erbaluna

B.ta Pozzo, 43
12064 La Morra (CN)
tel. 0173/50800

Erbaluna has won a reconfirmation in the Guide with its fine range of wines, which will be expanded next year. Barbera and Dolcetto will be presented in two versions, to satisfy, with their different styles, different tastes. But let's get down to this year's wines. The Dolcetto has a violet color; fruit does not take the lead on the nose, but, on the palate, an agreeable bite makes the wine a pleasure to drink. The Barbera is more closed on the nose, which offers almost musky aromas, and is even a little timid on the palate: here the main features are the warmth of the alcohol and the characteristic varietal acidity, responsible in part for the vivacity of the color. The standard Barolo, forward in color (garnet) and bouquet (licorice and leather), and abundantly round on the palate, is not altogether overshadowed by their star wine, the Barolo Rocche, which has a distinct garnet hue and a pruney bouquet. It comes into its own in the mouth, where the fruit and the young tannins live up to expectation and culminate in a clean, fruity finish.

Wine	Glasses	Price
● Barbera d'Alba La Bettola '97	▼	3*
● Barolo '94	▼	5
● Barolo Rocche '94	▼	5
● Dolcetto d'Alba Le Ghiaie '97	▼	3*
● Barolo Rocche '93	▽	4

LA MORRA (CN)

Silvio Grasso

Cascina Luciani, 112
Fraz. Annunziata
12064 La Morra (CN)
tel. 0173/50322

This estate, comprising seven and a half hectares of vineyard between Luciani and Manzoni, near La Morra, is brilliantly run by Federico and Marilena Grasso. Over the years the improvement in their wines has been remarkable, as has the increase in demand for them, particularly abroad. We greatly admired the cool cellars of the Cascina Luciani, once a convent full of nuns, and now filled with bottles arranged with great care, and with a constantly increasing number of barriques. During 1998 we tasted a number of good wines, diminished only by the difficult '94 vintage, from which the Grassos produced three different Barolos: the Ciabot Manzoni, the Bricco Luciani and the standard version, which costs relatively little. The Ciabot Manzoni pleased us most; it is oakier, but also more rounded and softer, with smooth tannins and a sweet finish. The other two are only just correct; the Bricco Luciani, whose palate is made to toe the line by the austere tannins, suffers from somewhat disjointed aromas, and the standard Barolo, with a simple, nebbiolo-like nose, and not enough fruit or softness on the palate. Moving on to better years, we find the Langhe Nebbiolo '95 quite satisfying: its bouquet is toasty and spicy (vanilla, incense and pepper); you'd think you were drinking a Barolo, such is its power and character, with its clear notes of violet and licorice. The good Dolcetto '97, dark of hue, has a fruity and mature nose; it is still hard on the palate, but direct and a delight to drink. As usual, the Barbera d'Alba Fontanile is very good, and the '96 is more powerful than it has ever been.

Wine	Glasses	Price
● Barbera d'Alba Fontanile '96	▼▼	5
● Barolo Ciabot Manzoni '94	▼▼	5
● Langhe Nebbiolo '95	▼▼	4
● Barolo '94	▼	4
● Barolo Bricco Luciani '94	▼	5
● Dolcetto d'Alba '97	▼	3
● Barolo Bricco Luciani '90	▽▽▽	5
● Barbera d'Alba Fontanile '93	▽▽	4
● Barolo Bricco Luciani '91	▽▽	5
● Barolo Bricco Luciani '92	▽▽	5
● Barolo Bricco Luciani '93	▽▽	5
● Barolo Ciabot Manzoni '90	▽▽	5
● Barolo Ciabot Manzoni '93	▽▽	5

LA MORRA (CN)

GROMIS
VIA DEL LAGHETTO, 1
12064 LA MORRA (CN)
TEL. 0173/50137

After a hiatus imposed by natural causes - because of the poor vintage, the Barolo '92 was not produced - Gromis is back in the Guide. The wine they've presented, the Barolo '93, confirms that Angelo Gaja knows how to make a mean Barolo too. It is a very good wine indeed: its deep color gives you your first hint of the powerful structure that lies in wait. The varied bouquet offers youthful aromas of fruit pervaded by more complex toasty and coffee notes; on the palate it is powerful, velvety and enormously full-bodied. We owe these qualities to the Cerequio vineyard, some 22 hectares with a south/southeasterly exposure and one of the historic crus of La Morra, which Angelo Gaja bought in 1995 from the Marengo Marendas. The estate is now run by the young oenologist Alessandro Albarello, who, under the watchful eye of Guido Ravella, the wine technician who has made Gaja's wines great in these last 30 years, is realizing the new range dictated by Angelo. In fact in the next few years (a new vineyard of about eight hectares in the area of Silio di Santa Maria di la Morra has already been acquired), the winery will be equipped to satisfy the demands of a market increasingly bewitched by Barolo.

	Wine	Glasses	Price
●	Barolo Conteisa Cerequio '93	🍷🍷	6
●	Barolo Conteisa Cerequio '91	♀♀	6

LA MORRA (CN)

MARCARINI
P.ZZA MARTIRI, 2
12064 LA MORRA (CN)
TEL. 0173/50222

The legendary cellar of the Poderi Marcarini, now run by Luisa and Manuel Marchetti, is in the first square you come to in La Morra. The estate boasts 12 hectares in the celebrated vineyards of Brunate, La Serra and Boschi di Berri. This last is unique in these parts: located in the part of Berri that slopes down from La Morra to the Tanaro river, it is a dolcetto vineyard, some of whose vines are more than a hundred years old, which was miraculously spared the scourge of phylloxera at the beginning of this century, and is hence ungrafted. Old vines, as we know, naturally have a low yield, and wine made from their grapes is particularly good. The Boschi di Berri '97, deep ruby tinged with violet, offers fruity aromas of bitter cherry and almond; on the palate it is concentrated, with soft tannins and a long finish. The surprising Barbera Ciabot Camerano '97, very dark in color, reveals hints of jam and flowers which carry through onto the palate and linger there, thanks to the richness of the dense and succulent fruit. The Barolo Brunate '94, with its penetrating notes of strawberry, aromatic herbs and tobacco, wins Two Glasses: although a little harder on the palate than La Serra, it is very likely to improve a lot with bottle age. The last wines in the series are the Nebbiolo Lasarin, from a good vintage and showing sizable bitterish tannins, the Dolcetto Fontanazza, a little green and not very straightforward on the nose, and the well-balanced Moscato d'Asti.

	Wine	Glasses	Price
●	Barbera d'Alba Ciabot Camerano '97	🍷🍷	3*
●	Dolcetto d'Alba Boschi di Berri '97	🍷🍷	4
●	Barolo Brunate '94	🍷	5
●	Barolo La Serra '94	🍷	5
●	Langhe Nebbiolo Lasarin '97	🍷	3
○	Moscato d'Asti '97	🍷	3
●	Dolcetto d'Alba Fontanazza '97		3
●	Barolo Brunate Ris. '85	♀♀♀	6
●	Dolcetto d'Alba Boschi di Berri '96	♀♀♀	4
●	Barolo Brunate '90	♀♀	6
●	Barolo Brunate '93	♀♀	5
●	Barolo La Serra '93	♀♀	5

Mauro Molino

B.ta Gancia, 111
Fraz. Annunziata
12064 La Morra (CN)
tel. 0173/50814

What a shame that Molino's excellent wines almost all end up abroad: 95%, in fact, is exported, leaving little more than 1,500 bottles to satisfy Italian wine lovers! Mauro Molino, a calm man and a careful taster, explains that when he decided to follow his father's profession, he had no choice but to export what he produced, since the estate was small and totally unknown (his father did not bottle wine, and supplied grapes to large wineries). This year's range is stupendous: three wines easily win Two Glasses, and the Barbera d'Alba Vigneto Gattere, its first time out, has nonchalantly walked off with Three. It is a red with a great structure and admirable elegance. The balanced aromas, not dominated by wood, display notes of dark cherry with licorice and coffee. There is an explosion of sensations on the broad, harmonious palate and the finish is long and satisfying. The Acanzio '96 is no disappointment either, and only just missed its second Three Glasses; nebbiolo and barbera play equal parts in this wine, which offers aromas of raspberry, minty herbs and pepper; on the palate it is succulent and fat, with tannins in evidence but soft. The Barolo Vigna Conca '94, of a lively deep color, successfully blends vanilla and licorice with its fruit. The golden Chardonnay '97, fermented and aged in barriques for several months, offers notes of honey and vanilla followed by a generous body which makes it seem almost dense. The series ends with the Barolo '94, a good nebbiolo which is, however, a bit harsh, and the Dolcetto, fruity and good to drink.

	Wine	Glasses	Price
●	Barbera d'Alba Vigna Gattere '96	▼▼▼	5
●	Barolo Vigna Conca '94	▼▼	5
○	Langhe Chardonnay Livrot '97	▼▼	4
●	Langhe Rosso Acanzio '96	▼▼	5
●	Barolo '94	▼	5
●	Dolcetto d'Alba '97	▼	3*
●	Acanzio '95	▽▽	4
●	Barolo Vigna Conca '93	▽▽	5
○	Langhe Chardonnay Livrot '96	▽▽	4

Monfalletto Cordero di Montezemolo

Fraz. Annunziata, 67/bis
12064 La Morra (CN)
tel. 0173/50344

The cellar of the Cordero di Montezemolo family is near Monfalletto, in the hamlet of Annunziata di La Morra. The 26 hectares of vineyard surrounding the cellar are planted to nebbiolo, dolcetto, barbera, chardonnay and small quantities of arneis and pinot noir. There are a further three hectares in the Villero di Castiglione Falletto vineyard, which gives rise to the Barolo Enrico VI. In recent years Gianni and Enrico have fomented a sort of revolution in the cellar, in an attempt to modernize their wines. For Barolo, '95 represents a turning point in the history of the estate, while '94 is a transitional year, with deeper color, less hardness and more wood. Between the two Barolos presented this year, the Enrico VI is unquestionably better. It has distinct spicy, almost balsamic notes of mint and fennel seed; on the palate it shows clear tannins and a fairly long finish. The particularly interesting Nebbiolo '97 shows promise, despite its youth, of a good future, thanks to a substantial body and a long finish. The Dolcetto '97 is very dark in color, still headily grapey on the nose and rich in sweet fruit on the palate. The list ends with the Montezemolo Brut, a Metodo Classico sparkling wine made from chardonnay, and with a quite individual softness, and the Langhe Bianco '97, made from arneis, which contains 13.5° of alcohol. The Barbera '97, the Pinot Nero '96 and the Chardonnay Elioro '97 had not yet been bottled, so we'll review them next year.

	Wine	Glasses	Price
●	Barolo Enrico VI '94	▼▼	5
●	Langhe Nebbiolo '97	▼▼	4
●	Barolo Monfalletto '94	▼	5
●	Dolcetto d'Alba '97	▼	3
○	Langhe Bianco '97	▼	3
○	Montezemolo Brut	▼	4
●	Barolo Enrico VI '90	▽▽	6
●	Barolo Enrico VI '92	▽▽	5
●	Barolo Enrico VI '93	▽▽	5
●	Barolo Monfalletto '90	▽▽	6
●	Barolo Monfalletto '93	▽▽	5
●	Barolo Monfalletto '92	▽	5

LA MORRA (CN)

ANDREA OBERTO
VIA G. MARCONI, 25
12064 LA MORRA (CN)
TEL. 0173/509262

Andrea Oberto, now assisted in the cellar by his son, takes home a tray full of Glasses this year; he also has won his first Three Glasses with his Barbera Giada '96, and has almost earned another with the new wine dedicated to his son Fabio. The Barbera Giada, which comes from almost 60-year-old vines in the Boiolo vineyard and is aged in barriques for 18 months, shows a deep ruby color and concentrated aromas of ripe red fruit and sweet spice; the palate, supported by almost 14° of alcohol, is soft and fruity, with silky tannins and a long finish. It's a great success, this Barbera, crowning years of effort. The '95 is also very impressive, but not quite as rich, and more dominated by oak. The Langhe Rosso Fabio '96 has made a fine debut: a blend of nebbiolo (60%) and barbera (40%), it offers a toasty nose and a palate reminiscent of a Barolo in its great body and austere tannins. Of the two Barolos, the Vigneto Rocche is less colorful than the standard version, which originates in the San Francesco and Albarella vineyards and is distinctly fruity (raspberry), and delicately floral (rose) in bouquet, but lacks the depth on the palate of the Rocche. After so much praise, we must offer one criticism of the '97s: they are satisfying on the palate but show a certain rusticity on the nose. Nevertheless, of the Dolcettos, we preferred the Vantrino Albarella for a fullness and power in the mouth characteristic of a real thoroughbred, while the Barbera '97, elegant and soft on the palate, almost suggests a pinot noir with its fruity nuances of raspberry and red currant.

	Wine	Rating	Price
●	Barbera d'Alba Giada '96	🍷🍷🍷	5
●	Barbera d'Alba Giada '95	🍷🍷	5
●	Barolo Vigneto Rocche '94	🍷🍷	5
●	Dolcetto d'Alba Vantrino Albarella '97	🍷🍷	3*
●	Langhe Fabio '96	🍷🍷	5
●	Barbera d'Alba Vigneto Boiolo '97	🍷	3*
●	Barolo '94	🍷	5
●	Dolcetto d'Alba '97	🍷	3
●	Dolcetto d'Alba S. Francesco '97	🍷	3
●	Barbera d'Alba Giada '93	🍷🍷 (white)	4
●	Barolo Vigneto Rocche '90	🍷🍷 (white)	6
●	Barolo Vigneto Rocche '93	🍷🍷 (white)	5

LA MORRA (CN)

F.LLI ODDERO
VIA S. MARIA, 28
12064 LA MORRA (CN)
TEL. 0173/50618

The Barolo made by the brothers Giacomo and Luigi Oddero comes out of the historic winery in La Morra, thanks to the careful attention of a team of vineyard and cellar adepts, young and not so young, with the advice of renowned technical consultants and the supervision of Cristina Oddero. The Barolo is the most representative of the many wines of the estate, partly because it constitutes about 70% of the 250 thousand bottles produced. To deal with the tricky '94 vintage, they decided to use the grapes from various vineyards, so as to create just one wine, but a good one, only a little more modest than the splendid special selections of recent years. Its intense bouquet alternates between fruity fragrances (peach, prune and hazelnut) and balsamic notes to form a broad and intriguing ensemble which, however, is taken over, as time passes, by cruder tones. The limits of the year, such as medium body and a limited finish, can be sensed on the palate, but the abundant tannins are exceptionally well integrated and the acidity is sound. A pleasing newcomer is the Barbera d'Asti, from the historic vineyards of Vinchio and Vaglio. With its grapey freshness and slightly acidic taste, it is a good example of the Asti style as compared with that of Alba, which is fruitier and meatier. The Dolcetto makes no compromises; it has a dark, rich color, and a full, fruity nose with dumb moments; the palate, which is tannic and almost hard, is supported by lots of body. The innovative wines are more predictable; these are a balanced Chardonnay and a Langhe cabernet which still wants improvement.

	Wine	Rating	Price
●	Barbera d'Alba '97	🍷	3
●	Barolo '94	🍷	5
●	Dolcetto d'Alba '97	🍷	3
○	Langhe Chardonnay Collaretto '97	🍷	3
●	Langhe Furesté '96	🍷	4
●	Barbera d'Asti '97		3
●	Barolo Vigna Rionda '89	🍷🍷🍷 (white)	6
●	Barolo Vigna Rionda '90	🍷🍷 (white)	6
●	Barolo Vigna Rionda '93	🍷🍷 (white)	5
●	Barolo Rocche dei Rivera '93	🍷 (white)	5

LA MORRA (CN)

F.LLI REVELLO
FRAZ. ANNUNZIATA, 103
12064 LA MORRA (CN)
TEL. 0173/50276 - 50139

It's amazing to see the giant steps taken, in just a few years, by Enzo and Carlo Revello, hardly more than adolescents. It is true that at the outset they enjoyed the invaluable support of real giants, such as Elio Altare, but now that they have learned to stand on their own four feet, no mountain seems too high for them. The winning hallmarks of their cellar are short maceration (since '95 they have been using the famous rotofermenter), intense colors, intelligent use of wood, and elegant wines. With the '95 vintage they will start releasing special cru Barolos from the family property (the Rocche, Gattera and Giachini vineyards). This year we must be satisfied with the Barolo Vigna Giachini '94, with its lively ruby-verging-on-garnet color. Clear aromas of red fruit and spice emerge on the nose; the entry on the palate is intense, and then a balanced progression leads to a licorice finish. The more modest standard Barolo offers spicy aromas of dried herbs and fennel seed; the less rich palate seems lacking in fruit, but it's really only what is to be expected from that vintage. The surprising Barbera Ciabot du Re '96, aged for 18 months in wood where it undergoes its malolactic fermentation, has a deep ruby color; the aromas are of rare elegance, almost aristocratic in quality (with spicy notes of vanilla and citrus fruit perfectly blended with the varietal fruity tones). On the palate too, the wine is more elegant than strong, with not much acidity in evidence. The standard '97 Dolcetto and Barbera round off the list with style: they are both rich in structure yet soft, and can be drunk straight through dinner; indeed they are so easy and pleasant to drink that you'll find yourself wanting more of them.

●	Barbera d'Alba Ciabot du Re '96	🍷🍷	4
●	Barolo Vigna Giachini '94	🍷🍷	5
●	Dolcetto d'Alba '97	🍷🍷	3*
●	Barbera d'Alba '97	🍷	3
●	Barolo '94	🍷	5
●	Barolo '93	🍸🍸🍸	5
●	Barbera d'Alba Ciabot du Re '95	🍸🍸	4

LA MORRA (CN)

ROCCHE COSTAMAGNA
VIA VITTORIO EMANUELE, 12
12064 LA MORRA (CN)
TEL. 0173/50230 - 509225

Creating the identity of a wine, by blending qualities typical of its origins with a personality of its own, is a never-ending process. Alessandro Locatelli, a young and enthusiastic explorer of Piedmontese grape varieties, is more than likely to find the right way, despite some disconcerting reactions from his varied customers who are not always pleased by the wines to which he devotes most of his energy. This is the case with the Barolo Bricco Francesco. Both of his Barolos are good, even in tricky years; the Bricco originates in the highest and finest part of the estate's nebbiolo cru, the Rocche. The Barolo Bricco Francesco has an intense pruney bouquet and behaves like a young wine on the palate, because of the green tannins. The Barolo Rocche is of a garnet color, more brilliant than intense; the aromas of flowers and vine leaves are more exciting than the palate, which is balanced and without bitter surprises. The two Barberas differ much more from each other: the Annunziata, which has taken on a light and carefree style since '96, and the Rocche delle Rocche, a new arrival with a decidedly grander style; it is, however, still aging, so we shall write about it next year. As we expected, the Barbera Annunziata is heady and fresh, thanks to an acidity reminiscent of citrus fruit and to an undemanding finish. The Dolcetto, conceived in the same style, has a little more aromatic richness this time.

●	Barbera d'Alba Annunziata '96	🍷	4
●	Barolo Bricco Francesco '94	🍷	6
●	Barolo Rocche dell'Annunziata '94	🍷	5
●	Dolcetto d'Alba '97	🍷	3
●	Barbera d'Alba Annunziata '95	🍸🍸	4
●	Barolo Rocche dell'Annunziata '93	🍸🍸	5
●	Barolo Vigna Francesco '93	🍸	5

LA MORRA (CN)

Aurelio Settimo

Fraz. Annunziata, 30
12064 La Morra (CN)
tel. 0173/50803

In a part of the Langhe now dedicated to Barolo sold at increasingly startling prices, here is a small producer who is traditionalist and conservative to his roots, even in his prices (which are among the most reasonable to be found). The attachment of Aurelio, and of his daughter Tiziana, to those six hectares of vineyard in the Rocche (one of the finest crus), is an example to many winegrowers who are trying to resist the blandishments of the big wineries hunting for grapes and bulk wine. After exhausting efforts to produce a good wine even in a mediocre year like '94, it's hard to find the courage to sell it, once you've pasted on a label with your own name, at a reasonable price. The Barolo Rocche di Settimo has a fairly transparent appearance, but with exceptionally lively ruby highlights brightening the classic garnet. Its youthful bouquet promises a broad complexity, based on notes of plum and peach, accompanied by captivating woodier nuances of laurel and pepper. This is all reflected on the long finish on the palate, preceded by a tannin-derived austerity which is not amplified by the well-judged acidity. The standard Barolo is a simplified version of this: it has a very light aroma of plum, but the body is a little dilute. The Nebbiolo '96 would be surprising in its capacity to combine nonchalance and commitment only to those who forget that it is a déclassé Rocche; it offers aromas of peach, grass and spice, complex for this type of wine. The entry on the palate (firm but not aggressive) is characterized by plentiful (but smooth) tannins, and a long aromatic note of cherry. The Dolcetto is simpler and without particular personality; it is rich in alcohol but less attractive than usual.

Wine	Glasses	Price
● Barolo Rocche '94	🍷🍷	5
● Langhe Nebbiolo '96	🍷	3
● Barolo '94		4
● Dolcetto d'Alba '97		3
● Barolo '93	🍸🍸	5
● Barolo Rocche '89	🍸🍸	6
● Barolo Rocche '93	🍸🍸	5
● Barolo Rocche '90	🍸	6
● Barolo Rocche Ris. '90	🍸	6

LA MORRA (CN)

Mauro Veglio

Loc. Cascina Nuova, 50
12064 La Morra (CN)
tel. 0173/509212

While in the past Mauro Veglio was known as the young and promising winegrower next door to the great Elio Altare, he can now be described simply as the owner of one of the finest wineries in La Morra. Shy, well-mannered and capable, Veglio has presented a series of exciting wines this year. From his ten hectares of vineyards divided between La Morra (Rocche, Arborina, Gattera and Cascina Nuova) and Monforte (Castelletto), he produces about 50 thousand bottles. The Cascina Nuova '96 is one of the best Barberas of the Langhe: the deep ruby color already bodes well. On the concentrated nose, there are aromas of jam covered by the still distinct tones derived from 18 months in barriques. The palate is fascinatingly intense, powerful, warm and elegant. It's an extraordinary wine that certaintly deserves its first Three Glasses. The two Barolo crus, impeccably made in a difficult year, had no trouble winning their Two Glasses. The Vigneto Rocche, aged in new barriques, has muted aromas of licorice and chocolate, and a powerful palate with evident tannins that need further integration. The Vigneto Arborina, in its first appearance, is fruitier (raspberry and strawberry), with notes of minty herbs. On the palate it is elegant and soft, and seems readier than the Rocche. The Barolo '94, a little less intense and long-lasting, is not as big as its elder brothers, but it's still a fine specimen, particularly for its price. Of the two '97s we preferred the Barbera, with its aromas of cherry jam and its full body, to the fresh and floral Dolcetto.

Wine	Glasses	Price
● Barbera d'Alba Cascina Nuova '96	🍷🍷🍷	5
● Barolo Vigneto Arborina '94	🍷🍷	5
● Barolo Vigneto Rocche '94	🍷🍷	5
● Barbera d'Alba '97	🍷	3
● Barolo '94	🍷	5
● Dolcetto d'Alba '97	🍷	3
● Barbera d'Alba Cascina Nuova '94	🍸🍸	4
● Barbera d'Alba Cascina Nuova '95	🍸🍸	4
● Barolo Vigneto Rocche '93	🍸🍸	5

LA MORRA (CN)

Eraldo Viberti

B.ta Tetti, 53
Fraz. S. Maria
12064 La Morra (CN)
tel. 0173/50308

Eraldo Viberti's goal of making great wine and nothing else seems disarmingly simple, but it finds concrete expression in wines that are elaborate, complex and fascinating. His idea of a vineyard leaves no room for special crus: he owns various parcels of land in Santa Maria, but he produces only one Barolo. The quality of a vintage is central to his way of thinking about his wine, so in '94, a notoriously difficult year, he decided to halve his production, in an attempt to repeat the concentration of his magical '93 (which, by the way, was in glorious form when we tasted it recently). According to Eraldo, the secret lies in ruthless pruning, an operation which he personally performs throughout all his five hectares of vineyards. (Luigi and Olga, although they have gotten used to their son's bizarre fancies, would never dream of throwing away all that natural goodness.) However, the result is a Barolo with youthful ruby highlights, but an already formed complex bouquet that offers cherry and rose blended with more marked aromas of cinnamon and juniper derived from the new wood of the barrels (which in poorer years tends to make itself felt). On the palate alcoholic warmth, acidity and fruit all play a part, while the smooth and active tannins play their supporting role. The Barbera, even more satisfying, is so concentrated that it does not rush to reveal its aromas of wild berries, red currant and blackberry; there then follows a procession of sensations (cherry, laurel and clove) that seems inexhaustible. You almost expect a mouthful of jam when you taste it, but instead all the riches on the palate are released gradually, with very smooth tannins, right into a long, lightly sour finish. The Dolcetto, exuberant but brief, offers an equable mixture of varietal and heady aromas.

	Wine	Glasses	Price
●	Barbera d'Alba Vigna Clara '95	▼▼	4
●	Barolo '94	▼▼	5
●	Dolcetto d'Alba '97	▼	3*
●	Barolo '93	▽▽▽	5
●	Barbera d'Alba Vigna Clara '91	▽▽	4
●	Barbera d'Alba Vigna Clara '93	▽▽	4
●	Barolo '90	▽▽	5
●	Barolo '91	▽▽	5
●	Barolo '92	▽▽	5
●	Barbera d'Alba Vigna Clara '94	▽	4

LA MORRA (CN)

Gianni Voerzio

Reg. Loreto, 1/bis
12064 La Morra (CN)
tel. 0173/509194

Would you like a barrique-aged wine to be identified as such by means of the image of a little barrel on its label? Gianni and Franca Voerzio think you might, and have correspondingly adorned the labels of those of their wines that age in new 500-liter barrels. We especially liked the Barbera, with its dark violet color and its broad and elegant bouquet of flowers and fruit. The wine offers perfect acidity on the palate, supporting a firm structure and a remarkably long finish. The Barolo holds its own despite the poor year: the color is mature but lively; the nose displays a slightly animal nuance as well as notes of walnut; on the palate it wants only enough concentration to act as a mediator between the notable acidity and the rich alcohol. In contrast, the Serrapiù, a blend of nebbiolo and barbera, has plenty of body; the concentrated bouquet blends wild blueberry and sweet raspberry, which re-emerge distinctly on the finish. The less lingering Nebbiolo, fresh and a little grassy, shows a particularly intense and lively ruby color. The Dolcetto, only slightly less excellent than usual, is pleasingly rustic and redolent of sour cherry; it has a cheering delicate freshness. The Freisa offers a bright color (unlike most of its kind), and a lively mousse which makes it pleasanter to the palate than to the nose. Gianni Voerzio completes his wide range with an Arneis and a Moscato.

	Wine	Glasses	Price
●	Barbera d'Alba Ciabot della Luna '96	▼▼	4
●	Langhe Rosso Serrapiù '96	▼▼	4
●	Barolo La Serra '94	▼	5
●	Dolcetto d'Alba Rocchettevino '97	▼	3
●	Langhe Freisa Sotto I Bastioni '97	▼	4
●	Langhe Nebbiolo Ciabot della Luna '96	▼	4
○	Roero Arneis Bricco Cappellina '97	▼	4
●	Barbera d'Alba Ciabot della Luna '95	▽▽	4
●	Barolo La Serra '93	▽▽	5
●	Serrapiù '95	▽▽	4

LA MORRA (CN)

ROBERTO VOERZIO
LOC. CERRETO, 1
12064 LA MORRA (CN)
TEL. 0173/509196

We learn something new about Roberto Voerzio every year. By observing him work we have understood that he does not simply own his vineyards, but feels that they are a part of him. His dedication pays off even in tricky vintages, witness the Barolo Brunate '94. Its color is a rich garnet; the bouqet opens up gradually, and, while never well-defined, displays remarkable richness. The development on the palate is also gradual, underpinned by lots of fruit. This year, however, Roberto Voerzio has produced a sensational wine, the Vignaserra '96, a model of density and elegance: the vivid deep color is almost creamy; the broad and layered bouquet opens the debate between the typical Langhe grapes (barbera and nebbiolo) and a small proportion of non-native varieties: red currant, blackberry, violet, cinnamon and pepper emerge most clearly. The oak, a wonderful element in the bouquet, also sustains the balance on the palate, which is notable for body and a triumphal finish. Although the Cerequio and La Serra Barolos don't have the rich extract of the Brunate, they still manage to put on quite a good show. The Dolcetto displays Voerzio's customary care; indeed he does not seem to understand the concept of a "minor" wine: its deep violet hue and generous fragrance confirm the youthfulness of the Priavino; on the palate, fruit, balsamic notes and hints of walnut skin are exuberantly repeated. The barriqued Chardonnay is harmonious and invitingly succulent.

	Wine	Rating	Price
●	Vignaserra '96	🍷🍷🍷	5
●	Barolo Brunate '94	🍷🍷	6
●	Barolo Cerequio '94	🍷🍷	6
●	Dolcetto d'Alba Priavino '97	🍷🍷	4
○	Langhe Chardonnay Fossati e Roscaleto '97	🍷🍷	5
●	Barolo La Serra '94	🍷	6
●	Barolo Brunate '89	🍸🍸🍸	6
●	Barolo Brunate '90	🍸🍸🍸	6
●	Barolo Brunate '93	🍸🍸🍸	6
●	Barolo Cerequio '88	🍸🍸🍸	6
●	Barolo Cerequio '90	🍸🍸🍸	6
●	Barolo Cerequio '91	🍸🍸🍸	6
●	Barolo Cerequio '93	🍸🍸	6
●	Barolo La Serra '93	🍸🍸	6

LERMA (AL)

ABBAZIA DI VALLECHIARA
LOC. CASCINA ALBAROLA, 16/B
15070 LERMA (AL)
TEL. 0143/877618

The wines of Elisabetta Currado, the dynamic oenologist of the Abbazia di Vallechiara, have a vibrant style, based on the richness of the grapes and an intelligent interpretation of traditional vinification techniques. These are wines that mature over time, and do not disdain a rustic touch that adds to their decided character. The Dolcetto di Ovada '96 is a fine example: its density is already apparent in the ruby-garnet color with a compact, youthful rim. The captivating and complex nose offers aromas of blackberry and black cherry, with fascinating spicy tones; on the palate it is full and substantial, with notable acidity and an intense, dry finish with fruity and balsamic notes. The Due Donne (a blend of dolcetto, barbera and lancillotta) has a concentrated ruby-garnet hue; the slightly forward nose offers aromas of jam and dried fruit, with mineral hints. On the robust palate the slightly excessive acidity makes itself felt, but should be integrated by a few months in the bottle. The Torre Albarola '95, a blend of dolcetto, barbera and lancillotta that spends some time in barriques, was not yet ready when we went to press, so we shall consider it next year.

	Wine	Rating	Price
●	Dolcetto di Ovada '96	🍷🍷	3*
●	Due Donne '95	🍷	4
●	Dolcetto di Ovada '95	🍸🍸	3
●	Torre Albarola '93	🍸	5

LESSONA (VC)

Sella

Via IV Novembre, 110
13060 Lessona (VC)
tel. 015/99455

This estate, which has belonged to the Sella family since the 19th century, consists of 16 hectares of vineyards (two of which are rented) and produces 60 thousand bottles a year of typical local wines, such as the Lessona and the Bramaterra (made mostly from nebbiolo, which is known as spanna in these parts), but also the Orbello (a blend of the native barbera with the international cabernet). Giancarlo Scaglione is the consultant oenologist and the manager, Pietro Marocchino, plays a leading role. The Lessona San Sebastiano allo Zoppo '93 shows notable finesse and freshness and has earned One quite full Glass; the slightly faded ruby color with some orange on the rim is followed by a nose that offers aromas of raspberry, wild strawberry, and fading flowers. On the palate the wine shows fair body, which is given austerity by a clear vein of tannin; the finish displays notes of red fruit and caramel. The less demanding Coste della Sesia Rosso Orbello has a ruby hue of medium intensity with garnet highlights, and a bouquet of jam, dried flowers and leather. The palate is medium-bodied and succulent, with a corresponding finish. The Piccone has a forward nose, with notes of raspberry, hazelnut and custard; it is pleasingly rustic and dry in the mouth. Finally, the white La Doranda is not completely straightforward in fragrance, but the crisp, well-balanced palate quite makes up for it.

●	Coste della Sesia Rosso Orbello '96	🍷	3
●	Lessona S. Sebastiano allo Zoppo '93	🍷	4
●	Piccone '96	🍷	2*
○	La Doranda		3

LOAZZOLO (AT)

Forteto della Luja

Casa Rosso, 4 - Reg. Bricco
14050 Loazzolo (AT)
tel. 0141/831596

Moscato and Brachetto are Giancarlo Scaglione's real fortes, and with the Loazzolo he has done it again, but the aromatic red came awfully close to getting its own Three Glasses, and we'll discuss it first. The attractive varietal aromas are expressed and blended with an unparalleled finesse, which has no relation to the sort of soda pop which is widely sold as Brachetto and the despair of real devotees. The Pian dei Sogni displays all the aristocratic richness of this grape. The cherry-red color is tinged with orange and there's an entire botanical garden in the floral aromas on the nose, but fruity notes are not behindhand. On the palate, which is already complex and lingering, there is an enthralling confrontation between the restrained sugars and the dry tannins. The Piasa Rischei can take on the best Italian sweet wines with the strength of its delicacy; its vibrant gold color precedes an intoxicating variety of aromas: notes of aromatic herbs, yellow-fleshed fruit, sage and exotic citrus nuances form a classic ensemble, which contrives to seem new every year. The sweetness is more marked than the '94's, but in general the palate seems improved, as does the harmony that the acidity contributes to establishing, all of which makes for an unusually delectable wine. The Monferrato Le Grive, apparently unable to take advantage of the fine '96 vintage, is the only discordant note this year.

○	Loazzolo Piasa Rischei '95	🍷🍷🍷	6
●	Piemonte Brachetto Pian dei Sogni '95	🍷🍷	5
○	Moscato d'Asti Piasa San Maurizio '97	🍷	3
●	Monferrato Rosso Le Grive '96		4
○	Loazzolo Piasa Rischei '93	🍸🍸🍸	6
○	Loazzolo Piasa Rischei '94	🍸🍸🍸	6
●	Piemonte Brachetto Pian dei Sogni '94	🍸🍸	5
●	Monferrato Rosso Le Grive '95	🍸	4

MANGO (CN)

Cascina Fonda

Loc. Cascina Fonda, 45
12056 Mango (CN)
tel. 0173/677156

The partially fermented must from aromatic grapes (so the label of the Vendemmia Tardiva reads): in a word, Moscato. The decision not to bring it out as a DOCG was dictated by prudence in presenting a wine whose typical nature may be disputed, but which will leave no room for argument about its quality. The grapes are harvested from an old vineyard two weeks late. Its warm almost golden color is enlivened by green highlights, and you get most pleasure from the complex bouquet if you give it a while to express itself. Then there are delightful forward notes of walnut skin, ripe apricot and coconut, enriched by fresh hints of anise and apple. The palate is another surprise; it is fat but not too sweet, thanks in part to the velvety mousse; it continues to offer new aromatic notes, such as pear, on the long finish. The standard Moscato is a smaller wine, but it shows the same breeding. The fragrance, while not exuberant, is lingering and elegant; perfect handling of carbon dioxide and sugars give harmony to the palate, which culminates in a long, herby finish. The Asti seems a lesser wine only when compared with giants; it has a brilliant color, a green fragrance of apple and bread, and a fully corresponding taste. Not content with Moscato alone, Secondino and Maria Barbero (together with their sons Massimo and Marco) are also producing red wines, represented for the time being by a fruity and fresh Dolcetto.

Wine	Rating	Price
○ Vendemmia Tardiva '97	🍷🍷	3*
○ Asti '97	🍷	3
○ Moscato d'Asti '97	🍷	3
● Dolcetto d'Alba '97	🍷	3

MANGO (CN)

Cascina Pian d'Or

Fraz. Bosi, 15/bis
12056 Mango (CN)
tel. 0141/89440

Walter Barbero has become the proprietor of the Cascina Pian d'Or this year, taking over from his father Giuseppe, who established the winery ten years ago. And this year too the cellar was given its finishing touch: a temperature-controlled room for the storage of bottles. Walter explains, in fact, that it is very important to them to be able to supply this very delicate type of wine in perfect condition. And freshness seems to be one of the main problems for their Moscato. The Bricco Riella has always been a Moscato for those who seek, even in this kind of wine, something fat and a little forward, with, at times, quite unusual aromas; it's not for lovers of up-front immediacy. This year, there are notes of hazelnut and coffee custard on the nose, and, in the mouth, a sweet roundness leading to a finish of overripe apples. The same style and the same mature aromas can be found in the Asti Spumante, although here they are more complex. The characteristic fragrance is accompanied by sweet aromas of apricot and coconut, while the abundant gas, although it escapes rather quickly, provides freshness to the palate and leaves room for a sweet aromatic finish.

Wine	Rating	Price
○ Asti Acini '97	🍷	3
○ Moscato d'Asti Bricco Riella '97	🍷	3

MANGO (CN)

SERGIO DEGIORGIS
VIA CIRCONVALLAZIONE, 3
12056 MANGO (CN)
TEL. 0141/89107

Sergio Degiorgis, who received a degree in oenology from the wine institute in Alba, conducts his family estate with passion and competence, cultivating the typical local grapes moscato and dolcetto. From their eight hectares (six and a half of which are planted to moscato) of vineyard they produce 35 thousand bottles a year. So there's always plenty to do, especially since the family does just about everything. Invaluable assistance is provided by Sergio's wife Patrizia, who learned to love these hills when, as a little girl, she used to come here on holiday from Genoa. When we visited they were in the midst of redoing the cellar, which will be much easier for them to work in when it is finished. Their range of wines, more than half of which is sold abroad, consists of two Moscatos, the standard one and the Sorì del Re cru, and two Dolcettos, standard and Bricco Peso. This last is matured for four or five months in second-season barriques. The result is encouraging: the Bricco Peso offers fruity aroma with notes of cherry and violet. On the palate it shows good fruit, energy and a distinctive personality. The basic Dolcetto is less intense, beginning with the color; the nose is redolent of dark cherry, blueberry and pepper, and the palate is full and substantial but less long-lasting than the cru. The Moscato Sorì del Re, with its clear straw color tinged with green, presents aromas of peach, pear, sage and crusty bread, with some finesse; the smooth, light and well-balanced palate offers a finish of moderate length.

	Wine	Rating	Price
●	Dolcetto d'Alba Bricco Peso '97	🍷🍷	3*
●	Dolcetto d'Alba '97	🍷	3
○	Moscato d'Asti Sorì del Re '97	🍷	3

MOASCA (AT)

PIETRO BARBERO
V.LE SAN GIUSEPPE, 19
14050 MOASCA (AT)
TEL. 0141/856012

Massimo Barbero's ambition is to give his winery not only an image, but also real quality. His most recent investments in vineyard and cellar have given rise this year to a Barbera Vignassa, which is not only the finest of his many wines, but has also never been so good. The '96 vintage doubtless played a part, but the old vineyard from which it springs has an extremely low yield, and this always makes for a high concentration. Barrique aging adds to its balance and the charm and power of the bouquet. The deep ruby hue is the prelude to a nose which offers distinctly perceptible oak, although the rich fruit is in the foreground. The decided palate shows a clear acidic vein, but rich extract is an effective counterpoise and adds zest to the finish as well. The Barbera Camparò, made from grapes gathered at two different times in order to maximize their ripeness, has a resultant bouquet of sweet fig jam and hazelnut. The palate is soft, silky and quite long. The Bricco Verlenga vineyard has given rise to a lively and interesting Barbera; tones of oak, perhaps too evident, do not get in the way of the harmonious progression on the palate. Only the Barbera Piagé is still a simple wine. Among the whites, we noted the successful performance of the Gavi di Rovereto, to which Barbero wants to give even more character. The Sivoy (a blend of cortese with a little chardonnay and even less sauvignon), shows great promise.

	Wine	Rating	Price
●	Barbera d'Asti Sup. La Vignassa '96	🍷🍷	5
○	Monferrato Bianco Sivoy '96	🍷🍷	3*
○	Gavi di Rovereto Vigna Il Poggio '97	🍷	3
●	Barbera d'Asti Sup. Bricco Verlenga '96	🍷	4
●	Barbera d'Asti Sup. Camparò '96	🍷	3*
●	Barbera del M.to Piagé '96		3
●	Barbera d'Asti Sup. Camparò '95	🍷🍷 (outline)	3
●	Barbera d'Asti Sup. La Vignassa '94	🍷🍷 (outline)	4
●	Barbera d'Asti Sup. Bricco Verlenga '95	🍷 (outline)	3

MOMBELLO M.TO (AL)

FELICE COPPO

Cascina Coste, 15
15020 Mombello M.to (AL)
tel. 0142/944503

Felice Coppo continues to be a determined and tireless winegrower. His Bastiàn Cuntrari (now a DOC Barbera di Monferrato) is a wine which has been gradually gaining definition, changing a bit as regards cellar technique, but still made from grapes of the same excellence. This red is the result of the severity with which Felice tends his roughly four hectares of vineyards, imposing very low yields on vines that are already of quite a good age (and hence not abundant producers) by means of ruthless pruning. A mid-October harvest means that the grapes are slightly overripe, and produce a very concentrated must, from which one can make a great wine. That leaves only modifications in cellar technique, as we were saying, which, with constant experimentation, will eventually hit upon the right method for this wine. Felice is assisted here by the well-known wine-taster and writer Luca Maroni. The biggest change has been in the use of barriques: until '94 the wine spent a period in wood; the '95 vintage did not stay there for such a long time, and in '96 Felice started to do without wood altogether. We now review the '97, of which only 4,500 bottles were made; it is aged exclusively in stainless steel, and has won Two full Glasses. A very dense garnet-ruby color is followed by a sumptuous nose with aromas of cherry, blackberry, tobacco leaf, custard and licorice; the palate is concentrated and broad, thanks to a very low acidity which allows it to expand, with appropriate succulence, right into a long soft finish.

Wine	Glasses	Price
● Barbera del M.to Bastiàn Cuntrari '97	🍷🍷 (full)	5
● Bastiàn Cuntrari '93	🍷🍷 (empty)	5
● Bastiàn Cuntrari Tipe III '95	🍷🍷 (empty)	5

MONCHIERO (CN)

GIUSEPPE MASCARELLO & FIGLIO

Via Borgonuovo, 108
12060 Monchiero (CN)
tel. 0173/792126

In a year in which the Monprivato doesn't show its usual intensity, Mauro Mascarello has presented a pair of Barolos that are a worthy substitute, maintaining estate standards. The wines come from two important crus of Castiglione and Monforte: Villero and Santo Stefano di Perno. They have in common the cellar technique that formed them, which was inspired by Langhe tradition, but are very interestingly different. The Villero is complex and austere; the moderately intense garnet color is followed by a slowly opening fragrance revealing distinct tones of licorice and tobacco and, after a while, floral and jammy notes. The tannins underpin the development on the palate, and the other components fall in line, showing a not yet perfect integration. In the mature and intriguing Santo Stefano notes of cherries in spirits and sweet spice have their way with the bouquet. The attack on the palate is soft; the tannins show a surprising sweetness and the structure is not overwhelming. The Barolo Monprivato, with its customary forward tone in color and bouquet, doesn't show the body of a great wine, and it soon finishes. The Barbera d'Alba Codana, although vigorously heady, is not a paragon of elegance; however, the excellence of the grapes is evident. The same rustic expressiveness characterizes the Nebbiolo Langhe '95; in this wine the vitality of color and flavor contrasts with the thorough sweetness of the bouquet. The pleasing and harmonious Nebbiolo d'Alba San Rocco is drier and more delicate.

Wine	Glasses	Price
● Barolo Villero '93	🍷🍷 (full)	5
● Barbera d'Alba Codana '95	🍷 (full)	5
● Barolo Monprivato '93	🍷 (full)	6
● Barolo Santo Stefano di Perno '93	🍷 (full)	6
● Langhe Nebbiolo '95	🍷 (full)	4
● Nebbiolo d'Alba San Rocco '96	🍷 (full)	4
● Barolo Monprivato '85	🍷🍷🍷 (empty)	6
● Barbaresco Marcarini '88	🍷🍷 (empty)	5
● Barolo Monprivato '89	🍷🍷 (empty)	6
● Barolo Monprivato '90	🍷🍷 (empty)	6

MONDOVÌ (CN)

Il Colombo - Barone Riccati
Via dei Sent, 2
12084 Mondovì (CN)
tel. 0174/41607 - 43022

For some years Carlo and Anna Riccati, leaving frenetic city life behind them (or almost: Carlo still teaches philosophy at the Univerity of Turin), have devoted themselves heart and soul to restoring a venerable farmstead, entirely surrounded by vineyards, which dominates the plain of Cuneo. Having overcome the architectural problems (assisted by Giuseppe Giusta, Adriana's brother) they have now focussed their energies on their almost four hectares of vineyards. In just a few years, their prescience and enthusiasm have paid off: not only have they become the standard-bearers of the Langhe Monregalese (a relatively easy task, given the diastrous state of viticulture in the area), but they are now among the best producers of Dolcetto altogether. After two vintages, which could be considered a trial period, they had identified the viticultural and oenological methods needed to create great wines: they sell the grapes from the less sunny vineyards, they vinify the Vignone and Vigna della Chiesetta grapes separately (the former is planted with old and splendidly exposed vines which produce their best grapes), they keep yields low with hard pruning and, when necessary, green harvests. With the '97 vintage, the Vigna della Chiesetta too, usually a fresh, quaffable Dolcetto, has become dense in color and fragrance, with rich aromas of red berries. The Colombo '97 is fantastic: the almost impenetrable violet hue is followed by an explosion of dark berry aromas (blackberry in particular) and cocoa. The palate is incredibly rich, velvety and chewy, pervaded by very smooth tannins. It's a great Dolcetto that fully deserves its Three Glasses.

	Wine	Glasses	Price
●	Dolcetto delle Langhe Monregalesi Il Colombo '97	🍷🍷🍷	3*
●	Dolcetto delle Langhe Monregalesi Vigna Chiesetta '97	🍷🍷	3*
●	Dolcetto delle Langhe Monregalesi Il Colombo '95	🍷🍷 (white)	3
●	Dolcetto delle Langhe Monregalesi Il Colombo '96	🍷🍷 (white)	3

MONFORTE D'ALBA (CN)

Gianfranco Alessandria
Loc. Manzoni, 13
12065 Monforte d'Alba (CN)
tel. 0173/78576 - 787222

It was clear from our first visit to his winery that Gianfranco meant to make great wine, even when he was crammed into a sort of back room where there was hardly space for the absolute minimum of necessary equipment he had at his disposal. He was spurred on further by his friendship with Mauro Veglio and the brothers Enzo and Carlo Revello, which inspired an amicable spirit of competition. So his lightning rise is in some way comprehensible. Today Gianfranco, who looks after his four hectares of vineyards in Monforte practically on his own, is already considered to be one of the virtuosos of wine-making in the Langhe. After last year's Three Glasses for the Barolo '93, not many people imagined that he could show the same magic touch with a barbera. But the Vittoria '96 has won top honors in its turn. Its depth of color is astonishing, as is the power of its concentrated bouquet, offering clear notes of sour cherry, sweet spice and elegant hints of damp earth. The palate shows extraordinary body and harmony. The Barolo '94, although not like the '93, still has a place among the best of the year; it doesn't have an overwhelming structure, although the tannins do make their presence clear; but the nose (intense and stylish, with spicy and heady aromas) is immediately fascinating. The standard Barbera '97 (still very young, but already so dense as to seem edible as well as drinkable), is a great pleasure to drink. The Dolcetto '97, which is not altogether typical of this estate, is fresh and fruity.

	Wine	Glasses	Price
●	Barbera d'Alba Vittoria '96	🍷🍷🍷	5
●	Barbera d'Alba '97	🍷🍷	3*
●	Barolo '94	🍷🍷	5
●	Dolcetto d'Alba '97	🍷🍷	3*
●	Barolo '93	🍷🍷🍷 (white)	5

Bussia Soprana

Loc. Bussia Soprana, 87
12065 Monforte d'Alba (CN)
tel. 039/305182

Silvano Casiraghi has a long and distinguished career as a selector and distributor of great wines behind him; he was the first, for instance, to import the "little great" Burgundian wines into Italy. If a person of this stature takes it into his head to produce wines, he immediately does it on a grand scale: his 18 hectares in Bussia and Mosconi, two of the best hillside sites in Monforte d'Alba, will give him over 100 thousand bottles a year. In a mediocre vintage like '94 it's hard to pull off a miracle, even for Silvano Casiraghi and his partner Guido Rossi; although they decided to release only a Barolo '94 (selecting the best grapes and bottling only 11 thousand bottles from Bussia instead of the usual 30 thousand, divided between Bussia and Vigna Colonnello) the result was a little disappointing. The Barolo Bussia '94 is garnet-colored, and offers a bouquet reminiscent of salt water and dried flowers, and a palate which is characteristic of the year but not perfectly clean. The Barbera d'Alba '95, produced from their youngest vines, also gets One Glass; a little faded in color, it displays uncomplicated green but pleasant aromas and a medium body. This year's star is undoubtedly the Barbera d'Alba Vin del Ross '96. Silvano has dedicated this to his late father, who was known by this nickname because of his ginger hair. The wine, made from their oldest vines (in Bussia and Mosconi) is of a deep ruby color; its complex nose (aromas of cherry, with spicy and balsamic tones, well-integrated with toasty notes of oak) leads to a rich and long palate.

Wine	Glasses	Price
● Barbera d'Alba Vin del Ross '96	🍷🍷	5
● Barbera d'Alba '95	🍷	3
● Barolo Bussia '94	🍷	5
● Barolo Vigna Colonello '93	🍸🍸	6
● Barolo Bussia '93	🍸	5

MONFORTE D'ALBA (CN)

★ Domenico Clerico

Loc. Manzoni, 67
12065 Monforte d'Alba (CN)
tel. 0173/78171

Arte is making history. It has shown us the noble qualities of nebbiolo (but not as it appears in Barolo), and has revealed that this Langhe grape can blend with others without being overwhelmed, producing something new and wonderful. Clerico has not added barbera and cabernet in order to "improve" his nebbiolo (which would have produced a wine without personality), but has regarded them as equals in creating the wine he has always had in mind. The Arte '96 is a synthesis of all the best versions from the last ten years, and, starting with the not very intense ruby color, the nebbiolo rules the roost. The succession of aromas and their extraordinarily pleasing articulation can be attributed to a perfect maturation in wood, but also to the austere and layered richness that only a great nebbiolo can provide. The other grapes contribute to a lively interaction that unites bouquet and palate in a magnificent seamless progression. The expressively delicate and profoundly satisfying palate subtly rings the changes in its gradual and harmonious development. Of the two '94 Barolos we preferred the Pajana: its characteristic softness mitigates the aggressiveness of a lean year. The Mentin, with its thin sharpness, could not give more than it did. The Barbera '96 finally possesses an openness worthy of its warmth and body, as do the Freisa and the Dolcetto, which are both light, but not commonplace.

Wine	Glasses	Price
● Langhe Arte '96	🍷🍷🍷	5
● Barbera d'Alba '96	🍷🍷	4
● Barolo Pajana '94	🍷🍷	5
● Barolo Ciabot Mentin Ginestra '94	🍷	5
● Dolcetto d'Alba '97	🍷	3
● Langhe Freisa La Ginestrina '97	🍷	3
● Arte '90	🍸🍸🍸	5
● Arte '93	🍸🍸🍸	5
● Barolo Ciabot Mentin Ginestra '85	🍸🍸🍸	6
● Barolo Ciabot Mentin Ginestra '86	🍸🍸🍸	6
● Barolo Ciabot Mentin Ginestra '89	🍸🍸🍸	6
● Barolo Ciabot Mentin Ginestra '92	🍸🍸🍸	5
● Barolo Pajana '90	🍸🍸🍸	6
● Barolo Pajana '91	🍸🍸🍸	6
● Barolo Pajana '93	🍸🍸🍸	5

MONFORTE D'ALBA (CN)

★ Poderi Aldo Conterno

Loc. Bussia, 48
12065 Monforte d'Alba (CN)
tel. 0173/78150

The Langhe are now graced by a proper château. Near Bussia on the road to Monforte from Castiglione Falletto is one of the loveliest wineries in the area. Its style is reminiscent of Bordeaux, with great wooden doors adorned by a sort of tympanum in white stone. This is where the great wines of the Conterno family come into being. Aldo, assisted by his sons, Franco Giacomo and Stefano, has presented a fine series of wines that range from Barolo to Chardonnay, with other typical Langhe specialties along the way. This year, when their historic Barolo crus did not appear because of the troublesome '94 vintage, we got a chance to taste the Barolo Romirasco cru, which is produced rarely. The '93 is of a garnet hue lightly tinged with orange. The intense bouquet offers notes of tobacco and coffee, and the palate is full-bodied, with austere tannins in need of further integration. The very interesting Chardonnay Bussiador '96 is better than ever. The delightfully sweet oak-derived hints of spice and vanilla still partly dominate the other aromas (hazelnut and pineapple), while an almost chewable fatness fills the whole mouth without cloying. The Barbera '96, with its intense toasty notes and hints of damp earth, recalls the glories of the Conca Tre Pile from the late '80s. The Barolo Bussia Soprana '94 is thin and delicate (but somewhat forward on the nose), without, however, having smoothed the roughness on the palate. The Chardonnay Printanié and the Dolcetto, both '97s, are simple and correct wines.

	Wine	Rating	Price
●	Barbera d'Alba '96	🍷🍷	4
●	Barolo Romirasco '93	🍷🍷	6
○	Langhe Chardonnay Bussiador '96	🍷🍷	5
○	Langhe Bianco Printanié '97	🍷	4
●	Barolo Bussia Soprana '94	🍷	6
●	Dolcetto d'Alba '97	🍷	3
●	Barolo Bussia Soprana '85	ΥΥΥ	6
●	Barolo Gran Bussia Ris. '88	ΥΥΥ	6
●	Barolo Gran Bussia Ris. '89	ΥΥΥ	6
●	Barolo Gran Bussia Ris. '90	ΥΥΥ	6
●	Barolo Vigna Colonnello '88	ΥΥΥ	6
●	Barolo Vigna Colonnello '89	ΥΥΥ	6
●	Barolo Vigna Colonnello '90	ΥΥΥ	6
●	Barolo Cicala '93	ΥΥ	6
●	Langhe Favot '95	ΥΥ	5

MONFORTE D'ALBA (CN)

★ Giacomo Conterno

Loc. Ornati, 2
12065 Monforte d'Alba (CN)
tel. 0173/78221

Giovanni Conterno has not had a really good vintage for Barolos since the beginning of the '90s (not counting '93). After a series of hailstorms that devastated the magnificent La Francia vineyard, drastically reducing production, Giovanni had to deal with the devilish '94 vintage. He can comfort himself with the wines from the subsequent vintages, which, under his watchful eye, are aging in wood, and acquiring characteristics of which he can more wholeheartedly approve. Despite the most ruthless selection, both at the outset (he discards the grapes he considers unworthy of crushing), and at the end of aging in wood (the lots not up to Conterno standards are sold in bulk to wholesalers), the result has earned only One Glass. Everything about the Barolo Cascina Franca '94 recalls the dreadful weather that attended its birth: from the cold faded garnet color to the intense (but rather simple) strawberry fragrance, finishing with the hardness on the palate, where the sweet alcoholic fruit provided by ripe grapes only partly succeeds in covering the underlying tannic and acidic backbone. All of his usually less important wines are more enjoyable, but then they are '97s, so it's no surprise. The most promising at the moment is the Freisa, which enchants both nose and palate with intense notes of plum and inviting peppery aromas; the long finish includes the characteristic slight bitterness. The fruity and heady Dolcetto and the fresh, succulent Barbera are both very good too, if not quite as striking.

	Wine	Rating	Price
●	Barbera d'Alba '97	🍷🍷	4
●	Dolcetto d'Alba '97	🍷🍷	4
●	Langhe Freisa '97	🍷🍷	4
●	Barolo Cascina Francia '94	🍷	6
●	Barolo Cascina Francia '85	ΥΥΥ	6
●	Barolo Cascina Francia '87	ΥΥΥ	6
●	Barolo Cascina Francia '89	ΥΥΥ	6
●	Barolo Cascina Francia '90	ΥΥΥ	6
●	Barolo Monfortino Ris. '74	ΥΥΥ	6
●	Barolo Monfortino Ris. '82	ΥΥΥ	6
●	Barolo Monfortino Ris. '85	ΥΥΥ	6
●	Barolo Monfortino Ris. '87	ΥΥΥ	6
●	Barolo Monfortino Ris. '88	ΥΥΥ	6
●	Barolo Monfortino Ris. '90	ΥΥΥ	6

MONFORTE D'ALBA (CN)

Paolo Conterno
Via Ginestra, 34
12065 Monforte d'Alba (CN)
tel. 0173/78415

Interest in the wines of the Langhe, particularly Barolo, is now worldwide. Nevertheless, in the Barolo zone one can still, amazingly enough, discover little-known wineries that produce excellent wines. The best example is run by Paolo Conterno and his son Giorgio, and it has claimed a place for itself in the Guide this year. The family, which has been bottling Barolo for several generations, owns just over six hectares under vine in the splendid sunny Ginestra vineyard. The total production is about 40 thousand bottles, almost all of which are filled with either Barolo or Barbera (just a few are conceded to Dolcetto). Although the cellar has recently been redone, it is still distinctly traditional: maceration time is never hurried, and the period devoted to aging in 35-hectoliter barrels of French oak is always a good bit longer than the regulation two years. Their range, which they limit to the classic wines of these hills, includes a remarkable Dolcetto '97 which is redolent of wild strawberries and the typically varietal almond. The seductive palate offers softness and succulent fruit. The Barbera '96 is less generous: the nose is still somewhat closed, and there is not yet enough fruit on the palate to stand up to the very lively acidity. The Barolo Ginestra '94 is noteworthy for the power it manages to display in this substandard vintage. The wine needs to breathe before it opens on the nose, but the palate shows a good balance between fruit and spice, and between alcohol and tannins. Hence we eagerly await the Barolo '95 and the Barolo Riserva '93, both still aging in wood.

●	Barolo Ginestra '94	🍷🍷	5
●	Dolcetto d'Alba Ginestra '97	🍷🍷	3
●	Barbera d'Alba Ginestra '96	🍷	4

MONFORTE D'ALBA (CN)

Conterno Fantino
Via Ginestra, 1
Loc. Bricco Bastia
12065 Monforte d'Alba (CN)
tel. 0173/78204

Although there are no Three Glass wines in their range this year, Conterno Fantino has again shown that it is one of the best wineries in the Langhe. With the purchase of another eight hectares of nebbiolo vineyard in Castiglione Falletto, and the definitive reorganization of the ample and efficient cellar, the winery is well able to continue its excellent work, characterized by the attentive care lavished on the vineyards by the brothers Claudio and Diego Conterno, and by the knowing hand of Guido Fantino in the cellar. The Monprà '96, excellent as usual, missed its Three Glasses by a hair. A blend of 45% each of barbera and nebbiolo and 10% cabernet sauvignon, it has a dark ruby color; the bouquet, still somewhat closed, nevertheless distinctly shows red fruit and floral notes, together with a faint vegetal hint from the cabernet. The palate reveals a wine still young, with very well-judged wood, and capable of opening with time. The two Barolos, both '94s, to their cost, are of course not as good as usual, but clearly display the skill with which they were tended in vineyard and cellar. We preferred the Ginestra, which has greater structure and complexity on both the nose and the palate, but the Gris is readier, not at all harsh and quite elegant. The Chardonnay continues to be one of the best in the Langhe, and will probably age well. The heady and fruity Dolcetto is as good as ever; the Barbera Vignota shows its customary straightforwardness.

○	Langhe Chardonnay Bastia '97	🍷🍷	5
●	Barolo Sorì Ginestra '94	🍷🍷	5
●	Langhe Rosso Monprà '96	🍷🍷	5
●	Barbera d'Alba Vignota '97	🍷	4
●	Barolo Vigna del Gris '94	🍷	5
●	Dolcetto d'Alba Bricco Bastia '97	🍷	3
●	Barolo Sorì Ginestra '86	ΥΥΥ	6
●	Barolo Sorì Ginestra '90	ΥΥΥ	6
●	Barolo Sorì Ginestra '91	ΥΥΥ	5
●	Langhe Rosso Monprà '95	ΥΥΥ	5
●	Monprà '94	ΥΥΥ	5
●	Barolo Sorì Ginestra '93	ΥΥ	5
●	Barolo Vigna del Gris '93	ΥΥ	5

MONFORTE D'ALBA (CN)

ALESSANDRO E GIAN NATALE FANTINO
VIA G. SILVANO, 18
12065 MONFORTE D'ALBA (CN)
TEL. 0173/78253

Although you can find some barbera, dolcetto and freisa in the estate's vineyards, it's clear that the hearts of the Fantino brothers belong to nebbiolo. Alessandro worked at one time with Bartolo Mascarello; Gian Natale and he look after their roughly six hectares under vine, as well as the cellar, and produce just over 20 thousand bottles. The vineyards are in Dardi, near Bussia, and have a fine southern exposure. The Nebbiolo Passito, their prize, is made from grapes gathered two weeks before the nebbiolo used for Barolo; they are carefully selected and left to dry on racks for three months, then fermented and aged in large barrels. The Nebbiolo Passito is produced only in particular years; the one they have just released, the '94, offers an array of intense and lingering aromas (spice, chocolate, licorice and orange peel); on the palate it is dry, well-structured and properly tannic and acidic. The Barolo Vigna dei Dardi '94, with a pleasing but not very deep nose, suffers from its vintage; although somewhat dilute in the mouth, it shows characteristic nebbiolo notes. The Barbera d'Alba is also well executed and interesting, especially on the nose.

● Nebbiolo Passito Vigna dei Dardi '94	🍷🍷	5
● Barbera d'Alba Vigna dei Dardi '96	🍷	3
● Barolo Vigna dei Dardi '94	🍷	5
● Barolo Vigna dei Dardi '93	🍷🍷 (white)	5
● Nebbiolo Passito Vigna dei Dardi '90	🍷🍷 (white)	5
● Nebbiolo Passito Vigna dei Dardi '93	🍷 (white)	4

MONFORTE D'ALBA (CN)

ATTILIO GHISOLFI
REG. BUSSIA, 27
CASCINA VISETTE
12065 MONFORTE D'ALBA (CN)
TEL. 0173/78345

The Ghisolfi estate has more than a century of experience: the family has been cultivating the vine since 1896. Gian Marco, who calls the shots in the cellar, has decided to dedicate himself to the family property together with his father Attilio. Only four and a half of their six hectares are under vine. Gian Marco, with the expert advice of Beppe Caviola, produces about 22 thousand bottles of Barolo, Barbera, Dolcetto and (as of this year) a Langhe Rosso called Carlin (made from separately vinified nebbiolo and freisa assembled in the barrique). The Barbera Vigna Lisi, of a concentrated ruby color, is particularly good; it offers intense and lingering aromas of red berries and dark cherry with fresh spicy tones. On the palate it has not yet achieved full balance, but there is lots of body. The Carlin did very well thanks to its good, varied and open bouquet (balsamic, floral and fruity notes); it shows a restrained authority on the velvety and clean palate. The Barolo, however, is, alas, a '94; a faint bouquet with hints of violet and plum is followed by a somewhat fragile structure. The good standard Barbera is characteristically varietal in its fruity and heady aromas, and the Dolcetto is properly tannic, direct, well-proportioned and lots of fun to drink.

● Barbera d'Alba Vigna Lisi '96	🍷🍷	4
● Langhe Rosso Carlin '96	🍷🍷	4
● Barbera d'Alba '96	🍷	3*
● Barolo Bricco Visette '94	🍷	5
● Dolcetto d'Alba '97	🍷	3*
● Barbera d'Alba Vigna Lisi '93	🍷🍷 (white)	3
● Barolo Bricco Visette '90	🍷🍷 (white)	5
● Barolo Bricco Visette '93	🍷🍷 (white)	5
● Barbera d'Alba Vigna Lisi '95	🍷 (white)	4
● Barolo Bricco Visette '91	🍷 (white)	5
● Barolo Bricco Visette '92	🍷 (white)	5

MONFORTE D'ALBA (CN)

ELIO GRASSO

LOC. GINESTRA, 40
12065 MONFORTE D'ALBA (CN)
TEL. 0173/78491

Elio Grasso has finally inaugurated his new cellar, a model of attractive efficiency. His experience in recent vintages has been put to use in designing a technically up-to-the-minute but also optimally comfortable working environment. But it would be worth the trip just to see the view from the winery. As for this year's wines, we can report no overwhelming excitement, but then they are almost without exception from miserable years. One can however, sense in them all Elio's capable hand, which has let them show at their best, without pushing them to extremes. The Barolo '94, from the Chiniera and Casa Maté crus, is at its peak. The fairly intense garnet color is followed by a complex and nuanced bouquet, not identifiable in its particulars. The palate, pleasantly balanced, displays well-integrated tannins and a finish that clearly mirrors the nose. The Barbera della Vigna Martina doesn't have the '94's brilliance; the color is dense and vivid; the fruity aromas, completely blended with the notes of oak, seem to bode well, but the palate never opens as it should, and the finish is short. The Chardonnay '96 is not yet properly harmonious, but shows a fleshiness to which the oak adds density. The Dolcetto is agreeably fresh.

	Wine	Glasses	Price
●	Barolo '94	🍷🍷	5
●	Barbera d'Alba Vigna Martina '95	🍷	4
●	Dolcetto d'Alba Gavarini Vigna dei Grassi '97	🍷	3
○	Langhe Chardonnay Educato '96	🍷	4
●	Barolo Gavarini Vigna Chiniera '89	🍷🍷🍷 (prev.)	6
●	Barolo Ginestra Vigna Casa Maté '90	🍷🍷🍷 (prev.)	6
●	Barolo Ginestra Vigna Casa Maté '93	🍷🍷🍷 (prev.)	5
●	Barolo Gavarini Vigna Chiniera '90	🍷🍷 (prev.)	6
●	Barolo Gavarini Vigna Chiniera '93	🍷🍷 (prev.)	5
●	Barolo Ginestra Vigna Casa Maté '89	🍷🍷 (prev.)	6
○	Langhe Chardonnay Educato '95	🍷🍷 (prev.)	4

MONFORTE D'ALBA (CN)

GIOVANNI MANZONE

VIA CASTELLETTO, 9
12065 MONFORTE D'ALBA (CN)
TEL. 0173/78114

The estate vineyards, planted to the traditional nebbiolo, dolcetto and barbera, as well as the venerable rossese bianco, are cultivated organically. Until recently, Giovanni's cramped cellar was the source of his problems, but now that it has been completely redone, things should improve, although his courageous refusal to filter or fine his wines means that they can seem less clean on the nose. This is why they have to be released late. The Barbera d'Alba La Serra '94, for example, has only just appeared. Its age is apparent, especially to the eye, whereas the nose and palate, although complex (leather and licorice) and harmonious, still display a youthful acidity. The Bricco Serra '95 (from white rossese) is very particular: an aged white that some may find puzzling. It shows a lovely deep gold color and a pleasing palate (it seems almost tannic!), both powerful and lingering. The nose, however, does not show all the freshness of a really good vintage. This year Giovanni decided to make two separate Barolos out of his two parcels of land on the Gramolere hill, but at different altitudes, with all the other differences that follow. The Gramolere '94 is at its best on the nose, thanks to an enviable cleanness and complexity (aromas of licorice and resin). The palate, though pleasant enough, lacks character. The Briccat '94, which wins Two Glasses, is somewhat richer and younger-seeming in bouquet (red fruit and toasty notes). Giovanni's new wine, the Langhe Rosso '95 (equal parts of nebbiolo, barbera and dolcetto) needs a little more work.

	Wine	Glasses	Price
○	Bricco Serra '95	🍷🍷	4
●	Barolo Gramolere Bricat '94	🍷🍷	5
●	Barbera d'Alba La Serra '94	🍷	4
●	Barolo Gramolere '94	🍷	5
●	Langhe Rosso Tris '95	🍷	4
●	Barolo Gramolere '90	🍷🍷 (prev.)	5
●	Barolo Gramolere '91	🍷🍷 (prev.)	5
●	Barolo Gramolere '93	🍷🍷 (prev.)	5
●	Barolo Gramolere Ris. '90	🍷🍷 (prev.)	6

MONFORTE D'ALBA (CN)

ARMANDO PARUSSO
TIZIANA E MARCO PARUSSO
LOC. BUSSIA, 55
12065 MONFORTE D'ALBA (CN)
TEL. 0173/78257

We had been waiting, with some trepidation, for a great Parusso wine: for at least three years we could tell that the fruit was there, but ideal conditions somehow contrived to appear by turns. Now that they've won their Three Glasses, we can say that all this time Marco and Tiziana have never wavered in the pursuit of their ideal of quality. They resisted the temptation to produce just a few bottles of exceptional wine, but wanted any success to correspond to their habitual volume of production: one shining star, however dazzling, would not have helped them. And so they have made 12 thousand bottles of the masterful Bricco Rovella '96, which pays homage to both a fine vintage and a new interpretation of the Langhe style, which need not shun tannins in order to charm. The deep ruby hue introduces an enticing depth of fragrance: subtle nuances and clearer tones all find their place in an ordered ensemble. The closely knit tannins appear first on the palate, overtaken by the pervasive fruit which leads into a triumphal finish. The '94 Barolos are worthy of attention: they have been cleverly made to be well-structured and currently drinkable wines, which perfectly corresponds to the potential of that vintage. The Rocche offers an intriguing bouquet and a well-articulated progression on the palate. The Munie has a captivating floral nose and a soft and supple body. The extremely successful Dolcetto d'Alba '97 shows rich and varietal aromas and a firm and lingering palate. The Barbera and the Bricco Rovella Bianco are harmonious and very quaffable.

	Wine	Glasses	
●	Langhe Rosso Bricco Rovella '96	▼▼▼	5
●	Barolo Bussia Vigna Munie '94	▼▼	5
●	Barolo Bussia Vigna Rocche '94	▼▼	5
●	Dolcetto d'Alba '97	▼▼	3
●	Barbera d'Alba Ornati '97	▼	4
○	Langhe Bianco Bricco Rovella '97	▼	4
●	Barolo Bussia '90	▽▽	5
●	Barolo Bussia Vigna Munie '92	▽▽	4
●	Barolo Bussia Vigna Munie '93	▽▽	5
●	Barolo Bussia Vigna Rocche '92	▽▽	5
●	Barolo Bussia Vigna Rocche '93	▽▽	5
●	Barolo Mariondino '90	▽▽	5
●	Langhe Rosso Bricco Rovella '95	▽▽	5
○	Langhe Bianco Bricco Rovella '96	▽▽	4

MONFORTE D'ALBA (CN)

PODERE ROCCHE DEI MANZONI
LOC. MANZONI SOPRANI, 3
12065 MONFORTE D'ALBA (CN)
TEL. 0173/78421

Barely six years ago, Valentino Migliorini completely overhauled his production methods (which took some courage) and acquired the up-to-date equipment that would allow him to make the most of the considerable viticultural investments he was making. While this immediately energized the '89 and '90 Barolos and led to the birth of the Spumante Brut Zero (still the winery gem), it was too soon for it to set its definitive stamp on the estate's style. The most surprising wine is the Barbera '96 from the Mosconi vineyard, which very nearly won itself Three Glasses with its overwhelming vigor; the enchanting fragrance makes the rich color and full body pleasurable, and the attractively lively sensations linger. The Qatr Nas, this year's knock-out, is a model of finesse and length. It's a blend of nebbiolo (50%), barbera, pinot noir and cabernet, and the whole is definitely greater than the sum of its parts; its balance rests on substantial extract and the exemplary smoothness of the tannins. The Brut Zero is a stranger to minor years: broad, dense and developed, it progresses with charm, revealing an extraordinary underpinning (quite apart from the perfect mousse). In addition to these three champions, there are a well-defined, fruity and full-bodied Barolo '94, the Bricco Manzoni '95 (a blend of nebbiolo and barbera), which is mature, harmonious and long-lasting, and another deep and generous Barbera. The barriqued Chardonnay is making some progress, but the Pinot Nero and the Sauvignon seem a little tired.

	Wine	Glasses	
●	Langhe Rosso Quatr Nas '96	▼▼▼	6
●	Barbera d'Alba Sorito Mosconi '96	▼▼	5
●	Barbera d'Alba Vigna La Cresta '96	▼▼	5
●	Barolo Rocche '94	▼▼	6
●	Bricco Manzoni '95	▼▼	5
○	Valentino Brut Zero Ris. '94	▼▼	5
○	Langhe Chardonnay L'Angelica '96	▼	5
●	Barolo Vigna Big Ris. '89	▽▽▽	6
●	Barolo Vigna Big Ris. '90	▽▽▽	6
●	Barolo Vigna d'la Roul Ris. '90	▽▽▽	6
○	Valentino Brut Zero Ris. '92	▽▽▽	5
○	Valentino Brut Zero Ris. '93	▽▽▽	5
●	Barolo Cappella di Santo Stefano '93	▽▽	6
●	Barolo Vigna Big '93	▽▽	6

MONFORTE D'ALBA (CN)

FERDINANDO PRINCIPIANO

VIA ALBA, 19
12065 MONFORTE D'ALBA (CN)
TEL. 0173/787158

After its triumphant debut in the Guide last year (the spectacular Barolo Boscareto '93 launched this winery into the higher realms of Italian wine-making and seemed a miracle), Ferdinando Principiano has not let us down despite the tricky '94 vintage. He has succeeded in preserving the essence of the Boscareto cru, one of the best (but also least known) vineyards in Barolo territory, near the birthplace of the legendary Monfortino. The oak, (which characterizes the bouquet of this Barolo '94, producing intense toasty and spicy notes which blend with the more classic leather and dried herbs), does not completely succeed in taming the well-known tannic structure of the Serralunga nebbiolo, so the wine is still a little aggressive. This estate, which is on the rise, vinifies an increasing proportion of grapes from their seven already producing hectares (two more, in Boscareto, are about to be planted), and is slowly increasing the number of bottles produced annually. Thus, for example, the Barolo Boscareto, only 1,300 bottles in '93, will fill 13 thousand in '97, and this year's release, the '94, totals 2,500 bottles. For the millennium, they will be presenting a Barolo Le Coste '96, which ought to be a suitable companion for the Boscareto. The Barbera Pian Romualdo '95, which comes from a historic barbera sub-zone, fully confirms expectations: its almost black opacity is a harbinger of the toasty and cherry jam notes that invade the nostrils, and the incredible richness on the palate, which needs further balance. The good, fruity Dolcetto goes down quite easily.

	Wine	Glasses	Price
●	Barbera d'Alba Pian Romualdo '95	🍷🍷	5
●	Barolo Boscareto '94	🍷🍷	5
●	Dolcetto d'Alba Sant'Anna '97	🍷	3
●	Barolo Boscareto '93	⚲⚲⚲	5
●	Barbera d'Alba Pian Romualdo '93	⚲⚲	4
●	Barbera d'Alba Pian Romualdo '94	⚲⚲	4

MONFORTE D'ALBA (CN)

FLAVIO RODDOLO

LOC. S. ANNA, 5
BRICCO APPIANI
12065 MONFORTE D'ALBA (CN)
TEL. 0173/78535

Ever since we stumbled, a few years ago, on a Dolcetto d'Alba '90 of incredible power and breeding, this winery has never put a foot wrong with this wine. Certainly, each year there are some wines that outshine it, but it always displays an excellence based on respect for its terroir. Flavio, who has been a winegrower all his life, has a unique familiarity with the vineyards of this corner of the Langhe, between Monforte and Roddino, where vines gradually give way to meadows and hazelnut groves. His hand shows no want of skill; the only problem is the micro-climate, which does not produce wines that are much fun to drink when they're young: they need time for their aromas and palates to develop their inherent richness. Flavio has been forced to adapt to market needs, but if left to himself he would wait at least another year before releasing each of his wines. The Barolo '94, from Ravera, is still a little reluctant to display all the balsamic and licorice aromas clearly hovering in the background; the palate gives a hint of future harmony, but the tannins are still too noticeable at the moment. As is usual during our tasting time, the Dolcetto showed its muscles particularly on the palate, where the important tannic structure still dominates the fruit, rich though it is. On the nose, the raspberry notes are already delightful. The very good Barbera '96 has taken advantage of an especially good year, and of a well-judged barrique aging. The Nebbiolo d'Alba '96, with its broad and austere palate, is excellent, as is its wont.

	Wine	Glasses	Price
●	Barbera d'Alba '96	🍷🍷	3*
●	Nebbiolo d'Alba '96	🍷🍷	4
●	Dolcetto d'Alba '97	🍷🍷	3*
●	Barolo '94	🍷	5
●	Barolo '93	⚲⚲	5

MONFORTE D'ALBA (CN)

F.LLI SEGHESIO

FRAZ. CASTELLETTO, 20
12065 MONFORTE D'ALBA (CN)
TEL. 0173/78108

From this winery, in a very beautiful and relatively isolated spot, you can get a breathtaking view: the Barolo vineyards of the Serralunga valley, in an enchanting play of light and shadow, seem like a painted backdrop. Riccardo and Aldo Seghesio's wines also provide seductive sensual pleasures. The Barolo performs well even in a mediocre year; it has a deep garnet ruby hue; the not very complex aromas are open, broad and fruity, with hints of sweetness and dried roses; the rounded and ripely fruity palate displays soft but lively tannins and a long, satisfying finish. The Barbera Vigneto della Chiesa is worthy of the estate from which it springs; broad aromas of well-judged, sweet wood, with notes of red berries and mint, precede a warm, soft, lively palate with good acidity and well-balanced final tannins. The simpler standard Barbera commends itself for its clean fragrance and overall balance. We like the Dolcetto for the directness of its intense aromas and the balance on the heady, sound and full palate. This year's novelty is the Bouquet, mostly merlot with some cabernet sauvignon and nebbiolo, each separately aged for a year in wood before assemblage. It has a soft impact on the nose, which offers well-behaved wood and notes of cherry, violet and geranium with slightly grassy undertones: on the palate, although further balance is needed, it is delightfully mouth-filling, with rich alcohol perfectly blended with the fruit.

●	Barbera d'Alba Vigneto della Chiesa '96	🍷🍷	4
●	Barolo Vigneto La Villa '94	🍷🍷	5
●	Bouquet '96	🍷🍷	5
●	Barbera d'Alba '97	🍷	3
●	Dolcetto d'Alba Vigneto della Chiesa '97	🍷	3
●	Barolo Vigneto La Villa '91	🍸🍸🍸	5
●	Barolo Vigneto La Villa '90	🍸🍸	5
●	Barolo Vigneto La Villa '93	🍸🍸	5

MONLEALE (AL)

VIGNETI MASSA

P.ZZA G. CAPSONI, 10
15059 MONLEALE (AL)
TEL. 0131/80302

This outpost of Piedmont on the edge of the province of Pavia (the Colli Tortonesi) seems to have been specially created to produce barbera. This grape, with its exuberant acidity, needs a warm climate to ripen enough to offer its characteristic breadth of taste, and these hills are among the warmest in Piedmont, witness the flourishing olive tree which, indifferent to the far from mild Piedmontese winters, so unlike those of olive-friendly Liguria, stands, for all to admire, near the church of Monleale. Add to the climate Walter Massa's particular empathy with the barbera grape, and you can pretty much understand the recent successes of his Bigolla and the Vecchia Cerreta, a barbera with some croatina, cabernet and nebbiolo. We were particularly impressed by the richness of the Vecchia Cerreta, shown first by the very dense ruby-garnet color, then by the bouquet, in which clear notes of blackberry and cherry open the way to complex nuances of toasty oak, pepper and fig leaf, and the palate, with its breadth and softness, completed and harmonized by the tannins. The Bigolla '96 has a dense color with a compact violet rim; its composite aromas of cherry, blueberry, coffee and menthol are enriched by earthy tones. It is sumptuous and well-rounded on the palate, leading into a pleasantly dry and long finish. The good Timorasso '96 offers aromas of ripe exotic fruit, and a broad and structured palate.

●	Bigolla '96	🍷🍷	5
●	Vecchia Cerreta '96	🍷🍷	5
○	Piemonte Cortese Dueterre '97	🍷	3
○	Timorasso '96	🍷	4
○	Piemonte Cortese Casareggio '97		3
●	Piemonte Barbera Campolungo '97		3
●	Bigolla '95	🍸🍸	4
●	Vecchia Cerreta '95	🍸🍸	4
●	Colli Tortonesi Monleale '95	🍸	4

MONTÀ D'ALBA (CN)

Giovanni Almondo

Via S. Rocco, 26
12052 Montà d'Alba (CN)
tel. 0173/975256

The wines of Domenico Almondo are again excellent this year. His two gems, the Roero Bric Valdiana and the Arneis Bricco delle Ciliegie, fully express the elegance and personality which have long characterized them. We particularly liked the former, a '96, which has a ruby-garnet color with a faintly orange rim, and a complex nose that offers notes of strawberry, raspberry, violet and vanilla. It is soft, warm, substantial and firm on the palate, if not very powerful. A decided tannic vein gives the finish dryness and grip. The Bricco delle Ciliegie, of a luminous straw color with light green highlights, offers a fresh and delicate nose with subtle notes of apple, lemon, white flowers and aromatic herbs. The silky, soft, persistent and rounded palate leads into a slightly almondy finish. The Arneis Vigne Sparse '97, quite light straw yellow tinged with green, displays fresh notes of apricot and very ripe apple, and a fairly substantial palate, underpinned by a tonic acidity that enlivens the finish. The Fosso della Rosa, a brachetto, has a lovely purplish ruby color; notes of rose and raspberry emerge on the characteristically varietal nose; the sweet palate is balanced by a decided effervescence.

	Wine	Glasses	Price
○	Roero Arneis Bricco delle Ciliegie '97	▼▼	3
●	Roero Bric Valdiana '96	▼▼	4
●	Fosso della Rosa '97	▼	3
○	Roero Arneis Vigne Sparse '97	▼	3
○	Roero Arneis Bricco delle Ciliegie '96	▽▽	3
●	Roero Bric Valdiana '95	▽▽	4

MONTEGROSSO D'ASTI (AT)

Tenuta La Meridiana

Fraz. Tana, 5
14048 Montegrosso d'Asti (AT)
tel. 0141/956172 - 956250

Giampiero Bianco steadfastly runs this ten-hectare estate, where his family has been making wine since last century, together with his wife Grazia, his father Edoardo and his mother Romilda. Montegrosso d'Asti is especially suited to barbera, which grows in more than half the vineyards of La Meridiana. So we start with the two Barberas. Produced from an old vineyard, the Barbera Bricco Sereno (whose pomace, skins and seeds are used to make a small amount of grappa) is garnet-ruby in color with a mature rim and an interesting (though somewhat forward) nose, with aromas of cherries in spirits, walnut skin, coffee and clove; on the palate it is balanced and restrained, and the finish is moderately long and faintly bitter. The Barbera Le Gagie, simple and undemanding, has a somewhat dark ruby hue, aromas of sour cherry and violet, and an agreeably cheering palate with an almondy finish. The Bianco Vigneti Delizia e Collina (a blend of chardonnay, favorita and cortese) is again very good; the straw color is followed by a fragrance of flowers and white-fleshed fruit with undertones of overripeness; on the palate it is smooth, crisp and moderately persistent. One Glass goes also to the Grignolino Vigna Maestra, with its aromas of almond, pepper and peanut; on the rounded palate it reveals a typical tannic note. A curiosity offered by this estate is a small production of Malaga (one dry, one sweet). In the recently restructured cellar a new wine made from barbera and nebbiolo (with a little cabernet franc) is completing its maturation in barriques; we shall be tasting it for next year's Guide.

	Wine	Glasses	Price
○	Monferrato Bianco Vigneti Delizia e Collina '97	▼	3
●	Barbera d'Asti Le Gagie '96	▼	3
●	Barbera d'Asti Sup. Bricco Sereno '95	▼	4
●	Grignolino d'Asti Vigna Maestra '97	▼	3
●	Vigneti del Papa Malaga Dolce '97		3
●	Vigneti del Papa Malaga Secco '96		3
●	Barbera d'Asti Sup. Bricco Sereno '94	▽	3

MONTELUPO ALBESE (CN)

CA' VIOLA
VIA LANGA, 17
12050 MONTELUPO ALBESE (CN)
TEL. 0173/617570 - 617119

Beppe Caviola is a perfect example of a modern wine producer. He has, first of all, a great palate, and the enthusiasm this has bred for the wines of others has helped him realize the potential of his own. He has also understood that the future of the Langhe lies in its native varieties, and in a very short time he has revealed their staggering possibilities. In his hands and in those of Maurizio Anselma who assists him in the vineyards, Dolcetto and Barbera have become more interesting and complex, partly because these two winegrowers know how to combine rigorous vine-tending and up-to-date cellar technique. In short, Caviola, apart from being an excellent consultant to various budding wineries, has shown, as a producer, an uncommon ability to make intelligent use of really good vintages. This is notably the case with the '96, from which, first of all, he made a fantastic Dolcetto (which was suitably honored last year), and then a memorable Bric du Luv. The grapes (mostly barbera) for this wine are macerated for only a few hours and then finish their fermentation and mature in new wood. The color is really impressive; the nose (deep and complex) has the virtue of being splendidly indescribable, a progression of delicate nuances and warmer notes; the palate starts with a dense attack and expands with confident power; the well-regulated typical exuberance of this grape provides elegance and satisfaction. The Dolcetto Barturot (irresistible, dense and pleasurable) has that little touch of severity in the mouth which makes it vivid and never commonplace. The creamy, mouth-filling standard Dolcetto is reassuringly immediate. We shall have to keep our eye on the warm and elegant Pinot Nero as it develops.

●	Langhe Rosso Bric du Luv '96	▼▼▼	5
●	Dolcetto d'Alba '97	▼▼	3
●	Dolcetto d'Alba Barturot '97	▼▼	4
●	Langhe Rosso Rangone '96	▼▼	5
●	Dolcetto d'Alba Barturot '96	▽▽▽	3
●	Langhe Rosso Bric du Luv '95	▽▽▽	5
●	Bric du Luv '93	▽▽	4
●	Bric du Luv '94	▽▽	4
●	Dolcetto d'Alba '96	▽▽	3
●	Langhe Rosso Rangone '95	▽	5

MONTEU ROERO (CN)

ANGELO NEGRO & FIGLI
FRAZ. S. ANNA, 1
CASCINA RIVERI
12040 MONTEU ROERO (CN)
TEL. 0173/90252

Some old documents preserved in the historical archives of the town council at Monteu Roero testify to the centuries-old involvement of the Negro family in viticulture; in 1670 one Giovanni Domenico Negro is listed as the owner of a house (with an oven, courtyard, cellar and vines) more or less where the Perdaudin vineyard now lies. The Negro estate has been growing uninterruptedly ever since, and now includes about 41 hectares under vine, passionately tended by the current owner, Giovanni Negro, with the help of his sons Angelo and Gabriele. This year, among the many wines presented, the Barberas stand out. As usual, the Barbera Bric Bertu is excellent; it shows a concentrated ruby-garnet hue with a compact violet rim. The broad, deep nose offers aromas of black cherry, mint, pepper, vanilla and coffee. The palate is rich, full, soft and broad, harmonized by subtle and noble tannins on a fruity long finish. The Barbera Nicolon, which is excellent value for money, is deep ruby tinged with garnet; the bouquet displays notes of violet, red currant and blackberry, with a hint of pennyroyal; it is full-bodied and distinctly acidic in the mouth. The well executed Roero Prachiosso, of a fairly intense ruby-garnet hue, offers notes of red currant, raspberry, licorice and tobacco; the palate is balanced and substantial. The Arneis Perdaudin displays pleasing aromas of fruit, herbs, wildflowers and green hazelnut. When we tasted it, although it seemed full-bodied, an exuberant acidic vein got in the way of perfect balance. Finally, the Bonarda Bric Millon '96 is also successful.

●	Barbera d'Alba Bric Bertu '96	▼▼	4
●	Barbera d'Alba Nicolon '96	▼▼	3*
●	Roero Prachiosso '96	▼	3
●	Piemonte Bonarda Bric Millon '96	▼	3
○	Roero Arneis Perdaudin '97	▼	4
○	Roero Arneis '97	▼	3
●	Barbera d'Alba Bric Bertu '95	▽▽	4
●	Barbera d'Alba Nicolon '95	▽	3

MORIONDO (TO)

TERRE DA VINO
VIA ROMA, 50
10020 MORIONDO (TO)
TEL. 011/9927070

This is the first time that the red wines have really taken the lead at the Terre da Vino. Recently their various Gavis and Chardonnays had done almost as well as the classic Langhe and Monferrato wines; this time the difference is greater, largely because of the improvement of the Barberas and the appearance of a new Langhe Rosso, La Malora (a blend of barbera, nebbiolo and non-native varieties). It offers a deep violet ruby hue and sweet aromas of red fruit and vanilla which pave the way for hints of geranium, mint and green peppercorns. The entry on the palate is inviting and succulent, and then the silky substance of the tannins characterizes the structure and the delightful finish. The Barbera La Luna e il Falò brims over with attractive, heady aromas; a stimulatingly bitter finish and excellent correspondence are the pleasures of the palate. The San Nicolao, although it doesn't have all the body of the last version, is nevertheless a bright and energetic Barbera: a delicate toasty note helps define the bouquet of damson, sour cherry and licorice. The confrontation between acidity and a lovely softness is counterpoised by a fairly long finish. The two lightly fizzy red '97s are successful: both the Freisa and the Barbera are enjoyably open without being over-simple or cloying. Only the Grignolino and the Dolcetto di Ovada are a bit murky on the nose and disjointed on the palate. The only white which stands out from the rather tame correctness of the others is the delicate Chardonnay Rocche di Ricaldone; wood has, however, made inroads on the good fruit of the Chardonnay della Tenuta Magnona.

	Wine	Glasses	Price
●	Barbera d'Asti La Luna e I Falò '96	🍷🍷	4
●	Barbera d'Asti San Nicolao '96	🍷🍷	3*
●	Langhe Rosso La Malora '96	🍷🍷	4
●	Barbera del M.to Vivace Tenuta Cannona '97	🍷	3
●	Freisa d'Asti Vivace Abbazia di Vezzolano '97	🍷	3
○	Piemonte Chardonnay Rocche di Ricaldone '97	🍷	3
●	Dolcetto di Ovada Tenuta Magnona '97		3
○	Gavi di Gavi Ca' da Bosio '97		3
●	Grignolino d'Asti Cascina Spinarola '97		3
●	Barbera d'Asti La Luna e I Falò '93	YY	4
●	Barbera d'Asti La Luna e I Falò '94	YY	3
●	Barbera d'Asti La Luna e I Falò '95	YY	4

MORSASCO (AL)

LA GUARDIA
REG. LA GUARDIA
15010 MORSASCO (AL)
TEL. 0144/73076

Franco Priarone and his five children (Graziella, Bruna, Mariangela, Ottavio and Giorgio, all employed in the family winery) have been waiting for some time for a vintage like '96 to give them first-class grapes to work with. Not that La Guardia's wines from difficult vintages disappointed our high expectations for this estate, but a range of wines like those presented for this edition of the Guide gives us the real measure of their abilities. Among the Dolcettos, we particularly admired the Gamondino and the Villa Delfini. The former, of a quite dark ruby hue, offers aromas of violet, cherry and spice; on the palate it shows all the elegance and nobility of its aged vines. The barrique-aged Villa Delfini is redolent of cherry, red currant jam and spice; the full and harmonious palate displays a long, fruity finish with an austerity provided by well-judged tannins. Two Glasses go to the Chardonnay Butàs, 30% of which is fermented in wood. The wine, of a clear, dark straw color, has a wide-ranging bouquet with notes of hazelnut and acacia blossom honey and fresh undertones of grapefruit and mandarin oranges; the silky and rich palate offers body and crispness leading to a fruity finish on which a note of vanilla emerges. The good Gavi Villa Delfini shows complex and singular aromas and, in the mouth, body and breadth. The Bricco Riccardo '96, which has a really remarkable structure, should achieve balance after a few more months in the bottle. The list concludes with the Gavi Camghé, the Barbera Ornovo, the Sacro e Profano (cabernet sauvignon and barbera) and the Figlio di un Bacco Minore, made from brachetto.

	Wine	Glasses	Price
●	Dolcetto di Ovada Il Gamondino '96	🍷🍷	4
●	Dolcetto di Ovada Villa Delfini '96	🍷🍷	4
○	Piemonte Chardonnay Butàs '96	🍷🍷	4
○	Gavi Villa Delfini '97	🍷	4
○	Gavi Camghé '97	🍷	4
●	Barbera del M.to Ornovo '96	🍷	3
●	Dolcetto di Ovada Sup. Vigneto Bricco Riccardo '96	🍷	3
●	Figlio di un Bacco Minore '97	🍷	4
●	Monferrato Rosso Sacro e Profano '95	🍷	4
●	Dolcetto di Ovada Villa Delfini '94	YY	4
●	Dolcetto di Ovada Sup. Vigneto Bricco Riccardo '95	Y	3

NEIVE (CN)

PIERO BUSSO
B.TA ALBESANI, 8
12057 NEIVE (CN)
TEL. 0173/67156

It has quickly become common knowledge that the wines from this small family estate are consistently good, so Piero Busso has to deal with requests from all over the world. The cellar, which they redid a few years ago, soon proved to be too small, and thus Piero has energetically contrived, by digging into the hillside, to create new spaces for maturing in wood: barriques are small, but take up more space than the traditional barrels. The vineyards too have grown, particularly so as to increase the amount of nebbiolo for their Barbaresco. Recently Piero Busso has shown all his skill in the Langhe Bianco, made from an assemblage of more or less equal parts of chardonnay and sauvignon: both the '96 and the '97 are excellent. The latter is even more elegant, concise and less oaky than the '96, which was already very good; the sauvignon adds a complex and stylish varietal character to the fat richness of the chardonnay. The Barbaresco '95, which certainly needs some time in the bottle if it is to offer more of a bouquet, is perfectly respectable, if not as rich as we had hoped. The Barbera '96, which has an appealing nose and a rustic palate, is perhaps too mouth- puckering. The correct and pleasant Dolcetto '97 has a green, slightly bitter note that acts as a counterweight to the power of this much touted vintage.

	Wine	Glasses	Price
○	Langhe Bianco '96	🍷🍷	4
○	Langhe Bianco '97	🍷🍷	4
●	Barbaresco Vigna Borgese '95	🍷🍷	5
●	Barbera d'Alba Vigna Majano '96	🍷	4
●	Dolcetto d'Alba Vigna Majano '97	🍷	3*
●	Barbaresco Vigna Borgese '93	YY	4
●	Barbaresco Vigna Borgese '94	YY	4
●	Barbaresco Vigna Borgese '91	Y	4
●	Barbaresco Vigna Borgese '92	Y	4

NEIVE (CN)

F.LLI CIGLIUTI
VIA SERRA BOELLA, 17
12057 NEIVE (CN)
TEL. 0173/677185

Once again this year Renato Cigliuti has presented a range of impeccable wines. His vineyards (mostly old and all located in Serra Boella, not far from Bricco di Neive) enjoy excellent exposure and produce splendid grapes, rich in aromatic substances, alcohol and tannins. We were hoping that the Barbaresco Serraboella '95, the fruit of quite a good vintage, would be another of Renato's stupendous wines, like the '83 and the '90; however, although it easily won Two Glasses, it does not provide the sensations that those two do. The color is ruby red with a distinct garnet cast; the nose, still a little closed, offers a preponderance of spicy notes to which fascinating suggestions of tobacco and light fruity undertones add complexity. At the moment, the palate suffers a little from rough tannins, which do not meet with sufficient resistance from the sweetness of the alcohol and glycerin; however, the long fruity finish bodes well for the future. The Dolcetto d'Alba Serraboella '97, with the aid of a very warm and sunny end of season, is already very satisfying with its quite dense violet ruby color, opulent but never overripe aromas of blackberry jam, and, especially, a dense, succulent palate with smooth and velvety tannins. The Langhe Rosso Bricco Serra '96 needs greater balance between the tannins of the wood and those of the nebbiolo grapes. Unfortunately we were unable to taste the Barbera d'Alba '97, which was still resting in its vat during our tastings, so we shall have to wait until next year.

	Wine	Glasses	Price
●	Barbaresco Serraboella '95	🍷🍷	5
●	Dolcetto d'Alba Serraboella '97	🍷🍷	3*
●	Langhe Rosso Bricco Serra '96	🍷	5
●	Barbaresco '83	YYY	5
●	Barbaresco Serraboella '90	YYY	5
●	Barbaresco Serraboella '92	YY	5
●	Barbaresco Serraboella '93	YY	5
●	Barbaresco Serraboella '94	Y	5
●	Bricco Serra '95	Y	5

NEIVE (CN)

FONTANABIANCA
FRAZ. BORDINI, 15
12057 NEIVE (CN)
TEL. 0173/67195

Fontanabianca is a small estate with an annual production of about 50 thousand bottles which draw on 11 hectares of vineyard; its fine range of wines has won it this debut in the Guide. The partners Aldo Pola and Bruno Ferro, who share the responsibility for this production, eagerly strive (with the invaluable help of their families) to achieve what has long been their aim: excellence. These likeable "vignerons" have the assistance of two exceptional consultants: Beppe Caviola as oenologist and Silvano Formigli for marketing. Among the wines they have presented, the Barbaresco Sorì Burdin and the Barbera d'Alba are outstanding for their well-defined bouquets and solid structures. The Barbaresco shows a deep ruby color with an orange rim, and a complex, balanced nose with aromas of red berries, vanilla and coffee and a light, intriguing mineral undertone; on the palate it is rich and soft, with sinew underpinning the progression up to a finish where fruit and spice re-emerge. The Barbera, of a dark garnet-ruby hue with a youthful, compact violet rim, offers notes of violet, dark cherry, red currant and mint. The well-articulated palate has considerable breadth, and tannic grip that reappears on the intense and corresponding finish. The good Chardonnay wants better balance between wood and fruit, but it is already rounded and satisfying in the mouth. The Arneis displays fruity aromas with hints of rhubarb, and a not very demanding but fairly full palate. The last in the list is the Dolcetto '97, which has a fine fragrance of violet, blackberry and almond, and a palate of medium structure, with tannins pleasantly in evidence on the fruity finish.

●	Barbaresco Sorì Burdin '95	TT	5
●	Barbera d'Alba '96	TT	3*
●	Dolcetto d'Alba Bordini '97	T	3
○	Langhe Arneis '97	T	3
○	Langhe Chardonnay Montesommo '97	T	4

NEIVE (CN)

BRUNO GIACOSA
VIA XX SETTEMBRE, 52
12057 NEIVE (CN)
TEL. 0173/67027

This great expert on the vineyards of the Langhe does not like fuss and concentrates on facts. In his cellar, Bruno has for some years had all the equipment and space necessary for making whites as well; if you go, you shouldn't miss the subterranean storage rooms for the Spumante. However, it is the great reds of the Langhe which are Giacosa's passion, and Barbaresco comes first. The S. Stefano, the estate's most important special selection, is, as usual, better on the palate than on the nose during its first years in the bottle; the nose has a certain charm but is still a little closed, while there is lots of succulent fruit on the palate, with decided but not bitter tannins promising a long future. When we tasted the '78 S. Stefano again recently, the complexity of the bouquet and the richness of the palate were extraordinarily moving. The Arneis, well-made as usual, has soft floral aromas; on the palate it is simpler and smoother than earlier versions. The correct standard Barbaresco '95 reveals almost sweet notes on the palate, and still rather mouth-puckering tannins. The proverbial caution of this great wine-maker prevented us from tasting either the special selections of Barbaresco or the Spumante Bruno Giacosa '95, which will be released in the spring of 1999. These are all eagerly awaited, and you should taste them as soon as possible: the Barbaresco comes from newly acquired vineyards in a historic site, and the Spumante is always one of the best in Italy. The Nebbiolo di Valmaggiore, admirable as usual, comes from a highly regarded Roero cru and serves as a further confirmation of Bruno Giacosa's gifts when it comes to understanding vineyards.

●	Barbaresco S. Stefano '95	TT	6
●	Barbaresco '95	T	6
●	Nebbiolo d'Alba Valmaggiore '96	T	4
○	Roero Arneis '97	T	4
●	Barolo Collina Rionda Ris. '82	YYY	6
●	Barolo Rocche di Castiglione Falletto '85	YYY	6
●	Barbaresco S. Stefano '90	YY	6
●	Barbaresco S. Stefano '93	YY	6
●	Barolo Collina Rionda '93	YY	6
●	Barolo Collina Rionda Ris. '90	YY	6
●	Barolo Falletto '90	YY	6
●	Barolo Falletto '93	YY	6
●	Barolo Villero '90	YY	6

NEIVE (CN)

Giacosa Fratelli

Via XX Settembre, 64
12057 Neive (CN)
tel. 0173/67013

The brothers Valerio and Silverio Giacosa (with their respective sons Maurizio, who has a degree in economics and business studies, and Paolo, with his diploma from the oenological institute in Alba), manage what counts as a very large winery in the Langhe (600 thousand bottles a year). Their ability to maintain quality, even at that volume and in moderately-priced wines, is a particular point of pride for the family. A concrete proof of this ability can be found in the Barbera Maria Gioana and the standard Barbaresco. This year their range is greatly enriched by the Barbaresco Rio Sordo '95, which lords it over all the other wines from the height of its Two Glasses. It has a deep ruby color with an orange-tinged rim; the broad bouquet displays aromas of red fruit, cocoa and clove, and on the palate it shows good substance and fine, well-tamed tannins that add dryness to the long finish with notes of wild berries and licorice. The simpler standard Barbaresco has a slightly faded color, aromas of ripe cherry and raspberry with hints of dried flowers and sweet pastry, and medium structure on the palate. The Barbera Maria Gioana '96, garnet-ruby in hue with a slightly faded rim, offers aromas of cherry and roasted coffee with mineral undertones. There is good grip on the palate, and a pleasing acidic note on the finish. Among the whites, we liked the Arneis, with its fairly deep straw color and notes of apricot and very ripe exotic fruit; it is soft and easy to drink.

●	Barbaresco Rio Sordo '95	🍷🍷	5
●	Barbaresco '95	🍷	4
●	Barbera d'Alba Maria Gioana '96	🍷	4
○	Roero Arneis '97		3
●	Barbera d'Alba Maria Gioana '95	Y	3
●	Barolo Bussia '93	Y	5

NEIVE (CN)

Paitin

Via Serra Boella, 20
12057 Neive (CN)
tel. 0173/67343

In the last few years the Pasquero Elias have hit their stride. In this edition of the Guide, whether because of the greater cellar experience of Secondo and his two sons Silvano and Giovanni, or because of a year that was quite mean with quantity (although the family has always been rigorous on this point), the Barbaresco '95 has won Three Glasses. The estate has established its definitive size of 15 hectares: about ten of them are on the slopes of the splendid Neive hill known as Serra Boella (and about five of these are planted to nebbiolo for Barbaresco). The new five hectares are near Alba in Rivoli, where a country inn has recently been opened. The Barbaresco Sorì Paitin '95 is one of the greatest Piedmontese wines in this year's Guide; even to the eye it reveals its imposing character. The bouquet has an exceptional elegance; the aromas of red fruit and licorice meet the spice from the new wood and enrich each other. On the palate, the tightly knit tannins give density and sweetness without diminishing the wine. The Dolcetto '97 and more especially the Langhe Paitin '96 (an assemblage of nebbiolo with small amounts of barbera, cabernet and syrah), although they do not show the complexity and breeding of the Sorì Paitin, are extremely pleasurable. The first produces an explosion of heady fruit and lots of fresh softness, while the second, more austere, offers complexity and depth. The Campolive Bianco '96 (a mixture of equal amounts of sauvignon matured in stainless steel and barrique-aged chardonnay) and the Barbera d'Alba Campolive '96 are a step down; they are both in need of greater harmony between fruit and wood.

●	Barbaresco Sorì Paitin '95	🍷🍷🍷	5
●	Dolcetto d'Alba Sorì Paitin '97	🍷🍷	3
●	Langhe Paitin '96	🍷🍷	5
●	Barbera d'Alba Campolive '96	🍷	4
○	Campolive Bianco '96	🍷	4
●	Barbaresco Ris. '90	YY	6
●	Barbaresco Sorì Paitin '93	YY	5
●	Barbaresco Sorì Paitin '94	YY	5
●	Langhe Paitin '95	YY	5

NEIVE (CN)

SOTTIMANO
LOC. COTTÀ, 21
12057 NEIVE (CN)
TEL. 0173/635186

The '95 vintage made it possible for Rino's winery to achieve an excellence which it had only rarely reached with its Barbaresco. There are three Barbarescos this year: they correspond to three estate vineyards, all in excellent but different positions, and otherwise diverse. We'll start with the Brichet, made from grapes grown around the winery: the color is transparent garnet: the bouquet, not very well-defined, offers a clean, gradual development; it is full, ready and not very demanding in the mouth, straightforward also on the finish. The Pajorè provides an interestingly mature version of Barbaresco: to the eye it has the classic concentrated garnet hue; hints of plum and sour cherry jams open the bouquet to nuances of cocoa and rose. Full development characterizes the palate as well which, if not very dense, does progress harmoniously. The best performance is given by the Barbaresco Currà: captivating, full and distinct in its aromas, it clearly states, despite its innovative style, its close links with its terroir. The Pajorè is the Barbaresco with the greatest promise of future development. Sottimano's successful season is further confirmed by the Casa Maté, a dry Brachetto with fresh floral aromas and a straightforward taste. The Dolcetto Bric del Salto and the Barbera Pairolero resemble each other: they both offer hints of fermentation and a rustic, simple palate.

●	Barbaresco Currà '95	🍷🍷	5
●	Barbaresco Pajorè Vigna Lunetta '95	🍷🍷	5
●	Barbaresco Brichet '95	🍷	5
●	Barbera d'Alba Pairolero '96	🍷	3
●	Dolcetto d'Alba Bric del Salto '97	🍷	3*
●	Langhe Rosso Maté '97	🍷	3
●	Dolcetto d'Alba Cottà '97		3
●	Barbaresco Brichet '90	🍷 (white)	5
●	Barbaresco Brichet '93	🍷 (white)	4
●	Barbaresco Pajoré Vigna Lunetta '94	🍷 (white)	4
●	Barbaresco Seiranera '93	🍷 (white)	4

NEVIGLIE (CN)

F.LLI BERA
CASCINA PALAZZO, 12
12050 NEVIGLIE (CN)
TEL. 0173/630194

The Beras produce 90 thousand bottles of Moscato and 15 thousand of red wines annually. Since they are among the best producers of Moscato, the disparity is not just a matter of quantity; nevertheless it will be interesting to see whether their Barbera, which keeps improving, will acquire greater importance. For the moment their star (for which Attilio and Walter, as well as Sisto and Maria, are responsible) is still the Moscato Su Reimond: very broad in its aromas, which range from huisache to sandalwood, it is soft and velvety rather than sweet in the mouth. The standard Moscato, not as broad and with a little more sweetness than usual, is characteristically reminiscent of marzipan on the finish. The Asti is not as good as usual: it seems overripe, and it quickly releases its gas, but it does have a lovely, long sugared almond finish. The family skill can also be seen in the Spumante Brut, a specialty made from chardonnay and pinot noir from an old vineyard. New-mown grass and Golden Delicious apple have their way with the nose, leaving the mousse, rather than the extract, the task of enriching the palate. The Barbera Sassisto has an impenetrable dark violet hue; the blackberry fragrance is simple, but concentrated and captivating; the rich flavor of fruit in spiritis accompanies the acidity right up to the pleasingly bitter finish. The standard Barbera, headier and less intense, is very good, as is the correct and balanced Dolcetto.

○	Moscato d'Asti Su Reimond '97	🍷🍷	3
○	Asti Cascina Palazzo '97	🍷	3
○	Bera Brut	🍷	4
○	Moscato d'Asti '97	🍷	3
●	Barbera d'Alba '96	🍷	3
●	Barbera d'Alba Sassisto '95	🍷	4
●	Dolcetto d'Alba '97	🍷	3

NIZZA M.TO (AT)

Bersano Antiche Cantine Conti della Cremosina

P.zza Dante, 21
14049 Nizza M.to (AT)
tel. 0141/721273

After years of routine production, this historic winery (which could return to being a reference point for Monferrato), is showing distinct signs of improvement, and has presented a very interesting range of wines. This is thanks to the owners, and in particular to Ugo Massimelli, who wants to produce really good wines and has given the general manager Domenico Conta carte blanche to that end. This year's wines were very successful, especially those from the recently acquired Generala estate in Agliano. The Barbera d'Asti Generala '96 has a violet ruby color, a nose of spice, red berries and vanilla and a succulent, juicy, vigorous palate rich in extract. The Pomona '96, an assemblage of barbera and cabernet sauvignon, has an almost impenetrable bluish hue; the imposing bouquet is dominated by pepper and green tones, with a nuance of Peruvian bark; the palate suggests licorice and ripe red fruit. The Gavi Tenuta Marchese Raggio is still one of the best of its kind: the '97, of a green-tinged straw color, has an elegant and lingering fragrance of orange blossom, yeasts and toast. On the palate it is vivid, vigorous and rich in ripe fruit. The Brachetto d'Acqui Vigna Castelgaro has never been this good: the '97 has a deep pink shade, dense and brilliant, and a perfectly varietal nose, with rose and honey emerging (but without the excesses of some mawkish Brachettos); it has an aristocratic palate, dense and fruity. It's worth noticing the house Brut and the Barbera Cremosina '96, which we would like to see a little more concentrated and expressive of its terroir.

	Wine	Glasses	Price
○	Gavi di Gavi Marchese Raggio '97	🍷🍷	4
●	Barbera d'Asti Sup. Generala '96	🍷🍷	5
●	Brachetto d'Acqui Castelgaro '97	🍷🍷	4
●	Barbera d'Asti Cremosina '96	🍷	4
●	Pomona '96	🍷	6
○	Spumante Arturo Bersano Ris. '94	🍷	4
●	Barbera d'Asti Vigna Cremosina '95	(white glass)	4

NIZZA M.TO (AT)

Cascina La Barbatella

Strada Annunziata, 55
14049 Nizza M.to (AT)
tel. 0141/701434

The Vigna di Sonvico and the Vigna dell'Angelo have both made it over 90 points: a great triumph for these two wines, conceived and worked for by the dedicated Angelo Sonvico, and realized thanks to the knowledge and skill of Giuliano Noè. With its deep intense color, the Vigna di Sonvico has a captivating bouquet, where, after a few moments, the initial aroma of fresh grass gives way to intense notes of blackberry, raspberry, coffee and balsamic and spicy tones (pepper and clove). The palate is commanded with authority by various elements that have struck a balance, and the excellent correspondence between nose and mouth accompanies an intense and persistent flavor. La Vigna dell'Angelo, a barbera, is of a clear and concentrated ruby color; the delicate and elegant aromas display perfectly blended fruity (particularly dark cherry) and toasty notes; on the palate it is silky, rounded and harmonious, offering a pleasing (as well as typical) vein of freshness on the long finish. The good La Barbatella '97 carries through its fresh fruity bouquet (cherry) onto the warm and striking palate. The Bianco Noè (cortese and sauvignon), with a crisp palate and a pleasantly almondy finish, is redolent of grass and flowers, in addition to oak. Angelo and Giuliano, never complacent, continue to try out new ideas; we look forward to further successes.

	Wine	Glasses	Price
●	Barbera d'Asti Sup. La Vigna dell'Angelo '96	🍷🍷🍷	5
●	La Vigna di Sonvico '96	🍷🍷🍷	6
●	Barbera d'Asti '97	🍷	4
○	Monferrato Bianco Noè '97	🍷	4
●	Barbera d'Asti Sup. La Vigna dell'Angelo '89	(3 white glasses)	6
●	La Vigna di Sonvico '90	(3 white glasses)	6
●	La Vigna di Sonvico '91	(3 white glasses)	6
●	La Vigna di Sonvico '93	(3 white glasses)	5
●	La Vigna di Sonvico '94	(3 white glasses)	5
●	La Vigna di Sonvico '95	(3 white glasses)	5
●	Barbera d'Asti Sup. La Vigna dell'Angelo '95	(2 white glasses)	5

NIZZA M.TO (AT)

Scarpa - Antica Casa Vinicola

Via Montegrappa, 6
14049 Nizza M.to (AT)
tel. 0141/721331

While the world of wine is always on the move, and not always in the right direction, this estate seems to live in another dimension: it tends its splendid vines with old-fashioned care, and wines are entrusted to the cellar for long periods of aging. Monferrato specialties like Rouchet and Brachetto have an innate aromatic quality, never mediated by sugars. Mario Pesce is a man of another age - and this is not just idle rhetoric; we can see it in his consideration for his colleagues, and in his professional rigor; he shares the credit for Scarpa's success with his nephew, Carlo Castino, who oversees production. It cannot be said that their wines make for easy drinking: made to last, but not in the modern sense of the term, they do not have an immediate depth of color and bouquet, and they reveal their qualities with a slow deliberation adored by real (and patient) connoisseurs. The Nebbiolo d'Alba '96 has structure, grip and persistence; the bouquet shows a singular mineral vein, and the tannins on the palate blend actively with the fruit. The Barbera Bogliona comes from the complicated '95 vintage, and after a period in which it seemed to have gotten stuck, it is now beginning to display its mature and typical nose. The acidity calls the tune on the palate, and bodes well for future development. The Dolcetto d'Acqui, fresh and fruity, and the peppery and floral Grignolino are clearly characteristic. The Barbera di Castelrocchero, on the other hand, is still a mysterious and almost inexpressive wine. The dry and silky Freisa is surprising in its winning gradual development. The hailstorms of April '95 put an end to that year's Barbaresco.

	Wine	Rating	Price
●	Barbera d'Asti Sup. La Bogliona '95	🍷🍷	5
●	Nebbiolo d'Alba Ca' du Nota '96	🍷🍷	5
●	Rouchet Bricco Rosa '97	🍷🍷	6
●	Dolcetto d'Acqui La Selva di Moirano '96	🍷	4
●	Grignolino d'Asti S. Defendente '96	🍷	4
●	Monferrato Freisa Secco La Selva di Moirano '96	🍷	5
●	Rouchet Bricco Rosa '90	🍷🍷🍷 (past)	5
●	Barbera d'Asti La Bogliona '89	🍷🍷 (past)	5
●	Barolo Tettimora '88	🍷🍷 (past)	6
●	Rouchet Bricco Rosa '96	🍷🍷 (past)	5
●	Barolo Tettimora '90	🍷 (past)	6

NIZZA M.TO (AT)

Franco e Mario Scrimaglio

Via Alessandria, 67
14049 Nizza M.to (AT)
tel. 0141/721385 - 727052

At the Scrimaglio winery they keep their eye on the market. The wines, designed to express brilliance, rarely have a substantial body and always have a fair price. The winery shows the lighter and more carefree side of Piedmontese wines, conquering markets at some remove from the traditional ones. Since the Barbera Croutin, their real gem, was not presented, our attention was caught by the RoccaNivo '96 version. The color is fairly concentrated; at first the bouquet is just heady, then delicate notes of red fruits emerge; on the palate the inevitable acidity takes the lead, and the structure is supple and of medium length. We hoped for a lot from the Barbera Bricco Sant'Ippolito, but it is no more than correct; although well made, it would need more personality on the nose and more density on the palate to rise above its peers. The Gavi, another carefully made wine, shows a delightful zest in its fruity aromas as well as a long, satisfying palate. The subtler Gavi di Gavi reveals its customary elegance together with a delicate vitality of flavor. The lightly sparkling and attractive Cortese Vivace is a witness to the excellent care in cellar technique which is shown to all 800 thousand bottles that this winery annually produces.

	Wine	Rating	Price
●	Barbera d'Asti Bricco S. Ippolito '96	🍷	4
●	Barbera d'Asti Sup. Vigneto RoccaNivo '96	🍷	3
●	Barbera del M.to Vivace Il Matto '97	🍷	3
○	Gavi '97	🍷	3
○	Gavi di Gavi '97	🍷	4
○	Cortese dell'Alto M.to Vivace Il Matto '97		2
●	Dolcetto d'Alba '97		3
●	Barbera d'Asti Sup. '95	🍷🍷 (past)	3
●	Barbera d'Asti Sup. Croutin '90	🍷🍷 (past)	5
●	Barbera d'Asti Sup. Croutin '95	🍷 (past)	4

NOVELLO (CN)

ELVIO COGNO
LOC. RAVERA, 2
12060 NOVELLO (CN)
TEL. 0173/731405

Walter Fissore and his wife Nadia, from Novello, have taken up the reins of Elvio Cogno's winery and have shown themselves worthy of this distinguished heritage by producing an enviable range this year. The wines, all very distinct, have an unusual openness and a modern fleshy fruit. In the Barbera, Walter and Nadia, with the help of Beppe Caviola, have taken full advantage of the '96 vintage; its concentration is evident from its hue, and the aromas of red fruit mingle with the oak-derived tones; on the equally intense palate, alcoholic warmth, extract and woody tannins are in the process of blending with the fresh acidity. The Dolcetto '97, too, shows considerable length; it has at last gone beyond its habitual pleasant correctness to take on a vivid intensity. A dark ruby color precedes aromas of blackberry and almond; the palate is broad, with densely woven tannins and a triumphant finish. The Langhe Rosso Montegrilli '96 (complex, intriguing and very slightly mineral) seems to suggest that some non-native grape has been keeping company with its nebbiolo; it is in any case a successful and carefully made wine. The color is vivid and uniform, and varietal characteristics are fused with the notes of new oak on the nose; the palate is very warm, dense and long. Only the Barolo '94 failed to stir up enthusiasm, but how could it, from a year like that? There is also a white wine, Nas-Cetta, made from that obscure local variety.

	Wine	Glasses	Price
●	Barbera d'Alba Bricco del Merlo '96	▼▼	4
●	Dolcetto d'Alba Vigna del Mandorlo '97	▼▼	3*
●	Langhe Rosso Montegrilli '96	▼▼	4
●	Barolo Ravera '94	▼	5
○	Nas-Cetta '97		4
●	Barbera d'Alba Bricco del Merlo '95	▽▽	4
●	Barolo Ravera '93	▽▽	5
●	Barbera d'Alba Bricco del Merlo '94	▽	4

NOVI LIGURE (AL)

CASCINA DEGLI ULIVI
STRADA MAZZOLA, 12
15067 NOVI LIGURE (AL)
TEL. 0143/744598

Stefano Bellotti's winery is on the boundary of Gavi territory and has finally been officially declared to be on the right side of the border, so his wines again proudly sport Gavi DOC labels. In any case, the vineyards themselves were never in question, since they are clearly within the Gavi zone, some, indeed, lying in particularly prized sites such as the cru Filagnotti di Tassarolo, the source of the first wine we're about to discuss. It is of a fairly deep green-tinged straw color and offers intense aromas of flowers, peach and apple, together with light mineral notes. Good fruit is immediately evident on the palate and is gradually animated by a refreshing acidity, leading into the lightly bitter notes on the finish. The standard Gavi, brilliant in color, displays agreeable fruity aromas that are slightly disturbed by somewhat unbalanced vegetal notes, but it redeems itself on the soft, well-balanced palate. The Montemarino, clear gold in color, is redolent of flowers and shows good fruit on the not perfectly harmonized palate. The white A Demua and the dessert wine L'Amoros are correctly executed. A re-tasting of the Dolcetto Nibiô '96 confirmed last year's assessment and its ability to last: an almost transparent ruby hue; a frank fragrance with notes of cherry; a fairly robust and pleasingly dry taste.

	Wine	Glasses	Price
○	Gavi Ulivi '97	▼	2*
○	Gavi I Filagnotti '97	▼	3
○	Monferrato Bianco Montemarino di Tassarolo '96	▼	2
○	A Demua '96		4
●	L'Amoroso '97		3
●	Monferrato Dolcetto Nibiô '96	▽	3

OTTIGLIO (AL)

CAVE DI MOLETO
REG. MOLETO, 4
15038 OTTIGLIO (AL)
TEL. 0142/921468 - 921455

The vineyards of this winery, which belongs to the Merone Holderbank group, are expanding; from the eight hectares owned in 1992, it has grown to the present 26, planted to barbera (a good eleven hectares), cabernet sauvignon, merlot, nebbiolo, cortese, chardonnay and grignolino. The rest of the property consists of 40 hectares of arable land and four of apple orchards, the latter including an experimental section in which some old local varieties are grown. But let's get back to the wines: we should say at once that the Barbera Mülej '95 confirmed the excellent impression made by last year's version. The rich dark garnet-ruby color precedes a broad, complex nose with notes of cherry and ripe red currant and elegant undertones of grass and coffee custard. In the mouth it is full and rich, with a distinct acidic vein and a fruity and spicy finish underpinned by delicate tannins. The very good standard Barbera very nearly won Two Glasses for its elegance and balance; its color is ruby verging on garnet, and notes of black berries, anise, clove and fig leaf emerge on the nose. The successful and even palate has a corresponding finish. The Rosso delle Cave, a merlot, also only just missed Two Glasses. You can already sense its possibilities, but it needs the additional concentration and power that older vines will be able to give it. The enchanting bouquet displays aromas of red fruit and varietal notes of green leaf with undertones of spice and dried flowers; the palate is balanced and pleasingly dry. The last on the list is the agreeable Bianco delle Cave, which offers the aromatic notes of the moscato grape with some finesse; the sweet palate is gracefully fizzy.

	Wine	Glasses	Price
●	Barbera del M.to Mülej '95	🍷🍷	4
●	Barbera del M.to '96	🍷	3
●	Rosso delle Cave '95	🍷	2
○	Bianco delle Cave '97	🍷	4
●	Barbera del M.to Mülej '94	🍸🍸	4

PIOBESI D'ALBA (CN)

TENUTA CARRETTA
LOC. CARRETTA, 2
12040 PIOBESI D'ALBA (CN)
TEL. 0173/619119

The Miroglio family's Tenuta Carretta, 52 hectares of vineyards divided between the Langhe and Roero zones, produces a wide range of wines typical of each side of the Tanaro river, including, on the Langhe side, Barolo and Barbaresco, with which we begin our review. The Barolo is ruby-hued with a faded rim, and displays a slightly faint nose of some finesse, with notes of violet, wild berries and leather; on the palate it is medium-bodied and well-balanced, with a corresponding finish. The Barbaresco, ruby in the glass and lightly orange-rimmed, offers notes of violet, raspberry and spice with a delicately mineral undertone. It is more structured than the Barolo, in part because it's a '95, not a '94. The Dolcetto d'Alba Vigna Tavoleto, with youthful violet highlights in its ruby hue, has a distinctive nose, with notes of red currant, earth and violet, and vegetal nuances. On the palate it is robustly substantial and pleasantly rustic. Two of the Roero wines have won Two Glasses: the Roero Superiore Bric Paradiso and the Arneis Vigna Canorei. The first has a deep garnet-ruby color and a broad bouquet with notes of blackberry, strawberry, tobacco and black pepper; the palate is well-balanced, soft, even and rounded, if not very powerful. The dry finish reveals hints of coffee. The richly straw-colored Arneis offers aromas of banana, peach, white flowers and yeasts; on the palate it is crisp and silky, with a not extremely long but intense finish. The Bric Quercia shows aromas of dark cherry and cocoa, good body, and notes of caramel on the finish.

	Wine	Glasses	Price
○	Roero Arneis Vigna Canorei '97	🍷🍷	4
●	Roero Sup. Bric Paradiso '96	🍷🍷	4
●	Barbaresco Cascina Bordino '95	🍷	5
●	Barolo Vigneti Cannubi '94	🍷	5
●	Dolcetto d'Alba Vigna Tavoleto '97	🍷	3
●	Langhe Bric Quercia '96	🍷	5
○	Langhe Favorita '97	🍷	3
●	Barolo Vigneti Cannubi '93	🍸🍸	5
●	Barbaresco Cascina Bordino '93	🍸	5
●	Nebbiolo d'Alba Bric Tavoleto '94	🍸	3

PRASCO (AL)

Verrina - Cascina Tornati

Via S. Rocco, 14
15010 Prasco (AL)
tel. 0144/375745

The Dolcetto di Ovada Vigna Oriali has established itself as a Two Glass winner. The '97 offers the same rich fruit we admired last year, but with greater finesse. Nicolò Verrina, not content with having produced this gem, has acquired two and a half hectares of vineyard near Cremolino in a first-rate site on the crest of a hill called Bricco Tulle. But let's consider the Vigna Oriali: its density and concentration can be seen from its intense ruby hue. The broad and fruity nose offers aromas of raspberry, red currant and strawberry enriched by almond and pepper nuances. On the palate it is full-bodied and robust, with noble tannins and a long, balanced finish that mirrors the bouquet. The characteristic and inviting Semonina wins One overflowing Glass; ruby tinged with purple in color, it presents fresh aromas of dark cherry and raspberry with vegetal hints of green peppercorns; on the palate it is faultlessly pleasing and leads into an agreeably bitterish finish. The pleasant Barbera di Monferrato is definitely a step up from last year's. Of a garnet-ruby color, it has heady but frank aromas with notes of violet and raspberry, and good body. The correct straw-colored Cortese is full-flavored; the nose shows moderate finesse and the wine goes down very easily.

	Wine	Glasses	Price
●	Dolcetto di Ovada Vigna Oriali '97	🍷🍷	3
●	Barbera del M.to '97	🍷	1*
●	Dolcetto di Ovada Podere Semonina '97	🍷	3
○	Cortese dell'Alto M.to '97		1
●	Dolcetto di Ovada Vigna Oriali '96	🍷🍷 (outline)	2

PRIOCCA (CN)

Cascina Val del Prete

Strada Santuario, 2
12040 Priocca (CN)
tel. 0173/616534

In 1977 Bartolomeo Roagna and his wife Carolina took over the Casina Val del Prete, where they had worked for many years as share-croppers. It was a few hectares of land planted with grains and fruit, in the amphitheater which lies above the farmhouse. Subsequently they have frequently added contiguous pieces of land, so the estate now covers eight hectares. Bartolomeo increased the area under vine, but like so many Roero farms of that period, it produced a variety of crops. The Roagna sons Luigi and Mario have, in the past few years, been taking care of the vineyards, while Bartolomeo looks after the orchards and the cattle. Val del Prete's debut in the Guide is the result of Mario's firm determination to make great wine. After a brief period of readjustment, the estate has produced an excellent series of wines from the '96 and '97 vintages. The two whites, which have overcome the problems caused by a very hot year, reveal Mario's experienced hand in the winery. La Favorita offers a fat and full palate and a fragrance that includes notes of apple and inviting mineral hints. The Arneis is a little less developed on the nose, but very rich in the mouth. Among the reds, the barrique-aged wines are outstandingly elegant. The Barbera d'Alba Carolina, which has already succeeded in integrating its wood, displays aromas of cherry, smoke and licorice, which carry through onto the palate. The Nebbiolo d'Alba Vigna di Lino has more body; in addition to an extremely aristocratic bouquet, it offers, on the palate, powerful tannins that are still somewhat rough (and bode well for a long maturation). The very fruity Barbera '97 is also worthy of note.

	Wine	Glasses	Price
●	Barbera d'Alba Sup. Carolina '96	🍷🍷	4
○	Langhe Favorita '97	🍷🍷	2*
●	Nebbiolo d'Alba Sup. Vigna di Lino '96	🍷🍷	4
●	Barbera d'Alba '97	🍷	3
○	Roero Arneis '97	🍷	3

ROCCHETTA TANARO (AT)

Braida
Via Roma, 94
14030 Rocchetta Tanaro (AT)
tel. 0141/644113

The Bologna family's attractive and technically up-to-the-minute cellar will soon also accommodate sweet wines for their vinification, which used to take place elsewhere. All 350 thousand of their bottles are made with extreme care, as you can tell from this year's results. The most interesting, the Barbera Ai Suma, is late-harvested and aged in new barriques. The '96 vintage has given it remarkably dense fruit. Its color provides the first in a series of rich and deep sensations; the bouquet has an intense, rustic tone, and the palate offers well-distributed alcoholic warmth, and an acidity that is well-integrated into the structure. With just a touch more elegance Ai Suma would be unstoppable. The Barbera Bricco della Bigotta presents a color of medium intensity, and a well-defined fruity bouquet; both the entry and the progression on the palate are delicate. The Barbera Bricco dell'Uccellone, similar in style, has a subdued fragrance of dark cherry and spice; the palate reveals the contribution made by the oak in the backbone it has given to the structure. The Bacialé, a blend of pinot noir and barbera, was designed to combine freshness and complexity; although it is wood-fermented, it should be drunk soon. La Monella, also vivid and immediate, (with the characteristic qualities of a lightly fizzy Barbera and the frank style of a modern wine) shows a surprising fullness. The best of the Serra dei Fiori wines this year is not the Dolcetto, which is somewhat evanescent, but the white Il Fiore (riesling and chardonnay), in market terms the most important of their wines.

	Wine	Rating	Price
●	Barbera d'Asti Ai Suma '96	🍷🍷	6
●	Barbera d'Asti Bricco dell'Uccellone '95	🍷🍷	6
●	Barbera d'Asti Bricco della Bigotta '95	🍷	6
●	Barbera del M.to La Monella '97	🍷	3
●	Dolcetto d'Alba Serra dei Fiori '97	🍷	3
●	Monferrato Rosso Il Bacialé '97	🍷	4
○	Langhe Bianco Il Fiore '97	🍷	3
○	Langhe Chardonnay Asso di Fiori '97		5
●	Barbera d'Asti Ai Suma '89	YYY	6
●	Bricco dell'Uccellone '91	YYY	6
●	Barbera d'Asti Ai Suma '95	YY	6
●	Bricco dell'Uccellone '94	YY	5

RODELLO (CN)

Viticoltori Associati di Rodello
Via Montà, 13
12050 Rodello (CN)
tel. 0173/617159 - 617318

The various Dolcettos from the Viticoltori Associati are variations on the theme of the cru: the same grape, the same use of stainless steel, and the same style; the only variable is the vineyard of origin. For example, the very deep hue and decided taste of the Vigna Deserto can be traced to the clayey soil and the not very high site; this best of the year's wines wins us over with its broad if rather forward fragrance and pleasingly clean finish. The Vigna San Lorenzo is a vineyard (on the summit of a hill) which has traditionally produced paler-hued Dolcettos that are youthful, heady, acidic and fairly lingering. The less straightforward Vigna Buschin does not succeed this time in providing either the usual fresh, light sensations or the complexity and concentration of the '96. Lastly, some news: after a hiatus of 10 years the Viticoltori are again making a Dolcetto from the Bricco Campasso, a very interesting wine, which will be a fine addition to their collection of crus. Its fuchsia hue is lively if not intense; the simple but clean fragrance is reminiscent of sour cherry; on the palate it is balanced and shows an admirable aromatic persistence; furthermore it is thirst-quenching. The makers of these admirable wines (Renzo and Valentino Drocco, Massimo and Maurizio Anselmo, and Gianni Nada) manage, with a genuinely cooperative spirit, their 12 hectares of vineyard, producing 50 thousand bottles a year, two thirds of which contain their basic Dolcetto.

	Wine	Rating	Price
●	Dolcetto d'Alba Vigna Deserto '97	🍷🍷	3*
●	Dolcetto d'Alba Vigna Buschin '97	🍷	3
●	Dolcetto d'Alba Vigna Campasso '97	🍷	3
●	Dolcetto d'Alba Vigna San Lorenzo '97	🍷	3

ROSIGNANO M.TO (AL)

VICARA
CASCINA MADONNA DELLE GRAZIE, 5
15030 ROSIGNANO M.TO (AL)
TEL. 0142/488054

Every year Diego Visconti, Carlo Cassinis and Domenico Ravizza present a wide range of very good wines. From their 40 hectares of vineyards, they produce all the typical Monferrato wines in a variety of versions, to satisfy a variety of tastes. Their top wine is the Rubello, which, from the '96 vintage, has a deep ruby color shot through with garnet. Its complex and balanced bouquet offers aromas of cherry, peach skin, roasted coffee and green leaf; on the palate it is full, even and soft, with a dry finish suggestive of fruit and licorice. The three Barberas made a good showing at our tastings: the Cantico della Crosia, the Volpuva and the Superiore. The first, mature and reserved, is redolent of red fruit and coffee; there is a decided vein of tannins on the savory palate and the finish is somewhat dominated by the wood. The Volpuva shows, right from its dense, youthful color, the rich fruit of the '97 vintage; the direct and intense nose offers aromas of cherry, pepper and violet, and it is full and frank in the mouth, with a pleasingly dry finish. The Barbera Superiore '96, more moderate, offers notes of red fruit, violet and spice on the nose; the palate, if not very powerful, is harmonious and graceful. The Airales (a blend of cortese, chardonnay and sauvignon) has a fruity nose and a smooth, dry palate. The aggressive spicy tones of the characteristic Grignolino are tempered by soft notes of red fruit. The long list ends with the Nettare del Paradiso, which displays the varietal tones of moscato and a sweet palate with a decided, full effervescence.

	Wine	Glasses	Price
●	Monferrato Rubello '96	🍷🍷	4
●	Barbera del M.to Cantico della Crosia '96	🍷	4
●	Barbera del M.to Sup. '96	🍷	3
●	Barbera del M.to Volpuva '97	🍷	3*
●	Grignolino del M.to Casalese '97	🍷	3
○	Monferrato Bianco Airales '97	🍷	3
○	Nettare del Paradiso '97	🍷	3
●	Monferrato Rubello '95	🍷🍷 (prev.)	3
●	Rubello di Salabue '93	🍷🍷 (prev.)	3

S. GIORGIO CANAVESE (TO)

ORSOLANI
VIA MICHELE CHIESA, 12
10090 S. GIORGIO CANAVESE (TO)
TEL. 0124/32386

Gianluigi Orsolani believes in the potential of Caluso Passito: you have only to taste his La Rustìa to get an idea of how much he is doing to revive a rather neglected wine which was, until relatively recently, very well known, even abroad. (For example, the interesting research on this dessert wine conducted by Garino Canina, Capris and Passera in 1951 is mentioned in the celebrated Traité d'Oenologie by Ribéreau-Gayon and Peynaud.) But to return to the excellent La Rustìa: it has a clear light amber color, and a captivating bouquet composed of walnut and candied orange peel with complex undertones of noble rot. On the palate it is full, round, sweet and glycerin-rich, with a refreshing acidity that perfectly harmonizes the progression to the intense, corresponding finish. Two Glasses also go to the Erbaluce, which has a pale straw color tinged with green. Well-defined notes of white-fleshed fruit, hay, the sea and flint precede a silky, even, beautifully balanced and thoroughly satisfying palate. The Caluso Vignot S. Antonio, made from erbaluce, has a deep straw hue and aromas of hazelnut, dried herbs and citron. The robust palate shows vigor and body. The last offering, the Brut Nature Cuvée '92, displays a characteristic nose with distinct notes of hazelnut, apple and crusty bread and, in the mouth, crispness and fruit.

	Wine	Glasses	Price
○	Caluso Passito La Rustìa '93	🍷🍷	5
○	Erbaluce di Caluso La Rustìa '97	🍷🍷	3*
○	Brut Nature Cuvée '92	🍷	4
○	Caluso Bianco Vignot S. Antonio '96	🍷	4
○	Caluso Passito La Rustìa '88	🍷🍷 (prev.)	5

S. MARTINO ALFIERI (AT)

MARCHESI ALFIERI
CASTELLO ALFIERI
14010 S. MARTINO ALFIERI (AT)
TEL. 0141/976288

There is an important gap in Marchesi Alfieri's range of wines this year: the Monferrato Rosso San Germano was not presented. Since we were unable to taste the '95 version of this always outstandingly elegant pinot noir, we had another taste of the '94, and can confirm last year's assessment, adding only that the bouquet has achieved a subtle complexity. However the heart of this San Martino estate's production is Barbera, as you can tell from the care that they have lavished in vineyard and cellar to turn a normally reliable, simple red into an important wine. In good years like '96 they succeed, witness the Barbera La Tota, usually an immediate, invigorating wine, in which we now find depth on nose and palate. The lively deep ruby color precedes an expressive fragrance of varietal sour cherry with a sweet constant undertone of spice; the typical acidity is perfectly blended into the structure on the palate, so that what you sense is a voluptuous and long-lasting fullness, capped by a reflection of the bouquet on the frank finish. If this is what the lesser '96 Barbera can do, just imagine what awaits us in the Alfiera! This year they have released the '94, however, from which we were not expecting great things. It is correctly executed and past its peak. The Grignolino Sansoero is typical and pleasant, while the two Monferratos, the Bianco and Rosso dei Marchesi, are delightful bargains.

	Wine	Rating	Price
●	Barbera d'Asti La Tota '96	🍷🍷	4
●	Barbera d'Asti Alfiera '94	🍷	5
○	Monferrato Il Bianco dei Marchesi '97	🍷	3
●	Monferrato Il Rosso dei Marchesi '96	🍷	3*
●	Piemonte Grignolino Sansoero '97		3
●	Barbera d'Asti Alfiera '93	YY	5
●	Monferrato Rosso San Germano '94	YY	5
●	Barbera d'Asti La Tota '95	Y	4

S. MARZANO OLIVETO (AT)

ALFIERO BOFFA
VIA LEISO, 50
14050 S. MARZANO OLIVETO (AT)
TEL. 0141/856115

This winery ceaselessly seeks the right combination of factors to turn Barbera into an exemplary wine. Alfiero Boffa looks after his vineyards (some his own, others leased) as if they were his garden. His cellar style is traditional, with medium-long maceration, and aging in large barrels or barriques; the 200 thousand bottles produced annually are then aged in the cellar of the castle of San Marzano. The four Barbera crus, the top of the line, have in common the expression of their bouquets, which is traditionally gradual: they don't open at once, but slowly reveal their notes of sour cherry steeped in alcohol, walnut, licorice and tar. The Barbera Vigna More is the only one with a fresh immediacy, found again on the palate (mouth-filling, long and balanced). The Collina della Vedova, released a year later than the others, and made from grapes from all the crus, vaunts a more marked and essential structure; the intensity of its color suggests the wine might age well, and the lively fruit is evenly distributed. The Muntrivé, a 35-year-old vineyard, produces a more austere Barbera; its bouquet includes an animal nuance and an almost earthy note; on the palate subtle tannins are well integrated with the fruit. The Vigna Cua Longa is the one most nearly resembling a normal Barbera, dry and not very demanding. Boffa is planning a new important Barbera, called Testimonium, and a pinot noir from an experimental vineyard

	Wine	Rating	Price
●	Barbera d'Asti Vigna More '96	🍷🍷	3
●	Barbera d'Asti Collina della Vedova '95	🍷🍷	4
●	Barbera d'Asti Vigna Cua Longa '96	🍷	3
●	Barbera d'Asti Vigna Muntrivé '96	🍷	3
●	Barbera d'Asti Vigna Cua Longa '93	YY	4
●	Barbera d'Asti Vigna Cua Longa '95	YY	3
●	Barbera d'Asti Collina della Vedova '93	YY	4
●	Barbera d'Asti Vigna More '95	Y	4
●	Barbera d'Asti Collina della Vedova '94	Y	4

S. MARZANO OLIVETO (AT)

CASCINA L'ARBIOLA
REG. SALINE, 56
14050 S. MARZANO OLIVETO (AT)
TEL. 0141/856194

This lovely estate on the hills of San Marzano Oliveto has been given new life by the Terzano family in a very few years. Excellent professional advice (from, among others, the oenologist Giuliano Noè), has enabled them to perfect a plan (which involves extending the vineyards, planting new vines, some of which are international varieties, and building an efficient, modern cellar) which should make Arbiola one of the top wineries in an already distinguished zone. The wines we tasted are the first results of the general reorganization and are quite encouraging. The Arbiolin '97, a well-made Barbera di Monferrato Vivace, is inviting and pleasing. The moderately deep color precedes a richly fruity nose and a crisp and balanced palate with just the right amount of fizz. The elegant and austere La Romilda '96, a Barbera d'Asti Superiore, clearly aims higher; of a dark, dense garnet hue, it has an intense bouquet, with fruit enhanced by sweet oak-derived notes. The palate does not show overwhelming structure, but is notably balanced and round, with a reprise of the fruit on the finish. The last wine is Le Clelie '97, a Monferrato Bianco made from cortese that reflects the Arbiola style, which prefers elegance to power. It has a pale straw color and delicate, almost evanescent aromas that reveal the presence of good oak. The palate shows depth and a vein of acidity that emphasizes the not very densely woven structure.

●	Barbera d'Asti Sup. La Romilda II '96	🍷🍷	4
○	Monferrato Bianco Le Clelie II '97	🍷	4
●	Barbera del M.to L'Arbiolin '97		3

S. STEFANO BELBO (CN)

CA' D'GAL
STRADA VECCHIA, 108
FRAZ. VALDIVILLA
12058 S. STEFANO BELBO (CN)
TEL. 0141/847103

One duty and several fancies act as spurs to the dynamic Alessandro Boido. Not surprisingly for a wine-maker in this zone, the duty is to produce good Moscato; the fancies are his other wines, which are in part for the delectation of the guests of the family country inn, and in part oenological curiosities. He now produces 30 thousand bottles of Moscato, but if he wished he could make lots more: he sells half the grapes, and actually uses only those bunches that he, his father Riccardo and his sister Laura have carefully selected. The result can be enjoyed at its best in the Moscato Vigna Vecchia, which stimulates without overwhelming and lingers for a good long time; the aromas of tangerine, apple and green leaf carry through onto the palate, to which the persistent fine perlage lends a velvety softness. The citrus theme reappears in the standard Moscato, which is muskier on the nose and softer but less lingering on the palate. But Alessandro focuses particular attention on the Pian del Gäje, a blend in which freisa, the other historic Santo Stefano grape, takes the lead. The addition of barbera and dolcetto and the use of new medium-sized barrels should, he feels, reinforce the structure of the freisa without obscuring its characteristics. The result is successful, without suggesting superlatives. It has a somewhat pale but brilliant ruby hue and a very intense, almost aromatic bouquet with heady, vegetal aromas and a clear sharp strawberry note, characteristic of the freisa. The entry on the palate is delicate, enlivened by a zesty acidity and young tannins; the body is not very full and the finish is of moderate length.

○	Moscato d'Asti Vigneti Ca' d' Gal '97	🍷	3
○	Moscato d'Asti Vigna Vecchia '97	🍷	3
●	Langhe Pian del Gäje '96	🍷	4
●	Dolcetto d'Alba '97		3
○	Langhe Chardonnay '97		3

S. STEFANO BELBO (CN)

PIERO GATTI
LOC. MONCUCCO, 28
12058 S. STEFANO BELBO (CN)
TEL. 0141/840918

This year Piero again refused a DOCG label so that he could harvest a week earlier than those regulations permit. This proved an excellent decision for the hot, early autumn of '97, in which moscato winegrowers ran the risk of seeing the fragrance of this delicate and aromatic grape burnt up. His Moscato is fragrant, and the characteristic varietal aromas are fused with notes of lime and Golden Delicious apple. The body, although it's lean, is delightfully crisp (but not citric) and leads into a long and corresponding finish. The Freisa is also worthy of mention, with its sweet, intense aroma of fruit-flavored candy; the semi-sweetness in the mouth is balanced by acidity and well-judged effervescence. This year we did not get a chance to taste the Brachetto, which is generally anything but commonplace, because it was sold out before our tastings. But be of good cheer: although they produce only a few thousand bottles of Freisa and Brachetto, there are 35 thousand bottles of the Moscato! Three and a half hectares of their own vineyards, all near the winery, are the source of its grapes.

○	Piemonte Moscato '97	🍷🍷	3
●	Langhe Freisa La Violetta '97		3

S. STEFANO BELBO (CN)

SERGIO GRIMALDI - CA' DU SINDIC
LOC. SAN GRATO, 15
12058 S. STEFANO BELBO (CN)
TEL. 0141/840341

The inimitable Ilario is still here, among the knotty vines which he himself planted 60 years ago on the dizzying slopes near Santo Stefano. Today, however, the Ca' du Sindic is confidently run, with lots of modern technology, by his son and daughter-in-law, Sergio and Angela, who are also passionately devoted to this inestimable viticultural patrimony. In fact, it is precisely from this patrimony, in the form of the oldest vines, that the best results are to be had: this is Sergio's conclusion, and he consequently has no desire to replace the older vines, because they are the ones that yield the best grapes. From their seven hectares of vineyard in San Grato they make 33 thousand bottles of Moscato, 3 thousand of Brachetto and a few more of Chardonnay. The Moscato has a deep straw color; its generous bubbles accompany an exuberant array of aromas, with apple and hay keeping a fermentative note of nail polish from emerging too clearly. The palate, while not thoroughly entrancing, blends a sound acidity with the sugars, making the wine agreeable even to those who are not very fond of sweetness. The Chardonnay, redolent of banana and Golden Delicious apple, still displays rather fermentative aromas, but it has color and body and fair length. The Brachetto is more notable for its intense and vivid cherry-red hue than for its heady aroma of blackberry, which also gives zest, however briefly, to the sweet palate. A rustic Barbera Vivace is also worthy of mention.

●	Piemonte Brachetto Ca' du Sindic '97	🍷	3
○	Moscato d'Asti Ca' du Sindic '97	🍷	3
○	Langhe Chardonnay Zamblino '97		2
●	Piemonte Barbera Vivace '97		2

S. STEFANO BELBO (CN)

TENUTA IL FALCHETTO
VIA VALLE TINELLA, 16
12058 S. STEFANO BELBO (CN)
TEL. 0141/840344

Adriano, Chiara, Cinzia, Fabrizio, Giorgio, Raffaella and Roberto: all the Fornos are here again this year. And all the wines are here too, but the list is so long that we don't have room for the whole of it, so we're just describing the most important ones, starting with the reds. The surprising Dolcetto fully exploits the concentration of its fine vintage, first in its very intense color, then in an almost succulent fruity fragrance and finally in its powerful but harmonious structure. The Barbera Lurei (from a cru in Costigliole) does not quite live up to expectations; its desirable characteristic qualities are expressed without much conviction. The Barbera dedicated to Zio Rico was still aging when we went to press. The heart and soul of their production, however, is their Moscato, 50 thousand bottles strong, and made from two different crus, friendly rivals in a contest they seem to take turns in winning. With the '97 vintage the Ciombi comes out on top, thanks to its irresistible acerbic grip; it has some raw notes (sour fruit and green leaf) that enhance the sweet varietal aromas; on the (not very sweet) palate, it displays perfect acidity and fair persistence. The Fant puts up a good fight with the intensity of its aromas (ripe Golden Delicious apple and banana) and the balance of its moderate palate. As for the dry whites, it is worth trying the agreeable and aromatic Arneis, with its fragrance of mint and green apple and its very soft palate with an almondy finish. Lastly, a rarity: 2,000 bottles of a Chardonnay called Incompreso which they make only when a great vintage and ruthless pruning produce grapes that can stand up to a bit of oak.

	Wine	Glasses	Price
○	Langhe Chardonnay Incompreso '96	🍷	4
○	Langhe Arneis '97	🍷	3
○	Moscato d'Asti Tenuta dei Ciombi '97	🍷	3
○	Moscato d'Asti Tenuta del Fant '97	🍷	3
●	Dolcetto d'Alba Soulì Braida '97	🍷	3*
●	Barbera d'Asti Sup. Lurei '96		3
●	Barbera d'Asti Vigna Zio Rico '95	🍷 (white)	4

S. STEFANO BELBO (CN)

I VIGNAIOLI DI S. STEFANO BELBO
FRAZ. MARINI, 12
12058 S. STEFANO BELBO (CN)
TEL. 0141/840419

The results of this year's rigorous blind tastings should please both I Vignaioli and lovers of good Moscato. The Passito, which is produced only in the best years, did beautifully. But the Asti and, to some extent, the Moscato too, the classics of this zone of the Langhe, were enchanting. Behind it all, perforce, is the great skill of the Vignaioli, who have shown their bravura in two radically different interpretations of the same category of wine. The Passito has two major virtues: it is absolutely consistent throughout every phase of tasting, and it succeeds in combining elegance and concentration, which is no common feat. Its warm golden color with bright green highlights is followed by an elegant bouquet which ranges from mint to ripe apricot and fig, continuing then with notes of cherries in spirits. On the palate the sweetness avoids sickly unctuousness, blending instead into the structure, rich in alcohol and extract, and perfectly balanced by acidity. On the complex finish sweet and bitter notes of vanilla and green walnut skin emerge. The Asti, at the other end of the spectrum, shows the verve of fresh moscato, accompanied by a distinct fragrance of unripe pear and more intrusive fermentative notes. On the palate it is even and displays a clean finish. The less graceful Moscato offers aromas of sage and more musky and earthy notes; on the palate, however, its fatness is not counterpoised by the complexity of its brother wines.

	Wine	Glasses	Price
○	Asti '97	🍷🍷	4
○	Piemonte Moscato Passito	🍷🍷	5
○	Moscato d'Asti '97	🍷	3

SCURZOLENGO (AT)

CANTINE SANT'AGATA
REG. MEZZENA, 19
14030 SCURZOLENGO (AT)
TEL. 0141/203186

In the heart of Monferrato wine country the Cavallero family, which has been working here since the beginning of this century, now owns some 20 hectares of vineyard planted to the traditional local varieties. They reach their annual production of about 100 thousand bottles and a certain amount of wine sold in bulk with the addition of grapes acquired, for the most part, from reliable neighbor growers. In the past few years Claudio, in the cellar, and his brother Franco, in administration and marketing, have started to assist their father Giuseppe. We have noticed a distinct increase in quality, which seems to go hand in hand with a decrease in the number of different wines on offer; their fine results have also won them marketing successes abroad where they now sell 60% of what they produce. Their enthusiasm and energy, together with the new vines and the necessary modernization of the cellar, bode very well for the future. Returning to the present, we begin with the Cortese Alto Monferrato Ciarea, which astonished us with the intensity and definition of its aromas, and the structure and presence it offers in the mouth. The Grignolino Miravalle is very successfully characteristic. The elegant and refreshing Barbera d'Asti Superiore '96 is rich in fruity aromas and substantial on the palate. The Barberas come from two different crus, the Piatin and the Cavalé, and are both matured in barriques. We preferred the second, which has a fresher fragrance and more succulence and persistence on the palate, but they are both interesting. The Ruché 'Na Vota, the Sant'Agata gem, certainly has few rivals; the intense color precedes a delightful nose, dominated by typical notes of pepper and spice; on the palate the wine is rich, full and long.

	Wine	Rating	Price
●	Barbera d'Asti Sup. Cavalé '96	🍷🍷	4
●	Ruché di Castagnole M.to 'Na Vota '97	🍷🍷	4
●	Barbera d'Asti Sup. '96	🍷	3
●	Barbera d'Asti Sup. Piatin '96	🍷	3
○	Cortese dell'Alto M.to Ciarea '97	🍷	3
●	Grignolino d'Asti Miravalle '97	🍷	2*

SERRALUNGA D'ALBA (CN)

LUIGI BAUDANA
FRAZ. BAUDANA, 43
12050 SERRALUNGA D'ALBA (CN)
TEL. 0173/613354

History repeats itself: in the bleak years for agriculture, in the Langhe and elsewhere, children often decided not to continue the difficult and not very remunerative work of their farming forebears, who for decades had grown a variety of crops so as to keep their large families from starving. The Baudanas were no exception: after working for a long time as a blacksmith, and then running the Grinzane wine shop for 11 years, Luigi and his wife Fiorina, long-time members of the Terre del Barolo cooperative winery, decided they would themselves vinify the grapes from their approximately four hectares under vine, all in the splendid Baudana cru, and divided as follows: two and a half hectares planted to dolcetto, one and a half to nebbiolo for Barolo, and the odd barbera and chardonnay vine. Unfortunately, in 1989, when he was doing a lot of new planting, Luigi chose to put dolcetto into some of the best sites in Baudana, since it was then selling for more than nebbiolo. This is why they now make more Dolcetto than anything else. The Sorì Baudana is distinctly the better of the two Dolcettos. It shows a deep violet-ruby color and the intense and fruity aromas suggest blackberry and cherry. Its impressive palate has a great tannic structure, typical of Serralunga, which is well balanced by the sweetness of the alcohol and the glycerin. The standard Dolcetto is less powerful, and more simply quaffable. The rich, fruity Chardonnay is good, and the Barbera '97 is even better. The Barbera d'Alba Donatella '96, matured for 14 months in new large casks and barriques, is special; it is, in fact, one of the best Barberas of this excellent vintage. In addition to an intense, complex nose (aromas of cherry, tobacco, cocoa and vanilla), it has a dense and elegant palate which offers long, velvety sensations.

	Wine	Rating	Price
●	Barbera d'Alba Donatella '96	🍷🍷	3*
●	Dolcetto d'Alba Sorì Baudana '97	🍷🍷	3*
●	Barbera d'Alba '97	🍷	3
●	Dolcetto d'Alba '97	🍷	3
○	Langhe Chardonnay '97	🍷	3

GIUSEPPE CAPPELLANO

Via Alba, 13
Fraz. Bruni
12050 Serralunga d'Alba (CN)
tel. 0173/613103

In the debate between tradition and innovation that has characterized the recent oenological history of the Langhe, Giuseppe Cappellano is willing to give each side its due. While his Barolos, with their long cellar times, are clearly in the classic camp, Cappellano has now presented at least two wines of a more modern style, that could favorably influence his whole range: a Langhe Rosso and a Barbera d'Alba. The latter has changed in an interesting way in the last few years: it has acquired greater balance by integrating the dominant acidic vein, and it shows greater order in its bouquet, which adds to its charm. At this point all it wants is more richness to make it outstanding. The Langhe Rosso, a blend of Langhe grapes and, probably, an imported variety, is already quite complete: the concentrated color precedes a nose with an unmistakable mineral note that gives way to aromas of red fruit, oak and spice, and it is all attractively mirrored on the palate, which is further distinguished by density, an inviting liveliness, and elegance. The Nebiolo (sic) d'Alba '94, is surprisingly expressive, apparently unaffected by the troublesome vintage. Its color and bouquet both suggest autumnal maturity (aromas of petals steeped in alcohol and quince jam); the palate is underpinned by tannins and the finish is attractively fruity. Two Barolos were presented this year, but we consider only the classic Otin Fiorin, a really elegant and harmonious wine, although within the limits of the '94 vintage. Next year we shall review the one that comes from ungrafted vines.

	Wine	Rating	Price
●	Barolo Chinato	🍷🍷	5
●	Langhe Rosso Augusto '96	🍷🍷	4
●	Barbera d'Alba Gabutti '96	🍷	4
●	Barolo Otin Fiorin Collina Gabutti '94	🍷	5
●	Nebiolo d'Alba '94	🍷	3
●	Barolo Otin Fiorin Collina Gabutti '90	ΥΥΥ	6
●	Barolo '91	ΥΥ	5
●	Barolo '92	ΥΥ	5
●	Barolo Otin Fiorin Collina Gabutti '91	ΥΥ	5
●	Barbera d'Alba Gabutti '95	Υ	4
●	Barolo Otin Fiorin Collina Gabutti '93	Υ	5

SERRALUNGA D'ALBA (CN)

FONTANAFREDDA

Via Alba, 15
12050 Serralunga d'Alba (CN)
tel. 0173/613161

In the last edition of the Guide we rejoiced in the excellent results of this winery that belongs to the Monte dei Paschi bank. This year, the release of wines from not very propitious vintages and the concomitant absence of some of their best wines have lowered the average. Despite everything that could be provided by the care of the excellent oenological professionals who have been at the helm here for some years, the Barolo '94 did not soar. Tasting it serves to remind you that Serralunga, which is capable of bringing forth wines that are full-bodied yet austere and tannic, needs first-class grapes to do so; otherwise the results are discouraging: it is as if the terroir refused to accept compromises. The Barolo di Serralunga has, however, well-defined aromas and a pleasing balance, but the structure has suffered. The firmer Barolo La Villa '93 shows, with its complexity, that vintage matters. We were hoping for something more from the Barolo Vigna La Delizia '93, which seems closed still, and aggressive. We felt better off with the frankness and vitality of the Barbaresco Coste Rubin '95 and the mature and succulent density of the Nebbiolo d'Alba Marne Brune, which finally shows backbone and incisiveness. It's a surprising wine, because the entry on the palate is quite delicate, and only thereafter does it bring out its big guns. Youthful simplicity characterizes the two dry whites, the Chardonnay and the Gavi, which should be drunk within the year if you want to have the best of their fragrance and lightness. The Dolcetto di Diano Vigna La Lepre, not up to the '96, is rather dumb and evanescent.

	Wine	Rating	Price
●	Barolo La Villa '93	🍷🍷	5
●	Barbaresco Coste Rubìn '95	🍷	4
●	Barolo di Serralunga '94	🍷	5
●	Barolo Vigna La Delizia '93	🍷	5
○	Gavi di Gavi '97	🍷	3
○	Langhe Chardonnay Ampelio '97	🍷	3
●	Nebbiolo d'Alba Marne Brune '96	🍷	3
●	Diano d'Alba Vigna La Lepre '97		3
●	Barolo di Serralunga '93	ΥΥ	4
●	Barolo Vigna La Rosa '90	ΥΥ	6
●	Barolo Vigna Lazzarito Ris. '90	ΥΥ	6
○	Contessa Rosa Brut '92	ΥΥ	4
○	Gatinera Brut '89	ΥΥ	5
○	Gatinera Gran Riserva '85	ΥΥ	6
●	Barolo Galarey '93	Υ	5

SERRALUNGA D'ALBA (CN)

Gabutti - Franco Boasso

B.ta Gabutti, 3/a
12050 Serralunga d'Alba (CN)
tel. 0173/613165

The Gabutti winery produces just under 30 thousand bottles a year. It owns four hectares in the Gabutti and Parafada crus, two of the very best sites in Serralunga. Despite the excellent position of the vineyards, a vintage like the '94, plagued by constant rain, makes really great wine rather unlikely. The Boassos, skilled winegrowers, did what they could by producing a fairly simple Barolo, rather like a big Nebbiolo, rich in fruity and lactic notes. It is easy to drink and has no pretensions to ageworthiness. The standard Dolcetto '97, fair in structure, is not aggressive on the nose; on the palate it is austere, tannic and even a little bitter. The Dolcetto Parafada '97 is richer in fragrance and has an attractively soft and intense body, but was diminished somewhat, when we tasted it, by some residual carbon dioxide, which caused a conflict in the mouth between good succulent fruit and some unwanted bubbles. It is sure to improve with a few months' time. The Barbera d'Alba, definitely over-mature, seems to have suffered from the hot season of '97: sweet, stewed notes are in evidence, rather than freshness. Apropos of Barbera, we recently re-tasted the Superiore '90, a monument of fruit and alcohol, which still has an astonishing power and a delightfully rustic personality, without any signs of decline.

	Wine	Glasses	Price
●	Barolo '94	▼	5
●	Dolcetto d'Alba Vigna Parafada '97	▼	3
●	Dolcetto d'Alba '97		3
●	Barolo Gabutti '90	▽▽	5
●	Barolo Gabutti '93	▽▽	5
●	Barolo Gabutti '92	▽	5

SERRALUNGA D'ALBA (CN)

Ettore Germano

B.ta Cerretta, 1
12050 Serralunga d'Alba (CN)
tel. 0173/613528 - 613112

In a very short time this firm has made great strides, changing from a sort of laboratory which experimented with a few bottles of many different types of wine into a first-class winery with a character of its own (based on excellent vineyards and remarkable cellar skills). Germano's ability can be seen in the Barolo Ceretta '94; since he did not have very rich grapes at his disposal, he concentrated his efforts on producing a notably elegant and attractive wine, making use of a brief aging in wood to enrich the bouquet with the freshness of new oak. Tannins have the upper hand on the palate, which is not very long but should age well. The Dolcetto Vigneto Lorenzino, fresh and redolent of hay, has a pleasing bitterness in a not very muscular body. The more successful Dolcetto Vigneto Pra di Po, with a broad but not aggressively heady nose, displays a rich palate which should be quite harmonious in a few months' time. The good Balàu '96, an unconventional assemblage of 90% barbera and a little dolcetto, offers an attractive nose with light notes of oak; it is still a little hard and sharp on the palate, but a few more months in the bottle should take care of that. The Barbera Vigna della Madre '96, similar in bouquet (correct and simple aromas, with non-intrusive wood), has a light acidic note that detracts from the roundness of the palate. The Chardonnay '97 is clean if not complex in fragrance; the sweetish palate shows good structure.

	Wine	Glasses	Price
●	Barolo Cerretta '94	▼▼	5
●	Dolcetto d'Alba Vigneto Pra di Po '97	▼▼	3
●	Barbera d'Alba Vigna della Madre '96	▼	4
●	Dolcetto d'Alba Vigneto Lorenzino '97	▼	3
○	Langhe Chardonnay '97	▼	3
●	Langhe Rosso Balàu '96	▼	4
●	Barolo '91	▽▽	4
●	Barolo '93	▽▽	4
●	Barolo Cerretta '93	▽▽	5
●	Barbera d'Alba Vigna della Madre '95	▽	3
●	Langhe Rosso Balàu '95	▽	4

SERRALUNGA D'ALBA (CN)

VIGNA RIONDA - MASSOLINO

P.ZZA CAPPELLANO, 8
12050 SERRALUNGA D'ALBA (CN)
TEL. 0173/613138

Every year the Massolinos acquire more confidence and mastery, a process that began with the new era some ten years ago. One particularly good sign is their willingness to let their wines age in barrel or bottle just that little while longer, avoiding the release of wines that show raw edges or unintegrated wood. With the now customary and altogether appropriate delay, then, here is the Dolcetto Vigna Barilot '96: still heady and full of fruit, it shows the characteristic varietal bitter note and tannins that have a little bite left. The Nebbiolo '95 displays easy, immediate and enchanting aromas which introduce a fairly simple palate (both a little sweet and mouth-puckering). The problematic standard Barolo '93 has a sea-water nose, and a tannic, bitter and pugnacious palate; we shall try tasting it again later on. There seems to be an extra dimension in the Barolo Vigna Rionda '93; an additional year in the bottle has greatly improved the very promising palate (which still has noticeable, but no longer aggressive tannins). The nose is fresh and still rather closed, but this vineyard is well-known for taking its time. The Barolo Vigneto Margheria '93 is currently muffled by a not sufficiently clean bouquet. The standard Barolo '94, on the other hand, is well above average. It offers aromas of fruit and tar and a particularly fruity and balanced palate that wants just a little more length. It is one of the most successful Barolos produced in that ticklish year.

	Wine	Glasses	Price
●	Barolo '94	🍷🍷	4
●	Barolo Vigna Rionda '93	🍷🍷	5
●	Dolcetto d'Alba Vigneto Barilot '96	🍷	3
●	Langhe Nebbiolo '95		3
●	Barolo Parafada Ris. '90	🍷🍷🍷 (white)	5
●	Barolo Vigna Rionda Ris. '90	🍷🍷🍷 (white)	5
●	Barolo '90	🍷🍷 (white)	5
●	Barolo Parafada '90	🍷🍷 (white)	5
●	Barolo Parafada '91	🍷🍷 (white)	5
●	Barolo Vigna Parafada '93	🍷🍷 (white)	5
●	Barolo Vigna Rionda '90	🍷🍷 (white)	5
●	Barolo Vigneto Margheria '90	🍷🍷 (white)	5
●	Barolo Vigneto Margheria Ris. '90	🍷🍷 (white)	5

SERRALUNGA DI CREA (AL)

TENUTA LA TENAGLIA

STRADA SANTUARIO DI CREA, 6
15020 SERRALUNGA DI CREA (AL)
TEL. 0142/940252

Delfina Quattrocolo's fine estate has presented, with the help of the excellent '96 and '97 vintages, a remarkably good range of wines. The secrets of her success are her splendid vineyards, in enviable sites, which are kept to low yields, and a cellar technology which allows her to get the very best from her grapes. We start with an excellent syrah, the Paradiso, which has a very dense garnet-ruby color, and a deep and complex nose with aromas of wild berries, fig, pepper, almond and vanilla. On the palate the wine is substantial, broad, with an even and confident progression to a very long finish enriched by noble tannins. The Barbera Emozioni, deep ruby-red tinged with garnet, offers aromas of red fruit and violet on a delicately spicy and balsamic background. The palate shows a sturdy structure and some acidic sinew and then settles into a warm, lingering finish. The Barbera Giorgio Tenaglia, matured starting this year in large barrels of new wood, offers an intense color, and notes of dark cherry, red currant, toasty oak and mint; the palate displays an acidic zest, and a finish slightly dominated by the wood. The Grignolino, shows, as is its wont, its varietal characteristics with clear definition and balance; aromas of white pepper and dried herbs alternate with suggestions of almond and fading rose; the palate has grip and savor. The Chardonnay is crisp and clear, with notes of banana and green hazelnut; it is balanced and light in the mouth. Lastly, the good Barbera Bricco Crea is simple and open.

	Wine	Glasses	Price
●	Barbera d'Asti Emozioni '96	🍷🍷	5
●	Paradiso '96	🍷🍷	5
●	Barbera d'Asti Bricco Crea '97	🍷	3
●	Barbera d'Asti Giorgio Tenaglia '97	🍷	4
●	Grignolino del M.to Casalese '97	🍷	3
○	Piemonte Chardonnay '97	🍷	4
●	Barbera d'Asti Emozioni '95	🍷🍷 (white)	5
●	Emozioni '94	🍷🍷 (white)	5
●	Paradiso '94	🍷🍷 (white)	5
●	Paradiso '95	🍷🍷 (white)	5

SPIGNO M.TO (AL)

CASCINA BERTOLOTTO
VIA PIETRO PORRO, 70
15018 SPIGNO M.TO (AL)
TEL. 0144/91223 - 91551

The Traversa family, which owns Cascina Bertolotto, offers a very interesting version of Dolcetto d'Acqui, based on richness of extract and a vigorous palate. Giuseppe Traversa, his children Fabio and Marida and his son-in-law Raffaello Rovera are running a winery that is on the rise. New land was purchased not long since, and this year one and a half hectares were planted to dolcetto and barbera. The Dolcetto La Muïètte '96, which is excellent as usual, shows a dark ruby color and a bouquet based on the freshness of the fruit, with hints of red currant, cherry and almond on a lightly spicy background. The palate is rich without being heavy, even and full up to an intensely fruity finish. La Cresta is the name of a vineyard planted in 1963, which gives rise to the Dolcetto of the same name; this has a more delicate character than the Muïètte; its ruby red color sports a youthful rim, and its fragrance is clean and balanced, with notes of dark cherry, red currant and pepper. The palate, soft and structured, shows well-judged acidity and a warm and fruity finish. The Brachetto Il Virginio, purplish red in hue, offers characteristic varietal aromas, but wants finesse; it is sweet and easy drinking, with refreshing effervescence. Our re-tasting of the Barbera I Cheini '96 (ruby-red with garnet highlights, bouquet of red and black berries, soft and persistent palate) confirmed that this is a wine that will age well.

	Wine	Glasses	Price
●	Dolcetto d'Acqui La Muïètte '96	🍷🍷	3*
●	Dolcetto d'Acqui La Cresta '97	🍷	3
●	Piemonte Brachetto Il Virginio '97		3
●	Dolcetto d'Acqui La Muïètte '95	🍸🍸	3
●	Barbera del M.to I Cheini '96	🍸	3

STREVI (AL)

BANFI VINI
VIA VITTORIO VENETO, 22
15019 STREVI (AL)
TEL. 0144/363485

Banfi Vini has presented a rich and inviting array of good wines, a testimony to the admirable efficiency of this winery. The recently enlarged modern cellar is equipped with the up-to-the-minute technology that makes such a performance possible. The Dolcetto Argusto '96, which was aged in barriques for six months, has won Two Glasses for its rich fruit. Of a garnet-ruby color, it offers aromas of violet, raspberry and cherry with balsamic undertones. The vigorous palate progresses steadily to an intensely fruity finish. The Asti, also very well made, shows a subtle and extremely elegant fragrance suggestive of lemon, elder blossom, sage and peach. On the palate it is perfectly harmonious, crisp and well-defined. The two Metodo Classico vintage sparkling wines, '92 and '93, are good as well. The first, which came very close to Two Glasses for its elegance and substance, is redolent of hazelnut, grapefruit, fruit and crusty bread, and is balanced and full in the mouth. The '93 has a fruity nose with notes of smoke and yeasts, and is fairly energetic on the palate. The agreeable Brachetto di Vigneto la Rosa, purplish ruby in color, offers aromas of fresh pear and rose and is sweet and refreshing on the palate. The admirable Moscato Strevi has a fragrance of grapefruit, peach and sage; the hot summer of '97 has made inroads on its customary freshness, but the palate is rich and broad. Both the Gavis are good. The Vigna Regale is reminiscent of peach and sage on the nose; the palate, full and soft, finishes with a note of caramel. The Principessa Gavia has a fresh and fruity nose and a crisp palate.

	Wine	Glasses	Price
○	Asti '97	🍷🍷	3*
●	Dolcetto d'Acqui Argusto '96	🍷🍷	4
●	Acqui Brachetto d'Acqui Vigneto La Rosa '97	🍷	4
○	Banfi Brut Metodo Classico '92	🍷	4
○	Banfi Brut Metodo Classico '93	🍷	4
○	Gavi Principessa Gavia '97	🍷	3
○	Gavi Vigna Regale '96	🍷	4
○	Strevi Moscato d'Asti '97	🍷	3
○	Spumante Brut Tener '97		3
●	Dolcetto d'Acqui Argusto '95	🍸	4

STREVI (AL)

MARENCO
P.ZZA VITTORIO EMANUELE, 10
15019 STREVI (AL)
TEL. 0144/363133

The Marenco family's modern winery, with its recently enlarged and notably well-equipped cellar, has now presented admirable versions of all the typical Acqui wines. This must be a real satisfaction for the Marenco family, which is large, fortunately, as it does everything that needs to be done: from pruning to bottling, with all the technical and commercial decisions thrown in. This year we particularly liked the Barbera Ciresa and the Dolcetto Marchesa. The first offers an intense garnet-ruby color with a purple rim and a pleasing, quite broad nose with notes of black cherry, cocoa and vanilla played over a balsamic bass. On the palate it shows substance and softness, and light tannins give dryness to the fruity finish. The Dolcetto, vivid ruby in color with a youthful rim, displays aromas of red currant, dark cherry and almond; the round, smooth palate shows a pleasing note of tannin. The dessert wines are impeccable, as usual: the Moscato Scrapona, pale gold in color, has intense aromas of ripe peach and rose, and the sweetness on the palate is well balanced by a decided effervescence, leading into a richly aromatic finish. The Brachetto Il Pineto displays a characteristic delicately aromatic nose and a fresh and well-balanced palate. The clean and agreeable Cortese Valtignosa, with secondary aromas of moderate finesse and an enlivening delicate sparkle, goes down quite easily. We end our review with the simple Barbera Bassina and the Carialoso, with a light fragrance that includes vegetal hints, and a correct but not lingering taste.

●	Barbera d'Asti Ciresa '96	🍷	4
●	Brachetto d'Acqui Il Pineto '97	🍷	4
○	Cortese dell'Alto M.to Valtignosa '97	🍷	3
●	Dolcetto d'Acqui Marchesa '97	🍷	3
○	Moscato d'Asti Scrapona '97	🍷	3
●	Barbera d'Asti Bassina '96		3
○	Carialoso '97		3

TASSAROLO (AL)

CASTELLO DI TASSAROLO
CASCINA ALBORINA
15060 TASSAROLO (AL)
TEL. 0143/342248

Marquis Paolo Spinola runs his winery with the help of the oenologist Agostino Berruti, and together they maintain a consistently high standard even in the most difficult vintages. The Castello di Tassarolo wines have always done well at our tastings, and it can't be said that they have done badly this year, although the fine '97 vintage, with its beneficent effects on the proverbially acidic cortese, rather made us hope for something more. The good Vigneto Alborina has a green-tinged straw color and a fragrance of fruit, coffee and vanilla; the full-bodied and silky palate is, however, slightly dominated by the wood. Our re-tasting of the '95 gives us some idea of the potential longevity of the Ambrogio Spinola; its straw color still shows light greenish highlights, and the bouquet offers notes of banana, fruit candy and vanilla with a faint vegetal undertone. On the palate it is silky and crisp, and there is a note of caramel on the fairly intense finish. The good Rosso '95, of a pale ruby hue tinged with orange, offers aromas with balsamic and mineral undertones; the palate is well constructed and harmonious. One Glass goes to the Gavi di Tassarolo, fruity and floral on the nose, with evident secondary nuances. The fruity body leads to a pleasingly almondy finish. The Tassarolo has a somewhat murky nose, but it picks up on the palate, which shows its usual pleasing lightness.

○	Gavi Castello di Tassarolo '97	🍷	3
○	Gavi Vigneto Alborina '96	🍷	4
●	Rosso '95	🍷	4
○	Gavi Tassarolo S '97		2
○	Gavi Vigneto Alborina '93	🍸🍸	4
○	Ambrogio Spinola '95	🍸	4
○	Gavi Vigneto Alborina '95	🍸	4

TASSAROLO (AL)

La Zerba

Strada Francavilla, 1
15060 Tassarolo (AL)
tel. 0143/342259 - 744413

La Zerba, which has belonged to the Lorenzi family since 1972, is a small family-run estate with about eight hectares under vine near Tassarolo which produces just under 40 thousand bottles a year. Ida and Livio Lorenzi look after production, while their son Luigi and son-in-law Andrea Mascherini divide their time and enthusiasm between the vineyards, the well-equipped cellar and the marketing of the wines (a substantial proportion of which is sold abroad). The pomace left after vinification is turned into a small amount of Gavi grappa called La Zerba. But let's consider the wines: there are two, both very good, straightforward and cleanly executed. The Gavi Terrarossa, from their best vineyard, is macerated on the skins (although not for as long as it was last year). The rich straw color is shot through with light green; the fresh and citric nose offers aromas of fruit, citrus fruit, white flowers and wild herbs. There is good structure on the palate with tonic acidity and a not very well-integrated note of sweetness. The standard Gavi, light straw tinged with green, displays a fragrance of lime, apricot and wildflowers; it is balanced, undemanding and satisfying.

	Wine	Glasses	Price
○	Gavi La Zerba '97	🍷	3
○	Gavi Terrarossa '97	🍷	3

TORINO

Franco M. Martinetti

Via S. Francesco da Paola, 18
10123 Torino
tel. 011/8395937

Franco Martinetti is a wine producer in the strictest sense of the term: not, in other words, a mere producer of bottles, but a perfectionist who wants his grapes to give their best, and he goes about his work with the constantly inquiring spirit of a creative scientist. The Barbera d'Asti Montruc displays the vivid brilliance of its grape and an overwhelming irrepressibility (what a change from the usual well-mannered immediacy!). You can tell how carefully and with what passion it was made. It has cast aside the customary slightly rough-hewn character of Barbera to become an exquisitely refined and dense wine. The richness of its bouquet is enhanced by what the oak contributes, but we were really overwhelmed by the progression on the palate, its exciting and harmonious pace. The same continuity characterizes Sul Bric, another of Martinetti's major wines, made by adding 30% of cabernet sauvignon to barbera. An intense ruby color precedes the characteristic mineral note, blended with the fruit and hints of spice. The entry on the palate doesn't have the power of the '95, but the development is graceful and the finish completely winning. The '96 vintage enabled Martinetti to make the Gavi he had been planning for a long time: elegant and long, but also so confidently distinctive that it provokes comparison with much more celebrated whites. The Barbera Bric dei Banditi, (juicy, straightforward and not very demanding) is a perfect wine for everyday drinking.

	Wine	Glasses	Price
●	Barbera d'Asti Sup. Montruc '96	🍷🍷🍷	5
●	Barbera d'Asti Bric dei Banditi '97	🍷🍷	3
●	Monferrato Rosso Sul Bric '96	🍷🍷	5
○	Gavi Minaia '96	🍷🍷	4
●	Sul Bric '94	☐☐☐	5
●	Sul Bric '95	☐☐☐	5
●	Barbera d'Asti Sup. Montruc '93	☐☐	5
●	Barbera d'Asti Sup. Montruc '94	☐☐	5
●	Barbera d'Asti Sup. Montruc '95	☐☐	5
●	Sul Bric '93	☐☐	5
○	Gavi Minaia '95	☐	4

TREISO (CN)

Orlando Abrigo
Fraz. Cappelletto, 5
12050 Treiso (CN)
tel. 0173/630232

The Abrigo family runs this 11-hectare estate (40 thousand bottles a year) with great balance. Modern techniques are wedded to more traditional methods to produce consistently excellent wine. Thus, for example, modern rotary fermenters are used in conjunction with more classical vinifying methods, and lovely barriques share cellar space with the medium-capacity barrels dear to the Langhe. The results can be seen in two very well constructed wines: the Barbaresco '95 and the Barbera Roreto '96. The first has a rich ruby-garnet color with a very slightly orange rim, and a concentrated and fascinating nose (hints of red currant, fig, cocoa, tar and spice). On the palate it is full and broad, with a solid tannic structure and a long finish that echoes the theme of fruit and spice. The Barbera, of an intense ruby hue crowned by a vivid purple rim, offers captivating aromas of strawberry, cherry, mint and rosemary with elegant mineral undertones. The well-constructed palate shows lively acidity, and a decided tannic note on the finish. Lastly, the nose of the good '97 Dolcetto displays green notes of grass and geranium together with red fruit; the color is a fairly intense ruby with a purple rim; on the palate it shows medium body and good balance, with tannins in evidence and a pleasingly bitter finish.

	Wine	Glasses	Price
●	Barbaresco '95	🍷🍷	5
●	Barbera d'Alba Vigna Roreto '96	🍷	3
●	Dolcetto d'Alba Vigna dell'Erto '97	🍷	3
●	Barbaresco Vigna Pajoré '93	♀♀	5
●	Barbaresco Vigna Pajoré '94	♀♀	5
●	Barbera d'Alba Mervisano '94	♀	4
●	Barbera d'Alba Vigna del Campo della Fontana '94	♀	3

TREISO (CN)

Cà del Baio
Via Ferrere, 33
12050 Treiso (CN)
tel. 0173/638219

The Grasso family's estate consists of 13 hectares under vine, including a vineyard in the legendary Asili cru in Barbaresco. Ernesto Grasso, his wife Fiona, their son Giulio and their daughter-in-law Luciana all work together. Giulio and Luciana have three daughters, the eldest of whom, Paola, is studying at the oenological institute in Alba, and seems to have caught the bug too. We particularly liked the two '95 Barbarescos, both called Asili; one matures in traditional barrels, while half of the other is barrique-aged. Starting next year there will be only one Asili, (barriqued), and the traditional version will be called Valgrande. The barrique-aged Barbaresco is richer and more structured; it has a garnet ruby color with some orange at the rim, and a complex nose with notes of raspberry, blackberry, pepper and cedar. On the palate the wine is full and broad, with a solid tannic structure and a long corresponding finish. The other Barbaresco, of a fairly deep ruby hue, presents aromas of blackberry and red currant with balsamic and spicy background notes. In the mouth it reveals concentration, an austere character and a long-lasting finish. The Langhe Chardonnay, of an intense straw color, shows that it is partly barrique-aged; it has a frank fragrance with hints of banana, vanilla, hazelnut and butter. The medium-bodied palate is enlivened by a refreshing acidity and the finish offers notes of caramel and rhubarb. The Moscato d'Asti provides a stylish and balanced interpretation of the aromatic varietal fragrance; its decided effervescence is an effective counterpoise to its sweetness. Last on the list, the correct Dolcetto presents heady aromas and is quite quaffable.

	Wine	Glasses	Price
●	Barbaresco Asili '95	🍷🍷	4
●	Barbaresco Asili Barrique '95	🍷🍷	5
●	Dolcetto d'Alba Vigna Lodali '97	🍷	3
○	Langhe Chardonnay '96	🍷	3
○	Moscato d'Asti '97	🍷	3

TREISO (CN)

FIORENZO NADA
LOC. ROMBONE
12050 TREISO (CN)
TEL. 0173/638254

Since work is under way to enlarge the Nada family's cellar, we took advantage of a six-meter deep excavation to examine the composition of the soil in these wonderful hills. It is a greyish calcareous shaley marl, rich in tufa, compact when moist, but tending to crumble into fine dust if completely dry. It is a real glory, and indeed Bruno, the owner of the estate, plans to leave a small part of the earth wall of the new subterranean cellar exposed to view just as it is. But let's get to the wines. We tasted the most interesting version yet of the Seifile, the '95, of which about 3,000 bottles were produced. It is a blend of 70% barbera from over 70-year-old vines and nebbiolo. Of a dark, vivid ruby color, it offers very elegant aromas of dark cherry, licorice and flowers; the attack on the palate is powerful and sure, the tannins are well integrated and the acidity is balanced by the alcohol. This is a great Langhe blend which should age beautifully for a long time and has, furthermore, not been distorted by the use of small barrels. The 6,600 bottles of the Barbareso '95 (more are promised for next year) were swept up in no time, leaving many regular customers empty-handed. It reminded us, when we tasted it, of the '93; the aromas of raspberry and strawberry are intense; the palate shows the hard tannins, which want only time to integrate. The Dolcetto '97, splendidly elegant as usual, displays an attractive lively purplish ruby color, a characteristic fragrance of almond and red fruit and a satisfying palate, full and balanced.

● Langhe Rosso Seifile '95	🍷🍷🍷	6
● Barbaresco '95	🍷🍷	5
● Dolcetto d'Alba '97	🍷🍷	4
● Seifile '93	♢♢♢	6
● Barbaresco '90	♢♢	6
● Barbaresco '91	♢♢	5
● Barbaresco '92	♢♢	5
● Barbaresco '93	♢♢	5
● Barbaresco '94	♢♢	5
● Seifile '92	♢♢	6
● Seifile '94	♢♢	6

TREISO (CN)

PELISSERO
VIA FERRERE, 19
12050 TREISO (CN)
TEL. 0173/638136 - 638430

With the last three vintages Giorgio has really pulled out all the stops. A tireless worker, he looks after his own vines (almost 15 hectares of them) with the help of his father and his uncle, producing nearly 100 thousand bottles a year. But it would seem that this isn't enough for him to do, and he is therefore enlarging his cellar so as to improve the order and efficiency of all the phases of wine-making. This year he has presented an excellent range, with some peaks he had never previously reached. The Barbaresco Vanotu '95 repeatedly came out at the top of its category in our blind tastings and has won Three Glasses: of a lively, intense ruby-garnet color, it offers an ample and rich bouquet, with lovely fruit punctuated by very delicate sweet spicy and floral aromas. The palate, full-bodied and harmonious, shows well-integrated tannins which persist into the fruity finish. From the over 70-year-old Casot vine in the I Piani vineyard the Pelisseros have produced a very great and irresistibly drinkable Barbera which has spent nine months in new barriques. It looks black and opaque in the glass and vaunts an aristocratic nose of rare perfection and a dense, velvety palate with silky tannins. The Augenta, among the best Dolcettos of '97, has a color that rejects compromise: it is practically black. Distinct aromas of jam are followed by a powerful and warm entry on the palate; the wine then spreads and develops, showing fruit and length. The Nebbiolo, the Dolcetto Munfrina and the Barbera I Piani also get Two Glasses each; these are rich satisfying wines, and bargains as well. The Langhe Favorita '97, with toasty notes of hazelnut and spice, is almost golden in color; it is, however, the least interesting of the wines.

● Barbaresco Vanotu '95	🍷🍷🍷	5
● Barbaresco '95	🍷🍷	5
● Barbera d'Alba Casot '97	🍷🍷	4
● Barbera d'Alba I Piani '97	🍷🍷	3*
● Dolcetto d'Alba Augenta '97	🍷🍷	3*
● Dolcetto d'Alba Munfrina '97	🍷🍷	3*
● Langhe Nebbiolo '97	🍷🍷	4
○ Langhe Favorita '97	🍷	3*
● Barbaresco Vanotu '90	♢♢	5
● Barbaresco Vanotu '92	♢♢	5
● Barbaresco Vanotu '93	♢♢	5
● Barbaresco Vanotu '94	♢♢	5

TREVILLE (AL)

Livio Pavese

Regione Bettola
15030 Treville (AL)
tel. 0142/487215

Livio Pavese's fine winery is back in the Guide; this year, apart from his usual reliable range, he is also presenting some exciting wines of excellent quality. One of these is the Montarucco, a barbera and cabernet sauvignon blend. It has an intense ruby-garnet color and a broad bouquet including blackberry, cherry, violet and balsamic and spicy notes. On the palate it is full and even, with a generous character, sweet tannins and a long and intense finish. Another very attractive wine is the Grignolino '97, whose characteristic qualities are presented in an unusually rich context. Of a light and transparent ruby hue, it offers a fragrance of delicately faded rose, geranium petals and pepper against a light balsamic background. On the palate it is fat and rich in glycerin, with a tonic acidity and the varietal tannins kept in check by the fullness of the body. The Barbera d'Asti Superiore '96, ruby-colored with garnet highlights, displays aromas of red fruit with notes of custard, hay and tobacco. It has balance and good structure, and the dry finish reflects the bouquet. The pleasing and harmonious Chardonnay is of a light greenish straw color; the simple nose displays secondary and varietal aromas enriched by notes of banana, apricot and hazelnut; on the palate it is simple, smooth and balanced. The two correct and agreeably rustic '97 Barberas, the Asti and the Monferrato are unpretentious examples of their respective categories.

	Wine	Glasses	Price
●	Monferrato Rosso Montarucco '95	🍷🍷	4
●	Barbera d'Asti Sup. Podere S. Antonio '96	🍷	3
●	Grignolino del M.to Casalese Podere S. Antonio '97	🍷	3
○	Piemonte Chardonnay Podere S. Antonio '97	🍷	3
●	Barbera d'Asti Podere S. Antonio '97		3
●	Barbera del M.to Podere S. Antonio '97		3

VERDUNO (CN)

F.lli Alessandria

Via Beato Valfré, 59
12060 Verduno (CN)
tel. 0172/470113

Gian Alessandria's Barolo Monvigliero '94 suffers somewhat from its troublesome vintage; it is certainly well-made and fully satisfying, but it lacks the extra charge of power it has in the best years. It has a garnet-tinged ruby color with an orange rim, and a bouquet that offers restrained notes of jam, pepper, cinnamon and dried flowers. The fairly substantial palate has distinct tannins and a corresponding finish. If the Monvigliero Barolo is "only " good, the Pelaverga '97 is particularly admirable for its personality, and the finesse of its varietal characteristics. Fairly intense ruby-garnet in color, it displays notes of pepper, red fruit and geranium (with haunting marine nuances); on the palate it is soft and underpinned by noble tannins, which add dryness to the long finish with a spicy aftertaste. The good Dolcetto '97, intense in color with youthful purple highlights, displays distinct notes of blackberry and red currant (on a light mineral ground). The robust and intense palate shows an acidic vein and light tannins. The Barbera '96, garnet-ruby with a lightly faded rim, is redolent of violet, dark cherry, vanilla and almond. On the palate it is substantial and soft, with an intense if not particularly long finish. Our review closes with a straightforward and quaffable Favorita.

	Wine	Glasses	Price
●	Verduno Pelaverga '97	🍷🍷	3
●	Barbera d'Alba '96	🍷	3
●	Barolo Monvigliero '94	🍷	5
●	Dolcetto d'Alba '97	🍷	3
○	Langhe Favorita '97		3
●	Barolo Monvigliero '90	🍷🍷 (outline)	5
●	Barolo Monvigliero '93	🍷🍷 (outline)	5

VERDUNO (CN)

Bel Colle

Fraz. Castagni, 56
12060 Verduno (CN)
tel. 0172/470196

Once again this year Paolo Torchio's range of wines reflects the style of the winery, which was established in 1968; although it is essentially traditional Langhe in inspiration, it does not disdain modern improvements if they improve general quality. This year, many of their top wines are missing; in fact, in poor years they don't make either the Barolo Monvigliero or the whole Le Masche range, apart from the Chardonnay. Their selection is interesting all the same, starting with the Barbaresco '95. The ruby color with a lightly faded rim precedes aromas of jam, red fruit, dried fig and spice. The palate shows fair structure, balance and a corresponding finish, to which a pleasing tannic layer gives dryness. The standard Pelaverga, typical and frank as usual, has a limpid ruby color and hints of black pepper and geranium; it is pleasingly rustic and goes down easily; its balanced finish mirrors the bouquet. The Chardonnay Le Masche '97, 30% of which is barrique-aged, reveals delicate green shading on a straw-colored background; subtle notes of banana, hazelnut and lemon emerge on the nose, and it is silky and light on the palate. The Dolcetto Borgo Castagni, of a moderately dark ruby hue, unites heady aromas with notes of grass and spice; it is soft and simple in the mouth. The Arneis is good, as we expected, while La Favorita is unpretentious in fragrance and undemandingly quaffable.

	Wine		
●	Barbaresco '95	🍷	5
●	Dolcetto d'Alba Borgo Castagni '97	🍷	3
●	Verduno Pelaverga '97	🍷	3
○	Langhe Chardonnay Le Masche '97	🍷	3
○	Roero Arneis '97	🍷	3
○	Langhe Favorita '97		3
●	Barolo Vigna Monvigliero '90	🍸🍸	5
●	Barolo Vigna Monvigliero '93	🍸🍸	5
●	Verduno Pelaverga Le Masche '95	🍸🍸	4

VERDUNO (CN)

Commendator G. B. Burlotto

Via Vittorio Emanuele, 28
12060 Verduno (CN)
tel. 0172/470122

This year Marina Burlotto, Giuseppe Alessandria and their son Fabio (an oenologist, like his father) have presented an excellent range of wines; two Barolos and the Sauvignon Dives scored more than 80 points, while the other three won One Glass each without any trouble. Year after year the style of this faithfully traditional winery seems to acquire greater definition. A good example is the Barolo Cannubi '94: it shows a deep ruby color and a captivating nose with aromas of cherry, raspberry, mint and hay; the palate immediately reveals substantial body, with a broad progression, a somewhat austere character and a lingering finish. The standard Barolo '93, with orange highlights, offers a bouquet of admirable intensity with notes of strawberry, raspberry and clove. On the palate it shows a fairly full body with somewhat noticeable tannins and a faintly sharp acidity that is softened on the intense and warm finish. The Barolo Monvigliero '93 has a bouquet of wild berries and a balanced palate which is less rich than the wines we just discussed. The very successful Dives has found a perfect balance between fruit and wood this time. The golden hue precedes a varietal nose with characteristic notes of tomato flower and grapefruit. The palate, rich, fat and well articulated, does not disappoint. The delicate aromas of the Barbera Boscato range from blackberry to cherry and pepper; the palate is well-modulated, balanced and soft. The Pelaverga is typical and rich in fruit.

	Wine		
○	Langhe Dives '96	🍷🍷	4
●	Barolo '93	🍷🍷	5
●	Barolo Vigneto Cannubi '94	🍷🍷	5
●	Barbera d'Alba Vigneto Boscato '96	🍷	3
●	Barolo Vigneto Monvigliero '93	🍷	5
●	Verduno Pelaverga '97	🍷	3
●	Barolo Vigneto Monvigliero '88	🍸🍸	5
●	Barolo Vigneto Monvigliero '89	🍸	5
●	BaroloVigneto Neirane '88	🍸	5
●	Barolo Vigneto Neirane '89	🍸	5
●	Barolo Vigneto Neirane '90	🍸	5

VERDUNO (CN)

Castello di Verduno
Via Umberto I, 9
12060 Verduno (CN)
tel. 0172/470125 - 470284

Gabriella and Franco Bianco's vineyards are divided between Verduno and Barbaresco, so their wines are from the two most renowned zones of the Langhe (Barolo and Barbaresco). Barolo accounts for a good part of their 35 thousand bottles. This year, however, because of the tricky '94 vintage, no crus were produced. So here is the lone remaining Barolo, admirable for its frankly typical character. A pale ruby color with a fairly wide orange rim precedes a delicate but clearly defined nose, with suggestions of red fruit jam, rosemary and white pepper; there is not a lot of structure on the palate, which does have a notable tannic vein and a corresponding and long finish. The Barbaresco Rabajà '95, of a slightly faded ruby hue with a light orange rim, has a delicate and forward bouquet with notes of raspberry jam and dried flowers (and complex undertones of leather and tar). There is a medium body underpinned by fine tannins, leading up to a warm finish that mirrors the bouquet. The good Palaverga, richly ruby-hued, boasts a fragrance of red fruit and black pepper; the robust and balanced palate shows firm tannins and a pleasingly bitter finish. Last of the series, the Barbera Bricco del Cuculo is ruby tinged with garnet; notes of blackberry and spice emerge on the nose and it is dry and smooth in the mouth.

Wine	Glasses	Price
● Barbaresco Rabajà '95	🍷🍷	5
● Verduno Pelaverga '97	🍷🍷	4
● Barbera d'Alba Bricco del Cuculo '96	🍷	4
● Barolo '94	🍷	5
● Barbaresco Rabajà '93	YY	5
● Barolo Monvigliero '90	YY	5
● Barolo Monvigliero '93	YY	5
● Barbaresco Vigna Faset '93	Y	5
● Barolo Massara '93	Y	5

VIGNALE M.TO (AL)

Giulio Accornero e Figli
Ca' Cima, 1
15049 Vignale M.to (AL)
tel. 0142/933317

We welcome the Accornero family to the Guide this year, with their estate, in the midst of the glorious Monferrato hills, which celebrated its centenary in 1997. The brothers Ermanno and Massimo devote themselves to vineyard and cellar, conferring on their wines a style that has been constantly gaining in definition in recent years. It is now quite distinctive, inspired by tradition and realized by means of up-to-the-minute cellar technique. The Barbera Bricco Battista '96 is outstanding; it has a deep ruby-garnet color, and a broad, complex nose with notes of red currant, cherry, tobacco leaf and leather. On the palate it displays the richness of structure that the good vintage and skilled hands have given it; it's very soft and satisfying, with a long finish that reveals notes of caramel and licorice. The Centenario displays a dense color, a fragrance of black berries, green leaf and hay, and a full and vigorous palate with noble tannins adding dryness to the long finish. The Barbera Giulin, named after Massimo and Ermanno's grandfather, is pleasantly rustic and full-bodied and redolent of cherry, violet and dried hay. The Bricco del Bosco is a Grignolino which is perfectly varietal. The two malvasias, the Brigantino and the sparkling wine, are both distinctly aromatic; they are two excellent examples of dessert wine. The correctly executed Mattacchiona and Bernardina are, respectively, a Barbera and a fizzy Freisa.

Wine	Glasses	Price
● Barbera d'Asti Bricco Battista '96	🍷🍷	4
● Monferrato Rosso Centenario '95	🍷	5
● Barbera del M.to Sup. Giulin '96	🍷	3
● Casorzo Brigantino '97	🍷	3
● Grignolino del M.to Casalese Bricco del Bosco '97	🍷	3
● Malvasia di Casorzo Spumante Vigneto S. Martino '97	🍷	4
● Barbera del M.to La Mattacchiona '97		3
● Monferrato Freisa La Bernardina '97		3

VIGNALE M.TO (AL)

BRICCO MONDALINO

REG. MONDALINO, 5
15049 VIGNALE M.TO (AL)
TEL. 0142/933204

What we most admire in Mauro Gaudio is his exceptional ability to interpret a difficult wine: Grignolino. Bellini's "Casta Diva" comes to mind, an aria of an extraordinary nuanced subtlety, (far from the power of Verdi or Puccini's lushness), which only the genius of Maria Callas, in our time, could do justice to. We are certainly not suggesting that we'd like to see Mauro on the stage of La Scala, but we are delighted to find him in his cellar whenever we go. The Grignolino Bricco Mondalino, made from very slightly overripe grapes, is, year after year, a little masterpiece. The '97 shows a vivid cherry color with a rim only just tinged with orange; the nose is broad, with hints of rose, red fruit, white pepper and peanut. On the palate it is succulent and soft, with the characteristic tannic vein kept in check by the richness of the body. The good standard Grignolino, transparently cherry-colored, has a fresh fragrance of rose, strawberry and almond; the palate is frank and firm. The Barbera Il Bergantino '96, slightly under par, is of a garnet-tinged ruby color; cherry and raspberry aromas emerge on a fascinating background of leather and mint. The palate doesn't have the power shown in other years, but its admirable balance quite makes up for it. The fragrance of the Malvasia Molignano (rose and fresh pear) is delicate and harmonious; sweetness and effervescence achieve a balance on the palate. To round off the list there are the pleasant Barbera Vivace, a sort of easy bubbling holiday, and the Ciaret with its fruity fragrance and inviting palate.

	Wine	Rating	Price
●	Grignolino del M.to Casalese Bricco Mondalino '97	🍷🍷	3*
●	Barbera d'Asti Il Bergantino '96	🍷	3
●	Barbera del M.to Vivace '97	🍷	2*
●	Grignolino del M.to Casalese '97	🍷	3
●	Malvasia di Casorzo Molignano '97	🍷	3
●	Barbera d'Asti Il Bergantino '95	🍷🍷 (outline)	3
●	Grignolino del M.to Casalese Bricco Mondalino '96	🍷🍷 (outline)	3

VIGNALE M.TO (AL)

COLONNA

CA' ACCATINO, 1
FRAZ. S. LORENZO
15049 VIGNALE M.TO (AL)
TEL. 0142/933239

Alessandra Colonna's commitment to defending and improving viticulture in Monferrato is equalled only by her dedication to her own estate, which she runs with unquestionable entrepreneurial skill. Vice-President of the Enoteca Regionale del Monferrato, Alessandra is tireless in promoting familiarity with local wines, and in bringing tourists to Monferrato. Indeed this is beautiful country, alternating between forests and vineyards and offering a symphony in green. But let's turn to the wines. The Mondone '95 (a blend of barbera, pinot noir, bonarda and cabernet sauvignon) has a quite intense garnet-ruby color, and a broad bouquet with notes of cherry, roasted coffee and dark leaf. On the palate it is balanced and consistent, although it might be the better for a little more power. The Bigio, a monovarietal pinot noir, has a pale ruby hue and aromas of wild berries, enhanced by mineral and leather notes; the pleasing palate has moderate structure. The Grignolino succeeds in presenting its typical characteristics with style and balance; it has a translucent purplish ruby color with a youthful rim; the delicate nose offers hints of rose on a spicy background; the rounded palate leads into a finish with well-judged tannins. The Chardonnay, of a rich straw color with distinct greenish highlights, offers aromas of banana, apple and apricot, and a broad and quite full palate with an intense and balanced finish. The fragrance of the Barbera '96, which shows fruit and grip on the palate, is forthright and clean.

	Wine	Rating	Price
●	Barbera del M.to '96	🍷	3
●	Grignolino del M.to Casalese '97	🍷	3
●	Monferrato Rosso Il Bigio '96	🍷	3
●	Monferrato Rosso Mondone '95	🍷	4
○	Piemonte Chardonnay '97	🍷	3

VINCHIO (AT)

CANTINA SOCIALE
DI VINCHIO E VAGLIO SERRA
REG. S. PANCRAZIO, 1
14040 VINCHIO (AT)
TEL. 0141/950138

The Cantina Sociale is in the process of doing over most of its cellar. Having perfected the new bottling plant, which will be a great help, they have acquired other equipment to make the most of their grapes. They will be producing about 260 thousand bottles, made from the best fruit supplied by their member growers. The '96 and '97 vintages produced some very good wines, beginning with the Grignolino d'Asti, which has never been better. It has the usual not very deep ruby color; the piquant tone of the bouquet is made more enticing by notes of flowers and red berries. The fruit on the palate is in keeping with the vigor of the structure. The Barbera Vivace (pleasing, inviting and well made) is well above average for its lightly fizzy category, and is unabashedly immediate and quaffable. The Cortese, although it doesn't have the same character, is delightfully delicate. The only '97 we were doubtful about was the Dolcetto di Monferrato: it seemed a bit too forward, although we could tell good grapes had gone into it. The Barbera Vigne Vecchie '96 (15 thousand bottles, once again as excellent as it was a couple of years ago) fully lived up to our expectations. The intensity of the color suggests the classic vigor of this wine; the aromas of dark cherry, strawberry and raspberry steeped in alcohol have integrated with the new oak, which has added to their charm. On the palate the wine is generous, and the finish is stimulating. The characteristic standard version of the Barbera d'Asti '97, while not very long-lasting, progresses evenly on the palate.

	Wine	Glasses	Price
●	Barbera d'Asti Sup. Vigne Vecchie '96	🍷🍷	4
●	Barbera d'Asti '97	🍷	2*
●	Barbera d'Asti Sup. '96	🍷	3
●	Grignolino d'Asti '97	🍷	3
●	Barbera del M.to Vivace '97		2
○	Cortese dell'Alto Monferrato '97		2
●	Dolcetto del M.to '97		2
●	Barbera d'Asti Sup. Vigne Vecchie '90	ΥΥ	5
●	Barbera d'Asti Sup. Vigne Vecchie '91	ΥΥ	5
●	Barbera d'Asti Sup. Vigne Vecchie '94	ΥΥ	5
●	Barbera d'Asti Sup. Vigne Vecchie '93	Υ	5
●	Barbera d'Asti Sup. Vigne Vecchie '95	Υ	4

VIVERONE (BI)

LA CELLA DI SAN MICHELE - ENRIETTI
VIA CASCINE DI PONENTE, 21
13040 VIVERONE (BI)
TEL. 0161/98245

The Enrietti family, owners of eight hectares of vineyards in a splendid position overlooking Lake Viverone, maintains its place among the best interpreters of Erbaluce di Caluso, by no means an easy wine because of the high acidity and sometimes aggressively vegetal aromas that this grape can produce. But with sufficiently ripe grapes, low yields and modern cellar techniques excellent results can in fact be obtained even in these parts and with the grape in question, to which the Enriettis bear witness. Once again the two house wines, the Erbaluce di Caluso and the sparkling Cella Grande di San Michele Brut, did very well at our tastings, winning One very full Glass each. The first shows a clear light straw color and a delicate and graceful fragrance with notes of peach, apple and hazelnut against a light, attractive background of dried aromatic herbs. On the palate it shows good body, enlivened by a crisp acidic vein, and a balanced finish with hints of peach and lime. The Cella Grande di San Michele, made from erbaluce and given its sparkle by the long Charmat method, has a not very deep straw color and a fruity and floral nose. The aromas of white- and yellow-fleshed fruit are joined by notes of peach blossom and lily of the valley. This wine is fun to drink and if the effervescence gets just a touch out of hand, the crisp and corresponding finish makes up for it.

	Wine	Glasses	Price
○	Brut Cella Grande di San Michele	🍷	3
○	Erbaluce di Caluso Cella Grande '97	🍷	3

OTHER WINERIES

The following producers obtained good scores in our tastings with one or more of their wines:

PROVINCE OF ALESSANDRIA

Ca' Bianca, Alice Bel Colle, tel. 0144/55843, Barbera d'Asti '97

La Slina, Castelletto d'Orba, tel. 0143/830542, Dolcetto di Ovada Vigneto Pianterasso '97

La Merlina, Gavi, tel. 0143/682150, Gavi di Gavi La Merlina '97

Produttori del Gavi, Gavi, tel. 0143/642786, Gavi di Gavi Etichetta Nera '97

Santa Seraffa, Gavi, tel. 0143/643600, Gavi di Gavi Le Colombare '97

Tenuta S. Sebastiano
Lu M.to, tel. 0131/741353, Barbera del M.to Risà '95

Cantina Sociale Tre Castelli
Montaldo Bormida, tel. 0143/85136, Dolcetto di Ovada Sup. Colli di Carpeneto '96

Isabella, Murisengo, tel. 0141/693000, Barbera d'Asti Truccone '96

Il Vignale, Novi Ligure, tel. 0143/72715, Gavi Vigne Alte '97

La Marchesa, Novi Ligure, tel. 0143/743362, Gavi Etichetta Nera '97

Tenuta Rombetta, Novi Ligure, tel. 0143/321451, Gavi '97

Vigna del Pareto,
Novi Ligure, tel. 010/8398776, Gavi Vigna del Pareto '97

Rossi Contini, Ovada, tel. 0143/833696, Dolcetto di Ovada Vigneto Ninan '96

Cantine Valpane
Ozzano M.to, tel. 0142/486713, Barbera d'Asti Valpane '95

Brezza, S. Giorgio M.to, tel. 0142/781761, Barbera del M.to Vigna Galavagna '97

Cascina Alberta, Vignale M.to, tel. 0142/933313, Grignolino del M.to Casalese '97

PROVINCE OF ASTI

Roberto Ferraris
Agliano Terme, tel. 0141/954234, Barbera d'Asti Nobbio '96

La Giribaldina
Calamandrana, tel. 0141/718043, Barbera d'Asti Cala delle Mandrie '96

Vittorio Bera, Canelli, tel. 0141/831157, Moscato d'Asti '97

Cascina Barisel, Canelli, tel. 0141/824849, Barbera d'Asti La Cappelletta '95, Barbera d'Asti Barisel '97

Cantina Sociale Barbera Sei Castelli,
Castelnuovo Calcea, tel. 0141/957137, Barbera d'Asti Sup. Bricco Vignole '96

Cantina Sociale del Freisa,
Castelnuovo Don Bosco, tel. 011/9876117, Malvasia di Castelnuovo Don Bosco '97

Renaldo Graglia
Castelnuovo Don Bosco, tel. 011/9874708, Freisa d'Asti Secco Sup. '96

Corte del Cavaliere, Fontanile, tel. 0141/739355, Barbera d'Asti Sup. '95

Cantina Sociale di Mombaruzzo
Mombaruzzo, tel. 0141/77019, Barbera d'Asti Vigneti Storici '95

Luigi Spertino, Mombercelli, tel. 0141/959098, Grignolino d'Asti '97

Cascina Orsolina, Moncalvo, tel. 0141/917277, Barbera d'Asti Sup. Bricco dei Cappuccini '96

Antonia Gazzi, Nizza M.to, tel. 0141/793512 Barbera d'Asti Praiot '97

Clemente Guasti e Figli
Nizza M.to, tel. 0141/721350, Barbera d'Asti Fonda S. Nicolao '95

Castello del Poggio
Portacomaro, tel. 0141/202543, Barbera d'Asti '97, Grignolino d'Asti '97

Franco Mondo
S. Marzano Oliveto, tel. 0141/834096, Barbera d'Asti Vigna del Salice '96

PROVINCE OF CUNEO

Gianluigi Lano, Alba, tel. 0173/286958, Barbaresco '94, Barbera d'Alba Fondo Prà '95

La Ca' Nova, Barbaresco, tel. 0173/635123, Barbaresco Montefico '95

Ronchi, Barbaresco, tel. 0173/635156, Barbaresco '95

Bricco del Cucù Bastia Mondovì, tel. 0174/60153, Dolcetto di Dogliani Bricco S. Bernardo '97

Cornarea, Canale, tel. 0173/979091, Roero Arneis '97

Ca' du Russ, Castellinaldo, tel. 0173/213069, Roero Arneis Costa delle Rose '97

Gigi Rosso, Castiglione Falletto, tel. 0173/262369, Barolo Arione Sörì dell'Ulivo '93, Dolcetto di Diano d'Alba Moncolombetto '97

Cantina Sociale del Dolcetto di Clavesana, Clavesana, tel. 0173/790451, Dolcetto di Dogliani Pensieri '97

Casavecchia, Diano d'Alba, tel. 0173/69205, Diano d'Alba Sorì Bruni '97

Il Palazzotto, Diano d'Alba, tel. 0173/69234, Diano d'Alba Sörì Cristina '97

Paolo Monte, Diano d'Alba, tel. 0173/69231, Diano d'Alba Cascina Flino Vigna Vecchia '96

Mario Cozzo, Dogliani, tel. 0173/70571, Dolcetto di Dogliani Vigna Pregliasco '97

La Fusina, Dogliani, tel. 0173/70488, Dolcetto di Dogliani Vigna Muntà '97

Aldo Marenco, Dogliani, tel. 0173/721090, Dolcetto di Dogliani Surì '97

Bruno e Claudio Porro, Dogliani, tel. 0173/70371 Dolcetto di Dogliani Ribote '97

Anna Maria Abbona Farigliano, tel. 0173/797228, Dolcetto di Dogliani Sorì dij But '97

Eraldo Revelli, Farigliano, tel. 0173/797154, Dolcetto di Dogliani '97

Ciabot Berton, La Morra, tel. 0173/50217, Barbera d'Alba Bricco S. Biagio '96

Mario Marengo, La Morra, tel. 0173/50127, Barolo Brunate '94

Cascina Pellerino Monteu Roero, tel. 0173/978171, Barbera d'Alba Sup. Bricco della Salute '96

Cantina del Castello, Neive, tel. 0173/67171, Barbaresco Santo Stefano '95

Cantina del Glicine, Neive, tel. 0173/67215, Barbaresco Curà '95, Barbaresco Marcorino '95

Cascina Crosa, Neive, tel. 0173/67376, Dolcetto d'Alba Cascina Crosa '97

Cascina Vano, Neive, tel. 0173/677705, Barbaresco '95

Parroco di Neive, Neive, tel. 0173/67008, Barbaresco Vigneto Gallina '95

Punset, Neive, tel. 0173/677423, Barbaresco Campo Quadro '95

Giovanni Stra, Novello, tel. 0173/731214, Dolcetto d'Alba '97

Mossio F.lli, Rodello, tel. 0173/617149, Dolcetto d'Alba Bricco Caramelli '97

Luigi Pira, Serralunga d'Alba, tel. 0173/613106, Barolo Vigneto Margheria '93

Ada Nada, Treiso, tel. 0173/638127, Barbaresco Valeirano '95

Vignaioli Elvio Pertinace Treiso, tel. 0173/442238, Barbaresco Marcarini '95, Dolcetto d'Alba Nervo '97

PROVINCE OF NOVARA

Luigi Dessilani e Figlio Fara Novarese, tel. 0321/829252, Fara Caramino '93,

PROVINCE OF TORINO

Cooperativa della Serra Piverone, tel. 0125/72166, Erbaluce di Caluso '97

LIGURIA

1997 in Liguria was not the much-hyped "vintage of the century"; the year was definitely, however, a good one, even if sometimes the high sugar levels in the grapes were not skillfully handled during fermentation. Of the wines we tasted, the quality of the whites was on the whole higher than that of the reds, confirming Liguria's vocation for white wines. The Pigatos and the Vermentinos of the Riviera del Ponente took the lion's share of awards, but the Levante certainly did not miss out either. Those producers who had the foresight and courage to invest in technology and modernize their vineyards and wineries have been rewarded with notable results. Experimentation (still the preserve of a select few) to discover how to make the most of the grapes available has had a positive effect on the white wines, making them more richly aromatic and also longer-lived; this should make producers think twice about releasing their wines too young and thus ignoring their potential for developing with bottle age. It is perhaps time for at least those producers who no longer merely make easy-drinking wines to take up the challenge. As regards the wines in the glass, the question of how to distinguish between wines made from vermentino and pigato (grape varieties which are in some way related), is not much closer to being answered, since the particular characteristics of each tend to be neutralized by standardized vinification techniques. Wines with more distinct individual character will certainly be created through research, experimentation and the efforts of individual producers. On the other hand, producers are gradually, with plantings of new varietals, moving towards expanding their ranges to include wines of internationally known kinds. This is not, in itself, a negative step, as long as the identities of the various areas within the region are not compromised. But let us look at the situation as it stands. Riccardo Bruna confirms the positive trend of the last few years with his Pigato Le Russeghine. Also at Ranzo, La Maccia (an estate run by women) is making the most of the potential of its Pigato. Tommaso and Angelo Lupi have earned themselves a healthy collection of Two Glass awards, while Arnold Schweizer's Tenuta Giuncheo has excelled with the splendid Vermentino Le Palme. Emanuele Trevia, at Diano, has presented a praiseworthy Pigato and an intriguing Eretico (barrique-aged vermentino). Terre Bianche presented the excellent Arcana Bianco and Rosso (two blends) and also makes its presence felt with the Rossese di Dolceacqua Bricco Arcagna. Cane's Rossese di Dolceacqua Vigneto Morghe is outstanding, as is the Rossese of Rodolfo Biamonti, which definitely steps into the limelight. In the Albenga zone, the Pigato of the ageless Pippo Parodi comes back with a vengeance, but also La Vecchia Cantina's example of the same varietal is notable. In the province of Genoa, it is once again the Enoteca Bisson which flies the flag with its standard Vermentino. In the Levante, Walter De Battè stands out from the crowd with two Cinque Terres (a Secco and a Sciacchetrà) which both earn Two Glasses. Following close behind are the Cooperativa delle Cinque Terre with their very good Sciacchetrà and single-vineyard Costa da Sera, and Lambruschi, who once again proves himself an excellent producer of Vermentino.

ALBENGA (SV)

Anfossi

Via Paccini, 39
Fraz. Bastia
17030 Albenga (SV)
tel. 0182/20024

To say that Mario Anfossi is just a skilled winegrower would be doing him a great injustice. At this handsome estate, he makes the very most of his land. One only has to cite the example of his basil, principal ingredient in that most Ligurian of sauces, pesto; here there is just one sowing, but the plants sprout about ten times to give a total yield of 150 thousand kilograms of basil, enough for 280 thousand kilos of basil paste. These numbers give an idea of the production capacity of the estate which, in addition, also makes preserves, oil, cheese and, naturally, wine. This year we tasted only the standard versions of Vermentino and Pigato: the two single-vineyard wines were deemed still to need a little more aging before they showed the full potential of the vintage. The '97 Pigato is at first delicate on the nose, but then opens up to reveal vegetal, floral and fruity (peach skin and apple) tones. On the palate it is dry and straightforward, with just a light structure, but easy and uncomplicated to drink. The Vermentino, with its lively, bright, pale color, offers fragrant, discreet and elegant aromas (sage, basil and wildflowers); the fruit on the palate is underpinned by a highly attractive vein of acidity.

	Wine	Glasses	Price
○	Riviera Ligure di Ponente Pigato '97	🍷	3
○	Riviera Ligure di Ponente Vermentino '97	🍷	3
○	Riviera Ligure di Ponente Pigato Le Caminate '96	🍸	3

ALBENGA (SV)

Cascina Feipu dei Massaretti

Loc. Massaretti, 8
Fraz. Bastia
17030 Albenga (SV)
tel. 0182/20131

Well done, Pippo! Here at last is the vintage we were waiting for, to remind us of past glories. The '97 is a really top-notch Pigato: entirely fermented in stainless steel, it displays a straw-yellow color; on the nose it is broad, with good depth and persistence, and offers clean vegetal (sage) and fruity (citrus, peach and apricot) hints. On the palate it is dry (yet soft and pleasantly alcohol-rich) and a perfect recapitulation of the nose. It is appealingly rounded but well-balanced and savory, with a long, persistent finish. The slightly less characterful Due Anelli is a blend of 60% stainless steel- and 40% barrique-aged pigato. The oak, which still needs to integrate somewhat with the fruit, at the moment covers light perfumes of grass and wildflowers, which combine with an undertone of fruit (peach); on the palate it is neither powerful nor fine, but it does reveal reasonable intensity, even if it is a little lacking in body. Lastly, the pleasant Rossese Riviera Ligure di Ponente offers slightly heady delicate notes of raspberry and cherry, and a hint of roses; its flavor is dry, tasty and reasonably persistent, although the alcohol is a little out of balance. As of this year, Pippo Parodi has the full-time assistance not only of his wife, Bice, but also of his daughters and sons-in-law. With his vast experience, he guides them in a constant quest for greater quality. In future the Due Anelli, made to celebrate Pippo and Bice's Golden Wedding anniversary, will be replaced by another, more carefully selected barrique-aged wine. Cascina Feipu currently produces about 50 thousand bottles a year.

	Wine	Glasses	Price
○	Riviera Ligure di Ponente Pigato '97	🍷🍷	4
○	Due Anelli '97	🍷	4
●	Riviera Ligure di Ponente Rossese '97		3

ALBENGA (SV)

La Vecchia Cantina

Via Corta, 3
Fraz. Salea
17030 Albenga (SV)
tel. 0182/559881

The only old features of this winery, which is well-sited, skillfully integrated into the original structure, functional, well-equipped and extremely clean, are its thick, substantial walls surmounted by elegant vaulting. The affable Umberto Calleri, owner of and guiding spirit behind the estate, greets his visitors and is very happy to talk about his wines, about how strongly he believes in Pigato (which enjoys a particularly favorable microclimate at Salea) and about the arrival of that varietal (right in the Albenga zone, it would seem) from the Middle East at the beginning of the 17th century. It is no accident that his Pigato should repeat the success of the previous vintage and obtain our Two Glass accolade. The intense, aromatic and complex nose displays scents of wildflowers, musk and ripe peach. The wine is rich and soft on the palate, with good balance and a long, typically bitter-almondy finish. The second wine of the estate is the Vermentino. Though initially a bit dumb, the nose opens up to reveal ripe fruit notes and lightly vegetal tones; on the palate it has a certain depth and good evolution of flavor: we are not talking about a complex wine, but rather one that is well-made and eminently quaffable. The estate also produces a small quantity of Rossese which, in the near future, will begin to be bottled and sold. Our general impression is that these are sound, reliable wines, in line with what one might expect from a serious-minded and conscientious producer who makes about 19 thousand bottles from his four hectares of vineyards.

	Wine	Glasses	Price
○	Riviera Ligure di Ponente Pigato '97	🍷🍷	3
○	Riviera Ligure di Ponente Vermentino '97	🍷	3

CAMPOROSSO (IM)

Tenuta Giuncheo

Loc. Giuncheo
18033 Camporosso (IM)
tel. 0184/288639

This year the wines of Tenuta Giuncheo, which have always been notably reliable, performed very well. This success stems, to a large degree, from the great passion that Marco Romagnoli puts into his work, as well as from the technical skills of the oenologist Donato Lanati and from the considerable investments made by the owners, Arnold and Monica Schweizer. Everything at this estate has been planned with care, from the completely renovated winery to the up-to-the-minute wine-making equipment, state-of-the-art agricultural machinery, and new plantings of "top-secret" grape varieties. Here, then, is a range of good wines which are attractive, clean and modern in style. We particularly liked the Vermentino Le Palme, 50% of which was barrique-fermented. A bright straw-yellow in color, it offers a broad, intense bouquet (hints of Mediterranean underbrush, pear and plum). In the mouth one finds good plump fruit, but also crisp acidity and a long, elegant finish. The basic Vermentino is less complex: it has a straightforward, delicate bouquet whose main tones are of fruit and flowers. On the palate it is crisp, and its flavor corresponds admirably with the nose. The basic Rossese, an example of a correct but less complex style, displays a fragrant, fruity bouquet and a light, not very intense palate, with slightly over-evident alcohol. Appealing complexity on the nose (a hint of vanilla, balsamic scents and fruity notes) and a soft, medium-bodied, crisp palate are the principal characteristics of the excellent Rossese Vigneto Pian del Vescovo.

	Wine	Glasses	Price
○	Riviera Ligure di Ponente Vermentino Le Palme '97	🍷🍷	4
○	Riviera Ligure di Ponente Vermentino '97	🍷	3
●	Rossese di Dolceacqua Vigneto Pian del Vescovo '97	🍷	4
●	Rossese di Dolceacqua '97		3

CASTELNUOVO MAGRA (SP)

Il Torchio
Via Provinciale, 202
19030 Castelnuovo Magra (SP)
tel. 0187/674075

Giorgio Tendola is a likeable fellow who is well worth getting to know in person; you should make a point of visiting his small, charming winery, a model of neatness and tidiness. There have been farmers in the family since 1920, although Giorgio's background is quite different: at one time he also tended olive groves and, in fact, the estate took on its name (meaning press) because it used to be the site of an olive press. The excellently sited vineyards are guyot-trained on predominantly clayey soil, and have a low number of grape bunches per vine. With the aid of Giorgio Bacigaluppi, an expert oenologist from the Riviera di Levante, the estate has produced a wine that received unanimous praise at our tastings and very nearly won Two Glasses. The limpid, transparent Vermentino '97 has a rather deep straw-yellow color (as a result of just a little maceration on the skins) and reasonably evident "legs". On the nose it confirms what the eyes suggest: it displays a broad, enticing, characterful bouquet, with scents of flowers and of ripe fruit (peach skin and apricot), as well as aromatic, honeyed notes. It follows through on the palate with fat, persistent and well-balanced fruit; the slightly almondy finish is very typical of the variety. The estate produces a total of some 30 thousand bottles, including a number filled with a good, straightforward red made from sangiovese and merlot.

○	Colli di Luni Vermentino '97	🍷	2
●	Colli di Luni Rosso '97		2

CASTELNUOVO MAGRA (SP)

Ottaviano Lambruschi
Via Olmarello, 28
19030 Castelnuovo Magra (SP)
tel. 0187/674261

Ottaviano and Fabio Lambruschi's estate succeeds, even in lesser years, in making wines that are worthy of recommendation, so you can imagine the results they managed to obtain in a year like '97, with its particularly fine, ripe and healthy grapes. Their range of wines is, in general, of a high standard. The basic Vermentino has a good deep straw-yellow color. Its attractive bouquet offers well-defined scents of Mediterranean underbrush delightfully intertwined with fresh fruity notes. On the palate, the wine is appealing, soft and well-balanced; it mirrors the bouquet and lingers pleasingly. The "older" of the two special selections of Vermentino, the Costa Marina, (the first to be planted), is similar to the standard wine in color; it offers a broad if still somewhat closed nose, which is nicely aromatic and complex, topped off by enticing floral, honeyed notes. On the palate it is soft, rich, silky and well-balanced. The Sarticola, on the other hand, is not quite so impressive. It has a slightly lighter straw-colored hue, and displays an appealing freshness on the nose, which, though less perfumed than that of the other "cru", does offer immediate sensations of grass and wildflowers, which carry through onto the reasonably elegant and well-balanced palate; here more personality would be welcome, but the finish is fresh and typically almondy. We still have some reservations about the Ottaviano Lambruschi, the estate's barriqued wine: although it offers aromas (flowers, honey and underbrush) reminiscent of the style of Lambruschi's Vermentinos, the oak is still rather overbearing.

○	Colli di Luni Vermentino '97	🍷🍷	3*
○	Colli di Luni Vermentino Costa Marina '97	🍷	3
○	Colli di Luni Vermentino Sarticola '97	🍷	3
○	Ottaviano Lambruschi		4

CHIAVARI (GE)

ENOTECA BISSON
C.SO GIANELLI, 28
16043 CHIAVARI (GE)
TEL. 0185/314462

Of the many different types of wine produced by Piero Lugano, not all, unfortunately, are worthy of a listing here. This energetic wine merchant and grower has a secret dream: to dedicate himself full-time to working in the vineyards. But let's get down to the wines. The standard Vermentino scored highest in our blind tastings, earning Two Glasses. This wine has a bright straw-yellow color and fresh, elegant rather than powerful scents of flowers, citrus fruit and pear, enriched by light resinous and aromatic notes. On the palate it is well-balanced, with a fresh and typical bitterish finish. Though they both earn One Glass, the two "crus", Monte Bernardo and Vigna Erta, are less impressive. The Marea (a blend of bosco, vermentino and albarola) is good; it has quite a complex and gently captivating nose with notes of herbs, dried flowers, chamomile and vine flowers. On the palate it is rounded, elegant and nicely savory. The Bianchetta U Pastine is characterized by light scents of Mediterranean underbrush and resin; in the mouth it is dry and not particularly structured but balanced. We also liked the Musaico, made from dolcetto grapes: a lively ruby in color, on the nose it offers heady fruity aromas (almond and cherry), carrying through onto the palate, which also displays well-judged tannins and a pleasant aromatic finish. The two sweet wines are a little disappointing. The Caratello is the better of the two: it has a golden color and light scents of chestnut and dried fruit (apricot and peach); the fruit on the palate, though not cloying, is nevertheless rather simple. Of the two vintages of Acinirari (the other dessert wine) we prefer the '95.

○	Golfo del Tigullio Vermentino '97	🍷🍷	2*
○	Acinirari '95	🍷	5
○	Caratello '96	🍷	4
○	Golfo del Tigullio Bianchetta Genovese U Pastine '97	🍷	3
●	Golfo del Tigullio Rosso Musaico '97	🍷	3
○	Golfo del Tigullio Vermentino Monte Bernardo '97	🍷	3
○	Golfo del Tigullio Vermentino Vigna Erta '97	🍷	3
○	Marea '97	🍷	3
○	Acinirari '96		5

DIANO CASTELLO (IM)

MARIA DONATA BIANCHI
VIA DELLE TORRI, 16
18010 DIANO CASTELLO (IM)
TEL. 0183/498233

Emanuele Trevia decided to give the name "Eretico" (heretical) to the two wines he ferments and ages in small Allier oak barrels, to underline the "unheard-of excess", according to purists, of which he is guilty in making wines in this manner. They are a Vermentino and a Pigato, both monovarietal; to differentiate between the labels, which are otherwise identical, he uses different colors, green for the former, brown for the latter. Our opinion is that making the most of a grape variety's potential by improving not only vineyard husbandry but also wine-making techniques is merely a sign that the wine-maker is fully aware of the value of the progress that has been made in vinification. This is particularly true here, as these wines do not substitute, but complement the traditional versions. The Eretico Vermentino is quite the best example of its type: it has a brilliant golden yellow color and aromas of ripe apple, flowers and wild herbs; an initial crispness on the palate is joined by a soft complexity and persistence; the lovely fruit recalls the bouquet, with toasty notes of oak. In the Eretico Pigato, which is more aggressively flavored and in fact a bit overbearing, the oaky tones are more marked and dominate the varietal notes both on the nose and in the flavor, which, however, is rounded and concentrated. The excellent standard Pigato is elegant, broad and fruity on the nose; it evolves well on the palate, the fruit echoing the bouquet, with a pleasant fresh vegetal touch as well. The basic Vermentino impressed us with its direct nose and substantial palate; together with excellent balance of its various components it also offers reasonable body and a long finish.

○	Eretico Vermentino '96	🍷🍷	5
○	Riviera Ligure di Ponente Pigato '97	🍷🍷	4
○	Eretico Pigato '96	🍷	5
○	Riviera Ligure di Ponente Vermentino '97	🍷	4

DOLCEACQUA (IM)

GIOBATTA MANDINO CANE
VIA ROMA, 21
18035 DOLCEACQUA (IM)
TEL. 0184/206120

Mandino Cane is an affable man, a gifted communicator with a knack for making instant friendships, and this is reflected in his wines. In fact his two single-vineyard Rossese di Dolceacquas have conquered the palates of wine experts and wine lovers with equal ease. These are wines of great breeding which are real expressions of their terroir (the soil and microclimate of a given vineyard site) and to which Mandino, in typically deft and meticulous manner, has given structure and body by carefully selecting his grapes and by skillful wine-making. The gem is the Vigneto Morghe, a real star with a knock-out palate. It has a handsome rich ruby color and an intriguing, well-knit bouquet: on a lightly spicy background there emerge notes of blackberry, red currant and crushed rose petals. The concentrated fruit on the palate perfectly echoes that on the nose, and is soft, full-bodied and well-structured; the finish is long and velvety. The excellent Vigneto Arcagna almost rated Two Glasses as well. This is ruby red in color; though initially rather closed on the nose, it opens up to reveal red fruit scents and more delicate aromatic tones; on the palate, we found good vigorous concentrated fruit, an attractive succulence, satisfying weight and a long, clean finish. These wines benefited from the propitious vintage, both as regards the harvest itself (which took place when the grapes were perfectly ripe) and in the vinification process, supervised by Mandino with his habitual care and conscientiousness.

●	Rossese di Dolceacqua Sup. Vigneto Morghe '97	TT	4
●	Rossese di Dolceacqua Sup. Vigneto Arcagna '97	T	4

DOLCEACQUA (IM)

TERRE BIANCHE
LOC. ARCAGNA
18035 DOLCEACQUA (IM)
TEL. 0184/31426

When this Guide appears, months will already have passed since the death of Claudio Rondelli, creator of rich, full-bodied wines to which he succeeded in imparting all the pathos of a restless and resolute "vigneron". The reins of the company now pass to Claudio's brother Paolo and his brother-in-law Franco Laconi (who was already involved in the running of the estate); Marco Ronco, a young oenologist with a Piedmontese background, is their technical consultant. Given the range of wines presented this year, the winery achieved notable success and there were some outstanding offerings. Of the Pigatos the standard version is the more persuasive. This satisfyingly structured and well-balanced wine has a fruity and slightly vegetal nose, as well as well-modulated, persistent fruit on the palate. The Vigna Arcagna, a bit closed and not altogether clean on the nose, displays good mouth-filling fruit, but offers few other interesting sensations. Among the Vermentinos, the Vigna Campetto has a delicate fruity bouquet and reasonable structure on the palate, whereas the basic version is less appealing, in both aroma and flavor. The Arcana Bianco (pigato and vermentino) and the Arcana Rosso (rossese and cabernet sauvignon) are the fruits of a new - and successful - project. The white displays complex varietal aromas which are well integrated with the toastiness of the oak, and then satisfying density on the palate; the red offers skillfully used oak, an attractive vein of acidity and just the right amount of tannin. The Rossese di Dolceacqua Bricco Arcagna is the epitome of elegance and offers an enticing nose, with a slightly spicy tone which leads on into the fruit. The palate reflects the bouquet and is well-articulated and rounded. The finish is long. The good basic Rossese is full-bodied and savory, with an underlying flavor of almonds.

○	Arcana Bianco '96	TT	5
●	Arcana Rosso '96	TT	5
●	Rossese di Dolceacqua Bricco Arcagna '96	TT	5
○	Riviera Ligure di Ponente Pigato '97	T	4
○	Riviera Ligure di Ponente Pigato Vigna Arçagna '97	T	4
○	Riviera Ligure di Ponente Vermentino Vigna Campetto '97	T	4
●	Rossese di Dolceacqua '97	T	4
○	Riviera Ligure di Ponente Vermentino '97		4
●	Rossese di Dolceacqua Bricco Arcagna '95	YY	5

FINALE LIGURE (SV)

CASCINA DELLE TERRE ROSSE
VIA MANIE, 3
17024 FINALE LIGURE (SV)
TEL. 019/698782

The Cascina delle Terre Rosse is one of the most prestigious wineries in Liguria. But the wines we tasted did not, frankly, live up to our expectations, which had been high. The always reliable Pigato, which does show good varietal character, is the best of the '97 vintage. It has the color of straw and a delicately fruity bouquet with scents of peach and hints of sage, herbs and resin. On the palate it is soft and well-balanced, with a full and reasonably concentrated flavor. The less persuasive Vermentino has a somewhat dumb nose and is generally rather dilute. The lumassina-based L'Acerbina is a more interesting example of its type and has a cold straw color; its nose is persistent and characteristic, with delicate scents of wildflowers, apple, hay and lemon balm. On the palate it is fresh and lively; a vein of acidity is both typical and appealing; it is not especially full-bodied, but does have a certain elegance. The Rossese is fuller in the mouth than on the nose; on the palate we found a pleasantly bitter tone and a long finish. The final wine in the range is the '95 Passito: a deep golden yellow in color, it has a faint aroma of dried fruit, toasted almonds and candied citrus peel; on the palate it lacks the concentration of the '93, but it corresponds to the nose and is well-balanced and full-bodied, and its finish is nothing to be ashamed of.

○	L'Acerbina '97	🍷	3
○	Passito Terre Rosse '95	🍷	6
○	Riviera Ligure di Ponente Pigato '97	🍷	4
●	Riviera Ligure di Ponente Rossese '97	🍷	4
○	Riviera Ligure di Ponente Vermentino '97		4

IMPERIA

TENUTA COLLE DEI BARDELLINI
VIA FONTANAROSA, 12
LOC. S. AGATA
18100 IMPERIA
TEL. 0183/291370

The U Munte vineyard, the Vermentino "cru" of the Colle dei Bardellini estate, thrives and bears fruit in its splendid location, situated on a plateau, on a sun-drenched plain, in the midst of Mediterranean maquis, with a fine view of the sea. This well-ventilated site requires very little spraying because the grapes are less affected by humidity here, but it also makes cultivation considerably more difficult. The Vigna U Munte '97 wins One Glass. It has a clear and intense straw color followed by elegantly fragrant, delicately aromatic floral and fruity scents (hints of white peach, citron and pear); on the palate it is stylish, lean, warm, soft and persistent. The Pigato Vigna La Torretta also did well: it is limpid and fragrant (underbrush, citrus fruit, wildflowers and apple). On the palate, it is stylish and pleasing, not imposing or well-structured but crisp and persistent. It can whet the appetite, served as an aperitif, or be drunk with a light (perhaps fish-based) meal. With the assistance of the experienced oenologist Giuliano Noè, Colle dei Bardellini produces 70 thousand bottles annually from its own grapes and from those purchased from reliable neighboring winegrowers.

○	Riviera Ligure di Ponente Pigato Vigna La Torretta '97	🍷	4
○	Riviera Ligure di Ponente Vermentino Vigna U Munte '97	🍷	4

PIEVE DI TECO (IM)

Tommaso e Angelo Lupi
Via Mazzini, 9
18026 Pieve di Teco (IM)
tel. 0183/36161 - 291610

We greatly enjoyed the wines produced by the Lupis because of their complexity and their inviting and particularly attractive quaffability; in addition they were produced with a technical purity rarely found elsewhere, in keeping with the standards of their cellar, which has few rivals in the region. The Lupis have not yet come up with an absolute champion, but several of their wines easily won Two Glasses. Their Pigato Le Petraie, undoubtedly the best of the range, offers an elegant nose with a broad array of aromas ranging from aromatic and balsamic notes to fruit; the palate corresponds, and is succulent, rich, mouth-filling and persistent. The excellent standard Pigato, crisp and varietal, reveals sound structure, excellent balance and a long finish. The Vermentino Le Serre, with its inviting deep straw color, shined at our tastings: on the well-expressed nose one finds hints of underbrush, flowers and wild herbs. The palate is rich, soft and substantial, with just the right amount of acidity and reasonable structure. The basic Vermentino shows a complex amalgam of floral and fruity scents; it offers similar notes on the palate enriched by a firm structure and an attractive bitterish finish. The Ormeasco Superiore Le Braje is fruity on the nose (blackberry, red currant and violets) and repeats these sensations on the palate, where it is rich, full-bodied, warm and persistent, underpinned by light tannins on a delicately bitter background. The interesting Rossese di Dolceacqua reveals a typically varietal nose; the well-balanced palate is attractively savory and fruity; the wine also offers reasonable concentration and a good, long finish.

	Wine	Glasses	Price
●	Riviera Ligure di Ponente Ormeasco Sup. Le Braje '96	🍷🍷	4
○	Riviera Ligure di Ponente Pigato '97	🍷🍷	3
○	Riviera Ligure di Ponente Pigato Le Petraie '97	🍷🍷	4
○	Riviera Ligure di Ponente Vermentino Le Serre '97	🍷🍷	4
○	Riviera Ligure di Ponente Vermentino '97	🍷	3
●	Rossese di Dolceacqua '97	🍷	4

RANZO (IM)

A Maccia
Via Umberto I, 56
Fraz. Borgo
18028 Ranzo (IM)
tel. 0183/318003

This year, the wines produced by the Maccia winery, run by the determined and hardworking Loredana Faraldi and her mother, Fernanda Fiorito, surpassed all our expectations. We had thought that this tiny estate (a mere spot on the map, as its name suggests) in the heart of the Albenga area was continuing to work in a slow, steady way, without offering any major surprises. But the '97 Pigato decided to astound us. In the space of just a few years, an enterprise which started up almost by accident has been pursued with great dedication and constancy, "without ever biting off more than we can chew", as Loredana emphasizes, and has now made a name for itself, not to mention a market. Production has increased a little and now stands at around 17 thousand bottles, with the help of the grapes they used to give to the cooperative. Cellar technique has also improved and barriques are not altogether unknown here. Even the building which houses the winery has been smartened up, with a legible new sign and a minute but functional shop where, in addition to wine, they sell extra-virgin olive oil, olive paste and olives in brine. The Pigato shows a definite personality: of a lively deep straw-yellow color, it is broad and persistent on the nose, which is attractively vegetal, with fruity tones and subtle hints of resin and aromatic herbs. The succulent and direct palate is supported by a well-balanced structure which combines finesse and complexity. The range also includes a Rossese, which is fruity on the nose and headily enjoyable on the palate.

	Wine	Glasses	Price
○	Riviera Ligure di Ponente Pigato '97	🍷🍷	3
●	Riviera Ligure di Ponente Rossese '97		3

RANZO (IM)

BRUNA
VIA UMBERTO I, 81
FRAZ. BORGO
18028 RANZO (IM)
TEL. 0183/318082

Bruna has won hands down in the Pigato stakes, rewarding Riccardo's years of dedicated labor. Even now, when Pigato generally speaking is a much better wine than it used to be, Bruna's versions are still touchstones for all the other producers. Tradition skillfully brought up to date, constancy and vitality are all reflected in the small range of characterful and inviting wines that have succeeded in resisting the blandishments of the barrique. Let's begin with the Pigato Le Russeghine, a very impressive white with a deep straw color. Its broad, complex bouquet includes notes of aromatic herbs, chamomile, resin and citrus fruit; in the mouth, the fruit flavor is well blended with acidity and alcohol, and the palate as a whole, with its homogeneous structure, perfectly echoes the sensations of the nose. The less important-seeming Villa Torrachetta combines a lightly resinous, musky note on the nose with scents of peach and honey. The wine is soft and well-balanced on the palate; it has reasonable concentration, a delectable tastiness and an attractive bitterish finish. The Rossese, consistent in quality, with a charming pale ruby color, happily combines a persistence of aromas and fruity flavors. The grappa made from pigato is also decidedly interesting: this is distilled for the estate by the Rovero brothers at San Marzanotto d'Asti.

	Wine	Glasses	Price
○	Riviera Ligure di Ponente Pigato Le Russeghine '97	🍷🍷	3*
○	Riviera Ligure di Ponente Pigato Villa Torrachetta '97	🍷	3
●	Riviera Ligure di Ponente Rossese '97		3
○	Riviera Ligure di Ponente Pigato Le Russeghine '96	ΥΥ	3

RIOMAGGIORE (SP)

COOPERATIVA AGRICOLA
DI RIOMAGGIORE, MANAROLA,
CORNIGLIA,VERNAZZA E MONTEROSSO
LOC. GROPPO - FRAZ. MANAROLA
19010 RIOMAGGIORE (SP)
TEL. 0187/920435

After the below par performance noted in last year's edition of the Guide, the Cooperativa delle Cinque Terre has promptly returned to form with the '97 wines. Despite their wide assortment of wines the average performance was very good. The single-vineyard Costa da Posa, with its vivid straw-yellow color, offers fairly intense and persistent perfumes with, initially, aromatic and balsamic notes. The harmonious and well-balanced palate leads to a pleasing and crisp finish corresponding nicely to the nose. The good Costa de Sèra, less intense and persistent on the nose (with its hints of aromatic herbs, eucalyptus and vine flowers) than the Costa da Posa, is savory and attractive on the palate. The Costa de Campo is less engaging, with its somewhat repressed notes of underbrush; on the palate it is a bit disjointed and lacking in structure: indeed the basic version seems better. This has a straw color of reasonable depth; on the nose, though the sulphur is still noticeable, one finds underlying suggestions of conifers, aniseed and other aromatic notes. The palate corresponds nicely, but its relative lack of body detracts from its balance. The Cinque Terre Sciacchetrà is a Two Glass winner: it has a golden hue lightly tinged with amber; its bouquet is delicate and elegant (hints of apricot jam, dried figs and honey), followed by a corresponding, generous, velvety and well-balanced palate with a long, clean finish.

	Wine	Glasses	Price
○	Cinque Terre Sciacchetrà '96	🍷🍷	5
○	Cinque Terre '97	🍷	3
○	Cinque Terre Costa da Posa di Volastra '97	🍷	3
○	Cinque Terre Costa de Sèra di Riomaggiore '97	🍷	3
○	Cinque Terre Costa de Campo di Manarola '97		3

RIOMAGGIORE (SP)

WALTER DE BATTÈ
VIA PECUNIA, 168
19017 RIOMAGGIORE (SP)
TEL. 0187/920127

By way of homage to Burgundy, the inspiration for the wine-making methods of this winery, the "Hock" bottles of former years have been replaced by "Burgundy" bottles: the quality of the wine, however, remains unchanged. The dry version of Cinque Terre wasn't bottled until August, because Walter, in keeping with the intentions he expressed last year, has decided to release his wine only when he feels it is properly mature. We cannot refrain from thoroughly approving this policy, particularly after another tasting of the '95 and '96 vintages, which are delightfully improved after a further rest in the bottle. The '97, which we had a taste of before its release, shows a family likeness to its elder brothers. Its color is intense, and the fine, complex bouquet offers fruity and floral aromas delicately blended with a toasty note. On the palate it is well-balanced and harmoniously meaty. The Cinque Terre Sciacchetrà is outstanding; indeed it came within a hair of winning Three Glasses and is unquestionably the best sweet wine from Liguria we tasted this year. It has a warm amber hue and clear, delicate perfumes of dried apricot, cocoa and walnut skins. On the aristocratic and perfectly corresponding palate it is beautifully harmonious and not at all cloying, with smooth tannins and a backbone of acidity in exquisite balance. It is enticingly drinkable and characterful, with a personality of its own. High marks for this young "vigneron" who, while keeping abreast of technical advances, does not forget the experience and efforts of those who have done this work here before him.

O	Cinque Terre Sciacchetrà '95	ΨΨ	6
O	Cinque Terre '97	ΨΨ	4

S. BIAGIO DELLA CIMA (IM)

RODOLFO BIAMONTI
VIA A. MOLINARI, 7
18030 S. BIAGIO DELLA CIMA (IM)
TEL. 0184/289461

Reserved; calm in word and deed; an excellent host and a traditionalist as far as viticulture and wine-making are concerned: these are the salient characteristics we discovered on first meeting Rodolfo Biamonti, a youthful sixty-three-year-old whose whole life has been engaged, body and soul, with the earth. His wife Clelia, a lively and energetic lady who knows what she's about, helps him run this tiny estate which produces just a few thousand bottles. Until the early '80s the wine was sold in bulk, as it had been in Rodolfo's father's time; thereafter, partly to show off a wine pleasing to all the senses, Rodolfo decided to change tack. His vineyards are called Novilla, Pinella and Luvaira (the most highly prized), and they harbor some very old vines. These are mainly of rossese and, to a lesser extent, massarda, a grape variety of ancient and uncertain origin which was once widely cultivated near Imperia. In the winery, stainless steel long ago replaced the old barrels, and the wine-making equipment is modest but perfectly adequate. The vinification procedure is of a straightforward simplicity: ten to twelve days' maceration; natural malolactic fermentation; rackings, but no fining. The results are astonishing. The '97 Rossese di Dolceacqua really is exceptional: it has an inviting ruby red color, and is fragrant on the nose, with well-defined scents of ripe berries (including blackberry and black currant) and light hints of tamarind tisane, all mirrored on the palate which is powerful as well as soft and well-balanced: a Rossese that is definitely among the best we tasted this year.

●	Rossese di Dolceacqua '97	ΨΨ	3*

SOLDANO (IM)

ENZO GUGLIELMI
C.SO VERBONE, 143
18030 SOLDANO (IM)
TEL. 0184/289042

Soldano is one of the towns that rebelled against Ventimiglia in 1686 and founded an independent republic (the "Magnifica Comunità degli Otto Luoghi") which lasted until 1797, when the Ligurian Republic was formed. The town, rich in wine-making history and traditions, has always been "primus inter pares" for the quality of its Rossese. Enzo Guglielmi is an experienced winegrower: it's in his blood, and he continues to earn his living by the sweat of his brow among the rows of vines of his estate, as his forebears did. An important reason for his success is the two-hectare vineyard he owns (in a particularly favorable site by virtue of its climate, soil and position) in the most highly prized zone of Soldano, I Pini, renowned for extremely seductive Rosseses. The vines are of a perfect age for producing good grapes, which are then vinified by means of techniques judiciously combining modernity and tradition. Enzo's labors have once again been rewarded this year, confirming the constantly improving quality of his wines, which is also due to the continued assistance of the oenologist Giampaolo Ramo. The DOC regulations about Rossese Superiore require that the wines be released the November of the year following the harvest, so some wines were not altogether ready for our tastings. Such was in fact the case with this Rossese, which is still a bit dumb on the nose but already very attractive on the palate, which is succulent, warm, deep and concentrated, with a subtle and restrained bitterish undertone.

● Rossese di Dolceacqua Sup. '97 ꝉ 4

VENDONE (SV)

CLAUDIO VIO
FRAZ. CROSA, 16
17030 VENDONE (SV)
TEL. 0182/76338 - 76297

By an odd quirk of fate, Claudio Vio has not yet succeeded in taking his two wines, Vermentino and Pigato, simultaneously over the Two Glass threshold. This strange state of affairs continues with the '97 vintage. The excellent Vermentino is a deep straw-yellow in color with delicate green highlights, and has an intense, persistent and clean bouquet with delicate and varied aromas of herbs, wildflowers (broom, anise) and citrus fruit, as well as woodland scents: in the mouth it reveals a good grip; it is soft, and rich in alcohol well balanced by a refreshing vein of acidity; it evolves well on the palate, with a pleasing faintly bitter undertone. The Pigato, though, is slightly below par. Like all of Claudio's wines it displays the winery's trademark depth of color. The nose is less immediate than that of the Vermentino, but it does give indications of future richness with its unusual initially floral (rose) tones which then give way to vegetal, aromatic notes and hints of orange peel, all reflected on the pleasantly crisp and dry palate. Finesse rather than power is its strong suit, and its evolution on the palate could be improved. The finish leaves one's mouth clean and dry, and enlivened by a lightly lemony tone. This family-run estate consists of about five hectares divided into various particular vineyards almost entirely planted with white grapes; there is also a very small production of red grapes of the indigenous croetto variety, from which Claudio makes just a few bottles of a refreshing red wine.

○ Riviera Ligure di Ponente Vermentino '97 ꝉꝉ 3*
○ Riviera Ligure di Ponente Pigato '97 ꝉ 3

OTHER WINERIES

The following producers obtained good scores in our tastings with one or more of their wines:

PROVINCE OF GENOVA

Domenico Barisone
Genova-Coronata, tel. 010/6516534,
Bianco di Coronata '97

Andrea Bruzzone
Genova-Bolzaneto, tel. 010/7455157,
Bianchetta Genovese '97,
Valpolcevera Rosso '97

F.lli Parma
Ne, tel. 0185/337073,
Golfo del Tigullio Vermentino '97,
Golfo del Tigullio Vermentino I Canselé '97

PROVINCE OF IMPERIA

Laura Aschero
Pontedassio, tel. 0183/293515,
Riviera Ligure di Ponente Pigato '97,
Riviera Ligure di Ponente Vermentino '97

Montali e Temesio
Diano Marina, tel. 0183/495207,
Riviera Ligure di Ponente Vermentino '97,
Riviera Ligure di Ponente Vermentino Vigna Sorì '97

Antonio Perrino
Dolceacqua, tel. 0184/206267,
Rossese di Dolceacqua '97

Lorenzo Ramò
Pornassio, tel. 0183/33097,
Riviera Ligure di Ponente Ormeasco '97,
Riviera Ligure di Ponente Ormeasco Sciac-trà '97

PROVINCE OF LA SPEZIA

Forlini e Cappellini
Riomaggiore, tel. 0187/920496,
Cinque Terre '97

Luciana Giacomelli
Castelnuovo Magra, tel. 0187/674155,
Colli di Luni Vermentino '97

Fattoria Il Chioso
Arcola, tel. 0187/986620,
Colli di Luni Vermentino Stemma '97,
Colli di Luni Ciliegiolo '97

Il Monticello
Sarzana, tel. 0187/621432,
Colli di Luni Rosso '97,
Colli di Luni Vermentino '97

Santa Caterina
Sarzana, tel. 0187/610129,
Colli di Luni Vermentino '97

PROVINCE OF SAVONA

Filippo Ruffino
Varigotti, tel. 019/698522,
Riviera Ligure di Ponente Pigato '97,
Mataossu '97

LOMBARDY

Lombardy reaches a record with this issue of the Guide: a good nine wines have won our highest award, a result that only a few years ago would have seemed more like science fiction than reality. What is behind this performance, this unprecedented success? We can assure you that our standards haven't changed one iota since the Guide's first edition. We still taste all samples blind, with tasting panels made up of expert tasters. The top-rated wines then undergo a further series of control tastings and only those that retain the highest of scores throughout are awarded the prized Three Glasses. All this explanation serves merely to emphasize that behind Lombardy's achievement is an indisputable stride forward in quality throughout the region. Oltrepò Pavese, for example, where numerous estates have, in these past few years, been turning out increasingly fine wines, missed having one in our top category by a hair. Its fine rieslings, good pinot noirs, notable Oltrepò Pavese Rossos and its Metodo Classico sparkling wines of merit paint a rich, fascinating picture of the spirit of revitalization and the dedication to experimentation which abound. But the real star of Lombardy remains Franciacorta, this year decorated with six top-level awards. There is little left to say about estates such as Ca' del Bosco and Bellavista: these names are always to be found in lists of leading wine producers. Ca' del Bosco's Franciacorta Cuvée Annamaria Clementi and its Chardonnay are two wines of international standing. And Bellavista's Riserva Vittorio Moretti '91 is as good as, if not better than, the previous vintage, which was stupendous. Then there's Uberti, showing pure class with Magnificentia, a wine that continues to prove itself great year after year. There were surprises too. Among the most rewarding was the return of Cavalleri to the gold medallists' list with a Franciacorta Collezione '93 of supreme elegance. But the zone's real debutant this year is Monte Rossa. Its Franciacorta Cabochon '93, a wine of the most elegant refinement, is the best the estate has ever produced. In Valtellina, Nino Negri's Sfursat 5 Stelle '96 is no longer the only wine to hold the banner aloft in this core of Alpine winemaking: it is now partnered by Sfursat Ca' Rizzieri '95 from Rainoldi of Chiuro, a wine of remarkable depth and complexity. However the awards list would not be complete without the Garda area and this year, for the first time, its vineyards have given birth to a top-ranking wine. The prize goes to an estate in Sirmione, Ca' dei Frati, whose wines of impeccable style have long been hovering around the top of the tree. Their Il Pratto '96 captures all the attributes one could ever wish to find in a great white wine: full structure, breadth, intense fragrances and great aromatic length. In short, it has a fabulous balance sheet and we ardently hope this success will not be just a fluke. Such an array of wines surely demonstrates without doubt that wine-making in Lombardy has come of age. Even so we firmly believe that it will improve even further.

ADRO (BS)

COLA
VIA SANT'ANNA, 22
25030 ADRO (BS)
TEL. 030/7356195

Battista and Stefano Cola, father and son, and true "vignerons", run their estate in Adro with great dedication and commitment. It boasts 12 hectares of well-exposed vineyard lying on the rocky slopes of Monte Alto, where the use of tractors or other mechanization is well-nigh impossible. Assisted by consultant oenologist Alberto Musatti (Stefano is still at college studying agronomy), they are producing an attractive series of still wines and Franciacortas. This year the most interesting of the latter is without doubt the Franciacorta Extra Brut '94, which announces its fullness and intensity even in its color, a good deep straw flecked with gold. It has a rich nose with notes of ripe fruits, yeast and toasted bread which give way to appealing spicy tones that are reflected on the palate too. The mouth-feel of the mousse is soft and gentle and the wine is deep, full and well-balanced. The non-vintage Brut has youthful aromas and good character, underlined by fresh fruity notes together with an attractive softness, although we would have appreciated a touch more structure. The still white wines are as good as ever, particularly Terre Bianco Tinazza, although the '96 is possibly a little over-evolved and over-ripe. We will defer judgment on the red Tamino '96 until the next edition of the Guide.

○	Franciacorta Extra Brut '94	▼▼	4
○	Franciacorta Brut	▼	4
○	T. d. F. Bianco '97	▼	2*
○	T. d. F. Bianco V. Tinazza '96	▼	3
○	Franciacorta Brut	♀♀	4
○	Franciacorta Extra Brut '92	♀♀	4
○	T. d. F. Bianco V. Tinazza '95	♀♀	3
●	Franciacorta Rosso '93	♀	3
●	T. d. F. Rosso '95	♀	2
●	T. d. F. Rosso Tamino '95	♀	3

ADRO (BS)

CONTADI CASTALDI
VIA COLZANO, 52
25030 ADRO (BS)
TEL. 030/7450126

This up-and-coming Franciacorta estate is rapidly consolidating its position in our Guide after its first appearance last year. The winery forms part of Gruppo Terre Moretti, whose main estate is Bellavista. Its operation is in the sure hands of Martino De Rosa, who has entrusted the technical side to a gifted oenologist, Mario Falcetti. As well as managing around 30 hectares of leased vineyard, the estate buys a goodly part of the grapes for its numerous cuvées in the manner of a "négociant-manipulant". This allows Falcetti to select from some of the best parcels of land in the Franciacorta zone each year, and as a result he creates blends of particular opulence. We can do no less than pay tribute to his meticulousness and competence, and what better way than by raising a toast with a glass of his Franciacorta Brut? Indeed, this standard estate wine is particularly rich and attractive this year. A very fine perlage and a complex, sweet nose with notes of vanilla, white peaches, yeasts and toffee lead to a creamy, soft taste, with bubbles that lightly caress the palate before ceding their place to the wine itself: fully structured, well fruited and finishing with long-lasting honeyed tones. Not bad for a "simple" Brut. The Satèn is just as fascinating, with entrancing spicy notes, delicate aromas and well-judged "dosage". The Rosé seemed a little too slim and slightly over-evolved, but Zero, the Extra Brut, maintained its good standard. The still wines were good too.

○	Franciacorta Brut	▼▼	4
○	Franciacorta Satèn	▼▼	5
⊙	Franciacorta Rosé	▼	5
○	Franciacorta Zero	▼	5
○	T. d. F. Bianco '97	▼	3
●	T. d. F. Rosso '96	▼	3
○	Franciacorta Brut	♀♀	4*
⊙	Franciacorta Rosé	♀♀	5
○	Franciacorta Satèn	♀♀	5
○	T. d. F. Bianco '96	♀♀	3*

ADRO (BS)

CORNALETO
VIA CORNALETO, 2
25030 ADRO (BS)
TEL. 030/7450507 - 7450565

After several years in which the wines of Cornaleto gave us the impression of being somewhat below the estate's potential, we can now celebrate the return to the Guide of this fine estate, ideally with a magnum of its first-rate Brut '89 that we tasted this year. When we say "first-rate", though, we don't mean simply very good: this Franciacorta came perilously close to reaching our very highest category. Here's why: it has a beautifully bright greenish straw color, a long-lasting, fine perlage and refined, intense aromas giving scents of ripe white fruits, vegetal hints and the most elegant touches of vanilla. It is soft, balanced, mouth-filling, round and harmonious on the palate with plentiful (although not exceptional) length. In short, it is a gem. Its style and attractiveness are echoed in the Extra Brut, a broadly nuanced, full, soft wine that few in this category can match. Its class leaves no doubt about the high quality of the grapes used, the determination of the Lancini brothers to make wines of note and the abilities of Cesare Ferrini, the estate's consultant oenologist. The two still white wines are also of good standard: Saline '96, despite a slight imbalance of oak, and Terre di Franciacorta '97, which offers fresh aromas of ripe melon but on the palate finishes slightly citric and a touch short. Currently the two '95 reds, Baldoc and Poligono, are somewhat less convincing and so we are holding their evaluation over to the next edition.

○	Franciacorta Brut '89	🍷🍷	5
○	Franciacorta Extra Brut	🍷🍷	4
○	T. d. F. Bianco '97	🍷	3
○	T. d. F. Bianco V. Saline '96	🍷	4
○	Franciacorta Extra Brut	YY	4
●	Franciacorta Rosso Cornaleto '90	YY	3
●	Franciacorta Rosso Poligono '90	YY	3
○	Franciacorta Brut '88	Y	4
●	Franciacorta Rosso Poligono '91	Y	3
○	T. d. F. Bianco V. Saline '95	Y	3

CAMIGNONE (BS)

CATTURICH DUCCO
VIA DEGLI EROI, 5
25040 CAMIGNONE (BS)
TEL. 030/6850566

With over half a million bottles produced each year and a history stretching back to the late 1960s when Franciacorta production was in its infancy, the estate of Count Piero Catturich Ducco is one of the most significant in the area. In recent years the quality of its production has been improving consistently, and today the estate can offer a carefully honed range, with the bonus of being good value for money. The 'starter' wine, non-vintage Franciacorta Brut, gains plaudits for its bright, light straw color, its creamy mousse and its clean, fresh aromas that are perfectly matched on the palate. The "dosage" is well-integrated, the flavors well fruited and it is round, balanced and of decent length. The Brut selection Torre Ducco almost gained a Two Glass score (a target it is quite capable of reaching, as last year proved). It has well-knit aromas of yeasts and toasted bread, reveals good structure on the palate and has an excellent mousse, but its style is just slightly over-evolved. The Rosé Demi-Sec is attractive and full of soft tones although we would have appreciated a deeper color and more decisive perfumes; the Pas Dosé '93 has a good, bright, greenish straw color, fine, fresh, intense perfumes, and an elegant palate suggestive of white fruits with vegetal tones, yet it lacks length. The two still wines are perfectly correct but would benefit from further fine-tuning.

○	Franciacorta Brut	🍷	4
○	Franciacorta Brut Torre Ducco	🍷	4
○	Franciacorta Pas Dosé '93	🍷	4
⊙	Franciacorta Rosé Démi-Sec	🍷	4
○	T. d. F. Bianco '97		2
●	T. d. F. Rosso '96		2
○	Franciacorta Brut Torre Ducco	YY	4
○	Franciacorta Pas Dosé '92	Y	4

CANNETO PAVESE (PV)

BRUNO VERDI
VIA VERGOMBERRA, 5
27044 CANNETO PAVESE (PV)
TEL. 0385/88023

Verdi's winery has so far always shown reliable consistency of quality. It is situated at Vergomberra in Canneto Pavese, on the first slopes of the Oltrepò Pavese hills, lands which are particularly suited for red wine production, although the whites are not at all bad either. Every so often the estate produces a Two Glass wine (for instance, its Riesling Renano Vigneto Costa '96 last year), and as a rule it maintains a level of quality that is more than respectable. In this edition it has several wines that easily attain One Glass and there are clear signs of further improvements on the way. Paolo Verdi, Bruno's son, has expanded the estate's already impressive technological apparatus with a modern pneumatic press and a crusher-destemmer. Given the good grapes their vineyards yield, this will enable them to produce whites of greater character without problems with polyphenols, and softer, more rounded reds. The first results are already to be seen with the '97 vintage: a Bonarda Vivace, dark ruby in color, savory and redolent of blackberry and violet, is very good; the Moscato, with an inviting aroma of orange flowers, risks being almost too rich; the Riesling Renano is delightful, even though a touch more acidic backbone would have helped; the Pinot Nero is full and rounded. From previous vintages a dry, spicy Rosso Oltrepò Pavese Riserva '93 from the Cavariola vineyard stands out.

	Wine	Glasses	
●	O. P. Bonarda Vivace '97	🍷	3
○	O. P. Moscato '97	🍷	2
○	O. P. Pinot Grigio '97	🍷	3
○	O. P. Riesling Renano '97	🍷	3
●	O. P. Rosso Ris. Cavariola '93	🍷	4
●	O. P. Barbera '90	YY	3
●	O. P. Bonarda '93	YY	3
○	O. P. Moscato '95	YY	2*
○	O. P. Riesling Renano Vign. Costa '96	YY	3
●	O. P. Rosso Ris. Cavariola '90	YY	4
●	O. P. Bonarda Vivace '96	Y	3
○	O. P. Brut Cl. Vergomberra '95	Y	4
○	O. P. Moscato '96	Y	2
●	O. P. Rosso Ris. Cavariola '91	Y	4

CAPRIOLO (BS)

LANTIERI DE PARATICO
VIA PARATICO, 50
25031 CAPRIOLO (BS)
TEL. 030/736151

Lack of space forced us to consign this estate to the sidelines last year and it had to be satisfied with a mere mention at the end of the Lombardy section. Such treatment would be impossible this year, given the quality of the Franciacortas sent to our tastings, in particular a vintage and an Extra Brut. Neither has ever merited fewer than Two Glasses, a confirmation of stylistic and technical know-how that places the estate among Franciacorta's best. The vintage, Franciacorta Brut '94 has a delightful, greenish-tinged color and excellently formed bubbles, but it is in its bouquet that it particularly excels. This evokes a large array of fruits including some of tropical origin, plus subtle hints of citrus, mint and vanilla. On the palate it demonstrates that a marriage of structure and elegance is more than possible; and that's not all: it has great length as well. The Extra Brut is among the most attractive of the wines made in this style and has sweet, elegant perfumes with a full, creamy palate of good acidity. The Brut is also good, with everything playing on the freshness of its fruity aromas and its citrus, floral overtones, which reveal a sure hand in the amount of "liqueur d'expédition" used. Both the fresh white Terre di Franciacorta '97 and the two '96 red versions are well made and of interest.

	Wine	Glasses	
○	**Franciacorta Brut '94**	🍷🍷	5
○	**Franciacorta Extra Brut**	🍷🍷	4
○	Franciacorta Brut	🍷	4
○	T. d. F. Bianco '97	🍷	3
●	T. d. F. Rosso '96	🍷	3
●	T. d. F. Rosso Colzano '96	🍷	4

CAPRIOLO (BS)

Ricci Curbastro

Via Adro, 37
25031 Capriolo (BS)
tel. 030/736094

In the past few years the Ricci Curbastro estate has made significant steps forward and today finds itself among Franciacorta's best. The power behind this family-run house (whose annual production hovers around 80 thousand bottles) is Riccardo Ricci Curbastro, a dynamic, passionately dedicated and enterprising producer, who also finds time to act as president of numerous organizations, including the Consorzio Vini Franciacorta (Franciacorta Wine Consortium). The standard of the Franciacortas that Riccardo makes together with his consultant oenologist Alberto Musatti can best be judged from the Satèn. This has a bright straw color with intense greenish tinges. It offers a broad sweep of aromas which range from damsons to white plums and from sage to vanilla and yeasts. The mouthfeel of the effervescence is gentle; the palate is delicate and refined, with dominant flavours of ripe white fruits which give way to a captivating note of vanilla. The Franciacorta Demi-Sec has an attractive balance and reveals very fine nuances of fruits and herbs on the nose, while its palate is broad, soft and full, with fresh acidity and fruitiness. We also liked the Extra Brut '94, despite its being slightly over-evolved for its vintage, and the basic Brut, which is characterized by its customary fruity freshness. Among the still wines, produced with the aid of the New Zealand oenologist Owen J. Bird, an excellent barrique-matured Pinot Nero stands out. It is rich and elegant, perfumed and characteristically varietal, and has fine tannins and good length: it is probably the most interesting of its type that we tasted in Franciacorta this year.

	Wine	Glasses	Price
○	Franciacorta Satèn '93	🍷🍷	4
●	Pinot Nero Sebino '95	🍷🍷	4
○	Franciacorta Brut	🍷	4
○	Franciacorta Démi Sec	🍷	4
○	Franciacorta Extra Brut '94	🍷	5
○	T. d. F. Bianco '97	🍷	3
○	T. d. F. Bianco Vigna Bosco Alto '96	🍷	4
●	T. d. F. Rosso Santella del Gröm '95	🍷	4
○	Franciacorta Brut Magnum '91	🍸🍸	5
○	Franciacorta Extra Brut '93	🍸🍸	4*
○	Franciacorta Satèn	🍸🍸	4*
○	Franciacorta Satèn '92	🍸🍸	4*
○	T. d. F. Bianco '96	🍸	2
○	T. d. F. Bianco Vigna Bosco Alto '95	🍸	3

CASTEGGIO (PV)

Frecciarossa

Via Vigorelli, 141
27045 Casteggio (PV)
tel. 0383/804465

Frecciarossa has prestige, history, well-sited vineyards and well-equipped cellars; moreover it boasts the consultancy of Franco Bernabei, an oenologist of proven abilities and notable experience. And yet the estate somehow fails to express its great potential to the full. Let there be no mistake: the wines are good, and if they came from any other estate they would probably be more than good enough. But we are talking about Frecciarossa. From an estate whose buildings go back to the 18th century and which obtained an official national export permit as early as 1934, it is surely reasonable to expect somewhat more. Indeed, it should be a case of "noblesse oblige". This year One Glass is awarded to the Riesling Renano '97: its color is bright green-gold, there are fresh fragrances of apples and lemon balm with light mineral scents, but it is a little unripe on the palate; the wine is played for finesse more than vigor. The Oltrepò Pavese Rosso Le Praielle '96 is elegant and spicy yet already clearly in its tertiary stage of development. A bright garnet color; delicate perfumes of black currant jam, toasty oak and sweet spices; mature, savory flavors with good length mark out the Pinot Nero '94, matured for twelve months in French oak barriques. On the other hand the Villa Odero '93 Rosso Oltrepò Pavese is already too mature: the development of both bouquet and taste is practically at its limit.

	Wine	Glasses	Price
●	O. P. Pinot Nero '94	🍷	4
○	O. P. Riesling Renano '97	🍷	4
●	O. P. Rosso Le Praielle '96	🍷	4
●	O. P. Rosso Villa Odero Ris. '93		4
●	O. P. Pinot Nero '91	🍸🍸	5
●	O. P. Rosso '90	🍸🍸	5
●	O. P. Rosso Ris. Villa Odero '90	🍸🍸	5
●	O. P. Rosso Villa Odero '89	🍸🍸	5
●	O. P. Rosso Villa Odero '91	🍸🍸	4
●	O. P. Pinot Nero '90	🍸	5
●	O. P. Pinot Nero '93	🍸	4
●	O. P. Rosso Villa Odero '92	🍸	3
●	O. P. Rosso Villa Odero Ris. '91	🍸	4

CASTEGGIO (PV)

LE FRACCE
VIA CASTEL DEL LUPO, 5
27045 CASTEGGIO (PV)
TEL. 0383/804151

For some time Francesco Cervetti, the oenologist who directs this organically farmed estate owned by Lina Branca Bussolera and the Fondazione Ferdinando, has produced better whites than reds. In the 1998 Guide it was the Riesling Renano that stood out, this year it is the Pinot Grigio, one of the best in the Oltrepò, while the reds (apart from Bohemi, one of the more important Riservas) seem somewhat overshadowed. Let's start with the Pinot Grigio '97, produced, as is the custom at Le Fracce, from grapes grown without any use of herbicides, insecticides or anti-rot treatments. The grapes, hand-picked, were ripe and healthy and gave over 13% of alcohol while retaining good acidity (5.8 gr/l). The resultant wine is bright and pale straw-colored, with full aromas of acacia blossom, apples and pears, and with a rich, round, long-lasting taste: it fully deserves its Two Glasses. The Riesling Renano is also good, with flavors of lemon balm and wild peach; it is still slightly sharp but will improve in bottle. The Rosso Oltrepò Cirgà '96 (whose name derives from a hilltop site beside a small circular rose garden whose form recalls a "chierica" or monkish tonsure) is interesting but has more power than elegance. The Rosso '97 Villa Rajna (named after the old manor house of Mairano) is worthy of note: when tasted it was developing nicely.

○	O. P. Pinot Grigio '97	🍷🍷	4
○	O. P. Riesling Renano '97	🍷	4
●	O. P. Rosso Cirgà '96	🍷	5
●	O. P. Rosso Villa Rajana '97		4
●	O. P. Bonarda '94	🍷🍷	4
●	O. P. Bonarda '95	🍷🍷	4
○	O. P. Pinot Grigio '93	🍷🍷	4
○	O. P. Pinot Grigio '95	🍷🍷	4
○	O. P. Riesling Renano '96	🍷🍷	4
●	O. P. Rosso Bohemi '90	🍷🍷	5
●	O. P. Rosso Cirgà '90	🍷🍷	5
●	O. P. Rosso Cirgà '91	🍷🍷	5
○	O. P. Extra Brut Cuvée Bussolera '95	🍷	4
○	O. P. Pinot Grigio '96	🍷	4

CAZZAGO S. MARTINO (BS)

CASTELFAGLIA
FRAZ. CALINO
LOC. BOSCHI, 3
25040 CAZZAGO S. MARTINO (BS)
TEL. 059/908828

The range of wines from CastelFaglia is growing. This promising new estate is owned by Cavicchioli, one of the most noted names in classic Lambrusco production. The Cavicchioli family, which follows Castelfaglia personally, currently produces something like 130 thousand bottles split between Franciacortas and still wines. It all comes from grapes grown exclusively on their 15 hectares of well-exposed, well-sited hillside vineyard. The debut of Franciacorta Monogram Brut '91 has been a fortunate one thanks to the good vintage. That and the technical abilities of Sandro Cavicchioli, the estate's oenologist, have produced a wine of bright, greenish straw color, tiny, tightly-packed bubbles and intense, soft aromas of yeast and toasty oak. The palate is round, fresh, rich in flavors of fruit and toasted bread, finishing with elegant vanilla traces. The non-vintage Brut Monogram is pale straw in color with aromas of fresh almonds and white flowers, while on the palate it is pleasingly creamy and floral. We felt, though, that both the Brut, with its positive notes of yeast and fruits, and the Extra Brut, with its slightly inexpressive aromas and its somewhat thin body, were correct but less exciting. Among the still wines we found the Terre di Franciacorta Bianco '97 and Rosso '96, both from the Castelletto line, interesting; while of the two standard wines we had a distinct preference for the red.

○	Franciacorta Brut Monogram '91	🍷🍷	5
○	Franciacorta Brut	🍷	4
○	Franciacorta Brut Monogram	🍷	4
○	Franciacorta Extra Brut	🍷	4
○	T. d. F. Bianco Vigneti del Castelletto '96	🍷	3
○	T. d. F. Bianco Vigneti del Castelletto '97	🍷	3
●	T. d. F. Rosso '96	🍷	3
●	T. d. F. Rosso Vigneti del Castelletto '96	🍷	3
○	T. d. F. Bianco '97		3
○	Franciacorta Brut	🍷🍷	4*
●	T. d. F. Rosso Castello di Calino '95	🍷	3

CAZZAGO S. MARTINO (BS)

GUARISCHI

FRAZ. CALINO
VIA PAOLO VI, 62
25040 CAZZAGO S. MARTINO (BS)
TEL. 030/7250838 - 775005

For several years now Guarischi, located in Calino, an outlying part of Cazzago San Martino, has been producing carefully honed, impeccable wines which sit comfortably among Franciacorta's best. This year we award the honors to an excellent Franciacorta Brut '92 which comes close to joining "la crème de la crème". It has a lovely bright greenish straw color and thickly-packed, long-lasting bubbles of great finesse, but perhaps its aromas are its most fascinating feature. They are intense, incredibly fresh for a vintaged wine and evocative of sage and spices, candied peel and yeasts. The palate is soft, well-fruited, pleasantly redolent of vanilla, full and long. The non-vintage Brut is also good: round, harmonious, soft, enticing and suggestive of yeasts and crusty bread, yet not without a certain body. Terre Rosso Le Solcaie '95, a barrique-aged blend of cabernet franc, merlot, barbera and nebbiolo, has a deep ruby color and notable concentration; on the palate it reveals spicy notes, refined vegetal nuances, soft tannins and great attractiveness despite still being a little closed. Among the whites it is the Terre di Franciacorta Bianco Le Solcaie '96 that stands out, with its complex aromas of peaches, pears and ripe Golden Delicious apples, its elegantly vegetal notes and its very carefully judged hint of oak. The palate is notably firm and balanced, and yields the same aromatic sensations found on the nose. Congratulations to the oenologist, Signor Azzolini, who has also produced two worthy standard Terre di Franciacorta wines.

	Wine	Glasses	Price
○	Franciacorta Brut '92	🍷🍷	5
○	T. d. F. Bianco Le Solcaie '96	🍷🍷	4
●	T. d. F. Rosso Le Solcaie '95	🍷🍷	4
○	Franciacorta Brut	🍷	4
○	T. d. F. Bianco '97	🍷	3
●	T. d. F. Rosso '96	🍷	3
○	Franciacorta Bianco Le Solcaie '93	YY	3
○	Franciacorta Brut	YY	4*
○	Franciacorta Brut Selezione '91	YY	5
●	Franciacorta Rosso Le Solcaie '92	YY	3
●	Franciacorta Rosso Le Solcaie '93	YY	3
○	T. d. F. Bianco Le Solcaie '95	YY	4
●	T. d. F. Rosso Le Solcaie '94	YY	4

CAZZAGO S. MARTINO (BS)

MONTE ROSSA

FRAZ. BORNATO
VIA MARENZIO, 14
25040 CAZZAGO S. MARTINO (BS)
TEL. 030/725066

After moving ever closer over the past three years, Monte Rossa has finally reached a goal of great importance. In blind tastings of the vintage sparkling wines of Franciacorta and all Italy, their Franciacorta Brut Cabochon '93 lined up with the absolute top of the tree and consequently received the fabled Three Glasses. It is a success for the entire estate, which works with commitment and professionalism and which has always sat easily among Franciacorta's best. We hope that Paolo Rabotti, who, with his wife Paola, owns this fine house, will not be offended if we say that we consider this also a personal success for his son Emanuele, who has given Monte Rossa a decided nudge forward in quality since his arrival at the estate. The '93 Cabochon, a gem if there ever was one, has a deep straw color, a creamy mousse and the finest of bubbles. The richness and complexity of its aromas, which range from white-fleshed fruit such as apples, peaches and plums, to more exotic ones, and its final floral, spicy tones are enthralling enrapturing. Its creamy effervescence entices and there is great breadth on the palate, which is complex, full, balanced and of great length. In short, it's marvelous. But Cabochon is only the peak of a top-quality range which, unfortunately, we have to review summarily for reasons of space. The Satèn is a seductive wine, with its fresh, fruity softness and its elegant, vanilla-studded flavors. The Extra Brut '93 has all the structure, elegance and fullness befitting a vintage wine from a good year, but expressed with the typical Monte Rossa refinement. Finally, the Brut and the Terre Bianco Ravellino '97 are also very good.

	Wine	Glasses	Price
○	Franciacorta Brut Cabochon '93	🍷🍷🍷	5
○	Franciacorta Brut Satèn	🍷🍷	5
○	Franciacorta Extra Brut '93	🍷🍷	5
○	Franciacorta Brut	🍷	4
○	T. d. F. Bianco Ravellino '97	🍷	2
○	Franciacorta Brut	YY	4*
○	Franciacorta Brut Cabochon '90	YY	5
○	Franciacorta Brut Cabochon '92	YY	5
○	Franciacorta Brut Satèn	YY	5
○	Franciacorta Brut Satèn	YY	5
○	Franciacorta Extra Brut '92	YY	5
○	Franciacorta Sec	YY	4
●	T. d. F. Rosso Cèp '95	YY	3*

CENATE SOTTO (BG)

Monzio Compagnoni
Via degli Alpini, 3
24069 Cenate Sotto (BG)
tel. 030/9884157 - 940311

For reasons of space we are combining the listings of Marcello Monzio Compagnoni's two estates, the "historic" one in Valcalepio and the new Franciacorta branch. This latter, which from its first appearance in the Guide last year fitted right in among the area's best, is leased from the heirs of the Barons Monti della Corte. The Franciacorta Brut is excellent, even though not as full and structured as the previous release. It is rich in aromas of honey and ripe fruit, round and soft on the palate, and it finishes with a lightly bitter tang. However, in our judgment, the best wine of the estate this year is Ronco della Seta '97, a Terre di Franciacorta with a good greenish straw color, a nose rich in aromas of tropical fruit and herbs (sage, mint), and a palate that demonstrates uncommon levels of structure and balance. It is harmonious in the true sense of the word and remarkably long. The barrique-matured Bianco della Seta '95 has aromas of ripe fruit and flavors rich in vanilla but is a little over-evolved, while Ronco della Seta Rosso '96 seemed reasonable enough. Among the Valcalepio wines an excellent Rosso di Nero '95 from 100% pinot noir stands out: it is concentrated, harmonious and has a perfect balance of varietal flavors and more spicy ones acquired from the new wood. It is backed by a range of enviable level, from Monzio Compagnoni Brut, a round, vanilla-rich Metodo Classico sparkling wine, to Colle della Luna Bianco '97, a floral blend of chardonnay and pinot blanc of good length, to Colle della Luna Rosso '96, a warm, fruited Bordeaux blend. A final excellent red is Rosso di Luna '95, a concentrated, barrique-aged cabernet sauvignon with notably elegant tannins.

●	Rosso di Luna '95	▼▼	4
●	Rosso di Nero '95	▼▼	4
○	T. d. F. Bianco Ronco della Seta '97	▼▼	3*
○	Colle della Luna Bianco '97	▼	3
●	Colle della Luna Rosso '96	▼	3
○	Franciacorta Brut	▼	4
○	Monzio Compagnoni Brut M. Cl.	▼	4
○	T. d. F. Bianco della Seta '95	▼	4
●	T. d. F. Rosso Ronco della Seta '96	▼	3
●	Moscato di Scanzo Passito Don Quijote '95	▽▽	5

CHIURO (SO)

Nino Negri
Via Ghibellini, 3
23030 Chiuro (SO)
tel. 0342/482521

Casimiro Maule, recently appointed president of the new Valtellina Wine Consortium, has long been at the helm of this, the most important estate of the zone. The winery is well rooted in the territory, both culturally and economically, and is fitted out with the ultimate in modern cellar equipment. It also owns stupendous vineyards in some of the best sites of the zone. Strangely, though, it has only recently gone over to trial guyot-pruned plantings: three and a half hectares, all nebbiolo. If we now add that Negri is part of Gruppo Italiano Vini (GIV), you can begin to understand the continued qualitative growth of this exemplary wine-making set-up. In this edition of the Guide it once more wins Three Glasses for a supremely elegant version of Sfursat 5 Stelle '96. Less linear than usual in style, it is full and juicy on the nose, with well-integrated new oak and intense aromas of alcohol-steeped wild berries. Its palate is soft and diffuse, with rounded, ripe tannins and a dense and concentrated but velvety finish. Sfursat '96, regarded as more traditional because it's aged in large Slavonian oak casks, is as good as ever. The white Ca' Brione '97, made mainly from sauvignon, is surprising for the breadth of its aromas and the density of its flavors, and is the first white from Valtellina to be awarded Two Glasses. Sassella and Inferno Botti d'Oro '95 are both as correct, clean and drinkable as ever; lower down the scale is Fracia '95, slightly lacking in precision and with tannins that are a touch bitter.

●	Valtellina Sfursat 5 Stelle '96	▼▼▼	5
●	Valtellina Sfursat '96	▼▼	4
○	Vigneto Ca' Brione Bianco '97	▼▼	4
●	Valtellina Sup. Inferno Botti d'Oro '95	▼	3
●	Valtellina Sup. Sassella Botti d'Oro '95	▼	3
●	Valtellina Sup. Fracia '95		3
●	Valtellina Sfursat 5 Stelle '89	▽▽▽	5
●	Valtellina Sfursat 5 Stelle '94	▽▽▽	5
●	Valtellina Sfursat 5 Stelle '95	▽▽▽	5
●	Valtellina 1897 Centenario '95	▽▽	5
●	Valtellina Sfursat '95	▽▽	4
●	Valtellina Sfursat 5 Stelle '88	▽▽	5
●	Valtellina Sfursat 5 Stelle '90	▽▽	6

CHIURO (SO)

ALDO RAINOLDI
VIA STELVIO, 128
23030 CHIURO (SO)
TEL. 0342/482225

Giuseppe Rainoldi's great merit, which deserves wide recognition, is not simply that he had the courage to modernize the style of his wines, but that he did so with the sensitivity and care of one who has a clear understanding both of the markets in which they circulate and of the specific characteristics of the Valtellina's climate and grapes. This led to the need for high standards of technology in the cellar, investment in wood of the highest quality and comparative tasting and updating in Italy and abroad. Both Sfursat Ca' Rizzieri '95 and Crespino '95 show signs of the turnaround in this dynamic company. In the former we have an extraordinary wine, obtained from exquisitely semi-dried grapes which are then fermented and matured in new wood. Dense and syrupy, it is strikingly suggestive of alcohol-steeped black cherries with seductive hints of chocolate. Its richly soft taste is harmonious, majestic and long, with smooth, well-integrated tannins. An easy Three Glasses. The Crespino, another nebbiolo, is also macerated more briefly than tradition dictates. On the nose, fruity aromas stand out, but still in harmony with oak and spice; the palate is broad, with a fluid finish, deep and immensely pleasing. In some ways it is rather Burgundy-like. The Inferno and Sassella, both '95s, are characteristic and well made, with clean perfumes and attractive drinkability, while the Inferno Riserva '94 is well structured, spicy and warmly aromatic. Ghibellino '96 is as reliable as ever, with its singular citrus aromas and notable intensity on a well-rounded palate.

●	Valtellina Sfursat Ca' Rizzieri '95	🍷🍷🍷	5
●	Valtellina Sup. Crespino '95	🍷🍷	4
●	Valtellina Sup. Inferno Ris. '86	🍷🍷	4
●	Valtellina Sup. Inferno Barrique Ris. '94	🍷🍷	4
●	Valtellina Sup. Inferno '95	🍷	3
●	Valtellina Sup. Sassella '95	🍷	3
○	Bianco Ghibellino '96		4
●	Valtellina Sfursat '88	YY	5
●	Valtellina Sfursat '94	YY	4
●	Valtellina Sup. Inferno Ris. '89	YY	4
●	Valtellina Sup. Inferno Barrique Ris. '89	YY	5
●	Valtellina Sup. Inferno Barrique Ris. '86	YY	4
●	Valtellina Sup. Inferno Barrique Ris. '90	YY	4
●	Valtellina Sup. Sassella '90	YY	4

COCCAGLIO (BS)

TENUTA CASTELLINO
VIA S. PIETRO, 46
25030 COCCAGLIO (BS)
TEL. 030/7721015

Tenuta Castellino, owned by the Bonomi family, has given us some of the best bottles produced in Franciacorta in the last few years. This edition of the Guide, however, doesn't offer much that is new because after the excellent performance of the '93s reported on last year (and confirmed at each tasting since), the following year's vintage wines had not yet been released by the time of our tastings. Castellino's standard-bearer this year is an excellent Terre di Franciacorta Bianco '96 from the Solicano vineyard, an easy Two Glass winner. It has a good pale straw color and a nose rich in notes of Golden Delicious apples and white peaches, underpinned by delicate nuances of toasty oak. It is soft, stylish and balanced in the mouth, and the finish is particularly long. We found the Brut good: fragrantly yeasty and pleasantly crisp, and the two Terre di Franciacorta wines, the fresh, fruity Bianco '97 and the full and meaty Rosso '96, rich in smooth tannins, are both pleasing.

○	T. d. F. Bianco Solicano '96	🍷🍷	4
○	Franciacorta Brut	🍷	4
○	T. d. F. Bianco '97	🍷	3
●	T. d. F. Rosso '96	🍷	3
○	Franciacorta Brut '93	YY	5
○	Franciacorta Satèn '92	YY	4*
○	Franciacorta Satèn '93	YY	5
○	T. d. F. Bianco Solicano '95	YY	3*
●	Capineto '94	Y	4
○	T. d. F. Bianco '96	Y	3
●	T. d. F. Rosso '95	Y	3

COCCAGLIO (BS)

LORENZO FACCOLI & FIGLI
VIA CAVA, 7
25030 COCCAGLIO (BS)
TEL. 030/7722761

If Faccoli is, in size, one of Franciacorta's minor estates (four hectares of vineyard and an annual production of 40 thousand bottles), its quality is anything but, and we always find its wines among the high rankers. Lorenzo Faccoli is a man who lives and breathes vineyards and he is out in them daily. His sons Gian Mario and Claudio, who have long been helping him run the estate, have caught the bug as well. The Faccolis are specialists in white grapes and this year have a Franciacorta Brut to offer that takes your fancy from the moment you see its brilliant greenish straw color stippled with the tiniest of long-lasting bubbles. It has intense, remarkably complex fragrances: ripe fruit and citrus peel sitting beside delicate notes of incense and aromatic herbs. In the mouth it is perfectly balanced, full and reflective of the nose. One step below (but only a tiny step) is the classic Brut which suffers, we reckon, from too high a "dosage", which reduces its freshness. Nevertheless it is soft and attractive overall. The Terre di Franciacorta Bianco is as good and excellently priced as ever. We tasted the '97.

	Wine	Glasses	Price
○	Franciacorta Extra Brut	▼▼	4
○	Franciacorta Brut	▼	4
○	T. d. F. Bianco '97	▼	3
○	Franciacorta Brut	YY	4*
○	Franciacorta Extra Brut	YY	4
○	T. d. F. Bianco '96	Y	2

CODEVILLA (PV)

MONTELIO
VIA MAZZA, 1
27050 CODEVILLA (PV)
TEL. 0383/373090

On the occasion of its 150th anniversary this historical wine estate returns to the Guide. It has been owned by the Mazza Sesia family since 1802, but winegrowing didn't start until 1848. Out of a total landholding of 78 hectares there are now 27 hectares of vineyard surrounding the small hexagonal house on the top of Montelio (the sun is evoked by the second and Greek part of the name), and from them the current owner, Maria Rosa Sesia, working with the estate's oenologist, Mario Maffi, produces various fine wines. The pick of the lot this year turned out to be Comprino '95, a 100% merlot vinified with about ten days' maceration and matured for ten months in 25-hectoliter casks. Marketed in a special bottle like one in use a century and a half ago, the wine has a brilliant deep garnet hue, aromas of wild berry jam, clove and vanilla and a warm, harmonious, elegant flavor. Comprino '96, this time from 85% merlot together with other local varieties but without oak, is still developing but already looks promising. The Solarolo Rosso Riserva '94, a blend of barbera, croatina, uva rara and pinot noir, is elegant, spicy and well matured, while the Müller Thurgau '97 La Giostra is full and complex, with attractive varietal aromas. Brut La Stoppa '97 ("cuve close"), from chardonnay and cortese in equal proportions, is clean, floral, fruity and savory.

	Wine	Glasses	Price
●	Comprino Rosso '95	▼▼	4
○	Brut La Stroppa '97	▼	4
●	Comprino Rosso '96	▼	3
○	Müller Thurgau La Giostra '97	▼	4
●	O. P. Rosso Solarolo Ris. '94	▼	4
●	Comprino Rosso '90	YY	4
●	Comprino Rosso '90	YY	4
●	O. P. Pinot Nero '90	YY	4
●	O. P. Pinot Nero '93	YY	4
●	Comprino Rosso '91	Y	3
●	O. P. Barbera '90	Y	3
●	O. P. Bonarda La Costuma '91	Y	4
●	O. P. Pinot Nero '90	Y	4
●	O. P. Rosso '94	Y	3
●	O. P. Rosso Ris. Solarolo '90	Y	4

CORTEFRANCA (BS)

Barone Pizzini Piomarta

Loc. Timoline
Via Brescia, 5
25050 Cortefranca (BS)
tel. 030/984136

This estate has over a century of wine-making history behind it and is among those that have shown particular determination in matters of quality and notable business sense in the past few years. With its orientation, up-to-date equipment and excellently sited vines (25 hectares between Timoline and Borgonato di Cortefranca), this is one estate that we would put money on. It's easy to sound wise about the future, but you would be tempted to do so as well after trying the terrific Franciacorta Bagnadore I Brut '93. It is quite simply one of the best we have tasted this year. It has a brilliant greenish straw color, a fine, continuous perlage, and a whole raft of fragrances that unfurl on the nose: spices, ripe fruit, yeast and delicate notes of thyme and aromatic herbs. On the palate it is rich, full and long. As for the Franciacorta Brut, even by itself it could support the reputation of the estate; its color is straw tinged with gold; its nose is fresh and redolent of ripe white-fleshed fruit and flowers; its palate excels in depth, elegance of structure and finely judged "dosage". On the other hand, the Franciacorta Bagnadore V Extra Brut '93 seemed a little under par: it has quite reasonable finesse on the nose but lacks similar balance on the palate. We found the Terre di Franciacorta Bianco '97 attractive and well fruited, and the Terre Rosso '96 nicely spicy and full-bodied, but somewhat dominated by a grassy note. The debut of San Carlo, a Bordeaux blend, with the '96 vintage, was interesting: it has a deep ruby hue, intense aromas of red fruit with balsamic notes and hints of chocolate and spice, and a rich palate with fine tannins and remarkable length.

○	Franciacorta Brut	🍷🍷	4
○	Franciacorta Brut Bagnadore I '93	🍷🍷	5
●	San Carlo '96	🍷🍷	4
○	Franciacorta Extra Brut Bagnadore V '93	🍷	3
○	T. d. F. Bianco '97	🍷	3
●	T. d. F. Rosso '96	🍷	3
○	Franciacorta Brut	ΥΥ	4
○	Franciacorta Extra Brut Bagnadore V '92	ΥΥ	5
○	T. d. F. Bianco '96	ΥΥ	3*
○	T. d. F. Bianco Pulcina '95	ΥΥ	3*
●	T. d. F. Rosso '95	Υ	3

CORTEFRANCA (BS)

F.lli Berlucchi

Loc. Borgonato
Via Broletto, 2
25040 Cortefranca (BS)
tel. 030/984451

With an annual production of about 30 thousand bottles, all of consistently good quality year after year, the Fratelli Berlucchi winery is an important presence in Franciacorta. The credit for this is shared between Pia Donata Berlucchi, who is the family member most closely involved in running the estate, and Cesare Ferrini, Berlucchi's long-standing consultant oenologist. Obviously there are extraordinary vintages, like '92, in which Franciacorta seems to have an extra dimension and allows us to have a glimpse of what this estate could be capable of. Yet even in an unexciting vintage like '94 the Franciacorta from this winery is still among the highest rankers, as it fully deserves to be. This Franciacorta Brut '94 has an attractive golden straw color, small, long-lasting bubbles, a soft, truly enticing nose with scents of ripe fruit, butter, hazelnut and toasted bread and a dense, well-structured somewhat fat palate that closes very softly (possibly a little too softly). The Rosé from the same vintage partners it well, revealing an attractive salmon color, good aromas of wild berry jam and "patisserie" and a fresh, pleasing palate, although it doesn't have the fullness and roundness of the Bianco. We feel, however, that the estate's still wines could still be significantly improved. We found the Terre di Franciacorta Bianco '97 correct and very drinkable, but the '96 Rosso was one step down: not completely clean on the nose and a little dilute.

○	Franciacorta Brut '94	🍷🍷	4
⊙	Franciacorta Rosé '94	🍷	3
○	T. d. F. Bianco '97	🍷	3
●	T. d. F. Rosso '96		3
○	Franciacorta Brut '91	ΥΥ	4
○	Franciacorta Brut '92	ΥΥ	4*
○	Franciacorta Brut '93	ΥΥ	4
⊙	Franciacorta Rosé '92	ΥΥ	4
○	T. d. F. Bianco '96	Υ	3
○	T. d. F. Bianco Dossi delle Querce '95	Υ	4
●	T. d. F. Rosso '95	Υ	2

CORTEFRANCA (BS)

GUIDO BERLUCCHI & C.
LOC. BORGONATO
P.ZZA DURANTI, 4
25040 CORTEFRANCA (BS)
TEL. 030/984381 - 984293

Guido Berlucchi is one of the most important wineries in Italy. Its heart and soul is Franco Ziliani and has always been so, right from the company's foundation in 1958. The first bottles of sparkling wine he produced, in 1961, bore the name Pinot di Franciacorta. Since then times have changed: the Franciacorta zone has become the heart of Italian sparkling wine production and Berlucchi, with almost five million bottles produced each year, is one of the bastions of the country's wine industry. Not to mention the fact that for many Italians the name is synonymous with excellence in sparkling wine. Berlucchi's range is vast and well honed, but Brut Cellarius is the pride of the line. Made from a blend of chardonnay, pinot blanc and pinot noir, Cellarius spends about three years on its yeasts. In the glass it has a brilliant straw color, a rich mousse and a fine, long-lasting perlage. Its perfumes are floral and yeasty, and on the palate it offers lovely structure, excellent freshness, a creamy mousse and a good fruity finish. Brut Extrême is agreeable for its pleasing notes of yeasts and ripe fruit, and the Rosé for its attractive red fruit flavors. Cuvée Imperiale Brut is, as ever, a very well-made wine, characterized by good yeasty perfumes, full flavor and an excellent mousse. There is also a splendid Franciacorta Brut produced from the estate called Antica Cantina Fratta di Monticelli Brusati. This has a deep straw color and intense aromas; the delightful palate is richly soft with engaging fruitiness and a fine aftertaste. Among the still wines we particularly mention the crisp and quaffable Terre di Franciacorta Bianco '97.

	Wine	Glasses	Price
○	Cellarius Brut Ris.	▼▼	5
○	Franciacorta Brut Antica Cantina Fratta	▼▼	4
○	Cuvée Imperiale Brut	▼	4
○	Cuvée Imperiale Brut Extrême	▼	4
⊙	Cuvée Imperiale Max Rosé	▼	4
○	T. d. F. Bianco Antica Cantina Fratta '97	▼	3
○	Bianco Imperiale		3
○	Cellarius Brut Ris.	▽▽	5
○	T. d. F. Bianco Antica Cantina Fratta '96	▽▽	3*
○	Cuvée Imperiale Brut '93	▽	5
○	Cuvée Imperiale Brut Extrême	▽	4
○	T. d. F. Bianco Antica Cantina Fratta '95	▽	3

ERBUSCO (BS)

BELLAVISTA
VIA BELLAVISTA, 5
25030 ERBUSCO (BS)
TEL. 030/7760276

Franciacorta Riserva Vittorio Moretti is only produced in the best vintages, and for some years we have been eagerly awaiting a Franciacorta with the complexity and elegance of the great '88. Let there be no misunderstanding: Bellavista has never begrudged us great wines (do you remember the splendid '93 Brut showered with accolades last year?), but Riserva Moretti is quite simply unforgettable. And now the '91, released this year and enthralling us all, proves the point. Its perlage is extraordinarily fine, the mousse is supremely creamy, the color is straw, both pale and bright. On the nose one first notices yeast and toasted crusty bread, then succulent white-fleshed fruits, vanilla, white flowers... The palate is delicately balanced and of remarkable finesse. In short, it goes without saying that it more than merits our top score. But the owner, Vittorio Moretti, and Mattia Vezzola, the manager and oenologist, have other strings to their bow. One is Gran Cuvée Brut '94. To describe this Franciacorta as refined and elegant is a gross understatement. Then there is the soft, creamy Satèn, with perfumes of vanilla and fruit, both tropical and citrus; and the delicate, rounded Franciacorta Cuvée Brut, one of the best standard Franciacortas ever. The Pas Operé '92, however, did not excite us: its flavors were a little too forward and ripe, but Gran Cuvée Rosé '94 is appealing for its delicate, wild berry nuances. The still wines that stand out are the Bianco del Convento dell'Annunciata '95, one of its best versions yet, and the chardonnay Uccellanda '95, stunningly fresh, fruity, elegant and long and with the note of oak perfectly judged (at last!). The red Solesine '95, a successful Bordeaux blend, is excellent; all the other wines are very good too.

	Wine	Glasses	Price
○	Franciacorta Extra Brut Vittorio Moretti Ris. '91	▼▼▼	6
○	Franciacorta Cuvée Brut	▼▼	4
○	Franciacorta Cuvée Brut '94	▼▼	5
○	Franciacorta Gran Cuvée Satèn	▼▼	5
●	Solesine '95	▼▼	5
○	T. d. F. Bianco Convento dell'Annunciata '95	▼▼	5
○	T. d. F. Uccellanda '95	▼▼	5
○	Franciacorta Gran Cuvée Pas Operé '92	▼	5
⊙	Franciacorta Gran Cuvée Rosé '94	▼	4
○	T. d. F. Bianco '97	▼	4
●	T. d. F. Rosso '95	▼	4
○	Franciacorta Gran Cuvée Brut '93	▽▽▽	5

Ca' del Bosco

Via Case Sparse, 20
25030 Erbusco (BS)
tel. 030/7760600

It is hard to find new ways each year of describing Ca' del Bosco, the estate masterfully run by Maurizio Zanella, who is, worldwide, one of the best known and most highly regarded figures on the Italian wine scene. This year Ca' del Bosco has presented another pair of unforgettable wines. For the third year running the Franciacorta Cuvée Annamaria Clementi walks off with Three Glasses, this time with the '91. It is one of the best sparkling wines ever produced in Italy and one of the few that can glance across to France with an air of challenge. And here's why: the color is a brilliant deep golden straw; the intense and complex bouquet is dominated by elegant floral scents supported by fresh citrus notes of yeasts and vanilla. In the mouth it is simply a marvel of glyceric richness, balance, creaminess of mousse, fruit and length. Then there is the '96 Chardonnay, as good as the exceptional '93 lauded by us in previous years. It is a white of great concentration with inviting perfumes full of ripe fruit and delicate aromatic notes elegantly blended with notes of new oak; in the mouth it is just as enchanting in its finesse and concentration. But the rest of Maurizio's range is no let-down either: the Satèn is his best of recent years, and the Brut '94 and the excellent and perfectly clean Dosage Zéro '94 are equally charming. Among the '95 still wines the Bordeaux blend, Maurizio Zanella, and the elegant, varietal Pinèro are top-notch, as is their wont. The rest of the large range of wines from this splendid house is excellent.

	Wine	Glasses	
○	Franciacorta Cuvée Annamaria Clementi '91	🍷🍷🍷	6
○	T. d. F. Chardonnay '96	🍷🍷🍷	6
○	Franciacorta Brut '94	🍷🍷	5
○	Franciacorta Dosage Zéro '94	🍷🍷	5
○	Franciacorta Satèn '93	🍷🍷	5
●	Maurizio Zanella '95	🍷🍷	6
●	Pinèro '95	🍷🍷	6
○	T. d. F. Bianco '97	🍷🍷	4
○	Franciacorta Brut	🍷	4
●	T. d. F. Rosso '96	🍷	4
○	Franciacorta Chardonnay '93	YYY	6
○	Franciacorta Cuvée Annamaria Clementi '90	YYY	6
○	Franciacorta Dosage Zéro '92	YYY	5

Cavalleri

Via Provinciale, 96
25030 Erbusco (BS)
tel. 030/7760217

Cavalleri of Erbusco is one of the Franciacorta names that savvy wine buffs tend to know. The quality of the wines, produced entirely from their own splendid vineyards, has in the past been at the top locally and, for sparkling wines, in Italy as a whole. There were, however, several comparatively less successful years. Neither the house's still wines nor its Franciacortas excited us as much as, for example, the rich, elegant Franciacorta Collezione '82 had done, and our criticisms were not always well received by the Cavalleri family. But last year it was clear that the estate was once more moving forward with renewed spirit. The '93 Collezione quells any doubt: it is quite simply a stunner. It has a straw hue shot through with lively greenish tones, excellent perlage, an intense, complex and extremely elegant bouquet featuring yeasts, ripe pear and peach, hints of vanilla and a toasty oak note of great finesse. The palate is creamy, harmonious, bewitching and fruity, with notes of vanilla on the finish. Nor is this an isolated success. Cavalleri's Pas Dosé '93 is almost as good, with its intriguing fragrances of dried figs and raisins, and a soft elegance on the palate. The Satèn is among the best of its type, the Blanc de Blancs reveals good ripe fruit aromas and great finesse, and the Rosé Collezione '93 scores for its delicate notes of wild berries and, once more, of vanilla. Among the still wines we preferred the structured, round white from the Seradina vineyard, but the entire range is of a very high quality. It all just goes to show that the Cavalleri star is shining more brightly than ever.

	Wine	Glasses	
○	Franciacorta Collezione Brut '93	🍷🍷🍷	6
●	Corniole Merlot '95	🍷🍷	4
○	Franciacorta Brut	🍷🍷	5
⊙	Franciacorta Collezione Rosé '93	🍷🍷	6
○	Franciacorta Pas Dosé '93	🍷🍷	5
○	Franciacorta Satèn	🍷🍷	5
○	T. d. F. Bianco Seradina '96	🍷🍷	5
○	T. d. F. Bianco '97	🍷	4
○	T. d. F. Bianco Rampaneto '96	🍷	4
●	T. d. F. Rosso '96	🍷	4
●	T. d. F. Rosso Tajardino '95	🍷	5
○	Franciacorta Collezione '86	YYY	6
○	Franciacorta Collezione '91	YY	5
○	Franciacorta Nondosato '92	YY	5
○	T. d. F. Bianco Rampaneto '96	YY	3*

ERBUSCO (BS)

Ferghettina
Via Case Sparse, 4
25030 Erbusco (BS)
tel. 030/7760120 - 7268308

Roberto Gatti knows what he wants; he also knows Franciacorta's terroir and production techniques like the back of his hand. He is totally committed to his work, which has always been in wine cellars, initially for some of the area's most noted estates. In 1992 he decided to set up on his own, and ever since the first bottles from Ferghettina, his farm in Erbusco, started to arrive we have always found his wines worthy of more than favorable ratings, and have noticed that they were to be had for comparatively little. But Roberto did not create all this simply to produce "good" wines; his estate, which now controls over twenty hectares of vineyards sited in various parts of the zone, has greater ambitions. We are just leading up to the fact that this year Ferghettina has brought out some wines that are truly impressive both for their technical competence and their personality. The Franciacorta Brut is better than it has ever been: it has a greenish straw color, intense, fresh perfumes with hints of aromatic herbs, white flowers and vanilla, and a soft, creamy palate of great elegance and length. Superb! Among the still wines the Merlot '95 could convince any skeptic of the suitability of the zone for red wine production. It has a dark ruby color and an intense, concentrated nose, rich in wild berry notes, while its palate is fleshy, rounded and elegantly tannic. Excellent use of new wood is also discernible in the chardonnay, Favento, which wins us over by the opulence of its tropical fruit and vanilla scents, and by its freshness and balance on the palate. There is no doubt that we shall be hearing more of these wines.

○	Franciacorta Brut	🍷🍷	4
○	T. d. F. Bianco Favento '97	🍷🍷	4
●	T. d. F. Merlot '95	🍷🍷	4
○	T. d. F. Bianco '97	🍷	3
●	T. d. F. Rosso '96	🍷	3
○	Franciacorta Brut	🍸🍸	4*
○	Franciacorta Brut	🍸🍸	4*
○	T. d. F. Bianco '95	🍸🍸	2*
○	T. d. F. Bianco '96	🍸	2
○	T. d. F. Bianco Favento '96	🍸	3
●	T. d. F. Rosso '95	🍸	2*

ERBUSCO (BS)

Enrico Gatti
Via Metelli, 9
25030 Erbusco (BS)
tel. 030/7267999 - 7267157

Each year we look forward to tasting good Franciacortas and still wines from this estate and so far we have not been disappointed. The brothers-in-law Lorenzo Gatti and Enzo Balzarini, helped by Sonia and Paola, their respective wives, work with enthusiastic commitment, and year after year the estate's reputation lines up with the best of the area. This standing is due mainly to the Franciacorta Brut (a vintage version is due imminently, we hear), which has a bright straw color, a dense, fine perlage and a complex nose with elegant notes of yeasts and toasted bread, scents of ripe peach and apricot, and vanilla nuances. The sensations carry through onto the palate, with its soft and delicate mousse and notable pervasive freshness. From the '96 vintage, Gatti Rosso, a cabernet sauvignon matured in small barrels, also shows well: a deep ruby color and intense, spicy perfumes of pencil lead and red fruit lead to a concentrated, elegant and finely tannic palate. Having retasted the '95 Gatti Rosso, which we first assessed last year, we can confirm that it's excellent, which can also be said of the Gatti Bianco '96. This is without doubt one of Franciacorta's best whites. It has a greenish straw hue and intense, full fragrances of exotic fruit, vanilla, spices and aromatic herbs; its palate is fleshy, crisp and very long. Both the Terre di Franciacortas, the Bianco '97 with its lively acidity and the Rosso '96 with a well-rounded fruitiness, are of very good quality, as they are every year.

○	Franciacorta Brut	🍷🍷	4
○	Gatti Bianco '96	🍷🍷	4
●	Gatti Rosso '96	🍷🍷	4
○	T. d. F. Bianco '97	🍷	3
●	T. d. F. Rosso '96	🍷	3
○	Franciacorta Bianco '94	🍸🍸	2*
○	Franciacorta Brut	🍸🍸	4*
●	Gatti Rosso '91	🍸🍸	4
●	Gatti Rosso '95	🍸🍸	4
○	T. d. F. Bianco '95	🍸🍸	2*
○	T. d. F. Bianco '96	🍸🍸	2*
●	T. d. F. Rosso '95	🍸🍸	2*

ERBUSCO (BS)

Principe Banfi

Via Iseo, 20
25030 Erbusco (BS)
tel. 030/7750387

Once again the Franciacortas from Principe Banfi have done very well. It is the Brut that impresses us most: it has a good, bright, greenish straw color, extremely fine perlage and delicate but notably elegant aromas distinguished by soft tones of ripe fruit and delicate floral nuances. On the palate the first sensation is of lively acidity, giving way to a commanding structure tempered by a fine effervescence and soft fruitiness. It is long-lasting, leaving the mouth pleasantly full of fruit flavors. The Extra Brut is very good this year too. It is quite similar to the Brut on the nose, but its palate is drier yet just as soft, caressing and persistent. The special selection Pio IX (named after the 19th century Pope who received this estate as a gift) of the Terre di Franciacorta Chardonnay '97 is interesting but not as exciting as in previous vintages: it is fruity, round and harmonious, but we would have preferred a little more acidic backbone. We found the two Terre di Franciacortas, the '97 Bianco and '96 Rosso, correct but not at the level of some previous years.

○	Franciacorta Brut	▼▼	4
○	Franciacorta Extra Brut	▼▼	5
○	T. d. F. Chardonnay Pio IX '97	▼	4
○	T. d. F. Bianco '97		3
●	T. d. F. Rosso '96		3
○	Franciacorta Brut	▽▽	5
○	Franciacorta Extra Brut	▽▽	4
○	T. d. F. Bianco '96	▽▽	3*
○	T. d. F. Chardonnay Pio IX '96	▽▽	4

ERBUSCO (BS)

Uberti

Via E. Fermi, 2
25030 Erbusco (BS)
tel. 030/7267476

There seems to be no stopping the legendary Magnificentia, which this year is again one of the best sparkling wines in all of Italy. With a perverse persistence we really tried to put it at a disadvantage. We held comparative tastings with certain well-known sparkling wines from the other side of the Alps, we served it warm, we served it almost frozen, we poured it into non-stemmed glasses, but all to no avail. Magnificentia virtually burst from the glass and bowled us over. Its brilliant color is bewitching, as are its complex and unmistakable perfumes with ripe fruit alternating with aromatic herbs and vanilla. Not to mention the palate, "crémant" from head to toe yet dense, full, crisp and of fine length. And its delights never pall. In short, it is a small masterpiece. The Ubertis, together with their consultant oenologist Cesare Ferrari, also produce a captivating Franciacorta Brut, balanced, soft and long, and an Extra Brut rich in scents of yeasts, toasted bread and ripe fruit, and unusually elegant on the palate. While we wait for the release of the new vintage, we can continue to drink the '91, which is still delicious and has several years ahead of it. The '96 vintage is one of the best yet for Terre di Franciacorta Bianco dei Frati Priori. It has a deep straw color with elegant greenish tinges, a nose with fruity notes wrapped in elegant oak and a taste that is structured and full without sacrificing crispness or drinkability. The Rosso dei Frati Priori '95, from cabernet sauvignon, has a deep ruby color and enticing perfumes of red fruit, tobacco and spice, while in the mouth it reveals firm body, soft tannins, concentration and good length.

○	Franciacorta Magnificentia	▼▼▼	5
○	Franciacorta Brut Francesco I	▼▼	4
○	Franciacorta Extra Brut Francesco I	▼▼	4
○	T. d. F. Bianco dei Frati Priori '96	▼▼	4
●	T. d. F. Rosso dei Frati Priori '95	▼▼	4
○	T. d. F. Bianco '97	▼	3
○	T. d. F. Bianco Maria dei Medici '96	▼	4
●	T. d. F. Rosso '96	▼	3
○	Franciacorta Magnificentia	▽▽▽	5*
○	Franciacorta Magnificentia	▽▽▽	5
○	Franciacorta Brut Comarì del Salem '91	▽▽	5
○	Franciacorta Francesco I Extra Brut	▽▽	4
○	T. d. F. Bianco dei Frati Priori '95	▽▽	4
○	T. d. F. Bianco Maria dei Medici '95	▽▽	4
●	T. d. F. Rosso dei Frati Priori '94	▽▽	4

GODIASCO (PV)

CABANON

LOC. CABANON
27052 GODIASCO (PV)
TEL. 0383/940912

The most interesting wine from the Cabanon estate, owned by the Mercandelli family, is, like last year, Cabanon Blanc Opera Prima, a sauvignon that easily earns Two Glasses. The '97 does not have the complexity of the '96, but is really admirable for its exotic fruit aromas and its full, elegant, balanced palate. On the other hand, the Vigna Vignassa Pinot Grigio '97 is better than last year's: pale straw hue, cleanly varietal scents (flowers, hay, honey), dry but soft taste, clean and full. Among the reds, the oak-aged Bonarda '95 is good: it has an attractive ruby color flecked with light garnet, a perfume of blackberry jam and spices (vanilla, clove) and an open, generous taste. The Bonarda Vivace '97 is simpler but equally enjoyable with its light refermentation in the bottle and fruity drinkability. The Barbera Vivace '97 (with 20% freisa) is worthy of note for its pleasingly rustic full body. However, the Rosso Oltrepò Infernot '93 is over-evolved; perhaps it lingered in the barrel a little longer than it should have.

	Wine	Rating	Price
○	Opera Prima Cabanon Blanc '97	TT	4
●	O. P. Bonarda '97	T	4
●	O. P. Bonarda Vivace '97	T	3
○	O. P. Pinot Grigio Vigna Vignassa'97	T	3
●	O. P. Barbera Vivace '97		3
●	O. P. Rosso Ris. Infernot '93		5
●	O. P. Bonarda Ris. '91	YY	4
○	O. P. Pinot Grigio '93	YY	4
○	O. P. Riesling Renano '93	YY	4
●	O. P. Ris. Bonarda '90	YY	4
●	O. P. Rosso Ris. Infernot '91	YY	5
●	O. P. Rosso Ris. Infernot '90	YY	5
●	O. P. Rosso Vino Cuore '91	YY	4
○	Opera Prima Cabanon Blanc '93	YY	4
○	Opera Prima Cabanon Blanc '96	YY	4

GRUMELLO DEL MONTE (BG)

CARLOZADRA

VIA GANDOSSI, 13
24064 GRUMELLO DEL MONTE (BG)
TEL. 035/832066 - 830244

Carlo Zadra, a native of Trentino who has adopted Bergamo as his home, produces wines of admirably consistent quality. The most noteworthy are the Extra Dry Tradizionale, made for those who like a softer wine (an Extra Dry has between 12 and 20 grams/liter of residual sugar and is less dry than a Brut) and the Nondosato, for those who prefer a bone-dry palate. The Extra Dry, vintage '91, "dégorgement" February '98, is from chardonnay and Trentino pinot noir and pinot meunier. It has alluring scents of sweet pastries, vanilla and ripe red currant, and on the palate it is full, graceful but firm, ripe and tasty. The Nondosato (vintage '92, "dégorgement" February '98, 5 thousand bottles) is made from pinot noir and Trentino chardonnay only, and is dry without being sharp, very clean and underpinned by a note of toasted almonds. Each wins Two Glasses. The Brut '94 ("dégorgement" '98) is elegant and tasty, if not very complex. The Extra Dry Liberty, a blanc de blancs from chardonnay and pinot blanc with 22 months on its yeasts, is fruity and attractive. The very pleasing Don Ludovico Pinot Nero '96 offers a light garnet hue, intense perfumes of black currant jam and spice and a particularly harmonious taste. The original Donna Nunzia '97, from Trentino moscato giallo, is dry, crisp and lively, with a marked aroma of rosewood.

	Wine	Rating	Price
○	Carlozadra Cl. Brut Nondosato '92	TT	5
○	Carlozadra Cl. Extra Dry Tradizione '91	TT	5
○	Carlozadra Cl. Brut '94	T	4
○	Carlozadra Cl. Extra Dry Liberty	T	4
●	Don Ludovico Pinot Nero '96	T	4
○	Donna Nunzia Moscato Giallo '97	T	3
○	Carlozadra Cl. Brut '93	YY	5
○	Carlozadra Cl. Brut '92	YY	4
○	Carlozadra Cl. Brut Nondosato '91	YY	4
○	Carlozadra Cl. Extra Dry Tradizione '89	YY	4
○	Carlozadra Cl. Gran Ris. '87	YY	6

GRUMELLO DEL MONTE (BG)

TENUTA CASTELLO
VIA FOSSE, 11
24064 GRUMELLO DEL MONTE (BG)
TEL. 035/830244 - 4420817

The "castello" is the 12th century castle of Grumello, perched on the Val Calepio hills between Bergamo and Lake Iseo, and the estate named in its honor produced a chardonnay in '96 which is more than worthy of respect, the Chardonnay della Bergamasca Aurito. The soil of the Aurito vineyard is clayey limestone and the vines are guyot-trained; the grapes are fermented in new Allier barriques, where the wine also undergoes its malolactic fermentation and then remains for a further eight months' maturation. The wood is perhaps too noticeable, but the underlying wine is excellent: a light golden color, a broad, spicy (vanilla) nose with scents of musk, apple and almond blossom, a full, decided, vigorous but elegant flavor. This '96 is more harmonious than the '95 and hence reclaims its Two Glasses. The Colle di Calvario '95 Valcalepio Rosso comes from the estate's best vineyards, where grapes yield no more than 50 quintals per hectare, but it is "merely" good. It has notable finesse and complexity on the nose, with some forward aromas, and its palate displays more elegance than vigor. It is maturing faster than the '93, which is still holding up perfectly well. The Valcalepio Rosso '96 is attractive, as is the Bianco '97 (which may be just a bit forward). The Moscato Nero Passito '94 seems to have improved: its time in bottle has been useful, particularly for harmony on the palate.

	Wine	Glasses	Price
○	Chardonnay della Bergamasca Aurito '96	🍷🍷	4
●	Valcalepio Rosso Colle del Calvario '95	🍷	4
○	Valcalepio Bianco '97		3
●	Valcalepio Rosso '96		3
●	Valcalepio Rosso Colle del Calvario '90	♀♀	4
○	Chardonnay della Bergamasca Aurito '95	♀	4
●	Valcalepio Moscato Nero Passito '94	♀	6
●	Valcalepio Rosso Colle del Calvario '93	♀	4

MARIANA MANTOVANA (MN)

STEFANO SPEZIA
VIA MATTEOTTI, 90
46010 MARIANA MANTOVANA (MN)
TEL. 0376/735012

Stefano Spezia is a producer and wine merchant in Mariana in the province of Mantova, viticultural territory whose potential, so far, has been exploited only minimally. For years Spezia has been offering attractive, naturally "frizzante" (semi-sparkling) Lambrusco fermented in a tank (Etichetta Rossa) or in the bottle (Etichetta Blu). Both are worth more than they cost. Recently, however, he has begun to experiment with a deeply colored, vigorous and slightly rough red, Ancellotta. By means of barrique maturation he has produced some surprisingly good results. The Ancellotta Barrique '95 mentioned in last year's Guide struck us as sound when we tasted it, despite being a little sharp and green. It has now improved in the bottle and gained balance. The '96 version is a wine of notable structure and seems readier than the '95. It has a dark purple color, fragrances of jam, toasty oak and spices and a full, vigorous taste with a strong acidic backbone: a few months' aging will do it good even though it is more than good already. The straightforward, fruity Ancellotta '97 in its "frizzante" version (metodo italiano) is also much to be admired. Last but not least the Rosso Spezia '96 is of great interest. Made from 100% merlot grown in the Colli Morenici Mantovani, it has an intense ruby hue, generous aromas of raspberry jam, cherry brandy and roasted cocoa and a warm, full, firm palate with good aromatic length.

	Wine	Glasses	Price
●	Ancellotta Barrique '96	🍷	4
●	Ancellotta Frizzante '97	🍷	1*
●	Rosso Spezia Merlot '96	🍷	3
●	Lambrusco Etichetta Blu '97		1
●	Lambrusco Etichetta Rossa '97		1
●	Ancellotta Barrique '91	♀♀	4
●	Ancellotta Barrique '93	♀♀	4
●	Ancellotta '92	♀	3
●	Ancellotta '93	♀	3
●	Ancellotta Barrique '92	♀	3
●	Ancellotta Barrique '95	♀	4

MONIGA DEL GARDA (BS)

COSTARIPA
VIA CIALDINI, 12
25080 MONIGA DEL GARDA (BS)
TEL. 0365/502010

We know that Costaripa is working hard to improve his wines, and we wish his best were better, but we continue to have faith in vintages yet to come, especially since few things require as much patience as wine-making, particularly when it comes to seeing the results of the changes you have made. The estate's two Chiarettos, both '97s, are likeable but no more: Rosamara is soft and pleasantly fruited but not completely clean on the nose; the standard Chiaretto is cleaner but also simpler and not really very aromatic. The most attractive of the reds was the Marzemino Le Mazane '97, we felt. It has a good ruby color, a fragrant aroma of wild berry jam and a warm and tasty palate with a lingering undertone of blueberry and blackberry. The interesting Gropello Le Castelline '97 reveals a distinctly vegetal and fruited (black cherry) nose and a reasonably concentrated palate. Campo delle Starne '97, although not up to our expectations, is still worthy of note: it offers notes of spice, red fruit jam, fur and leather on a rapidly evolving nose. To finish, the Lugana '97 is soft, appealing, crisp and lively, with distinct varietal notes of bitter white flowers and citrus blossom and a faint background of green almonds.

●	Campo delle Starne '97	🍷	3
●	Groppello Le Castelline '97	🍷	3
○	Lugana '97	🍷	3
●	Marzemino Le Mazane '97	🍷	3
⊙	Garda Bresciano Chiaretto '97		3
⊙	Garda Bresciano Chiaretto Rosamara '97		3

MONTALTO PAVESE (PV)

DORIA
CASA TACCONI, 3
27040 MONTALTO PAVESE (PV)
TEL. 0383/870143

There is no question about the dedication to excellence of the Doria di Montalto family, but the results continue to disappoint, particularly considering that the vineyards are overseen by the Department of Agriculture of the University of Milan, and that the oenologist Bruno Bassi supervises cellar operations. In contrast to recent years, no wine earned Two Glasses this time, not even the Pinot Nero Querciolo, the estate's standard-bearer. The '96 version is fairly deep in color; the maturation in French barriques (Nevers and Allier) has added spicy notes to the nose, which is interesting but not very complex; the palate is full, warm and firm, showing more structure than finesse. It may well need another year of bottle-aging. Speaking of pinot noir, the white version (fermented without the skins), Pinot Nero in bianco Le Briglie '97, is attractive, full and fruity. The Riesling Italico '97, also from the Le Briglie range, gains One Glass for its intensely aromatic fragrance and its crisp, stylish flavor. The Roncorosso '96 Oltrepò Pavese Vigna Siura (barbera, croatina, uva rara) is good: a dark ruby color, an intense aroma of jam and a full, firm taste. It is not unlike the '94 we reviewed last year. The clean, fruity Bonarda Vivace '97 is an agreeable wine.

●	O. P. Pinot Nero Querciolo '96	🍷	5
○	O. P. Riesling Italico Le Briglie '97	🍷	4
●	O. P. Rosso Roncorosso V. Siura '96	🍷	4
●	O. P. Bonarda Vivace '97		4
○	O. P. Pinot Nero in bianco Le Briglie '97		4
●	O. P. Pinot Nero Querciolo '91	🍷🍷	5
●	O. P. Pinot Nero Querciolo '93	🍷🍷	5
●	O. P. Pinot Nero Querciolo '95	🍷🍷	5
○	O. P. Riesling Renano Roncobianco V. Tesi '94	🍷🍷	4
●	O. P. Rosso Roncorosso V. Siura '93	🍷🍷	4
●	O. P. Rosso V. del Masö '91	🍷🍷	4

MONTECALVO VERSIGGIA (PV)

CASA RE
FRAZ. CASA RE
27047 MONTECALVO VERSIGGIA (PV)
TEL. 0383/99986

Casa Re, in Valle Versa, some 20 hectares under vine cultivated with a minimal use of chemicals, is owned by the Casati family. It first appeared in the Guide last year and its wines have made further progress since. Two of them, for which the oenologist Donato Lanati is in large part responsible, are particularly noteworthy. The first is the pale gold Chardonnay '96 from the property called Il Fossone, and it offers a rich, varietal bouquet (musk, artemisia, almond blossom) with undertones of spice (vanilla), and a vigorous, soft, pleasantly long-lasting flavor. The other is the Riesling Italico '94, which tastes very like a Rhein riesling. It is decidedly mature but perfectly firm. The color is greeny gold, the fragrances broad and complex with mineral (flint), floral (dried rose) and spicy (vanilla) scents and the taste is very full and harmonious, with elegant aromatic length. The Brut Classico '89 is also mature, but could easily keep longer; it has a good perlage, a clear golden color, aromas of crusty bread, toasted hazelnut, apple and black currant jam and a firm, well-balanced palate. The Pinot Nero '94, on the other hand, with its ether-rich, very forward aroma, is already sliding downhill. The Bonarda is a '94 that has held up better, but the wood is too noticeable.

	Wine	Rating	Price
○	O. P. Chardonnay Il Fossone '96	🍷🍷	4
○	O. P. Riesling Italico Il Fossone '94	🍷🍷	4
○	O. P. Brut Classico '89	🍷	4
●	O. P. Bonarda '94		3
●	O. P. Pinot Nero '94		4
○	O. P. Riesling Italico Il Fossone '96	🍸	3
○	Valle Versa Chardonnay '94	🍸	4

MONTICELLI BRUSATI (BS)

CASTELVEDER
VIA BELVEDERE, 4
25040 MONTICELLI BRUSATI (BS)
TEL. 030/652308

Castelveder is one of those "small" Franciacorta estates (its annual production has now reached 100 thousand bottles) that were started almost as a hobby but that with time and the gradually increasing competence and enthusiasm of their owners have started to turn out some of the still and sparkling wines that have forged the reputation of Franciacorta. With the '94 vintage the duo consisting of Renato Alberti, the owner, and Teresio Schiavi, the oenologist, has recreated the glories of the excellent '92 vintage. The Franciacorta Brut '94 shows a bright straw color with elegant greenish tinges, a creamy mousse and fine perlage. On the nose it is fresh, fruity, intense and elegant, all of which can be said of the palate, which is also fat, soft and rich in fruited notes, with a creamy development of the mousse and a long and harmonious finish. We found the non-vintage Franciacorta Brut good, although it lacked the concentration and richness of last year's: it is clean-cut and has attractive yeasty aromas and a crisp, fruity and balanced palate. The Terre di Franciacorta Bianco '97 is correct, fruity and good drinking, but there is nonetheless room for improvement, especially when it is compared with the rest of Castelveder's range.

	Wine	Rating	Price
○	Franciacorta Brut '94	🍷🍷	5
○	Franciacorta Brut	🍷	4
○	T. d. F. Bianco '97	🍷	3
○	Franciacorta Brut	🍸🍸	4*
○	Franciacorta Brut '91	🍸🍸	4
○	Franciacorta Brut '92	🍸🍸	4
●	Franciacorta Rosso '93	🍸	2
○	T. d. F. Bianco '96	🍸	2*

MONTICELLI BRUSATI (BS)

LA MONTINA
VIA BAIANA, 17
25040 MONTICELLI BRUSATI (BS)
TEL. 030/653278

Once more this year La Montina, the fine estate owned by the Bozza brothers, has brought home a shelfful of Glasses. Last year the vintage Brut, the '93, more or less left us cold, but this year we have the excellent '94 and it leaps to the head of our review. It has an attractive, brilliant golden straw color, a particularly fine mousse and tiny, long-lasting bubbles. The nose is dominated by fresh and elegant aromas of the white flesh of pear and peach, with delicate vegetal hints. And fresh notes, evocative of flowers and new-mown grass, together with great finesse and attractiveness, characterizes the palate. Fullness and length of taste are also attributes of the excellent Franciacorta Brut, which has a faint hint of rose in its hue and pleasant fruited tones on the nose. The palate is delicately alluring and of fair length. But what to say about the Satèn? This year it is again one of the best to have been made, and it makes a very convincing argument for this category of Franciacorta wine. Greenish straw in color, it has sweet perfumes of ripe and exotic fruit, and it melts in the mouth with further evocations of exotic fruit. The Extra Brut and the Rosé do not match its alluring grace, but each is nevertheless exemplary of its type. The two Terre di Franciacorta special selections, the white Palanca '97 and the Rosso dei Dossi '96, are also good. A correct Terre di Franciacorta Rosso '96 is worthy of note.

	Wine	Glasses	Price
○	Franciacorta Brut '94	🍷🍷	5
○	Franciacorta Satèn	🍷🍷	4
○	Franciacorta Brut	🍷	4
○	Franciacorta Extra Brut	🍷	4
⊙	Franciacorta Rosé	🍷	4
○	T. d. F. Bianco Palanca '97	🍷	3
●	T. d. F. Rosso dei Dossi '96	🍷	3
●	T. d. F. Rosso '96		3
○	Franciacorta Brut	🍷🍷 (empty)	4
○	Franciacorta Brut	🍷🍷 (empty)	4*
○	Franciacorta Brut '91	🍷🍷 (empty)	4*
○	Franciacorta Crémant	🍷🍷 (empty)	4
○	Franciacorta Extra Brut	🍷🍷 (empty)	4*
○	Franciacorta Extra Brut	🍷🍷 (empty)	4
○	Franciacorta Satèn	🍷🍷 (empty)	4*

MONTICELLI BRUSATI (BS)

LO SPARVIERE
VIA COSTA, 2
25040 MONTICELLI BRUSATI (BS)
TEL. 030/652382

The Gussalli Beretta family has owned this attractive estate near Monticelli Brusati for over twenty years. Started as just an artisanal concern, it has grown to control about thirty hectares of vineyard and an annual production of over 100 thousand bottles. The oenologist Francesco Polastri produces a full range of still and sparkling wines, DOC and DOCG, and although this year's Franciacorta Extra Brut does not have the force and weight of last year's, the Franciacorta Brut has done beautifully. It has a fine deep straw color and intense aromas dominated by scents of yeasts, butter and toasted hazelnut, which carry through onto the fat and structured palate, further graced by a soft and long-lasting mousse. The Extra Brut is paler in hue, and notes of face powder join the fruit and yeasts on the nose; the palate is somewhat forward, perhaps even a touch overripe. The Terre di Franciacorta wines are good, and we particularly liked the red Vino del Cacciatore '95, made from the traditional blend of cabernet, merlot, barbera and nebbiolo.

	Wine	Glasses	Price
○	Franciacorta Brut	🍷🍷	4
○	Franciacorta Extra Brut	🍷	4
○	T. d. F. Bianco '97	🍷	3
●	T. d. F. Rosso Vino del Cacciatore '95	🍷	3
○	Franciacorta Brut	🍷🍷 (empty)	4
○	Franciacorta Extra Brut	🍷🍷 (empty)	4
○	T. d. F. Bianco Ris. '95	🍷🍷 (empty)	3
○	T. d. F. Bianco '96	🍷 (empty)	2

MONTICELLI BRUSATI (BS)

VILLA
FRAZ. VILLA
25040 MONTICELLI BRUSATI (BS)
TEL. 030/652329 - 6852305

Once more Alessandro Bianchi's position as one of the best exponents of this area's wines is confirmed. Indeed, Villa brings a good three Franciacortas to the noble Two Glass ranks, and all the rest of the range is well-made and of notably high quality. The oenologist Corrado Cugnasco selects the grapes for Franciacorta Extra Brut '94 from the best-exposed slopes of the 25 hectares of estate-owned vineyard. It is one of those sparkling wines that you could just drink and drink. It has a pale straw color shot through with greenish tinges, fresh, intense aromas of ripe fruit and yellow flowers and a creamy, soft palate with good acidity and length. These are gifts shared by the other '94, the Brut, which has a slightly softer outline and aromas more freshly herby than fruity. The '92 vintage, for its part, is enviably endowed with freshness and scores in particular for its notes of well-ripened fruit and elegant mineral tones. On the palate it reveals, with its youthful freshness, the hallmark of the Villa Franciacortas: a creamy mousse, balance and roundness, as well as a delightful fruited note on the finish. Finally, Cuvette is one of the most successful of Extra Drys: it is soft, fat and full without losing its balance. Among the Terre di Franciacortas we particularly enjoyed the fresh, smooth and fruited Pian della Vigna '97 with its well-balanced if not imposing structure. The red Gradoni '95 is very good although it doesn't repeat the success of the previous vintage: there is a good use of wood and it has well-defined aromas but it seems a little thin on the palate. All the other wines are good.

	Wine	Rating	Price
○	Franciacorta Brut '94	🍷🍷	4
○	Franciacorta Brut Sel. '92	🍷🍷	6
○	Franciacorta Extra Brut '94	🍷🍷	4
○	Franciacorta Extra Dry Cuvette	🍷	5
○	T. d. F. Bianco Marengo '96	🍷	4
○	T. d. F. Bianco Pian della Vigna '97	🍷	3
●	T. d. F. Rosso '96	🍷	3
●	T. d. F. Rosso Gradoni '95	🍷	4
○	T. d. F. Bianco '97		3
○	Franciacorta Brut '93	🍷🍷 (prev. year)	4
○	Franciacorta Brut Ris. '91	🍷🍷 (prev. year)	5
○	Franciacorta Cuvette '93	🍷🍷 (prev. year)	5
●	Franciacorta Rosso Gradoni '93	🍷🍷 (prev. year)	4
●	T. d. F. Rosso Gradoni '94	🍷🍷 (prev. year)	4

MONTÙ BECCARIA (PV)

VERCESI DEL CASTELLAZZO
VIA AURELIANO, 36
27040 MONTÙ BECCARIA (PV)
TEL. 0385/60067

With the Pinot Nero Luogo dei Monti the Vercesi family has repeated its success of last year: the '95 vintage has also easily carried off Two Glasses. Made from various French clones and aged for a year in medium-toasted Allier barriques, it is brilliant ruby in color and displays distinct aromas of black currant jam, vanilla and undergrowth, followed by a supremely elegant, full palate, with undertones of licorice and toasted cocoa. The Gugiarolo '96 (named after a plot owned by the family since the 17th century) is also a pinot noir, but is fermented off the skins to make a white wine. Its color is straw, it smells of apples, peaches and wildflowers and has a fresh, fruity taste. The red Vespolino '97 deserves a special entry. It is made from the vespolina grape, also known as ughetta, which was grown widely in Oltrepò before phylloxera struck. At the time it was considered an essential component of any blend to which one wished to impart character. Vinified with just a brief maceration, the vespolina produces a wine of a light ruby hue and a fresh, penetrating aroma dominated by scents of green peppercorns and ginger, with vegetal hints (bell pepper, tomato leaf); the palate is very savory, almost salty, with a lightly bitter note of green almonds. It's a terrific little wine, dry and not very different from a Piedmontese Grignolino, and quite delightful drunk young, at cellar temperature, right through the meal. We wind up with the Oltrepò Rosso Pezzalunga '97, which is still a touch sharp, the Bonarda Fatila '94, which in contrast is mature and forward, and the attractive white Pinot Nero "in bianco" Le Marghe '97, with its fruit and pleasing freshness and effervescence.

	Wine	Rating	Price
●	O. P. Pinot Nero Luogo dei Monti '95	🍷🍷	4
●	O. P. Bonarda Fatila '94	🍷	4
○	O. P. Pinot Nero in bianco Gugiarolo '96	🍷	4
●	O. P. Rosso Pezzalunga '97	🍷	4
●	Vespolino Rosso '97	🍷	3
○	O. P. Pinot Nero in bianco Le Marghe Vivace '97		3
●	O. P. Bonarda Fatila '90	🍷🍷 (prev. year)	4
●	O. P. Bonarda Fatila '91	🍷🍷 (prev. year)	4
●	O. P. Pinot Nero Luogo dei Monti '91	🍷🍷 (prev. year)	4
●	O. P. Pinot Nero Luogo dei Monti '94	🍷🍷 (prev. year)	4

MONZAMBANO (MN)

Prendina
Loc. La Prendina
46040 Monzambano (MN)
tel. 045/516002

The admirably consistent quality of the wines from La Prendina, owned by the Piona family, earns it an individual entry in the '99 Guide. Previously the wines were always reviewed with those of La Calvalchina (in the Custoza zone in the Veneto), the other estate owned by the Pionas. Among the wines presented this year the Falcone '95 Cabernet Sauvignon dell'Alto Mincio (containing 10% merlot) stands out. Matured for 12 months in small oak casks, it has a good dark ruby color and an intense, elegant nose (cherry brandy, ripe hay, vanilla, toasted cocoa beans); the taste is still evolving but is dry and warm, with still evident but attractive tannins. Time in the bottle should improve it. The Garda Merlot '96 (containing 15% cabernet franc, aged for a year in barrique) is of great interest: it is full, concentrated, pleasantly grassy and fruity, with enticing notes of spice. The Garda Colli Mantovani Rosso '97 is simple but clean and attractive. The most successful of the whites is the Garda Riesling '97, redolent of roses and flint. It is dry but not excessively so, racy and balanced and has good aromatic length. The Sauvignon Garda '97, a good white, is full and soft but crisp, and, on the nose, reminiscent of tropical fruit (pineapple, lychee) and minerals. To round off, the agreeable Pinot Bianco Garda '97 is delicate and flowery.

●	Cabernet Sauvignon Alto Mincio Il Falcone '95	▼▼	4
○	Garda Riesling '97	▼▼	3
●	Garda Merlot '96	▼	3
○	Garda Pinot Bianco '97	▼	2
○	Garda Sauvignon '97	▼	3
●	Garda Colli Mantovani Rosso '97		2
●	Cabernet Vigneto Il Falcone '93	▽▽	4
○	Garda Riesling '96	▽▽	3
○	Garda Sauvignon '96	▽▽	3*
●	Cabernet Vigneto Il Falcone '94	▽	4
○	Garda Pinot Bianco '96	▽	1*

MORNICO LOSANA (PV)

Ca' di Frara
Fraz. Casa Ferrari
27040 Mornico Losana (PV)
tel. 0383/892299

Ca' di Frara's best wine from the 1997 vintage is unquestionably the Pinot Grigio Vendemmia Tardiva. Produced from overripe grapes, it is quite individual in style, which may be a function of the soil, a medium-grained crystalline chalk resting on sandy subsoil. But quite apart from any considerations of particularity it is a wonderful wine: green-gold in color, with a rich bouquet, featuring rose, tropical fruit and linden blossom, and a powerful, full, velvety palate. The Chardonnay '97, with its perfumes of honey, pineapple and gooseberry, and its firm structure and balance, is excellent too. The Riesling Renano '97, good as it is (aromas of apple, lemon balm and pineapple), is not up to the level of the '95 reviewed last year. With the reds things are different. The barrique is one of the tools an oenologist has at his disposal to enhance certain wines. It must, however, be used wisely, because too much wood is counterproductive. This is exactly what has happened to Frater '97, a Rosso Oltrepò Pavese (barbera, pinot noir, uva rara and croatina): an excellent foundation for a wine has been suffocated by an overdose of oak. A great pity: it's a wine that could have cut a very good figure.

○	O. P. Chardonnay '97	▼▼	3
○	O. P. Pinot Grigio V. T. '97	▼▼	4
○	O. P. Riesling Renano '97	▼	3
●	O. P. Rosso Il Frater '97		3
○	O. P. Pinot Grigio V. T. '95	▽▽	4
○	O. P. Riesling Renano '95	▽▽	3
●	O. P. Bonarda '96	▽	3
○	O. P. Chardonnay '96	▽	3
●	O. P. Pinot Nero I Rari '94	▽	4

PASSIRANO (BS)

MARCHESI FASSATI DI BALZOLA

PASSIRANO (BS)
TEL. 030/8692132

Named after its owners, the Marquises Fassati di Balzola, this winery has been based in the fine castle of Passirano since the end of the last century. Leonardo Fassati is advised by their consultant oenologist Corrado Cugnasco for their small-scale production of attentively made Franciacortas and still wines: 30 thousand bottles per year from grapes grown on their own approximately six hectares of vineyard. The pride of this small house is the Franciacorta Extra Brut, made from the classic Franciacorta blend of chardonnay and pinot blanc and matured for more than two years on its yeasts before "dégorgement". It has a brilliant pale straw color and fine and continuous perlage, and the nose, of notable finesse, opens to evolved scents of ripe fruit, yeasts and toasted bread. On the palate everything is played for elegance and balance and the resultant wine is stylish, crisp and long-lasting. The Brut is slightly leaner and has a somewhat sulphurous nose, but its almond-nuanced finish is most attractive. The Terre di Franciacorta Bianco '95 from the Medes vineyard almost reaches the Two Glass level. It is dense and structured, crisp and harmonious, and offers succulence and reasonable length. The Terre Bianco '97 is good; the '96 Rosso is no more than correct.

	Wine	Glasses	
○	Franciacorta Extra Brut	🍷🍷	4
○	Franciacorta Brut	🍷	4
○	T. d. F. Bianco '97	🍷	3
○	T. d. F. Bianco Vigna Medes '95	🍷	4
●	T. d. F. Rosso '96		3
○	Franciacorta Brut		0
●	T. d. F. Rosso '95		0

PASSIRANO (BS)

IL MOSNEL

FRAZ. CAMIGNONE
VIA BARBOGLIO, 14
25040 PASSIRANO (BS)
TEL. 030/653117 - 654236

Giulio and Lucia Barzanò have been assisting their mother, Emanuela Barboglio, in running this family-owned estate for the past five vintages now. These have been critical years, taking the estate through the extension of its range and, more importantly, an upswing in the overall quality of its wines. Today Il Mosnel has about ten different labels, which some may consider too many. However the quality of these wines, both sparkling and still, remains excellent and continues to benefit from ongoing experimentation with the terrain and its potential. While waiting for the release of the latest vintage, we retasted the Brut '91 and found it still excellent. It is supported by a good Extra Brut, which, although we would like to see it a little fleshier, has fair balance, and by a very well-executed Brut, which is, however, a bit too forward. This year the estate's standard-bearer is the Brut Nouvelle Cuvée, a Franciacorta of a lovely brilliant hue and soft, enchanting aromas; on the palate it is crisp, rounded and fruity, just as it should be. The Terre Bianco Sulìf '97 is one of the best we tasted this year. It has a good deep straw color, intense aromas of ripe fruit with a touch of vanilla and a fruity palate of good body with a carefully judged dose of new wood. The Campolarga '97, another white DOC, is light and enjoyable, while Pienne '96 Pinot Nero del Sebino displays elegantly varietal aromas.

	Wine	Glasses	
○	Franciacorta Brut Nouvelle Cuvée	🍷🍷	4
○	T. d. F. Bianco Sulìf '97	🍷🍷	4
○	Franciacorta Brut	🍷	4
○	Franciacorta Extra Brut	🍷	4
●	Pienne Pinot Nero Sebino '96	🍷	4
○	T. d. F. Bianco '97	🍷	3
○	T. d. F. Bianco Campolarga '97	🍷	3
○	Franciacorta Brut	🍸🍸	4
○	Franciacorta Brut '90	🍸🍸	5
○	Franciacorta Brut '91	🍸🍸	5
○	Franciacorta Brut Nouvelle Cuvée	🍸🍸	4
●	T. d. F. Rosso Fontecolo '93	🍸🍸	4

POZZOLENGO (BS)

TENUTA ROVEGLIA
LOC. ROVEGLIA, 1
25010 POZZOLENGO (BS)
TEL. 030/918663

Although the wines produced by this Lake Garda estate received no more than Honorable Mention in last year 's Guide, this year's tastings indicated that they had made significant progress, so here they are with a profile of their own. Not surprisingly for a winery in this part of the country, they produce a varied range of Luganas; each is well made and well worth the attention of both wine enthusiast and everyday drinker. Let 's start with Lugana Vigne di Catullo, the best of the range. The '97 displays a vivid gold color; its bouquet is intense and complex, with elegant mineral notes of flint and aromas of dried apricot, linden blossom and vanilla, followed by sweet citrus fruit and "patisserie ". It is full, powerful, long and elegant on the palate with a distinct undertone of ripe white peach, and good structure as well. Both the Lugana Filo di Arianna '96 and the standard Lugana '97 are admirable. The former has a well-evolved, mineral and floral bouquet and a decided and harmonious if slightly short taste; while the latter, redolent of citron and almond, has a tasty and clean palate with a distinctly bitterish finish. The fresh, open, well-balanced Lugana Brut is worthy of mention.

○	Lugana Vigne di Catullo '97	🍷🍷	4
○	Lugana '97	🍷	2
○	Lugana Filo di Arianna '96	🍷	4
○	Lugana Brut		3
○	Lugana Vigne di Catullo '96		4

PROVAGLIO D'ISEO (BS)

BERSI SERLINI
VIA CERRETO, 7
25050 PROVAGLIO D'ISEO (BS)
TEL. 030/9823338

The headquarters of the Bersi Serlini estate is a fine group of farm buildings, dating from the 15th century and impeccably restored. They were once owned by the monks of the nearby convent of San Pietro in Lamosa and it was the monks who brought viticulture to the morainal hills stretching towards Lake Iseo, where the estate's 30 hectares of vineyards are situated. The vines, which yield primarily white grapes, are tended according to the European Union's rules for environmental protection. Their best offering this year is Franciacorta Brut, one of the most reliable of the denomination. It has a bright, pale straw color; the nose offers soft, complex aromas; and the palate is admirable for its soft effervescence, its acidic drive and its attractive, long, fruity finish. The Extra Brut '92, reviewed last year and reassessed now, is still excellent, but the Brut from the same vintage seemed a little under par. It is slightly inharmonious on the nose and although its palate is correct and balanced we would have liked greater length. Bersi Serlini 's Demi Sec, the soft, fruity Nuvola, is as good as ever: a sparkling wine that goes well with pastries or crème caramel. We found the Terre di Franciacorta Bianco '97 fair, while the red from the same vintage rather puzzled us: it seemed thin and roughly tannic.

○	Franciacorta Brut	🍷🍷	4
○	Franciacorta Brut '92	🍷	5
○	Nuvola Démi Sec	🍷	4
○	T. d. F. Bianco '97	🍷	3
●	T. d. F. Rosso '97		3
○	Franciacorta Brut	🍸🍸	4*
○	Franciacorta Brut '91	🍸🍸	5*
○	Franciacorta Brut '91	🍸🍸	4
○	Franciacorta Extra Brut '92	🍸🍸	5
●	T. d. F. Rosso '94	🍸	3
●	T. d. F. Rosso '95	🍸	5

ROCCA DE' GIORGI (PV)

Anteo

Loc. Chiesa
27043 Rocca de' Giorgi (PV)
tel. 0385/48583 - 99073

In last year 's Guide we expressed the wish that Anteo would come closer to realizing the potential of its vineyards (30 well-sited hectares) and its modern, well-equipped cellar. And suddenly there are signs of just that: Two Glasses for Ca' dell 'Oca '95 Pinot Nero in bianco, their white-fermented pinot noir (with 20% chardonnay) matured for six months in barriques. It has an attractive and brilliant golden hue, perfumes of vanilla, pineapple and banana and a soft, harmonious, fruited, spicy flavor. The sparkling wines are not quite so sensational but they are still worthy of serious attention: first of all the non-vintage Brut Classico (36 months on its yeasts), with a fine fragrance of crusty bread and spice and just a hint of citrus; then the bone-dry Brut Nature (also three years on the yeasts), now at its peak. Freshness, fruitiness (apple, pineapple) and intriguing scents of dry toast characterize the Pinot Nero Brut Metodo Martinotti. (It 's high time to stop calling the closed-vat procedure for making wines sparkling "Charmat ": this method is Italian in origin.) Quattro Marzo (the 4th of March, the date of bottling), a white table wine made from chardonnay, pinot noir and Rhein riesling, is fragrant and stylish. However the red Ca ' dell 'Oca Pinot Nero in Rosso '93, matured in small oak casks from the Massif Centrale, has rather dominant tannins: it could improve with time.

○	O. P. Pinot Nero in bianco Ca' dell'Oca '95	🍷🍷	4
○	O. P. Pinot Nero Brut Cl.	🍷	5
○	O. P. Pinot Nero Brut Martinotti	🍷	4
●	O. P. Pinot Nero Ca' dell'Oca '93	🍷	4
○	O. P. Pinot Nero Cl. Nature	🍷	5
●	O. P. Bonarda Vivace '97		3
○	Quattro Marzo Bianco '97		3
○	O. P. Nature Extra Brut '91	🍸	5
○	O. P. Pinot Nero Brut	🍸	4
○	O. P. Pinot Nero Brut Cl.	🍸	5
○	O. P. Pinot Nero Brut Cl. Sel. Gourmet	🍸	5
○	O. P. Pinot Nero Extra Brut Cl.	🍸	5

RODENGO SAIANO (BS)

Mirabella

Via Cantarane, 2
25050 Rodengo Saiano (BS)
tel. 030/611197

Mirabella is owned by quite a number of partners. Some of these, like the oenologist Teresio Schiavi, have wine-linked interests; others come from different backgrounds, such as the set designer Enrico Job, who happens to be married to film director Lina Wertmüller. This is how the name Wertmüller has come to appear on the labels of two (non-DOCG) sparkling wines produced by this winery. At this year's tastings we tried a delightful Wertmüller Brut that came very close to getting Two Glasses. It has a pale straw color and a bead of some finesse in the glass; admirably clean aromas of fruit and toasted bread distinguish the nose. A well-judged "dosage" can be sensed on the palate, which is soft and caressing and finishes with lingering fruity notes. The Franciacorta Non Dosato '91 is Mirabella 's best offering: it has a brilliant greenish straw color; its fresh bouquet is redolent of white-fleshed fruit and tropical fruit, with delicate hints of aromatic herbs; the palate is round, dense, full and long. The Franciacorta Brut, lean of body and attractively yeasty on the nose, has an excellent perlage and a good general balance. Of the two Terre di Franciacorta wines, the good Bianco '97 has sweet perfumes but a somewhat acidic palate and the Rosso '96 is correctly made.

○	Franciacorta Non Dosato '91	🍷🍷	5
○	Franciacorta Brut	🍷	4
○	Terre di Franciacorta Bianco '97	🍷	3
○	Wertmüller Brut	🍷	4
●	Terre di Franciacorta Rosso '96		3
○	Franciacorta Brut	🍸🍸	4
○	Franciacorta Brut '90	🍸🍸	5
○	Terre di Franciacorta Bianco Barrique '95	🍸🍸	4
○	Terre di Franciacorta Bianco '96	🍸	3
●	Terre di Franciacorta Rosso Barrique '95	🍸	4

ROVESCALA (PV)

F.LLI AGNES
VIA CAMPO DEL MONTE, 1
27040 ROVESCALA (PV)
TEL. 0385/75206

A debut in the Guide for the young Agnes brothers of Rovescala and their estate in the foothills of the Oltrepò! This is the birthplace of Bonarda: the wine was already being produced in the area 800 years ago, as we learn from a notary's deed of the 12th century in which a certain Count Anselmo of Rovescala, in payment of a debt, agrees to supply 600 "congi " (around 20 hectoliters) "de puro vino suarum vinearum de Revascalla de meliori quod habuerit super locum " (of the very best pure wine from his vines in Rovescala). The Agnes family have been winegrowers since time immemorial: even they do not know exactly how long. It is Cristiano and Sergio, the sons of Giovanni, who are currently running the estate; Cristiano is an agronomist and looks after the vines and the cellar; Sergio handles business and promotion. The grapes grown on the estate's 10 hectares of vineyard are vinified in its well-equipped cellar. Most of them (90%) are bonarda; there is a little barbera and there are some encouraging experiments under way with pinot noir and cabernet sauvignon. The four Bonardas presented for tasting are remarkable. The oak-matured Campo del Monte '97 is of a deep purple hue, with fragrant perfumes of blackberry and almond; it reveals a powerful palate with just a touch of sweetness that shades off into lightly bitter notes of the little peach known as pêche de vigne. The full-bodied and harmonious Bonarda Vignazzo '97 has a hint of bubble. The Bonarda '97 which is called Possessione del Console, from the title of the former owner of the vineyard, who was Consul in Switzerland and Holland, comes from a particular clone known as "pignolo " and is as rich and powerful as the bottle 's label is ugly. Bonarda Cresta del Ghiffi '97 is a straightforward, genuine wine, made from late-harvested grapes.

●	O. P. Bonarda Campo del Monte '97	🍷🍷	3
●	O. P. Bonarda Possessione del Console '97	🍷🍷	3
●	O. P. Barbera '97	🍷	2
●	O. P. Bonarda Cresta del Ghiffi '97	🍷	3
●	O. P. Bonarda Vignazzo '97	🍷	3

S. COLOMBANO AL LAMBRO (MI)

PANIGADA-BANINO
VIA DELLA VITTORIA, 9/13
20078 S. COLOMBANO AL LAMBRO (MI)
TEL. 0371/89103

The Panigada family's Banino estate, which produces San Colombano, the only DOC in the province of Milan, makes a triumphal return to the Guide. Since the '50s the Panigadas have had vineyards (five hectares, around the hamlets of La Merla and San Pietro) and cellars in San Colombano al Lambro, between the Plain of Lodi and the lowlands of Pavia, roughly halfway between Milan and Pavia. The village was named after an Irish monk who found his way to Italy in the 6th century and reintroduced the cultivation of the vine after the barbarian invasions. The inhabitants of San Colombano are known as "banini " and Banino is the name the Panigadas have given their wines, which they produce in a rigorously traditional way: these are wines that speak in dialect, as they say. The best one is the red Riserva '93, a blend of croatina (60%) and barbera matured for 20 months in 750-liter oak barrels. Of a deep ruby color, it is redolent of wild blackberry, tobacco and spices (clove, vanilla), and has a dry, full, vigorous taste with a lightly bitter finish of pêche de vigne, those little peaches that often grow near grapevines: a good, attractively well-balanced wine that should keep beautifully (the Banino Riserva '90, for example, now no longer available, is still in perfect condition). The very successful red Banino '97 La Merla is fragrant and straightforward and has a light sparkle from secondary bottle fermentation. Both the Bianco '97 (80% riesling italico and some local varieties) and the Rosato '97, from 100% uva rara, are agreeable.

●	San Colombano Banino Ris. '93	🍷🍷	3
●	San Colombano Banino Vigna La Merla '97	🍷	1
○	Banino Bianco '97		1
⊙	Banino Rosato '97		1
●	San Colombano Banino Vigna La Merla '90	🍸🍸	4
○	San Colombano Banino Vigna La Merla '92	🍸	3
●	San Colombano Banino Vivace '93	🍸	3

S. GIULETTA (PV)

ISIMBARDA
FRAZ. CASTELLO
27046 S. GIULETTA (PV)
TEL. 0383/899256

The Isimbarda farm (named after the Marquises Isimbardi who founded Santa Giuletta at the end of the 17th century) is owned by the Meroni family and first appeared in the Guide last year. They produce several wines of interest and are more than likely to be making even better ones in future, given the care and attention lavished on their 33 hectares of vineyard. The cellar equipment is in itself quite promising but, as we all know, and should never forget, quality depends on the grapes. The vintage '97 of the Riesling della Vigna Belvedere (the riesling in question is mostly italico, but there is some Rhein) was vinified with 50% of the grapes cold-macerated on the skins for 24 hours at 4°C, followed by a controlled fermentation with selected yeasts. The result is a wine of a greenish yellow straw color with distinct perfumes of apricot, peach and linden blossom, and a crisp and soft but decided flavor. The most notable of the reds is the Bonarda Vivace '97, made from croatina grapes from the Ronco de ' Torti vineyard near Mornico Losana. It has a 4-5-day maceration and is refermented in the spring in pressure tanks to give it a light fizz. It is a lively wine, purple in color with a violet tinge; it offers heady aromas of wild cherry, ripe grape and bitter almond and reveals well-judged tannins on a palate with a distinct lightly bitter undertone. The white Pinot Nero in bianco '97 from the Selva Grande vineyard is dry and tasty, clean and crisp, with a slightly sharp, almost citric finish.

●	O. P. Bonarda Vivace '97	🍷	3
○	O. P. Riesling V. Belvedere '97	🍷	3
○	O. P. Pinot Nero in bianco '97		3
○	O. P. Pinot Nero in bianco '96	🍸	3
○	O. P. Riesling Italico '96	🍸	3

SCANZOROSCIATE (BG)

LA BRUGHERATA
VIA MEDOLAGO, 47
24020 SCANZOROSCIATE (BG)
TEL. 035/655202

A newcomer to the Guide, Patrizia Merati 's La Brugherata is a small estate with a great desire to make good wines. It lies seven kilometers east of Bergamo, the heart of the zone where the legendary Moscato Nero Passito is produced. The wines from the estate, which was purchased in 1985, did not appear on the market until 1992. They come from just four hectares of vineyard, but another one and a half recently replanted hectares should be producing shortly. The vines are cultivated by the agronomist Bruno Marengoni together with Signora Merati. The modern cellar is furnished with the most up-to-date equipment. We were astonished by the harmony and concentration of the Doglio Valcalepio Rosso Riserva '94, made from cabernet sauvignon and merlot matured for three years in a new 16-hectoliter Allier barrel. It is dark ruby in color and displays an intense bouquet of black cherry and vanilla, and a full-bodied palate, soft but firm, with smooth, mature tannins. This is the first Riserva released by the estate, and there's an Italian proverb that says you can tell from the morning if the day is going to be fine. The Valcalepio Rosso '95 is also good, but we were particularly interested in the Valcalepio Bianco Vescovado '97, a blend of chardonnay, pinot blanc and pinot gris with a clear gold color, distinct floral and fruited varietal notes and a full, crisp and tasty palate. Rounding off the range is an attractive Moscato di Scanzo Passito '96. The technical advice of Sergio Cantoni, an oenologist of sound experience, has done much to realize the potential of Brugherata 's grapes; now the challenge is to maintain the level achieved or, better yet, improve it.

●	Valcalepio Rosso Doglio Ris. '94	🍷🍷	4
○	Valcalepio Bianco Vescovado '97	🍷	3
●	Valcalepio Rosso '95	🍷	3
●	Valcalepio Moscato di Scanzo Passito Doge '96		6

SIRMIONE (BS)

CÀ DEI FRATI
FRAZ. LUGANA
VIA FRATI, 22
25010 SIRMIONE (BS)
TEL. 030/919468

Ca' dei Frati has been the best estate in the Garda area for years. Their perfectly clean and impeccable Luganas represent an innovation in wine-making in the area. But the Dal Cero family is not given to resting on its laurels, and has continued to invest and experiment. And, at last, with the stunning Pratto '96, a white from oak-matured chardonnay and sauvignon, they have won their first Three Glasses, joining the best wineries in the country. Pratto is an astonishing wine: it has a deep straw color elegantly tinged with green; its intense and complex bouquet offers aromas of rosewood, honey, musk, sugared almonds, ripe pineapple, banana, wisteria, vanilla, sweet pastry and goodness knows what else; on the palate it is dry, soft, crisp, lively and harmonious, with an elegant undertone of rose jam. It was impossible to give it less than our highest award. As for the others, the Lugana Il Brolettino '96 is living up to the Two Glasses it received last year, as is the excellent Tre Filer '95, a sweet white dessert wine. The appealing Chiaretto del Garda '97 has a delicate floral nose and a very savory, clean, racy palate, perhaps a bit lean, but crisp and attractive. The '97 Lugana I Frati, with its subtle fragrance of white flowers and citrus, graceful and well-balanced in the mouth, is quite good. We find this year 's Lugana Brut Cuvée dei Frati only worthy of mention, with its citron peel and crusty bread on the nose, green lemon on the palate and not much leneth.

	Wine	Glasses	
○	Pratto '96	🍷🍷🍷	4
⊙	Garda Bresciano Chiaretto '97	🍷	3
○	Cuvée dei Frati Brut		4
○	Lugana I Frati '97	🍷	3
○	Lugana Il Brolettino '95	YY	4
○	Lugana Il Brolettino '96	YY	4
○	Pratto '94	YY	4
○	Pratto '95	YY	4
○	Tre Filer '89	YY	5
○	Tre Filer '90	YY	5
○	Tre Filer '92	YY	5
○	Tre Filer '94	YY	5
○	Tre Filer '95	YY	5

TEGLIO (SO)

FAY
LOC. S. GIACOMO
VIA PILA CASELLI, 1
23030 TEGLIO (SO)
TEL. 0342/786071

Apart from Sforzato, which is the most highly prized wine in the Valtellina, our tastings have now revealed that another wine is improving by leaps and bounds: Sassella, which comes from the most renowned of the four Valtellina Superiore subzones. Sandro Fay's interpretation, Sassella Glicine '94, was one of the two top Sassellas we tasted this year. It has a lovely deep garnet color, and a strikingly clean bouquet which blends well-judged hints of toasty oak and licorice with its characteristic fruitiness. It shows off its distinct personality on a rounded palate, the tannins are smooth, the finish silky and long. The '94 and '95 vintages of the Valgella Ca ' Morei are less successful, and certainly not like the great versions of this wine that Fay, a fine oenologist, had made us think we could count on. In both cases, despite a good breadth of structure on the palate, we found oak-derived aromas of imperfect purity. The Sforzato '95 has an unmistakable individual style: lots of ripe fruit and jam on the nose lead to a sweet palate with smooth tannins, a deep finish and an aftertaste suggestive of over-ripe fruit.

	Wine	Glasses	
●	Valtellina Sup. Sassella Il Glicine '94	🍷🍷	4
●	Valtellina Sforzato '95	🍷	5
●	Valtellina Sup. Valgella Ca' Morei '94	🍷	4
●	Valtellina Sup. Valgella Ca' Morei '95	🍷	4
●	Valtellina Sforzato '89	YY	5
●	Valtellina Sforzato '94	YY	4
●	Valtellina Sup. Sassella Glicine '89	YY	4
●	Valtellina Sup. Valgella Ca' Morei '90	YY	5
●	Valtellina Sup. Valgella Ca' Morei '92	YY	4

TIRANO (SO)

CONTI SERTOLI SALIS
P.ZZA SALIS, 3
23037 TIRANO (SO)
TEL. 0342/710404

The Sertoli Salis range presented for the '99 edition of the Guide is remarkable. In a way this doesn 't surprise us, given the steady improvement seen in the last few years and, more importantly, the rock-solid determination of Claudio Introini, the oenologist and manager of the estate, and of Cesare Sertoli Salis, its owner, to go all out for excellence. One wine in particular absolutely fascinated us: the Sforzato Canua '95. Its bouquet combines spicy and balsamic notes with intense tones of syrup and tea. It is warm and very soft in the mouth, with dense flavors in the long finish: a splendid red that verges on the very highest of scores. Corte della Meridiana '95 is a red of great breeding with an important nose featuring aromatic notes of tobacco and in some ways suggestive of a Barolo. It is soft, full-bodied and velvety on the smooth and fascinatingly tannic palate. The rounded Saloncino '96 offers lots of fruit on the nose and a delightful quaffability; and the classic, well-made Sassella '95 gets a similar appraisal: appealing scents of raspberries emerge on the nose and the palate is moderately structured and well-balanced. The white Torre della Sirena '97 is very good, as usual; its nose is characterized by the finest of mineral notes and the palate is round and long-lasting.

●	Valtellina Sforzato Canua '95	🍷🍷	5
●	Valtellina Sup. Corte della Meridiana '95	🍷🍷	4
●	Il Saloncello '96	🍷	4
○	Torre della Sirena '97	🍷	3
●	Valtellina Sup. Sassella '95	🍷	3
●	Valtellina Sforzato Canua '90	♀♀	5
●	Valtellina Sforzato Canua '92	♀♀	5
●	Valtellina Sforzato Canua '93	♀♀	5
●	Valtellina Sforzato Canua '94	♀♀	5
●	Valtellina Sup. Corte della Meridiana '90	♀♀	5
●	Valtellina Sup. Corte della Meridiana '94	♀♀	4

TORRICELLA VERZATE (PV)

MONSUPELLO
VIA SAN LAZZARO, 5
27050 TORRICELLA VERZATE (PV)
TEL. 0383/896043

Monsupello is beginning to create problems... of space; in just one column it is not easy to summarize all the noteworthy wines produced by Carlo and Pierangelo Boatti with their viticultural consultant, the agronomist Paolo Fiocchi. The care taken in the vineyards is practically maniacal, the dedication to quality is total. The legendary Three Glasses are just around the corner, but for now the estate will have to make do, so to speak, with seven Two Glass awards and four One Glasses. And bear in mind that some of their wines weren't ready in time for the tastings. So, let 's begin. The Riesling Renano '97 is splendid, rich and harmonious; the Chardonnay '97 is varietal and very full-bodied; the Chardonnay Senso '96, a barriqued version, has uncommon structure and harmony; La Cuenta Passito Giallo '95, a mystery blend, is already impressive even before its bottle aging. The three classic method sparkling wines are all admirable, particularly the Nature, but the Pinot Nero Brut Classese '93 and the non-vintage Brut don 't mess around either. Among the reds the Oltrepò La Borla '95, still and partially barrique-matured; the Great Ruby Vivace '97 and the new Croatina Dolce Carlotta '97, slightly bubbly and sweet, stand out. The Pinot Nero in bianco I Germogli '97, an excellent white-vinified pinot noir, brings the series to a close.

○	La Cuenta Passito Giallo '95	🍷🍷	6
○	O. P. Chardonnay '97	🍷🍷	3
○	O. P. Chardonnay Senso '96	🍷🍷	4
○	O. P. Pinot Nero Brut Cl.	🍷🍷	4
○	O. P. Pinot Nero Cl. Nature	🍷🍷	4
○	O. P. Pinot Nero Classese '93	🍷🍷	4
○	O. P. Riesling Renano '97	🍷🍷	3
●	Croatina Dolce Carlotta Vivace '97	🍷	3
○	O. P. Pinot Nero in bianco I Germogli '97	🍷	3
●	O. P. Rosso Great Ruby Vivace '97	🍷	3
●	O. P. Rosso La Borla '95	🍷	4
○	La Cuenta Passito Giallo '93	♀♀	6
○	O. P. Brut Classico '92	♀♀	4
○	O. P. Chardonnay '96	♀♀	3

VILLA DI TIRANO (SO)

Triacca

Via Nazionale, 121
23030 Villa di Tirano (SO)
tel. 0342/701352

Domenico Triacca has recently completed the enlargement and modernization of his vinification cellar. We won't even go into his ceaseless efforts and experimentation in his vineyards, where the single-minded passion of this oenologist seems at times to verge on madness. He has, for example, been trying out new ways of planting that allow him to mechanize much of the necessary work between rows of vines, significantly reducing both time and labor. The results of his meticulous planning are available for all to see and this year's wines are the proof of the pudding. Prestigio '95, made from nebbiolo, reveals superb elegance: it has complex perfumes with characteristic fruited notes; on the palate, it reveals significant structure and softness, with well-judged and integrated oak: one of the most interesting Valtellina wines we tasted. The Riserva Triacca '94 has a little less elegance on the nose, with its characteristic aromas of new-mown hay and mushrooms, but a comparable palate, soft, balanced and long. The Sforzato '95 is obviously made from excellent grapes; it offers aromas of slightly over-ripe fruit with clear tobacco notes, and a structured palate, though not yet as dense as one might expect. The Valtellina La Gatta '95 (still undergoing bottle aging) is well executed, fresh and broad, and its tannins are balanced and elegant. The correct white La Contea '97 displays a linear, floral nose and a clean and expressive palate.

	Wine	Glasses	Price
●	Valtellina Prestigio '95	▼▼	4
●	Valtellina Sup. Ris. Triacca '94	▼▼	4
○	La Contea '97	▼	3
●	Valtellina Casa La Gatta '95	▼	3
●	Valtellina Sforzato '95	▼	4
●	Valtellina Prestigio '89	▽▽	4
●	Valtellina Prestigio '94	▽▽	4
●	Valtellina Sforzato Il Corvo '94	▽▽	4
●	Valtellina Sup. Ris. Triacca '90	▽▽	4
●	Valtellina Sup. Ris. Triacca '91	▽▽	4
●	Valtellina Sup. Sassella '89	▽▽	4
●	Valtellina Tradizione '91	▽▽	3
●	Valtellina Prestigio '91	▽	4
●	Valtellina Sforzato '94	▽	4

ZENEVREDO (PV)

Tenuta Il Bosco

Loc. Il Bosco
27049 Zenevredo (PV)
tel. 0385/245326

Zonin's model estate on the Oltrepò hills has recently increased its vineyard holding to about 125 hectares and has introduced two new reds: a Bonarda Vivace from the Poggio Pelato vineyard and the still Barbera Teodote, both made under the supervision of the Gruppo Zonin's new head oenologist, Franco Giacosa, long a renowned figure on the Italian wine scene. Teodote '96 is made from 100% barbera vinified in modern roto-vats with very light skin maceration. The wine is then matured in French barriques. It is deep ruby in color, with spicy, varietal perfumes and a vigorous sinewy palate with a distinctly bitterish finish. It almost reached the Two Glass level but still needs time in bottle; it will doubtless improve. The Bonarda '97 Poggio Pelato undergoes a slight secondary fermentation in a pressure tank. It is better than the more traditional Bonarda Il Bosco, richer and more perfumed. A new sparkling wine has appeared as well: the Brut Classico Regal Cuvée, which has taken the place of the Extra Dry Il Bosco. It is a blend of pinot noir and chardonnay with four years of maturation. It shows an excellent perlage and broad perfumes of artemesia, bay and crusty bread; it's dry without being harsh and is perfectly mature. The Philéo, a tank-method bubbly made from pinot noir, is softer, fresher and fruitier after its long time under pressure. The three mildly bubbly ("vivace") whites, the Riesling Renano, the Pinot Nero in bianco and the slightly more anonymous Cortese, are all attractive and easy drinking.

	Wine	Glasses	Price
●	O. P. Barbera Teodote '96	▼	4
●	O. P. Bonarda Vivace Poggio Pelato '97	▼	2
○	O. P. Brut Cl. Regal Cuvée	▼	4
○	O. P. Cortese Vivace '97	▼	2
○	O. P. Philéo Brut	▼	3
○	O. P. Pinot Nero in bianco Vivace '97	▼	2
○	O. P. Riesling Renano Vivace '97	▼	2*
●	O. P. Bonarda Vivace '97		2
○	O. P. Brut Cl. '92	▽▽	2
○	O. P. Moscato '95	▽▽	2*
●	O. P. Bonarda '95	▽	2*
○	O. P. Extra Dry Il Bosco	▽	4
○	O. P. Pinot Spumante Philéo	▽	3

OTHER WINERIES

The following producers obtained good scores in our tastings with one or more of their wines:

PROVINCE OF BERGAMO

Cantina Sociale Val San Martino
Pontida, tel. 035/795035,
Valcalepio Bianco '97,
Valcalepio Rosso '95,
Valcalepio Rosso Sel. '94

Cantina Sociale Bergamasca
San Paolo d'Argon, tel. 035/951098,
Merlot della Bergamasca '97,
Valcalepio Bianco Orologio '97,
Valcalepio Rosso Orologio '96,
Valcalepio Rosso Ris. '94

Pecis
San Paolo d'Argon, tel. 035/959104,
Valcalepio Bianco '97,
Valcalepio Bianco Dolce '97,
Valcalepio Rosso '95

Bonaldi - Cascina del Bosco
Sorisole, tel. 035/571701,
Bonaldi Brut Classico,
Cantoalto '91,
Valcalepio Bianco '97,
Valcalepio Rosso Ris. '94

La Tordela
Torre de' Roveri, tel. 035/580172,
Valcalepio Bianco '97,
Valcalepio Rosso '95

PROVINCE OF BRESCIA

Cooperativa Vitivinicola Cellatica Gussago
Cellatica, tel. 030/2522418,
Franciacorta Brut

La Boscaiola
Cologne, tel. 030/7156386,
Franciacorta Brut

Barboglio de' Gaioncelli
Cortefranca, tel. 030/9826831,
Franciacorta Brut,
T. d. F. Rosso '96

Visconti
Desenzano del Garda, tel. 030/9120681,
Lugana Brut,
Lugana S. Onorata '97

Boschi
Erbusco, tel. 030/7703096,
Franciacorta Brut

Longhi de Carli, Erbusco, tel. 030/7760280,
T. d. F. Bianco '97

San Cristoforo, Erbusco, tel. 030/7760482,
T. d. F. Rosso '96

Sit del Toni, Erbusco, tel. 030/7722422,
Franciacorta Brut

Berardi, Mazzano, tel. 030/2620152,
Franciacorta Brut

Ca' dei Colli
Monticelli Brusati, tel. 030/3756043,
Franciacorta Brut

Vezzoli, Palazzolo, tel. 030/7386177,
Franciacorta Brut

Bredasole, Paratico, tel. 035/910407,
Franciacorta Extra Brut

Le Marchesine, Passirano, tel. 030/657005,
Franciacorta Brut '93,
Franciacorta Non Dosato '94

La Pertica
Polpenazze del Garda, tel. 0365/651471,
Garda Bresciano Rosso Le Sincette '97,
Le Zalte Rosso '95

Comincioli
Puegnago del Garda, tel. 0365/651141,
Garda Bresciano Chiaretto '97

Leali di Monteacuto
Puegnago del Garda, tel. 0365/651291,
Riviera del Garda Groppello '97

PROVINCE OF MANTOVA

Cantina Sociale di Quistello
Quistello, tel. 0376/618118,
Lambrusco Mantovano Banda Blu '97,
Lambrusco Mantovano Banda Rossa '97

PROVINCE OF PAVIA

Cantina Sociale Intercomunale di Broni
Broni, tel. 0385/51505,
O. P. Brut Classico,
O. P. Buttafuoco '95,
O. P. Moscato Spumante '97,
O. P. Rosso '97,
O. P. Sangue di Giuda '97

Maga Lino, Broni, tel. 0385/51212,
O. P. Rosso Barbacarlo '97,
O. P. Rosso Montebuono '97,
O. P. Rosso Ronchetto '97

Fiamberti
Canneto Pavese, tel. 0385/88019,
O. P. Bonarda '97,
O. P. Buttafuoco Solenga '97,
O. P. Pinot Nero in bianco '97

Quacquarini
Canneto Pavese, tel. 0385/60152,
O. P. Bonarda '97

Riccardo Albani
Casteggio, tel. 0383/83622,
O. P. Riesling Italico '96,
O. P. Rosso Vigna della Casona '95

Cantina Sociale Casteggio
Casteggio, tel. 0383/890696,
O. P. Malvasia '97

Clastidio - Ballabio
Casteggio, tel. 0383/82724,
O. P. Bonarda '97,
O. P. Pinot Nero in bianco Fior di Pesco '97,
O. P. Rosso Narbusto '95

Ruiz de Cardenas
Casteggio, tel. 0383/82301,
O. P. Pinot Nero Brumano '96

Tenuta Pegazzera
Casteggio, tel. 0383/804646,
O. P. Pinot Nero '97,
O. P. Pinot Nero Brut '96,
O. P. Pinot Nero in bianco '97

Travaglino, Casteggio, tel. 0383/872222,
O. P. Riesling Italico '97

Ca' Montebello
Cigognola, tel. 0385/85182,
O. P. Chardonnay '97,
O. P. Pinot Nero '97

Monterucco, Cigognola, tel. 0385/85151,
O. P. Bonarda Il Modello '97,
O. P. Pinot Nero in bianco '97

Ca' del Gè
Montalto Pavese, tel. 0383/870179,
O. P. Barbera '97,
O. P. Barbera Vigna Varmasi '97,
O. P. Moscato '97,
O. P. Pinot Nero in bianco '97,
O. P. Riesling Italico '97

La Piotta
Montalto Pavese, tel. 0383/870178,
O. P. Barbera '97,
O. P. Riesling Italico '97

La Costaiola,
Montebello della Battaglia,
tel. 0383/83169,
O. P. Pinot Nero in bianco '97

Torti Pietro
Montecalvo Versiggia, tel. 0385/99763,
O. P. Bonarda '97

Cascina Gnocco
Mornico Losana, tel. 0383/873226,
Bianco Ambrogina '97,
O. P. Rosso Nibbio '95

Martilde
Rovescala, tel. 0385/756280,
O. P. Barbera '96

San Giorgio
Santa Giuletta, tel. 0383/899168,
Castelsangiorgio Bianco '95,
O. P. Pinot Nero '95

La Versa
Santa Maria della Versa, tel. 0385/798411,
O. P. Brut Classico '92,
O. P. Bonarda '97,
O. P. Moscato '97,
O. P. Pinot Nero in bianco '97

Il Fontanino
Stradella, tel. 0385/49920,
O. P. Bonarda '97

PROVINCE OF SONDRIO

Nera
Chiuro, tel. 0342/482631,
Valtellina Sup. Grumello Ris. '94,
Valtellina Sup. Inferno '94

Mamete Prevostini
Mese, tel. 0343/41003,
Valtellina Sup. Inferno '95,
Valtellina Sup. Sassella '95

AR.PE.PE.
Sondrio, tel. 0342/214120,
Valtellina Sup. Grumello Buon Consiglio '91,
Valtellina Sup. Sassella Vigna Regina '91

La Castellina
Sondrio, tel. 0342/512954,
Valtellina Sup. Sassella '95

F.lli Bettini
Teglio, tel. 0342/786068,
Valtellina Sforzato '94,
Valtellina Sup. Sassella Reale '94

TRENTINO

Much work has been done in recent years to revitalize viticulture and wine-making in this beautiful province in northern Italy. With a millennium of vine cultivation to its credit, this land has now been traversed far and wide by expert agronomists, and local production has achieved notable results. Quantity too has expanded phenomenally, with more than a million hectoliters produced. Not at all bad! A great part of this wine, furthermore, comes from cooperatives which have created consortiums for marketing and export. The results are enormously positive. It is thanks to them that jobs have been created, and that a great part of the Dolomites' splendid vineyards are still productive. And some of them have turned out excellent wine. On the other hand the cooperatives, despite having organized and sustained production of notable quality and quantity, seem to have lost some of the zeal required in the creation of a great wine. Their products, in other words, are properly made, and even, most of the time, very good. But they seem to be soulless. The commercial decisions that have been made seem, in many cases, to favor the globalization of wine production (joint ventures to set up wineries in China, for example), and the conquest of foreign markets, rather than protecting and developing local resources. And this is a pity, because the wealth of native grape varieties available calls out for further research and experimentation so as to produce wines of a more distinctive personality, reflecting the distinctive character of this fascinating Italian region. Trentino, however, is not only a land of giant wineries. It also belongs to small producers who cultivate their own vines and make only a few thousand bottles a year. Trentino, these wine-makers assure us, will be different in the coming millennium. It will be characterized by the rediscovery of local grapes, long forgotten; there will be Dolomitic wines, rich in character, side by side with pockets of internationally famous varietals. It will be clear that this region, with its thousand years of oenological experience, needs fear no rivals. Meanwhile, we present the three labels that have earned our Three Glasses. First, one of the subtlest, most elegant and long-lived of Italian sparkling wines, the Giulio Ferrari Riserva del Fondatore '90. It is a perfect expression of everything that Chardonnay from the best vineyards in the province can offer. Elisabetta Foradori's Granato '96 is probably the best wine she has ever made, and successfully combines depth and solid structure with a lovely drinkability and incredible finesse. Guerrieri Gonzaga's '95 San Leonardo wins its umpty-umpth Three Glasses. It's a grand wine in every sense, demonstrating once again that in the presence of a great wine all quibbling about grapes, barrels and technology seems immaterial.

AVIO (TN)

CANTINA SOCIALE DI AVIO
VIA DANTE, 14
38063 AVIO (TN)
TEL. 0464/684008

It is a pleasure to include the Cantina Sociale di Avio in our guide. This cooperative has for some years been making a name for itself because of the distinctive personality of its wines and also because of its courageous innovations in vineyard and cellar for the purpose of developing and relaunching the best that the Campi Sarni can offer. These are highly desirable lands, which a few estates that had in the past devoted most of their efforts to making spumante or white wines have set aside for the planting of red grapes. Their idea is that by using what are generally held to be the best locations in the province, they will be in a position to compete with really great red wines. Under these circumstances the local wine cooperative, which has 450 members, could hardly sit on its hands. Its young director, Alfonso Iannielli, together with the equally enthusiastic Eugenio Rosi, an enologist with firm convictions, has put together a decidedly attractive list of wines. The Bordeaux blend Trentino Rosso '96, in which the cabernet is softened by a merlot of great finesse, is easy to drink and a bit jammy; it's full-bodied, with a touch of grassiness and a fascinating finish. And it's very good value for money. Unusual because fruity and almost too easy to drink, the Pinot Nero '96 was made in answer to a local challenge. The Marzemino '97, with a taste that overwhelms its aroma, is an indication of the potentiality of this area for reds. The Trentino Pinot Grigio '97 and Trentino Bianco '96 are both good if unremarkable wines.

●	Trentino Rosso '96	🍷🍷	3*
○	Trentino Bianco '96	🍷	2
●	Trentino Marzemino '97	🍷	2
○	Trentino Pinot Grigio '97	🍷	2
●	Trentino Pinot Nero '96	🍷	3

AVIO (TN)

TENUTA SAN LEONARDO
LOC. SAN LEONARDO, 3
FRAZ. BORGHETTO
38060 AVIO (TN)
TEL. 0464/689004 - 689000

Coming into this wine estate, a haunting spot just made for vineyards, in a fascinating corner of Trentino, is really quite moving. The Marquises Guerrieri Gonzaga know how to yoke their aristocratic polish to a genuine rural simplicity. They do it spontaneously, directly involving all the people they work with at the Tenuta San Leonardo. As a result the vineyards, home only to cabernet and merlot, become more and more beautiful, and the grapes ever more delicious. It's sufficient to sip the San Leonardo '95 in order to understand how Marquis Carlo's approach is in tune not only with the peculiarities of the Campi Sarni (a micro-zone in the southernmost part of Trentino which is waiting for official recognition as an independent wine area) but also with the dedication of its makers. This is a really remarkable red wine, starting with its color, an almost impenetrable ruby. The nose presents a dense impression of ripe fruits and a delightful hint of wild herbs, a hallmark of this thoroughbred. And it fills the mouth with a taste that seems an enticing velvety caress. The Merlot '95 is, of course, different from its more famous older brother. It is pleasing both to the eye, with its rich garnet reflections, and in the mouth, where it is easy, full and fruity, and has an elegant texture. More so here, perhaps, than in any other cellar — class tells...

●	San Leonardo '95	🍷🍷🍷	5
●	Trentino Merlot '95	🍷🍷	3*
●	San Leonardo '88	YYY	5
●	San Leonardo '90	YYY	5
●	San Leonardo '93	YYY	5
●	San Leonardo '94	YYY	5
●	San Leonardo '91	YY	5
●	Trentino Cabernet '93	YY	3*
●	Trentino Cabernet '94	YY	3*
●	Trentino Merlot '92	YY	3*
●	Trentino Merlot '95	YY	3*
●	Villa Gresti '93	YY	3*

AVIO (TN)

VALLAROM
LOC. MASI DI VO' SINISTRO, 21
38063 AVIO (TN)
TEL. 0464/505070 - 684297

Perhaps we were harsh, but it seems that our criticism of this estate in the last edition of the Guide was right on the mark. Professor Attilio Scienza's wines this year show a distinct improvement. Naturally they were helped by good harvests, but also by the revived enthusiasm that this most appealing and expert wine-maker has succeeded in directing to his vines and hence to his wines. The vintage '97 Pinot Bianco and Marzemino have all the vigor of youth, particularly the latter, which was made according to criteria quite different (was there perhaps a brief carbonic maceration?) from those governing traditional local practices, in order to capture all the fragrances and the exquisite delicacy of the most famous wine of the Vallagarina. The other white, Campi Sarni, has a decided character and is what the Scienza family (management is soon going to pass to young Michele, who has studied oenology, acquired experience internationally and got a degree in agricultural science) has devised to make the best possible use of the vines in Avio. There's a touch of wood, lovely fruit and a long finish. Its qualities are mirrored in the Chardonnay Riserva, which has well-judged wood and plenty of taste and goes down easily. Of the other two red Riservas, both '95s, we prefer the Cabernet Sauvignon, which is rounded, engaging and well-balanced, while the Pinot Nero, although unquestionably well made, has too much of a grassy accent, something one finds increasingly in this wine in Trentino as well as elsewhere.

	Wine	Glasses	Price
○	Campi Sarni '96	🍷🍷	4
●	Trentino Cabernet Sauvignon Ris. '95	🍷🍷	4
○	Trentino Chardonnay Ris. '96	🍷🍷	4
●	Trentino Marzemino '97	🍷🍷	3
○	Trentino Pinot Bianco '97	🍷	3
●	Trentino Pinot Nero Ris. '95	🍷	4
●	Trentino Cabernet '90	YY	5
●	Trentino Cabernet Sauvignon Ris. '94	YY	4
○	Trentino Chardonnay '95	YY	4
○	Trentino Chardonnay Ris. '90	YY	4
○	Trentino Chardonnay Ris. '93	YY	4
○	Trentino Chardonnay Vendemmia Tardiva '92	YY	5

CALLIANO (TN)

VALLIS AGRI
VIA VALENTINI, 37
38060 CALLIANO (TN)
TEL. 0464/834113

SAV is a name to be reckoned with in Trentino agriculture. It's the acronym of the Società Agricola Vallagarina, a cooperative consortium that pursues a variety of activities, from dairy and cheese-making to producing wine, fruit, feed and farm equipment. Intent upon carving out a place for themselves in the world of wine, they have, for the past ten years, been operating Vallis Agri (the Latin root of Vallagarina), a winery in a charming grange from the turn of the century in Calliano. They are meticulous in their selection of grapes, especially for their Marzemino, the prime mover of local wine-making. Both the normal version and the special Ziresi are very inviting, full and fruity, and also well-balanced, in part because they have been released after a year's aging in the bottle. The same is true of the Trentino Rosso, a Bordeaux-style red, which has, however, a slightly muted nose, although there is substance there for the palate. The white Aura is a delightful wine, complex, generous and harmonious. The Arcadio is good too, a lagrein rosé that at first seems just easy drinking, but in fact reveals considerable structure. Both the Nosiola (a grape you find a lot in these parts) and the Pinot Grigio are simple but well made. The Moscato Giallo seems more of a success. It has lovely color and mineral aromas combined with a fruity fragrance: a dry and pleasing wine.

	Wine	Glasses	Price
●	Trentino Marzemino dei Ziresi '96	🍷🍷	3
○	Trentino Moscato Giallo '97	🍷🍷	3
⊙	Arcadio '97	🍷	3
○	Aura '97	🍷	3
●	Trentino Rosso '94	🍷	4
○	Trentino Pinot Grigio '97		3
●	Paris '93	Y	4
●	Trentino Cabernet '90	Y	4
●	Trentino Cabernet '92	Y	4
●	Trentino Marzemino dei Ziresi '93	Y	4
●	Trentino Rosso '91	Y	4

CIVEZZANO (TN)

MASO CANTANGHEL
LOC. FORTE
VIA MADONNINA, 33
38045 CIVEZZANO (TN)
TEL. 0461/859050

Yes, it's true: Merlot Tajapreda '97 is a really good wine. Once again Piero Zabini has given his personal stamp to the wine of the future. This red is bottled very young, so as to make the most of the immediate charm of a fresh, tenacious wine with a vast range of red berry scents. It's also the product of what was a fantastic vintage for the small and charming Maso Cantanghel estate as well. Now that they have finished converting their Austro-Hungarian fortress into a winery, they have at last been able to concentrate all their attention on their wines, and with what results! The Chardonnay Vigna Piccola '97 is very concentrated, stylish, fragrant and well-structured. We found a distinct personality also in the white wine named after the fortress where it's made: Forte di Mezzo, a blend of chardonnay, pinot bianco and sauvignon. And now for the reds. Piero Zabini was one of the first to bet on pinot nero. He insisted on planting it on the higher slopes in a marginal area, going against received local opinion. And he has been proven right, by a red wine of lovely elegance and great intensity, with a structure that perhaps could do with more balance but is already a pleasure. The Rosso di Pila '96 is exemplary: it's among the most concentrated and powerful cabernet sauvignons we tasted in the Trentino, with notes of rich spice and even bittersweet chocolate on the palate. These are wines one could call, given the location of the winery, solid bulwarks for the defense of the best traditions of Trentino wine-making.

	Wine	Glasses	Price
○	Trentino Bianco Forte di Mezzo '97	🍷🍷	3*
●	Trentino Cabernet Sauvignon Rosso di Pila '96	🍷🍷	5
○	Trentino Chardonnay Vigna Piccola '97	🍷🍷	4
●	Trentino Merlot Tajapreda '97	🍷🍷	3*
●	Trentino Pinot Nero Piero Zabini '96	🍷	5
●	Trentino Cabernet Sauvignon Rosso di Pila '95	🍷🍷 (white)	5
○	Trentino Chardonnay Vigna Piccola '96	🍷🍷 (white)	4
●	Trentino Merlot Tajapreda '96	🍷🍷 (white)	3*

FAEDO (TN)

GRAZIANO FONTANA
VIA CASE SPARSE, 9
38010 FAEDO (TN)
TEL. 0461/650400

Chardonnay and Sauvignon: a duo this small producer can enter in any race, even against the old favorite thoroughbreds, thanks in part to a fantastic vintage, but most of all to the meticulous care lavished on his lovely vines on the Faedo hillsides, and to the equal competence at work in the cellar. We tried a crisp Chardonnay '97, with unbelievable structure, a fascinating acidulous motif and clear, focussed substance on the palate. The Sauvignon too is very typical of its grape, concentrated, full-bodied and well-balanced, perhaps the most successful white offered by this fine wine-maker, who is attempting to capture in his wines the characteristic fragrance of his highland vineyards. This is true also of both his Müller Thurgau, redolent of hay and fresh fines herbes, with a wonderfully pleasing rustic touch in the finish, and of his delightfully peppery Traminer Aromatico. We know the whites are really good, but so are the two reds from this estate, Lagrein and Pinot Nero. We were particularly happy with the former, vintage '96, which has much more structure and a deep, translucent color. Perhaps we were swayed by the medley of sensations provoked by a light hint of vanilla and a great density, together with a fruity, youthful elegance.

	Wine	Glasses	Price
○	Trentino Chardonnay '97	🍷🍷	3
●	Trentino Lagrein di Faedo '96	🍷🍷	3
○	Trentino Müller Thurgau '97	🍷🍷	3
○	Trentino Sauvignon di Faedo '97	🍷🍷	3
●	Trentino Pinot Nero di Faedo '96	🍷	4
○	Trentino Traminer Aromatico '97	🍷	3
○	Sauvignon di Faedo '94	🍷🍷 (white)	3*
○	Sauvignon di Faedo '95	🍷🍷 (white)	3*
●	Trentino Lagrein di Faedo '95	🍷🍷 (white)	3*
○	Trentino Müller Thurgau '96	🍷🍷 (white)	3*
●	Trentino Pinot Nero '94	🍷🍷 (white)	4*
○	Trentino Sauvignon di Faedo '96	🍷🍷 (white)	3*

FAEDO (TN)

Pojer & Sandri

Loc. Molini, 6
38010 Faedo (TN)
tel. 0461/650342

Mario Pojer and Fiorentina Sandri should be well pleased because their entire range of wines is successful. Their Rosso Faye, even though it doesn't come up to the level of preceding years, is persuasively attractive and well-balanced, with lots of vanilla. Citron, eucalyptus and graphite enhance the dominating flavors of red currants and chocolate which this wine offers, although not with such clear focus as formerly. Its satisfying aromatic length makes it a distinguished and very enjoyable wine. All the other wines are dependable, and two stand out: the Essenzia and the Pinot Nero Riserva '95. They are both highly individual, the fruit of time well spent among the vines and in the cellar. The Müller Thurgau, thanks to an up-to-the-minute approach to wine-making, is a prototype of the new "mountain wines". Then there's the Spumante (made from wines of two different years) with its hint of toast and bread fresh from the oven, its tiny elegant bubbles, and its suave and entrancing finish. The Pinot Nero Riserva differs from others of this category in its fresh note of cherries and deliberate lightness of body. We also found their soft and succulent Sauvignon above the Trentino average, as we did the Chardonnay (the "wooded" version, called Bianco Faye, is good too).

	Wine	Rating	Price
●	Rosso Faye '95	▼▼	5
○	Bianco Faye '95	▼▼	4
○	Essenzia Vendemmia Tardiva '97	▼▼	4
○	Spumante Cuveé Brut Ris.	▼▼	5
○	Trentino Chardonnay '97	▼▼	4
○	Trentino Müller Thurgau '97	▼▼	4
●	Trentino Pinot Nero Ris. '95	▼▼	5
○	Trentino Sauvignon '97	▼▼	4
●	Rosso Faye '93	▽▽▽	5
●	Rosso Faye '94	▽▽▽	5
○	Essenzia Vendemmia Tardiva '96	▽▽	4
●	Trentino Pinot Nero Ris. '93	▽▽	5

FAEDO (TN)

Villa Piccòla

Loc. Villa Piccola, 4
38010 Faedo (TN)
tel. 0461/650420 - 0335/5732463

A map in the shape of a wine bottle, supported by old winepresses, indicates the lanes that lead to some microscopic cellars in Faedo. As one climbs up towards the best-known viticultural hill in Trentino one immediately notices Villa Piccola. After passing a few dozen meters of trellised vines overlooking the Rotalian plain, here we are at Walter Rossi's estate. A great beech adorns his sign, as well as his label, indicating that we are in a part of the country devoted to this noble tree. With modesty and much courtesy, the owner offers us those wines they're proudest of in these parts, from Müller Thurgau to Pinot Nero, Nosiola and Chardonnay, finishing with Traminer and Sauvignon. In our tasting, his Pinot Nero stood out, giving Villa Piccola full title to inclusion in the Guide. It is graceful and fragrant, more elegant on the nose than on the palate, where it is nevertheless satisfying, well blended and persistent. The white wines are generally good and quite distinctive, especially the Chardonnay. But the Traminer has a crisp spiciness, the Müller Thurgau is fragrant, the Sauvignon has about it that freshness typical of a very young vine, and the Nosiola has a pleasing touch of hazelnut, in keeping with its name, its grape and the wines of Faedo.

	Wine	Rating	Price
●	Trentino Pinot Nero '96	▼▼	4
○	Trentino Chardonnay '97	▼	3
○	Trentino Müller Thurgau '97	▼	3
○	Trentino Nosiola '97	▼	3
○	Trentino Sauvignon '97	▼	3
○	Trentino Traminer '97	▼	3

ISERA (TN)

CANTINA D'ISERA
VIA AL PONTE, 1
38060 ISERA (TN)
TEL. 0464/433795

This long-established wine cooperative is undergoing a moment of radical change. They want to spread the word that excellent wines are being made in Trentino, and that the Cantina is among those making them. And the wine market is saying to them, "You're right!". The winery has become a construction site: the part where wine is made is enlarged; the part where the barrels are stored, rebuilt; and a guest house has been built for visitors. It is, however, in the marzemino vineyards that the most important decisions are being made. New clones have been selected, and the vines have been replanted after careful consideration of both exposure and the nature of the soil. An enormous amount of intelligent effort, including important progress in vinification, has already produced significant results, as we immediately perceived in the tastings. The Marzeminos, both the normal one and the special Etichetta Verde, are even fruitier and more attractive. The other reds have increased in body, particularly the Bordeaux blend, Novecentosette (named after the year, 1907, in which the cellar was founded). Both the Merlot, a very worthy effort, and the Cabernet can count on improvement in the bottle. The whites are distinguished by their raciness and delicate aromas, quince in the case of the Pinot Grigio, which finishes with a pleasing note of bitterness. The Moscato Giallo is completely different. It's dry and intriguing to sip, splendidly fruity, intense and captivating. Of course this grape has always done well in Vallagarina, even though its full potential has yet to be realized.

	Wine	Glasses	Price
●	Trentino Marzemino Etichetta Verde '97	2 black glasses	3*
○	Trentino Moscato Giallo '97	2 black glasses	3
●	Trentino Rosso Novecentosette '95	2 black glasses	3
●	Trentino Cabernet '96	1 black glass	2
●	Trentino Marzemino '97	1 black glass	2
●	Trentino Merlot '96	1 black glass	2
○	Trentino Pinot Grigio '97	1 black glass	2
●	Trentino Marzemino Etichetta Verde '96	2 white glasses	3*
●	Trentino Merlot '95	2 white glasses	2*

ISERA (TN)

DE TARCZAL
LOC. MARANO
38060 ISERA (TN)
TEL. 0464/409134

1997 was an exceptional year for Marzemino, the wine that symbolizes the whole of the Vallagarina, and Isera in particular. Hence Ruggero de Tarczal decided to surprise us with a new special selection, its label dedicated to an officer of the Hussars in honor of his family connections with the Austro-Hungarian dynasty. His Husar Marzemino, with its beautiful purple color and its progression of extraordinarily pleasurable tastes, is complex and elegantly balanced to the nose, with suggestions of preserved fruits and Parma violets. Our compliments also for his traditional Marzemino, notable for its fragrance and concentration, and an easy drinkability rarely found in this wine so dearly loved by the local inhabitants. This was generally proclaimed a phenomenal vintage, and its benefits are to be found in this year's whites as well. The Chardonnay and Pinot Bianco are both straightforward and richly colored, with a high concentration of sugars and perfumes, and excellent balance. The Pinot Bianco, especially supple, light but persistent, offers a complex bouquet of ripe apples and a lively personality.

	Wine	Glasses	Price
●	Trentino Marzemino di Isera Husar '97	2 black glasses	4
○	Trentino Chardonnay '97	1 black glass	2
●	Trentino Marzemino di Isera '97	1 black glass	3
○	Trentino Pinot Bianco '97	1 black glass	2*
●	Trentino Marzemino di Isera '96	2 white glasses	3*
●	Trentino Cabernet Sauvignon '95	1 white glass	3
●	Trentino Merlot d'Isera '95	1 white glass	3

ISERA (TN)

ENRICO SPAGNOLLI
VIA G. B. ROSINA, 4/A
38060 ISERA (TN)
TEL. 0464/409054

Spagnolli is a winery that functions as if it were a small farm, dedicating most of its attention to its tiny plots of vines scattered here and there on the hills above the right bank of the Adige. The young owner, Luigi Spagnolli, a wine technician, takes personal care of his own vines and those of the growers who for scores of years have entrusted their grapes to the expertly run cellars of his family. Luigi, whose expertise includes viticulture and viniculture, has decided not to concentrate only on Marzemino (although he makes a good one in the local manner), the wine most acclaimed and heavily produced in the Vallagarina, but to diversify his list and emphasize his personal style. So it was not a matter of chance that he produced for our tasting four whites and two reds, which did not include a Marzemino. His Tebro '96, a Bordeaux blend, notable for its full body and caressing harmony, is not excessively vegetal or tannic and has a long and tasty finish. The Pinot Nero seems soft and supple but still mute. Of the whites, the rich Traminer has lots of spice for nose and palate, and a hint of ginger. The Moscato Giallo Secco is successful, the Müller Thurgau fragrant and drinkable, and we found an enjoyable freshness in the light Nosiola.

●	Trentino Rosso Tebro '96	🍷🍷	4
○	Trentino Traminer Aromatico '97	🍷🍷	3
○	Trentino Moscato Giallo '97	🍷	3
○	Trentino Müller Thurgau '97	🍷	3
○	Trentino Nosiola '97	🍷	3
●	Trentino Pinot Nero '96	🍷	4

LASINO (TN)

PRAVIS
VIA LAGOLO, 28
38076 LASINO (TN)
TEL. 0461/564305

The Pravis estate produces enjoyable simple wines that are nevertheless highly personal. Here, with a stubborn persistence, they cultivate tiny terraces scattered among the lakes and mountains that surround the Dolomites of Brenta, to obtain a wide range of wines, Nosiola first of all, but also wines that make the most of old-fashioned grapes (gropello and franconia) as well as some new experimental varieties. The trio of owners, Chisté, Pedrini and Zambarda, bet on the syrah grape and came up with a winner, their Syrae '96, of a dense, deep garnet color, with distinct aromas of wild blackberries, red currants and sour cherries and a characteristic spicy touch of white pepper. In the mouth it seems round, well made, tasty and youthfully persistent. It's a wine with breeding, as is its companion, the cabernet Fratagranda '95, the best version made so far. Harmonious to nose and palate, it presents a complex array of aromas (including the grassy note usually found locally) dominated by suggestions of blueberries, vanilla and chocolate, which pop up again in the mouth, where the wine's well-balanced acidity makes itself felt, and it has a long, silky, enchanting finish. Much more of a simple immediacy is to be found in the Nosiola Le Frate, Müller Thurgau St. Thomà and the Pinot Nero Madruzzo, which has more elegance than structure. Fullness of body isn't wanting in their Moscato Giallo Portéle, on the other hand, and especially in their most recent arrival, Soliva '97, a vendange tardive blend of various aromatic grapes. Both perfumed and flavorful, its acidity is balanced by a luscious taste of sweet ripe fruit.

○	Soliva '97	🍷🍷	4
●	Syrae '96	🍷🍷	4
●	Trentino Cabernet Fratagranda '95	🍷🍷	4
○	Trentino Nosiola Le Frate '97	🍷🍷	3
○	Trentino Moscato Giallo Le Portéle '97	🍷	3
○	Trentino Müller Thurgau St. Thomà '97	🍷	3
●	Trentino Pinot Nero '96	🍷	3
●	Syrae '95	🍸🍸	4
●	Trentino Cabernet Fratagranda '92	🍸🍸	4
○	Trentino Nosiola Le Frate '96	🍸🍸	3*
○	Trentino Nosiola Le Frate '95	🍸🍸	3
○	Vino Santo Le Arele '83	🍸🍸	5

LAVIS (TN)

Nilo Bolognani

Via Stazione, 19
38015 Lavis (TN)
tel. 0461/246354

We had been hoping to see some red wines from this producer, but he has postponed their debut. Diego Bolognani doesn't look for easy praise. A patient man, he's willing to wait until his oenological gems are quite ready, and most particularly until his hillside vineyards produce grapes he deems worthy. So this year too we can only consider his whites, the fruit of the efforts and decisions of a wine-maker who is ever more intent on building up his already excellent reputation. And in '97 he cetainly has succeeded! His battalion of six Trentino whites marches out with all the power of a memorable vintage, each of them round, full, and persistent. They have a nearly explosive power in the mouth, coupled with an inviting and captivating delicacy of aroma differing noticeably from wine to wine, according to the original grape variety. Young Bolognani has always given particular attention to his Müller Thurgau, grown in the nearby Valle di Cembra. With its greenish tinge, a faint mineral aroma and lots of character, it's a very elegant wine. The other pride of the estate, the Moscato Giallo, also quite stylish, is aromatic, dry, inviting and very easy to quaff. The Sauvignon is noteworthy as well: more concentrated than it has been in recent years, it is very varietal, rich, potent and long. The Chardonnay makes a similar impression but it has notes of ripe fruit and its flavors are more striking than its perfumes. Although we felt less enthusiastic about the Pinot Grigio and the Nosiola, they are nonetheless well-made, distinct and delicate, as is to be expected from Diego Bolognani.

	Wine	Rating	Price
○	Trentino Moscato Giallo '97	TT	3
○	Trentino Müller Thurgau '97	TT	3
○	Trentino Sauvignon '97	TT	3
○	Trentino Chardonnay '97	T	3
○	Trentino Nosiola '97	T	3
○	Trentino Pinot Grigio '97	T	3
○	Müller Thurgau della Val di Cembra '95	YY	3
○	Müller Thurgau della Val di Cembra '96	YY	3*
○	Trentino Moscato Giallo '95	YY	3
○	Trentino Moscato Giallo '96	YY	3*
○	Trentino Pinot Grigio '95	YY	3
○	Trentino Pinot Grigio '96	YY	3*

LAVIS (TN)

Cesconi

Loc. Pressano
Via Marconi, 39
38015 Lavis (TN)
tel. 0461/240355

This family-run estate continues to go from strength to strength. The Cesconis still produce only white wines, but they have planted red grapes in Ceniga di Drò, in the Basso Sarca, which are tended daily by the young Franco, Roberto, Lorenzo and Alessandro under Paolo's paternal eye. They have slightly increased their production, to about 30,000 bottles, and added a newcomer, Nosiola, to their list, with which they have already had a noticeable success. But the wine we liked most is their Pinot Bianco, particularly fat, very concentrated, and with a complicated array of aromas. The Nosiola, though, is a bit rustic to the nose, with a suggestion of raw hazelnut ("nocciola", hence Nosiola), while in the mouth it has a pleasant peachiness and a touch of mint. The Traminer is a fairly good white in which we would have preferred more distinctive notes of citrus fruit and spices. This is in line with other local whites this year, which have somehow been suppressed aromatically, while being enhanced structurally. The Chardonnay is charming - a successful ensemble of fruit and succulence, and its palate has continued to improve. The Pinot Grigio is good too, with coppery reflections and a fragrance of pear, while the Sauvignon is still closed and has an unfortunate hint of sulfur, despite a distinct alcohol base. We look forward confidently to their reds.

	Wine	Rating	Price
○	Trentino Chardonnay '97	TT	3
○	Trentino Pinot Bianco '97	TT	3
○	Trentino Pinot Grigio '97	TT	3
○	Trentino Traminer Aromatico '97	TT	3
○	Trentino Nosiola '97	T	3
○	Trentino Sauvignon '97	T	3
○	Sauvignon Atesino '96	YY	3*
○	Trentino Pinot Bianco '96	YY	3*
○	Trentino Pinot Grigio '96	YY	3*
○	Trentino Traminer Aromatico '96	YY	3*
○	Trentino Chardonnay '96	Y	3

LAVIS (TN)

La Vis
Via Carmine, 12
38015 Lavis (TN)
tel. 0461/246325

This year you won't find Three Glasses at the bottom of this column. But don't let this fool you. The quality of the whole range of wines we tasted, including those that don't appear in the Guide for reasons of space, is simply amazing. These are full-bodied, faultlessly made wines with distinctive personality. From the ordinary Chardonnay '96 (produced, by the way, in massive quantities) to their special selections for the more demanding (who will, nevertheless, not have much trouble finding them because lots have been made), they are exemplary. This clearly shows that this splendid wine cooperative dedicates its strength and skill to the optimal development of Trentino wine-making. The Ritratto '96 is excellent: it has a bewitchingly intense deep ruby hue and a panoply of ripe berries and spice. Equal praise for the Cabernet Sauvignon Ritratti '96 (on the labels are "ritratti" or portraits by the Trentino artist Giovanni Segantini), the Merlot Ritratti '96, which has thrilled a number of our tasting panels, and the Pinot Nero Ritratti '96, lovingly and carefully made. The Sorni Rosso '97 is easily approachable, but bids fair to become a far more important wine than present appearances suggest. The reds are good, but the whites are even better. In the Ritratti series, the Chardonnay and the Pinot Grigio, both '97, are rivals in excellence, but the Müller Thurgau '97, very well-made and fragrant, shouldn't be overlooked.

	Wine	Glasses	Price
●	Ritratto '96	▼▼	5
●	Trentino Cabernet Sauvignon Ritratti '96	▼▼	4*
○	Trentino Chardonnay Ritratti '97	▼▼	4
●	Trentino Merlot Ritratti '96	▼▼	4*
○	Trentino Müller Thurgau '97	▼▼	2*
○	Trentino Pinot Grigio Ritratti '97	▼▼	4
●	Trentino Pinot Nero Ritratti '96	▼▼	4
●	Trentino Sorni Rosso '97	▼▼	3
●	Ritratto '91	YYY	4
○	Trentino Pinot Grigio Ritratti '95	YYY	4*
●	Ritratto '95	YY	5
●	Trentino Cabernet Sauvignon Ritratti '95	YY	4*

MEZZOCORONA (TN)

Marco Donati
Via Cesare Battisti, 41
38016 Mezzocorona (TN)
tel. 0461/604141

The Associazione Vignaioli del Trentino, an association of local wine-makers, has been going from strength to strength in championing good wine-making in this province. It started as a small group of determined wine-makers who then brought in another hundred or so growers. Marco Donati is one of the leaders, and he seems to develop more skill and firmness of purpose with each year that passes. As is natural in these parts, he concentrates his efforts on the Teroldego Rotaliano. A small selection of his 1996 version, fermented in wood and now available, goes under the name of Sangue di Drago (dragon's blood) in honor of the legendary local dragon. The wine is dark, intense and indeed blood-red. Powerful to the nose, it is both strong and austere on the palate, satisfyingly mouth-filling and in no way cloying. The regular version of his Teroldego has also profited from an excellent year and offers this time a more complex nose of herbs and berries, and really remarkable concentration in the mouth. Another notable red is the Vino del Maso, basically a teroldego with some lagrein and merlot, with aromas ranging from mature fruit to freshly ground pepper. His Terre del Noce '97, a blend of chardonnay and sauvignon, is good; the other whites, which are simpler than usual, rate a simple listing.

	Wine	Glasses	Price
●	Teroldego Rotaliano Sangue di Drago '96	▼▼	4
○	Bianco Terre del Noce '97	▼	3
●	Rosso Vino del Maso '97	▼	4
●	Teroldego Rotaliano '97	▼	3
○	Trentino Müller Thurgau '97		2
○	Trentino Pinot Grigio '97		2
○	Bianco Terre del Noce '95	YY	3*
○	Bianco Terre del Noce '96	YY	3*
●	Moscato Rosa Atesino '94	Y	4
●	Moscato Rosa Atesino '95	Y	4
●	Rosso Vino del Maso '96	Y	4
○	Sauvignon Atesino '96	Y	3
●	Teroldego Rotaliano '96	Y	3

MEZZOCORONA (TN)

F.LLI DORIGATI
VIA DANTE, 5
38016 MEZZOCORONA (TN)
TEL. 0461/605313

No one who knows them would be surprised to hear that the Dorigati brothers, Carlo and Franco, are not in any kind of hurry when it comes to making their wines. So the latest vintage of their Spumante Methius is not yet ready to be released. Ah, well! We can console ourselves with the new Teroldego Riserva, Diedri '96, a great red and one of the most interesting wines our panels tasted this year. It has that garnet hue that only the best Teroldegos achieve. The concentration of the color is matched by that of the palate: the tannins are sweet and the finish satisfyingly long, and there's a well-judged toasty touch. The young, normal Teroldego '97 is once again a very good wine, with a deep ruby color and a wide range of aromas including a hint of tar often found in the Dorigatis' wines. And when it hits the palate there's all the force of a fantastic vintage. All the other wines are interesting, starting with the Rebo '96, a racy mix of marzemino and merlot. The whites make a good showing too, although it's red country up here. The '97 Chardonnay has a lovely golden color tinged with green, aromatic finesse and an unctuous persistence. The Pinot Grigio, equally well-made, with a characteristic coppery glow, is the result of a traditional wine-making style that respects the vine and its seasons. The Dorigatis, with their patient, self-sacrificing labors, have for generations been showing this sort of respect.

●	Teroldego Rotaliano '97	🍷🍷	3*
●	Teroldego Rotaliano Diedri Ris. '96	🍷🍷	5
○	Trentino Chardonnay '97	🍷	2
○	Trentino Pinot Grigio '97	🍷	2
●	Trentino Rebo '96	🍷	3
●	Teroldego Rotaliano Diedri '90	🍷🍷 (empty)	5
●	Teroldego Rotaliano Diedri Ris. '92	🍷🍷 (empty)	5
●	Teroldego Rotaliano Diedri Ris. '94	🍷🍷 (empty)	5
○	Trentino Chardonnay Le Alte '94	🍷🍷 (empty)	4
○	Trento Methius '90	🍷🍷 (empty)	5
○	Trento Methius Ris. '91	🍷🍷 (empty)	5

MEZZOCORONA (TN)

MEZZACORONA
VIA IV NOVEMBRE, 127
38016 MEZZOCORONA (TN)
TEL. 0461/605163

Improvement pays. MezzaCorona has been shipping more wine and getting better reviews, and they want things to keep on that way. The 1300 members of this cooperative, which is nearly a hundred years old, are ready for the challenge. With their 2,000 hectares of vineyards producing almost 30,000 quintals of grapes every autumn, they certainly can make an impact on the market. And they do make it by following the course set by their directors, Fabio Rizzoli and his associate and young son, Claudio, whose efforts extend throughout Italy, Northern Europe and the USA. Quality and effective marketing are their two intertwined guiding principles, particularly evident in the case of their bubbly wines. Recent dégorgements of their Rotari range have proved the point. The '94 Riserva has a brilliant straw-like color. To the nose it offers a wide range of enticing aromas both fresh and mature, and in the mouth it is deliciously harmonious and velvety, with an extremely fine perlage. But the Rotari Arte Italiana does well too. There's backbone in this spumante. Its nose suggests slightly under-ripe fruit (Val di Non apples come to mind), and it reveals both depth and finesse. And the still wines are very good indeed. The Teroldego Riserva '96 is a thoroughbred that typifies its grape, which is also true of the Lagrein and the Marzemino. This last is emblematic of MezzaCorona's efforts to present all the Trentino wines, not just their local ones, to the world market. Of the whites, we liked the Traminer Aromatico '97 best, as it's fuller-bodied than the Müller Thurgau and the Pinot Grigio.

●	Teroldego Rotaliano Ris. '96	🍷🍷	3
○	Trentino Traminer Aromatico '97	🍷🍷	3
○	Trento Rotari Brut Arte Italiana	🍷🍷	3
○	Trento Rotari Brut Ris. '94	🍷🍷	4
●	Trentino Lagrein '96	🍷	3
●	Trentino Marzemino '97	🍷	3
○	Trentino Müller Thurgau '97	🍷	2
○	Trentino Pinot Grigio '97	🍷	2
●	Teroldego Rotaliano Ris. '94	🍷🍷 (empty)	3*
●	Trentino Cabernet Sauvignon Oltresarca '94	🍷🍷 (empty)	3*
○	Trentino Traminer Aromatico '96	🍷🍷 (empty)	3*
○	Trento Rotari Brut Arte Italiana	🍷🍷 (empty)	3*

MEZZOLOMBARDO (TN)

Cantina Rotaliana

C.so del Popolo, 6
38017 Mezzolombardo (TN)
tel. 0461/601010

With a little help from 1997, a good year in these parts, the Cantina Rotaliana continues to garner awards. Their success, of course, is due not only to the weather. Luciano Lunelli, the enthusiastic director, and his whole staff got right down to it, both in the vineyards of their hundreds of member growers, and in the cellar where they clearly know what they're about. Nearly all the "novello" wine made in the Trentino, for example, is made here. Furthermore, work is about to begin on a completely new, up-to-the-minute winery. Luciano Lunelli is more or less the Great Red Father of Teroldego, as this year's results demonstrate. Both in the normal '97 version and in the '95 Riserva, this red wine, which is emblematic of the Rotaliano, is sound, inviting, intense in color and delicately fruity; best of all, it develops delightfully in the mouth. The whites do not lag far behind, and are an excellent interpretation of their grape varieties. As usual the Pinot Bianco '97, with its aromas of apples and pears and a full and generous vitality on the palate, has defended its reputation (and very well too). The notably aromatic Müller Thurgau maintains standards, and we found the Chardonnay to be already highly developed and forward. In fact for wine-makers who supposedly know only about red wines, these are good whites. They continue to concentrate on their Teroldego (and on its "twin" Lagrein, the result of carefully-made grape selection) and, because the year was extraordinary, they have made a delicious Moscato Rosa '97 from some recently planted vines, which hints already at the wonderful wine it will become in the future.

	Wine	Glasses	Price
●	Teroldego Rotaliano '97	▼▼	2*
●	Teroldego Rotaliano Ris. '95	▼▼	3
○	Trentino Chardonnay '97	▼	2
●	Trentino Moscato Rosa '97	▼	4
○	Trentino Müller Thurgau '97	▼	2
○	Trentino Pinot Bianco '97	▼	2
●	Teroldego Rotaliano Ris. '93	▽▽	3
○	Trentino Pinot Bianco '96	▽▽	2*
●	Teroldego Rotaliano '96	▽	2
●	Teroldego Rotaliano '94	▽	2*
●	Teroldego Rotaliano Ris. '94	▽	3
○	Trentino Chardonnay '95	▽	2
○	Trentino Chardonnay '96	▽	2
●	Trentino Lagrein Tait '95	▽	3
○	Trentino Müller Thurgau '96	▽	2

MEZZOLOMBARDO (TN)

Foradori

Via Damiano Chiesa, 1
38017 Mezzolombardo (TN)
tel. 0461/601046

Elisabetta Foradori returns triumphantly and with clearer ideas than ever before of what she wants to do. Starting next year, she is going to offer only three wines: two teroldegos and one wine blended from her white grapes. There will be a Teroldego Rotaliano Foradori, (with no special selections such as the Sgarzon or Morei), and a Granato only in excellent years. There could also be, conditions permitting, two other "exotic" reds, Karanar and Ailanpa, which were not made in 1996, because she didn't consider their grapes good enough. Myrto will be the only white, and will still be made with chardonnay, pinot bianco and sauvignon. But let's consider this year's production. The Granato '96 is, to put it mildly, marvelous. It has that splendid depth of color that all wine-makers would like to achieve. Its perfumes, intensely seductive, have an extraordinary finesse which suggests both wild berries and a delicate incense. Then it explodes in the mouth, sweetly and powerfully demonstrating its velvety structure, its captivating touch of oak and, unforgettably, its length. It is a great wine, maybe the best so far produced by our independent-minded Elisabetta. Congratulations, indeed our heartiest congratulations, for her Sgarzon '96 too, full-bodied and subtly tannic, but especially for her Teroldego '97, an incredibly solid wine that perfectly exemplifies the power this grape can offer. The Myrto '97, which has already been blended but is still maturing after its vinification in wood and steel, is a curious and unusual yet certainly good white wine.

	Wine	Glasses	Price
●	Granato '96	▼▼▼	5
○	Myrto '97	▼▼	3
●	Teroldego Rotaliano '97	▼▼	3
●	Teroldego Rotaliano Sgarzon '96	▼▼	4
●	Granato '91	▽▽▽	5
●	Granato '93	▽▽▽	5
●	Teroldego Rotaliano Sgarzon '93	▽▽▽	4*
●	Teroldego Rotaliano Sgarzon '94	▽▽▽	4*
●	Granato '90	▽▽	5
●	Granato '95	▽▽	5
●	Karanar '95	▽▽	4

NOGAREDO (TN)

CASTEL NOARNA
FRAZ. NOARNA - VIA CASTELNUOVO, 1
38060 NOGAREDO (TN)
TEL. 0464/413295 - 167/348809

Castel Noarna is one of the most beautiful and well-known castles in the Trentino. Growing grapes and making wine there were begun without fanfare by Marco Zani, who comes from a famous family of hotel-keepers. Formerly a computer expert and tour operator, Marco has become a rabid, committed wine-maker, and his wines stand out in the Trentino wine world. While waiting for his Cabernet Romeo '95 to mature, we very happily tasted the '94, which continues to improve: the sweet spiciness of the oak rounds off its rich, complex and burstingly balsamic structure. His Chardonnay Campo Grande '96, fermented in barriques, is another important wine and among the few whites from Trentino that could compete internationally. It's concentrated and powerful in the mouth, with lots of luscious fruit. The white blend Bianco di Castelnuovo '96 is first-class: it's a wine of complex nuances, with a fruity bouquet and fat succulence that set each other off. The Chardonnay Reno needs more time, as usual, and will be dealt with in next year's edition, but the Nosiola '97 is well-made and easy to drink, as is the Schiava Scalzavacca '97. According to legend, three young women were tried for witchcraft at Castel Noarna in the 1600s and then burnt at the stake. To one of these unfortunates, Mercuria, a cabernet, fresh and very fruity, and redolent of pepper, tobacco and mountain hay, has been dedicated.

○	Bianco di Castelnuovo '96	**TT**	3
●	Trentino Cabernet Romeo '94	**TT**	4
●	Trentino Cabernet Sauvignon Mercuria '97	**TT**	3
○	Trentino Chardonnay '97	**TT**	3
○	Trentino Chardonnay Campo Grande '96	**TT**	4
○	Trentino Nosiola '97	**T**	3
●	Valdadige Schiava Scalzavacca '97	**T**	3
●	Trentino Cabernet Romeo '93	YY	4
○	Trentino Nosiola '96	YY	3*
○	Trentino Sauvignon '96	YY	3*
●	Valdadige Schiava Scalzavacca '95	YY	3

NOGAREDO (TN)

LETRARI
PALAZZO LODRON, 4
38060 NOGAREDO (TN)
TEL. 0464/411093 - 414147

How can one reconcile an infatuation with the heady sparkle of a classic spumante with a passion for full-bodied red wines? Without, let's say, giving up one's devotion to white wines and the occasional rarity as well? The Letrari family resolved this quandary years ago, in the days when Lionello, Letrari senior, made wines for others-sparkling wines here and Bordeaux-style reds there. At the same time, he made important experiments at home, which led to a risky but eventually successful venture in which his children, the young Lucia, in particular, have become involved as well. Hence the following battery of extraordinarily well-made wines. First we have a classic spumante, the Trento Brut Letrari '94, a nicely rounded example of a Trentino bubbly. Then comes the '97 Sauvignon, which is known for its remarkable concentration and a telling touch of green pepper. And we could hardly omit the elegant and aromatic Bianco Saccardo '96, a pinot bianco and chardonnay blend. Now for their reds, which for the Letraris mean principally Marzemino. They have made a normal version and a Selezione '97, and they are both well above average in quality, very approachable and full of fruit, with a lovely hint of cherry. We were intrigued by the Maso Lodron too, a Bordeaux blend that is lightly grassy and richly tasty. Their Moscato Rosa '95 is quite delicious, with a marvelous bouquet of roses, but perhaps just a touch too sweet.

○	Trentino Bianco Saccardo '96	**TT**	3
●	Trentino Marzemino Sel. '97	**TT**	3
●	Trentino Moscato Rosa '95	**TT**	6
●	Trentino Rosso Maso Lodron '95	**TT**	3
○	Trentino Sauvignon '97	**TT**	3
○	Trento Brut Letrari '94	**TT**	4
●	Trentino Marzemino '97	**T**	2*
●	Trentino Cabernet Sauvignon Ris. '94	YY	3*
●	Trentino Marzemino '96	YY	2*
●	Trentino Marzemino Sel. '96	YY	3*
●	Trentino Moscato Rosa '93	YY	6
●	Trentino Moscato Rosa '94	YY	6
○	Trentino Pinot Bianco '94	YY	3
○	Trentino Sauvignon '96	YY	3*

NOMI (TN)

LUCIANO BATTISTOTTI
VIA III NOVEMBRE, 21
38060 NOMI (TN)
TEL. 0464/834145

For almost half a century the Battistotti family, however large their winery, has continued to work with the steadfast care of wine growers. These days the brothers Enzo, Elio and Luciano not only make their grape selections in the vineyards, going from row to row, but also pass on to their friends, the vineyard owners who supply them, the latest and best viticultural techniques. Although they are red-wine loyalists, Marzemino being dearest to their hearts, they nonetheless make a few thousand bottles of white. Once again their Müller Thurgau '97 is incredibly fruity, savory, attractive and persistent. The Merlot '97 is simpler, a fresh young wine for immediate consumption. Their Bordeaux blend, the Rosso Savignam '96, has breeding and structure without losing its drinkability. But it is with their Marzeminos that the Battistottis assert their authority, producing wines that serve as benchmarks at many comparative tastings, including ours. This edition is dry, harmonious and seductive, as is the rare Moscato Rosa '97 which Luciano Battistotti offers as if just to prove that even when he turns his hand to growing (the vines are on his land) he is without equal.

	Wine	Glasses	Price
●	Trentino Marzemino '97	▼▼	3
●	Trentino Moscato Rosa '97	▼▼	5
○	Trentino Müller Thurgau '97	▼▼	3
●	Rosso Savignam '96	▼	3
●	Trentino Merlot '97		3
●	Trentino Marzemino '96	▽▽	3*
●	Trentino Cabernet '96	▽	3
○	Trentino Chardonnay '96	▽	3
●	Trentino Merlot '96	▽	3

ROVERETO (TN)

BALTER
VIA VALLUNGA ILA, 26
38068 ROVERETO (TN)
TEL. 0464/430101

Nicola Balter is the beating heart of this winery and has instituted a new approach, increasing the involvement of his co-workers in running operations in both vineyard and cellar, and encouraging criticism so as to increase his understanding of how his wines and those round about evolve. He has done this with unassuming intelligence, and has regularly made himself available to wine-makers who are just starting out. This is how the Casa del Vino, uniting thirteen wine producers with one philosophy ñ to make better wine without losing the best of local traditions ñ got started at Isera. Nicola is their president, and the friendly competition among the members stimulates improvement, as all his wines demonstrate. His three jewels, the Trentino Cabernet Sauvignon '95, his classic spumante, the Trento Balter Brut, and the imaginative white Clarae '96, are all delicious. While the Bordeaux-style red is more austere and important, with its delicately complex nose (one notes among the fragrances the tarry accent of a great wine) and beautiful deep ruby color, the Clarae blend is elegantly floral and musky in aroma and offers a mouth-filling experience of apples, peaches, pears and spice. The Brut is brilliant in color and has a very fine perlage. It's redolent of citron and both dried and tropical fruits, and has a creamy effervescence that dissolves softly in the mouth. His Traminer Aromatico has an intriguing touch of ginger, the Sauvignon is good, the classic Chardonnay enjoyable, and the Rossinot '97, simple and ready to drink, is not to be sneezed at, benefiting as it does from the contribution of lagrein and pinot noir.

	Wine	Glasses	Price
○	Clarae '96	▼▼	4
●	Trentino Cabernet Sauvignon '95	▼▼	4
○	Trentino Chardonnay '97	▼▼	3
○	Trento Balter Brut	▼▼	4
●	Rossinot '97	▼	2*
○	Trentino Sauvignon '97	▼	3
○	Trentino Traminer Aromatico '97	▼	3
○	Clarae '95	▽▽	4
○	Sauvignon Atesino '94	▽▽	3
●	Trentino Cabernet Sauvignon '91	▽▽	4
○	Trentino Sauvignon '96	▽▽	3*
●	Trentino Cabernet Sauvignon '93	▽	4
○	Trento Balter Brut	▽	4

ROVERETO (TN)

CONTI BOSSI FEDRIGOTTI
VIA UNIONE, 43
38068 ROVERETO (TN)
TEL. 0464/439250

An increase in production and an eye to expanding distribution have brought the desired commercial results to the Conti Bossi Fedrigotti winery. But basically they have never abandoned their allegiance to the goals of a small winery intent on quality. The owners have in Rosanna Grigoletto a very competent director who, with her new technical staff, has left her stamp on recently made wines. With the help of an excellent vintage, this estate has proven its merit. Mention must of course be made first of their Fojaneghe Rosso, which was already legendary throughout Italy in the '60s (it was virtually the first decidedly Bordeaux-style blend vinified in small casks to be produced in Italy). The '96 has a beautiful dark ruby color, and a good nose, although it seems a bit thin and slightly vegetal on the palate, with a bitterish finish. The Marzemino '97 is dark red and fruity. Though not an important wine, it is decidedly well made. Among the whites, their Traminer Aromatico '97 seemed successfully varietal, spicy and savory, with a surprisingly long finish. The other whites, the Pinot Grigio, Pinot Bianco and the white version of Fojaneghe have perhaps been affected by vastly increased production: they don't really come out or differ distinctly from one another.

	Wine	Rating	Price
●	Trentino Marzemino '97	🍷	2
○	Trentino Pinot Bianco '97	🍷	3
○	Trentino Traminer Aromatico '97	🍷	3
●	Vallagarina Fojaneghe Rosso '96	🍷	3
○	Trentino Pinot Grigio '97		2
○	Vallagarina Fojaneghe Bianco '97		3
●	Conte Federico '88	🍸🍸	5
○	Fojaneghe Bianco '94	🍸	3
●	Fojaneghe Rosso '90	🍸	4
●	Fojaneghe Rosso '92	🍸	3
●	Trentino Cabernet '90	🍸	3
●	Trentino Merlot '91	🍸	3
○	Trentino Pinot Bianco '94	🍸	3
○	Trentino Traminer Aromatico '94	🍸	3

ROVERETO (TN)

LONGARIVA
LOC. BORGO SACCO
VIA ZANDONAI, 6
38068 ROVERETO (TN)
TEL. 0464/437200

We knew we would find big, important red wines, but we tasted whites of amazing structure as well. Hats off to Marco Manica, whose wines once again prove him to be one of the best wine-makers in the region. All of his wines have distinctive personalities. The Cabernet Marognon '95 is a very fine wine indeed, with its notes of spices and oak properly blended; it's well-balanced, mouth-filling and very long on structure. The Pinot Nero Zinzele '94 is one of the best from Trentino, but in the shadow of the Dolomites this grape always seems to sacrifice complexity for rotundity and to pay for easy drinking with the finesse that one can find in a good Burgundy. The Chardonnay Praistel '96, which was fermented in barrique, is clearly a wine with breeding. It has lots of body and its oaky tones are held in check by the richness of its aromas and its elegant, dynamic and well-paced structure. The Pinot Grigio Graminè '97 is also interesting and delightful. It is so made as to keep the coppery tint and the other attractive hallmarks of the ruländer, as the locals here and in Alto Aldige call this grape. The Pinot Bianco '97, and the traditional Cabernet '95 are both very good, but Marco Manica decided not to present his Sauvignon Cascari '97 because he felt it wasn't good enough to bear the Longariva label.

	Wine	Rating	Price
●	Trentino Cabernet Sauvignon Marognon Ris. '95	🍷🍷	4
○	Trentino Chardonnay Praistel '96	🍷🍷	4
●	Trentino Merlot Tovi Ris. '95	🍷🍷	4
○	Trentino Pinot Grigio Graminè '97	🍷🍷	4
●	Trentino Cabernet '95	🍷	3*
○	Trentino Pinot Bianco '97	🍷	3
●	Trentino Pinot Nero Zinzele Ris. '94	🍷	4
●	Trentino Cabernet Sauvignon Marognon Ris. '94	🍸🍸	4
●	Trentino Merlot Tovi '93	🍸🍸	4
●	Trentino Pinot Nero Zinzele Ris. '93	🍸🍸	4

ROVERETO (TN)

ARMANDO SIMONCELLI
LOC. NAVESEL, 7
38068 ROVERETO (TN)
TEL. 0464/432373

The dedicated Trentino winemaker Armando Simoncelli has concentrated on his reds this year. He has thrown aside, so to speak, his classic whites and prepared us a Lagrein that, while easy to drink, has a distinct personality and a deep garnet color, and is as grapey, lively and pleasurable as a classic Alto Adige Lagrein. But that's Armando: an apparent simplicity concealing stunning surprises. Every year he brings out wines that are better, more mature and more interesting. Red wines, we were saying: in addition to his Marzemino, which has always been considered an exemplary version of this Vallagarina specialty, he has selected some lots of his Cabernet Franc and Merlot and made a blend to show off his technical proficiency. Hence his Navesel, named after the farm where he lives, with vineyards blessed with fertile soil and glorious exposure. Like any Trentino Cabernet it has a hint of greens, but there's a consistent soft fruitiness, its tannins are harmonious, its taste well-balanced and its finish long. This same eminent drinkability, accompanied by notes of red berries and undercurrents of spice, characterizes the Cabernet Franc and the Merlot, which are bottled immediately without aging time in the wood. Good, but not as good as usual was our verdict on the Pinot Bianco and the Chardonnay. They are easy enough to drink, but have a touch of the over-ripe grape about them. The '97 vintage, in other words, was kinder to the reds than the whites, and permitted Simoncelli to return, with a firm hand, to making wines from his best local grapes.

	Wine	Glasses	Price
●	Trentino Lagrein '97	**ΨΨ**	3
●	Trentino Marzemino '97	**ΨΨ**	3
●	Trentino Rosso Navesèl '97	**ΨΨ**	3*
●	Trentino Cabernet '97	**Ψ**	3
○	Trentino Chardonnay '97	**Ψ**	3
●	Trentino Merlot '97	**Ψ**	3
○	Trentino Pinot Bianco '97		3
○	Trentino Chardonnay '94	ΨΨ	3
○	Trentino Chardonnay '95	ΨΨ	3*
●	Trentino Marzemino '96	ΨΨ	3*
○	Trentino Pinot Bianco '95	ΨΨ	3
●	Trentino Rosso Navesel '91	ΨΨ	3
○	Trentino Chardonnay '96	Ψ	3
●	Trentino Merlot '96	Ψ	3
●	Trentino Rosso Navesèl '94	Ψ	3

S. MICHELE ALL'ADIGE (TN)

AZIENDA VITIVINICOLA
DELL'ISTITUTO AGRARIO PROVINCIALE
VIA EDMONDO MACH, 2
38010 S. MICHELE ALL'ADIGE (TN)
TEL. 0461/615252

The wines that this school, a guiding light for Trentino wine- making, has made this year are even better than their recent offerings. Although there is still, perhaps, some room for improvement, the results are certainly noteworthy. The reds are more concentrated, and the whites have more character. All the wines we tasted were very well received. We particularly enjoyed the Merlot '96, which we found clean and well-defined in nose and palate, and their Bordeaux blend, the Castel San Michele '95, a fresh wine attractively redolent of wild berries, and fairly long in the mouth. Their Rebo '97 (a traditional hybrid of merlot and marzemino developed in the 1930s by Rebo Rigotti, who was a research botanist at this first-rate institute), has good structure in its bouquet and palate. The Moscato Giallo '97 is well-focused and tasty drinking, and the Moscato Rosa '96, which has captured the aromatic essence of its grape, is equally worthy. Their Prepositura '96 a white blend, stakes its all on fragrance and is pleasantly quaffable. Their other offerings are also properly made and agreeable.

	Wine	Glasses	Price
○	Prepositura Atesino '96	**ΨΨ**	3
●	Trentino Castel San Michele '95	**ΨΨ**	4
●	Trentino Merlot '96	**ΨΨ**	4
●	Trentino Rebo '97	**ΨΨ**	3
○	Trentino Moscato Giallo '97	**Ψ**	3
●	Trentino Moscato Rosa '96	**Ψ**	5
●	Castel San Michele '93	ΨΨ	4
○	Prepositura Atesino '93	ΨΨ	4*
●	Trentino Merlot '95	ΨΨ	4
○	Trentino Pinot Bianco '94	ΨΨ	3
○	Trentino Pinot Bianco '95	ΨΨ	3*
○	Trentino Riesling Renano '94	ΨΨ	4

ENDRIZZI

LOC. MASETTO
38010 S. MICHELE ALL'ADIGE (TN)
TEL. 0461/650129

This is the first year for Christine and Paolo Endrici's newest wine, a pinot nero. Its grapes are grown in the Pian di Castello vineyard adjacent to Monreale, the hillside castle of Faedo, and it's very promising. It has an elegant color and a rich berry bouquet, but its finish falls somewhat short, which could however be due to the youth of the vines or to the fact that it had only just been bottled when we tasted it. Their other new wine, the Teroldego Rotaliano Superiore Selezione '96, whose grapes come from the Camorz vineyard, also needs more time in the bottle. Fermented partly in barriques and partly in great 40-hectoliter barrels, this is another red that could make it to the top. The Endricis have dedicated two blends, one red and one white, to their "maso" (family farm). The Masetto Nero won't be ready until next year, but we tasted the Bianco Masetto '97, made from chardonnay, pinot bianco, sauvignon and a bit of traminer, and we were won over right away. Its highly individual floral bouquet seems more concentrated than immediate. In the mouth, roundness and acidity appear to promise perfect balance to those who are patient enough to put off the pleasure of drinking it. Their normal range of wines, like the Teroldego Rotaliano '97, are all interesting, as are the tasty new versions of the Moscato Rosa '95 and their Dulcis in Fundo '96, a sweet dessert wine.

	Wine	Rating	Price
●	Teroldego Rotaliano Sup. Sel. '96	▼▼	4
○	Trentino Bianco Masetto '97	▼▼	4
○	Dulcis in Fundo '96	▼	4
●	Teroldego Rotaliano '97	▼	3
●	Trentino Moscato Rosa '95	▼	5
●	Trentino Pinot Nero Sup. Sel. '96	▼	4
○	Trentino Chardonnay Tradizione '95	▽▽	3
●	Trentino Moscato Rosa Collezione '94	▽▽	5
○	Trento Masetto	▽▽	4
○	Dulcis in Fundo '95	▽	4
●	Teroldego Rotaliano '96	▽	3
●	Trentino Cabernet Collezione '93	▽	4

S. MICHELE ALL'ADIGE (TN)

ZENI

FRAZ. GRUMO
VIA STRETTA, 2
38010 SAN MICHELE ALL'ADIGE (TN)
TEL. 0461/650456

They were leaders during the initial phase of Trentino's oenological modernization, and now the Zeni brothers are back again in the forefront of wine-makers whose aim is to produce wines of high quality. Andrea and Roberto have concentrated their efforts on very few traditional grape types, and this year they are presenting only four wines, all mono-varietal, which palpably demonstrate the skill the Zenis have applied both in their cellar and in their small vineyards scattered on the slopes towards Lavis and in the heart of the Campo Rotaliano. The Teroldego Rotaliano '97 fills the glass with all the vigor of an extraordinary vintage. It's a wine that will age gracefully, although its enjoyable grapiness is there from the start, together with its violet hue, rich scents of wild berries and an attractive youthful rusticity and dense texture on the palate. Then there are the two good whites, the Müller Thurgau La Croce and the Pinot Bianco Sortì. The former is just as fragrant as it ought to be, and the latter, a very elegant tipple indeed, is delicate, dry and harmonious, with some Golden Delicious notes. The Moscato Rosa gets better every year. It has a fragrance of wild roses and a spiciness all its own which the Zeni brothers have developed a way, known to them only, of bringing out perfectly.

	Wine	Rating	Price
●	Teroldego Rotaliano '97	▼▼	4
○	Trentino Müller Thurgau La Croce '97	▼▼	4
●	Trentino Moscato Rosa '97	▼	4
○	Trentino Pinot Bianco Sortì '97	▼	4
●	Teroldego Rotaliano Pini '93	▽▽	4
●	Teroldego Rotaliano '96	▽	3
●	Trentino Moscato Rosa '96	▽	4
○	Trentino Riesling Renano Reré '96	▽	3
○	Trentino Sauvignon '96	▽	3

TRENTO

CAVIT
CONSORZIO DI CANTINE SOCIALI
FRAZ. RAVINA
VIA PONTE, 31
38040 TRENTO
TEL. 0461/381711

Cavit is a consortium formed years ago to promote and sell Trentino wines. This it has done astutely, making dynamic choices with an eye on the market. This wine giant's commercial success (it bills more than 200 billion lire, 55% of which is in export) has permitted its members, almost six thousand in all, a certain satisfaction - good prices for their grapes, a guaranteed return (no small accomplishment, this), and wines of an ever-improving quality. Cavit is at work in China and California, diversifying its production and conquering distant territories, and is about to open a new bottling plant with a thirty million bottle capacity. But it doesn't lose sight of the Dolomites. The Riserva of the Trento Brut, Graal '94, is once again one of the three best sparkling wines from the area. It's mellow and inviting, and has a creamy foaminess and excellent length. This time it doesn't get Three Glasses but it didn't miss by much and only, probably, because of the capriciousness of the weather that year. Their Brut Firmato, however, is a decided success in its category. And now for the still wines. A round of applause for their Vino Santo '91, thick, sweet and unctuous, smelling and tasting of dried figs, distinctly Mediterranean in its intense golden color, with a long, enchanting finish. The Sauvignon Maso Torresella is the most notable of the whites, and the Bordeaux-type Quattro Vicariati, a powerful and luscious delight with an intense violet hue, is our choice among the reds. The Marzemino is characteristic of its varietal and is a selection of grapes harvested from the highly prized Ziresi vineyards in Vallagarina.

	Wine	Glasses	Price
●	Trentino Marzemino dei Ziresi '97	🍷🍷	3
●	Trentino Rosso Quattro Vicariati '94	🍷🍷	4
○	Trentino Sauvignon Maso Torresella '96	🍷🍷	4
○	Trentino Vino Santo '91	🍷🍷	5
○	Trento Brut Firmato	🍷🍷	3*
○	Trento Graal Brut Ris. '94	🍷🍷	4
○	Trento Graal Brut Ris. '93	🍸🍸🍸	4*
○	Trentino Vino Santo '89	🍸🍸	5
○	Vendemmia Tardiva Collezione '95	🍸🍸	4

TRENTO

CESARINI SFORZA
FRAZ. RAVIN
VIA STELLA, 9
38040 TRENTO
TEL. 0461/382200

The Cesarini Sforzas are among the few wine-makers in the area who dedicate themselves almost exclusively to making sparkling wines. They choose their grapes with care: only those they consider bubble-worthy make it to their cellar. In recent years they have had to keep one eye on what the competition is up to (the winery is in Ravina, the "golden triangle" of spumante-making which includes two other legendary giants of classic Italian spumante production) and the other on an increasingly selective market. For these reasons, the Cesarini Sforzas have developed their own technique for making first-rate spumante, based on the so-called "cuves closes" system, which uses large specially constructed and equipped containers for the initial stages of wine-making before bottling. And this "Cesarini Sforza Lungo" method has now produced its first and very promising results. The Riserva dei Conti is once again a spumante with a very fine perlage, a characteristic and enticing intensity on the nose and a well-balanced flavor of ripe yeasts. The white-labeled Brut Riserva is lighter, readier and pleasantly easy to drink. Smooth and frisky, and with an unusual youthful vigor, their Blanc de Blancs is made completely from chardonnay grapes. In keeping with what one would expect from the best sort of classic spumante, the Brut Riserva Aquila Reale '95 has considerable finesse in its aromas and its flavors are mouth-filling.

	Wine	Glasses	Price
○	Brut Riserva dei Conti	🍷🍷	4
○	Blanc de Blancs	🍷	4
○	Brut Riserva	🍷	4
○	Brut Aquila Reale Ris. '95	🍷	5
○	Trento Classico Brut	🍸🍸	5
●	Trentino Lagrein Villa Graziadei '94	🍸	3
○	Brut Aquila Reale Ris. '92	🍸	5

TRENTO

Ferrari

Fraz. Ravina
Via del Ponte, 15
38040 Trento
tel. 0461/972311 - 922500

Never before have the Lunellis presented such a strong and really exciting list as this one, confirming a general excellence which is almost unrivalled. Their consistently high performance includes an offering deservedly crowned by our Three Glasses. Three of their sparkling wines, along with their Sauvignon and a new Bordeaux-style blend, have scored champion-level points, and are without any doubt among the very best of Trentino wines. The legendary Riserva del Fondatore, vintage '90, is a wine in a class of its own. It's a dense, creamy, seductive spumante with a thrilling elegance and perfect balance: it yields yeasty toasty scents that finish with white flowers, hazelnuts and mountain honey, and a wonderfully complex dense texture on the palate. The Perlé '94 is excellent too, maybe the best one so far, and the Maximum, soft and complex, is no less successful. Together with the Incontri and the Trento Brut it easily wins two very full glasses. There are also positive results on the still wine front, with bottles bearing the Fratelli Lunelli label. Their newest offering is a red, Maso Le Viane '95, from young vines (mostly cabernet, with merlot, syrah and a few experiments). Since it is already vigorous, full and peppery, with lovely tannins, we expect to hear a good deal more of it in the future. You can still count on the Villa Margon and the Villa Gentilotti, two admirable chardonnays (the second is wood-fermented). And finally, the Villa San Nicolò, a compelling Sauvignon both exotic and typical, revealing exceptional balance, rounds off a really extraordinary group of wines.

	Wine	Glasses	
○	Giulio Ferrari '90	🍷🍷🍷	6
●	Lunelli Maso Le Viane '95	🍷🍷	4
○	Lunelli Villa Gentilotti '96	🍷🍷	4
○	Lunelli Villa Margon '96	🍷🍷	4
○	Lunelli Villa San Nicolò '97	🍷🍷	4
○	Trento Brut	🍷🍷	4
○	Trento Brut Maximum	🍷🍷	4
○	Trento Brut Perlé '94	🍷🍷	5
○	Trento Ferrari Incontri	🍷🍷	3*
○	Giulio Ferrari '86	🍷🍷🍷 (outline)	6
○	Giulio Ferrari '88	🍷🍷🍷 (outline)	6
○	Giulio Ferrari '89	🍷🍷🍷 (outline)	6
○	Giulio Ferrari '87	🍷🍷 (outline)	6
○	Trento Brut Perlé '91	🍷🍷 (outline)	5
○	Trento Brut Perlé '93	🍷🍷 (outline)	5

TRENTO

Le Meridiane

Loc. Casteller, 6
38100 Trento
tel. 0461/920811

Trento came by its name because its river, the Adige, in carving out the valley, created three hills, the "tridentum", or triple tooth, which the first settlers found a suitable place to stay. Well, one of these "teeth" lies to the south of the city, and is completely covered with vines. This hill is the Casteller, sacred in Trentino wine history. It is the most photographed spot in the province and graces a high percentage of viticultural publicity shots for the region. Le Meridiane is on this beautiful hill, and is determined to do its best and live up to the glory of its surroundings. After its triumph of last year with a series of exceptional wines indeed, Le Meridiane (sundials in English) still indicates that the time is right. We tasted four of their wines, two reds and two whites. Three were well over the threshold of two glasses and a fourth was on the point of joining them. Let's start with the Cabernet Vigneto San Bartolomeo '95 and the Merlot San Raimondo '95, both of which make an immediate impact with their elegance and importance. Thanks to the efforts of Giorgio Flessati, the director of Concilio Vini, who manages Le Meridiane himself and uses mostly grapes grown in his family vineyards, these are two very stylish reds, both with ample bouquets that combine a delicate vegetable note with an aroma of chocolate, accompanied by a long and clear progression of tastes. Then comes the delicious Chardonnay Vigneto Fontana Santa, rich in fruit and structure, followed by the savory Sauvignon Vigneto Al Poggio, fragrant and characteristically varietal. These are successful whites, carefully kept, already bottled, for a year, so as to develop a certain weight and complexity on the palate instead of going for the simpler pleasures of an immediate characteristic aroma and little else.

	Wine	Glasses	
●	Trentino Cabernet Sauvignon Vigneto San Bartolomeo Ris. '95	🍷🍷	4
○	Trentino Chardonnay Vigneto Fontana Santa '96	🍷🍷	3
●	Trentino Merlot Vigneto San Raimondo Ris. '95	🍷🍷	4
○	Trentino Sauvignon Vigneto Al Poggio '96	🍷	3
●	Trentino Cabernet Sauvignon Vigneto San Bartolomeo Ris. '94	🍷🍷 (outline)	3
○	Trentino Chardonnay '95	🍷🍷 (outline)	3*
●	Trentino Merlot Vigneto San Raimondo Ris. '94	🍷🍷 (outline)	4
○	Sauvignon Atesino '95	🍷 (outline)	3
○	Trentino Müller Thurgau '95	🍷 (outline)	3

TRENTO

Maso Martis

Loc. Martignano
Via dell'Albera, 52
38040 Trento
tel. 0461/821057

Initially the goal of this Martignano winemaker was simple. These dozen or so hectares on a residential hill in Trento would serve to grow grapes to make bubbly with. Antonio Stelzer, in fact, wanted to make good spumante. After years of viticultural ups and downs, he has done it. His sparkling wines are decidedly good. Both the Riserva and the classic Trento Brut make a very favorable impression, while the Chardonnay and two sweet treats (about which we shall speak in closing) are distinctly above average. The Brut Trento dégorgement '98 has a lovely fragrance, a mysterious aroma that is reminiscent of citron and exotic fruit. A rather rich wine, on the palate its attack is soft, elegant and tasty. These same sensations are present, but with greater vigor and complexity, in the Brut Riserva '94. Many-faceted in its range of aromas and even creamier in the mouth, it displays the finish of a great wine. Our compliments for the traditional Chardonnay with its golden brilliance, its distinct appley fragrance and its firm, unwavering persistence in the mouth. The two rarities from this producer, whose farm is dedicated to the god Mars, are the Moscato Rosa, delicate in its suggestion of roses, smooth, lively and with elegantly structured body, and the Sole d'Autunno, a late vintage with a chardonnay base. It's a fascinating sweet wine that seems to have captured and bottled the suave intensity of over-ripe grapes.

	Wine	Rating	Price
○	Trentino Chardonnay '97	🍷🍷	3
○	Trento Brut Riserva '94	🍷🍷	5
●	Trentino Moscato Rosa '97	🍷	5
○	Sole d'Autunno '97	🍷	5
○	Trento Brut	🍷	4
○	Trentino Chardonnay '94	♀♀	3
○	Trentino Chardonnay '95	♀♀	3*
○	Trento Brut Ris.	♀♀	4
○	Trento Brut Riserva '92	♀♀	5
○	Chardonnay Sole d'Autunno	♀	5
○	Sole d'Autunno	♀	5
●	Trentino Moscato Rosa '95	♀	5
○	Trento Brut '92	♀	4
○	Trento Brut Riserva '93	♀	5

VOLANO (TN)

Concilio Vini

Via Nazionale, 24
38060 Volano (TN)
tel. 0464/411000

Concilio Vini is a wine colossus whose wines get better as it gets bigger. We say "colossus" because Concilio Vini, Inc. owns four other labels as well: Grand Bleu, Lagaria, Clarius and Concilio Spumanti. To confirm their improvement we need only point to one fact: all 18 of the wines they presented to our tasting panels this year received at least One Glass. Their best wine, in our opinion, is the Merlot Novaline Riserva '95: its touch of noble oak and a round softness make it one of the most interesting reds from Trentino. The Cabernet Sauvignon Riserva '95 is of a similar quality, with its tannins already softened, its acidity well-balanced and a good long finish. These are both, along with the Marzemino Selezione Mozart '97 and the Teroldego Braide '96, reds that give many a more expensive wine strong competition. The Trentino Chardonnay Riserva '95 suffers slightly, but only slightly, from excessive striving to be true to type, which has resulted in aromas which diverge somewhat from flavors. The Pinot Grigio is pleasantly fresh, and the Nosiola full-bodied. These are whites that are likely to give a boost to the stock of this dynamic wine company, the pride not only of the Vallagarina.

	Wine	Rating	Price
●	Trentino Cabernet Sauvignon Ris. '95	🍷🍷	4
●	Trentino Marzemino Mozart '97	🍷🍷	3
●	Trentino Merlot Novaline Ris. '95	🍷🍷	4
●	Teroldego Rotaliano Braide '96	🍷	3
○	Trentino Chardonnay Ris. '95	🍷	4
○	Trentino Nosiola '97	🍷	3
○	Trentino Pinot Grigio '97	🍷	3
●	Trentino Merlot Novaline Ris. '91	♀♀	4
●	Trentino Merlot Novaline Ris. '94	♀♀	4
○	Trento Angelo Grigolli Ris.	♀♀	5
●	Trentino Cabernet Sauvignon Ris. '93	♀	4
●	Trentino Pinot Nero Ris. '94	♀	3

OTHER WINERIES

The following producers in the province of Trento obtained good scores in our tastings with one or more of their wines:

Madonna delle Vittorie
Arco, tel. 0464/505542,
Trentino Chardonnay '97

Maso Roveri
Avio, tel. 0464/684396,
Trentino Pinot Grigio '97

Cantina Sociale di Toblino,
Calavino, tel. 0461/564168
Trentino Cabernet '96,
Trentino Nosiola '97

Cantina Valle di Cembra
Cembra, tel. 0461/680010,
Trentino Müller Thurgau '97,
Trentino Pinot Nero '96

Nicolodi
Cembra, tel. 0461/683020,
Cimbrus '97,
Trentino Müller Thurgau '97

Zanotelli
Cembra, tel. 0461/683134,
Trentino Müller Thurgau '97,
Trentino Pinot Nero '96

Arcangelo Sandri
Faedo, tel. 0461/650935,
Schiava di Faedo '97,
Trentino Müller Thurgau '97

Abate Nero
Gardolo, tel. 0461/246566,
Trento Brut,
Trento Extra Brut

Castel Warth - Francesco e Diego Moser
Giovo, tel. 0461/684140,
Trentino Müller Thurgau '97,
Trentino Riesling '97

La Vigne
Isera, tel. 0464/434600,
Trentino Marzemino '97

F.lli Pisoni
Lasino-Pergolese, tel. 0461/564106,
Trentino Nosiola '97
Trento Brut '90

Cantina Sebastiani
Lavis, tel. 0461/246315,
Trentino Chardonnay '97

Casata Monfort
Lavis, tel. 0461/241484,
Trentino Lagrein '96,
Trentino Traminer Aromatico '97

Équipe Trentina
Lavis, tel. 0461/246325,
Trento Brut

Vignaioli Fanti
Lavis, tel. 0461/241000
Incrocio Manzoni 6.0.1.3 '97,
Trentino Nosiola '97

Baron de Cles
Mezzolombardo, tel. 0461/601081,
Teroldego Rotaliano '97

Conti Martini
Mezzocorona, tel. 0461/603932,
Teroldego Rotaliano '97

Cantina Sociale di Mori - Colli Zugna,
Mori, tel. 0464/918154
Trentino Marzemino '97,
Trentino Sauvignon '97

Cantina Sociale di Nomi
Nomi, tel. 0464/834195,
Trentino Marzemino '97

Grigoletti
Nomi, tel. 0464/834215,
Trentno Marzemino '97

Maso Lock
Povo di Trento,
tel. 0461/810071,
Trentino Chardonnay '97,
Trentino Merlot '97

Gaierhof
Roveré della Luna,
tel. 0461/658514,
Trentino Pinot Grigio '97

Vigneto Dalzocchio
Rovereto, tel. 0464/413664,
Pinot Nero Atesino '95,
Trentino Chardonnay '96

Cadalora
Santa Margherita di Ala,
tel. 0464/696540,
Trentino Pinot Nero '95

Maso Bergamini
Trento, tel. 0461/983079,
Trentino Lagrein '97

ALTO ADIGE

In terms of wine production Alto Adige is not a big region. Cultivation of the vine is restricted to the rather limited plain country and to the hillsides, which are hardly more common. And yet it is now a benchmark for quality and one of the most interesting wine-producing areas in Europe. It is characterized by a happy mixture of small but extremely competent cooperatives and a collection of private producers, themselves usually active throughout the phases of wine-making, with up-to-the-minute cellars and first-class oenologists. Then too there are both native grapes, such as lagrein, schiava and gewürztraminer, and a selection of international varietals which have been growing here for scores of years. Pinot blanc perhaps comes to mind first, but sauvignon, riesling, chardonnay, merlot, cabernet and particularly pinot noir have also now come into their own. The upshot is that we seem to have to devote more space to this region every year. In this edition we have dedicated profiles to 48 wineries, and another 17 have received honorable mention at the end. There are not many regions that can be so thoroughly examined with such satisfying results. Indeed we feel that Alto Adige has now earned a place in the "Who's Who" of the top Italian wine-producing areas, together with the Langhe, central Tuscany, Friuli and some parts of the Veneto. It's extraordinary, yet perhaps not so surprising, given the manpower engaged in the enterprise. But behind it all is what must be the best assortment of wine cooperatives in the world. Wineries like the Cantine Produttori of San Michele Appiano/St. Michael Eppan, of Colterenzio/Schreckbichl, of Cornaiano/Girlan, of Caldaro/Kaltern, of Termeno/Tramin, of Cortaccia/Kurtatsch, of Burgraviato/Burggräffler, of the Valle Isarco/Eisacktaler and of Prima & Nuova/Erste & Neue, just to name the most prominent, are exemplary for both their efficiency and the high general quality of even their run-of-the-mill products. Among the private producers, since Lageder, one of the great founding fathers of wine-making in this region, was out of the running because we were able to taste only one of his wines this year before going to press, the most distinguished wineries were Paolo and Martin Foradori's Hofstätter, Elena Walch, Cantina Convento di Muri Gries and Cantina dell'Abbazia di Novacella, the last of which has made an astonishing comeback after some rather lean years. Very high marks, even if they missed Three Glasses by a hair, go to Josephus Mayr and Andreas Menz for their two splendid versions of Lagrein Scuro, to Franz Pratzner and his Tenuta Falkenstein for an exceptional Riesling, to Peter Plieger's Kuen Hof for an excellent Veltliner and to Franz Haas for a spectacular Moscato Rosa.

ANDRIANO/ANDRIAN (BZ)

CANTINA PRODUTTORI ANDRIANO
VIA DELLA CHIESA, 2
39010 ANDRIANO/ANDRIAN (BZ)
TEL. 0471/510137

The Cantina Produttori Andriano, while not among the most famous cooperatives in Alto Adige, has been known for some years for the consistently high quality of its wines. Dating from 1893, it is also the oldest wine-growers' cooperative in the region. Every year the Andriano producers draw our attention to a couple of really exciting wines. This year it's the Chardonnay Tor di Lupo '95 and the Lagrein Tor di Lupo '95. The former, a barriqued wine, has a complex and fruity bouquet which goes very well with its elegant hint of toasty oak and good structure. On the palate it's concentrated and fresh, and we find it eminently drinkable. Their second triumph, Lagrein Tor di Lupo '95, is of an intensely, almost purplish red color. The nose releases a vast range of fruity aromas and a note of perfectly integrated oak. On the palate it's meaty and clean and has admirable structure and extract. High marks also for the Schiava Santa Giustina '97, fresh and elegant and a perfect example of wine made from this native grape. Finally, there are several well-made and attractive whites: the Terlano Pinot Bianco Classico, Terlano Müller Thurgau, Terlano Sauvignon Preciosa and the Gewürztraminer. These are all '97's and very interesting, not least of all because they are remarkably good value for money.

○	A. A. Chardonnay Tor di Lupo '95	🍷🍷	4
●	A. A. Lagrein Scuro Tor di Lupo '95	🍷🍷	4
●	A. A. Schiava S. Giustina '97	🍷🍷	2*
○	A. A. Gewürztraminer '97	🍷	3
○	A. A. Terlano Müller Thurgau '97	🍷	2
○	A. A. Terlano Pinot Bianco Cl. '97	🍷	2
○	A. A. Terlano Sauvignon Preciosa '97	🍷	3
○	A. A. Chardonnay Tor di Lupo '93	🍸🍸	4
○	A. A. Chardonnay Tor di Lupo '94	🍸🍸	4
●	A. A. Lagrein Scuro Tor di Lupo '94	🍸🍸	4
○	A. A. Terlano Sauvignon Cl. '95	🍸🍸	3*
○	A. A. Terlano Sauvignon Cl. '96	🍸🍸	3

APPIANO/EPPAN (BZ)

CANT. PROD. S. PAOLO
KELLEREIGENOSSENSCHAFT ST. PAULS
VIA GUARDIA, 21
39050 APPIANO/EPPAN (BZ)
TEL. 0471/662183

Their Exclusiv range consists of wines made from selected grapes grown in a number of small sub-zones which they believe to be specially suited to the grape in question. Thus Plötzner is the "cru" for their Pinot Bianco, Egg-leitn for Pinot Grigio and Gries, obviously, for the Lagrein. It is thanks to these three wines, the top of their line, that the Cantina Produttori di S. Paolo has regained its profile in the Guide. All three are very interesting wines and among the finest in their categories in the region. The Pinot Bianco stands out as an interpretation of the best qualities of that grape. Aromas of pineapple, Golden Delicious apple and green banana are a prelude to a soft and satisfyingly concentrated flavor. The dominant fruits in the Pinot Grigio Egg-Leitn's bouquet, on the other hand, are Williams pear and rennet apple, and the palate is more decidedly structured and succulent. We also liked the Lagrein Scuro, a classic Gries wine, which is redolent of berries, particularly blueberries and raspberries, and doesn't fudge its attack on the palate, where tannins are in evidence and the finish is just faintly bitterish.

●	A. A. Lagrein Scuro Exclusiv Gries Ris. '95	🍷🍷	4
○	A. A. Pinot Bianco Exclusiv Plötzner '97	🍷🍷	4
○	A. A. Pinot Grigio Exclusiv Egg-Leitn '97	🍷🍷	4
●	A. A. Lagrein Scuro Exclusiv Gries Ris. '94	🍸	4

APPIANO/EPPAN (BZ)

CANTINA PRODUTTORI SAN MICHELE
APPIANO/ST. MICHAEL EPPAN
VIA CIRCONVALLAZIONE, 17/19
39057 APPIANO/EPPAN (BZ)
TEL. 0471/664466

No one will be surprised. The consistent excellence of everything produced by this winery is, after all, no longer open to question. The wines will change, of course, from year to year, because harvests vary, but their wine-making technique is always very nearly perfect. This is thanks to the amazing skill of their kellermeister Hans Terzer, but also to the farsightedness of the member growers and the president of this cooperative who are with him all the way. Thus, in just a few years, the wines that bear the Sanct Valentin label have become almost legendary. In particular the Sauvignon, which in its '97 version once again receives Three Glasses, is a benchmark for other Italian wines of its kind. But also the Chardonnay '96, the Pinot Grigio '96 and the Gewürztraminer '97 (the first two kept a while in the barrique) are all winners. As of two years ago there are some reds in the family: the Cabernet '95, for example, but also a couple of Pinot Neros, a grape that seems to come naturally to Hans Terzer. Then there are excellent performances this year from the Sauvignon Lahn '97, which is almost the equal of the Sanct Valentin for varietal character, and the Pinot Bianco Schulthauser '97, a particularly important wine here. To conclude, there is the Riesling Montiggl '97, which is very interesting but a little forward in its aromas. These are wines in their secondary range that cost much less than the Sanct Valentins, but occasionally do not suffer at all in comparison with their bigger brothers.

	Wine	Glasses	Price
○	A. A. Sauvignon St. Valentin '97	▼▼▼	5
●	A. A. Cabernet St. Valentin '95	▼▼	5
○	A. A. Chardonnay St. Valentin '96	▼▼	5
○	A. A. Gewürztraminer St. Valentin '97	▼▼	5
○	A. A. Pinot Bianco Schulthauser '97	▼▼	3
○	A. A. Pinot Grigio '96	▼▼	5
○	A. A. Sauvignon Lahn '97	▼▼	3*
●	A. A. Pinot Nero Ris. '96	▼	5
○	A. A. Riesling Montiggl '97	▼	3
○	A. A. Pinot Grigio St. Valentin '95	▽▽▽	5
○	A. A. Sauvignon St. Valentin '95	▽▽▽	5
○	A. A. Sauvignon St. Valentin '96	▽▽▽	5
●	A. A. Pinot Nero St. Valentin '95	▽▽	5

APPIANO/EPPAN (BZ)

KÖSSLER - PRAECLARUS
SAN PAOLO/ST. PAULS
39057 APPIANO/EPPAN (BZ)
TEL. 0471/660256 - 662182

If you want to taste this year's best spumante from the Alto Adige, all you have to do is lay your hands on a bottle of Praeclarus Noblesse '90, chill it in a bucket full of water and ice, and then enjoy it to the last drop. Its pleasant fruity aromas and easy quaffability are seconded by its excellent balance and bead. It's almost a Three Glass wine, and misses only because it is not quite, perhaps, as rich in concentration as one might hope. It is certainly, however, a great technical success. Their non-vintage Brut is a little lighter, but still a very respectable effort. The other bottles presented to us by this winery are still wines and, for the most part, red ones. Last year we liked the Lagrein Scuro '95 particularly. The '96 version is less convincing: less drinkable, less body, less fruity to the nose, and only One Glass. As usual, the Cabernet-Merlot Cuvée St. Pauls, now the '96, is very interesting, and this year is the best of their reds. It is full, rich and powerful in the mouth and typically varietal to the nose. It's not a champion, but it is exceedingly good. The '96 version of the Tschiedererhof Merlot is pretty good, but it hasn't found itself yet. It does not have the balance and smooth tannins that are to be found in a great merlot. The Pinot Nero Herr von Zobel Riserva '96 is disappointingly thin and vegetal in its aroma, while the Schiava Weingut St. Justina '97 is pleasingly up-front, honest and unpretentious.

	Wine	Glasses	Price
●	A. A. Cabernet-Merlot St. Pauls '96	▼▼	5
○	A. A. Spumante Praeclarus Brut	▼▼	5
○	A. A. Spumante Praeclarus Noblesse '90	▼▼	5
●	A. A. Lagrein Scuro '96	▼	4
●	A. A. Merlot Tschiedererhof '96	▼	5
●	A. A. Schiava St. Justina '97	▼	2
●	A. A. Pinot Nero Herr von Zobel Ris. '96		4
●	A. A. Lagrein Scuro '95	▽▽	4
●	A. A. Cabernet-Merlot S. Pauls '95	▽	5
○	A. A. Spumante Praeclarus Noblesse '89	▽	5

APPIANO/EPPAN (BZ)

STROBLHOF
VIA PIGANO, 25
39057 APPIANO/EPPAN (BZ)
TEL. 0471/662250

A number of years have gone by since Josef Hanny, the founder of this excellent winery, passed away. Time had to pass before things could return to their former state in the cellar. But now Rosmarie and Christine Hanny, Josef's daughters, with the indispensable assistance of Andreas Nicolussi-Leck, Rosmarie's husband, and the friendly advice of Hans Terzer, director of the Cantina Produttori di San Michele Appiano, are definitely back on track. Perhaps that Pinot Nero Riserva '90 which had everyone talking about Stroblhof a few years back has not yet been equaled. But this year all their wines are decidedly satisfactory. Their Pinot Bianco Strahler '97 is elegant and extremely pleasurable, both in its appropriate aromas and in the great ease with which it goes down. It's a perfect wine of its kind. The very good Gewürztraminer '97 does not have a great deal of body (we're in Appiano, not Termeno, after all), but it offers finely delineated varietal aromas to the discerning nose. The somewhat neutral Chardonnay '97 is decently made, but less representative of its grape than the two wines just described. Not quite ready to drink, so still a little bumptious, the Pinot Nero Riserva '95 reminds us of the legendary '90, but has neither its body nor its complexity.

○	A. A. Gewürztraminer '97	▼▼	4
○	A. A. Pinot Bianco Strahler '97	▼▼	3*
○	A. A. Chardonnay '97	▼	4
●	A. A. Pinot Nero Ris. '95	▼	5
●	A. A. Pinot Nero Ris. '91	▽▽	4
●	A. A. Pinot Nero Strahler Ris. '90	▽▽	5
○	A. A. Pinot Bianco Strahler '95	▽	3
●	A. A. Pinot Nero Ris. '93	▽	4

BOLZANO/BOZEN

CANTINA CONVENTO MURI-GRIES
P.ZZA GRIES, 21
39100 BOLZANO/BOZEN
TEL. 0471/282287

The monks in this ancient monastery have been making wine ever since the 11th century. This continuity of tradition is, obviously, an excellent basis for high quality, so it comes as no surprise that we now have the pleasure of awarding them Three Glasses for a top-ranking and very important wine, their Lagrein Abtei Riserva '96. Christian Werth, their young oenologist, is definitely one of the best interpreters of this deep-colored local grape, from which he produces wines that are always rich in character and expressive power. His father, who was the oenologist before him in this cellar, had a profound understanding of lagrein, and one is tempted to say that a passionate love for this grape is stored in the family genetic code. The '96 vintage of the Lagrein Abtei Riserva is, at last, a perfect expression of this wine. Its deep color, ruby red verging on dark garnet, precedes a complex range of intense aromas, particularly violets and wild berries; in the mouth it's soft, full-bodied, velvety and lightly astringent. Round and harmonious in structure, it is further blessed with a long finish. It's a gem. The excellent Lagrein '97 is simpler but equally juicy, and the Lagrein Kretzer '97 is a charming rosé version, fresh, fruity and vivacious.

●	A. A. Lagrein Abtei Ris. '96	▼▼▼	5
●	A. A. Lagrein Scuro Gries '97	▼▼	2*
⊙	A. A. Lagrein Rosato '97	▼	2
●	A. A. Cabernet Ris. '91	▽▽	5
●	A. A. Lagrein Abtei Ris. '94	▽▽	5
⊙	A. A. Lagrein Rosato '96	▽▽	3
●	A. A. Lagrein Ris. '90	▽▽	4
●	A. A. Lagrein Ris. Abtei '92	▽▽	5
●	A. A. Lagrein Scuro Gries '95	▽▽	4
●	A. A. Lagrein '91	▽	4
●	A. A. Lagrein '92	▽	4
○	A. A. Pinot Grigio '96	▽	3

BOLZANO/BOZEN

Cantina di Gries

P.zza Gries, 2
39100 Bolzano/Bozen
tel. 0471/270909

Gries has always been one of the best makers of Lagrein, a red wine which is produced almost entirely in the area around Bolzano. Lagrein is a traditional wine. It has a very concentrated ruby color, a strong, fruity nose which reveals blackberry and black currant, and a taste that can be somewhat aggressive and bitter at the end. The Cantina di Gries took up the challenge of eliminating the excessively rustic nature of this wine, and has already succeeded in part. Their two Grieser Lagreins, one from the Prestige Line and the other Baron Carl Eyrl, both '95 Riservas and produced at least in part in small barrels, have excellent body and are soft and elegant. They are not very much like the rough Lagreins of the past that it took some determination to drink. They also bode very well for the future of this kind of wine. The Mauritius '95, made from the interesting mixture of lagrein and merlot, is the inaugural version of an already important wine. The other traditional wine, the Santa Maddalena Classico Tröglerhof '97 is pleasant, medium-bodied and well made. Their Sauvignon '97 is a delightful surprise, considering that it comes from a winery that specializes in reds. Only the Merlot Graf Huyn Riserva '95 is again somewhat disappointing. Although correctly made, it does not have the elegance and concentration that a wine of its pretensions and, especially, price ought to have.

●	A. A. Lagrein Grieser Baron Carl Eyrl Ris. '95	🍷🍷	5
●	A. A. Lagrein Grieser Prestige Line Ris. '95	🍷🍷	5
●	Mauritius '95	🍷🍷	5
●	A. A. Merlot Graf Huyn Ris. '95	🍷	5
●	A. A. Santa Maddalena Cl. Tröglerhof '97	🍷	3
○	A. A. Sauvignon '97	🍷	3
●	A. A. Lagrein Grieser Baron Carl Eyrl Ris. '93	🍷🍷 (outline)	5
●	A. A. Merlot Siebeneich Prestige Line Ris. '95	🍷🍷 (outline)	5
●	Mauritius '94	🍷🍷 (outline)	5

BOLZANO/BOZEN

Cantina Produttori Santa Maddalena

Via Brennero, 15
39100 Bolzano/Bozen
tel. 0471/972944

Santa Maddalena is still among the best of the Alto Adige wine cooperatives. After its great successes of the past few years, it doesn't really matter that Three Glasses haven't come their way this time. Eight of their wines have received Two Glasses, and that tells you just about all you need to know about their commitment to quality. Once again it was the Cabernet Mumelterhof, the '96, that excited us most. It has an intense ruby color, a richly fruity and delicate bouquet, both elegant and complex, and, in the mouth, softness and full body. Their kellermeister, Stephan Filippi, has demonstrated once again the excellence of his vines and his abilities in the cellar. The two Lagreins, the Riserva Taberhof and the Perlhof, both '96s, are splendid examples of what this good local grape can do. The first has a more decided and fuller structure, but both offer delicate aromas of violets and are velvety, pleasantly tannic, and well-balanced in the mouth. Their principal breadwinner, the Santa Maddalena '97, made a good impression in all three of its versions: the Classico, the Huck am Bach and the Stieler. They are full, fragrant wines, highly suggestive of berries and cherries both to the nose and on the delicate palate, and are fresh and elegant. 1997 was a wonderful year in Alto Adige both for Santa Maddalena and for Schiava. The whites are interesting. The two we particularly mention, the Chardonnay Kleinstein '97 and the Valle Isarco Müller Thurgau '97, are crisp and full of character.

●	A. A. Cabernet Mumelterhof '96	🍷🍷	4
○	A. A. Chardonnay Kleinstein '97	🍷🍷	3*
●	A. A. Lagrein Perlhof '96	🍷🍷	3*
●	A. A. Lagrein Scuro Taberhof Ris. '96	🍷🍷	4
●	A. A. Santa Maddalena Cl. '97	🍷🍷	2*
●	A. A. Santa Maddalena Cl. Huck am Bach '97	🍷🍷	3*
●	A. A. Santa Maddalena Cl. Stieler '97	🍷🍷	2*
○	A. A. Valle Isarco Müller Thurgau '97	🍷🍷	3*
●	A. A. Cabernet Mumelterhof '95	🍷🍷🍷 (outline)	4
●	A. A. Lagrein Scuro Taberhof Ris. '95	🍷🍷🍷 (outline)	4

BOLZANO/BOZEN

EGGER-RAMER
VIA GUNCINA, 5
39100 BOLZANO/BOZEN
TEL. 0471/280541

Toni Egger and his wife Cristina Furgler are the owners of this small winery and its 14 hectares of vineyards in the classic zone for Santa Maddalena and Lagrein. We have given them a profile of their own this year because the three wines they presented literally astonished us. The Lagrein Grieser Kristan Riserva '95 was one of the best reds we tasted and it only missed getting Three Glasses by a hair. It is a traditional Lagrein, aged in large barrels, and indeed does not have any aroma of vanilla. Instead the bouquet offers distinct and well-defined fragrances of berries. The taste is perhaps a little rough just at first, but the concentration and persistence are those of a really great wine. Their standard Lagrein, the Kristan '96, is very good too. The nose is less intense and complex and the body lighter, but we recognize the same technical mastery in its production. Their Santa Maddalena Classico '97 is a delicious red, extraordinarily easy to drink and fruitily fragrant, with hints of berries and undergrowth.

	Wine	Glasses	Price
●	A. A. Lagrein Grieser Kristan '96	▼▼	3*
●	A. A. Lagrein Grieser Kristan Ris. '95	▼▼	5
●	A. A. Santa Maddalena Cl. '97	▼▼	3

BOLZANO/BOZEN

FRANZ GOJER - GLÖGGLHOF
FRAZ. ST. MAGDALENA
VIA RIVELLONE, 1
39100 BOLZANO/BOZEN
TEL. 0471/978775

In the Santa Maddalena area, Franz Gojer is considered a master of the vine and of wine. Everything he produces has about it the romantic aura that only an artisan in the grand tradition can give it, and his wines are unique. All of which is even more admirable, considering that Gojer's vines are schiava and lagrein, two grapes that are hard to make concentrated and harmonious wines from. So, if you get a chance to taste his Santa Maddalena Classico '97, the best version we've tasted for years, think of his attentive care during fermentation, his painstaking labor among the vines, all the expense of experience and effort needed to produce such a result. And from schiava! You can get a good rosé from schiava, but where else would you find a red of such suave concentration? The Santa Maddalena Rondell '97, a special selection which should in theory be better than the Classico, was not as convincing. This may have been because we tasted the wine too soon, when it wasn't really ready. The two Lagrein Scuros are all right, but not as good as the two from last year. The '97 is direct and not very complicated and the '96 Riserva has concentration but not the richness and opulence of the '95 Riserva. Taken all in all, this was a good year for this small but prestigious winery.

	Wine	Glasses	Price
●	A. A. Santa Maddalena Cl. '97	▼▼	3
●	A. A. Lagrein Scuro '97	▼	3
●	A. A. Lagrein Scuro Ris. '96	▼	4
●	A. A. Santa Maddalena Rondell '97	▼	3
●	A. A. Lagrein Scuro Ris. '95	▽▽	4
●	A. A. Santa Maddalena Cl. '95	▽▽	3
●	A. A. Santa Maddalena Rondell '93	▽▽	4
●	A. A. Santa Maddalena Rondell '95	▽▽	3
●	A. A. Santa Maddalena Rondell '96	▽	3

BOLZANO/BOZEN

H. LUN
V.LO SABBIA/TAFELGRIES 5/7
39100 BOLZANO/BOZEN
TEL. 0471/976583

Lun is one of the best-known wine producers in Alto Adige, and the excellent performance of their wines this year is responsible for this debut in the Guide. We particularly liked the Riesling Sandblichler '97, a complex and aristocratic white, and one of the very best of its category. It has refined, varietal aromas, and a full and harmonious taste unblemished by excessive acidity or other roughness. The interesting Cabernet Riserva '95 from their Albertus line has excellent body, like the best cabernets, but does not have the concentration on nose or palate that a real champion would display. It's a good wine, though, and excellent value for money, which is a particular strong point of H. Lun in general. The Lagrein Scuro Riserva '95, another Albertus wine, is medium/good in body, a little forward on the nose, well-balanced, and without any harsh tannins. The straightforward Pinot Bianco Lun Line '97, with its fruity fragrance, is a light, pleasantly drinkable wine.

	Wine	Glasses	Price
●	A. A. Cabernet Albertus Ris. '95	▼▼	4
○	A. A. Riesling Sandblicher '97	▼▼	3*
●	A. A. Lagrein Scuro Albertus Ris. '95	▼	4
○	A. A. Pinot Bianco Lun Line '97	▼	3

BOLZANO/BOZEN

THOMAS MAYR E FIGLIO
VIA MENDOLA, 56
39100 BOLZANO/BOZEN
TEL. 0471/281030

This is another satisfactory year for Thomas Mayr's winery, and with a more limited range of wines. The Lagrein Scuro Riserva '96, even though it is not from an easy year, earns its Two Glasses without much difficulty. The fairly intense bouquet offers characteristic aromas of blackberry, raspberry and black currant. The palate displays good concentration and that bitter aftertaste, so typical of Lagrein, is only just suggested, and not overdone. It's a successful wine, quite in keeping with the style of the house, which is known for its good Lagrein. The standard Lagrein '97 is quite decent, but we are curious to see, next year, how the Riserva of this excellent and promising vintage comes out. The Santa Maddalena Classico Rumplerhof '97 is pretty good, but we think they could have done better: we'd prefer it softer and more concentrated, and also without those greenish tones that we found in the '96 version as well, although we must admit that the '97 is vastly superior.

	Wine	Glasses	Price
●	A. A. Lagrein Scuro Ris. '96	▼▼	4
●	A. A. Lagrein Scuro '97	▼	3
●	A. A. Santa Maddalena Cl. Rumplerhof '97	▼	3
●	A. A. Lagrein Scuro '93	▽▽	3
●	A. A. Lagrein Scuro '95	▽▽	3
●	A. A. Lagrein Scuro Ris. '92	▽▽	4
●	A. A. Lagrein Scuro Ris. '94	▽▽	4
●	Creazione Rosa '95	▽▽	5
●	A. A. Lagrein Scuro '94	▽	3
●	A. A. Lagrein Scuro '96	▽	3
●	A. A. Santa Maddalena Cl. Rumplerhof '95	▽	3
●	A. A. Santa Maddalena Cl. Rumplerhof '96	▽	3

BOLZANO/BOZEN

HEINRICH PLATTNER - WALDGRIESHOF

SANTA GIUSTINA, 2
39100 BOLZANO/BOZEN
TEL. 0471/973245

There is no longer any doubt that the Waldgries winery in Sancta Justina and its proprietor, Heinrich Plattner, are among the best interpreters of the cabernet sauvignon grape in Alto Adige. We tried the '94 and the '95 last year, and now here's the sensational '96. It very nearly received Three Glasses, and demonstrated very clearly that such an award is well within its reach. It's only a question of the vintage, and '97 could be it. A glance at their vines and at their figures explains everything. They eschew the pergola system for that of guyot. Their yield is only 5 thousand kilos per hectare. They use small barrels of new French oak for aging. They have made the right choices, and our enthusiasm is well-grounded. And the Cabernet is not their only good wine. The Lagrein Scuro Riserva '96 is, of its kind, a little gem. Complex and rich to the nose, powerful and decided on the palate, this wine is the measure by which others of its kind will be judged. The Santa Maddalena Classico '97 is also very good, while the Pinot Bianco di Terlano '97 is not up to the others. Under the circumstances this seems a very minor misdemeanor indeed.

	Wine	Glasses	Price
●	A. A. Cabernet Sauvignon '96	🍷🍷	5
●	A. A. Lagrein Scuro Ris. '96	🍷🍷	4
●	A. A. Santa Maddalena Cl. '97	🍷	3
○	A. A. Terlano Pinot Bianco '97		3
●	A. A. Cabernet Sauvignon '94	ΥΥ	5
●	A. A. Cabernet Sauvignon '95	ΥΥ	5
●	A. A. Lagrein Scuro '93	ΥΥ	4
●	A. A. Lagrein Scuro '95	ΥΥ	4
○	A. A. Terlano Pinot Bianco '94	ΥΥ	4
●	A. A. Lagrein Scuro '94	Υ	4
●	A. A. Moscato Rosa '96	Υ	5
○	A. A. Pinot Grigio '96	Υ	3
●	A. A. Pinot Nero '95	Υ	4
●	A. A. Santa Maddalena '95	Υ	3
○	A. A. Terlano Pinot Bianco '95	Υ	4

BOLZANO/BOZEN

GEORG RAMOSER

LOC. S. MADDALENA
39100 BOLZANO/BOZEN
TEL. 0471/975481

This is another small but excellent winery making its maiden appearance in the Guide with a limited number of wines that are, however, of exceptionally fine quality. The proprietor and "soul" of the estate is Georg Ramoser, who owns the Untermoserhof vineyard, and it is from these vines that he makes a small amount of excellent wine. His Merlot '96 is a gem. It has smooth tannins, good body, and aromas of tobacco and berries without an overdose of vanilla. Particular care was obviously lavished on both the fermentation and aging, which took place in small oak barrels. The Lagrein Riserva '96 is also very interesting, not least because this year was generally such a poor one. It has perhaps less concentration and is thus a bit leaner than the '95 version, but the clarity of its aromas and its elegance on the palate easily earn it Two Glasses. His Santa Maddalena Classico '97 scores just as high: a light wine, with a delicately fruity fragrance, and quite exciting to drink. It's a splendid young red from our "deep" north, to be drunk by the bucketful.

	Wine	Glasses	Price
●	A. A. Lagrein Scuro Untermoserhof Ris. '96	🍷🍷	4
●	A. A. Merlot Untermoserhof '97	🍷🍷	5
●	A. A. S. Maddalena Cl. Untermoserhof '97	🍷🍷	3*
●	A. A. Lagrein Scuro Untermoserhof Ris. '95	ΥΥ	4

BOLZANO/BOZEN

HANS ROTTENSTEINER
VIA SARENTINO, 1/A
39100 BOLZANO/BOZEN
TEL. 0471/282015

As we write this entry, we still have in our nose and mouth the scents and savors of an authoritative version of Lagrein Scuro, the Grieser Select Riserva '95, which Anton Rottensteiner presented this year for tasting. It is a great and typical example of its kind. Almost opaque in the glass, it has characteristically fruity fragrance. On the palate it is powerful and just a touch rough, but overwhelmingly fascinating. We might borrow a phrase from our colleagues of the Guide Hachette, "un coup de coeur", to describe its effect. However it is just shy of receiving Three Glasses, precisely because of those slightly aggressive tannins which are typical of lagrein but also its major defect. To balance them, more richness, more fat in the mouth and more glycerin are needed. These are all things that it is not always possible to attain. The wine, as is, however, is a great one, a little rustic but captivating. And we take our hats off to Rottensteiner. The rest of this year's wines are not on the same level. Whites (Pinot Bianco and Pinot Grigio) do not seem to be a specialty of the winery. The Santa Maddalena Classico Premstallerhof '97 is certainly decent but not exceptional. The Cabernet Select Riserva '95 is somewhat disappointing, since the '93 was so good. Frankly it's a bit rough and deficient in concentration. The Lagrein Rosato '97 is fruity and easy to drink but in no way an ambitious wine.

	Wine	Rating	Price
●	A. A. Lagrein Grieser Select Ris. '95	▼▼	4*
●	A. A. Cabernet Select '95	▼	5
⊙	A. A. Lagrein Rosato '97	▼	2
○	A. A. Pinot Grigio '97	▼	3
●	A. A. Santa Maddalena Cl. Premstallerhof '97	▼	3
○	A. A. Pinot Bianco '97		3
●	A. A. Cabernet Select Ris. '90	▽▽	5
●	A. A. Cabernet Select Ris. '91	▽▽	5
●	A. A. Cabernet Select Ris. '93	▽▽	5
●	A. A. Lagrein Grieser Select Ris '94	▽▽	4
●	A. A. Pinot Nero Mazzon Select Ris. '93	▽▽	5

BRESSANONE/BRIXEN (BZ)

KUEN HOF - PETER PLIEGER
LOC. MAHR, 110
39042 BRESSANONE/BRIXEN (BZ)
TEL. 0472/850546

Peter Plieger's winery, Kuen Hof, is back in the Guide after a couple of years. He is one of the most interesting wine-makers in the Valle Isarco, the northernmost wine-producing area in Alto Adige. Around here it is very hard for grapes to ripen completely. If one goes even a few yards beyond the area of benign influence of the Isarco River it is no longer possible to grow vines. But for zones like this, '97 was a godsend. A very hot, dry summer led to an early harvest of fully ripened grapes. The results are surprising, to say the least. Plieger's Veltliner '97 has an aromatic concentration which was hardly possible in other years. It has grassy and citrus-fruity aromas of rare finesse and intensity. It's full-bodied and has an extremely pleasant slight harshness that adds to the wine's complexity and will help it age well. The Sylvaner '97 is almost as good. It has a delightful nose rich in alfalfa and wildflowers, and on the excellent palate offers the complexity and structure of a wine of international stature. His Kaiton '97, a riesling aged in large barrels, has delicate fruity aromas and an excellent structure. The Gewürztraminer '97 is the only fly in the ointment for Plieger this year, but just because it is quite good, not exceptional.

	Wine	Rating	Price
○	A. A. Valle Isarco Sylvaner '97	▼▼	4
○	A. A. Valle Isarco Veltliner '97	▼▼	4
○	Kaiton '97	▼▼	4
○	A. A. Valle Isarco Gewürztraminer '97	▼	4
○	A. A. Valle Isarco Veltliner '93	▽▽	4
○	A. A. Valle Isarco Gewürztraminer '92	▽	4
○	A. A. Valle Isarco Gewürztraminer '93	▽	4
○	A. A. Valle Isarco Sylvaner '92	▽	4
○	A. A. Valle Isarco Sylvaner '93	▽	4
○	A. A. Valle Isarco Veltliner '92	▽	4

CALDARO/KALTERN (BZ)

Cantina Viticoltori di Caldaro/Kaltern

Via delle Cantine, 12
39052 Caldaro/Kaltern (BZ)
tel. 0471/963149

The Cantina Viticoltori di Caldaro, its cellar surrounded by vineyards, is one of the leading Alto Adige wine cooperatives. Helmuth Zozin is its director and cellar master. He has demonstrated his enormous competence as a wine-maker many times in the recent past. Last year his splendid Gewürztraminer Campaner '96 received Three Glasses, underlining the cooperative's resources and potential in the field of white wines. The '97 just missed Three Glasses, but it's still a magnificent wine, mature and tasty, with stupendous structure and great concentration. The Chardonnay Wadleith '97 is a classic Alto Adige white, with well-defined aromas, an elegant crispness and succulent substance. The fresh Pinot Bianco Vial '97 is pleasantly easy to drink. But their reds are, if anything, even better. The magnificent Cabernet Sauvignon Riserva '95 towers over the others. This is the third time that it has received Three Glasses. Once again it won us over with its imposing structure, abundant fruit, featuring black currant with well-judged notes of spice, and its rich and extremely elegant body. The Cabernet Sauvignon Campaner '95, soft and juicy, did almost as well as its big brother. Their red made from schiava is the cornerstone of their wine production, and the Lago di Caldaro Scelto Pfarrhof '97 is typically easy to drink, clean, and fruity. And a happy ending too: their Serenade '97, made from semi-dried moscato giallo, is a wine of rare finesse and body.

	Wine	Glasses	Price
●	A. A. Cabernet Sauvignon Ris. '95	🍷🍷🍷	5
●	A. A. Cabernet Sauvignon Campaner Ris. '95	🍷🍷	4
○	A. A. Chardonnay Wadleith '97	🍷🍷	4
○	A. A. Gewürztraminer Campaner '97	🍷🍷	4
●	A. A. Lago di Caldaro Pfarrhof '96	🍷🍷	3
●	A. A. Lago di Caldaro Pfarrhof '97	🍷🍷	3
○	A. A. Serenade '97	🍷🍷	5
○	A. A. Pinot Bianco Vial '97	🍷	2
○	A. A. Sauvignon '97	🍷	3
●	A. A. Cabernet Ris. '92	🍸🍸🍸	5
●	A. A. Cabernet Sauvignon Ris. '93	🍸🍸🍸	5
○	A. A. Gewürztraminer Campaner '96	🍸🍸🍸	4

CALDARO/KALTERN (BZ)

Castel Sallegg - Graf Kuenburg

V.lo di Sotto, 15
39052 Caldaro/Kaltern (BZ)
tel. 0471/963132

This historic winery is known particularly for its Moscato Rosa, a rare and precious wine. But things have changed here, and as if to emphasize the fact that all of its wines, not only the Moscato Rosa, are now important, the Moscato Rosa itself is not among those we tasted. Two of these, even if just barely, have been awarded Two Glasses. One is the Gewürztraminer '97, one of the best so far, and the other is their Cabernet '95, made in a fairly good year in a zone reputed to be one of the best in Alto Adige for important reds. The Merlot Riserva '95 is also good, but strangely we preferred last year's standard version. The Lago di Caldaro Scelto Bischofsleiten '97, one of their most traditional wines, is quite acceptable. The whites, with the exception of the Chardonnay '97, which is typically varietal and pleasant, are less fun. The Sauvignon '97 was the victim of a conspiracy between a very hot season and an area somewhat inimical to whites. The Terlano Pinot Bianco '97 lacks body. As a result these are two well-made but somewhat anonymous wines. We expect a lot more from such a distinguished producer.

	Wine	Glasses	Price
●	A. A. Cabernet '95	🍷🍷	5
○	A. A. Gewürztraminer '97	🍷🍷	3*
○	A. A. Chardonnay '97	🍷	3
●	A. A. Lago di Caldaro Scelto Bischofsleiten '97	🍷	4
●	A. A. Merlot Ris. '95	🍷	5
○	A. A. Sauvignon '97	🍷	3
○	A. A. Terlano Pinot Bianco '97		3
●	A. A. Cabernet '90	🍸🍸	5
●	A. A. Merlot '95	🍸🍸	5
●	A. A. Moscato Rosa '90	🍸🍸	6
●	A. A. Cabernet '95	🍸	5
●	A. A. Moscato Rosa '93	🍸	6

CALDARO/KALTERN (BZ)

Prima & Nuova/Erste & Neue

Via delle Cantine, 5
39052 Caldaro/Kaltern (BZ)
tel. 0471/963122

If anything really surprised us among the Alto Adige wines we tasted this year it was the exceptional Gewürztraminer Puntay '97 from Prima & Nuova (Erste & Neue in German). Word had reached us that the kellermeisters round about, who are in the habit of gathering to compare the wines of the local cooperatives, were speaking very well of it, so it was not a bolt out of the blue, but until this year, Prima & Nuova was essentially one of those wineries that produce reliable bottles at a reasonable price, not anything one would think of crowning with Three Glasses. And the fact that they have produced a wine of just that caliber seems to us to be good news for the wine world of Alto Adige. The "Three Glass Club" has a new member, a good, large cooperative that makes trustworthy wines. The wine itself is a dream. It is very aromatic, with a distinct fragrance of rose hips, and a full persistent palate with only a slight bitterness in the aftertaste. This is one of the best from a year that was extremely kind to this category. The Cabernet Puntay '95 and the classic Lago di Caldaro Scelto Leuchtenburg '97 are both excellent. The latter is the best of its type this year, and one of the best wines made anywhere from this grape. The Lago di Caldaro Scelto Puntay, the Sauvignon Stern and the Pinot Biancos Brunar and Puntay are all '97s and all very interesting. Their entire range is excellent, demonstrating that those Three Glasses are not a fluke.

	Wine	Glasses	Price
○	A. A. Gewürztraminer Puntay '97	🍷🍷🍷	4
●	A. A. Cabernet Puntay '95	🍷🍷	5
●	A. A. Lago di Caldaro Scelto Leuchtenburg '97	🍷🍷	4
○	A. A. Chardonnay Salt '97	🍷	3
●	A. A. Lago di Caldaro Scelto Puntay '97	🍷	3*
○	A. A. Pinot Bianco Brunar '97	🍷	3
○	A. A. Pinot Bianco Puntay '97	🍷	3
○	A. A. Sauvignon Stern '97	🍷	3*
●	A. A. Cabernet Puntay '94	YY	5
●	A. A. Lago di Caldaro Scelto Leuchtenburg '95	YY	4
○	A. A. Pinot Bianco Brunar '96	YY	4
○	A. A. Gewürztraminer Puntay '96	Y	4

CARDANO/KARDAUN (BZ)

Josephus Mayr

Erbhof Unterganzner
Via Campiglio, 15
39053 Cardano/Kardaun (BZ)
tel. 0471/365582

Once again Josephus Mayr's wines are excellent. Perhaps the '96 reds are not quite as rich in concentration as the '95s, but the difference is very slight indeed. The Cabernet '96 is, as usual, a knockout. Its bouquet is intense and varietal and not very vegetal at all. The touch of wood is well dosed and not overbearing. The concentration in the mouth is more than a match for its slight note of acidity, the only reminder of this year's relative weakness. The situation of his Lagrein Scuro Riserva '96 is similar. It seems excellent to us, and very nearly on the same level as the formidable '95. It is full, powerful, rich but not too aggressively polyphenolic. It's a little masterpiece; it hasn't received Three Glasses only because it could have used a little more concentration. Now for a surprise. The Lagrein Rosato Vendemmia Tardiva '97 is, perhaps, the best rosé we tasted this year, and not just in Alto Adige. It's a stunning wine with intensely fruity aromas and a lovely soft body. It's a delicious example of its kind. The Lagrein Scuro '97, the Lagrein Rosato '97 and the Santa Maddalena '97 are all good, honest, workaday wines.

	Wine	Glasses	Price
●	A. A. Cabernet Sauvignon '96	🍷🍷	5
⊙	A. A. Lagrein Rosato V. T. '97	🍷🍷	4
●	A. A. Lagrein Scuro Ris. '96	🍷🍷	5*
⊙	A. A. Lagrein Rosato '97	🍷	2
●	A. A. Lagrein Scuro '97	🍷	3
●	A. A. Santa Maddalena '97	🍷	3
●	A. A. Cabernet Sauvignon '95	YY	5
●	A. A. Lagrein Scuro Ris. '93	YY	5
●	A. A. Lagrein Scuro Ris. '94	YY	5
●	A. A. Lagrein Scuro Ris. '95	YY	5
●	Composition Reif '95	YY	5
●	A. A. Cabernet '94	Y	4
●	A. A. Cabernet Sauvignon '94	Y	4
●	A. A. Santa Maddalena '96	Y	3

CERMES/TSCHERMS (BZ)

Graf Pfeil Weingut Kränzel
Via Palade, 1
39010 Cermes/Tscherms (BZ)
tel. 0473/564549

Count Franz Pfeil, a young and enthusiastic winegrower, is not a slave to fashion. In his 14th-century cellar he works according to his own notions. Wine, he maintains, is an important part of a country's heritage, and should therefore be carefully looked after. Furthermore it takes time, and then more time, to make and age it properly. Thus his versions of Schiava, a wine which locally is usually ready to drink as soon as it is bottled, reach their full complexity and expressiveness after two or three years. This year we were particularly excited by his Sagittarius '96, a cabernet sauvignon and merlot blend. Dark and concentrated ruby in color, it has a rich, complex and stylish bouquet. In the mouth, it reveals great and elegant structure and a stupendously long finish. It's a spectacular wine that only just missed Three Glasses. The other wine we liked enormously is the Dorado '95, made from semi-dried pinot blanc. Its harmonious and concentrated bouquet, rich in aromas and finesse, is followed by a full, distinct and fairly complex palate. A number of other wines are not reviewed this time: the dry whites, Pinot Bianco and Sauvignon, were not ready in time for our tastings, and the Pinot Nero, which delighted us last year, will be available next year. The Meranese Hügel '97, made from schiava and bottled shortly before our tastings, is an excellent example of what can be done with this grape.

○	Dorado '95	TT	5
●	Sagittarius '96	TT	5
●	A. A. Meranese Hügel '97	T	3
○	A. A. Dorado '94	YY	5
○	A. A. Pinot Bianco '95	YY	4
○	A. A. Pinot Bianco '96	YY	4
●	A. A. Pinot Nero '95	YY	5
○	A. A. Sauvignon '95	YY	4
●	Sagittarius '95	YY	5
●	A. A. Meranese Hügel '95	Y	3

CHIUSA/KLAUSEN (BZ)

Cantina Produttori
Valle Isarco/Eisacktaler
Loc. Coste, 60
39043 Chiusa/Klausen (BZ)
tel. 0472/847553

If you take the highway towards the Brenner Pass you'll find yourself, after Bolzano, in the narrow valley of the Isarco, and in a few miles you'll reach the small, romantic, medieval town of Chiusa. On the precipitous slopes defining the valley the vines cling for dear life. Someone who knew about life in these parts once wrote, "Farming the land here is a gamble; producing wine gets you time off Purgatory." The local growers formed the Cantina Produttori Valle Isarco in 1961. They do not have to worry about over-producing with their vines, as the process of selection is taken care of by the vines themselves. This natural phenomenon gives their white grapes the aromatic fragrance that has made the wines of the Cantina Produttori famous. At our tastings this year two of their wines did not seem quite ready to be judged, so we shall be trying them again. But their Valle Isarco Müller Thurgau Aristos '97 was excellent. It has a singularly powerful nose with touches of new-mown hay, sage and fruit, and, in the mouth, a lovely complexity. The Valle Isarco Kerner '97 is also very convincing. It is lively, crisp, and elegantly aromatic. The Sylvaner Dominus '96, aged for eight months in barriques, is worthy of note. Enhanced by restrained notes of vanilla, it displays a very rich body, and an appealing freshness. Their Veltliner, Chardonnay, Pinot Grigio, Gewürztraminer and Sylvaner are all simple, fresh, and fruity white wines, typical of their zone of production, and also excellent bargains. The Klausner Laitacher is an interesting combination of schiava, lagrein, and portugieser.

○	A. A. Valle Isarco Kerner '97	TT	2*
○	A. A. Valle Isarco Müller Thurgau Aristos '97	TT	3*
○	A. A. Chardonnay '97	T	2
○	A. A. Valle Isarco Gewürztraminer Aristos '97	T	3
●	A. A. Valle Isarco Klausner Laitacher '97	T	2
○	A. A. Valle Isarco Pinot Grigio '97	T	2
○	A. A. Valle Isarco Sylvaner Aristos '97	T	3
○	A. A. Valle Isarco Sylvaner Dominus '96	T	3
○	A. A. Valle Isarco Veltliner '97	T	2

CORNAIANO/GIRLAN (BZ)

CANTINA PRODUTTORI
COLTERENZIO/SCHRECKBICHL
STRADA DEL VINO, 8
39050 CORNAIANO/GIRLAN (BZ)
TEL. 0471/664246

Colterenzio has put on an amazing performance this year. Their entire line has few competitors in any part of Italy, and their whites are among the very best of their area. Three of their wines made it to our finals, and one, the fantastic Cabernet Sauvignon Lafoa '95, the best version ever of this wine, easily won Three Glasses. We were enchanted by its elegant balsamic aromas, the clear definition of the notes of blueberry and black currant and the perfectly dosed touch of barrique-derived oak completely integrated into the bouquet, as well as by its firm palate with dense velvety tannins and imposing body. Superb as it is, it is only the tip of the iceberg of a list of wines that has never been so completely convincing as this year. The Sauvignon Lafoa '97 is formidable. The Caberbet-Merlot Cornelius Rosso '95, a mixture of cabernet and merlot, is the best it has ever been. The Chardonnay Contessa Coret '97, even though it is on the inferior list, is better than nearly all its competitors in the region. Their Cornelius Bianco, a blend of pinot blanc, pinot gris and chardonnay, only suffers the consequences of an inferior year, as does the Chardonnay Cornell. The Pinot Bianco Weisshaus and the Sauvignon Prail, both '97s, are fine examples of their varietals. Lack of space forces us not even to list three wines that received a Glass each. What can we say? Our compliments to Luis Raifer, who for years has been in charge of this extraordinary winery.

●	A. A. Cabernet Sauvignon Lafoa '95	▼▼▼	6
●	A. A. Cabernet-Merlot Cornelius '95	▼▼	6
○	A. A. Chardonnay Coret '97	▼▼	4
○	A. A. Chardonnay Cornell '97	▼▼	5
○	A. A. Pinot Bianco Weisshaus '97	▼▼	4
○	A. A. Sauvignon Lafoa '97	▼▼	5
○	A. A. Sauvignon Prail '97	▼▼	4
○	Cornelius Bianco '96	▼▼	5
●	A. A. Cabernet Sauvignon Lafoa '92	▽▽▽	6
●	A. A. Cabernet Sauvignon Lafoa '94	▽▽▽	6

CORNAIANO/GIRLAN (BZ)

CANTINA PRODUTTORI
CORNAIANO/GIRLAN
VIA S. MARTINO, 24
39050 CORNAIANO/GIRLAN (BZ)
TEL. 0471/662403

We are very pleased with the wines from the Cornaiano/Girlan winery this year. It is in all probability the best selection that they have offered us, and this is to the credit of their charismatic president Spitaler. Let's start at once with one of the best Gewürztraminers of '97, which reached our finals and very nearly received Three Glasses. It has an intensely aromatic nose, typical of the grape, and a soft and mouth-filling taste barely interrupted by a slightly bitter aftertaste. It is indeed delicious. Their Schiava von Alten Reben aus Gschleier is, in this '96 version, its usual fascinating self. It is without the shadow of a doubt the best wine in its category and indeed seems to inhabit a different world from the others. It has a complexity of bouquet which approaches that of the pinot nero, and is extraordinarily long-lived. Its little sister, the Schiava Fass n° 9 '97, doesn't approach its soft balance and extraordinary concentration. Their Cabernet Sauvignon, this time the Riserva '96, is very good, as usual. It is not either so rich or so powerful as the '95, but it is an excellently made wine. And now for the remaining whites. The quite good Riesling '96 is varietal and has good structure. The Pinot Bianco Plattenriegl '97 is less fragrant but fuller-bodied than in the past, and the Chardonnay '97 is an honest, well-made wine that, however, does not seem to have been made from any particular grape.

●	A. A. Cabernet Sauvignon Ris. '96	▼▼	5
○	A. A. Gewürztraminer '97	▼▼	4*
●	A. A. Schiava Gschleier '96	▼▼	5
○	A. A. Chardonnay '97	▼	3
○	A. A. Pinot Bianco Plattenriegl '97	▼	3
○	A. A. Riesling '96	▼	4
●	A. A. Schiava Fass n° 9 '97	▼	3
●	A. A. Cabernet Optimum '90	▽▽	5
●	A. A. Cabernet Optimum '92	▽▽	5
●	A. A. Cabernet Optimum '93	▽▽	5
●	A. A. Cabernet Optimum '95	▽▽	5
○	A. A. Pinot Bianco Plattenriegl '93	▽▽	4
●	A. A. Schiava Fass N. 9 '93	▽▽	4
●	A. A. Schiava Gschleier '95	▽▽	4
○	Strahler '95	▽▽	4

CORNAIANO/GIRLAN (BZ)

K. Martini & Sohn

Via Lamm Weg, 28
39050 Cornaiano/Girlan (BZ)
tel. 0471/663156

There are more successes than not this year for Gabriel Martini's cellar. His Chardonnay Palladium '97 is made with considerable artistry: it displays elegant and delicate varietal aromas and it tastes delicious, thanks in part to its remarkable balance. This is a wine to keep in mind when you want a fruity Chardonnay from the Alto Adige. The Lago di Caldaro Classico Felton '97 is good as well. It may not have great body but it's pleasantly soft and easy to drink. The Lagrein Scuro Maturum '96, the house specialty, is not the marvelous wine that last year's version was. Of course, in general terms, '96 was no '95 either. Nevertheless the wine does quite respectably, offering finesse on the nose and concentration on the palate, even if Two Glasses are beyond its reach this year. We have re-tasted the Cabernet-Lagrein Palladium Coldirus '95. Last year we were critical of the wine, having tried a not yet bottled sample. For this reason we make an exception and change our evaluation, giving it Two Glasses. Our former judgment is, as it were, expunged. The wine is excellent and deserves it.

	Wine	Glasses	Price
●	A. A. Cabernet-Lagrein Palladium Coldirus '95	▼▼	5
○	A. A. Chardonnay Palladium '97	▼▼	3*
●	A. A. Lago di Caldaro Cl. Felton '97	▼	4
●	A. A. Lagrein Scuro Maturum '96	▼	5
●	A. A. Cabernet-Lagrein Palladium Coldirus '94	▽▽	5
●	A. A. Lagrein Scuro Maturum '95	▽▽	5
●	A. A. Lagrein Scuro Rueslhof '95	▽▽	5
●	A. A. Lagrein Scuro Maturum '93	▽	5
●	A. A. Lagrein Scuro Rueslhof '94	▽	5

CORNAIANO/GIRLAN (BZ)

Josef Niedermayr

Via Casa di Gesù, 15
39050 Cornaiano/Girlan (BZ)
tel. 0471/662451

This producer's wines have become a sure thing. Josef Niedermayr and his young oenologist Lorenz Martini have shown year after year that they mean to make reliability a hallmark of their line. This year, although there is no absolute masterpiece, all the wines presented have made at least a creditable showing. The Gewürztraminer Lage Doss '97 is among the best of its category in a year in which good and even excellent wines of this type are thick on the ground. The Lagrein Gries Riserva '95 is a splendidly full-bodied, concentrated red that proudly represents an excellent vintage. Their Aureus '96 is a sweet wine made from chardonnay, pinot blanc and sauvignon. Though it does not show the depth and aromatic complexity of its predecessor from last year, it is still a concentrated and well-balanced wine. The Sauvignon Lage Naun '97 is as good as ever, and has become one of their classics. The Terlano Hof zu Pramol '97 is better than last year's, showing more body and better aromatic definition. Only the fair Cabernet Riserva '95 can be said to be a little disappointing, but this may be because we tasted it together with a number of superb cabernets and it suffered in comparison. The Lago di Caldaro Ascherhof '97 and the Santa Maddalena Egger-Larcherhof '97 are decent and correct, period.

	Wine	Glasses	Price
○	A. A. Gewürztraminer Lage Doss '97	▼▼	4
●	A. A. Lagrein Gries Ris. '95	▼▼	4
○	A. A. Sauvignon Lage Naun '97	▼▼	4
○	Aureus '96	▼▼	5
●	A. A. Cabernet Ris. '95	▼	5
●	A. A. Lago di Caldaro Scelto Cl. Sup. Ascherhof '97	▼	4
●	A. A. Lagrein Gries Blacedelle '97	▼	3
●	A. A. Santa Maddalena Cl. Egger-Larcherhof '97	▼	3
○	A. A. Terlano Hof zu Pramol '97	▼	4
○	Aureus '95	▽▽▽	5
●	A. A. Lagrein Gries Ris. '94	▽▽	4

CORNAIANO/GIRLAN (BZ)

IGNAZ NIEDRIST
VIA RONCO, 4
39050 CORNAIANO/GIRLAN (BZ)
TEL. 0471/664494

Ignaz Niedrist has done more than just make the best of two difficult vintages. 1997 was not a good year, generally, for either Rhine riesling or pinot blanc. In these parts, an early hot summer and speedily ripened grapes tended to lead to a loss of primary aromas in the white wines. His Riesling Renano '97, however, has done very well. Though it does not have the almost mineral tones of the '95 and, to some extent, the '96, it has full varietal aromas and a surprising degree of structure. This is a very good wine indeed, and easily deserves its Two Glasses. The Terlano Pinot Bianco '97, a less convincing example of its category, is nevertheless very interesting. The primary aromas have faded, but it has good body, and is not overly acidic as whites from this part of Alto Adige can too often be. The Pinot Nero '96 was another tough row to hoe for Niedrist. The year was just the opposite of '97, cold and rainy. But we think this is one of the best Pinot Neros Ignaz has ever made. Who knows? Perhaps the grapes were reminded of the somewhat inhospitable climate of their native Burgundy. In any case this wine stood out at our tastings because of its balance on the palate and its great fidelity to varietal characteristics, which is not found every day in Alto Adige. The general excellence of his wines leads us to hope that a Three Glass winner is just around the corner. The passionate seriousness with which he makes his wines merits, in itself, such a distinction.

	Wine	Rating	Price
●	A. A. Pinot Nero '96	▼▼	4
○	A. A. Riesling Renano '97	▼▼	4
○	A. A. Terlano Pinot Bianco '97	▼	4
●	A. A. Pinot Nero '91	▽▽	4
●	A. A. Pinot Nero '92	▽▽	4
●	A. A. Pinot Nero '93	▽▽	4
●	A. A. Pinot Nero '95	▽▽	4
○	A. A. Riesling Renano '93	▽▽	4
○	A. A. Riesling Renano '95	▽▽	4
○	A. A. Riesling Renano '96	▽▽	4
○	A. A. Pinot Bianco '96	▽	3
●	A. A. Pinot Nero '94	▽	4
○	A. A. Riesling Renano '94	▽	4
○	A. A. Terlano Sauvignon '95	▽	4

CORTACCIA/KURTATSCH (BZ)

CANTINA PRODUTTORI CORTACCIA
STRADA DEL VINO, 23
39040 CORTACCIA/KURTATSCH (BZ)
TEL. 0471/880115

The Cantina Produttori di Cortaccia carries off Three Glasses again this year, and a quick glance at the list at the bottom of the page shows that seven of their wines get Two Glasses. And some of these wines are better than they have ever been before. A typical case is their Chardonnay Eberlehof '96, which is matured in small barrels. Never before has it presented such an elegant array of aromas, such a well-judged touch of wood, or a balance worthy of a top-flight Chablis. Perhaps it could do with a little more weight in the mouth, but it is nonetheless a superbly made wine. The Sauvignon '97 from their standard line is also excellent. It too could use a little more body, but it is a formidable wine, and a great bargain as well. And now for the big reds. Their Cabernet Freienfeld '95, although it's still a bit on the young side, is a wine that we are very happy to bet on. It has intense and balsamic aromas, and the structure of a champion. It is easily worth its Three Glasses. The Cabernet Kirchhügel '96, one of our favorites, is still a bit harsh, perhaps because of the unpropitious year. The Merlot Brenntal '96 gets Two Glasses, but barely, and is not a patch on its illustrious predecessor, that full-bodied and elegant aristocrat, the '95. The best of the '96s is doubtless the Pinot Nero Vorhof, which is varietal and quite harmonious. The Lagrein Forhof '95 is very good: powerful and concentrated if a bit rough in the mouth. The Schiava Grigia Sonntaler '97 is really superb, fully profiting from a magical year for schiava. The two simpler wines, the Müller Thurgau Hofstatt '97 and the Chardonnay Felsenhof '97, are both quite decent.

	Wine	Rating	Price
●	A. A. Cabernet Freienfeld '95	▼▼▼	6
●	A. A. Cabernet Kirchhügel '96	▼▼	4*
●	A. A. Chardonnay Eberlehof '96	▼▼	4*
●	A. A. Lagrein Scuro Forhof '95	▼▼	4*
●	A. A. Merlot Brenntal '96	▼▼	5
●	A. A. Pinot Nero Vorhof '96	▼▼	5
○	A. A. Sauvignon '97	▼▼	3*
●	A. A. Schiava Grigia Sonntaler '97	▼▼	3*
○	A. A. Chardonnay Felsenhof '97	▼	3
○	A. A. Müller Thurgau Hofstatt '97	▼	3
●	A. A. Cabernet Freienfeld '92	▽▽▽	5
●	A. A. Cabernet Freienfeld Ris. '90	▽▽▽	6
●	A. A. Merlot Brenntal '95	▽▽▽	5
●	A. A. Cabernet Kirchhügel '95	▽▽	4

CORTACCIA/KURTATSCH (BZ)

Tiefenbrunner

Loc. Niclara
Via Castello, 4
39040 Cortaccia/Kurtatsch (BZ)
tel. 0471/880122

After the 25th anniversary of their Feldmarschall, one of their most renowned wines, Herbert Tiefenbrunner and his son Cristof are celebrating an even more important anniversary. Their winery was started in 1848 so this is the 150th birthday jubilee, celebrated with a list of wines which are, as usual, well-made and dependable, and this year include some stars. The Chardonnay Linticlarus '96, which spends some time in small barrels, improves from version to version and this one is even better than the '95, which comes from what was supposed to be a better year. This suggests that they selected the grapes with greater care. It also suggests that they are increasingly committed to producing wines of the highest quality. Two reds, the Cabernet Sauvignon Linticlarus '95 and the Linticlarus Cuvee '96, a blend of lagrein, cabernet sauvignon and pinot noir, are both excellent. Their very good Gewürztraminer '97, a house specialty, is in great form this year. The remaining wines are a little less good. The Feldmarschall von Fenner '97 is just a little forward in its aromas, and the Merlot '96 and the Chardonnay '97 from their standard line are merely correct. The Pinot Nero Linticlarus Riserva '95 does not seem to us to be worth its high price. The Lagrein Scuro '96 Jubiläumswein, on the other hand, is quite good, especially considering that this wasn't much of a year for reds.

●	A. A. Cabernet Sauvignon Linticlarus '95	🍷🍷	5
○	A. A. Chardonnay Linticlarus '96	🍷🍷	5
○	A. A. Gewürztraminer '97	🍷🍷	3*
●	Linticlarus Cuvée '96	🍷🍷	5
○	A. A. Chardonnay '97	🍷	3
●	A. A. Lagrein Scuro '96	🍷	4
●	A. A. Merlot '96	🍷	4
●	A. A. Pinot Nero Linticlarus Ris. '95	🍷	5
○	Feldmarschall von Fenner '97	🍷	5
●	A. A. Cabernet Sauvignon Linticlarus '94	♀♀	5

CORTACCIA/KURTATSCH (BZ)

Baron Widmann

Via Im Feld, 1
39040 Cortaccia/Kurtatsch (BZ)
tel. 0471/880092

We have succeeded in tasting two wines that eluded us last year: the Cabernet Feld '95 and the Rot '95, basically a syrah, with a bit of cabernet and merlot. Any doubts we had had before are resolved by these two wines. It's not that there was any question about the commitment or capacities of the young Baron Andreas Widmann, but he seemed always to send us minor wines for our tastings. Certainly his Schiava is always an extremely enjoyable light red wine, and the '97 version is no exception. And the Cabernet-Merlot '96, the fruit of a tricky vintage, is not at all bad. But those other two reds are another matter, and the Rot '95 is proof that some serious experimentation is going on: a syrah up here (and it should do very well too)! It displays lightly spiced aromas and a very impressive structure, and it is not without elegance. The Cabernet Feld '95 is still very young and has some rough bits in need of further smoothing, but it's just a question of more time in the bottle: the stuff is there. The whites on his list are less interesting. The Sauvignon '97 is decent, while the Pinot Bianco is a bit forward, although correct. But in Cortaccia, the heart of red country, this is quite normal.

●	A. A. Cabernet Feld '95	🍷🍷	5
●	A. A. Schiava '97	🍷🍷	2*
●	Rot '95	🍷🍷	5
●	A. A. Cabernet-Merlot '96	🍷	5
○	A. A. Sauvignon '97	🍷	3
○	A. A. Pinot Bianco '97		3
●	A. A. Cabernet Feld '91	♀♀♀	5
●	A. A. Merlot '93	♀♀♀	5
●	A. A. Cabernet Feld '90	♀♀	5
●	A. A. Cabernet Feld '93	♀♀	5
●	A. A. Merlot '91	♀♀	4
●	A. A. Merlot '92	♀♀	5
●	A. A. Merlot '94	♀♀	5
●	A. A. Merlot '95	♀♀	5
●	A. A. Schiava '96	♀♀	2*

CORTINA/KURTINIG (BZ)

Peter Zemmer

Strada del Vino, 24
39040 Cortina/Kurtinig (BZ)
tel. 0471/817143

One can count on Peter Zemmer to make good wines. But this year, in addition to his well-made wines at excellent prices, he has also made a little gem, his Chardonnay Barrique '96, a white of great breeding which shows excellent structure with first-class execution. Its aromas are well-defined, with varietal notes perfectly fused with oak-derived vanilla; ripe pineapple, banana, and plum are to the fore. It is full-bodied and perfectly balanced by a slight vein of acidity. This is a wonderful Chardonnay from the Alto Adige, and one of the very best of the year. The standard Chardonnay '97 is fruity, varietal, easy to drink and easy to pay for. His Cabernet-Lagrein '95, a blend that could profitably be more widely used in these parts, is a very interesting wine. It could do with a bit more weight and complexity, but it seems to us to be an almost completely successful experiment. The Merlot '96 is not so successful but its year was extremely difficult. The Pinot Grigio '97 is very well made. This pleasantly simple wine has a nice nose and good body.

	Wine	Rating	Price
●	A. A. Cabernet-Lagrein '95	🍷🍷	5
○	A. A. Chardonnay '97	🍷🍷	3*
○	A. A. Chardonnay Barrique '96	🍷🍷	4*
●	A. A. Merlot '96	🍷	3
○	A. A. Pinot Grigio '97	🍷	3
○	A. A. Chardonnay '96	🍸🍸	3*
○	A. A. Pinot Grigio '96	🍸	3
○	A. A. Riesling '96	🍸	3
○	A. A. Sauvignon '96	🍸	3

EGNA/NEUMARKT (BZ)

Peter Dipoli

Via Villa, 5
39055 Egna/Neumarkt (BZ)
tel. 0471/954227

Peter Dipoli is not overly diplomatic. He's a perfectionist, and a ferocious critic of every wine he tastes, even his own, but always in a direct and forthright manner. It may at times seem an awkward way to behave, but it's altogether legitimate and worthy of respect. This time, however, it's his turn to be criticized. (And we feel he'll understand.) In any case we are among his most enthusiastic supporters, particularly now that he has his own cellar and doesn't have to depend on the hospitality of others when he wants to vinify or age his wines. Of course one wouldn't expect his Merlot-Cabernet Sauvignon Yugum, the jewel of his collection, to be, in a troublesome year like '96, as intense or concentrated as his '95. His Sauvignon Voglar '97 is less varietal, if fuller in body, than both the '96 and the '95. We feel sure that Dipoli, a great connoisseur, would be the first to admit these slight limitations, but his wines are still very good, if not at the moment exceptional. These things happen.

	Wine	Rating	Price
●	A. A. Merlot-Cabernet Sauvignon Yugum '96	🍷🍷	5
○	A. A. Sauvignon Voglar '97	🍷🍷	4
●	A. A. Merlot-Cabernet Sauvignon Yugum '95	🍸🍸	5
○	A. A. Sauvignon Voglar '93	🍸🍸	4
○	A. A. Sauvignon Voglar '94	🍸🍸	4
○	A. A. Sauvignon Voglar '95	🍸🍸	4
○	A. A. Sauvignon Voglar '96	🍸🍸	4

CANTINA PRODUTTORI BURGGRÄFLER

VIA PALADE, 64
39020 MARLENGO/MARLING (BZ)
TEL. 0473/447137

The Pinot Nero Tiefenthalerhof has become a classic of the Alto Adige. Even in the '96 version, it confirms its quality and its ranking among the very best of its fellows. Its only limitation is to be found in a slight lack of concentration. This is due both to the year, which was quite rainy, and to its zone of origin, the Burgraviate near Merano, one of the northernmost parts of the area. This did not keep it from reaching our finals, and doing well in them, for the third year in a row. The rest of their line this year is also admirable. The Cabernet-Lagrein MerVin '96 is very nearly as good as the '95, which is saying a lot. Its aromas are only slightly vegetal, its taste is well balanced, and its tannins are not overly aggressive. The excellent MerVin '97, made from semi-dried pinot blanc, is better than ever, and does not have that too forward nose that it has sometimes shown in the past. The Moscato Giallo '97 is delicately aromatic, and the Meranese '97, made mostly from schiava, is a light and fragrant red. Indeed, in its category, it's a little gem.

	Wine	Glasses	Price
●	A. A. Cabernet-Lagrein MerVin '96	🍷🍷 (black)	5
●	A. A. Meranese Schickenburg '97	🍷🍷 (black)	3*
●	A. A. Pinot Nero Tiefenthalerhof '96	🍷🍷 (black)	5
○	MerVin '97	🍷🍷 (black)	5
○	A. A. Moscato Giallo '97	🍷 (black)	3
●	A. A. Lagrein-Cabernet MerVin '95	🍷🍷 (white)	5
●	A. A. Pinot Nero Tiefenthalerhof '94	🍷🍷 (white)	5
●	A. A. Pinot Nero Tiefenthalerhof '95	🍷🍷 (white)	5

POPPHOF - ANDREAS MENZ

MITTERTERZERSTRASSE, 5
39020 MARLENGO/MARLING (BZ)
TEL. 0473/447180

One of our most pleasant surprises this year came from Andreas Menz's little winery in Marlengo. Popphof is an historic wine estate. They were already making wine here in 1592 and selling it in bulk in 1722, and they began bottling it last century, as Menz's old-fashioned labels testify. The vineyards are on land rich in slate and clay, and the Merano basin, opening towards the south, (Merlengo is only three kilometers from Merano), has a climate that is mild enough to foster great full-bodied reds. And Menz has presented a wine of just this sort. His aristocratic Cabernet '95, 70% cabernet sauvignon and 30% cabernet franc, came within an eyelash of receiving Three Glasses. It has elegantly varietal aromas, not at all too vegetal, and is velvety, concentrated and harmonious in the mouth, its tannins particularly suave and its touch of wood masterfully judged. Its Two Glasses don't really do it justice. The excellent Pinot Bianco '97, the best of its class this year, in our opinion, unites a wonderfully varietal character with an amazing bargain price. Only two wines, as you can see, but they have certainly earned Menz a place in the Guide.

	Wine	Glasses	Price
●	A. A. Cabernet '95	🍷🍷 (black)	5
○	A. A. Pinot Bianco '97	🍷🍷 (black)	3*

MELTINA/MÖLTEN (BZ)

VIVALDI - ARUNDA
CIVICO, 53
39010 MELTINA/MÖLTEN (BZ)
TEL. 0471/668033

Joseph Reiterer's "mountain-grown" sparkling wines are excellent this year too. They are made from chardonnay grapes grown in his Meltina vineyards just above Terlano at the dizzying height of nearly 1,000 meters. The wines made from those grapes are the perfect base for good spumante, as they are aromatic and acidic enough to keep their fragrance and elegance after going through the "prise de mousse ". This is the reason why the bubblies that bear the Vivaldi and Arunda labels are always among the best in the area. ("Arunda" is the label used in Alto Adige.) Our favorite this year is the Arunda Spumante Extra Brut Riserva '93. It has splendidly elegant and intense fragrances, with a very well-expressed yeasty note. In the mouth it is decided and persistent, underpinned by its well-judged and integrated carbon dioxide. The Spumante Extra Brut '95 Vivaldi is very interesting too, but is still perhaps a little bit on the young side, although already starting to come out. It's less complicated than the wine we just described, but its bubbles are about as good as you can get. The Spumante Extra Brut Cuvée Marianna is softer and has a delicately fruity nose with delectable undertones of white plums. Their standard offering, the Spumante Brut Vivaldi is simple, enjoyable and easy to drink, if perhaps a bit monotonous.

○	A. A. Spumante Extra Brut Arunda Ris. '93	▼▼	5
○	A. A. Spumante Extra Brut Vivaldi '95	▼▼	5
○	A. A. Spumante Extra Brut Vivaldi Cuvée Marianna	▼▼	5
○	A. A. Spumante Brut Vivaldi	▼	4
○	A. A. Spumante Brut Vivaldi '93	▽▽	5
○	A. A. Spumante Extra Brut Vivaldi Ris. '87	▽▽	5
○	A. A. Spumante Extra Brut Vivaldi Ris. '89	▽▽	5
○	A. A. Spumante Extra Brut Vivaldi '93	▽	5

MONTAGNA/MONTAN (BZ)

FRANZ HAAS
VIA VILLA, 6
39040 MONTAGNA/MONTAN (BZ)
TEL. 0471/812280

There's a slightly subdued review for Franz Haas this year: some wines were not ready, some vintages were not exceptional. Indeed we are discussing only two of their wines, which are both excellent, but don't really give you an accurate picture of Haas' much vaster and more varied range. No Merlot, no Pinot Nero, no Gewürztraminer. Instead the splendid Moscato Rosa Schweizer '96 is left to man the fort. For the second year in a row, it is the best wine of its kind, in our opinion. Its aromas are deliciously spicy and aromatic, with the presence of rose hips very clear, and its sweet taste is elegant and not at all cloying. This is a rare and exceptional wine. The Mitterberg Manna '96, made from chardonnay, gewürztraminer, sauvignon and riesling, has excellent structure, concentration, and aromatic length, with very interesting herbal notes. Then it is mouth-filling, and a delicate acidity ties it all together and makes it refreshing to drink. It's a wine to try, and very nearly as good as the '95, which had the assistance of a much more favorable vintage.

●	A. A. Moscato Rosa '96	▼▼	5
○	Mitterberg Manna '96	▼▼	5
○	A. A. Gewürztraminer '95	▽▽	4
●	A. A. Merlot '91	▽▽	5
●	A. A. Merlot Schweizer '93	▽▽	4
●	A. A. Moscato Rosa '90	▽▽	6
●	A. A. Moscato Rosa '92	▽▽	6
●	A. A. Moscato Rosa '94	▽▽	5
●	A. A. Moscato Rosa Schweizer '95	▽▽	5
●	A. A. Pinot Nero '90	▽▽	4
●	A. A. Pinot Nero Ris. '91	▽▽	5
●	A. A. Pinot Nero Schweizer '95	▽▽	5
○	Mitterberg Manna '95	▽▽	5
○	A. A. Gewürztraminer '96	▽	3
●	A. A. Pinot Nero Schweizer '93	▽	5

NALLES/NALS (BZ)

CANT. PROD. NALLES NICLARA MAGRÈ
KG NALS, MARGREID, ENTIKLAR
VIA HEILINGENBERG, 2
39010 NALLES/NALS (BZ)
TEL. 0471/678626

The spectacular Terlano Sauvignon Classico Mantele '97 is the best of the year's offerings from this wine cooperative uniting producers from Nalles, between Bolzano and Merano, and from Magrè and Niclar in the southern part of Alto Adige. This really exciting Sauvignon has very intense and slightly forward varietal aromas, in which touches of sage and elder blossom can be found among the smoky and mineral tones. All this is mirrored on the palate, which is soft, intense and quite long. The Pinot Bianco Sirmian '97 and the Chardonnay '97 are both varietal, but lacking in concentration. The quite good Santa Maddalena Classico Rieserhof '97 is delicately fruity. Their two important reds, the Cabernet-Merlot Anticus '95 and the Cabernet Riserva '95, both in their Ansitz von Menz Baron Salvadori line, are both a little disappointing. They are correctly made, but both stand much in need of more weight and concentration.

○	A. A. Terlano Sauvignon Cl. Mantele '97	▼▼	4*
●	A. A. Cabernet Baron Salvadori Ris. '95	▼	5
●	A. A. Cabernet-Merlot Baron Salvadori Anticus '95	▼	5
○	A. A. Chardonnay '97	▼	3
○	A. A. Pinot Bianco Sirmian '97	▼	3
●	A. A. Santa Maddalena Cl. Rieserhof '97	▼	3
●	A. A. Cabernet Baron Salvadori '92	▽▽	5
●	A. A. Pinot Nero Baron Salvadori Ris. '90	▽▽	5
●	Anticus '90	▽▽	5
●	A. A. Santa Maddalena '95	▽	3

NALLES/NALS (BZ)

CASTELLO SCHWANBURG
VIA SCHWANBURG, 16
39010 NALLES/NALS (BZ)
TEL. 0471/678622

The Cabernet Castel Schwanburg is perhaps the only important red wine in the Alto Adige which has been produced for several decades. It is made from the vines that surround the splendid Schloss Schwanburg near Terlano, halfway between Bolzano and Merano. Here in the northern part of Alto Adige it is difficult to produce wine in years that are less than exceptionally favorable. Fortunately 1995 was a good vintage and offered reds that have good structure, but are slow to develop in the bottle. This is particularly the case with the Cabernet '95, so we have decided to put off evaluating it until next year's Guide. Meanwhile we tasted an admirable Riesling '97, in our opinion the best of the wines in their standard line. Its delicate varietal aromas have classic hints of minerals, and in the mouth it has elegance and even a bit of length. We found the Moscato Rosa '97 very interesting, but we'll review it next year. Our sample was from the barrel, and we prefer to base our judgments on wines in their final, bottled, stage. The other wines on their list are all decent. The Cabernet Riserva '95, the Santa Maddalena '97 and the Pinot Grigio '97 are better-balanced and more characteristic of their category than both the Schiava Schlosswein '97 and, especially, the Sauvignon '97, which is more neutral than past versions.

○	A. A. Riesling '97	▼▼	3*
●	A. A. Cabernet Ris. '95	▼	4
○	A. A. Pinot Grigio '97	▼	3
●	A. A. Santa Maddalena '97	▼	3
●	A. A. Schiava Schlosswein '97	▼	2*
○	A. A. Terlano Sauvignon '97	▼	3
●	A. A. Cabernet Castel Schwanburg '90	▽▽▽	6
●	A. A. Cabernet Castel Schwanburg '93	▽▽	5
●	A. A. Cabernet Castel Schwanburg '94	▽▽	5
●	A. A. Cabernet Ris. '90	▽▽	5

NATURNO/NATURNS (BZ)

TENUTA FALKENSTEIN
FRANZ PRATZNER
VIA ARGINE, 2
39025 NATURNO/NATURNS (BZ)
TEL. 0473/666054

Franz Pratzner has come up with three fantastic wines this year, without doubt among the best whites of the entire region. They come from vineyards on the outer border of vine-friendly territory, in the heart of the Val Venosta, near Merano, at an altitude of 650 meters. The Riesling '97 is extraordinary and almost won Three Glasses. This wine is not far from the top Italian whites, and gives us hope that we may soon have wines that are comparable to those of the Wachau and the Mosel. To the nose, it reveals distinct varietal characteristics with elegant hints of minerals and grapefruit. It is even more elegant in the mouth, its acidity balanced by its body: a delectable white wine worth drinking with attention. The very interesting Pinot Bianco '97 is delicate and recognizably varietal, if not particularly structured. The Falkensteiner '97 is a very successful sauvignon, distinctly characteristic, with hints of sage and elder blossom. It has a medium body and is delightfully drinkable. We have put off reviewing the Pinot Nero '96, because it is developing so slowly.

○	A. A. Val Venosta Pinot Bianco '97	🍷🍷	3*
○	A. A. Val Venosta Riesling '97	🍷🍷	3*
○	Falkensteiner '97	🍷🍷	5
○	A. A. Val Venosta Pinot Bianco '96	ΥΥ	3
●	A. A. Val Venosta Pinot Nero '95	ΥΥ	5
○	A. A. Val Venosta Riesling '96	ΥΥ	3

ORA/AUER (BZ)

CLEMENS WALDTHALER
VIA DEL RIO, 4
39040 ORA/AUER (BZ)
TEL. 0471/810182

Ora, along with Gries near Bolzano, are the best zones for growing lagrein, as the gravelly land in these parts makes this grape feel right at home. The Lagrein Scuro Raut '95 makes this point very clearly. We were already very pleased by the version presented last year, which was from a much less propitious vintage, '94. The '95 is a powerful and full-bodied wine with intensely fruity aromas of blueberry and black currant, and a hint of balsamic wood. In the mouth its generous concentration and grip predominate, reducing the typical bitterish aftertaste to the merest suggestion. This is the star player from the Waldthaler family winery this year. The other wines are unquestionably good, but they haven't got the Lagrein's breeding. The correct Bianco Grigio Raut '97, made from a number of different grapes, has a pleasant impact in the mouth but is not very interesting to the nose. The Pinot Bianco '97 is also properly made, and characteristically varietal, but it doesn't have an overwhelming structure.

●	A. A. Lagrein Scuro Raut '95	🍷🍷	4
○	Bianco Grigio Raut '97	🍷	4
●	A. A. Pinot Bianco '97	🍷	3
●	A. A. Cabernet Raut '95	ΥΥ	4
●	A. A. Lagrein Scuro Raut '94	ΥΥ	4
●	A. A. Cabernet '95	Υ	3
●	A. A. Merlot Raut '95	Υ	4
○	A. A. Pinot Bianco '96	Υ	3

SALORNO/SALURN (BZ)

HADERBURG

POCHI, 31
39040 SALORNO/SALURN (BZ)
TEL. 0471/889097

Work like ours involves expressing judgments, sometimes of a general nature, and it can happen that, in the space of a year, our judgment is proven wrong. This is what has occurred with Luis Ochsenreiter's Haderburg. Last year we stated that we did not altogether agree with the way they made their non-bubbly wines. And at this year's tastings it was two of their still wines that quite stole the scene, the Sauvignon '96 and the Pinot Nero '95, both from the Hausmannhof vineyard. The Sauvignon has elegant varietal aromas with a pleasant light undertone of toasty oak, all reflected on the not very concentrated palate with finesse and balance. The Pinot Nero offers both good body and elegance, and ranks high among its peers. On the other hand, his other wines, the Pinot Nero, Chardonnay and Sauvignon from the Stainhauser line, are not as convincing, mainly in that they all are somewhat lacking in structure, even though they are technically very well made. Their Spumante Pas Dosé '93 is good, but as its position here at the end of the article indicates, Haderburg can no longer be considered primarily a maker of spumante. It has become a wine producer of considerable importance and variety here in Alto Adige.

	Wine	Rating	
●	A. A. Pinot Nero Hausmannhof '95	▼▼	5
○	A. A. Sauvignon Hausmannhof '96	▼▼	5
○	A. A. Chardonnay Stainhauser '97	▼	4
●	A. A. Pinot Nero Stainhauser '96	▼	5
○	A. A. Sauvignon Stainhauser '97	▼	4
○	A. A. Spumante Haderburg Pas Dosé '93	▼	5
○	A. A. Sauvignon Stainhauser '96	▽▽	4
○	A. A. Spumante Haderburg Pas Dosé '91	▽▽	5

STAVA/STABEN (BZ)

TENUTA UNTERORTL-CASTEL JUVAL

JUVAL, 1B
39020 STAVA/STABEN (BZ)
TEL. 0473/667580

Reinhold Messner, the well-known explorer and mountain climber, is the owner of the Tenuta Unterortl in Stava with its five hectares of vineyard over 600 meters high. It is run, however, by the Aurich family, which has been renting it for some years now, and is responsible both for producing the wine and for selling it. Martin Aurich, the oenologist who plays an important role on the technical staff of the Istituto Laimburg (about which you can read a few pages hence), naturally enough also plays the leading role here. This year they have presented three wines, their Pinot Bianco and Riesling, both '97s, and the Pinot Nero '96, all labeled Castel Juval. They all seemed to us a little bit less good than the versions presented last year. The Pinot Bianco in particular has paid a particularly heavy price for a year that was rather hostile to this grape. The Riesling Val Venosta '97 has fared better, and is in the process of becoming, perhaps, their leading wine. Its aromas are clearly varietal, and have notes of minerals and citrus fruits, and in the mouth it shows its excellent body accompanied, however, by a slight residual roughness. Though it is not up to the level of the '96, it is certainly among the best of its year. The Pinot Nero '96 is decent, but is far from having that lovely softness which caused us to admire the '95 version.

	Wine	Rating	
○	A. A. Val Venosta Riesling '97	▼▼	4
○	A. A. Val Venosta Pinot Bianco '97	▼	4
●	A. A. Val Venosta Pinot Nero '96	▼	5
●	A. A. Val Venosta Pinot Nero '95	▽▽	5
○	A. A. Val Venosta Riesling '96	▽▽	4
○	A. A. Val Venosta Pinot Bianco '96	▽	4

TERLANO/TERLAN (BZ)

CANTINA DI TERLANO
VIA SILBERLEITEN, 7
39018 TERLANO/TERLAN (BZ)
TEL. 0471/257135

In recent years we have not infrequently been at a loss about what to say of the Cantina di Terlano's wines. This year, however, we have not only found most of their wines satisfactory but, in two cases, really exciting. These two made it all the way into our final round at the national level, and only barely missed receiving Three Glasses. Our compliments to the technical specialists of this cellar, therefore, and to the young and ambitious cellar master, Hartmann Donà, for the great progress that they have made. The two extraordinary wines are their Terlano Pinot Bianco '88 (yes, 1988: in Alto Adige only this winery comes up with white wines so long-lived) and the Lagrein Riserva '95 Porphyr. The first is a wine of amazing aromatic richness and opulence. In the mouth it offers mature depth and notable elegance. The Lagrein has intense aromas of wild berries, and displays on the palate an admirable balance and richness of extract. The Gewürztraminer Lunare '96, with its typical aromatic complexity, the Terlano Cl. Sauvignon Quarz '96, a big fat wine with a distinctly mineral bouquet and the Terlano Vorberg '97, very fresh, fruity and soft, are all definitely worthy of mention.

○	A. A. Gewürztraminer Lunare '96	🍷🍷	4
●	A. A. Lagrein Porphyr Ris. '95	🍷🍷	5
○	A. A. Terlano Pinot Bianco '88	🍷🍷	5
○	A. A. Terlano Sauvignon Quarz '96	🍷🍷	5
●	A. A. Pinot Nero Montigl Ris. '95	🍷	5
●	A. A. Santa Maddalena Haüslerhof '97	🍷	3
○	A. A. Terlano Cl. Vorberg '97	🍷	4
○	A. A. Terlano Nova Domus '96	🍷	5
○	A. A. Terlano Pinot Bianco '79	YYY	5
○	A. A. Pinot Grigio Klaus '95	YY	4
○	A. A. Terlano Classico '95	YY	5
○	A. A. Terlano Sauvignon Cl. '93	YY	6

TERMENO/TRAMIN (BZ)

CANTINA PRODUTTORI DI TERMENO
STRADA DEL VINO, 122
39040 TERMENO/TRAMIN (BZ)
TEL. 0471/860126

The Cantina Produttori di Termeno has just celebrated its centenary, and we send our best wishes. But we offer our particular congratulations to their wine-maker Willi Stürz for having created a really extraordinary wine. Their Cabernet Riserva Terminum '95 has aroused enthusiasm in all who tasted it, and held its own with all the great reds of Italy. Made from cabernet sauvignon with 20% cabernet franc, harvested from very low-yielding vines, it was kept in barriques for 17 months. The resulting wine is a very noble one, stylish, intense and deep on the nose, with its distinct traces of oak perfectly judged. In the mouth, it shows its size and strength, but is never inelegant. It fully deserves its Three Glasses. Their Gewürztraminer Nussbaumerhof '97 is also remarkable. With its intensely fruity aromas, its elegant structure and its full and pleasing body, it is clearly one of the best wines of its kind in Alto Adige. The other whites are also excellent. The Chardonnay Glassien '97 is tasty, the Sauvignon '97 is crisp, and the Pinot Grigio Unterebnerhof '97 very convincing. The Pinot Nero Riserva Schiesstandhof '96 and the Lagrein Urbanhof '96 are both very good, complexly varietal and expressive wines. Their Schiavas should not be neglected either. The Schiava Freisingerhof '97 is very fruity, fresh and elegant, while the Schiava Hexenbichler '97 is a good wine.

●	A. A. Cabernet Terminum Ris. '95	🍷🍷🍷	5
○	A. A. Chardonnay Glassien Renomée '97	🍷🍷	4
○	A. A. Gewürztraminer Nussbaumerhof '97	🍷🍷	4
●	A. A. Lagrein Urbanhof '96	🍷🍷	3*
○	A. A. Pinot Grigio Unterebnerhof '97	🍷🍷	4
●	A. A. Pinot Nero Schiesstandhof Ris. '96	🍷🍷	4
○	A. A. Sauvignon '97	🍷🍷	4
●	A. A. Schiava Freisingerhof '97	🍷🍷	3*
●	A. A. Schiava Hexenbichler '97	🍷	3
○	A. A. Chardonnay Glassien Renomée '96	YY	4

TERMENO/TRAMIN (BZ)

**Poderi Castel Ringberg
e Kastelaz Elena Walch**
Via A. Hofer, 1
39040 Termeno/Tramin (BZ)
tel. 0471/860172

We welcome Elena Walch to our Three Glass club. She has earned her entrée with a Gewürztraminer made from grapes grown in the splendid Kastelaz vineyard on an almost vertical hillside above Termeno, whose guyot-trained vines are planted 6 thousand to the hectare. It is a spectacular vineyard and an extraordinary wine of its kind. Its varietal aromas are wonderfully evident, and include rose hips and honey in mingled intensity. Its taste is soft, intense and only very lightly bitter at the end. It is, however, not the only impressive wine on her list. The Cabernet Sauvignon Riserva '95 from Castel Ringberg near Caldaro was itself just shy of Three Glasses. Much more concentrated and convincing than in previous versions, it has a very intense nose and is even a bit forward in the mouth. There follow a series of wines which are simpler, perhaps, but also simply delicious. The Chardonnay Cardellino '97 combines a nose that is fruity and fragrant with an extremely pleasurable ease in drinking. It is also a great bargain. The '97 Pinot Bianco has aromas of ripe fruit and is softly elegant and balanced on the palate. The Pinot Grigio '97 has pleasant fragrances of pear and excellent balance in the mouth. The only disappointment, and certainly not a great one, is that the Sauvignon '97 is merely good. But heavens, to have made five such excellent wines is no mean accomplishment, but is an incontrovertible proof that the great progress made in recent years was no fluke.

○	A. A. Gewürztraminer Kastelaz '97	🍷🍷🍷	4
●	A. A. Cabernet Sauvignon Ris. '95	🍷🍷	5
○	A. A. Chardonnay Cardellino '97	🍷🍷	3*
○	A. A. Pinot Bianco Kastelaz '97	🍷🍷	4
○	A. A. Pinot Grigio Castel Ringberg '97	🍷🍷	4
○	A. A. Sauvignon Castel Ringberg '97	🍷	4
●	A. A. Cabernet Sauvignon Castel Ringberg Ris. '92	YY	5
●	A. A. Cabernet Sauvignon Castel Ringberg Ris. '93	YY	5
○	A. A. Chardonnay Castel Ringberg '94	YY	4

TERMENO/TRAMIN (BZ)

Hofstätter
P.zza Municipio, 5
39040 Termeno/Tramin (BZ)
tel. 0471/860161

It was easy to give oneself prophetic airs last year, predicting a triumph for Hofstätter: they have the enthusiastic hard-working Martin Foradori at the helm, and a completely renovated and up-to-date cellar. And then they had the benefit of two excellent years, '95 for their Pinot Nero and Cabernet Sauvignon, and '97 for their Gewürztraminer. The end result is overwhelmingly successful. Their Pinot Nero Sant'Urbano '95 has been awarded Three Glasses for the fourth time ('90, '91 and '93 being its illustrious predecessors), confirming its position as far and away the best Italian pinot noir. It is an elegant wine of an international level, refined in its inviting display of red currant and vanilla on the nose. But there's more to come. The Gewürztraminer Kolbenhof '97 appears in its best version yet, and almost received Three Glasses. Their Yngram '95, mostly cabernet sauvignon with small amounts of petit verdot, malbec, merlot and syrah as well, is a wine of great breeding; it needs only more concentration in order to be really outstanding. But the wines from their standard range have done very well too. The Reisling '97 is excellent and the Chardonnay '97 and the Cabernet Sauvignon '95 are both very good. Only the Lagrein Scuro '96 was a little below par, and that must be put down to the year. All in all this is their most outstanding performance in about a decade and it has brought it the big tray full of Glasses it deserves.

●	A. A. Pinot Nero S. Urbano '95	🍷🍷🍷	6
●	A. A. Cabernet Sauvignon '95	🍷🍷	4
○	A. A. Chardonnay '97	🍷🍷	3*
○	A. A. Gewürztraminer Kolbenhof '97	🍷🍷	4
○	A. A. Riesling '97	🍷🍷	3*
●	Yngram '95	🍷🍷	5
●	A. A. Lagrein Scuro '96	🍷	4
●	A. A. Pinot Nero S. Urbano '91	YYY	6
●	A. A. Pinot Nero S. Urbano '93	YYY	6
●	A. A. Pinot Nero S. Urbano '90	YYY	6
●	A. A. Pinot Nero S. Urbano '92	YY	6
●	A. A. Pinot Nero S. Urbano '94	YY	6

VADENA/PFATTEN (BZ)

Istituto Sperimentale Laimburg
Loc. Laimburg, 6
39051 Vadena/Pfatten (BZ)
tel. 0471/969210

The Istituto Sperimentale Laimburg can be trusted to make excellent wines. For many years now almost every wine they've made has won Two Glasses, (once, with the '94 Gewürztraminer, they got Three) and their wines continue to serve as a touchstone for the area. This year is no exception (apart from the Cabernet Riserva '95 and the Pinot Nero '96, about which we are deferring judgment until next year). The Gewürztraminer '97 is again the most successful. It does not have the body of the greatest wines of its kind this year, which is a particularly splendid one for this grape, but it is very good and wonderfully well-balanced. We liked the Riesling '97 very much too. It has pleasant citrus aromas with hints of minerals, and an enjoyably full if still slightly sharp taste. The Merlot '96 is delicious. From a difficult vintage, it doesn't have a lot of body, but it is masterfully made. The Lagrein Scuro Riserva '95, which is good and strong, is a notable wine, while the Moscato Rosa, this year in the '96 version, continues to seem unexciting. It is sweet but not much else.

	Wine	Glasses	Price
○	A. A. Gewürztraminer '97	🍷🍷	4
●	A. A. Lagrein Scuro Ris. '95	🍷🍷	5
●	A. A. Merlot '96	🍷🍷	5
○	A. A. Riesling '97	🍷🍷	4
○	A. A. Sauvignon '97	🍷🍷	4
●	A. A. Moscato Rosa '96	🍷	6
○	A. A. Gewürztraminer '94	YYY	4
●	A. A. Cabernet Ris. '93	YY	5
●	A. A. Cabernet Ris. '94	YY	5
○	A. A. Gewürztraminer '95	YY	4
○	A. A. Gewürztraminer '96	YY	4
○	A. A. Riesling Renano '93	YY	4
○	A. A. Riesling Renano '94	YY	4
○	A. A. Riesling Renano '95	YY	4
○	A. A. Riesling Renano '96	YY	4

VARNA/VAHRN (BZ)

Cantina dell' Abbazia di Novacella
Via dell'Abbazia, 1
39040 Varna/Vahrn (BZ)
tel. 0472/836189

Wine has been at home here at the Novacella Abbey for centuries. The Augustinian Fathers have been making their famous Val d'Isarco white wines near Novacella and Brixen on the steep sunny slopes, at the outer limit of viticulture, for 800 years. Theirs are the northernmost vines in Italy. Some years ago they underwent a difficult period. Recently, however, with the arrival of Urban von Klebelsberg, many changes have been made in both vinification and aging . The new cellar master, Celestino Lucin, who for years was the oenologist for the Colterenzio cooperative, has played an important role in these changes. The difference is enormous. The '97 wines are clean and fresh, rich in the aromas that typify the big whites of the Val d'Isarco. The Sylvaner and the Gewürztraminer, as well as the Müller Thurgau and the Kerner (a cross between riesling and schiava, very popular up here) all do well. But their Sauvignon '97 is, this year, the clear winner. Elegant to look at with its green and gold highlights, it offers fresh, ripe fragrances of nettles, elder blossom and sage, and a remarkable structure on the palate. Our compliments for the first wine from the Abbazia di Novacella to receive Three Glasses. The red wines this year are quite good, particularly the Pinot Nero '97 and also the Moscato Rosa '97. Neither, however, was able to repeat previous, more positive, results.

	Wine	Glasses	Price
○	A. A. Sauvignon '97	🍷🍷🍷	4
○	A. A. Valle Isarco Gewürztraminer '97	🍷🍷	4
○	A. A. Valle Isarco Sylvaner '97	🍷🍷	3*
●	A. A. Moscato Rosa '97	🍷	5
●	A. A. Pinot Nero '97	🍷	4
○	A. A. Valle Isarco Kerner '97	🍷	3
○	A. A. Valle Isarco Müller Thurgau '97	🍷	3
●	A. A. Lagrein '93	YY	3
●	A. A. Pinot Nero '95	YY	4
○	A. A. Valle Isarco Gewürztraminer '93	YY	4
●	A. A. Moscato Rosa '94	YY	5
●	A. A. Moscato Rosa '95	YY	5

OTHER WINERIES

The following producers in the province of Bolzano obtained good scores in our tastings with one or more of their wines:

Viticoltori Alto Adige/Südtiroler Weinbauernverband
Appiano/Eppan, tel. 0471/666060,
A. A. Terlano Sauvignon Classico '97

Hans Berger - Turmhof
Bolzano/Bozen, tel. 0471/288460,
A. A. Cabernet Sauvignon Weinegg Ris. '95

Eberlehof
Bolzano/Bozen, tel. 0471/978607,
A. A. Cabernet Komposition '95,
A. A. Lagrein Scuro '95

Malojer Gummerhof
Bolzano/Bozen, tel. 0471/972885,
A. A. Chardonnay Gummerhof '97,
A. A. Lagrein Rosato Weingutt Rahmhütt '97,
A. A. Lagrein Scuro Gummerhof '95,
A. A. Lagrein Scuro Weingutt Rahmhütt '96

Georg Mumelter
Bolzano/Bozen, tel. 0471/973090,
A. A. Lagrein Scuro Griesbauerhof '97,
A. A. Pinot Grigio Griesbauerhof '97,
A. A. Santa Maddalena Griesbauerhof '97

Heinrich Rottensteiner
Bolzano/Bozen, tel. 0471/973549,
A. A. Lagrein Scuro Obermoser Grafenleiten '96

Anton Schmid - Oberrautner
Bolzano/Bozen, tel. 0471/281440,
A. A. Lagrein Grieser '97,
A. A. Lagrein Rosato Grieser '97,
A. A. Lagrein Scuro Ris. '95

Loacker Schwarhof
Bolzano/Bozen, tel. 0471/365125,
A. A. Cabernet Kastlet '96,
A. A. Lagrein Scuro Pîz Thurù '96,
A. A. Santa Maddalena Classico Morit '97

Soini Quinto & Figli
Bronzolo/Branzoll, tel. 0471/967044,
A. A. Cabernet '96

Baron Dürfeld de Giovannelli
Caldaro/Kaltern, tel. 0471/962072,
A. A. Cabernet Sauvignon Panholzerhof '94,
A. A. Lago di Caldaro Scelto Classico '97,
A. A. Lago di Caldaro Scelto Keil '97

Peter Sölva & Sohn - Paterbichl
Caldaro/Kaltern, tel. 0471/964650,
A. A. Gewürztraminer Kühebene '97,
A. A. Lago di Caldaro Scelto Cl. Sup. Peterleiten '97,
A. A. Merlot Desilvas '95

Kettmeir, Caldaro/Kaltern, tel. 0471/963135,
A. A. Pinot Grigio Maso Reiner '97

Josef Brigl
Cornaiano/Girlan, tel. 0471/662419,
A. A. Gewürztraminer '97,
A. A. Lagrein Rosato '97,
A. A. Lago di Caldaro Cl. Sup. Schloss Kaltenburg '97,
A. A. Merlot '95,
A. A. Pinot Grigio '97,
A. A. Pinot Nero '95,
A. A. Santa Maddalena Rielerhof Monika Brigl '97,
A. A. Sauvignon '97

Lorenz Martini
Cornaiano/Girlan, tel. 0471/664136,
A. A. Comitissa Brut Ris. '92

Kupelwieser
Cortina/Kurtinig, tel. 0471/817143,
A. A. Cabernet '95,
A. A. Chardonnay '97,
A. A. Lagrein Scuro Intenditore '96,
A. A. Sauvignon '97

Alois Lageder
Magré/Margraid, tel. 0471/809500,
di questa importante azienda abbiamo potuto assaggiare soltanto:
A. A. Chardonnay Löwengang '95

Cantina Produttori Merano/Meraner Kellerei
Merano/Meran, tel. 0473/235544,
A. A. Chardonnay Graf Von Meran '97,
A. A. Gewürztraminer Graf Von Meran '97,
A. A. Cabernet-Merlot Graf Von Meran '95

VENETO

The Veneto is trying hard to climb to the top of the quality ladder: the region's wines are winning ever more accolades and, although the path that lies ahead can hardly be without problems, producers here are at least heading in the right direction. The most significant wineries are trying to combine more convinced quality-led decisions with the region's real vocation, that of producing large volumes of wine. In the Veneto, thanks to the large area under vine, excellent wines can be produced in reasonable quantities rather than being unfindable rarities. It is just a matter of forgetting the viticultural practices of the '60s and '70s and of adapting traditional training systems like the "Verona pergola", bringing the yield per vine down to the levels found in Friuli, Piedmont and Tuscany. The success of some red wines (like Amarone) and the critical worldwide slackening in the consumption of white wine are two faces of the same coin. Today, thanks to the commercial success that has breathed new life into the Valpolicella zone, producers must become more aware that the only way to ensure a future for the area is to invest in their vineyards, from the point of view of both quality and ecology; it is not enough for them merely to smarten up their wineries and buy a few barriques. In the Soave zone and in all of the eastern Veneto, the gap grows ever wider between the best producers, who are continuing to improve, and numerous wineries which, year in, year out, continue to produce mediocre wines whose prices go on rising without reflecting any improvement in quality. If the former are relatively secure because consumers drink less but choose better, the others will have to pull their socks up if they do not wish to see their inventory rise further. In presenting this year's leading players, we should like to point out that the Veneto has never before won so many Three Glass awards. The Valpolicella zone is once again in the region's vanguard: Allegrini and Dal Forno are the shining stars, while Speri, Nicolis, Bussola and Tedeschi have followed their example with intelligence and skill. After a few years' absence, Masi has once again produced a Three Glass wine: they have hit the mark with an Amarone that is deeply bound to tradition. Amongst the many emerging wineries, we find, with scores very close to the Three Glass threshold, Novaia and Tenuta Sant'Antonio, two small producers with large ambitions. Bertani, with a good handful of Two Glass wines, is returning to its rightful level. Anselmi, Pieropan, Gini and Portinari take Soave and the dessert wines of the zone into the realms of Italy's great wines, while La Cappuccina has come up with a stunning Cabernet. Heading eastwards, a Three Glass award again goes to Vignalta: the company merits this honor not only for the wines it presented, but also because it represents a model for those wineries in the Colli Euganei which still have to awaken from their slumbers. Vignalta is joined by a company which is used to receiving our highest distinction, Serafini & Vidotto. Excellent wines, even if they did not succeed in scoring absolutely top marks, come from the Prosecco area: Ruggeri, Bisol, Adami and Le Colture have attained a level of reliability which was undreamt of a mere five years ago.

ARQUÀ PETRARCA (PD)

VIGNALTA
VIA MARLUNGHE, 7
35032 ARQUÀ PETRARCA (PD)
TEL. 0429/777225

Fresh, clean aromas and fruit which evolves on the palate, gradually filling the mouth, are the fundamental features of the white Sirio and of the red Gemola. The former represents the brighter and livelier face of the Colli Euganei: it is rather like a photograph taken here in spring, when the Colli are at their most inviting, verdant, and fragrant. The Gemola shows us the twilight tones of autumn: its colors, aromas and balance all suggest something that has experienced life, has matured, and is ready to be picked. These sensations of an enchanting affinity with the area from which the wines come conceal great efforts, consisting of research and selection involving the entire zone. Franco Zanovello looks after, and darts around between, the numerous vineyards which are either owned by the estate or controlled by it, and which are in stunning locations. His hectic days invariably end up at the winery where, quite apart from just reorganizing his ideas, he seeks the energy with which to confront ever increasing new commitments. It has taken five years to replace, in our collective memory, that wonderful '90 Cabernet Riserva. Now Franco has succeeded in doing so with the '95 Gemola. This barrique-aged red, made from merlot (70%) and cabernet franc, has a deep yet brilliant color; the nose and palate share a rare finesse, and both display elegance, good evolution and length. The Sirio, a dry moscato bianco, boasts a very rich panoply of aromas. At the moment it still merely expresses a sort of ingenuous simplicity but soon it will become more complex and intriguing: the palate perfectly echoes the sensations on the nose, and the flavor is vigorous, yet harmonious. The Colli Euganei Bianco from the Marlunghe range is characteristic and dependable, while the Pinot Bianco Agno Casto continues to improve.

	Wine	Rating	Price
●	Colli Euganei Rosso Gemola '95	🍷🍷🍷	5
○	Colli Euganei Pinot Bianco Agno Casto '97	🍷🍷	4
○	Sirio '97	🍷🍷	4
○	Colli Euganei Bianco Marlunghe '97	🍷	2*
●	Colli Euganei Merlot Marlunghe '97	🍷	3
○	Colli Euganei Pinot Bianco '97	🍷	3
●	Colli Euganei Cabernet Ris. '90	🍸🍸🍸	5
●	Colli Euganei Rosso Gemola '94	🍸🍸	4
●	Gemola '93	🍸🍸	4
○	Sirio '96	🍸🍸	4

BARDOLINO (VR)

GUERRIERI RIZZARDI
P.ZZA GUERRIERI, 1
37011 BARDOLINO (VR)
TEL. 045/7210028

Costeggiola, one of the prime sites in the whole of the Soave area, lies in the extreme western part of the Soave Classico zone. This wine expresses very well the satisfying and juicy qualities of the garganega grape and is endowed with considerable structure: it is, yet again, the best wine from Guerrieri Rizzardi. Even from its color we are aware of its rich structure. Sweet pineapple and hazelnut hints are initially evident on the nose, and these sensations are wonderfully reproduced on the palate as well. The estate's other white, the Dogoli, a blend that combines aromatic varieties with indigenous grapes, attained almost as high a score. Its color is a deep straw. What particularly impressed us is the way its broad, quite complex nose leads on into refined, persistent fruit on the palate, creating a harmonious whole of rare and seductive quaffability. The Amarone Classico is fairly good, considering the poor quality of the '94 vintage, and displays a relatively delicate, forward style. This is not a wine with ambitions for long aging, but at the moment the pleasantly jammy fruit on the nose and its warm, soft flavor make it a perfect red to accompany mature cheeses. The winery's property near Lake Garda provides a pleasant Bardolino Chiaretto, the Bardolino Tacchetto '97 and the Bardolino Superiore Munus '95, which reveals excellent fruit but should perhaps have been released a year earlier. The Castello Guerrieri Rosso seems to promise well, especially its attractive progression on the palate; the nose is, in fact, still slightly overshadowed by the oak so we don't yet quite know what it will have to offer.

	Wine	Rating	Price
○	Dogoli Bianco '97	🍷🍷	3
○	Soave Cl. Costeggiola '97	🍷🍷	3*
●	Amarone della Valpolicella Cl. '94	🍷	5
⊙	Bardolino Chiaretto '97	🍷	3
●	Bardolino Sup. Munus '95	🍷	4
●	Castello Guerrieri Rosso '93	🍷	4
●	Bardolino Tacchetto Cl. '97		3
●	Amarone della Valpolicella Cl. Calcarole '91	🍸	5

BARDOLINO (VR)

F.LLI ZENI
VIA COSTABELLA, 9
37011 BARDOLINO (VR)
TEL. 045/7210022

After last year, when we tasted mostly the lighter and more youthful wines in Zeni's range, we return this time to the company's big guns. The Amarone, even though '94 was not the best of vintages, is once again the leading player, and this goes for all three of their usual versions. It is difficult to choose between the one aged in barrique and the Vigne Alte: both have an impressive structure, whereas their aromas vary considerably. In the barrique-aged Amarone, one finds an immediately striking nose with, in addition to a distinct oaky note, a fragrance of hazelnuts, flowers and red fruit. The Vigne Alte reveals its charms in a gentler, more intriguing manner: it offers very appealing nuances of spice, and its hints of apricot and cherry seem to be enveloped in a cocoa veil. These two wines, which combine substance with drinkability, both show good evolution and elegant length on the palate. The standard Amarone has a simpler, more rustic style, but the quality of the fruit is undeniable. The '95 Recioto is sweet and mouth-filling, while displaying good balancing acidity: though not a Zeni specialty, it got a very high score. The basic Valpolicella Superiore was admired more than the Vigne Alte version because its fruit is better-knit on the palate. Amongst Zeni's many wines from Lake Garda, we recommend the Chiaretto and Bardolino from the Vigne Alte, which both combine aging capacity with character. The Bianco di Custoza shows a nice balance between acidity and fleshy fruit, while the corvina-based red, Cruino, is clean and pleasant. The Soave and the Garda reds are decent and well-made, and the Garganega is quite interesting.

	Wine	Glasses	Price
●	Amarone della Valpolicella Cl. '94	🍷🍷	5
●	Amarone della Valpolicella Cl. Barrique '94	🍷🍷	6
●	Amarone della Valpolicella Cl. Vigne Alte '94	🍷🍷	5
●	Recioto della Valpolicella Cl. '95	🍷🍷	5
⊙	Bardolino Chiaretto Cl. Vigne Alte '97	🍷	2
●	Bardolino Cl. Vigne Alte '97	🍷	2
○	Bianco di Custoza '97	🍷	2*
●	Cruino '94	🍷	5
○	Garda Garganega '97	🍷	2*
●	Valpolicella Cl. Sup. '96	🍷	3
○	Soave Cl. Sup. '97		3
●	Valpolicella Cl. Sup. Vigne Alte '96		3
●	Amarone della Valpolicella Cl. '88	🍷🍷🍷 (previous year)	5

BASSANO DEL GRAPPA (VI)

VIGNETO DUE SANTI
V.LE ASIAGO, 84
36061 BASSANO DEL GRAPPA (VI)
TEL. 0424/502074

As you climb from Bassano towards the Asiago plateau, you can't help noticing how the gentle, hilly landscape is dotted with handsome, excellently-sited vineyards. It is here that we find the Vigneto Due Santi estate, which Stefano Zonta runs with a sure hand and an increasing awareness of its potential. Gradually he has brought the vineyard plantings and winery equipment up to date, so that the estate is now a well-established entity and can look forward to making even greater improvements in the future. The Breganze Bianco (100% tocai) has a bouquet of citrus fruit and banana, and is crisp and quaffable, with a touch of melon on the finish. The Malvasia Campo dei Fiori returns to its usual high standard: its aromas of ripe peach and apricot, citrus fruit and almond are echoed on the palate, whose length and liveliness temper the notable level of alcohol. Half of the Sauvignon spends some time in oak, and you can tell: the nose is dominated by aromas of vanilla and exotic fruit, and leads on to a fresh palate and a peppery finish. The wine still seems to be searching for precise definition, but the basic structure is all there. We like the aromatic clarity and the balance of the well-made Prosecco. The reds are from the difficult '96 vintage which Zonta admirably interprets by not seeking great extraction at all costs, but rather by concentrating on the fresh aspects of the fruit, and on balance and elegance. The basic version of Cabernet is up-front, well-balanced and fairly long on the palate. The Riserva, whose greater ambitions are evident even from its deep, dark color, combines hints of spice, hazelnut and vanilla with typical black berries. The wine also evolves firmly on the palate (with the tannins playing a substantial role), is by no means lacking in meat and has a long, rich finish.

	Wine	Glasses	Price
●	Breganze Cabernet Vigneto Due Santi '96	🍷🍷	4
○	Breganze Bianco '97	🍷	3
●	Breganze Cabernet '96	🍷	3
●	Breganze Rosso '96	🍷	3
○	Malvasia Campo dei Fiori '97	🍷	3
○	Prosecco Spumante Extra Dry	🍷	3
○	Breganze Sauvignon Vigneto Due Santi '97	🍷	4
●	Breganze Cabernet Vigneto Due Santi '95	🍷🍷 (previous year)	4
●	Breganze Cabernet '95	🍷 (previous year)	3

BREGANZE (VI)

MACULAN
VIA CASTELLETTO, 3
36042 BREGANZE (VI)
TEL. 0445/873733

Of the many interesting wines offered this year by Fausto Maculan, the real surprise was a wood-aged Chardonnay which is decidedly lively and well-balanced. After several years in which the oak held the fruit hostage, we actually found the weight and character of the Burgundian varietal were enhanced by barrel-aging in this version of the Riale, the '96. The color is a deep straw; aromas of apple and pear assert themselves positively, underpinned by a richness deriving from the wood. The entry on the palate is elegant, and the flavor is succulent and long. The Chardonnay from the Ferrata range, on the other hand - in theory a wine that aims higher than the Riale - seems to belong to the past. The Sauvignon was fairly unexciting but the Vespaiolo impressed us with its delicacy. We now shift our focus to the estate's five red wines: we draw your attention to the successful, mouth-filling yet fresh and incisive Merlot Marchesante, as well as to the sound performance of the dependable - if unexciting - Cabernet Palazzotto. We now come, at last, to the much-awaited Cabernet Sauvignon Ferrata, offered this year in the '95 and '96 versions. It is difficult to choose between them: we tasted them both many times and their scores were always very similar. However, the '95 does have greater length and aging potential. The '96 is more immediate and, naturally, more youthful: if this helps it to show off its vitality, it does take a toll in terms of balance and depth. Both have notably deep, opaque colors; mineral tones and black berry notes characterize their respective bouquets and both show remarkable body and structure, even if the oak-derived tannins add some dryness to the flavor.

	Wine	Rating	Price
●	Breganze Cabernet Sauvignon Ferrata '95	YY	5
●	Breganze Cabernet Sauvignon Ferrata '96	YY	5
○	Breganze Chardonnay Riale '96	YY	4
●	Breganze Cabernet Fratta '95	Y	5
●	Breganze Cabernet Fratta '96	Y	5
●	Breganze Cabernet Palazzotto '96	Y	4
●	Breganze Merlot Marchesante '96	Y	5
○	Breganze Vespaiolo '97	Y	3
○	Breganze Chardonnay Ferrata '96		5
○	Breganze Sauvignon Ferrata '97		4
○	Acininobili '91	YYY	6
●	Cabernet Sauvignon Ferrata '90	YYY	5
●	Cabernet Sauvignon Ferrata '94	YYY	5

CAVAION VERONESE (VR)

TENUTA VALLESELLE - TINAZZI
LOC. POLICCHIA
37010 CAVAION VERONESE (VR)
TEL. 045/7235394

Tinazzi is one of those large Veneto wineries that purchase parcels of grapes, or wines, from regular suppliers. The positive symbiosis between the old and the new generations has led first to stricter grape selection, and then on to the purchase of the Valleselle estate, where the ambitions of this winery to produce top-quality wines are destined to be put into practice. The results of our tastings were reassuring: among the many wines presented, we prefer the ones from the Valleselle estate. The Bardolino Superiore '96, conceived in a traditional style, is rich, and displays not only considerable body, but also a mature complexity. The Bardolino '97 is more lively: it has good fruit on the nose and a singularly attractive presence on the palate. The Sauvignon I Seregni and the Chardonnay Arnasi express their different varietal characteristics very well: the former is greener and more vivacious, the latter reveals greater breadth on the nose and palate. In both cases, oak-aging has made their taste profile more satisfying. The exemplarily elegant Cabernet Sauvignon is really interesting. It is quite complex on the nose, and the palate is not particularly mouth-filling, but offers enticing, nuanced fruit. The Ca' de Rocchi line includes a Cabernet Sauvignon in which the herbaceous aspects combine well with the black berry fruit tones. Of the two Valpolicella Superiores presented, the '96 and the '95, we preferred the younger because it shows more definition and better balance. The Merlot and the Chiaretto are minor wines, though by no means unpleasant. The Chardonnay and the Sauvignon are well-made and, again from the Ca' de Rocchi line, the Prato del Faggio, a blend of red Veronese varietals and cabernet sauvignon, is well worth watching.

	Wine	Rating	Price
●	Bardolino Cl. Sup. Pieve S. Vito Valleselle '96	YY	3
●	Cabernet Sauvignon Ca' de Rocchi '96	YY	3*
●	Cabernet Sauvignon Bastia S. Michele Valleselle '96	YY	3
●	Bardolino Cl. Valleselle '97	Y	3
○	Chardonnay Arnasi Valleselle '97	Y	3
○	Chardonnay Ca' de Rocchi '97	Y	3
●	Prato del Faggio Ca' de Rocchi '92	Y	5
○	Sauvignon Ca' de Rocchi '97	Y	3
○	Sauvignon I Seregni Valleselle '97	Y	3
●	Valpolicella Sup. Ca' de Rocchi '96	Y	3
⊙	Bardolino Cl. Chiaretto Valleselle '97		3
●	Merlot Ca' de Rocchi '97		3

COLOGNOLA AI COLLI (VR)

Tenuta S. Antonio
Via Ceriani, 23
Fraz. S. Zeno
37020 Colognola ai Colli (VR)
tel. 045/7650383

The Castagnedi family has been involved in wine for over forty years: after the father, Antonio, had dedicated his viticultural career to the Cantina Sociale di Colognola ai Colli (as a founding member grower), his children decided to create an estate that also vinifies the grapes it grows. The vineyards they own are to the east of Verona, and cover some 40 hectares, equally divided between two zones: the first, near the winery, is completely devoted to Soave; the second comprises innovative planting and training systems for both indigenous Veronese varietals and imported grape types, and produces the more important wines. Looking forward to the release of a promising '95 Amarone, we appreciated a warm and intense Valpolicella Superiore '96: the oak has a slightly overdominant role in the wine at present, but the fruit is all there and Celestino Gaspari, consultant oenologist to the estate, will no doubt be able to strike a better balance in the future. Barrique-aging has, on the other hand, been entirely successful in the Cabernet Sauvignon Vigna Capitello: its nose is concentrated, deep and complex, with mineral tones that mingle with herbal and fruity notes; on the palate it is robust, vigorous and long. The extremely concentrated and evocative chardonnay-based Passito Colori d'Autunno displays a brilliant amber color and a classic bouquet of ripe raspberries. It reveals immediate and voluptuously sweet fruit on the palate, underpinned by an imposing structure. The range also includes a lesser, but nevertheless successful, Cabernet Sauvignon, the Torre dei Mellotti, which is in effect the "second wine" of the Vigna Capitello. The only wine that did not convince us was the barriqued Chardonnay.

	Wine	Glasses	Price
●	Cabernet Sauvignon Vigna Capitello '95	🍷🍷	5
○	Passito Bianco Colori d'Autunno '95	🍷🍷	5
●	Cabernet Sauvignon Torre dei Mellotti '96	🍷	3
●	Valpolicella Sup. '96	🍷	3
○	Chardonnay Vigna Capitello '96		4

CROCETTA DEL MONTELLO (TV)

Astoria
Viale Antonini, 9
31035 Crocetta del Montello (TV)
tel. 0423/665042

This newcomer to the Guide is a winery whose name, until a few years ago, was linked to well-made but undeniably commercial wines. However, a desire to make the most of the viticultural potential of the zone has encouraged the Polegato family to improve the quality of their wines and, in fact, after not very long at all, they have produced some very interesting results. The heart of this renewed enthusiasm is the Val de Brun estate, from which come noteworthy prosecco-based sparkling wines and some still wines that still have room for improvement. Of these the best is definitely the Prosecco Tranquillo, which just missed its Two Glasses. It has a deep color and rich aromas with apple and pear notes; in the mouth, the fruit is broad, balanced and long. The Pinot Grigio and the Cabernet have less character and are merely sound, but unexciting. The Prosecco Extra Dry is another matter altogether: it lacks neither aromatic personality nor balance, and is impeccably executed. The Prosecco Dry Grande Cuvée is rounded and mouth-filling, as befits its style, and is easily recognized by its squat, big-bellied bottle. This sparkling wine aims to compete with the best in the zone and, even if certain aspects, like the integration of the carbon dioxide and the definition on the nose, are faultless, it really needs to offer greater all-round breadth if it is to establish a place for itself in the very top rank. These qualities are already to be found in the Cartizze, where the creamy mousse and complex bouquet lead on seamlessly to mellow, barely sweet fruit on the palate and an extremely fresh and lively finish.

	Wine	Glasses	Price
○	Cartizze	🍷🍷	3
○	Prosecco di Conegliano Dry Grande Cuvée	🍷	4
○	Prosecco di Valdobbiadene Extra Dry Millesimato '97	🍷	3
○	Prosecco di Valdobbiadene Tranquillo '97	🍷	3
○	Pinot Grigio del Piave '97		2
●	Cabernet del Montello '97		2

CUSTOZA (VR)

CAVALCHINA
LOC. CAVALCHINA
37060 CUSTOZA (VR)
TEL. 045/516002

Luciano Piona, the driving force behind the new Garda DOC, has not limited himself to playing an important organizational role, but has also produced wines that amply demonstrate the validity of this new denomination. As the owner of two estates on the border between the provinces of Verona and Mantua, Piona produces the classic DOC wines of both areas: in the Veneto he makes those of the Cavalchina estate, and the wines of La Prendina come from Lombardy. In this section we discuss only the wines from the Verona area, where the winery is located. The Amedeo, the best custoza in Cavalchina's range, is less rich than last year but is still one of the most representative wines of its category. Its color is of medium depth and its perfumes are spicy and well-defined, and the fruit evolves pleasantly on the palate. The standard version also earns One Glass for its attractively quaffable style. The Bardolino is well-made, fresh and eminently drinkable. Luciano Piona has also started to show some skill with sweet wines: we draw your attention to the elegant and floral moscato-based La Rosa, while Le Pergole del Sole, made from semi-dried müller thurgau grapes from the difficult '96 vintage, doesn't offer much more than a fresh sweetness.

○	Bianco di Custoza '97	🍷	3
○	Bianco di Custoza Amedeo '97	🍷	3
⊙	La Rosa '97	🍷	4
○	Le Pergole del Sole '96	🍷	6
●	Bardolino '97	🍷	3

FAEDO DI CINTO EUGANEO (PD)

CA' LUSTRA
VIA S. PIETRO, 50
35030 FAEDO DI CINTO EUGANEO (PD)
TEL. 0429/94128

The wine-making philosophy of this estate is pretty straightforward: to improve the quality of its wines while keeping prices low and, at the same time, to try to bring out the enormous viticultural potential of the Colli Euganei, in the hope that other producers in the zone will follow suit. That the wines presented by Ca' Lustra this year are better than those of past years was not only due to the quality of the vintage and the great efforts of Franco Zanovello, but also to the assistance of Francesco Polastri, who has succeeded in fine-tuning the wine-making procedures so that none of the grapes' original quality is lost. We find evidence of this in the Bianco Colli Euganei, whose deep color and delicate floral tones, combined with more intense fruity aromas, are in perfect, elegant balance with the evolving fruit on the palate and with the satisfyingly long and corresponding finish. The Incrocio Manzoni, with its characteristic aromatic hints, is a restrained and soft white of medium length. The more immediately appealing Chardonnay Vigna Marco is not particularly rich, but captures one's attention with its spontaneous, charming fruit. Another pleasingly simple wine is the Sauvignon, very slightly herbaceous on the nose, and underpinned by a light vein of acidity on the palate. We find greater richness and depth than formerly in the Cabernet Girapoggio, which indicates that the reds, too, are on the right path. Its color is a reasonably deep ruby, and its nose displays promising complexity, with balsamic notes and hints of red berries. The wine shows decisive attack on the palate and has good aromatic length. The basic Pinot Bianco and Chardonnay are both honest, well-made wines.

○	Colli Euganei Bianco '97	🍷🍷	2*
●	Colli Euganei Cabernet Girapoggio '95	🍷🍷	3*
○	Colli Euganei Chardonnay Vigna Marco '97	🍷	4
○	Incrocio Manzoni Vigna Linda '97	🍷	4
○	Sauvignon '97	🍷	3
○	Colli Euganei Chardonnay '97		3
○	Colli Euganei Pinot Bianco '97		2

FARRA DI SOLIGO (TV)

MEROTTO
VIA TREVISET, 68
FRAZ. COL S. MARTINO
31010 FARRA DI SOLIGO (TV)
TEL. 0438/898195

The results of our tastings of Merotto's wines are somewhat contradictory: in the last few years some wines have achieved excellence, while others make do with a correct but characterless style. Wines such as the Prosecco Tranquillo Olchera or the Spumante Dry Colle Molina, which in the past had expressed considerable personality, gave us no more this year than decidedly simple aromas, as well as lackluster fruit on the palate. The Prosecco Primavera di Barbara, which is a Dry (in other words, a sweeter style) is altogether more charming. Even its appearance announces its intensity and the finesse of its perlage: its nose is fresh, soft and broad; the fruit on the palate is rendered intriguing by the balance between restrained sweetness and a lively acidulous note, while its finish is stylish, if not especially long. The Prosecco Extra Dry is even better, with its particularly attractive balance. Appley aromas are evident on the nose, which broadens out to reveal considerable complexity; the fine and creamily well-integrated mousse diffuses the fruit on the palate with notable elegance. The Cartizze also performs well: its color has good depth and its bubbles offer a fine, persistent bead; the nose is initially appealingly positive but then becomes more toned down and straightforward. A slightly sweet vein characterizes the flavor, which is not very long, but is distinct and clean.

	Wine	Rating	Price
O	Prosecco di Valdobbiadene Extra Dry	ŶŶ	2*
O	Cartizze	Ŷ	3
O	Prosecco di Valdobbiadene Dry Primavera di Barbara '97	Ŷ	3
O	Prosecco di Valdobbiadene Dry Colle Molina		3
O	Prosecco di Valdobbiadene Tranquillo Olchera '97		2

FUMANE (VR)

★ ALLEGRINI
CORTE GIARA, 7
37022 FUMANE (VR)
TEL. 045/6801171 - 7702306

Franco Allegrini has been carefully studying the Valpolicella zone, in order to take hold of its good qualities and, when necessary, to overcome its obstacles. He knew that the wines from Valpolicella made fifteen years ago did not do justice to their extraordinary reputation, but the terroir was there to bear witness to its tradition and potential. Today he and the zone are as one: it inspires him and follows his lead, and Franco honors it by investing ever more of his energy in the vineyards, whose tremendous potential has never been fully exploited. His wines this year are exemplary and are absolute paradigms of the very best of their various styles. The Amarone is faultless: its perfect color attests to the fact that the drying process has really augmented the potential of the grapes. Floral aromas, hints of vanilla and cocoa, and succulent notes of cherry are all to be found in the seductively complex nose. The elegant and well-knit fruit on the palate offers a magnificent and persistent sensation of balance. La Poja, made exclusively from corvina, reveals deep and evolving sweet fruit. Its aristocratic color is complemented by the lively richness of its gamut of aromas; its soft black berry fruit vein matches perfectly with the dense richness on the palate, and an essential mineral note underpins firm structure-yielding tannins. The Recioto offers, above all, masterly balance: the nose, color and flavor are all of equal intensity and just leave you to watch their intriguing interplay. The Valpolicellas are all splendid and are ideal models of a wine quite separate from Amarone.

	Wine	Rating	Price
●	Amarone della Valpolicella Cl. '93	ŶŶŶ	6
●	La Poja '93	ŶŶŶ	6
●	Recioto della Valpolicella Cl. Giovanni Allegrini '95	ŶŶ	5
●	Valpolicella Cl. Sup. La Grola '95	ŶŶ	4
●	Valpolicella Cl. Sup. Palazzo della Torre '95	ŶŶ	4
●	Valpolicella Cl. '97	ŶŶ	3*
●	La Poja '90	ΥΥΥ	5
●	Recioto della Valpolicella Amarone Cl. Sup. '90	ΥΥΥ	5
●	Recioto della Valpolicella Amarone Cl. Sup. '91	ΥΥΥ	5
●	Recioto della Valpolicella Cl. Giovanni Allegrini '93	ΥΥΥ	5

FUMANE (VR)

LE SALETTE
VIA PIO BRUGNOLI, 11/C
37022 FUMANE (VR)
TEL. 045/7701027

In the last few years Franco Scamperle has been one of the major players in Valpolicella, particularly when the vintages were less than good. This year his range includes some really first-class wines. The Amarone Le Pergole Vecie offers all the richness and explosive vitality of the '93 vintage, to which Franco Scamperle has added some complexity and elegance to produce a firm, rich and persistent red in keeping with the traditional alcoholic warmth of the style: it is a wine that shows the many-faceted richness typical of a modern red. The only slightly less successful Amarone Marega '94 stands up extremely well, particularly for the standard version from a lesser vintage: its color is intense; on the nose, we liked the clean blend of oak, flowers and red fruit. On the palate, it has plenty of fleshy fruit, traditional alcohol and good length. The Recioto Le Traversagne shows exemplary balance and hamony, and is concentrated even in appearance; it offers among its aromas an inviting balsamic note, while the flavor is an intriguing balancing act of sweetness and tannins. The Valpolicella Superiore I Progni rounds out this top-quality range; designed to have its own niche, independent of the market success of Amarone or Recioto, this wine displays the potential of the corvina grape when it is not semi-dried: it is mouth-filling, lively and vigorous. Apart from the Passito Bianco Cesare, rustic although made from good fruit, we draw your attention to the easy but well-made Recioto Le Pergole Vecie. Only the Valpolicella Ca' Carnocchio is lean and rather lacking in character, whereas the '97 Classico again shows this wine's light, fresh and undemanding style.

	Wine	Rating	Price
●	Amarone della Valpolicella Cl. La Marega '94	▼▼	5
●	Amarone della Valpolicella Cl. Le Pergole Vecie '93	▼▼	6
●	Recioto della Valpolicella Le Traversagne '95	▼▼	5
●	Valpolicella Cl. Sup. I Progni '95	▼▼	3*
○	Bianco Passito Cesare '95	▼	4
●	Recioto della Valpolicella Le Pergole Vecie '95	▼	5
●	Valpolicella Cl. Sup. Ca' Carnocchio '95		4
●	Valpolicella Cl. '97		2
●	Amarone della Valpolicella Cl. La Marega '93	▽▽	4

GAMBELLARA (VI)

LA BIANCARA
C.DA BIANCARA, 8
36053 GAMBELLARA (VI)
TEL. 0444/444244

Angiolino Maule has entered what can be considered the second phase of his career. After having demonstrated his skills as a winegrower by freeing garganega from the oblivion of overproduction into which it had fallen, he has now given a precise direction to the vinification and aging of his wines. The first result is a great improvement in the Gambellara Sassaia, a white which is not only intense and well structured (made as it is from a special selection of his grapes), but which also offers a graceful freshness. Its color is a bright straw; its nose displays a well-knit fragrance, while its mouth-filling fruit evolves well on the palate and yields a satisfyingly long finish. The Gambellara I Masieri is a sort of standard version of the category, to which Maule gives a touch of personality that makes it very appealing. The Recioto di Gambellara '95 is really successful, its most satisfying quality being the balance between its sweet, ripe white-fleshed fruit, spicy notes and hints of oak. Its warm golden color is echoed by the roundness of its attack; it is not at all cloying in the mouth and has an extremely elegant finish. The Pico de Laorenti, the estate's experimental wine, is a white made from garganega and aged in oak: the '96 version is not yet ready and we therefore prefer to withhold judgment until next year's Guide. For the time being we can say that, after numerous comparisons with the wines of other producers and many experiments in his own winery, Maule has perhaps found the right aging system for increasing the expressiveness of garganega without diminishing its finesse.

	Wine	Rating	Price
○	Gambellara Cl. Sup. Sassaia '97	▼▼	3*
○	Recioto di Gambellara '95	▼▼	5
○	Gambellara I Masieri '97	▼	1*
●	Rosso La Biancara '96	▼	4
●	Rosso La Biancara '95	▽	3

GAMBELLARA (VI)

ZONIN
VIA BORGOLECCO, 9
36053 GAMBELLARA (VI)
TEL. 0444/640111

Among the giant wineries of Italy, Zonin is the one that is making the greatest effort to bring the quality level of its wines in line with new market demands. Thus the range produced at Ca' Bolani, Zonin's estate in Friuli, shows constant improvement, there is some progress in the Gambellara and Valpolicella wines, and the Prosecco Brut has again done well. But let's get down to detail. The Tocai Aquileia - clean, intense and well-structured - also offers a fair correspondence between its appearance, nose and palate. This Friulian varietal contributes, together with chardonnay, in making another attractive white, the Opimio, which has an elegant nose with peach and almond notes, while on the palate its delicate fruit also evolves well. The Traminer and Riesling are well-made; their spicy aromas are in perfect counterpoint to the lively fruitiness on the palate. Both display very good balance and length. The other whites, such as the Pinot Grigio, Sauvignon and Pinot Bianco, are pleasant, even if they cannot boast the same personality as the wines mentioned above. The reds were not quite as good as we had expected. The most interesting ones are those from Valpolicella. The Valpolicella itself showed surprisingly good evolution on the palate, allied with positive, satisfying aromas. We could not expect great things from the '94 Amarone, but its cleanness and reasonable fruit earned it One Glass. The straightforward and inviting Gambellara Il Giangio and the mouth-filling, mellow, and fragrant Prosecco Brut also got a Glass apiece.

	Wine	Glasses	Price
●	Amarone della Valpolicella '94	🍷	4
○	Friuli Aquileia Bianco Opimio '97	🍷	3
○	Friuli Aquileia Riesling Ca' Bolani '97	🍷	2
○	Friuli Aquileia Tocai Ca' Bolani '97	🍷	2
○	Friuli Aquileia Traminer '97	🍷	2
○	Gambellara Cl. Podere Il Giangio '97	🍷	2*
○	Prosecco Spumante Brut	🍷	2*
●	Valpolicella Cl. '96	🍷	2*
●	Amarone Podere Il Maso '92	Y	4
●	Berengario '93	Y	4

ILLASI (VR)

ROMANO DAL FORNO
VIA LODOLETTA, 4
FRAZ. CELLORE
37030 ILLASI (VR)
TEL. 045/7834923

Romano Dal Forno must be numbered amongst the legendary ranks of the great "vignerons": tough farmers who have written memorable pages in the oenological annals throughout the ages. These men, used to facing up to nature with a mixture of indomitable will and healthy resignation, are individuals who, inevitably, stand alone. Their solitude does not mean that they are not sociable (they are, in fact, usually friendly and helpful), but that other people can only be spectators of the journey that life has mapped out for them. Dal Forno has, in this sense, made his wine an expression of his independent spirit: though remaining a true son of the Valpolicella area, he has created an Amarone that is absolutely outstanding among its peers. It is no longer a question of tradition or innovation: this wine does not stoop to any form of compromise, but is a sort of revelatory beacon in which one senses the glowing aura of the fruit itself. When you taste the wine you are simply not aware that it comes form a lesser year: indeed, the '91 vintage seems to have given it a new dynamism. The bouquet bursts forth with its beautiful force, and modulates the depth of the wine by unraveling into aromas of spice, flowers and fruit. The connection between the fruit on the nose and that on the palate manifests itself quite clearly: they are merely two expressions of the same being. The structure on the palate is overwhelming: we admired its vein of sweetness, and the accompanying masterful thrust that barely gives one time to catch one's breath. The finish conveys a sensation-laden, almost overblown echo of the nose, seeming to reiterate the uniqueness of this unforgettable Amarone. The Recioto boasts balance, finesse on the nose and a sweetness that is so well amalgamated that it becomes part and parcel of the tannic structure. The '93 Valpolicella Superiore is also excellent.

	Wine	Glasses	Price
●	Amarone Vigneto di Monte Lodoletta '91	🍷🍷🍷	6
●	Recioto della Valpolicella Vigneto di Monte Lodoletta '90	🍷🍷	6
●	Valpolicella Sup. '93	🍷🍷	5
●	Amarone Vigneto di Monte Lodoletta '86	YYY	6
●	Amarone Vigneto di Monte Lodoletta '87	YYY	6
●	Amarone Vigneto di Monte Lodoletta '88	YYY	6
●	Amarone Vigneto di Monte Lodoletta '89	YYY	6
●	Amarone Vigneto di Monte Lodoletta '90	YYY	6

ILLASI (VR)

F.lli Giuliari
Loc. Santa Giustina, 3
37031 Illasi (VR)
tel. 045/7834143

The area to the east of Verona continues to yield pleasant surprises. The Giuliaris, "vignerons" for generations and skilled, hard-working farmers, have for some time now been making the most of their fine grapes and producing rich, intense wines. They have made great efforts to improve their own ten hectares under vine, and they fill out their production by buying grapes from vineyards they keep a close eye on. A leap in quality has come about also because of their improved cellar technique, a development which was absolutely crucial to giving a consistent level of quality to all 200 thousand bottles they produce. The splendid '93 Amarone, a red that reflects both tradition and innovation, accounts for 10% of their production. Its deep color displays homogeneity of tone and suggests firmness: its nose offers floral aromas with undertones of ripe raspberry. The entry on the palate shows the usual exuberant level of alcohol, but the evolution shows a modern balance that lifts the flavor, making it satisfying and long. The '96 Recioto was not adversely affected by its unfortunate vintage; indeed, it seems to have gained a more modulated and attractive style. The wine starts displaying its charms right away, even in its color; the bouquet is open but not overblown, yielding notably fresh, fruity notes; the perfect restraint of the sweetness allows all of the components to express themselves on the palate, creating an inviting sense of harmony. Lastly, the sparkling version of the Recioto di Soave deserves attention: in this wine, the Giuliaris aim to keep wine-making technology to a minimum, thus preserving as far as is possible the excellent fruit at their disposal.

●	Amarone della Valpolicella Cl. '93	🍷🍷	5
●	Recioto della Valpolicella '96	🍷🍷	5
○	Recioto di Soave Spumante '93	🍷	5

ILLASI (VR)

Santi
Via Ungheria, 33
37031 Illasi (VR)
tel. 045/6520077

Santi represents the traditional face of the Gruppo Italiano Vini. It has a lot in common with another historic winery that forms part of GIV, Nino Negri, and, even if it has not yet reached the same heights as its sister company in the Valtellina zone, this Illasi-based winery should be well pleased by the most recent performances of its wines. The first major achievement was giving the two million bottles it produces a tiny bit more character, so that even the simplest wines (those intended for the extremely competitive low-priced market) have a recognizable personality. Then there are the more ambitious wines, and here too there are positive notes. The two Soaves both received high scores and are good examples of two different interpretations of this white wine. The Monteforte is fresh and quaffable, and displays immediately appealing fruit. We particularly liked this wine because its characteristic grace does not keep its personality (and the quality of the grapes) from showing through. The more modulated and, we imagine, partly oak-aged Sanfederici displays a captivatingly sweet nose; on the palate we liked its elegance and nice balance. What really surprised us was the excellence of the Valpolicella Superiore Le Solane, a satisfyingly complete wine. Its bouquet combines concentrated red fruit aromas with fresh, lightly floral notes; its well-structured palate also offers perfectly balanced fruit. On the other hand, we prefer to suspend our judgment of the '95 Amarone Proemio, since it is still maturing. The Bardolino and the Chiaretto are decently made and quaffable.

○	Soave Cl. Monteforte '97	🍷🍷	2*
●	Valpolicella Sup. Le Solane '96	🍷🍷	3*
○	Soave Cl. Sanfederici '97	🍷	3
●	Bardolino Ca' Bordenis '97		2
⊙	Bardolino Chiaretto L'Infinito '97		2
●	Amarone della Valpolicella '90	🍷🍷 (outline)	5
●	Amarone della Valpolicella '91	🍷 (outline)	5

ILLASI (VR)

TRABUCCHI
VIA MONTE TENDA, 3
37031 ILLASI (VR)
TEL. 045/7833233-049/8755455

Trabucchi, too, like any recently-founded winery, has to take great pains to make wines of a consistently high quality and to give them a style of their own. And the undeniably quality-led options taken by this winery are beginning to bear fruit, as is demonstrated by this year's selection. Making good wines from the '95 vintage was not a difficult task, but the quality achieved here pleased us beyond our expectations. The Recioto is the best ever produced by Trabucchi and displays uncompromisingly its "eastern" origins: it in fact comes from the so-called "extended" part of the Valpolicella zone to the east of Verona. From that light, stony soil this wine has açquired elegant concentration as well as considerable complexity on the nose, which encompasses both floral aromas and typical black berry fruit notes. On the palate, the sweetness is not at all cloying and the structure of the wine is firm and persistent. The Amarone has benefited from careful aging in new oak, which has contributed to bringing out very appealing, complex fruit. The nose has become broader and more interesting; on the palate we found - and appreciated - its elegant, measured style which does not, however, detract at all from the immediate and lively character typical of Amarone. The Valpolicella Superiore, which has never before been so clean and attractive, is spicy, with good fruit concentration and reasonable length. The Passito Bianco Sparavieri, the real surprise of the entire range, is medium-sweet, graceful and, most notably, shows delightlful harmony on the palate.

●	Amarone della Valpolicella '95	🍷🍷	5
○	Passito Bianco Sparavieri '96	🍷🍷	4
●	Recioto della Valpolicella '95	🍷🍷	5
●	Valpolicella Sup. '95	🍷	4
●	Amarone '90	🍸🍸	5
●	Amarone '93	🍸	6
●	Valpolicella Sup. Terre di San Colombano '94	🍸	4

LAZISE (VR)

LAMBERTI
VIA GARDESANA
37017 LAZISE (VR)
TEL. 045/6770233

This Lazise-based winery has created a position for itself in the marketplace thanks to a happy combination of marketing, attractive prices and constant improvement in quality. The organization of the winery is really fairly segmented: the headquarters incorporate the aging cellars, in which the older barrels are gradually being replaced by new oak casks of various sizes; La Preella, in the heart of the Bardolino area, is a 50-hectare property where the classic Garda wines are vinified, whereas the wines from Valpolicella are produced on the Pule estate at San Pietro in Cariano. Everything is then bottled at their plant at Pastrengo. This year, too, we noticed the care with which all the wines are made and, even if there are no outstanding highlights, the average quality is good. The Soave Santepietre once again proves itself to be more than just a straightforward, pleasant white by offering complexity and refinement. It is an attractively deep straw in color; its bouquet reveals pineapple and hazelnut notes and it develops well in the mouth with fresh succulent fruit following through from the entry right to the finish. The reliable Lugana, with its clean bouquet and definition on the palate, and a particularly appealing dryness, is a perfect wine for fish. The Bianco di Custoza is a more straightforward wine, with a barely aromatic fragrance and a delicate flavor. We were quite surprised by how well the Amarone Corte Rubini showed, since it is from a not especially inspiring vintage: it reveals cleanness and balance, reasonably full fruit on the palate and a long, broad finish. The '97 Bardolino and Valpolicella are decent and well made.

○	Soave Santepietre '97	🍷🍷	2*
●	Amarone Corte Rubini '94	🍷	5
○	Bianco di Custoza Orchidea Platino '97	🍷	3
○	Lugana Oro '97	🍷	3
●	Bardolino Santepietre '97		2
●	Valpolicella Cl. Santepietre '97		2
●	Amarone Corte Rubini '93	🍸	4

LAZISE (VR)

Le Tende di Fortuna e Lucillini

Loc. Le Tende
Fraz. Colà
37010 Lazise (VR)
tel. 045/7590748

Le Tende's aim is to produce, to the best of its ability, those light wines which have made Lake Garda famous while at the same time coming up with some more serious and substantial bottles which fulfill the owners' yearning to make really excellent wines. The best wine in this "superior" range is the Passito Bianco Amoroso, made from garganega and a small proportion of imported varietals. The warmth of the '95 vintage has given the Amoroso a richness and a depth that had been lacking for a few years; in addition, the wine retains the balance and finesse that make a dessert wine truly irresistible. Its notes of honey and candied peel, its warm flavor and modulated sweetness are the salient aspects of its taste profile. The Cicisbeo, a blend of cabernet sauvignon and cabernet franc, did not repeat last year's fine showing, and perhaps one should not have expected it to in a vintage like '96. It is an agreeable, well-made red, but lacks the breadth of a great wine. The Sorbo degli Uccellatori, made from a combination of the Bordeaux blend and corvina, reveals its usual delicate style. The '97 Bardolino, on the other hand, is a pleasant surprise: it displays exemplary élan on the nose and richness on the palate. The Bardolino Superiore is also a well-made wine, with riper aromas and mouth-filling fruit on the palate. The Custozas performed less well, with just the Lucillini distinguishing itself by means of its more positive character.

○	Passito Bianco Amoroso '95	🍷🍷	4
●	Bardolino Cl. Sup. '96	🍷	2*
●	Bardolino Cl. '97	🍷	2
○	Bianco di Custoza Lucillini '97	🍷	3
●	Cicisbeo '96	🍷	4
●	Sorbo degli Uccellatori '96	🍷	3
⊙	Bardolino Cl. Chiaretto '97		2
○	Bianco di Custoza Oro '97		2
●	Cicisbeo '95	🍸🍸	4

MARANO DI VALPOLICELLA (VR)

Paolo Boscaini e Figli

Via Cadeloi, 2
Fraz. Valgatara
37020 Marano di Valpolicella (VR)
tel. 045/6800840

The Amarone Ca' de Loi continues to keep the average standard of the Boscaini wines high. The '93 vintage is interesting because it has the same richness as the '90 without displaying the latter's excessive level of alcohol. For this reason the flagship wine of this Marano-based winery seems even better then the version presented last year. This true and elegant Amarone reveals its notable potential in a slow, understated manner. Its color is clear and homogeneous, while hints of licorice, flowers and red fruit give it attractive complexity on the nose. The palate, after a perfect attack, becomes soft and well-balanced, and is nicely underpinned by the alcohol. In the rest of the range we find a general correctness, but also insufficient personality. To tell the truth, the '96 and '94 vintages, from which the Recioto and the Amarone hail, were not of any great moment, and consequently these wines are pleasant but in a minor - and rather light - key. The Valpolicella Classico San Ciriaco is sound, but definitely lacks that spark of liveliness which could turn it into an example of succulent quaffability. The Valpolicella Superiore seems a bit below par. The whites (Lugana, Soave and Custoza) are linear and delicate.

●	Amarone della Valpolicella Cl. Ca' de Loi '93	🍷🍷	5
●	Amarone della Valpolicella Cl. Marano '94	🍷	5
●	Recioto della Valpolicella Ca' Nicolis '96	🍷	5
○	Bianco di Custoza Carmina '97		3
○	Lugana Lunatio '97		3
○	Soave Cl. Sup. Monteleone '97		3
●	Valpolicella Cl. Sup. Marano '96		3
●	Valpolicella Cl. San Ciriaco '97		3
●	Amarone della Valpolicella Ca' de Loi '90	🍸🍸	5
●	Amarone della Valpolicella Vigneti di Marano '93	🍸	4

Giuseppe Campagnola

Via Agnella, 9
Fraz. Valgatara
37020 Marano di Valpolicella (VR)
tel. 045/7703900

Campagnola fully confirms the success that earned it a place in the Guide for the first time last year. The wine-making strategy of this winery in Valgatara remains the same: to ensure a reliable standard of quality for the approximately three million bottles turned out annually, while so improving the more important wines that they become competitive at the top level. The former objective has definitely been reached: the so-called "everyday" wines, such as the standard Soave and Valpolicella, are undoubtedly well-made. The second goal is more complicated, since it is not enough to have good grapes if you then only draw out part of their potential. The only fault in the first wine to emerge in this surperior range, an encouraging '96 Recioto, is that it has been released too soon. The wine is by no means lacking in richness and complexity; it has a bright, concentrated color, and its nose offers notes of aromatic herbs alongside well-defined notes of fruit and a youthful headiness. On the palate, the sensation of sweetness is immediately evident and, for the moment, overwhelms the other components, such as the fruit and tannins. The Soave Le Bine earns Two Glasses thanks to its fragrant, complex style: elegant and long, it displays good fruit on the nose and well-balanced breadth on the palate. The Valpolicella Superiore shows that it has been made with great care even if it cannot hide the fact that it is from a less than successful vintage. The '95 Amarone does not reach any great heights of quality, whereas we admired the light Bianco di Custoza. The Merlot-Corvina and Garganega-Chardonnay blends were decent, frank and inexpensive.

	Wine	Glasses	Price
○	Soave Cl. Sup. Le Bine '97	🍷🍷	2*
●	Amarone della Valpolicella '95	🍷	5
○	Bianco di Custoza '97	🍷	2*
●	Recioto della Valpolicella Casotto del Merlo '96	🍷	4
●	Valpolicella Cl. Sup. Le Bine '96	🍷	3
○	Garganega Chardonnay '97		1
●	Merlot Corvina '97		1

MARANO DI VALPOLICELLA (VR)

Michele Castellani e Figli

Via Granda, 1
Fraz. Valgatara
37020 Marano di Valpolicella (VR)
tel. 045/7701253

After the split between brothers Sergio and Giuseppe, the Castellani winery (with its I Castei labels) remains in the hands of the former, while the latter has founded a new winery under the Ca' La Bionda trademark. So far the range from this source are no more than simple and well-made, but the Castellani wines have lived up to their good performances over the last few years, proving that a combination of estate-owned vineyards and careful selection of bought-in grapes can give good results even in difficult vintages. The '94 Amarone earns high marks thanks to its completeness and elegance. It displays an attractively deep, opaque color, as well as a fairly marked oakiness on the nose which does not, however, mask the fruit. The entry on the palate is firm but restrained, and the development proceeds in crescendo to a really enjoyable and long finish. The exuberant and lively '96 Recioto offers a very deep color, aromatic finesse and an immediately appealing, well-balanced sweetness. Moreover, even though it is delicious right now, it gives the impression of having the potential to mature and take on the complexity of a great dessert wine. The success of this fortunate year for the Castellani winery is completed by a Valpolicella Superiore which only just missed getting Two Glasses. It has a reasonably deep color, its bouquet evolves attractively, displaying a floral tone, and it reveals supple structure, if no great depth, on the palate.

	Wine	Glasses	Price
●	Amarone della Valpolicella I Castei '94	🍷🍷	5
●	Recioto della Valpolicella I Castei '96	🍷🍷	5
●	Valpolicella Cl. Sup. I Castei '96	🍷	3

F.LLI DEGANI
VIA TOBELLE, 9
FRAZ. VALGATARA
37020 MARANO DI VALPOLICELLA (VR)
TEL. 045/7701850

This small estate, which seems like Tom Thumb amongst the giants of Valpolicella, continues to make marked progress. Its specialty is Amarone, which comes out well both when the vintage is not particularly favorable (as in '92), and when weather conditions are excellent. Indeed, in this case, the wine becomes outstanding. The '93, in fact, offers exceptional structure and is rich, long and firm. Semi-drying the grapes has made this red more seductive and rounded, and one notices this even in the concentration and homogeneity of its color. The nose, whose deep fruit is tempered by the richness of the alcohol, offers precise notes of black berry fruits that gradually become more complex, giving way to hints of licorice and cocoa. The fruit on the palate is vigorous on entry, and deliciously mouth-filling and long. Aldo and Angelo Degani have the character and temperament of true "vignerons" and are therefore particularly sensitive to the character of their grapes, which they attempt to express in each of their wines. Thus the Recioto, too, is powerful and sweet: it could really do with a bit more aging before being released, so it is a little rustic. Nevertheless, the wine by no means lacks cleanness, refreshing acidity, or the silky tannins to suggest interesting aging potential. We must, however, point out the backward step taken by the Valpolicella Superiore in comparison with last year's: it did not really take advantage of the very good '95 vintage. The '97 Valpolicella is a simple and immediate wine.

●	Amarone della Valpolicella '93	🍷🍷	4*
●	Recioto della Valpolicella '96	🍷🍷	4
●	Valpolicella Cl. Sup. '95		3
●	Valpolicella Cl. '97		2
●	Amarone della Valpolicella '92	🍷🍷 (white)	4
●	Recioto della Valpolicella '95	🍷🍷 (white)	4

GIUSEPPE LONARDI
VIA DELLE POSTE, 2
37020 MARANO DI VALPOLICELLA (VR)
TEL. 045/7755154

Giuseppe Lonardi divides his passion and his efforts between his estate and his "trattoria". Both operations are small-scale: thr whole family helps him, but what strikes one most of all is the different philosophies with which he deals with these activities. The restaurant is a point of reference for the purest of local culinary traditions, whereas the winery bears the hallmarks of intelligent and well-thought-out innovation, as the wines presented for tasting this year demonstrate. The first wine in the range to deserve Two Glasses this year is the Privilegia, a red (now in its second vintage) made from cabernet franc - and not rondinella as we had erroneously written - and corvina grapes which have been lightly sun-dried. The barrique-aged wine seems to have married well with the oak. Its color is a not very deep ruby-garnet, but it is charming because of the balance struck between the nose and the palate. The lively and succulent Recioto is perhaps just a bit too sweet, but is undoubtedly the product of outstanding fruit: the aromas are perfectly characteristic, and the palate is full and long. The fruit of the '93 Amarone opens up in an extremely attractive way, although we have the impresison that the wine has suffered a little from its sojourn in wood, instead of gaining in breadth and complexity. The '97 Valpolicella is fresh and eminently quaffable, whereas the Valpolicella Superiore seems to us less exciting.

●	Privilegia '95	🍷🍷	5
●	Recioto della Valpolicella '96	🍷🍷	4
●	Amarone della Valpolicella '93	🍷	5
●	Valpolicella Cl. '97	🍷	2
●	Valpolicella Cl. Sup. '95		3
●	Recioto della Valpolicella '95	🍷 (white)	4

MARANO DI VALPOLICELLA (VR)

Novaia

Via Novaia, 2
37020 Marano di Valpolicella (VR)
tel. 045/7755129

Cesare and Gianpaolo (known as Paolo) Vaona dedicate themselves to their five-hectare estate with the undaunted spirit of true "vignerons": the former looks after the vineyards, the latter runs the cellar. This spirit is a sine qua non, as both have other jobs. However, when Cesare and Paolo have a little spare time on their hands, they almost invariably spend it at their small winery in Marano. Here the grapes, which come from vines that are, on average, fairly old, are vinified; this after a long, slow drying process which takes place in one of the most favorable microclimates in the whole of Valpolicella. The result of this patient work of selection and maturation is a stunning Amarone, which is strong yet refined, with a complex bouquet of outstanding beauty. The dark garnet color contrasts with its fresh aromas of flowers and aromatic herbs, which overlay the juicy fragrance of the still very lively, ripe fruit. The entry on the palate has a lovely elegance and restraint which is thoroughly enjoyable without the wine's ever becoming cloying; the firm and rounded flavor develops on the palate, balanced by a tannic vein, and finishes splendidly. The Vaonas are planting some new vineyards in order to increase their volume a little, as production at present is really too small. The grapes from their younger vines end up, for now, in a pleasant and easy-drinking Valpolicella Superiore.

●	Amarone della Valpolicella '91	🍷🍷	5
●	Valpolicella Sup. '96	🍷	3

MARANO DI VALPOLICELLA (VR)

San Rustico

Via Pozzo, 2
Fraz. Valgatara
37020 Marano di Valpolicella (VR)
tel. 045/7703348

The positive signs we found last year have been amply confirmed. San Rustico steps back into the limelight, bucking the trend of the difficult '94 vintage with a really well-made wine, a modern and elegant Amarone whose qualities are not those of exuberance or muscle-bound structure, but rather of clean readiness. This does not mean that the wine is in any sense feeble or light; instead, it displays a delightful spontaneity and offers delectable taste sensations. Its deep ruby color precedes a nose characterized by sweetness; the palate is well-structured and the finish is long and broad. The '95 Valpolicella Superiore is made in an exemplary manner, and is meaty and mouth-filling; the wine is particularly attractive because of the ripe and spicy tones on the nose, a long way from the tiredness one often finds in this category. The wine is by no means disappointing on the palate either and, although it does not display great length, it does offer clean, well-defined fruit. This '95 Valpolicella has another merit: it does not seem to have been adversely conditioned by the rush for Amarone of that vintage which swept through the zone, leaving many Valpolicellas rather gutless; it is of independent origin and represents an interesting preview of the '95 Amarone rather than its by-product. From the estate's great cru, Il Gaso, we have the '93 Amarone, which only partly lives up to our expectations: though well-modulated and harmonious, it had accustomed us to more intense sensations and emotions. Lastly, the good performance of the '97 Valpolicella is well worth noting: it happily combines inevitable fermentative notes with attractive suggestions of red fruit.

●	Amarone della Valpolicella Cl. '94	🍷🍷	4
●	Valpolicella Cl. Sup. Vigneti del Gaso '95	🍷🍷	3
●	Amarone della Valpolicella Cl. Vigneti del Gaso '93	🍷	5
●	Valpolicella Cl. '97	🍷	2*
●	Amarone della Valpolicella Cl. Vigneti del Gaso '90	🍷🍷 (outline)	5
●	Amarone della Valpolicella Cl. Vigneti del Gaso '91	🍷🍷 (outline)	5
●	Amarone della Valpolicella Cl. '93	🍷 (outline)	4

MEZZANE DI SOTTO (VR)

CORTE SANT'ALDA
VIA CAPOVILLA, 28
LOC. FIOI
37030 MEZZANE DI SOTTO (VR)
TEL. 045/8880006

Marinella Camerani has not just sat back after her prize-winning '90 Amarone, but has let her own style evolve: she has succeeded in overcoming the temptation to let everything, subsequent vintages and her decisions about vinification, be carbon copies of those for that magnificent wine. Instead, she has adopted a new wine-making philosophy that reflects, as far as is possible, her conception of what wine is all about. This is revealed in the '93 Amarone, from which we naturally expected a full structure and the usual warmth of alcohol: in addition to these sensations, we also found notable elegance, which lifts the wine and makes it absolutely delicious. Its color is a deep ruby, and the nose displays really inviting freshness and cleanness, with an excellently integrated oaky tone that gives it added complexity. The evolution of the fruit on the palate does not need to be overwhelming; instead it is gradual, silky and long, and clearly echoes the aromas on the nose. We also tasted the '90 Amarone from the Mithas line, a red which is now fully mature and therefore showing at its absolute best: the fine, overripe aromas give way to delicate fruit on the palate, which is particularly noteworthy for its balance and the elegant persistence of its flavor. The Valpolicella Superiore '95, a juicy foretaste of what the same year's Amarone could be, is big, rich and firm, and, although a little less refined than the wines described above, nonetheless very close to Two Glasses. If the '97 Valpolicella is merely simple and well-made, and therefore somewhat below its usual level, we really enjoyed the ripe fruit of the Valpolicella Superiore '97, which is still maturing in the cellar.

	Wine	Glasses	Price
●	Amarone della Valpolicella '93	🍷🍷	5
●	Amarone della Valpolicella Mithas '90	🍷🍷	6
●	Valpolicella Sup. '95	🍷	4
●	Valpolicella di Mezzane '97		3
●	Amarone della Valpolicella '90	YYY	5
●	Amarone della Valpolicella '92	YY	5
●	Recioto della Valpolicella '94	Y	4
●	Valpolicella Sup. Mithas '94	Y	4

MIANE (TV)

GREGOLETTO
VIA S. MARTINO, 1
FRAZ. PREMAOR
31050 MIANE (TV)
TEL. 0438/970463

We have written on a number of occasions that Gregoletto had the courage, when no one else was doing so, to broaden his range beyond Prosecco and create a very varied selection of wines. So the results of our tastings gave rise to a number of considerations: some wines, which in the past few years had seemed a little below par, performed well, whereas the reds, the star wines in recent years, were not helped by the '96 vintage. In any case, we are convinced that spreading one's efforts over several wines in order to maintain them all at a high level - and not just to offer a number of commercial alternatives - is an exemplary and worthy approach. Let us begin with the Prosecco Extra Dry, which once again successfully offers an almost forgotten traditional style: its color reveals gold highlights and its perlage is very fine; on the nose we find a ripeness accompanied by broad and constantly evolving aromas. On the palate, the attack is soft and the structure mouth-filling. The lively, almost exuberant Prosecco Tranquillo has a very clean succession of yeasty aromas followed by fruit. The Colli di Conegliano, designed to give a sensation of straightforward fresh fruit, is also well-defined if without any great depth. The Cabernet did not repeat last year's performance: it shows rather too much typical herbaceous character on the nose, and is not very long on the palate. The Merlot, on the other hand, seemed a little unknit, whereas the Chardonnay evolves very appealingly in the mouth.

	Wine	Glasses	Price
○	Prosecco di Valdobbiadene Extra Dry	🍷🍷	3*
●	Cabernet '96	🍷	3
○	Chardonnay '97	🍷	3
○	Colli di Conegliano Albio '97	🍷	3
○	Prosecco di Valdobbiadene Tranquillo	🍷	3
●	Merlot '96		3
○	Verdiso '97		3
●	Cabernet '95	YY	3
●	Rosso Gregoletto '93	YY	4

MONTEBELLO (VI)

Domenico Cavazza & F.lli
Via Selva, 22
36054 Montebello (VI)
tel. 0444/649166

When you visit the splendid cellar, recently redone, and consider the huge sums invested in wine-making equipment, you can't help admiring the efforts Cavazza has made over the last few years. The clearly implemented strategy of this winery is to exploit the full potential of its "terroir" and to improve the standard of its vineyards. Thus, alongside simple wines destined for rapid consumption, we find Cavazza's two more representative ranges: Cicogna, from grapes grown in the Colli Berici denomination, and Capitel Santa Libera from the Gambellara DOC. Going on to this year's wines, we give an honorable mention to the correctly-made Gambellara Monte Boccara '97: it is relatively dumb on the nose, and soft on the palate with an almondy note on the finish. Softness is the main characteristic of the '97 whites, in which the ripeness of the fruit outweighs the acidity. However, greater crispness would have benefited both the clean Incrocio Manzoni Capitel Santa Libera and the Sauvignon from the same range. We would have expected to find a more marked personality in the Recioto, which is still a bit green. The '95 vintage reds, however, gave excellent results. The Cabernet Capitel has a herbaceous, spicy nose, and is of medium depth; the tannins are not dominant and the wine is easy to drink because of its fresh acidity. The greater potential of the Cabernet Cicogna can be perceived even from its color: the wine has a complex nose, in which one finds black berry fruits, pepper and a mineral note; on the palate it is full, well-balanced and echoes the sensations on the nose. It was worth waiting for the Merlot Cicogna '95, which turns out to be Cavazza's best wine. Its bouquet is intense and notably complex, with red berry fruits, tobacco, vanilla and menthol notes; the elegant, soft entry on the palate is followed by a full, long flavor.

	Wine	Glasses	Price
●	Colli Berici Cabernet Cicogna '95	▼▼	4
●	Colli Berici Merlot Cicogna '95	▼▼	4
●	Colli Berici Cabernet Capitel S. Libera '95	▼	3
○	Colli Berici Sauvignon Capitel S. Libera '97	▼	2
○	Gambellara Cl. Monte Boccara '97	▼	1
○	Incrocio Manzoni 6.0.13 Capitel S. Libera '97		2
○	Recioto di Gambellara '95		4
●	Colli Berici Cabernet Capitel S. Libera '93	▽▽	3
●	Colli Berici Cabernet Cicogna '94	▽▽	4
●	Colli Berici Cabernet Capitel S. Libera '94	▽	3

MONTEFORTE D'ALPONE (VR)

Roberto Anselmi
Via S. Carlo, 46
37032 Monteforte d'Alpone (VR)
tel. 045/7611488

Roberto Anselmi has succeeded in his efforts to bring out, to the greatest possible degree, the aromas that develop during and immediately after fermentation, enhancing their cleanness and richness so as to make his wine as enjoyable and complex as it is in them to be. The garganega grape is hardly aromatic at all: what we can smell in a Soave comes from the complex chemical relationship of the pulp and skin of the grape in the various phases of vinification. The optimal expression of this process is the noble goal Roberto Anselmi has attained in his constant search for new challenges. His Soave Capitel Foscarino has a faultless, regal demeanor, and its aristocratic style can best be appreciated when its entire gamut of aromas emerges to gratify the taster, allowing him to appreciate the wine's great vitality. When you taste this Soave you note a dry, firm, long-lived style, with a perfect balance between ripeness and freshness. The Recioto, on the other hand, seems to have been made to show the other face of garganega. Its instinctive generosity reflects that of the producer who, in the depth of winter, dedicates himself to making this warm, Mediterranean wine. The amber tone of its color, the rich oriental spiciness from the semi-dried grapes and the marked creaminess of the fragrance add a deep, concentrated harmony to the sweetness of the wine, making it more seductive than ever before: this Recioto fully deserves its Three Glasses. The Realda also showed very well. This cabernet sauvignon-based red has a deep color and a concentrated and mineral nose, with ripe fruit notes in evidence. On the palate, it is mouth-filling, well-balanced and long.

	Wine	Glasses	Price
○	Recioto di Soave I Capitelli '96	▼▼▼	5
○	Soave Cl. Sup. Capitel Croce '96	▼▼	4
○	Soave Cl. Sup. Capitel Foscarino '97	▼▼	4
○	Soave Cl. Sup. San Vincenzo '97	▼▼	3*
●	Realda Cabernet Sauvignon '96	▼▼	4
○	Recioto dei Capitelli '87	▽▽▽	6
○	Recioto dei Capitelli '88	▽▽▽	6
○	Recioto di Soave I Capitelli '93	▽▽▽	6
○	Recioto di Soave I Capitelli '95	▽▽	5
○	Soave Cl. Sup. Capitel Foscarino '96	▽▽	4

MONTEFORTE D'ALPONE (VR)

Ca' Rugate

Via Mezzavilla, 12
Fraz. Brognoligo
37032 Monteforte d'Alpone (VR)
tel. 045/6175082

Harmony on the nose and palate, personality and a precise expression of all their components: these are the salient characteristics of Ca' Rugate's Soaves. There is, however, a particular detail which unites them all, a territorial quality that suggests the excellence of the vineyards and of the grapes themselves: this is a note on the nose which evokes the skin of the garganega grape, a nuance that is slightly verdant but at the same time warm and ripe. This quality is most intensely demonstrated by the Soave from the Monte Fiorentine vineyard, whose captivating nose is composed of fresher, more fragrant aromas and of sweet hints that add to its overall complexity. On the palate, one finds the dense and lively fruit that comes from ripe grapes, and this evolves into a long and corresponding finish. The improvement over last year's version in the standard Soave clearly shows the Tessari brothers' commitment to qualilty: this is a light, lively white, but it is certainly not insipid; indeed, it has surprising depth on the nose and a lively and balanced impact on the palate. Our expectations of the Monte Alto were amply satisfied by a white of remarkable quality. As a result of a judicious use of oak, this rich and full-bodied Soave should prove to be long-lived. This impressively intense and balanced wine clearly shows the two faces of garganega: its elemental juicy freshness and its ripe, solid structure. The '95 harvest also presented the Tessaris with the grapes to make a delicate Recioto, not yet as full of personality as the dry whites, but definitely getting better and better.

O	Soave Cl. Sup. Monte Alto '97	🍷🍷	3*
O	Soave Cl. Sup. '97	🍷🍷	3*
O	Soave Cl. Sup. Monte Fiorentine '97	🍷🍷	3
O	Recioto di Soave La Perlara '95	🍷	4
O	Soave Cl. Sup. Monte Alto '96	🍷🍷🍷	3

MONTEFORTE D'ALPONE (VR)

Fattori & Graney

Via Zoppega, 14
37032 Monteforte d'Alpone (VR)
tel. 045/7460041

One of the most promising wineries in the Soave zone makes its first appearance in the Guide. The Fattori family's production has for years helped boost the base wines of a number of local industrial wineries, improving wines which would otherwise have remained anonymous. The reasons for this success lay in the Fattoris' skill in controlling the various phases of vinification and in the reliable quality of the fruit itself. At a certain point, however, this high-quality as a supplier activity was not enough to satisfy the ambitions of the brothers Giovanni and Antonio, who own a 25-hectare estate just outside the Classico area. Aware that on soil of volcanic origin and at an altitude of 250-300 meters one can obtain really interesting results with garganega, they reduced their yields, identified the most suitable sites on the property and, finally, vinified the individual lots separately. An exemplary Soave has emerged: a white which is able to match up to the best in its category. Its clean straw color indicates the liveliness of the fruit; its aromas are revealed with great elegance and freshness. These volatile delights are not limited to the notes of white flowers and almonds on the nose but are echoed on the palate, where harmony of flavor is central to our enjoyment. The latest technological improvements to the already modern cellar at Terrossa di Roncà and the involvement of Sarah Graney, Antonio's wife, in the work of selection and marketing of the wines bear witness to the Fattoris' desire to pursue an activity which is certainly more demanding than before, but which will no doubt provide far greater rewards.

O	Soave Sup. '97	🍷🍷	3*

MONTEFORTE D'ALPONE (VR)

Sandro e Claudio Gini
Via G. Matteotti, 42
37032 Monteforte d'Alpone (VR)
tel. 045/7611908

Their disarming fragrance, a quality of all Gini Soaves, transforms itself into an exuberant wealth of aromas and flavors which are easy to appreciate but never run-of-the-mill. It takes determination and sensitivity, care and delicacy to combine pleasing fruity spontaneity with rich extract: one must have an intimate knowledge of the fruit at one's disposal and be able to gauge its potential. The objective is not to sacrifice the fragile but decisive balance that is set up between the nose and the palate. This is an intriguing relationship in which the former leads us into the wine and stimulates our expectations with its broad and layered spectrum of aromas; the latter, without any interruption, has to take up this lead, consolidate its characteristics and give added enjoyment by means of its fullness. And this is what we find in the La Froscà and Salvarenza Soaves. The former is open and inviting on the nose, and displays highly attractive, very fresh and succulent fruit on the palate. Gini prevents the malolactic fermentation from taking place, thus leaving all the vitality that garganega can express; at the same time, he does not give up all the structure and complexity his 35-year-old vines provide. La Salvarenza is part of the Froscà vineyard, a strip of pale tufa halfway up the slope with 55- to 60-year-old vines. Gini aims for extreme ripeness in the grapes, so he harvests late; he then barrique-ferments and ages a must which, along with garganega, also contains a little chardonnay. This golden-colored and sumptuously elegant Soave marries perfectly with the oak; on the palate it echoes precisely the aromas on the nose and fills the mouth with beautifully-balanced fruit, enlivened with a touch of acidity. Do not miss out on the standard Soave, one of the best ever produced.

	Wine	Glasses	Price
○	Soave Cl. Sup. La Froscà '97	▼▼▼	3*
●	Pinot Nero Sorai Campo alle More '95	▼▼	5
○	Recioto di Soave Col Foscarin '95	▼▼	5
○	Soave Cl. Sup. Contrada Salvarenza Vecchie Vigne '97	▼▼	4
○	Soave Cl. Superiore '97	▼▼	3*
○	Sauvignon Maciete Fumé '97	▼	4
○	Soave Cl. Sup. Contrada Salvarenza Vecchie Vigne '95	▽▽▽	4
○	Soave Cl. Sup. Contrada Salvarenza Vecchie Vigne '96	▽▽▽	4
○	Recioto di Soave Col Foscarin '93	▽▽	4
○	Recioto di Soave Renobilis '93	▽▽	5
○	Soave Cl. Sup. La Froscà '96	▽▽	3

MONTEFORTE D'ALPONE (VR)

La Cappuccina
Via San Brizio, 125
Fraz. Costalunga
37030 Monteforte d'Alpone (VR)
tel. 045/6175840-6175036

Soave represents the main interest of La Cappuccina, but available space, the quality of their land and their desire to explore the varied potential of the zone have prompted the Tessari family to experiment with other wines. Success has come with a red, the Campo Buri, which is surprising in its intensity and balance: it is a Cabernet Franc whose style goes a long way beyond the often encountered monotonous herbaceous note, since it is characterized by aromatic complexity and depth on the nose. On the palate, the wine claims your attention with the vigor of its tannins, accompanied by unquestionably fine fruit leading to a long finish which vividly echoes the sensations on the nose. This is a wine of extraordinary balance which deserves its Three Glasses. Continuing with the "alternative" wines, the fresh and satisfying Sauvignon also scored well. The standard Soave and the Fontégo are garganega-based wines fermented and aged in stainless steel, and are both of considerable interest. The former demonstrates that just outside the Classico zone, on a light soil in the plain and from a carefully tended vineyard, one can obtain a well-structured white with an enchanting nose and lively flavor. From the Fontégo vineyard comes a white with depth, rich aromas and aging potential. The '96 Soave San Brizio has attained a notable point of maturation thanks to barrique aging and to the addition of 10% of chardonnay; on the nose it expresses varietal charcteristics, with notes of pineapple, hazelnut and pear, while the sweet spiciness of the oak adds extreme elegance. On the palate it displays the length of a fine white wine. Our closing note is on the Recioto Arzìmo, which is silky, rounded and caressing.

	Wine	Glasses	Price
●	Cabernet Franc Campo Buri '95	▼▼▼	4
○	Recioto di Soave Arzìmo '95	▼▼	4
○	Soave Cl. Sup. San Brizio '96	▼▼	4
○	Soave Sup. Fontégo '97	▼▼	3*
○	Soave Sup. '97	▼▼	3*
●	Cabernet Sauvignon Madégo '96	▼	3
○	Sauvignon '97	▼	3

MONTEFORTE D'ALPONE (VR)

UMBERTO PORTINARI

VIA S. STEFANO, 2
FRAZ. BROGNOLIGO
37030 MONTEFORTE D'ALPONE (VR)
TEL. 045/6175087

Portinari's Soaves have a special relationship with the "terroir" from which they come: firstly, because they are a true reflection of the many-faceted vigorousness that is the principal characteristic of the garganega grape; and secondly, because they seem to emerge directly from the country culture which animates these hills. These wines win us over with their healthy rusticity, which never slips into mere boring and monotonous simplicity; they also offer rich and homogeneous fruit on both the nose and palate. Each wine's appearance, bouquet and flavor interreact and mingle with each other; these characteristics take time to express themselves, thus reflecting the production philosophy of Portinari himself, who is not given to rushing. In fact, the shy and controlled initial impression the wines make always gives way to rich and winning sensations. The Soave Albare, made from partially dried grapes, convinced us from the very beginning: it is one of the best Soaves of the vintage and deserves its Three Glasses. The sweet fragrance of ripe grape skins is perfectly matched by the full, warm, deep flavor: it is a concentrated and very well-balanced Soave. The other single-vineyard selection, the Vigna Ronchetto, is made not only from garganega but also from chardonnay and trebbiano. It offers an attractively fresh and agile style, as well as a long and enjoyable finish. Though the Chardonnay '96 is merely lively and correctly made, the Recioto is a pleasant surprise: it has a bright golden color, and a bouquet of great finesse, and on the palate it is broad and sweet, with medium length but extraordinary balance.

	Wine	Glasses	
O	Soave Vigna Albare Doppia Maturazione Ragionata '97	🍷🍷🍷	3*
O	Recioto di Soave '95	🍷🍷	4
O	Soave Cl. Vigna Ronchetto '97	🍷🍷	2*
O	Chardonnay Albare '96	🍷	2
O	Soave Cl. Vigna Ronchetto '96	🍷🍷 (white)	2

MONTEFORTE D'ALPONE (VR)

F.LLI PRA

VIA DELLA FONTANA, 31
37032 MONTEFORTE D'ALPONE (VR)
TEL. 045/7612125

It is difficult to make a wine that's fermented and aged in wood: the process offers occasional encouraging and positive signs and, more often, major disappointments. Apart from selecting and caring for the grapes, one must also have a searching mind, long experience and great patience: these are all gifts which have aided Graziano Pra in making his Soave S. Antonio. If the first vintages were over-oaked or did not benefit from their aging, the last few years have seen clear improvements, which have come to fruition in the '96 vintage. It has given us a rich white wine, golden in appearance and exuberantly redolent of flowers, vanilla, apple and pear. The wine is powerful in its attack on the palate, and then shows a full body and a long finish; it is perhaps a little lacking in elegance, but it's captivating all the same. The very graceful basic Soave with its appealing freshness is perfectly characteristic. It has a delicate straw color, and a fresh nose with developing floral tones; on the palate, it has a lively balance and medium length. The more complete Soave from the Monte Grande vineyard does not show much complexity on the nose, but does offer clear, homogeneous sensations: its nose and palate share a subtle fragrance and show a pleasing correspondence. Only the '96 Recioto did not entirely convince us, so we've decided to wait a year before reviewing it.

	Wine	Glasses	
O	Soave Cl. Sup. S. Antonio '96	🍷🍷	4
O	Soave Cl. Sup. Vigneto Monte Grande '97	🍷🍷	3*
O	Soave Cl. '97	🍷	3

NEGRAR (VR)

Cav. G.B. Bertani
Loc. Novare
Fraz. Arbizzano di Valpolicella
37020 Negrar (VR)
tel. 045/6011211

Bertani is improving the quality of all of its wines: for now, the innovative ones show the best results, whereas for the traditonal wines, because of the length of time before their release, the improvement will come to light only in the future. Emilio Pedron has added to the long-standing staff of the company, in the person of Flavio Peroni; he, along with Paolo Grigolli and Gian Matteo Baldi, will form an efficient team capable of bettering the style of the wines. The most interesting of these is a concentrated Cabernet Sauvignon from a vineyard at the Novare estate. It has an opaque ruby color, and mineral aromas which blend with black berry fruit notes, enriched with hints of leather and coffee; on the palate, the lively and slightly mouth-puckering tannins are contrasted by warm, soft fruit, guaranteeing good evolution of flavor. The surprising Catullo Bianco, made from pinot gris and sauvignon, rises above the profile of a simple white wine with its added succulence and persistence. The more gradual and complex Bianco Le Lave, made from chardonnay and garganega, is improved and given a rounded elegance by its oak aging. The Catullo Rosso, made from cabernet and local varietals, is similarly attractive, and lacks only suitable length. Among the classic Veronese wines, the Soave (which has never been so good) and the Lugana showed well. We also mention the mature and reasonably full-bodied Valpolicella Superiore and the good, clean and lively '97 Valpolicella, whereas the Secco Bertani did not convince us. The much-awaited Amarone '90 merits Two Glasses for its mature, complete style; nevertheless, in view of the quality of the year, we expected greater élan and richness from it.

	Wine	Glasses	Price
●	Amarone della Valpolicella Cl. Sup. '90	🍷🍷	6
○	Le Lave '96	🍷🍷	4
●	Cabernet Sauvignon Villa Novare '96	🍷🍷	5
○	Catullo Bianco '97	🍷🍷	3*
●	Catullo Rosso '95	🍷	3
○	Lugana '97	🍷	2*
○	Soave Cl. '97	🍷	2
●	Valpolicella Cl. '97	🍷	2
●	Valpolicella Sup. '95	🍷	3
●	Amarone della Valpolicella Cl. Sup. '89		6
●	Valpantena Secco Bertani '96		4
●	Amarone della Valpolicella '85	🍸🍸🍸	6

NEGRAR (VR)

Tommaso Bussola
Via Molino Turri, 30
Fraz. S. Peretto
37024 Negrar (VR)
tel. 045/7501740

Tommaso Bussola has an insatiable thirst for experimentation: he has a burning desire to see just how much he can draw out of his beloved Valpolicella area, and especially to know if he will be able to make the wine of his dreams. Bussola maintains that with each passing year he gets closer to his goal, which he may well have fulfilled this year with the release of the extraordinary '95 Recioto which, for the first time, wins him Three Glasses. This wine, from a very successful vintage, has a distinctive aromatic complexity that combines Mediterranean hints of oregano and thyme with more concentrated notes of blackberries and black cherries. The impressive concentration on the palate echoes that of the color; the sweetness melds with the thrust and structure of the fruit; the flavor is powerful and long, with a pleasantly rustic spontaneity. We would have expected greater concentration from the nevertheless well-made and attractive Valpolicella Superiore; it has a bright ruby color and aromas of red berries; the fruit on the palate is delicate and elegant. The '97 Valpolicella is of a similar style, but naturally differs through being fresher and more youthful: it is essentially a light red, but is certainly not lacking in character. The '94 vintage was not a particularly good one for Amarone; Bussola's version displays evolving and mouth-filling fruit but is a long way off from the intensity and persistence of other vintages. On the other hand, there are wines from later years, now resting in the cellar, which will yield much greater rewards.

	Wine	Glasses	Price
●	Recioto della Valpolicella '95	🍷🍷🍷	5
●	Amarone della Valpolicella '94	🍷	5
●	Valpolicella Cl. Sup. '95	🍷	4
●	Valpolicella Cl. '97	🍷	2*
●	Amarone '93	🍸🍸	6
●	Recioto della Valpolicella '94	🍸🍸	5
●	Valpolicella Cl. Sup. '93	🍸	3

NEGRAR (VR)

Cantina Sociale Valpolicella
Via Ca' Salgari, 2
37024 Negrar (VR)
tel. 045/7500070

The wine cooperative of Negrar is a fine example of the good fortune that currently characterizes the Valpolicella wine world. Great quantities of wine are, as usual, being produced, but the standard of the wines of the Cantina, like that of the whole area around Verona, has improved; there is in fact a greater balance between the large scale of certain wineries and the market's demand for quality. In particular, Daniele Accordini and his staff are exercising greater control over the harvest, and convincing the growers who supply them to pick their grapes at the right time, a crucial condition for obtaining excellent final results. The promising outcome of their efforts will only really become clear after some time, but the wines available today are already quite good. The Recioto Vigneti di Moron is possibly even better than the more hyped '95 version, and again got a very high score. It has a notably concentrated ruby-violet color, and an elegant nose with notes of blackberry, hazelnut and pine needles. It is full and rich on the palate, and the sweetness combines well with the considerable presence of tannins which give it balance and length. The Amarone Vigneti di Jago is traditional and satisfying, and is a special selection from the '93 vintage: the '94 Amarone Domini Veneti, on the other hand, is merely satisfactory. The Valpolicella Superiore La Cresta earns One Glass: it has a mature nose and full fruit on the palate. We expected more from the Valpolicella Superiore Vigneti di Torbe, whose good fruit is somewhat overwhelmed by excessive oak, sapping the wine of some of its structure.

Wine	Glasses	Price
● Amarone della Valpolicella Cl. Vigneti di Jago Selezione '93	▼▼	5
● Recioto della Valpolicella Vigneti di Moron '96	▼▼	5
● Amarone della Valpolicella Cl. Dominii Veneti '94	▼	4
● Valpolicella Cl. Sup. La Cresta '95	▼	3
● Valpolicella Cl. Sup. Vigneti di Torbe '95	▼	3
● Recioto della Valpolicella Dominii Veneti '94	▽▽	4
● Recioto della Valpolicella Vigneti di Moron '95	▽▽	4
● Amarone della Valpolicella Cl. Dominii Veneti '93	▽	4

NEGRAR (VR)

Le Ragose
Via Ragose, 1
Fraz. Arbizzano
37024 Negrar (VR)
tel. 045/7513241

To describe the emotions which Le Ragose's Amarone provokes in us we have referred by turns to the soil from which it springs, the spare lines of the hills, the beauty of the Valpolicella zone and the passion of the people who produce it. This year, as never before, the wine communicates clearly its own essence and its own virtues. And this occurred in '94, a year that was anything but good, from which the wine seems, however, to have drawn all the energy it needed. Amarone tends by its very nature to exceed limits, and it does so with an ingenuous exuberance which is also its greatest virtue. Le Ragose's wine shares this intense spontaneity, but wins us over also with its intriguing style; it has a conentrated nose which offers, one after another, floral aromas, peppery nuances and licorice and coffee notes. One finds the same evolution at the basis of its flavor, which is really mouth-filling yet at the same time well-sustained by the acidity and tannins which make it taste lively and modern. This maturity of style not only means that we can enjoy it already, but also that the wine will be able to improve for some time to come. Of the other wines presented this year we point out the successful and elegant Cabernet and the pleasing '97 Valpolicella. The two '95 Valpolicella Superiores were less convincing: they were well-made but a little short on the nose and rather feeble on the palate. No news, on the other hand, about the Reciotos, which have unfortunately been missing from Le Ragose's list for at least three years now.

Wine	Glasses	Price
● Amarone della Valpolicella Cl. '94	▼▼	5
● Cabernet Le Ragose '95	▼▼	4
● Valpolicella Cl. '97	▼	2
● Valpolicella Cl. Sup. Le Sassine '95		3
● Valpolicella Sup. '95		3
● Amarone della Valpolicella Cl. '86	▽▽▽	5
● Amarone della Valpolicella Cl. '88	▽▽▽	5
● Amarone della Valpolicella Cl. '90	▽▽	5
● Amarone della Valpolicella Cl. '91	▽▽	5
● Recioto della Valpolicella '93	▽▽	4
● Cabernet Le Ragose '93	▽	4
● Cabernet Le Ragose '94	▽	4

NEGRAR (VR)

GIUSEPPE QUINTARELLI

VIA CERÈ, 1
37024 NEGRAR (VR)
TEL. 045/7500016

We first became wine lovers thanks to people like Giuseppe Quintarelli. Getting to know Amarone (and everything to do with Valpolicella, the drying of the grapes, the aging of the wines) through his bottles is an indelible memory for many of us. Every time we taste one of his wines, it is as if we were going back in our memories through a thousand such tastings: the intensity, the alcohol and the persistence all remain intact and still constitute today an extremely useful touchstone for quality. The '91 Amarone, protagonist of this year's tastings, demonstrates that Quintarelli faces good and more difficult vintages with equal aplomb: his is a sure hand which governs the fruit in such a way as to make it comform to his desires. In the glass the wine shows its customary hint of forwardness, which does not, however, affect one's appreciation of the wine's notable richness. The compactly emerging aromas are dominated by notes of black cherry, fig and walnut. These sensations linger even more than usual, and lead on into the equally long fruit on the palate, where the alcohol is surprisingly restrained. The other significant wines of the estate will only be released later, so we are unable to review the Amarone Riserva '90 or the Cabernet Alzero, from which we expect the warmth and depth which have always been their hallmark. Quintarelli did everything in his power to produce a good '92 Valpolicella; nevertheless it seemed tired and too forward.

● Amarone della Valpolicella '91	🍷🍷	6
● Valpolicella Sup. '92		4
● Alzero '90	🍷🍷🍷	6
● Amarone della Valpolicella Ris. '83	🍷🍷🍷	6
● Amarone della Valpolicella Ris. '85	🍷🍷🍷	6
● Amarone della Valpolicella '84	🍷🍷🍷	6
● Amarone della Valpolicella '86	🍷🍷🍷	6
● Alzero '91	🍷🍷	6
● Amarone della Valpolicella '90	🍷🍷	6

NEGRAR (VR)

VIVIANI

VIA MAZZANO, 8
37024 NEGRAR (VR)
TEL. 045/7500286

This small estate devotes equal attention to its Amarone and its Recioto: if last year the latter was the star wine of the range presented, in the '99 Guide we should like to tell you about two very particular Amarones. They are both from the '93 vintage which, as time goes on, is providing some very pleasant surprises. For the Amarone Casa dei Bepi, Claudio Viviani's signature wine, he has used a different selection of grapes and a different method of drying; also, aging takes place in new barriques. The wine, a power-packed red, displays its strong character starting with its deep garnet color; the nose offers fruity notes, made sweeter by the vanilla of the oak; the fruit fills the mouth; the tannins are well-integrated and guarantee a good balance with the meaty, attractive fruit. The other Amarone is an Ammandorlato, that is a wine made from semi-dried grapes in which not all the sugars have been turned into alcohol: it is therefore neither as sweet as a Recioto, nor as dry as an Amarone. In addition to its intense color, it yields broad and elegant aromas in which we can identify flowers and aromatic herbs; the fruit has an uncloying medium-sweet style, and it evolves in a delicious, unexpectedly gradual way. We think that drinking it with a mature pecorino cheese would best show off its mouth-filling roundness. The '96 Valpolicella offers a slightly warmer style than the average, and it amply deserves our One Glass rating. We do think, however, that Viviani's wines have the potential to improve quite a bit more in the future.

● Amarone della Valpolicella Cl. La Casa dei Bepi '93	🍷🍷	6
● Amarone della Valpolicella Cl. Ammandorlato '93	🍷	5
● Valpolicella Cl. '97	🍷	2*
● Amarone della Valpolicella Cl. '90	🍷🍷	5
● Amarone della Valpolicella Cl. '91	🍷🍷	5
● Recioto della Valpolicella La Mandrela '93	🍷🍷	5
● Recioto della Valpolicella '94	🍷	4
● Valpolicella Sup. '94	🍷	3

NERVESA DELLA BATTAGLIA (TV)

SERAFINI & VIDOTTO
VIA ARDITI, 1
31040 NERVESA DELLA BATTAGLIA (TV)
TEL. 0422/773281

The Rosso dell'Abazia '96 springs from the happy combination of perfect ripe grapes and Francesco Serafini's great sensitivity as a wine-maker. The result is therefore the fruit of an unusually happy marriage between human ability and the power of nature. Its color is deep and opaque, almost reminiscent of the bluish-violet shades of the grape skins; the seductive, warm nose expresses the perfect integration between fruit and oak; on the palate it is well-balanced and mouth-filling, representing as it does the very best that the Marca Trevigiana's top vineyards can produce. Thus the Rosso dell'Abazia shows once again this year that it is one of the best reds from the Veneto and indeed from Italy altogether, and it again earns our highest rating. But its long list of Three Glass awards should not make you think that it's the same old stuff, year in and year out; Francesco Serafini and Antonello Vidotto have, with the '96 vintage, gone beyond the already outstanding versions of previous years. The intense and determined passion of these "vignerons" has produced surprising effects in the Pinot Nero '96 too; this wine, with its mature, inviting and spicy bouquet, offers on the palate, by contrast, a dynamic vitality and a development of the taste that is sinewy and captivatingly drinkable. Serafini and Vidotto had almost decided to give up making the Prosecco and this wine has now mocked them by yielding its best vintage yet. It is the exact antithesis of the Phigaia After the Red, which is shy, refined, and, as always, ready to remind us that its place is "after the rosso" and that it knows it.

	Wine	Glasses	Price
●	Il Rosso dell'Abazia '96	🍷🍷🍷	5
●	Phigaia After the Red '96	🍷🍷	4
●	Pinot Nero '96	🍷🍷	5
○	Prosecco del Montello	🍷🍷	3*
○	Il Bianco dell'Abazia '97	🍷	4
●	Il Rosso dell'Abazia '93	🍷🍷🍷 (previous)	5
●	Il Rosso dell'Abazia '94	🍷🍷🍷 (previous)	5
●	Il Rosso dell'Abazia '95	🍷🍷🍷 (previous)	5
●	Il Rosso dell'Abazia '92	🍷🍷 (previous)	5
●	Phigaia After the Red '95	🍷🍷 (previous)	4

PESCHIERA DEL GARDA (VR)

OTTELLA
LOC. OTTELLA, 1
FRAZ. S. BENEDETTO DI LUGANA
37019 PESCHIERA DEL GARDA (VR)
TEL. 045/7551950

Francesco Montresor has every reason to be satisfied by his budding career as a wine producer; his decision to give up his legal career in order to dedicate himself to the family estate was right on the mark; indeed he has restored the white Lugana from the province of Verona to its old glory. But his satisfaction and his encouraging optimism hid a secret obsession: he lacked a red wine! Every white wine producer seeks a ne plus ultra against which to measure himself. Actually, Francesco has been producing a red for some years now, and has even succeeded occasionally in coming up with an interesting wine: never before, though, has he made such a convincing one as this year's. It is as if he had reached a turning point from which he can set off again to meet a new challenge. The Campo Sireso '96 is a really remarkable red: it has a supple yet solid style, and is complete, concentrated and dynamic; it represents an intriguing halfway house between the modern and international aspects provided by the merlot and the cabernet and the characteristic local softness of the corvina and croatina. The wine, which we believe will age well, has gone beyond the rustic completeness of the other vintages, taking on a silky depth. Returning to the estate's main wines, we point out the very successful performance of the two Luganas. At the time time of our tastings we preferred the standard version, a paradigm of pleasurable drinking, whereas the single-vineyard Le Creete is a more complex wine that still needs to open up. The Ottella estate's range also includes a lighter red, which nevertheless reveals an enchanting fragrance and succulent body.

	Wine	Glasses	Price
●	Campo Sireso '96	🍷🍷	4
○	Lugana '97	🍷🍷	2*
○	Lugana Le Creete '97	🍷	3
●	Rosso Ottella '96	🍷	2*
●	Campo Sireso '95	🍷🍷 (previous)	3

PESCHIERA DEL GARDA (VR)

ZENATO
VIA S. BENEDETTO, 8
FRAZ. S. BENEDETTO DI LUGANA
37019 PESCHIERA DEL GARDA (VR)
TEL. 045/7550300

Zenato does honor to the Three Glasses won last year with a really first-class range of wines this time. Although its Amarone Riserva '90 does not make it to the top, it came awfully close. Its color is extraordinarily concentrated; the well-defined bouquet opens in an enchanting progression with lively fruit aromas and a marked vanilla note. The palate, without the breadth of the '88, nevertheless evolves in a positive, intense and persistent manner. The other wine with a Sergio Zenato label is a barrel-aged Lugana: from the '96 vintage comes a fat, deep white, still perhaps a little too noticeably oaked, but with unusual fullness for its type; its aromas of apple and pear are evident nonetheless, and on the palate too one is aware of the fine, clean balance between alcohol and acidity. The Lugana San Benedetto is again a quaffable white, but it shows a surprising vigor on the palate. The Cabernet Sauvignon returns to the level of excellence which had marked it out a few years ago: Zenato aims to turn it into a really important red, and he probably will. For the moment, it offers an attractive purity: it has a lively color, and an invitingly complex nose (with red berry fruit notes and hints of spice); in the mouth, it is delicate on entry, but the fruit soon becomes more intense, quite dominating the structure of the wine. The Valpolicella Superiore Ripassa is beautifully made, representing an intelligent way of interpreting a method of refermenting on the pomace of the Recioto: the wine has taken on a greater complexity and has not lost its elegant fragrance.

	Wine	Glasses	Price
●	Amarone della Valpolicella Sergio Zenato Ris. '90	🍷🍷	6
●	Cabernet Sauvignon S. Cristina '95	🍷🍷	4
○	Lugana Sergio Zenato '96	🍷🍷	4
●	Valpolicella Cl. Sup. Ripassa '95	🍷🍷	3
○	Chardonnay Ris. '96	🍷	4
○	Lugana S. Cristina Vigneto Massoni '97	🍷	3
○	Lugana San Benedetto '97	🍷	3
●	Valpolicella Cl. Sup. Il Sole '95		2
●	Amarone della Valpolicella Cl. Sergio Zenato '88	🍸🍸🍸	6
●	Amarone della Valpolicella '90	🍸🍸	4
●	Amarone della Valpolicella '91	🍸🍸	4

PRAMAGGIORE (VE)

RUSSOLO
VIA LIBERTÀ, 36
30020 PRAMAGGIORE (VE)
TEL. 0421/799087

Russolo's decision to put off the release of his red wines, which shows a laudable consideration for his customers, did not have an adverse effect on his overall results at our tastings: his whites really excelled. The winery is located at Pramaggiore, but the grapes come from his estate in the Grave zone, at San Quirino del Friuli. Here the vineyards have been reorganized and are finally yielding the desired results. So, the Tocai rates Two Glasses thanks to its rich and inviting aromas and a palate that combines succulent fruit, liveliness and depth: this is a wine that is delicious now but should also evolve well in the bottle. The nose of the Sauvignon is green and exotic, with admirable aromatic persistence and tightness on the palate. Another wine that doesn't let you down is the Müller Thurgau, and Russolo is one of the few growers who devote considerable attention to producing it. The color has evident hints of green; the nose is floral and very lightly balsamic, while the fruit is remarkably forceful, with excellent balance tbetween extract and acidity. The Malvasia Istriana '97 surprised us with its delectable balance: the success of this wine despite the difficulties inherent in producing it bears witness to the overall quality of the vintage. If the Pinot Grigio and Pinot Bianco only gained honorable mentions, the Chardonnay closes the ranks of the wines aged in stainless steel with its customary stylish aromas, balance and length on the palate. Of the two wines aged in oak we draw your attention to the Sauvignon which, even within the simple style of the '96 vintage, put up a pretty good show.

	Wine	Glasses	Price
○	Friuli Grave Sauvignon Ronco Calaj '97	🍷🍷	3*
○	Friuli Grave Tocai Ronco Calaj '97	🍷🍷	3*
○	Müller Thurgau Mussignaz '97	🍷🍷	3*
○	Friuli Grave Chardonnay Ronco Calaj '97	🍷	3
○	Malvasia Istriana '97	🍷	3
○	Friuli Grave Sauvignon I Legni '96	🍷	4
○	Friuli Grave Chardonnay I Legni '96		4
○	Friuli Grave Pinot Bianco '97		3
○	Friuli Grave Pinot Grigio '97		3
●	Friuli Grave Merlot I Legni '95	🍸🍸	4
●	Friuli Grave Cabernet I Legni '95	🍸	4

Aleardo Ferrari

Via Giare, 15
Fraz. Gargagnago
37010 S. Ambrogio di Valpolicella (VR)
tel. 045/7701379

In last year's Guide we wrote that the recent string of poor vintages had had quite an adverse effect on the wines of Aleardo Ferrari, stripping them of the character and personality which they had displayed for some time. The wines presented this year, though not from particularly propitious vintages, nevertheless did very well. The one we liked best of all was the '94 Amarone, a model of cleanness and elegance, in which Ferrari has also skillfully brought out a well-modulated richness. Its color is a medium-deep garnet; the bouquet opens up to display the characteristic notes of cherries in brandy and chocolate; the palate reveals a satisfying balance and, even though the finish is not especially long, the fruit leaves a really delicious aftertaste. In the wake of a difficult year like '94, the winery has had to deal with an even trickier vintage, '96, from which we have a direct Recioto, rich in color and red fruit aromas, but perhaps a little too simple in its evolution on the palate; it is, at any rate, another good example of an honest and eminently drinkable wine. With the Valpolicella '97 Ferrari has fully succeeded in his attempt to make a youthful, succulent red. This wine is deeply colored, and displays fruity rather than heady aromas which are then echoed on the palate and sustain the wine's easy, supple structure. The '95 Valpolicella Superiore is sound; it has an intriguing savory flavor but is, on the whole, a bit too straightforward.

●	Amarone della Valpolicella Cl. '94	🍷🍷	5
●	Recioto della Valpolicella '96	🍷	4
●	Valpolicella Cl. '97	🍷	1*
●	Valpolicella Cl. Sup. '95		3
●	Amarone della Valpolicella '93	🍸	5
●	Pelara '96	🍸	2

S. AMBROGIO DI VALPOLICELLA (VR)

Masi

Via Monteleone
Fraz. Gargagnago
37010 S. Ambrogio di Valpolicella (VR)
tel. 045/6800588

Many of Masi's wines are worthy of mention for their character and intensity, but before going into greater detail there is a misunderstanding to be cleared up. Conti Serego Alighieri, which we merely thought to be a separate lable of Sandro Boscaini's winery, is in fact a separate and independent estate whose wines are bottled and distributed by Masi. We begin our report with Count Alvise's white wine (the Bianco Serego Alighieri '97), made from garganega and sauvignon, which is enjoyable and lively, with a herbaceous, tangy nose; it is not especially long on the palate, but offers a mouth-filling progression of juicy flavors. The '91 Amarone Vajo Armaron is a perfect example of the traditional style, and is noteworthy for its particularly broad nose which mingles mature tones with fresher notes, and for its elegant fruit on the palate. The Recioto is less exciting than usual, too straightforward and up-front really to stand out from the pack. So, now for the Masi wines. The '93 Amarone Campolongo di Torbe displays richness, depth and length in sufficient measure to saunter off with Three Glasses; this wine possesses authority but also such finesse that it can be considered a paradigm of elegance. The Osar, too, is very good: this is a blend of oseletta and corvina released for the first time. Its color is bright and deep in tone; the nose reveals notes of preserves and vanilla, while its flavor is warm, lively and long, underpinned by a subtle tannic texture. Two vintages of Campofiorin were presented: the '94 was better, more positive, vigorous and persistent than the '95. The Soave is an improvement on past versions, and the Bardolino is again very satisfying. The '94 Amarone does not earn more than an honorable mention, whereas the '95 is not a blockbuster, but makes pleasant drinking.

●	Amarone della Valpolicella Cl. Campolongo di Torbe '93	🍷🍷🍷	6
●	Amarone della Valpolicella Cl. Serego Alighieri Vajo Armaron '91	🍷🍷	6
○	Bianco Serego Alighieri '97	🍷🍷	3
●	Campofiorin Ripasso '94	🍷🍷	4
●	Osar '95	🍷🍷	4
●	Amarone della Valpolicella Cl. '95	🍷	5
●	Bardolino Cl. La Vegrona '97	🍷	3
●	Campofiorin Ripasso '95	🍷	4
●	Recioto della Valpolicella Serego Alighieri Casal dei Ronchi '95	🍷	6
○	Soave Cl. Sup. Colbaraca '97	🍷	3
●	Toar '94	🍷	4
●	Amarone della Valpolicella Cl. '94		5

S. BONIFACIO (VR)

Giuseppe Inama

Via IV Novembre, 1
37047 S. Bonifacio (VR)
tel. 045/6101411

It is not one of any producer's main intentions to provoke a heated debate in his or her wine-making zone; however, when a winegrower chooses a new path, it implies opening up to question the very style of the wine he is making and the culture and traditions that lie behind it. Stefano Inama has stimulated an open debate about Soave and the results are clear for all to see: his winery has made great forward strides and this grower's colleagues, who have been making important changes, albeit in a rather quieter way, for some time, have, as it were, come out into the open, declaring forcefully the way in which they conceive of Verona's primary white wine. The estate's two premium Soaves, the Du Lot and the Vigneti di Foscarino, stand out not only for their barrique-aging, but also because of other peculiarities such as the extreme ripeness of the grapes, their concentration, and their particular softness on the nose. Moreover, maceration on the skins gives the palate an incisive density which in turn brings out a flavor reminiscent of the rustic power of white wines of a bygone age. If the Vigneti di Foscarino shows a muscular structure and warm, mouth-filling fruit, the Du Lot displays a more gradual style that wins us over in a slightly more subtle way. We shall have to write about Inama's other passion, his Sauvignon, next year, since '97 is a vintage that requires longer aging, both for the standard Vulcaia which is kept in stainless steel and the oak-aged Fumé. The two Chardonnays are both very well made indeed: the version aged in stainless steel is more straightforward and quaffable; the barrique-aged wine called Campo dei Tovi is warm, succulent and long. The only slight disappointment from this estate is the basic Soave, which does not yet reveal sufficient character.

	Wine	Glasses	Price
○	Chardonnay '97	🍷🍷	3*
○	Chardonnay Campo dei Tovi '97	🍷🍷	5
○	Soave Cl. Sup. Vigneti di Foscarino '97	🍷🍷	4
○	Soave Cl. Sup. Vigneto Du Lot '97	🍷🍷	5
○	Soave Cl. Sup. Vin Soave '97	🍷	3
○	Sauvignon Vulcaia Fumé '96	🍸🍸🍸	4
○	Soave Cl. Sup. Vigneto Du Lot '96	🍸🍸🍸	4
○	Soave Cl. Sup. Vigneti di Foscarino '96	🍸🍸	4

S. FIOR (TV)

Masottina

Via Bradolini, 54
Loc. Castello di Roganzuolo
31010 S. Fior (TV)
tel. 0438/400775

Masottina was started up in the period immediately following the Second World War by Epifanio Dal Bianco and his brothers: since then, a lot of water has flowed under the bridge (and wine has flowed from the cellars). Masottina's wines have undergone a constant process of evolution, and are now quite successful. Though it is difficult to combine quantity with quality, today the winery produces over two million bottles a year, all at a praiseworthy level of quality. This is due to the skilled management of Masottina, which is controlled personally by the sons of the head of the clan: Renzo in the vineyards and Adriano and Valerio in the cellar. Vinification is carefully carried out under the expert guidance of Marzio Pol, and it is he who has, in recent years, helped realize the Dal Biancos' aspirations. One of the cardinal points of this change is the adoption of a more rigorous system of vineyard husbandry, with a drastic reduction in the yield per vine. The first wine to emerge, a white Incrocio Manzoni of considerable breadth, shows well-defined floral aromas; its concentrated and lively fruit evolves well on the palate, and finishes in crescendo. The Prosecco Extra Dry offers a rare fullness and a soft elegance, revealing not only fruit of excellent quality, but also state-of-the-art sparkling wine production methods. Though easy to drink, the Prosecco Frizzante expresses surprising personality and succeeds in combining this wine's typical immediacy with fruit of a certain power and depth. The Spumante Brut and the Colli di Conegliano Bianco are both very well made; however, the latter should improve even further in the future. The Pino Bianco and the Cabernet Franc are correct, but lacking in definition.

	Wine	Glasses	Price
○	Incrocio Manzoni 6.0.13 '97	🍷🍷	3*
○	Prosecco di Conegliano Extra Dry	🍷🍷	3
●	Colli di Conegliano Bianco '97	🍷	3
○	Prosecco di Conegliano Frizzante	🍷	2
○	Spumante Brut	🍷	3
●	Grave del Friuli Cabernet Franc '96		3
○	Piave Pinot Bianco '97		3

S. GERMANO DEI BERICI (VI)

Villa dal Ferro - Lazzarini

Via Chiesa, 23
36040 S. Germano dei Berici (VI)
tel. 0444/868025

The Lazzarini sisters' winery once again merits its own full listing, after a few years in which the wines seemed to have gone into a sort of hibernation. The renaissance of the winery began with the arrival of the top-flight oenological consultant Donato Lanati, and positive results followed almost immediately. Wine lovers have always known Villa dal Ferro for a Merlot, the Campo del Lago, whose principal characteristics were its breadth and opulence; today, we have yet to return to the great heights of yore, but the winery, aware that oenology has changed a good deal since the '70s, has started to give this wine a new style. The color of the '95 version is a medium deep ruby; the nose displays notes of black cherry, cinnamon and coffee; on the palate, it shows the usual softness, and the fruit is expansive rather than authentically deep. It is an elegant wine with surprisingly good length and it has the potential to become more complex on the nose with time. In the Cabernet '94, a wine which has, on the other hand, already reached an optimum state of maturity, the herbaceous note which has always characterized its bouquet finds the support of red fruit aromas as well as attractive floral tones. The entry on the palate is positive, the tannins make a clear contribution and the finish is satisfyingly long. The Pinot Bianco stands out amongst the whites. It is no longer merely neutral and correct, as it has been over the last few years, but is gaining in personality: its aromas are interestingly varied, while its flavor is still dominated by an acidulous vein. The Riesling is lighter, though it does not lack zest.

	Wine	Rating	Price
●	Colli Berici Cabernet Le Rive Rosse '94	🍷🍷	3*
●	Colli Berici Merlot Campo del Lago '95	🍷🍷	4
○	Riesling Renano Busa Calcara '97	🍷🍷	3
○	Colli Berici Pinot Bianco del Rocolo '97	🍷	3

S. PIETRO DI FELETTO (TV)

Bepin de Eto

Via Colle, 32/a
31020 S. Pietro di Feletto (TV)
tel. 0438/486877

The enthusiasm with which Ettore Ceschin and his consultant oenologist Marzio Pol are dedicating themselves to their new project (to produce a great red which will give added luster to the winery and at the same time demonstrate the great potential of the zone) is praiseworthy. This wine, which comes within the scope of the Colli di Conegliano denomination, is made form merlot, cabernet franc, cabernet sauvignon and marzemino, all grown with the aim of obtaining an excellent wine: hence a high density of vines per hectares, low yield per vine and thinning of the bunches. The wine is fermented in new barriques, in which it is also aged for almost 18 months, and then undergoes a brief period of bottle aging before being released. It has remarkable structure and balance on the palate, fully satisfying the expectations aroused by the great concentration of its color; the rich bouquet hints at an enticing complexity in the future: there are already aromas of blackberry, black cherry and sweet spice. The Colli di Conegliano Bianco reveals the same qualities of intensity and character: herbaceous, floral and with a lively evolution of succulent fruit, it has the rare ability to reveal the grapes from which it is made while maintaining an attractively supple and homogeneous style. The winery's successful performance this year is completed by the admirable Incrocio Manzoni 6.0.13, with its immediate yet elegantly aromatic style. Its long, full flavor makes it the best of its type that we tasted. We did not find any particularly marked personality in the three decent versions of Prosecco, but they were certainly not lacking in balance or clarity. The Cabernet is typically varietal and easy, while the well-made Novello is a fine example of its type.

	Wine	Rating	Price
○	Colli di Conegliano Bianco Il Greccio '96	🍷🍷	2*
●	Colli di Conegliano Rosso '96	🍷🍷	4
○	Incrocio Manzoni 6.0.13 '97	🍷🍷	2*
●	Cabernet '97	🍷	1*
○	Prosecco di Conegliano Extra Dry	🍷	2
○	Prosecco di Conegliano Frizzante	🍷	1*
○	Prosecco di Conegliano Tranquillo '97	🍷	1*

S. PIETRO IN CARIANO (VR)

Stefano Accordini

Via Alberto Bolla, 9
Fraz. Pedemonte
37029 S. Pietro in Cariano (VR)
tel. 045/7701733

The '94 vintage did not do much to help the Accordini family repeat their splendid performance of last year. In spite of this, and in spite of the fact that they did not present an Amarone Il Fornetto (the '93 of which won Three Glasses last year), their overall result is very good. The winery has shown maturity in its quality-led decisions: after passing though a difficult period without suffering too many ill effects, it is now getting ready to make the most of the great potential which is currently maturing in the cellars. The '94 Amarone is the result of very rigorous selection (only a small part of the total production was eventually bottled) and it represents a blueprint for modern Amarone. Its color is a bright medium-deep ruby, while on the nose one finds above all a satisfying cleanness, an indication of the care taken during the various phases of the wine-making process. Its aromas of cherries macerated in alcohol (with floral hints) are echoed on the palate, where we find moderate alcoholic warmth, adequately structured fruit, and a really satisfying balance of the wine's various components. Although the '96 vintage was not especially successful in Valpolicella, Stefano and Tiziano Accordini managed once again to come up with a good wine. Their Recioto offers less depth and exuberance than the '95, but it nevertheless has a rich, varied nose and good fruit on the palate; only the sweetness needs to become better integrated. The tightness and weight of the garganega-based Passito Bricco delle Bessole are notable; it has a concentrated, mature color and expansive aromas of preserves and spices, and it offers a forceful evolution on the palate. The two Valpolicellas are not yet totally convincing and deserve slightly more care and attention.

●	Amarone della Valpolicella Cl. Acinatico '94	🍷🍷	5
○	Passito Bricco delle Bessole '96	🍷🍷	4
●	Recioto della Valpolicella Acinatico '96	🍷🍷	4
●	Valpolicella Cl. '97		2
●	Valpolicella Cl. Sup. '96		3
●	Amarone della Valpolicella Cl. Vigneto Il Fornetto '93	🍸🍸🍸	5
●	Amarone della Valpolicella Cl. Acinatico '91	🍸🍸	4
●	Amarone della Valpolicella Cl. Acinatico '93	🍸🍸	5
○	Passito Bricco delle Bessole '95	🍸🍸	4

S. PIETRO IN CARIANO (VR)

Lorenzo Begali

Fraz. Cengia di Negarine, 10
37029 S. Pietro in Cariano (VR)
tel. 045/7725148

Cengia, a little hamlet near San Pietro in Cariano, lies almost hidden halfway up the side of a hill which is renowned for giving great grapes for Recioto. We are not talking only about sugar concentration, but also about aromas, balance and length. A site with this sort of potential deserves a grower who is committed to keeping its fruit from being diluted, in vinification, by inferior grapes. Lorenzo Begali has been working at it for five years; inspired by the magic moment the zone is enjoying, he has started bottling his own wines and is bringing his small winery up to date, as well as purchasing a few more good vineyards. He already has a recognizable style: great power, even at the cost of finesse, and an exuberant profusion of aromas and flavors which encapsulate all the warmth of the Valpolicella zone. The Recioto is sweet, mouth-filling and structured; black berries are not the only notes of the bouquet, whose richness is increased by aromas of hazelnut, vanilla and cocoa. If the Recioto is relatively (indeed almost disarmingly) easy to drink, Begali's Amarone evolves with mature complexity, displaying aromas reminiscent of walnut, fig and licorice. On the palate, the pleasingly tightly knit tannins are perfectly balanced by the lovely deep fruit. When this estate's wines start to show greater elegance Begali's fantastic grapes will be all the more enjoyable. In the summer of 1997 his vineyards were badly hurt by hail: hence he will be releasing only a limited number of bottles of Amarone and Recioto.

●	Amarone della Valpolicella Cl. '93	🍷🍷	5
●	Recioto della Valpolicella '96	🍷🍷	5
●	Amarone della Valpolicella Cl. '92	🍸🍸	4
●	Recioto della Valpolicella '95	🍸🍸	4
●	Valpolicella Cl. '96	🍸	1

Brigaldara

Via Brigaldara, 20
Fraz. S. Floriano
37029 S. Pietro in Cariano (VR)
tel. 045/7701055

This estate, which has only just finished a complete re-structuring of its vineyards - a choice it was more or less forced to make, but which will definitely have a positive effect on its future wines – has already presented an excellent range. From now on Stefano Cesari will be able to harvest grapes from nearly all of his vineyard holdings and will therefore have a greater choice of fruit to select from. The '93 Amarone, though not yet a product of the process of renewal, starts off this positive period with a really successful performance, showing just the right amount of maturity but also good aging potential. Its color is a medium-deep garnet; its nose opens up slowly, yielding aromas which are initially not very well-defined, but which gradually offer ever clearer notes of sour cherry, cocoa and spice; the wine shows at its best on the palate, with its rich, mouth-filling harmony and excellent aromatic length. Another pleasant surprise is the Garganega: this white has lost the rustic character which it once had, now expressing its undoubted potential in supple and extremely attractive fruit. It is a fresh, youthful wine, but with a rich, decided character as well. Il Vegro is a correct example of a traditional Valpolicella Superiore, but we would have expected a bit more from it, especially since it is the '95 version, and also because once upon a time it had a very different intensity; in any case, it is a delicate, mature red. We shall be providing news of the eagerly awaited '95 Recioto, which is currently maturing, in next year's Guide.

	Wine	Glasses	Price
●	Amarone della Valpolicella Cl. '93	🍷🍷	5
○	Garda Garganega '97	🍷	2*
●	Valpolicella Cl. Sup. Il Vegro '95	🍷	3
●	Amarone della Valpolicella Cl. '90	🍷🍷 (white)	4
●	Recioto della Valpolicella '93	🍷🍷 (white)	5
●	Amarone della Valpolicella Cl. '91	🍷 (white)	5
●	Recioto della Valpolicella '94	🍷 (white)	5

Luigi Brunelli

Via Cariano, 10
37029 S. Pietro in Cariano (VR)
tel. 045/7701118

Luigi Brunelli's Amarone is once again this year a model of breeding and power, as well as an excellent representative of the quality of the '95 vintage and of the impeccable planning and wine-making behind its successful execution. Brunelli has a sort of veneration for Amarone: you can tell it from the way he talks about it, from the way he looks after it, and also from the difference between its quality and that of his other wines. The '95 has a lively dense color; on the warm and seductive nose we find a gamut of well-defined yet mature and elegant aromas; on the palate it displays deep creamy fruit and good balance between the firm tannins and the softness provided by the alcohol. If Brunelli has, in the past, occasionally released his top wine too early - in order to meet pressing market demand - we think that this time he has chosen just the right moment: you can start enjoying it immediately, but it undoubtedly also has a glowing future ahead of it. Of Brunelli's other wines, we noted a slight improvement in the Valpolicellas: the Superiore offers pleasantly youthful sensations, whereas the Pa' Riondo version is for those who like a traditional warm style. The '96 vintage seems to have had a more marked effect on the Recioto: a simple sweetness is the main characteristic of a wine that, in good years, has offered greater complexity. The straighforward '94 Valpolicella and the white Pa' Riondo, made from garganega, are worthy of mention.

	Wine	Glasses	Price
●	Amarone della Valpolicella Cl. '95	🍷🍷	5
●	Recioto della Valpolicella '96	🍷	4
●	Valpolicella Cl. Sup. '96	🍷	1*
●	Valpolicella Cl. Sup. Pa' Riondo '96	🍷	3
○	Pa' Riondo Bianco '97		2
●	Valpolicella Cl. '97		1
●	Amarone della Valpolicella Cl. '93	🍷🍷 (white)	5
●	Amarone della Valpolicella Cl. Corte Cariano '90	🍷🍷 (white)	5
●	Amarone della Valpolicella Cl. '94	🍷 (white)	5
●	Recioto della Valpolicella '95	🍷 (white)	4
●	Recioto della Valpolicella Corte Cariano '95	🍷 (white)	4

 S. PIETRO IN CARIANO (VR)

Angelo Nicolis e Figli

Via di Villa Girardi, 29
37029 S. Pietro in Cariano (VR)
tel. 045/7701261

Beppe Nicolis, one of the brightest (and most surprising) stars of this new edition of the Guide, is on the right road in his bid to make his wines stand out from the crowd. He has succeeded by first of all convincing his family to follow him along a difficult path - but one which promises great satisfaction - and finally by drawing up a very precise blueprint for his top wines (and not just letting them come about because circumstances were favorable). This is demonstrated by the standard '93 Amarone: this wine, a model of elegance and warmth, comes from a good vintage, but one that was not easy to handle. Its bouquet is made up of vivid dark cherry and red currant notes intermingled with sweet nuances of hazelnut and cinnamon. The palate offers a successful balance between dense fruit and tannins; it does not have great structure, but it is mouth-filling. The vigorous and strong Amarone Ambrosan is so rich that its nose does not open up straightaway; its dark opacity and succulent fruit on the palate will more than satisfy those who love concentration and depth; refined aromas are also evident on the finish, and this delightful aspect helped push this wine, deservedly, over our Three Glass threshold. The Valpolicella Superiore Seccal does not have great length but it shows its usual mature style. The winery's Lake Garda wines showed well, while the youthful Valpolicella could do with a bit of fine-tuning. The Recioto, from which we could not have expected last year's spectacular performace, drew sufficient good fruit from the '96 vintage to offer a simple but pleasant profile.

	Wine	Glasses	Price
●	Amarone della Valpolicella Cl. Ambrosan '93	🍷🍷🍷	5
●	Amarone della Valpolicella Cl. '93	🍷🍷	4
⊙	Bardolino Cl. Chiaretto '97	🍷	2*
●	Bardolino Cl. '97	🍷	2*
○	Garda Chardonnay '97	🍷	2*
●	Recioto della Valpolicella '96	🍷	5
●	Valpolicella Sup. Seccal '95	🍷	4
●	Amarone della Valpolicella Cl. '91	🍷🍷 (outline)	5
●	Amarone della Valpolicella Cl. Ambrosan '90	🍷🍷 (outline)	5
●	Recioto della Valpolicella '94	🍷🍷 (outline)	4
●	Recioto della Valpolicella '95	🍷🍷 (outline)	4

Santa Sofia

Via Ca' Dedé, 61
Fraz. Pedemonte
37020 S. Pietro in Cariano (VR)
tel. 045/7701074

The Amarone is back to being Santa Sofia's best wine. Last year the reds had merely marked time, leaving the stage open to the various Custozas and Soaves produced by the winery: it was therefore high time for a red to emerge and show the result of the efforts to improve quality that the Begoni family is making (especially for its Valpolicella wines). If the simpler wines do not yet reveal the effects of this care, the '93 Amarone Gioé wins us over completely: traditional and powerful in character, it has a good, concentrated color; its nose displays the classic notes of fruit macerated in alcohol together with spicy, mature tones. A firm attack is followed by a tight progression on the palate, where the alcohol is quite marked but should integrate well with the passage of time. Of the two Valpolicellas presented we preferred the '97, which is certainly more straightforward but also more defined and enjoyable than the Superiore, which showed little substance and a slightly unknit style. Of the wines from Lake Garda, we admired the Chiaretto and the Bardolino, whose spontaneous light style also displays this year just the right élan on both nose and palate. The two thin and evanescent Custozas were less successful; the Soave Costalta is again reliable: its lively style is supported by an attractive variety on the nose and by supple, persistent fruit on the palate. The same satisfying immediacy is to be found in the Croara, a blend of garganega, trebbiano, chardonnay and pinot blanc. In the other wine in the Selezione line, the Predaia, Veronese varietals are enriched by cabernet sauvignon; despite this attractive blend, the wine is not really seriously engaging.

	Wine	Glasses	Price
●	Amarone della Valpolicella Cl. Gioé '93	🍷🍷	6
●	Bardolino Cl. '97	🍷	2
⊙	Bardolino Cl. Chiaretto '97	🍷	2
○	Croara '97	🍷	4
●	Predaia '95	🍷	3
○	Soave Cl. Costalta '97	🍷	3
●	Valpolicella Cl. '97	🍷	2
○	Bianco di Custoza Montemagrin '97		2
○	Soave Cl. Monte Foscarino '97		2
○	Recioto di Soave '95	🍷 (outline)	4

S. PIETRO IN CARIANO (VR)

F.lli Speri
Via Fontana, 14
Fraz. Pedemonte
37029 S. Pietro in Cariano (VR)
tel. 045/7701154

We visited Paolo Speri on a muggy day in July and he, kind as ever, showed us around the recently modernized estate headquarters: the new offices, the tasting room, but especially the new barrels in the cellar and the efforts that his entire family (and particularly Marco, Alberto and Pietro) is putting into the vineyards. This all just went to back up what his wines had already told us: the story of a family that believes in what it is doing, that transmits its love for the land to its wines, that never stops reevaluating its methods, and that has made the pursuit of quality a moral duty. The most recent result of this passion is the '93 Amarone Sant'Urbano, which has won another Three Glasses for the Speris. The wine is deep and concentrated even in color, and offers impressive breadth on the nose, with notes of overripe fruit and hazelnut butter, as well as hints of spice, coffee and cocoa. On the palate it is compact, warm and seductive; the fruit echoes sensations on the nose and is underpinned by the tannic backbone which gives vigor and cleanness to the finish. As the '95 Recioto La Roggia is not yet ready we enjoyed the more straightforward version, called I Comunai: this wine displays aromas of preserves and spice and, on the palate, reveals good balance between full, sweet fruit and elegant acidity. The Valpolicella Sant'Urbano '94 is starting to behave as the Speris would like it to: clean and pleasantly complex on the nose, sinuous and well-defined in the mouth. At the moment it just lacks that bit of vigor which will make it absolutely stunning. The Valpolicella La Roverina, on the other hand, seems rather old-fashioned. The '97 Valpolicella fully realizes its ambition to be pleasant easy drinking.

	Wine	Glasses	Price
●	Amarone della Valpolicella Cl. Vigneto Monte Sant'Urbano '93	🍷🍷🍷	5
●	Recioto della Valpolicella I Comunai '95	🍷🍷	5
●	Valpolicella Cl. Sup. Vigneto Monte Sant'Urbano '94	🍷	4
●	Valpolicella Cl. Sup. La Roverina '96		3
●	Valpolicella Cl. '97		2
●	Amarone della Valpolicella Cl. Vigneto Monte Sant'Urbano '90	🍸🍸🍸	5
●	Recioto della Valpolicella Cl. La Roggia '94	🍸🍸🍸	4
●	Amarone della Valpolicella Cl. Vigneto Monte Sant'Urbano '91	🍸🍸	5

S. PIETRO IN CARIANO (VR)

F.lli Tedeschi
Via Verdi, 4/a
Fraz. Pedemonte
37029 S. Pietro in Cariano (VR)
tel. 045/7701487

Tedeschi steps back into the limelight, and in particularly fine style, with its most important wines: these represent just the first results of a signficant period of transformation the company has undergone in the last five years. All the phases of the wine-making process have seen changes: greater care during the drying of the red grapes in order to prevent mould and to have healthier fruit; more intense maceration in order to achieve greater extraction of the polyphenols and aromatic substances in the grapes; and finally, the gradual replacement of the barrels so as to give wines with such high ambitions the ideal environment in which to mature. The results of this beneficial process are well exemplified by the exceptional '95 Amarone Monte Olmi, which has won its first Three Glasses. It has a traditional style, with deep aromas which open up slowly to become warm and expansive with spicy and almost balsamic notes. On the palate it is firm and vigorous, with a long, lingering finish. The '95 Recioto Monte Fontana is only just behind it: it has a deep opaque ruby hue, and displays unusual intensity on the nose, which is floral and complex. The palate is sweet and lively, underpinned by tannins that guarantee balance and length. The Amarone della Fabriseria is also of high quality: it is broad and modern in its gradual expression of aromas, and its flavor is powerful and mouth-filling. The basic Amarone, to which the '95 vintage has given elegance and body, is more modulated. The '97 Valpolicella is well-made, and the elegant and well-balanced Bianco Passito '95 is worth watching.

	Wine	Glasses	Price
●	Amarone della Valpolicella Cl. Capitel Monte Olmi '95	🍷🍷🍷	5
●	Recioto della Valpolicella Cl. Capitel Monte Fontana '95	🍷🍷	5
●	Amarone della Valpolicella Cl. Capitel della Fabriseria '95	🍷🍷	6
○	Bianco Passito '95	🍷🍷	4
●	Amarone della Valpolicella Cl. '95	🍷	5
●	Valpolicella Cl. '97	🍷	2*
●	Capitel San Rocco Rosso '95		4
●	Valpolicella Sup. Capitel dei Nicalò '95		3
●	Recioto della Valpolicella Cl. Capitel Monte Fontana '91	🍸🍸	4
●	Amarone della Valpolicella Cl. '91	🍸	4

Tommasi F.lli

Via Ronchetto, 2
Fraz. Pedemonte
37029 S. Pietro in Cariano (VR)
tel. 045/7701266-7701437

Tommasi did not repeat its fine performance of last year, in which many of its wines came close to receiving some very high ratings indeed. The simultaneous presence of not particularly successful vintages in the ranges of all the wineries that make up the group made it impossible to express the improvement in quality which this San Pietro-based family is seeking. It seems that Tommasi is not yet able to exploit to the full the enormous potential it possesses. The wines are, naturally, all correctly executed, but some of them do not have the necessary élan on the nose and palate to make them stand out from the crowd. Of the more successful ones we draw your attention to the '95 Recioto Campo Fiorato, which gives us a comforting insight into the potential of the wines from that very good year. Its color displays interesting depth; the nose evolves in a not particularly complex manner, but is notably clean. Its notes of blackberry, mint and violets are echoed in a minor key on the palate, giving an attractively graceful tone to the flavor. The '93 Amarone Ca' Florian, though not offering the depth of the '90 version, displays warmth and reasonably meaty fruit. The basic version, again from the '93 vintage, showed complete maturity, becoming broad and mouth-filling on the palate and clean on the finish. To continue with the Amarones, the version from the Monte Masua vineyard of Il Sestante rates One Glass. On the other hand, the "ripasso" style of the '95 Valpolicella did not produce good results: it in fact seems slightly tired by the technique, which should, in theory, give better aromas and body to the wine. We also mention the Lugana from Il Sestante, which shows us again what excellent fruit was to be had from the '97 vintage.

	Wine	Rating	Price
●	Recioto della Valpolicella Cl. Campo Fiorato '95	▼▼	4
●	Amarone della Valpolicella Cl. Ca' Florian Tommasi '93	▼	5
●	Amarone della Valpolicella Cl. Monte Masua Il Sestante '93	▼	5
○	Lugana San Martino Il Sestante '97	▼	3
●	Valpolicella Cl. Sup. Ripasso Tommasi '95		4
●	Valpolicella Cl. Sup. I Pianeti Il Sestante '95		3
●	Valpolicella Cl. Sup. Bure Alto Villa Girardi '95		3
●	Amarone della Valpolicella Cl. Villa Girardi '93	▽▽	5

S. PIETRO IN CARIANO (VR)

Massimino Venturini

Via Semonte, 20
Fraz. S. Floriano
37020 S. Pietro in Cariano (VR)
tel. 045/7701331-770330

The Venturini family's real passion, their Amarone, is remarkably constant, whether the vintage be good or bad, and it always expresses the same warm and compact style: this is thanks to the selection of the grapes, which becomes more rigorous from year to year. The estate owns vineyards of unquestionable quality and succeeds in drawing out from them not just the usual concentration but also the elegant richness that the Monte Masua and Semonte Alto vineyards are capable of producing. The wine's appearance already gives us an idea of the depth and concentration of the '94 Amarone; the complex nose displays notes of hazelnut, rose and cherry, with which the spicy oak-derived nuances combine in masterly manner, prolonging the evolution of the aromas. Its fullness on the palate is as much to be expected as it is satisfying, while the alcoholic note is well balanced and supports the fruit throughout the long, soft finish. The Recioto has seen a distinct improvement over its monotonous perfomance of last year. The style that Daniele and Mirco give it is not that of a complex wine, but the '96 version has acquired an overriding sensation of depth that embraces every aspect, from the color through to the finish. The nose displays immediate black berry fruit aromas, while the palate is characterized by a clean sweetness. The frankess which we found in the two top wines was not evident in all the Valpolicellas. The Superiore, however, showed reasonable structure and therefore did well; the '97 Classico is only deserving of mention.

	Wine	Rating	Price
●	Amarone della Valpolicella Cl. '94	▼▼	5
●	Recioto della Valpolicella Cl. '96	▼▼	4
●	Valpolicella Cl. Sup. '95	▼	3
●	Valpolicella Cl. '97		2
●	Amarone della Valpolicella Cl. '93	▽▽	4
●	Recioto della Valpolicella Cl. '94	▽▽	4
●	Recioto della Valpolicella Le Brugnine '94	▽	4
●	Valpolicella Cl. Sup. Semonte Alto '93	▽	3

S. PIETRO IN CARIANO (VR)

VILLA BELLINI
VIA DEI FRACCAROLI, 6
LOC. CASTELROTTO DI NEGARINE
37029 S. PIETRO IN CARIANO (VR)
TEL. 045/7725630

To taste Cecilia and Marco Zamarchi's Amarone is to embrace the very spirit of the Valpolicella zone and its historical heritage: their wine bears witness to the intensity and contradictions that have sprung up from this land. The primordial intensity of their '93 Amarone is neither overbearing nor vigorous; instead its way of captivating us is gradual, succulent and uninterrupted. The color is not very deep and in fact led us astray. The nose, on the other hand, reveals surprising depth: there are no "international" notes here; instead we find mature and expansive floral tones. The palate is the best part of all: it offers an immediate balance as well as a finish remarkable in its length and finesse. The same taste profile underlies the Valpolicella Superiore Il Taso; it always takes its time to release its most aristorcratic aromas, but on the palate it opens up immediately to express its meaty succulence. The '93 Recioto, subtle, intriguing and understated in its sweetness, is not yet as the Zamarchis would like it to be, but it certainly constitutes another precious exhibit in this imaginary gallery of the emotions. The '97 Valpolicella Il Brolo is heady and refreshing.

	Wine	Glasses	Price
●	Amarone della Valpolicella Cl. '93	🍷🍷	5
●	Recioto della Valpolicella '93	🍷	5
●	Valpolicella Cl. Il Brolo '97	🍷	2*
●	Valpolicella Cl. Sup. Il Taso '95	🍷	3
●	Amarone della Valpolicella '90	🍷🍷 (outline)	5
●	Amarone della Valpolicella Ris. '90	🍷🍷 (outline)	5
●	Recioto della Valpolicella Amandorlato '90	🍷🍷 (outline)	4
●	Amarone della Valpolicella '92	🍷 (outline)	4
●	Recioto della Valpolicella '92	🍷 (outline)	4

SALGAREDA (TV)

ORNELLA MOLON TRAVERSO
VIA RISORGIMENTO, 40
FRAZ. CAMPODIPIETRA
31040 SALGAREDA (TV)
TEL. 0422/804807

Ornella Molon and Giancarlo Traverso have taken on the arduous task of pursuing quality in a zone which seems not to want even to question its dedication to quantity. In spite of everything, Ornella and Giancarlo soldier on like modern-day Don Quixotes of the Piave DOC, buoyed up by their indomitable spirit and their firm determination to combine enjoyment and age-worthiness in their wines. This is how the '95 Merlot came about, with its soft, deep aromas; this creamy and elegantly structured wine opens out without holding anything back. This is not yet the stunning Merlot that the Traversos hope one day to make, but they are at least working with the right raw material. The same may be said of the '97 Traminer: this white no longer has the thin and slightly pungent aromas of a few years ago, but offers, as it did last year, more succulent notes of peach, apricot, fully-opened flowers and spice. On the palate it is full-bodied and warm and displays a depth of fruit that counters the inevitable bitterish aftertaste. This year the Sauvignon lacks the concentration that has often distinguished it, and expresses its pungent varietal notes to the full. The '95 Vite Bianca blend, consisting mostly of barrique-aged chardonnay, is more complete. It displays well-integrated oak and complex aromas that are then echoed on the palate, where a clean gradual development is the thing. The Vite Rossa does not yet have a style of its own: sometimes it does almost as well as the Merlot, adding an interesting complexity of sensations to the mix; on other occasions (and this is one of them), it does not benefit from its aging and becomes prematurely tired. The '95 Cabernet is maintaining standards, while the floral sweet wine, the Bianco di Ornella, displays a fragrance of citrus fruit and delicate flavors on the palate.

	Wine	Glasses	Price
●	Piave Merlot Ornella '95	🍷🍷	4
○	Traminer '97	🍷🍷	4
○	Vite Bianca '95	🍷🍷	4
○	Bianco di Ornella '94	🍷	3
●	Piave Cabernet Ornella '95	🍷	4
○	Sauvignon '97	🍷	4
●	Vite Rossa '94	🍷	4
●	Piave Cabernet Ornella '94	🍷🍷 (outline)	4
●	Piave Merlot Ornella '94	🍷🍷 (outline)	4

SOAVE (VR)

Cantina del Castello

Corte Pittora, 5
37038 Soave (VR)
tel. 045/7680093

The Cantina del Castello enjoys a high reputation among the leading players in the Soave renaissance. The winery has not yet exploited its potential to the full, but this year one is aware of the happy combination of the excellent '97 vintage and a more adroit handling of the vinfication process. The best wine presented was the Soave from the Monte Pressoni vineyard, an attractive and immediately appealing white which is fruity, succulent and dynamic in its evolution on the palate. Its bright straw color precedes aromas of pineapple, medlar and a hint of peach; in the mouth, the balance between its vein of acidity and a good level of alcohol make the wine long and appealing. From the Monte Carniga vineyard comes a more delicate, fresh and traditional Soave; its color is again pale; the nose offers pleasant yeasty notes and the palate reveals crisp acidity. In the basic Soave one finds a traditional blend of garganega and trebbiano di Soave; it is an elegant wine even on the nose, with its appealing notes of white-fleshed fruit and almond. The progression in the mouth does not disappoint, for all that the wine's principal characteristic is lightness. Thus the Soaves already display excellent style, but the same cannot be said of the Reciotos, which lack the necessary personality to make their presence felt. The versions presented this year were from difficult vintages, so we look forward to more propitious years to get an idea of their true potential.

	Wine	Rating	Price
O	Soave Cl. Sup. Monte Pressoni '97	🍷🍷	3*
O	Soave Cl. Sup. '97	🍷	3
O	Soave Cl. Sup. Monte Carniga '97	🍷	3
O	Recioto di Soave Corte Pittora '96		5
O	Recioto di Soave Selezione '94		5

SOAVE (VR)

Coffele

Via Roma, 5
37038 Soave (VR)
tel. 045/7680007

Giuseppe Coffele owns some of the finest vineyards in Soave - his wife Giovanna is a Visco, a name well-known among Soave producers - and even though in the past he expended huge amounts of energy, dividing his efforts between teaching and viticulture, for many years his grapes were snapped up by other wineries in the zone. Today, as one looks into the eyes of this reserved man, one sees the satisfaction of someone who has succeeded in getting his own back, and in fulfilling his just aspirations. Coffele's wines are in fact among the best we tasted this year: if part of the merit can be attributed to his tenaciousness, another decisive factor is the skill of his son Alberto, a real rising star in the wine-making firmament of the Veneto. The main vineyard holding of the estate's 25 hectares is at Castel Cerino, a great high hillside cru with a limestone subsoil. It's from here that he gets the perfect blend of garganega and trebbiano di Soave to make up the standard Soave, a characterful and appealing wine that combines a beneficent crispness and the succulence of excellent grapes. It has rich fruity and floral aromas and, on the palate, progesses with elegance and length. The Soave Ca' Visco, which contains a small proportion of barrique-aged chardonnay, seduces us in a different way: it has a deeper color, while the aromas are attractively ripe and the apple and pear notes of the previous wine are replaced by aromas of ripe fruit and caramel hints. The entry on the palate is soft, and the enchanting development broadens gradually to a very long finish. The finesse of the Recioto di Soave is remarkable: its notes of pear, its gentle entry on the palate and its lively structure make it a dessert wine of exemplary elegance and balance.

	Wine	Rating	Price
O	Recioto di Soave Le Sponde '95	🍷🍷	4
O	Soave Cl. Sup. Ca' Visco '97	🍷🍷	3*
O	Soave Cl. Sup. '97	🍷🍷	2*

SOAVE (VR)

Monte Tondo di Gino Magnabosco

Via S. Lorenzo, 89
37038 Soave (VR)
tel. 045/7680347

Gino Magnabosco owns one of the finest vineyards in the entire Soave area. For many years he dedicated himself to farming it while following another profession; then, when he saw the opportunity to become a full-time wine producer, his life-style changed completely. He started to use more sophisticated bottling systems, and is in the process of fitting out a cellar that will be more in line with the demands of a modern winery. He has also bought more land so as to be able to increase the rigor of his grape selection and produce 100 thousand bottles a year. His wines immediately stand out for their crystalline cleanness, to which Gino has added, over the last few years, a more well-defined character, especially in the Soaves. The one from the Monte Tondo vineyard is really complete: it displays weight and vitality even in its straw color; its fragrance of white-fleshed fruit reveals attractive breadth and voluptuous depth. The entry on the palate is crisp and forceful, and we found the evolution of the fruit perfectly balanced, while the finish perfectly echoes the nose. The outstanding qualities of liveliness and quaffability are present also in the Soave Spumante Brut, one of the few wines in its category which are elegant and well-made. The Recioto Spumante, whose greatest appeal lies in its understated sugar content and its delicate, noncloying fragrance, is more enticing and, naturally, considerably sweeter. The rustic and slightly alcoholic Chardonnay offers good ripe fruit, but lacks the finesse and intensity of the other wines.

Wine	Glasses	Price
O Soave Cl. Sup. Monte Tondo '97	🍷🍷	2*
O Recioto di Soave Spumante	🍷	4
O Soave Spumante Brut	🍷	3
O Chardonnay '97		1
O Soave '97		1

SOAVE (VR)

Leonildo Pieropan

Via Camuzzoni, 3
37038 Soave (VR)
tel. 045/6190171

The La Rocca and the Calvarino reveal, in their radically different conceptions and styles, the real goal of the man who makes them: to produce ever better Soaves, which are innovative but also indissolubly linked to their "terroir". The garganega grape rules the roost in the wine from the La Rocca vineyard. Pieropan picks the grapes here at different times so as to blend together fruit of varying levels of ripeness, and then he ferments the must in small barrels, not all of which are new. His idea is that the oak should play a supporting role, blending into the soft, complex bouquet and the already substantial body on the palate. The result is a gloriously brilliant white wine that offers an exquisitely refined bouquet, mouth-filling and exciting fruit on the palate, and admirable length. The contribution of a certain amount of trebbiano di Soave is a decisive factor in the composition of the wine from the Calvorino vineyard. Here Pieropan stresses Soave's propensity for freshness, giving elegance and delicacy to the wine's floral aromas without neglecting breadth and depth on the palate. The wine that emerges is lively, sinuous and seductive with its succulent and measured fruit, demonstrating that a wine can be outstanding even if it is unoaked. Pieropan's dessert wines are immersed in the spirit of autumn: they evoke its colors and its melancholy sweetness. While the Vendemmia Tardiva displays a drier tone and recalls the elemental ripeness of grape skins, the Passito della Rocca yields its full body with an exotic sensuality, proving itself to be one of the best white dessert wines that Italy (but not only Italy) has to offer.

Wine	Glasses	Price
O Passito della Rocca '95	🍷🍷🍷	5
O Soave Cl. Sup. Vigneto La Rocca '96	🍷🍷🍷	4
O Recioto di Soave Le Colombare '95	🍷🍷	4
O Soave Cl. Sup. Vigneto Calvarino '97	🍷🍷	4
O Soave Cl. Sup. '97	🍷🍷	3*
O Vendemmia Tardiva Santa Lucia '95	🍷🍷	4
O Passito della Rocca '88	YYY	5
O Passito della Rocca '93	YYY	5
O Soave Cl. Sup. Vigneto La Rocca '95	YYY	3

SOAVE (VR)

Suavia
Via Centro, 14
Fraz. Fittà
37038 Soave (VR)
tel. 045/7675089

We really like the tenaciousness, the energy and the exemplary devotion to hard work of the owners of this small Soave estate, qualities which are symptomatic of their deep attachment to their area and its wines. We particularly, and quite naturally, like their top wine, a Soave. We are talking about the Monte Carbonare, which represents the meeting point between inevitable, and indeed desirable, technical progress in the winery and the undiluted typical character of the grape from which it is made. Garganega does not give to the producer the gratifying aromas of certain other varietals, nor does it offer their attractive range of taste sensations. For this reason it is more difficult to bring out the full quality of its fruit, but when a producer succeeds in doing so, he produces a white of rare and satistying complexity and vitality. The color of the Monte Carbonare is a bright, deep straw; the bouquet reveals an appealing background of secondary aromas, above which rise up delicate varietal hints of pear and almond; on the palate, the fruit evolves delicately, underpinned by a lively and persistent vein of acidity. The Soave Monte Carbonare has another quality, its capacity to age, and this was evinced this year when we tasted once again the '95 and '96 versions, which we had reviewed in the past. The standard Soave, on the other hand, did not repeat the successful performance of last year. We do not think that this is a question of the quality of the grapes themselves, but the wine does not offer its usual clarity on the nose, a factor which unfavorably influenced its entire taste profile: perhaps a further period of bottle-aging will improve the situation. The Recioto and the barrique-aged Soave Le Rive, on the other hand, were not presented this year.

	Wine	Glasses	Price
○	Soave Cl. Sup. Monte Carbonare '97	🍷🍷	3
○	Soave Cl. Sup. '97		2
○	Soave Cl. Sup. Monte Carbonare '96	🍷🍷 (prev. year)	3
○	Recioto di Soave La Boccara '95	🍷 (prev. year)	5

SOMMACAMPAGNA (VR)

Le Vigne di San Pietro
Via S. Pietro, 23
37066 Sommacampagna (VR)
tel. 045/510016

In a year in which Carolo Nerozzi did not have great fruit to work with for his innovative wines, the Refolà and the Moscato, he came out with the best classic Lake Garda wines of his career. The Chiaretto deserves its Two Glasses not so much because it has, unexpectedly, become a very well-structured wine, but because it represents the absolute ideal of its type. Its pink hue offers just the right combination of brightness and depth of color; the secondary aspects of the nose are held in check in a masterly manner by red berry fruit notes, and rendered more attractive by floral tones. This wine has really improved, however, on the palate. The flavor is no longer supported only by the acidity, as is the case with many Chiarettos, but by a supple and full body, in which all the components play their role and guarantee notable length. Nerozzi's other aim was to create a white which, along with its natural fragrance, would also display greater richness. He has certainly succeeded here too: the '96 vintage has given us the first edition of the San Pietro, a Custoza produced from grapes which were ripened longer than usual, and which was relased for sale at a later date than normal. Its color is a deep straw; on the nose one does not find simple and distinct notes, but rather a sensation of homogeneity and depth. In the mouth, the initial flavors amalgamate perfectly with the structure, which leads to a distinct fruit on the finish. The Refolà shows warmth, compactness and definite structure, although the oak has yet to integrate fully. The Moscato is still maturing and acquiring definition, so we are not reviewing it yet. As always, we were impressed by the Balconi Bianco, made from riesling and showing the classic mineral tones of that grape as well as its customarily lively palate.

	Wine	Glasses	Price
⊙	Bardolino Chiaretto '97	🍷🍷	3*
○	Bianco di Custoza San Pietro '96	🍷🍷	3
○	I Balconi Bianco '96	🍷🍷	4
●	Refolà Cabernet Sauvignon '94	🍷🍷	5
●	Bardolino '97		3
○	Bianco di Custoza '97		3
○	Sud '95	🍷🍷🍷 (prev. year)	5
○	Moscato Due Cuori '94	🍷🍷 (prev. year)	5
●	Refolà Cabernet Sauvignon '93	🍷🍷 (prev. year)	5

SONA (VR)

DANIELE ZAMUNER
VIA VALECCHIA, 40
37060 SONA (VR)
TEL. 045/6081090

This year, Zamuner's top wine is once again a bubbly. It is the '92 Brut, made from the classic blend of pinot noir (70%), pinot meunier (20%) and chardonnay. Though it is the fruit of a far from outstanding vintage, the wine still has the dynamic structure that will allow it to improve. The characteristic ripeness on the nose, which we find in all of this winery's sparkling wines, is here balanced by a surprising freshness; on the palate, the carbon dioxide lifts the fine, full fruit, giving it brightness and length. Our re-tasting of the Rosé confirmed the rating we gave it last year; we now look forward to the "dégorgement" of the promising '93s. The Rosso Valecchia, (a cabernet/merlot blend), returns to a style more consonant with its ambitions to be youthful and intensely fruity, after the rather wan and disjointed '95, which we sampled again in this year's tastings. The '96, on the other hand, is deep in color, herbaceous and mineral on the nose, with a lively attack and a dense and balanced progression on the palate. This is not a wine that aims at complexity, but its bracing immediacy is extremely satisfying. The Bianco Montespada, made from the classic grape blend of Custoza, offers enjoyably frank, direct fruit, whereas the light Rosso Montespada, (practically a Bardolino), is rather too delicate and evanescent. The Bianco Valecchia, released for the first time and made from barrique-aged chardonnay, displayed good fruit but lacked the necessary clarity of style.

●	Rosso Valecchia '96	▼▼	4
○	Spumante Metodo Classico Brut '92	▼▼	4
○	Bianco Montespada '97	▼	2*
●	Rosso Valecchia '94	▽▽	3
○	Spumante Metodo Classico '91	▽▽	4
⊙	Spumante Metodo Classico Brut Rosé '92	▽	4
○	Spumante Metodo Classico Extra Brut '91	▽	4

SUSEGANA (TV)

CONTE COLLALTO
VIA XXIV MAGGIO, 1
31058 SUSEGANA (TV)
TEL. 0438/738241

The Collalto estate again proves that it is one of the top producers in the Marca Trevigiana. It maintains a high level of quality thanks to its ever-improving exploitation of the notable potential of its vineyards, as well as to the slow but constant modernization of the winery. Even if this time around we did not find the surprising wines of last year (we refer in particular to the Incrocio Manzoni Rosso), we were aware of a generally higher standard throughout the range. Indeed, in the Prosecco Extra Dry, which has never before been so good, the inviting floral fragrance is in perfect harmony with the full fruit and well-integrated carbon dioxide on the palate. The appointment of Marzio Pol as consultant oenologist for the sparkling wines has clearly paid off. The Incrocio Manzoni Bianco offers a fresh, fruity nose; on the palate, the well-balanced acidity sets off the fruit, which shows a dry and long progression. The rich and mouth-filling Colli di Conegliano Bianco reveals ripe complexity on the nose, and notable softness on the palate. Only the Pinot Grigio and the Chardonnay were a bit lacking in personality. Among the reds, the Colli di Conegliano still does not really convince us: it seems a little fatigued by its sojourn in oak. The Incrocio Manzoni 2.15 and the Wildbacher are livelier: they offer herbaceous perfumes and are very attractive, although they cannot boast the richness of the '96 versions. The balance of the tannic and imposing Cabernet Torrai '94, with its positive, concentrated nose and depth of flavor, will no doubt improve as time goes on. The Cabernet Riserva is richer and more mature, with its evolved notes of pepper and macerated red berries. The wine is silky and gradual in its development on the palate which, although not very deep, is perfectly harmonious.

●	Cabernet Torrai '94	▼▼	4
○	Incrocio Manzoni 6.0.13 '97	▼▼	2*
●	Piave Cabernet Ris. '94	▼▼	4
○	Prosecco di Conegliano Extra Dry	▼▼	3
○	Colli di Conegliano Bianco '97	▼	3
●	Incrocio Manzoni 2.15 '97	▼	2
●	Wildbacher '97	▼	2
○	Chardonnay '97		2
○	Pinot Grigio '97		2
●	Colli di Conegliano Rosso '95		4
●	Incrocio Manzoni 2.15 '95	▽▽	2
●	Incrocio Manzoni 2.15 '96	▽▽	2
●	Piave Cabernet Ris. '93	▽▽	4
●	Wildbacher '95	▽▽	2
●	Cabernet Torrai '93	▽	4

DESIDERIO BISOL & FIGLI
VIA FOL, 33
FRAZ. S. STEFANO
31049 VALDOBBIADENE (TV)
TEL. 0423/900138

What makes the Prosecco Garnei a fine wine is not only its elegance and control, but those profound sensations which underpin its nose, giving it a sense of voluptuousness which evokes the scents and atmosphere of the vineyards themselves. The Garnei confirms that wine-making technology is not the only thing that counts: it is no accident that technical correctness is always overshadowed by the richness of the fruit itself, even if the grape variety is called prosecco. The Salis, like the Garnei, is a Prosecco Dry that combines richness and balance; its creamy perlage complements its delicate, softly sweet fruit; its aromas of flowers and pears are echoed on the clearly developing, articulated and persistent palate. The Prosecco Extra Dry Vigneti del Fol is absolutely the best of its type: it is full-bodied, complex and, at the same time, velvety, glossy and full of satisfying, vibrant fruit. The more understated and straightforward Colmei demonstrates, however, how Bisol never falls below a level of excellence. Breadth of style is the trump card of the Cartizze, a real dessert bubbly that admirably combines a restrained sugar level with the brio of acidity and carbon dioxide. The tangy, dry Prosecco Brut Crede reveals a crisp, straightforward nose which is perfectly echoed by the spicy suppleness of its flavor. The Tranquillo Molera, a still wine, closes the list of Proseccos: every year it gains in roundness and complexity. The Jeio is another fascinating sparkling wine, made from five different grapes, including prosecco and incrocio Manzoni. Among the Metodo Classico bubblies we can recommend the interesting Cuvée del Fondatore '92.

O	Cartizze	🍷🍷	4
O	Prosecco di Valdobbiadene Dry Garnei '97	🍷🍷	4
O	Prosecco di Valdobbiadene Dry Salis	🍷🍷	3
O	Prosecco di Valdobbiadene Extra Dry Colmei	🍷🍷	3
O	Prosecco di Valdobbiadene Extra Dry Vigneti del Fol	🍷🍷	3
O	Prosecco di Valdobbiadene Tranquillo Molera '97	🍷🍷	3
O	Talento Cuvée del Fondatore '92	🍷🍷	5
O	Prosecco di Valdobbiadene Spumante Brut Crede	🍷	3
O	Spumante Jeio	🍷	3

VALDOBBIADENE (TV)

F.LLI BORTOLIN SPUMANTI
VIA MENEGAZZI, 5
FRAZ. S. STEFANO
31049 VALDOBBIADENE (TV)
TEL. 0423/900135

The Bortolin family's winery has carved out a space for itself among the leading producers in the zone. There is certainly no lack of historical family tradition, since already at the beginning of the 1900s Valeriano Bortolin was taking part in exhibitions and winning awards for his wines, but it is really with the last two generations that the winery has really made its mark. It specializes in sparkling wines, which are always made with extraordinary care, so that they are good even in lesser vintages like last year, and remarkable in better years such as the one now available. The major characteristic of the Extra Dry version called Rù is the elegance and restraint of the sensations it offers; its straw color shimmers with a very fine perlage; the captivating aromas have a succulent tone which is echoed in the softness on the palate. The broad, floral and dynamic Cartizze is also enlivened by a fountain of minute bubbles; its aromas are distinct, seductive and complex; the full fruit on the palate just hints at sweetness and displays a wonderfully fresh balance. Delicacy, both on the nose and on the palate, is the salient characteristic of the Prosecco Extra Dry, which does not have a marked personality, but does show a clean continuity. The sparkling Vigneto del Convento is made from prosecco (70%) and chardonnay, and is dry but smooth. We found the same lightness and correct execution in the Prosecco Brut, which only lacks a touch of zest on the palate. The Prosecco Dry, however, was less impressive.

O	Cartizze	🍷🍷	4
O	Prosecco di Valdobbiadene Extra Dry Rù	🍷🍷	3*
O	Prosecco di Valdobbiadene Brut	🍷	3
O	Prosecco di Valdobbiadene Extra Dry	🍷	3
O	Spumante Brut Vigneto del Convento	🍷	3
O	Prosecco di Valdobbiadene Dry		3

BORTOLOMIOL
VIA GARIBALDI, 166
31049 VALDOBBIADENE (TV)
TEL. 0423/975794

Bortolomiol has confirmed its right to an individual entry after its debut in the Guide last year, and it has done so, like any large winery worth its salt, with a reprise of last year's results, showing that consistent quality is its forte. The wines from Giuliano and Maria Elena's winery do not stand out, in fact, for any marked characteristic; they are, instead, distinguished by respect for tradition and brilliant expression of varietal style. An excellent example is the Prosecco Extra Dry Banda Rossa: it is glowing in appearance, and offers clean, precise varietal aromas, and the gradual evolution on the palate is rounded and well-balanced. Like all of Bortolomiol's wines, it shows a masterly integration of carbon dioxide into the structure. The delicious and vividly fragrant Prosecco Extra Dry, the basic version, is not particularly complex, but shows a rare elegance. The still Prosecco Tranquillo shares a similar style: it has herbaceous notes on the nose and lively, positive fruit on the palate. The Prosecco Brut has a more restrained flavor, but its nose displays crystalline notes of green apple and almond. The Cartizze did not match up to our expectations for this great vintage, but this was a widespread phenomenon with Cartizze; this one revealed less richness and depth than usual.

O	Prosecco di Valdobbiadene Brut	🍷	3
O	Prosecco di Valdobbiadene Extra Dry	🍷	3
O	Prosecco di Valdobbiadene Extra Dry Banda Rossa	🍷	3
O	Prosecco di Valdobbiadene Tranquillo	🍷	3
O	Cartizze		4

VALDOBBIADENE (TV)

CANEVEL SPUMANTI
VIA CALPIANDRE, 25
31049 VALDOBBIADENE (TV)
TEL. 0423/975940

The Prosecco Extra Dry is Canevel's most successful wine, and one of the very best in its category. It is the sparkling wine with the highest production (400 thousand bottles) in their range; it is also the one that is trickiest to make, and the focus of attention for everyone, customers and experts alike; and then it is a wine whose true worth must be gauged by referring not merely to a single bottle but to its production as a whole. We therefore made an effort to taste various lots and different bottlings, and so we came to the conclusions outlined above. Its color is a brilliant straw, with a delicate and persistent perlage; the intense fragrance offers pineapple notes, hints of green apple and nuances of exotic spices. The entry on the palate is full, and gives way to a perfect balance between softness and lively acidity, with the carbon dioxide sustaining the flavor through to a long and satisfying finish. Their other wines did not match up to the Extra Dry, and seemed a little less exciting than usual. The Cartizze offers very varied aromas, ranging from floral to fruity notes, and including refreshing hints of green; we did not find the same continuity on the palate and the wine soon fades away. The more complete Prosecco Tranquillo did not earn last year's score (Two Glasses), but it did win us over with its restraint and the elegance of the sensations it offers; it is a very supple still white wine, with a long finish. We particularly appreciated the fine perlage of the well-made Prosecco Brut. Another wine we had looked forward to tasting was the Prosecco Extra Dry Millesimato (vintage), which had moments of exciting potential, but not clearly or consistently expressed.

O	Prosecco di Valdobbiadene Extra Dry	🍷🍷	3*
O	Cartizze	🍷	4
O	Prosecco di Valdobbiadene Brut	🍷	3
O	Prosecco di Valdobbiadene Millesimato '97	🍷	4
O	Prosecco di Valdobbiadene Tranquillo '97	🍷	3

VALDOBBIADENE (TV)

CANTINA PRODUTTORI DI VALDOBBIADENE
VIA PER S. GIOVANNI, 65
FRAZ. S. GIOVANNI
31030 VALDOBBIADENE (TV)
TEL. 0423/982070

This cooperative winery's Prosecco Extra Dry is one of the best we tasted this year. The Val d'Oca range has enjoyed a high reputation and marketing success for some time, but it has never been as good as this year, with the '97 vintage. The Extra Dry is refined yet rich: its aromas clearly reflect varietal characteristics (notes of pear and hazelnut with a hint of greens); the palate is defined by a perlage perfectly integrated with the supple fruit, and the finish is long and expansive. The Prosecco Tranquillo does not lag far behind; it is fruity on the nose and develops gradually on the palate, where we find more restrained acidity than in previous versions. The attractive finish reveals a lively echo of the nose. One should not expect depth and structure from the well-made Prosecco Frizzante, but rather an appealing cleanness on the nose and well-integrated carbon dioxide. The Prosecco Brut is effervescent, fresh, reasonably full-bodied and perfectly typical of its category. The Cartizze is the only one of their wines that does not live up to last year's performance. Its nose is promising, with its delicate floral notes, but one looks in vain for a proper softness and concentration on the palate.

	Wine	Rating	Price
O	Prosecco di Valdobbiadene Extra Dry Val d'Oca	🍷🍷	3*
O	Cartizze Val d'Oca	🍷	4
O	Prosecco di Valdobbiadene Brut Val d'Oca	🍷	3
O	Prosecco di Valdobbiadene Frizzante Val d'Oca	🍷	3
O	Prosecco di Valdobbiadene Tranquillo Val d'Oca	🍷	2*

VALDOBBIADENE (TV)

COL VETORAZ
VIA TRESIESE, 1
FRAZ. S. STEFANO
31040 VALDOBBIADENE (TV)
TEL. 0423/975291

Col Vetoraz is a place (which gives its name to the winery) in the heart of the Cartizze zone, and here one finds all the ideal conditions for growing the prosecco grape: a breathtaking vineyard site, a subsoil which is not very fertile but is rich in micro-elements, and a warm and breezy climate. Loris Dall'Acqua and his partners have taken full advantage of this favorable situation by keeping yields low and by combating parasites in an environment-friendly way. This old-fashioned style of viticulture is counterbalanced by avant-garde winery equipment, designed with maximum hygiene and respect for the grapes in mind. It is no surprise then that the wines here are among the best and that they have the rare quality of being recognizable. The Cartizze is stupendous: it offers concentrated aromas of ripe banana and citrus fruit, and a rich development and attractive balance on the palate: one almost forgets one is drinking a sparkling wine, the carbon dioxide is so well integrated. We find the same mouth-filling development of flavor in the Prosecco Dry Selezione, a real model of its type. Its color is a deep straw and it has a fine, persistent bead; on the nose the notes of apple, pear and almond reveal that it was made from perfectly ripened grapes. In the mouth it is characterful and persistent, with an enveloping semi-sweetness and a finish of great elegance. The dry definition of the Prosecco Brut reminds one just how fragrant a grape prosecco can be. The supple, delicate and highly varietal Prosecco Extra Dry offers its customary dependable quality. The Tranquillo Tresiese, a full and satisfying wine, is another small gem in the Col Vetoraz range.

	Wine	Rating	Price
O	Cartizze	🍷🍷	4
O	Prosecco di Valdobbiadene Brut	🍷🍷	3*
O	Prosecco di Valdobbiadene Dry Selezione '97	🍷🍷	3
O	Prosecco di Valdobbiadene Extra Dry	🍷	3
O	Prosecco di Valdobbiadene Tranquillo Tresiese '97	🍷	3

VALDOBBIADENE (TV)

LE COLTURE
VIA FOL, 5
FRAZ. S. STEFANO
31049 VALDOBBIADENE (TV)
TEL. 0423/900192

Le Colture is now reaping the benefits of the major restructuring that took place over the last few years. It is not easy to give one's best when one has to concentrate on several different objectives at once, but now that everything is in order, the potential exists for some really notable results. The wines presented this year were all very good and, apart from the excellent quality of the '97 vintage, we also noted enormous skill in the production of the sparkling wines. The Prosecco Extra Dry, the version recognized as classic, again earns Two Glasses, with an even better performance. It won us over gradually, with aromas slowly opening to reveal an unsuspected richness; the palate is lively, succulent and long. The Prosecco Dry Funer shows exemplary depth and has returned to the level which we expect of it. Its deep color, enlivened by a fine perlage, leads one on to fruity aromas that express the undoubted quality of the grapes used; the sweet fruit on the palate is given the necessary backbone by its richness and depth. The Cartizze, though it belongs to the same general style – that of the rounder, more mellow Drys - expresses itself in a different way: one is struck by its length and the subtle, medium-sweet fruit on the palate as well as by the persistence of its aromas which perfectly capture the gamut of fragrances that the prosecco grape can provide when it is grown with skill. The balance of the star-bright and crisp Prosecco Brut results from its lively taste and the brilliant tingle of its perlage. The Tranquillo Masaré is fruity, well-made and quaffable.

O	Cartizze	🍷🍷	4
O	Prosecco di Valdobbiadene Dry Funer	🍷🍷	3*
O	Prosecco di Valdobbiadene Extra Dry	🍷🍷	3*
O	Prosecco di Valdobbiadene Brut	🍷	3
O	Prosecco di Valdobbiadene Tranquillo Masaré '97	🍷	3
O	Incrocio Manzoni 6.0.13 '97		3

VALDOBBIADENE (TV)

ANGELO RUGGERI
VIA FOL, 18
FRAZ. S. STEFANO
31049 VALDOBBIADENE (TV)
TEL. 0423/900235

This small winery has for some time been making very good wines, and has now become a byword for reliability. Remigio in the cellar and Vittore in the vineyards honor their father's memory by dedicating themselves to their labors with unassuming passion. Technological improvements have not interfered with the frank yet refined character of their wines. The Cartizze, in which we find all the aromatic force of the prosecco grape, is a good case in point: its very lively fruity aromas are followed by a full, sweet structure. Good length and hints of complexity also characterize the Prosecco Dry Funer: the fragrance opens out to reveal citrus fruit and almond notes; on the palate its progression is more delicate than that of the Cartizze but is not any the less positive or characterful. These two Dry Proseccos have different functions: the former is more suitable for desserts, such as those made with puff pastry or sponge cake, whereas the Funer goes better with savory dishes of a spicy or sweet-and-sour kind. A measured, restrained style is a principal feature of the Extra Dry version, in which we find, in abundance, all the virtues of a classic Prosecco: perfect integration of the mousse, appealing soft fruit and, as expected, a delicious quaffability. A rounded style is also a characteristic feature of the Prosecco Brut, which is delicate and well-defined, but lacks the vitality of the above-mentioned wines. Our very positive overall rating of these wines is further substantiated by the prices here, which are among the most reasonable in the entire zone.

O	Cartizze	🍷🍷	4
O	Prosecco di Valdobbiadene Dry Funer	🍷🍷	3*
O	Prosecco di Valdobbiadene Brut	🍷	3
O	Prosecco di Valdobbiadene Extra Dry	🍷	3

VALDOBBIADENE (TV)

RUGGERI & C.
VIA PRA FONTANA
31049 VALDOBBIADENE (TV)
TEL. 0423/975716

Five years after transferring to his new cellar, Paolo Bisol has begun a new revolution, which will lead to the construction of two completely independent production lines for receiving the grapes; this will enable him to select his grapes by quality right at the outset, on the basis of the date of picking, the area of origin and the reliability of the supplier (and all this on the busiest days, too). Ruggeri, which vinified 1,350,000 kilos of grapes from the '97 vintage, is by far the largest private Prosecco producer as regards volume of grapes (other larger wineries work with musts and bought-in wines). For this reason, the separation of the lines is absolutely necessary for maintaining the quality achieved over the last few years. However, wine-making technology is not a sterile and soulless process: it is constantly guided by human choice, and hence informed by the experience and sensitivity of the people who perform it. And Paolo Bisol shows that he is a Prosecco craftsman, from the vine to the bottle. The Prosecco Extra Dry Oro, the result of this dedication, is rich and impressively lively, and also dependable, which is most striking, given the enormous quantity produced (600 thousand bottles). The well-defined Cartizze, one of the best in recent years, offers perfectly integrated carbon dioxide; on the palate pear flavors are combined with elegance and roundedness. The Prosecco Dry Santo Stefano is once again excellent; it is mouth-filling and graceful, aromatic and never cloying. The Colli di Conegliano Bianco, produced thanks to a new supplier in the Collalto zone, offers a floral nose and a balanced flavor well supported by a fresh acidity. The Prosecco Extra Dry Giustino B., the Tranquillo and the Frizzante all performed well, completing an enviable selection of wines.

Wine	Rating	Price
O Cartizze	🍷🍷	4
O Prosecco di Valdobbiadene Dry Santo Stefano	🍷🍷	3*
O Prosecco di Valdobbiadene Extra Dry Oro	🍷🍷	3*
O Colli di Conegliano Bianco Corte S. Anna '97	🍷	3
O Prosecco di Valdobbiadene Brut	🍷	3
O Prosecco di Valdobbiadene Extra Dry Giustino B. '97	🍷	4
O Prosecco di Valdobbiadene Frizzante Gentile	🍷	3
O Prosecco di Valdobbiadene Tranquillo Le Bastie '97	🍷	3

VALDOBBIADENE (TV)

S. EUROSIA DI GIUSEPPE GERONAZZO
VIA DELLA CIMA, 2
FRAZ. S. PIETRO DI BARBOZZA
31049 VALDOBBIADENE (TV)
TEL. 0423/973236

At first sight this winery, located on the crest of a hill from which one can make out Valdobbiadene in the distance, may seem somewhat isolated and almost indifferent to the hustle and bustle of the world of Prosecco. However, Giuseppe Geronazzo, a painstaking and meticulous wine-maker, leaves nothing to chance and just goes his own way, which is rather different from the way of many producers in the zone. Apart from frequenting markets rarely visited by his colleagues (such as Calabria), he dedicates a large part of the grapes he vinifies to the production not of Prosecco Extra Dry, but of Prosecco Brut, and the results are very interesting indeed. The wines may have new labels, but their outstanding quality is what we have come to expect. We start with the rounded and elegant Cartizze, which offers rich, mouth-filling fruit and a very creamy mousse. Naturally the Prosecco Brut, given all the attention devoted to it, is one of the best of its kind: its fresh, herbaceous nose leads on to fine fruit on the palate, which clearly mirrors the fragrance, and the wine displays a perfect integration of the carbon dioxide which is rare for its type. The dryness of the Prosecco Extra Dry is given definition by its appealing bitterish finish. It has ripe aromas of apple and pineapple and its flavor is delicate yet persistent. A testimony to Geronazzo's skill as a wine-maker is the large number of wineries which entrust the making of their standard wines to him and the quality of the sparkling wines he produces on behalf of others. Finally, we mention the quaffability and faultless execution of the Prosecco Tranquillo.

Wine	Rating	Price
O Cartizze	🍷🍷	4
O Prosecco di Valdobbiadene Brut	🍷	2*
O Prosecco di Valdobbiadene Extra Dry	🍷	2*
O Prosecco di Valdobbiadene Tranquillo '97	🍷	2

VALDOBBIADENE (TV)

TANORÈ
VIA MONT, 4/A
FRAZ. S. PIETRO DI BARBOZZA
31049 VALDOBBIADENE (TV)
TEL. 0423/975770

After their promising first appearance in the Guide last year, Sergio and Renato Follador's winery has shown that it can be counted on to offer reliable quality in its wines. The backbone of their operation is the intrinsic excellence of their vineyards: sites and subsoils are absolutely ideal, and the Folladors' diligent and intelligent husbandry ensures that they produce the very best results. Wine-making here tends to follow the book, with the addition of minor experiments that serve to give the wines greater personality. The Cartizze, in which we find the sweetly rich fruit which is the hallmark of this denomination, is deservedly their flagship wine. Its straw color is accompanied by a fine bead which is perfectly integrated in the concentrated structure. The wine is fruity and immediately positive on the nose, and subsequently reveals subtler hints of almond and mint. The sweetness on the palate is well balanced by the rest of the wine's components, which contribute to an excellent length. The Prosecco Extra Dry, though it does not share the Cartizze's concentration, is notable for the freshness of its bouquet, which leads into a satisfying and juicy development on the palate. The Prosecco Brut, conceived as a dry and lively wine, sets off its natural dryness with broad fragrances and an extraordinarily attractive almondy finish. Aromas of white flowers, in the Prosecco Tranquillo, are followed by a palate that perhaps wants more fruity succulence to balance an acidity which is pleasantly refreshing, but a little excessive.

○	Cartizze	ΨΨ	4
○	Prosecco di Valdobbiadene Brut	ΨΨ	3*
○	Prosecco di Valdobbiadene Extra Dry	Ψ	3
○	Prosecco di Valdobbiadene Tranquillo	Ψ	3

VALEGGIO SUL MINCIO (VR)

CORTE GARDONI
LOC. GARDONI, 5
37067 VALEGGIO SUL MINCIO (VR)
TEL. 045/7950382

The Passito Bianco I Fenili is a splendid dessert wine. Its consistent excellence has long since turned it into a sort of cult wine, but now, with the '94 vintage, this Valeggio-based estate offers a version with really extraordinary personality. Its grapes are almost exactly the varieties that go into Custoza, but it contains a significant proportion of garganega. I Fenili has a brilliant amber color, and its nose mingles elegant hints of almond with more pronounced notes of candied orange peel. These aromas are echoed throughout the development on the palate, giving a sensation of vigor and persistence. The infinitely patient efforts which Mattia and Stefano Piccoli devote to the Passito are dedicated to the other wines as well, making them touchstones of quality for the wines of Lake Garda. The two Custozas deserve their Two Glasses each, but for different reasons. The appeal of the basic version lies in the gentle immediacy of its nose together with its surprising body and satisfying length on the palate. The Bianco di Corte is more complex and serious: its deep straw color precedes floral aromas and, in the mouth, remarkable liveliness. The zestful Bardolino Le Fontane has aromas of red fruit and a flavor which is not limited to the usual lightness, but offers really attractive, vigorous and intense fruit. The only wine very slightly below par is the '96 Bardolino Superiore, which has not benefited either from its awkward vintage or from a year's extra aging. The successful Chiaretto easily earns One Glass.

○	Bianco di Custoza '97	ΨΨ	2*
○	Bianco di Custoza Bianco di Corte '97	ΨΨ	3*
○	Passito Bianco I Fenili '94	ΨΨ	4
⊙	Bardolino Chiaretto '97	Ψ	2*
●	Bardolino Cl. Le Fontane '97	Ψ	2
●	Bardolino Sup. '96		2
●	Rosso di Corte '92	ΥΥ (outline)	4

VERONA

Baltieri

Via Villa Piatti, 5
Loc. Mizzole
37030 Verona
tel. 045/557616

We invariably recognize the wines of this estate in our blind tastings: they are intense, concentrated and almost overwhelming in their amazing density of flavors and depth on the nose. To the enormous potential derived from semi-dried grapes, Baltieri adds complexity and richness by aging his wines in new oak. So there is no lack of excitement here, but a little more elegance would make the wines really complete and give them an indispensable gradual expressiveness. The Amarone Sortilegio overcomes the problems of the '94 vintage with élan, offering a heady traditional style; its sweet aromas of fruit and walnut skillfully walk the tightrope between semi-dried flavor and oxidation. On the palate, the tannins are evident and serve to hold the exuberance of the extract and of the alcohol in check, producing an evolution of flavor. The Recioto Praedium displays even more intensity and individual character. In the glass it looks almost like a fortified wine; on the nose we find a combination of oak (quite marked) and black berry jam; its sweet richness of flavor demonstrates the outstanding quality and ripeness of the grapes used. The wine is sumptuous, mouth-filling and incredibly long. In the way he produces his Valpolicella, Baltieri is certainly innovative: he dedicates a whole vineyard to it alone, rather than just using up the grapes left over from the production of Amarone, as many wine-makers do. The outcome is an attractive and evolved red, in which the alcohol is slowly integrating with the delicate fruit. The positive results coming from Baltieri and other producers in the "extended" Valpolicella zone should be enough to convince the last few absurdly conservative skeptics of the excellent potential of this area to the east of Verona.

	Wine	Rating	Price
●	Amarone della Valpolicella Sortilegio '94	🍷🍷	5
●	Recioto della Valpolicella Praedium '94	🍷🍷	5
●	Valpolicella Sup. Monte Paradiso '94	🍷	4
●	Amarone della Valpolicella '93	🍸🍸	5
●	Recioto della Valpolicella '93	🍸🍸	4
●	Valpolicella Sup. '93	🍸	3

VERONA

F.lli Bolla

P.zza Cittadella, 3
37122 Verona
tel. 045/8670911

The signs of a reawakening that we noted in last year's Guide have been confirmed in this year's wines. It is difficult for Bolla, as it is for any large-scale winery, to make changes rapidly, but we do think that they have set out on an irreversible and more determined quest for quality. Last year it was, not surprisingly, the '90 Amarone that ruled the roost. But the winery in Piazza Citadella has succeeded in producing, even from the lesser '91 vintage, an elegant if undemanding wine, an appealing Amarone that you can drink right now. Its color shows good depth; its bouquet is dominated by flowers and fruit steeped in alcohol; on the palate it is delicate and fairly persistent. For the Valpollicella Superiore Le Pojane, Bolla has made the most of the '95 vintage, giving back to this wine, of which they have always been rather proud, the richness and personality that rightfully belong to it. Admirable concentration is already apparent in its color and the bouquet is attractively complete, combining freshness and more mature tones, enhanced by an appealing hint of oak. It progresses well on the palate, sustained by full, well-structured fruit. This year's examples of the Cabernet Sauvignon Creso and the Merlot Colforte are less distinctive. The two wines certainly differ, but they share a not especially happy use of oak. The Creso is forward, while the Colforte seems the prisoner of its oak. The delicate and refreshing Sauvignon and the reasonably good Soave Tufaie are also worthy of mention.

	Wine	Rating	Price
●	Valpolicella Cl. Sup. Le Pojane '95	🍷🍷	3*
●	Amarone della Valpolicella '91	🍷	5
○	Sauvignon Lunaia '97	🍷	3
●	Merlot Colforte '97		3
○	Soave Cl. Sup. Tufaie '97		3
●	Amarone della Valpolicella '90	🍸🍸	4
●	Amarone della Valpolicella Ris. '89	🍸🍸	4
●	Creso Rosso '91	🍸	5

VERONA

GIACOMO MONTRESOR
VIA CA' DEI COZZI, 16
37124 VERONA
TEL. 045/913399

The quality of the range of wines presented by Montresor makes them one of the most delightful surprises in this year's Guide. We consider their performance a definite step forward compared to the merely pleasant and well-made standard of last year's wines: this time around, indeed, we noted a new richness and intensity. A wine we looked forward to tasting was the Amarone Capitel della Crosara, in which Montresor made the very most of the favorable '95 vintage. Its color is deep and the concentration of the wine is evident even on the nose, with its lively fruity notes, enhanced by hints of herbs, spices and undergrowth; on the palate it displays great power, considerable alcoholic warmth and vigor, and is thoroughly satisfying. From the same vintage the Montresor brothers have produced a meaty Recioto, an excellent compromise between an easy-drinking style and the new emphasis on more complex full-bodied wines. As regards the Cabernet Campo Madonna, we must apologize for an error. Last year we wrote about the '96, but this wine was only released this year and indeed amply deserves Two Glasses. This is an exuberant red, not particularly complex on the nose (which is nevertheless wonderfully fresh), but highly attractive even in its color and remarkably rich on the palate. The range of red wines is completed by a cabernet/merlot blend called Santomio which, although it is more delicate, is another confirmation of the skill at work in this winery. The Lugana is again one of the best of its type: it displays character on the nose, a positive, dry flavor and a particularly attractive correspondence between nose and palate. The Bianco di Custoza Montefiera is even better: it has a faintly aromatic fragrance and is authoritatively mouth-filling and well-balanced.

	Wine	Glasses	Price
●	Amarone della Valpolicella Capitel della Crosara '95	▼▼	6
○	Bianco di Custoza Montefiera '97	▼▼	3*
●	Cabernet Sauvignon Campo Madonna '96	▼▼	3
●	Recioto della Valpolicella Re Teodorico '95	▼▼	5
○	Lugana '97	▼	3
○	Valdadige Pinot Grigio '97	▼	3
●	Rosso Santomio '95	▼	5
●	Amarone della Valpolicella Capitel della Crosara '90	▽▽	5
●	Amarone della Valpolicella della Cantina Privata '90	▽	5

VERONA

F.LLI PASQUA
VIA BELVIGLIERI, 30
37131 VERONA
TEL. 045/8402111

Once again a Soave is Pasqua's best wine. This time around it is not called Montegrande but Sagramoso; on the other hand, it has maintained the same level of character and attractiveness which made us sit up and take notice last year. Its color is a bright straw yellow of good depth; its delicate fragrance opens out slowly but charms with its freshness. The palate too is gradual in its progress and elegant, with a long and corresponding finish. An encouraging sign also comes from another white, the Lugana, a wine which is less rounded and mouth-filling than the Soave, with more marked acidity and a distinct almondy fragrance. The red wines presented this year, on the other hand, were not as successful, partly because, with the difficult '94 vintage, some top wines were not released. The Amarone Casterna was therefore the only representative of its type. It has a deep garnet color, and a bouquet whose varied aromas are not sufficiently well-knit. The palate does better, with its admirable delicacy and balance. The Valpolicella Superiore, on the other hand, is below par: Pasqua does not seem to have been able to get a really remarkable red out of the '95 vintage. Indeed the wine is well-made, but lacks a well-defined personality.

	Wine	Glasses	Price
○	Soave Cl. Sup. Sagramoso '97	▼▼	3*
○	Lugana Vigneto Ca' Nova '97	▼	3
●	Amarone della Valpolicella Vigneti di Casterna '94	▼	6
●	Valpolicella Sup. Sagramoso '95		3
●	Amarone della Valpolicella Vigneti di Casterna '90	▽▽	5
●	Morago Cabernet Sauvignon '93	▽▽	5
●	Amarone della Valpolicella Vigneti di Casterna '93	▽	5
●	Valpolicella Sup. Vigneti di Casterna '94	▽	3

VIDOR (TV)

Adami

Via Rovede, 21
Fraz. Colbertaldo
31020 Vidor (TV)
tel. 0423/982110

It is significant that Franco and Alvaro Adami have changed their labels this year, with the aim of reinforcing still further their territorial connection, as if to underline the local origin and sense of belonging behind their way of making Prosecco. This is just the final choice in the Vidor-based brothers' fine-tuning of the quality of all of their wines. Helped by the recent run of good vintages, their range has grown in character and depth, while maintaining an unmistakable delicacy. The Prosecco Extra Dry dei Casel (named after the family's ancient nickname) displays a rich and succulently fruity fragrance, while a combination of liveliness and concentration is its hallmark on the palate, which also offers good structure, length and elegance. The broad, soft, well-balanced style of the Prosecco Dry Giardino is even more evident this year, and contributes to a sensation of richness and complexity. The Prosecco Brut Bosco di Gica (which takes its name from the historic spot where the Giardino vineyard is located) is vivacious and absolutely delicious, and has a perfect mousse; it offers notes of green apple which highlight its freshness, and is dry yet supple and graceful on the palate. The Cartizze, on the other hand, is a bit light, though clean, rounded and reasonably well-defined. The Incrocio Manzoni Le Portelle is much better than it was a few years ago and has acquired a bit more zip. The only wine under par in this otherwise impeccable range was the Prosecco Tranquillo.

	Wine	Glasses	Price
O	Prosecco di Valdobbiadene Brut Bosco di Gica	🍷🍷	3*
O	Prosecco di Valdobbiadene Dry Giardino '97	🍷🍷	3*
O	Prosecco di Valdobbiadene Extra Dry dei Casel	🍷🍷	3*
O	Cartizze	🍷	4
O	Incrocio Manzoni 6.0.13 Le Portelle '97	🍷	3
O	Prosecco di Valdobbiadene Tranquillo Giardino '97		3

VIDOR (TV)

De Faveri

Via G. Sartori, 21
Fraz. Bosco
31020 Vidor (TV)
tel. 0423/987673

Lucio De Faveri's wines have for some time now been among the most satisfying and well-made in the zone. This high standard has not always been easy to achieve, because he can't get equally good grapes from every vintage, and every year the grapes make different wines. He has needed professionalism, sensitivity and a cellar with adequate space and equipment to help him confront varying conditions. The '97 vintage, for example, gave wines which are rich in sugar but low in acidity, thus calling for particular care in the cellar in order to keep them as fresh as possible. The results of our tastings show that De Faveri's hard work has paid off. The Prosecco Dry, the estate's best wine, is full yet elegant on the palate, with an extrememly fine bead; its nose its rich and attractive, with irresistibly straightforward scents of banana and flowers. We should also like to underline the excellent balance between the wine's sweetness and its other components, a happy combination which also has a positive effect on the nose, which is not at all cloying. The Prosecco Brut in the black bottle, which indicates a special selection, is as captivating as ever, although it does lack its customary energy; it has a straw color and a persistent, fine-beaded mousse; on the nose, one finds a marked green apple note which immediately gives way to more delicate fragrances of hazelnut and flowers. The palate is notable for its harmony between the characteristic roundedness and an appealing freshness. The Prosecco Extra Dry is more delicate in tone, but its frank, characteristic style is undiminished. Only the standard Prosecco Brut was not as good as we had expected.

	Wine	Glasses	Price
O	Prosecco di Valdobbiadene Dry Etichetta Nera	🍷🍷	4
O	Prosecco di Valdobbiadene Brut Selezione Etichetta Nera	🍷	4
O	Prosecco di Valdobbiadene Extra Dry	🍷	3
O	Prosecco di Valdobbiadene Brut		3

VIDOR (TV)

Sorelle Bronca

Via Martiri, 20
Fraz. Colbertaldo
31020 Vidor (TV)
tel. 0423/987201 - 987009

Having established a place among the leading estates of the area, the Bronca sisters' winery has begun a period of change which will result in its having a larger area under vine and a new vinification cellar. The primary goal of Piero Balcon, Ersiliana and Antonella is to give a consistent level of quality to their wines, and the old cellar was not ideal for the purpose. Also, their range of wines will enable them to gain a fuller understanding of their zone and will give them greater experience. From the recently-acquired Rua di Feletto vineyard come two new wines which fall within the Colli di Conegliano DOC. The Bianco '97 is a good reflection of the grapes from which it is made, displaying both the delicate aromatic nature of incrocio Manzoni and the fleshy elegance of pinot blanc. A deep straw in color, the wine offers well-defined notes of pineapple and pear shot through with hints of white flowers; on the palate its mouth-filling elegance and pleasing persistence are most striking. The '96 Rosso displays good ripe fruit, although compared to the Bianco it still seems quite some way from finding its true style. The Prosecco Tranquillo Delico shows exemplary finesse and all the attractive elements of its particular category: its lively nose leads into a supple, smooth and persistent body. The Prosecco Brut is remarkably open in aroma and flavor but it lacks the richness which won it Two Glasses last year. So it is the Prosecco Extra Dry which has the most marked personality, with the satisfying richness of its fragrance and the successful combination of its perlage with the fruit.

	Wine	Glasses	Price
○	Prosecco di Valdobbiadene Extra Dry	🍷🍷	3
○	Colli di Conegliano Bianco Ser Bele '97	🍷	3
○	Prosecco di Valdobbiadene Brut	🍷	3
○	Prosecco di Valdobbiadene Tranquillo Delico '97	🍷	3*
○	Spumante Livio Bronca Brut	🍷	3
●	Colli di Conegliano Rosso '96	🍷	4
○	Prosecco di Valdobbiadene Frizzante		2

VIDOR (TV)

Spumanti Dal Din

Via Montegrappa, 31
31020 Vidor (TV)
tel. 0423/987295

For the second year running we register the fact that Dal Din seems more at home making still wines. The bubblies did not show the expressive difficulties of last year's and are in fact more than well made, but they do not have the vigor and character of the bottles without bubbles. The most striking example is the Prosecco Tranquillo, which rates as one of the most elegant in its category: its color is a deep straw with green highlights; its fragrance is extremely clean, with notes of almond and pineapple; these sensations are excitingly echoed on the palate, and lead on into an outstandingly attractive finish. The Colli di Conegliano, making its first official appearance, is also very elegant. This white, made from a variety of grapes including incrocio Manzoni and pinot blanc, has subdued aromatic notes combined with yeasty hints; the palate is admirable for its surprising structure. Another wine with a stimulating and dynamic progression on the palate is the Incrocio Manzoni Bianco; paler in color and rather reticent on the nose, it reveals a supple body and all the breadth it needs. The Prosecco Brut is the most convincing of the sparkling wines, especially as far as its flavor is concerned: the carbon dioxide is very elegantly integrated and the aromatic persistence is also very fine, and emphasized by a pleasantly bitter finish. The Prosecco Extra Dry and the Cartizze display overly forward aromas, and even on the palate they do not offer the requisite liveliness. The Verdiso, on the other hand, is dependable and characteristic.

	Wine	Glasses	Price
○	Colli di Conegliano Bianco '97	🍷	3
○	Incrocio Manzoni 6.0.13 '97	🍷	3
○	Prosecco di Valdobbiadene Spumante Brut	🍷	3
○	Prosecco di Valdobbiadene Tranquillo '97	🍷	3
○	Cartizze		4
○	Prosecco di Valdobbiadene Extra Dry		3
○	Verdiso		3

OTHER WINERIES

The following producers obtained good scores in our tastings with one or more of their wines:

PROVINCE OF PADOVA

La Roccola
Cinto Euganeo, tel. 0429/94298,
Moscato Fior d'Arancio '97

Borin, Monselice, tel. 0429/74384,
Serprino '97

La Montecchia
Selvazzano Dentro, tel. 049/637294,
Moscato Fior d'Arancio '97,
Rosso Godimondo '97

PROVINCE OF TREVISO

Carpené Malvolti
Conegliano, tel. 0438/410575,
Prosecco di Conegliano
Tranquillo Bianco dei Carpené '97

Loggia del Colle
Conegliano, tel. 0438/23719,
Prosecco di Conegliano Brut

Zardetto, Conegliano, tel. 0438/208909,
Cartizze,
Prosecco di Conegliano Extra Dry

La Gioiosa
Crocetta del Montello, 0423/665043,
Piave Pinot Grigio Villa Sandi '97,
Cartizze Villa Sandi

Dall'Armellina
Mareno di Piave, tel. 0438/308878,
Incrocio Manzoni 6.0.13 '97

Moletto
Motta di Livenza, tel. 0422/860576,
Piave Pinot Grigio '97,
Tocai Rosso '97

Cantina Sociale La Marca
Oderzo, tel. 0422/814681,
Prosecco di Valdobbiadene Extra Dry

Nardin
Ormelle, tel. 0422/851002,
Lison Pramaggiore Merlot '97,
Lison Pramaggiore Pinot Grigio Vigna Melonetto '97,
Incrocio Manzoni 6.0.13 Borgo Molino '97

Vincenzo Toffoli
Refrontolo, tel. 0438/894240,
Rosso Amaranto dei Vanai '97

Vigna Dogarina
Salgareda, tel. 0422/804129,
Passito Bianco Il Prelato

Bernardi, Susegana, tel. 0438/781022,
Prosecco di Valdobbiadene Frizzante '97

Montesel
Susegana, tel. 0438/781341,
Prosecco di Valdobbiadene Tranquillo '97

Bruno Agostinetto
Valdobbiadene, tel. 0423/972884,
Prosecco di Valdobbiadene Tranquillo '97

Bellussi, Valdobbiadene, tel. 0423/982147,
Cartizze

Ciodet, Valdobbiadene, tel. 0423/973131,
Prosecco di Valdobbiadene Extra Dry,
Prosecco di Valdobbiadene Tranquillo '97

Col de' Salici
Valdobbiadene, tel. 055/291424,
Prosecco di Valdobbiadene Brut,
Prosecco di Valdobbiadene Extra Dry

Franco
Valdobbiadene, tel. 0423/972051,
Prosecco di Valdobbiadene Rustico

Valdo, Valdobbiadene, tel. 0423/972403,
Prosecco di Valdobbiadene
Extra Dry Cuvée del Fondatore,
Prosecco di Valdobbiadene Extra Dry Oro

PROVINCE OF VERONA

Lenotti, Bardolino, tel. 045/7210484,
Soave Vigna Capocolle '97

Valetti, Bardolino, tel. 045/7235075,
Bardolino Cl. '97

Villabella, Bardolino, tel. 045/7236448,
Amarone della Valpolicella '91,
Bianco di Custoza Fiordaliso '97

Corte S. Arcadio
Bussolengo, tel. 045/7575331,
Bianco di Custoza La Boschetta '97,
Cabernet Sauvignon '93

Le Fraghe, Cavaion Veronese, tel. 045/7236832, Valdadige Chardonnay '97, Bardolino '97

Fasoli, Colognola ai Colli, tel. 045/7650741, Soave Sup. '97

Vicentini
Colognola ai Colli, tel. 045/7650539
Soave '96

Armani, Dolcé, tel. 045/7290033, Sauvignon Campo Napoleone '97, Rosso Foja Tonda '96

Coati, Marano di Valpolicella, tel. 045/7702153, Amarone Corte Rugolin '95

Villa Erbice
Mezzane di Sotto, tel. 045/8880086
Recioto della Valpolicella '95

Cantina Sociale di Monteforte
Monteforte d'Alpone, tel. 045/7610110, Soave Cl. Sup. Il Vicario '97

Mazzi, Negrar, tel. 045/7500136, Valpolicella Cl. Sup. Pojega '95, Recioto della Valpolicella Calcarole '95

Sartori, Negrar, tel. 045/7513200, Recioto di Soave '95, Soave Cl. '97

Villa Spinosa, Negrar, tel. 045/7500093, Amarone della Valpolicella '93, Recioto della Valpolicella '95

Marcato, Roncà, tel. 045/7460070, Colli Berici Merlot dell'Asinara '95, Soave '97

Aldegheri
S. Ambrogio di Valpolicella, tel. 045/6861356, Valpolicella Sup. Ripasso '96

Villa Monteleone
S. Ambrogio di Valpolicella tel. 045/7704974, Amarone della Valpolicella '94, Recioto della Valpolicella '95

Luigi Vantini
S. Floriano di Valpolicella, tel. 045/7701374, Recioto della Valpolicella '95

Fornaser
S. Pietro in Cariano, tel. 045/7701651, Passito Bianco Bure Alto '96, Amarone Monte Faustino '93

Bisson
Soave, tel. 045/7680775,
Soave '97,
Soave Cl. Sup. '97

Arcadia, Verona, tel. 045/8204466, Merlot '97, Amarone della Valpolicella '95, Pinot Grigio Cantarelle '97

Cantina Sociale della Valpantena
Verona, tel. 045/550032, Amarone della Valpolicella '95, Valpolicella Sup. '96

Cecilia Beretta
Verona, tel. 045/8402021, Amarone Terre di Cariano '94

PROVINCE OF VENEZIA

Tenuta S. Anna
Annone Veneto, tel. 0422/769812, Colli Orientali del Friuli Verduzzo '96

Santa Margherita
Fossalta di Portogruaro, tel. 0421/246111, Laudato di Malbech '93, Müller Thurgau dell'Alto Adige '97

Teracrea
Portogruaro, tel. 0421/287041, Malvasia di Teracrea '97

PROVINCE OF VICENZA

Bartolomeo da Breganze
Breganze, tel. 0445/873112, Vespaiolo Sup. Savardo '97

Dal Maso
Montebello, tel. 0444/649104, Gambellara Cl. Vigneti Ca' Cischele '97, Recioto di Gambellara '97

Conte Alessandro Piovene Porto Godi
Villaga, tel. 0444/885142, Colli Berici Tocai Rosso '97

FRIULI VENEZIA GIULIA

In 1997 Friuli Venezia Giulia was blessed with an exceptionally favorable vintage in which, although very high temperatures were recorded during the summer months, there was no significant drought.

The extremely hot and unvaried weather from the end of August until harvest-time, while penalizing fragrance, especially in aromatic varieties such as sauvignon, riesling and traminer, encouraged accumulation of sugar, which is necessary for the formation of body and alcohol (occasionally too much of the latter). Many wines benefited: Tocai Friulano, Pinot Grigio, Pinot Bianco and Ribolla Gialla among the whites, and, of the reds, the Cabernets. After a record 1,500 tastings in Friuli we can confirm a further rise in wine-making standards throughout the region. There are now 112 wineries with an individual profile in the Guide, compared with the 92 of two years ago, more wines have been awarded Three Glasses, and several estates offering premium wines have had to be relegated to the "Honorable Mention" section. But nevertheless the fact is that Friuli excites little interest in the Italian public because it fails to "project an image". Many winegrowers, accustomed to working hard on their own, underrate the importance of promotion in boosting not only their own wines but also the region as a whole. And, although local producers seem to be able to sell just about every bottle they fill, we still maintain that there should be more concerted action on the part of both the regional government and consortiums of growers to develop the image of a wine-making area that is rising to new heights. These heights are evident from the number of wines that received Three Glasses, but even more from the number of new estates to which this award was presented, proof that the pursuit of supreme quality is becoming more widespread. Enzo Pontoni confirms his status as "enfant terrible" of Friuli's wineries with both his Bianco and Rosso Miani, sharing the honors with an old master, Mario Schiopetto, who is back with his Pinot Bianco Amrità and Sauvignon. The classic winners are present: Livio Felluga with his Terre Alte, Silvio Jermann with Vintage Tunina, and Villa Russiz with their Sauvignon de La Tour. The Livon estate has proved its worth with a stunning white, the Braide Alte, and Edi Keber has made a come-back with his Tocai Friulano. Russiz Superiore repeats last year's success with the Rosso Riserva degli Orzoni '94, and Venica & Venica has pulled an old winner out of the hat, their Sauvignon Ronco delle Mele. And don't forget the women winemakers: Ivana Adami of Ronco delle Betulle and her Rosso Narciso '94, and Roberta Borghese of Ronchi di Manzano with the Merlot Ronc di Subule. The Castello di Spessa is a newcomer with its Pinot Bianco. Last but not least, the Isonzo boys are out in practically full force: Gianfranco Gallo of Vie di Romans with his Flors di Uis, Alvaro Pecorari of Lis Neris with the Sauvignon Dom Picòl, Pierpaolo Pecorari with the Sauvignon Kolàus, and finally Mauro and Alessandra Mauri of Borgo San Daniele and Giorgio Badin of Ronco del Gelso, each with a Tocai Friulano.

BAGNÀRIA ARSA (UD)

TENUTA BELTRAME
LOC. ANTONINI, 6/8
FRAZ. PRIVANO
33050 BAGNÀRIA ARSA (UD)
TEL. 0432/923670

The Tenuta Beltrame consists of about 40 hectares, of which 25 are vineyard. The team working on the farm and in the cellar is led by the oenologist Giuseppe Gollino, with Cristian Beltrame gaining experience and ability at his side. The cellar, which is situated in part of the beautifully restored old farmhouse, is really impressive. The amazing successes of this year are due to skilful vineyard management and the availability of working space. The unexpected Sauvignon '97 has lots of personality, offering an intense, complex and balanced nose with well-defined aromas of tomato leaves, elderberry and rue, which follow through on a mouth-filling, long palate. The Pinot Bianco is even more satisfying: notes of citrus mingle with elegant scents of apple, while the palate is complex, broad and fresh with apple and summer fruits lingering on the finish. This brings us to the extensive range of One Glass wines. The Chardonnay '97 displays a nose reminiscent of apple, honey and yeast; the fruit is repeated on the palate, which reveals good acidity and length. The characteristic Pinot Grigio is a broad, complex wine with hints of apple and pear and a mineral streak. The Tocai Friulano, whose rather sweet perfumes detract from its varietal character, is nevertheless well-structured, warm and harmonious. The Cabernet Franc, which fully deserves its One Glass rating, reveals ripe plum on the nose and herbaceous undertones with an elegant spiciness and notes of tobacco; the palate is rich, broad and long, with a good balance of tannins and acidity. The intensely colored Refosco dal Peduncolo Rosso has attractive aromas of spices, pencil lead and compote of cherries. Two other of the estate's reds deserve a mention, the Merlot and the Cabernet Sauvignon '97.

	Wine	Glasses	Price
○	Friuli Aquileia Pinot Bianco '97	🍷🍷	3*
○	Friuli Aquileia Sauvignon '97	🍷🍷	3*
○	Friuli Aquileia Chardonnay '97	🍷	3
○	Friuli Aquileia Pinot Grigio '97	🍷	3
○	Friuli Aquileia Tocai Friulano '97	🍷	3
●	Friuli Aquileia Cabernet Franc '97	🍷	3
●	Friuli Aquileia Refosco P. R. '96	🍷	3
●	Friuli Aquileia Cabernet Sauvignon '97		3
●	Friuli Aquileia Merlot '97		3

BAGNÀRIA ARSA (UD)

MULINO DELLE TOLLE
VIA ROMA, 29
LOC. SEVEGLIANO
33050 BAGNÀRIA ARSA (UD)
TEL. 0432/928113

The Mulino delle Tolle estate belongs to the Bertossi cousins, Giorgio and Eliseo, with 17 hectares under vine all situated at the northern edge of the Friuli Aquileia DOC zone. Oenologist Giorgio and agronomist Eliseo took the big decision of bottling their own wine in 1988. The emblem of the cellar is a small Roman votive head found in the area, where ancient wine vessels have also been discovered, proof of a centuries-old wine-making tradition. We particularly enjoyed the highly representative Cabernet Franc '97 and awarded it Two Glasses: warm and grassy on the nose, in the mouth it is full, round and distinctly varietal with characteristic overtones of hay and spices. The Malvasia, another excellent wine, is obtained from local clones and is a blend of which one third is aged in five-hectoliter casks and two thirds are unoaked. Pineapple and orange emerge over the underlying vanilla on the nose and are repeated on the palate which is dry, harmonious, with a faint hint of pink peppercorn. The Chardonnay, which comes close to winning Two Glasses, has toffee aromas mingling with notes of tropical fruit, pear and carruba; on the palate it is intensely fruity and harmonious, with good structure and length. The Refosco '96 offers a rich, elegant nose of ripe red fruit followed by a well-balanced palate with soft, fruity structure and hints of spiciness. Herbaceous notes mingling with ripe fruit characterize the Merlot '97.

	Wine	Glasses	Price
●	Friuli Aquileia Cabernet Franc '97	🍷🍷	2*
○	Malvasia '97	🍷🍷	2*
○	Friuli Aquileia Chardonnay '97	🍷	2
●	Friuli Aquileia Refosco P. R. '96	🍷	3
●	Friuli Aquileia Merlot '97		2

BERTIOLO (UD)

CABERT
VIA MADONNA, 27
33032 BERTIOLO (UD)
TEL. 0432/917434

Cabert is the label used by the Cantina del Friuli Centrale of Bertiolo for the line reserved for restaurants, while Cavaliere di Bertiolo is the name of their other line. This large winery, handling over 30,000 quintals of grapes from 290 hectares of vineyard, is supervised with unquestionable competence by the oenologist Daniele Calvazara. For the production of their Cabernet Franc, two consultants from the antipodes are called in: Australian John Worontschak and Duncan Killiner from New Zealand. This team is of recent formation but is already giving excellent results. The Cabernet Franc l'Arco '97 is a down-under sort of wine offering a soft nose with hints of cherries, prunes, licorice and spices and a palate with pronounced tannins and a fruit partly dominated by the acidity. It has come out well, especially considering the not exactly ideal conditions of the vintage. We were also impressed by the first wines created with the partial use of wood. The best is the Chardonnay with aromas of vanilla, peaches and apricots. These are repeated on the palate, slightly diminished by a touch of acidity which, however, gives it backbone. Just below it is the Sauvignon Barrique, where sweet wood and sage emerge in a wonderful nose. The palate reveals good complexity with balance and adequate structure. The Rosso del Cavaliere '95 is also a successful wine, creamy and fruity on the palate with just a little too much acidity and a broad, balanced nose with spices, mushrooms and compote of sour cherries. Of the Riserva wines reviewed last year, we are glad to report how well the '93 Merlot and Cabernet Sauvignon have evolved.

	Wine		Rating
●	Friuli Grave Cabernet Franc l'Arco '96	🍷	2*
○	Friuli Grave Chardonnay Barrique '97	🍷	3
○	Friuli Grave Sauvignon Barrique '97	🍷	3
●	Rosso del Cavaliere '95	🍷	3
●	Friuli Grave Cabernet Sauvignon '97		2
○	Friuli Grave Pinot Grigio '97		3
○	Friuli Grave Sauvignon '97		3
○	Friuli Grave Tocai Friulano '97		2
○	Friuli Grave Verduzzo Friulano '97		3

BUTTRIO (UD)

CONTE D'ATTIMIS - MANIAGO
VIA SOTTOMONTE, 21
33042 BUTTRIO (UD)
TEL. 0432/674027

When visiting the Conte d'Attimis - Maniago estate one is immediately aware of how the whole place is steeped in history and tradition. The family manor has maintained the architectural character of former times; the 15th century cellars and the estate records bear witness to the viticultural heritage of the family. The vineyards are in an excellent positon and this year's production shows great promise, although from such a combination of tradition, know-how and optimum terroir we expect a further rise in quality. The long series of One Glass wines begins with the Chardonnay, which reveals personality both on the nose, with prominent apple and pineapple, and on the palate which is rich and fruity with a well-judged acidity. The two barrique-aged Vignaricco blends are enjoyable wines. The '92 white, from chardonnay and pinot bianco, is a golden color with complex aromas of milky coffee, vanilla, apricots in spirit and herbal tea, with ripe pineapple and citrus emerging on the palate. The '94 red, from cabernet sauvignon, merlot and schioppettino, is impressive for its warm, concentrated scents of summer fruit, cherries and hay and its flavors of licorice and plum. A lively spiciness and balanced fruit characterize the Merlot, while the Malvasia Istriana has delicate, intense, appley notes. The Verduzzo Friulano Tore delle Signore is clean on the nose with echoes of barley sugar, apricot and peaches in syrup; supple in the mouth, it reveals the right note of sweetness and good tannins. The Pinot Grigio, Tocai Friulano, Schioppettino and Refosco are all reliable wines.

	Wine		Rating
○	COF Chardonnay '97	🍷	3
○	COF Malvasia '97	🍷	3
○	COF Tocai Friulano '97	🍷	3
○	COF Verduzzo Friulano Tore delle Signore '97	🍷	4
○	Vignaricco '92	🍷	4
○	COF Pinot Grigio '97	🍷	3
●	COF Merlot '96	🍷	3
●	COF Refosco P. R. '97	🍷	3
●	COF Schioppettino '97	🍷	4
●	Vignaricco '94	🍷	4

BUTTRIO (UD)

GIROLAMO DORIGO
VIA DEL POZZO, 5
33042 BUTTRIO (UD)
TEL. 0432/674268

Dorigo is a well-established estate, built up by dint of years of hard work on the land and in the cellar, and it maintains its high standards even when faced with sudden changes in management. This is proved by the tasting results of the wines of Dorigo, now run by Girolamo and Alessio, father and son. Rather than rushing to present extremely promising but still immature wines (such as the Chardonnay and the Picolit Passito '97) they have chosen to wait for them to evolve, and have postponed assessment until next year. They mean to let the wines mature in the cellar and release them only when they are ready. The most recent whites are of surprisingly good quality, fresh and structured. The Pinot Grigio offers fruit salad aromas followed by a rich, close-knit, long palate with hints of pear, damson and licorice. The Ribolla Gialla recalls wild flowers and apple on the elegant nose. Very successful in a difficult year, the Sauvignon preserves its varietal aromas of tomato leaves and elderberry and displays a perfect harmony of nose and palate. The Tocai Friulano is very slightly diminished by an over-generous touch of acidity. The estate's top wine is unquestionably the Montsclapade '94, which offers a full, complex, alcohol-rich nose with notes of spices and pennyroyal mingling with berries. The close-textured palate has plenty of body with hints of chocolate, sour cherries and blueberries; time is needed to soften the pronounced tannins. The dense, alcohol-rich Verduzzo Friulano '96 offers pronounced notes of dried apple.

	Wine	Glasses	Price
○	COF Pinot Grigio '97	🍷🍷	4
○	COF Ribolla Gialla '97	🍷🍷	4
○	COF Sauvignon '97	🍷🍷	4
○	COF Tocai Friulano '97	🍷🍷	4
○	COF Verduzzo Friulano Vigneto Ronc di Juri '96	🍷🍷	5
●	Montsclapade '94	🍷🍷	6
●	Schioppettino '94	🍷	4
●	COF Refosco P. R. '97		4
●	Montsclapade '92	YYY	5
●	Pignolo di Buttrio '89	YYY	6
○	COF Chardonnay Vigneto Ronc di Juri '96	YYY	4
○	COF Verduzzo Friulano Vigneto Ronc di Juri '91	YYY	5

BUTTRIO (UD)

DAVINO MEROI
VIA STRETTA DEL PARCO, 1
33042 BUTTRIO (UD)
TEL. 0432/674025 - 673421

Paolo Meroi works both on the farm and in the cellar with Enzo Pontoni, the renowned grower and producer of Miani wines: this helps explain the quality we have found in Paolo's wines, which all the same have a personality of their own. The estate, just to give a few details, consists of nearly seven hectares of vineyards, located partly in Buttrio and partly on the slopes of Rosazzo. The yield per vine is kept very low, in the cellar the wines go into barrique and the whites as well as the reds undergo malolactic fermentation. The novelty this year is the Dominin '96, a blend of merlot, cabernet sauvignon and refosco dal peduncolo rosso, which has been given the Friuli dialect name of Paolo's grandfather, Domenico. Smokey notes and hints of berry tarts, undergrowth and laurel are evident on the nose, followed by a dense, powerful structure with the fruit and tannins wonderfully balanced on a rich, mouth-filling palate with a long finish. The Picolit '97 is golden in color with ripe figs and almond milk apparent on the nose; the palate is sweet but not cloying, rich in alcohol and glycerin with notes of figs, apples and dried pears with honey. Because of the very hot summer and malolactic fermentation the Sauvignon loses some of its varietal character but earns credit for good structure and breadth. The Refosco dal Peduncolo Rosso '96 is more appealing on the nose than on the palate, while the Chardonnay suffers from a presence of wood that was still too marked at the time of tasting. The Ribolla and Tocai went into bottle when our tastings were over.

	Wine	Glasses	Price
●	Dominin '96	🍷🍷	5
○	COF Picolit '97	🍷🍷	6
○	COF Sauvignon '97	🍷	4
○	COF Chardonnay '97		4
●	COF Refosco P. R. '96		5
●	Dominin '95	YY	4
○	COF Picolit '96	YY	5
○	COF Ribolla Gialla '96	YY	4
○	COF Tocai Friulano '96	YY	4
○	COF Verduzzo Friulano '95	YY	4

BUTTRIO (UD)

MIANI
VIA PERUZZI, 10
33042 BUTTRIO (UD)
TEL. 0432/674327

People are always talking about Enzo Pontoni, his cultivation methods, his wines and the awards he receives. Miani's vineyard practices are by all accounts extreme: two or four bunches per vine mean a reduction in yield which is impossible to compensate economically. We ask ourselves if we can really give Three Glasses to wines produced in such limited quantities, equating them with wines turned out in tens of thousands of bottles. Be that as it may, we certainly cannot ignore Enzo's champions: this year yet again he has twice hit the mark with the Bianco '97, from chardonnay, pinot grigio and riesling, and the Rosso '96, a blend of merlot, the cabernets franc and sauvignon, and tazzelenghe. And his other wines only just miss Three Glasses. The Bianco Miani has a nose redolent of milk, vanilla, apricot, banana and lemon tea while the palate is mouth-filling, rich and warm, with a lingering fruity finish. The Rosso Miani offers concentrated fruit on the nose with overtones both wild and velvety and a hint of tar, while the well-oaked, full-bodied, generous palate reveals sun-warmed berries and hints of sandalwood on a powerful structure. The Tocai Friulano has custardy notes with nuances of herb butter and citrus on the nose, and evolves well on the soft, broad, warm palate. The Sauvignon displays notes of vanilla, elderberry, sage and cream on the nose and a fresh fruitiness on the palate which is satisfyingly long and mouth-filling. The Ribolla Gialla discloses ripe yellow fruit and toastiness on the nose, while tropical fruits, apricot and notes of freshness emerge on the glycerin-rich, velvety, expanding palate.

	Wine	Glasses	Rating
●	COF Rosso Miani '96	🍷🍷🍷	5
○	COF Bianco Miani '97	🍷🍷🍷	5
○	COF Ribolla Gialla '97	🍷🍷	5
○	COF Sauvignon '97	🍷🍷	5
○	COF Tocai Friulano '97	🍷🍷	5
○	COF Bianco '96	🥂🥂🥂	4
○	COF Sauvignon '96	🥂🥂🥂	4
○	COF Tocai Friulano '96	🥂🥂🥂	4
●	COF Merlot '94	🥂🥂🥂	5
●	COF Merlot '93	🥂🥂	5
●	Rosso Miani '95	🥂🥂	5
○	COF Ribolla Gialla '96	🥂🥂	4
○	COF Sauvignon '94	🥂🥂	4

BUTTRIO (UD)

LINA E PAOLO PETRUCCO
VIA MORPURGO, 12
33042 BUTTRIO (UD)
TEL. 0432/674387

The estate of Paolo Petrucco and his wife Lina is living up to its excellent reputation. The Petruccos have about 20 hectares under vine and an annual production of around 100,000 bottles, evidence of admirable ruthlessness in both restriction of yields in the vineyards and selection in the cellar. This is a winery where the oenologist Flavio Cabas, surrounded by all the necessary technical equipment, has found working conditions for achieving the highest levels of quality. In the superbly harmonious Chardonnay '97, the partial malolactic fermentation and a brief sojourn in barrique were entirely imperceptible at tasting. Elegant notes of apple and yeast emerge on the nose and are repeated on the palate, whose dense, close-knit structure is nevertheless long and supple. The Merlot Vigna del Balbo, aged in small casks, scores very high. The entry on the nose is elegant and complex with aromas of undergrowth and a hint of tar, and the impact on the palate is full, followed by a solid structure, dense texture and a very long, fruity finish. The Pinot Grigio fully deserves a Glass for its aromas of apple and other fruits, with hints of banana. Two other convincing whites are the Sauvignon, mainly because of its palate, where rue is dominant in the midst of the varietal flavors, and the Ribolla Gialla, with green apple and flowers on the finish. A final mention for the Tocai Friulano (honey, dried pear and apple), the Refosco dal Peduncolo Rosso '96 (spices, cherries and rough tannins) and the Cabernet Franc '96 (herbaceous and vegetal).

	Wine	Glasses	Rating
○	COF Chardonnay '97	🍷🍷	3*
●	COF Merlot Vigna del Balbo '96	🍷🍷	4
○	COF Pinot Grigio '97	🍷	3
○	COF Ribolla Gialla '97	🍷	3
○	COF Sauvignon '97	🍷	3
●	COF Cabernet Franc '96		3
●	COF Refosco P. R. '96		3
○	COF Tocai Friulano '97		3
●	COF Cabernet Franc '95	🥂🥂	3
○	COF Ribolla Gialla '96	🥂🥂	3

BUTTRIO (UD)

FLAVIO PONTONI
VIA PERUZZI, 8
33042 BUTTRIO (UD)
TEL. 0432/674352

Flavio Pontoni, an agronomist from Buttrio who is just over forty, describes his winery as a big little estate. The family has been involved in wine-making since the beginning of the century; now it is Flavio and his father Giuseppino who look after the four and a half hectares of vineyard, distributed among the Colli Orientali and Grave del Friuli DOCs. The average annual output is from 25 to 30 thousand bottles, and, in accordance with the custom in Friuli, which it is our custom to criticize, they comprise 12 different wines. We do feel obliged to admit that the market responds positively (as it tends to do when quality is excellent, as is the case here). Last year Pontoni received Honorable Mention, and now that his consistency of quality has been confirmed he has his own profile in the Guide. His outstanding Braidès Bianco '97, made mainly from chardonnay matured in small oak barrels, offers vanilla, banana and apricot on the nose, carrying through on the palate, which opens out in a continuing profusion of new aromas and lingers delightfully on the finish. The Picolit, golden with greenish tints, has typical scents of apple and lavender followed by a medium-sweet, dense, fruity palate with breadth and continuity. A fresh appley aroma pervades the fruit in the Pinot Grigio, which has plenty of acidity. The Tocai has an elegant nose typically evocative of apple seeds, and follows through nicely on the palate, with a touch of acidity in the finish. The Verduzzo Friulano, a medium-sweet wine with a long finish, has a nose that offers aromas of fresh and dried apple; the follow-through on the palate is excellent. A final mention among the One Glass wines for the Merlot with its scents of blackberry and cherry tart and solid tannins.

	Wine	Glasses	Price
○	Braidès Bianco '97	🍷🍷	3
○	COF Picolit '97	🍷	5
○	COF Pinot Grigio '97	🍷	2*
○	COF Tocai Friulano '97	🍷	2*
○	COF Verduzzo Friulano '97	🍷	3
●	COF Cabernet '97		3
●	COF Merlot '97	🍷	2*

BUTTRIO (UD)

GIGI VALLE
VIA NAZIONALE, 3
33042 BUTTRIO (UD)
TEL. 0432/674289

Gigi Valle's winery, admirably arranged and extraordinarily well equipped, deals without difficulty with the vast quantities of grapes that pile in from its own various hillside DOC properties and from those of other growers. Last year we grumbled about the absence of really first-rate wine, although the overall picture was of undoubted merit, and this year our assessment is unfortunately the same. The wine we liked most, the Rosso L'Araldo '95, has exceptional balance, apart from the high acidity on the palate; ripe nuances detectable on the nose give way to red fruit preserves, red berry tarts and tar; in the mouth licorice, coffee and spices mingle with the fruit. The oak in the Chardonnay San Blâs '96 has been so well measured that it is only faintly perceptible in the background, while well-ripened fruit and an echo of milky coffee are evident on the nose. The palate follows through perfectly, enriched by flavors of juniper berries, tropical fruits and a fresh bite of acidity on the finish. Elegance is the overall characteristic of the Pinot Bianco, which offers fresh apple and wildflowers on the nose; the same aromas are repeated on the palate, accompanied by a good acidity. The Rosso Florean '96, from merlot, refosco dal peduncolo rosso and cabernet sauvignon, recalls raspberries and morello cherries on the nose, followed by a moderately rich palate with an adequate acidity and hints of very ripe red fruits. The medium-sweet Picolit reveals original notes of baked apple and almond milk, while residual sugar is the dominating feature of the Ambrosie. The Ribolla Gialla San Blâs, the Refosco '96 and the Pinot Grigio '97 are all reliable wines.

	Wine	Glasses	Price
●	COF Rosso Florean Linea Valle '96	🍷	3
●	COF L'Araldo Rosso Selezione Araldica '95	🍷	4
○	COF Pinot Bianco Linea Valle '97	🍷	3
○	Collio Chardonnay Barrique Selezione San Blâs '96	🍷	4
○	COF Picolit Selezione San Blâs '97		5
○	Ambrosie Selezione San Blâs		4
○	COF Pinot Grigio Selezione Araldica '97		4
○	COF Ribolla Gialla Selezione San Blâs '96		4
●	COF Refosco P. R. Linea Valle '96		3

CAPRIVA DEL FRIULI (GO)

CASTELLO DI SPESSA

VIA SPESSA, 1
34070 CAPRIVA DEL FRIULI (GO)
TEL. 0481/639914

"A glorious estate and great wines" could be the slogan of the Castello di Spessa, whose range is limited but always of premium quality. The winery is in the center of an estate of 57 hectares, 25 of which are under vine, on the ground floor of a splendid country house redone in 1881. The incredible barrel cellar is in an underground chamber without any direct link to the outside, so that it maintains a constant temperature all the year round. Two of the wines of Loretto Pali, the owner, were in the running for Three Glasses this year and one of them, the Pinot Bianco '97, made the grade. Its intense and complex fruity aromas recall apple and banana on the nose and follow through on a full, satisfying palate with just the right amount of acidity to offset the dense texture and underpin the long finish. The Pinot Grigio '97, another outstanding wine, with faint highlights of onion-skin in the color, comes just below it. The elegant nose, dominated by notes of pear, leads into a powerful, warm, palate with a continuous unfolding of new fruity sensations and an exceptionally long, satisfying finish. The Rosso Conte di Spessa '93, a Bordeaux-style blend with a long maturation in small oak casks, fully deserves Two Glasses: the entry on the nose is broad and concentrated, with tarry notes in the background, while the palate is soft and round in spite of the hefty tannins, with well-balanced fruit and plenty of body. Finally the Sauvignon, in a year that didn't do much for this grape, offers varietal flavors of elderberry, rue and tomato leaves on the palate, with a good acidity and rich alcohol.

	Wine	Rating	Price
○	Collio Pinot Bianco '97	🍷🍷🍷	4
○	Collio Pinot Grigio '97	🍷🍷	4
●	Collio Rosso Conte di Spessa '93	🍷🍷	4
○	Collio Sauvignon '97	🍷	4
○	Collio Pinot Bianco di Santarosa '91	♀♀	4
●	Collio Rosso Conte di Spessa '92	♀	4

CAPRIVA DEL FRIULI (GO)

GIOVANNI PUIATTI

VIA AQUILEIA, 30
34070 CAPRIVA DEL FRIULI (GO)
TEL. 0481/809922

Giovanni Puiatti, son of the great Vittorio, already takes his place in the Guide at only his second vintage. Last year we were sufficiently impressed by some of his wines to accord him Honorable Mention. Giovanni is aware that, to give of their best, vineyards need the constant attention that only their owner can give them; he has therefore augmented the four hectares bought several years ago at Ruttars, in the Collio appellation, with the purchase of 24 hectares in the Isonzo DOC. The tasting results were very encouraging, starting with an excellent Pinot Grigio whose complex and elegant aromas of moss, aniseed and green apple are repeated on a rich, broad palate with a well-balanced acidity. The Chardonnay '97 wins a Glass for its aromas of barley sugar, custard, yeasts and well-ripened fruit, in perfect harmony with a palate which is equally satisfying, with a bite of acidity on the finish. The Cabernet Franc '97 earns the same rating for its unusually stylish nose (with notes of hay, grass and black currant) and its concentrated, long, rich chewy palate, loaded with ripe fruit and spices. Lastly, the Merlot gets a Glass: red fruits and baked pear are discernible on the nose, cherries and prunes on the palate in nice balance with the tannins and acidity. With a start like this, Giovanni Puiatti has not only our good wishes but also our confident prediction of his future success.

	Wine	Rating	Price
○	Friuli Isonzo Pinot Grigio '97	🍷🍷	3*
○	Friuli Isonzo Chardonnay '97	🍷	3
●	Friuli Isonzo Merlot '97	🍷	3
●	Friuli Isonzo Cabernet Franc '97	🍷	3

CAPRIVA DEL FRIULI (GO)

Roncùs

Via Mazzini, 26
34070 Capriva del Friuli (GO)
tel. 0481/809349

If Marco Perco, the young owner of the Roncùs estate, can keep going the way he started, he will be much talked about in the future. After last year's striking entry into the Guide, he has now presented a range of top-notch wines which, although slightly muffled in bouquet by very recent bottling, passed the tastings with excellent marks. Despite his youth, Marco sticks to his guns, making highly individual decisions both in the vineyard, with late harvests, and in the cellar, with special maceration techniques. It is no coincidence that his wines display a marked personality. The most convincing is the Tocai: fresh and stylish on the nose with an attractive appley overtone, it has a vigorous impact on the palate, which is enjoyably soft with a long fruity finish. The Roncùs Bianco, from pinot, malvasia and ribolla, is another excellent wine. It has an elegant note of fresh apple on the nose, picked up again on the harmonious, full, warm palate, and ends with a lingering fruitiness on the finish. The Pinot Bianco, of a golden yellow hue delightful to the eye, offers pleasing aromas of fresh fruit and yeast which give way to soft, fruity, lingering flavors in the mouth, enhancing the wine's appeal. The Sauvignon, almost as good, evolves nicely on the moderately long, lactic palate. This list of reliable wines includes no reds, since at the time of our tastings they were not yet bottled.

Wine	Glasses	Price
○ Pinot Bianco '97	▼▼	4
○ Roncùs Bianco '97	▼▼	4
○ Tocai Friulano '97	▼▼	4
○ Sauvignon '97	▼	4
○ Sauvignon '96	▽▽	4
○ Pinot Bianco '96	▽	4
○ Roncùs Bianco '96	▽	4
○ Tocai Friulano '96	▽	4

CAPRIVA DEL FRIULI (GO)

Russiz Superiore

Via Russiz, 7
34070 Capriva del Friuli (GO)
tel. 0481/80328 - 92237

Russiz Superiore has once again presented lovers of fine wines with a superb Rosso Collio Riserva named after the Conti Orzoni family who once owned these vineyards. Marco Felluga and his daughter Patrizia have flanked it with two other worthy reds, the Cabernet Franc and the Merlot '96. But let's get right to the Three Glasses winner, the Orzoni '94. It's almost entirely cabernet sauvignon, matured in barrique for 18 months and aged for at least a year in bottle. The entry on the nose is intense and concentrated with aromas of cherries, both sweet and sour, and woodland berries; the soft, mellow impact on the palate unfolds in a mouth-filling fruit while retaining its solid structure, and ends with a good tannic grip. In the Merlot '96 the entry on both the nose and the palate is vigorous, full and intense, presenting a rich array of well-ripened red fruits and good structure, and only on the finish do the tannins reveal a certain harshness which will mellow with time. Again the tannins jar on the finish of the Cabernet Franc '96, which is otherwise commendable for its concentrated aromas, with hints of cherry tart on the nose, while the smooth palate has a lingering aftertaste. The Pinot Grigio '97 offers a wonderfully complex nose with pears, apples and a hint of sweet pepper, and a palate with rich fruit and a long finish. This year did not promise well for the Sauvignon, but against all expectation it has turned out to be a superb wine, with elderberry, rue and sweet pepper on the nose leading into a rich, full, well-structured palate with good acidity. The Tocai Friulano '97 is broad and complex, only just shy of Two Glasses. To end with, the Pinot Bianco has complex perfumes of vanilla and custard; fruit is the most prominent feature on the nicely structured palate.

Wine	Glasses	Price
● Collio Rosso Riserva degli Orzoni '94	▼▼▼	5
● Collio Cabernet Franc '96	▼▼	4
○ Collio Pinot Grigio '97	▼▼	4
○ Collio Sauvignon '97	▼▼	4
● Collio Merlot '96	▼▼	4
○ Collio Pinot Bianco '97	▼	4
○ Collio Tocai Friulano '97	▼	4
● Collio Rosso Riserva degli Orzoni '93	▽▽▽	5
● Collio Cabernet Franc '95	▽▽	4
● Collio Rosso Riserva degli Orzoni '92	▽▽	5
○ Collio Pinot Bianco '96	▽▽	4
○ Collio Tocai Friulano '96	▽▽	4
○ Collio Pinot Grigio '96	▽▽	4

CAPRIVA DEL FRIULI (GO)

MARIO SCHIOPETTO

VIA PALAZZO ARCIVESCOVILE, 1
34070 CAPRIVA DEL FRIULI (GO)
TEL. 0481/80332

Much has been written and said about Mario Schiopetto, grand master of wine-making in Friuli. Because of the state of his health everybody thought that his creations would no longer cause a stir, but with the help of his children, Maria Angela, Carlo and Giorgio, a series of stunning wines has appeared. Some of these have been produced with a technique commonly thought to be despised by Schiopetto - the use of wooden barrels for whites. The superb Pinot Bianco '96 Amrità, (the name given by the Chaldeans to the potion of immortality), easily wins Three Glasses. The wine offers an elegant, full and faintly lactic nose with a distinct appley scent; this carries through on the wonderfully well-balanced palate, with notes of fresh fruits and a hint of vanilla underneath. The Pinot Bianco '97 has scents of apple, fresh fruit salad and apricot, while the broad, mouth-filling palate winds up with banana and apple on the finish. The other champion, the Sauvignon '97, is full and elegant, with aromas of elderberry and rue; the stylish palate has a long, lingering finish. The second oaked white, the Tocai Friulano '96 Pardes (meaning paradise or center of the world in Chaldean) is only just behind it: intense aromas of pear, smoke, wood, dried flowers and citrus fruit emerge on the nose, and the palate is exceptionally long and fruity. The Pinot Grigio recalls acacia blossom and apple, and displays mineral notes and a fresh acidity, while the Malvasia offers scents of green apple, yeasts, violets and fresh fruits. The Blanc des Rosis evokes sour apples, lemon and mint, the Merlot has an attractive balance of fruit and tannins, and the Rivarossa reveals red fruits and notes of tar.

	Wine	Glasses	Price
○	Collio Pinot Bianco Amrità '96	🍷🍷🍷	5
○	Collio Sauvignon '97	🍷🍷🍷	5
○	Blanc des Rosis '97	🍷🍷	4
○	Collio Malvasia '97	🍷🍷	4
○	Collio Pinot Bianco '97	🍷🍷	4
○	Collio Pinot Grigio '97	🍷🍷	4
○	Collio Tocai Friulano '97	🍷🍷	4
○	Collio Tocai Friulano Pardes '96	🍷🍷	5
●	Collio Merlot '96	🍷🍷	4
●	Rivarossa '96	🍷🍷	4
○	Collio Pinot Bianco '94	(🍷🍷🍷)	4
○	Collio Sauvignon '89	(🍷🍷🍷)	4
○	Collio Tocai Friulano '93	(🍷🍷🍷)	4
○	Collio Tocai Friulano '94	(🍷🍷🍷)	4
○	Collio Tocai Friulano '95	(🍷🍷🍷)	4

CAPRIVA DEL FRIULI (GO)

VIDUSSI GESTIONI AGRICOLE

VIA SPESSA, 18
34070 CAPRIVA DEL FRIULI (GO)
TEL. 0481/80072

Signora Antonietta Causero Vidussi, with the assistance of the oenologist Paolo Fornasiero, has given yet further proof of the reliability of her winery. The grapes are all from her own vineyards, which are mostly in the Collio DOC zone, with a smaller part in the Colli Orientali del Friuli appellation. This year two reds vye for first place. The Refosco dal Peduncolo Rosso, from the Ipplis vineyards in the Colli Orientali zone, undergoes a short spell of maturation in used barriques. The wine is dense and concentrated both in color and on the nose, with distinct notes of blackberry. The palate follows through well and is structured, full-bodied and very long, with nicely judged oak. The Ronc dal Rol, a blend of merlot, cabernet sauvignon and cabernet franc aged for 15 months in both new and used small oak casks, has an assertive oak on the nose enriched by ripe fruit and underbrush; it carries through perfectly on the palate, which is warm and rounded despite rather acidity-roughened tannins. The wide range of One Glass wines begins with the Bianco Croce Alta, made from malvasia, sauvignon and tocai friulano grapes and named after the vineyard they come from: the nose is rich, fresh and broad, while the fairly structured palate displays good alcohol, acidity and length. The Chardonnay is attractive in its unusual elegance, correct acidity and long fruity finish. The intense Pinot Bianco has a wonderfully rich nose evoking apple, medicinal herbs and tea; the apple is repeated on the palate but an over-assertive acidity on the finish detracts from the wine's appeal. Elegance is also the keynote in the Tocai Friulano. The rich, broad, long Boan is made with grapes from Pradis di Cormons.

	Wine	Glasses	Price
●	COF Refosco P. R. '97	🍷🍷	3
●	Ronc dal Rol '96	🍷🍷	4
○	Collio Bianco Croce Alta '97	🍷	3
○	Collio Chardonnay '97	🍷	3
○	Collio Pinot Bianco '97	🍷	3
○	Collio Tocai Friulano '97	🍷	3
○	Il Boan '97	🍷	3
○	COF Verduzzo Friulano '97		3
○	Collio Sauvignon '97		3
●	COF Schioppettino '97		3
●	Ronc dal Rol '95	(🍷🍷)	4
○	Collio Chardonnay '96	(🍷🍷)	3

CAPRIVA DEL FRIULI (GO)

VILLA RUSSIZ
VIA RUSSIZ, 6
34070 CAPRIVA DEL FRIULI (GO)
TEL. 0481/80047

The quality of this estate's wines can be seen at a glance from the list below, but although these details would be sufficient we feel our readers should have some additional information. The Sauvignon de La Tour '97 was unhesitatingly awarded Three Glasses, while the merits of Gianni Menotti's other most extraordinary wines, the Graf de La Tour '95 and the Pinot Bianco '97, were discussed at length. An astonishing structure backs up the rich aromas of the Sauvignon de La Tour '97, where delicate tomato leaf, elder blossom and rue emerge elegantly on a full, broad, concentrated palate with echoes of citrus fruit. The Merlot Graf de La Tour offers a warm, intense nose, soft and stylish, with notes of talcum and prunes, sour cherry tart and sweet cherries in spirit; the wine is long and full-bodied with vigorous tannins masked by the abundant fruit and then a note of bitter chocolate on the finish. The Pinot Bianco, whose nose offers aromas of green apple with underlying lactic nuances, has tremendous impact on the palate, which is concentrated, dense, mouth-filling, wonderfully rich, and long in the finish. Among the other Two Glass wines is the Tocai Friulano, whose key features, surprisingly, are elegance and length, rather than body. The Malvasia Istriana stands out for its harmonious mingling of fruit and wild flowers, while the Pinot Grigio reveals fresh, vegetal notes which lend refinement to a concentrated, close-knit wine. The Ribolla Gialla has delicate tones of apple, banana and pear; it is stylish and inviting, with length and freshness. The Sauvignon '97 and the Merlot '96 both come close to Two Glasses.

	Wine	Glasses	Price
○	Collio Sauvignon de La Tour '97	🍷🍷🍷	4
○	Collio Malvasia Istriana '97	🍷🍷	4
○	Collio Pinot Bianco '97	🍷🍷	4
○	Collio Pinot Grigio '97	🍷🍷	4
○	Collio Tocai Friulano '97	🍷🍷	4
○	Collio Ribolla Gialla '97	🍷🍷	4
●	Collio Merlot Graf de La Tour '95	🍷🍷	6
●	Collio Merlot '96	🍷	4
○	Collio Sauvignon '97	🍷	4
○	Collio Riesling '97		4
●	Collio Merlot Graf de La Tour '93	𝖸𝖸𝖸	5
●	Collio Merlot Graf de La Tour '94	𝖸𝖸𝖸	5
○	Collio Sauvignon de La Tour '91	𝖸𝖸𝖸	4
○	Collio Sauvignon de La Tour '94	𝖸𝖸𝖸	4
○	Collio Tocai Friulano '95	𝖸𝖸𝖸	4

CIVIDALE DEL FRIULI (UD)

DAL FARI
VIA DARNAZZACCO
33043 CIVIDALE DEL FRIULI (UD)
TEL. 0432/731219 - 706711

Since Renzo Toffolutti, an industrialist with a passion for wine, decided to revise and upgrade the overall running of his estate, the results have been definitely encouraging. Under the skilled and careful guidance of the oenologist Fabio Coser, who makes optimum use of the advanced technological equipment in the cellar, the wines are of increasingly reliable and attractive quality. This year two blends, the Bianco delle Grazie and the Rosso d'Orsone, have scored high marks. The first, from chardonnay, sauvignon, tocai friulano and riesling, has immediate impact on the nose with buttery scents, acacia blossom and tropical fruit: the entry on the palate is positive and the wine evolves well, with a fresh, delightful acidity on the long finish. The second, a barrique-aged blend of cabernet franc, cabernet sauvignon, merlot and schioppettino, has an ample nose with hints of jam, plums, coffee and tar, and reveals good complexity on the palate, but is slightly diminished by the harshness of the tannins which stop it from getting an even higher score. The Merlot, another fine red, has complex aromas of coffee and red fruits, repeated in the mouth with tannins which still need to soften. The Cabernet displays a delightful toastiness with aromas of coffee and red currants; the palate has balance, length and good structure with an agreeable fruitiness.The Chardonnay is the best of the varietal whites, with a crusty, yeasty, appley nose and a nicely-structured, mouth-filling, almost lactic palate revealing warmth and well-evolved flavors. The Pinot Grigio and the Tocai Friulano are technically correct and worthy of notice.

	Wine	Glasses	Price
○	COF Bianco delle Grazie '96	🍷🍷	4
●	Rosso d'Orsone '93	🍷🍷	4
●	COF Cabernet '96	🍷	4
●	COF Merlot '96	🍷	4
○	COF Chardonnay '97	🍷	4
○	COF Pinot Grigio '97		4
○	COF Tocai Friulano '97		4
●	COF Cabernet '95	𝖸𝖸	4
●	Rosso d'Orsone '90	𝖸	4
●	Rosso d'Orsone '91	𝖸	4

LUCIA GALASSO
STRADA DI PLANEZ, 32
FRAZ. SPESSA
33043 CIVIDALE DEL FRIULI (UD)
TEL. 0432/730292 - 701462

Lucia Galasso, wife of Giovanni Crosato, an oenologist from the Veneto who settled in Friuli many years ago, has with a touch of irony named two of the estate's wines, the Bianco Don Giovanni and the Rosso Don Giovanni, after her husband, with a picture of him holding a wineglass reproduced on the label. The winery cultivates five hectares of vineyards with vines over 35 years old. Since it used to be the custom to grow a variety of grapes, Lucia decided to make a virtue of necessity and concentrate largely on blends. This is how we come to have the Bianco Don Giovanni, from tocai, sauvignon and pinot bianco, a wine of great elegance with an attractive nose of juniper berries which follows through on the warm, tasty, structured palate. The Colli Orientali del Friuli Rosso DOC, four parts merlot to one of refosco, spends three months in barrique: this wine very nearly won Two Glasses for its balanced oak on the nose and the softness and fruity structure of the palate. The Rosso Don Giovanni '96, a blend of merlot, cabernet sauvignon, cabernet franc, refosco and schioppettino which spends nine months in small oak barrels, shows greater complexity; the nose is redolent of warm plums and cherry preserve which carry through on the palate, whose softness is undisturbed by its acidity. The Merlot and Cabernet of the last vintage both deserve our mention.

	Wine	Glasses	Price
○	Il Bianco Don Giovanni '96	🍷🍷	4
●	COF Rosso '97	🍷	3*
●	Il Rosso Don Giovanni '96	🍷	4
●	COF Cabernet '97		3
●	COF Merlot '97		3

PAOLO RODARO
VIA CORMONS, 8
FRAZ. SPESSA
33040 CIVIDALE DEL FRIULI (UD)
TEL. 0432/716066

In the '96 Guide we wrote that this estate was the surprise of the '94 vintage in Friuli. Several harvests have gone by since then and Paolo Rodaro's wines have continued to display a consistently high quality, placing the winery firmly among the top rank of producers in Friuli. This year too Rodaro can boast a wide range of excellent wines, with the Tocai Friulano and the Verduzzo Pra Zenâr nearly achieving Three Glasses. The Tocai Friulano (45,000 bottles) is the traditional flagship of the estate (probably the microclimate of the Bosco Romagno is well suited to this grape). The wine is a deep, brilliant straw-yellow in color, with intense almondy aromas and scents of crusty bread following through on a vigorous palate, which, mouth-filling, buttery and very long as it is, still reveals a delightful finesse. The Verduzzo Pra Zenâr, although tasted just after bottling, was striking in its complex nose of figs, sultanas and candied orange and its balanced density and sweetness. The golden Picolit, with lovely fragrances of pineapple, tropical fruit, peaches in syrup and chocolate, has exceptional concentration and length on the palate, with an attractive lavender note on the finish. Intense and harmonious scents of banana and tropical fruits characterize the Ribolla Gialla, which is powerful and lingering on the palate. The Tocai Bosc Romain, the fruit of rigorous thinning in the vineyard, has consequently more alcohol and opulence. The Pinot Bianco and the Pinot Grigio are both worthy of a full Glass. The first has pleasant aromas of apple and pear, the second a satisfying complexity on the palate. Lastly, a mention for the correct and typical Verduzzo Friulano.

	Wine	Glasses	Price
○	COF Picolit '97	🍷🍷	5
○	COF Ribolla Gialla '97	🍷🍷	3
○	COF Tocai Friulano '97	🍷🍷	3*
○	COF Tocai Friulano Bosc Romain '97	🍷🍷	4
○	COF Verduzzo Friulano Pra Zenâr '97	🍷🍷	5
○	COF Pinot Bianco '97	🍷	3
○	COF Pinot Grigio '97	🍷	3
○	COF Verduzzo Friulano '97	🍷	3
○	COF Chardonnay '97		3
○	COF Sauvignon Bosc Romain '96	🍷🍷🍷 (prior)	3
○	COF Verduzzo Friulano Pra Zenâr '96	🍷🍷 (prior)	5

CORMONS (GO)

TENUTA DI ANGORIS
LOC. ANGORIS, 7
34071 CORMONS (GO)
TEL. 0481/60923

The Tenuta di Angoris was originally granted to Locatello Locatelli of Friuli by the Austrian Emperor Ferdinand III in 1648. After many vicissitudes the property, which was bought by Luciano Locatelli in 1963, now comprises 540 hectares, of which 90 are under vine. The vineyards in the Collio DOC, from which the Ronco Antico range is produced, and those of the Podere Rocca Bernarda, in the Colli Orientali del Friuli appellation, are also part of the estate. Annual output is about one million bottles, of which 100,000 are special selections. Luciano's daughter, Claudia, looks after sales and marketing, and the oenologist Natale Favretto is in charge of the technical side. The Sauvignon Podere Rocca Bernarda has distinctly toasty aromas with underlying hints of elderberry, rue and tomato leaf, while the warm, mellow palate reveals a full structure and varietal notes only lightly masked by the wood. The Pinot Bianco Podere Ronco Antico also fully deserves its Glass: subtle, elegant scents of apple, flowers and citrus fruit lead into a palate with notes of tea and summer fruits. The Podere Rocca Bernarda gives further pleasure with the Refosco '96, characterized by rich aromas and a seductive palate with berries and spices. The Cabernet Sauvignon '96 Podere Larghi, from the vineyards surrounding the cellar, is more satisfying in the mouth than on the nose, with flavors of concentrated red fruits, a full but fresh structure and tannins noticeable only on the finish. The Spumante Angoris Nature Metodo Classico '94, from pinot nero with a little pinot bianco and chardonnay, will be appreciated particularly by fans of ripeness. The Ravòst '96, from schioppettino and some refosco, is worthy of notice.

	Wine	Glasses	Price
○	Angoris Nature Metodo Classico '94	🍷	4
○	COF Sauvignon Podere Rocca Bernarda '97	🍷	3
○	Collio Pinot Bianco Podere Ronco Antico '97	🍷	3
●	COF Refosco P. R. Podere Rocca Bernarda '96	🍷	3
●	Friuli Isonzo Cabernet Sauvignon Podere Larghi '96	🍷	3
●	Ravòst '96		3
●	Collio Merlot Ronco Antico '95	🍸	3
○	COF Picolit '96	🍸	5
○	Spìule '96	🍸	3

CORMONS (GO)

BRUNO & MARIO BASTIANI
VIA SAVAIAN, 36
34071 CORMONS (GO)
TEL. 0481/60725

Mario and Marinella Bastiani's estate is one of the most interesting small wineries of the area. Its seven hectares of vineyards are situated on the hillsides and the plains of Cormons and consequently belong to two different DOCs, Collio and Isonzo. They are cultivated according to a mixture of traditional methods, such as using natural fertilizer and dense plantings, and modern practices, such as careful restriction of the yields per vine, with highly positive results. The Pinot Bianco '97 has gold tints, an indication of its concentration; the nose is warm and redolent of apple and custard, while the entry on the palate is soft with a wonderful broad fruit, good acidity, a rich dense texture and echoes of lemon rind and pear on the finish. The Tocai Friulano, with notes of pear and apple seeds evolving well on the nose, is a wine of exceptional balance and harmony of nose and palate. The Ribolla Gialla evokes unripe fruit and meadow herbs on the nose, while the palate is broad and complex with distinct notes of apple and yellow plum, a well-judged acidity and a long fruity finish. The Pinot Grigio's most attractive feature is the nose, with pear and elegant hints of nail polish, while the palate displays a certain leanness due to the acidity which, however, freshens it up. The very hot summer was hard on the aromas of the Sauvignon but it also imparted greater structure, enriched with notes of apple and citrus fruit.

	Wine	Glasses	Price
○	Collio Pinot Bianco '97	🍷🍷	2*
○	Collio Pinot Grigio '97	🍷	3
○	Collio Ribolla Gialla '97	🍷	3
○	Collio Tocai Friulano '97	🍷	2*
○	Friuli Isonzo Sauvignon '97	🍷	3
●	Friuli Isonzo Cabernet '97		2

CORMONS (GO)

BORGO DEL TIGLIO
VIA S. GIORGIO, 71
FRAZ. BRAZZANO
34070 CORMONS (GO)
TEL. 0481/62166

Nicola Manferrari's winery, Borgo del Tiglio, produces a range of top-flight wines, and some are really exceptional. We were very impressed, for example, by the Rosso della Centa '93 with its outstanding structure and intense, concentrated nose, and a palate that offers a rich ensemble of wild berries, red fruit tart and attractive hints of tar, underpinned by an unusually powerful body. Our only reservation: a faintly overripe note gives the impression that it may have been at its best a year ago. In the highly appealing Chardonnay '96 the unobtrusive oak is very finely judged, lending elegance to the aromas and enhancing the soft, warm palate in which banana is the keynote in a composition of fresh apple and medicinal herbs. The Collio Rosso '94 is another excellent wine, not so much because of its nose, reminiscent of red fruits and a hint of green rind, as on the palate, which has lots of body and breadth with warm red berries, sandalwood and spices; the long, generous finish is slightly compromised by rough-edged tannins. The stylish Bianco '96, despite a marked toastiness which will tone down with time, also earns Two Glasses; the aromatic, flinty nose leads into a broad, creamy palate with a good, fresh acidity backing up the length. The Studio di Bianco, still distinctly toasty, nearly got Two Glasses, whereas the Tocai '96, both the basic version and the Ronco della Chiesa, are not up to their usual standard.

●	Collio Rosso '94	🍷🍷	5
●	Rosso della Centa '93	🍷🍷	6
○	Bianco '96	🍷🍷	5
○	Collio Chardonnay '96	🍷🍷	5
○	Collio Tocai Friulano Ronco della Chiesa '96	🍷	6
○	Collio Sauvignon Selezione '96	🍷	5
○	Collio Tocai Friulano '96	🍷	4
○	Studio di Bianco '96	🍷	5
○	Collio Tocai Ronco della Chiesa '90	🍸🍸🍸	4
○	Collio Sauvignon '95	🍸🍸	4
●	Collio Rosso '92	🍸🍸	5
●	Collio Rosso '93	🍸🍸	5

CORMONS (GO)

BORGO SAN DANIELE
VIA S. DANIELE, 16
34071 CORMONS (GO)
TEL. 0481/60552

The Mauri siblings of Borgo San Daniele, an estate with land in the Collio and Isonzo DOC zones, are never satisfied with their efforts: every year sees them, with the stubbornness of youth, making alterations, carrying out renovations and developing new ideas in the endless pursuit of higher quality. This year Mauro, in charge of viticulture and wine-making, wanted to make wines with a richer, more international style, and used wood to enhance them without standardizing them. In accordance with the advice of Alessandra, who looks after the commercial side, the estate has also reduced its range of wines, channelling the grapes from the Collio vineyards into the production of blends. Everyone knows that big changes do not always have immediate and positive results, but for Borgo San Daniele the vintage has turned out to be sensational for a whole range of premium wines, with the Tocai even garnering Three Glasses. This white is distinguished by aromas of pear well blended with scents of fruit compote, lemon, chamomile and medicinal herbs, all of which re-emerge on the warm, broad palate and lead into a long, almondy finish. The Lucky Red '94, which scored only slightly less, is a barrique-aged Merlot offering warm, concentrated, plum tart aromas and tarry notes which carry through on a full palate with lots of generous fruit. The Arbis Bianco '97, from tocai, sauvignon and müller thurgau, has elegant, intense herbal, fruity and elderberry aromas followed by a wonderfully rich palate. The Pinot Grigio '97 offers scents of golden delicious apples which reappear on the palate and on the long, delightful finish. Lastly a Glass goes to the Arbis Rosso '96, cabernet franc and cabernet sauvignon, and to the Chardonnay '97.

○	Friuli Isonzo Tocai Friulano '97	🍷🍷🍷	4
○	Arbis Bianco '97	🍷🍷	4
○	Friuli Isonzo Pinot Grigio '97	🍷🍷	4
●	Lucky Red '94	🍷🍷	4
●	Arbis Rosso '96	🍷	4
○	Friuli Isonzo Chardonnay '97	🍷	4
○	Isonzo Chardonnay '96	🍸🍸	4
●	Gortmarin '94	🍸🍸	4

CORMONS (GO)

BORIS E DAVID BUZZINELLI
LOC. PRADIS, 22/BIS
34071 CORMONS (GO)
TEL. 0481/62272

Work continues without a break in the big, new winery of the Buzzinelli brothers, Boris and David. After the opening of the tasting room, the next job is completion of the place for maturing the reds for the two labels, Carlo Buzzinelli and BorDavi. The '97 Merlot is maturing in wood, but the new wine from this vintage, the Collio Bianco, from tocai friulano, sauvignon, ribolla gialla and malvasia istriana, was marred by its strong toasty flavor of new barriques. At our tastings we particularly liked a superb Pinot Bianco with an intense, clean appley perfume carrying through on the palate, which is mouth-filling, fresh, and fruity with a long aftertaste. The Tocai Friulano has well-defined aromas of pear and apple seeds; the impact on the palate is vigorous, warm and full and leads into a satisfying finish with plenty of acidity. The Pinot Grigio is rather undefined on the nose, but the palate is fresh and continuous, revealing good structure, and enjoyable notes of aromatic herbs emerge on the finish. The excellent Merlot '95, characterized by well-judged oak, offers cherry tart and licorice on the nose; the palate evolves well but the tannins are too pronounced. Both the Merlot '96 and the Sauvignon '97 deserve mention.

	Wine	Glasses	Price
○	Collio Pinot Bianco Vigneti di Pradis '97	🍷🍷	3*
○	Collio Pinot Grigio Vigneti di Pradis '97	🍷	3
○	Collio Tocai Friulano Vigneti di Pradis '97	🍷	3
●	Collio Merlot Vigneti di Pradis '95	🍷	4
●	Collio Merlot Vigneti di Pradis '96		4
○	Collio Sauvignon Vigneti di Pradis '97		3
●	Collio Merlot Carlo Buzzinelli '94	♈♈	4

CORMONS (GO)

PAOLO CACCESE
LOC. PRADIS, 6
34071 CORMONS (GO)
TEL. 0481/61062

Weather conditions in the past year, especially the extremely hot summer, have led to reduced production, on top of which the vineyards of the appealing and sociable Paolo Caccese, a wine-maker from Gorizia who moved with his family to Cormons, suffered from a frost which further depleted the crop. The resulting grapes were very high in sugar content which fermentation transformed into a powerful alcohol. We especially enjoyed the Pinot Bianco, the Pinot Grigio and the Malvasia, wines which in the '97 vintage had over 13.5% of alcohol. The Pinot Grigio has a long entry on the palate, which is warm, fruity, broad and mouth-filling, offering a continuous succession of soft, enjoyable sensations and culminating in a fresh and delightful finish. The Pinot Bianco is subtly reminiscent of tobacco leaf and apple on the nose; in the mouth it is full-flavored and structured, displaying good evolution and length. Caccese has made a Malvasia Istriana, (which in other hands is usually delicate and fresh), of exceptional body, warm, enticing and glycerin-rich with notes of apple and pear. The Tocai Friulano only just failed to get Two Glasses: it was full and mellow on the palate but slightly sulphurous at our tastings; we are, however, confident that it will acquire balance with a little more time. The Sauvignon was more convincing on the palate than on the nose, likewise the two reds which have become classics for Paolo Caccese, the Merlot and the Cabernet Franc, the former displaying good body, the latter a marked spiciness.

	Wine	Glasses	Price
○	Collio Malvasia Istriana '97	🍷🍷	4
○	Collio Pinot Bianco '97	🍷🍷	4
○	Collio Pinot Grigio '97	🍷🍷	4
●	Collio Cabernet Franc '97	🍷	4
●	Collio Merlot '97	🍷	4
○	Collio Sauvignon '97	🍷	4
○	Collio Tocai Friulano '97	🍷	3
○	Collio Riesling '97		3
●	Collio Cabernet Franc '96	♈♈	4

CORMONS (GO)

Cantina Produttori di Cormons

Via Vino della Pace, 31
34071 Cormons (GO)
tel. 0481/60579-62471

Hats off to the Cantina Produttori di Cormons for the steady rise in quality which we have observed over the last few years. If you bear in mind that the wines assessed were 20 and the member growers over 200, their vineyards scattered around the hills and the plain, you can get some idea of the efforts made, particularly by the small growers, to raise the level of the wines produced. The excellent results can be traced in large part to the tenacity of Luigi Soini, the Cantina's forceful, feisty manager. The intense nose of the Chardonnay del Collio unfolds in subtle, elegant aromas of banana, melon, crusty bread and yeasts, leading into a fresh, structured palate with wonderful balance and length. In the Pinot Grigio Collio, notes of mango, fresh apple, banana and wildflowers emerge on the nose, while in the mouth it is rich, broad, and full-flavored with good acidity and a delicious lingering fruitiness at the end. The Collio Bianco offers notes of muscat, apple, roses and ripe apricot, while macaroons are the keynote among the aromas of the Pinot Bianco Collio. The Ribolla Gialla presents typical aromas of green apple and wildflowers. The Picolit deserves to be discussed in fuller detail: amber-gold in color, it has aromas of dried figs, apricot, chocolate and lavender leading into a sweet but not cloying palate, enriched with notes of sultanas. There is an interesting method of production for the Isonzo Vendemmia Tardiva Vino degli Angeli: the bunches of grapes, nipped in the stalk with special pincers in mid-August, begin to shrivel. The harvest takes place in early October, and the grapes come out low in the tartaric acid which often detracts from the taste of wines made from sun-dried grapes.

	Wine	Glasses	Price
○	Collio Chardonnay '97	🍷🍷	3*
○	Collio Pinot Grigio '97	🍷🍷	3*
○	Collio Collio '97	🍷	3
○	Collio Picolit '96	🍷	5
○	Collio Pinot Bianco '97	🍷	3
○	Collio Ribolla Gialla '97	🍷	3
○	Friuli Isonzo Pinot Grigio '97	🍷	3
●	Friuli Isonzo Refosco P. R. '97	🍷	3
○	Friuli Isonzo V. T. Vino degli Angeli '96	🍷	4
○	Passito di Cormons	🍷	4

CORMONS (GO)

Mauro Drius

Via Filanda, 100
34071 Cormons (GO)
tel. 0481/60998

This estate, whose vineyards lie partly on the slopes of Monte Quarin, in the Collio DOC, and partly in the low-lying zone around Cormons, in the Isonzo DOC, has had a successful vintage. When we tasted them the wines were not in the most attractive stage of their evolution and, although they nearly all scored well, we had been expecting even better from them. This year's best is the Isonzo Tocai Friulano, offering pear, russet apples and hints of elderberry on the nose; the right amount of acidity emerges on the long, balanced palate, whose generous fruit finishes off with notes of pear and banana. The same grape but from the Collio zone only just misses Two Glasses: its elegant, appley aromas are repeated on the palate, which evolves well and reveals a good acidity. The Isonzo Riesling has varietal notes of petroleum and unripe plums, while its firm structure is backed up by an adequate acidity and the re-emergence of the plummy aromas on the finish. The Isonzo Malvasia has a flowery, fruity nose and an equally attractive palate. The entry on the nose in the Isonzo Cabernet is warm and delightful, with spices, vanilla and fruit; the palate has good structure and fruit but lacks complexity. We know that they are working hard on the white blend Vìgnis di Sìris, from tocai, sauvignon partially fermented in barrique and a small amount of pinot bianco. This year the promising nose offers intense, elegant fruity perfumes, but the palate is somewhat diminished by the acidity. The Isonzo Pinot Bianco and the Collio Sauvignon are both correctly made wines that deserve mention.

	Wine	Glasses	Price
○	Friuli Isonzo Tocai Friulano '97	🍷🍷	3*
○	Collio Tocai Friulano '97	🍷	3
●	Friuli Isonzo Cabernet '96	🍷	3
○	Friuli Isonzo Malvasia '97	🍷	3
○	Friuli Isonzo Riesling '97	🍷	3
○	Collio Sauvignon '97		3
○	Friuli Isonzo Bianco Vìgnis di Sìris '97		3
○	Friuli Isonzo Pinot Bianco '97		3
○	Friuli Isonzo Tocai Friulano '96	🍷🍷 (previous edition)	3

CORMONS (GO)

Livio Felluga

Via Risorgimento, 1
Fraz. Brazzano
34071 Cormons (GO)
tel. 0481/60203

The successful creation of the Rosazzo subzone, lying in the Colli Orientali del Friuli DOC and recently recognized by the authorities, is largely due to Livio Felluga's estate, and now there is a Rosazzo DOC wine that has won Three Glasses: Livio Felluga's Terre Alte '96. This outstanding wine has been remarkably consistent for many years. Of exceptional longevity, it is made from a blend of sauvignon, pinot bianco and tocai friulano vinified in stainless steel. The varietal aromas of the sauvignon are the keynote on the nose, with echoes of elderberry, citrus peel, fresh vegetal scents and green apple. The palate opens out in a continuous succession of fresh fruits and herbal infusions which, backed up by the acidity and alcohol, linger on the wonderfully long finish. The Merlot Sossò increases in appeal every year: the '95 vintage offers a nose with hints of cherries in spirit, black currants, tea, undergrowth, balsam and a streak of tar, carried through onto the palate, which has loads of fruit and slightly over-assertive tannins. The much softer Refosco offers a round, complex bouquet of warm red fruits, blackberry and raspberry jam and an insistent spicy note, but it doesn't have the body of the Sossò. The Picolit was the subject of lively discussion: the nose of candied citrus, figs and almonds leads into a wonderfully balanced, sweet palate with hints of white chocolate, ripe fruit and wildflowers. The Pinot Grigio and the Tocai Friulano almost got Two Glasses, the former for complexity of nose and palate and the latter for marked varietal character. Lastly the Esperto line, with its Chardonnay as well as its other wines, is excellent value for money.

	Wine	Glasses	Price
○	COF Rosazzo Bianco Terre Alte '96	🍷🍷🍷	5
●	COF Merlot Rosazzo Sossò Ris. '95	🍷🍷	5
●	COF Refosco P. R. '95	🍷🍷	5
○	COF Picolit '94	🍷🍷	6
○	Chardonnay Esperto '97	🍷	3*
○	COF Pinot Grigio '97	🍷	4
○	COF Tocai Friulano '97	🍷	4
○	COF Sauvignon '97		4
○	COF Bianco Terre Alte '95	YYY	5
○	Terre Alte '89	YYY	5
○	Terre Alte '90	YYY	5
○	Terre Alte '92	YYY	5
○	Terre Alte '93	YYY	5

CORMONS (GO)

Edi Keber

Loc. Zegla, 17
34071 Cormons (GO)
tel. 0481/61184

Edi Keber, a warm, calm, staunch wine-maker from Cormons, has again won Three Glasses for his Tocai Friulano. Alas, his father Pepi will not be here this time to celebrate. Generous and exemplary to the very end, he participated wholeheartedly in all his son's innovations, including the decision to keep on only two varietal labels (the Tocai and the Merlot) and two blends, produced with the best of the other grapes. But life goes on, and Edi's decisions are receiving approval from critics and wine-buying public alike, and we hope that others will be persuaded to join him in the strategy that some of the most important wineries have devised and that promises to be the success of the future. The intense, delightful aromas of the Tocai '97 are redolent of apple, lemon and citron; the full, opulent, broad, warm nose is almost reminiscent of the wines of Alsace, while russet apple and apple seeds emerge on the palate. The Bianco '97, from tocai, ribolla, malvasia and pinot bianco, again offers apple and citrus fruit on the nose, but is even more convincing in the mouth with its warm, soft structure and perfect harmony of fruit and acidity in the long finish. Edi has created a stunning Rosso from merlot and cabernet franc: fresh, herbaceous notes mingle with echoes of cherry tart on the nose, followed by a broad, chewy, densely-textured palate with attractive, supple body. The Merlot '96 has sour cherries and blueberries on the nose, which then reappear on a seductive, glycerin-rich palate with a complex structure.

	Wine	Glasses	Price
○	Collio Tocai Friulano '97	🍷🍷🍷	3*
○	Collio Bianco '97	🍷🍷	3*
●	Collio Rosso '97	🍷🍷	3*
●	Collio Merlot '96	🍷	4
○	Collio Tocai Friulano '95	YYY	4
○	Collio Bianco '96	YY	3
●	Collio Merlot '95	YY	4
○	Collio Pinot Bianco '96	YY	3
○	Collio Tocai Friulano '96	YY	3
●	Collio Cabernet '96	Y	3

The International Slow Food Movement

Slow Food is an international movement which was founded in 1989 and is active in 35 countries worldwide, with 60,000 members and about 475 Convivia (chapters).

Slow Food has a cultural agenda:
It promotes a **philosophy of pleasure**, protects small food producers who make quality products, counters the degrading effects of industrial and fast food culture which standardize tastes, has a **taste education** program for adults and children, works towards **safeguarding** traditional food and wine heritage, provides **consumer information**, promotes tourism that respects and cares for the environment.

Slow Food Events:
Each year Slow Food puts on important food and wine events for food enthusiasts and professionals: the biennial **Salone del Gusto** (the Hall of Taste) in Turin; the biennial **Cheese** in Bra; the **Luebeck Festival**, a food and drink event which celebrates German fare; **Wine Conventions; Tasting Sessions**.

Each **Convivium** organizes social meetings, tastings, cooking courses, trips, visits to restaurants, and lectures for its members. The twinning of Convivia from different countries promote the exchange of tastes and knowledge of different cultures.

An Ark to safeguard products and the planet of tastes:
An important project aimed at safeguarding and benefitting small-scale agricultural and food production, which risks dying out. Thousands of different kinds of *charcuterie*, cheeses, animal breeds and plants are in danger of disappearing forever: the homologation of tastes, the excessive power of industrial companies, distribution difficulties and disinformation are the causes of a process which could lead to the loss of an irreplaceable heritage of traditional recipes, knowledge and tastes. The Ark is a scientific research and documentation program which works towards relaunching businesses and outfits with important cultural and economic value.

Education of Taste:
The Slow Food Movement has taken action to realize one of the objectives of the **Ark Manifesto** to promote taste education in grade schools. Along with putting on numerous conferences on this subject, Slow Food published an instructional manual for teachers and parents on how to best teach children about enjoying and understanding their taste culture. Slow Food plans many more educational activities around the world during **"Weeks of Taste"**.

Fraternal Tables to feed those who need assistance:
Slow Food funds three **Fraternal Tables** dedicated to increasing international solidarity. The **Hekura Project** involves monthly support to the kitchen of a native American hospital for infectious diseases in Brazil. The **Zlata Project** funds two lunch programs to help resolve food emergencies, in particular concerning children, in Bosnia. **Project Colfiorito** is dedicated to the reconstruction of a cheese manufacturing plant that was destroyed during an earthquake in Colfiorito in the region of Umbria in 1997.

Slow

Slow features in-depth and often off-the-wall stories about food culture across the globe, with related lifestyle topics of a truly international scope, unlike anything you've seen before on the newsstand... 160 well-designed pages in full color, with exciting photography and articles by top authors, gourmets, wine experts, and food & travel writers worldwide. Just take your pick: English, German, French, Spanish or Italian…

Italian Wines 1999

For the first time in English, the most complete, reliable and influential guide to the best Italian wines. Published by Slow Food and Gambero Rosso, it is now in its twelth edition. It describes the history and production of 1536 vineyards, describes and evaluates 10120 wines, awards 154 wines with "Tre Bicchieri" (Three Glasses): the élite of the great Italian wine-making tradition.
Price £15.99 or $ 24.95

Registration Form

Slow Food is aimed at food and wine enthusiasts, those who do not want to lose the myriad of tastes in traditional foodstuffs from around the world, and those who share the snail's wise slowness. Annual membership includes:
- a personal membership card
- four issues of the quarterly magazine, *Slow*
- the right to attend all events organized by the Slow Food movement throughout the world
- a 20% discount on all Slow Food publications

If you have any questions, please feel free to contact us. We are only a FAX, phone call or e-mail away. Phone: ++39 172 419611 - FAX: ++39 172 421293
E-mail: international@slow-food.com

I would like to:
❑ start a convivium ❑ become a member ❑ subscribe to "Slow"

....
Full Name

....
(of company or restaurant or other)

....
Street Address City

....
State/Prov./County Country Postal Code

....
Home Tel. Day Tel. Fax

....
Profession

I would prefer to receive Slow in: ❑ English ❑ German ❑ French ❑ Spanish ❑ Italian

	Subscription fees to receive *Slow* only	membership fees to join *Slow Food*
U.K.	£26.00	£33.00
U.S.	$44.00	$60.00

Method of Payment

❑ Cash ❑ Eurocheque (in Italian lire) - no personal checks, please
❑ Credit Card: ❑ Visa ❑ AmEx ❑ Mastercard

\# |__|__|__|__||__|__|__|__||__|__|__|__||__|__|__|__|

|__|__/__|__| ✗ ....
Exp. Date Signature

....
Cardholder Total Amount

Toll-free number in U.S. and Canada: 1-877-SLOW FOOD (756-9366)

CORMONS (GO)

KURTIN
LOC. NOVALI, 9
34071 CORMONS (GO)
TEL. 0481/60685

We are always pleased when a producer returns to the Guide in top form, and especially so when a friendly, genial man like Alberto Kurtin reappears, presenting decidedly convincing wines. The winery was founded in 1903 by the present owner's great-grandfather, and for 20 years it has been producing wines with the Kurtin label. Eleven hectares are under vine, the most recent plantings having a density of over 4,000 vines per hectare. The Chardonnay '97 is a real success, with a nose redolent of tropical fruits and toffee and a long, fruity palate with a lively acidity. Among the wines awarded One Glass the Tocai Friulano stands out. Medicinal herbs, chamomile, tea, apple and pear mingle harmoniously on the nose, leading into a mouth-filling palate. The Pinot Bianco has typical aromas of wildflowers and apple and the palate is fresh-tasting with lots of fruit. In the Pinot Grigio, more interesting on the nose than the palate, scents of chamomile and pear are in evidence, while the Sauvignon, characterized by notes of sweet pepper rather than of elderberry, has a well-evolved, consistent structure.

O	Collio Chardonnay '97	🍷🍷	3*
O	Collio Pinot Bianco '97	🍷	3
O	Collio Pinot Grigio '97	🍷	3
O	Collio Sauvignon '97	🍷	3
O	Collio Tocai Friulano '97	🍷	3

CORMONS (GO)

MAGNÀS
ANDREA E LUCIANO VISINTIN
VIA CORONA, 47
34071 CORMONS (GO)
TEL. 0481/60991

This small, traditional estate run by Luciano Visintin and his son Andrea continues to hold onto its place in the Guide. The wines selected for this year's tastings made an excellent impression with their elegance of both nose and palate. The Chardonnay offers aromas of ripe fruit and apples and the warm, broad, mouth-filling, fat palate has good continuity and texture with hints of honey, barley-sugar and candied orange peel. The Pinot Grigio is a complex wine with intense aromas of beeswax, apple and tea, and a corresponding fresh palate with notes of russet apples and a bitterish twist on the finish. In the Pinot Bianco green apple and very persistent notes of citrus fruit emerge on the nose, while the complex, aromatic palate has good structure and acidity. The Tocai Friulano has an appley nose with faint traces of sulphur, possibly due to recent bottling, following through on a fairly fresh, straightforward, bitterish palate with almonds and licorice on the finish.

O	Friuli Isonzo Chardonnay '97	🍷🍷	4
O	Collio Pinot Bianco '97	🍷	4
O	Collio Pinot Grigio '97	🍷	4
O	Collio Tocai Friulano '97		4

CORMONS (GO)

ROBERTO PICECH
LOC. PRADIS, 11
34071 CORMONS (GO)
TEL. 0481/60347

Roberto Picech's five hectares of vineyards, splendidly situated on the grape-friendly hills of the Pradis di Cormons zone, are tended by their owner with rare devotion. In the 1920s the family worked the same land under the sharecropping system, but Roberto's father Egidio, aptly named "the rebel" because of his part in the farmers' struggles for their rights, succeeded in becoming the owner. The Passito di Pradis '96, glorious as usual, is made from malvasia istriana grapes left on racks until February, when they are crushed and put into barrique to ferment on the skins and yeasts for six months; the wine is then transferred into different barriques where it matures for another six months. A clear amber in color, the wine has a bouquet of almond milk and figs in spirit and a luscious, long palate with new hints of citrus and chocolate. The Collio Bianco '97, from tocai friulano, malvasia istriana and ribolla gialla, is 40% barrique-fermented, a procedure imparting toasty aromas with a complex fruit on the nose, while in the mouth it is harmonious and balanced with good acidity and a long finish. The nicely-structured Merlot '96 scored well. Fermented in steel, it spent a year in small barrels where it acquired a notable aromatic complexity, with red fruit tart, blueberries and blackcurrants, but the palate does not altogether correspond. The Cabernet Sauvignon '96 has also been aged for about a year in wood, partly barrique and partly medium-sized barrels, resulting in a nose evoking blueberries, spices and concentrated red fruits, with a wonderfully fruity entry on the palate continuing through to the long, balanced finish. The Malvasia '97 is very enjoyable drinking, offering aromas of dried figs and walnuts.

○	Collio Bianco '97	🍷🍷	4
○	Passito di Pradis '96	🍷🍷	6
●	Collio Cabernet Sauvignon '96	🍷	4
●	Collio Merlot '96	🍷	4
○	Collio Malvasia '97	🍷	3
○	Collio Pinot Bianco '97		3
○	Collio Tocai Friulano '97		3
●	Collio Cabernet Sauvignon '95	🍸🍸	4
●	Collio Merlot '95	🍸🍸	4
○	Passito di Pradis '94	🍸🍸	5

CORMONS (GO)

ISIDORO POLENCIC
LOC. PLESSIVA, 12
34071 CORMONS (GO)
TEL. 0481/60655

This winery, with 18 hectares of vineyards in the Collio zone and a couple in the Isonzo, has kept up the standard of previous vintages with a fine range of whites. The one which impressed us most was the Oblìn Blanc '96, named after the stream running beside the vineyard. Made from ribolla gialla, chardonnay and sauvignon, it undergoes fermentation and a long maturation in small oak casks which lend it a pleasant background note of coffee, while the nose offers cream, custard, white chocolate and banana. These are repeated on the rich, mellow palate, with the chocolate reappearing on the long finish, accompanied by the fresh acidity of the ribolla grape. Appley and yeasty fragrances dominate the nose in the Chardonnay, following through on the soft palate, which has a delightful fruity finish. In the Pinot Bianco hints of chestnut honey with undertones of green apple emerge on the nose and reappear on the nicely evolved palate. The more complex Pinot Grigio offers a bouquet of apples, citrus, apricots and sugared almonds, while green apple and plums emerge on the palate, whose mellow structure is excellently balanced by the acidity. The Tocai Friulano comes close to earning Two Glasses, with distinct notes of pear, medicinal herbs and a hint of basil on the nose and a typical echo of peach leaf on the soft, concentrated palate. Doro, Elisabetta and Michele, Isidoro's children, contributed to the success of these wines.

○	Oblin Blanc '96	🍷🍷	5
○	Collio Chardonnay '97	🍷	3
○	Collio Pinot Bianco '97	🍷	3
○	Collio Pinot Grigio '97	🍷	3
○	Collio Tocai Friulano '97	🍷	3
○	Collio Pinot Bianco '96	🍸🍸	3
○	Collio Pinot Grigio '96	🍸🍸	3
○	Collio Sauvignon '96	🍸🍸	3
○	Collio Chardonnay '96	🍸	3

CORMONS (GO)

Alessandro Princic
Loc. Pradis, 5
34071 Cormons (GO)
tel. 0481/60723

Once again Sandro Princic has come within a hair of getting Three Glasses. The easygoing Sandro with his unexpected flashes of wit is one of the most charismatic personalities of Cormons. He learned from his father Doro, a living myth, how to make first-class wines by restricting the yield per vine and vinifying the grapes when they're really ripe. Although his wines are notable for their bouquet, what Princic really goes after is structure. The highly enjoyable Pinot Bianco '97 has distinct aromas of apple on the nose, and the entry on the palate is fat and full, following through with softness, echoes of apple and pear and mouth-warming alcohol. It is well-balanced and consistent in structure, lingering in the mouth well after taking its leave. His other top wine, for the second year running, is the Malvasia, whose golden tints in the glass are followed by an elegant, appley nose with smoky, dusty overtones. The impact on the palate is opulent and powerful, followed by an acidity immediately overwhelmed by the structure and dense fruit; the finish is long and fresh. In the Pinot Grigio, characterized by a very seductive finish, the rich alcohol is again offset by the fresh appley fruit. The Sauvignon has an aristocratic nose of elderberry, honey and mint, followed by a full, glycerin-rich palate with notes of ripe pineapple and grapefruit and a balanced acidity. The classic Tocai Friulano offers almond leaf, pear and mint on the nose, followed by structure and firmness on the palate, with typical notes of bitter almonds on the finish. Last of all, the Merlot '97, better on the nose than on the palate, is going to be a challenge for Sandro.

	Wine	Glasses	Price
○	Collio Malvasia '97	▼▼	4
○	Collio Pinot Bianco '97	▼▼	4
○	Collio Pinot Grigio '97	▼▼	4
○	Collio Sauvignon '97	▼▼	4
○	Collio Tocai Friulano '97	▼▼	4
●	Collio Merlot '97	▼	4
○	Collio Pinot Bianco '95	▽▽▽	4
○	Collio Tocai Friulano '93	▽▽▽	4
○	Collio Pinot Bianco '96	▽▽	3
○	Collio Tocai Friulano '96	▽▽	4

CORMONS (GO)

Dario Raccaro
Via S. Giovanni, 87/b
34071 Cormons (GO)
tel. 0481/61425

This has definitely been a good year for Dario Raccaro, whose new tocai vineyard is beginning to give excellent results. Dario is a small-scale producer whose reliability and professional authority make him well suited to act as president of the group of growers from Cormons who run the municipal wine museum and tasting center. But let's get down to his masterpiece, the Tocai Friulano '97: the aromas are both elegant and intense, with a wonderful mingling of apple and pear perfectly mirrored on the palate, where the concentrated structure, rich alcohol and fresh acidity lend it even greater complexity. The superb Cabernet Franc, usually rather a rustic wine, has undoubtedly gained from the hot, dry summer which allowed the grapes to ripen perfectly. The intense, herbaceous nose has undertones of black cherries, and the palate is rounded, displaying a satisfying fruit with the tannins emerging on the finish. The Malvasia offers scents of apple and linden flowers on the nose, following through nicely on the refreshingly crisp palate. The first edition of Collio Bianco, a blend of tocai, malvasia, sauvignon and pinot bianco, promises well on the nose with its enjoyable, elegant notes of pear and apricot, but the palate is overwhelmed by acidity. The Sauvignon, with its typical faint hints of tomato leaf, is worthy of mention.

	Wine	Glasses	Price
●	Friuli Isonzo Cabernet Franc '97	▼▼	3
○	Collio Tocai Friulano '97	▼▼	3
○	Collio Malvasia '97	▼	3
○	Collio Bianco '97		3
○	Collio Sauvignon '97		3
○	Collio Malvasia Istriana '96	▽▽	3
○	Collio Tocai Friulano '96	▽	3

CORMONS (GO)

Ronco dei Tassi

Loc. Monte, 38
34071 Cormons (GO)
tel. 0481/60155

When Fabio Coser won Three Glasses last year, nobody supposed that it was just a flash in the pan, since his skill is recognized by all who know him. This year that success was not repeated, but we can safely confirm that his Collio Bianco Fosarin is once again outstanding, a pearl in a top-flight range from an estate which has never made a wine below the One Glass rating. This oaked white, from tocai friulano, ribolla gialla, malvasia istriana and pinot bianco, has subtle, elegant aromas of fresh fruit and herbal infusions, and offers a soft palate with attractive fruit and the right acidity, leading into an exceptionally long finish. The Pinot Grigio reveals banana, vanilla and apple on the nose, while the palate is complex, balanced, rich and very long. The Tocai Friulano is another stunning white, with dominant notes of pear, apple and peach over a very faint undertone of chives; the palate displays a welcome, fresh acidity backing up a fruity, close-knit structure that opens out onto a broad finish. The Cjarandon '96, a Bordeaux blend, is a big red wine which can be kept for years but is already lovely drinking. The elegant nose reveals scents of pennyroyal and ripe red fruits, followed by a fresh palate with solid tannins and concentrated fruit.

	Wine	Rating	Price
●	Collio Rosso Cjarandon '96	▼▼	4
○	Collio Bianco Fosarin '97	▼▼	4
○	Collio Pinot Grigio '97	▼▼	4
○	Collio Tocai Friulano '97	▼▼	4
○	Collio Bianco Fosarin '96	▽▽▽	3
○	Collio Pinot Grigio '96	▽▽	3
○	Collio Tocai Friulano '96	▽▽	3
●	Collio Rosso Cjarandon '94	▽▽	4
●	Collio Rosso Cjarandon '95	▽	4

CORMONS (GO)

Ronco del Gelso

Via Isonzo, 117
34071 Cormons (GO)
tel. 0481/61310

Giorgio Badin's Tocai has again walked off with Three Glasses. Now that his cellar techniques have been perfected, he will no longer meet with the problems which last year kept him from top scores for his Tocai. At our tastings, in fact, his wines often suffer from sulphur which can hardly be dissipated in a few minutes, and only if one knows them is it possible to make a reliable assessment of how they will evolve. Try tasting the Tocai Friulano '96 now and you'll believe us! But let's consider the Tocai Friulano '97: it is gold-colored with lemon tints, and full and elegant on the nose, where a complex fruit emerges with notes of aniseed and spices. These are all repeated on the palate, accompanied by a warm full body and a long finish. The Bianco Làtimis '97, from tocai and chardonnay, was very close to getting Three Glasses. The nose offers pineapple, citrus and fresh apple, followed by an exceptionally rich palate continually unfolding new sensations right through to the long, fruity finish. The Sauvignon '97, another excellent wine, offers a nose of elderberry, mint and sage, which follow through on a fresh, fat palate with delightful echoes of citrus. The Sauvignon Sot lis Rivis '97, partially aged in wood, gets a slightly lower score due to a faintly overripe note. The Cabernet Franc '97 fully deserves its Two Glasses for its array of aromas and superbly full-bodied, rich palate. One is reminded of Chablis when tasting the Chardonnay '97 with its green nuances on the nose and the structure, acidity and fresh fruit of its palate. The Merlot '96 stands out for its chewy palate but is somewhat disappointing on the nose.

	Wine	Rating	Price
○	Friuli Isonzo Tocai Friulano '97	▼▼▼	4
○	Friuli Isonzo Bianco Làtimis '97	▼▼	4
○	Friuli Isonzo Sauvignon '97	▼▼	4
●	Friuli Isonzo Cabernet Franc '97	▼▼	4
●	Friuli Isonzo Merlot '96	▼	4
○	Friuli Isonzo Chardonnay '97	▼	4
○	Friuli Isonzo Sauvignon Sot lis Rivis '97	▼	4
●	Isonzo Merlot '91	▽▽▽	5
○	Isonzo Tocai Friulano '94	▽▽▽	4
○	Friuli Isonzo Tocai Friulano '95	▽▽▽	4
○	Friuli Isonzo Bianco Làtimis '96	▽▽	4
○	Friuli Isonzo Tocai Friulano '96	▽▽	4

CORMONS (GO)

Ronco di Zegla

Loc. Zegla, 12
34071 Cormons (GO)
tel. 0481/61155

This small recently established winery, which we've had our eye on since its first bottling, is now in the Guide for the first time. Management is in the hands of Maurizio Princic, aged 27, whose grandfather Pepi, born in 1908, was brother to Doro Princic of the estate in Pradis. The cellar has been entirely renovated and Maurizio has produced 18 thousand bottles of white wine, vintage '97. It has been traditional to produce many different varieties, and Maurizio's aim is to reduce their number gradually. We didn't get a chance to try the reds, Merlot and Cabernet, at our tastings, because they were still in the barrel awaiting release in 1999, but we were very favorably impressed by the four wines we sampled, which reached scores nearly justifying Two Glasses. The Ribolla Gialla has a light toastiness and notes of apple on the nose, carrying through to an enjoyably supple, refreshing, long palate. The Pinot Grigio has greenish gold tints and an elegant nose of apple and mixed fruit, followed by a full, tasty palate with a long finish. The extremely interesting Tocai Friulano is concentrated and pleasantly appley on the nose, followed by a complex, broad, full-flavored palate with the right acidity and a long finish. Finally, the golden-tinted Chardonnay has distinct aromas of yeast and ripe apples, which are echoed on the full-flavored palate with its chewy fruit and hints of lemon. After this encouraging start we wish Maurizio and his father Giuseppe every future success.

○	Collio Chardonnay '97	🍷	3
○	Collio Pinot Grigio '97	🍷	3
○	Collio Ribolla Gialla '97	🍷	3
○	Collio Tocai Friulano '97	🍷	3

CORMONS (GO)

Oscar Sturm

Loc. Zegla, 1
34071 Cormons (GO)
tel. 0481/60720

The Sturm family, originally from Graz, capital of the Styrian province of Austria, has lived for over two centuries in these hills that are so admirably suited to viticulture. The estate, managed by Oscar Sturm, has undergone extensive modernization during the last few years, and the quality of its wines has been constantly improving. With a fully equipped cellar, which boasts a modest stock of barriques, Oscar has all he needs to make the best of what is painstakingly harvested from his twelve hectares of vineyards. The sauvignon clones at his disposal have produced very satisfying results, as is annually evident from the consistently high level of the wine he makes from them. The first-rate Sauvignon '97 offers aromas of vanilla, with overtones of elderberry and grapefruit, and a creamy, fat, mouth-filling palate laced with sage, pineapple and grapefruit. The rich alcohol, almost excessive at 14.5%, can be traced to the excellent vintage. The Chardonnay Andritz, one of the barrique-aged wines named after the Austrian village the family originally came from, is a golden color and reminiscent of fresh bread, dried fruit and citrus on the nose, which is followed by a palate where fresh apple, licorice, leather and tobacco form a harmonious whole with structure and acidity. The Bianco Andritz '96, from pinot grigio, chardonnay and sauvignon, came very close to Two Glasses. Vanilla, banana, apricot and tropical fruits emerge on an alcohol-rich nose and are repeated on the palate where the impact is powerful, but lacking in grip on the finish. The Tocai Friulano has cleanly defined aromas of pear, apple and mixed fresh fruit with a tasty palate and an almondy finish; the Pinot Grigio, while worthy of mention, is more convincing on the nose than in the mouth.

○	Chardonnay Andritz '97	🍷🍷	3*
○	Collio Sauvignon '97	🍷🍷	3*
○	Bianco Andritz '96	🍷	3
○	Collio Tocai Friulano '97	🍷	3
○	Collio Pinot Grigio '97		3
○	Collio Tocai Friulano '96	YY	3

CORMONS (GO)

Subida di Monte

Loc. Monte, 9
34071 Cormons (GO)
tel. 0481/61011

This family-run estate is well on the way to becoming a top-rank winery, with the praiseworthy efforts of Gigi Antonutti and his sons Cristian and Andrea already producing rewarding results. The Bianco Sotrari '97, an excellent Collio DOC from riesling, traminer and sauvignon, has an elegant nose offering a profusion of fresh fruits, and a warm, opulent palate with acidity and fruit in wonderful balance and a long, clean finish. The Pinot Grigio '97, another high scorer, is fresh and fruity on the nose, with hints of banana. This is echoed on the continually unfolding palate which also shows excellent structure. The Chardonnay '97 cru Vigna delle Acacie offers a yeasty, buttery nose with notes of banana and tropical fruits, while the palate reveals caramel, mixed fruit and a slightly excessive acidity. The inviting Tocai Friulano '97 is gold-tinted in color and aromatic on the nose, with pear in the foreground, but the enjoyable fruitiness in the mouth gives way to an acidity which detracts from the finish. We were very impressed by the reds, starting with the Cabernet Franc '97, which discloses spices, cherries and a light smokiness on the nose, followed by a palate offering sweet fruits, good body and adequate tannins. The Cabernet Franc Riserva '95 has ripe red fruits with a touch of green and echoes of very ripe orange on the nose, leading into a full-bodied palate with firm structure, a hint of chocolate and good length. Lastly, the Merlot Riserva '95 has a complex, concentrated nose in which fresh notes mingle with ripe red fruits, carrying through to a nicely structured palate rich in a variety of fruit.

	Wine	Rating	Price
○	Collio Bianco Sotrari '97	🍷🍷	4
●	Collio Cabernet Franc '97	🍷🍷	4
●	Collio Cabernet Ris. '95	🍷🍷	5
●	Collio Merlot Ris. '95	🍷🍷	4
○	Collio Pinot Grigio '97	🍷🍷	3*
○	Collio Chardonnay Vigna delle Acacie '97	🍷	4
○	Collio Tocai Friulano '97	🍷	3
●	Collio Merlot Ris. '94	🍸🍸	4
○	Collio Tocai Friulano '96	🍸	3

CORMONS (GO)

Franco Toròs

Loc. Novali, 12
34071 Cormons (GO)
tel. 0481/61327

Reliability characterizes this winery owned by Franco Toròs, a producer in Novali di Cormons. The reason for this lies in the nine hectares of vineyards, partly replanted a few years ago, which bear the marks of a desire to increase quality by reducing the yield per vine, and in the cellar, which was expanded to facilitate the vinification cycle. Franco has also built a passage underneath the courtyard of his house to connect the old cellar with the new, thus creating extra space for aging his wines at a naturally constant temperature. Despite an unpropitious harvest, Franco Toròs produced an excellent Sauvignon with elegant, stylish perfumes repeated on an attractive palate of unusual structure and length. The Pinot Grigio has a nose redolent of apple, pear and ripe fruits, and is dense and warm on the lingering palate, where the glycerin is nicely offset by the fresh fruit. The Chardonnay '97 scores points for breadth and suppleness, but the oaked Chardonnay Riserva '96 deserves more of our attention. The wonderfully enticing nose recalls milk, licorice, toffee, mint and ripe fruits, but a marked acidity detracts from the palate. The alcoholic, glycerin-rich Pinot Bianco has lots of fruit with apple in the lead. The Tocai is characterized by delicate scents of apple, while the Cabernet Franc '97 offers ripe plums and prunes on the nose and is fleshy, soft and concentrated on the palate.

	Wine	Rating	Price
○	Collio Pinot Grigio '97	🍷🍷	4
○	Collio Sauvignon '97	🍷🍷	4
○	Collio Chardonnay '97	🍷	4
○	Collio Chardonnay Ris. '96	🍷	4
○	Collio Pinot Bianco '97	🍷	3
○	Collio Tocai Friulano '97	🍷	3
●	Collio Cabernet Franc '97	🍷	4
●	Collio Merlot Ris. '96		4
●	Collio Merlot '95	🍸🍸	3
○	Collio Pinot Grigio '96	🍸🍸	3
○	Collio Tocai Friulano '96	🍸🍸	3

CORMONS (GO)

Vigna del Lauro

Loc. Monte, 38
34070 Cormons (GO)
tel. 0481/60155

Fabio Coser, whose oenological skill is well known, produces excellent wines when he can manage the vineyards in his own way. This is just what happened with Vigna del Lauro, the estate he rented for some time in San Floriano del Collio. Fabio has not renewed his contract with the Tacco countesses for 1998, so, starting with the next vintage, other wines will bear the Vigna del Lauro label. Fabio does not choose to produce all the varieties which are often included by Friuli's wineries in their range of wines, but prefers to concentrate on a few of them. In our opinion the top wine of the superb range presented is the Sauvignon. Notes of elderberry and sage emerge on the intense, elegant nose, which is repeated on the warm, mellow palate with good length and terrific grip. The unusually stylish Pinot Grigio has aromas of pear and apple following through on the full, balanced, rich palate with a long, fruity finish. The Pinot Bianco, elegant as usual, offers delicate fruit on the nose, with a dominant note of apples, and the closely-textured palate is warm, rich, subtle and long. The Merlot, a big, complex wine, has aromas of ripe oranges which then mingle with peaches in wine and unfold to disclose clove, rosemary, juniper and pine. It has great firmness on the palate, with soft tannins emerging. The Tocai Friulano is characterized on the nose by pear, apple and a touch of green faintly reminiscent of celery, leading into a long, mouth-filling, textured palate.

	Wine	Rating	Price
●	Collio Merlot '96	🍷🍷	4
○	Collio Pinot Bianco '97	🍷🍷	3
○	Collio Pinot Grigio '97	🍷🍷	3
○	Collio Sauvignon '97	🍷🍷	3
○	Collio Tocai Friulano '97	🍷	3
○	Collio Bianco '96	🍸🍸	3
○	Collio Sauvignon '96	🍸🍸	3

CORNO DI ROSAZZO (UD)

Ca' di Bon

Via Casali Gallo, 1
33040 Corno di Rosazzo (UD)
tel. 0432/759316

This year's vintage has been distinctly rewarding for the small estate belonging to Gianni and Ameris Bon. The '97 harvest from eight hectares of vineyards distributed among various DOCs has yielded a range of well-made, dependable wines of which two, the Refosco dal Peduncolo Rosso and the Sauvignon, obtained from the Grave del Friuli vineyards, are of premium quality. The former, of an intense ruby color, displays the typical spicy nose of this grape mingling with hints of morello cherries, followed by a palate of commendable concentration and body with a broad, rich fruit and soft tannins. The Sauvignon, with its varietal aromas recalling elderberry, peach and sage, is close-knit and full-flavored, with a wonderfully balanced palate ending in a long, rich finish. The highly typical Tocai offers an intense nose of apple seeds and almonds with notes of vanilla, leading into a palate which evolves well but is rather short in the finish. The Pinot Grigio is more convincing on the nose than on the palate, but it still rates One Glass. Of the reds, we found the Merlot very attractive in its concentration and wide array of fruit on the nose, with prunes dominating, and in the softness and complexity encountered on the palate. This vintage, with its well-ripened grapes, was certainly a boon to the Cabernet Franc, and the Bons have produced a mouth-filling, herbaceous wine with nicely judged alcohol, less rustic in character than this variety usually is. The Verduzzo Friulano has has good varietal aroma but is hurt by too much acidity.

	Wine	Rating	Price
○	Friuli Grave Sauvignon '97	🍷🍷	3*
●	COF Refosco P. R. '97	🍷🍷	3*
●	COF Merlot '97	🍷	3
●	Friuli Grave Cabernet Franc '97	🍷	3
○	COF Pinot Grigio '97	🍷	3
○	COF Tocai Friulano '97	🍷	3
○	COF Verduzzo Friulano '97		3

CORNO DI ROSAZZO (UD)

EUGENIO COLLAVINI
LOC. GRAMOGLIANO
33040 CORNO DI ROSAZZO (UD)
TEL. 0432/753222

Several of Collavini's wines from the Collio DOC zone and his sweet wines from the Colli Orientali del Friuli show a marked improvement in quality. Such success is an important achievement for an estate which has an annual output of over 30,000 hectoliters of wine and is also a leading producer of sparkling wines in Friuli, since it can make a real, and positive, difference to the whole region's winemaking image. The Chardonnay dei Sassi Cavi '96 is light in color but reveals its complexity with the entry on the nose, where notes of vanilla and banana emerge. The palate is equally satisfying, being well-balanced, rich and long. The Tocai Friulano has elegant, intense aromas of apple, pear and white flowers, which are reflected on the palate, where, with a delightful harmony, broad firm structure and long finish, it is at its best. The Ramandolo is a typical, intense gold color with an apparent but elegant oak accompanying aromas of dried fruit and sultanas on the nose. On the palate it is full, sweet and nicely balanced. The Picolit, offering barley sugar and vanilla on the nose and marzipan on the palate, is let down by the acidity on the finish. The Merlot Conte di Cuccanea '96, with a spicy, fruity, alcohol-rich nose, is mouth-filling, concentrated and rich on the palate, with a firm structure but a rather sharp acidity that accentuates the harsh edge of the tannins. Spices and cherry dominate the nose of the Cabernet Franc, which, although perhaps atypical, has nicely rounded structure in the mouth. The Ribolla Gialla Brut '95 has great elegance and freshness and displays nuances of crusty bread and white fruit, while the Applause Brut '93 is more straightforward.

	Wine	Glasses	Price
○	Collio Chardonnay dei Sassi Cavi '96	🍷🍷	4
○	Collio Tocai Friulano '97	🍷🍷	4
○	Applause Brut '93	🍷	5
○	Ribolla Gialla Brut '95	🍷	4
○	COF Ramandolo '96	🍷	4
●	Collio Cabernet Conte di Cuccanea '96	🍷	4
●	Collio Merlot Conte di Cuccanea '96	🍷	4
○	COF Picolit '96		6
○	Collio Pinot Grigio '97		4

CORNO DI ROSAZZO (UD)

ADRIANO GIGANTE
VIA ROCCA BERNARDA, 3
33040 CORNO DI ROSAZZO (UD)
TEL. 0432/755835

Adriano Gigante, under pressure from the demands of the market, has had to change his bottling time, bringing it forward to early summer, which is why we found ourselves tasting two vintages, the '96 and the '97, simultaneously. We found the general level of this small estate very good and have given out lots of Glasses. The Chardonnay '97 is many-faceted, with a nose redolent of honey, yeast and barley sugar, while the palate offers juniper, alcohol, a faint, bitterish hint of gentian and an abundance of fresh ripe fruit. The Pinot Grigio '96, with a tint of onion-skin pink in the glass, has a nose ranging from green apple to ripe melon, leading into a mouth-filling, opulent palate with a fresh bite of acidity on the finish. Pear mingled with peach are the key aromas of the Tocai Friulano '97, whose palate is mellow and concentrated with echoes of yellow plums on the long finish. The Picolit '96 releases aromas of noble rot with peach, honey and juniper, echoed on a sweet, oily, glycerin-rich palate. The two Sauvignon vintages deserve a full Glass, the '96 being more varietal in aroma, and the '97 performing better on the palate. Both vintages of the Cabernet Franc are markedly varietal in their grassy, fruity aromas, the younger wine being more textured as a result of a warmer and drier season. The Verduzzo Friulano '96 is old gold in color and nearly rates Two Glasses for its aromatic structure, with notes of dried apricots and white chocolate, echoed by the medium-sweet, mouth-filling, fresh, long palate.

	Wine	Glasses	Price
○	COF Chardonnay '97	🍷🍷	3
○	COF Picolit '96	🍷🍷	6
○	COF Pinot Grigio '96	🍷🍷	3
○	COF Tocai Friulano '97	🍷🍷	3
●	COF Cabernet Franc '96	🍷	3
●	COF Cabernet Franc '97	🍷	3
○	COF Sauvignon '96	🍷	3
○	COF Sauvignon '97	🍷	3
○	COF Verduzzo Friulano '96	🍷	3
●	COF Refosco P. R. '96	🍷	3
●	COF Schioppettino '96		4
○	COF Tocai Friulano '95	🥂	3

PERUSINI

VIA TORRIONE, 13
LOC. GRAMOGLIANO
33040 CORNO DI ROSAZZO (UD)
TEL. 0432/675018 - 759115

Teresa Perusini's winery and what it produces have long been an object of interest for us. In the 1990 edition of the Guide there was an entry devoted to their Ribolla Gialla '88, the premier wine of this estate, which belongs to one of the oldest and most prestigious wine-making families in Friuli. In the 1995 Guide the winery received Honorable Mention for the Ribolla Gialla and the Pinot Grigio '93. Last year we did not review the '96 wines because they were distinctly sulphurous at our tastings; when we had occasion to taste them again a few months later we found them clean and fresh. (The old vinification methods used to aim at producing longer-lived wines at the cost of freshness.) Now cellar practices have been revised, and here is a series of delicious, drinkable wines. The Ribolla Gialla '97, from plantings of clones carefully selected a few decades ago by Teresa's father, Giampaolo Perusini, is a wine of premium quality. Dried flowers, tobacco and dried apple emerge on the nose, with the apple reappearing on the palate, where nicely-judged acidity backs up the long finish. The '96 Merlot Nero, (black being the color of its label), is another excellent wine, matured in 500 liter casks of Allier oak. It offers complex, elegant aromas of sour cherries and licorice, while a similarly rich palate has pronounced tannins on the finish. The Pinot Bianco easily deserves a Glass for its close-knit yet fresh structure. The same rating goes to the Pinot Grigio, with russet apple flavors and coppery glints in the color, to the Picolit, dense and continuous on the palate with hints of citrus, apple and peach leaf, and lastly to the warm, generous Merlot '97 with its sour cherries, spices and adequate tannins.

	Wine	Rating	Price
○	COF Ribolla Gialla '97	🍷🍷	3*
●	COF Merlot Nero '96	🍷🍷	4
●	COF Merlot '97	🍷	3
○	COF Picolit '97	🍷	5
○	COF Pinot Bianco '97	🍷	3
○	COF Pinot Grigio '97	🍷	3
●	COF Cabernet '97		3

LEONARDO SPECOGNA

VIA ROCCA BERNARDA, 4
33040 CORNO DI ROSAZZO (UD)
TEL. 0432/755840

The products of man often reflect the personality of their creators and this is certainly the case with Graziano Specogna's wines. Graziano is a robust, candid man, honest and generous, at times impetuous, and he transmits all these traits to his wines, which with one exception have all done extremely well this year. In the last Guide we wrote that Specogna considered his zone to be suited to reds, and in fact the two best wines of the vintage are red. The superb Cabernet offers a wonderfully enticing nose where complex, toasty coffee aromas harmonize with notes of red fruit compote. The entry on the palate is soft and warm, opening out with delightful fruity flavors and ending with mellow tannins on the finish. The excellent Refosco, made from a grape that has always been considered rough and aggressive, startled us with its wonderfully harmonious nose and palate, its attractive fruit and its length. The Merlot displays a marked spiciness on the nose which mingles nicely with intense perfumes of red fruits, but the palate, inadequately structured, is something of a letdown. The Verduzzo Friulano is golden in color and delicately perfumed with honey, vanilla and apple, all of which reappear harmoniously on the palate with the right touch of sweetness. The oaked Chardonnay discloses warm scents of banana, crusty bread and vanilla, but is disappointing on the palate. The traditionally well-made Tocai is characterized by intense fruity aromas, with hints of apple seeds, and by warm, full flavors in the mouth. The varietal Sauvignon has aromas of vanilla, ripe tomato and dry bread, which are rather impaired on the palate by excessive wood. The Pinot Grigio, looking as usual almost like a rosé, is characterized by richness and good fruit.

	Wine	Rating	Price
●	COF Cabernet '96	🍷🍷	3*
●	COF Refosco P. R. '96	🍷🍷	3*
○	COF Chardonnay '96	🍷	3
●	COF Merlot '96	🍷	3
○	COF Pinot Grigio '97	🍷	3
○	COF Sauvignon '97	🍷	3
○	COF Tocai Friulano '97	🍷	3
○	COF Verduzzo Friulano '97	🍷	3
●	COF Cabernet '95	🍸🍸 (empty glasses)	3
●	COF Merlot '95	🍸 (empty glass)	3

CORNO DI ROSAZZO (UD)

ANDREA VISINTINI
VIA GRAMOGLIANO, 27
33040 CORNO DI ROSAZZO (UD)
TEL. 0432/755813

We were amazed by the number of Glasses awarded to Andrea Visintini's winery in the last edition of the Guide, but now we hardly blink an eye as we observe that there are even more. This consistently high standard is due to Oliviero, his father Andrea and the steady commitment with which they look after 17 hectares of vineyards. The two Collio wines, the Pinot Bianco and the Tocai Friulano, both earn Two Glasses. The first, with a fresh nose offering nuances of toffee which almost suggest the presence of chardonnay, is rich and mouth-filling, with distinct aromas of apple and fruit salad, ending in a lively finish. The Tocai Collio, perfectly typical in its aromas of pear and apple seeds, has a concentrated, intense impact on the palate, with the ripe pear and alcohol leading through to a harmonious finish where the acidity nicely offsets the rich glycerin. The pick of this year's vintage is, however, the Colli Orientali Sauvignon. Elderberry, pineapple and rue emerge on the nose, the palate is soft and powerful, with acidity attractively subdued by the fruit, and the finish is long and inviting. And now a quick run-through of the One Glass wines: the Pinot Grigio, fresh and agreeable with tints of onion-skin pink in the glass, has aromas of pear on both nose and palate, while the Ribolla Gialla has an original touch of aniseed mingling with the classic aromas of apple and pear. The Colli Orientali Tocai recalls the Collio wine of the same variety, without the latter's rich texture on the palate. The Traminer Aromatico, one of the best of this variety, has a typical nose with notes of citrus and rose and is lean but firm on the palate, and the Merlot '97 is warm and chewy with a good balance of ripe red fruits and acidity. The Cabernet Franc is well worth noting.

	Wine	Glasses	Price
○	COF Sauvignon '97	🍷🍷	3*
○	Collio Pinot Bianco '97	🍷🍷	3*
○	Collio Tocai Friulano '97	🍷🍷	3*
●	COF Merlot '97	🍷	2
○	COF Pinot Grigio '97	🍷	3
○	COF Ribolla Gialla '97	🍷	3
○	COF Tocai Friulano '97	🍷	2
○	COF Traminer Aromatico '97	🍷	3
●	COF Cabernet Franc '97		3
●	COF Merlot '96	🍷🍷 (prev. ed.)	3
○	COF Tocai Friulano '96	🍷🍷 (prev. ed.)	3
○	Collio Pinot Grigio '96	🍷🍷 (prev. ed.)	3

CORNO DI ROSAZZO (UD)

ZOF
VIA GIOVANNI XXIII, 32/A
33040 CORNO DI ROSAZZO (UD)
TEL. 0432/759673

In 1984 Alberto Zof and his wife Angela began making wine, from little more than a hectare and a half of vineyard, to serve to guests in their country hotel. The profits from the business were ploughed back into the land, which now comprises almost ten hectares. In 1990 their son Daniele completed his course in oenology at Cividale and then met Donato Lanati, the well-known Piedmontese professor who became the estate's consultant. The results were prompt and rewarding, and Alberto was able to hand over management of the cellar to his son, while he himself looks after the land. The Va' Pensiero '96 is a very fine wine made from merlot, cabernet franc and a small percentage of cabernet sauvignon and aged in oak. It has inviting aromas of cinnamon, baked apple, spices and sour cherry, all reflected on the broad, full-bodied palate with soft tannins. The gold-tinted Tocai '97 has aromas of pear followed by a well-evolved fruity palate and a long finish with hints of toffee. The Pinot Grigio has unusual, delightful scents of apple, damp grass and wild flowers, while the palate is rich and mellow with a nicely judged acidity and lots of fruit in the lingering finish. The Pinot Bianco recalls ripe apples with underlying yeasty notes and evolves well on the palate, where sweet, fresh fruits emerge with appropriate alcohol. The Sauvignon offers varietal aromas of elderberry and tomato leaf, joined by pineapple on the palate. Raspberry, sour cherry, undergrowth and herbaceous notes characterize the Merlot, but we are withholding judgment on the Cabernet Franc, tasted at different times and provoking very divergent opinions.

	Wine	Glasses	Price
○	COF Pinot Grigio '97	🍷🍷	2*
○	COF Tocai Friulano '97	🍷🍷	2*
●	Va' Pensiero '96	🍷🍷	4
●	COF Merlot '97	🍷	2
○	COF Pinot Bianco '97	🍷	2
○	COF Sauvignon '97	🍷	2
●	COF Schioppettino '97		2
○	COF Pinot Grigio '96	🍷🍷 (prev. ed.)	2
○	COF Sauvignon '96	🍷🍷 (prev. ed.)	2

DOLEGNA DEL COLLIO (GO)

Ca' Ronesca
Loc. Lonzano, 27
34070 Dolegna del Collio (GO)
tel. 0481/60034

Paolo Bianchi, the young and determined manager of Ca' Ronesca, has very clear ideas about wine, which he does not view as a cult object, but as an enjoyable accompaniment at mealtimes or while chatting with friends. It should therefore be correctly made, varietal, pleasant without going to extremes, neither over-demanding nor over-priced. He has stuck to these principles in his management of vineyard and cellar. The estate owns vineyards both on the wild hillsides of Dolegna in the Collio DOC region and at Ipplis in the Colli Orientali DOC. The Collio Tocai Friulano is of outstanding quality and personality. The entry on the nose is impressive in its elegant, complex notes of pear and citrus, then echoed on the long, round palate, to which the citrus lends a sunny, Mediterranean tone. Another excellent wine, the Collio Pinot Bianco, displays an overall elegance and finesse and is delightfully scented with white fruit and acacia blossom. The attack on the palate is pleasing, and good balance and continuity are soon evident. The estate's two oaked blends are both reliable wines. The Marnà, from malvasia istriana, pinot bianco and chardonnay, has an intense and complex bouquet with vanilla, tea and apricot which are nicely repeated on the palate, but it is slightly impaired by an imperfect balance of wood and fruit. The Sariz, from pinot nero, cabernet franc, refosco and merlot, has elegant fruity flavors and well-judged tannins. The Collio Pinot Grigio, in which delicate mineral notes and green apple emerge on an enjoyably fat palate, wins One very full Glass. The Refosco dal Peduncolo Rosso makes a good impression as it avoids this variety's typical harshness.

○	Collio Tocai Friulano '97	🍷🍷	3
○	Collio Pinot Bianco '97	🍷🍷	3*
○	Collio Pinot Grigio '97	🍷	3
○	Marnà '96	🍷	4
●	COF Refosco P. R. '96	🍷	3
●	Sariz	🍷	4
○	Collio Malvasia '97		3
○	Collio Chardonnay '97		3
○	COF Pinot Grigio Podere di Ipplis '97		4
○	COF Picolit '96	🍷🍷 (white)	5
○	Marnà '95	🍷🍷 (white)	4

DOLEGNA DEL COLLIO (GO)

La Rajade
Loc. Restocina, 12
34070 Dolegna del Collio (GO)
tel. 0481/639897

For some time Romeo Rossi, the young and dedicated wine-maker who runs La Rajade, has had at his disposal the means for an upward leap in quality, as well as the assistance of Professor Zironi from the University of Udine. Romeo has almost seven hectares of estate vineyard to work with and some more that he rents. They are on very steep slopes, right on the Slovenian border, and they take a lot of hard work, but they guarantee excellent results. The white Caprizzi di Marceline (referring to a whim of Marcellina, his grandmother) is obtained from malvasia, ribolla, tocai, sauvignon and verduzzo. It has a mellow structure and remarkable length, the nose is dominated by the sweet pepper aromas of the sauvignon, while fresh apple emerges on the broad fruit of the palate, with notes of white chocolate. A distinct but delicate mingling of tobacco leaves and pear emerges on the nose of the Tocai Friulano, but it really scores points with the palate, which is mouth-filling, chewy and rich, with a streak of crisp acidity and firm structure. The Sauvignon performs unusually well for this vintage, with its aromas of elderberry, green pepper and fresh apple on the nose as well as on the rich, complex palate. The Cabernet Franc easily earns One Glass. It has concentrated aromas of ripe red fruit and spices and is continuous, full-bodied and chewy on the palate, with rounded tannins. The Stratin '96, from cabernet sauvignon and merlot, is nearly as good, characterized by a bouquet of sour cherry, blueberries and blackberries, with a dense fruity structure in the mouth and slightly rough-edged tannins. Finally, One Glass, full to the brim, goes to the Chardonnay whose yeasty nose with tobacco and fresh fruit carries through on the concentrated, silky palate with a citrus finish.

○	Caprizzi di Marceline	🍷🍷	4
○	Collio Sauvignon '97	🍷🍷	4
○	Collio Tocai Friulano '97	🍷🍷	3*
○	Chardonnay '97	🍷	3
●	Collio Cabernet Franc '97	🍷	3
●	Stratin '96		4

DOLEGNA DEL COLLIO (GO)

VENICA & VENICA

VIA MERNICO, 42
LOC. CERÒ
34070 DOLEGNA DEL COLLIO (GO)
TEL. 0481/60177 - 61264

If out of the ten wines presented by a producer not a single one scores less than 70 out of 100, then that winery is definitely top-rank. The Venica brothers Gianni and Giorgio regularly achieve highly satisfactory results, by dint of constant effort in cellar and vineyards. Their success is all the more appealing because of Gianni's wife, Ornella, who gives a warm reception to visitors and guests. This year the Three Glass wine is the Sauvignon Ronco delle Mele '97, from vineyards with a northwesterly exposure. It has stylish aromas of elderberry, rue and green leaves, while the broad, fresh palate has mouth-filling structure with peach and grapefruit on the finish. The normal Sauvignon, only slightly less elegant, offers elderberry and rue on the nose and a peach-flavored palate with a good bite of acidity and a long finish. Vanilla emerges on the bouquet of the Chardonnay, with the yeasty, fresh-cream notes of the malolactic fermentation, while vanilla, banana and custard emerge on the fresh yet full palate. The Pinot Bianco, elegant as always, has appley aromas, both rennet and golden delicious, on the nose, with the complex palate evolving smoothly and ending on a long, fruity note. The Tocai Friulano, with typical and elegant nuances of apple seeds on the nose, is well-structured and concentrated, crisp and long. A brief run-through of the One Glass wines: the Pinot Grigio is harmonious and consistent, the Ribolla Gialla elegant and nicely crisp, while the Vignis, from sauvignon, tocai and chardonnay, is mellow and very fruity. The Merlot Perilla '94 loses points because of its astringent tannins, while the Rosso delle Cime ends the list.

	Wine	Glasses	
○	Collio Sauvignon Ronco delle Mele '97	🍷🍷🍷	4
○	Collio Chardonnay '97	🍷🍷	4
○	Collio Pinot Bianco '97	🍷🍷	4
○	Collio Sauvignon '97	🍷🍷	4
○	Collio Tocai Friulano '97	🍷🍷	4
○	Collio Pinot Grigio '97	🍷	4
○	Vignis '96	🍷	4
○	Collio Ribolla Gialla '97	🍷	4
●	Rosso delle Cime '94	🍷	5
●	Collio Merlot Perilla '94	🍷	5
○	Collio Pinot Bianco '96	♀♀♀	4
○	Collio Sauvignon '88	♀♀♀	5
○	Collio Sauvignon '90	♀♀♀	5
●	Collio Merlot Perilla '93	♀♀	4

DUINO-AURISINA (TS)

EDI KANTE

LOC. PREPOTTO, 3
FRAZ. S. PELAGIO
34011 DUINO-AURISINA (TS)
TEL. 040/200761

However his wines turn out, Edi Kante is a myth for many wine-makers and for anyone who knows his wines and his cellar. The latter is an amazing tunnel dug out of the karstic rock, with bare, colorful walls punctuated by occasional openings leading nobody quite knows where. Not everyone in these parts manages to make wine, let alone wines of premium quality, and we take our hats off to Edi and his success in this almost impossible undertaking. As usual, the Chardonnay and the Sauvignon are at the top of the range, but the Vitovska, from the native variety of this name, is also an excellent wine. Limpid in appearance, the Chardonnay '96 offers a bouquet in which yeasty notes, crusty bread, banana, elderberry and ripe pineapple mingle harmoniously, followed by a concentrated palate with fresh acidity, firm structure and a long finish. The Sauvignon, with golden glints in the glass, has a complex nose with honey, cream, toasty notes, pineapple and tropical fruits. These, with the addition of elderberry, are repeated on the palate with an unassertive acidity which balances nicely with the softness of the malolactic fermentation. The Vitovska, partially aged in the barriques previously used for the Sauvignon, recalls elderberry, sage, citrus, muscat and ripe fruit. It has a marked acidity which is slightly out of key with the oak-derived vanilla, but nevertheless it's a lovely wine.

	Wine	Glasses	
○	Carso Chardonnay '96	🍷🍷	4
○	Carso Sauvignon '96	🍷🍷	4
○	Carso Vitovska '96	🍷	4
○	Chardonnay '90	♀♀♀	4
○	Chardonnay '94	♀♀♀	4
○	Sauvignon '91	♀♀♀	4
○	Sauvignon '92	♀♀♀	4
○	Chardonnay '95	♀♀	4
○	Sauvignon '95	♀♀	4
●	Carso Terrano '94	♀	4

FAEDIS (UD)

PAOLINO COMELLI
VIA DELLA CHIESA - LOC. COLLOREDO
33040 FAEDIS (UD)
TEL. 0432/711226 - 504973

Pierluigi Comelli, a notary, is the head of the family estate, situated on some hills with a wonderful view of the Friuli plain. The results of our blind tastings confirm a steady rise in quality. Top of the crop is the Chardonnay. Gold in color, it has a complex bouquet recalling toffee, pear, apple and wildflowers, while the attack on the palate is crisp and followed by buttery notes mingling with tropical fruits; the oak is perfectly judged and hints of citrus appear in the long lingering finish. The Pinot Grigio with tints of onion-skin pink also earns Two Glasses. It has aromas of apple and pear and a full, complex palate with just a touch too much acidity on the finish. The Tocai Friulano, which scores a Glass, impresses most for its intense fruity bouquet, while the palate has less concentration but a wonderful almondy finish. Another full Glass goes to the Sauvignon Superiore, from a yield of less than 80 quintals of grapes per hectare. Golden-hued, it offers complex aromas of pineapple and medicinal herbs, mingling on the palate with grapefruit and rue. The Cabernet Sauvignon is also an excellent wine. The Rosso Soffumbergo, derived mainly from merlot with some cabernet sauvignon and a dash of cabernet franc, has had a long maceration followed by barrique aging, and is mellow with pronounced herbaceous overtones. The Bianco Locum Nostrum, from four parts chardonnay and one sauvignon fermented and matured in barrique, has good complexity but is over-crisp in character.

	Wine	Glasses	Price
○	COF Chardonnay '97	🍷🍷	3
○	COF Pinot Grigio '97	🍷🍷	3
○	COF Sauvignon Sup. '97	🍷	3
○	COF Tocai Friulano '97	🍷	3
●	COF Cabernet Sauvignon '97	🍷	3
●	COF Rosso Soffumbergo '96	🍷	4
●	COF Schioppettino '96		3
○	COF Bianco Locum Nostrum '96		4

FARRA D'ISONZO (GO)

BORGO CONVENTI
STRADA COLOMBARA, 13
34070 FARRA D'ISONZO (GO)
TEL. 0481/888004

1997 has been a year of progress for Gianni Vescovo's winery. Although the leading wines of this vintage have not reached last year's stratospheric scores, all the estate selections (Borgo Conventi, La Colombara and I Fiori) are of admirably consistent unfailing quality. We were very impressed by the powerful structure of the Braida Nuova '95, a Bordeaux-style blend of outstanding merit. Wild berries, toffee and vanilla emerge with fresh notes on the nose; the nuances of vanilla are repeated on the palate with attractive fruit and robust tannins. The Chardonnay has a warm appley bouquet, following through well on a straightforward palate with a distinct crispness. The Chardonnay cru Colle Russian has toasty aromas with milky notes, ripe fruit and honey, all echoed on the palate, which is slightly lacking in balance and diminished by the acidity. The Chardonnay I Fiori, with a fresh appley bouquet and supple, attractive palate, is lean and lively and easy to drink. The Pinot Grigio I Fiori offers a nose with green notes on a fruity background and a harmonious palate with a good fresh acidity. The other Pinot Grigio, the Collio DOC, is a lovely onion-skin pink, reminiscent of dried fruit and russet apples on the nose, with adequate structure and length on the palate. The golden-tinted Pinot Bianco has an intense, elegant bouquet of apples and aromatic herbs repeated on a clean palate with fresh acidity on the finish. To end with, the Cabernet Sauvignon La Colombara has complexity of aroma and surprisingly good structure in the mouth.

	Wine	Glasses	Price
●	Braida Nuova '95	🍷🍷	5
●	Collio Merlot '97	🍷	4
●	Friuli Isonzo Cabernet Sauvignon La Colombara '97	🍷	3
○	Collio Chardonnay '97	🍷	4
○	Collio Chardonnay Colle Russian '96	🍷	4
○	Collio Pinot Bianco '97	🍷	4
○	Collio Pinot Grigio '97	🍷	4
○	Friuli Isonzo Chardonnay I Fiori '97	🍷	3
○	Friuli Isonzo Pinot Grigio I Fiori '97	🍷	3
○	Collio Tocai Friulano '97		4
●	Braida Nuova '91	YYY	5
●	Braida Nuova '93	YY	5
●	Braida Nuova '94	YY	5

FARRA D'ISONZO (GO)

CASA ZULIANI
VIA GRADISCA, 23
34070 FARRA D'ISONZO (GO)
TEL. 0481/888506

The excellent reviews of Casa Zuliani's wines in this edition of the Guide are a confirmation of their laudably constant high quality. Our congratulations to Signora Bruna Zuliani for having now dedicated the entire estate to the production of wine. There are 14 hectares under vine, part in the Collio and part in the Isonzo zone. Vineyard management aims at restricting yields, which are limited to 60 quintals of grapes per hectare for the Collio and 70 for the Isonzo. Claudio Tomadin, in charge of marketing, has brought out some experimental wines this year which he has envisaged musically. Thus we found ourselves tasting the Collio Bianco Swing, from chardonnay partially aged in barrique, tocai and sauvignon. It has a bouquet of pear, apple and fruit salad and is broad and mellow in the mouth, with fresh acidity and a delightfully fruity finish. When it has a little more grip on the palate it will carry off Two Glasses. The Cabernet Franc Habanera comes from vineyards with a yield of 45 quintals per hectare and is aged in six-hectoliter casks for a year. It is mellow, fruity and soft, with rounded tannins and a full structure. The Merlot Gospel has a similar origin but is partly aged in barriques. The bouquet offers notes of various cherries and plums (with hints of ripe blueberries), while the rich, rounded palate has unobtrusive tannins and attractive citrusy notes on the finish. The other wines we've listed as worthy of your attention are inviting and correctly made, alcoholic but pleasantly crisp.

	Wine	Glasses	Price
●	Collio Cabernet Franc '97	🍷	3
●	Collio Cabernet Franc Habanera '96	🍷	3
●	Collio Merlot '97	🍷	3
●	Collio Merlot Gospel '96	🍷	4
○	Collio Bianco Swing '97	🍷	3
○	Collio Pinot Grigio '97	🍷	3
○	Collio Tocai Friulano '97	🍷	3
○	Friuli Isonzo Sauvignon '97	🍷	3
○	Collio Pinot Bianco '97		3
○	Collio Sauvignon '97		3
○	Collio Pinot Bianco '96	🍷🍷 (outline)	3

FARRA D'ISONZO (GO)

COLMELLO DI GROTTA
VIA GORIZIA, 133
FRAZ. VILLANOVA
34070 FARRA D'ISONZO (GO)
TEL. 0481/888445

Last year lack of space obliged us to put Luciana Bennati's winery, managed by Fabio Coser, into the Honorable Mention section, although it had earned One Glass ratings for two wines (Isonzo Pinot Grigio and Sauvignon '96). This year their range of excellent wines leaves us with no option but to devote a full entry to Colmello di Grotta. We will begin with the Collio Bianco Rondon, a blend of chardonnay, pinot grigio and sauvignon. Gold-tinted in color, it has sweet fruity aromas combined with a stylish toastiness, and enters the mouth with rich fruit, buttery notes, yeast and citrus, unfolding on the palate and leading into a warm, elegant finish. It easily earns Two Glasses, as do the Collio Tocai Friulano and Chardonnay. The first offers aromas of apple seeds, aniseed and pear merging with hints of lavender, and a broad palate with lots of fruit and good length. The second has a typical nose with vanilla, banana and milk, and an even more exciting palate with wonderful grip and continuity, leading into a broad finish with a harmonious blending of honey, toasty coffee and fresh apple. The Isonzo Chardonnay (half of the vineyards being in the Isonzo zone and the other half in Collio) is another Two Glass scorer. It relies more on elegance than the other Chardonnay, and less on power. An intense, broad, appley fruit emerges on the nose, mingling with smokey notes, while the closely-structured palate offers hints of honey, peach and yeast. The Collio Sauvignon has more distinct and varietal aromas (elderberry, sage and grapefuit) than the same variety from the plain, just as the Collio Pinot Grigio reveals more mellowness of structure than the Isonzo variety.

	Wine	Glasses	Price
○	Collio Bianco Rondon '97	🍷🍷	3
○	Collio Chardonnay '97	🍷🍷	3
○	Collio Tocai Friulano '97	🍷🍷	3
○	Friuli Isonzo Chardonnay '97	🍷🍷	3*
○	Collio Pinot Grigio '97	🍷	3
○	Collio Sauvignon '97	🍷	3
○	Friuli Isonzo Pinot Grigio '97	🍷	3
○	Friuli Isonzo Sauvignon '97	🍷	3

FARRA D'ISONZO (GO)

★ VINNAIOLI JERMANN
VIA MONTE FORTINO, 21
FRAZ. VILLANOVA
34070 FARRA D'ISONZO (GO)
TEL. 0481/888080

Silvio Jermann's genius has once again created a magnificent white of incredible longevity, his Vintage Tunina, from chardonnay and sauvignon. The golden-hued '96 vintage, redolent of banana, orange, syrupy peaches and elderberry, is powerful on the palate, rich, broad, long and continually evolving. In our opinion it is the most stunning of the estate's wines, which are all unrivalled in charm. The Capo Martino is again superb. The oak on the nose is overlaid with scents of honey, banana, pear and yellow plum which carry through onto a structured palate offering notes of citrus and honey; its rich glycerin lends its such smoothness that it almost seems sweet. The Vinnae '97, mostly ribolla gialla, gains complexity from the addition of riesling and malvasia, a demonstration of Silvio's ability to create a white in which richness combines with freshness, structure with suppleness. Dreams has changed its name to Were Dreams, Now It Is Just Wine!, indicating its evolution, not an abandoned goal. It is a stylish and intense wine, crisp and long with lots of rich fruit. The Pinot Bianco has a fresh bouquet of fruit salad leading into a complex, harmonious palate where acidity, apple and pear are nicely balanced on the long finish. The Chardonnay '97 is a fresh, long wine with exceptional firmness on the palate. The Pinot Grigio, with a faint coppery glow, discloses notes of ripe melon balanced by the freshness its acidity provides. The Riesling Afix, named after his youngest son, Alojz Felix, is strongly varietal, displaying typical aromas of apples, plums, lemon rind and a delicate mineral streak.

	Wine	Glasses	Price
○	Vintage Tunina '96	🍷🍷🍷	5
○	Capo Martino '96	🍷🍷	6
○	Pinot Bianco '97	🍷🍷	4
○	Vinnae '97	🍷🍷	4
○	Were Dreams, Now It Is Just Wine! '96	🍷🍷	6
○	Chardonnay '97	🍷	4
○	Pinot Grigio '97	🍷	4
○	Riesling Afix '97	🍷	4
○	Sauvignon '97		4
○	Capo Martino '91	🍷🍷🍷 (previous)	5
○	Capo Martino '93	🍷🍷🍷 (previous)	5
○	Vintage Tunina '90	🍷🍷🍷 (previous)	5
○	Vintage Tunina '93	🍷🍷🍷 (previous)	5
○	Vintage Tunina '94	🍷🍷🍷 (previous)	5
○	Vintage Tunina '95	🍷🍷🍷 (previous)	5

FARRA D'ISONZO (GO)

TENUTA VILLANOVA
VIA CONTESSA BERETTA, 29
FRAZ. VILLANOVA
34070 FARRA D'ISONZO (GO)
TEL. 0481/888593

This historic estate, which in 1999 will celebrate its fifth century of existence, has further strengthened its position in the Guide. While it is true that the '97 harvest favored reds, it was equally advantageous for whites where people knew what to do in the vineyard. We were therefore not surprised to find that the Tocai Friulano '97 is an excellent wine, with aromas of flint, pear and sugared almonds, and typical almondy notes on the full, generous silky palate. Of the Monte Cucco range we liked the Chardonnay '96. Its golden hue precedes a toasty, lactic bouquet with broad, concentrated fruit; the palate is close-knit and continuous with nuances of licorice and fresh honey and a long finish. The Sauvignon '97 reveals atypical fruit on the nose, a common characteristic of the variety this vintage, while on the palate the wine is mouth-filling, warm and very well-structured, with notes of tropical fruits. Of the two blends we particularly liked the Menj Bianco '97, from malvasia istriana, pinot bianco and tocai. Lemon-gold in color with scents of white peaches, it is broad and lingering on the palate, with echoes of banana and citrus fruit on the full, rich finish. The good Menj Rosso '95, from merlot, the cabernets franc and sauvignon and petit verdot, has a herbaceous nose on which red fruits emerge, leading into a remarkably full palate with forceful tannins and plums and blueberries on the finish. The Pinot Bianco '97, an uncomplicated wine with balanced acidity, has enjoyable green apple on the nose followed by a fresh, fruity palate.

	Wine	Glasses	Price
○	Collio Chardonnay Monte Cucco '96	🍷🍷	4
○	Collio Tocai Friulano '97	🍷🍷	3*
○	Menj Bianco '97	🍷🍷	3*
○	Collio Pinot Bianco '97	🍷	3
○	Collio Sauvignon Monte Cucco '97	🍷	4
●	Menj Rosso '95	🍷	3
○	Montecucco Spumante Brut		4
○	Collio Ribolla Gialla Montecucco '96	🍷🍷 (previous)	4
○	Collio Sauvignon Montecucco '96	🍷🍷 (previous)	4

GONARS (UD)

Di Lenardo
Via Battisti, 1
Fraz. Ontagnano
33050 Gonars (UD)
tel. 0432/928633

Massimo Di Lenardo increasingly identifies with the new, emerging breed of wine-maker. He pays close attention to the market, particularly abroad, for which international-style wines such as the Chardonnay Woody are produced; he seeks technical advice from various sources, including university research departments; marketing and pricing policies are under his direct supervision. All this efficiency may seem a bit soulless, but it certainly guarantees results. One result is the wonderful Pinot Grigio, which impressed us with its elegant, flowery, fruity bouquet, suggesting pear, citrus fruit and pineapple; the entry on the palate is vigorous, and it continues at length, revealing fullness of body and the right amount of refreshing acidity. The Chardonnay Woody, partially fermented in wood, releases wonderful aromas of vanilla and melon, with stylish licorice and vanilla on the palate, but it misses Two Glasses because of over-prominent oak. The soundly made Chardonnay Musque offers aromas of elderberry, banana and apple, carried through onto a complex palate. The reliable Tocai, by now a tradition of the estate, displays varietal aromas of bitter almonds and green apple on both nose and palate. In an unfavorable year for this grape, the estate's Sauvignon stands out for its notes of sweet pepper on the nose and palate, backed up by a good length. The Pinot Bianco, highly varietal with its aromas of green apple, reveals interesting almondy notes. Among the reds, the Ronco Nolè, a blend of merlot, cabernet franc and cabernet sauvignon, draws attention with its nicely-mingled scents of grass and red fruit compote, while attractive notes of coffee appear on the palate together with rather raw tannins.

	Wine	Glasses	Price
○	Friuli Grave Pinot Grigio '97	🍷🍷	3*
○	Friuli Grave Chardonnay Musque '97	🍷	3
○	Friuli Grave Chardonnay Woody '97	🍷	3
○	Friuli Grave Pinot Bianco '97	🍷	3
○	Friuli Grave Sauvignon '97	🍷	3
○	Friuli Grave Tocai Friulano '97	🍷	3*
●	Ronco Nolè '96	🍷	3
●	Friuli Grave Merlot '97		3
○	Friuli Grave Tocai Friulano '96	ΥΥ	2
●	Ronco Nolè '95	Υ	3

GORIZIA

Fiegl
Loc. Lenzuolo Bianco, 1
Fraz. Oslavia
34170 Gorizia
tel. 0481/31072

For some years now quality has been steadily on the rise in this estate. The three Fiegl brothers, Alessio, Giuseppe and Rinaldo, have been working eagerly to improve both the vineyards and the cellar, which is undergoing a program of remodernization and expansion. The results are immediately apparent in the high scores of the wines. The Leopold Cuvée Blanc, from sauvignon, tocai, pinot bianco and ribolla, has a stylish bouquet of dried flowers and fruit, with the palate repeating the fruit, here accompanied by an enjoyable, refreshing acidity. The Leopold Rosso, 80% merlot and 20% cabernet franc, partially aged in barrique, is outstanding for its complex aromas of prunes and red flowers and its broad palate. The Tocai Friulano discloses scents of apple, elderberry and apple seeds on the nose, followed by a nicely structured, continuous palate with attractive sweet notes, fresh herbs and an inviting fruity finish. The Sauvignon, which has pronounced varietal character, offers an intense, broad nose with tomato leaf and elderberry, leading into a warm palate backed up by adequate acidity. The Chardonnay also scores well: it is characterized by fruity aromas, particularly banana and melon, leading into a long palate with refreshing acidity. The Pinot Grigio loses points for its bitterish notes and a lack of balance on the finish, but reveals an elegant, complex fruit salad on the nose. The simple, straightforward Ribolla Gialla offers typical scents of fruit and flowers, while the Pinot Bianco, with its hints of pear and wildflowers on the nose, has a fruity palate with marked notes of ripeness.

	Wine	Glasses	Price
○	Collio Chardonnay '97	🍷🍷	3*
○	Collio Sauvignon '97	🍷🍷	3*
○	Collio Tocai Friulano '97	🍷🍷	3
○	Leopold Cuvée Blanc '96	🍷🍷	4
●	Leopold Rosso '93	🍷🍷	5
○	Collio Pinot Bianco '97	🍷	3
○	Collio Pinot Grigio '97	🍷	3
○	Collio Ribolla Gialla '97	🍷	3
○	Collio Pinot Grigio '96	ΥΥ	3
○	Leopold Cuvée Blanc '95	ΥΥ	4
●	Collio Merlot '95	ΥΥ	4

GORIZIA

★ JOSKO GRAVNER
LOC. LENZUOLO BIANCO, 9
FRAZ. OSLAVIA
34170 GORIZIA
TEL. 0481/30882

In the last few years Josko Gravner has been hit more than once by dreadful weather which has significantly diminished both the quantity and the quality of his harvests. He has, however, also played a part himself. He has revolutionized his winery, (and, as we know, revolution generally includes excess) in his attempt to return to the old ways of making wine. You mustn't imagine that by "old" he means 50 or 100 years ago: the glory of Greece and the grandeur of Rome would appear to be more like what he has in mind, as he is reverting to earthenware amphorae, and abandoning barriques in favor of large barrels. This may perhaps explain the unexciting results of recent years. The Ribolla Gialla has again achieved excellence: of an almost golden hue, its aromas recall ripe yellow fruits, vanilla custard and malaga; it offers a balanced, mellow palate with lots of fruit and a dry finish. The Rosso '93 almost got Two Glasses: vegetal notes emerge on a background of warm strawberries and berry tart on the nose, but the full fruit of the palate is cut short by heavy, raw tannins. The Breg '95, a blend of native white grapes and sauvignon, riesling italico and pinot grigio, with aromas ranging from vanilla, butter and tea to wood and ripe fruit, lacks blance.

	Wine	Glasses	Price
○	Collio Ribolla Gialla '95	🍷🍷	6
●	Rosso '93	🍷	6
○	Breg '95		6
○	Chardonnay '83	YYY	6
○	Chardonnay '87	YYY	6
○	Chardonnay '88	YYY	6
○	Chardonnay '92	YYY	6
○	Chardonnay '93	YYY	6
○	Collio Chardonnay '90	YYY	6
○	Collio Chardonnay '91	YYY	6
○	Collio Ribolla Gialla '92	YYY	6
○	Collio Sauvignon '89	YYY	6
○	Sauvignon '93	YYY	6
○	Chardonnay '94	YY	6
○	Sauvignon '94	YY	6

GORIZIA

LA CASTELLADA
FRAZ. OSLAVIA, 1
34170 GORIZIA
TEL. 0481/33670

Giorgio and Nicolò Bensa were among the first in Friuli to prune the profusion of wines they offered, concentrating on Ribolla Gialla, emblematic of the region, and two estate blends, one white and one red. We entirely agree with this decision, an example which many producers from Friuli and elsewhere would do well to follow. But back to La Castellada: their Three Glass winning streak was bound to be interrupted sooner or later, and it seems that this was the year, although our tasting panels were by no means unanimous about denying them this accolade. The candidate was the Bianco della Castellada '96, from barrique-fermented tocai friulano, pinot grigio, sauvignon and ribolla gialla. The concentrated nose offers notes of honey and butter followed by ripe fruit and cane sugar, leading into a warm, rich, broad palate with soft fruit, and a dried flower and caramel finish. Production is so consistent that for the Ribolla Gialla '96 we can repeat last year's review: delicate and fruity, its appeal lies in the equilibrium achieved between its fresh green notes and the creamier toastiness of the wood. The Rosso della Castellada '94, from cabernet sauvignon and merlot, is distinctly redolent of warm berry tart with a hint of tar, licorice, candied orange peel and spice. The palate corresponds, supported by tannins and acidity that are kept properly in check, with a note of sour cherries on the fruity finish, almost as if pinot nero were present in the blend.

	Wine	Glasses	Price
●	Rosso della Castellada '94	🍷🍷	6
○	Bianco della Castellada '96	🍷🍷	5
○	Collio Ribolla Gialla '96	🍷🍷	5
○	Bianco della Castellada '92	YYY	5
○	Bianco della Castellada '94	YYY	5
○	Bianco della Castellada '95	YYY	5
○	Collio Chardonnay '94	YYY	5
○	Collio Sauvignon '93	YYY	5
○	Bianco della Castellada '93	YY	5
○	Collio Chardonnay '93	YY	5
○	Collio Pinot Grigio '93	YY	5
○	Collio Ribolla Gialla '95	YY	5
●	Rosso della Castellada '90	YY	6
●	Rosso della Castellada '91	YY	6
●	Rosso della Castellada '92	YY	6

GORIZIA

PRIMOSIC

VIA MADONNINA DI OSLAVIA, 3
FRAZ. OSLAVIA
34170 GORIZIA
TEL. 0481/535153

The Primosic winery of Oslavia has achieved even better results with its selection than it did last year. Marko has presented a range of wines which easily reached high scores, with nothing below 75 out of 100. The Chardonnay Gmajne, Two overflowing Glasses, has undergone a long period of aging in stainless steel and bottle after fermentation and six months of barrique maturation. Dried fruit is the keynote on the nose, followed on the palate by tropical fruits, milky coffee, a rich medley of other fruit and a soft finish. The Ribolla Gialla is also aged in oak, but this time in 15-hectoliter barrels. It offers sweet scents of wild flowers and yellow plums, followed by acidity and fruit in perfect balance on the palate, whose rich structure reveals a dominant appley flavor. The barrique-aged Klin '95, another Two Glass white, is obtained from sauvignon, chardonnay and ribolla gialla. Straw-yellow with greenish-gold tints, it reveals a bouquet of elegant oak-derived toastiness and well-ripened fruit, while vanilla, banana and pineapple are evident on the palate. The Merlot Riserva '95 spends six months in barrique, followed by 18 months of barrel maturation. The ripe red fruit and spice on the nose are followed by a closely-knit, lingering palate with a dense fruity structure displaying notes of steeping cherries. The Pinot Grigio is broad and elegant, with an attractive nose but a palate that is perhaps a bit lean, despite the fact that the wine is one third barrique-aged. The Sauvignon has distinct varietal character with the classic aromas of elderberry and rue.

	Wine	Rating	
●	Collio Merlot Ris. '95	🍷🍷	4
○	Collio Chardonnay Gmajne '97	🍷🍷	4
○	Collio Ribolla Gialla Gmajne '97	🍷🍷	4
○	Klin '95	🍷🍷	4
○	Collio Pinot Grigio Gmajne '97	🍷	4
○	Collio Sauvignon Gmajne '97	🍷	4
○	Collio Ribolla Gialla Gmajne '96	YY	4
○	Collio Sauvignon Gmajne '96	YY	4

GRADISCA D'ISONZO (GO)

MARCO FELLUGA

VIA GORIZIA, 121
34072 GRADISCA D'ISONZO (GO)
TEL. 0481/99164-92237

This winery in Gradisca supervises a group of small growers through every stage of vineyard management in order to obtain grapes capable of producing wines of premium quality. One of these is unquestionably the Collio Merlot '97, redolent of mulberries mingling with ripe red fruits, with a broad, solid, long palate. The Moscato Rosa is excellent, the best we tasted this year in Friuli, pink in color, redolent of roses, strawberries and raspberry cordial, and medium-sweet on a palate reminiscent of fresh orange juice with elegant hints of clove. The two blends, the red Carantan '95 and the white Molamatta '97, also performed well. The first, from merlot, cabernet sauvignon and cabernet franc, displays intense, harmonious aromas of fresh fruit and wild berries carrying through on the palate, with a good tannic grip on the finish. The Molamatta, made from ribolla gialla, tocai and pinot bianco, offers a bouquet of apple, tea and wildflowers. The palate has depth, a fresh acidity and intense, varied fruit. The Chardonnay has a generous, rich, long palate, more clearly defined than the nose, whereas the opposite is true of the Sauvignon, with its attractive nose evoking elderberry, tomato leaf and rue. The substantial Ribolla Gialla offers fresh notes of medicinal herbs. To conclude, the Cabernet '96 displays typical grassy aromas with a soft entry on the palate and adequate tannins on the finish.

	Wine	Rating	
●	Collio Merlot '97	🍷🍷	4
●	Moscato Rosa '97	🍷🍷	5
●	Carantan '95	🍷	5
●	Collio Cabernet '96	🍷	4
○	Collio Chardonnay '97	🍷	3
○	Collio Ribolla Gialla '97	🍷	4
○	Collio Sauvignon '97	🍷	3
○	Molamatta '97	🍷	4
○	Collio Pinot Grigio '97		3
○	Collio Tocai Friulano '97		3
●	Collio Merlot '95	YY	3
○	Collio Pinot Bianco '96	YY	3
○	Collio Tocai Friulano '96	YY	3
○	Marco Felluga '96	YY	4

MANZANO (UD)

BANDUT

VIA ORSARIA, 32
33044 MANZANO (UD)
TEL. 0432/299208 - 740524

This year's range of wines from the Bandut estate, which belongs to a well-known consortium of pharmacists in Udine with a long-standing passion for viticulture, is rather inconsistent. Some wines are really excellent, while others are so disappointing that we prefer not to mention them. Their vineyards lie in a greatly sought-after hillside area, and for this reason as well we expect that they will soon be turning out wines worthy of their zone of origin and of Colutta traditions. This year the Pinot Grigio and Tocai Friulano are the pick of the bunch. The latter's merit is already apparent from the bouquet, characterized by pear and elderberry; then the warm, structured palate offers delightful notes of ripe pear which linger on the long finish. The stylish Pinot Grigio displays a rich, complex nose, leading into a palate which unfolds to reveal appley, citrusy notes mingling with honey and apricot. The Nojâr, which means walnut in Friuli and is named after its vineyard in Buttrio, is a blend of ribolla gialla and chardonnay distinguished by the finesse of its perfumes, in which apple and fresh fruits are dominant, while the notes of citrus and stewed apple on the palate have a hint of honey indicating a faint overripeness. The Chardonnay, much fresher, has aromas of banana, vanilla and cream with green notes, which all reappear on the palate together with unripe plums, citrus and tropical fruits. The Merlot '97 displays the herbaceous aromas typical of the variety and is a very quaffable wine.

	Wine	Glasses	Price
○	COF Pinot Grigio '97	🍷🍷	3*
○	COF Tocai Friulano '97	🍷🍷	3*
○	COF Bianco Nojâr '97	🍷	4
○	COF Chardonnay '97	🍷	3
●	COF Merlot '97		3

MANZANO (UD)

NICOLA E MAURO CENCIG

VIA SOTTOMONTE, 171
33044 MANZANO (UD)
TEL. 0432/740789

Last year we were impressed by what this estate, belonging to the Cencig brothers Nicola and Mauro, produced. The wines were well made in general and excellent in some particular cases. This year they've done it again, thus earning a profile in the Guide. The cellar is essentially innocent of up-to-date technology (apart from the bladder press and the crusher-destemmer for the whites), and Mauro, the oenologist, works with equipment that has been around for a while. However, with Nicola's skilful laboring in the vineyard, the grapes are first-rate and Mauro succeeds in making something of them. The Cencigs look after seven hectares of vineyards on the hills of Manzano and for fifteen years have been bottling a part of their average annual production of 400 hectoliters. We liked the Sauvignon, which is remarkable for its overall structure and texture rather than its varietal character. The nose, in fact, is distinctly appley, followed by pear and fresh aromatic herbs on a closely-knit, mellow, mouth-filling palate with good length. The Tocai Friulano very nearly got Two Glasses. It offers aromas of pear, apple and almonds, perfectly mirrored on the palate, with just the right acidity and echoes of bitter almonds, typical of this grape, on the finish. The gold-tinted Pinot Grigio has a yeasty bouquet and a full, broad, balanced palate with fresh sweet fruit salad lingering on the finish. The Verduzzo Friulano has the more intense gold color characteristic of its grape, and typical baked apple on the nose, with notes of vanilla and banana. In the mouth it is medium-sweet, rich, and lingering. The estate's reds will be released at the end of the year, so we shall review them in the next edition of the Guide.

	Wine	Glasses	Price
○	COF Sauvignon '97	🍷🍷	3
○	COF Pinot Grigio '97	🍷	3
○	COF Tocai Friulano '97	🍷	3
○	COF Verduzzo Friulano '97	🍷	3

MANZANO (UD)

WALTER FILIPUTTI
P.ZZA DELL'ABBAZIA, 15
LOC. ROSAZZO
33044 MANZANO (UD)
TEL. 0432/759429

With the '97 vintage Walter and Patrizia Filiputti have regained full control of the vineyards and cellar of the Abbazia di Rosazzo, owned by the Curia of Udine. This is still a period of adjustment, so it's no wonder if there are some ups and downs. What matters is that the wines with Walter Filiputti's label show a marked rise in quality. Walter's winery produced 953 hectoliters in the last vintage, filling 127,000 bottles, half of which come from the grapes of the Abbazia vineyards. Walter has great hopes for the Pignolo '95, which, although still a young wine, struck us very favorably. Distinct aromas of blackberries and woodland fruit with cherry tart lead into a full-bodied palate, but the finish is masked by over-boisterous young tannins. Elegant charm distinguishes the Bianco Ronco del Monastero, a blend of tocai, malvasia and ribolla gialla, whose fruity softness and balanced acidity we found very attractive. The Ribolla Gialla, vinified as a monovarietal, scores points for its harmonious freshness, suppleness and fragrance. The Bianco Poiesis '97, made from tocai, pinot bianco, chardonnay and a dash of picolit, offers rich aromas of apple, pear and citrus, followed by a warm, fruity structure on the palate, with nuances of white chocolate. In the red Broili di Filip, "bròili" being a plot cultivated near home, merlot is the main grape, with decreasing percentages of refosco, cabernet sauvignon and cabernet franc. It is an easy, undemanding wine just right for everyday drinking.

●	Pignolo '95	ΨΨ	6
○	COF Bianco Poiesis '97	Ψ	4
○	COF Bianco Ronco del Monastero '97	Ψ	4
○	COF Ribolla Gialla '97	Ψ	4
○	COF Pinot Grigio '97		4
○	COF Sauvignon '97		4
●	Broili di Filip '97		4

MANZANO (UD)

RONCHI DI MANZANO
VIA ORSARIA, 42
33044 MANZANO (UD)
TEL. 0432/740718

We are extremely pleased to welcome Roberta Borghese and her winery, Ronchi di Manzano, to the exclusive ranks of Three Glass winners. This success is in part the result of years of hard work in the vineyards (with emphasis on the replanting of selected clones and tireless efforts to find the proper balance between density per hectare and yield per vine) and the cellar, which is extraordinary for its up-to-the-minute technology and its imposing collection of barrels of all sizes. The Merlot Ronc di Subule '96 is intense and concentrated on a nose that features red fruits, licorice and tar; the warm, harmonious, powerful palate is velvety and complex with a long finish and nicely judged tannins on a toasty background. Two other wines were runners-up for Three Glasses. The first, Le Zuccule, is a red from merlot and cabernet. Wild berries, tar, licorice and chocolate on the nose are followed by ripe red fruits and milky coffee flavors in the mouth, with a weighty structure backed up by good tannins and a wonderfully long finish. The second, the Picolit Rosazzo '96, is amber and old gold in color, with a bouquet of baked apples, raisins, custard and white chocolate. The entry on the palate is soft, leading into a sweet, velvety finish. The Rosazzo Bianco '97 is extraordinary in its structure, close texture and elegant perfumes of ripe tropical fruits, while the Chardonnay '97 offers buttery aromas with vanilla, tropical fruit and almonds. The amber-gold Verduzzo Ronc di Rosazzo has a flowery, almondy nose with candied orange peel, leading into a medium-sweet, viscous, warm palate disclosing pleasant citrusy notes on the sweet finish. Two Glasses go to the Cabernet Sauvignon '96, with a broad fruity aroma over a background of toasty, tarry notes and a palate offering chocolate, vanilla and lively tannins.

●	COF Merlot Ronc di Subule '96	ΨΨΨ	4
●	COF Cabernet Sauvignon '96	ΨΨ	3
○	COF Chardonnay '97	ΨΨ	3
○	COF Rosazzo Bianco '97	ΨΨ	4
○	COF Rosazzo Picolit '96	ΨΨ	5
○	COF Verduzzo Friulano Ronc di Rosazzo '96	ΨΨ	4
●	Le Zuccule '96	ΨΨ	4
●	COF Cabernet Franc '96	Ψ	3
●	COF Merlot '96	Ψ	3
○	COF Pinot Grigio '97	Ψ	3
○	COF Tocai Friulano '97	Ψ	3
●	COF Merlot Ronc di Subule '95	ΨΨ (outline)	4

MANZANO (UD)

RONCO DEI ROSETI - ZAMÒ
VIA ABATE CORRADO, 55
LOC. ROSAZZO
33044 MANZANO (UD)
TEL. 0432/759693

Ronco dei Roseti, the Zamò family's new estate, is destined to become the headquarters of their three properties in the Colli Orientali. The administration, the new guest-house and the tasting rooms are here and, as soon as bureaucratic requirements permit, it will be the home of a new vinification cellar for all three holdings. The 15 hectares of vineyard feature high-density plantings, and the varieties grown are chardonnay, pinot grigio, sauvignon and ribolla gialla. Meanwhile, in the Zamò family cellars the wines produced during their management of the Abbazia di Rosazzo are maturing, and can be sold under this label through the '96 vintage. The Ronco dei Roseti wines have the defects typical of young vines, but results are already remarkable, an example being the Chardonnay '97. Its nose reveals an elegant, fruity complexity, while the glycerin-rich palate has a lively acidity underpinning the finish. The Ronco delle Acacie, one of the estate's classics, is made from chardonnay, tocai and pinot bianco. Vanilla, almonds, apricot, banana and spice mingle on the nose, while the palate evolves nicely with a wonderfully long, rich finish. The Pignolo '94, a great red from a local grape, is redolent of ripe plums, cherry jam, licorice and tar, while the palate displays fruit jam, leather, licorice and undergrowth, lightly masked by robust tannins. The Ronco dei Roseti '93, a blend of cabernet sauvignon, merlot, cabernet franc, refosco and tazzelenghe, has a bouquet of warm, ripe red fruits enriched with notes of tar and licorice, but unfortunately diminished by rather harsh tannins on the finish. We liked the harmonious palate of the Sauvignon, the abundant flowery, fruity aromas of the Ribolla Gialla and the sweet balance of the Picolit '94.

○	COF Chardonnay '97	▼▼	4
○	COF Ronco delle Acacie Abbazia di Rosazzo '95	▼▼	4
●	Pignolo Abbazia di Rosazzo '94	▼▼	5
●	Ronco dei Roseti Abbazia di Rosazzo '93	▼▼	5
●	COF Picolit Abbazia di Rosazzo '94	▼	6
○	COF Ribolla Gialla '97	▼	4
○	COF Sauvignon '97	▼	4
○	COF Pinot Grigio '97		4
●	Ronco dei Roseti '88	▽▽▽	5
●	Ronco dei Roseti '90	▽▽▽	5
●	Ronco dei Roseti '92	▽▽▽	5
○	Ronco delle Acacie '93	▽▽▽	4
○	Ronco di Corte '87	▽▽▽	4
○	COF Chardonnay '96	▽▽	4

MANZANO (UD)

RONCO DELLE BETULLE
VIA A. COLONNA, 24
LOC. ROSAZZO
33044 MANZANO (UD)
TEL. 0432/740547

The Narciso '94, 85% cabernet sauvignon and 15% merlot aged in barrique for two years, is the first wine to win Three Glasses in the history of Ronco delle Betulle. The wine is a deep ruby-red in color and has rich and beautifully balanced aromas of ripe red fruits, herbs, spices, chocolate and coffee and a rich, lingering palate with vigorous but attractive tannins. The award-winner in question comes from an estate which has always pursued quality and is personally managed in every detail by Ivana Adami. The following wide range of really top-rank wines bears witness to the high standard of production. The golden Rosazzo Picolit has a complex bouquet of herbal teas (mint and chamomile), white flowers and pineapple, followed by a long, dense, harmonious palate ending on an elegant almondy note. The Franconia, another of Friuli's rare wines, is spicy, flowery and herbal on the nose; the palate follows through with sweet creamy notes and green bark. The Pinot Bianco stands out among the whites for its intense, elegant and complex aromas recalling golden delicious apples and flowers, all of which are slightly diminished on the palate by excessive acidity. The Pinot Grigio is characterized by intense aromas of candied peel, wildflowers, melon and apple on both nose and palate. The Sauvignon offers a concentrated nose revealing sage and elderberry. The full palate is warm, creamy and salty, with lingering, well-balanced notes of sweet pepper and sage. The characteristically varietal Tocai Friulano offers fresh aromas of green apple and almond and a long, soft, fruity finish. The Ribolla Gialla, with its customary pale hue, is enjoyable for its flowery, fruity sensations on the nose and palate, its slight acidity and an attractive note of green apple in the finish.

●	Narciso Rosso '94	▼▼▼	5
●	Franconia '96	▼▼	3
○	COF Pinot Bianco '97	▼▼	3
○	COF Pinot Grigio '97	▼▼	3
○	COF Rosazzo Picolit '97	▼▼	6
○	COF Sauvignon '97	▼▼	3
○	COF Tocai Friulano '97	▼▼	3
○	COF Bianco Narciso '96	▼	4
○	COF Rosazzo Ribolla Gialla '97	▼	3
○	COF Pinot Bianco '96	▽▽	3
○	COF Tocai Friulano '96	▽▽	3

MANZANO (UD)

Torre Rosazza
Loc. Poggiobello, 12
33044 Manzano (UD)
tel. 0432/750180

Our congratulations for the wines presented this year by the Torre Rosazza estate, one of the Friuli wineries belonging to Genagricola, part of the Assicurazioni Generali insurance group. We were anticipating a coup from the Altromerlot '94, instead of which the Cabernet Sauvignon Ronco della Torre '95 was in the running for Three Glasses. The bouquet offers chocolate and red fruit compote blending with the perfectly judged oak, while the full, fruity palate has lingering grip and power. The excellent Altromerlot '94 offers ripe, concentrated fruit with coffee and cocoa on the nose, but the toastiness and raw-edged tannins are not yet assimilated on the palate and detract from its rich fruit. The barrique-derived vanilla in the Pinot Bianco Ronco delle Magnolie lends elegance to the fresh, appley nose; the palate is firm and mellow with nicely balanced acidity. The Pinot Grigio, another of the premium wines, displays an intense but stylish nose with white fruits and flowery notes repeated on the palate together with a hint of macaroons, good acidity and pleasant vegetal notes on the finish. The gold-tinted Verduzzo Friulano '96 also earns Two Glasses. Apple, dried apricot and raisin emerge on the nose and follow through perfectly on the slightly sweet, elegantly-oaked palate. We lift high One Glass to the Ribolla Gialla for the intensity of its bouquet, the elegance of its palate and its fruity complexity. The Tocai Friulano offers pear, apricot and a delightfully harmonious yeasty note on the nose. Ripe apple and pineapple are the keynotes in the Pinot Bianco '97, but it is let down by a marked acidity, also present in the Chardonnay.

	Wine	Glasses	Price
●	COF Cabernet Sauvignon Ronco della Torre '95	🍷🍷	4
●	COF Merlot L'Altromerlot '94	🍷🍷	5
○	COF Pinot Bianco Ronco delle Magnolie '96	🍷🍷	4
○	COF Pinot Grigio '97	🍷🍷	3*
○	COF Verduzzo Friulano '96	🍷🍷	4
○	COF Chardonnay '97	🍷	3
○	COF Pinot Bianco '97	🍷	3
○	COF Ribolla Gialla '97	🍷	3
○	COF Tocai Friulano '97	🍷	3
●	COF Pinot Nero Ronco del Palazzo '96		4
●	COF Refosco P. R. '96		3
●	COF Merlot L'Altromerlot '95	🍷🍷 (white)	4

MANZANO (UD)

Zamò & Zamò
Via Abate Corrado, 55
Loc. Rosazzo
33044 Manzano (UD)
tel. 0432/759693

Under the Zamò & Zamò label the brothers Pierluigi and Silvano Zamò market the wines deriving from the vineyards on the Ronchi di Buttrio, some of which are very old and therefore yield grapes with a high natural concentration. This year's most outstanding wines are the blends, first of which comes the ironically named Vino di Lâ which in Friuli dialect means "must we go?" and refers to the transfer of the Zamò family to their new estate, Ronco dei Roseti. The wine is made from tocai friulano, sauvignon, pinot grigio and chardonnay vinified entirely in stainless steel. The result is a superb wine, delicately perfumed with apple and ripe yellow fruit. It offers a complex palate, rich, broad and soft, with considerable acidity masked by the concentrated fruit. The Bianco TreVigne '96 is an oaked blend of tocai, chardonnay and sauvignon grapes, of which a small percentage is sun-dried, from the Buttrio, Rosazzo and Rocca Bernarda vineyards. The nose offers elegant aromas of fresh and well-ripened fruit with notes of citrus, while the broad, harmonious, alcohol-rich palate is closely-textured and very long, with fruit and acidity balancing each other. The Merlot '96 has a warm, concentrated nose recalling cooked red fruits and a hint of licorice and tar, while the palate has slightly unsettled tannins on the finish. The Merlot Vigne Cinquant'Anni, although it's a '95, seems younger than the Merlot '96 because of its astringent tannins and the freshness on the finish. The Tocai Friulano, with notes of barley sugar on the nose, is worthy of mention.

	Wine	Glasses	Price
○	COF Bianco TreVigne '96	🍷🍷	4
○	COF Bianco Vino di Lâ '97	🍷🍷	3*
●	COF Merlot '96	🍷🍷	4
●	COF Merlot Vigne Cinquant'Anni '95	🍷	5
○	COF Tocai Friulano '97		4
○	COF Bianco TreVigne '95	🍷🍷 (white)	4
○	COF Tocai Friulano Vigne Cinquant'Anni '96	🍷🍷 (white)	4
●	COF Cabernet '95	🍷🍷 (white)	4

MARIANO DEL FRIULI (GO)

★ VIE DI ROMANS
LOC. VIE DI ROMANS, 1
34070 MARIANO DEL FRIULI (GO)
TEL. 0481/69600

In this edition of the Guide many members of what we call the band of Isonzo Boys have been awarded Three Glasses and it would be impossible not to include the one who led the way. Gianfranco Gallo, the owner of the Vie di Romans winery, has once again pulled a winner out of the hat, his stunning Flors di Uis '96 (meaning scent of flowering grapes), a blend of malvasia, chardonnay and riesling. If Gianfranco's aim was to express to perfection the acidity, the rich balance and the aromatic character of the three varieties, he has undoubtedly hit the mark. The Flors di Uis has gotten better and better during the period of our tastings, achieving an extraordinary richness and elegance of structure and fruit, recalling apple and hawthorn, while losing none of its freshness. The Sauvignon Vieris reveals oak-derived notes of tobacco with varietal aromas of tomato leaf on the nose, followed by vanilla and milky coffee mingling with fresh grapefuit on the palate. The unoaked Sauvignon Piere is one of Gianfranco's classics, displaying original hints of goats' cheese underlying a distinct aroma of elderberry, while the closely-knit, mouth-filling palate is broad and fresh. The toastiness of the barrique is still evident in the Pinot Grigio Dessimis, but is covered by the full fruit which lends it suppleness on the palate. In the Chardonnay Vie di Romans the wood is only just discernible, owing to the rich, complex fruit; vanilla and banana emerge on the palate with a fresh acidity. The Chardonnay Ciampagnis Vieris has the toffee-like aromas typical of the variety, with toasted, nutty flavors on a remarkably well-structured palate.

	Wine	Rating	Price
○	Friuli Isonzo Bianco Flors di Uis '96	🍷🍷🍷	4
○	Friuli Isonzo Chardonnay Vie di Romans '96	🍷🍷	4
○	Friuli Isonzo Pinot Grigio Dessimis '96	🍷🍷	4
○	Friuli Isonzo Sauvignon Piere '96	🍷🍷	4
○	Friuli Isonzo Sauvignon Vieris '96	🍷🍷	4
○	Friuli Isonzo Chardonnay Ciampagnis Vieris '96	🍷	4
○	Chardonnay '86	☐☐☐	4
○	Friuli Isonzo Chardonnay '91	☐☐☐	4
○	Friuli Isonzo Piere Sauvignon '93	☐☐☐	4
○	Friuli Isonzo Sauvignon Vieris '95	☐☐☐	4
○	Friuli Isonzo Vieris Sauvignon '90	☐☐☐	4
○	Friuli Isonzo Vieris Sauvignon '92	☐☐☐	4
○	Friuli Isonzo Vieris Sauvignon '93	☐☐☐	4

NIMIS (UD)

DARIO COOS
VIA RAMANDOLO, 15
33045 NIMIS (UD)
TEL. 0432/790320

Although Ramandolo was launched by others, Dario Coos has definitely turned it into a nectar more than worthy of a place among the world's sweet wines. The Verduzzo grape, which adapted itself to the bitter cold of Ramandolo that gave the wine its name, is thick-skinned and rich in tannins, so that even the briefest period of maceration gives it the mouth-puckering quality that makes it instantly recognizable. Dario in fact harvests the grapes when they are extremely ripe and leaves some of them to dry out in crates, after which the must is fermented in barriques. The Longhino is the unoaked version, old-gold and amber in color, followed by a fragrances of stewed apples, chocolate and raisins. The entry on the palate is soft and sweet and there is apple juice on the full, mellow finish. The amber-gold Ramandolo '96 releases aromas of dried apple, almond-milk and apricots in spirit. The palate is elegant and medium-sweet, with notes of apple and honey leading into a long, delightful finish. Try it with cheese or paté de foie gras, or sip it slowly on its own.

	Wine	Rating	Price
○	COF Ramandolo '96	🍷🍷	5
○	COF Ramandolo Il Longhino '97	🍷	4
○	COF Ramandolo '95	☐☐	5
○	COF Ramandolo Il Longhino '96	☐	4

PAVIA DI UDINE (UD)

PIGHIN F.LLI
V.LE GRADO, 1
FRAZ. RISANO
33050 PAVIA DI UDINE (UD)
TEL. 0432/675444

The 22 wines we tasted from the Pighin estate give the impression of a winery capable of achieving above average quality in almost its entire range. All but three of the wines were approved by our tasting panels, and many of them earned One Glass. It is true that none of them reached peaks of excellence, but this is not easy when you're working 140 hectares in the Grave DOC and 30 in Collio, which means oceans of wine. The Chardonnay Collio '97 has appley, yeasty aromas and a full, structured, long palate. Pear and almonds emerge on the nose of the Tocai Friulano, which has a supple palate and notes of pear and apple mingling harmoniously with the acidity on the finish. The elegant, fruity Pinot Grigio '97 has a splendid bouquet with notes of macaroons; it is mouth-filling, warm and bracing and underpinned by good acidity. The Picolit '95 is redolent of apple and peach preserves, which reappear on the palate with sweet apple and almondy notes. The Cabernet Collio '96 offers sour cherry and undergrowth aromas on a soft, full palate, while the Pinot Grigio displays unusual elegance on both nose and palate, dominated by apple and aromatic herbs. The varietal Sauvignon Grave '97 offers typical aromas of sage, rue and sweet pepper. The Sauvignon Vigna Casette '96, from ungrafted rootstock (one of the many experiments carried out by the Pighin brothers with their expert wine technician Paolo Valdesolo), is more reminiscent of tomato leaf. To round off the list, the Soreli (sun), from tocai, pinot bianco and sauvignon del Collio, is refined and elegant.

	Wine	Rating	Price
●	Collio Cabernet '96	🍷	3
○	Collio Chardonnay '97	🍷	3
○	Collio Picolit '95	🍷	6
○	Collio Pinot Bianco '97	🍷	3
○	Collio Pinot Grigio '97	🍷	3
○	Collio Tocai Friulano '97	🍷	3
○	Friuli Grave Pinot Grigio '97	🍷	3
○	Friuli Grave Sauvignon '97	🍷	3
○	Friuli Grave Sauvignon Vigna Casette '96	🍷	3
○	Soreli '96	🍷	4
○	Collio Tocai Friulano '96	🍸🍸	3
○	Soreli '95	🍸🍸	4
●	Collio Merlot '96	🍸🍸	3
●	Baredo '91	🍸	4

PAVIA DI UDINE (UD)

SCARBOLO - LE FREDIS
V.LE GRADO, 4
FRAZ. LAUZACCO
33050 PAVIA DI UDINE (UD)
TEL. 0432/675612 - 675150

Le Fredis, owned by Walter Scarbolo, who is a farmer and pork butcher as well as a wine-maker, was established ten years ago. Its wines are known to us and were in the Guide for a few years, until Walter became too taken up with other commitments to be able to devote enough time to the winery. For a couple of years now the production of good wines has become his ruling passion and he is back in the Guide with the Scarbolo label. For the moment he has about eight hectares of vineyard in Grave del Friuli, but from the next vintage we shall also be tasting wines from the Colli Orientali del Friuli. Emilio del Medico is the house wine technician and the consultant oenologist is Maurizio Castelli. We very much liked the Merlot '97, intensely fruity and spicy on the nose, with a palate of rare complexity in which cherries, blueberries and woodland fruit nicely offset the tannins. The Merlot Campo del Viotto '95 unfortunately loses points because of a slight touch of volatile acidity, but it definitely deserves One Glass for texture and good ripe fruit. The Tocai Friulano, offering enjoyable notes of pear with underlying rue and almonds on the nose, has a full palate with crisp acidity on the finish. The Chardonnay '97 has distinct varietal character on the nose, with hints of melon, banana, yeasts and toffee, and a fresh yet generous palate. The Pinot Grigio '97, with typical faint tints of onion-skin pink, displays a rich and various composition of aromas, and supple structure in the mouth.

	Wine	Rating	Price
●	Friuli Grave Merlot '97	🍷🍷	3*
●	Friuli Grave Merlot Campo del Viotto '95	🍷	4
○	Friuli Grave Chardonnay '97	🍷	3
○	Friuli Grave Pinot Grigio '97	🍷	3
○	Friuli Grave Tocai Friulano '97	🍷	3
○	Friuli Grave Sauvignon '97		3

PINZANO AL TAGLIAMENTO (PN)

ALESSANDRO VICENTINI ORGNANI
VIA SOTTOPLOVIA, 1
FRAZ. VALERIANO
33090 PINZANO AL TAGLIAMENTO (PN)
TEL. 0432/950107

In last year's Guide, our comment on this estate's range of wines was that despite his skill Alessandro had not come up to everyone's expectations. This year he has succeeded, and what a triumph! Two wines, the Merlot '96 and the Pinot Bianco Braide Cjase '97, win Two Glasses, and there's an impressively long list of One Glass wines. This year's results are due to Alessandro's increased experience, and he is now firmly established as a major player on the wine-making scene in Friuli. After years of effort, experiments and investments he has reached a level of professional accomplishment which will stand him in good stead for the future. There are two production lines, the Braide Cjase, with partially barrique-aged wines, and the standard range. The Pinot Bianco Braide Cjase offers intense, fruity perfumes in which ripe apple stands out, and a delicate, stylish, long palate with a lingering fruity finish. The Merlot '96 is a classic of the estate and an excellent wine, offering a spicy nose with complex, harmonious aromas of blackberries,cherries and blueberries. The palate is structured and long with slightly rough-edged tannins. The Chardonnay and Pinot Grigio are both soundly made wines of the Braide Cjase line. The first is distinguished by its full, fruity aromas, in particular banana, and its balanced palate where a refreshing acidity mingles pleasantly with the fruit and the oak-derived vanilla. The second has delicate fragrances of vanilla, yellow plums and apricots and an excellent harmony of nose and palate. The Sauvignon, reliable as ever, offers rue on the nose and attractive notes of grapefruit and sweet lemon on the palate. We found the Tocai, with its characteristic almondy aromas, and the Pinot Grigio, with onion-skin tints and scents of dried flowers, also well up to standard.

	Wine	Glasses	Price
●	Friuli Grave Merlot '96	🍷🍷	3*
○	Friuli Grave Pinot Bianco Braide Cjase '97	🍷🍷	3*
○	Friuli Grave Chardonnay Braide Cjase '97	🍷	3
○	Friuli Grave Pinot Grigio '97	🍷	3
○	Friuli Grave Pinot Grigio Braide Cjase '97	🍷	3
○	Friuli Grave Sauvignon '97	🍷	3
○	Friuli Grave Tocai Friulano '97	🍷	2*
●	Friuli Grave Pinot Nero '97		3
●	Friuli Grave Merlot Braida Cjase '92	🍸🍸	3

POVOLETTO (UD)

TERESA RAIZ
VIA DELLA ROGGIA, 22
LOC. MARSURE DI SOTTO
33040 POVOLETTO (UD)
TEL. 0432/664144

This estate, belonging to the Tosolini brothers Paolo and Giovanni who are also first-rate distillers, has had a rather disappointing vintage. A transitional period, in which new, high-density plantings have been made near the cellar, is reflected in the wines, but we are speaking of defects in a context of overall reliability. The Ribolla Gialla is a soundly made wine, as often in previous years. It is intense but elegant on the nose with distinct notes of fresh apple, followed by a fruity palate which displays this variety's typical acidity backing up the long finish. Although very pale in the glass, the Tocai Friulano offers intense aromas of apple seeds with hints of almonds and pears, while on the palate it is fresh and supple, revealing fruity notes that linger on the finish. The Refosco dal Peduncolo Rosso is wonderfully harmonious in aroma, displaying rich fruit with marked notes of morello cherries and very ripe plums on both nose and palate, where it is underpinned by a firm structure that gives length to the finish. The Sauvignon dei Colli Orientali del Friuli is attractive in its aromas reminiscent of elderberry, sage, lemon and pineapple, but it does not score so well on the palate because of its pronounced acidity. To end with, the Sauvignon Rovel, the Chardonnay and the Querciolo di Torbaia are simpler wines worthy of note.

	Wine	Glasses	Price
●	Friuli Grave Refosco P. R. '97	🍷	2*
○	COF Ribolla Gialla '97	🍷	3
○	COF Tocai Friulano '97	🍷	3
○	COF Sauvignon '97		3
○	Friuli Grave Chardonnay '97		2
○	Friuli Grave Sauvignon Le Marsure Rovel '97		3
●	Querciolo di Torbaia '96		3
●	Decano Rosso '93	🍸🍸	4
●	Decano Rosso '94	🍸🍸	4
●	Decano Rosso '95	🍸	4

PRADAMANO (UD)

Fantinel Vini
Via Cussignacco, 80
33040 Pradamano (UD)
tel. 0432/670444

If we had to sum up the recent evolution of this winery in one phrase, it would be: from quantity to the arduous pursuit of quality. The quality of the wines had not been superlative in the past, but in the last few vintages we have observed some successful attempts at improvement, which resulted in a modest appearance in the Honorable Mention section last year, and a full profile in this year's Guide. Marco Fantinel, the young and determined general manager, is working to improve quality and we wish him all the best in this important undertaking and hope that it continues. The estate covers 90 hectares of the superb Scriò and Vencò zones in Collio and about 100 hectares in the Spilimbergo zone in Grave. The annual output of almost two million bottles of wine and spumante is divided into various ranges. The wine that impressed us most is the Grave Cabernet Sauvignon, with its moderately intense fragrances of ripe red fruits and tobacco and its stylish, subtle palate, where the grassy notes harmonize with the fruit and well-judged tannins. The Collio Cabernet Franc Vigneti Santa Caterina reveals sweet and mild aromas followed by a soft, warm, ripe fruit in the mouth. Intriguing scents of mint and tea distinguish the Collio Sauvignon Vigneto Sant'Helena, with nectarines on the palate. The reliable Grave Pinot Grigio Borgo Tesis reveals a delicate mingling of light, toasty notes with the fruit on the nose, leading into a broad, harmonious palate with hints of macaroons. The Fantinel Brut Spumante has a fine perlage and good tertiary aromas reminiscent of figs, raisins and dates (which will appeal to lovers of this type of wine), but the palate, although enjoyable, is rather short.

	Wine	Rating	Price
○	Collio Sauvignon Vigneti Sant'Helena '97	🍷	4
○	Fantinel Brut	🍷	4
○	Friuli Grave Pinot Grigio Vigneti Borgo Tesis '97	🍷	3
●	Collio Cabernet Franc Vigneti Santa Caterina '97	🍷	3
●	Friuli Grave Cabernet Sauvignon Vigneti Sant'Helena '96	🍷	4
●	Friuli Grave Refosco P. R. Paron Mario '97		3

PRATA DI PORDENONE (PN)

Vigneti Le Monde
Via Garibaldi, 2
Loc. Le Monde
33080 Prata di Pordenone (PN)
tel. 0434/626096 - 622087

Piergiovanni Pistoni, the energetic, enterprising president of the Friuli Grave Consortium, has as usual come up with a reliable range of wines, but premium quality, a tradition of the estate, is lacking. The clayey soils of Le Monde are well-suited for the production of fine red wines for aging, which make up half of the annual output of 200,000 bottles, an unusual choice in Friuli. Nevertheless the wine which impressed us most this vintage is the Pinot Grigio, in which aromas of apple and pineapple are in perfect harmony with the variety's typical mineral notes. The palate follows through well, enhanced by a refreshing acidity on the finish that makes it very easy to drink. Two of the reds are good scorers, the Refosco dal Peduncolo Rosso and the Querceto '94. The first, a clear ruby in color, has a spicy nose with overtones of hay typical of the estate's reds; its long, fruity palate is particularly attractive. The Querceto, a blend of cabernet sauvignon with some cabernet franc, stands out for its aromas of prunes and spice, followed by a rich, complex, fruity palate with good length. The Cabernet Sauvignon Riserva '94 is characterized by appealing, complex aromas of ripe fruit well blended with spicy undertones, but a marked acidity and rather raw tannins lose it points on the palate. The soundly made Chardonnay discloses banana and apricot on the nose, nicely repeated on the palate.

	Wine	Rating	Price
○	Friuli Grave Pinot Grigio '97	🍷	3
●	Friuli Grave Refosco P. R. '97	🍷	3
●	Querceto '94	🍷	5
○	Friuli Grave Chardonnay '97		3
●	Friuli Grave Cabernet Sauvignon Ris. '94		4
●	Friuli Grave Cabernet Franc '96	🍷🍷	3
●	Friuli Grave Cabernet Sauvignon '96	🍷	3
●	Querceto '93	🍷	5

PREMARIACCO (UD)

DARIO E LUCIANO ERMACORA

VIA SOLZAREDO, 9
FRAZ. IPPLIS
33040 PREMARIACCO (UD)
TEL. 0432/716250

This was another fine vintage for the Ermacora brothers who, aided by the advice of the oenologist Flavio Zuliani, have released a range of first-rate wines. They all scored well at our tastings, confirming the reliability of the winery. We are now eager to see what Dario, president of the Consorzio Colli Orientali del Friuli, and his brother Luciano will come up with in the future. The estate has been extended from 14 hectares to the current 18, with a production of 80,000 bottles. In a year in which this variety performed very well, the Pinot Grigio presented by the Ermacora brothers is of superb quality, displaying intense mineral notes, yellow flowers and fruit on the nose, and a rich, full-flavored palate with good balance and length. The Pinot Bianco offers sensations of banana and mango with a vigorous entry on the warm, broad palate, where it expands and lingers. The Verduzzo Friulano reveals typical aromas of baked apple and dates, repeated on a fresh, elegant, moderately sweet palate with a delightful note of apple on the finish. The long, stylish Tocai Friulano came very close to Two Glasses; its delicate scents of almonds and ripe pear are followed by a palate which lacks complexity. Despite an unpropitious vintage the Sauvignon offers delicate aromas with notes of rue and tomato leaf, leading on to an elegant and refreshingly crisp palate.

	Wine	Glasses	Price
○	COF Pinot Bianco '97	🍷🍷	3*
○	COF Pinot Grigio '97	🍷🍷	3*
○	COF Verduzzo Friulano '97	🍷🍷	3*
○	COF Sauvignon '97	🍷	3
○	COF Tocai Friulano '97	🍷	3
○	COF Pinot Grigio '96	🍸🍸	3
○	COF Sauvignon '96	🍸🍸	3

PREMARIACCO (UD)

ROCCA BERNARDA

VIA ROCCA BERNARDA, 27
FRAZ. IPPLIS
33040 PREMARIACCO (UD)
TEL. 0432/716273

The wines of this estate are getting better every year, thanks to the concerted efforts of the enthusiastic manager, Marco Zuliani, and Marco Monchiero, skilled consultant oenologist from Piedmont. The 40 hectares of vineyard are well situated on the hills sloping down from the impressive sixteenth century fortress (the Rocca), and the optimum exposure is backed up by careful vineyard management, which has shown remarkable improvement in recent years. And of course they are not exactly hurt by the tradition in the air one breathes on this beautiful estate. (Most of what one knows about the cultivation of the picolit grape in the 19th century is based on documentation relative to these vineyards.) This year the Merlot Centis only just missed getting Three Glasses. It is deep ruby in color, and offers elegant aromas of mint, wild rose, chocolate and ripe fruit echoed on the rich, harmonious palate with a wonderful dense texture and balance. The Pinot Grigio scores well for its rich, lingering aromas recalling apple and ripe pear, which follow through well on a complex palate. The very varietal Tocai Friulano, with fine, delicate, lingering sensations in the mouth, echoing the appley, almondy aromas of the nose, is of like quality. The Chardonnay, delightful on the nose with its hints of coffee, apricot and vanilla, is diminished on the palate by the heavy oak that overwhelms the fruit. The varietal tomato leaf aromas of the Sauvignon mingle with toasty notes, leading into a fresh, tasty and continuous palate, and the typical Ribolla Gialla is worthy of mention. The estate is devoting considerable attention to its Picolit, a great local tradition, as we mentioned above. The '96 version, which will be released this autumn, showed great promise when we tasted it from the vat.

	Wine	Glasses	Price
●	COF Merlot Centis '96	🍷🍷	4
○	COF Pinot Grigio '97	🍷🍷	3
○	COF Tocai Friulano '97	🍷🍷	3*
○	COF Chardonnay '97	🍷	3
○	COF Sauvignon '97	🍷	3
○	COF Ribolla Gialla '97		3
●	COF Merlot Centis '93	🍸🍸	4
●	COF Merlot Centis '94	🍸🍸	4
●	COF Merlot Centis '95	🍸🍸	4
○	COF Picolit Ris. '94	🍸🍸	6

PREMARIACCO (UD)

SCUBLA

Via Rocca Bernarda, 22
Fraz. Ipplis
33040 Premariacco (UD)
tel. 0432/716258

We have tried several times to convince the likeable Roberto Scubla to reduce the number of his labels, but he remains an incorrigible experimenter with new styles in the wine-making adventure he plunged into a few years ago. With eight hectares of vineyard to work with, the estate at the moment has a range of at least twelve wines. An excellent one is the Bianco Pomédes, a blend of pinot bianco, tocai and semi-dried riesling, fermented and matured in new barriques. The wine has aromas of banana, apricot and tropical fruits that follow through on the broad, mouth-filling palate. Another high scorer is the Bianco Speziale, from tocai, sauvignon and very ripe pinot bianco. The nose is soft and slightly sweet but fresh at the same time, leading into a full, broad palate with lots of fruit on the finish. The Merlot '96 offers a nose with hints of mould on ripe, concentrated red fruit, while the complex palate includes chocolate and toasty notes. The vigorous but restrained tannins merge on the finish with berries and cherry and damson preserve. The Pinot Bianco, whose vines suffered from a frost in April, has a broad, complex bouquet with a hint of yeasts and fresh ripe fruits, while crisp acidity lends backbone to the palate. The Tocai Friulano, with intense perfumes of green apple and peach, is full and inviting on the palate, followed by a finish with typical notes of bitter almond. The warm, herbaceous, highly varietal Cabernet Franc '97 offers a fresh palate with unaggressive tannins.

	Wine	Rating	Price
○	COF Bianco Pomédes '97	🍷🍷	4
○	COF Bianco Speziale '97	🍷🍷	4
●	COF Merlot '96	🍷🍷	4
●	COF Cabernet Franc '97	🍷	4
○	COF Pinot Bianco '97	🍷	4
○	COF Tocai Friulano '97	🍷	4
○	COF Riesling '97		4
○	COF Sauvignon '97		4
○	COF Verduzzo Friulano '97		4
○	COF Bianco Pomédes '96	ΥΥ	4
○	COF Verduzzo Friulano Graticcio '96	ΥΥ	5

PREMARIACCO (UD)

VIGNE DAL LEON

Via Rocca Bernarda, 38
Fraz. Ipplis
33040 Premariacco (UD)
tel. 0432/759693

It is now 20 years since Vigne dal Leon was bought by Tullio Zamò, an industrialist converted to wine-making. His sons, Pierluigi and Silvano, caught his enthusiasm and they now run the estate. Starting next year Vigne dal Leon, Ronco dei Roseti and Zamò & Zamò will be under a single management with the brand Le Vigne di Zamò. Their consultant is the renowned oenologist Franco Bernabei, who has also had some notable successes with the wines produced by the Zamò family. Barbara Maniacco, a graduate in forestry sciences who has specialized in oenology, is devoting increasingly close attention to the vineyards and cellar, as well as managing the commercial department. The Pinot Bianco is once again the estate's premier wine in both the barrique-aged version, Tullio Zamò '94, and the non-oaked version. The latter, displaying its usual standard of excellence, is fresh and elegant, with nuances of green apple on the nose followed by a rich, spicy palate with nicely-judged acidity and a long finish. The Tullio Zamò '94 underwent both the alcoholic and the malolactic fermentations in wood, and a long bottle aging after a year in barrique. It offers an intense, elegant nose with hints of banana and vanilla, leading into a powerful, mouth-filling, broad palate with ripe fruit and acidity in perfect balance. The Schioppettino '94, one of the best wines of this variety, has a bouquet of sour cherries, spice and leather with elegant oak in the background, followed by a spicy palate with good structure and body. A delicate fragrance of apple and wildflowers distinguishes the Malvasia, but a rather marked acidity detracts from the palate.

	Wine	Rating	Price
○	COF Pinot Bianco '97	🍷🍷	4
○	COF Pinot Bianco Tullio Zamò '94	🍷🍷	4
○	COF Schioppettino '94	🍷🍷	6
○	COF Malvasia Istriana '97		4
○	COF Malvasia Istriana '96	ΥΥ	4
○	COF Pinot Bianco '96	ΥΥ	4
○	Tullio Zamò '92	ΥΥ	4
○	Tullio Zamò '93	ΥΥ	4
●	Rosso Vigne dal Leon '90	ΥΥ	5

PREPOTTO (UD)

La Viarte
Via Novacuzzo, 50
33040 Prepotto (UD)
tel. 0432/759458

This beautiful estate, whose vineyards and cellar are both meticulously cared for, was founded in 1973 by Giuseppe Ceschin, known as Franco. Having moved to Friuli from the Veneto to work as a professional oenologist, Franco found a wife and settled in this sometimes inhospitable region. He now has the daily assistance of his son Giulio, who has inherited his father's knowledge and thoroughness. A really impressive number of glasses has been awarded to La Viarte, which means spring in the Friuli dialect, starting with the pride of the house, the Liende (legend). It is a blend of tocai, pinot bianco, sauvignon, riesling and a dash of ribolla gialla. The '96 version has a bouquet of yeast, honey and crusty bread, followed by an inviting palate with a rich, full structure, well-judged acidity and good length. It is a long-lived wine which will follow an upward curve in quality for at least five or six years, if you find you can wait. Another very successful wine is the red blend Roi '94, mainly merlot and cabernet with a long spell in barrique. The concentrated red fruit and light smokey notes on the nose are followed by a full-bodied, broad palate with a harmonious mingling of the tannins and the fruit, and a lingering finish. The Siùm (dream) is a well-calibrated sweet wine from verduzzo friulano and picolit fermented in barrique. It stays for 18-20 months on its lees and goes into bottle two years after the harvest. Amber in color, it has a rich, broad and complex bouquet with aromas of fruit preserved in spirit, while the luscious, rounded and well-balanced palate has an almondy finish. The Tocai Friulano reveals superb structure on the palate, while the Sauvignon, although rich in glycerin, offers greater freshness with notes of elderberry, grapefruit and mint on the long finish. To end the list, the Pinot Grigio well merits Two Glasses for its outstanding elegance.

	Wine	Glasses	Price
○	COF Bianco Liende '96	🍷🍷	4
○	COF Pinot Grigio '97	🍷🍷	4
○	COF Sauvignon '97	🍷🍷	4
○	COF Tocai Friulano '97	🍷🍷	4
●	Roi '94	🍷🍷	4
○	Siùm '95	🍷🍷	5
○	COF Pinot Bianco '97	🍷	4
○	COF Ribolla Gialla '97	🍷	4
●	COF Schioppettino '95	🍷	4
●	Tazzelenghe '94	🍷	4
○	COF Pinot Bianco '96	♀♀	4
○	Siùm '94	♀♀	5

PREPOTTO (UD)

Le Due Terre
Via Roma, 68/b
33040 Prepotto (UD)
tel. 0432/713189

Flavio Basilicata and his wife Silvana are sticking to their policy of reducing the number of labels they present every year. They own a small winery near the Judrio, the river which separates the Colli Orientali del Friuli and Collio appellations, and have about seven hectares under vine. Their production consists of two blends, one white and one red, and, in particularly favorable vintages, they also make the Picolit Implicito and the Pinot Nero. We especially liked the Sacrisassi Rosso, from refosco and schioppettino, of which about 7,000 bottles have been produced. Made with well-ripened grapes and matured for a long period in 550-liter casks of French and Slavonian oak, it has a creamy, fruity nose with distinct notes of spice. The complex palate has a marked acidity that slightly accentuates the tannins, but the densely-textured, enveloping red fruit lends overall harmony. The golden Picolit Implicito is as usual a superb wine, with aromas of sweet apple, honey, semi-dried fruit and apricot tart perfectly mirrored on the palate, which is slightly sweet because of the residual sugar. Its powerful natural alcohol (14.5°) is offset by the acidity. The Sacrisassi Bianco '96 is not up to its usual standard, mostly because of the marked acidity of the palate which detracts from the fruitiness of the tocai, sauvignon and ribolla. It does, however, offer elegant aromas of fresh apple, citrus and roses. The Pinot Nero is highly typical in color and aroma, but at our tastings it was handicapped by very aggressive tannins, so it earns only a well-merited mention.

	Wine	Glasses	Price
○	Implicito '96	🍷🍷	5
●	Sacrisassi Rosso '96	🍷🍷	4
●	COF Pinot Nero '96		4
○	Sacrisassi Bianco '96		4
○	Implicito '94	♀♀	5
○	Sacrisassi Bianco '95	♀♀	4
●	Sacrisassi Rosso '95	♀♀	4
●	Sacrisassi Rosso '94	♀	4

PREPOTTO (UD)

PETRUSSA
VIA ALBANA, 49
33040 PREPOTTO (UD)
TEL. 0432/713192

The estate owned by the Petrussa brothers Gianni and Paolo is in continual expansion, since besides vinifying the crop from their own five hectares of vineyard they also buy in grapes from outside growers, whose vines are kept under close supervision. They have thus reached an annual output of over 40,000 bottles, mainly of very high quality. In this edition of the Guide it is the reds that win Two Glasses, and if '97 is the year for Cabernets, the Petrussa version is among the best. The complex, warm, intensely fruity nose is followed by a well-evolved palate, with notes of spice, cherries and licorice, ending in a long, mellow finish. The Rosso Petrussa '95, from merlot with a long maturation in wood, is its usual excellent self. The toastiness on the nose gives way to sweet fruit and undergrowth, while the amazingly youthful, promising palate displays good underlying tannins and acidity. Although they did not win Two Glasses, we were very taken with the '97 Tocai Friulano and Pinot Bianco and the Bianco Petrussa '96, from tocai, pinot bianco, sauvignon and chardonnay. The first is rich and structured with typical bitter almonds on the finish; the second offers aromas of bananas, tropical fruits and fresh pennyroyal, while the third displays a light toastiness with rich fruit and glycerin. The Merlot '97 came close to getting One Glass, particularly for its concentrated herbal and red fruit aromas; the palate fizzles out on a rather flat finish. We had an advance tasting of the Pensiero '96, a monovarietal verduzzo to be released at the beginning of 1999, which is already an outstanding sweet wine.

●	COF Cabernet '97	▼▼	3*
●	COF Rosso Petrussa '95	▼▼	4
○	COF Bianco Petrussa '96	▼	4
○	COF Pinot Bianco '97	▼	3
○	COF Tocai Friulano '97	▼	3
●	COF Merlot '97		3
○	Pensiero '95	▽▽	4
●	COF Merlot '96	▽	3

PREPOTTO (UD)

RONCHI DI CIALLA
FRAZ. CIALLA, 47
33040 PREPOTTO (UD)
TEL. 0432/731679

We must admit that the Ronchi di Cialla wines we tasted this year left us feeling somewhat puzzled. This estate, managed by Dina and Paolo Rapuzzi with the increasingly close collaboration of their two sons Pierpaolo and Ivan, is a landmark in the history of the last 20 years of wine-making in Friuli. It is a well-known fact that it was the first in the region to use barriques and the first in the whole of Italy to use them for whites. But a state of inertia seems to have set in, unjolted even by the novelties of the most recent vintages, the Ciallabianco and the Ciallarosso. Briefly, this top-rank winery seems to be content with resting on its laurels. The Ciallabianco '96, a blend of verduzzo friulano, ribolla gialla and picolit fermented and aged in barriques for about a year, has aromas of unripe banana, acacia blossom and vanilla, followed by a creamy palate with notes of apple and citrus on the soft, elegant finish. The Ciallarosso '95, made from more or less equal quantities of refosco and schioppettino, is only partially matured in casks. The complex nose recalls strawberries, raspberries, mulberries and fresh sweet fruit, which are repeated on a supple palate that offers further hints of strawberry, ripe orange and spice. The Refosco di Cialla '94 has quite prominent oak-derived aromas on both nose and palate, but attractive notes of spice, strawberry and raspberry do emerge. The Schiopettino di Cialla, a somewhat simpler wine, reveals sour cherries and spice with tannins on the finish. The last wine we reviewed, the golden Verduzzo di Cialla '95, recalls almond milk on the nose, while a marked acidity detracts from the slightly sweet palate.

●	Ciallarosso '95	▼	4
●	COF Refosco di Cialla '94	▼	5
○	COF Cialla Ciallabianco '96	▼	4
○	COF Verduzzo di Cialla '95		5
●	COF Schioppettino di Cialla '94		5
○	COF Picolit di Cialla '94	▽▽	6
●	COF Refosco P. R. di Cialla '90	▽▽	5
●	COF Schioppettino di Cialla '90	▽▽	5
●	COF Refosco P. R. di Cialla '91	▽	5
●	COF Refosco P. R. di Cialla '92	▽	5
●	COF Schioppettino di Cialla '91	▽	5

RONCHI DEI LEGIONARI (GO)

TENUTA DI BLASIG
VIA ROMA, 63
34077 RONCHI DEI LEGIONARI (GO)
TEL. 0481/475480

This estate is under the confident management of Elisabetta Bortolotto Sarcinelli, who in the last few years has undertaken to relaunch it. The cellar and the property of the Blasigs (Elisabetta's ancestors on her mother's side, to whom she is dedicating her wines) around Ronchi dei Legionari are of venerable age. About ten hectares are under vine and the grapes are vinified in the cellar at Ronchi, which was rebuilt in 1892 on older foundations. Here, next to the great old Slavonian oak barrels, Elisabetta has placed modern stainless steel tanks, more suitable for modern vinification. We especially liked the Bianco, based on chardonnay with malvasia and tocai friulano, whose fruity nose recalls dried flowers and tobacco and is followed by a broad, rich, fresh palate with apple and yellow plums on the lingering finish. The Chardonnay '97 achieves premium quality with just ten percent of barrique-aging. Fresh, broad aromas with hints of yeast, coffee and dried apricots lead into a mellow, crisp palate offering ripe grapefruit and vanilla on the lingering finish. The Spumante Brut, a delightful tank-fermented bubbly, mingles green notes with ripe pear and crusty bread on the nose, while freshness dominates the palate. The Tocai offers a very attractive nose with pear and apple seeds but disappoints on the palate, just missing One Glass. The Malvasia is of similar quality.

	Wine	Glasses	Price
○	Falconetto Bianco '97	🍷🍷	4
○	Friuli Isonzo Chardonnay '97	🍷🍷	3*
○	Vino Spumante Brut	🍷	3
○	Friuli Isonzo Malvasia '97		3
○	Friuli Isonzo Tocai Friulano '97		3
○	Falconetto Bianco	🍷🍷 (previous edition)	4

S. CANZIAN D'ISONZO (GO)

LORENZON
VIA CA' DEL BOSCO, 6
LOC. PIERIS
34075 S. CANZIAN D'ISONZO (GO)
TEL. 0481/76445

This year the Lorenzon estate, composed of almost 160 hectares of vineyards in addition to its orchards, celebrates 25 years of wine-making. The present owner, the appealing Enzo Lorenzon, has divided the wines into two ranges, Feudi di Romans and Borgo dei Vassalli, whose vineyards are closer to the modern cellar. He and his son Davide, who is an oenologist and assists him in the cellar, work together to improve quality. The results are confirmed by the increasing number of glasses awarded to the wines with the Feudi di Romans label. The Isonzo del Friuli DOC Alfiere Bianco, a blend of tocai, malvasia, pinot bianco and chardonnay harvested when very ripe, has a deep, elegant, rich nose with flowers and fresh fruit, while the full, generous palate shows good acidity and wonderful balance. The Cabernet Franc, generally a rather rustic wine, is delightfully complex and harmonious; the entry on the palate is dense, and as it evolves it becomes fruity and faintly herbaceous, while the tannins on the finish are just a little too pronounced. One Glass, highly merited, goes to the Refosco for its spicy, cherry tart aromas and warm, inviting palate with hints of sour cherries. The correctly made Merlot also deserves an award, although with its notes of herbs, spices and geranium reminiscent of other varieties it is not very representative. In contrast the Chardonnay is perfectly characteristic, revealing yeasty and crusty bread aromas on the nose and toffee and apricots on the palate. The Tocai Friulano earned marks for its close-knit structure, complexity and length on the palate, while the elegant Pinot Bianco offers attractive appley, smokey notes.

	Wine	Glasses	Price
○	Friuli Isonzo Alfiere Bianco I Feudi di Romans '97	🍷🍷	3*
●	Friuli Isonzo Cabernet Franc I Feudi di Romans '97	🍷🍷	3*
●	Friuli Isonzo Merlot I Feudi '97	🍷	3
●	Friuli Isonzo Refosco P. R. I Feudi di Romans '97	🍷	3
○	Friuli Isonzo Chardonnay I Feudi di Romans '97	🍷	3
○	Friuli Isonzo Tocai Friulano I Feudi di Romans '97	🍷	3
○	Friuli Isonzo Pinot Bianco I Feudi di Romans '97	🍷	3
○	Friuli Isonzo Sauvignon I Feudi di Romans '97		3

S. FLORIANO DEL COLLIO (GO)

Ascevi

Via Uclanzi, 24
34070 S. Floriano del Collio (GO)
tel. 0481/884140

Mariano Pintar works almost 30 hectares of vineyards, all hilly. In 1993 he bought a 10-hectare farm and decided to give the name Luwa to the range coming from the new property, to emphasize continuity. Luwa stands in fact for his daughter Luana, a graduate in oenology who works in the cellar, and his son Walter, who is expert with vines. This year Pintar has again come up with a range of highly reliable wines, with the Chardonnay and the Pinot Grigio showing real excellence. The first offers a nose of tropical fruits with hints of apricots in spirit, while Golden Delicious apples and a fresh acidity are the dominant features on the palate. The second is impressive in its elegant fragrances with hints of mineral and fresh apple. The well-structured palate is backed up by appropriate acidity and offers a delightfully long, fruity finish. Of the numerous One Glass wines, the blends deserve detailed description. The Vigna Verdana, from sauvignon with a substantial percentage of chardonnay and ribolla gialla, is fresh and supple after maceration on the skins in barrique. Sauvignon, tocai and pinot grigio are the grapes in the Col Martin Luwa, a much more complex wine. It is soft and elegant, with very fruity aromas leading into a broad, harmonious palate, enlivened on the finish by enjoyable notes of green apple. The white blend Grappoli Shaden, from sauvignon, riesling and moscato giallo, undergoes a maceration of 48 hours at about freezing temperature, after which it matures in wood. This is reflected in its golden color and its aromas of ripe peaches, banana and vanilla, but not so much on the palate, which is close-textured but attenuated by the acidity. The Sauvignon Ascevi, with its characteristic notes of elderberry and rue, almost got Two Glasses.

	Wine	Glasses	Price
○	Collio Chardonnay '97	🍷🍷	3
○	Collio Pinot Grigio '97	🍷🍷	3
○	Col Martin Luwa '97	🍷	4
○	Collio Pinot Grigio Luwa '97	🍷	3
○	Collio Ribolla Gialla Luwa '97	🍷	3
○	Collio Sauvignon '97	🍷	3
○	Collio Tocai Friulano '97	🍷	3
○	Grappoli Shaden	🍷	4
○	Vigna Verdana '97	🍷	4
○	Collio Sauvignon Luwa '97		3
●	Le Vigne '94	🍷	4

S. FLORIANO DEL COLLIO (GO)

Borgo Lotessa

Loc. Giasbana, 23
34070 S. Floriano del Collio (GO)
tel. 0481/390302

This is a proper family estate, run by father, mother and two children (Roberto, an oenologist who is gaining experience at the side of their consultant Giovanni Crosato, and Raffaella, engaged in marketing) and they are united in their desire to improve quality and shed glory on the name of Borgo Lotessa. The enthusiasm their father Salvatore radiated when he talked to us bodes very well for the future. From the 13 hectares under vine, partly in the Collio DOC and partly in Isonzo, 60,000 bottles are produced, mostly of white wine. However the highlight this year, which walked off with Two Glasses, was the Isonzo Cabernet Sauvignon. It has a complex nose recalling spices, especially cloves, red fruits and licorice, followed by a concentrated palate with tremendous body and robust tannins on the finish. The Collio Pinot Grigio is well made and displays a complex, intense nose of flowers and fruit leading into a palate with a good crisp acidity. The Collio Pinot Bianco offers delicate perfumes of green apple and rue; the palate is warm and long with lots of fruit on the finish, but it is slightly deficient in overall structure. The Margravio Bianco is a barrique-aged blend of sauvignon, pinot grigio and chardonnay characterized by intense, rich aromas recalling herb tea, dates and hay. These are echoed on the palate, which is crisp and rich in fruit, followed by a rather short finish. The other blend, the barrique-aged Margravio Rosso, from schioppettino, merlot and cabernet sauvignon, is disappointingly dull on the palate despite the promise of an important nose with notes of coffee and sour cherry preserve. The Collio Chardonnay and Collio Sauvignon are both reliable wines that deserve mention.

	Wine	Glasses	Price
●	Friuli Isonzo Cabernet Sauvignon '96	🍷🍷	3*
○	Collio Pinot Bianco '97	🍷	3
○	Collio Pinot Grigio '97	🍷	3
○	Il Margravio Bianco '96	🍷	4
○	Collio Chardonnay '97		3
○	Collio Sauvignon '97		3
●	Il Margravio Rosso '96		4
○	Collio Pinot Bianco '96	🍷🍷 (white)	3

S. FLORIANO DEL COLLIO (GO)

CONTI FORMENTINI

VIA OSLAVIA, 5
34070 S. FLORIANO DEL COLLIO (GO)
TEL. 0481/884131

The Conti Formentini estate, founded in 1520, was bought a few years ago by the Gruppo Italiano Vini. The leadership of its team of experts has been entrusted to the Piedmontese consultant Marco Monchiero, who shows increasing skill with Friuli's whites. Their Wine Museum is well worth a visit, as is the extensive cellar, which turns out over 300,000 bottles a year. The wine is made from grapes bought in the Collio zone, where they are carefully selected for quality. The exciting Ribolla Gialla '97 is both elegant and intense on the nose, with delicate hints of linden blossom, and has a broad, full palate with appley notes unfolding on the long, balanced finish. The Chardonnay Torre di Tramontana, already intense and brilliant in the glass, discloses aromas of toasty coffee over tropical fruits which open out on the palate and mingle with honey, yeast and white chocolate. The Pinot Grigio is at its best on the palate, where it reveals a close-knit fruity texture with echoes of banana and pear, but a bitterish note on the finish unfortunately detracts from this otherwise excellent wine. The Sauvignon performs better on the palate than on the nose, a frequent characteristic of the variety this vintage, offering typical flavors of sage and rue through to the finish. A good balance of tastiness, acidity and appley fruit, with notes of pear, is the key feature of the Tocai Friulano. We long to know about the reds, but we shall not be tasting them until next year.

	Wine	Rating	Price
○	Collio Chardonnay Torre di Tramontana '97	🍷🍷	4
○	Collio Ribolla Gialla '97	🍷🍷	3*
○	Collio Pinot Grigio '97	🍷	3
○	Collio Sauvignon '97	🍷	3
○	Collio Tocai Friulano '97	🍷	3
●	Collio Cabernet Franc '95	🍷🍷 (white)	3

S. FLORIANO DEL COLLIO (GO)

MUZIC

LOC. BIVIO, 4
34070 S. FLORIANO DEL COLLIO (GO)
TEL. 0481/884201

The debut appearance of Giovanni Muzic's estate in the Guide last year is not just a record of its one brief moment of glory, but is rather a sign of determination to achieve premium quality and a name to reckon with in a region that already boasts numerous top-flight wineries. This year's tastings were a clear confirmation of this fact. Two wines are outstanding, the Tocai Friulano and the Pinot Grigio. The first offers a nose with fruity aromas and apple seeds that carries through nicely onto the complex, broad palate with typical bitter almonds on the finish. The elegant appley aromas of the second reappear on the glycerin-rich palate with notes of apple. Their other wines are all interesting. The Sauvignon has an intense, varietal nose of elderberry and sage, followed by a mouth-filling palate again revealing elderberry, but finishing rather quickly. The Chardonnay has lingering aromas of ripe fruit and a complex, opulent, continuous palate of a pleasing crispness. Of the reds we tasted we particularly liked the Cabernets. The deep ruby-red Cabernet Franc offers aromas of hay and ripe fruit which are nicely repeated on a full, warm, structured palate with notes of blackberries and sour cherries. The Cabernet Sauvignon recalls juniper, undergrowth, red fruit and spice on a nose followed by a palate with slightly aggressive tannins that do not, however, detract from the fruit.

	Wine	Rating	Price
○	Collio Pinot Grigio '97	🍷🍷	3*
○	Collio Tocai Friulano '97	🍷🍷	3*
○	Collio Chardonnay '97	🍷	3
○	Collio Sauvignon '97	🍷	3
●	Collio Cabernet Sauvignon '96	🍷	3
●	Friuli Isonzo Cabernet Franc '96	🍷	3
●	Collio Merlot '96		3
○	Collio Ribolla Gialla '97		3

S. FLORIANO DEL COLLIO (GO)

MATIJAZ TERCIC
VIA BUKUJE, 9
34070 S. FLORIANO DEL COLLIO (GO)
TEL. 0481/884193

Matijaz Tercic's small winery is developing as it should, by small stages. The family has increased in number, with the addition of a lovely baby daughter called Klara, and so have the estate's vineyards. Plantings are always of a high density and yields are kept low, as it is quality that interests them. The decision to delay the release of the Chardonnay '97 until next year met with our warm approval, since this wine still needs time to age. The same goes for the Merlot '96, which will be released in 1999 after 18 months in barrique. Among the wines presented this year we were particularly struck by the Vino degli Orti, a white blend from tocai friulano, malvasia istriana and riesling, which displays a fruity, elegant nose, notes of peach, almond and apple seeds on the palate and a rich, mellow structure. The Pinot Grigio offers mineral notes on a background of green apple and yeasty aromas carrying through on a rounded palate with an ample finish. The Ribolla Gialla '97 easily scores One Glass for its elegant, flowery nose enriched with fresh fruit dominated by peach aromas. Elegance is again the key feature, this time with echoes of elderberry, on the well-structured palate. We conclude with the respectable Sauvignon, which offers typical, somewhat broad aromas of elderberry and rue, and a glycerin-rich, salty palate which rather fades out on the finish.

	Wine	Glasses	Price
○	Vino degli Orti '97	🍷🍷	3*
○	Collio Pinot Grigio '97	🍷	3
○	Collio Ribolla Gialla '97	🍷	3
○	Collio Sauvignon '97		3
○	Collio Chardonnay '96	🍷🍷 (empty)	3
●	Collio Merlot '95	🍷 (empty)	3

S. FLORIANO DEL COLLIO (GO)

FRANCO TERPIN
LOC. VALERISCE, 6/A
34070 S. FLORIANO DEL COLLIO (GO)
TEL. 0481/884215

Every year the Terpin estate gradually increases the amount of wine it bottles with its own label. We tasted four wines, and the results can be seen from the list below. But something else is cooking in the cellar: Franco's experiment with a barrique-aged white blend from some of the grapes of the '97 harvest. At our tastings we liked the Sauvignon '97, a clear straw-yellow in color with a sweet, aromatic nose revealing elderberry and sage, perfectly mirrored on the rich, tasty, satisfying palate with added echoes of peach. The Tocai Friulano, straw-yellow with greenish tints, offers a fragrances of pears and bananas in a rich fruity ensemble; the palate is almondy with a bitterish finish, a distinctly varietal feature. The Chardonnay has slightly unbalanced aromas which will harmonize after a time, while the palate, to which the acidity lends a youthful freshnes, has a distinct appley flavor. The Pinot Grigio, straw-yellow with faint coppery highlights, offers a rather unsettled but promising nose disclosing original notes of hay and macaroon. The palate follows through well with notes of walnuts shading to almonds on the finish.

	Wine	Glasses	Price
○	Collio Chardonnay '97	🍷	3
○	Collio Pinot Grigio '97	🍷	3
○	Collio Sauvignon '97	🍷	3
○	Collio Tocai Friulano '97	🍷	3
○	Collio Chardonnay '96	🍷 (empty)	3
○	Collio Pinot Grigio '96	🍷 (empty)	3
○	Collio Ribolla Gialla '96	🍷 (empty)	3

FORCHIR

VIA CIASUTIS, 1
FRAZ. PROVESANO
33095 S. GIORGIO DELLA RICHINVELDA (PN)
TEL. 0427/96037

The Forchir estate is not really a newcomer to the Guide. Already included in the Honorable Mention section of last year's Guide, it has been the major share-holder of the Durandi estate for years and at the beginning of 1998 took over the property entirely, marketing the entire production under a single label. As before, the cellar is in the hands of Gianfranco Bianchini, who is both oenologist and one of the owners. The other owner, Enzo Deana, who has had experience managing other wineries, looks after the commercial side. This major establishment has 290 hectares of vineyards in the Grave DOC in the provinces of Udine and Pordenone, a large vinification cellar at Flumignano and a modern bottling plant at San Giorgio della Richinvelda, with an annual output of about 800,000 bottles. With any kind of change, even a minor one, there is generally a danger that the wines will pay the price, for a time at least, but the Forchir estate has kept up its standards, presenting a range of wines of sound quality. The traditionally reliable Sauvignon offers tomato leaf on the nose followed by attractive fruit and fresh acidity on a nicely balanced palate. Appley and flowery aromas characterize the Chardonnay, but a slightly sharp acidity in the mouth reduced one's pleasure. The Bianco del Martin Pescatore, a blend of riesling, chardonnay and traminer, is golden in color with an intense bouquet of ripe fruits and yeasts. This follows through nicely on the palate, which is enhanced by the contrasting fruit and acidity. We were struck by the Cabernet Sauvignon Rojuzza with its lingering taste of fruit and coffee in the mouth. The Bordeaux-style blend, the Rosso di San Gerolamo, has aromas of spices and red currants, with still rather raw tannins on the palate.

	Wine	Glasses	Price
●	Friuli Grave Cabernet Sauvignon Rojuzza '96	🍷	3
○	Friuli Grave Chardonnay '97	🍷	2*
○	Friuli Grave Sauvignon '97	🍷	2*
○	Martin Pescatore Rojuzza '96	🍷	3
●	Rosso di San Gerolamo Rojuzza '95	🍷	3
●	Friuli Grave Merlot '97		2
○	Friuli Grave Pinot Grigio '97		2
●	Friuli Grave Refosco P. R. '97		2
○	Friuli Grave Tocai Friulano '97		2

ALFIERI CANTARUTTI

VIA RONCHI, 9
33048 S. GIOVANNI AL NATISONE (UD)
TEL. 0432/756317

Antonella Cantarutti, helped by her husband Fabrizio Ceccotti in the vineyards, has taken over the management of the estate founded by her father Alfieri. Marketing policy is carefully aimed at keeping prices competive even when the wines concerned are of premium quality. There are 48 hectares of vineyards, 32 in Colli Orientali del Friuli and the rest in Friuli Grave. The two blends are successes. The white is called Solivo, meaning out in the sun, and the red Poema, meaning "epic poem" and referring to the lengthy experimentation preceding its final release. The excellence achieved by the latter, made from merlot, cabernet franc and two local grapes, schioppettino and the rustic tazzelenghe, is really remarkable. After a vigorous entry it unfolds on the palate, evolving with broad, fruity sensations. These are underpinned by a full-bodied, dense structure carrying through on a long finish. The Soliva is from a blend of pinot bianco fermented and aged in new barriques, with tocai friulano and riesling vinified in steel. The nose reveals banana, vanilla and custard, which carry through onto a structured, fruity, buttery palate with a very delicate freshness on the faintly toasty finish. One Glass goes to the Colli Orientali Tocai, with aromas of sage, and the same to the Colli Orientali Pinot Grigio, with distinct onion-skin highlights in the glass and aromas of pear and macaroon. The aromatic herbs and licorice of the Cabernet Sauvignon '95 are marred by harsh tannins which whisk away its second Glass from under its nose. The Grave Chardonnay has lots of varietal character with its aromas of banana and toffee.

	Wine	Glasses	Price
○	COF Bianco Solivo '96	🍷🍷	4
●	COF Rosso Poema '96	🍷🍷	4
●	COF Cabernet Sauvignon '95	🍷	3
○	COF Pinot Grigio '97	🍷	3
○	COF Tocai Friulano '97	🍷	3
○	Friuli Grave Chardonnay '97	🍷	2
○	COF Ribolla Gialla '97		3
○	COF Sauvignon '97		3
○	Friuli Grave Pinot Grigio '97		2
○	Friuli Grave Tocai Friulano '97		2
●	COF Merlot Carato '93	🍷 (outline)	4

LIVON

VIA MONTAREZZA, 33
FRAZ. DOLEGNANO
33048 S. GIOVANNI AL NATISONE (UD)
TEL. 0432/757173-756231

In order to have a fair idea of the quality of all the wines produced by the Livon brothers Tonino and Valneo, we decided to consider their standard range as well as the special selections this year. The results are a credit to their oenologist Rinaldo Stocco. The superb Braide Alte '96, from chardonnay, sauvignon, picolit and moscato giallo harvested when very ripe and aged for quite a while in barrique, was one of the highest scorers in the final selection for Three Glasses. The nose offers a symphony of fruity, flowery aromas, with tones of vanilla and elderberry, followed by a palate of extraordinary breadth, texture and continuity with a succession of fruity notes on the long finish. A brief outline of the Two Glass wines: the elegant, well-structured Chardonnay Tre Clas offers a rich abundance of tropical fruit on the palate, while the Sauvignon Valbuins is full and fat, with varietal aromas of tomato leaf and sweet pepper. The broad, complex Tocai Ronc di Zorz reveals a fruitiness dominated by apple and pear both on the palate and in the long finish. Spicy notes, warm fruit and herb tea emerge in the Tiareblù '94, with good robust tannins. The Verduzzo Casali Godia spends ten months maturing in 225-liter barriques: hence its amber hue. It is a delightful sweet wine with a luscious palate leading into a fresh finish. The normal line includes a very stylish Pinot Bianco with an inviting appley finish, to which Two Glasses were awarded. The Tocai Friulano earned the same rating, recalling apple, lemon rind and moss on the nose, followed by a fresh, mouth-filling palate. The Sauvignon received only slightly lower marks.

	Wine	Glasses	Price
○	Braide Alte '96	▼▼▼	5
○	Collio Tocai Friulano '97	▼▼	3*
○	COF Verduzzo Friulano Casali Godia '96	▼▼	4
○	Collio Chardonnay Tre Clas '97	▼▼	3
○	Collio Pinot Bianco '97	▼▼	3*
○	Collio Sauvignon Valbuins '97	▼▼	4
○	Collio Tocai Friulano Ronc di Zorz '97	▼▼	4
●	Tiareblù '94	▼▼	4
○	Collio Sauvignon '97	▼	4
○	COF Verduzzo Friulano Casali Godia '94	▽▽▽	4
○	Collio Sauvignon Valbuins '96	▽▽▽	4
○	Collio Chardonnay Braide Mate '96	▽▽	5
●	Collio Merlot Tiare Mate	▽▽	5

S. GIOVANNI AL NATISONE (UD)

RONCO DEL GNEMIZ

VIA RONCHI, 5
33048 S. GIOVANNI AL NATISONE (UD)
TEL. 0432/756238

It is a real pleasure for us to taste the wines Serena Palazzolo offers her guests: all the care and devotion she and Gabriele put into their work are revealed in them. This year once again there was a lively debate about the Chardonnay '96, perhaps still too young to merit unqualified praise. Some of our panel considered it outstanding, starting with its clear gold color. The perfectly measured oak on the nose discloses notes of vanilla overlying tropical fruits and toffee, which lead into a rich, broad, complex palate with good grip and a long finish. You can't find a Müller Thurgau this good anywhere else in Friuli. Its elegant aromas recall apple and herbs, while the fresh acidity of the palate mingles with green apple and nearly ripe plum. When we tasted their Schioppettino '95 we believed for the very first time that it's possible to make a great wine from this native varietal. The creation of this superlative curiosity, full-bodied and spicy, started with a very late harvest, partially-dried grapes and barrique fermentation and maturation. Two vintages of the Rosso del Gnemiz, '94 and '95, were presented, of which the second is definitely more interesting. Its nose offers the intense, fruity aromas typical of merlot and cabernet sauvignon, mingling with custard and green notes, followed by a mellow, fruity palate with wonderful body. The '94 version offers aromas more reminiscent of plums, licorice and tar, and aggressive tannins on the palate. The Pinot Grigio will be getting better, and its evolution will be sustained by its lively acidity. The Tocai Friulano '97, with a nose that outperforms the palate, ends our review.

	Wine	Glasses	Price
○	COF Chardonnay '96	▼▼	5
○	Müller Thurgau '97	▼▼	4
●	COF Schioppettino '95	▼▼	5
●	Rosso del Gnemiz '95	▼▼	6
●	Rosso del Gnemiz '94	▼	5
○	COF Pinot Grigio '97	▼	4
○	COF Tocai Friulano '97	▼	4
○	COF Sauvignon '97		4
○	Chardonnay '90	▽▽▽	5
○	COF Chardonnay '91	▽▽▽	5
○	COF Chardonnay '94	▽▽	5
○	COF Chardonnay '95	▽▽	4
○	COF Picolit '94	▽▽	6
●	Rosso del Gnemiz '93	▽▽	5

S. GIOVANNI AL NATISONE (UD)

VILLA CHIOPRIS
VIA MONTAREZZA, 33
FRAZ. DOLEGNANO
33048 S. GIOVANNI AL NATISONE (UD)
TEL. 0432/757173

The Villa Chiopris estate, with 50 hectares under vine in the heart of the Grave del Friuli DOC, was bought a few years ago by Tonino and Valneo Livon, whose first action was to devote all their energies to modifying and improving the vineyards to meet their standards of quality. Vinification is carried out in the cellars at Dolegnano, with the sole use of stainless steel vessels. For anyone who knows the Livon brothers and their oenologist Rinaldo Stocco, it is no surprise to find such a high standard throughout the entire range. The only wine not to win at least One Glass was the Pinot Grigio, over which tasters' opinions were divided: at one reviewing it received One Glass, and at another just an enthusiastic mention. The Tocai Friulano is a superb wine with lemon-yellow tints and fresh perfumes of apple and flowers. The well-structured palate, with notes of pears, sweet flowers and aniseed, has good acidity and flavor and a very long finish. The Sauvignon, typical in its aromas of elderberry, grapefruit and pineapple which follow through on a rich palate with nicely judged acidity, very nearly got Two Glasses. The Chardonnay also reveals distinct varietal character, offering a nose of toffee and yeasts followed by a complex, broad palate with adequate acidity that lends it backbone. The Merlot, recalling sour cherries on the nose, has a vigorous entry on the palate where it unfolds with tannins and sweet fruit on the finish. The Cabernet Sauvignon discloses a bouquet of spices, ripe plums and cherries leading onto a firm, chewy palate whose rich fruit, acidity and tannins are nicely balanced. Although not without elegance, the Pinot Grigio suffers from an over-assertive acidity in the mouth which detracts from the hints of apple.

	Wine	Glasses	Price
○	Friuli Grave Tocai Friulano '97	🍷🍷	3
●	Friuli Grave Cabernet Sauvignon '97	🍷	3
○	Friuli Grave Chardonnay '97	🍷	3
●	Friuli Grave Merlot '97	🍷	3
○	Friuli Grave Sauvignon '97	🍷	3
○	Friuli Grave Pinot Grigio '97		3

S. LORENZO ISONTINO (GO)

LIS NERIS - PECORARI
VIA GAVINANA, 10
34070 S. LORENZO ISONTINO (GO)
TEL. 0481/80105

In past editions of the Guide several wines from this estate have missed Three Glasses by a hair's breadth. This year two were in the running, but only the Sauvignon Dom Picòl '96 passed the final test. Our congratulations to Alvaro Pecorari for this stunning wine. The nose is redolent of syrupy pineapple, rue, elderberry, banana and custard, followed by a complex, mouth-filling, varietal palate where elderberry, pineapple and sweet lemon rind emerge over the toastiness of the wood and conclude in a long, fresh finish. The Chardonnay St. Jurosa '96, also matured in French oak casks of 225 to 500 liters, very nearly won Three Glasses for its rich complexity, generous oak and admirable texture and structure. Another high scorer is the Sauvignon Picòl '97, which has not undergone malolactic fermentation. It displays clean aromas of elderberry and tomato leaf, repeated with hints of pineapple on a full, soft, fresh palate with a lingering finish. The Tal Lûc '96 is from verduzzo friulano fermented in new barriques after being left to dry for 70-80 days. The wonderful bouquet recalls wild roses, muscat and dried pears, while in the mouth it is sweet, soft and generous, distinguished by an exciting note of herb tea. The Pinot Grigio '97, another Two Glass winner, offers a deep nose marked by hints of pear and followed by a broad, round, dense palate with good balance and evolution. The over-generous oak in the Gris '96 diminishes it, while the Chardonnay has a striking long finish. The Isonzo Rosso Lis Neris '95, a blend of merlot and cabernet sauvignon, is youthful, full-bodied and fruity, although it still reveals a marked toastiness.

	Wine	Glasses	Price
○	Friuli Isonzo Sauvignon Dom Picòl '96	🍷🍷🍷	4
○	Isonzo Chardonnay St. Jurosa '96	🍷🍷	4
○	Friuli Isonzo Pinot Grigio '97	🍷🍷	4
○	Friuli Isonzo Sauvignon Picòl '97	🍷🍷	4
○	Tal Lûc '96	🍷🍷	6
○	Friuli Isonzo Chardonnay '97	🍷	4
○	Friuli Isonzo Pinot Grigio Gris '96	🍷	4
●	Isonzo Rosso Lis Neris '95	🍷	5
●	Isonzo Rosso Lis Neris '94	🍸🍸	5
○	Isonzo Pinot Grigio Gris '95	🍸🍸	4
○	Isonzo Sauvignon Dom Picòl '95	🍸🍸	4

S. LORENZO ISONTINO (GO)

PIERPAOLO PECORARI
VIA TOMMASEO, 36/C
34070 S. LORENZO ISONTINO (GO)
TEL. 0481/808775

Pierpaolo Pecorari is a newcomer, in some ways unexpected, to the Mount Olympus of Three Glass winners. Although of premium quality, the wines presented every year did not lead us to guess that this producer had the ability to come up with a really superlative creation. But here we are celebrating the arrival of his Sauvignon Kolàus '96, fermented and matured in 500-liter casks. Golden in color with marked greenish tints, it offers distinct aromas of custard and elderberry, followed by a palate of tremendous impact, soft, structured and broad with notes of pineapple and a wonderfully long finish. This splendid wine is not the only success from the Pecorari cellar, being flanked by a whole range of Two Glass winners, starting with the oak-aged Pinot Grigio Olivers '96. It is amber-tinted in color, with suggestions of vanilla and apple on the nose, carrying through on a rich, structured but supple palate with the fruit emerging triumphantly in the finish. Intense aromas of pear and citrus mark the Tocai Friulano '97, whose powerful entry on the palate is followed by a soft expansion, leading into a warm yet fresh finish. The Pratoscuro '96, a blend of oaked riesling and unoaked müller thurgau, offers a nose of plums and apples followed by a warm palate with lots of fruit and a flinty note in the finish. The Sauvignon '97, with aromas of tomato leaf and a fresh, integrated palate, is halfway between One and Two Glasses. The same is true of the Pinot Grigio '97, characterized by good balance, nicely-judged acidity and faint hints of coffee on the nose. The Malvasia came close to winning One Glass but was hurt by an over-pronounced acidity. We end our list with the Chardonnay.

	Wine	Rating	Price
O	Friuli Isonzo Sauvignon Kolàus '96	🍷🍷🍷	5
O	Friuli Isonzo Pinot Grigio Olivers '96	🍷🍷	5
O	Friuli Isonzo Tocai Friulano '97	🍷🍷	4
O	Pratoscuro '96	🍷🍷	4
O	Friuli Isonzo Pinot Grigio '97	🍷	4
O	Friuli Isonzo Sauvignon '97	🍷	4
O	Friuli Isonzo Chardonnay '97		4
O	Malvasia '97		4
O	Friuli Isonzo Chardonnay Soris '95	♡♡	4
O	Friuli Isonzo Pinot Bianco '96	♡♡	4
O	Friuli Isonzo Tocai Friulano '96	♡♡	4
O	Pratoscuro '95	♡♡	4

SACILE (PN)

VISTORTA
VIA VISTORTA, 87
33077 SACILE (PN)
TEL. 0434/71135

Just outside the ancient village of Vistorta, on the border between Friuli and the Veneto, is the beautiful country villa with its outbuildings and farmhouses built in the last century by the Brandolini d'Adda family. The present-day owner Brandino manages the 200 hectares of land around the villa, devoting special care to the 16 hectares planted with merlot. This is the only wine made in Friuli by the estate, which in the neighboring Veneto produces several varietals, red and white, under a different label. The merlot vineyards are a mixture of old vines and recently planted ones from Bordeaux. Georges Pauli, the estate's oenologist, is also from Bordeaux, where he performs similar services for Château Gruaud-Larose. Clay soils similar in type to those found in some parts of Bordeaux, dense plantings and the extensive use of wood in the cellar result in a new style of wine for Friuli. A mediocre vintage contributed to the below-average performance of the Merlot '96, although its prospects for improvement are good. The nose offers herbaceous scents and notes of hay on a concentrated background of berries, baked cherries and prunes, while the satisfying, broad palate has a fruity finish and mellow tannins.

	Wine	Rating	Price
●	Friuli Grave Merlot '96	🍷	4
●	Friuli Grave Merlot '95	♡♡	4

SAGRADO (GO)

CASTELVECCHIO
VIA CASTELNUOVO, 2
34078 SAGRADO (GO)
TEL. 0481/99742

The following was written by Gianni Bignucolo, the estate manager and oenologist, in the letter introducing his wines: "...the reds are of the '95 vintage, which we consider excellent since the grapes had the advantage of four or five weeks of sunshine before the harvest, which ended on 27/10/95". This opinion, given by an expert, matches our assessment and confirms that Castelvecchio is particularly suited to the making of red wines. The care lavished on them in the cellar, where they first spend a year in small French oak casks and then another year in 15-25-hectoliter barrels of Slavonian oak, contributes further to their excellence. This is true of the whites as well, which, although quite good, have no real winners amongst them this year. The structure and complexity of the superb Cabernet are immediately apparent from its deep ruby color and find confirmation in its rounded, elegant aromas of ripe morello cherries, juniper, pencil lead and coffee, which follow through on the palate with delightful flavors of hay and licorice. The Turmino, a blend of 70% terrano and 30% cabernet, has vinous aromas with typical varietal notes and a long, well-evolved, elegant palate. One Glass, highly deserved, goes to the Terrano '95, a typical grape of the Carso plateau which is rustic in youth but softens with age. The '97 version is an incredibly dense ruby color and offers cherry, red currant and tobacco on the nose, while its varietal harshness is nicely toned down by the wood on a concentrated, fruity palate. The moderately complex Cabernet Franc has aromas of ripe baked fruit and coffee which are repeated on the palate.

	Wine	Glasses	Price
●	Cabernet Sauvignon '95	🍷🍷	4
●	Carso Rosso Turmino '95	🍷🍷	3*
●	Cabernet Franc '95	🍷	4
●	Terrano '95	🍷	3
●	Terrano '97	🍷	3
●	Refosco P. R. '95		4
○	Carso Malvasia Istriana '97		3
○	Carso Pinot Grigio '97		3
○	Carso Sauvignon '97		3
○	Carso Traminer Aromatico '97		3
●	Cabernet Franc '93	🍷🍷 (outline)	3

SPILIMBERGO (PN)

PLOZNER
VIA DELLE PRESE, 19
FRAZ. BARBEANO
33097 SPILIMBERGO (PN)
TEL. 0427/2902

The level of the wines released this year is, with a few exceptions, such as to warrant the return to the Guide of this winery run by Valeria Plozner. It is a typical estate of the Grave area, with poor, gravelly soils that require irrigation and punishing variation between the temperatures at night and during the day. These conditions tend to produce lightly structured but highly varietal, richly perfumed wines that demand ceaseless care at every stage of their production. The care provider is the extremely competent and equally taciturn Francesco Visentin, who has been the estate's oenologist for years. The really excellent Sauvignon shows great varietal character with delicate aromas of elderberry and pennyroyal, followed by sweet pepper and grapefruit flavors on the palate, which is pleasantly crisp. The Chardonnay, concentrated, broad and stylish on the nose with notes of mint and tea, only just misses Two Glasses. It offers a rich palate with good fruit and yeasty notes on the finish. The Cabernet Sauvignon Riserva '92, after two years in barrique followed by a period of bottle aging, offers aromas of hay and cherries. The initial correspondence on the palate is good, but it rather fades out on the finish. The younger version of this wine, the '96 vintage, offers similar sensations on nose and palate and is fairly mouth-filling, with tannins still rather rough-edged. The well-structured Pinot Bianco reveals pear and apple on the nose and enjoyable freshness on the palate. One Glass also goes to the Tocai Friulano for its intense, lingering fruity aromas with apple emerging on the finish. The Merlot and the Traminer Aromatico are both well-made wines.

	Wine	Glasses	Price
○	Friuli Grave Sauvignon '97	🍷🍷	3*
○	Friuli Grave Chardonnay '97	🍷	3
○	Friuli Grave Pinot Bianco '97	🍷	3
○	Friuli Grave Tocai Friulano '97	🍷	2*
●	Friuli Grave Cabernet Sauvignon '96	🍷	3
●	Friuli Grave Cabernet Sauvignon Ris. '92	🍷	4
●	Friuli Grave Merlot '97		2
○	Friuli Grave Traminer Aromatico '97		3

TALMASSONS (UD)

MANGILLI
VIA TRE AVIERI, 12
FRAZ. FLUMIGNANO
33030 TALMASSONS (UD)
TEL. 0432/766248

This old-established firm offers a range of highly reliable wines as a sideline to its principal concern, the distillery. The vineyards are for the most part rented, which explains why they produce wines from three different Friuli DOC zones. Adriano Teston is in charge of the cellar and the wines are all well made and in some cases excellent. Unfortunately when we tasted the Progetto '90 it was not performing at its best and we gave it rather low marks. Made from cabernet franc, cabernet sauvignon and merlot, it spends a year in 25-hectoliter oak barrels and six months in barrique, followed by the blending in 50-hectoliter oak barrels and finally a long spell of bottle aging. We found it complex, herbaceous and somewhat overpowered by heavy tannins in the finish. The successful Grave del Friuli Pinot Grigio '97 offers aromas of pear and wildflowers with mineral notes, which are perfectly echoed on the palate and accompanied by a glycerin-rich structure and good acidity backing up the finish. In the Collio Pinot Bianco '97 we found an array of perfumes including damp grass, apple and slightly underripe apricot, followed by a palate offering wonderful balance and a nicely judged acidity. The Grave del Friuli Chardonnay '97 reveals varietal character with its nuances of banana and tropical fruits, and complex structure in the mouth. The golden Ramandolo '95 has notes of stewed apple on the nose which reappear on the medium-sweet, opulent palate. The Collio Sauvignon '97 and the Grave del Friuli Cabernet '95 are soundly made wines and both nearly score a Glass.

○	COF Ramandolo '95	🍷	5
○	Collio Pinot Bianco '97	🍷	3
○	Friuli Grave Chardonnay '97	🍷	3
○	Friuli Grave Pinot Grigio '97	🍷	3
●	Progetto '90	🍷	5
●	COF Refosco P. R. '96		3
●	Collio Cabernet Franc '96		3
○	Collio Sauvignon '97		4
●	Friuli Grave Cabernet '95		3
●	Friuli Grave Merlot '95		3
○	Friuli Grave Sauvignon '97		3

TORREANO DI CIVIDALE (UD)

SANDRO & ANDREA IACUZZI
V.LE KENNEDY, 39/A
LOC. MONTINA
33040 TORREANO DI CIVIDALE (UD)
TEL. 0432/715147

Sandro and Andrea Iacuzzi are keenly committed to their small winery, looking after the vineyards and the cellar themselves in a hands-on, distinctly non-industrial fashion. Although the estate is only eight hectares, with an output of 40,000 bottles, they are experimenting with the use of barriques in their search for new styles and higher quality in their wines. Experiments are often a failure, especially at first, but the Iacuzzi brothers have had a success with their Lindi Uà, a white blend of pinot bianco, sauvignon and tocai friulano, fermented separately for seven months in barriques. This wine, which earned Two Glasses with no trouble, offers stylish, delicate perfumes of ripe mixed fruit with prominent banana and apple and underlying toasty notes. These are mirrored on the full, warm palate, where the fruit nicely offsets the toastiness of the wood. The other blend, La Torca, from equal percentages of müller thurgau and the Manzoni hybrid, does not score quite so well but is definitely a good wine. It has a fruity fragrance, recalling apple and yellow plum, which reappears in the mouth accompanied by depth and good length. Both the Pinot Bianco and the Tocai Friulano fully deserve One Glass. The first displays a refined, stylish nose with scents of ripe apple, followed by a harmonious, long palate where a touch of excess acidity loses it points. The second is distinguished by good structure and personality, with enjoyable appley sensations. We were impressed by the balanced, spicy aromas and ripe fruit of the Merlot but it disappoints on the finish, which has a bitterish twist.

○	COF Bianco Lindi Uà '96	🍷🍷	4
○	COF Pinot Bianco '97	🍷	3
○	COF Tocai Friulano '97	🍷	3
○	La Torca '97	🍷	3
●	COF Merlot '96		3
○	COF Sauvignon '96	🍸🍸	3
○	La Torca '96	🍸	3

Valchiarò

Via Casali Laurini, 3
33040 Torreano di Cividale (UD)
tel. 0432/712393

The secret of this estate's success lies in the friendly charm of the Valchiarò partners, who are always a pleasure to meet, combined with the reliable quality and competitive prices of their wines. In a vintage considered especially favorable for reds, they have come up with a really commendable range of whites. The Pinot Bianco only just misses Two Glasses because of an agreeable but over-pronounced acidity on the palate. It offers a complex nose with hints of honey, citrus, apple and fruitiness that reappear with the glycerin and alcohol on the palate. The Torre Quâl '95, similarly good, is from merlot, cabernet franc and refosco. Plums, raspberries and blackberries together with spice emerge on the nose and are nicely repeated on the palate, where the structure, sweet tannins and softness of this wine are revealed. The Pinot Grigio also scores a full Glass with its aromas of freshly sliced apple followed by a tasty, long palate with hints of pear and licorice. The varietal Sauvignon reveals typical notes of elderberry, apple and tomato leaf on the nose as well as the palate, which is mellow, warm, and lingering. Aromas of elderberry, with dried flowers, are also evident in the Tocai, with a moderately-structured, salty palate disclosing a highly typical flavor of apple seeds. The Verduzzo Friulano shows good varietal aromas of baked apple that reappear on the finish of the sweet, supple palate. Excessive acidity diminishes the Cabernet '96, which has intense ripe fruit aromas and a note of tar.

	Wine	Glasses	Price
○	COF Pinot Bianco '97	🍷	3
○	COF Pinot Grigio '97	🍷	3
○	COF Sauvignon '97	🍷	3
○	COF Tocai Friulano '97	🍷	3
○	COF Verduzzo Friulano '96	🍷	3
●	Torre Quâl '95	🍷	3
●	COF Cabernet '96		3

Volpe Pasini

Via Cividale, 16
Fraz. Togliano
33040 Torreano di Cividale (UD)
tel. 0432/715151

Emilio Rotolo, the new owner of Volpe Pasini, is charming, good-natured and determined to restore to its former glory an estate which is part of Friuli's wine-making history. A doctor and real estate broker, he has made enormous investments in constructing a modern cellar (as well as beautifully restoring the historic one), a guest house and a small conference center. Rosa Tomaselli assists him with marketing and public relations and Flavio Zuliani is the expert oenologist. The results can be seen from the list below. The Bianco Le Roverelle is a superb wine, made from several different grape varieties including a fairly large percentage of picolit. Fermented and matured in new barriques, it offers lactic notes mingling with sweet fruit on the nose, while the broad, long, well-constructed palate has wonderful softness, warmth and lots of very ripe fruit. The Pinot Grigio has faint greyish tints in the glass and elegant, rounded, generous aromas of ripe apple. After an initial fruity impact the acidity emerges on the palate, with nuances of apple and pear reappearing and lingering on the finish. The Chardonnay Zuc di Volpe is partially barrique-fermented and offers a harmonious nose in which nuances of vanilla, crusty bread and dried apricot mingle attractively. The palate is notable for the close-knit fruit of its structure, which is just grazed by a touch of pronounced acidity. In addition to the Zuc di Volpe range, some of the unoaked wines under the Villa Volpe label scored well: the Chardonnay, the Tocai Friulano and the Pinot Grigio, all '97s, were particularly appreciated.

	Wine	Glasses	Price
○	COF Bianco Le Roverelle Zuc di Volpe '96	🍷🍷	5
○	COF Chardonnay Zuc di Volpe '97	🍷🍷	4
○	COF Pinot Grigio Zuc di Volpe '97	🍷🍷	4
○	COF Chardonnay Villa Volpe '97	🍷	3
○	COF Pinot Bianco Zuc di Volpe '97	🍷	4
○	COF Pinot Grigio Villa Volpe '97	🍷	3
○	COF Pinot Grigio Zuc di Volpe '96	🍷	4
○	COF Ribolla Gialla Zuc di Volpe '97	🍷	4
○	COF Sauvignon Zuc di Volpe '97	🍷	4
○	COF Tocai Friulano Zuc di Volpe '97	🍷	4
●	Moscato Rosa Zuc di Volpe '97	🍷	5
○	COF Tocai Friulano Villa Volpe '97		3
○	COF Chardonnay Zuc di Volpe '96	🍷🍷 (previous edition)	4

OTHER WINERIES

The following producers obtained good scores in our tastings with one or more of their wines:

PROVINCE OF GORIZIA

Maurizio Buzzinelli
Cormons, tel. 0481/60902,
Collio Tocai Friulano '97,
Collio Tocai Friulano Ronc dal Luis '97

Colle Duga, Cormons, tel. 0481/61177,
Collio Chardonnay '97,
Collio Tocai Friulano '97

La Boatina, Cormons, tel. 0481/60445,
Collio Pinot Bianco '97

Stanislao Mavric
Cormons, tel. 0481/60660,
Collio Bianco Rosa Mistica '97,
Collio Tocai Friulano '97

Laura Srednik, Cormons, tel. 0481/61943,
Collio Pinot Grigio '97

Roberto Ferreghini
Dolegna del Collio, tel. 0481/60549,
Collio Pinot Bianco '97,
Collio Pinot Grigio '97

Vittorio Puiatti
Farra d'Isonzo, tel. 0481/888304,
Collio Ribolla Gialla '97,
Collio Chardonnay '97

Radikon, Gorizia, tel. 0481/32804,
Collio Ribolla Gialla '95, Oslavje '95

Luisa Eddi
Mariano del Friuli, tel. 0481/69175,
Friuli Isonzo Sauvignon '97,
Friuli Isonzo Pinot Bianco '97

Draga
S. Floriano del Collio, tel. 0481/884182,
Collio Pinot Grigio Miklus '97,
Collio Tocai Friulano '97

Il Carpino,
S. Floriano del Collio, tel. 0481/884097,
Collio Pinot Grigio '97,
Collio Sauvignon Vigna Runc '97

Marega
S. Floriano del Collio, tel. 0481/884058,
Collio Merlot '97, Collio Tocai Friulano '97

PROVINCE OF PORDENONE

Borgo Magredo
Spilimbergo, tel. 0427/51444,
Friuli Grave Chardonnay Braida Longa '97,
Moscato Rosa '97

PROVINCE OF UDINE

Livio e Claudio Buiatti
Buttrio, tel. 0432/674317,
COF Sauvignon '97,
COF Tocai Friulano '97

Ronchi di Fornaz
Cividale del Friuli, tel. 0432/701462,
COF Pinot Grigio '97,
Il Bianco Diverso '96

Rubini
Cividale del Friuli, tel. 0432/716141,
COF Ribolla Gialla Linea Classica '97,
COF Tocai Friulano Linea Classica '97

Valentino Butussi
Corno di Rosazzo, tel. 0432/759194,
COF Cabernet Franc '97,
COF Pinot Grigio '97

Midolini, Manzano, tel. 0432/754555,
COF Merlot '97,
COF Pinot Grigio '97

Aquila del Torre
Povoletto, tel. 0432/666428,
COF Bianco Canticum '97,
COF Merlot Canticum '96

Ronco del Castagneto
Prepotto, tel. 0432/713072,
COF Chardonnay '97,
COF Pinot Bianco '97,
Il Falco di Castellamonte Rosso '96

Altran F.lli, Ruda, tel. 0431/96230,
Friuli Aquileia Pinot Bianco '97,
Friuli Aquileia Pinot Grigio '97,
Friuli Aquileia Tocai Friulano '97

Tenuta Ronc Alto
S. Giovanni al Natisone, tel. 0432/757173,
Collio Ribolla Gialla '97

Brojli - Franco Clementin
Terzo di Aquileia, tel. 0431/32642,
Friuli Aquileia Merlot '97,
Friuli Aquileia Refosco P. R. '97

EMILIA ROMAGNA

The success of Emilia Romagna wines this year has, in many ways, exceeded our rosiest expectations. No fewer than five estates have been awarded Three Glasses, and another couple only just missed out. At this point we feel we may claim to have been the first to spot the enormous potential of these wines, and also, indeed, to criticize the shortcomings of a production and marketing policy which had long been based on quantity at the expense of quality. So we feel justified in underlining yet again that these outstanding results confirm an irreversible trend: only farsighted investment in vineyards, clonal research and experiments in the cellar, and the assistance of qualified oenologists, together with judicious expenditure on the latest advances in vinification technology, can guarantee a resultant high quality. And this is the only possible road to success. You cannot hope to promote the wine production of a region simply by introducing new DOC categories, or by stubbornly insisting on maintaining the old varietals and time-honored traditions which have seen their day and can't even be recommended as economically sound. In any case the results are there for all to see and (even more important) this year's highest scorers are representative of viticulture in a region on the point of becoming a national byword for the production of wines of high quality. The Colli Piacentini area has made a glorious debut in the Guide with La Stoppa's magnificent Cabernet Sauvignon '96. Together with the usual admirable production of estates like La Tosa, it now plays a leading role in enhancing the image of the vineyards near Piacenza. If Romagna has excelled in Three Glasses, it is thanks to estates like La Palazza (with a superb Cabernet Sauvignon Magnificat '94), Tre Monti (with the excellent Colli d'Imola Boldo '97) and Zerbina (with their Marzieno '95). Boldo and Marzieno are two great wines obtained from the French-Romagna blend of cabernet and sangiovese. The area around Bologna known as the Colli Bolognesi also scores high; this year a Cabernet Sauvignon (Bonzarone '96 produced by Francesco Lambertini at his Tenuta Bonzara) bears the palm. We could hardly fail to note the astonishing leap forward of Vallona, which has produced such excellent wines as their Sauvignon and two Chardonnays. Finally (apart from noting the splendid performance yet again of Casteluccio and of Vallania, or the vast improvement in the wines, now rich in substance, offered by Cesari), we must also mention the most representative wine of the region, Albana. In addition to providing an agreeable secco, this wine can be first-rate as a passito, or sun-dried grape wine, as is amply borne out by bottles from such estates as Conti, Ferrucci, Tre Monti and Zerbina.

BERTINORO (FO)

VINI PREGIATI CELLI
V.LE CARDUCCI, 5
47032 BERTINORO (FO)
TEL. 0543/445183

For the last few years this promising winery in Bertinoro has had grapes from its own vineyards to add to the local grapes with which it makes wine. We can expect interesting results from this estate, which is clearly now passing through a transitional stage. However their entire range is well-made, indicative of the general high quality they have achieved. The admirable Poggio Ferlina '97, from trebbiano grapes, offers an array of pleasing fruity aromas; on the palate it reveals unusual structure and finesse. The Croppi '97, is no disappointment; it has a good deep color together with sweet and properly alcoholic notes. The residual sugar of Albana Dolce Le Querce satisfies the palate without assaulting it, while Le Grillaie '97 (broad, clean and vinous scents) is strikingly harmonious and pleasant. The bouquet of Grillaie Sangiovese Superiore'96 is more traditional: bitterish and reminiscent of dry leaves and classic wine-making methods; however there is no lack of character and intensity in this wine. The more ambitious Le Grillaie Reserve '95 is well-balanced, concentrated and rich; the right touch of acidity gives it a youthful zest.

○	Albana di Romagna Dolce Le Querce '97	🍷	2*
○	Albana di Romagna Secco I Croppi '97	🍷	2*
●	Sangiovese di Romagna Le Grillaie Ris. '95	🍷	3
●	Sangiovese di Romagna Sup. Le Grillaie '96	🍷	2*
●	Sangiovese di Romagna Sup. Le Grillaie '97	🍷	2*
○	Trebbiano di Romagna Poggio Ferlina '97	🍷	1
○	Albana di Romagna Passito Solara '95	🍸	4

BERTINORO (FO)

FATTORIA PARADISO
VIA PALMEGGIANA, 285
47032 BERTINORO (FO)
TEL. 0543/445044

When the various wine-makers who are now making the wines of Romagna great were still in short pants, Cavalier Pezzi of Fattoria Paradiso was already well launched on the road to high-quality wine production and had wholeheartedly devoted himself to preserving what most typified the area. This was no easy matter in those years, when oenology in the region was almost always represented by bulk wine sold in demijohns. Today his daughter Graziella runs the estate, fully aware of her heritage as mediator between the traditional and the modern. The Fattoria Paradiso wine that made most impression on us was the Albana Passito Gradisca '92. Even if it's not perfectly harmonious, it is a wine with an indisputable charm of its own. It has a handsome deep gold color and dense heady aromas; on the palate it is full-bodied and mellow and long in the finish. The Barbarossa '94, made from a local cousin of the sangiovese grape, is completely in line with the traditions of this estate: here too it isn't its harmony that distinguishes the wine, but rather its robustness, a rich structure and a rustic but complex nose; it only just misses our Two Glasses. For a hot summer afternoon we recommend their legendary Pagadebit '97, which is fresh and agreeably acidic.

○	Albana di Romagna Passito Gradisca '92	🍷🍷	5
●	Barbarossa '94	🍷	3
○	Pagadebit '97		2

BOMPORTO (MO)

Francesco Bellei
Via per Modena, 80
41030 Bomporto (MO)
tel. 059/818002

Beppe Bellei's ambition is to move, together with his cellars, into the midst of the Riccò vineyards along the slopes of the hills near Modena, where the pinot nero and chardonnay grapes are grown , the bases of his sparkling wines. So great are the dedication and competence he has devoted to his bubbles that when people now talk about Bellei and his wines the famous Lambrusco produced in his Bomporto winery hardly gets a mention. Extensive experience in France, study tours and an irrepressible passion for champagne have turned Bellei into a grand master of spumante. At this year's tastings we found his stars were the two Cuvée Speciale '93s, which have only just become available. The Brut in particular is as good as any spumante in the country. Its intense straw-yellow color has a fine perlage and delightful aromas with complex spicy nuances; it is soft on the palate and displays fascinating personality and length. The Cuvée Rosé has an impressively beautiful color with intense and fine fruity scents evolving towards toasty tones; on the palate it reveals balance, succulence and a pleasing freshness. The Extra Cuvée Brut is harmonious and delicately flavored in the mouth, and fruity on the nose. Nor should we forget the Sorbara, fermented in the bottle, with a subsequent "dégorgement", and characterized by highly individual fresh vegetal aromas.

	Wine	Glasses	Price
○	Spumante Brut Cuvée Speciale '93	🍷🍷	5
○	Bellei Extra Cuvée Brut	🍷	4
●	Lambrusco di Sorbara	🍷	3
⊙	Spumante Extra Cuvée Rosé Brut '93	🍷	5
○	Spumante Brut Cuvée Speciale '92	♈♈	5
○	Spumante Extra Cuvée Brut '94	♈♈	4

BORGONOVO VAL TIDONE (PC)

Tenuta Pernice
Loc. Pernice
Fraz. Castelnovo Val Tidone
29010 Borgonovo Val Tidone (PC)
tel. 0523/860050

Seventeen different types of wine may perhaps seem somewhat ambitious. However, the Tenuta Pernice has not only opted for this technical and managerial challenge, but is also making an impact on the market, thanks to the exceptional care devoted to the production of sparkling wines. This estate has always produced wines notable for their consistency, cleanness and contemporary style. The most tried and true are the Ortrugo and the Gutturnio. About 60,000 bottles of Ortrugo were produced in 1997. It is slightly aromatic to the nose, anticipating a palate of well-balanced acidity backed up by a proper effervescence. The Gutturnio Frizzante (pleasant, fruity and vinous) is flavorsome and refreshing. Another of the bubblies worthy of note is the Chardonnay, characterized by a pleasing bouquet of exotic fruits, a lively palate and an attractive softness. Now for the still wines: we find the Gutturnio '97 convincing. It has an intense violet hue and makes a good impression from start to finish thanks to its remarkable body and discreet finesse (tannins well under control) and its fresh and elegant aromas. The '96 version of Collare Rosso, a blend of cabernet sauvignon and bonarda, falls a little below last year's. Aged in oak, this wine is still mute to the nose and somewhat dominated by the toasty notes of the wood; on the palate its body does not overwhelm, and it goes down easily without harshness.

	Wine	Glasses	Price
●	Collare Rosso '96	🍷	3
●	Colli Piacentini Gutturnio '97	🍷	2*
●	Colli Piacentini Gutturnio Frizzante '97	🍷	2*
○	Colli Piacentini Chardonnay Frizzante '97		2
○	Colli Piacentini Ortrugo Frizzante '97		2
●	Collare Rosso '95	♈	3

BRISIGHELLA (RA)

La Berta
Via Pideura, 48
48013 Brisighella (RA)
tel. 0546/84998

Costantino Giovannini's estate lies in the hills beyond Faenza near Brisighella, and has an absolutely superb view. Astute investment and a passion for hard work are the ingredients of the increasing success of this small but enterprising winery which has reaped the benefit of sound advice (both friendly and professional) from the distinguished oenologist Stefano Chioccioli. The few wines produced here are all correctly executed and extremely interesting. At the top of the list, especially thanks to its delightful taste, is the Sangiovese Riserva Olmatello '95. The aromas are an agreeable cocktail of wood, ripe fruit and a note of lavender; its deep ruby color is followed by a full-bodied taste, with appropriate tannins, concentration and length. The fine Solano '96, a Sangiovese Superiore with an intense bouquet of cherries and red berries, offers the palate an elegant note of wood that softens what might have been an overwhelming structure. The warm and alcoholic Pieve di Tho '97, made from chardonnay grapes, has still some way to go towards balance. The Infavato '95, a malvasia wine, is very pleasing and harmonious; it is characterized by good residual sugar and a delicately aromatic note.

●	Sangiovese di Romagna Olmatello Ris. '95	🍷🍷	3*
○	Infavato '95	🍷	4
○	Pieve di Tho '97	🍷	3
●	Sangiovese di Romagna Sup. Solano '96	🍷	3

CASTELBOLOGNESE (RA)

Stefano Ferrucci
Via Casolana, 3045/2
48014 Castelbolognese (RA)
tel. 0546/651068

This year we welcome to the Guide an estate we have been watching closely as it evolved and improved. Proudly administered by the singular Stefano Ferrucci (who invariably adds a touch of creativity to traditional wine-making), the winery was built on the ruins of an ancient Roman military post. This accounts for the Latin names of some of his wines, such as Domus Caia. We tasted the '95 version and found it, for all its apparent rusticity, rich in characteristic bouquet, mouth-filling and full-bodied, with noble tannins agreeably evident. The elegance of the Bottale '93, another sangiovese wine, was a complete surprise. Its fine nose rich in licorice and chocolate is followed by a soft, harmonious and long-lasting palate. The rather interesting Sangiovese Superiore '97 offers a clean fragrance, a pleasing taste and easy quaffability. The two Albanas, Secco and Dolce, both '97s, are notable wines. The former is pleasantly fresh and fruity and the latter reveals restrained raisin tones. The fine Albana Passito '95 with its warm and sustained taste releases a honeyed scent. The Vino Bianco Passito from the same vintage, made from malvasia, is particularly fresh and agreeable on the palate; its aromas are enticing and aromatic.

○	Albana di Romagna Passito '95	🍷🍷	4
●	Bottale '93	🍷🍷	5
●	Domus Caia '95	🍷🍷	4
○	Vino Bianco Passito '95	🍷🍷	5
○	Albana di Romagna Dolce '97	🍷	3
○	Albana di Romagna Secco '97	🍷	2
●	Sangiovese di Romagna Sup. '97	🍷	3

CASTEL S. PIETRO (BO)

Umberto Cesari

Via Stanzano, 1120
Fraz. Gallo Bolognese
40050 Castel S. Pietro Terme (BO)
tel. 051/941896 - 940234

This winery has made an almost unbelievable leap forward. It took only two harvests to raise the Cesari estate to the top ranks of wine-makers in the region. Unquestionably much of this is due to the brilliant young oenologist, Vito Piffer, back on home territory after a time as an itinerant expert in other regions. The extraordinarily well-equipped cellar Cesari has put at his disposal has allowed him to give the very best of himself. This explains the quality of the barrique-fermented and aged Laurento '96 with its complex aromas, in which one distinguishes varietal perfumes together with notes of vanilla, almond and coffee. It fills the mouth with its structure and softness and an elegance all its own. The Liano '95, which should get better with time, also scored very well; a blend of cabernet sauvignon and sangiovese, it offers rich and fascinating aromas of spices and cocoa; on the palate it is silky, long-lasting and aristocratic. The Sangiovese Riserva '95 shows great intensity and concentration, while the Sangiovese Superiore Ca' Granda '97 is fresh, resinous and very easy to drink. The Sangiovese di Romagna '97 has a traditional nose but a good structure. The Albana Passito Colle del Re, soft and delicately redolent of peaches, is absolutely delicious. The bouquet of the dry version of Albana Colle del Re is mature but flawed; the interesting Malise, however, is a felicitous blend of pignoletto and chardonnay.

○	Albana di Romagna Passito Colle del Re '95	🍷🍷	4
○	Laurento '96	🍷🍷	3*
●	Liano '95	🍷🍷	4
○	Malise '97	🍷	3*
●	Sangiovese di Romagna '97	🍷	2*
●	Sangiovese di Romagna Ris. '95	🍷	3
●	Sangiovese di Romagna Sup. Ca' Granda '97	🍷	2*
○	Albana di Romagna Secco Colle del Re '97		2
●	Liano '94	🍸🍸	3

CASTELLO DI SERRAVALLE (BO)

Vallona

Via S. Andrea, 203
Loc. Fagnano
40050 Castello di Serravalle (BO)
tel. 051/6703058 - 6703066

A particularly good vintage for Maurizio Vallona, whose wines score high for elegance, structure and impact on the nose. The whites are the best this area has ever produced. The Chardonnay Selezione '96, fermented in wood, has a rich nose in which fruit and oak are well blended; the rich palate is succulent, rounded and fresh. The Chardonnay '97, fermented in stainless steel, has a bouquet of ripe fruit with almost exotic nuances; its taste is elegant and concentrated and keeps right on going; this is an exemplary wine for those who like their whites innocent of oak. The Sauvignon '97 has lots of personality, particularly on the nose, complex and dense with penetrating notes of sage and elder flowers; on the palate the attack is full and lively, and the finish caressing and harmonious. As for the reds, the Cabernet Sauvignon '96 offers a broad array of intense aromas; it is rich on the palate as well, where it reveals concentration, elegance and a very individual style. The Pignoletto '97 is a fruity wine in which what you smell is what you taste. The Vivace di Pignoletto version is an agreeable and well-made wine; the green apple notes are clean and clear-cut; it is light on the palate with a fairly long and tasty finish. The nose of the Barbera in this its debut year is still rather closed, but it's soft on the palate and goes down with remarkable ease.

●	Colli Bolognesi Cabernet Sauvignon '96	🍷🍷	3*
○	Colli Bolognesi Chardonnay '97	🍷🍷	3*
○	Colli Bolognesi Chardonnay Selezione '96	🍷🍷	3*
○	Colli Bolognesi Sauvignon '97	🍷🍷	3*
●	Colli Bolognesi Barbera '97	🍷	3
○	Colli Bolognesi Pignoletto '97	🍷	3
○	Colli Bolognesi Pignoletto Vivace '97	🍷	2
●	Colli Bolognesi Cabernet Sauvignon '95	🍸	3

CASTELVETRO (MO)

VITTORIO GRAZIANO
VIA OSSI, 30
41014 CASTELVETRO (MO)
TEL. 059/799162

Vittorio Graziano is a producer who has always combined a dedication to quality with a passion for the grasparossa grape and its possibilities. His style includes hard pruning, minimal vineyard intervention, no irrigation and absolute avoidance of chemical fertilizers. As a result he has discovered that the grasparossa was once a much more interesting grape than what we usually see today. Graziano has also been experimenting for some time with still wines and the first results are promising. For the present, however, Grasparossa remains the pick of the lot and once again justifies its excellent reputation: its lovely ruby color is the prelude to a nose with penetrating notes of red berries; on the palate the well-balanced carbon dioxide and moderate tannins help create a soft and altogether elegant Lambrusco. The semi-sparkling white Spargolino, made from seven different varieties of grapes, is "dégorgé" after two years' contact with the yeasts. The wine has personality: an intense straw-yellow color and fine, persistent effervescence lead to agreeable aromas of ripe fruit and crusty bread. Very dry but by no means thin on the palate, it reveals a distinctly toasty finish.

●	Lambrusco Grasparossa di Castelvetro '97	🍷	2
○	Spargolino Frizzante	🍷	2

CIVITELLA DI ROMAGNA (FO)

PODERI DAL NESPOLI
VIA STATALE, 49
LOC. NESPOLI
47012 CIVITELLA DI ROMAGNA (FO)
TEL. 0543/989637

If you are driving up the Bidente valley towards Tuscany you are sure to come across the handsome buildings that frame this estate and you may also feel like sampling the famous "piadina" (a local rather fluffy type of pizza) in the recently created farmhouse pensione (part of the agricultural tourism movement which is catching on so quickly). Up here, where they really far from the madding crowd, the Ravaioli brothers carry on producing their traditional wines without bothering too much about the waves of fashion that wash over the wine world of today. The Borgo dei Guidi '95 (a blend of sangiovese, cabernet sauvignon and raboso del Pieve aged at length in barriques, and then in old casks) is up to the level of vintage '94. What it has perhaps lost in concentration it has certainly gained in elegance, finesse and balance: its ample nose, including oak and ripe fruit, reveals uncommon tobacco nuances, and it is mouth-filling, full- bodied and satisfying. The Santodeno '97 is very good value; it tastes fresh, vinous and fruity, with uncommon structure and length. The Nespoli '97, made from late-harvested sangiovese, was tasted much too soon: it won't be on the shelves until December 1999. This is an intensely ruby-red wine with violet tints that suggest a very high level of extract; ripeness and sweetness are just as one would wish, but at the moment a certain lack of harmony reveals that it is under age; hence we suspend judgment until next year. The Prugneto '97, on the other hand, is already mature and well-developed.

●	Borgo dei Guidi '95	🍷🍷	4
●	Sangiovese di Romagna Sup. Santodeno '97	🍷🍷	2*
●	Sangiovese di Romagna Sup. Il Prugneto '97		3
●	Borgo dei Guidi '93	🍷🍷 (white)	4
●	Borgo dei Guidi '94	🍷🍷 (white)	4
●	Il Nespoli '95	🍷🍷 (white)	3
●	Il Nespoli '93	🍷 (white)	3

FAENZA (RA)

Leone Conti

Via Pozzo, 1
Tenuta S. Lucia
48018 Faenza (RA)
tel. 0546/642149 - 27130

For some years Leone Conti has been managing the family vineyards and winery himself. And every year this reserved yet friendly producer has some special surprises in store for us, all demonstrating the enormous potential of this estate. Take the Non ti Scordar di Me '95, really a unique wine in its category. This is an exemplary version of Albana Passito, extraordinarily elegant, warm and succulent, with delicate oaky aromas that do not overwhelm scents of yellow-fleshed fruit and honey; for a long time the palate retains a delightfully sweet sensation that charms without cloying. We were less enthusiastic about his Vignapozzo Albana Secco '97, which presented a flawed nose; the wine turns up trumps on the palate, however, displaying structure, roundness and a long finish. We found more harmony and finesse, although supported by a flimsier structure, in the Albana Dolce Vignacupa '97, a thoroughly pleasing wine with its characteristic residual sugars. The Sangiovese Superiore Riserva '95, ripe and agreeable on the palate, for this reason as well as for its sweet tannins earns a very full Two Glasses. The Sangiovese di Romagna '97 has a red berry fragrance. Finally the Capanno '97, made from ciliegiolo grapes, is a likeable curiosity.

○	Albana di Romagna Passito Non ti Scordar di Me '95	🍷🍷	5
●	Sangiovese di Romagna Sup. Conti Ris. '95	🍷🍷	4
○	Albana di Romagna Dolce Vignacupa '97	🍷	3
○	Albana di Romagna Secco Vignapozzo '97	🍷	3
●	Il Capanno '97		3
●	Sangiovese di Romagna '97		2
●	Sangiovese di Romagna Sup. Ris. '93	🍸🍸	3
○	Albana di Romagna Passito Non ti Scordar di Me '94	🍸	5

FAENZA (RA)

Fattoria Zerbina

Via Vicchio, 11
Fraz. Marzeno
48010 Faenza (RA)
tel. 0546/40022

Fattoria Zerbina's wines are, as usual, without rivals and continue to come out on top in comparative tastings. But this year they've really outdone themselves. For the first time Cristina Giminiani's estate (with the help of the Tuscan Vittorio Fiore, one of the best oenologists in the country) has been awarded our Three Glasses. The highly deserving winner is the Marzieno '95, a legendary Zerbina wine. This version is an intriguing and perfect aromatic mixture of oak, licorice, wild berries and chocolate. Its blend of cabernet and sangiovese, tradition yoked to innovation, produces a full-bodied, velvety taste of great breeding. This is a wine that's clearly first-class from the moment you see its almost opaque color. The Scacco Mato '94 is not its inferior by much: an Albana Passito that doesn't suffer by comparison with the great Sauternes. It has a captivating intense gold color and a delightful honeyed and fruity bouquet with a delicate hint of wood; on the palate it's very elegant, soft, warm and intense, with a touch of acidity and a bitterish aftertaste typical of noble rot. It is elegance strength and concentration that characterize the Pietramora '95 as well, a Sangiovese di Romagna Superiore Riserva, with a memorably intense and spicy nose. Great structure and agreeable oak are to be found in the Torre di Ceparano '96 which carried off its customary Two Glasses despite being tasted too young. Floral and vanilla tones are prominent in the Tergeno '96, a white sauvignon and chardonnay blend that we found soft and particularly harmonious. The Trebbiano Dalbiere '92 is quite crisp and very drinkable, while the Ceregio '97 had already matured and seemed a bit thin.

●	Marzieno '95	🍷🍷🍷	5
○	Albana di Romagna Passito Scacco Matto '94	🍷🍷	5
●	Sangiovese di Romagna Sup. Pietramora Ris. '95	🍷🍷	5
●	Sangiovese di Romagna Sup. Torre di Ceparano '96	🍷🍷	4
○	Tergeno '96	🍷🍷	4
○	Trebbiano di Romagna Dalbiere '97	🍷	2
●	Sangiovese di Romagna Sup. Ceregio '97		2
○	Albana di Romagna Passito Scacco Matto '93	🍸🍸	5
●	Marzieno '93	🍸🍸	3

FORLÌ

DREI DONÀ TENUTA LA PALAZZA
VIA DEL TESORO, 23
MASSA DI VECCHIAZZANO
47100 FORLÌ
TEL. 0543/769371

Claudio Drei Donà's passion for wine is as white-hot as ever. You see it in the continuous innovations on the estate, and in a brand new home for the barriques, further enriching an already quite well-equipped winery. Now Franco Bernabei, the oenologist who has guided this estate since its infancy, has at his disposal the most up-to-date cellar technology together with vines providing really extraordinary grapes. The Cabernet Sauvignon Magnificat '94 is once again a thoroughbred of international standing. A stupendous garnet color, a fascinatingly rich nose including chocolate, spice and vanilla and a round, silky, full-bodied palate with significant but uninvasive tannins make up an aristocratic wine to which one needn't begrudge cellar space for some years: an easy Three Glasses. The Pruno '94, pure sangiovese, is one of the most successful of its kind; delicate aromas of oak blend with wild berry, violet and licorice nuances; its deep color anticipates a full-bodied, powerful, meaty taste and an imposing finish. Another of their reds is the Notturno '96, a sangiovese with 10% of cabernet sauvignon; it's simpler than the Pruno but is nonetheless well-balanced, clean and soft. The Tornese '96, although it doesn't have all the flesh of last year's glorious specimen, is still a fine example of a complex and elegant white wine with an intense and harmonious palate.

	Wine	Glasses	Price
●	Magnificat Cabernet Sauvignon '94	▼▼▼	5
○	Il Tornese Chardonnay '96	▼▼	4
●	Notturno Sangiovese '96	▼▼	3*
●	Sangiovese di Romagna Sup. Pruno Ris. '94	▼▼	5
○	Il Tornese Chardonnay '95	▽▽▽	4
●	Magnificat Cabernet Sauvignon '92	▽▽	4
●	Magnificat Cabernet Sauvignon '93	▽▽	5
●	Sangiovese di Romagna Sup. Pruno Ris. '93	▽▽	4
●	Notturno Sangiovese '95	▽	3

FORMIGINE (MO)

BARBOLINI
VIA FIORI, 40
FRAZ CASINALBO
41041 FORMIGINE (MO)
TEL. 059/550154

This small estate, managed with passion and expertise by the Buffagnis, husband and wife, is attracting increasing notice in the somewhat chaotic world of Lambrusco production. As always, their wines are properly made. Il Maglio, first of all, is one of the most interesting Lambruscos to be found in the Modena area. They use a selection of sobara grapes with 15% malbo gentile, and the result is a wine of an intensely deep ruby color and an evanescent froth; it is fruity and persistent on the nose, and, for the palate, instead of a too aggressive carbon dioxide, there is structure supported by the right degree of acidity. The Grasparossa, mildly effervescent, has an attractive violet hue; in its clean bouquet jammy and toasty aromas stand out, and on the palate it is vigorously full and well-balanced. The classic Sorbara with its lively froth and sweet violet scent, is soft on the palate with a rich finish of ripe fruit. Civolino is a pleasing semi-sparkling white with a base of trebbiano scarsafoglia; it is fruity to the nose, soft to the palate and fairly long. The salamino-based Rosa della Molina has a fine deep pink color and delicately fruity aromas; it's ripe on the palate, with a refreshing and exciting effervescence.

	Wine	Glasses	Price
●	Lambrusco di Modena Il Maglio '97	▼	1*
●	Lambrusco di Sorbara '97	▼	2*
●	Lambrusco Grasparossa di Castelvetro '97	▼	1*
○	Bianco Il Civolino '97		2
⊙	Lambrusco di Modena Rosa della Molina '97		2

IMOLA (BO)

TRE MONTI
VIA LOLA, 3
40026 IMOLA (BO)
TEL. 0542/657122 - 657116

After getting off to a rather slow start the Navacchia family - young Vittorio and David, and the inimitable grand old man, Sergio - have begun to function smoothly as a team, coached by the eminent oenologist Donato Lanati. First came came an overhauling of the family vineyards, then a thorough updating of the cellar and the casks, and finally results of really astonishing quality. Today there is not a single wine on the Tre Monti list that fails to interest, at the very least, and some of their reds are absolutely first-class. At the top of the list is the Boldo '97, a sangiovese and cabernet sauvignon blend: stupendous fruity and youthful aromas are the prelude to a succulent, full-bodied and intriguing palate with a marvelous long finish; this is one of the best Emilian wines we tasted this year; a hearty Three Glasses are the deserved result of the Navacchias' years of well-judged effort. Their other outstanding wine is Turico, just cabernet sauvignon, which walks off with a brim-full Two Glasses for its vintage '97. It has unusual structure, and is robust and rounded, with an intense and extremely elegant bouquet. The Sangiovese Riserva '95 is a surprisingly successful combination of ancient and modern. The whites scored high as well. The Ciardo may not be particularly long in the finish, but it is very harmonious, its oak is kept in check, and it's lots of fun to drink. In the Albana Passito '95 we were struck by a fragrance of peach and apricot and a discreet sweetness. The Albana Dolce is delicate, while the Trebbiano Vigna del Rio is probably the best wine of its category. The appealing Albana '97 has a rich and elegant palate. A blend of albana and chardonnay that they call Salcerella is an agreeable wine.

	Wine	Glasses	Price
3●	Colli d'Imola Boldo '97	🍷🍷🍷	4
○	Albana di Romagna Passito '95	🍷🍷	4
●	Colli d'Imola Cabernet Turico '97	🍷🍷	3*
○	Colli d'Imola Chardonnay Ciardo '97	🍷🍷	3*
●	Sangiovese di Romagna Ris. '95	🍷🍷	3*
○	Albana di Romagna Dolce '97	🍷	2
○	Albana di Romagna Secco '97	🍷	2*
○	Albana di Romagna Secco Vigna della Rocca '97	🍷	3
○	Colli d'Imola Salcerella '97	🍷	3
●	Sangiovese di Romagna Sup. '97	🍷	2
○	Trebbiano di Romagna Vigna del Rio '97	🍷	3

LANGHIRANO (PR)

ISIDORO LAMORETTI
STRADA DELLA NAVE, 6
LOC. CASATICO
43013 LANGHIRANO (PR)
TEL. 0521/863590

Isidoro Lamoretti is the owner of twenty hectares of vineyards in an enviable position in the Casatico zone, which seems created for the cultivation of the vine. From these, with the help of the oenologist Mario Zanchetta, he produces around 140,000 bottles a year. Let's get straight to the new arrival: the Vignalunga 71, vintage '96. This is a still red (cabernet sauvignon with just a touch of merlot) aged in French oak. At only its second appearance in society this wine carries off One Glass filled to the brim. It has a very concentrated brilliant ruby hue, a nose of ripe fruit with notes of plum jam and coffee only partly muffled by the still prevalent oak, and a palate that, while not very deep, is fresh, well-balanced and satisfactorily thick. The excellent Vigna di Montefiore '96 may well be the best Colli di Parma Rosso we have tasted in recent years: a lively froth dances on a brilliant purple ground; the nose offers sweet and intense aromas of wild berries; thanks to a perfect balance between alcohol, acidity and tannins, the fruit emerges on the palate in all its fresh succulence. The Vigna del Guasto cru is a still version of the Colli di Parma Rosso, but not quite as good, at least the '97 vintage. The Malvasia and Sauvignon '97s are as good as ever, as is the agreeable Moscato Dolce, a partially fermented grape must.

	Wine	Glasses	Price
●	Colli di Parma Rosso Vigna di Montefiore '96	🍷🍷	3
○	Colli di Parma Malvasia '97	🍷	2*
●	Colli di Parma Rosso Vigna del Guasto '96	🍷	3
○	Moscato Dolce	🍷	3
●	Vignalunga 71 '96	🍷	3
○	Colli di Parma Sauvignon '97		3

MODIGLIANA (FO)

Castelluccio
Via Tramonto, 15
47015 Modigliana (FO)
tel. 0546/942486

This renowned estate is now simply blazing ahead under new ownership. First, they have sought the advice of the oenologist Attilio Pagli, and have consequently changed their wine-making style, producing wines that are less imposing but much more elegant. Next, they have revolutionized their sales policy, reducing, for instance, the price of the legendary Ronco del Re, version '96, (pure sauvignon) without reducing the quality. Indeed this wine, complex and buttery on the nose, and revealing a full, warm and engrossing palate rich in glycerine, with pleasing echoes of the oak in the aftertaste, definitely presents itself as an important wine that will be all the better for long aging. The Lunaria '96 (another sauvignon) is less ambitious and intellectual; redolent of almonds and vanilla, it is soft, long-lasting and delightfully fresh. As for the reds, only two of their traditional sangiovese crus have come out this year. The Ronco della Simia '95 with its complex and delicate aromas of ripe fruit (with the odd grassy note) is extemely pleasing to the palate, full-bodied and satisfying with a long finish. The Ronco dei Ciliegi '95 is more developed: a bouquet of wild berries introduces a full and important palate with aristocratic tannins in perfect balance. Le More '95, also sangiovese, has a somewhat bitter aftertaste.

○	Lunaria '96	🍷🍷	3*
○	Ronco del Re '96	🍷🍷	5
●	Ronco dei Ciliegi '95	🍷🍷	4
●	Ronco della Simia '95	🍷🍷	5
●	Sangiovese Sup. Le More '95	🍷	3
●	Ronco delle Ginestre '90	YYY	5
●	Ronco dei Ciliegi '92	YY	5
●	Ronco dei Ciliegi '93	YY	5
●	Ronco della Simia '92	YY	5
●	Ronco della Simia '93	YY	5
●	Ronco delle Ginestre '93	YY	5
●	Ronco delle Ginestre '92	YY	5

MONTE S. PIETRO (BO)

Tenuta Bonzara
Via S. Chierlo, 37/a
40050 Monte S. Pietro (BO)
tel. 051/6768324

The team that Francesco Lambertini has put together, with the winning combination of the oenologist Stefano Chioccioli and Mario Carboni, the expert cellarman, is going full steam ahead. Now that the cellar has been entirely re-equipped, attention is focused on the vineyards, and indeed next year two more hectares will start producing merlot and cabernet sauvignon. Once again the two stars of the estate, Cabernet Sauvignon Bonzarone and Merlot Rocca di Bonacciara, came entirely up to expectations and won unanimous approval. This time the Bonzarone '96 has deservedly usurped the place of Merlot Rocca di Bonacciara and walked away with Three Glasses. We found it an absolutely enchanting wine. The depth of its color anticipates a dense bouquet of berries both red and black; its powerful concentrated palate boasts a superbly soft, engrossing tannic texture: altogether a remarkably elegant wine that can stand up to the best Cabernets in Italy. The '96 version of Rocca di Bonacciara, aged in oak for 18 months, has an elegant and rich bouquet (with characteristic vegetal notes combined with wild berries). Although slightly inferior to last year's version, it is still vigorous and harmonious on the palate, its oak well-judged. The Merlot '97 presents distinct fruity aromas; it is round and moderately textured on the palate, with tannins correctly displayed. The Sauvignon Le Carrate '97 offers a pleasing bouquet of peaches and sage, and proper structure in the mouth, although the alcohol wants curbing. The Pinot Bianco, agreeable to the nose, is rather thin on the palate.

●	Colli Bolognesi Cabernet Sauvignon Bonzarone '96	🍷🍷🍷	4
●	Colli Bolognesi Merlot Rocca di Bonacciara '96	🍷🍷	5
●	Colli Bolognesi Merlot '97	🍷	3
○	Colli Bolognesi Sauvignon Le Carrate '97	🍷	3
○	Colli Bolognesi Pinot Bianco Borgo di Qua '97		3
●	Colli Bolognesi Merlot Rocca di Bonacciara '95	YYY	4
●	Colli Bolognesi Cabernet Sauvignon Bonzarone '95	YY	4
●	Colli Bolognesi Merlot Rocca di Bonacciara '94	YY	4

MONTE S. PIETRO (BO)

ISOLA
VIA BERNARDI, 3
40050 MONTE S. PIETRO (BO)
TEL. 051/6768428

Marco Franceschini coordinates the work on this small family-run estate. In recent years they have invested wisely in cellar and vineyard, with new equipment in the former and new hectares of vines in the latter. They had produced some good wines in the past, but this year they make their debut in the Guide with a whole fine range of wines, all vinified in stainless steel. Their Chardonnay '97, we note with pleasure, is among the best whites in the entire region. This wine, which is, by the way, excellent value for money, has an original bouquet (notes of melon and exotic fruits) and is succulent and well-balanced on the palate, with a long finish. The still version of the Pignoletto has for years been amongst the best of its category. It is quite characteristic, delicate and well-balanced to the nose, and then pleasingly tasty and soft on the palate. The well-made Cabernet Sauvignon '97 stands out among the reds: a fine ruby color, varietal bouquet and an immediately agreeable palate. The Pignoletto Frizzante is noteworthy for its genuine straightforwardness. It is made in the traditional manner and goes down very easily indeed.

○	Colli Bolognesi Chardonnay '97	🍷🍷	2*
●	Colli Bolognesi Cabernet Sauvignon '97	🍷	2
○	Colli Bolognesi Pignoletto Sup. '97	🍷	3
○	Colli Bolognesi Pignoletto Frizzante '97		2

MONTEVEGLIO (BO)

CANTINA DELL'ABBAZIA
VIA ABÈ, 33
40050 MONTEVEGLIO (BO)
TEL. 051/6702069

Silvia Morara, with the assistance of Giorgio Mena, is determined to have a formative influence on the wines she produces. In this year's tastings we could perceive, particularly among the reds, the results of painstaking research and experiment, and of the special attention given to controlling the ripeness of the grapes at harvest. The outcome is only partly convincing at this point, but extremely promising for the future. The Merlot '97, in its first year in the bottle, seemed still rather closed and indistinct to the nose when we tasted it, but its appearance and taste give reason for hope. The color is dense and vivid, the palate rich and full-bodied, with soft and noble tannins. Their version of Pignoletto Frizzante is original and interesting: a light froth accompanies its deep straw-yellow color, the fruity nose is clean and well-defined, and on the palate it is pleasing and round, without excessive acidity . The Sauvignon '97 has some structure and interesting vegetal aromas with original notes of hay and dried herbs. The still version of the Pignoletto is well-made and quaffable.

●	Colli Bolognesi Merlot '97	🍷	3
○	Colli Bolognesi Pignoletto Frizzante '97	🍷	2*
○	Colli Bolognesi Pignoletto '97		3
○	Colli Bolognesi Sauvignon '97		3
●	Colli Bolognesi Cabernet Sauvignon '95	🍸🍸	3
●	Colli Bolognesi Barbera '95	🍸	4

MONTEVEGLIO (BO)

SAN VITO
VIA MONTE RODANO, 6
FRAZ. OLIVETO
40050 MONTEVEGLIO (BO)
TEL. 051/964521

After years engaged in other activities, Aldo Mazzanti is now devoting himself and his resources to the making of wine. His aim is to restore his historic estate to the first ranks of producers of wine of the highest quality, and his chosen method of achieving this aim involves up-dating his cellars, high-density planting and giving San Vito a revamped contemporary image. The results are already quite encouraging, judging by the wines presented this year. Consider, for starters, the interesting Cabernet Sauvignon: a very personal bouquet with a decided vegetal accent followed by a pleasing round palate with lots of body and restrained tannins. The well- executed Chardonnay '97 has a nose with light, clean, toasty notes of fruit; the wine is soft and of good consistency, with a fairly long finish. The Pignoletto Frizzante presents a distinctly floral bouquet and a characteristic fresh, balanced acidity: you won't have trouble drinking it. The still version of the Pignoletto is soft and well-balanced in the mouth; its nose, however, is neither here nor there. It probably needs more time.

●	Colli Bolognesi Cabernet Sauvignon '97	🍷	3
○	Colli Bolognesi Chardonnay '97	🍷	2
○	Colli Bolognesi Pignoletto Frizzante '97	🍷	2
○	Colli Bolognesi Pignoletto Sup. '97		2

OSPEDALETTO DI CORIANO (RN)

SAN PATRIGNANO - TERRE DEL CEDRO
VIA S. PATRIGNANO, 53
47852 OSPEDALETTO DI CORIANO (RN)
TEL. 0541/756436 - 362362

The winery of the Comunità di San Patrignano is striking out in new directions: further proof, not that we really needed it, of their determination to produce good wine. On an estate that makes leather goods, cheese, carpentry and pork products, and where some of Europe's prize horses are raised, wine is especially dear to their hearts. This recent great reorganization has involved their questioning their absolute faith in the exclusive use of stainless steel, so you can now see wood in these cellars, particularly wood worked into the form of small casks. The firebrand who started this "revolution" was their new oenologist, Riccardo Cotarella, a name that is hardly new to lovers of Italian wine. The results of all this change will be easier to read from future vintages, but there are some clear signs already. The wine that is emblematic of their conversion is the Vintàn '97, a barrique-fermented trebbiano with interesting, harmoniously blended oaky and floral aromas; the palate, full and warm, is not particularly long but very well balanced. The normal Trebbiano also has a clean fruity nose. The reds seem more stimulating, starting with the Sangiovese di Romagna Zarricante '95: the color is less than intense but the taste, with its blend of chocolate, wild berries and well-integrated tannin, is delicious. The elegant Sangiovese Aulente '97 is less tannic, more like a Bordeaux in style, and redolent of Parma violets. The Sangiovese di Romagna '97, mature but not without grace and attractiveness, is decidedly lighter.

●	Sangiovese di Romagna Terre del Cedro Zarricante Ris. '95	🍷🍷	3*
●	Sangiovese di Romagna Sup. Terre del Cedro '97	🍷	1*
●	Sangiovese di Romagna Sup. Terre del Cedro Aulente '97	🍷	3
○	Trebbiano di Romagna Terre del Cedro '97	🍷	1*
○	Vintàn Terre del Cedro '97	🍷	3
●	Sangiovese di Romagna Terre del Cedro Zarricante Ris. '94	🍸🍸 (outline)	3
●	Sangiovese di Romagna Sup. Terre del Cedro Aulente '95	🍸 (outline)	2

OZZANO TARO (PR)

MONTE DELLE VIGNE
VIA COSTA, 25-27
43046 OZZANO TARO (PR)
TEL. 0521/809105

Andrea Ferrari, the young owner of Monte delle Vigne, firmly believes that good wine starts with good vines. Hence he has recently acquired the Buca della Volpe property at Cafragna, planted with malvasia di Candia, giving Monte delle Vigne a total of 25 hectares of splendid vineyards, both owned and rented. With the help of advice from the oenologist Giulio Armani and with the assistance of the agronomist Daniele Dosualdo, Andrea Ferrari has yet again presented a range of first-rate wines. The Nabucco '96, a still barbera and merlot blend aged in French oak, gets Two Glasses, even though it's not quite up to the level of the '93. The nose is sweet and intense, with the oak not yet entirely integrated; then it's mouth-filling and consistent on the palate, and its tannins are lively. An appealing varietal freshness insures that the Colli di Parma Sauvignon Tenuta Bottazza is, as usual, very good, in fact one of the best in the area. The Lambrusco, redolent of raspberry and notable for body, and the Malvasia Dolce, a partially fermented grape must, are both particularly attractive. The Colli di Parma Malvasia Tenuta Bottazza, which we didn't like as much as their standard Malvasia, is below par for once, because of a somewhat sulphurous nose.

●	Nabucco '96	🍷🍷	4
●	Colli di Parma Rosso Tenuta Bottazza '97	🍷	3
○	Colli di Parma Sauvignon Tenuta Bottazza '97	🍷	3
●	Lambrusco '97	🍷	2*
○	Malvasia Dolce '97	🍷	2*
○	Colli di Parma Malvasia Tenuta Bottazza '97		3
●	Nabucco '93	🍸🍸	4
●	Nabucco '95	🍸	4

RIVERGARO (PC)

LA STOPPA
FRAZ. ANCARANO
29029 RIVERGARO (PC)
TEL. 0523/958159

If today's wines from the Colli Piacentini are being praised to the skies, and not only the skies over Piacenza, much of the credit must go to La Stoppa. This winery has always been able to get the utmost out of its terroir and its grapes, disproving the accepted wisdom according to which the area is good only for bubbles. This year it has topped all its previous performances by winning Three Glasses for the first time ever. The Cabernet Sauvignon Stoppa, a real Grand Cru from the Colli Piacentini, is an outstanding example of what this land is capable of producing when people know exactly what they're doing. The vintage '96 has just enough oak, almost all of it new, to enhance the delicate nose and palate and contribute to a rich and elegant finish; the roundness of its attack, the noble tannins, the depth all help make this a wine of international standing. The successful Barbera '96 earns its Two Glasses. Its vivid color precedes a nose of sour cherry and raspberry; on the palate it's dense with fruit, and acidity is kept in check. The red Macchiana '95, aged in large casks, is a wine with structure, but its nose wants definition, and its palate, although full-bodied, is slightly rough. The Alfeo '95, a pinot nero, combines a balsamic fragrance with a palate of moderate weight and rather harsh tannins. The positive impressions made by the Vigna del Volta '95 at its debut are now fully confirmed. It is a particularly successful passito made from malvasia di Candia grapes. Wonderful aromas of ripe peach and apricot enchant the nose, while the liqueur-like sensation in the mouth slides perfectly into a long aromatic finish.

●	Cabernet Sauvignon Stoppa '96	🍷🍷🍷	4
●	Colli Piacentini Barbera '96	🍷🍷	3
○	Vigna del Volta Malvasia Passito '96	🍷🍷	4
●	Colli Piacentini Pinot Nero Alfeo '95	🍷	4
●	Macchiona '95	🍷	4
●	Colli Piacentini Cabernet Sauvignon Stoppa '95	🍸🍸	4
●	La Stoppa '91	🍸🍸	4
○	Vigna del Volta Malvasia Passito '95	🍸🍸	4
●	Macchiona '93	🍸	4

RUSSI (RA)

TENUTA UCCELLINA
VIA GARIBALDI, 51
48026 RUSSI (RA)
TEL. 0544/580144

Tenuta Uccellina, a winery on the hillside near Bertinoro which is back in the Guide after a few years' absence, fully deserves the recognition it has won for quiet, conscientious and telling efforts. The estate includes about twenty hectares, divided between olive trees and vineyards. Their cellar now boasts the very best technological equipment they could find. From a winery in the most hide-bound traditional town in Romagna, a pinot nero is something of a surprise as the top of the line. The intense and resinous nose of this Ruchetto dell'Uccellina '93 is perhaps slightly imperfect, but its palate is full, round, long-lasting and satisfying, and its garnet color is extraordinary for a pinot nero. The good Sangiovese Superiore '97 has a vinous fruity scent and a pleasantly ripe taste. The Sangiovese Riserva '95, a more structured and serious wine, makes up for a rather rustic, albeit interesting, nose with unsuspected power and elegance. The very pleasing Albana Passito '96 has fresh scents of peach and, even more, of apricot; the taste is warm and the alcohol well-judged. And another thing: their wines are really excellent buys.

○	Albana di Romagna Passito '96	🍷🍷	4
●	Ruchetto dell'Uccellina '93	🍷🍷	4
●	Sangiovese di Romagna Ris. '95	🍷	3
●	Sangiovese di Romagna Sup. '97	🍷	1*

S. ILARIO D'ENZA (RE)

MORO RINALDO RINALDINI
VIA PATRIOTI, 47
FRAZ. CALERNO
42040 S. ILARIO D'ENZA (RE)
TEL. 0522/679190

The new appellation of Colli di Scandiano e Canossa has brought some innovations to this winery. Thus, on his first time out with the Charmat Method, Rinaldini has produced a rather special Pinot Frizzante. The wine, half pinot grigio and half pinot bianco, has a potent nose with pleasing fruity notes; there's finesse on the palate, and, an original touch, a hint of residual sugar. The Pjcol Ross, which has gradually become the standard-bearer of this estate, has a vivid ruby color; its vinous bouquet includes characteristic vegetal nuances; on the palate it is round and mouth-filling, with an interesting long finish. The Malvasia Brut is very promising: the product of low-temperature maceration followed by Metodo Classico vinification, it has a beautiful straw-yellow color with coppery glints; on the nose it is intense and particularly aromatic, and in the mouth it is dry and well-balanced. The Spumante Rinaldo Brut, of a deep straw-yellow hue, has a fine effervescence and scents of ripe fruit and generous yeast; on the palate it is soft and tastily, lastingly succulent. We also noted the Lambrusco Rio Rubino, with its singular aromatic nose, and the Grasparossa Vecchio Moro, which is slightly effervescent and moderately structured.

○	Colli di Scandiano e di Canossa Pinot Frizzante	🍷	1*
●	Lambrusco Spumante Metodo Classico Pjcol Ross	🍷	2*
○	Spumante Metodo Classico Malvasia Secco Brut	🍷	2
○	Spumante Metodo Classico Rinaldo Brut '94	🍷	3
●	Colli di Scandiano e di Canossa Lambrusco Grasparossa Vecchio Moro		2
●	Lambrusco Reggiano Rio Rubino		1

S. PROSPERO (MO)

CAVICCHIOLI
P.ZZA GRAMSCI, 9
41030 S. PROSPERO (MO)
TEL. 059/908828

The Cavicchioli winery is trying something new and interesting: the Tre Medaglie range. Indeed the best Sorbara at our tastings turned out to be the Tre Medaglie, which takes the place of Tradizione. It has a handsome color and a fine effervescence; the nose, pronounced and elegant, is followed by a clean, concentrated and vigorous palate. The Grasparossa Col Sassoso is a brilliant deep ruby red, shot through with a light fine froth; the nose may lack finesse but it's rich in flowery and vegetal tones; the palate is dry and slightly tannic and the finish is somewhat bitter. On the whole it is a curious Grasparossa, which bespeaks a desire to make something more of this grape than an easy tipple. The Lambrusco di Modena, in its second version, is a technically well-made wine: the color is an intense ruby; the nose abounds in delightful flowers and fruit; it is soft on the palate with fruity notes that return in the finish. The Grasparossa Amabile, with its fine effervescence and purplish ruby hue, is still a bit closed, although the nose seems original; the taste is vinous, the acidity well-balanced. Vigna del Cristo is usually better than this year's. The Salamino Semisecco, made with great care, has aromas of bonbons, and agreeable residual sugar on the palate.

●	Lambrusco di Modena	🍷	1*
●	Lambrusco di Sorbara Tre Medaglie '97	🍷	1
●	Lambrusco Grasparossa di Castelvetro Amabile Tre Medaglie	🍷	1*
●	Lambrusco Grasparossa di Castelvetro Col Sassoso '97	🍷	2*
●	Lambrusco di Sorbara Vigna del Cristo '97		2
●	Lambrusco Salamino di S. Croce Semisecco Tre Medaglie		2

SCANDIANO (RE)

CASALI
VIA SCUOLE, 7
FRAZ. PRATISSOLO
42019 SCANDIANO (RE)
TEL. 0522/855441

This historic estate near Reggio Emilia always produces a vast range of well-made wines. We particularly enjoyed the Casino dei Greppi, a blend of sangiovese and cabernet: it has an intense nose with a jammy accent accompanied by clean, well-integrated oak; on the palate it is elegantly and harmoniously nuanced, and its fine tannins add to the pleasure. With the Roggio del Pradello, Casali has made a very good case for using the Metodo Classico for a Lambrusco: this is a wine with a fine effervescence and fruity scents; the palate is round with a dry and elegant finish. The Malvasia Secca Acaia goes beautifully with prosciutto and salami; it has a crystalline appearance and a clean, aromatic nose; on the palate it is big and succulent and delightfully fresh. The unwary often underrate the Casali Rosa because of its color, a very pale pink, but in fact it's delicious: aromas of flowers and apple are followed by a succulent palate with equal parts of crispness and softness. The two Sauvignons, however, are paying the price for a harvest in great heat: they are well executed and balanced on the palate, but the nose is weak and lacks the the varietal fruity notes. By the way, the Prà di Bosso, a pleasing Lambrusco, is good value for money.

○	Acaia Malvasia dell'Emilia '97	🍷	2*
⊙	Casali Rosa '97	🍷	1*
●	Casino dei Greppi '95	🍷	3
●	Lambrusco Metodo Classico Roggio del Pradello	🍷	3*
○	Colli di Scandiano e di Canossa Sauvignon La Dogaia '97		2
○	Colli di Scandiano e di Canossa Sauvignon Vivace Altobrolo '97		2
●	Lambrusco Reggiano Prà di Bosso '97		1

TRAVERSETOLO (PR)

Villa Bianca

Via Ronconi, 7
Loc. Guardasone
43029 Traversetolo (PR)
tel. 0521/842680

Villa Bianca has fifteen hectares of vineyards in the district of Traversetolo on the hills above the Valle dell'Enza, (the valley marking the border between the provinces of Parma and Reggio Emilia). The owner, Ferrante Cavalli, with the invaluable assistance of the oenologist Mario Zanchetta, has turned Villa Bianca into one of the most interesting wineries of the Colli di Parma. They produce about 130 thousand bottles a year, divided between two ranges of wines, Villa Bianca and the much less numerous Vigna dei Cavalli. This year the two Malvasias, the Vigna Caveriot, of the Villa Bianca range, and the Vigna dei Cavalli were definitely among the best. These are two effervescent whites that are recognizably malvasia, rich in aromas of fresh fruit and characterized by a succulent and consistent palate that corresponds nicely to the nose. The Colli di Parma Rosso Vigna dei Cavalli, a blend of barbera, bonarda and croatina, is an interesting wine of its type: a fizzy red with some intensity, verve and character. To conclude, there are the Spumante Brut, its forwardness well balanced by acidity, and the pleasing Malvasia Dolce Vigna dei Cavalli, a partially fermented grape must.

○	Colli di Parma Malvasia Vigna Caveriot '97	🍷	1
○	Colli di Parma Malvasia Vigna dei Cavalli '97	🍷	2
●	Colli di Parma Rosso Vigna dei Cavalli '97	🍷	2
○	Malvasia Dolce Vigna dei Cavalli '97		2
○	Spumante Brut		2

TRAVO (PC)

Il Poggiarello

Fraz. Scrivellano di Statto
29020 Travo (PC)
tel. 0523/957241 - 571610

Despite its youth, Paolo and Stefano Perini's estate has already achieved an enviable consistency of quality. Splendidly situated on the hills of the Val Trebbia, it now comprises 13 hectares of vineyards from which, by means of a painstaking cultivation of the vine and careful, up-to-the-minute vinification techniques, they produce the five wines that make up their entire range. The white Sauvignon Perticato Il Quadri '97 did very well at our tastings: aged for six months in medium-toasted Allier and Nevers oak, it has a varietal nose that goes well with the mineral and vanilla notes on the palate; a soft attack leads to an interesting array of crisp, opulent and aromatic sensations. The Chardonnay Perticato La Piana '97 is a newcomer: aromas of citron and pear with well-integrated wood greet the nose, and the palate reveals a moderately full body backed up by proper acidity. The red Gutturnio Riserva Vigna Valandrea '95, redolent of red fruit and spice, and well-constructed, balanced and fresh on the palate, is already a classic of this winery. The Cabernet Sauvignon Perticato del Novarei '96 displays a lovely density of color and a nose of vanilla and spice punctuated by green peppers; the moderately intense palate echoes the aromas. The Pinot Nero Perticato Le Giastre '96 is a delightful surprise (but word had gotten out): Two Glasses, filled to the brim, for this tour de force with a notoriously ticklish grape. It's aged for 12 months in new oak and then for a further five in vats and offers balsamic and berryish aromas and a soft fruity palate; the tannins are properly controlled and the finish long.

●	Colli Piacentini Pinot Nero Perticato Le Giastre '96	🍷🍷	4
○	Colli Piacentini Sauvignon Perticato Il Quadri '97	🍷🍷	3*
●	Colli Piacentini Cabernet Sauvignon Perticato del Novarei '96	🍷	4
○	Colli Piacentini Chardonnay Perticato La Piana '97	🍷	3
●	Colli Piacentini Gutturnio Vigna Valandrea Ris. '95	🍷	3
●	Colli Piacentini Cabernet Sauvignon Perticato del Novarei '95	🍸🍸	4
●	Colli Piacentini Gutturnio Vigna Valandrea Ris. '94	🍸	2

VERNASCA (PC)

LURETTA
LOC. PAOLINI, 3
FRAZ. BACEDASCO ALTO
29010 VERNASCA (PC)
TEL. 0523/895465

Carla Asti and Felice Salamini's Luretta winery fully deserves its place in the Guide. Since they took it over in 1994 they have used their 15 hectares scattered about the countryside near Piacenza to produce an annual 90 thousand bottles subdivided into six different wines (two Metodo Classico bubblies and four still wines). This was a bold decision based on the conscious desire to avoid following local tradition, which calls for the production of effervescent wines and provides a market for them too. It was a problematic move, involving the pursuit of outside markets, with the increased competition, but also greater stimulation, that that implies. Three white wines were presented in 1998, including the Sauvignon '96 with its aromas of citrus fruit shot through with greenery; on the palate it seems original and rustic, and moderately dense. The Chardonnay '97, partially barrique-aged, has a fruity nose that hints at banana and apple; in the mouth it seems well-made and soft, with a fresh finish. The feminine Malvasia Bocca di Rosa '97 (dedicated to the singer and composer Fabrizio De André) is enjoyable and intriguing: a lovely sweet nose with suggestions of pear and peach introduces a soft and appealing palate suggestive of residual sugars. The only red on offer at the moment is the Bonarda '95, which starts off well on the nose and in the mouth, where it initially reveals a good structure, soft and spicy, but is then thrown off course by a slightly acid note at the finish.

	Wine	Rating	Price
●	Colli Piacentini Bonarda '95	🍷	3
○	Colli Piacentini Chardonnay '97	🍷	3
○	Colli Piacentini Malvasia Bocca di Rosa '97	🍷	4
○	Colli Piacentini Sauvignon '96	🍷	3

VIGOLZONE (PC)

CONTE OTTO BARATTIERI DI SAN PIETRO
FRAZ. ALBAROLA
29020 VIGOLZONE (PC)
TEL. 0523/875111

The time-hallowed tradition of noble sweet wines "da meditazione" is, in Italy, represented by just a few estates, of which this is unquestionably one. Hence we are turning our tasting notes upside down and starting with a couple of sweet wines. With a fine disregard for commercial logic, the Barattieri family has always allowed some grapes to dry on the vine, in order to make minute quantities of really extraordinary wine. Such is the case with their Vin Santo, which was not even on sale until last year, and which is now clearly one of the very best wines of its kind. It is made from sun-dried malvasia grapes through the agency of a "mother" (in something like a solera system) that started out in 1846. This procedure periodically gives birth to a few hundred bottles of genuine nectar. The wine is opaque and amber-colored and offers fascinating scents of tamarind and candied fruit, with notes of noble rot; the extraordinarily dense and opulent palate reveals a vast array of aromas. Fagio, their other unusual sweet wine, is made from sun-dried brachetto grapes grown on old vines on the estate and aged for two years in the barrel. It has a sweet fragrance of sour cherry and rose petals; on the palate it's chewy, long-lasting and pleasingly refreshing. Among the normal wines there is a good Cabernet Sauvignon '96, with a clean nose reminiscent of red fruit; it has a grassy palate and appropriate tannins. Lastly, we note the agreeable Barbera Vignazza '96 and the Chardonnay Arzana, which has some body but is slightly unbalanced in the finish.

	Wine	Rating	Price
○	Colli Piacentini Vin Santo '88	🍷🍷	6
●	Il Faggio	🍷🍷	5
●	Colli Piacentini Cabernet Sauvignon Barattieri Rosso '96	🍷	4
○	Colli Piacentini Chardonnay Arzana '96	🍷	4
●	Colli Piacentini Barbera Vignazza Alta '96		4
○	Colli Piacentini Vin Santo '87	🍷🍷 (previous edition)	5
●	Colli Piacentini Barbera Vignazza Alta '95	🍷 (previous edition)	3
●	Colli Piacentini Cabernet Sauvignon Barattieri Rosso '95	🍷 (previous edition)	4
●	Colli Piacentini Cabernet Sauvignon Barattieri Rosso '93	🍷 (previous edition)	4

VIGOLZONE (PC)

La Tosa
Loc. La Tosa
29020 Vigolzone (PC)
tel. 0523/870727

IIn every area of the vast wine-making world of Italy there are producers who strike out on their own and spur all the others to change and develop, at times even to take risks and defy tradition. Such a one is Stefano Pizzamiglio, who for years has been experimenting in vineyard and cellar in the pursuit of wine with a unique, indeed an inimitable, personal style. Sorriso di Cielo '97, his partially barrique-fermented malvasia di Candia wine, is a perfect example. The fruit of extremely rigorous grape selection and of almost obsessive attention to the process of vinification, this wine has a concentration and body which seem paradoxically excessive. The enormously intriguing and suggestive nose is not followed by an equally successful palate: the attack is meaty, but overwhelmed by alcohol (15%!), which is, however, powerless against the bitter finish. In the Sauvignon '97, which is much better balanced, the green and varietal notes blended with sweeter aromas are harmoniously restated on the palate. The red Luna Selvatica '95, a blend of cabernet and merlot, still has an unresolved nose; in the mouth, however, are ripe raspberries and spice, with a rich tannic structure that needn't fear aging. Finally, after four years' absence, the Vignamorello Gutturnio has returned in triumph, with two vintages appearing almost simultaneously. The '96, which became available at the end of 1998, has a concentrated violet hue with an immediate bouquet rich in red fruit fused with well-integrated oak; the succulent and sweet palate is enriched by delectable balsamic and fruity notes.

	Wine	Glasses	Price
●	Colli Piacentini Cabernet Sauvignon Luna Selvatica '95	🍷🍷 (black)	5
●	Colli Piacentini Gutturnio Vignamorello '96	🍷🍷 (black)	4
○	Colli Piacentini Sauvignon '97	🍷🍷 (black)	4
○	Colli Piacentini Malvasia Sorriso di Cielo '97	🍷 (black)	4
●	Cabernet Sauvignon Luna Selvatica '91	🍷🍷 (white)	4
●	Colli Piacentini Cabernet Sauvignon Luna Selvatica '93	🍷🍷 (white)	4
●	Colli Piacentini Cabernet Sauvignon Luna Selvatica '94	🍷🍷 (white)	4
○	Colli Piacentini Malvasia Sorriso di Cielo '95	🍷🍷 (white)	4

ZIANO PIACENTINO (PC)

Gaetano Lusenti e Figlia
Loc. Case Piccioni di Vicobarone
29010 Ziano Piacentino (PC)
tel. 0523/868479

The phase of constant development which had come to seem the natural condition of this estate has slowed more or less to a halt in the last two years. But we should not like to be misunderstood: their wines are still excellent, but we can't help feeling that they could do better, particularly for their more important wines. We include in this category the Cabernet Sauvignon Villante '95, which has less density and length of finish than the splendid '93. It is nevertheless a wine with a fine garnet hue, well-balanced and consistent on the palate, with a pleasing bouquet of ripe fruit and aromatic herbs. The extremely enjoyable Gutturnio Frizzante '97, definitely their best wine, is one of the most successful of the entire appellation: vinous and spicy on the nose, it's tasty and succulent in the mouth, with a fresh and slightly astringent finish. Among the fizzy whites the Pinot Grigio and the Ortrugo are outstanding for their straightforward execution; the former has delicate floral aromas and a clean and clearly defined palate with a distinctly soft finish. The Ortrugo, on the other hand, has mature aromas, lightened in the mouth by a genuine and refreshing vivacity. Among the sweet wines we noted the agreeable Filtrato di Malvasia with its deep yellow color, fresh, youthful aromas, and attractive notes on the palate which make it quite easy to drink.

	Wine	Glasses	Price
●	Colli Piacentini Gutturnio Frizzante '97	🍷 (black)	2*
●	Il Villante Cabernet Sauvignon '95	🍷 (black)	4
○	Colli Piacentini Ortrugo '97		2
○	Colli Piacentini Pinot Grigio '97		3
○	Filtrato Dolce di Malvasia '97		2
●	Il Villante Cabernet Sauvignon '93	🍷🍷 (white)	4
●	Colli Piacentini Gutturnio Sup. '95	🍷 (white)	2
●	Pinot Nero La Picciona '94	🍷 (white)	4

ZOLA PREDOSA (BO)

Maria Letizia Gaggioli
Vigneto Bagazzana
Via Raibolini, 55
40069 Zola Predosa (BO)
tel. 051/753489

An ancient document penned by the Benedictines of the Abbey of Nonantola reveals that in the year 1030 someone was already making good wine on the slopes just beyond Zola Predosa. The Gaggiolis, proud of this venerable tradition, are carrying it on in accordance with their firm belief in the salutary effects of a thoroughgoing knowledge of vinification techniques. This year the Pinot Bianco is once again the estate's best wine: the '97 is delicate and flowery in fragrance, pleasing and harmonious in the mouth. The Pignoletto Frizzante '97 with its fine exuberant froth, has characteristically floral aromas and a pleasantly dry palate with a bitterish finish, just as it should. The still version of the Pignoletto '97 is agreeably fruity and faintly redolent of celery; on the palate it reveals some body, good balance and a refreshing finish. The Sauvignon '97, whose more developed nose is punctuated by green pepper, is soft and crisp on the palate. The correctly executed Chardonnay Lavinio '97 has faint white fruit aromas and is lean and fresh in the mouth.

	Wine	Glasses	Price
○	Colli Bolognesi Pignoletto Frizzante '97	🍷	3
○	Colli Bolognesi Pignoletto Sup. '97	🍷	3
○	Colli Bolognesi Pinot Bianco Crilò '97	🍷	3
○	Colli Bolognesi Sauvignon '97	🍷	3
○	Colli Bolognesi Chardonnay Lavinio '97		3
●	Colli Bolognesi Cabernet Sauvignon '96	Y	3

ZOLA PREDOSA (BO)

Vigneto delle Terre Rosse
Via Predosa, 83
40069 Zola Predosa (BO)
tel. 051/755845

The Vallanias, who were in the vanguard in Emilia Romagna in the production of wine of the highest quality, have succeeded in establishing a decidedly personal oenological style . All of their wines have always lived up to their excellent reputation, and the last wines we tasted were no exception. The Rosso di Enrico Vallania Cabernet '94, a ruby red shading to garnet, offers elegant, rich and concentrated aromas; on the palate it reveals the body and extraction of the great Cabernets, and a staggeringly long finish. The Cuvée '93, although in some ways similar, has a rather closed nose and less personality on the palate, but it's still an excellent wine. The Riesling Malagò Cuvée '95 is unique: the fruity bouquet is still developing; the palate, which is at once imposing, harmonious and powerful, is soft and sweet in the finish. The Chardonnay Cuvée, characterized by fine scents with lingering and varied fruity accents, is rich, round and well-balanced in the mouth. The Malagò '97 is still very young but shows some resemblance to the Cuvée, with concentration and finesse on the palate. The Malvasia is well-made: a characteristic nose, and a fresh palate with just the right amount of sweetness. The Chardonnay '97 is not exceptional: a penetrating and very varietal nose is followed by a dominant sweetness of taste caused by excessive residual sugars.

	Wine	Glasses	Price
○	Colli Bolognesi Giovanni Vallania Chardonnay Cuvée '95	🍷🍷	4
●	Colli Bolognesi Il Rosso di Enrico Vallania '94	🍷🍷	4
●	Colli Bolognesi Il Rosso di Enrico Vallania Cuvée '93	🍷🍷	5
○	Colli Bolognesi Riesling Malagò Vendemmia Tardiva Cuvée '95	🍷🍷	4
○	Colli Bolognesi Malagò Riesling Italico '97	🍷	3
○	Malvasia Adriana Vallania '97	🍷	3
○	Chardonnay '97		3
●	Il Rosso di Enrico Vallania Cuvée '87	YYY	5

OTHER WINERIES

The following producers obtained good scores in our tastings with one or more of their wines:

PROVINCE OF BOLOGNA

Beghelli
Castello di Serravalle, tel. 051/6704786,
Colli Bolognesi Barbera '96

Erioli, Bazzano, tel. 051/830103,
Colli Bolognesi Chardonnay '96

La Mancina, Monteveglio, tel. 051/832691,
Colli Bolognesi Cabernet Sauvignon '97

Luigi Ognibene, Monteveglio, tel. 051/830265,
Colli Bolognesi Pinot Bianco '97

Santarosa, Monte S. Pietro, tel. 051/969203,
Colli Bolognesi Pinot Bianco '97

PROVINCE OF FORLÌ

Fattoria Casetto dei Mandorli
Predappio, tel. 0543/922361,
Passolo

Colombina, Bertinoro, tel. 0543/460658,
Sangiovese di Romagna Sup. Ris. '94

Giovanna Madonia
Bertinoro, tel. 0543/444361,
Sangiovese di Romagna Sup. Ris. '96

PROVINCE OF MODENA

Roberto Balugani, Castelvetro, tel. 059/791546,
Lambrusco Grasparossa di Castelvetro '97

Chiarli 1860, Modena, tel. 059/310545,
Lambrusco di Modena Vecchia Modena

Maletti, Soliera, tel. 059/563876,
Lambrusco di Sorbara Selezione '97

Manicardi, Castelvetro, tel. 059/799000,
Lambrusco Grasparossa di Castelvetro
Ca' Fiore '97

PROVINCE OF PARMA

Cantine Ceci, Torrile, tel. 0521/810134,
Malvasia Brut Corti della Duchessa

Forte Rigoni, Pilastro, tel. 0521/637678,
Colli di Parma Sauvignon '97

Vigneti Calzetti
Sala Baganza, tel. 0521/830117,
Malvasia Dolce '97

PROVINCE OF PIACENZA

Giulio Cardinali
Castell'Arquato, tel. 0523/803502,
Montepascolo Dolce '97

Pusterla, Castell'Arquato, tel. 0523/896105,
Colli Piacentini Chardonnay '97

Romagnoli, Vigolzone, tel. 0523/870129,
Colli Piacentini Gutturnio
Vigna del Gallo Ris. '94

Solenghi
Borgonovo Val Tidone, tel. 0523/860352,
Colli Piacentini Barbera l'Attesa '95

La Torretta, Nebbiano, tel. 0523/997008,
Dionisio '96

Cantina Sociale Valtidone
Borgonovo Val Tidone, tel. 0523/862168,
Colli Piacentini Bonarda Secco '97

Villa Peirano, Vigolzone, tel. 0523/875146,
Colli Piacentini Gutturnio Frizzante '96

PROVINCE OF RAVENNA

Cooperativa Agricola Brisighellese
Brisighella, tel. 0546/81103,
Sangiovese di Romagna Sup. Brisigliè '95

Casa Chiara, Brisighella, tel. 0546/85765,
Sangiovese di Romagna Vir '97

Treré, Faenza, tel. 0546/47034,
Albana di Romagna Vigna della Calunga '97

PROVINCE OF REGGIO EMILIA

Ermete Medici & Figli
Reggio Emilia, tel. 0522/942135,
Lambrusco Reggiano Concerto '97

Venturini e Baldini
Quattro Castella, tel. 0522/887080
La Papessa Bianco '97

PROVINCE OF RIMINI

San Valentino, Rimini, tel. 0541/752231
Sangiovese di Romagna Ris. '95

TUSCANY

Tuscany is one of the two principal wine-making regions in Italy (the other being Piedmont) engaged in the making of wine of high quality. Much of this success can be attributed to extensive investment of capital from other local enterprise. It was thanks to just such investment that, beginning at the end of the 1970s, many Tuscan wine-makers were able to set up shop, and others, who were on the verge of closing, were saved. Many wineries were founded by settlers from abroad, with the Germans, the Swiss and the British weighing in heavily. But that now seems like ancient history. Today, Tuscan wineries are at a turning point in their history. The worldwide success of some of the best Tuscan labels is causing a great stir, and the effects of the resulting commotion are by no means only positive. In fact, prices of the best-known Tuscan wines have gone sky-high: buyers are crawling over each other to get their hands on Brunellos, the so-called super-Tuscans are selling like hotcakes, and the average asking price for a Chianti Classico has practically doubled over the past five years. This takes place against the backdrop of a less than rosy period for wine producers. The vines themselves have aged, and no definitive answer has been found as to which sangiovese clones should be planted to replace them. The yields are lower, decimated by touchwood fungus. What's more, the price of wine grapes has risen four- and five-fold in six years' time, creating great difficulties for all those who, like giant wineries, are not self-sufficient. And then there's the fact that the 1995 and 1997 vintages were among the smallest ever seen in Italy, with Tuscany being no exception. So there's ever less wine and it costs ever more money. As for quality, the top labels maintain their footing, but problems are cropping up down market. So let's enjoy the best of the super-Tuscans from '95 and also from '96, which is providing some delightful surprises. Another good bet is Chianti Classico Riserva, vintage '95. As far as the '93 vintage Brunello di Montalcino is concerned, on the other hand, the buyer would be wise to proceed with caution. Of course, we do not mean to shed doubt on the Montalcino zone and its potential. However, producers should bear in mind that if they ask 40 thousand lire or more for a bottle at the winery, they simply cannot skimp on quality, even though at the moment demand is such that they could produce ten times as much and still not have any wine left over. The change in Brunello regulations which lowers the minimum time for cask-aging from three years to two provides a unique opportunity for this zone's winemakers to replace old "vintage" casks that may still be in use. And it would not be a bad thing if limits were placed on vine and hectare yields. But the most interesting news this year comes from relatively young wine-making zones, especially from Bolgheri, as well as from parts of the Maremma region near Grosseto. Newer, modern vineyards are producing low yields of exceptional quality. The next frontier in Tuscan wines seems to be forming in the hills of Scansano and Manciano, where many great Chianti Classico producers, among others, are purchasing vineyards or refurbishing semi-abandoned family properties. Montelpulciano is also a bright spot, because they have made so much headway in cellar techniques.

BARBERINO VAL D'ELSA (FI)

CASA EMMA
FRAZ. CORTINE
50021 BARBERINO VAL D'ELSA (FI)
TEL. 055/8072859

This winery has hit a third consecutive bull's-eye, and is becoming one of the most interesting Chianti producers. This time the Chianti Classico Riserva has re-emerged as a Three Glasses winner in its '95 version. Softness and concentration are the hallmarks of this red wine, whose blend has a touch of the modern and international about it but is basically faithful to the best characteristics of the sangiovese of the subzone between San Donato and Barberino Val d'Elsa, as the typical aromas of cherry and red currant attest. The tannins are smooth, sweet and dense, the finish long and elegant. This small masterpiece is the work of the Bucalossi family, in cooperation with the respected oenologist Nicolò d'Afflitto. At Casa Emma this year we tasted two other very fine wines. The Chianti Classico '96 proves that even a difficult harvest can yield a happy ending. This Chianti Classico should be held two to three years at the most, and the resulting complexity will lend it uncommon class and elegance. Its delicate fruity fragrance and its grip together with a slight acidity that supports the body and bodes well for the future, are this wine's most evident pluses. The 1995 vintage Soloìo, made from merlot, is also a decidedly appealing wine. It has neither the power nor the softness of the '94 and will probably not age as gracefully, but it is true to form, and offers satisfying, concentrated taste.

	Wine	Glasses	Price
●	Chianti Classico Ris. '95	🍷🍷🍷	4
●	Chianti Classico '96	🍷🍷	3*
●	Soloìo '95	🍷🍷	5
●	Chianti Classico Ris. '93	ΥΥΥ	4
●	Soloìo '94	ΥΥΥ	5
●	Chianti Classico '90	ΥΥ	3*
●	Chianti Classico '93	ΥΥ	3
●	Chianti Classico Ris. '90	ΥΥ	4
●	Chianti Classico Ris. '94	ΥΥ	4
●	Chianti Classico '94	Υ	3
●	Chianti Classico '95	Υ	3

BARBERINO VAL D'ELSA (FI)

ISOLE E OLENA
LOC. ISOLE, 1
50021 BARBERINO VAL D'ELSA (FI)
TEL. 055/8072763

It is a particularly pleasant task this year to write about Isole e Olena and its creator, Paolo De Marchi, first of all because De Marchi is among the top winegrowers in Italy. More over, he has probably never given us such good wines as those he is presenting this year. The most exciting bottle on offer is the Cabernet Sauvignon '95 from the Collezione De Marchi. This is a wine of extraordinary breeding with a definite international style. It is, in fact, comparable to the best that Bordeaux or California have to offer from the same vintage, despite its outspoken Tuscan character. Intense, complex aromas, without grassy notes and rich in stylish fruity tones, with black currant and tobacco against a background of india ink and pencil lead, precede a wonderful palate with a decisive but elegant attack and extraordinarily elegant tannins supporting a rich but not excessive succulence. The finish lasts and lasts. The Cepparello '95 is also excellent: the very model of a sangiovese for its varietal character and the consistency of flavor and aroma. It doesn't have an imposing structure, but you can't expect the concentration to be found in Monti in Chianti, for example, from a wine made in Isole e Olena's subzone. The same goes for the Chianti Classico '96, a smaller wine but one that could give lessons in its neighborhood. The Syrah '95 is slightly less satisfactory: an interesting wine, but one with a nebulous nose in which the classic varietal tones are somewhat obscured. The Vin Santo '93, a modern version of an age-old wine, is as exceptional as ever.

	Wine	Glasses	Price
●	Cabernet Sauvignon '95	🍷🍷🍷	6
●	Cepparello '95	🍷🍷	5
●	Chianti Classico '96	🍷🍷	4*
●	Syrah '95	🍷🍷	6
○	Vin Santo '93	🍷🍷	6
●	Cabernet Sauvignon '88	ΥΥΥ	6
●	Cabernet Sauvignon '90	ΥΥΥ	6
●	Cepparello '86	ΥΥΥ	6
●	Cepparello '88	ΥΥΥ	6
●	Cabernet Sauvignon '94	ΥΥ	5
●	Cepparello '90	ΥΥ	5
●	Cepparello '93	ΥΥ	5
●	Cepparello '94	ΥΥ	5
○	Chardonnay '95	ΥΥ	5
○	Vin Santo '91	ΥΥ	5

Le Filigare

Loc. San Donato
in Poggio Via Sicelle
50020 Barberino Val d'Elsa (FI)
tel. 055/8072796

The Filigare estate is right in the middle of fairly wild countryside, and reachable only after you've negotiated myriad curves and innumerable small dirt roads. The border between the regions of Siena and Florence cuts right through the vines, along the ancient traces of the medieval road known as Via Francigena, which today could not even be called a cow-path, and is, of course, unpaved. This is the very heart of Chianti Classico country, between Barberino, San Donato and the northernmost reaches of Castellina in Chianti. The wines produced here are true to their geographical origins. The force and acidity typical of the sangiovese grapes grown in upper Castellina are slightly toned down by the softer, broader nature of a mid-Barberino Val d'Elsa Chianti Classico. The results of this combination can sometimes be interesting indeed, and so they are in the Chianti Classico '96, a well-balanced and particularly well-made wine, and proof that this vintage is better than you might think, rather like the '86, slandered at first, but now holding its own, in many cases, more than the much-touted '85. The Chianti Classico Riserva '95 is less appealing, more 'vertical' in structure and rather closed aromatically. It's painful to have to say it, given past successes, but this year the Podere Le Rocce '95 is also a disappointment. We found this sangiovese and cabernet sauvignon blend too forward on the nose and insufficiently concentrated in flavor.

●	Chianti Classico '95	🍷🍷	4
●	Chianti Classico Ris. '95	🍷	5
●	Podere Le Rocce '95	🍷	5
●	Podere Le Rocce '88	ỸỸỸ	5
●	Chianti Classico '88	ỸỸ	4
●	Chianti Classico Ris. '87	ỸỸ	5
●	Chianti Classico Ris. '88	ỸỸ	5
●	Chianti Classico Ris. '90	ỸỸ	5
●	Chianti Classico Ris. '91	ỸỸ	5
●	Chianti Classico Ris. '93	ỸỸ	5
●	Podere Le Rocce '90	ỸỸ	5
●	Podere Le Rocce '91	ỸỸ	5
●	Podere Le Rocce '93	ỸỸ	5
●	Podere Le Rocce '94	ỸỸ	5
●	Podere Le Rocce '92	Ỹ	5

Monsanto

Via Monsanto, 8
50021 Barberino Val d'Elsa (FI)
tel. 055/8059000

The Castello di Monsanto is one of the key Chianti Classico producers. Its cellars have brought forth some of the most august bottles in this wine's recent history. Thrilling tastings of the Chianti Classico Riserva '64, '71, '72, and more recently of the '88 and '90 vintages come to mind. These are big, deep, full-bodied reds, full of charm and character despite tannins which are slightly on the harsh side. Having said this, we must also admit that this year we were a bit disappointed to note that the best wines from this cellar were not the Chianti Classicos. What's more, the Chianti Classico Riserva '95, which should be the very backbone of this estate's production, seemed a bit below par. With its rather forward aromas and only moderate body, it is quite a different wine from the one we had been expecting to taste. Thumbs up, however, for the Fabrizio Bianchi Chardonnay '96 and the Nemo '95, primarily cabernet sauvignon. The Chardonnay is an excellent white, with almost smokey aromas and a rich, unctuous structure reminiscent of certain of its Californian counterparts. Nemo '95 is the sort of aristocratic red wine Monsanto had taught us to expect. Perhaps the nose is a bit forward, but lots of body helps make for concentrated flavor on the palate. We look forward to future excellence from Monsanto, particularly in its traditional fortes: sangiovese and Chianti Classico wines. Il Poggio Riserva has not yet been released, and this may in some way explain this year's diminished performance.

○	Fabrizio Bianchi Chardonnay '96	🍷🍷	5
●	Nemo '95	🍷🍷	6
●	Chianti Classico Ris. '95		4
●	Chianti Classico Il Poggio Ris. '88	ỸỸỸ	5
●	Chianti Classico Il Poggio Ris. '86	ỸỸ	5
●	Chianti Classico Il Poggio Ris. '90	ỸỸ	5
●	Chianti Classico Il Poggio Ris. '93	ỸỸ	5
●	Fabrizio Bianchi Chardonnay '93	ỸỸ	5
●	Nemo '90	ỸỸ	5
●	Nemo '93	ỸỸ	5
●	Nemo '94	ỸỸ	5

BARBERINO VAL D'ELSA (FI)

CASTELLO DELLA PANERETTA
STRADA DELLA PANERETTA, 37
50021 BARBERINO VAL D'ELSA (FI)
TEL. 055/8059003

Given that the Chianti Classico '95 tickled our tastebuds and our fancy last year, imagine our delight this time round, with not one but two '95 vintages to taste. Both the Chianti Classico Riserva and the Chianti Classico Torre a Destra Riserva are delicious, lacking only a bit of "weight" on the palate, a little more concentration, to win its third glass. These are two supremely drinkable wines with seductive fresh aromas. The Chianti Classico Riserva is somewhat more austere, with a bit of an edge and a bouquet that mixes openly fruity tones with whiffs of something almost animal. The Torre a Destra Riserva, more modern and finer in its polyphenols, with its red berry aromas and soft and beautifully balanced flavor, quickly cast its spell on us. The Chianti Classico '96 is a good but slightly lean wine, which pales in the shadow of the '95 vintage released last year. The Quattrocentenario '95, a pure sangiovese made in celebration of the 400th anniversary of the estate castle, is a splendid wine. It is redolent of fruit and new wood and is notably soft and full-bodied. We remain unimpressed by the super-Tuscan Le Terrine, made from a blend of sangiovese and cabernet sauvignon. This year the '95 vintage took the stage, but our applause was muted. We found it a bit forward on the nose, in fact too much so, reflecting a search for concentration which risks producing jammy aromas and excessive softness on the palate. We sincerely hope that we were just unlucky in our bottles, which is a possibility, given the consistent success of this estate's other wines.

Wine	Glasses	Price
● Chianti Classico Ris. '95	▼▼	4
● Chianti Classico Torre a Destra Ris. '95	▼▼	4
● Quattrocentenario '95	▼▼	5
● Chianti Classico '96	▼	3
● Le Terrine '95		5
● Chianti Classico '95	▽▽	4
● Chianti Classico Ris. '90	▽▽	4*
● Chianti Classico Ris. '93	▽▽	4
● Chianti Classico '93	▽	3
● Chianti Classico '94	▽	3
● Chianti Classico Ris. '94	▽	4
● Le Terrine '90	▽	4
● Le Terrine '93	▽	5

BARBERINO VAL D'ELSA (FI)

I BALZINI
LOC. PASTINE
VIA COMUNALE DI PONETA
50021 BARBERINO VAL D'ELSA (FI)
TEL. 055/8075503

The collective efforts of Vincenzo D'Isanto and Walter Filiputti are starting to bear fruit. Formerly sole owner of this lovely Barberino Val d'Elsa estate, D'Isanto has been joined by the celebrated Friuli wine-maker Filiputti in its management. Their avowed aim is to produce a red wine of great character which could hold its own with the best Tuscan and international bottles. This is why they asked us at I Balzini not to include a review of their wine in last year's Guide, as the '95 vintage which had just been bottled at the time was not yet at its best. Almost exactly a year later, we were able to taste the I Balzini '95, which is officially a Colli della Toscana Centrale Rosso IGT. This wine was unsettled and inexpressive in the first weeks after bottling, and D'Isanto and Filiputti were entirely justified in begging us to be patient: today's wine is an excellent, soft, well-balanced red, made, as you can read from the label, from sangioveto and cabernet sauvignon grapes and aged in small barrels. It has an intense ruby hue, with garnet nuances shading to brown. Seductive aromas of black currants and ripe plum alternate with contained, discreet notes of oak. This is a bouquet that reminds us distinctly of the noble and austere nose of a Bordeaux. Its elegance is repeated on the palate, where judicious fruit and fine hints of wood again take turns. This is an excellent wine, lacking only a bit of structure in mid-palate. It was certainly worth the wait.

Wine	Glasses	Price
● I Balzini Rosso '95	▼▼	6
● I Balzini Rosso '94	▽	5

Tenuta Belvedere

Loc. Belvedere, 140
57020 Bolgheri (LI)
tel. 0565/749735

The wines produced at the Tenuta Belvedere of the Marquises Antinori are becoming increasingly identifiable. For once, we would like to begin our review with this estate's "standard", i.e. simpler wines, since Belvedere has been making a particular effort in recent years on its Vermentino, which has been planted extensively, as well as on its Rosato Scalabrone, which has been revolutionized in style and taste. The underlying strategy of this vast estate is quite comprehensible: it is not enough just to make great wines for the select few; they should also be producing reliable wines that are neither scarce nor expensive. There is no doubt in our minds that, in terms of quality, they have attained their goal this year. The Vermentino '97 is a great success: it is a flavorful and well-balanced wine with intense, distinct aromas of apricots, peaches, yellow flowers and roses. The Scalabrone '97 is no less impressive. Obtained through rosé vinification of cabernet grapes, it has an intensity of color and nose which is well above average. The aromas are pleasingly direct and fragrant, suggesting raspberry and other red fruit. The liveliness of the palate coexists with surprising substance. And now for Belvedere's most important wine, Guado al Tasso. The '95 vintage is extremely good, in keeping with its predecessors, and displays its characteristic bouquet of sour cherry preserves, blackberries, bell pepper and spice. Mouth-filling and soft on the palate, it has a notable tannic content, which is more marked on the finish.

	Wine	Glasses	Price
⊙	Bolgheri Rosato Scalabrone '97	▼▼	3
●	Bolgheri Rosso Sup. Guado al Tasso '95	▼▼	6
○	Bolgheri Vermentino '97	▼	3
●	Guado al Tasso '90	▽▽▽	6
●	Guado al Tasso '92	▽▽	4
●	Guado al Tasso '93	▽▽	6
●	Guado al Tasso '94	▽▽	6
○	Bolgheri Bianco Belvedere '96	▽	2
⊙	Bolgheri Rosato Scalabrone '96	▽	3
●	Bolgheri Rosso Belvedere '95	▽	2
●	Bolgheri Rosso Belvedere '96	▽	2
●	Fattoria Belvedere '93	▽	1

Le Macchiole

Via Bolgherese
57020 Bolgheri (LI)
tel. 0565/763240

"Color: concentrated ruby; nose: ample, very intense, a background of fruit with notes of red currant preserves, roasted coffee, and a faint vegetal suggestion; palate: hot, intriguing, dense, progressive and very profound." These are our tasting notes for the Paleo Rosso '95, which, after various attempts with earlier vintages, has at last earned its Three Glasses. Eugenio Campolmi deserved nothing less for his consistent dedication over the last few years, backed up by the recent purchase and planting of new vineyards. But we also found the Paleo Bianco '96 better than ever. With its deep, rich aromas, serving up just the right blend of smokey and fruity tones, this is a satisfying, mouth-filling wine with excellent follow-through. The Le Contessine range also performed well, which proves that all this success has not come about by chance. The monovarietal vermentino Bianco almost garnered Two Glasses. This wine offers whistle-clean aromas, with tones of apricot, peach and citrus, and fresh, full, well-balanced flavor. The Bolgheri Rosso Le Contessine appears to good advantage as well, thanks to its mellow structure, concentrated flavor and intense fruity aroma. The last feather in their cap this very fine year is the Rosato, which walks off with One Glass.

	Wine	Glasses	Price
●	Bolgheri Rosso Sup. Paleo '95	▼▼▼	6
○	Bolgheri Sauvignon Paleo '96	▼▼	4
○	Bolgheri Bianco Le Contessine '97	▼	3
⊙	Bolgheri Rosato '97	▼	3
●	Bolgheri Rosso Le Contessine '97	▼	3
○	Bolgheri Vermentino Le Contessine '97	▼	3
○	Bolgheri Sauvignon Paleo '95	▽▽	4
●	Bolgheri Rosso Sup. Paleo '94	▽▽	5
○	Paleo Bianco '94	▽▽	3*
●	Paleo Rosso '91	▽▽	5
●	Paleo Rosso '92	▽▽	2
●	Paleo Rosso '93	▽▽	5

BOLGHERI (LI)

TENUTA DELL' ORNELLAIA
VIA BOLGHERESE, 191
57020 BOLGHERI (LI)
TEL. 0565/762140 - 762141

It won't be long before the countryside around Bolgheri looks like one giant vineyard. Given the frenetic rate at which new vines are being planted, be it by new arrivals or by old hands, the first years of the next millennium should deliver at least three times as much Bolgheri Superiore as is currently on offer. Behind all of this development is the far-sighted wisdom of Marquis Lodovico Antinori, a quality that was mistaken for capriciousness and even insanity when the first vines were planted at the Tenuta dell'Ornellaia. Today, it is the most important estate on the entire coast, and not just because of the number of bottles it produces. And there's no back-sliding here either, as the quality of the Masseto, pocketing its Three Glasses for the third year in a row, clearly demonstrates. Ornellaia's vintage '95 merlot still has all the qualities that made it justly famous, and it seems on the point of becoming a veritable Tuscan coastal cult wine. With its concentrated color and fragrance, neither of which is yet fully developed but which are both already rich in nuance, this wine displays magnificent notes of roasted coffee, chocolate and lead pencil with delicate mineral hints against a solid fruity background. The palate, in fine-tuned balance, is extremely soft and dense, with a very long finish. The Ornellaia '95, a masterfully executed wine with a structure both rich and well-balanced, is nearly as good. We were very pleased by the sauvignon, Poggio alle Gazze '97, which in the past few years has acquired a distinct and recognizable character all its own, admirable both for its aromatic expressiveness and for its full, round and mellow palate. Last of all, the Rosso Le Volte '96 is a well-made wine.

	Wine	Glasses	
●	Masseto '95	**YYY**	6
●	Ornellaia '95	**YY**	6
○	Poggio alle Gazze '97	**YY**	4
●	Le Volte '96		3
●	Masseto '93	YYY	6
●	Masseto '94	YYY	6
●	Ornellaia '93	YYY	6
●	Masseto '89	YY	6
●	Masseto '92	YY	6
●	Ornellaia '88	YY	6
●	Ornellaia '90	YY	6
●	Ornellaia '91	YY	6
●	Ornellaia '92	YY	6
●	Ornellaia '94	YY	6
○	Poggio alle Gazze '96	YY	4

BOLGHERI (LI)

TENUTA SAN GUIDO
LOC. CAPANNE, 27
57020 BOLGHERI (LI)
TEL. 0565/762003

Sassicaia is back amongst the Olympians with its '95, a harvest distinguished by high overall quality. This is a wine that never falsifies the results obtained in the vineyard: its characteristics vary with the quality of the grapes from year to year, but it is remarkably consistent in style. Anyone making wine in Italy should pause to consider this basic point: seeking rich and concentrated flavor is important, but not if the search is conducted to the detriment of a clearly defined style which confers the personality of the terroir to the wine. These are the characteristics sought by wine tasters in countries where they are used to finding them in their great wines. Consider, for example, the Revue du Vin de France, whose assessment of Sassicaia we should like, unusually, to quote: "Even if at first the nose seems dominated by oak and toasty tones, the fruit comes through upon aeration. The nose continues to increase in complexity even after the wine has been left to breathe for a few hours, releasing notes of prunes, leather and ever more evident fruit. The palate, rich and unctuous, almost sumptuous, shows uncommon refinement. This wine will require a few more years' aging to mature fully and reveal the full intensity of its fruit". It goes without saying that they gave it a very high score indeed. We would add only that, even if the palate did not seem quite so rich to us, we are in full agreement with these notes. Let skeptics be reminded that '96 and '97 were quite simply magnificent years…

	Wine	Glasses	
●	Bolgheri Sassicaia '95	**YYY**	6
●	Sassicaia '83	YYY	6
●	Sassicaia '84	YYY	6
●	Sassicaia '85	YYY	6
●	Sassicaia '88	YYY	6
●	Sassicaia '90	YYY	6
●	Sassicaia '92	YYY	6
●	Sassicaia '93	YYY	6
●	Bolgheri Sassicaia '94	YY	6
●	Sassicaia '86	YY	6
●	Sassicaia '87	YY	6
●	Sassicaia '89	YY	6
●	Sassicaia '91	YY	6

BUCINE (AR)

Fattoria Santa Maria di Ambra

Loc. Ambra
52020 Bucine (AR)
tel. 055/996806

The proprietor of this historic estate, Vincenzo Zampi, whose family has owned the Fattoria di Santa Maria di Ambra since the 15th century, divides his time between his professorship at the University of Florence and his passion for wine. Tastings of the red wines he produces reveal his quest for a style accenting elegance and understatement, while fully respecting the characteristics particular to this zone. Reasonable as they seem, these ideals are neither as obvious nor as widely followed as one might imagine. We were particulary impressed by the results that this approach lent to Casamurli, a blend of sangiovese and malvasia nera. The '95 vintage delivers elegantly contoured flavor and aroma, and excellent structure, not in the least heavy. Ruby-hued, with marked notes of oak that the next few months should succeed in integrating, it has an elegant base of ripe fruit. Its attack on the palate is soft and woody, its tannins well developed and noble. The Gavignano is also worthy of note, a blend of cabernet (roughly 60%) and sangiovese, in which apparent care has been taken to limit vegetal notes on nose and palate. With deeper color than the Casamurli, it offers intense, distinct aromas of ripe blackberries. On the palate its richness in extract compensates for its lesser overall complexity. The Chardonnay '97, with its clearly varietal banana fragrance and forthright drinkability, and the Chianti Riserva La Bigattiera '96, a pleasant wine, though a bit below our expectations, are both simpler wines but very good value for money.

	Wine	Rating	Price
●	Casamurli '95	🍷🍷	5
●	Gavignano '95	🍷🍷	4
○	Chardonnay '97	🍷	3
●	Chianti V. La Bigattiera Ris. '96	🍷	3
●	Gavignano '92	♀♀	3
●	Gavignano '93	♀♀	3
○	Chardonnay '93	♀	3
○	Chardonnay '94	♀	3
●	Chianti Ris. '88	♀	3*
●	Chianti V. La Bigattiera Ris. '95	♀	3
●	Chianti V. La Bigattiera Ris. '92	♀	2
●	Gavignano '90	♀	4
●	Gavignano '94	♀	3

BUCINE (AR)

Fattoria Villa La Selva

Loc. Montebenichi
52021 Bucine (AR)
tel. 055/998203 - 998200

The consultant oenologist Vittorio Fiore needs no introduction, so widespread is his fame in the Italian wine world. Sergio Carpini, the owner of the estate, is a talented and determined wine-maker. Both the vineyards and the equipment in the cellar are as one would wish. The new consultant Stefano Chioccioli is much admired in Tuscany. And yet the wines of Villa La Selva have yet to realize their tremendous potential. It can't be denied that they are wines of high quality, but they have yet to make us sit up and take notice. It seems that their reliability is their greatest virtue. But one can just hear in the background a thoroughbred champion pawing the ground. Meanwhile their two top offerings are once again excellent. The Selvamaggio '95, a cabernet sauvignon and sangiovese blend, vaunts aromatic finesse (with a faint vegetal tone, however) and is clean, substantial and soft on the palate. The Felciaia of the same vintage, a notably elegant pure sangiovese, is equally successful: light red in color, it is delicately oaky on the nose, and fairly full-bodied, with smooth tannins. The Chianti '96 is straightforward, fruity and clean, as a good Chianti should be. Two versions of Vin Santo are on offer this year. The first is the Fiore di Luna '93, of traditional style, providing intense walnut and leather tones on a medium-weight structure. The second is the more modern Vigna del Papa '94, which displays an interesting nose of candied fruits and raisins, and a leaner, lighter palate.

	Wine	Rating	Price
●	Felciaia '95	🍷🍷	5
●	Selvamaggio '95	🍷🍷	5
●	Chianti '96	🍷	3
○	Fiore di Luna '93	🍷	6
○	Vigna del Papa '94	🍷	5
●	Chianti Ris. '93	♀♀	5
●	Felciaia '93	♀♀	4
●	Felciaia '94	♀♀	5
○	Fiore di Luna Ris. '90	♀♀	6
●	Selvamaggio '90	♀♀	5
●	Selvamaggio '91	♀♀	5
●	Selvamaggio '92	♀♀	5
●	Selvamaggio '93	♀♀	5
●	Selvamaggio Ris. '90	♀♀	6
○	Vin Santo '93	♀	5

CAPANNORI (LU)

TENUTA DI VALGIANO
FRAZ. VALGIANO
55010 CAPANNORI (LU)
TEL. 0583/402271

The Tenuta di Valgiano estate is growing apace. The old and new vines already permit them to make an excellent selection of grapes, and further plantings are in the works. The wines we tasted this year confirmed our previous good impressions, but our highest expectations are reserved for a wine which has not yet made it out of the cellar, Scasso dei Cesari '97. Its '96 vintage does make a good showing though, and all in all is quite a satisfying wine. Unfortunately, for a variety of reasons, less of this wine than usual was produced, but this had no impact on quality. Vivid ruby in hue, Scasso dei Cesari '96 has pleasant red currant, vanilla and minerally notes on the nose. It is soft, concentrated and well-balanced on the palate, with lively tannins and an appealing finish. The Giallo dei Muri '97, trebbiano with a small proportion of oak-fermented chardonnay, gets Two Glasses. Intensely straw-yellow in color, this wine is redolent of both fruit and flowers, with notes of vanilla. It is fairly full, juicy and well-articulated on the palate, if not very generous on the finish. The last of the line is the Rosso dei Palistorti, which for a 'standard' red is not at all bad. Well-made, lively and straightforward, it boasts great balance and intriguing aromas of red fruits, pepper, violets and faint vegetal notes.

	Wine	Glasses	Price
○	Colline Lucchesi Bianco Giallo dei Muri '97	▼▼	3*
●	Scasso dei Cesari '96	▼▼	4
●	Colline Lucchesi Rosso dei Palistorti '96	▼	3
●	Scasso dei Cesari '95	▽▽	4
○	Colline Lucchesi Bianco Giallo dei Muri '95	▽	2*
○	Colline Lucchesi Bianco Giallo dei Muri '96	▽	2
●	Colline Lucchesi Rosso dei Palistorti '95	▽	2*
●	Scasso dei Cesari '94	▽	3*

CAPRAIA E LIMITE (PO)

TENUTA CANTAGALLO
VIA VALICARDA, 35
50050 CAPRAIA E LIMITE (PO)
TEL. 0574/574323

A good showing for this winery, owned by Enrico Pierazzuoli, a young producer who knows what he's after. The range of wines offered is quite wide, in part because Cantagallo comprises three different estates: Matroneo in Chianti Classico, le Farnete in Carmignano and Cantagallo in the Montalbano zone. The only white wine provided for official tasting is probably the most interesting and original of the wines we tasted from this producer. Called Carleto '97, it is a monovarietal riesling that has managed to blend its lively varietal character with a taste of Tuscan terroir, giving rise to a wine that combines the aromatic freshness and crisp acidity of this grape with the ripe fruitiness and full structure typical of this zone. Another high scorer is the Carmignano Riserva Le Farnete '94, firm and consistent on the palate, with a lasting finish and intense aromas, but somewhat overwhelmed by oak. The Chianti Montalbano Riserva '94 fully deserves its Two Glasses for its soft, mellow flavor, sweet finish and expressive bouquet with vegetal notes and coconut. We raise One Glass to the Montalbano '96, with its fairly profound aromas of black fruit and its dense palate. Another Glass for the Gioveto, whose interesting aromatic structure reveals traces of blackberries, pepper, fruit preserves and toasty oak. The palate has some substance, but the finish is cut a bit short. Both the Chianti Classico '95 and the Carmignano '95 are more than respectable.

	Wine	Glasses	Price
○	Carleto '97	▼▼	4
●	Carmignano Le Farnete Ris. '94	▼▼	4
●	Chianti Montalbano Ris. '94	▼▼	4
●	Carmignano Le Farnete '95	▼	3
●	Chianti Classico Matroneo '95	▼	3
●	Chianti Montalbano '96	▼	2*
●	Gioveto '96	▼	3
○	Carleto '96	▽▽	4
●	Carmignano Ris. '92	▽▽	4
●	Carmignano Ris. '93	▽▽	4
●	Chianti Ris. '93	▽▽	3
○	Vin Santo Millarium '92	▽	4

CARMIGNANO (PO)

FATTORIA AMBRA

VIA LOMBARDA, 85
50042 CARMIGNANO (PO)
TEL. 055/486488 - 8719049

The modernization of production techniques still so urgently needed in many Italian wine-making areas is old hat at this dependable Carmignano estate. The owner, Beppe Rigoli, has for years now offered proof of the merits of vinifying single lots of vines, in keeping with his attempt to express the characteristics of individual crus. Hence he bottles three different Carmignano wines, each with its own personality. The Carmignano Santa Cristina in Pilli '95 is a masculine wine, in both its extract and its alcohol content. A bit muffled on the nose but intensely fruity, it offers a fresh palate with well-judged acidity and a long, straightforward finish. The Riserva Le Vigne Alte of the same vintage was, at our tasting, still far behind in its development, but with obvious future potential. Although its nose is mute, its palate is more open, with firm tannic structure, and fruit awaiting fuller expression. The latest arrival, the Riserva Elzana, delivers on the promise it showed last year: fragrant and appetizing, with slight green nuances, it has full, very well-balanced flavor, tending towards the austere rather than the expansive. The Barco Reale '97 is faithful to the fresh, fruity style of its kind, with a succulent entry on the palate and a truly pleasing peppery finish.

●	Carmignano Elzana Ris. '95	🍷🍷	4
●	Barco Reale '97	🍷	3
●	Carmignano Le Vigne Alte Ris. '95	🍷	4
●	Carmignano Vigna S. Cristina in Pilli '95	🍷	4
●	Carmignano '89	🍸🍸	3
●	Carmignano Le Vigne Alte Ris. '94	🍸🍸	4
●	Carmignano Le Vigne Alte Ris. '90	🍸🍸	4
●	Carmignano Ris. '88	🍸	4
●	Carmignano Vigna S. Cristina in Pilli '94	🍸	4

CARMIGNANO (PO)

CAPEZZANA

LOC. SEANO
VIA CAPEZZANA, 100
50042 CARMIGNANO (PO)
TEL. 055/8706005 - 8706091

Wine enthusiasts have grown to expect from Capezzana a rigorous, austere style that honors age-old local traditions. Moderation in dealings with customers, together with a sober and unembroidered approach to vinification continue to make Capezzana a benchmark estate for the entire Carmignano zone. But even a legendary cellar must evolve. Capezzana is no exception, and has recently undergone a reorganization. One of the estate's best vineyards, the Villa di Trefiano, has now been entrusted to the care of Vittorio Contini Bonacossi, son of the founder, Ugo. Stefano Chioccioli, a promising young oenologist who has already made quite a name for himself, is directing operations in the cellar. As often happens in times of transition, the quality of the wines produced at Capezzana right now varies. Of the Carmignanos we tasted we found the Villa di Capezzana Riserva '95 was good but not up to its own high standards. A clean red wine with subtle fruity aromas, it is pleasing on the palate but a bit unsteady in structure, lacking the richness in extract characteristic of the best vintages. The Carmignano Villa di Trefiano '95 was also flawed, perhaps because it has not yet hit its stride, so we have put off our review until next year. The Barco Reale '97 is up to par, with its fresh and slightly vegetal aromas, its full body, liveliness and persistence. The Bordeaux blend Ghiaie della Furba, customarily one of the top wines from this estate, was not available for tasting.

●	Barco Reale '97	🍷	3
●	Carmignano Villa di Capezzana Ris. '95	🍷	5
●	Carmignano Villa di Capezzana Ris. '90	🍸🍸	5
●	Carmignano Villa di Trefiano '88	🍸🍸	5
●	Carmignano Villa di Trefiano '90	🍸🍸	5
●	Ghiaie della Furba '90	🍸🍸	5
●	Ghiaie della Furba '94	🍸🍸	5
●	Ghiaie della Furba '95	🍸🍸	5
○	Vin Santo di Carmignano Ris. '89	🍸🍸	5
○	Vin Santo di Carmignano Ris. '90	🍸🍸	5

CASTAGNETO CARDUCCI (LI)

GRATTAMACCO

LOC. GRATTAMACCO
57022 CASTAGNETO CARDUCCI (LI)
TEL. 0565/763840

The '95 vintage was celebrated in Tuscany as one of the most successful and promising of the entire decade. But what is true for the region in general is capable of variation as one moves from subzone to subzone and from one grape variety to another. Around Bolgheri and all along the coast, vintages tend not to differ enormously, and a really bad one is a rarity, so variation is usually not extreme. At Grattamacco, however, there was an appreciable difference between '94 and '95, although it's hard to say whether this depends on the vintages themselves or on the way they were handled. To dispel any lingering doubts, we'll say right out that we definitely liked the Grattamacco '95. Pleasing to the eye with its rich, intense color, it has an aroma that is still veiled by smoky, animal scents, but the flavor makes up for it: it is powerful and vigorous on the attack, and follows right through to a characterful finish. As always, this wine is the highly personal creation of Piermario Meletti Cavallari, and it resists easy categorization. The other wines, briefly: the Bolgheri Rosso '96 is simple but pleasant; the Bianco '96 is somewhat less successful; the Bianco '97, on the other hand, has come out very well, with a clearly defined, intense and rather rich aromatic structure featuring notes of acacia flowers and chamomile, as well as apricot and melon. The flavor is full, backed up by a refreshing crispness.

	Wine	Glasses	
●	Bolgheri Rosso Sup. Grattamacco '95	🍷🍷	6
○	Bolgheri Bianco '97	🍷	3
●	Bolgheri Rosso '96	🍷	3
○	Bolgheri Bianco '96		3
●	Grattamacco '85	🍷🍷🍷 (white)	5
●	Grattamacco '90	🍷🍷 (white)	5
●	Grattamacco '91	🍷🍷 (white)	5
●	Grattamacco '92	🍷🍷 (white)	4
●	Grattamacco '93	🍷🍷 (white)	5

CASTAGNETO CARDUCCI (LI)

MICHELE SATTA

LOC. VIGNA AL CAVALIERE
57020 CASTAGNETO CARDUCCI (LI)
TEL. 0565/763894

Another banner year for Michele Satta, a wine-maker dedicated to his art if ever there was one. His wines have by now taken on their own style and personality, together with a certain substance achieved after years of hard work. It all goes to show that a vineyard needs time to express itself, and that this producer has grown with his experience, both good and bad. The Vigna al Cavaliere '96 represents a milestone for this wine and for Satta himself: it confirms last year's success, retaining the characteristic features of this sangiovese, but the fruit is denser this year, a sine qua non for binding together alcohol content and tannins in a harmonious whole. Thumbs up as well for Piastraia '96, a "Bolgheri blend" with syrah added. There seems to be the right amount of everything: concentration drinkabilty, softness and oak. It's an excellent achievement, but why stop here? Increased complexity and a more intense flavor would make it even better. Good marks for the Vermentino Costa di Giulia '97 too, a fruity, fragrant, substantial wine which suffers from being tasted before its time. In fact, with each month that passes we like it more. The Bolgheri Bianco, on the other hand, can be enjoyed at once, with its fresh aromas and well-balanced palate. The Rosato, characteristically redolent of raspberries, also did well, and the pleasant, simple Diambra came very close to One Glass.

	Wine	Glasses	
●	Bolgheri Rosso Piastraia '96	🍷🍷	4
●	Vigna al Cavaliere '96	🍷🍷	5
○	Bolgheri Bianco '97	🍷	3
⊙	Bolgheri Rosato '97	🍷	2
○	Bolgheri Vermentino Costa di Giulia '97	🍷	3
●	Bolgheri Rosso Diambra '97		2
●	Bolgheri Rosso Piastraia '95	🍷🍷 (white)	3*
●	Vigna al Cavaliere '90	🍷🍷 (white)	5
●	Vigna al Cavaliere '95	🍷🍷 (white)	4
○	Bolgheri Vermentino Costa di Giulia '96	🍷 (white)	3
●	Vigna al Cavaliere '92	🍷 (white)	4
●	Vigna al Cavaliere '93	🍷 (white)	4
●	Vigna al Cavaliere '94	🍷 (white)	4

CASTELLINA IN CHIANTI (SI)

TENUTA DI BIBBIANO
VIA BIBBIANO, 106
53011 CASTELLINA IN CHIANTI (SI)
TEL. 0577/743065

We must admit the error of our ways in having only just included this estate in the Guide. Tenuta di Bibbiano has been in existence for more than a century, and has recently attracted attention for the range of very respectable wines it produces. In '95 they made two especially interesting Chianti Classicos, which are recognizably products of the western sub-zone of Castellina in Chianti (where Lilliano and Rodano come from, for example). These two wines, the Chianti Classico Montornello and especially the Chianti Classico Vigna del Capannino Riserva, made from a special sangiovese grape resembling the Montalcino variety, were created with the expert advice of Giulio Gambelli, an oenologist who has long been prized in Tuscany. But let's proceed in an orderly fashion. The first wine is obviously simpler and more immediate, but should not be underestimated. It is among the most powerful on the palate and most concentrated in polyphenols of the non-"riserva" Chianti Classicos. The tannins are perhaps a little rough and the nose may be a bit forward, but you really feel you're drinking a full-bodied wine with lots of character. The Chianti Classico Vigna del Capannino Riserva '95 is quite simply magnificent: it made it all the way to the Three Glass finals. One senses immediately from the balsamic, toasty aromas that accompany the sour cherry notes that this wine was aged in small oak barrels. It's intense, closely woven and long-lasting on the palate, with dense and delicate tannins.

● Chianti Classico Montornello '95	🍷🍷	3
● Chianti Classico Vigna del Capannino Ris. '95	🍷🍷	5

CASTELLINA IN CHIANTI (SI)

CASTELLARE DI CASTELLINA
LOC. CASTELLARE
53011 CASTELLINA IN CHIANTI (SI)
TEL. 0577/740490

The inauguration of a lovely new cellar coincides with one of the best performances ever by this famous estate's wines. In our view they have yet to produce a real gem which could compete at the highest levels, but they clearly know what they're about and Paolo Panerai, the owner and "soul" of the estate, has reason to be proud, and has done very well to avail himself of the advice of the highly respected oenologist Maurizio Castelli. But let's get down to the wines. The best of the range is, we feel, the new Chianti Classico Vigna al Poggiale '95, an elegant red with a structure that allows it to take its place among its peers without fear of disgrace. It displays the typical sangiovese aromas of Parma violets and sour cherry. It has an aristocratic palate, dominated by a slightly acidic touch that supports a full body, rich in polyphenols. The Coniale '94, mostly cabernet sauvignon, is very interesting. With its very slightly vegetal aromas, it offers a fairly long finish and excellent balance. The Chianti Classico Riserva '95 and especially the Chianti Classico '96 are more diluted and less full as a result of more noticeable acidity. The '96 is the result of a very irregular year. No news is available on this estate's most representative wine, I Sodi di San Nicolò, a monovarietal sangiovese. Our last tasting of it, in its '91 incarnation, goes back three years.

● Chianti Classico Vigna al Poggiale '95	🍷🍷	5
● Coniale '94	🍷🍷	6
● Chianti Classico '96	🍷	4
● Chianti Classico Ris. '95	🍷	5
● Chianti Classico '90	🍸🍸	4
● Chianti Classico '95	🍸🍸	4
● Chianti Classico Ris. '90	🍸🍸	5
● Coniale '90	🍸🍸	6
● I Sodi di San Niccolò '88	🍸🍸	6
● I Sodi di San Niccolò '91	🍸🍸	5
● I Sodi di San Nicolò '86	🍸🍸	5
● Chianti Classico '94	🍸	3
● Chianti Classico Ris. '93	🍸	4
● Coniale '91	🍸	6

Cecchi - Villa Cerna

Loc. Casina dei Ponti
53011 Castellina in Chianti (SI)
tel. 0577/743024

Let's hope this is the last year we're obliged to combine the reviews for Cecchi and Villa Cerna, the winery owned by the Cecchi family and located just a hop, skip and jump away from their own headquarters. Our hand was forced in this choice because Villa Cerna offered us only one wine for tasting, the Chianti Classico Riserva '95, insufficient for a separate listing. This is a fairly good red, though a bit disappointing both in concentration and in character. Paradoxically, it was Cecchi, the more "commercial" enterprise, that harbored the greatest surprises. The Vigneto La Gavina '95, largely cabernet sauvignon, is a small wonder. It offers characteristic complex aromas, with balsamic tones, and a definite yet elegant palate, without a hint of harshness, dominated by dense, velvety tannins. The Spargolo '95, a monovarietal sangiovese, was very good, as usual. It is somewhat diminished by a heavy hand with acidity, but the aromas are clear and distinct and from a technical standpoint this is almost a perfect wine. The Chianti Classico Messer Piero di Teuzzo '96 is rather less dense, a well-made wine but nothing more.

	Wine	Glasses	Price
●	Spargolo '95	**YY**	4
●	Vigneto La Gavina '95	**YY**	5
●	Chianti Classico Messer Piero di Teuzzo '96	**Y**	4
●	Chianti Classico Villa Cerna Ris. '95	**Y**	4
●	Cabernet Sauvignon '94	YY	4
●	Chianti Classico Messer Piero di Teuzzo '93	YY	3*
●	Chianti Classico Messer Piero di Teuzzo '95	YY	4
●	Spargolo '85	YY	5
●	Spargolo '88	YY	5
●	Spargolo '90	YY	4
●	Spargolo '91	YY	4
●	Spargolo '94	Y	4

Rocca di Cispiano

Loc. Cispiano
53011 Castellina in Chianti (SI)
tel. 0577/740961

Another good performance from the wines of Rocca di Cispiano, the estate owned by the Milanese financial journalist Guido Busetto and his wife Nobuko Hashimoto. Especially high marks go to the flag-bearer, Rocca di Cispiano '95, which made it to the finals and only just missed Three Glasses. This is one of the finest sangiovese wines made in '95 and has all the best traits of its zone of origin, Castellina's Conca d'Oro. From these slopes, which face south-west, one can see the famous towers of San Gimignano on the hilltops opposite, about 15 kilometers as the crow flies. This is a notably concentrated and at the same time soft red wine, altogether innocent of tannic or acidic harshness. The expressive bouquet is dominated by balsamic and ripe fruity notes. Altogether an important wine. The Chianti Classico '96 is also very interesting, and similar in other ways, though less dense and concentrated. The Chianti Classico Riserva '95 was less impressive and too forward on the nose, but as the tasting sample probably came straight from the barrel, we"ll reserve judgment until next year. We are further inclined to wait by the fact that a further tasting of the standard Chianti Classico '95 proved it to be holding its own, and it hardly seems likely that the riserva would be a lesser wine.

	Wine	Glasses	Price
●	Chianti Classico '96	**YY**	4
●	Rocca di Cispiano '95	**YY**	5
●	Chianti Classico '95	YY	4
●	Chianti Classico Ris. '90	YY	4*
●	Rocca di Cispiano '94	YY	5
●	Chianti Classico '90	Y	4
●	Chianti Classico '91	Y	4

CASTELLINA IN CHIANTI (SI)

★ Castello di Fonterutoli

Loc. Fonterutoli Via Rossini, 5
53011 Castellina in Chianti (SI)
tel. 0577/740476

Big changes at Fonterutoli: with a farsighted, almost drastic decision they have struck two of their classic wines from their list. As of this year Concerto and Chianti Classico Ser Lapo are no more. In their place we find a Chianti Classico Riserva, called Castello di Fonterutoli, which is destined to be their "grand vin" from now on. It is a modern wine, sangiovese-based with 10% cabernet sauvignon, which is about as much as DOC regulations will allow. More than 100 thousand bottles were produced, enough to make it a contender on the international market. In quality, it falls somewhere between its predecessors, Concerto and Ser Lapo. It's a little less concentrated than Concerto, and has a little more grip and character than Ser Lapo. The aromas reveal the presence of the cabernet, which is neither dominant nor vegetal. The acidity conferred by the sangiovese is a significant presence on the palate, but it underpins a really noteworthy body. Three Glasses its first time out: not a bad beginning. But the real show-stopper once again this year is the Siepi '96, an equal mix of sangiovese and merlot. It doesn't have quite the explosive power of the '95 vintage, which was perhaps last year's best Tuscan wine, but it is softer than ever on the palate and wonderfully concentrated. With these two wines, the Fonterutoli estate earns a star for its more than ten Three Glasses. The "standard" Chianti Classico '96 is excellent, a smaller wine than the Riserva, but simply delicious, love at first sip. The other newcomer, the Morellino di Scansano '97, is surprising as well. It hails from the Tenuta di Belguardo, which also belongs to the Mazzei family. It is an extremely fruity red, simple and immediate, but with excellent concentration. You'll be wanting barrels of it.

	Wine	Glasses	Price
●	Chianti Classico Castello di Fonterutoli Ris. '95	**YYY**	5
●	Siepi '96	**YYY**	6
●	Chianti Classico '96	**YY**	4
●	Morellino di Scansano Belguardo '97	**YY**	3*
●	Chianti Classico Ser Lapo Ris. '90	YYY	5
●	Concerto '86	YYY	5
●	Concerto '90	YYY	5
●	Concerto '93	YYY	5
●	Concerto '94	YYY	5
●	Siepi '93	YYY	5
●	Siepi '94	YYY	6
●	Siepi '95	YYY	6
●	Concerto '88	YY	5

CASTELLINA IN CHIANTI (SI)

Podere La Brancaia

Loc. Brancaia
53011 Castellina in Chianti (SI)
tel. 0577/743084

No repeat this year of last year's stunning performance with the '94 vintage Brancaia, a sangiovese-based red with a touch of added merlot, which took our breath away. Brancaia '95 is a more austere and leaner wine, and lacks the enticing smoothness of the '94 vintage, one which is often dismissed as minor but is providing quite a number of surprises. Most importantly, Brancaia '95 is not as well-balanced, though the concentration is there. The tannic and acid components are more jostlingly apparent, the aromas are elegant, with characteristic sangiovese fruitiness in evidence, but it's not as easy to drink, and the complexity on the palate is not yet harmonious. Predicting the development of a wine like this one is about as easy as picking the winning lottery ticket. The Chianti Classico '96 is less of a mystery. This is a simpler wine, of course, but an extremely elegant and well-balanced one, with delicate fruity aromas, in which sour cherries and plums emerge. The tannins are right on target: they underpin the wine's body and don't make your mouth pucker. With its tannins not emphasized by the acidity, this wine is soft and stylish. These two wines finally got almost the same score. What we'd like to know is what we can expect of the Brancaia '96, which will be out in a few months.

	Wine	Glasses	Price
●	Brancaia '95	**YY**	6
●	Chianti Classico '96	**YY**	4
●	Brancaia '94	YYY	6
●	Brancaia '88	YY	6
●	Brancaia '90	YY	6
●	Brancaia '91	YY	6
●	Brancaia '93	YY	5
●	Chianti Classico '95	YY	4

Castello di Lilliano

Loc. Lilliano
53011 Castellina in Chianti (SI)
tel. 0577/743070

This standard-bearer of Chianti tradition has partly given up its role this year and has just missed getting Three Glasses with a somewhat untraditional wine. Anagallis '95 is a sangiovese-based red with a small amount of canaiolo (no offense to tradition so far), but matured in small barrels and unembellished by a Chianti Classico DOCG on its label, which suggests that the time-honored canons have not been strictly observed. We could hardly care less. We like a wine to reflect its terroir and Anagallis certainly does just that. In the aromas you can just about recognize the fragrant flowering linden trees lining the road at the entrance to the Castello di Lilliano. The flavor is lively and sinewy, which is as Chianti-born a characteristic as one can find, and the concentration excellent. But one does rather wonder why in the name of heaven this magnificent Chianti Classico, (because that is what it really is), doesn't call itself that. This is the question we would ask Giulio Ruspoli Berlingieri, prince and farmer, and proud possessor of that little corner of heaven called Lilliano. The other two wines presented for tasting were less striking. The Chianti Classico '96 was a bit old-fashioned. We found the Chianti Classico Riserva '95 somewhat thin, but really not at all bad, and in the end it holds its own against the memory of that delicious standard Chianti Classico of the same vintage which we reviewed in the last edition of the Guide. High marks for what could be considered the alter ego of Lilliano's wines, the very modern merlot, Vigna Catena '95, which is aged in small oak barrels. Its aromas are characteristic and elegant and its palate is soft, with delicate sweet tannins.

	Wine	Glasses	Price
●	Anagallis '95	TT	5
●	Chianti Classico Ris. '95	TT	4*
●	Vigna Catena '95	TT	5
●	Chianti Classico '96		3
●	Chianti Classico E. Ruspoli Berlingieri Ris. '85	YYY	6
●	Anagallis '88	YY	5
●	Anagallis '90	YY	5
●	Chianti Classico E. Ruspoli Berlingieri '88	YY	4
●	Chianti Classico '88	YY	3*
●	Chianti Classico '90	YY	3*
●	Chianti Classico '95	YY	3*
●	Chianti Classico Ris. '90	YY	4*
●	Chianti Classico Ris. '94	YY	4

Fattoria Nittardi

Loc. Nittardi
53011 Castellina in Chianti (SI)
tel. 0577/740269

The fabled elegance of Peter Femfert's Fattoria di Nittardi Chianti Classico wines is again in evidence this year. But we feel a little disappointed. We had felt sure that, with its Riserva '95, this estate would put up a good fight for Three Glasses, which it has often come close to winning. But, though a very interesting wine, the Riserva '95 is just a bit lacking in concentration, which keeps it back once again from rising to the top. It is, however, an excellent Chianti Classico Riserva, with wonderfully elegant, well-articulated aromas including toasty and mineral notes against a clear fruity background. On the palate, however, somewhat disagreeable rough-edged tannins and acidity get in the way of easy drinking. The Chianti Classico Casanuova di Nittardi '96, an extremely pleasant wine which makes no claims to greatness and is much more approachable, almost seems a better wine. So Fattoria Nittardi is still on our waiting list for the time being, although they have again produced an excellent range of wines. But we expect something greater from Femfert and his oenologist Carlo Ferrini, and we feel sure that in '96 or '97 we'll get it.

	Wine	Glasses	Price
●	Chianti Classico '96	TT	4
●	Chianti Classico Ris. '95	TT	5
●	Chianti Classico '91	YY	4
●	Chianti Classico '93	YY	4
●	Chianti Classico '95	YY	4
●	Chianti Classico Ris. '88	YY	4
●	Chianti Classico Ris. '90	YY	5
●	Chianti Classico Ris. '93	YY	4
●	Chianti Classico Ris. '94	YY	5
●	Chianti Classico '90	Y	3
●	Chianti Classico '92	Y	4
●	Chianti Classico '94	Y	3

CASTELLINA IN CHIANTI (SI)

Rocca delle Macìe

Loc. Macìe
53011 Castellina in Chianti (SI)
tel. 0577/7321

We were again favorably impressed by the performance of Rocca delle Macìe. Hence this profile in the Guide for Italo and Sergio Zingarelli's big and important winery, a profile dominated by the best version ever of their most significant wine, the monovarietal sangiovese Ser Gioveto '95. This is a majestically imposing red, intensely fruity on the nose, with vanilla and sour cherries rising to the fore, and a broad, rich, soft palate, in the best tradition of Rocca delle Macìe wines. But that's not all. The two Chianti Classico Riserva '95s on offer, the standard version and especially the Fizzano selection, more concentrated and substantial in the mouth, also do very well. The Roccato '95 isn't bad: a sangiovese/cabernet sauvignon blend that could be faulted for excess simplicity, but is a correctly executed wine. To finish, the two '96 Chianti Classicos, the standard version, well made and pleasing but nothing more, and the Tenuta Sant'Alfonso, which we found more convincing. Rocca delle Macìe gives the overall impression of a reliable winery offering good value for money, and which is starting to propose wine (the Ser Gioveto) that's good, period. It is all very encouraging, and an indication of the enormous progress made here, particularly in vinification technique.

Wine	Rating	Price
● Ser Gioveto '95	🍷🍷	5
● Chianti Classico '96	🍷	2*
● Chianti Classico Fizzano Ris. '95	🍷	4
● Chianti Classico Ris. '95	🍷	3*
● Chianti Classico Tenuta S.Alfonso '96	🍷	3
● Roccato '95	🍷	4
● Chianti Classico Fizzano Ris. '93	🍷🍷 (white)	5
● Chianti Classico Tenuta S. Alfonso '95	🍷🍷 (white)	3*
● Roccato '93	🍷🍷 (white)	5
● Ser Gioveto '85	🍷🍷 (white)	5
● Ser Gioveto '86	🍷🍷 (white)	5
● Ser Gioveto '88	🍷🍷 (white)	5
● Ser Gioveto '94	🍷🍷 (white)	5

Rodano

Loc. Rodano
53011 Castellina in Chianti (SI)
tel. 0577/743107

This estate is listed once again after a year's absence. Its owner, Vittorio Pozzesi, was president of the Consorzio del Chianti Classico in a very important period in its history, when the new DOCG regulations were adopted. His son Enrico oversees the vineyards and the cellar, while Enrico's brother Alberto focuses on the business end of the operation. There are a number of novelties in store for the next few years: thanks to the new Italian law assisting young entrepreneurs, Enrico will be able to plant an additional seven hectares of vineyards, which will be added to the twenty hectares already under vine, while the monovarietal merlot harvested in '97 is set for its debut (we'll be tasting it for next year's edition). Turning to this year's results, the Chianti Classico '96 was the least convincing of the Rodano wines we tasted. It has pleasant, intensely fruity aromas, but the meek entry on the palate hints immediately at a certain thinness, which is confirmed by a short finish. The Riserva Viacosta '95 did better. It is of a deep ruby hue, with lovely cherry and black currant tones on the nose. The attack on the palate is full and juicy, backed up by densely woven and well-integrated tannins. The finish is long and smooth. Finally, and best of all, the Monna Claudia '95, a sangiovese/cabernet blend. Its color is a rich and definite ruby red. On the nose, after the first pleasing fruity fragrance, an array of complex and deep aromas emerges. The attack on the palate is not imposing, but then the wine opens up and displays considerable complexity, with tannins and alcohol harmoniously integrated.

Wine	Rating	Price
● Chianti Classico Viacosta Ris. '95	🍷🍷	4
● Monna Claudia '95	🍷🍷	4
● Chianti Classico '96		3
● Chianti Classico Viacosta Ris. '86	🍷🍷 (white)	4
● Chianti Classico Viacosta Ris. '88	🍷🍷 (white)	4
● Chianti Classico Viacosta Ris. '90	🍷🍷 (white)	4
● Monna Claudia '88	🍷🍷 (white)	5
● Chianti Classico '90	🍷 (white)	3
● Chianti Classico '93	🍷 (white)	3
● Chianti Classico '94	🍷 (white)	3*

CASTELLINA IN CHIANTI (SI)

San Fabiano Calcinaia

Loc. Cellole
53011 Castellina in Chianti (SI)
tel. 0577/979232

For some time at San Fabiano, Three Glasses were only just beyond their reach. Such was the case with the Chianti Classico Riserva from the Cellole vineyard, and again with their sangiovese-based red with 30% cabernet sauvignon, Cerviolo. But it had to happen eventually. And, as is always the case, it couldn't happen until the time was ripe. It took a quirky and surprising vintage like '96. And it also took Carlo Ferrini, who started work as consulting oenologist here that very year. But it particularly took that touch of madness so characteristic of Guido Serio, the Milan-based Florentine financier with a passion for the vineyards of Chianti Classico. This year's is the first bull's-eye, the first of many, we are sure, and it goes to the magnificent Cerviolo '96. This is a red with complex, intensely fruity aromas, its new oak tones nearly perfectly blended (it's just a question of a little more time in the bottle) in an aristocratic and refined bouquet. Its palate is almost magically harmonious, with sweet tannins part and parcel of a dense, long-lasting structure. A true masterpiece. The Chianti Classico Cellole Riserva '95 came awfully close to a bull's-eye too. It's very impressive, and with a little more concentration it would have hit it. And, in its category, the standard Chianti Classico '96 is no sluggard. It's a smaller wine, of course, but very drinkable and quite charming. Altogether their range of wines is of an excellence that few other Chianti estates can equal this year.

	Wine	Glasses	Price
●	Cerviolo Rosso '96	🍷🍷🍷	5
●	Chianti Classico '96	🍷🍷	3*
●	Chianti Classico Cellole Ris. '95	🍷🍷	4*
●	Cerviolo Rosso '91	🍷🍷 (white)	5
●	Cerviolo Rosso '95	🍷🍷 (white)	5
●	Chianti Classico '95	🍷🍷 (white)	3
●	Chianti Classico Cellole Ris. '90	🍷🍷 (white)	4
●	Chianti Classico Cellole Ris. '93	🍷🍷 (white)	4
●	Cerviolo Rosso '93	🍷 (white)	4
●	Cerviolo Rosso '94	🍷 (white)	5
●	Chianti Classico '91	🍷 (white)	4

CASTELLINA IN CHIANTI (SI)

Tramonti

Loc. Tramonti
53011 Castellina in Chianti (SI)
tel. 0577/741205

The fact that we add new estates to this section of the Guide each year is another sign of the vitality of Tuscan viticulture. Tramonti has just started out, and very well too, so it seemed natural to devote a profile to it. The American husband and wife team of Martin and Kile Kolk, under the well-known spell of Tuscany and of the Chianti countryside in particular, purchased the estate in 1995. It is located in the sought-after Castellina in Chianti zone and comprises 60 hectares, most of which are occupied by woods and olive groves. It is the small vineyard, however, which is of most interest. An additional five acres will probably be planted next year, a testimony to their growing commitment. The young Marco Mazzarrini is in charge of both vineyard and cellar, and his passion and talent shine through in the estate's first wine, released this year. The Chianti Classico '96, a monovarietal sangiovese, underwent relatively long maceration and then spent a year in barriques from Allier and Nevers, where it naturally completed its malolactic fermentation. Light clarification took place before assemblage, so the wine was bottled without filtration. We found the result outstanding. The aromas are dense and concentrated, with characteristic notes of sour cherry and violets. The palate provides further evidence that this is a traditional Chianti Classico: the entry is sweet and inviting, the tannins mature, all following through to a classic and elegant finish.

	Wine	Glasses	Price
●	Chianti Classico '96	🍷🍷	4

CASTELLINA MARITTIMA (PI)

TENUTA DEL TERRICCIO
LOC. LE BADIE
VIA BAGNOLI
56100 CASTELLINA MARITTIMA (PI)
TEL. 050/699709

Let us be frank: it has become extremely difficult for us to invent anything new to write about the Tenuta del Terriccio. What can we possibly say about an estate which, with disarming regularity, offers up wines that win Three Glasses with the unanimous votes of our merciless tasting panels, and with an average score well above the minimum requirement for pinning down the prize? Needless to say, the Lupicaia '96 is the latest jewel in Terriccio's collection. Lovely to look at, seductive to sniff, it has those well-known balsamic notes (eucalyptus to the fore) providing distinction and distinguishability to this cabernet and merlot blend, but never until now so harmoniously mixed with the rich untouched freshness of the fruit. The palate is entrancing and in continuous progression, with deep, silky tannins. A similar blend, but with a significant addition of sangiovese, goes into the Tassinaia '96, which is very good as usual, with its perfectly balanced palate and intense, multifaceted aromas. The Rondinaia '97, a chardonnay/sauvignon blend, does not let down the side: an exemplary nose with lots of fruit, and then sweetly round and mouth-filling, further proof that oak isn't indispensable for an excellent white wine. The Sauvignon Con Vento '97 is also vinified in steel containers to keep the varietal aromas fresh and pure. The flavor is well-articulated and pleasing but it doesn't have the structure of the Rondinaia. In conclusion, we note that the Saluccio, their only oak-fermented white, will not be ready until next year, but if it's as good as it promises to be...

	Wine	Glasses	
●	Lupicaia '96	3 (black)	6
○	Rondinaia '97	2 (black)	4
●	Tassinaia '96	2 (black)	5
○	Con Vento '97	1 (black)	4
●	Lupicaia '93	3 (white)	5
●	Lupicaia '95	3 (white)	6
○	Con Vento '94	2 (white)	3
●	Lupicaia '94	2 (white)	6
○	Rondinaia '96	2 (white)	4
○	Saluccio '96	2 (white)	4
●	Tassinaia '93	2 (white)	4
●	Tassinaia '94	2 (white)	5
●	Tassinaia '95	2 (white)	5
●	Le Tassinaie '92	1 (white)	3*
●	Lupicaia '91	1 (white)	5*

CASTELNUOVO BERARDENGA (SI)

FATTORIA DELL'AIOLA
LOC. VAGLIAGLI
53010 CASTELNUOVO
BERARDENGA (SI)
TEL. 0577/322615

The vineyards of the Fattoria dell'Aiola estate are located in the southernmost part of Chianti Classico country, just a few miles from Siena's city walls. This area, bordering Chianti and the Crete Senesi, is a magical one for grape- and olive-growing, with a landscape that is not easily forgotten. The wines produced here, almost exclusively sangiovese-based reds, are powerful and generous, with aromas of sour cherry and leather more reminiscent of Brunello than of the northern reaches of the Chianti Classico zone, with its elegant floral and fruity bouquets. The wines of Maria Grazia Malagodi, daughter of the late Senator Giovanni Malagodi, one of the great fathers of the Italian Republic, are no exception to this rule. With the help of the expert oenologist Nicolò d'Afflitto, the estate has presented a range of excellent reds this year. The best of them, we found, was the Chianti Classico Riserva '95, with the freshest, fruitiest aromas of the bunch, and the liveliest and most elegant palate. We enjoyed the Logaiolo '94 too, a sangiovese-based red with some cabernet sauvignon. We reviewed it last year, and it seems to be holding its own, apart from a slightly gamey note on the nose that we'd prefer to notice less. The Rosso del Senatore '95 is not bad either, a sangiovese with a little merlot and colorino. It's a wine that was made with higher things in mind, but to us it seemed a bit simple and dominated by slightly vegetal aromas. The Chianti Classico '96 is an honest, well-made wine that delivers what it promises.

	Wine	Glasses	
●	Chianti Classico Ris. '95	2 (black)	4
●	Chianti Classico '96	1 (black)	3
●	Rosso del Senatore '95	1 (black)	5
●	Chianti Classico Ris. '90	2 (white)	5
●	Chianti Classico Ris. '94	2 (white)	4
●	Chianti Classico '91	1 (white)	4
●	Chianti Classico '93	1 (white)	3
●	Chianti Classico '94	1 (white)	3
●	Chianti Classico '95	1 (white)	3
●	Chianti Classico Ris. '88	1 (white)	5
●	Logaiolo '91	1 (white)	5
●	Logaiolo '94	1 (white)	5
●	Rosso del Senatore '90	1 (white)	5

Castello di Bossi

Loc. Bossi in Chianti
53010 Castelnuovo
Berardenga (SI)
tel. 0577/359330

This is one of the most magical parts of the Chianti Classico region. Here the Crete Senesi meet the confines of the characteristic rocky terrain of Chianti. The hills are gentler and the landscape much more open than in the heart of Chianti. This is real Siena countryside, between San Gusmè and Vagliagli, northwest of Castelnuovo Berardenga and just a stone's throw from Piazza del Campo. And here are the Castello di Bossi and its vineyards, precisely where the sangiovese grape does best, if it is treated properly both on the vine and in the cellar. And the treatment is certainly proper if it's dispensed by the able hands of the expert oenologist Andrea Mazzoni. Proof is available this year in the form of an outstanding Chianti Classico Riserva '95, called Berardo. This is a splendid wine that came very close to earning Three Glasses, having been eliminated only in the final round of tasting. It features ripe fruit aromas with hints of vanilla and pencil lead, together with big, rich, mellow, lasting flavor, dominated by sweet tannins and a Brunello-like structure. It was a great surprise, and really outstanding in its category. We can but suggest you taste it, and that you keep an eye on this estate, which is clearly capable of other wonders in the future. The less interesting Chianti Classico '96 has over-developed aromas and a slightly flabby taste. They have not yet released the Coniale '95, so we shall have to wait until next year.

Wine	Glasses	Price
● Chianti Classico Berardo Ris. '95	**YY**	5
● Chianti Classico '96		3
● Chianti Classico Ris. '94	YY	4
● Corbaia '94	YY	5
● Chianti Classico '94	Y	3
● Chianti Classico '95	Y	3*

CASTELNUOVO BERARDENGA (SI)

Fattoria di Dievole

Loc. Dievole
53019 Castelnuovo
Berardenga (SI)
tel. 0577/322613

The Dievole estate weighs in with a fine performance again this year: the five wines presented were all on target. We have yet to taste a really exceptional wine from this winery, but they have produced one of the best and most interesting collections in Chianti. The pick of the bunch this time was the Broccato '95, a monovarietal sangiovese red with intense aromas, featuring mildly vegetal notes against a characteristic and distinct fruity background. The palate is dominated by an acidity that is, however, well-integrated into the structure of the wine. The finish is long, and the polyphenolic concentration satisfactory. The Chianti Classico Riserva '95 was not dissimilar, but was probably aged differently. It's a bit less intense in both taste and aroma, but it is certainly well-made and does not belie its origins. The Chianti Classico Novecento '95 offers elegant and very fruity aromas, is soft on the palate and rather resembles the two Chiantis described above, so that one rather wonders about the point of making three separate wines that differ so little. The Rinascimento '95, a sangiovese/cabernet sauvignon blend, is definitely of a different stripe, but it is the wine we liked the least of the batch. It is a bit too oaky on the nose, and has a body that fails to impress. However, from a technical standpoint we have no complaints. Finally, the Chianti Classico '96 is an excellent wine of its kind, simple but well-articulated and highly drinkable.

Wine	Glasses	Price
● Broccato '95	**YY**	4
● Chianti Classico '96	**YY**	3*
● Chianti Classico Novecento '95	**YY**	4
● Chianti Classico Ris. '95	**YY**	4
● Rinascimento '95	**Y**	4
● Chianti Classico Novecento '93	YY	4
● Chianti Classico Novecento '94	YY	4
● Chianti Classico Ris. '93	YY	4
● Broccato '93	Y	4
● Broccato '94	Y	4
● Chianti Classico '93	Y	3
● Chianti Classico '95	Y	3
● Chianti Classico Dieulele '93	Y	4
● Rinascimento '93	Y	4
● Rinascimento '94	Y	4

★ Fattoria di Felsina

Strada Chiantigiana, 484
53019 Castelnuovo
Berardenga (SI)
tel. 0577/355117

The Fattoria di Felsina maintains its position as Tuscany's Three Glass leader, with 12 top ratings to its credit on the occasion of the guide's twelfth edition. The winner this year is a wine whose praises we had already sung in the past, but one which is rather unusual for an estate that has always shown a preference for big sangiovese-based reds. The wine in question, Maestro Raro '93, made from cabernet sauvignon, was easily the best that the "art director" Giuseppe Mazzocolin and Franco Bernabei, the consultant oenologist, provided for tasting. Maestro Raro '93 is a profound and complex red, in which you would have trouble finding vegetal or grassy hints, so apparent are the notes of fruit, tobacco, leather and new oak on the nose. The tannins almost fool the palate into thinking it is tasting a Bordeaux. They are dense, compact and velvety, already well-blended into a rich, concentrated structure. As for sangiovese wines, on the other hand, we tasted good ones, but no real thoroughbred. The Chianti Classico Rancia Riserva '95 is a bit closed on the nose, with acidity taking over on the palate. The Fontalloro '94 is immediately pleasing, even soft on the palate and easily drinkable thanks to its being less concentrated than is its wont. The Chianti Classico Riserva '95 is acceptable, but a bit thin, and its nose is not all it should be . But the Chianti Classico '96 is an excellent, full-bodied and surprisingly rich wine. It is certainly among the best of its vintage.

	Wine	Glasses	Price
●	Maestro Raro '93	🍷🍷🍷	6
●	Chianti Classico '96	🍷🍷	4
●	Chianti Classico Rancia Ris. '95	🍷🍷	5
●	Fontalloro '94	🍷🍷	6
●	Chianti Classico Ris. '95	🍷	4
●	Chianti Classico Rancia Ris. '86	YYY	5
●	Chianti Classico Rancia Ris. '88	YYY	5
●	Chianti Classico Rancia Ris. '90	YYY	5
●	Chianti Classico Rancia Ris. '93	YYY	5
●	Chianti Classico Ris. '90	YYY	4*
●	Fontalloro '86	YYY	5
●	Fontalloro '88	YYY	5
●	Fontalloro '90	YYY	5
●	Fontalloro '93	YYY	6
●	Maestro Raro '91	YYY	5

Le Trame

Loc. Le Bonce
53010 Castelnuovo
Berardenga (SI)
tel. 0577/359116

We are delighted to be reviewing Giovanna Morganti's minuscule winery once again. At last we have managed to taste the Chianti Classico '95, and can now give it the space it deserves. We had been warned by Giovanna that it might seem harsh, as it is a monovarietal sangiovese, and she was afraid this would put us off. But we, who are by no means cabernet freaks, will surprise her this time. We didn't like her wine, we loved it. The '95 vintage is still a bit rough around the edges, but this is par for the course as far as '95 goes, so no surprises here. As always, what's most important is the wine's balance, and in this case there are no faults to be found. Le Trame's Chianti Classico '95 is a mouth-filling, full-bodied wine. Its tannins are still apparent, but time and a bottle can work miracles. The aromas are well-articulated and characteristic of sangiovese. This is a stunning reappearance by Le Trame, proof positive of Giovanna Morganti's ability to meet the challenges both of that recalcitrant and feisty sangiovese vine and of an equally difficult terrain, the southernmost part of the Chianti Classico zone.

	Wine	Glasses	Price
●	Chianti Classico '95	🍷🍷	4
●	Chianti Classico '90	YY	4
●	Chianti Classico '92	YY	4
●	Chianti Classico '93	YY	4
●	Chianti Classico '94	YY	4

CASTELNUOVO BERARDENGA (SI)

PACINA

LOC. PACINA
53019 CASTELNUOVO
BERARDENGA (SI)
TEL. 0577/355044 - 0577/355037

Giovanna Tiezzi's appealing estate is back in these pages after a year's absence. Pacina is extraordinary in that it straddles the border of the Chianti Classico zone: the river Malena, which gives its name to Pacina's newest offering, separates the winery from its vineyards. Because of a few yards' distance, Pacina's labels must read "Colli Senesi" instead of the more prestigious "Chianti Classico". However the intelligent director of the estate has chosen to glory in the difference, rather than regard it as a disadvantage. Indeed, despite the merciless borders that separate the Chianti Classico zone from the land of lesser mortals, the Chianti dei Colli Senesi di Pacina '95 is more classic than many a Classico. Perhaps we should simply say that it is the best Colli Senesi wine we have had the pleasure of tasting this year. It has a vivid ruby hue, its intense aromas suggest sour cherry, blackberry and violets, with a light touch of toasty wood. Its sangiovese characteristics re-emerge on the palate, with a good level of alcohol-induced warmth complemented by typical sinewy acidity. The fruit, the softness of the tannins and the long finish complete the picture, which can hardly fail to please. The Malena, a 50-50 sangiovese/syrah blend, is a very interesting debutant. Its color is of moderate intensity, and blackberries and cherries dominate the nose, though there are also some not yet perfectly blended notes of oak. The palate is particularly successful: the sweet and slightly over-ripe syrah notes are delightfully balanced by the lively acidity of the sangiovese, forming an impressive whole.

	Wine	Glasses	Price
●	Chianti Colli Senesi '95	🍷🍷	4
●	Malena '96	🍷	5
●	Chianti Colli Senesi '88	YY	3
●	Chianti Colli Senesi '90	YY	4
●	Chianti Colli Senesi '89	Y	3
●	Chianti Colli Senesi '91	Y	3
●	Chianti Colli Senesi '93	Y	3
●	Chianti Colli Senesi '94	Y	3

CASTELNUOVO BERARDENGA (SI)

FATTORIA DI PETROIO

LOC. QUERCEGROSSA
VIA DI PETROIO, 43
53010 CASTELNUOVO
BERARDENGA (SI)
TEL. 0577/328045

If you should ever succeed in getting hold of a real Chianina steak, the kind that should be grilled over slow-burning oak embers and then seasoned with extra virgin olive oil and a dash of salt, don't forget to open a bottle of Chianti Classico '96 from Gian Luigi and Pamela Lenzi's Fattoria di Petroio. It may not be the best there is, but if we had to choose a fruity, immediately pleasing, drinkable but not commonplace Chianti Classico, this would be one of the first to come to mind. This year the nose seems even better, as if some older barrels had been replaced, and the fragrant cherry and plum aromas are clearer than ever. The Riserva '95 is also an excellent wine, but then it comes from a wonderful vintage, especially wonderful for those who could wait until the end of October to harvest their grapes. In the case of Petroio it was the oenologist/agronomist Carlo Ferrini who gave the sign to start picking, and there are some things he never gets wrong. As a result, this wine is full and concentrated on the palate, with aromas revealing ripe fruit of good complexity. Overall, this is one of the best showings ever for this winery virtually on Siena's doorstep.

	Wine	Glasses	Price
●	Chianti Classico '96	🍷🍷	3*
●	Chianti Classico Ris. '95	🍷🍷	4
●	Chianti Classico '90	YY	3*
●	Chianti Classico '91	YY	3*
●	Chianti Classico '93	YY	2*
●	Chianti Classico '95	YY	3*
●	Chianti Classico Ris. '90	YY	4*
●	Chianti Classico '94	Y	3*
●	Chianti Classico Ris. '93	Y	4

CASTELNUOVO BERARDENGA (SI)

SAN FELICE
LOC. SAN FELICE
53019 CASTELNUOVO
BERARDENGA (SI)
TEL. 0577/359087 - 359088

All of the wines that this important and lovely Chianti estate presented this year were simply wonderful, a further sign of their commitment and also that they knew how to get the best out of the extraordinary '95 vintage. The Chianti Classico Poggio Rosso Riserva '95 is a truly great wine on an international level and is quite simply a masterful interpretation of what is best about the terroir of San Felice. On the nose we found slightly spicy aromas with tones of red and, in the background, balsamic wood. The palate is extremely well-balanced, with sweet, dense tannins and an acidity which is entirely blended into the structure, together with persistence and concentration. A Three Glass winner, without a doubt. The Vigorello '95 makes up in large part for its minor setback of '94. A blend of sangiovese and cabernet sauvignon, its balsamic aromas reveal faint vegetal notes and hints of Jesuits' bark. In the mouth it's soft and concentrated. The velvety tannins have no puckering effect. The Chianti Classico '96 is excellent of its kind, very drinkable and fragrant, and, incidentally, a very good buy. The Chianti Classico Il Grigio Riserva '95 is as good as ever, a wine you can count on. The fruit on the nose is riper than the Poggio Rosso's, and its palate is rich and soft, but somewhat lacking in variation. Hats off to the entire staff of San Felice, and especially to their master oenologist Leonardo Bellaccini.

	Wine	Glasses	Price
●	Chianti Classico Poggio Rosso Ris. '95	🍷🍷🍷	5
●	Chianti Classico '96	🍷🍷	3*
●	Chianti Classico Il Grigio Ris. '95	🍷🍷	4
●	Vigorello '95	🍷🍷	5
●	Chianti Classico Poggio Rosso Ris. '90	♀♀♀	4
●	Vigorello '88	♀♀♀	5
●	Chianti Cl. Poggio Rosso Ris. '86	♀♀	4
●	Chianti Cl. Poggio Rosso Ris. '93	♀♀	4
●	Chianti Cl. Poggio Rosso Ris. '94	♀♀	5
●	Chianti Classico Il Grigio Ris. '90	♀♀	4
●	Vigorello '90	♀♀	5
●	Vigorello '93	♀♀	5
●	Chianti Classico Il Grigio Ris. '93	♀	4

CASTIGLIONE DELLA PESCAIA (GR)

HARALD BREMER
PODERE SAN MICHELE
LOC. VETULONIA
58040 CASTIGLIONE
DELLA PESCAIA (GR)
TEL. 0564/939060

He's been called a trouble-maker and an inflexible despot. Others find him haughty and rather sure of himself. Whatever he's like, it's Harald Bremer's wines that interest us. With the help of his son Bodo, Harald has been making wine in Tuscany, in the hilly region of Vetulonia near Grosseto, for decades. His yields per hectare are low, he is a stickler for scrupulous care in the cellar (well beyond the legendary Teutonic passion for precision), and he makes shrewd use of small oak barrels for aging. Somehow it all works together to produce great results. The Vetluna Cabernet Sauvignon '95 is really excellent. Incredibly deep and intense in its lively bright ruby hue, it has a nose with intriguing ripe, full wild berry notes, backed up by well-articulated new oak which is innocent of vulgar excess. With its distinct, meaty, concentrated, elegant palate, this is a wine of international status. If the term were not rather hackneyed, we might even have called this wine a real super-Tuscan. We didn't get a chance this year to taste the estate's second red, the Montereggio di Massa Marittima Rosso.

	Wine	Glasses	Price
●	Vetluna Cabernet Sauvignon '95	🍷🍷	5
●	Vetluna Cabernet Sauvignon '94	♀♀	5
●	Monteregio di Massa Marittima Rosso Vetluna '94	♀	3

CHIUSI (SI)

FICOMONTANINO
LOC. FICOMONTANINO
53043 CHIUSI (SI)
TEL. 0578/21180 - 06/5561283

Among the lesser-known Tuscan wineries, the Ficomontanino estate deserves special mention. Despite its less than aristocratic-sounding name, it holds its own with august titles in the world of wine. Its vineyards grow along the eastern reaches of the province of Siena, and include both traditional local grapes, most notably sangiovese, and such fashionable varietals as cabernet and sauvignon blanc. This year once again the range of wines on offer provides reassuring proof of technical expertise and constant quality. We'll begin with the Chianti Colli Senesi Tutulus, a red wine with a nose dominated by new oak tones and a sweet, spicy palate full of fruit. Two to three years of bottle age should help this wine to reabsorb at least a part of the overly-present wood. The Lucumone, this estate's most ambitious red, is a monovarietal cabernet sauvignon. The rather grassy aromas are more typical of cabernet franc. Clean, fresh and fruity, it has moderate extract and a long finish. In conclusion, we salute the white Porsenna '97, a fragrant sauvignon less rich in barrique-derived tones than the '96, but perhaps also more successful both in extract and in the fine balance on the palate.

	Wine	Glasses	Price
●	Chianti Colli Senesi Tutulus '96	🍷🍷	3
●	Porsenna '97	🍷🍷	4
●	Lucumone '96	🍷	5
●	Chianti Colli Senesi Tutulus '95	🍷🍷 (white)	3
●	Lucumone '95	🍷🍷 (white)	5
●	Porsenna '96	🍷 (white)	4

COLLE VAL D'ELSA (SI)

IL PALAGIO
LOC. CASTEL S. GIMIGNANO
53034 COLLE VAL D'ELSA (SI)
TEL. 0577/953004

The Palagio estate, which is owned by the giant winery Zonin, is located in Castel San Gimignano, bordering the territory of Colle Val d'Elsa, of which it is considered part for administrative purposes, although it has recently been counted as belonging to th Vernaccia di San Gimignano zone. It includes the 25 hectares of vernaccia vineyards of the Abbazia di Monteoliveto, in the shadow of San Gimignano and its celebrated medieval towers. The business strategy of the winery is clear, and has indeed made the Zonin brothers famous. The most surprising wine on offer was again the Sauvignon '97: the many varietal characteristics it displays were such as comfortably to earn it Two Glasses. Furthermore, the sauvignon was mechanically harvested, which could even be the reason that its aromatic, vegetal notes are so intense. It's a wine you could use at a tasting to illustrate the qualities of this grape. Straw-yellow in color, it has an intense nose with characteristic aromas of tomato leaves and mint that are echoed on the palate and all the way through the finish, with a fairly full and balanced body. Its tasters and drinkers will certainly be talking about it. The '97 version of the Vernaccia La Gentilesca, obtained from the vines that grow near the old Monteoliveto church at San Gimignano, is excellent. A pale straw-yellow color is followed by floral and fruity aromas with a background note of vanilla. It is fairly persistent and fat in the mouth and its finish is good. The Vernaccia Abbazia di Monteoliveto '97 is interesting as well. It is pale straw-yellow in color, with faint aromas of flowers and fruit, and it doesn't have much of a finish, but it is a lean, balanced, well-made wine.

	Wine	Glasses	Price
○	Il Palagio Sauvignon '97	🍷🍷	2*
○	Vernaccia di S. Gimignano Abbazia di Monteoliveto '97	🍷	2
○	Vernaccia di S. Gimignano Abbazia Monteoliveto La Gentilesca '97	🍷	4
●	Chianti Colli Senesi Il Palagio '95	🍷 (white)	2
○	Il Palagio Sauvignon '95	🍷 (white)	2
○	Vernaccia di S. Gimignano Abbazia Monteoliveto La Gentilesca '95	🍷 (white)	3

CORTONA (AR)

TENIMENTI D'ALESSANDRO
LOC. CAMUCIA
VIA DI MANZANO, 15
52044 CORTONA (AR)
TEL. 0575/618667

There are few Tuscan estates that can vaunt such a tangible leap in quality as the one taken by Tenimenti D'Alessandro (formerly the Fattoria di Manzano) over the last few years. After a well-intentioned beginning practically from scratch in terms of grape-growing and wine-making techniques, the D'Alessandro brothers have drawn on their intuition and financial courage to create a winery of the highest quality in an astoundingly short time. Their star has risen rapidly, with a series of national and international distinctions including our Three Glasses for their syrah Podere del Bosco in the last edition of the Guide. The most recent vintages offer proof positive of this happy trend, though there are signs here and there that further progress is needed. One wine in particular seems more opaque than usual this year: the Podere Il Vescovo, a gamay-based red whose '97 version shows various defects on both nose and palate. Their top wine, the much more successful Podere del Bosco, has the rare ability to unite great elegance with imposing structure. The '96 offers very satisfying extract underlying a broad aromatic structure including woodland fruit, white pepper and spice; there is a full tannic taste which is at the moment somewhat bitter and in need of further blending. Perhaps it doesn't have all the refinement of the '95, but it's a success nonetheless. Their sauvignon, Le Terrazze '97, an intense, clean wine with delightful notes of tropical fruit, and the Podere Fontarca (chardonnay and viognier), an eminently approachable white just a bit low in acidity, are both very good.

●	Podere Il Bosco '96	🍷🍷	5
○	Le Terrazze '97	🍷	3
○	Podere Fontarca '97	🍷	4
●	Podere Il Vescovo '97	🍷	3
●	Podere Il Bosco '95	YYY	5
○	Podere Fontarca '94	YY	4
●	Podere Il Bosco '94	YY	5
●	Vigna del Bosco '92	YY	5
●	Vigna del Bosco '93	YY	4
○	Le Terrazze '94	Y	3
○	Le Terrazze '95	Y	3
○	Le Terrazze '96	Y	3
○	Podere di Fontarca '93	Y	4
●	Podere Il Vescovo '95	Y	3
●	Podere Il Vescovo '96	Y	3

FAUGLIA (PI)

FATTORIA DELL'UCCELLIERA
VIA PROVINCIALE
LORENZANA CUCIGLIANA, 1
56043 FAUGLIA (PI)
TEL. 050/662747

The Uccelliera estate is by now an established member of the small coterie of top-flight Colline Pisane winemakers, as this year's tastings yet again demonstrate. Though there were no real stars, the consistency and reliability of their wines was very evident, despite the presence of representatives of the quirky '96 vintage. The Castellaccio Rosso doesn't manage to repeat its feat of '95 (an even better bottle today), but it is well above average. Its lovely color is intense and brilliant, and it is characterized by lots of fresh fruit, clean aromas and excellent balance, making for a lean and very pleasing quaffability. They didn't try to force the issue of structure or complexity which the '96 vintage did not naturally provide. For those of us who have followed the progress of this estate over the years, it is reassuring to note that the other wines in its range maintain a high standard. The well-made Chianti '96 has a satisfying density that goes well with its aromas. The Castellaccio Bianco '97 is a tightly woven wine, with well-judged vanilla on the nose. Finally, we were surprised by the Ficaia '97, with its intense pear and tropical fruit aromas. The tasty palate is no less captivating and it has a convincing finish. The Rosato was perfectly acceptable.

●	Castellaccio Rosso '96	🍷🍷	4
○	Castellaccio Bianco '97	🍷	4
●	Chianti '96	🍷	3
○	Ficaia '97	🍷	3
⊙	Rosaspina '97		2
○	Castellaccio Bianco '96	YY	4
●	Castellaccio Rosso '93	YY	4
●	Castellaccio Rosso '95	YY	4*
○	Castellaccio Bianco '94	Y	4
●	Castellaccio Rosso '92	Y	4
●	Chianti '94	Y	3
●	Chianti '95	Y	3

FIRENZE

Marchesi Antinori
P.zza degli Antinori, 3
50123 Firenze
tel. 055/23595

Beginning this year, Renzo Cotarella is not just the oenologist in charge of production at Marchesi Antinori. He has been named general manager of this legendary firm, a kind of vice-Marquis Piero Antinori, as it were, and he has already started coordinating the various branches that combine to form this vast and renowned winery in the Chianti Classico. It is not a simple task. It involves producing and selling 15 million bottles worldwide, and managing almost 1,500 hectares of vineyards divided among three regions, Tuscany, Umbria and Piedmont, quite apart from the joint ventures under way in Hungary and the United States. This is a level of responsibility that would set anyone's knees to shaking. But Renzo is a man of character, and one of the most capable organizers on the Italian wine scene, so we feel he will be up to it. This year he has presented yet another series of top-flight wines, which is nothing new for Antinori. But the Solaia '95 is a real stunner, probably even better than the magnificent '94 we tasted last year. The nose is of extraordinary elegance, its cabernet notes almost masquerading as Bordeaux, but its intensity really gave us pause. The palate features sweet, dense tannins underpinning a deep, rich body. The Tignanello is back in the spotlight with its '95 vintage as well. It is not as concentrated as we would have liked, but producing more than 25,000 cases of such a stellar wine is a very tall order. The two Chianti Classico Riserva wines on offer, the Tenute del Marchese, which seems an attenuated version of the Tignanello, and the Badia a Passignano, soft and concentrated, are very good . The two '96s, Chianti Classico Badia a Passignano and Pèppoli, are pleasant if a bit simple, right on target for their intended markets.

	Wine	Glasses	
●	Solaia '95	▼▼▼	6
●	Chianti Classico Badia a Passignano Ris. '95	▼▼	5
●	Chianti Classico Tenute del Marchese Ris. '95	▼▼	5
●	Tignanello '95	▼▼	6
●	Chianti Cl. Badia a Passignano '96	▼	3
●	Chianti Classico Pèppoli '96	▼	4
●	Solaia '86	▽▽▽	6
●	Solaia '88	▽▽▽	6
●	Solaia '90	▽▽▽	6
●	Solaia '94	▽▽▽	6
●	Tignanello '83	▽▽▽	6
●	Tignanello '93	▽▽▽	6
●	Tignanello '94	▽▽	6

FIRENZE

Marchesi de' Frescobaldi
Via S. Spirito, 11
50125 Firenze
tel. 055/27141

The range of wines offered by Marchesi De' Frescobaldi this year is truly magnificent, demonstrating how lively such a monumental and historical winery can be. This august estate is quick on its feet in responding to the challenges posed by today's market. We start with the wonderful Mormoreto '95, a cabernet-based red that delivers clean, intense aromas and a full-bodied, well-balanced, tannic palate with a good finish. The Chianti Rufina Nipozzano Riserva '95 was a bit slower off the mark and less convincing. Its nose is fresh and grassy, but at tasting time the wine was a bit hard. Doubtless a few years in the bottle will produce a marked improvement. The Pomino Rosso is, as usual, reliable: the '95 offers rich fruit aromas and a fresh and tonic palate. It is a straightforward, drinkable wine, and its sister, the Pomino Bianco '97 is even better. It's a brilliant yellow in the glass, there are aromas of tropical fruit, and the palate displays great softness, harmony and limpidity. The equally enjoyable Pomino Il Benefizio '96 has characteristic but understated notes of oak on the nose and satisfying continuity on the palate, which is rich in hints of citrus. But the real top of the line this year is the Montesodi, a splendid Chianti Rufina Riserva. It is an object lesson in style, with its purity, depth and clarity. Redolent of wild berries, it is incredibly intense, and offers splendid extract and a wonderful progression on the palate, together with a remarkable finish. The Pater '97, a red at the other end of the line, is clean and grassy and elementary, but tasty. Finally, the reliable Albizzia and Nubis, both '97s, are good white wines.

	Wine	Glasses	
●	Chianti Rufina Montesodi Ris. '95	▼▼▼	6
●	Mormoreto '95	▼▼	6
○	Pomino Bianco '97	▼▼	4
○	Pomino Il Benefizio '96	▼▼	5
○	Albizzia '97	▼	2
●	Chianti Rufina Nipozzano Ris. '95	▼	4
○	Nubis '97	▼	2
●	Pater '97	▼	3
●	Pomino Rosso '95	▼	4
●	Chianti Rufina Montesodi Ris. '88	▽▽▽	6
●	Chianti Rufina Montesodi Ris. '90	▽▽▽	6
●	Pomino Rosso '85	▽▽▽	5
●	Mormoreto '94	▽▽	6

FUCECCHIO (FI)

Fattoria di Montellori
Via Pistoiese, 5
50054 Fucecchio (FI)
tel. 0571/260641

The Nieri family has always found a certain pioneering pleasure in creating wines in an area beyond the pale of major wine-growing zones. We should note that their choice was conditioned by their conviction that the Montellori vineyards are capable of great things. The best representative of what they can do is without doubt the Salamartano, a cabernet sauvignon/merlot blend which made a very convincing showing in its '95 vintage. Dark and dense in aspect, this wine is still evolving, and we believe it shows great potential for improvement in the bottle. The nose is richly fruity, if still a bit muffled, with toasty notes of oak. The palate is fuller, nice and meaty, but reveals its youth on the finish, which is tannic and not yet as broad as it could be. The Castelrapiti Rosso '95 is a far cry from the unassuming '94 vintage. A sangiovese with 25% cabernet, (and once the flagship of Montellori), it has ripe fruit on the nose with distinct sweet vanilla tones. The palate is concentrated, well-balanced and not without a certain style. The remaining bottles in the vast range produced by this estate are all good, particularly the Vinsanto '94 and the Brut. The Castelrapiti Bianco '95, the Chianti Vigna del Moro '96, the La Costa di Sant'Amato '97 and the viognier, Bonfiglio '97, are all interesting.

●	Castelrapiti Rosso '95	🍷🍷	4
●	Salamartano '95	🍷🍷	5
○	Bonfiglio '97	🍷	4
○	La Costa di Sant'Amato '97	🍷	4
○	Montellori Brut	🍷	5
○	Vin Santo dell'Empolese '94	🍷	5
○	Castelrapiti Bianco '95		5
●	Chianti Vigna del Moro '96		3
○	Bonfiglio '94	♀♀	4
●	Castelrapiti Rosso '92	♀♀	5
●	Castelrapiti Rosso '90	♀♀	5
●	Castelrapiti Rosso '93	♀♀	5
●	Salamartano '92	♀♀	5
●	Salamartano '93	♀♀	5
●	Salamartano '94	♀♀	5

GAIOLE IN CHIANTI (SI)

Agricoltori
del Chianti Geografico
Via Mulinaccio, 10
53013 Gaiole in Chianti (SI)
tel. 0577/749451

When a wine-growing cooperative is well managed, it can yield fantastic results, a reproach to all detractors of a system theoretically second to none, but occasionally given to churning out colorless average wine. The Agricoltori del Chianti Geografico is an extraordinary example of what a co-op can do when it functions well. For years now, this estate has been offering well-made and sometimes really interesting wines. All their bottles always cost amazingly little for what they are, and everything they make is exceptionally reliable, produced under the watchful eye of the distinguished oenologist Vittorio Fiore. This year we tasted three wines that were exemplary in their respective categories. The Capitolare di Biturica I Vigneti del Geografico '95, a blend of sangiovese and cabernet sauvignon, is, as usual, the best. Rich and concentrated on the palate, it displays complex aromas of red fruit with pleasant balsamic and vanilla notes in the background. The Chianti Classico Montegiachi Riserva '95 is more convincing than its earlier versions. Its aromas are still a bit overripe, but its richness and especially its soft entry on the palate make it definitely noteworthy. The Chianti Classico '96, simpler, of course, is a pleasant, light and quaffable wine. The Contessa di Radda selection, another '96, is an elegant and very typical Chianti Classico, with a refreshing dose of acidity underpinning a full body.

●	Chianti Cl. Montegiachi Ris. '95	🍷🍷	4*
●	I Vigneti del Geografico '95	🍷🍷	5
●	Chianti Classico Contessa di Radda '96	🍷	3
●	Chianti Classico '96	🍷	2*
●	Chianti Cl. Montegiachi Ris. '87	♀♀	3*
●	Chianti Cl. Montegiachi Ris. '88	♀♀	4*
●	Chianti Cl. Montegiachi Ris. '90	♀♀	3*
●	Chianti Cl. Montegiachi Ris. '94	♀♀	4*
●	Chianti Classico '90	♀♀	2*
●	Chianti Classico '95	♀	2*

GAIOLE IN CHIANTI (SI)

★ Castello di Ama
Loc. Ama
53010 Gaiole in Chianti (SI)
tel. 0577/746031

We continue to taste Castello di Ama's wines a few months late, as we are unable to obtain samples before their commercial release. We apologize to our readers for the inconvenience, but this state of affairs is the result of a decision at the estate which we're obliged to respect. Hence this year we are reviewing the Vigna l'Apparita '94, the Chianti Classico La Casuccia and the Chianti Classico Bellavista, also both '94s, and their standard Chianti Classico '96. Vigna l'Apparita '94 is its usual self, a true champion of a wine. In this vintage it offers balsamic, herbal aromas, including notes of rosemary and eucalyptus. It has balance and finesse on the palate, with sweet, well-integrated tannins. It lacks perhaps the concentration of earlier versions, and the nose, although striking, is a bit atypical. The Chianti Classico Bellavista '94 is uncontestably a well-made wine, and helps one to forget how difficult this vintage was for the zone as a whole. The tannins may slightly overpower the structure, but it's very successful. The Chianti Classico La Casuccia '94 delivers more sweetness and complexity, and one wonders whether there wasn't a small quantity of merlot added to the blend. The aromas are spicy and slightly vegetal, against a distinct and well-articulated fruity background. It is full-flavored, with notably sweet and elegant tannins and a fairly long finish. The Chianti Classico '96 is slightly less impressive, well-made but a bit faint on the nose, with an immediate and straightforward taste.

	Wine	Glasses	
●	Chianti Classico Bellavista '94	▼▼	6
●	Chianti Classico La Casuccia '94	▼▼	6
●	Vigna l'Apparita Merlot '94	▼▼	6
●	Chianti Classico '96	▼	5
●	Chianti Classico Bellavista '85	▽▽▽	6
●	Chianti Classico Bellavista '86	▽▽▽	6
●	Chianti Classico Bellavista '90	▽▽▽	5
●	Chianti Classico Bertinga '88	▽▽▽	6
●	Chianti Classico La Casuccia '88	▽▽▽	6
●	Vigna l'Apparita Merlot '88	▽▽▽	6
●	Vigna l'Apparita Merlot '90	▽▽▽	6
●	Vigna l'Apparita Merlot '91	▽▽▽	6
●	Vigna l'Apparita Merlot '92	▽▽▽	6
●	Chianti Classico Bellavista '93	▽▽	5
●	Vigna l'Apparita Merlot '93	▽▽	6

GAIOLE IN CHIANTI (SI)

Badia a Coltibuono
Loc. Badia a Coltibuono
53013 Gaiole in Chianti (SI)
tel. 0577/749498

An absolutely unbeatable Sangioveto '95 has garnered the first Three Glasses for this well-known estate in Gaiole in Chianti. This is a wine which at last justifies their reputation, and, most importantly, a big red wine that expresses its terroir. The vineyards are in Monti, a southern sub-zone of Gaiole, which divides the two wings of the Castelnuovo Berardenga zone like a wedge. These lands are the birthplace of big red wines with ample structure and imposing polyphenol concentration, as well as tremendous aging potential. The Sangioveto '95 has all these qualities, and also manages to offer extraordinarily elegant aromas and Chianti character. The nose is intensely fruity, with sour cherry, vanilla and balsamic wood notes. The palate has extremely stylish tannins, dense but not mouth-puckering, and a full body leading into a long, concentrated finish. The Chianti Classico Riserva '95 is almost as good, but there's less denseness and body, and the tannins are a bit rough. It is certainly an excellent wine, but not a champion. Both the Chianti Classico '96 and the '96 selection are respectable wines. The latter was created by Roberto Stucchi, co-owner of the estate, and is slightly more fortunate in its wood, and clearer on the nose. In conclusion, we can't hide a certain satisfaction in having been able to reward an estate that is so representative of its zone. Hats off to Roberto and to Emanuela Stucchi, as well as to their celebrated oenologist Maurizio Castelli.

	Wine	Glasses	
●	Sangioveto '95	▼▼▼	6
●	Chianti Classico Ris. '95	▼▼	5
●	Chianti Classico '96	▼	3
●	Chianti Classico R. S. '96	▼	3
●	Chianti Classico Ris. '82	▽▽	5
●	Chianti Classico Ris. '85	▽▽	4
●	Chianti Classico Ris. '88	▽▽	4
●	Chianti Classico Ris. '90	▽▽	4
●	Sangioveto '83	▽▽	6
●	Sangioveto '85	▽▽	6
●	Sangioveto '86	▽▽	6
●	Sangioveto '88	▽▽	6
●	Sangioveto '90	▽▽	6
●	Sangioveto '94	▽▽	6
●	Chianti Classico Ris. '93	▽	4

GAIOLE IN CHIANTI (SI)

CASTELLO DI BROLIO - RICASOLI

LOC. BROLIO
53013 GAIOLE IN CHIANTI (SI)
TEL. 0577/7301

The Blue Bloods of Castello di Brolio strike again. The estate that just three short years ago seemed destined for bankruptcy is now on its way to a major entry in the Who's Who of Italian winemaking. The engine behind this success is Francesco Ricasoli, the young agricultural manager who also happens to belong to a family that virtually invented Chianti. The top performance this year comes from the Casalferro '96, the best sangiovese of the year. This is a great red, modern in style, with typical varietal aromas and an uncommonly elegant palate featuring tannins that are sweeter than those of many a merlot, and a concentration worthy of a Bordeaux premier cru. Simply stupendous. Francesco was ably assisted by the oenologist Carlo Ferrini, who has really hit his stride here, and to his capable and intelligent counsellor, Filippo Mazzei from Fonterutoli. This winning team is completed by Maurizio Ghiori, a top marketing man with years of experience, who has, since last year, been helping the estate to recover its glorious image. And the other wines? They are formidable, in their categories. The Chianti Classico Riserva Castello di Brolio '95 is a small Casalferro, and the standard '96 is soft and drinkable, just as a young Chianti Classico should be. The Formulae '96 from the Ricasoli line is a young, delicious and very affordable monovarietal sangiovese. The Torricella '96, an oak-aged chardonnay, is only good. Not a bad collection, one might say. More innovations are on the way, including what is slated to become the "grand vin" of Brolio. But more about that next year.

	Wine	Rating	Price
●	Casalferro '96	🍷🍷🍷	5
●	Chianti Classico Castello di Brolio Ris. '95	🍷🍷	4*
●	Chianti Classico '96	🍷🍷	3*
●	Formulae '96	🍷🍷	3*
○	Torricella '96	🍷	4
●	Casalferro '95	YYY	5*
●	Casalferro '94	YY	5
●	Chianti Classico Castello di Brolio Ris. '90	YY	4
●	Chianti Classico Castello di Brolio Ris. '93	YY	4
●	Chianti Classico Castello di Brolio Ris. '94	YY	4
●	Formulae '95	YY	3*

GAIOLE IN CHIANTI (SI)

CASTELLO DI CACCHIANO

FRAZ. MONTI IN CHIANTI
LOC. CACCHIANO
53010 GAIOLE IN CHIANTI (SI)
TEL. 0577/747018

We must begin by correcting an error: the wine that we tasted and reviewed last year as the Chianti Classico '95 was actually a barrel sample of the Riserva Millennio of the same year which has not yet been released. This correction is particularly needful, because Cacchiano never released its standard Chianti Classico '95, choosing instead to reserve the entire yield for the Riserva, which we have reviewed this year. This is an excellent wine, with balsamic, characteristic tones on the nose and notable density. It is perhaps still a bit austere and sharp, but this is not unusual for wines that emerge from this famous Monti in Chianti winery. The RF '95 is also quite convincing, a monovarietal sangiovese aged in small barrels. This gives it more vanilla on the nose than large barrels produce, but also some assertive tannins and a certain hardness on the palate. This did not, however, keep it from doing very well; indeed it made it to the finals, thanks to its really remarkable density. The last on the roster is the Chianti Classico '96, a decidedly smaller wine, because of both its role and its vintage. It is slightly harsh on the palate, mostly due to the characteristic acidity that sangiovese often produces in non-banner years.

	Wine	Rating	Price
●	Chianti Classico Millennio Ris. '95	🍷🍷	5
●	RF Castello di Cacchiano '95	🍷🍷	5
●	Chianti Classico '96	🍷	3
●	Chianti Cl. Millennio Ris. '90	YYY	5
●	Chianti Cl. Millennio Ris. '88	YY	5
●	Chianti Classico '88	YY	3*
●	Chianti Classico '90	YY	3*
●	Chianti Classico '93	YY	3*
●	RF Castello di Cacchiano '88	YY	5
●	RF Castello di Cacchiano '90	YY	5
●	RF Castello di Cacchiano '93	YY	4
○	Vin Santo '86	YY	5
○	Vin Santo '91	YY	5
●	Chianti Classico '94	Y	3

S. M. Lamole & Villa Vistarenni

Loc. Vistarenni
53013 Gaiole in Chianti (SI)
tel. 0577/738186

The Codirosso '95, a pure sangiovese, symbolizes the comeback of the famous Gaiole estate Villa Vistarenni. It reveals elegant fruity aromas, a particularly well-balanced palate, stylish densely woven tannins, and an elegant finish. This may well be the beginning of a new direction for this cellar, which together with the Lamole estate now belongs to the Gruppo Marzotto. The Chianti Classico Riserva '94 is acceptable, but its nose is decidedly thinner and more forward and it doesn't have much of a finish. But the Chianti Classico Assolo '96 is interesting, not particularly structured but well made and very modern, smooth on the palate and pleasantly fruity on the nose. The standard Villa Vistarenni Chianti Classico '96 is also a light and pleasant wine. It is similar to the Assolo, but without its concentration. If Villa Vistarenni is the innovative winery, Lamole, named after the Greve sub-zone, is the respecter of tradition. Perhaps it was the infelicitous vintages, especially the '94, but we found their results less encouraging. The Chianti Classico Lamole di Lamole Riserva '94 is not bad, though a bit too simple to have a starring role. The Riserva Campolungo '93 is extremely old-fashioned, balsamic on the nose but not quite mouth-filling enough, and dominated by an acidity that seems divorced from the rest of the body. The real test will come next year with the release of their Riserva wines from '95, which should really reflect the change in management.

Wine	Glasses	Price
● Codirosso '95	2 black	5
● Chianti Cl. Lamole di Lamole Ris. '94	1 black	4
● Chianti Cl. Villa Vistarenni Ris. '94	1 black	4
● Chianti Classico '96	1 black	3
● Chianti Classico Assolo '96	1 black	3
● Chianti Cl. Campolungo Ris. '93		4
● Chianti Cl. Villa Vistarenni '95	2 white	4
● Chianti Cl. Lamole di Lamole '94	1 white	4
● Codirosso '93	1 white	5

GAIOLE IN CHIANTI (SI)

Riecine

Loc. Riecine
53013 Gaiole in Chianti (SI)
tel. 0577/749098

Important news from Riecine: John Dunkley, the legendary founder (with his late wife) of this small and wonderful winery, has given up the reins. He has sold the estate, and is today probably enjoying his well-deserved retirement on a boat anchored in some lovely Mediterranean cove. However Sean O'Callaghan, his right hand in recent years and chief wine technician, together with Carlo Ferrini, is still there. So Riecine's philosophy remains the same, as do their viticulture and wine-making methods. Indeed we have never been so impressed by Riecine's wines as we were this year. Best of all is La Gioia '95, a monovarietal sangiovese. It is a "gioia" (joy) in name and in fact, a breath-taking wine that manages to retain the rich polyphenol concentration typical of Riecine's great reds, (that can at times be a bit hard), integrated with, or even tamed by a succulent and rich softness. Of course, a hint of austerity and some rough tannins remain. But it is an enormous and powerful wine, one of the best sangioveses we have ever tasted. It is worth every penny of its steep price. The Chianti Classico Riserva '95 is, of course, also a very good wine, though at the moment tannins and acidity make it a little too hard. The Chianti Classico '96 is deliciously fruity, and bodes well for the more important wines of this vintage to be released next year.

Wine	Glasses	Price
● La Gioia '95	3 black	6
● Chianti Classico '96	2 black	5
● Chianti Classico Ris. '95	2 black	6
● Chianti Classico Ris. '86	3 white	5
● Chianti Classico Ris. '88	3 white	6
● Chianti Classico '95	2 white	4
● Chianti Classico Ris. '90	2 white	6
● Chianti Classico Ris. '93	2 white	5
● Chianti Classico Ris. '94	2 white	5
● La Gioia '86	2 white	5
● La Gioia '88	2 white	6
● La Gioia '90	2 white	6
● La Gioia '91	2 white	5
● La Gioia '93	2 white	5
● La Gioia '94	2 white	5

ROCCA DI MONTEGROSSI

LOC. MONTI IN CHIANTI
53010 GAIOLE IN CHIANTI (SI)
TEL. 0577/747267

The differentiation between Marco Ricasoli's Rocca di Montegrossi estate and the Castello di Cacchiano is becoming clearer and clearer. The vineyards have already been divided, and the technical management of the harvest and vinification is also separate now. They still share the cellar underneath the Castello di Cacchiano, but even this "umbilical cord" will soon be cut, perhaps even this year, and Rocca di Montegrossi will then be fully independent. Meanwhile their wines are beginning to be distinguishable from Cacchiano's, in part for their more modern style. Newer and smaller oak barrels, less hardness and more fruit on the nose, suggesting some concessions to the American market (and who's to blame them?). Indeed the Geremia '95 seems to have emerged from a dream of Robert Parker's. It is a monovarietal sangiovese aged in Allier oak barriques and is intensely fruity on the nose, with vanilla and toasty wood notes coming to the fore. Full and rich on the palate, it harbors some residual rough, unblended tannins and an oaky aftertaste. The Chianti Classico '96 comes from a more difficult vintage, and is much frailer in structure, revealing an excess of acidity- and tannin-induced harshness that will be difficult to resolve through bottle aging. This is definitely a version in a minor key, but it may serve as a warm-up for this young estate. Unsurprisingly, the Chianti Classico Riserva '95 is a much better wine, rich and well-balanced on the palate, with just the right dose of oak.

●	Chianti Classico Ris. '95	🍷🍷	4
●	Geremia '95	🍷🍷	5
●	Chianti Classico '96	🍷	3
●	Chianti Classico Vigneto S. Marcellino '93	ΥΥ	4
●	Chianti Classico '93	ΥΥ	3*
●	Chianti Classico '95	ΥΥ	3*
●	Vin Santo '88	ΥΥ	5
○	Vin Santo '91	ΥΥ	5
●	Chianti Classico '94	Υ	4
●	Geremia '93	Υ	5

SAN GIUSTO A RENTENNANO

LOC. MONTI IN CHIANTI
53010 GAIOLE IN CHIANTI (SI)
TEL. 0577/747121

Of the three wines presented this year by San Giusto a Rentennano it was, not surprisingly, the Percarlo '95 that stood out: it came very close indeed to winning Three Glasses. It has remarkable richness of color, and the intensity of the bouquet announces a concentrated wine, still quite young, with delightful black fruit and rich spicy tones. Its attack is dense and powerful, and it displays great balance and structure as it develops on the palate, with a finish not yet free of rough edges. This is a very impressive wine, more contemporary and much less austere in style than in the past, and none the worse for that. We liked the Chianti Classico Riserva '95, but we had expected something more. Volatile alcohol with hints of leather and tobacco dominate the aromas, while the palate is firm and full of character, its alcohol well set off by tannins. Denser fruit would probably have helped to improve the overall balance. The Chianti Classico '96 is a simpler wine, but it lives up to expectations.

●	Percarlo '95	🍷🍷	6
●	Chianti Classico '96	🍷	4
●	Chianti Classico Ris. '95	🍷	5
●	Percarlo '88	ΥΥΥ	6
●	Chianti Classico '92	ΥΥ	3*
●	Chianti Classico Ris. '88	ΥΥ	5
●	Percarlo '85	ΥΥ	6
●	Percarlo '87	ΥΥ	6
●	Percarlo '90	ΥΥ	6
●	Percarlo '91	ΥΥ	6
●	Percarlo '92	ΥΥ	6
●	Percarlo '93	ΥΥ	6
●	Percarlo '94	ΥΥ	6
○	Vin Santo '90	ΥΥ	6

San Vincenti

Podere di Stignano
53013 Gaiole in Chianti (SI)
tel. 0577/734047

After three years of silence, we now have reason to mention the San Vincenti estate and its wines once again. Its picturesque vineyards are surrounded by woods that reach the southeastern border of the Chianti Classico DOCG zone, and the danger of wild boar attack at harvest time was so great that the estate's owners had to build special fences to keep the boar at bay. An apparent change of direction accounts for San Vincenti's reappearance in the Guide. Carlo Ferrini has been signed on as consultant oenologist, but this only partly explains the distinct improvement in their wines this year. They can now begin to build on experience (and learn from mistakes) which they simply didn't have a few years ago. Hence these good results. The Chianti Classico Podere di Stignano '96 is among the best of its peers. It has complex aromas, revealing red fruit, leather and oak tones. The palate is full and powerful, perhaps a bit monotonous, but the finish is impressively long. A slightly bitter aftertaste somewhat disturbs one's enjoyment, but it is a price one often pays for high tannic content. The Chianti Classico Riserva '95 is also a very good wine: it has less grip and is a bit forward on the nose; in the mouth it is soft and intense, with a long, elegant finish. So two lovely wines for a start, and great hope for the future.

Wine	Glasses	Price
● Chianti Classico Podere di Stignano '96	2 (black)	3
● Chianti Classico Ris. '95	2 (black)	4
● Chianti Classico '88	2	3
● Chianti Classico Ris. '85	2	4
● Chianti Classico Ris. '88	2	4*
● Chianti Classico '90	1	3*
● Chianti Classico '91	1	4
● Chianti Classico Ris. '91	1	3

GAIOLE IN CHIANTI (SI)

Fattoria Valtellina

Loc. Castagnoli
53013 Gaiole in Chianti (SI)
tel. 0577/731005

If we really wanted to be sticklers, the only fault we could find with Cristoph Schneider and his wines this year is that the difference in quality between Valtellina's two leading bottles, Convivio and Chianti Classico Riserva, and its standard Chianti Classico is simply too great. True, the first two wines are from the exceptional '95 vintage, while the third is just a '96. But a justly celebrated estate like Valtellina ought to produce a standard red as excellent in its way as their premier wines. This said, we must admit that the two thoroughbreds mentioned above are splendid. The Convivio '95, a barrique-aged red made from sangiovese (75%) and cabernet sauvignon (25%), is in one of its best incarnations ever, and missed its Three Glasses by a hair. This is a superb wine, with intensely fruity aromas revealing sour cherries and plums against an especially elegant vanilla background. On the palate it is full-flavored with sweet, dense tannins that are not in the least aggressive or mouth-puckering. Overall it seems an extremely well-made wine, but just a bit monotonous, which is what lost it its Third Glass. The Chianti Classico Riserva '95 is excellent and seems to be a restatement of the Convivio with the soft pedal down: less intensity and concentration, but otherwise quite familiar. Next to these champions the Chianti Classico '96 seems like a poor relation with its structural limitations and lower-than-expected concentration.

Wine	Glasses	Price
● Chianti Classico Ris. '95	2 (black)	5
● Convivio '95	2 (black)	6
● Chianti Classico '96	1 (black)	4
● Convivio '91	3	6
● Chianti Classico '90	2	4
● Chianti Classico '91	2	4
● Chianti Classico '93	2	4
● Chianti Classico Ris. '90	2	5
● Chianti Classico Ris. '93	2	5
● Convivio '90	2	6
● Convivio '93	2	6
● Convivio '94	2	6
● Chianti Classico '88	1	4
● Chianti Classico '94	1	3
● Convivio '88	1	6

GAMBASSI TERME (FI)

VILLA PILLO
VIA VOLTERRANA, 26
50050 GAMBASSI TERME (FI)
TEL. 0571/680212

Another memorable year for this young winery in Gambassi. We found many interesting wines among the multitude presented, with impressive overall tasting scores. But we feel that, with their excellent technical management in both vineyard and cellar, they could do even better if they were willing to give up producing such quantities, at least for the most promising wines. A case in point is the Merlot '96, a superior wine with elegant, well-articulated aromas, rich in fruit, with spicy, grassy undertones. It is round, well distributed and balanced on the palate. Superior richness of extract would make a great wine of it. Much the same can be said of the Cabernet Sauvignon '96, less limpid in bouquet but with an enchanting palate, thanks to an excellent progression and sweet, silky tannins. The nose of the Syrah '96, however, is of an exemplary purity and absolutely characteristic: red fruit, hints of flowers and lots of pepper. Its entry on the palate is elegant and refreshing, and it develops well but, once again, if it had only been a bit more concentrated... The long list continues with a Chardonnay '97 that offers pleasantly characteristic banana and citrus aromas and simple, refreshing balance on the palate. The acceptable Vivaldaia '96, a further confirmation of the technical know-how behind Villa Pillo's wines, is well-made, lively and immediate in its straightforward appeal. The Vin Santo '92 is more convincing on the palate than on the nose, and the Borgoforte could stand some improvement.

	Wine	Glasses	Price
●	Cabernet Sauvignon '96	🍷🍷	5
●	Merlot '96	🍷🍷	5
●	Syrah '96	🍷🍷	5
○	Chardonnay '97	🍷	5
●	Vivaldaia '96	🍷	5
●	Borgoforte '96		4
○	Vin Santo '92		6
●	Merlot '95	🍷🍷 (prev.)	5
●	Vivaldaia '95	🍷🍷 (prev.)	6
●	Borgoforte '94	🍷 (prev.)	4
○	Chardonnay '95	🍷 (prev.)	5
○	Chardonnay '96	🍷 (prev.)	5
●	Syrah '95	🍷 (prev.)	5
○	Vin Santo '91	🍷 (prev.)	6

GHIZZANO DI PECCIOLI (PI)

TENUTA DI GHIZZANO
VIA DELLA CHIESA, 1
56030 GHIZZANO DI PECCIOLI (PI)
TEL. 050/20596 - 0587/630096

The wines of the Tenuta di Ghizzano never fail to impress us, In fact, this year they are better than ever. The Veneroso '95, sangiovese with some cabernet sauvignon and merlot, continues its heady climb, getting ever closer to the Olympian heights of Three Glasses. Its color is an intense ruby, and the nose conveys a firm, lively base of fruit embroidered with sweet, oak-derived vanilla tones. In keeping with the Ghizzano style, the palate is not overwhelmingly powerful, but it develops in an impressively confident progression: an elegant and profound wine. Similar in profile, but more intense in both color and fruit, the Nambrot '96, a monovarietal merlot, makes its first entrance on the scene this year. It displays excellent aromas, with black woodland fruit over traces of cocoa, and an impressive palate, with acidity - unusual for a merlot - that tones down the fullness from the fruit and tannins. The debut of the Vin Santo '94 is a further example of the dynamism of this estate; it is also about as close to a white wine as the young Countess Ginevra, a known red partisan, is willing to get. The intense and stylish aromas with their traces of sour cherry preserves, prunes and violets, suggest in fact that some red grapes found their way into the blend. The palate fulfils the promise of the bouquet and is sweetly mouth-filling and of a juicy concentration. The list ends with the highly successful Chianti, an eminently quaffable wine of noteworthy structure.

	Wine	Glasses	Price
●	Nambrot '96	🍷🍷	6
●	Veneroso '95	🍷🍷	5
○	Vin Santo Germano '94	🍷🍷	5
●	Chianti '97	🍷	2*
●	Veneroso '85	🍷🍷 (prev.)	5
●	Veneroso '86	🍷🍷 (prev.)	5
●	Veneroso '88	🍷🍷 (prev.)	5
●	Veneroso '90	🍷🍷 (prev.)	5
●	Veneroso '91	🍷🍷 (prev.)	4
●	Veneroso '93	🍷🍷 (prev.)	4
●	Veneroso '94	🍷🍷 (prev.)	4
●	Chianti '93	🍷 (prev.)	2*
●	Chianti '94	🍷 (prev.)	2
●	Chianti '95	🍷 (prev.)	2*
●	Chianti '96	🍷 (prev.)	2*

GREVE IN CHIANTI (FI)

CARPINETO
FRAZ. LUCOLENA
LOC. DUDDA
50022 GREVE IN CHIANTI (FI)
TEL. 055/8549062

This important Chianti winery has made a very good showing this year. As usual, the Cabernet Sauvignon Farnito '95 passed its test with flying colors, easily winning Two Glasses. Intensely dark red but limpid in the glass, it offers a varied array of intriguing if not intense aromas: faint animal notes blend with tobacco and delightful fruit. The attack is not imposing, but the structure is soon apparent: alcohol effectively counters hardness, producing an effect of excellent balance. The Riserva '95 is interesting, but not as good as it has been in other years. Its pleasant aromas mix hints of vanilla with black currant preserves and an appetizing final spice. After an entry on the palate of moderate intensity, the relatively mature and substantial tannins make their presence felt. The Chianti Classico '96 is light in structure, with pleasant but muted fruity aromas and not much persistence on the palate. We had never tasted the Vino Nobile di Montepulciano Riserva '94 before, so it came as a real surprise. It is intensely fruity on the nose, with mineral and oaky tones, and has a big palate with lots of grip. The tannins are dense and mellow, and the finish is long.

Wine	Rating	Price
● Farnito Cabernet Sauvignon '95	▼▼	5
● Vino Nobile di Montepulciano Ris. '94	▼▼	4*
● Chianti Classico Ris. '95	▼	4
● Chianti Classico '96		3
● Chianti Classico Ris. '85	♀♀	4
● Chianti Classico Ris. '88	♀♀	4
● Chianti Classico Ris. '91	♀♀	4
● Chianti Classico Ris. '93	♀♀	4
● Chianti Classico Ris. '94	♀♀	4
● Dogaiolo '95	♀♀	3*
● Farnito Cabernet Sauvignon '90	♀♀	5
● Farnito Cabernet Sauvignon '91	♀♀	5
● Farnito Cabernet Sauvignon '93	♀♀	5
● Farnito Cabernet Sauvignon '89	♀♀	5

GREVE IN CHIANTI (FI)

CASTEL RUGGERO
LOC. ANTELLA
50011 GREVE IN CHIANTI (FI)
TEL. 055/6819237

Castel Ruggero's vineyards lie between Strada and San Polo in Chianti, in one of the northernmost areas of the Chianti DOCG zone. Nicolò d'Afflitto, the estate owner, is a renowned oenologist, and works as a consultant for the Marchesi Frescobaldi estate, as well as for the joint venture between Frescobaldi and the Mondavi family that produces Luce in Montalcino. Somehow, this busy man manages to find time to dedicate to his family estate as well, and, judging from the results, he does a fine job of it. His wines always do well at our tastings. The Chianti Classico Riserva is generally a sure bet, and its price is eminently reasonable for a wine of such quality. The '95 is no exception. It is an extremely well-made wine, with clean, intense, even complex aromas, revealing distinct fruity notes. The palate is substantial, the tannins fairly sweet and the finish good. The Chianti Classico '96 is obviously not of the same density, but it's an agreeable, quaffable red, with simple but pleasingly well-executed fruity aromas.

Wine	Rating	Price
● Chianti Classico Ris. '95	▼▼	4
● Chianti Classico '96	▼	3
● Chianti Classico '90	♀♀	4
● Chianti Classico '93	♀♀	3*
● Chianti Classico Ris. '90	♀♀	4
● Chianti Classico Ris. '93	♀♀	4
● Chianti Classico Ris. '94	♀♀	4
● Chianti Classico '88	♀	4
● Chianti Classico '91	♀	4
● Chianti Classico '92	♀	4
● Chianti Classico '94	♀	3

GREVE IN CHIANTI (FI)

LA MADONNINA - TRIACCA

LOC. STRADA IN CHIANTI
V.LO ABATE, 1
50027 GREVE IN CHIANTI (FI)
TEL. 055/858003 - 0342/701352

Finding another estate with such tremendous potential for Chianti Classico production would be a difficult task: it comprises 100 hectares of vineyards, which the Triacca family is gradually replanting. For years now, their policy has been clear and simple: only three wines were produced, a standard Chianti Classico and a Riserva, together with a cabernet-based wine called Mandorlo. The oenological duo of Vittorio Fiore and Stefano Chioccioli selected a few crus from the most promising vineyards, and the first of them was presented this year. The only problem faced by Italian connoisseurs is the scarcity of these wines on the market, not, for once, because they don't exist, but rather because they exist elsewhere: more than 90% is exported. The Riserva '95 is a Two Glass wine. Of a glowing ruby color, it has intense aromas of tobacco and leather nicely amalgamated with ripe fruit. The attack is definite, followed by a fine balance between alcohol, acidity and tannins that makes for eminent drinkability. The Chianti Classico Vigna La Palaia '95, of a lovely ruby hue, has vegetal notes on the nose, with balsamic tones dissolving into an evident aroma of bell pepper. Its entry on the palate is good, and it is broad, engrossing and persistent once it gets there. The Chianti Classico '96 is somewhat less impressive: its color is a limpid ruby, and its fruity tones of cherry are very pleasing but rather evanescent. In the mouth it is refreshing, but only moderate in structure and finish. The Mandorlo '95 was not yet ready for tasting, so we shall just have to wait until next year.

Wine	Rating	Price
● Chianti Classico Ris. '95	▼▼	4
● Chianti Classico '96	▼	3
● Chianti Classico V. La Palaia '95	▼	4
● Chianti Classico '94	YY	3*
● Chianti Classico '95	YY	3
● Chianti Classico Ris. '94	YY	4
● Chianti Classico '93	Y	3
● Chianti Classico Ris. '91	Y	4
● Chianti Classico Ris. '93	Y	4
● Il Mandorlo '91	Y	4
● Il Mandorlo '93	Y	4
● Il Mandorlo '94	Y	4
● Vino Nobile di Montepulciano '93	Y	4

GREVE IN CHIANTI (FI)

LA TORRACCIA DI PRESURA

LOC. STRADA IN CHIANTI
VIA DELLA MONTAGNOLA, 130
50022 GREVE IN CHIANTI (FI)
TEL. 055/490563 - 489997

This estate has consistently struck us as having tremendous potential and the enthusiasm and determination, on the part of those responsible, to exploit it fully. This year's tastings confirmed our good impressions and particularly highlighted the newcomer, the Chianti Classico '96. Its main defect is the currently excessive presence of oak-derived spice and vanilla notes on both nose and palate, but its ripe black fruit and floral aromas and its lively, compact taste and juicy finish are worthy of note. It easily earned its Two Glasses, a good omen for the future. Their other wines didn't miss Two Glasses by much. The Chianti Classico Il Tarocco Riserva '94 has a recognizably La Torraccia palate: concentrated, a little hard and unyielding, but with distinct character. The aromas, on the other hand, would be more fully enjoyable without some slightly animal and dried fruit notes. Lastly the Lucciolaio, a sangiovese/cabernet blend, is also admirable. There are vegetal tones and volatile alcohol on the nose and a well-balanced, full-bodied palate, but it's bit short on the finish.

Wine	Rating	Price
● Chianti Classico Il Tarocco '96	▼▼	3
● Chianti Classico Il Tarocco Ris. '94	▼	4
● Lucciolaio '95	▼	5
● Chianti Classico Il Tarocco '92	Y	3
● Chianti Classico Il Tarocco '93	Y	3
● Chianti Classico Il Tarocco '94	Y	3
● Chianti Classico Il Tarocco '95	Y	3
● Chianti Classico Il Tarocco Ris. '90	Y	4
● Chianti Classico Il Tarocco Ris. '91	Y	4
● Chianti Classico Il Tarocco Ris. '93	Y	4
● Lucciolaio '94	Y	5

GREVE IN CHIANTI (FI)

TENUTA MONTECALVI
VIA CITILLE, 8
50022 GREVE IN CHIANTI (FI)
TEL. 055/8544665

Many changes have taken place over the years in the Chianti Classico zone. Once a flag-bearer of tradition, it is increasingly taking on the contours of a laboratory in which the Tuscan wine of the future is being created. The research is more practical than theoretical, and it is in fact what they are now doing to the vines that is changing the aspect of the sangiovese grape and determining what we shall all be drinking in the 21st century. Montecalvi is among the more forward-looking wineries, having understood in time just what to do to be able to produce excellent wines of recognizable character. Their vines are, almost entirely, selected sangiovese clones grafted onto unassertive rootstock and closely planted, and, after two drastic summer prunings, they yield less than one kilogram per vine. This is how both the literal and figurative roots of great sangiovese wines are produced. We shouldn't forget that we can probably count on further improvement when the vines have matured. Montecalvi's '95 wine encourages us to hope and is already awfully good. The color is very dense, and the aromas are not yet entirely open, with the oak a little too noticeable and black fruit, licorice, and not very elegant but distinctive mineral notes. The palate is characterized by density of extract and soft vital tannins, which are capable of embracing alcohol and acidity in a harmonious whole.

●	Montecalvi '95	**YY**	5
●	Montecalvi '94	YY	4
●	Montecalvi '93	Y	4

GREVE IN CHIANTI (FI)

FATTORIA DI NOZZOLE
VIA DI NOZZOLE, 12
LOC. PASSO DEI PECORAI
50022 GREVE IN CHIANTI (FI)
TEL. 055/858018

The villa at Nozzole, surrounded by vineyards and woods in the heart of a zone with an extraordinary microclimate, is a place of exceptional beauty. In this part of the northern Chianti Classico zone there's a history of producing wines of great worth that are certain to age well. The wine that inherited the mantle of the old, long-lived reds of Nozzole is the Chianti Classico La Forra Riserva, which walked off with Three Glasses for its vintage '90. This year the '95 made its debut and, although it did not reach the stratospheric heights of its elder brother, it showed a fairly traditional style and a little tannic roughness, but also a particularly delightful fullness of body and pleasurable drinkability. So much for the "Chianti" side of the estate. But there exists another side, whose expression is a great red wine made from pure cabernet sauvignon from more recent vines with a density of 5 thousand plants per hectare. It is called Il Pareto, which will hardly be news to wine-lovers throughout the world. Aged in small oak casks, it stakes its all on complexity and density, and this year it was the '95 we had for tasting. We must say at once that we had hoped for something more. The nose was complex but a bit forward, and balsamic and herbal notes, rosemary in particular, emerged at the end. In the mouth it seemed, if anything, too soft and ready, as if this were the moment to drink it. It is still a splendid wine, but a little more grip wouldn't have hurt it.

●	Chianti Classico La Forra Ris. '95	**YY**	4
●	Il Pareto '95	**YY**	6
●	Chianti Classico La Forra Ris. '90	YYY	4
●	Il Pareto '88	YYY	6
●	Il Pareto '90	YYY	6
●	Il Pareto '93	YYY	6
●	Chianti Classico La Forra Ris. '88	YY	4
●	Chianti Classico La Forra Ris. '93	YY	4
●	Chianti Classico La Forra Ris. '94	YY	4
●	Chianti Classico '95	YY	3*
●	Il Pareto '89	YY	6
●	Il Pareto '94	YY	6
○	Le Bruniche '96	YY	3*
○	Le Bruniche '95	Y	3

GREVE IN CHIANTI (FI)

Podere Poggio Scalette

Loc. Ruffoli
50022 Greve in Chianti (FI)
tel. 055/8549017

The Ruffoli zone is in the southern part of Greve. Lamole and Panzano are not far away, and all three areas enjoyed a terrific '94 vintage that in some cases yielded better results than the '95, which was universally considered superior. This background information helps to explain the state of affairs at Poggio Scalette, where this is more or less what happened. We preferred the Carbonaione, a monovarietal sangiovese, in its '94 version; the '95 seemed somewhat aggressively tannic and a bit closed on the nose. We should point out, however, that the distinguished critic Robert Parker disagrees totally, and considers the Carbonaione '95 one of the best Italian wines he has ever tasted, as demonstrated by the astronomic 94/100 rating he gave it. Taste is notoriously subjective, and we can but hope, given our great esteem for the oenologist Vittorio Fiore who is the owner of this estate, that it is we who are mistaken. It is however the case that the acidity was such as to interfere with our pleasure, although the palate was otherwise characterized by excellent concentration and length. This wine easily gets Two Glasses, but we must defer the pleasure of granting our highest award to Vittorio Fiore for the wine we know he is capable of making, and we're sorry.

Wine	Glasses	Price
● Il Carbonaione '95	🍷🍷	5
● Il Carbonaione '92	🍷🍷 (white)	5
● Il Carbonaione '93	🍷🍷 (white)	5
● Il Carbonaione '94	🍷🍷 (white)	5

GREVE IN CHIANTI (FI)

Castello di Querceto

Loc. Dudda
50020 Greve in Chianti (FI)
tel. 055/8549064

In September 1997 a celebration at the Castello di Querceto marked the hundredth anniversary of uninterrupted ownership by the François family. An extraordinary vertical tasting of all of the estate's most important Chianti vintages was part of the splendid festivities. We must admit that the most moving experience for us was tasting the 1904 vintage: a fantastic wine, still very much alive, in our gustatory memory as well. With this event in mind, we were very glad to see an indication of a return to their glorious past in the excellent wines they presented this year. The Sangiovese La Corte '94 seemed to have fully hit its stride. It is not a powerful wine, but it seems to find a just measure in all things: a wonderful structural balance, an elegance of bouquet with notes of blackberries, violets and judiciously dosed oak. The intensely ruby-hued Chianti Classico '95 is also splendid. It has extremely clean and stylish fruity and floral aromas, and a fresh, continuous and well-balanced palate that seemed more elegant than concentrated. To complete this happy picture, the Chianti Classico il Picchio Riserva '93 is also excellent. Of an intense garnet color, this wine displays a distinct personality on the nose with its hints of ripe fruit, preserves, leather and spice. In the mouth it is concentrated and dense, and is just slightly disjointed on its still rather tannic finish.

Wine	Glasses	Price
● Chianti Classico '95	🍷🍷	3
● Chianti Classico Il Picchio Ris. '93	🍷🍷	4
● La Corte '94	🍷🍷	5
● Chianti Classico '94	🍷🍷 (white)	3
● Chianti Classico Il Picchio Ris. '90	🍷🍷 (white)	4
● Chianti Classico Ris. '90	🍷🍷 (white)	4
● Cignale '88	🍷🍷 (white)	5
● Cignale '89	🍷🍷 (white)	5
● Cignale '90	🍷🍷 (white)	5
● La Corte '88	🍷🍷 (white)	5
● La Corte '90	🍷🍷 (white)	5
● Querciolaia '88	🍷🍷 (white)	5
● Querciolaia '90	🍷🍷 (white)	5

GREVE IN CHIANTI (FI)

AGRICOLA QUERCIABELLA
LOC. RUFFOLI
VIA S. LUCIA A BARBIANO, 17
50022 GREVE IN CHIANTI (FI)
TEL. 055/853834 - 853307

This is quite simply the best Chianti Classico estate of the year. No other words can do justice to the stupendous range of wines that Agricola Querciabella has presented. Of the four wines we tasted, four made it into the finals. This is a record, the result of an extraordinarily happy combination of factors. First, there is the far-sighted owner, Giuseppe Castiglioni, wine-lover first and winegrower second, who understands that certain decisions must be made, and, at times, great sums must be spent, to obtain certain results. Then there is his friend and advisor, Giacomo Tachis, supreme oenologist, who lends a hand because he wants to, and not for professional or financial reasons. Next there is the capable manager, Guido De Santi, who oversees all the parts and keeps them running together smoothly. Finally, there is Mother Nature, who really should have top billing, as she dispenses good years or bad, and lets the grapes ripen, as long as people have been laboring in the vineyard as they should. And so we get the Camartina '94, sangiovese and cabernet sauvignon, easily one of the best versions of this wine. Its aromas are concentrated and elegant, with hints of sour cherries, black currants and new oak. The palate has extraordinary finesse, the tannins are stylish and soft and the finish is of remarkable length. And so we also get (and we are fortunate) the Chianti Classico Riserva '95, which is perhaps a bit harder, but is an aristocratic wine with incredibly sweet tannins for a monovarietal (or very nearly) sangiovese. Thus Querciabella walks off with two Three Glasses, a rare honor. The Chianti Classico '96, among the best of its vintage, and the barrique-aged chardonnay Batàr '96, delightful as usual, although somewhat less complex than it has been, came close to making it to the top and bringing the total to four!

	Wine	Glasses	
●	Camartina '94	▼▼▼	5
●	Chianti Classico Ris. '95	▼▼▼	5
○	Batàr '96	▼▼	5
●	Chianti Classico '96	▼▼	4
●	Camartina '88	▽▽▽	5
●	Camartina '90	▽▽▽	5
●	Chianti Classico '95	▽▽▽	4
○	Batàr '95	▽▽	5
○	Batard '92	▽▽	5
●	Camartina '87	▽▽	5
●	Camartina '91	▽▽	5
●	Camartina '93	▽▽	5
●	Chianti Classico Ris. '90	▽▽	5
●	Chianti Classico Ris. '91	▽▽	4
●	Chianti Classico Ris. '93	▽▽	4

GREVE IN CHIANTI (FI)

RISECCOLI
VIA CONVERTOIE, 9
50022 GREVE IN CHIANTI (FI)
TEL. 055/853598

Though reaching a goal one has set for oneself is sure to provide satisfaction, the farsighted among us know that the real work begins once the celebration ends. Similarly, the listing of an estate in this Guide should be considered a starting point leading to further improvement. The Romanellis certainly don't intend to rest on their laurels. Having seen the family's wines gain an international reputation (more than 90% of their production is exported), Signora Ilaria Romanelli continues her successful collaboration with the oenologist Giorgio Marone and the agronomist Valerio Barbieri. Let's turn our attention to the tasting results: the Saeculum '95, a sangiovese/cabernet sauvignon blend, is the estate's premier bottle. Deep garnet ruby in color, it has very pleasing aromas, which include well-defined fruit fragrances, especially cherry, and clear balsamic tones. In the mouth it is clearly a wine with structure, soft in attack and harmoniously blending tannins and alcohol. The Riserva '95 makes a good impression; its color is a brilliant but not too intense ruby. It reveals elegant fragrances of fruit and vanilla, with light toasty undertones. Its entry on the palate is decisive, and the tannins are only partly mellowed. The Chianti Classico '96 is less convincing: its fruity aromas are too forward, and dominant tannins and acidity take their toll on overall balance.

	Wine	Glasses	
●	Saeculum '95	▼▼	5
●	Chianti Classico '96	▼	3
●	Chianti Classico Ris. '95	▼	4
●	Saeculum '94	▽▽	5
●	Chianti Classico '95	▽	3
●	Chianti Classico Ris. '94	▽	4

GREVE IN CHIANTI (FI)

Savignola Paolina
Via Petriolo, 58
50022 Greve in Chianti (FI)
tel. 055/853139

This small Greve winery is back in the Guide once again. Its name recalls both the village where the winery is located and Paolina Fabbri, grandmother of the present owner, Carlo, who has been managing the estate since 1988, intent on making better wine. Hence the overhaul of the estate's cellar and vat room was recently completed. Not too long ago, Carlo's daugther Ludovica began to devote herself full-time to the estate, in keeping with family tradition. The wines they presented this year were impressive indeed. Let's start with the Chianti Classico '96. Its color is an intense ruby red, and it offers a wonderfully elegant fruity bouquet in which cherry emerges clearly, opening into delicate balsamic notes. The attack on the palate is not very weighty, but excellent balance is soon evident. The finish is pleasant, albeit not very long. The Riserva '95 features a beautiful deep ruby hue and an impressive array of fragrances including ripe fruit in which blackberry and plum fuse, tertiary aromas and tobacco at the end. The palate, with its notable lovely concentration, is satisfying too, and the tannins are evident but not aggressive. The finish is pleasing and long.

Wine	Rating	Price
● Chianti Classico Ris. '95	🍷🍷	4
● Chianti Classico '96	🍷	3
● Chianti Classico Ris. '85	ŸŸ	5
● Chianti Classico Ris. '90	ŸŸ	5
● Chianti Classico Ris. '88	Ÿ	5
● Chianti Classico Ris. '91	Ÿ	4

GREVE IN CHIANTI (FI)

Terreno
Via Citille, 4
50022 Greve in Chianti (FI)
tel. 055/854001

The Terreno estate is located in Citille, just a few kilometers north of Greve in Chianti, between the Castello di Uzzano and Villa Calcinaia. This area is already quite far north for Chianti Classico, but is sometimes capable of producing elegant wines with surprising aging potential. We are convinced that this winery's Chianti Classicos belong to that category, especially the Riserva '95, which can hold its own with the best reds ever made in these parts. Of course the harvest was propitious, although some '95s were disappointing after what we had all been taught to expect from this vintage. But let's get back to the enchanting Chianti Classico Riserva '95: the nose is characterized by distinct fruity fragrances with emerging sour cherry and other red fruit, but also a complex mixture of mineral tones, ink and, particularly, pencil lead, which confer both depth and elegance. The palate, although not very well articulated, reveals elegance, especially in its unusually sweet and dense polyphenols. The finish is pleasantly protracted, the concentration merely average. The Chianti Classico '96 is not at all bad. It is a much simpler, fresh and easily drinkable wine which displays the manifold advantages of a wine made from healthy grapes by means of sound vinification techniques.

Wine	Rating	Price
● Chianti Classico Ris. '95	🍷🍷	4
● Chianti Classico '96	🍷	3

GREVE IN CHIANTI (FI)

CASTELLO DI VERRAZZANO
LOC. VERRAZZANO
50022 GREVE IN CHIANTI (FI)
TEL. 055/854243

They've done better than last year, but we expect yet more from this winery. For the moment, we note a substantial improvement in their special selections, both the Sassello '95 and the Bottiglia Particolare '95 being outstanding wines, whereas the Chianti Classico '95 seems just to be treading water and the Chianti Classico '96 was not much to our liking. But let's get back to what we did like. The Bottiglia Particolare '95, sangiovese with some cabernet sauvignon, is excellent. It does not have enormous body, but it's wonderfully drinkable, the tannins are elegant and the acidity well-judged. The aromas are outstanding: clearly defined and concentrated fruit on an excellent oaky background. All in all a very well-made wine and just what we expect from Castello di Verrazzano and its owner, Luigi Cappellini. The Sassello '95, pure sangiovese, is very interesting. It may not be so complex on the nose, but it does well on the palate with its remarkable balance and excellent structure. The Chianti Classico Riserva '95, however, is rather forward on the nose, and notes of toasty wood obscure the background fruit. The palate makes a better showing, where a certain elegance is in evidence, despite the somewhat thin body. Our final and least cheering comments concern the Chianti Classico '96. With an almost neutral palate and a quite forward nose, it is a wine of little character and not much body. It is true that the vintage was anything but exceptional, but we were hoping for something a bit better.

Wine	Glasses	Price
● Bottiglia Particolare '95	TT	5
● Sassello '95	TT	5
● Chianti Classico Ris. '95	T	4
● Chianti Classico '96		3
● Chianti Classico Ris. '90	YYY	5
● Bottiglia Particolare '90	YY	5
● Chianti Classico Ris. '88	YY	4
● Sassello '90	YY	5
● Sassello '93	YY	5
● Bottiglia Particolare '88	Y	5
● Chianti Classico '95	Y	3
● Chianti Classico Ris. '86	Y	4
● Chianti Classico Ris. '91	Y	4
● Chianti Classico Ris. '93	Y	4
● Chianti Classico Ris. '94	Y	4

GREVE IN CHIANTI (FI)

CASTELLO DI VICCHIOMAGGIO
VIA VICCHIOMAGGIO, 4
50022 GREVE IN CHIANTI (FI)
TEL. 055/854079

For some years Castello di Vicchiomaggio has done very well at our tastings. The wines show a consistency of quality that crowns the labors of John Matta, the estate's owner and oenologist. Hence we can hardly wait to sample what they're making at the newly acquired estate at Panzano, Villa Boscorotondo, from which a very interesting new wine is promised. Although none of the four wines presented at this year's tasting won Three Glasses, the general level of achievement was, as usual, very high. Let's begin with the Ripa delle More, which last year made it to the top: the '95 vintage didn't seem nearly as convincing. Although the fruity and lightly spicy bouquet was interesting, the palate was less structured, somewhat disjointed and dominated by the tannins. We once again preferred La Prima to the other Chianti Classico Riserva, Petri. We were impressed by La Prima's powerful bouquet, rich in tertiary aromas well blended with scents of ripe fruit and spice. On the palate the rich tannic component is not altogether balanced with the softer elements but there's a very pleasing finish. The Riserva Petri has a persistent bouquet of ripe fruit, but the palate is less elegant, with excess alcohol unbalancing the overall structure, and too short a finish. The Chianti Classico San Jacopo '96 is the least impressive of the bunch. The aromas are not altogether clean and feature hints of overripeness, and the structure, although correct, is light.

Wine	Glasses	Price
● Chianti Classico La Prima Ris. '95	TT	5
● Ripa delle More '95	TT	5
● Chianti Classico Petri Ris. '95	T	4
● Chianti Classico San Jacopo '96	T	3
● Ripa delle More '94	YYY	5
● Chianti Classico La Prima Ris. '86	YY	5
● Chianti Classico La Prima Ris. '90	YY	5
● Chianti Classico La Prima Ris. '93	YY	5
● Chianti Classico La Prima Ris. '88	YY	5
● Chianti Classico La Prima Ris. '94	YY	5
● Chianti Classico Petri Ris. '86	YY	5
● Chianti Classico Petri Ris. '90	YY	5
● Ripa delle More '90	YY	5

GREVE IN CHIANTI (FI)

FATTORIA DI VIGNAMAGGIO
VIA DI PETRIOLO
50022 GREVE IN CHIANTI (FI)
TEL. 055/853007 - 853559

Well, we said last year that sooner or later Vignamaggio would produce something superlative and lo and behold! Here is the Chianti Classico Monna Lisa Riserva '95, an easy Three Glass winner! This is Chianti Classico at its best: a wine of character and extremely drinkable. The nose reflects the terroir, with mineral, tobacco and undergrowth tones, as well as hints of oak fused with the generous fruit and hints of licorice. The palate is even more expressive, sweet and soft. Although the Monna Lisa is number one, we were more astonished by the Chianti Classico '96, given its category and vintage. The color is a wonderfully intense ruby, and the bouquet is unusually rich for a normal vintage Chianti: we found notes of blackberries, plums, cocoa and mint. Then it is mouth-filling, soft, dense and broad. In fact it very nearly won a second Three Glasses for this estate. The Gherardino '95, somewhat in the shadows because of these other two, is still an excellent wine. It's made from sangiovese with a little cabernet, and displays warm aromas reminiscent of sour cherry preserves. The palate is second to none in body, though it may not win prizes for elegance. We round off the list with their good Vin Santo '93, which follows the dry tradition and is crisp and fresh.

●	Chianti Cl. Monna Lisa Ris. '95	▼▼▼	4
●	Chianti Classico '96	▼▼	3
●	Gherardino '95	▼▼	5
○	Vin Santo '93	▼	5
●	Chianti Cl. Monna Lisa Ris. '85	▽▽	4
●	Chianti Cl. Monna Lisa Ris. '88	▽▽	5
●	Chianti Cl. Monna Lisa Ris. '90	▽▽	4*
●	Chianti Cl. Monna Lisa Ris. '94	▽▽	4
●	Chianti Cl. Monna Lisa Ris. '93	▽▽	4
●	Chianti Classico '90	▽▽	4
●	Chianti Classico Ris. '88	▽▽	4
●	Gherardino '88	▽▽	5
●	Gherardino '90	▽▽	5
●	Gherardino '93	▽▽	5
●	Vignamaggio '93	▽▽	5

GREVE IN CHIANTI

VITICCIO
VIA SAN CRESCI, 12/A
50022 GREVE IN CHIANTI (FI)
TEL. 055/854210

Please excuse us if we repeat ourselves, but the consistency of quality that distinguishes Viticcio, year after year, is no small matter. Our only criticism, which we offer in the friendliest possible spirit, is that this estate, like many others in Chianti Classico country, focuses more on its "table wines" than on DOCGs. Couldn't an excellent wine like the Prunaio '95, a monovarietal sangiovese, be put forward, perhaps a few years from now, as the Riserva or special selection of their Chianti Classico? But, as we said, the problem is widespread, and what interests us more at the moment is that the wine in question did very well indeed at our tastings. It's a pleasure to look at and its rich and intense bouquet includes prominent notes of black fruit, followed by hints of spice and toasty oak. The palate is every bit as good: the opening is dense, and the tannins are closely woven, making for general balance. It positively upstaged the fine Monile '95 for once. Said Monile has a rather vegetal nose and a smooth and well-balanced palate, not perhaps characterized by great concentration. The Chianti Classico Riserva '95 was probably not at its best, having just settled into the bottle when we tasted it, but it did display a good, sweet, concentrated and substantial palate. The Chianti Classico '96 is a reliable wine, with the brashness of youth.

●	Monile '95	▼▼	5
●	Prunaio '95	▼▼	5
●	Chianti Classico '96	▼	4
●	Chianti Classico Ris. '95	▼	4
●	Chianti Classico '95	▽▽	4
●	Chianti Classico Ris. '90	▽▽	4
●	Chianti Classico Ris. '91	▽▽	4
●	Monile '91	▽▽	5
●	Monile '93	▽▽	5
●	Monile '94	▽▽	5
●	Prunaio '90	▽▽	5
●	Prunaio '93	▽▽	5
●	Prunaio '94	▽▽	5
●	Chianti Classico '93	▽	3
●	Monile '90	▽	5

IMPRUNETA (FI)

Podere Lanciola II
Via Imprunetana, 210
50023 Impruneta (FI)
tel. 055/208324 - 352011

Slowly but surely Lanciola has been getting better and better. This year's wines are further proof, even if a defect here and there indicates the need for additional improvement. The Chianti Colli Fiorentini '96, a clean, crisp red with lots of good fruit, is an excellent example of what this kind of wine should be. The Riserva '95 aims higher: it features a distinctly oaky nose with pleasant hints of spice. The palate shows body, the appropriate tannins, softness and balance. The grander of their Chianti Classico selections more or less share the same merits and the same faults. The Chianti Classico di Greve '96 has a clean fruity bouquet with a faint accent of new wood. On the palate, together with quite noticeable tannins, the oak reappears more insistently. The Chianti Classico Le Masse di Greve Riserva '95 is not, whatever one might expect, really more distinguished. Oak dominates the nose, but it is clean and very spicy; it has gone somewhat overboard on acidity and the finish is tannic. Quality climbs with the reassuringly harmonious Terricci '95, a sangiovese and cabernet blend. Toasty oak notes appear in the clean bouquet and it is supple on the palate, although the structure is not very firm and the oak is still too noticeable.

	Wine	Rating	Price
●	Terricci '95	🍷🍷	4
●	Chianti Classico Le Masse di Greve '96	🍷	3
●	Chianti Classico Le Masse di Greve Ris. '95	🍷	4
●	Chianti Colli Fiorentini '96	🍷	2
●	Chianti Colli Fiorentini Ris. '95	🍷	3
●	Terricci '86	🍸🍸	4
●	Terricci '88	🍸🍸	4
●	Chianti Classico Le Masse di Greve Ris. '94	🍸	4
●	Chianti Colli Fiorentini '94	🍸	2
●	Chianti Colli Fiorentini Ris. '93	🍸	3
●	Terricci '93	🍸	4
○	Vin Santo '91	🍸	5

MAGLIANO IN TOSCANA (GR)

Le Pupille
Loc. Pereta
58051 Magliano in Toscana (GR)
tel. 0564/505129

More good news from Le Pupille: the wines are outstanding this year, and Elisabetta and Stefano are expecting another baby. These two form one of the most effective husband-and-wife teams in the wine world today: she with her sweet insistence on quality, and he with his valuable experience as a wine merchant in America. As you may have guessed they are passionate about winegrowing, and they have recently acquired much more land nearby. They also understand the market and respect their customers. It is this respect that leads them at times to make difficult decisions, such as when they decided not to produce a Saffredi '96, which should have appeared next year, because the vintage was not, they felt, up to par. Not many producers would have done the same. Some, indeed, would have pretended that nothing was wrong, perhaps even raising the price. But consider the silver lining: we had a taste from the barrel of something they are going to release in '99 and we now understand their master plan: staking everything on uncompromising quality. Speaking of newcomers, we tasted two vintages, '95 and '96, of a new sweet wine, Solalto, whose qualities will make its peers tremble in their bottles: balance and elegance, structure and length. And it will be sold at a very competitive price. As for the other family jewels, there is the Saffredi '95, an excellent wine as usual except for a slight aromatic defect. The Riserva di Morellino '95 is also a very good wine, but it needs to breathe. The Morellino '97 is simply outstanding and the new white, Poggio Argentato '97, a blend of sauvignon and traminer, is pleasing.

	Wine	Rating	Price
●	Morellino di Scansano '97	🍷🍷	3*
●	Saffredi '95	🍷🍷	5
○	Solalto '96	🍷🍷	3*
○	Solalto '95	🍷🍷	3*
●	Morellino di Scansano Ris. '95	🍷	4
○	Poggio Argentato '97	🍷	3
●	Saffredi '90	🍸🍸🍸	6
●	Morellino di Scansano Ris. '94	🍸🍸	4
●	Saffredi '87	🍸🍸	5
●	Saffredi '88	🍸🍸	5
●	Saffredi '89	🍸🍸	5
●	Saffredi '91	🍸🍸	5
●	Saffredi '93	🍸🍸	5
●	Saffredi '94	🍸🍸	5
○	Vin Santo di Caratello '90	🍸🍸	4

MANCIANO (GR)

LA STELLATA
VIA FORNACINA, 18
58014 MANCIANO (GR)
TEL. 0564/620190

Since the time of the Etruscans, the vine has been cultivated near Pitigliano, and Bianco di Pitigliano has been well-known for centuries. When the Jews were expelled from Spain at the end of the fifteenth century, an important Jewish community came into being here, and many of its members dedicated themselves to what became a flourishing wine-making industry, which still survives and specializes in the production of kosher wines. But this is not the only wine produced in these parts. The most refreshing, fruity and enjoyable white from Pitigliano is Lunaia, which Manlio and Clara Divizia have been producing for some years on their lovely estate, La Stellata. The classic Tuscan trebbiano is there, of course, but it's accompanied by greco, malvasia and a touch of verdello. This is not a wine of structure to be laid down in your cellar. It is round, soft, and redolent of Golden Delicious apples, and it just slips right down. It goes beautifully with the fishy cuisine of the coast near Grosseto. The price is good, the quality excellent – what more can you ask for?

	Wine	Rating	Price
○	Bianco di Pitigliano Lunaia '97	▼	3
○	Bianco di Pitigliano Lunaia '93	▽▽	3
○	Bianco di Pitigliano Lunaia '95	▽	3
○	Bianco di Pitigliano Lunaia '96	▽	3
●	Lunaia Rosso '93	▽	2

MASSA MARITTIMA (GR)

MASSA VECCHIA
PODERE FORNACE
LOC. ROCCHE, 11
58024 MASSA MARITTIMA (GR)
TEL. 0566/915522

Whether you want to dismiss it as winebar talk or the pointless sort of argument you run into at wine-tasting societies, the question remains: which is better, a wine made from native grapes or one produced from an "international" varietal, like cabernet or merlot? You will have to answer this one for yourself, letting your palate be the judge. Perhaps Europe was united long before Maastricht, by quantities of bottles of excellent wine. And perhaps the world is smaller than it seems, especially if you look at it from the perspective of a first-rate wine shop. Because wine, when it's good, is good, whatever grapes were used and whatever fashions were reigning when it was made. So a wine from the Maremma made from French varietals can be just as praiseworthy as a bottle whose grapes have never flourished anywhere but Scansano. These thoughts come to us with particular force after tasting La Fonte di Pietrarsa, the outstanding cabernet sauvignon produced by Masssa Vecchia, a winery that has become a regular in the Guide. It's an elegant, soft wine, with a hint of sweet oak, lovely tannins and a long finish: a classic in these parts. The good Terziere, made from alicante, reveals a delicate bouquet of cherries (although perhaps it's a bit too sweet on the palate). Finally, the Patrizia Bartolini, a tasty sweet wine made from sauvignon and vermentino, is perfectly acceptable.

	Wine	Rating	Price
●	La Fonte di Pietrarsa '95	▼▼	4
○	Patrizia Bartolini '96	▼	4
●	Terziere '96	▼	4
●	La Fonte di Pietrarsa '92	▽▽	4
●	La Fonte di Pietrarsa '93	▽▽	4
●	La Fonte di Pietrarsa '94	▽▽	4
●	Terziere '93	▽▽	4
●	Le Veglie di Neri '90	▽	4

MASSA MARITTIMA (GR)

MORIS FARMS
LOC. CURANUOVA
58024 MASSA MARITTIMA (GR)
TEL. 0566/919135

We have been praising this fine Maremma winery for ages. The vineyards owned by Gualtierluigi Moris cover almost 400 hectares of land divided into two estates: the larger is near Massa Marittima, and the smaller one, at Poggio a Lamozza, is dedicated entirely to the production of Morellino di Scansano. Twenty-five of its 56 hectares currently produce grapes, and the rest, only recently planted, will start bearing fruit in a few years. The winery is managed by Adolfo Parentini, who, with the expert aid of the oenologist Attilio Pagli and the agronomist Andrea Paoletti, produces 220,000 bottles of excellent wine annually. Their gem is the Avvoltore, which has become one of the great wines of the Maremma. The '95 is almost impenetrably dark. The dominant aromas are of dry mushrooms, kirsch and a very appealing ink, drawing one on to an almost overwhelming palate with an imposing structure and noble tannins very much present. It's almost too big, and still hard, but it promises great things for the future if bottle age succeeds in taming it. The Morellino di Scansano '97, which is meant to be very good, was not ready when we were, so we shall consider it next time.

●	Avvoltore '95	🍷🍷	5
●	Avvoltore '94	🍷🍷	5
●	Morellino di Scansano Ris. '94	🍷🍷	4
●	Avvoltore '93	🍷	5
●	Morellino di Scansano '94	🍷	2
●	Morellino di Scansano '95	🍷	2
●	Morellino di Scansano Ris. '93	🍷	4

MATRAIA (LU)

FATTORIA COLLE VERDE
LOC. CASTELLO
55010 MATRAIA (LU)
TEL. 0583/402256

Tired of life in the big city, Francesca Pardini and Piero Tartagni, like many others, left Rome and moved to the country. And what do you do in the country, particularly if it happens to be in Tuscany? You make wine and olive oil, of course. It is very much less a matter of course that the liquids in question will be reliably excellent year after year. Now it's not our place to pass judgment on the Colle Verde oil, but we can assure you that the wine is remarkable. The estate, located in a magnificent sort of hilly amphitheater near Matraia, presented a trio of extremely interesting wines this year. First of all, the Brania del Cancello '97, a white wine which is half trebbiano picked when slightly overripe and half chardonnay. It is fermented and matured in barriques and is an intense yellow with gold highlights. One is immediately struck by notes of toasty oak, which in fact predominate, but pleasing, if still rather meek, fruity aromas soon emerge. A couple of years in the bottle should go a long way towards taming the wood. The palate is stimulating, full-bodied, almost fat, and decidedly alcoholic. An excellent wine, and here's another: Brania delle Ghiandaie '95, a blend of sangiovese and 10% of syrah. Of a deep ruby hue, it too has very woody aromas, but the fruit (wild blackberries and raspberries) is able to stand up to it. There is dense extract, the tannins are substantial, the palate is very clean and the finish is long. We awarded Two Glasses to each Brania, (which means terracing in the local dialect). One Glass went to the Greco delle Gaggie, a monovarietal greco: it is a soft, sweet wine with delightful aromatic notes of candied apricot.

○	Brania del Cancello '97	🍷🍷	4
●	Brania delle Ghiandaie '95	🍷🍷	4
○	Greco delle Gaggìe '95	🍷	4

MERCATALE VALDARNO (AR)

FATTORIA PETROLO

LOC. GALATRONA
52020 MERCATALE VALDARNO (AR)
TEL. 055/9911322 - 992965

The two main wines produced at Petrolo reflect the spirit of an estate which, although solidly traditional, is willing to meet the future halfway. Torrione, a pure sangiovese with a classic taste and a well-defined style, symbolizes the traditional side, and Galatrona, a merlot with a rounder and more direct palate, is certainly a more modern wine. This year we preferred the Torrione '95, excellent even in appearance and quite characteristic in its bouquet that reveals black fruit and faint floral and mineral hints against a spicy background of oak. Wood is also evident on the palate, which progresses with excellent balance, pleasantly sweet at first and enlivened by tannins on the finish. As for the Galatrona, after its debut with the '94 vintage which we treated somewhat roughly, we expected rather more. The color of the '95 is not particularly concentrated, and on the nose, which is distinct and intense, vegetal and minty notes overwhelm the fruit. The palate is admirably well-balanced and evenly arranged, but there's a rather forward note and the tannins are a bit dry. At Petrolo they are perfectly well aware of the limitations of this good wine, so we feel certain that Lucia Sanjust will soon have some very pleasant surprises for us.

	Wine	Glasses	Price
●	Galatrona '95	🍷🍷	6
●	Torrione '95	🍷🍷	5
●	Chianti Titolato Ris. '90	ΥΥ	4
●	Torrione '90	ΥΥ	5
●	Torrione '94	ΥΥ	5
○	Vin Santo '93	ΥΥ	5
●	Chianti Ris. '91	Υ	3
●	Chianti Titolato '90	Υ	2*
●	Chianti Titolato '91	Υ	3
●	Galatrona '94	Υ	6
●	Torrione '88	Υ	5
●	Torrione '91	Υ	5
●	Torrione '93	Υ	5

MONTAGNANA VAL DI PESA (FI)

LE CALVANE

VIA CASTIGLIONI, 1
50020 MONTAGNANA
VAL DI PESA (FI)
TEL. 0571/671073

Le Calvane may not produce celebrated and fashionable wines, but it has a place in the Guide year after year for its constant reliability. The range is wide but once again the Cabernet Borro del Boscone is the pick of the lot. Usually its virtues are power and concentration, rather than elegance, but the '95 is fresher and even stylish. Its color is wonderfully intense, and distinct fruity aromas are punctuated by agreeable spice, leading to an excellent progression on the palate, which is succulent and soft. Although this wine may lack complexity, it shows off the best side of the cabernet: lots of fruit and hardly any vegetal hints. Among the other wines, we liked the Chianti Colli Fiorentini '97, with its lively ruby hue, simple but distinct red fruit aromas and dense and well-balanced palate with rounded tannins. The other wines presented by this estate are acceptable. The well-made Chianti Colli Fiorentini Quercione '96, characterized by aromas of cherry and a sprinkling of pepper, has a moderate amount of body and is quite drinkable. The Riserva Il Trecione '95 did not really live up to our expectations: its bouquet is clean but not very expressive, and it's a bit forward in taste. The Chardonnay Collecimoli '96 has good weight on the palate but is less limpid on the nose, while the Zipolo d 'Oro, an acceptable dessert wine, could be better.

	Wine	Glasses	Price
●	Borro del Boscone '95	🍷🍷	5
●	Chianti Colli Fiorentini Quercione '96	🍷	3
●	Chianti Colli Fiorentini Quercione '97	🍷	3
●	Chianti Colli Fiorentini Il Trecione Ris. '95		4
○	Collecimoli '96		3
○	Zipolo d'Oro '91		4
●	Borro del Boscone '91	ΥΥ	4
●	Borro del Boscone '94	ΥΥ	4
●	Chianti Colli Fiorentini Il Trecione Ris. '91	ΥΥ	4
●	Chianti Colli Fiorentini Quercione '95	Υ	2

MONTALCINO (SI)

ALTESINO
LOC. TORRENIERI
53028 MONTALCINO (SI)
TEL. 0577/806208

After a year's absence, the excellent Altesino returns to these pages. The estate comprises a total of 17 hectares in the DOCG zone mainly to the north of Montalcino, including the highly-prized Montosoli area. It's worth the few kilometers of dirt road after the highway to see this lovely estate and the well-equipped cellar with barrels of various sizes and woods. All of the many wines they presented this year were of notable quality.. There were two '93 Brunellos: the cru Montosoli and the "regular vintage ", and both easily earned Two Glasses. Strangely enough, we preferred the regular vintage, which we found more complete. To the nose it's intense and clean, and hints of violets in the fruity bouquet give it a particular elegance. It fills the mouth, the tannins are well-behaved and the finish is broad and impressive. The Brunello cru, on the other hand, features an initial vegetal nuance that gets in the way, although the bouquet then opens out convincingly. The palate is very refined and stylish, although a faintly bitter finish limits its depth. It should, however, get better in the bottle. The fragrant, clean and pleasing Quarto d 'Altesi seemed to us the best of their table wines.

Wine	Glasses	Price
● Brunello di Montalcino '93	🍷🍷	5
● Brunello di Montalcino Montosoli '93	🍷🍷	6
● Quarto d'Altesi '95	🍷🍷	6
● Alte d'Altesi '95	🍷	5
● Borgo d'Altesi '95	🍷	4
● Palazzo d'Altesi '95	🍷	4
● Brunello di Montalcino Ris. '88	♀♀	6
● Brunello di Montalcino Ris. '90	♀♀	6
● Brunello di Montalcino '89	♀	5
● Brunello di Montalcino '90	♀	5
● Brunello di Montalcino Montosoli '90	♀	5
● Rosso di Montalcino '94	♀	3
● Rosso di Montalcino '93	♀	3

MONTALCINO (SI)

TENUTA DI ARGIANO
LOC. S. ANGELO IN COLLE, 54
53020 MONTALCINO (SI)
TEL. 0577/864037

Argiano owns 18 hectares of vines for Brunello, along with other vineyards devoted to the production of such international varietals as cabernet sauvignon, syrah and merlot. This winery has always been on the lookout for innovative techniques to improve their Brunello. They were among the first to adopt barrique-aging, giving rise to heated but useful argument throughout the area about the best way to make this wine "comprehensible " abroad. Their decision, a good one as it happens, was based on the considerable experience of both Noemi Cinzano, owner of the estate, and Giacomo Tachis, the oenologist who virtually re-invented Tuscan wine towards the end of the '60s. There were three wines for us to taste this year: the Rosso di Montalcino '96, the Brunello '93 and the Solengo '96. This last was excellent, and serves as further proof that "alternative " grapes also do very well here. The color is intense ruby red with bluish glints and the broad bouquet offers distinct notes of wild berry preserve. In the mouth it is concentrated and the tannins are elegant, if perhaps a bit too noticeable. The finish is good, and corresponds perfectly to the aromas. The Brunello, modern in style, has a singular bouquet in which rich tones of minerals and orange peel cover the classic fruity aroma. The attack and progression on the palate are good, but the tannins should be less in evidence. Finally, the Rosso di Montalcino is not quite up to form this year.

Wine	Glasses	Price
● Brunello di Montalcino '93	🍷🍷	6
● Solengo '96	🍷🍷	6
● Rosso di Montalcino '96		3
● Brunello di Montalcino Ris. '85	♀♀♀	5
● Brunello di Montalcino Ris. '88	♀♀♀	6
● Solengo '95	♀♀♀	6
● Brunello di Montalcino '85	♀♀	5
● Brunello di Montalcino '87	♀♀	5
● Brunello di Montalcino '88	♀♀	5
● Brunello di Montalcino '90	♀♀	5
● Brunello di Montalcino '92	♀♀	6
● Brunello di Montalcino '91	♀♀	5
● Brunello di Montalcino Ris. '90	♀♀	6
● Brunello di Montalcino Ris. '91	♀♀	6
● Rosso di Montalcino '95	♀	4

MONTALCINO (SI)

Castello Banfi

Castello di Poggio alle Mura
53024 Montalcino (SI)
tel. 0577/840111

Castello Banfi is a leader in Montalcino both for its size (they own 150 hectares of vines for making Brunello, just for a start) and for the general quality of what they produce. There is not enough space to discuss all their the wines, but even their less expensive ones are well made. We always find a Three Glass winner among their large selection of top wines, and behind this consistently admirable performance is Ezio Rivella, one of the most brilliant managers on the Italian wine scene. In addition to directing the Banfi estate, which belongs to the Mariani brothers, American entrepreneurs, he is the president of several important oenological associations. This year, we were most impressed by the Summus '95, a barrique-aged blend of sangiovese, syrah and cabernet. This wine, which easily earned Three Glasses, embodies all the potential of Montalcino, which is friendly both to the native sangiovese and to imported varietals. The Summus '95 is very intense in color, almost purple. Its aromas are ample and intense with raspberry and blackberry softened by spicy oak. The palate is just as impressive, full and solid, with a long finish. In the Two Glass category are the succulent Mandrielle '96, a merlot, the Tavernelle '95, a well executed cabernet sauvignon, and the Fontanelle '96, an elegant chardonnay with characteristic delectable suggestions of ripe banana. We also very much liked the Moscadello '96, intensely sensual to the nose and soft and harmonious on the palate.

	Wine	Glasses	Price
●	Summus '95	▼▼▼	6
○	Fontanelle Chardonnay '96	▼▼	4
●	Mandrielle Merlot '96	▼▼	4
○	Moscadello di Montalcino '96	▼▼	5
●	Tavernelle Cabernet '95	▼▼	5
●	Brunello di Montalcino '93	▼	5
●	Rosso di Montalcino '96	▼	3
●	Brunello di Montalcino Poggio all'Oro '88	▽▽▽	6
●	Brunello di Montalcino Poggio all'Oro Ris. '90	▽▽▽	6
●	Excelsus '93	▽▽▽	6
●	Brunello di Montalcino '90	▽▽	5
●	Summus '93	▽▽	6
●	Summus '94	▽▽	6

MONTALCINO (SI)

Fattoria dei Barbi

Loc. Podernovi
53024 Montalcino (SI)
tel. 0577/848277

Fattoria dei Barbi, a historic Montalcino winery, has contributed significantly to the widespread success of Brunello ever since the end of the war, in part by following an enlightened pricing policy which has made it possible for many more people to get to know this wine. They have maintained local tradition in many ways, and still make all the products of a classic Tuscan farm. Thus excellent salamis and cheeses have their place beside the wines, which themselves are traditional in the best sense and very well made, as this year's range bears out. The first-rate staff includes the oenologist Luigi Casagrande and the agronomist Carlo Ferrini. The Brunello '93 is classic in color, hence not impenetrable, with a garnet glow. The aromas reveal a touch of tobacco, and fruit preserved in alcohol. It is satisfyingly drinkable, in part because of its excellent balance, free of excessive tannic astringency. The Rosso di Montalcino '96 is also very good. There are interesting earthy notes on the nose, together with cherry and a hint of india ink. The palate is pleasing, the acidity well-judged, and the finish fairly long. We can say nothing of their prize, the Brunello Vigna del Fiore, which they of course did not make in '92. The '93 will appear in these pages next year.

	Wine	Glasses	Price
●	Brunello di Montalcino '93	▼▼	5
●	Rosso di Montalcino '96	▼	3
●	Brunello di Montalcino Ris. '88	▽▽	6
●	Brunello di Montalcino Vigna del Fiore Ris. '88	▽▽	6
●	Brunello di Montalcino Vigna del Fiore Ris. '90	▽▽	6
●	Brunello di Montalcino Vigna del Fiore Ris. '91	▽▽	6
●	Brunello di Montalcino '89	▽	5
●	Brunello di Montalcino '90	▽	4
●	Brunello di Montalcino '91	▽	4
●	Brunello di Montalcino Ris. '90	▽	6
●	Rosso di Montalcino '93	▽	3
●	Rosso di Montalcino '94	▽	3

MONTALCINO (SI)

BIONDI SANTI
LOC. GREPPO
53024 MONTALCINO (SI)
TEL. 0577/847121 - 848087

Biondi Santi distributes the Montalcino wines of Il Greppo as well as those from the Poggio Salvi estate, and also the table wines of Jacopo Biondi Santi. Unfortunately the wines of Il Greppo were not ready in time for our consideration. However, our tastings of the Brunello Poggio Salvi '93 comfortingly indicated an improvement over earlier versions. Its classic color with garnet veining is followed by slightly forward aromas of tobacco and leather against good background fruit. It progresses well on the palate, all the elements are in excellent balance and the finish is satisfyingly long. Jacopo Biondi Santi's wines are of an enviably consistent quality, although a difference in vintages makes itself felt. The Schidione '94 won Two Glasses thanks to the softness given it by elegant tannins perfectly integrated into the not exactly monumental structure. The aroma is generous, with notes of tobacco and sour cherry blunting a rather vegetal tone. We preferred the Sassoalloro '95, which displays intense blackberries and dark cherries on an oak-derived balsamic base. In the mouth it's elegant and substantial, and the aromas are reflected on the finish. The Lavischio di Poggi Salvi '96, a merlot, is simpler but attractive.

● Brunello di Montalcino Poggio Salvi '93	🍷🍷	6
● Sassoalloro '95	🍷🍷	5
● Schidione '94	🍷🍷	6
● Lavischio di Poggio Salvi '96	🍷	4
● Brunello di Montalcino '83	ΥΥΥ	6
● Brunello di Montalcino '85	ΥΥ	6
● Brunello di Montalcino '88	ΥΥ	6
● Brunello di Montalcino '90	ΥΥ	6
● Brunello di Montalcino Il Greppo Ris. '90	ΥΥ	6
● Brunello di Montalcino Ris. '85	ΥΥ	6
● Brunello di Montalcino Ris. '88	ΥΥ	6
● Sassoalloro '94	ΥΥ	5
● Schidione '93	ΥΥ	6

MONTALCINO (SI)

CAMPOGIOVANNI
LOC. S. ANGELO IN COLLE
53024 MONTALCINO (SI)
TEL. 0577/864001 - 864001

This estate represents the Montalcino holdings of the distinguished San Felice winery in Chianti and comprises about 12 hectares under vine near Sant' Angelo in Colle to the south of Montalcino. Although they have not yet succeeded in fully exploiting these splendidly situated vineyards, they have begun replanting, and will be taking advantage of the experience gained in the experimental vineyards that San Felice owns near Castelnuovo Berardenga. Thus the number of vines per hectare will increase, and new clones grown and selected in Chianti will be used here. Then too, they will have more barriques for aging their Brunello, now that the regulations have changed and the minimum barrel time for the most famous local wine has been reduced to two years. Campogiovanni produces nothing but Brunello. The '93 is a moderately dense ruby shading to garnet. The nose is slightly forward, with notes of tobacco enriching the cherry jam and sour cherries in spirits. The palate goes for elegance and balance, rather than power, and the tannins are appropriate.

● Brunello di Montalcino '93	🍷	6
● Brunello di Montalcino '87	ΥΥ	5
● Brunello di Montalcino '88	ΥΥ	5
● Brunello di Montalcino '89	ΥΥ	5
● Brunello di Montalcino '90	ΥΥ	5
● Brunello di Montalcino Vigna del Quercione Ris. '90	ΥΥ	6
● Brunello di Montalcino '85	Υ	5
● Brunello di Montalcino '86	Υ	5

MONTALCINO (SI)

CANALICCHIO DI SOPRA DI FRANCO PACENTI

Via Canalicchio di Sopra
53024 Montalcino (SI)
tel. 0577/849277

In case all the "Pacenti " and "Canalicchio " labels that seem to proliferate in Montalcino tend to make your head swim, we can offer the reassuring news that this is not yet another variation on that theme, but instead the new name of "Franco e Rosildo Pacenti", who are father and son and the current representatives of this dynasty of Montalcino winegrowers. This news should be particularly reassuring to the faithful customers of this estate, used as they are to a consistent style and unvarying quality in their wines. Indeed, aromatic and structural elegance and harmoniousness, if not power, have been among the most evident merits of Franco Parenti's Brunello year after year, and are in part the result of the "northern " clime of the vineyards in Canalicchio di Sopra. They now have four and a half hectares under vine for Brunello production, but starting next year they will be expanding, in the hopes of starting the new millennium with a supply that more nearly meets the ever-growing demand. Their Brunello '93 is perfectly in keeping with their style and our positive expectations. The color is between ruby and garnet, and the intense bouquet reveals fresh notes of black fruit and sweet vanilla as well as floral hints. The palate, although not very concentrated, offers softness and outstanding balance, with perfectly integrated tannins. The Rosso '96 is of course a simpler wine, with aromas of dark cherry and raspberry: light, mellow and delightfully drinkable.

● Brunello di Montalcino '93	🍷🍷	5
● Rosso di Montalcino '96	🍷	4
● Brunello di Montalcino '92	🍸	5
● Rosso di Montalcino '95	🍸	4

MONTALCINO (SI)

CANTINA DI MONTALCINO

Loc. Val di Cava
53024 Montalcino (SI)
tel. 0577/848704

Here is something new and unusual in Montalcino: a wine cooperative dedicated to making first-class wines. They are taking advantage of a method successfully tried out by cooperatives in Alto Adige: the grapes of member growers are carefully analyzed and the payment meted out ranges from 30% more to 25% less than the going market rate, depending on their quality. This would appear to have a stimulating effect on winegrowers. Last year we were pleased with the Brunello '92, and the '93 now offers further proof of an admirable consistency in quality achieved thanks to the labors of their oenologist Pucci, who is assisted by the advice of the great Montalcino wizard Paolo Vagaggini. Their state-of-the-art facilities include steel tanks equipped with automatic treaders as well as temperature control during fermentation, and they have a brand-new collection of barrels of all sizes. The Brunello '93 is of an intense ruby hue with garnet veining, and the intense, persistent and classic bouquet is particularly redolent of both sweet and sour cherries. The palate is pleasantly rich in extract, the tannins are well-integrated and the alcohol does not disappoint: a well-made wine, elegant rather than powerful. Just a step down is the Rosso '96, with a successful bouquet featuring unexpected but appealing hints of rhubarb. There's a light acidity on the palate which makes this wine particularly quaffable, despite a slightly bitterish finish.

● Brunello di Montalcino '93	🍷🍷	6
● Rosso di Montalcino '96	🍷	4

MONTALCINO (SI)

TENUTA CAPARZO
LOC. TORRENIERI
53028 MONTALCINO (SI)
TEL. 0577/848390 - 0577/847166

Caparzo is managed by Nuccio Turone, with the assistance of the oenologist Vittorio Fiore. This seems to be a successful combination, since things are getting better and better. The estate comprises a total of 22 hectares devoted to Brunello, between Siena and Grosseto, including some particularly choice vineyards in Montosoli to the north and Castelgiocondo to the south. Their cru, Brunello La Casa '93 is a Montosoli selection, and it is back up at the dizzying heights of the legendary '88, another Three Glass wine. Its color is a deep and intense ruby, and the complex bouquet displays notes of red fruit, notably sour cherry, and warm cherry preserves, on a background of oak-derived vanillin and cocoa. The palate serves as proof of the theory that there need not be massive structure in a great wine. Its elegance, based on gentle and stylish tannins and well-judged acidity, leads to a broad, enchanting and very long finish.. It is a Brunello that reflects, even magnifies, its terroir. The interesting Brunello '93 is classic and very well-made. The bouquet is fruity but more forward, and opens after an initial moment of hesitation. The palate is decisive and opulent, with well-integrated tannins. The very tasty white Le Grance '95, a blend of chardonnay, sauvignon and gewürztraminer, displays intense aromas of citrus fruit and flowers, particularly roses; then it's full-bodied, well-balanced and persistent. Finally, the Rosso '96 is pleasantly fruity and fairly long-lasting on the palate.

●	Brunello di Montalcino La Casa '93	🍷🍷🍷	6
●	Brunello di Montalcino '93	🍷🍷	6
○	Le Grance '95	🍷🍷	3*
●	Ca' del Pazzo '94	🍷	5
●	Rosso di Montalcino '96	🍷	4
●	Rosso di Montalcino La Caduta '95	🍷	4
●	Brunello di Montalcino La Casa '88	🍷🍷🍷 (white)	6
●	Brunello di Montalcino '88	🍷🍷 (white)	6
●	Brunello di Montalcino La Casa '85	🍷🍷 (white)	6
●	Brunello di Montalcino La Casa '86	🍷🍷 (white)	6
●	Brunello di Montalcino La Casa '91	🍷🍷 (white)	5
●	Brunello di Montalcino Ris. '88	🍷🍷 (white)	6
○	Le Grance '93	🍷🍷 (white)	3*
●	Brunello di Montalcino La Casa '90	🍷 (white)	5
●	Brunello di Montalcino Ris. '90	🍷 (white)	6

MONTALCINO (SI)

CASANOVA DI NERI
LOC. TORRENIERI
53028 MONTALCINO (SI)
TEL. 0577/834029

The worldwide prestige enjoyed by Brunello is of course a temptation to its producers to rest on their laurels and cash in on the name, and some have done just that. We have, however, observed that there are now many who are engaged in seeking to produce wine that lives up to this extraordinary reputation, and Giacomo Neri is most certainly one of them. He is never content with his own wine and always eager to improve it. This can be seen, for a start, in the meticulous care he devotes to his vineyards, which cover more than 15 hectares in the northernmost part of Montalcino. Naturally, the winery also reflects this attitude: he has completely re-equipped his cellar with well-chosen barrels, large and small. He has sought to modify the style of his wines by softening the tannins and offering more evident and consistent fruit, without however changing their nature, i.e. alcoholic warmth and Chianti acidity, well covered by richness of extract. We found his excellent Brunello Tenuta Nuova '93 to be a perfect embodiment of these qualities, with the addition of intense dark cherry, blackberrry and sweet vanilla aromas. The "normal " Brunello is extremely good as well, riper and more classical in its bouquet, with notes of minerals, earth, leather and tobacco, and powerful and vigorous on the palate. The Rosso di Montalcino '96 is more easily approachable and very agreeable.

●	Brunello di Montalcino '93	🍷🍷	5
●	Brunello di Montalcino Tenuta Nuova '93	🍷🍷	6
●	Rosso di Montalcino '96	🍷	4
●	Brunello di Montalcino Cerretalto Ris. '88	🍷🍷🍷 (white)	6
●	Brunello di Montalcino '85	🍷🍷 (white)	5
●	Brunello di Montalcino '88	🍷🍷 (white)	6
●	Brunello di Montalcino '89	🍷🍷 (white)	6
●	Brunello di Montalcino '90	🍷🍷 (white)	5
●	Brunello di Montalcino '91	🍷🍷 (white)	6
●	Rosso di Montalcino '95	🍷🍷 (white)	4
●	Brunello di Montalcino Cerretalto Ris. '90	🍷 (white)	6
●	Casanova di Neri Rosso '96	🍷 (white)	3

MONTALCINO (SI)

FATTORIA DEL CASATO
DONATELLA CINELLI COLOMBINI
LOC. PODERNOVI
53024 MONTALCINO (SI)
TEL. 0577/848277

It is not often that a newly-established Montalcino winery appears in these pages, but when there is solid wine-making experience behind it, such a thing can happen. Donatella Cinelli Colombini used to direct the legendary Montalcino winery Fattoria dei Barbi, and is one of the most energetic "Women in Wine ", renowned for her managerial ability. The estate will soon have its own cellar, but for the moment their Brunello, the only wine they are presenting this year, albeit in two versions, is fermented and aged at the Fattoria dei Barbi. These two '93s differ in style but are both Two Glass winners. The normal Brunello '93 is decidedly classical, with its translucent ruby hue shading to garnet and its characteristic bouquet featuring distinct notes of tobacco and dark cherry preserve underpinned by alcohol. The palate is elegant and substantial and the finish mirrors the bouquet. The Brunello '93 Prime Donne is the result of an interesting project: the wines that go into the final assemblage are chosen by a panel of female tasters. It is a Brunello made by women, but certain to please men as well, given its outstanding quality. It is more modern in style, with a very intense ruby color. The bouquet is distinctly fruity with notes of sour cherry preserve underpinned by very fresh sweet cherry. The substantial palate progresses well to a finish with a light and inviting nuance of india ink.

Wine	Glasses	Price
● Brunello di Montalcino '93	**YY**	5
● Brunello di Montalcino Prime Donne '93	**YY**	6

MONTALCINO (SI)

CASTELGIOCONDO
LOC. CASTELGIOCONDO
53024 MONTALCINO (SI)
TEL. 055/27141

The Castelgiocondo estate is owned by the Marchesi de ' Frescobaldi, one of the most famous names in wine both for the amount of land they own in Tuscany and the for quality of the wines they produce there. In Montalcino they have 130 hectares of Brunello vineyards. After last year's quirky results, the estate has returned to its usual high standards with both the Brunello '93 and the merlot-based Lamaione '95. The Rosso di Montalcino Campo ai Sassi, however, rates no more than a mention because of its not quite clean aromas. The Brunello '93 is very concentrated in color, while the bouquet, although intense, displays wood-derived caramel and chocolate aromas that overwhelm the fruit. The palate progresses well and the extract is satisfactory, but somewhat untamed, although noble, tannins produce a slight astringency. The Riserva, which is scheduled for release next year, aims a great deal higher. The Lamaione is becoming their most reliable wine, and the '95 is no disappointment. Here too the nose is at first dominated by notes of roasted coffee, caramel and cocoa, and it is only later that tobacco and red fruit make their appearance. Perhaps this is the new Castelgiocondo style, but we 'd prefer less insistent wood. The palate, however, is very pleasant, intense and harmonious, leading up to a long, broad finish.

Wine	Glasses	Price
● Brunello di Montalcino '93	**YY**	5
● Lamaione '95	**YY**	5
● Rosso di Montalcino Campo ai Sassi '96		4
● Brunello di Montalcino Ris. '88	YYY	6
● Brunello di Montalcino Ris. '90	YYY	6
● Brunello di Montalcino '89	YY	5
● Brunello di Montalcino '90	YY	5
● Brunello di Montalcino '91	YY	5
● Lamaione '91	YY	5
● Lamaione '92	YY	5
● Lamaione '94	YY	5

MONTALCINO (SI)

Col d'Orcia
Loc. S. Angelo in Colle
53020 Montalcino (SI)
tel. 0577/808001

Traveling wine-lovers would be well advised to visit Col d 'Orcia, both for its physical beauty and for the opportunity of tasting its excellent wines. This year their Olmaia '94, a pure cabernet sauvignon, is the top of the list and has carried off Three Glasses, conquering us all and getting stratospheric scores. An impenetrable intense ruby with bluish nuances, it offers broad and long-lasting aromas of blueberry and black currant, with enticing faint toasty undertones and hints of cocoa. It is quite delightful on the palate, with a gentle attack and a really sublime progression including very elegant and perfectly integrated tannins, leading to a long, rich, unwavering finish: a very impressive performance with a grape often considered one of the true tests of greatness in the international arena. The DOCs were far less convincing: indeed the Brunello '93 got only One Glass. The bouquet is rather forward and offers animal and tobacco notes. There is not a great deal of body, and the acidity is not well integrated. The Rosso di Montalcino '96 is actually better: the nose is rich in dark and sour cherry aromas, and its palate is pleasingly fresh and fairly substantial. To close, the Ghiaie Bianche '96, an oak-aged chardonnay, is altogether agreeable.

●	Olmaia '94	▼▼▼	5
●	Brunello di Montalcino '93	▼	5
○	Ghiaie Bianche '96	▼	4
●	Rosso di Montalcino '96	▼	3
●	Brunello di Montalcino Poggio al Vento Ris. '85	YYY	6
●	Brunello di Montalcino Poggio al Vento Ris. '88	YYY	6
●	Brunello di Montalcino Poggio al Vento Ris. '90	YYY	6
●	Brunello di Montalcino '90	YY	5
○	Moscadello di Montalcino Vendemmia Tardiva Pascena '91	YY	5
●	Olmaia '92	YY	5
●	Olmaia '93	YY	5

MONTALCINO (SI)

Andrea Costanti
Loc. Colle al Matrichese
53024 Montalcino (SI)
tel. 0577/848195

This winery has always had a place in our pages thanks to the consistent quality of its high-scoring wines. Perhaps there has been no absolute show-stopper so far, but Andrea Costanti, the owner of the estate, can consider himself well rewarded for his labors by the success his wines enjoy on the market. Now that his term as President of the Consorzio del Brunello has expired, Andrea will have more time to dedicate to his own winery, which has, however, shown no signs of suffering from neglect. Costanti's wines are always nobly distinctive. But then, the raw material is outstanding, thanks to the scrupulous selection process in the vineyards, which are pampered like few others in Montalcino. (You can 't miss them if you go from Torrenieri up towards Montalcino: there's a rose bush at the top of each row of vines.) The Brunello '93 easily earns its Two Glasses: of a limpid and intense ruby hue, it offers a rich bouquet with distinct traditional hints of blackberry and dark cherry and a very discreet suggestion of oak-derived spice, a novelty for Costanti. The palate reflects these qualities, and adds rich extract and wonderfully elegant dense tannins. The excellent finish includes an interesting note of licorice. The Rosso did well too: it is very clean and has a light acidity that makes it quite refreshing without disturbing the continuity on the palate.

●	Brunello di Montalcino '93	▼▼	6
●	Rosso di Montalcino '96	▼	4
●	Brunello di Montalcino '88	YYY	6
●	Brunello di Montalcino '83	YY	6
●	Brunello di Montalcino '85	YY	6
●	Brunello di Montalcino '86	YY	6
●	Brunello di Montalcino '87	YY	6
●	Brunello di Montalcino '89	YY	6
●	Brunello di Montalcino '90	YY	6
●	Brunello di Montalcino '91	YY	6
●	Brunello di Montalcino Ris. '83	YY	6
●	Brunello di Montalcino Ris. '88	YY	6
●	Brunello di Montalcino Ris. '90	YY	6
●	Rosso di Montalcino '95	YY	4
●	Brunello di Montalcino '92	Y	6

MONTALCINO (SI)

DUE PORTINE - GORELLI
Via Cialdini, 53
53024 Montalcino (SI)
tel. 0577/848098

Giuseppe Gorelli seems to have hit his stride; his wines have acquired a distinctive style, which emphasizes harmony and elegance rather than power, a characteristic to which Montalcino wines seem almost genetically predisposed. The estate is rather small, though it has grown recently, and the young owner dedicates himself to his vineyards, while still running his wine shop in Montalcino. The Brunello '93 is a mature wine to be enjoyed right away, as its predominantly garnet color indicates, and as is confirmed by a bouquet that offers admirable hints of spice, preserves, licorice and herbs. The palate also reveals a specific design, with sweetly present notes of ripe fruit, good balance and an elegant finish. Giuseppe is just as careful with his Rosso di Montalcino, which we all considered worthy of Two Glasses. The lively ruby color with glints of violet reveals the youth of this wine, which offers distinct and simple but well-focused red fruit to the nose. This freshness is reflected on the palate, underscored by a pleasing acidity and accompanied by balance and smooth tannins, leading to an agreeable fruity finish.

	Wine	Glasses	Price
●	Brunello di Montalcino '93	♥♥ (black)	6
●	Rosso di Montalcino '96	♥♥ (black)	4
●	Brunello di Montalcino '88	♀♀	6
●	Brunello di Montalcino '89	♀♀	6
●	Brunello di Montalcino '90	♀♀	6
●	Brunello di Montalcino '92	♀♀	6
●	Rosso di Montalcino '90	♀♀	4
●	Rosso di Montalcino '91	♀♀	4
●	Rosso di Montalcino '92	♀♀	4
●	Rosso di Montalcino '93	♀♀	4
●	Rosso di Montalcino '95	♀	4
○	Vin Santo '89	♀	6

MONTALCINO (SI)

FANTI - LA PALAZZETTA
Fraz. Castelnuovo dell'Abate
B.go di Sotto, 25
53020 Montalcino (SI)
tel. 0577/835631

La Palazzetta is one of the small Montalcino estates: this is, in fact, unlike the rest of Tuscany, an area where very large estates and individual winegrowers with just a few hectares exist side by side. Flavio Fanti, the owner of La Palazzetta, has taken part in the development and growing success of Brunello with passion and a good sense of proportion. He has five hectares currently under vine off near Castelnuovo all 'Abate, perhaps the best location in Montalcino. Next year another five hectares will be planted at a density of about 5,000 vines per hectare, so both quantity and quality should be increasing. Flavio Fanti is very well aware of the great potential of these vineyards, and has been concentrating on improving cellar techniques, by acquiring excellent equipment and the expert advice of the noted oenologist Maurizio Castelli, in order to produce softer and more elegant wines. He already has good reason to be pleased with the Brunello '93. The bouquet is intense and well-focused, with notes of dark cherry, blackberry and well-judged oak. The palate is not powerful, but it develops very well, supported by a crisp acidity. The Rosso di Montalcino '96 is even more surprising, given its category: the nose is intense, fruity and very lively, and it has a sweetness at its entry on the palate, where it is then mouth-filling and inviting, with a long finish.

	Wine	Glasses	Price
●	Brunello di Montalcino '93	♥♥ (black)	5
●	Rosso di Montalcino '96	♥♥ (black)	4

MONTALCINO (SI)

FANTI - SAN FILIPPO
LOC. SAN FILIPPO
53020 MONTALCINO (SI)
TEL. 0577/835523

This has been an extremely successful year for Baldassare Fanti: his estate is making its debut in the Guide and he was elected President of the joint Consorzio del Brunello e del Rosso di Montalcino, a responsible position and a clear sign of the trust his fellow wine-makers place in his abilities. The estate comprises more than six hectares of Brunello vines, but recently several more hectares of vineyards have been planted between Castelnuovo and Castello della Velona. The cellar, which is in the village itself, is barely large enough to meet the estate's current needs. It includes a good collection of 25- to 40-hectoliter Slavonian oak barrels. We were very well impressed by both of the wines presented this year: the Brunello performs better, as you might expect from a wine of its lineage and vintage. Of a classic ruby color with a garnet glow, it offers a bouquet with distinct notes of tobacco and spice that enrich its fruit. It is pleasing in the mouth as well, and there is plenty of substance and fairly densely woven tannins typical of the year and the zone. The strong suit of the Rosso di Montalcino is a fresh fruitiness, with cherry in the foreground. The acidity is well-judged, neither dominating the extract nor exaggerating the tannins, but making the wine agreeable and soft to the taste, which is appropriately lingering.

●	Brunello di Montalcino '93	🍷🍷	5
●	Rosso di Montalcino '96	🍷🍷	4

MONTALCINO (SI)

TENUTA FRIGGIALI
LOC. FRIGGIALI
53024 MONTALCINO (SI)
TEL. 0577/849358 - 849454

Wine experts familiar with the area generally agree that Friggiali has one of the most favorable locations in all of Montalcino and consequently promises first-class wine. So we feel justified in expecting a decisive leap in quality sooner or later. Meanwhile it is encouraging to note that for some years the Peluso family has consistently produced very good wines, regularly earning a place in these pages, which is no mean feat, given the strength of the competition. The Brunello Pietranera '93 easily won its Two Glasses. A bouquet of fresh fruit, hints of flowers and well-judged oak are followed by a round, almost sweet attack on the palate, dense structure and a very pleasing finish: a modern Brunello, not very complex, but successful. The standard Brunello is also a worthy bottle, although it does not measure up to the Pietranera. Its nose features scents of slightly overripe fruit and evident oak, while there is much to be said for the succulence and general balance in the mouth. We were unable to try the Rosso di Montalcino, but we had another go at the sangiovese "table wine ", Pietrafocaia '93, to which we gave One Glass last year. We must admit that it tastes as though it deserved rather more: the formerly unfocused bouquet is clear and characterful now, although there is still some roughness on the palate.

●	Brunello di Montalcino '93	🍷🍷	5
●	Brunello di Montalcino Pietranera '93	🍷🍷	6
●	Brunello di Montalcino '90	🍷🍷 (previous edition)	5
●	Rosso di Montalcino '93	🍷🍷 (previous edition)	3
●	Brunello di Montalcino '92	🍷 (previous edition)	5
●	Pietrafocaia '93	🍷 (previous edition)	5
●	Rosso di Montalcino '95	🍷 (previous edition)	3
●	Rosso di Montalcino Pietranera '95	🍷 (previous edition)	4

MONTALCINO (SI)

EREDI FULIGNI
VIA S. SALONI, 33
53024 MONTALCINO (SI)
TEL. 0577/848039

The Fuligni wines keep getting better. Behind it all is Roberto Guerrini, nephew of the owner and man of multiple interests, university professor and music lover, for whom a certain elegance seems to come naturally, as it does in his wines. The estate vineyards are situated in the most favorable part of the north-east slopes of Montalcino on the way to Buonconvento. The cellar was recently refurbished and is now entirely temperature-controlled. The barrels for aging the wine are excellent, and small new ones are constantly being added. This year, not surprisingly, the Brunello outdid the Rosso di Montalcino, which was made from the estate cru, Ginestreto, and is a sort of winery proving ground for barrique aging. The Brunello '93 has a lovely "pigeon-blood" ruby color. A complex and intense bouquet with hints of sour cherry preserves is followed by a fairly sweet attack and a refreshing acidity which restores balance. On the finish the oak returns, and we wish it were subtler. The Rosso di Montalcino Ginestreto has a somewhat vegetal note that partially obscures the fruit of the bouquet, but it's more appealing in the mouth, and the finish is good and reasonably long.

● Brunello di Montalcino '93	🍷🍷	5
● Rosso di Montalcino Ginestreto '96	🍷	4
● Brunello di Montalcino '87	♀♀	5
● Brunello di Montalcino '88	♀♀	5
● Brunello di Montalcino '89	♀♀	5
● Brunello di Montalcino '90	♀♀	5
● Brunello di Montalcino Ris. '88	♀♀	6
● Brunello di Montalcino Ris. '90	♀♀	6
● Rosso di Montalcino Ginestreto '95	♀♀	4
● Brunello di Montalcino '92	♀	5
● Brunello di Montalcino '91	♀	5
● Rosso di Montalcino Ginestreto '93	♀	4

MONTALCINO (SI)

GREPPONE MAZZI
TENIMENTI RUFFINO
LOC. GREPPONE
53024 MONTALCINO (SI)
TEL. 055/8368307 - 849215

On the way up to Montalcino from Torrenieri, just at the level of the turning for Buonconvento, you can't fail to notice a fine villa on your left with a loggia on the upper floor. It is the headquarters of the Greppone Mazzi estate, which has for some time been part of the giant Tenimenti Ruffino winery. Surrounding the villa but a bit above it are about seven hectares of sangiovese vineyards with a wonderful exposure and a soil rich in stone (which makes it, according to tradition, the ideal environment for producing great wine). The expertise of the Ruffino staff is formidable and money has not been spared in equipping the cellar, but a real champion has not yet emerged. Of course the last year they had released, the '91, was not exactly an exceptional vintage, but we were hoping for rather more personality from the Brunello '93 presented this year. Since they do not make a Rosso di Montalcino and have only just begun to offer a standard Bunello, we can but hope that their Riserva '93, coming out in '99, will do justice to their enormous potential. The Brunello we sampled is undoubtedly well-made, very stylish and pleasingly well-defined and fruity in bouquet. The tannins are elegant and the acidity well-judged, but a great wine has more complexity.

● Brunello di Montalcino '93	🍷	5
● Brunello di Montalcino Ris. '82	♀♀	6
● Brunello di Montalcino Ris. '83	♀♀	6
● Brunello di Montalcino Ris. '90	♀♀	6
● Brunello di Montalcino '91	♀	5
● Brunello di Montalcino Ris. '85	♀	6
● Brunello di Montalcino Ris. '88	♀	6
● Brunello di Montalcino Ris. '91	♀	6

MONTALCINO (SI)

Il Poggione

Loc. S. Angelo in Colle
53020 Montalcino (SI)
tel. 0577/864029

An important change has recently taken place in the technical direction of this winery: Fabrizio Bindocci, after years of experience in the cellar, has taken the place of the oenologist Pierluigi Talenti, one of the grand masters of Montalcino wine. This transition is most unlikely to have any negative effect on the estate, as Bindocci is a sort of oenological son of Talenti, with whom he worked side by side for twenty years. A further distinction for Fabrizio (and for Il Poggione) is his election to the vice presidency of the joint Consorzio del Brunello e del Rosso di Montalcino. In their wines, however, we are pleased to report no changes: consistency of quality is still the main goal of this famous and reliable winery, together with an exemplary pricing policy. This year Il Poggione, which owns more than 47 hectares of Brunello vines, almost all south of Montalcino, presented two successful wines that perfectly reflect the characteristics of the terroir. The Brunello '93, ruby tending towards garnet in color, reveals a clean bouquet with hints of tobacco and a delicate spiciness. On the palate we found the traditional alcoholic presence, balanced by good tannins that still emerge too distinctly, but this is a vice of youth. The Rosso di Montalcino '96 did equally well: it is extremely pleasing to both nose and palate, but the acidity is just a bit excessive. We should like to think that they will consider making a special cru Brunello some time soon, with which they can show all they are capable of.

Wine	Rating	Price
● Brunello di Montalcino '93	🍷	5
● Rosso di Montalcino '96	🍷	3
● Brunello di Montalcino '88	♀♀	5
● Brunello di Montalcino '90	♀♀	5
● Brunello di Montalcino '92	♀♀	5
● Brunello di Montalcino Ris. '88	♀♀	6
● Rosso di Montalcino '92	♀♀	3
● Rosso di Montalcino '93	♀♀	3
● Rosso di Montalcino '95	♀♀	3
● Brunello di Montalcino '89	♀	5
● Brunello di Montalcino '91	♀	5
● Brunello di Montalcino Ris. '90	♀	6
● Rosso di Montalcino '94	♀	3

MONTALCINO (SI)

La Fiorita

Loc. Castelnuovo Abate
53020 Montalcino (SI)
tel. 0577/835521

The excellence of the wines it presented this year has won this small estate a debut appearance in the Guide. There is not even a full hectare under vine for Brunello, but with new vineyards starting to bear fruit, the '96 vintage should yield some 10 thousand bottles. This year's two wines, produced under the supervision of the noted oenologist Roberto Cipresso, are very interesting. The Quadratura del Cerchio ("squaring the circle") is, in the words of its creator, "a blueprint for oenological anarchy". This wine is made from different grape varieties each year, which is why instead of finding the vintage on the label we read the number of the "journey", both physical and philosophical, of which it is the fruit. We tasted the "second journey", a blend of sangiovese di Montalcino and primitivo di Manduria: a singular wine, which transports us beyond the limits of Montalcino to a kind of oenological frontier. A dense ruby with bluish highlights in the glass, it has a broad bouquet with distinct mint and cocoa lording it over the notes of blackberry and black currant preserve. It makes its presence felt in the mouth, and displays good acidity and tannins well integrated in the opulent structure. There is no faulting the strength of the sensations it provides, but it could perhaps do with just a little more elegance. The bouquet of the Brunello '93 is dominated by balsamic and spicy tones, and the palate reveals style and finesse as well as a certain depth. A successful debut!

Wine	Rating	Price
● Brunello di Montalcino '93	🍷🍷	6
● Quadratura del Cerchio secondo viaggio	🍷🍷	5

Podere La Fortuna

Loc. Podere La Fortuna
53024 Montalcino (SI)
tel. 0577/848308

After appearing in these pages for the first time last year, La Fortuna has not only confirmed our original good opinion but has, with the two wines now presented, shown itself capable of real excellence. Since, in addition to describing wines, we try to understand the people behind them, it is worth mentioning that this winery has made a very positive overall impression. Perhaps the size of the vineyard, less than three hectares, allows the winegrowers to devote painstaking care to every step of cultivation and harvesting, but in any case the results are there to be tasted. The Brunello '93 is among the best of its vintage. Its interesting personality is already apparent on the nose, where juicy dark fruit, with sour cherries to the fore, is followed by spice and cocoa, with hints of minerals. The entry on the palate is powerful, then dense, stylish and long, though a bit dry on the finish. Their Rosso di Montalcino is even more astonishing and may well be the best we tasted this year: a broad bouquet with lots of wonderfully ripe dark fruit leads to a fascinating, substantial and firm palate with very good tannins. This is an exemplary way to view the Rosso: not as the estate's second- or third-string wine, but one that is simply different from Brunello.

	Wine	Glasses	Price
●	Brunello di Montalcino '93	TT	6
●	Rosso di Montalcino '96	TT	4
●	Brunello di Montalcino '83	YY	6
●	Brunello di Montalcino '91	YY	6
●	Rosso di Montalcino '95	YY	4
●	Brunello di Montalcino '85	Y	6
●	Brunello di Montalcino '92	Y	6
●	Rosso di Montalcino '94	Y	4

La Gerla

Loc. Canalicchio
53024 Montalcino (SI)
tel. 0577/848599

In the past La Gerla has had some trouble staying in these pages, but things have got so much better recently, and all the wines are of such a quality as to warrant a second consecutive profile in the Guide. This is particularly admirable, considering the fact that they did not even release a Brunello Riserva, their pet bottle, this year. So hats off to the owner, Sergio Rossi, a Milanese advertising executive with a passion for viticulture, and to his staff, headed by the oenologist Vittorio Fiore. Along with a range of traditional wines, La Gerla makes the table wine Birba, an experiment in barrique-aged sangiovese. The '95 seemed particularly convincing and definitely better than last year's, a difference to be attributed only in part to a better vintage. It is of a lovely intense ruby color, and its broad array of aromas includes black cherry, blueberry and blackberry together with spice. It walked right off with Two Glasses. The Brunello '93 and the Rosso di Montalcino '96 were both good, although not as remarkable. We preferred the Brunello, which shouldn't be surprising. It displays a dense, concentrated color and notes of vanilla and incense that partially obscure the underlying fruit. The palate also reflects good raw material and mature tannins, but we would prefer less obvious wood. Finally, the Rosso is distinctly quaffable and has a certain personality.

	Wine	Glasses	Price
●	Birba '95	TT	5
●	Brunello di Montalcino '93	T	5
●	Rosso di Montalcino '96	T	4
●	Birba '90	YY	5
●	Brunello di Montalcino Ris. '88	YY	6
●	Brunello di Montalcino Ris. '90	YY	6
●	Brunello di Montalcino Ris. '91	YY	6
●	Brunello di Montalcino '88	Y	5
●	Rosso di Montalcino '95	Y	4

MAURIZIO LAMBARDI

PODERE CANALICCHIO DI SOTTO, 8
53024 MONTALCINO (SI)
TEL. 0577/848476

The new regulations governing the production of Brunello are certainly a boon for this famous wine and its producers. The reduction of the required minimum time the wine spends aging in the barrel makes greater flexibility possible and means that wine-makers will not have to resort quite so often to the (perfectly legal) process known as "rejuvenation", and will also be able to vary the size of barrels according to the quality of the grapes. Maurizio Lambardi has always shown a great sensitivity to the characteristics of different vintages and has usually been able to produce good wines without relying on trickery of any sort. So it was reasonable to expect an upward leap after the rather modest performance of the '92, and indeed his Brunello '93 is one of the best of its vintage and perfectly in keeping with the style of the estate. Its color is an intense ruby shading to garnet at the rim of the glass; the nose is concentrated, with notes of dark fruit well blended with oak-derived aromas. The palate is dense, compact and admirable in its progression and in its thickly woven tannins; the finish shows remarkable depth. The Rosso di Montalcino '96 is naturally a simpler and lighter wine, reflecting, once again, the characteristics of its vintage. It has a vivid ruby hue and sound fruity aromas and is, thanks to its excellent balance, very pleasing on the palate.

Wine	Rating	Price
● Brunello di Montalcino '93	🍷🍷	5
● Rosso di Montalcino '96	🍷	4
● Brunello di Montalcino '88	ΥΥ	5
● Brunello di Montalcino '90	ΥΥ	5
● Brunello di Montalcino '91	ΥΥ	5
● Rosso di Montalcino '90	ΥΥ	4
● Rosso di Montalcino '91	ΥΥ	4
● Rosso di Montalcino '92	ΥΥ	4
● Rosso di Montalcino '93	ΥΥ	4
● Rosso di Montalcino '95	ΥΥ	3
● Brunello di Montalcino '87	Υ	5
● Brunello di Montalcino '89	Υ	5
● Brunello di Montalcino '92	Υ	5

MONTALCINO (SI)

LISINI

FATTORIA DI S. ANGELO IN COLLE
53024 MONTALCINO (SI)
TEL. 0577/864040

It isn't easy to reach this estate, located in one of the wildest but also most beautiful parts of Montalcino, but if you don't pale before dirt paths, we recommend that you take the road that leads from Sant'Angelo in Colle to Castelnuovo dell'Abate. You will be able to admire not only the odd fawn and wild boar, but also the best zone for the production of Brunello. The ten hectares of vineyard owned by Lisini are all located here, so it is not too difficult to understand their success. Excellent raw material, the expertise of a great oenologist like Bernabei, a regular turnover of barrels and barriques: what a simple recipe (at least when you're just reciting it) and what a reliable one! This year's selection was once again very good, although it didn't include their gem, the Brunello Ugolaia: the '93 will be released next year. The "normal" Brunello '93, of a classic ruby hue with garnet highlights, and features a complex nose with fruity notes which emerge less clearly than usual. Unfortunately, its tannins do not entirely unfold. The Rosso di Montalcino '96 is also noteworthy, although this vintage will not go down in history. The bouquet displays a fruity aroma dominated by the typical marasca cherry scents yet partially overlaid by a bitter edge. The palate unfolds refreshingly and reveals an acidity which has not yet entirely merged into the body of this wine, which is nevertheless quite attractive.

Wine	Rating	Price
● Brunello di Montalcino '93	🍷🍷	6
● Rosso di Montalcino '96	🍷	4
● Brunello di Montalcino '88	ΥΥΥ	6
● Brunello di Montalcino '90	ΥΥΥ	6
● Brunello di Montalcino Ugolaia '91	ΥΥΥ	6
● Brunello di Montalcino '87	ΥΥ	6
● Brunello di Montalcino '89	ΥΥ	6
● Brunello di Montalcino '91	ΥΥ	6
● Brunello di Montalcino Ris. '85	ΥΥ	6
● Brunello di Montalcino Ris. '86	ΥΥ	6
● Brunello di Montalcino Ris. '88	ΥΥ	6
● Brunello di Montalcino Ugolaia '90	ΥΥ	6
● Rosso di Montalcino '95	Υ	4

MONTALCINO (SI)

Luce
Loc. Castelgiocondo
53024 Montalcino (SI)
tel. 0577/848492

We had felt quite enthusiastic about this joint venture between the very Tuscan Frescobaldi family and Mondavi, the most well-known wine dynasty in the United States, and indeed last year their Luce, a blend of sangiovese and merlot, won Three Glasses its first time out, with the '94 vintage. It seemed to be in the cards that the '95 vintage would do the same, but instead it is "only" an excellent wine, and not the champion we had expected, despite the superior vintage. Its color is dense but not impenetrable, and its aromas are of a moderate intensity, with notes of black cherry and tobacco. On the palate, acidity and tannins are not perfectly integrated in the structure, so the finish is slightly discordant. It is in any case a notable wine and probably some bottle age will do a lot towards harmonizing the tannins. Earlier in the year the winery presented a second wine, called Lucente. It too is a sangiovese and merlot blend, and two vintages appeared at the same time, the '95 and the '96, both of which did well at our tastings. In general they are very well made, but there is a falling off on the finish due to insufficient body. However, they are well-balanced wines that can be drunk with pleasure or kept with confidence for several years.

Wine	Glasses	Price
● Luce '95	🍷🍷 (black)	6
● Lucente '95	🍷🍷 (black)	5
● Lucente '96	🍷🍷 (black)	5
● Luce '94	♀♀♀	6
● Luce '93	♀♀	6

MONTALCINO (SI)

Mastrojanni
Poderi Loreto e S. Pio
Loc. Castelnuovo dell'Abate
53020 Montalcino (SI)
tel. 0577/835681

The estates of San Pio and Loreto are located near Castelnuovo dell'Abate, in an area that has recently attracted particular attention. In many ways Mastrojanni has been the leader of the local upward surge. This winery, directed by Antonio Mastrojanni with the expert help of the noted oenologist Maurizio Castelli and of Andrea Machetti, who has the wines constantly under his watchful eye as they mature, has in the past produced really exciting classic Brunellos, culminating in their glorious Brunello Schiena d'Asino '90. Consequently we were very eager to taste the '93 vintage of this cru, but printers are tyrants and we had to go to press without so much as seeing a bottle of it. We are, however, in a position to reveal that, tasted from the barrel, it seems very promising indeed and you can read all about it next year. Meanwhile we just had to "make do" with their normal Brunello '93, which perfectly reflects their way of thinking, according to which a wine should be substantial and perhaps somewhat hard in its youth. It is ruby-hued with garnet veining and has an austere bouquet, with notes of licorice and black cherries preserved in spirits. It is full-bodied and progresses well on the palate, but the tannins need more time in the bottle. The San Pio '95, a blend of sangiovese and cabernet sauvignon, is another Two Glass wine. It displays an interesting bouquet with fruity notes and hints of grass together with well-judged wood. The palate is good too, although there is a noticeable bitterish tinge on the finish. Their Rosso di Montalcino '96 is perfectly correct.

Wine	Glasses	Price
● Brunello di Montalcino '93	🍷🍷 (black)	5
● San Pio '95	🍷🍷 (black)	5
● Rosso di Montalcino '96	🍷 (black)	4
● Brunello di Montalcino '90	♀♀♀	6
● Brunello di Montalcino Ris. '88	♀♀♀	6
● Brunello di Montalcino Schiena d'Asino '90	♀♀♀	6
● Brunello di Montalcino '87	♀♀	6
● Brunello di Montalcino '88	♀♀	6
● Brunello di Montalcino '89	♀♀	6
● Brunello di Montalcino '91	♀♀	6
● Brunello di Montalcino Ris. '86	♀♀	6
● Brunello di Montalcino Ris. '90	♀♀	6
● San Pio '88	♀♀	5
● San Pio '93	♀♀	5

MONTALCINO (SI)

MOCALI
LOC. MOCALI, 273
53024 MONTALCINO (SI)
TEL. 0577/849485

Tiziano Ciacci's small estate is situated on the western slopes of Montalcino near the road to Castiglion del Bosco, a wonderful position, where the vines hardly ever suffer from drought and there are no extremes of temperature. The winery is, furthermore, atop a little hill facing Chiesa di S.Restituta and so well aired that very rainy seasons bring with them little risk of mould. From their two hectares under vine Mocali has produced two wines of contrasting quality. The Brunello '93 is a worthy descendant of the Riserva '91 and the non-Riserva '90 that carried Mocali on their shoulders into the Guide. Dense and concentrated in its garnet-veined ruby hue, it offers an intense bouquet with notes of sour cherry preserve. The palate is very traditional in style and balances acidity and young tannins with softer components. It bagged Two Glasses with no trouble at all. The Rosso di Montalcino is less successful, especially on the nose, which offers some less than agreeable aromas. It seems sound in the mouth, however, and goes down very easily. We can only suppose that barrels that have already seen their day have not done justice to the excellent grapes that went into them. The new temperature-controlled cellar will be furnished with new barrels of all sizes (the smallest will contain Riserva wines) made of Slavonian and French oak.

	Wine	Glasses	Price
●	Brunello di Montalcino '93	ŸŸ	5
●	Rosso di Montalcino '96		3

MONTALCINO (SI)

TENUTE SILVIO NARDI
LOC. CASALE DEL BOSCO
53024 MONTALCINO (SI)
TEL. 0577/808269

We note with pleasure that this estate has improved on a performance that had already earned it a return to these pages last year. They seem to be starting to reap the rewards of the changes in method they introduced a few years ago, although an estate as large as the Tenute Silvio Nardi always leaves plenty of room for improvement. The Brunello '93 did remarkably well, and it was particularly encouraging that the Rosso di Montalcino '96 easily won One Glass, quite resolving the problems the '95 had seemed to us to pose. But first things first: the Brunello is of an intense ruby hue and displays vivid aromas of red and black berries and hints of flowers. It is even more satisfying on the palate, where it shows a notable balance and concentration, and a long finish not without a certain elegance. The admirable Rosso, lively and dense in color, offers a sound bouquet with dark fruit and appropriate notes of wood. In the mouth it is full-bodied and seems quite supple, thanks to the presence of some acidity and vivacious tannins. A very good performance all around, that also bodes well for the future, when the new vineyards bear fruit.

	Wine	Glasses	Price
●	Brunello di Montalcino '93	ŸŸ	5
●	Rosso di Montalcino '96	Ÿ	4
●	Brunello di Montalcino '90	ŸŸ (previous years)	5
●	Brunello di Montalcino '92	Ÿ (previous years)	5
●	Rosso di Montalcino '93	Ÿ (previous years)	4
●	Rosso di Montalcino '95	Ÿ (previous years)	4

MONTALCINO (SI)

SIRO PACENTI

LOC. PELAGRILLI, 1
53024 MONTALCINO (SI)
TEL. 0577/848662

Giancarlo Pacenti is a determined and dynamic winegrower, but he is not satisfied with the success that he has already achieved with years of hard work. He continues with experiments to improve his wines yet further and he has such respect for those who will eventually drink them that he prefers to undergo financial sacrifice rather than blemish the reputation of his estate in any way. Having already given up on the Brunello '92, Giancarlo has decided not to produce a Riserva '93 either. He is still engaged in increasing the amount of land under vine for DOCG wines, which already extends over about eight hectares, and this should make the estate less vulnerable as a whole to local disasters like hailstorms. The wines we tasted this year were excellent. The Brunello '93 has great structure, with good tannins and a long finish, but just at first the bouquet is slightly muffled, covering the fruit. The Rosso di Montalcino '96 is also very successful, with good underlying structure and elegant, non-aggressive tannins that add to the density and weight on the palate without overwhelming the deep and satisfying finish. The aromas are intense and fruity, with notes of black cherry preserve.

●	Brunello di Montalcino '93	🍷🍷	6
●	Rosso di Montalcino '96	🍷🍷	4
●	Brunello di Montalcino '88	ΥΥΥ	6
●	Brunello di Montalcino '89	ΥΥ	6
●	Brunello di Montalcino '90	ΥΥ	6
●	Brunello di Montalcino '91	ΥΥ	6
●	Brunello di Montalcino Ris. '90	ΥΥ	6
●	Rosso di Montalcino '88	ΥΥ	4
●	Rosso di Montalcino '90	ΥΥ	4
●	Rosso di Montalcino '92	ΥΥ	4
●	Rosso di Montalcino '93	ΥΥ	4
●	Rosso di Montalcino '95	ΥΥ	4
●	Rosso di Montalcino '94	Υ	4

MONTALCINO (SI)

PIANCORNELLO

FRAZ. CASTELNUOVO ABATE
LOC. PIANCORNELLO
53020 MONTALCINO (SI)
TEL. 0577/370110

Silvana Pieri's Piancornello consists of little more than two hectares of Brunello vines in the southernmost part of the DOCG zone, which has been producing increasingly good results recently. The estate is family-run, and its small cellar is a model of the rational use of available space. New barrels are in the process of being introduced, which is good news, because some of the older ones somewhat cramped the estate style upon occasion. The Brunello '93 thus represents a transitional period, but the grapes were so good and the vinification so careful that it easily earned Two Glasses all the same. Ruby-hued with garnet nuances, it offers a bouquet that, after an initial mute moment, reveals red berry notes well conveyed on alcohol. Good structure and harmony are evident in the mouth, and the alcohol is kept in check. We would have preferred rounder and more integrated tannins, but the wine seems so substantial that we can confidently predict that it will improve in the bottle. The strong suit of the Rosso di Montalcino '96 is delightful quaffability. It is fresh and clean on the nose, with clear notes of fruit, and there is excellent balance on the palate.

●	Brunello di Montalcino '93	🍷🍷	5
●	Rosso di Montalcino '96	🍷	3

Agostina Pieri

Via Fabbri, 2
53014 Montalcino (SI)
tel. 0577/375785

Yet again Agostina Pieri has produced one of the very best Rosso's di Montalcino, although '96 was nothing like such a good year as '95, and so the Rosso '96 got only Two (and a half) Glasses instead of Three. It is of a uniformly intense ruby color, and offers aromas of blackberry and dark cherry with oak-derived eucalyptus, followed by a very appealing palate which is both complex and elegant, sweet at its entry and progressing well on the finish. The attractive and functional cellar of the winery houses barrels of quite a variety of sizes and woods. In addition to a large number of barriques, there are the more traditional 20- to 30-hectoliter barrels in which most of the Brunello is aging. Next year we shall be able to review the eagerly awaited '94, the first Brunello from this estate. We shall then see if Agostina Pieri can pass the acid test of every local producer with the high marks she has given us ample reason to expect. The technical advice of Paolo Vagaggini, a renowned Brunello expert, and the propitious southern position of the vineyards, where early ripening is the norm, should be particularly helpful in a difficult year like '94.

Wine	Glasses	Price
● Rosso di Montalcino '96	🍷🍷	4
● Rosso di Montalcino '95	YYY	4
● Rosso di Montalcino '94	YY	4

MONTALCINO (SI)

Pieve Santa Restituta

Loc. Chiesa di S. Restituta
53024 Montalcino (SI)
tel. 0577/848610

In 1994 Angelo Gaja, the famous Piedmontese wine-maker, and Roberto Bellini, the capable owner of these extraordinary vineyards, joined forces and transformed the old Chiesa di Santa Restituta estate into the Pieve di Santa Restituta, a new estate exclusively devoted to the production of Brunello. This was a risky decision financially (last year, for example, they did not produce a Brunello '92), but a comprehensible one. We were naturally very curious this year to see how the wines were taking to the new regime, but we were somewhat disappointed. The two '93 crus, Rennine and Sugarille, although perfectly adequate and well made, did not earn more than One Glass each. They have body and fragrance and are generally agreeable, but are not really distinctive in any way, a result well below the ambitions of the partners. We should emphasize that vinification took place before the partnership was formed. Nevertheless we feel that a more careful selection of the wine to be bottled could have improved the end result and justified the considerable expense incurred. For a proper idea of what they can do we shall have to wait for the release of the celebrated '95, the first vintage for which they share complete responsibility. The 15 hectares of vines for Brunello still enjoy a splendid exposure, and the bone-rich soil contributes to structure and rich bouquet in the wines. All this was evident in the Brunello Riserva '88 of the "ancien régime", and we hope to find it again in the wines the future has in store for us.

Wine	Glasses	Price
● Brunello di Montalcino Rennina '93	🍷	6
● Brunello di Montalcino Sugarille '93	🍷	6
● Brunello di Montalcino Ris. '88	YYY	6
● Brunello di Montalcino '88	YY	6
● Brunello di Montalcino Rennina '90	YY	6
● Brunello di Montalcino Rennina '91	YY	5
● Chiesa di S. Restituta loco detto Piano de Cerri '89	YY	6
● Chiesa di S. Restituta loco detto Piano de Cerri '90	YY	6

MONTALCINO (SI)

CASTELLO ROMITORIO
LOC. CASTELLO DI ROMITORIO
53024 MONTALCINO (SI)
TEL. 0577/897220

If you take the trouble to follow the unpaved road that leads to Castiglion del Bosco, you will come upon what started out as a convent, was turned into a fortress in the 14th century, is now the Castello Romitorio estate and still offers exceptionall views. The well-known artist Sandro Chia, who owns it, also designs the labels for his wines, giving rise to a collectors' rush reminiscent of what takes place with Château Mouton-Rothschild. The estate covers 187 hectares, 7.5 of which are under vine for Brunello, while another 12 are planted with such varieties as cabernet sauvignon and chardonnay. The well-equipped winery includes barrels of Slavonian oak as well as the sweeter-flavored French kind, and also barriques for the Romito del Romitorio, made from cabernet sauvignon and sangiovese. The '96 vintage of this blend displays intense aromas with distinct vegetal cabernet accents pleasingly amalgamated with the red fruit and blackberry of the sangiovese. On the palate it is dense and persistent. The excellent body of the Brunello '93 earned it Two Glasses, although the tannins are somewhat insistent. The fruity bouquet is enriched by delightful notes of tobacco and rhubarb. The interesting Rosso di Montalcino '96 offers lots of fruit without excessive acidity or tannins.

Wine	Rating	Price
● Brunello di Montalcino '93	🍷🍷	6
● Romito del Romitorio '96	🍷🍷	5
● Rosso di Montalcino '96	🍷	4
● Romito del Romitorio '90	🍷🍷 (white)	5
● Brunello di Montalcino '88	🍷 (white)	6
● Rosso di Montalcino '92	🍷 (white)	4

MONTALCINO (SI)

SALVIONI - LA CERBAIOLA
P.ZZA CAVOUR, 19
53024 MONTALCINO (SI)
TEL. 0577/848499

Small as it is, Giulio and Mirella Salvioni's La Cerbaiola is one of the estates most highly regarded by wine lovers both in Italy and abroad. Their Brunello and Rosso di Montalcino (when they make it) are fought over every year, and by the time the bottles are released they have already been snatched up, not only because there are so few of them, but also because Giulio and Mirella's wines are considered absolutely reliable. There is no mistaking the style of their Brunello, constant over the years, with its utterly original characteristic bouquet. The fusion of the fruitiness of the wine itself with the oak-derived aromatic components gives rise to an extremely rich mixture of nuances which, as tertiary aromas gradually develop, creates a further apparently endless variety of sensations. Tasting different vintages we find aromas that are unusual in other red wines, such as tropical fruit, peach and herbs, together with the sour and black cherry notes typical of Brunello. Over time, undertones of licorice, tobacco, leather and underbrush come into play. Their wine is distinctive on the palate as well: although hot and rich in extract, it almost never has a big attack, but progresses impressively, with great depth and balance. The Brunello '93 basically fits this description and is the most recent example of a wine with their highly characteristic style.

Wine	Rating	Price
● Brunello di Montalcino '93	🍷🍷	6
● Brunello di Montalcino '85	🍷🍷🍷 (white)	6
● Brunello di Montalcino '87	🍷🍷🍷 (white)	6
● Brunello di Montalcino '88	🍷🍷🍷 (white)	6
● Brunello di Montalcino '89	🍷🍷🍷 (white)	6
● Brunello di Montalcino '90	🍷🍷🍷 (white)	6
● Brunello di Montalcino '86	🍷🍷 (white)	6
● Brunello di Montalcino '91	🍷🍷 (white)	6
● Brunello di Montalcino '92	🍷🍷 (white)	6

MONTALCINO (SI)

TALENTI - PODERE PIAN DI CONTE

LOC. S. ANGELO IN COLLE
53020 MONTALCINO (SI)
TEL. 0577/864029

Pierluigi Talenti owns eight hectares near Sant'Angelo in Colle, south of Montalcino, but fairly high up. The winery is classic in its approach to cellar techniques, which is not surprising since Talenti worked for many years at the traditional winery Il Poggione, which he left only last year for reasons of health. He uses 25- to 40-hectoliter Slavonian oak barrels for aging his Brunello, after fermentation in temperature-controlled steel vats. Some evidence of innovation can, however, be found in the vineyards, where clonal experimentation has top priority, although the general aspect is traditional, with 3,500-4,000 vines per hectare. Talenti believes that dense planting is inappropriate for Montalcino, because it's so dry. More evident fruit would have been welcome in this year's wines. The Brunello '93 harmoniously blends its acid and tannic components. Extract and finish are acceptable. This is certainly not a wine that flexes its muscles, but it is quite drinkable. The finish reflects the Peruvian bark already noted on the nose. The Rosso di Montalcino '96 is only slightly less convincing, with its vegetal scents to the nose, while there is well-balanced acidity on the palate.

	Wine	Rating	Price
●	Brunello di Montalcino '93	🍷	5
●	Rosso di Montalcino '96	🍷	4
●	Brunello di Montalcino '88	YYY	5
●	Brunello di Montalcino '85	YY	5
●	Brunello di Montalcino '86	YY	5
●	Brunello di Montalcino '87	YY	5
●	Brunello di Montalcino '89	YY	5
●	Brunello di Montalcino '90	YY	5
●	Brunello di Montalcino Ris. '88	YY	6
●	Brunello di Montalcino Ris. '90	YY	6
●	Rosso di Montalcino '90	YY	4
●	Brunello di Montalcino '91	Y	5
●	Brunello di Montalcino '92	Y	5
●	Rosso di Montalcino '95	Y	4

MONTALCINO (SI)

UCCELLIERA

FRAZ. CASTELNUOVO ABATE
LOC. UCCELLIERA
53020 MONTALCINO (SI)
TEL. 0577/835729

Andrea Cortonesi should be pleased with the debut appearance of his estate in the Guide, which recognizes not only the quality of his wines but also his innovative efforts in his vineyards: he has introduced a density of about 6 thousand vines per hectare, almost unheard of for Brunello, at least in such a small estate. "It's the only way to get richer wines", says Andrea. Their first Brunello, the '91, certainly did not have a great year behind it, and they did not even produce a '92, having had such bad weather during the harvest. The Brunello '93 is the fruit of the three hectares the Cortonesi own near the pathway from Castelnuovo to Sant'Angelo in Colle. Although still somewhat dominated by raw oak, this wine shows considerable finesse. The Rosso di Montalcino '96 is very agreeable on the palate and delightfully fruity to the nose, with clear accents of sour cherry. The estate also produces Rapace, a red wine named after a local species of falcon. It is a blend of sangiovese, cabernet sauvignon and merlot aged for approximately 18 months in 500-liter French oak barrels, and is clean, fresh and well made, with moderate extract and a not very long finish.

	Wine	Rating	Price
●	Brunello di Montalcino '93	🍷🍷	5
●	Rapace '96	🍷	5
●	Rosso di Montalcino '96	🍷	4

MONTALCINO (SI)

VAL DI SUGA
LOC. VAL DI SUGA
53024 MONTALCINO (SI)
TEL. 0577/848701

Although we felt differently about the two Brunellos presented this year, we liked them both very much. And the Rosso di Montalcino '96, despite the not exactly brilliant vintage, earned One Glass. The estate cru, the Brunello di Montalcino Vigna del Lago '93, echoed the glorious '90 with a resounding Three Glasses. It vaunts a magnificent intense "pigeon's-blood" ruby color, and on its broad and persistent nose the oak-derived balsamic aromas do not overwhelm the substantial fruit (particularly dark cherry and blackberry). In the mouth it shows what a modern Brunello can do, with elegant tannins and well-judged acidity producing an eminently drinkable wine that still has richness of extract: a Brunello that makes us lick our lips. The standard Brunello '93, a Two Glass winner, is more traditional in style, starting with its garnet-veined ruby hue. The bouquet offers hints of cherry preserve together with quite enchanting notes of tobacco. On the palate, albeit pleasant, it seems somewhat undistinguished. The balance is excellent. We shall have to wait until next year for the Brunello '93 Vigna di Spuntali, but we're in a position to say that it is very promising.

Wine	Glasses	Price
● Brunello di Montalcino Vigna del Lago '93	🍷🍷🍷	6
● Brunello di Montalcino '93	🍷🍷	5
● Rosso di Montalcino '96	🍷	3
● Brunello di Montalcino Vigna del Lago '90	🍷🍷🍷 (prev.)	6
● Brunello di Montalcino '87	🍷🍷 (prev.)	5
● Brunello di Montalcino '90	🍷🍷 (prev.)	5
● Brunello di Montalcino Ris. '88	🍷🍷 (prev.)	6
● Brunello di Montalcino Vigna del Lago '87	🍷🍷 (prev.)	6
● Brunello di Montalcino Vigna Spuntali '89	🍷🍷 (prev.)	6
● Brunello di Montalcino Vigna Spuntali '90	🍷🍷 (prev.)	6

MONTALCINO (SI)

TENUTA VALDICAVA
LOC. VAL DI CAVA
53024 MONTALCINO (SI)
TEL. 0577/848261

After just a year's absence, Vincenzo Abbruzzese's Tenuta Valdicava has regained its rightful place in the Guide. The estate, currently seven and a half hectares producing grapes and soon to be almost ten, is located on the northern slopes of Montalcino, towards Siena, but this is not immediately evident from the wines, since the policy is to wait until the last possible moment for harvesting, to allow the grapes to ripen as much as possible. Abbruzzese's aim is to make soft, elegant wines with lots of fresh fruit that are still characteristic both of Brunello and of their terroir, which is particularly well expressed in the winery cru, Madonna del Piano. The Brunello '93 and the Rosso di Montalcino '96 did not disappoint, pushing their way to the fore amidst the increasingly tough competition. The Brunello is a wine with character, although the bouquet does not display great finesse, with its sour cherry preserve blending with rather less aristocratic animal notes, which, however, are dissipated if the wine is given a chance to breathe. On the palate it is more satisfactory: a sweet attack and a gradual, even and well-balanced progression. We particularly appreciated the direct and delightful liveliness of the fruit. The Rosso di Montalcino did equally well. An intense color between ruby and garnet is followed by a somewhat dumb nose with a fairly concentrated background fruit. Then it is soft and full-bodied, with a convincing finish.

Wine	Glasses	Price
● Brunello di Montalcino '93	🍷🍷	5
● Rosso di Montalcino '96	🍷🍷	4
● Brunello di Montalcino '90	🍷	5
● Brunello di Montalcino '91	🍷	5
● Rosso di Montalcino '92	🍷	4
● Rosso di Montalcino '93	🍷	4
● Brunello di Montalcino '88	🍷🍷 (prev.)	5
● Brunello di Montalcino '89	🍷🍷 (prev.)	5
● Brunello di Montalcino Madonna del Piano Ris. '88	🍷🍷 (prev.)	6
● Brunello di Montalcino Madonna del Piano Ris. '90	🍷🍷 (prev.)	6

MONTECARLO (LU)

FATTORIA DEL BUONAMICO
VIA PROVINCIALE, 43
55015 MONTECARLO (LU)
TEL. 0583/22038

If signs of oenological resurgence are perceptible around Lucca, a part of the credit must be given to the Fattoria del Buonamico. For years this estate has defended the reputation of the Montecarlo area, reminding us all, with the constant quality of its wines, of the past glories and future potential of this territory. Indeed they have an eye to the future at Buonamico, as is shown by their vineyards, newly replanted according to the most rigorous criteria. Their wines all did very well at our tastings this year, with their top line once again excellent and their standard range showing great improvement. The Syrah Fort'yrah '94, whose strong points are concentration and balance, is very good indeed. It has a dense and fairly complex bouquet, with aromas of dark berries and hints of cocoa. The Fortino, a blend of cabernet and merlot, is never a disappointment. At the moment its nose is dominated by wood, sweet vanilla notes in particular. In the mouth it is fresh, lively, juicy and not awfully complex but very appealing. A sweet, full, continuous flavor and a long, vanilla-tinted finish are the main characteristics of the Vasario, made from chardonnay and pinot bianco. The Rosso di Cercatoia '94 has an interestingly deep bouquet, with abundant lovely fruit to the fore; style and maturity are in evidence on the palate, and with a longer finish this wine would have won Two Glasses. The Bianco di Cercatoia '96 is also good, simple but balanced and fragrant. We conclude with the reliable performance of the two Montecarlos, both very well made and intensely fruity.

●	Fort'Yrah '94	🍷🍷	5
●	Il Fortino Cabernet/Merlot '94	🍷🍷	5
○	Vasario '96	🍷🍷	4
○	Bianco di Cercatoia '96	🍷	3
○	Montecarlo Bianco '97	🍷	2
●	Montecarlo Rosso '97	🍷	2
●	Rosso di Cercatoia '94	🍷	5
●	Il Fortino Cabernet/Merlot '91	🍷🍷 (outline)	5
●	Il Fortino Cabernet/Merlot '93	🍷🍷 (outline)	5
●	Il Fortino Syrah '92	🍷🍷 (outline)	5
●	Rosso di Cercatoia '90	🍷🍷 (outline)	5
○	Vasario '91	🍷🍷 (outline)	5
○	Vasario '95	🍷🍷 (outline)	5
●	Il Fortino Cabernet/Merlot '90	🍷 (outline)	5
●	Il Fortino Cabernet/Merlot '92	🍷 (outline)	5

MONTECARLO (LU)

FUSO CARMIGNANI
LOC. CERCATOIA
VIA DELLA TINAIA, 7
55015 MONTECARLO (LU)
TEL. 0583/22381

The wines of Gino Carmignani, known to his friends as "Fuso", had some real surprises for us this year. What struck us most was not the usual top of the line, For Duke, but the simple Montecarlo Rosso. This is a red that reminded us (although we hardly require such reminders) that wine is made to be drunk and not to be the object of endless academic discussion. The Montecarlo Sassonero '97 slips right down without any trouble; it is soft, concentrated and rich in fruit that expands in your mouth, with a dash of pepper: good enough to push the fine and theoretically superior For Duke down to second place. The merits of the two different vintages certainly play a decisive role: the '97 exhibits fully mature fruit and tannins, while the '96 presents a good but uneven structure, with some still unrounded edges. For Duke is unquestionably successful, but it lacks the energy of the '95. The bouquet is less complex, and there are vegetal notes and toasty hints of oak that the fruit cannot mask. It is agreeably sweet at its entry on the palate and expands fairly well thereafter, with good balance and a pleasant if somewhat simple finish. The other surprise was the former Vin Santo, now a table wine, Le Notti Rosse di Capo Diavolo '95, which has thrown off its customary oxidized style, and instead combines freshness and elegance with a full-bodied well-balanced sweetness. Finally, the Montecarlo Bianco is somewhat dumb on the nose but substantial in the mouth.

●	Montecarlo Rosso Sassonero '97	🍷🍷	2*
○	Vin Santo Le Notti Rosse di Capo Diavolo '95	🍷🍷	4
●	For Duke '96	🍷	4
○	Montecarlo Bianco Pietrachiara '97	🍷	2
●	For Duke '90	🍷🍷 (outline)	4
●	For Duke '94	🍷🍷 (outline)	4
●	For Duke '95	🍷🍷 (outline)	4
●	For Duke '93	🍷 (outline)	4
●	Montecarlo Rosso Sassonero '96	🍷 (outline)	2*
○	Vin Santo Le Notti Rosse di Capo Diavolo '93	🍷 (outline)	4
○	Vin Santo Le Notti Rosse di Capo Diavolo '94	🍷 (outline)	4

MONTECARLO (LU)

FATTORIA DI MONTECHIARI
VIA MONTECHIARI, 27
55015 MONTECARLO (LU)
TEL. 0583/22189

Perhaps the best news in Tuscany this year bears the name of Montechiari, an estate which has piled up an incredible series of records in one go: from its debut in the Guide to Three Glasses, incidentally the first ever awarded in the Province of Lucca. It must be pointed out that the winery was not born yesterday but has been in existence for almost twenty years, although the production of wines of high quality has only recently become its goal. Stefano Chioccioli's oenological management has been an essential ingredient of their success, as has the far-sighted determination of the owners, Moreno Panattoni and Catherine Pirmez. There are at present only five hectares under vine, but five more have just been planted at a density of 7 thousand vines per hectare. The Cabernet '95 managed to stand out in the crowded field of the best super-Tuscans thanks to its aromatic richness and, in particular, its superior depth of flavor. Even its deep ruby hue is very concentrated. Fresh and intense on the nose, with predominating tones of black currant combined with light vegetal and spicy hints, it reveals an extra dimension on the palate: softness, silky tannins and a long and elegant finish. The excellence of the other wines we tasted serves as proof that the Cabernet is not just a lucky shot. The Pinot Nero '95 succeeds in combining a typical varietal bouquet with a noteworthy body. The Rosso '95, a pure sangiovese, displays an admirable density produced by its thickly woven tannins; oak is still quite noticeable. The Montecarlo Rosso '96 has a truly surprising roundness and appeal, and the excellent Chardonnay '96 is distinguished by a full and vigorous palate supported by a fine acidity.

	Wine	Glasses	Price
●	Montechiari Cabernet '95	🍷🍷🍷	5
●	Montecarlo Rosso '96	🍷🍷	3*
○	Montechiari Chardonnay '96	🍷🍷	4
●	Montechiari Nero '95	🍷🍷	5
●	Montechiari Rosso '95	🍷🍷	4

MONTECARLO (LU)

FATTORIA DEL TESO
VIA POLTRONIERA
55015 MONTECARLO (LU)
TEL. 0583/286288

The Fattoria del Teso is another debutant in this year's Guide. It is the largest estate in the Montecarlo zone and is extremely well equipped. There are currently about thirty hectares under vine, with traditional local grapes predominating. Dr. Claudio Fucigna, the estate oenologist, calls the shots: the wines must be absolutely clean and correctly executed. But there has recently been a growing conviction that decisive intervention in the vineyards is a prerequisite for greater excellence in wines. At this year's tastings the well-made Riserva Anfiteatro di Lucca '95 stood out: a red whose intensity is apparent to eye and nose, with immediately pleasing fruity aromas. The appealing palate is well-balanced, with moderate concentration and length. It just missed getting Two Glasses. The equally successful Vin Santo '87 offers a bouquet of very interesting style, with mineral, vegetal, and dried flower notes. It has a restrained and classically dry character. The Stella del Teso '97 is a modern white, achieved by using low fermentation temperatures and a little cryomaceration. The results are noteworthy: clean, intense, very fresh aromas and a correspondingly straightforward, clearly defined palate, although perhaps there is too much evidence of the drawing board. The two Montecarlos are rather thin but perfectly respectable.

	Wine	Glasses	Price
●	Montecarlo Rosso Anfiteatro di Lucca Ris. '95	🍷	4
○	Stella del Teso '97	🍷	3
○	Vin Santo del Teso '87	🍷	5
○	Montecarlo Bianco '97		2
●	Montecarlo Rosso '97		2

MONTECARLO (LU)

Wandanna

Via Don Minzoni, 38
55015 Montecarlo (LU)
tel. 0583/228989 - 22226

After its debut in the Guide last year, we were curious to see if the winery owned by the Fantozzi family would withstand the test of time. Our tastings were more than reassuring: the level was even better than we had expected. Wandanna is an estate to keep one's eye on, both because of its size and because its owners are not resting on their laurels. The best of their wide range of wines is the Virente '95, an unusual mixture of merlot, syrah and ciliegiolo notable for an impeccably clean bouquet, a vivid genuine fruitiness, an elegant palate and good balance: Two full Glasses. But perhaps the most important development is the evident improvement in all their wines. The Montecarlo Rosso Terre dei Cascinieri '96 stands out in its category and did very well: it has an intense, lively ruby hue, while its nose, still somewhat dumb, displays dark berries with light vegetal and oaky hints. The entry on the palate is dense, the tannins are thickly woven and the finish is long. The appealing Montecarlo Bianco Terre dei Cascinieri '96 is soft and pleasing, while the Sauvignon '97 has a surprising aromatic impact revealing lots of lively fruit, with notes of peach skin combined with flowery and vegetal hints. The Vermentino '97, while not very crisp, has character; the Terre della Gioiosa Rosso '97 has substance and grip. Rounding off the list, the Terre della Gioiosa Bianco '97 and the fragrant rosé, Cerasello '97, are both properly made wines.

	Wine	Glasses	Price
●	Montecarlo Rosso Terre dei Cascinieri '96	🍷🍷 (black)	4
●	Virente '95	🍷🍷 (black)	5
○	Montecarlo Bianco Terre dei Cascinieri '96	🍷 (black)	4
●	Montecarlo Rosso Terre della Gioiosa '97	🍷 (black)	2*
○	Sauvignon '97	🍷 (black)	3
○	Vermentino '97	🍷 (black)	3
⊙	Cerasello '97		2
○	Montecarlo Bianco Terre dei Cascinieri '97		2
●	Virente '94	🍷🍷 (white)	5
●	Montecarlo Rosso Terre della Gioiosa '96	🍷 (white)	2

MONTECATINI VAL DI CECINA (PI)

Fattoria Sorbaiano

Via Provinciale Tre Comuni
56040 Montecatini
Val di Cecina (PI)
tel. 0588/30243

Sorbaiano is one of our "regulars": it has had its own profile in the Guide for years and, since this distinction must be fought for with each new edition, its constant presence indicates wines with a constancy of quality and reliability over a long period. This year we tasted five of them. The best, as is almost always the case, is the Rosso delle Miniere, which we found particularly successful in its '96 version. It has a lovely concentrated ruby hue and an intense bouquet featuring dark wild berries, toasty oak, and bell pepper. It is soft, supple and elegant on the palate, with quite a long finish on which vegetal notes reappear, thanks to the cabernet in the blend. It is a wine that perfectly reflects the freshness characteristic both of the '96 vintage and of the not insignificant altitude of the Sorbaiano vineyards. The Montescudaio Rosso '97 is a quite good wine, simple and immediate, but graced with good concentration and lots of fruit. The Montescudaio Bianco is correct but undistinguished. We found the Lucestraia curiously less convincing than usual. We tasted the '95 and '96, which both display unusual floral scents, rose in particular, reminiscent of traminer. On the palate the '95 seems a bit forward, while the '96 is full-bodied but slightly unbalanced.

	Wine	Glasses	Price
●	Montescudaio Rosso delle Miniere '96	🍷🍷 (black)	4
○	Montescudaio Bianco Lucestraia '96	🍷 (black)	3
●	Montescudaio Rosso '97	🍷 (black)	2*
○	Montescudaio Bianco '97		2
○	Montescudaio Bianco Lucestraia '95		3
●	Montescudaio Rosso delle Miniere '93	🍷🍷 (white)	4*
●	Montescudaio Rosso delle Miniere '94	🍷🍷 (white)	4*
●	Montescudaio Rosso delle Miniere '95	🍷🍷 (white)	4

MONTEFOLLONICO (SI)

Vittorio Innocenti
Via Landucci, 10/12
53040 Montefollonico (SI)
tel. 0577/669537

Vittorio Innocenti's winery is located in the center of Montefollonico, a small, splendidly restored medieval village. From the magnificent winery terrace you can enjoy one of the most enchanting views of the Montepulciano countryside. Once again this year Innocenti has made a good showing, a further confirmation of the value of the labors expended in both vineyard and cellar, where, in an ever more crowded barrel-room, increasing numbers of French oak casks of various sizes majestically reside. The Nobile di Montepulciano Riserva '94 is ruby red with garnet highlights, and has a nose redolent of flowers, particularly violet, and fruit. There is a certain hardness on the palate, but this is a characteristic of Innocenti's wines and is a function of the soil of his vineyards. In a difficult vintage like '94 one notices it all the more, and consequently it would be as well to wait a while before drinking this Riserva. For the same reason we did not review the flagship of the estate, the Sangiovese Acerone '93, in our last edition. After another year's aging it is a very interesting wine, and indeed has picked up Two Glasses without any trouble. Intensely ruby in color with suggestions of garnet, it vaunts a really captivating bouquet with tobacco and red fruit perfectly blended with the sweetness of the French oak; the palate is very successful as well, with tannin well integrated in the structure. Innocenti has also brought out a Vin Santo '90 that came close to winning Two Glasses. It has a fine amber color and offers aromas of green walnut and peanut, and some animal scents; its balance is excellent, as is its very long finish.

	Wine	Rating	Price
●	Acerone '93	🍷🍷	5
●	Vino Nobile di Montepulciano Ris. '94	🍷	5
●	Vino Nobile di Montepulciano Ris. '88	🍷🍷🍷	5
●	Acerone '90	🍷🍷	5
●	Vino Nobile di Montepulciano '93	🍷🍷	3
●	Vino Nobile di Montepulciano Ris. '90	🍷🍷	5
○	Vin Santo '90	🍷	5
●	Vino Nobile di Montepulciano Ris. '91	🍷	5
●	Vino Nobile di Montepulciano Ris. '93	🍷	5

MONTEMURLO (PO)

Tenuta di Bagnolo
dei Marchesi Pancrazi
Via Montalese, 168
50045 Montemurlo (PO)
tel. 0574/652058

For some years Marquis Vittorio Pancrazi has essentially been swimming against the tide in Tuscany. He does make red wine, but not from sangiovese or a more or less naturalized varietal like cabernet or merlot: his principal objective (at least for the moment) is to create a great red from pinot noir alone. This is like trying to get to the top of Mt. Everest, even if you're an experienced climber. The results, at least in a strictly Italian context, have been gratifyingly encouraging. The Pinot Nero Villa di Bagnolo in years like '89 and '93 has been a benchmark in Italy for a wine made from this notoriously tricky and unpredictable grape. The '96 vintage, however, was not quite up to our expectations. In a rather muffled bouquet with distinct sulphurous notes, a few nuances of wild berries timidly emerge, but too far in the background to overcome the initial lack of focus. Even after breathing for a good while, the wine does not really come out. Perhaps these are the vices of youth, which the right amount of bottle aging will temper. On the palate there is a prevalence (corresponding to the nose) of rather harsh, bitter tones, although there is considerable substance and structure. It is, in short, a rigid red that lacks the sensual elegance typical of the best pinot noir.

	Wine	Rating	Price
●	Pinot Nero Villa di Bagnolo '96	🍷	5
●	Pinot Nero Villa di Bagnolo '89	🍷🍷	5
●	Pinot Nero Villa di Bagnolo '91	🍷🍷	5
●	Pinot Nero Villa di Bagnolo '92	🍷🍷	5
●	Pinot Nero Villa di Bagnolo '93	🍷🍷	5
●	Pinot Nero Villa di Bagnolo '94	🍷🍷	5
●	Pinot Nero Villa di Bagnolo '95	🍷🍷	5
●	Pinot Nero Villa di Bagnolo '90	🍷	5

MONTEPULCIANO (SI)

Avignonesi

Via di Gracciano nel Corso, 91
53040 Montepulciano (SI)
tel. 0578/757872 - 757873

There are many innovations at Avignonesi this year: the new sangiovese and prugnolo gentile vines are interesting both in density (about 7 thousand vines per hectare) and in the way they are arranged (gobelet training). And in the cellar we observed that a series of wooden vats for red wine fermentation are replacing those in steel. So it seems reasonable to predict an ever brighter future for this winery, which the oenologist Paolo Trappolini directs. This year's wines did extremely well, and at last there was the thoroughbred champion we had long been looking for. The Vin Santo '88 is simply extraordinary. Its amber color has a rosy glow, and as one inhales one is almost intoxicated by the fragrances of candied peel, almonds and dried fruit. It is no less delightful on the palate, where it strikes a wonderful balance between sugars and acidity; it is very dense and its finish is counted in minutes. No fewer than three wines merit Two Glasses: the Nobile di Montepulciano '95, the Merlot Desiderio '95 and the Marzocco '96, a barrique-aged chardonnay. The Nobile di Montepulciano has a very agreeable palate with a good finish and a pleasing balance that makes it eminently drinkable. The Merlot has good structure, but the tannins are a bit harsh, and we would prefer more elegance of bouquet. The Marzocco is unquestionably better than ever: it is very varietal and elegant, with an excellent finish and a distinct personality. The Riserva Grandi Annate '93 is very much less impressive than we had hoped; it earned only One Glass.

	Wine	Glasses	
○	Vin Santo '88	🍷🍷🍷	6
○	Il Marzocco '96	🍷🍷	4
●	Merlot Desiderio '95	🍷🍷	6
●	Vino Nobile di Montepulciano '95	🍷🍷	5
●	Vino Nobile di Montepulciano Grandi Annate Ris. '93	🍷	5
●	Grifi '90	🍷🍷 (prev.)	5
●	Grifi '93	🍷🍷 (prev.)	5
●	Merlot '90	🍷🍷 (prev.)	5
●	Merlot '93	🍷🍷 (prev.)	6
○	Vin Santo '86	🍷🍷 (prev.)	6
●	Vino Nobile di Montepulciano Grandi Annate Ris. '90	🍷🍷 (prev.)	5
●	Vino Nobile di Montepulciano Ris. '90	🍷🍷 (prev.)	5

MONTEPULCIANO (SI)

Poderi Boscarelli

Loc. Cervognano
Via di Montenero, 28
53040 Montepulciano (SI)
tel. 0578/767277

This winery, which is located in the subzone of Cervognano, the pride of Montepulciano, is known for its powerful and elegant wines which have more than once garnered our highest award. The dynamic Paola De Ferrari runs the estate, with the help of her sons Luca and Niccolò, and the advice of Maurizio Castelli, one of the most renowned oenologists in Italy. Among this year's novelties is a new wine, the '96 De Ferrari, a blend of sangiovese and prugnolo gentile. The bouquet is pleasingly fruity, and its agreeable freshness makes it enchanting to drink. The Nobile di Montepulciano '95 is more complex; on the nose there are notes of blackberry and cherry sweetened by vanilla and other spices, while it is smooth and substantial in the mouth, with a light touch of tannin. But mindful of the past, Boscarelli has presented two quite significant wines: the Vino Nobile di Montepulciano Riserva del Nocio '95 and the Boscarelli of the same vintage. The former has a "pigeon's blood" ruby hue and an intense and persistent bouquet with aromas of sour cherry, red currant and blackberry; it seems important on the palate, where its attack is sweet and progression excellent, with stylish tannins perfectly balanced by its soft component. The finish is long and the correspondence between nose and palate is admirable. The Boscarelli '95 is of the same quality, with aromas of Peruvian bark and pencil lead that enhance the fruit; the excess of tannin that used in the past to dampen the finish has disappeared: this is the best Boscarelli ever.

	Wine	Glasses	
●	Boscarelli '95	🍷🍷	6
●	Vino Nobile di Montepulciano Ris. del Nocio '95	🍷🍷	5
●	De Ferrari '96	🍷	3
●	Vino Nobile di Montepulciano '95	🍷	4
●	Vino Nobile di Montepulciano Ris. '88	🍷🍷🍷 (prev.)	5
●	Vino Nobile di Montepulciano Ris. del Nocio '91	🍷🍷🍷 (prev.)	5
●	Boscarelli '90	🍷🍷 (prev.)	6
●	Vino Nobile di Montepulciano '92	🍷🍷 (prev.)	4
●	Vino Nobile di Montepulciano '93	🍷🍷 (prev.)	4
●	Vino Nobile di Montepulciano '94	🍷🍷 (prev.)	4
●	Vino Nobile di Montepulciano Ris. del Nocio '93	🍷🍷 (prev.)	5

CANNETO

VIA DEI CANNETI, 14
53045 MONTEPULCIANO (SI)
TEL. 0578/757737

This winery is Swiss-owned and has traditionally concentrated on Nobile di Montepulciano Riserva, which is greatly in demand among German-speakers. With the '94 vintage there was a change in policy, which led to the production of non-Riserva versions of the Nobile. Indeed, in 1994 no Riserva at all was produced, a decision we fully approve, given the problems posed by that vintage. A further innovation is the first appearance of their Rosso di Montepulciano '97. Unfortunately it wasn't bottled in time for our tasting, so we shall be reviewing it in the next edition of the Guide. There has been a change in the technical direction of the winery as well: it is now in the hands of Carlo Ferrini, one of the most celebrated agronomists and oenologists in Tuscany. There are currently about 18 hectares of vineyards in production, but some new non-native vines have been planted and should be bearing fruit for the '99 harvest. The cellar is completely temperature-controlled and the barrel-room, entirely overhauled, now also contains smaller (500-liter capacity) barrels. The only wine we can review this time is the Nobile di Montepulciano '95. It has a lovely concentrated ruby hue, and the blackberry fragrance is distinct, while its palate corresponds well, with a good balance between the soft and the acidic and tannic components: Two well-earned Glasses.

	Wine	Glasses	Price
●	Vino Nobile di Montepulciano '95	🍷🍷	4
●	Vino Nobile di Montepulciano Ris. '88	YY	4
●	Vino Nobile di Montepulciano Ris. '89	YY	4
●	Vino Nobile di Montepulciano Ris. '90	YY	4
●	Vino Nobile di Montepulciano '94	Y	4
●	Vino Nobile di Montepulciano Ris. '91	Y	4

MONTEPULCIANO (SI)

FATTORIA DEL CERRO

LOC. ACQUAVIVA
VIA GRAZIANELLA, 5
53040 MONTEPULCIANO (SI)
TEL. 0578/767722

The Fattoria del Cerro is one part of the tripartite Saiagricola wine domain, which also includes Poderina in Montalcino and the Umbrian Colpetrone in Montefalco. The vastness of the vineyards, which cover approximately 156 hectares, makes it possible to retire the oldest vines each year and put in new ones, which are being planted at a density of about 5 thousand vines (which will bear specially selected clones) per hectare. The technical staff has decided to limit the number of white wines to two: Cerro Bianco and Bravìolo. However, plans for the future call for a sweet wine if test results are positive. On the red front we have noticed some improvements, particularly in the Montepulcianos. The Rosso di Montepulciano '97 is very good, among the best in its category, and has won Two Glasses. It is of a very concentrated purple color with violet highlights. The ample and lingering nose reveals notes of chocolate, red currants and blueberries as well as the classic cherry. This complexity carries through to the palate, where its densely woven and soft texture makes it unusually delightful. Another but better Two Glass Wine is the Vino Nobile di Montepulciano '95. An interesting hint of ginger enriches the bouquet, in which a distinct note of tobacco accompanies the fruit. The palate is extremely well-balanced, with rich extract and noble tannins. The simpler but very well-made Chianti Colli Senesi '97 has staked its all on fruit and freshness. The Bravìolo, a trebbiano without the harshness typical of that grape, is excellent value for money.

	Wine	Glasses	Price
●	Rosso di Montepulciano '97	🍷🍷	3
●	Vino Nobile di Montepulciano '95	🍷🍷	4
○	Bravìolo '97	🍷	2*
○	Cerro Bianco '97	🍷	3
●	Chianti Colli Senesi '97	🍷	2
●	Vino Nobile di Montepulciano '90	YYY	4*
●	Rosso di Montepulciano '93	YY	2
●	Rosso di Montepulciano '96	YY	2*
○	Thesis '93	YY	4
●	Vino Nobiie di Montepulciano '91	YY	4
●	Vino Nobile di Montepulciano Ris. '93	YY	4*
●	Vino Nobile di Montepulciano Vigneto Antica Chiusina '90	YY	4

MONTEPULCIANO (SI)

CONTUCCI
VIA DEL TEATRO, 1
53045 MONTEPULCIANO (SI)
TEL. 0578/757006

Alamanno Contucci, the dynamic president of the Consorzio del Vino Nobile, is proceeding with the modernization of his historic winery, underneath his ancestral home on the main square in Montepulciano. This will mark the end of the ancient Montepulciano tradition of painting barrels for aging red and black, which made cellars quite picturesque. Both barriques and large wooden casks have begun to appear in this temple of oenology, changing not only the appearance of the cellar but also, starting with the '96 vintage, decisively transforming the characteristics of the wines produced. The '97 harvest has benefited also from the partial replacement of the old glazed-cement fermentation vats with new ones in steel. The estate has been expanded by four newly acquired hectares that should start producing grapes a few years hence. All in all, Contucci is on the move. Unfortunately, the wines we tasted this year have not yet benefited from these innovations and showed some shortcomings. The best was the estate's most traditional wine, the Vin Santo, fruit of the troublesome '92 vintage. Of a fine golden yellow color, it reveals a very clean bouquet with aromas of candied peel and dried fruit, and a delightful, fairly intense palate. The Vino Nobile '95 Pietrarossa does not rate more than a mention because of its muffled nose.

	Wine	Glasses	Price
○	Vin Santo '92	🍷	5
●	Vino Nobile di Montepulciano Pietrarossa '95		4
○	Vin Santo '86	YY	6
○	Vin Santo '90	YY	4
●	Vino Nobile di Montepulciano '90	YY	4
●	Vino Nobile di Montepulciano Pietrarossa '90	YY	5
●	Vino Nobile di Montepulciano Ris. '91	YY	4
○	Vin Santo '91	Y	5
●	Vino Nobile di Montepulciano '93	Y	3
●	Vino Nobile di Montepulciano '94	Y	4
●	Vino Nobile di Montepulciano Pietrarossa '94	Y	4

MONTEPULCIANO (SI)

DEI
LOC. VILLA MARTIENA
53045 MONTEPULCIANO (SI)
TEL. 0578/716878

Caterina Dei continues to expand her estate by acquiring new vineyards; the current total is almost 40 hectares. To our astonishment she still manages to do everything by herself. The wines themselves had mixed results. We did taste what we believe to be the best wine Dei has ever produced, but a few of the others fell short of expectations. The most traditional of her wines did not get more than One Glass because of unformed bouquets. Of the two versions of the Vino Nobile di Montepulciano presented, the Riserva '94 and the '95 non-Riserva, we preferred the second, the product of an unquestionably better vintage. This '95 offers a good progression of flavors, but the tannins are a little rough. The Riserva '94 suffers from its unimpressive vintage, but what it loses in power it gains in pleasing drinkability and elegance. The star of the estate is the Santa Catharina '95; in this its second time out, its high scores have catapulted it to the upper echelons of the Two Glass wines. Made from prugnolo gentile, syrah and cabernet sauvignon, it spends more than a year in French oak barrels before aging in the bottle. Its color is a highly concentrated ruby with violet nuances; the complex nose offers scents of citron, pencil lead and white pepper enriched by oak-derived notes of eucalyptus. There is a good attack on the palate and it progresses well to the rich long finish.

	Wine	Glasses	Price
●	Santa Catharina '95	🍷🍷	5
●	Vino Nobile di Montepulciano '95	🍷	4
●	Vino Nobile di Montepulciano Ris. '94	🍷	4
●	Rosso di Montepulciano '93	YY	3*
●	Rosso di Montepulciano '94	YY	3
●	Santa Catharina '94	YY	5
●	Vino Nobile di Montepulciano '90	YY	4
●	Vino Nobile di Montepulciano '91	YY	4
●	Vino Nobile di Montepulciano '93	YY	4
●	Vino Nobile di Montepulciano Ris. '90	YY	4
●	Vino Nobile di Montepulciano Ris. '93	YY	4

MONTEPULCIANO (SI)

Cav. Fanetti - Tenuta S. Agnese

Via Calamandrei, 29
53045 Montepulciano (SI)
tel. 0578/757266

Cavaliere Fanetti is the man who invented Vino Nobile di Montepulciano, in that it was he who patented the name. So innovations are not altogether welcome at the Tenuta Sant'Agnese, especially if they aim at altering this great red wine. White grapes are still used in the Cavaliere's Nobile di Montepulciano, and they do give it a personality all its own, but in our opinion they reduce the impact of both color and flavor. We tasted some pure prugnolo gentile which we found extremely interesting, but Fanetti maintains that this is not Vino Nobile, and if he ever gets around to bottling it he'll call it table wine. Such consistency is admirable, albeit difficult to comprehend. We continue to hope that the winery's splendid and impeccably kept vineyards will eventually produce the great red wine that is surely in them. At the moment the Cavaliere is refurnishing his barrel-room, and it could even happen that something new appears in this shrine of Montepulciano tradition. We found the Vino Nobile di Montepulciano '95 the most interesting of the wines presented this year. Ruby verging on garnet in color, it has a nose dominated by tobacco, with lightly vegetal accents. There is fair balance on the palate, tilting slightly towards the acidic, and tannins that tend to shorten the finish. The Riserva '94 del Nobile di Montepulciano isn't bad for that unpropitious vintage. The less interesting Rosso di Montepulciano '96 is really too simple to merit more than passing mention. The Santa Giuditta is better: there are notes of tobacco and oleander and a delightful quaffability.

	Wine	Glasses	
●	Santa Giuditta '95	▼	5
●	Vino Nobile di Montepulciano '95	▼	5
●	Vino Nobile di Montepulciano Ris. '94	▼	5
●	Rosso di Montepulciano '96		3
○	Vin Santo '71	▽▽	5
○	Vin Santo '75	▽▽	6
●	Vino Nobile di Montepulciano Ris. '88	▽▽	5
●	Vino Nobile di Montepulciano Ris. '90	▽▽	5
●	Aleatico '85	▽	4
●	Vino Nobile di Montepulciano '94	▽	5
●	Vino Nobile di Montepulciano Ris. '93	▽	5

MONTEPULCIANO (SI)

Fassati

Loc. Gracciano
Via di Graccianello, 3/a
53040 Montepulciano (SI)
tel. 0578/708708

Territorial expansion proceeds apace here, having already reached 75 hectares under vine, many of which are peculiarly suited to the production of Vino Nobile di Montepulciano. The cellar is also now in keeping with the requirements of Fassati, which belongs to the winery giant Fazi-Battaglia. All the wines presented are among the best in their categories, greatly to the honor of Dr. Porfiri, who directs the winery. The most notable this year was the Nobile di Montepulciano '95, an easy Two Glass winner and the best they've ever produced. It has an intense, almost impenetrable ruby hue, and a rather complex bouquet with fragrances of red fruit and black berries well amalgamated with French oak-derived nuances, all of which carry through onto the rich palate, progressing admirably, with tannins softened, to a broad finish. We tasted the '93 vintage of the new Fassati wine, Torre al Fante, a blend of prugnolo gentile and sangiovese aged in barriques and, after a brief stop in steel, for another 12 months or so in the bottle. Its captivating nose and good structure earned it Two Glasses, although the tannin seems somewhat astringent. We gave similar marks to the Nobile di Montepulciano Salarco '93 with its aromas of blackberry and tobacco and its harmonious palate. The Rosso di Montepulciano '97 Selciaia is very successful, one of the best of its kind this year.

	Wine	Glasses	
●	Torre al Fante '93	▼▼	5
●	Vino Nobile di Montepulciano '95	▼▼	4
●	Vino Nobile di Montepulciano Salarco '93	▼▼	5
●	Rosso di Montepulciano Selciaia '97	▼	3
●	Rosso di Montepulciano Selciaia '96	▽▽	3
●	Vino Nobile di Montepulciano '90	▽▽	4
●	Vino Nobile di Montepulciano '91	▽▽	4
●	Vino Nobile di Montepulciano '93	▽▽	4
●	Vino Nobile di Montepulciano '94	▽▽	4
●	Vino Nobile di Montepulciano Podere Graccianello '90	▽▽	4
●	Vino Nobile di Montepulciano Ris. '93	▽▽	5

MONTEPULCIANO (SI)

Gattavecchi
Loc. S. Maria
53045 Montepulciano (SI)
tel. 0578/757110

There are in Montepulciano some important wineries that have only recently taken to bottling all their wines. One of these is Gattavecchi, which produces about 250 thousand bottles a year. Their vineyards cover about 20 hectares, nine of which are dedicated to Nobile di Montepulciano. To satisfy demand, they have regularly purchased additional grapes from reliable local suppliers, but they have decided to separate their own and their neighbors' grapes in future, creating a new label to distinguish between them. Meanwhile, they are turning their attention to the barrel-room, acquiring new 35-hectoliter Slavonian oak casks; their 13th century cellar is already fitted out with barriques, in which the '97 vintage is reposing. Vinification equipment is also due for renewal, so temperature-controlled steel vats will be taking the place of traditional glazed-cement tanks. There is a rational division of labor on the estate, with Luca Gattavecchi focusing on the business end and his brother Gionata directing production with the help of their oenologist uncle Esposito, who worked for many years at Fassati. The wines presented this year still represent Gattavecchi's transitional stage and include acquired grapes, but they did very well nonetheless. The Nobile di Montepulciano '95 seemed awfully good and very nearly got Two Glasses, thanks to its complex palate, but the fruit of the bouquet was slightly disturbed by some rather "green" notes. In the same award category, but at a respectful distance, is the Rosso di Montepulciano '96, which offers lovely hints of red fruit and a delightful drinkability.

●	Rosso di Montepulciano '96	🍷	3
●	Vino Nobile di Montepulciano '95	🍷	4

MONTEPULCIANO (SI)

Tenuta di Gracciano Della Seta
Loc. Montepulciano Stazione
Via Umbria, 59
53040 Montepulciano (SI)
tel. 0578/708340

The Della Seta family has owned the Tenuta di Gracciano estate since the beginning of the century. The virtues of their land, oenologically speaking, include its south-southeast exposure, its altitude, around 300 meters, and the very poor, predominantly chalky soil. The owners have recently re-equipped the cellar, which is now bursting with 50-hectoliter French oak casks; space has also been found for a number of barriques, in which the merlot from the newly planted vines is aging. Ten of their thirteen hectares under vine produce Nobile di Montepulciano; the rest is dedicated to Rosso di Montepulciano and, to a small extent, merlot, producing a total of approximately 60,000 bottles. The land is of such natural excellence and the proprietors have invested so heavily that we rather think this estate will succeed in holding on to the space it conquered in the Guide this year. The wines we tasted revealed major progress: in fact the Rosso di Montepulciano '97 is more convincing than the Nobile di Montepulciano from the notable '95 vintage. The Rosso di Montepulciano is intensely ruby in hue with violet highlights; the very clean bouquet features lots of distinct and lingering fruit that carries through onto the palate, which progresses well thanks to its richness of extract, well-balanced by acidity. Although it is certainly well made, the Nobile di Montepulciano '95 is not complex enough on the palate or on the nose, where some less than clean notes emerge, probably due to the use of somewhat imperfect barrels.

●	Rosso di Montepulciano '97	🍷	3
●	Vino Nobile di Montepulciano '95	🍷	4
●	Vino Nobile di Montepulciano '90	YY	4
●	Vino Nobile di Montepulciano '91	Y	4
●	Vino Nobile di Montepulciano Ris. '91	Y	4

Podere Il Macchione

Via di Gracciano
53045 Montepulciano (SI)
tel. 0578/716493 - 758595

Last year this winery carried off Three Glasses for its Vino Nobile di Montepulciano Riserva '93, a distinctly well-made wine that is still stupendous a year later. This year they have presented their Nobile di Montepulciano '95, but no '94 version of the Riserva was produced since Robert Kengelbacher, the owner of the estate, didn't find the vintage up to his standards for a Riserva. From his four hectares of vineyards, Robert produces wines that stylishly succeed in combining elegance and power, and that give clear proof of his cellar skills, particularly his expert way of using wood for aging so that it enriches without dominating the fruit in the wine. In anticipation of the Riserva that will come out next year, the Vino Nobile di Montepulciano '95 made a good showing at our tastings. Of an extremely intense ruby hue, it really shines in its bouquet, which offers a broad array of aromas including sour cherry and violets; its entry on the palate is good, and it has enough substance to make it quite pleasurable to drink: Two Glasses on the mark. The delightful Rosso di Montepulciano '96 is all freshness and quaffability.

Wine	Glasses	Price
● Vino Nobile di Montepulciano '95	🍷🍷	5
● Rosso di Montepulciano '96	🍷	3
● Vino Nobile di Montepulciano Le Caggiole Ris. '93	ΥΥΥ	5
● Vino Nobile di Montepulciano '90	ΥΥ	5
● Vino Nobile di Montepulciano '91	ΥΥ	5
● Vino Nobile di Montepulciano Ris. '90	ΥΥ	5
● Vino Nobile di Montepulciano Ris. '91	ΥΥ	5
● Vino Nobile di Montepulciano '94	Υ	5
● Vino Nobile di Montepulciano '92	Υ	5

MONTEPULCIANO (SI)

Fattoria La Braccesca

Loc. Gracciano
S. S. 326,15
53040 Montepulciano (SI)
tel. 0578/707058

This winery, which belongs to Antinori, owns about 78 hectares of vineyards in the most highly prized zones of the appellation: the Vino Nobile vines near Nottola, Gracciano, and Cervognano, which are famous for their fragrant and long-lived wines. This year the winery presented two new labels: a Rosso di Montepulciano Sabazio '97, which is the best of the year, and the Merlot '96. These are both very interesting wines that reflect the expertise of the winery staff headed by Renzo Cotarella, general manager of Marchesi Antinori. The Rosso di Montepulciano Sabazio, which has earned Two Glasses, is intensely ruby in color with violet highlights; it displays dense fruit on the nose, with distinct notes of red currant and cherry, and an extremely pleasing palate with excellent balance between extracts and acidity. The attractive bouquet of the Merlot offers balsamic and toasty fragrances that blend well with the fruity and lightly vegetal nature of the grape. It is equally enchanting on the palate: the attack is sweet and the progression good, but the finish is slightly hampered by tannins. This is an excellent debut that more than merits Two Glasses and, in better vintages, will be in the running for a higher prize. The Vino Nobile di Montepulciano '95 is also very good. Intense and uniform ruby in color, it has lingering aromas distinctly suggestive of black cherry and blackberry. It is full-bodied, but lightly overstated tannins simplify the finish. This was, all in all, an excellent performance for a winery that seems to be getting better and better.

Wine	Glasses	Price
● Merlot '96	🍷🍷	5
● Rosso di Montepulciano Sabazio '97	🍷🍷	3
● Vino Nobile di Montepulciano '95	🍷🍷	4
● Vino Nobile di Montepulciano '90	ΥΥ	4
● Vino Nobile di Montepulciano '93	ΥΥ	4
● Rosso di Montepulciano '93	Υ	2
● Rosso di Montepulciano '96	Υ	2
● Vino Nobile di Montepulciano '92	Υ	4
● Vino Nobile di Montepulciano '94	Υ	4

La Calonica

Loc. Valiano
Via della Stella, 25
53040 Montepulciano (SI)
tel. 0578/724119

Federico Cattani's estate is different from other local wineries: the nearness of Lake Trasimeno guarantees comparatively mild winters and good humidity in the summer, preventing serious drought in hotter years. Of course, this means there are problems if the season is cold and rainy, but generally speaking the balance is positive. Another peculiarity of this winery is that it grows riesling, although they don't produce a monovarietal wine with it. The property consists of about 24 hectares under vine, including, in recent years, international varieties such as cabernet sauvignon and merlot, which are now legitimate components of Nobile di Montepulciano. The restocking of the barrel-room, begun several years ago, is not yet completed, especially in regard to the larger barrels; we believe that when they have finished this modernization process the winery will show further improvement. The wines presented this year performed well, confirming the reliability of this label. The Nobile di Montepulciano '95 just missed Two Glasses. A good palate with rich extract and perfect acidity contrasts with a less successful nose, where the fruity fragrances of blackberry and dark cherry are partially obscured by less pleasant notes. The same holds true for the Girifalco '96, a sangiovese. It displays an interesting knit of extracts, balance and a lingering finish, where its fine tannins are shown to good effect. The aftertaste reflects the minor uncertainties of the bouquet, with a dominant "green" accent.

	Wine	Rating	Price
●	Girifalco '96	▼	5
●	Vino Nobile di Montepulciano '95	▼	4
●	Girifalco '93	ΥΥ	5
●	Girifalco '95	ΥΥ	5
●	Rosso di Montepulciano '91	ΥΥ	3
●	Vino Nobile di Montepulciano '90	ΥΥ	4
●	Vino Nobile di Montepulciano '91	ΥΥ	4
●	Rosso di Montepulciano '95	Υ	3
●	Sangiovese '95	Υ	2*
●	Vino Nobile di Montepulciano '92	Υ	4
●	Vino Nobile di Montepulciano '93	Υ	4

Fattoria Le Casalte

Loc. S. Albino
Via del Termine, 2
53045 Montepulciano (SI)
tel. 0578/799138 - 06/9323090

Guido Barioffi has handed over the reins of this estate to his daughter Chiara. Her enthusiasm and competence during the past few years in developing and implementing a new policy that would bring the wines back up to the level of the vineyards merited this recognition. The recent complete refurbishment of the cellar and barrel-room is another reason why this winery is one of the most interesting in the area. Fermentation takes place in wooden vats, which are available in oak of various provenance, ranging from American to French, without neglecting the classic Slavonian. Size also varies: at one extreme are traditional barriques, at the other 30-hectoliter barrels. These investments should start to bear fruit with the '97 vintage; for the time being we have the wines produced during the transition period, which nonetheless did well at our tastings. The two wines presented this year are the Vino Nobile di Montepulciano '95 and the Rosso di Montepulciano '96. After their decision not to produce a Nobile di Montepulciano '94 because the vintage didn't meet their standards, there was some understandable curiosity about the '95 vintage, vinified by their new oenological consultant Roberto Cipresso. Intensely ruby-hued with garnet highlights, the wine is rather austere on the palate, where the tannin is somewhat divorced from the structure, reducing the breadth of the finish. The delightful Rosso di Montepulciano '96 has a pleasing fruity bouquet on the nose and a smooth palate.

	Wine	Rating	Price
●	Rosso di Montepulciano '96	▼	3
●	Vino Nobile di Montepulciano '95	▼	4
●	Rosso di Montepulciano '93	ΥΥ	3
○	Celius '93	Υ	3
○	Celius '95	Υ	3
○	Celius '96	Υ	3
●	Rosso di Montepulciano '95	Υ	3
●	Vino Nobile di Montepulciano '91	Υ	4
●	Vino Nobile di Montepulciano '92	Υ	4
●	Vino Nobile di Montepulciano '93	Υ	4

Tenuta Lodola Nuova

Tenimenti Ruffino
Loc. Valiano
Via Lodola, 1
53023 Montepulciano (SI)
tel. 0578/724032

This estate, which became part of the Tenimenti Ruffino a few years ago, (and is, by the way, a wonderful place to visit, just near the great 13th century Castello di Valiano after which the entire area is named), is still in the midst of a transitional period. Hence the wines do not yet show themselves at their best, which should be very good indeed, considering the excellent situation of the vineyards. Unfortunately, when the winery was purchased many vines were already rather old, and it was decided to replant them, further prolonging the waiting period for the new generation of wines. The new vineyards include several hectares of alternative varietals which are now permitted in Vino Nobile di Montepulciano. Down in the cellar, they have almost finished restocking the barrel-room, and under the beautiful cross-vaulting you can already see a great variety, in both Slavonian and French oak, of containers of different sizes, from barriques to the more traditional 60-hectoliter barrels. The Nobile di Montepulciano '95 did well at our tastings, winning Two Glasses. Of a concentrated ruby hue, it has a good nose with accents of pepper and black cherry enhanced by oak-derived notes. It is smooth in the mouth, with a moderate level of acidity, but we would have preferred a broader and longer finish. We feel confident that Lodola Nuova will make significant progress in the next few years, thus catching up with the other estates that constitute the Tenimenti of Ruffino and justifying the considerable investments made here.

Wine	Glasses	Price
● Vino Nobile di Montepulciano '95	🍷🍷 (black)	4
● Vino Nobile di Montepulciano '93	🍷🍷	4
● Vino Nobile di Montepulciano '94	🍷	4
● Rosso di Montepulciano '96		2

MONTEPULCIANO (SI)

Eredi Antonino Lombardo

Via Umbria, 59
53040 Montepulciano (SI)
tel. 0578/708321

The Eredi Antonino Lombardo estate has confirmed its right to a profile after its debut in the Guide last year. Work is proceeding at a furious rate here, and the transformation of what is to be the new winery building with connected tasting room and aging cellar is almost complete. The move from the rather anonymous current building to the new one, which started life as a Renaissance villa, should take place within a year. Under the beautiful cellar vaulting the new and much smaller barrels, holding about 750 liters each and indicating the new direction the winery is taking, will soon be installed. Innovation is also to be found in the vineyards, where cabernet and syrah now keep company with the prugnolo gentile. Francesco Lombardo and his brother Gino, the chief agronomist, are convinced that their increased rigor in the vineyard will further improve the quality of their wines over the next few years. The best of the wines presented this year was, in our opinion, the Nobile di Montepulciano '95, which is a joy to behold, although the palate is slightly muffled by tannin, which more bottle age should succeed in integrating in the structure of the wine. The interesting bouquet displays fruit harmoniously blended with notes of new oak. Although the Rosso di Montepulciano '97 is not quite as good, it still is a wine of admirable concentration for its category; it has a very intense and fruity nose and can be drunk at once with pleasure. The Vino Nobile di Montepulciano Riserva '94 and Chianti Colli Senesi '97 merit no more than a mention.

Wine	Glasses	Price
● Rosso di Montepulciano '97	🍷 (black)	3
● Vino Nobile di Montepulciano '95	🍷 (black)	4
● Chianti Colli Senesi '97		2
● Vino Nobile di Montepulciano Ris. '94		4
● Vino Nobile di Montepulciano '90	🍷🍷	3*
● Vino Nobile di Montepulciano Ris. '88	🍷🍷	4
● Vino Nobile di Montepulciano '91	🍷	3
● Vino Nobile di Montepulciano '94	🍷	4
● Vino Nobile di Montepulciano Ris. '93	🍷	4

MONTEPULCIANO (SI)

Nottola

Loc. Bivio Nottola
53045 Montepulciano (SI)
tel. 0578/707060 - 0577/685240

Big changes are taking place at this traditional Montepulciano estate. The owners have budgeted a huge amount of money for another great leap in quality. Their aim is to make the best possible use of excellent land and to become one of the local leaders in quality; in fact, Nottola is amongst the best crus in Montepulciano. The assistance of the famed oenologist Riccardo Cotarella and the total re- equipment of the cellar currently under way bode very well for the future wines of the Giomarelli family. Innovation is not limited to the cellar: new vineyards have been acquired, bringing the total of land under prugnolo gentile vine to ten hectares, not all of which are currently bearing fruit, because of ongoing replanting. While waiting for its new era, Nottola is maintaining its entirely respectable position. The Rosso di Montepulciano '96 wins One Glass thanks to its particularly delightful palate, but we should have liked a broader and more intense bouquet; the Nobile di Montepulciano '95 Vigna del Fattore is a very interesting wine: it has an intense ruby color with an attractive rim, and its nose offers intense notes of red fruit, with cherries to the fore; it is pleasing on the palate, dense and progressive with balanced acidity. The tannins are thickly knit and the finish is satisfying. The Vino Nobile di Montepulciano '95 seemed less convincing, betraying a certain roughness on the nose and a balanced but somewhat simple palate.

●	Vino Nobile di Montepulciano Vigna del Fattore '95	YY	5
●	Rosso di Montepulciano '96	Y	3
●	Vino Nobile di Montepulciano '95		4
●	Rosso di Montepulciano '93	(Y)	2*
●	Vino Nobile di Montepulciano '93	(Y)	4
●	Vino Nobile di Montepulciano '94	(Y)	4
●	Vino Nobile di Montepulciano Ris. '91	(Y)	4

MONTEPULCIANO (SI)

Redi

Via di Collazzi, 5
53045 Montepulciano (SI)
tel. 0578/757102

One of the most interesting discoveries of this series of tastings was a line of wines presented by Vecchia Cantina. Their technical staff, headed by the oenologist Valerio Coltellini, made good use of their considerable experience and chose the 40 best of the approximately 980 available hectares, to show what this winery can do. Redi represents the bridge Vecchia Cantina has erected between local tradition and oenological innovation, and for aging it uses a cellar of great architectural interest in the center of Montepulciano. Among the wines presented this year, we were particularly struck by the Vin Santo '90, fruit of a special selection kept for longer than usual in the traditional small casks. What has come out is the best Vin Santo ever presented by this winery and one of the best on the market today. Deep amber in color, it displays notes of green walnut, raisin, candied peel, dried fruit and chocolate; there is excellent balance on the palate, where the unexpected acidity provides an effective counterweight to the sugars, making it particularly pleasurable to drink; the broad and lingering finish reflects the bouquet. The good Vino Nobile di Montepulciano '95 Briareo has joined the Two Glass club its first time out. It has a very powerful bouquet with distinct notes of sour and black cherries; its flavor, although meaty, is discontinuous, a defect it could overcome with more time in the bottle, since its tannins are excellent. The Vino Nobile di Montepulciano '95 and the Rosso di Montepulciano '97 get One Glass apiece because they are agreeably quaffable and characterfully fragrant.

○	Vin Santo '90	YY	6
●	Vino Nobile di Montepulciano Briareo '95	YY	5
●	Rosso di Montepulciano '97	Y	3
●	Vino Nobile di Montepulciano '95	Y	4

MONTEPULCIANO (SI)

MASSIMO ROMEO
LOC. NOTTOLA DI GRACCIANO
VIA DI TOTONA, 29
53045 MONTEPULCIANO (SI)
TEL. 0578/716997

Massimo Romeo's little estate consists of two parts, Tortona, high on a hill 580 meters above sea level and covered with olive groves, and Corsica, some 450 meters high, where the vineyards are. The small cellar for aging is quite charming and the casks are in perfect condition. Recently some "tonneaux" were acquired for aging the Nobile di Montepulciano, more of which will be produced in the next few years. The top of the line, the Lipitresco '95, was not bottled in time for our tastings, so we shall speak of it next year. This year three wines were presented. The Vino Nobile di Montepulciano '95 is the best version Romeo has ever made. The fruit of classic wine-making, it is ruby-hued with garnet highlights and displays an intense and complex nose with aromas of tobacco, black cherry, and a suggestion of yellow-fleshed fruit. The palate is elegant and substantial and the very long finish mirrors what has gone before. The Vino Nobile di Montepulciano Riserva dei Mandorli '94 is also well constructed, although the vintage was not very exciting; fruity and floral notes dominate the bouquet, and the wine is soft in the mouth, but a more substantial finish would have been more to our liking. The Rosso di Montepulciano '97 performed better, confirming (should anyone require confirmation) that vintages count. It is fruity, simple and intense on the nose, with notes of sour cherry, and it's very drinkable and fairly long in its finish.

	Wine	Glasses	
●	Vino Nobile di Montepulciano '95	🍷🍷	5
●	Rosso di Montepulciano '97	🍷	3
●	Vino Nobile di Montepulciano Ris. dei Mandorli '94	🍷	5
●	Lipitiresco '90	🍷🍷	4
○	Vin Santo '83	🍷🍷	6
○	Vin Santo '86	🍷🍷	5
●	Vino Nobile di Montepulciano '91	🍷🍷	5
●	Vino Nobile di Montepulciano Ris. '88	🍷🍷	5
●	Lipitiresco '93	🍷	4
●	Lipitiresco '94	🍷	5
○	Vin Santo '89	🍷	5
●	Vino Nobile di Montepulciano '93	🍷	5
●	Vino Nobile di Montepulciano '94	🍷	5

MONTEPULCIANO (SI)

SALCHETO
VIA DI VILLA BIANCA, 15
53045 MONTEPULCIANO (SI)
TEL. 0578/799031

This year once again the winery owned by the Piccins, husband and wife, has earned itself a profile in the Guide with its fine range of wines. Already clearly reliable, Salcheto is, in our opinion, capable of achieving the highest quality in the near future. During our annual visit we noted with pleasure the attention to quality discernible in the barrel-room; the presence of "tonneaux" in addition to traditional casks shows a sensitivity to the market and an interest in experimentation. The property covers 26 hectares, of which about five are under vine; the most recent plantings are of clones they have themselves selected and are at a density of roughly 4 thousand vines per hectare. Of the wines they presented this time we particularly liked the Vino Nobile di Montepulciano Riserva '93, which was released later than is customary locally; it was worth waiting for, as they've come up with a Two Glass wine. It has an ample bouquet, in which the fruit is enhanced by floral fragrances, including a distinct note of violets; it is a pleasure to drink, with a slight astringency that should decrease with more bottle age. Both the Rosso di Montepulciano '96 and the Nobile di Montepulciano '95 amply exceed the requirements for One Glass. The former is an exemplary Rosso: a young wine with lots of fruit well supported by alcohol, well-balanced and agreeable. The Vino Nobile di Montepulciano '95 has a broad array of aromas with red fruit tones, a light oak-derived spice and a faint hint of almond, but its structure on the palate is a little weak, which cuts into the finish.

	Wine	Glasses	
●	Vino Nobile di Montepulciano Ris. '93	🍷🍷	5
●	Rosso di Montepulciano '96	🍷	3
●	Vino Nobile di Montepulciano '95	🍷	4
●	Salcheto '90	🍷🍷	4
●	Vino Nobile di Montepulciano '91	🍷🍷	4
●	Rosso di Montepulciano '92	🍷	3
●	Vino Nobile di Montepulciano '94	🍷	4

MONTEPULCIANO (SI)

TERRE DI BINDELLA
LOC. ACQUAVIVA
VIA DELLE TRE BERTE, 10/A
53040 MONTEPULCIANO (SI)
TEL. 0578/767777

A winegrower's work is never done, as the director of this estate, Matteo Mazzamurro, knows full well. He has started replanting the oldest vineyards, introducing the innovations already tested with success on new plots: high density planting, about 7 thousand vines per hectare, and clones chosen from the winery's best will maintain the excellent reputation this estate has earned in recent years. Renovation proceeds apace in the cellar as well: year by year the smaller barrels multiply; they have virtually squeezed out the traditional ones by now. On the production front they have decided to stop making a Riserva version of the Vino Nobile di Montepulciano. This involves a big financial sacrifice, for the sake of further improving the quality of the non-Riserva, of which more bottles will also be produced. The ultimate aim is to satisfy increasing customer demand. Thus two wines were presented for tasting: the Nobile di Montepulciano and the Vallocaia, both '95s. Sometime soon a sweet wine should also be appearing. The Nobile is of a deep ruby color with cardinal-red highlights; it vaunts good structure and excellent tannins that do not interfere with the elegance and agreeableness of the palate. The nose is slightly less successful because of a lactic note. The Vallocaia is a step up; this is the second year it has been presented unfiltered, and it is now clear for all to see that this was the right choice. It has a rich palate with admirable tannins that do not compromise the long finish. The enchanting prune and sour cherry fragrances are well blended with the oak-derived vanilla.

	Wine	Rating	Price
●	Vallocaia '95	🍷🍷	5
●	Vino Nobile di Montepulciano '95	🍷	4
●	Vallocaia '90	♀♀	5
●	Vallocaia '94	♀♀	5
●	Vino Nobile di Montepulciano '90	♀♀	4
●	Vino Nobile di Montepulciano '91	♀♀	4
●	Vino Nobile di Montepulciano '92	♀♀	4
●	Vino Nobile di Montepulciano '94	♀♀	4
●	Vino Nobile di Montepulciano Ris. '90	♀♀	5

MONTEPULCIANO (SI)

TENUTA TREROSE
FRAZ. VALIANO
VILLA BELVEDERE
53040 MONTEPULCIANO (SI)
TEL. 0578/724018

The Trerose estate near Valiano is part of the Tenimenti Angelini, which belongs to the Angelini pharmaceutical company. Over the last several years, their wines have improved to such an extent that the Nobile di Montepulciano La Villa '94 came within a hair of getting Three Glasses last year. The technical staff headed by Mario Calzolari has come even closer with the '95 version of the same wine. The deep ruby hue with "pigeon's blood" highlights heralds an important wine; the attack on the palate is soft and the progression excellent thanks to the balance between soft components and acidity and tannins. The finish is rich and long, reflecting the sensations of the bouquet with distinct notes of sour cherry enhanced by oak-derived balsamic and chocolate accents. The interesting Vin Santo '90 is rich in delicate white-fleshed fruit fragrances, with a pleasing sweetness and length on the palate, although it perhaps wants acidity. Each of the other wines earned One Glass, an indication of the eminent reliability of this winery. Of the whites, we thought the best was the Busillis, a pure barrique-fermented viognier. The bouquet displays a distinct fragrance of apricot enriched by the balsamic aroma of camphor; its rich palate is well balanced by acidity: an extremely promising wine that might benefit from less assertive wood. The Nobile di Montepulciano '95 has a delightful bouquet with elegant tobacco and almond aromas; it is well-balanced and pleasing in the mouth with appropriate tannins and acidity. The Flauto, a monovarietal sauvignon, is very agreeable but rather simple.

	Wine	Rating	Price
○	Vin Santo '90	🍷🍷	5
●	Vino Nobile di Montepulciano La Villa '95	🍷🍷	5
○	Busillis '96	🍷	4
○	Flauto	🍷	4
●	Vino Nobile di Montepulciano '95	🍷	4
●	Vino Nobile di Montepulciano '91	♀♀	4
●	Vino Nobile di Montepulciano '93	♀♀	4
●	Vino Nobile di Montepulciano La Villa '90	♀♀	5
●	Vino Nobile di Montepulciano La Villa '94	♀♀	4
●	Vino Nobile di Montepulciano Ris. '93	♀♀	4*
●	Vino Nobile di Montepulciano Simposio '93	♀♀	5

Tenuta Valdipiatta

Via della Ciarliana, 25/A
53045 Montepulciano (SI)
tel. 0578/757930

The Valdipiatta winery is a fixture of the Montepulciano wine scene. Ten additional hectares, some of which are rented and all of which are in excellent locations such as Poggio della Sala, have been added to the original thirteen dedicated to Vino Nobile. In the beautiful cellar carved out of the hill, the barriques and "tonneaux" are increasing in number, a clear sign that recent experiments with these casks have satisfied the technical staff and the owner. The Rosso di Montepulciano '96 easily wins One Glass thanks to its excellent body with soft and well-integrated tannins; the bouquet is less successful because of a green aroma that interferes with the fruit. The Nobile di Montepulciano Riserva '94 also earns One Glass, not bad going for a '94. The Tre Fonti '95, a barrique-aged blend of prugnolo, cabernet sauvignon and canaiolo, gets Two Glasses. Its cabernet-dominated nose is nonetheless intense and persistent; the attack on the palate is good, but untamed tannins limit the finish. The star this year, however, is the Nobile di Montepulciano '95, which approaches the triumph of the '90. It has a broad bouquet with balsamic and coffee fragrances that do not compromise the underlying fruit, with sour and sweet cherries to the fore. The rich palate displays succulence and good concentration, which stand up to the noble tannins. The finish is rather long and distinguished by a slightly bitter note.

	Wine	Rating	Price
●	Vino Nobile di Montepulciano '95	🍷🍷	4
●	Rosso di Montepulciano '96	🍷	3
●	Tre Fonti '95	🍷	5
●	Vino Nobile di Montepulciano Ris. '94	🍷	5
●	Vino Nobile di Montepulciano Ris. '90	🍷🍷🍷	5
●	Vino Nobile di Montepulciano '90	🍷🍷	4
●	Vino Nobile di Montepulciano '91	🍷🍷	4
●	Vino Nobile di Montepulciano '93	🍷🍷	4
●	Vino Nobile di Montepulciano '94	🍷🍷	4
●	Vino Nobile di Montepulciano Ris. '91	🍷🍷	4
●	Vino Nobile di Montepulciano Ris. '93	🍷🍷	5

MONTEPULCIANO (SI)

Villa S. Anna

Loc. Abbadia
53040 Montepulciano (SI)
tel. 0578/708017

Villa S. Anna is a winery with a feminine slant: the women of the Fabroni family are entirely set on improving their already good wines. They continue to make investments, particularly in the cellar, where new barrels and barriques constantly appear. Although it owns eight hectares under vine, Villa S. Anna is unable to satisfy the orders pouring in from all over the world. Now a solution to the problem is in sight: they have leased extra vineyards and hope to increase production. You would look in vain for Vallone, the flagship of the estate, amongst the wines released this year. Simonetta Fabroni, who is in charge of production, decided that the '94 was not up to standard. The '95 will be released in the course of the year and you can read all about it in our next edition. The Nobile di Montepulciano '95 has a good aromatic structure, clean and persistent, with distinct aromas of black cherry and cherries preserved in spirits. In the mouth it has some elegance, very smooth tannins and a good finish. It just misses Two Glasses. The Chianti Colli Senesi is in the same award category, but at a discreet distance. The '96 version is very agreeable, but a little too simple to aim higher.

	Wine	Rating	Price
●	Chianti Colli Senesi '96	🍷	3
●	Vino Nobile di Montepulciano '95	🍷	4
●	Chianti '94	🍷🍷	2
●	Chianti Colli Senesi '95	🍷🍷	2
●	Vino Nobile di Montepulciano '94	🍷🍷	4
●	Vino Nobile di Montepulciano '93	🍷🍷	4
●	Vigna Il Vallone '93	🍷	5
○	Vin Santo '90	🍷	5

Casale

Via di Nottola, 9
53045 Montepulciano
Stazione (SI)
tel. 0578/757737

A number of new wineries are establishing themselves in the vinous firmament of Montepulciano, managed by people who have only recently started to bottle but have been producing wine for ages. This is the case with Aldimaro Daviddi, who was praised in last year's Guide for the quality of his wines. The cellar has been completely renovated and the barrel-room restocked with 25-hectoliter French oak casks. The vineyards are in Gracciano and Valiano, renowned for structured and long-lived wines. About 30 thousand bottles are produced from about 13 hectares (some of which are rented). This year, Casale has earned a profile with its Nobile di Montepulciano '95. Of a classic ruby hue with garnet veining, the wine shows good concentration. Notes of spice, especially pepper, enhance the bouquet, which is dominated by the usual red berries, sour cherry and tobacco. It has a quite delightful palate that corresponds to the nose, and noble tannins which are well blended into the densely knit structure of the wine. Two Glasses hands down.

Wine	Glasses	Price
● Vino Nobile di Montepulciano '95	🍷🍷	5

MONTEPULCIANO STAZIONE (SI)

Poliziano

Via Fontago, 11
53040 Montepulciano
Stazione (SI)
tel. 0578/738171

Each year it is harder to find new adjectives to describe Federico Carletti's estate, which never makes a wrong move and is unanimously recognized as the benchmark for the area. Some very important decisions were made this year on the oenological and marketing fronts: they have chosen to reduce the range of wines, giving up some of their celebrated labels. Elegia is disappearing, its swan song having been the splendid '95, and the cru Vino Nobile di Montepulciano Caggiole is no more. Hence only four wines make up the entire range: the basic Vino Nobile, the cru Vino Nobile di Montepulciano Vigna dell'Asinone, produced only in the best years, the Rosso di Montepulciano and Le Stanze, which is changing identity, becoming a blend of cabernet sauvignon and merlot. The profusion of Glasses heaped on the winery yet again would seem to indicate that they chose well. The Vigna dell'Asinone '95 is excellent. Its color is an intense, almost impenetrable ruby; the bouquet is extremely complex with fruity fragrances enriched by spicy notes of cinnamon and cocoa; the entry on the palate is imposing, and in the dense and persistent structure the excellent tannins and acidity are perfectly integrated with the extract. Le Stanze '96 also struck us as very interesting. Dark violet in color, it offers an intense bouquet with notes of pencil lead and citron supported by fruit; the palate is rich and very elegant. The Vino Nobile di Montepulciano '95 is also well above a "mere" Two Glasses, elegant and eminently drinkable. The Rosso di Montepulciano '97 easily wins One Glass for its fresh fragrances and lingering flavor.

Wine	Glasses	Price
● Vino Nobile di Montepulciano Vigna dell'Asinone '95	🍷🍷🍷	5
● Le Stanze '96	🍷🍷	6
● Vino Nobile di Montepulciano '95	🍷🍷	4
● Rosso di Montepulciano '97	🍷	3
● Elegia '95	🍷🍷🍷 (previous years)	5
● Le Stanze '93	🍷🍷🍷 (previous years)	5
● Le Stanze '95	🍷🍷🍷 (previous years)	5
● Vino Nobile di Montepulciano '90	🍷🍷🍷 (previous years)	4*
● Vino Nobile di Montepulciano Vigna dell'Asinone '93	🍷🍷🍷 (previous years)	5
● Vino Nobile di Montepulciano Vigna dell'Asinone Ris. '90	🍷🍷🍷 (previous years)	5
● Vino Nobile di Montepulciano Vigna dell'Asinone Ris. '88	🍷🍷🍷 (previous years)	5

MONTESCUDAIO (PI)

Poggio Gagliardo

Loc. Poggio Gagliardo
56040 Montescudaio (PI)
tel. 0586/630775

Tastings this year of wines made by Poggio Gagliardo have confirmed the consistent quality offered by this winery. Nevertheless, in what could be interpreted as a stalled situation, the groundwork is being laid (specifically, new plantings in the vineyards) for improvement, as this large and traditionally important winery deserves. Our tastings indicated considerable progress in the white wines, particularly in the Montescudaio Bianco Vigna Lontana '97, which leapt to Two Glasses in a single bound. It is unmistakably a modern wine, fermented and aged in oak. The style may not be terribly original, but the wine certainly is well made and very delicious, with intense aromas of sweet vanilla, spice, and ripe fruit. It is soft, mild and very well-balanced on the palate. The Montescudaio Rosso Rovo '96 is also good, with distinct evidence in the bouquet of the time spent in oak, and light fruity and vegetal accents. Its flavor is well-balanced and fairly continuous, but lacks decided character. Among the other wines, we admired the clean crispness of the Montescudaio Bianco Linaglia '97, with its distinct notes of tropical fruit, pear and linden blossom on the nose, and a palate not without structure. The rest of the range (Montescudaio Bianco '97, Montescudaio Rosso Malemacchie '96, and Montescudaio Rosso '97) is perfectly correct; we should point out that the Montescudaio Rosso '97 is good value for money.

	Wine	Glasses	Price
○	Montescudaio Bianco V. Lontana '97	🍷🍷	4
○	Montescudaio Bianco Linaglia '97	🍷	3
●	Montescudaio Rosso Rovo '96	🍷	4
○	Montescudaio Bianco '97		2
●	Montescudaio Rosso '97		2
●	Montescudaio Rosso Malemacchie '96		3
●	Montescudaio Rosso Malemacchie '92	ΥΥ	3*
●	Montescudaio Rosso Rovo '93	ΥΥ	4
●	Montescudaio Rosso Rovo '94	ΥΥ	4
○	Montescudaio Bianco Linaglia '96	Υ	2*
○	Montescudaio Bianco V. Lontana '96	Υ	3
●	Montescudaio Rosso Rovo '95	Υ	4

MONTESPERTOLI (FI)

Castello di Poppiano

Via di Pezzana, 43
50025 Montespertoli (FI)
tel. 055/82315

For how long has there been a Castello di Poppiano? Since the Middle Ages, of course. Owned by the venerable Tuscan Guicciardini family since the middle of the 12th century, the estate, which lies on the hills between Florence and Siena, covers a good 270 hectares, including 120 under vine. Its range includes about a dozen different labels, from traditional local wines, Chianti dei Colli Fiorentini and Vin Santo in particular, to more innovative bottles. Indeed some blends might even be considered daring, such as, for example, Tricorno, the winery darling, made from sangiovese, nebbiolo, cabernet sauvignon, barbera, merlot and...have we got them all? The result of this exuberant varietal mix is worthy of note. Of a deep ruby hue, it offers a delightfully complete array of aromas, from the usual red berries to a perceptible but not overpowering note of toasty oak. The Tosco Forte '96, sangiovese with 10% of syrah, is good but less convincing. The bouquet is somewhat vegetal, the structure moderate; the dash of pepper on the finish is very welcome. A third red table wine, the Syrah '96 (which includes 10% of sangiovese), displays very sweet notes of wood in a clean and intense bouquet. Its flavor is fruity, full-bodied and focused, with a slightly green finish. Among the typical Chiantis we particularly liked the Chianti Colli Fiorentini Riserva '93, which is mature, alcoholic, noble, flavorful, and persistent: a classic, in fact. Finally, the non-Riserva Chianti Il Cortile is an agreeable wine.

	Wine	Glasses	Price
●	Chianti Colli Fiorentini Ris. '93	🍷🍷	3
●	Tricorno '93	🍷🍷	4
●	Chianti Colli Fiorentini Il Cortile '95	🍷	2
●	Syrah '96	🍷	3
●	Tosco Forte '96	🍷	3

MONTOPOLI VALDARNO (PI)

VARRAMISTA

LOC. VARRAMISTA
VIA RICAVO, 31
56020 MONTOPOLI VALDARNO (PI)
TEL. 0571/468121

A number of grape varieties that are not exactly traditionally Italian seem to settle in very well once they get here. A noteworthy example of such adaptability is the syrah, which is being made into some extraordinary wines in Tuscany. The Varramista estate, only a few hectares under vine looked after with painstaking care and competence, produces a version of it that has become a classic of its kind in very few years. But then, their declared ambition of competing with the best Syrahs, and not only from Australia but also from France, seemed in itself to indicate a high seriousness of purpose. The '96 vintage of this red Tuscan does not disappoint: of a very deep and vivid red color, it opens on the nose with intensely fruity aromas of mature blackberry and raspberry and then broadens to include subtle spicy accents of white pepper and vanilla. The palate is supported by substantial extract, softened by an uncommon elegance. Fruity, mature and clean, it is perhaps most praiseworthy for the finesse of its tannins. The very long finish only confirms the excellence of this wine. Congratulations to Federico Staderini, the oenologist responsible for the Varramista, and to his staff.

●	Varramista '96	🍷🍷 (filled)	5
●	Varramista '95	🍷🍷 (outline)	5

PALAIA (PI)

SAN GERVASIO

LOC. SAN GERVASIO
56036 PALAIA (PI)
TEL. 0587/483360

We are very pleased, if not at all surprised, to find Luca Tommasini's estate fully justifying our excellent impression a year after its debut in the Guide. And the new vineyards, planted according to the most rigorous criteria, seem to offer even brighter prospects for the future. The best wine on the San Gervasio list is the almost monovarietal sangiovese A Sirio '96, which has improved over last year's version. Aromatically well-defined, with notes of blackberry, pepper and a hint of spice, it is sweet and soft at its entry on the palate, where concentration is medium, but it gathers force for a fine progression on the finish. The Marna '97 is a very pleasant surprise: this wood-fermented blend of two parts vermentino and one of chardonnay has won Two Glasses. Its intense aromas of apricot and tropical fruit are followed by a sweet, full-bodied and lingering palate. It's not easy to find a better rosé than San Gervasio's Ostro: the distinct, intense aromas of raspberry and strawberry blend well with the roundness and crispness it offers in the mouth. The quite good Chianti Le Stoppie '97 is irreproachably clean and easy to drink, but not without depth. To wind up, the San Torpè is no more than correct, but what can you do with trebbiano?

●	A Sirio '96	🍷🍷 (filled)	4
○	Marna '97	🍷🍷 (filled)	4
●	Chianti Le Stoppie '97	🍷 (filled)	3
⊙	Ostro '97	🍷 (filled)	3
○	S. Torpè Casina de' Venti '97		2
●	A Sirio '95	🍷🍷 (outline)	4
●	Chianti Le Stoppie '96	🍷 (outline)	3
○	Marna '96	🍷 (outline)	4
⊙	Ostro '96	🍷 (outline)	3

PANZANO IN CHIANTI (FI)

Carobbio
Via S. Martino a Cecione, 26
50020 Panzano in Chianti (FI)
tel. 055/852136

Carobbio's wines embody the distinguishing characteristics of the Panzano zone while maintaining a style all their own, which adds to their attractiveness. Those who have witnessed any part of the great wood dispute in recent years may be interested to learn that all of these wines, with the sole (and only partial) exception of the non-Riserva Chianti Classico, are aged in barriques. This could be taken as evidence that with the proper care given to the raw material, i.e. the vines, small barrels help to give Chianti Classico a more modern style, by which we mean greater softness on the palate, without altering its basic character. The Riserva Chianti Classico '95, which did very well indeed at our tastings, is a perfect example: the nose is intense, although still partly dumb, with a fine fruity base; the palate is characterful and substantial, with the acidity typical of Panzano and slightly dry tannins. All this wine wants, to be really great, is a denser palate and a broader finish. The really noteworthy cabernet Pietraforte del Carobbio '95 also seems more an expression of its terroir than of its varietal: it is not remarkable for its power, but it is elegant, harmonious, even and long-lasting in the mouth, which corresponds to its bouquet with fruity and vegetal accents. The Chianti Classico '96 very nearly got Two Glasses, so is obviously very good: just at first the nose seems less than limpid, but when the wine has had a chance to breathe there are fragrances of fruit and jam. The palate is sound and acceptably concentrated.

Wine	Glasses	
● Chianti Classico Ris. '95	**YY**	5
● Pietraforte del Carobbio '95	**YY**	5
● Chianti Classico '96	**Y**	4
● Chianti Classico '88	YY	4
● Chianti Classico '90	YY	4
● Chianti Classico '93	YY	4
● Chianti Classico '94	YY	4
● Chianti Classico '95	YY	4
● Chianti Classico Ris. '88	YY	5
● Chianti Classico Ris. '90	YY	5
● Chianti Classico Ris. '93	YY	5
● Leone del Carobbio '93	YY	5
● Leone del Carobbio '94	YY	5
● Pietraforte del Carobbio '93	YY	5
● Pietraforte del Carobbio '94	Y	5

PANZANO IN CHIANTI (FI)

Fattoria Casaloste
Via Montagliari, 32
50020 Panzano in Chianti (FI)
tel. 055/852725

Giovan Battista and Emilia d'Orsi's estate is small but favorably situated. They used to sell their grapes to other winemakers, but now Giovan Battista personally oversees work in the vineyard and then in the cellar, assisted by the oenologist Gabriella Tani. And now they have acquired a further four hectares that should start producing in 2001. Three wines were presented this year, the Chianti Classico '96, the Riserva '95, and the Riserva Don Vincenzo '95. The first easily earned One Glass: of a fine deep ruby hue, the wine presents fruity aromas that move on to light spice before a pleasing final balsamic note. The decisive and intense entry on the palate is followed by medium body, good balance of flavor and a somewhat truncated finish. The Riserva, which we had been eagerly awaiting, does not disappoint. An intense, deep ruby hue is followed by a very expressive bouquet, with notes of vanilla and toasty oak perfectly blended with the fruit, cherry and plum in particular. Its complexity is immediately apparent in the mouth: the tannins, rich but not aggressive, are well balanced by the other components. The finish resonates with fruity aftertastes. Easily winning Two Glasses, it also bodes well for the future. The Riserva Don Vincenzo '95 is very good too, with a lovely concentrated ruby hue and intense aromas marked by minty wood and buttery notes. Its attack on the palate is full, broad and soft, with a finish still dominated by wood.

Wine	Glasses	
● Chianti Classico Don Vincenzo Ris. '95	**YY**	5
● Chianti Classico Ris. '95	**YY**	4
● Chianti Classico '96	**Y**	3
● Chianti Classico '95	YY	3
● Chianti Classico Ris. '94	YY	4
● Chianti Classico '93	Y	3
● Chianti Classico '94	Y	3

CENNATOIO

VIA DI SAN LEOLINO, 35
50020 PANZANO IN CHIANTI (FI)
TEL. 055/852134

The team made up of the owner Leandro Alessi and the highly competent oenologist Gabriella Tani is moving full steam ahead. Once again this year, the reds we tasted did very well. We are convinced that the constant high quality of Cennatoio wines is becoming a fact of life. The Rosso Fiorentino '95, mostly cabernet, put in a very good performance this year. Attractive deep ruby in color, it presents fruity, well-developed aromas with light hints of grass that quickly give way to pleasant balsamic notes. It is well-balanced on the palate, with tannins still in full attendance but counterpoised by softer elements, and a lingering, satisfying finish. Although it easily earns Two Glasses, the Sangiovese Etrusco '95 was unable to repeat its performance of last year. It has a rich ruby color and a nose dominated by a note of wood, with distinct aromas of nougat and vanilla. The attack on the palate is soft, followed by an appropriately continuous development and, yet again, lots of oak on the long finish. The excellent Chianti Classico Riserva '95 Oleandro has a rich, fruity and extremely agreeable bouquet. After a decisive entry on the palate, it reveals a certain elegance and good balance. The admirable Chianti Classico '96 is expressive on the nose, with a fruity fragrance of cherry and red currant, and on the palate, which is succulent and substantial, if a little short in the finish.

	Wine	Glasses	Price
●	Chianti Classico Ris. '95	TT	4
●	Etrusco '95	TT	5
●	Rosso Fiorentino '95	TT	5
●	Chianti Classico '96	T	3
●	Etrusco '94	YYY	5
●	Chianti Classico '93	YY	3*
●	Chianti Classico Ris. '91	YY	4
●	Chianti Classico Ris. '93	YY	4
●	Chianti Classico Ris. '94	YY	4
●	Etrusco '90	YY	5
●	Etrusco '93	YY	5
●	Mammolo '93	YY	6
●	Rosso Fiorentino '93	YY	5
●	Rosso Fiorentino '94	Y	5

PANZANO IN CHIANTI (FI)

★ TENUTA FONTODI

VIA SAN LEOLINO, 87
50020 PANZANO IN CHIANTI (FI)
TEL. 055/852005

The inauguration of a new, up-to-the-minute cellar carved out of the living rock is the most important news concerning Tenuta Fontodi and its young and dynamic owner, Giovanni Manetti, who may well be the best winegrowing executive of the new generation. The new cellar is just the latest of the investments that have propelled Fontodi, a standard-bearer for Panzano, to its current prominence in the region. This year one of Giovanni Manetti's wines struck us more than all the others: the Syrah Case Via '95, which beats every other Italian wine in its category. We are well aware that it is hardly typical of the zone, but it is a fine expression of the varietal characteristics of this singular and noble "cépage". It has intense, spicy aromas, with the classic note of pepper emerging on a background of red berries and Peruvian bark. On the palate it is full-bodied, soft and concentrated, with a dense but not drying polyphenolic component. His most celebrated wines, Flaccianello and Chianti Classico Vigna del Sorbo Riserva, both '95s, did not do quite as well, perhaps because this vintage was not in fact universally propitious, Panzano being one of these exceptions. In both of them we noted an excessive acidic and tannic roughness that will have some trouble, in our opinion, smoothing out completely over time. The admirable Chianti Classico '96 is an excellent representative of its vintage. It is fruity and a little forward on the nose, and has a pleasing acidity on the palate and just enough structure for what it is.

	Wine	Glasses	Price
●	Syrah Case Via '95	TTT	5
●	Chianti Classico '96	TT	4
●	Chianti Classico Vigna del Sorbo Ris. '95	TT	5
●	Flaccianello della Pieve '95	TT	5
●	Chianti Classico Vigna del Sorbo Ris. '86	YYY	5
●	Chianti Classico Vigna del Sorbo Ris. '90	YYY	5
●	Chianti Classico Vigna del Sorbo Ris. '94	YYY	5
●	Flaccianello della Pieve '88	YYY	6
●	Flaccianello della Pieve '90	YYY	6
●	Flaccianello della Pieve '91	YYY	5
●	Chianti Classico Ris. '94	YY	4

PANZANO IN CHIANTI (FI)

LA DOCCIA

LOC. CASOLE
50022 PANZANO IN CHIANTI (FI)
TEL. 055/8549049

We simply could not bring ourselves to consign this tiny Panzano estate to the Honorable Mention page. We feel as though we've adopted it, having discovered it several years ago when no one even imagined its existence, so we are allowing ourselves to stretch the rules a bit and keep it in these pages, even though something wasn't quite right this year. The Chianti Classico Riserva '95, their only wine, showed its habitual perfectly respectable structure. It was mouth-filling, with tannins that were neither aggressive nor mouth-puckering, and its balance was unimpeachable. The problem was the bouquet, which wasn't able to "come out" properly: some animal odors, a bit of leather, sulphur. But when you'd had it in your glass for a moment or two, these aromas vanished, making way for fruitier and more characteristic fragrances. Still, the initial impression was not positive, so instead of sailing up to its customary Two Glasses, the wine stopped short at One, too little for an inidividual winery profile. However, the great thing about rules, especially those you make yourself, is that they can occasionally be broken. Hence we are in a position to remind you that there is a tiny estate in Panzano called La Doccia, with little more than one hectare under vine, run by Isabella Cinuzzi and Renzo Pancani, and turning out fewer than 10 thousand bottles of excellent Chianti Classico each year. And we can forgive two such craftsmanlike wine-makers the occasional lapse.

Wine	Glasses	
● Chianti Classico Ris. '95	🍷	4
● Chianti Classico '90	🍷🍷	4
● Chianti Classico '91	🍷🍷	4
● Chianti Classico '92	🍷🍷	4
● Chianti Classico '93	🍷🍷	4
● Chianti Classico '94	🍷🍷	4

PANZANO IN CHIANTI (FI)

LA MASSA

VIA CASE SPARSE, 9
50020 PANZANO IN CHIANTI (FI)
TEL. 055/852701

"Crazy!" exclaims Giampaolo Motta, owner and winegrower, in pure Neapolitan dialect (he was born in Naples, so it comes naturally), commenting on the fact that, at La Massa, winning Three Glasses is stale news. For the fourth consecutive year, the Chianti Classico Giorgio Primo, the '96 this time, has come out a winner. Whatever you may think of the divergent qualities of these various vintages, this magnificent red manages to express a definite personality that gets stronger by the year, so that a number of us can hardly wait to see what the '97 will be like. A mental comparison of these vintages suggests that the latest is distinguished by a more harmonious blending of wine and wood. We would guess that this can be traced not only to increasing skill in vinification but also to ever richer and more balanced grapes. There are no surprises in our tasting notes, since the Giorgio Primo simply has the characteristics of a great wine, with an intriguingly complex palate: full-bodied, sensual, soft but substantial, it forms a harmonious whole. Even the "normal" Chianti Classico '96, fresh, succulent, rich but easy to drink, is excellent and delightful and is one of the "top ten" of its category for this vintage.

Wine	Glasses	
● Chianti Classico Giorgio Primo '96	🍷🍷🍷 (black)	5
● Chianti Classico '96	🍷🍷 (black)	4
● Chianti Classico Giorgio Primo '93	🍷🍷🍷	4
● Chianti Classico Giorgio Primo '94	🍷🍷🍷	5
● Chianti Classico Giorgio Primo '95	🍷🍷🍷	5
● Chianti Classico Giorgio Primo '92	🍷🍷	5
● Chianti Classico '90	🍷🍷	4*
● Chianti Classico '92	🍷🍷	4*
● Chianti Classico '93	🍷🍷	4
● Chianti Classico '94	🍷🍷	4
● Chianti Classico '95	🍷🍷	4*
● Chianti Classico Ris. '90	🍷🍷	5

LE BOCCE

VIA CASE SPARSE, 76
50020 PANZANO IN CHIANTI (FI)
TEL. 055/852153

The Fattoria Le Bocce is one of the most noted and representative wineries in the subzone of Panzano in Chianti. Up to a few years ago, it regularly appeared in the Guide, and the Chianti Classico vintages it presented were always easy to drink and freshly fragrant, if a bit simple. These were not the impressions we had this time: the wines seemed decidedly more complex, and in some cases more interesting as well. We particularly liked the Vigna del Paladino '95, a monovarietal sangiovese. Intensely fruity aromas with rather ripe notes of sour cherry, raspberry and red currant are followed by a concentrated palate with stylish dense tannins and a particularly elegant body that makes it pleasurably drinkable without excessive complexity. Aromas of new wood somewhat muffle the Chianti Classico '96, which offers somewhat forward tones of vanilla and fruit. The concentration is middling and there is a slightly bitter aftertaste. The more successful Chianti Classico Riserva '94 is the fruit of a harvest that produced better results in Panzano than in most of the rest of Chianti. The nose is a bit forward, but it is soft in the mouth, with a long and pleasing finish.

	Wine	Glasses	Price
●	Vigna del Paladino '95	🍷🍷	5
●	Chianti Classico '96	🍷	3
●	Chianti Classico Ris. '94	🍷	4

PANZANO IN CHIANTI (FI)

PODERE LE CINCIOLE

VIA CASE SPARSE, 83
50020 PANZANO IN CHIANTI (FI)
TEL. 055/852636

Not quite up to last year. This was our impression upon tasting the wines Le Cinciole presented this season. Much of this depends on the fact that the Chianti Classico '96 seemed a little weak compared to recent vintages. This time it is a simple, light red with a somewhat acidulous nature that is not effectively counterbalanced by softer components. Quite frankly, we were expecting more, which is also true, although not so worryingly, of the Chianti Classico Valle del Pozzo Riserva '95, the top of the line. We preferred the non-Riserva version of the same vintage that we reviewed in last year's Guide, which is something of a paradox. And yet we found the Riserva's aromas less distinct, with a quest for complexity that ended up in forwardness. The notes of ripe fruit were evident, as were balsamic tones and licorice. The palate was more successful, with its concentration and body, but the slight overripeness we had found on the nose was back again on the finish. It got Two Glasses by a hair, partly because of the respect and esteem that Luca Orsini and Valeria Viganò, the owners of the estate, have earned over the past years.

	Wine	Glasses	Price
●	Chianti Classico Valle del Pozzo Ris. '95	🍷🍷	4
●	Chianti Classico '96		3
●	Chianti Classico '93	🍷🍷 (previous)	3
●	Chianti Classico '94	🍷🍷 (previous)	3*
●	Chianti Classico '95	🍷🍷 (previous)	3*
●	Chianti Classico Valle del Pozzo Ris. '94	🍷 (previous)	4

PANZANO IN CHIANTI (FI)

Le Fonti
Via Le Fonti
50020 Panzano in Chianti (FI)
tel. 055/852194

After just one year's absence the Fattoria Le Fonti is back in the Guide. It has only four hectares under vine, but they are located in one of the most propitious areas of Chianti, the splendid subzone of Panzano. The vineyards are planted 400 to 500 meters above sea level in mostly marly soil. The overall output of this estate is limited, and the density of plantings (5,500 vines per hectare) suggests that the yield per vine is very low. So we have all the prerequisites for great wines and, quite apart from these calculations, we found confirmation at our tastings. We'll start with the Chianti Classico '96, which offers distinct but quite simple fruity aromas. An excellent softness, substance and a clean and pleasing finish contribute to the success of the palate. As you get to know the wines of Conrad Schmitt, the owner of the estate, you increasingly appreciate the extraordinary skill applied to vinification, which is evinced also by the Riserva '95, with its rich color, its still somewhat reticent bouquet with noticeable oak, and a very soft attack on a palate that develops well and finishes convincingly and at length. The head of the class is, without a doubt, the Fontissimo '95, a blend of sangiovese and cabernet that has distinct vegetal notes elegantly expressed, having been well blended with fruit and vanilla. The palate adheres to estate style, more elegant than powerful, with a lean, even body and considerable depth.

Wine	Glasses	
● Chianti Classico Ris. '95	▼▼	4
● Fontissimo '95	▼▼	5
● Chianti Classico '96	▼	4
● Fontissimo '91	YY	5
● Chianti Classico Ris. '90	Y	3
● Chianti Classico Ris. '91	Y	4
● Chianti Classico Ris. '93	Y	4
● Fontissimo '93	Y	5

PANZANO IN CHIANTI (FI)

Castello dei Rampolla
Via Case Sparse, 22
50020 Panzano in Chianti (FI)
tel. 055/852001

The wine of the year, i.e. the one that most pleased all the tasters at the final tasting, is La Vigna di Alceo '96. Did you follow our advice and reserve it last year? We hope so, because there isn't much of it and the wine is a dream. It is made from cabernet sauvignon and petit verdot and has a spicy, intense and extremely elegant bouquet and an explosive palate that manages to combine power and elegance. The tannins are so sweet and dense as to be an object lesson in how tannins should behave in a great red wine. Luca di Napoli and Giacomo Tachis must have put everything they had into it, to make a wine that would have satisfied Alcaeus, Prince of Naples and winegrower extraordinaire, who died after arranging for the planting of "his" vineyard just as he wanted, where he desired, and with the grapes he most loved. A story both sad and beautiful. But if he could now drink the wine from his vineyard, we are sure that he would be very well pleased. Beside this extraordinary wine, that Latour and Haut-Brion would have the devil's own time trying to beat in a comparative tasting, the Sammarco '95, cabernet sauvignon with a little sangiovese, almost fades into the background. It as not as powerful as the '94, but that happens in Panzano. It has intense, fruity aromas with notes of licorice and black currants, with a full-bodied, stylish palate and sweet tannins, that cannot be compared, however, to those of La Vigna di Alceo. Another excellent wine is the Chianti Classico Riserva '95, in accordance with winery tradition. It is an elegant and fragrant red with an unexceptional body. The Chianti Classico '96 is quite good, but the nose is a bit forward and the tannins are not quite tamed.

Wine	Glasses	
● La Vigna di Alceo '96	▼▼▼	6
● Chianti Classico Ris. '95	▼▼	5
● Sammarco '95	▼▼	6
● Chianti Classico '96	▼	4
● Sammarco '85	YYY	6
● Sammarco '86	YYY	6
● Sammarco '94	YYY	6
● Chianti Classico Ris. '85	YY	5
● Chianti Classico Ris. '86	YY	5
● Chianti Classico Ris. '88	YY	5
● Chianti Classico Ris. '90	YY	5
● Chianti Classico Ris. '93	YY	5
● Chianti Classico Ris. '94	YY	5
● Sammarco '88	YY	6
● Sammarco '93	YY	6

PANZANO IN CHIANTI (FI)

VECCHIE TERRE DI MONTEFILI
VIA S. CRESCI, 45
50022 PANZANO IN CHIANTI (FI)
TEL. 055/853739

Good results once again for the wines produced by Vecchie Terre di Montefili, an estate from which we actually expected rather more, given the high quality to which they had accustomed us. After the triumph, for example, of the '94 vintage, we were prepared to be overwhelmed by the Anfiteatro '95, which only partially fulfilled our expectations. We do not wish to be misunderstood: this is a wine with its own style, elegant, fruity and not wanting in complexity, a natural high scorer. But to be really great once again it needs, we feel, a jolt of energy. One ought to bear in mind that the '95 vintage, which ripened late, produced excellent results but nothing really exceptional in the Panzano area, which is wonderful for vineyards but higher than is normal in Chianti. The Bruno di Rocca '95, made from cabernet and sangiovese, is better than just good: it offers intense aromas with oak-derived vanilla to the fore. It is full-bodied and dense, but its tannins, a bit hard on the finish, need some smoothing. Once again there's the problem of the '95 vintage, which wants a bit more flesh and fruity richness. To conclude, the interesting Chianti Classico '96, with a good structure and decided taste, is still young and has a few rough edges to be taken care of, but we find it promising.

● Anfiteatro '95	🍷🍷	6
● Bruno di Rocca '95	🍷🍷	6
● Chianti Classico '96	🍷	4
● Anfiteatro '94	ΨΨΨ	6
● Chianti Cl. Anfiteatro Ris. '88	ΨΨΨ	6
● Chianti Classico Ris. '85	ΨΨΨ	6
● Anfiteatro '91	ΨΨ	6
● Anfiteatro '93	ΨΨ	6
● Bruno di Rocca '91	ΨΨ	6
● Bruno di Rocca '92	ΨΨ	6
● Bruno di Rocca '93	ΨΨ	6
● Bruno di Rocca '94	ΨΨ	6
● Chianti Classico '93	ΨΨ	4
● Chianti Classico '94	ΨΨ	4
● Chianti Classico '95	ΨΨ	4

PANZANO IN CHIANTI (FI)

VIGNOLE
VIA CASE SPARSE, 14
50022 PANZANO IN CHIANTI (FI)
TEL. 0574/592025 - 055/852197

Three years have passed since we last included this small but quite famous Panzano winery, owned by the Nistri family, in the Guide. Their technical consultant is Giorgio Marone, a young but already well-known oenologist and a student of Giacomo Tachis, having worked with him at Marchesi Antinori until a few years ago. Two wines were presented this year, and both are quite convincing. The Chianti Classico '96 shows an exemplary fidelity to the characteristics of its vintage. It displays delicate, elegant fruity aromas with notes of sour cherry and Parma violets. It has only medium body, with a noticeable but not excessive note of acidity and a not very long finish. It's pleasing, drinkable and not very complex, just as a non-Riserva Chianti Classico should be. The Chianti Classico Riserva '95 is much richer and more complex, indeed it exceeded our expectations. The bouquet displays sour cherry and red currant aromas with the faintest hint of vanilla, an indication that they knew what they were doing with the new oak they used for aging. The flavor is full and rich, with elegant tannins well-integrated, supporting the body without overwhelming it. The finish is long, and one is left with a sensation of soft balance. Not bad for a comeback.

● Chianti Classico Ris. '95	🍷🍷	4
● Chianti Classico '96	🍷	3

PANZANO IN CHIANTI (FI)

Villa Cafaggio

Via S. Martino in Cecione, 5
50020 Panzano in Chianti (FI)
tel. 055/8549094

All of Villa Cafaggio's wines were presented at our tastings this year, allowing us to form a picture of their production as a whole. In terms of quality, as you can see at the bottom of the page, our impressions were distinctly positive: all the wines were above average and two of them, Cortaccio and San Martino, were excellent. The Cortaccio '95, made from cabernet sauvignon with a small amount of sangiovese, is very good indeed, and is concentrated in color, bouquet and taste. The nose is still a bit dumb, but there are notes of black fruits and light vegetal hints; on the palate it is meaty, full-bodied and deep, with lively but not very aristocratic tannins. The San Martino '95 is on the same level and is made from the same grapes, but in inverse proportions. It displays fruit, flowers and vanilla on the nose, and has volume and weight in the mouth, where it develops with elegance and closes with a fair finish. The Riserva '94 Solatio Basilica landed a step lower but still in the Two Glass category. Vividly ruby in color, it offers a bouquet of fruit, jam, spice and balsamic wood. Its entry on the palate is powerful and broad; this is a wine with character and also with slightly rough tannins on the finish. The Riserva '95 wins One "high" Glass; the palate is definitely more successful than the not yet well-focused nose with its suggestions of fruit and oak and vegetal notes. Its flavor is soft and well-balanced, with a clear, sweet finish. The Chianti Classico '96 is more than respectable, offering well-blended scents and a simple but sound fruitiness, while the palate is fresh and well-balanced, with a medium-light body.

	Wine	Glasses	
●	Chianti Classico Solatio Basilica Ris. '94	▼▼	5
●	Cortaccio '95	▼▼	6
●	San Martino '95	▼▼	5
●	Chianti Classico '96	▼	4
●	Chianti Classico Ris. '95	▼	4
●	Cortaccio '93	▽▽▽	6
●	Chianti Classico '95	▽▽	4
●	Chianti Classico Ris. '93	▽▽	5
●	Cortaccio '90	▽▽	6
●	Cortaccio '94	▽▽	6
●	San Martino '90	▽▽	5
●	San Martino '93	▽▽	5
●	San Martino '94	▽▽	5
●	Solatio Basilica '90	▽▽	5

PIEVE AL BAGNORO (AR)

Villa Cilnia

Loc. Montoncello
52040 Pieve al Bagnoro (AR)
tel. 0575/365017

Although it has been making and bottling wine "only" since 1974, Villa Cilnia was for years a benchmark in the Arezzo area and the rest of Tuscany. Until not long ago, its most successful labels used to rival the best Tuscan wines. After an infelicitous period, Villa Cilnia reclaimed its own place in the Guide last year, and fully deserved it. Nevertheless the expectations raised by the '97 tastings have been partly disappointed by this year's. The wines are still well made, without serious defects, but they still lack the character necessary for a real leap upwards. The Chianti dei Colli Aretini '96 is faintly woody, clean, fresh, lightly structured and a little acidic. The Riserva '94 is good too: the oak-derived notes are still quite noticeable, but extract, especially tannin, is substantial. Of the non-DOC wines, the Vocato, which has long been the top of their line, is quite pleasant. A blend of sangiovese and cabernet, the '94 has alcoholic, delicately woody, clean fragrances and medium body with balanced tannins and a slightly acidic finish. This is a transitional year, which we hope is the prelude to further improvement.

	Wine	Glasses	
●	Chianti Colli Aretini '96	▼	2
●	Chianti Colli Aretini Ris. '94	▼	3
●	Vocato '94	▼	4
●	Vocato '93	▽▽	4
●	Chianti Colli Aretini '95	▽	2
●	Chianti Colli Aretini Ris. '93	▽	3
○	Mecenate '95	▽	4

POGGIBONSI (SI)

FATTORIA LE FONTI
LOC. S. GIORGIO
53036 POGGIBONSI (SI)
TEL. 0577/935690 - 035/711067

This farm belongs to the Imberti family, originally from the Bergamo area, who bought it in 1956. It's a big property, over 140 hectares, and much of it is planted with grains. The vineyards cover 15 hectares, ten of which fall within the Chianti Classico zone, but eight more hectares are slated for planting over the next few years. The tasting of their wines produced a pleasant surprise - the winery's debut in the Guide. Enologist Paolo Caciornia and agronomist Lorenzo Bernini are the technical experts in charge here. The Chianti Classico '96 has a fine, sparkling ruby hue. Its nose is dominated by spicy notes playing against a background of ripe fruit. The attack in the mouth is good but not overbearing, with its alcoholic side appearing afterwards, it too without being overbearing. The Riserva '95 immediately stands out thanks to its bold, endearing fruity aromas that blend well with light accents of menthol and spice. It has a good attack in the mouth, with solid but unassertive tannins; only a light acidic note contrasts with the other components. The finish is both satisfying and adequately long. The red table wine, named Vito Arturo and based on sangiovese, has earned the best ranking, making a good showing right from its visual impact, a vibrant, bold ruby. On the nose, vegetal notes blend very nicely with the fruity ones, highlighting cherry and plum. Its impact on the mouth is bold and soft, with its various components in perfect equilibrium. Engaging and full, it offers a long finish.

	Wine	Glasses	Price
●	Vito Arturo '95	🍷🍷	4
●	Chianti Classico '96	🍷	3
●	Chianti Classico Ris. '95	🍷	4

POGGIBONSI (SI)

MELINI
LOC. GAGGIANO
53036 POGGIBONSI (SI)
TEL. 0577/989001

Melini is among the great standard-bearers of Chianti Classico tradition. It is one of the numerous estates owned by the Gruppo Italiano Vini, and includes vineyards in different Chianti zones, specifically Poggibonsi, Castellina in Chianti, Radda and the southern part of Panzano, right on the border between the provinces of Florence and Siena. At the head of this historic house is Nunzio Capurso, who played a key role in the relaunching of Chianti Classico over the last fifteen years. Melini's hallmark wine is the Chianti Classico La Selvanella Riserva, made exclusively from sangiovese grapes grown in the vineyard of that name at Lucarelli, a hamlet halfway between Panzano and Radda. This year we tasted the '94, which is already available, and the '95, which will be released soon. Stylistically they are both typical traditional wines, but aged in large casks for much longer than is customary in these parts. The '94 is softer, with a more forward bouquet that includes notes of ripe plum and tamarind. The '95 still has some sharp acidic and tannic corners and a slightly muffled nose ascribable to recent bottling. However, both have structure and their usual style. The Vernaccia di San Gimignano Le Grillaie '97, as usual very interesting, is a full-bodied white which makes a good counterpart to La Selvanella. The Chianti Classico I Sassi '96 is quite good and a bargain, pleasant, soft and not too demanding.

	Wine	Glasses	Price
●	Chianti Cl. La Selvanella Ris. '94	🍷🍷	4*
●	Chianti Cl. La Selvanella Ris. '95	🍷🍷	4*
○	Vernaccia di S. Gimignano Le Grillaie '97	🍷🍷	3*
●	Chianti Classico I Sassi '96	🍷	2*
●	Chianti Cl. La Selvanella Ris. '86	🍷🍷🍷 (previous edition)	4*
●	Chianti Cl. La Selvanella Ris. '90	🍷🍷🍷 (previous edition)	4*
●	Chianti Cl. La Selvanella Ris. '85	🍷🍷 (previous edition)	4
●	Chianti Cl. La Selvanella Ris. '87	🍷🍷 (previous edition)	4
●	Chianti Cl. La Selvanella Ris. '88	🍷🍷 (previous edition)	4*
●	Chianti Cl. La Selvanella Ris. '91	🍷🍷 (previous edition)	4
●	Chianti Cl. La Selvanella Ris. '93	🍷🍷 (previous edition)	4*
○	Vernaccia di S. Gimignano Le Grillaie '96	🍷🍷 (previous edition)	3*

PONTASSIEVE (FI)

TENUTA DI BOSSI

VIA DELLO STRACCHINO, 32
50065 PONTASSIEVE (FI)
TEL. 055/8317830

First of all, a correction: in last year's Guide, we mistakenly identified the Vin Santo of the Tenuta di Bossi as a '93, whereas it was actually the fruit of the excellent '91 vintage. This year we did taste the '93, and we can assure you that it is by no means inferior to its big brother, in structure or drinkability. Given the excellence of past Vin Santo vintages, it's clear that Bonaccorso and Bernardo Gondi, with the help of the oenologist Carlo Corino, have developed a distinctive style and a consistent standard. This is also true for their other wines, although, with the brilliant exception of the Mazzaferrata, many could still be improved. The Chianti Rufina '96 is vinous and simple, with a typical almond fragrance; its palate, tannic and clean, has medium body and a slightly acidic finish. The Riserva Marchese Gondi '95, tasted in a preliminary sample drawn from the cask, revealed considerable structure, but also raw and astringent elements that are awaiting further smoothing. This is a full-bodied red wine that will undoubtedly come into its own over time. Notwithstanding the unimpressive quality of the '94 harvest, even the Chianti Rufina Villa Bossi Riserva is interesting, and yet, despite the softening effect of a pleasant background of oak, its flavor is a little empty. As usual, the best wine in the series was the Mazzaferrata, a powerful monovarietal cabernet. The '94 is robust and full-bodied (for a '94), with well-modulated nuances of wood and good ripe fruit.

	Wine	Glasses	Price
●	Mazzaferrata '94	▼▼	4
○	Vin Santo '93	▼▼	4
●	Chianti Rufina '96	▼	3
●	Chianti Rufina Ris. '94	▼	4
●	Chianti Rufina Ris. '90	▽▽	4
●	Mazzaferrata '90	▽▽	4
●	Mazzaferrata '92	▽▽	4
●	Mazzaferrata '93	▽▽	4
○	Vin Santo '85	▽▽	5
○	Vin Santo '86	▽▽	5
○	Vin Santo '91	▽▽	5
○	Vinsanto Bernardo Gondi '88	▽▽	4
●	Chianti Rufina Ris. '92	▽	4
●	Chianti Rufina Ris. '94	▽	4

PONTASSIEVE (FI)

RUFFINO

VIA ARETINA, 42/44
50065 PONTASSIEVE (FI)
TEL. 055/83605

Although we considered ourselves to be among the most loyal supporters of the new course taken by Ruffino, which has led this great and celebrated winery to form the Tenimenti and to relaunch Nozzole, we never imagined that the wines presented this year could be so good. It has racked up a real triumph, with Three Glasses twice and a veritable cabinetful of crystal to accompany them. But first things first. The Cabreo Il Borgo '96, sangiovese with a little cabernet sauvignon, is fantastic, a masterful interpretation of a decidedly difficult vintage, the result of merciless grape selection. It has a bouquet of red berries, dark cherries and black currants, as well as vanilla. The palate is soft but underpinned by delicate and elegant tannins and the finish is long and concentrated. The Romitorio di Santedame '96, a blend of prugnolo and colorino, is simply formidable: it's like one of Guigal's great syrahs. The nose is intense and complex, with distinct notes of spice and berries. Complexity and intensity also characterize the palate, where the tannins are dense and very stylish and the finish is of exceptional length: a real champion. Their pinot noir, the Nero del Tondo '96, is the best it has ever been and just misses Three Glasses. But even the less innovative wines are splendid: the Chianti Classico Riserva Ducale Oro '93, which is not very ample but beautifully made, the thoroughly enjoyable Chianti Classico Santedame '96, and the Chianti Classico Riserva Ducale '95 with Two Glasses that seem a stunning accomplishment for a wine produced in the millions of bottles. Finally, the Cabreo La Pietra '96, a chardonnay, is much less woody than it used to be.

	Wine	Glasses	Price
●	Cabreo Il Borgo '96	▼▼▼	6
●	Romitorio di Santedame '96	▼▼▼	5
○	Cabreo La Pietra '96	▼▼	5
●	Chianti Classico Ris. Ducale '95	▼▼	3*
●	Chianti Cl. Ris. Ducale Oro '93	▼▼	5
●	Nero del Tondo '96	▼▼	6
●	Chianti Cl. Santedame '96	▼	4
●	Cabreo Il Borgo '85	▽▽▽	6
●	Cabreo Il Borgo '95	▽▽▽	6
●	Chianti Cl. Ris. Ducale Oro '88	▽▽▽	5
●	Chianti Cl. Ris. Ducale Oro '90	▽▽▽	5
●	Romitorio di Santedame '94	▽▽	5
●	Romitorio di Santedame '95	▽▽	5

PONTASSIEVE (FI)

FATTORIA SELVAPIANA
LOC. SELVAPIANA, 43
50065 PONTASSIEVE (FI)
TEL. 055/8369848

This estate put the Rufina area on the wine map of the world. If we can now talk about steady improvement in the local wines, it is thanks in part to the Giuntini family, which has been making wine here since the 19th century. Their greatest achievement has been to combine modernization with respect for tradition. They presented us with four wines for tasting and we liked them all. The Chianti Rufina '96, a rich ruby in hue, offers clean, fruity scents of cherry and red currant. It makes an imposing entry on the palate, where the soft components nicely balance the underpinning unagressive tannins. The finish is fairly long and very pleasant. The Riserva '95 has a strikingly broad array of aromas, ranging from ripe fruit, plum in particular, to fresh notes of mint. In the mouth it shows firmness, with tannins still evident, and a clean, convincing finish. This year we were able to taste both the '94 and the '95 of their cru Bucerchiale. The former offers forward and nicely distinct aromas of well-blended ripe fruit. The palate, which is initially soft, reveals well-distributed tannins and perfectly balanced acidity, with a long finish. The '95 is definitely superior in complexity and breadth. Of a rich, dense ruby hue, it has coffee and tobacco fragrances that mix well with a mature fruitiness. In the mouth it's immediately engaging, with solid tannin counterpoised by softer components. The finish is very long and complex.

●	Chianti Rufina Bucerchiale Ris. '94	🍷🍷	5
●	Chianti Rufina Bucerchiale Ris. '95	🍷🍷	5
●	Chianti Rufina Ris. '95	🍷🍷	4
●	Chianti Rufina '96	🍷	3
●	Chianti Rufina '88	🍷🍷	3
●	Chianti Rufina '90	🍷🍷	3
●	Chianti Rufina '91	🍷🍷	3*
●	Chianti Rufina Bucerchiale Ris. '90	🍷🍷	5
●	Chianti Rufina Fornace Ris. '94	🍷🍷	5
●	Chianti Rufina Ris. '88	🍷🍷	4
●	Chianti Rufina Ris. '90	🍷🍷	4

PORTOFERRAIO (LI)

ACQUABONA
LOC. ACQUABONA
57037 PORTOFERRAIO (LI)
TEL. 0565/933013

We were really pleased with the wines presented this year by Acquabona. As we expected, there was a great performance from the Aleatico, on which they have lavished enormous care, with the declared aim of producing an important wine that properly expresses the uniqueness of the Isle of Elba. Unlike other producers on the island, Ugo Lucchini and Marcello Fioretti prefer to make a rather complex Aleatico that is already mature and balanced when they release it, so we just managed by the skin of our teeth to taste the '95. Despite long aging in oak, the wine has maintained its delightful freshness, with distinct intense aromas of sour cherry jam, wildflowers, herbs and spices. There is just the right sweetness on the well-structured palate, which evinces, with its rounded and well-judged tannins, excellent balance. But the wine that most surprised us and which we were tempted to rank even higher than we did, was the Ansonica '97. We have rarely encountered an Elban white that is so well-made: its clearly defined bouquet offers notes of ripe yellow fruit, chamomile and broom, with hints of almond, carrying through onto a succulent, fragrant and well-balanced palate. The Vermentino Acquabona was quite satisfactory, and the two Elba DOCs were properly made, but we wouldn't mind a little more character in the Rosso.

●	Aleatico dell'Elba '95	🍷🍷	6
○	Acquabona di Acquabona '97	🍷	3
○	Ansonica dell'Elba '97	🍷	4
○	Elba Bianco '97		3
●	Elba Rosso '97		3
●	Aleatico di Portoferraio '91	🍷🍷	6
●	Aleatico di Portoferraio '94	🍷🍷	6
●	Aleatico di Portoferraio '92	🍷	6
○	Ansonica Passito '92	🍷	5
●	Elba Rosso Ris. '94	🍷	4
●	Elba Rosso Ris. Camillo Bianchi '91	🍷	3*

PORTOFERRAIO (LI)

TENUTA LA CHIUSA
LOC. MAGAZZINI, 93
57037 PORTOFERRAIO (LI)
TEL. 0565/933046

Wine buffs visiting the Isle of Elba should not miss La Chiusa: they will always receive a splendid welcome and they will find a magnificent expanse of vineyards that seem to stop only a couple of feet from the sea. The name of the winery reflects the fact that the estate is in fact surrounded by a wall, like the "clos" of Burgundy. As for the wines, we must say that there is once again a disconcerting unevenness in quality, which seems to range from very good to mediocre. So we feel they should work on improving overall standards, since the potential for quality does exist. The first proof of this is provided by the very successful Aleatico '97. It has a lively deep ruby hue and a fresh, sound fruity bouquet, which is reflected on the sweet, concentrated, succulent and delightful palate with its well-calibrated tannins. The quite good Ansonica Passita '97 has a more oxidized style, with toasted hazelnuts on the nose and an alcoholic, enticing, almost unctuous palate. The Elba Rosso '97 is pleasant, a little lean perhaps but fruity and fragrant. The other passito, Goccia d'Oro, is not very convincing, and the Elba Bianco and the Rosato could definitely stand improvement.

	Wine	Glasses	Price
●	Aleatico dell'Elba '97	🍷🍷	5
○	Ansonica Passita '97	🍷	5
●	Elba Rosso '97	🍷	3
○	Goccia d'Oro '97		4
●	Aleatico dell'Elba '92	🍸🍸	5
●	Aleatico dell'Elba '95	🍸	5
○	Ansonica '92	🍸	4
○	Elba Bianco '96	🍸	3
●	Elba Rosso '96	🍸	3
○	Procanico '92	🍸	4

RADDA IN CHIANTI (SI)

CASTELLO DI ALBOLA
LOC. PIAN D'ALBOLA, 31
53017 RADDA IN CHIANTI (SI)
TEL. 0577/738019

Sooner or later it had to happen that one of the wines produced by one of Gianni Zonin's wineries would win Three Glasses. The wine that did it is the Acciaiolo '95, a blend of sangiovese and cabernet sauvignon, and is the fruit of the vineyards at Castello d'Albola in Radda. This is the cherry on the cake in this very important year for the Zonin Group. For one thing, this was the year of the arrival of Franco Giacosa, the renowned oenologist and manager. It could be pure coincidence, but the distinct general improvement in the wines of all the wineries held by Zonin seems to date from the start of his employment by the Group. But let's get back to the wines from Albola and particularly to the Acciaiolo '95, a wine that doesn't require much comment. It has an intense, engrossing bouquet, of great refinement, with distinct notes of fruit and new wood. On the palate, apart from a little acid and tannic roughness that goes with its tender age, it is notably full-bodied and persistent, with very densely knit tannins. As always, Le Fagge Chardonnay, the '96 this time, was very good. It continues to be one of the best whites in the area. It offers a depth of flavor that is rare in chardonnays from these parts, and its nose is dominated by notes of ripe fruit, pineapple and banana in particular, as well as vanilla. Finally, the Chianti Classico '96, a little, light red wine with a slight acidic bite, is certainly well made and better than many others from the same vintage.

	Wine	Glasses	Price
●	Acciaiolo '95	🍷🍷🍷	5
○	Le Fagge Chardonnay '96	🍷🍷	4
●	Chianti Classico '96	🍷	3
●	Acciaiolo '88	🍸🍸	5
●	Acciaiolo '93	🍸🍸	5
○	Le Fagge Chardonnay '91	🍸🍸	4*
○	Le Fagge Chardonnay '93	🍸🍸	4
○	Le Fagge Chardonnay '95	🍸🍸	4
●	Le Marangole '95	🍸🍸	4
●	Acciaiolo '90	🍸	5
●	Chianti Classico '95	🍸	3
●	Chianti Classico Ris. '93	🍸	4
●	Chianti Classico Ris. '94	🍸	4
○	Le Fagge Chardonnay '94	🍸	4
●	Le Marangole '94	🍸	5

RADDA IN CHIANTI (SI)

LIVERNANO
LOC. LIVERNANO
53017 RADDA IN CHIANTI (SI)
TEL. 0577/738353

Livernano came into being only recently, with very clear objectives right from the start, and it did beautifully at our tastings with all four wines it presented. The vineyards are at altitudes varying from 400 to 500 meters, with a density of almost 7 thousand vines per hectare and a very low yield. Nothing has been left to chance, and thus all the choices, from terrain to type of rootstock and the selection of clones and varietals, follow precise criteria. We were particularly delighted by the Puro Sangue '95, 100% sangiovese: its color is surprisingly deep, as is the bouquet, which has layers of black fruit and a still significant oak component. Its attack is full and powerful, with a dense progression to a long but still somewhat hard finish. This is a great wine, and it came within an inch of winning Three Glasses. The Nardina '95, made from cabernet and merlot, also put in an excellent performance: a very concentrated color is the prelude to an intense, richly fruity nose, which at the moment is still overly vanilla-laden. On the palate it is substantial and dense, with good tannic support and a relatively subdued finish. In years, like '96, that are not considered good enough for these two wines, a selection is made of two parts sangiovese and one of cabernet and merlot, and is called Livernano. The result is excellent. It has many characteristics in common with those two wines, and received a score that was exactly midway between theirs. The white Anima, 70% chardonnay, 20% sauvignon and 10% traminer, has a distinct personality, elegance, depth and structure.

○	Anima '96	🍷🍷	5
●	Livernano '96	🍷🍷	6
●	Nardina '95	🍷🍷	5
●	Puro Sangue '95	🍷🍷	6

RADDA IN CHIANTI (SI)

CASTELLO DI MONTERINALDI
LOC. LUCARELLI
53017 RADDA IN CHIANTI (SI)
TEL. 0577/733533

Thanks to the work of its owner and of the oenologist Paolo Vagaggini, this historic Radda estate has made a fine debut in the Guide with a series of quite interesting wines. This is a winery to keep an eye on: they are about to add more vineyards to the current 68 hectares, which will be sizable for these parts. Two wines were presented for tasting, the Chianti Classico '96 and the Riserva '95, but they also produce two table wines that can be easily distinguished from each other: the Gottizio, a quaffable wine that takes its name from the first Count of Monterinaldi, and the Pesanella, a cabernet sauvignon and sangiovese blend with great structure. We shall be getting to them next year, but meanwhile here are the Chiantis. The Chianti Classico '96, vivid ruby in color, has light fruity fragrances, notably cherry, somewhat dominated by fresh vegetal aromas. The entry on the palate is strong, with immediately evident but unaggressive tannins, and a silkiness that counterpoises the alcohol. The finish is pleasant and adequately long. It is clear from its rich color alone that the Riserva has excellent concentration. It has an intriguing nose, with balsamic tones at once evident, but blended with notes of resin and ripe fruit. In the mouth it is powerful and full-bodied, with the tannins already balanced by the other components. The finish is long and lovely.

●	Chianti Classico Ris. '95	🍷🍷	4
●	Chianti Classico '96	🍷	3

RADDA IN CHIANTI (SI)

Fattoria di Montevertine
Loc. Monte Vertine
53017 Radda in Chianti (SI)
tel. 0577/738009

In the last edition of the Guide we wrote about having to reassure Sergio Manetti every year of our enduring respect and fondness for him, a fondness such as one might feel for a somewhat cantankerous father. This year it is our turn to need reassurance that he hasn't started to think differently about making wine. We liked Le Pergole Torte '95, for example, less than we thought we would. It has fruity aromas with notes that almost suggest citrus. The typical fruit of the Sangiovese is there, well expressed. But it's all a little simple, lacking in great complexity. And this is also true on the palate, where there isn't enough flesh to balance a harshness from acidity and tannins. It is still a good, well-made wine, but it is not a great version of Le Pergole Torte. This somewhat grim picture is completed by the other '95s, which give the impression that this wasn't such a great vintage after all, at least not here. Both the Sodaccio and the Monte Vertine Riserva have forward bouquets and not much density. The Pian del Ciampolo '95 does yet less well, displaying very little body and rather simple fruity aromas. It was not intended to be great, but we are not used to the spectacle of a Montevertine wine that just wins One Glass by the skin of its teeth.

	Wine	Glasses	
●	Le Pergole Torte '95	▼▼	6
●	Il Sodaccio '95	▼	5
●	Montevertine Ris. '95	▼	5
●	Pian del Ciampolo '95	▼	4
●	Le Pergole Torte '83	YYY	6
●	Le Pergole Torte '86	YYY	6
●	Le Pergole Torte '88	YYY	6
●	Le Pergole Torte '90	YYY	6
●	Le Pergole Torte '92	YYY	6
●	Monte Vertine Ris. '85	YYY	5
●	Il Sodaccio '90	YY	6
●	Le Pergole Torte '85	YY	6
●	Le Pergole Torte '93	YY	6
●	Le Pergole Torte '94	YY	6
●	Monte Vertine Ris. '90	YY	6

Podere Capaccia
Loc. Capaccia
53017 Radda in Chianti (SI)
tel. 0577/738385

A year in the limbo of Honorable Mention seems to have been quite beneficial for the wines of Giampaolo Pacini's Podere Capaccia. At last year's tastings we had noticed a falling off. The wines were a bit forward, very soft but not as concentrated as we had expected. Thus we made the painful decision to drop the individual profile and relegate the winery to the back pages. We are happy to be able to make the opposite decision on the strength of one wine in particular, the Querciagrande '95, a monovarietal sangiovese, which seems to us to be a triumph. Here at last is a great red wine with intense aromas, dominated by notes of sour cherry and vanilla. It is full-bodied and firm, if a little monotonous, but wonderfully dense and substantial: a classic for this winery, thanks to Pacini's passionate commitment and the expert advice of Vittorio Fiore. We take our hats off to this wine and to Podere Capaccia, which has regained its rightful place among the best estates of Chianti Classico. Even the great Milan soccer team has occasionally found itself in the B league: these things happen. The Chianti Classico '95 is not as impressive, but perfectly acceptable. It is simpler and perhaps just slightly flabby in the mouth, where the polyphenolic concentration is not sufficient to balance the softer elements. Consequently it is not very exciting, although quite straightforward.

	Wine	Glasses	
●	Querciagrande '95	▼▼	6
●	Chianti Classico '95	▼	4
●	Querciagrande '88	YYY	6
●	Chianti Classico '90	YY	4
●	Chianti Classico Ris. '86	YY	5
●	Chianti Classico Ris. '88	YY	5
●	Querciagrande '86	YY	6
●	Querciagrande '87	YY	6
●	Querciagrande '90	YY	6
●	Querciagrande '91	YY	6
●	Querciagrande '92	YY	6
●	Querciagrande '93	YY	6
●	Chianti Classico Ris. '93	Y	5
●	Querciagrande '94	Y	6

RADDA IN CHIANTI (SI)

POGGERINO
VIA POGGERINO, 6
53017 RADDA IN CHIANTI (SI)
TEL. 0577/738232

Poggerino wines are always reliable and well made, which is rare for a small winery. This one has just eight hectares under vine that produce nothing but sangiovese of the highest quality. If it's true that it's hard to make an excellent wine in vast quantities, it is also true that big estates can pick and choose among their lots of wine, while small producers have just what their vineyard produces, and not one bunch more. Hence it's much more difficult for them to maintain a consistent level, and differences in weather have a much greater and more immediate impact on the quality of their wines. This is one of the reasons that the steady reliability of Poggerino wines is so admirable. The Chianti Classico Bugialla Riserva '95 is no exception to the rule. It is a well-made wine, and the barrique-derived wood component is perfectly judged. The vanilla and toasty oak aromas are not overpowering, it is substantial, if not extraordinarily so, on the palate, and while the tannins are noticeable, they are not aggressive. The Chianti Classico '96 is even better, in its category, and one of the best of its vintage. There are complex mineral hints in the intensely fruity bouquet, and on the palate it is even more balanced than the Riserva, with sweet, dense tannins and a finish that is a real surprise in a non-Riserva. Our compliments to Piero Lanza, young and passionate winegrower and owner of this wonderful little estate.

	Wine	Glasses	Price
●	Chianti Classico Bugialla Ris. '95	🍷🍷	5
●	Chianti Classico '96	🍷🍷	3*
●	Chianti Classico Ris. '90	ΥΥΥ	5
●	Chianti Classico Bugialla Ris. '94	ΥΥ	5
●	Chianti Classico '90	ΥΥ	3*
●	Chianti Classico '91	ΥΥ	3*
●	Chianti Classico '93	ΥΥ	3*
●	Chianti Classico '94	ΥΥ	3*
●	Chianti Classico '95	ΥΥ	3
●	Chianti Classico Ris. '88	ΥΥ	5
●	Vigna di Bugialla '88	ΥΥ	5
●	Vigna di Bugialla '90	ΥΥ	5
●	Vigna di Bugialla '91	ΥΥ	5
●	Vigna di Bugialla '93	ΥΥ	5
●	Chianti Classico '88	Υ	3

RADDA IN CHIANTI (SI)

FATTORIA TERRABIANCA
LOC. S. FEDELE A PATERNO
53017 RADDA IN CHIANTI (SI)
TEL. 0577/738544

Once again, just two wines from Roberto Guldener, who seems to measure out our samples with an eyedropper. But these are two Terrabianca champions: Piano del Cipresso, mostly sangiovese, and Campaccio, a blend of sangiovese and cabernet sauvignon. They are both '94s and both excellent, and with a little more density they would both have Three Glasses. They certainly have it in them, and with the right vintage the prize will be theirs. Indeed, the technical finish of the wines approaches perfection, so it is hard to ask for more. But let's get down to our tasting notes. The Piano del Cipresso '94 is a really good wine. The bouquet is intensely fruity, perhaps a bit forward, but delicate and well expressed. Although full-bodied and rich, it is easy to drink; the acidity nicely underpins the structure and avoids any unholy alliance with the tannins. The wine is soft, with good albeit unexceptional density, which applies to the finish as well. The Campaccio '94 is a splendid and very elegant wine. The nose is more intense and complex than its brother's, and the new wood is well blended with the particularly delicate fruit. The palate displays delicate, elegant tannins, but not very great depth. It's a well-made, consistent wine, but not an absolute champion.

	Wine	Glasses	Price
●	Campaccio '94	🍷🍷	5
●	Piano del Cipresso '94	🍷🍷	5
●	Campaccio '90	ΥΥ	5
●	Campaccio '91	ΥΥ	5
●	Campaccio '93	ΥΥ	5
●	Campaccio Sel. Speciale '91	ΥΥ	6
●	Campaccio Sel. Speciale '93	ΥΥ	6
●	Chianti Classico Vigna della Croce Ris. '88	ΥΥ	4
●	Chianti Classico Vigna della Croce Ris. '90	ΥΥ	5
●	Piano del Cipresso '91	ΥΥ	5
○	Piano della Cappella '95	ΥΥ	4
●	Chianti Classico Vigna della Croce Ris. '94	Υ	5

RADDA IN CHIANTI (SI)

Castello di Volpaia
Loc. Volpaia
P.zza della Cisterna, 1
53017 Radda in Chianti (SI)
tel. 0577/738066

We tasted only two wines at Castello di Volpaia. The '95 special selections Coltassala and Balifico were not yet ready when we went to press, so we "made do" with their standards, the Chianti Classico '96 and Chianti Classico Riserva '95. The former is a well-made, direct wine; it isn't extraordinarily full-bodied and perhaps it's a bit simple, but it is pleasurable and easy to drink. The Riserva is definitely in another class. It comes from an important vintage that in some cases gave rise to somewhat hard and closed wines. At Volpaia the wines tend to lean in that direction anyway, so a little excessive astringency in the '95 was to be expected. This is, however, the only fault we found in a wine that is generally correct. It has an intensely floral bouquet with fruity notes that were initially a little dumb. As we said, the palate is still dominated by a certain astringency caused by the combined force of tannins and acidity, but it does have body, and time should do wonders. So, while there may be some doubts this year, there is no question about the quality of Carlo Mascheroni and Giovannella Stianti's famous estate, which benefits from the assistance of the expert oenologist Maurizio Castelli.

	Wine	Rating	Price
●	Chianti Classico Ris. '95	TT	5
●	Chianti Classico '96	T	3
●	Balifico '86	YY	5
●	Balifico '87	YY	5
●	Balifico '88	YY	5
●	Balifico '91	YY	5
●	Chianti Classico Ris. '85	YY	5
●	Chianti Classico Ris. '86	YY	5
●	Chianti Classico Ris. '88	YY	5
●	Coltassala '85	YY	5
●	Coltassala '90	YY	5
●	Coltassala '91	YY	5
●	Coltassala '94	YY	5
●	Balifico '94	Y	5
●	Chianti Classico '95	Y	3

RAPOLANO TERME (SI)

Castello di Modanella
Loc. Serre
53040 Rapolano Terme (SI)
tel. 0577/704604

The village of Modanella dates back to the Middle Ages, which is hardly unusual in Tuscany: in 1339 it was already in the hands of the Piccolominis. The castle of Modanella dominates the estate vineyards, planted on the softly rolling hills of the Siena countryside. The property is vast: 645 hectares, 22 of which are under vine, including the traditional sangiovese, malvasia and canaiolo (particularly prized on the estate, which produces the interesting Poggio l'Aiole with it alone) and modern although no longer innovative varietals such as cabernet, chardonnay and sauvignon. Organic methods reign supreme, thanks to the supervision of the Istituto Sperimentale di Viticoltura in Arezzo. For its debut in the Guide we tasted three wines. We'll start with the Poggio Elci '96, an acceptable malvasia toscana that is worthy of mention, if nothing else. It is clean, not very characterful, light-bodied and quite quaffable. The Campo d'Aia '95, a monovarietal sangiovese aged in French oak barriques for 12-18 months, is more successful. Fragrant, clean, with a clearly defined note of toasty oak, it is full-bodied, although the wood is once again somewhat insistent. The wine we most liked was the Cabernet Sauvignon Le Voliere '95, a red with a distinct personality. Although its nose is a little muffled, there are delightful notes of roasting coffee and its entry on the palate is more decisive, indicating the presence of a solid structure. It is tannic, concentrated and clean, with a substantial and bitter finish: a lovely wine, which should be at its best a few years hence.

	Wine	Rating	Price
●	Campo d'Aia '95	TT	3
●	Le Voliere Cabernet Sauvignon '95	TT	4
○	Poggio Elci '96		2

ROCCALBEGNA (GR)

VILLA PATRIZIA
FRAZ. CANA
LOC. VILLA PATRIZIA
58050 ROCCALBEGNA (GR)
TEL. 0564/982028

As we wrote last year, there seems to be a wild rush to buy land in the Maremma. Financial syndicates, as well as wineries from other parts of Tuscany and Italy, the heavyweights in terms of quality and investments, have already landed in the neighborhood of Grosseto, eager to create big new wines (red, of course, given the zone). But lo!, like a bolt out of the blue, fact stranger than fiction, a great white wine has appeared on the Maremma scene. The credit goes to Romeo Bruni, who, together with his children Maurizio, Patrizia and Tiziano, owns the estate of Villa Patrizia, and makes good use of the inspired advice of the master oenologist Luca D'Attoma. The wine in question is Alteta, a highly successful blend of chardonnay (fermentation in new wood, followed by batonnage) and sauvignon, which rests for ten months in the bottle before its debut on the market. And what a debut! It has a deep straw color, a nose "exploding" with passion fruit and other exotic notes, a palate with perfect acidity and a finish of just the right length. A retasting of the Orto di Boccio '94 (sangiovese, merlot and cabernet) confirms its potential for improvement over time, while a taste from the cask of the '95 left us ecstatic. The Morellino and Villa Patrizia Rosso are, as usual, very good.

○	Alteta '96	🍷🍷	4
●	Morellino di Scansano '97	🍷	3
●	Villa Patrizia Rosso '96	🍷	3
●	Albatraia '96	🍸	1*
●	Morellino di Scansano '96	🍸	2
●	Orto di Boccio '94	🍸	4
○	Sciamareti '96	🍸	2

ROCCATEDERIGHI (GR)

MELETA
LOC. MELETA
58028 ROCCATEDERIGHI (GR)
TEL. 0564/567155

If you want to set up a winery from scratch, one whose startling wines will set people abuzz, arguing about the best vintages, in short a banner headline sort of wine, really all you need is...money. At this point investors with an extra billion lire or two to venture are either people who were born rich, giant wineries with a cash surplus, or industrial syndicates eager to invest in the wine world; this gives you an idea of what is happening now in the Maremma. If they're roses they'll blossom, as we say here. However, the person who continues to shower flowers and fruit on us is Erika Suter, a lady winegrower who has everything going for her: Austrian pragmatism, feminine sensitivity, first-rate vineyards, and a cellar and technical advice of the same sterling quality. And this is why her estate, Meleta, continues to prosper, moving our hearts and minds once again this year with her Rosso della Rocca '95. Its color is a vivid ruby and its elegant nose offers alternating notes of red berries and mint, with a perfectly judged touch of wood. On the palate it is soft and long, delicate and elegant. This is a great wine, and by its side are the pleasing Pietrello d'Oro and, most impressively, Erika's first Vin Santo, a very successful '94, thanks in particular to its fragrances reminiscent of white chocolate and almond paste. The Bianco della Rocca, which is becoming a little classic, is one of the few whites from the Maremma worthy of note, but there was no tasting it before we went to press, so we shall be writing about it next year.

●	Rosso della Rocca '95	🍷🍷	5
○	Vin Santo '94	🍷🍷	5
●	Pietrello d'Oro '96	🍷	4
●	Merlot '94	🍸🍸	6
●	Pietrello d'Oro '88	🍸🍸	4*
●	Pietrello d'Oro '90	🍸🍸	4*
●	Pietrello d'Oro '91	🍸🍸	4
●	Rosso della Rocca '85	🍸🍸	5
●	Rosso della Rocca '86	🍸🍸	5
●	Rosso della Rocca '88	🍸🍸	5
●	Rosso della Rocca '91	🍸🍸	5
●	Rosso della Rocca '92	🍸🍸	5
●	Rosso della Rocca '93	🍸🍸	5
●	Rosso della Rocca '94	🍸🍸	5

RUFINA (FI)

Fattoria di Basciano

V.le Duca della Vittoria, 159
50068 Rufina (FI)
tel. 055/8397034

In last year's Guide we noted that the Fattoria di Basciano has at least two strong points: the consistent quality of the wines it produces and its very fair prices. Indeed the last few vintages combine a reliable excellence with an affordability that has become a rarity in Tuscany. This year Paolo Masi, the young director of the estate, has released a series of even more successful wines, showing decided improvement. We'll begin with the standard Chianti Rufina '96, clean, fresh, fruity, with distinct "fumé" notes of oak, and soft and tasty: a simple red that starts you comfortably on your way to Baciano's more complex wines: the Chianti Rufina Riserva and the two top reds, I Pini and Il Corto. The Chianti Rufina Riserva '95 is sweet and tempting, with the enchanting aromatic notes typical of cabernet; on the palate it's refreshing and distinct, with medium body and a little grass on the finish. The '96 I Pini, a 50-50 blend of sangiovese and cabernet, is just as successful. Its intense and bewitching bouquet is distinctly characteristic of cabernet, and it reveals flawless character, firm and continuous, on the palate. It's a really excellent red, and the '96 Il Corto (90% sangiovese, 10% cabernet) that Masi is presenting beside it makes a showing that is every bit as good. Its aromas may not be quite so expressive and characterful, but it's without fault, full-bodied, with excellent alcohol, and tannins and acidity perfectly counterpoised. All in all, a veritable tour de force.

	Wine	Glasses	Price
●	Chianti Rufina Ris. '95	🍷🍷	2*
●	I Pini '96	🍷🍷	3
●	Il Corto '96	🍷🍷	3
●	Chianti Rufina '96	🍷	2
●	Chianti Rufina '95	Y	2
●	Chianti Rufina Ris. '93	Y	2
●	Chianti Rufina Ris. '94	Y	2
●	I Pini '94	Y	3
●	I Pini '95	Y	3
●	Il Corto '94	Y	3
●	Il Corto '95	Y	3

S. CASCIANO VAL DI PESA (FI)

Castelli del Grevepesa

Loc. Mercatale Val di Pesa
Via Grevigiana, 34
50024 S. Casciano Val di Pesa (FI)
tel. 055/821911

Wines from the Castelli del Grevepesa always keep their promises. Especially in their standard range, which is what we tasted this year, the level of quality is acceptable, as always. A big cooperative winery like this one stakes a lot on being able to produce a line of wines that are good value for money. This doesn't mean that good wines are not to be found in this category. The Chianti Classico Castelgreve Riserva '95, for example, has won back its Two Glasses after some years without, and you need look no farther than its bouquet and palate to discover the reason. It has intense characteristic sangiovese aromas with suggestions of violets, sour cherry and a light animal hint in the background. It is full-bodied, but shot through with an acidity that makes it refreshing and drinkable. A traditional wine, very well made. The quite good Chianti Classico L'Alberello di Lamole '96 is the product of a vineyard in Lamole planted in the "alberello" style (gobelet training). It has a simple fruity fragrance and a refreshing flavor dominated by a faintly acidic note. Last of all is the Chianti Classico Castelgreve '96, Grevepesa's standard wine, from which we would have liked a little more concentration. It is easy to drink but doesn't linger on the finish.

	Wine	Glasses	Price
●	Chianti Cl. Castelgreve Ris. '95	🍷🍷	4
●	Chianti Classico L'Alberello di Lamole '96	🍷	3
●	Chianti Classico Castelgreve '96		2
●	Chianti Cl. Castelgreve Ris. '88	YY	4
●	Chianti Cl. Castelgreve Ris. '90	YY	4
●	Chianti Classico Clemente VII '88	YY	5
●	Chianti Classico Montefiridolfi '90	YY	4
●	Chianti Classico Vigna Elisa '90	YY	5
●	Guado al Luco '93	YY	5
●	Chianti Classico Castelgreve '95	Y	2*
●	Chianti Cl. Castelgreve Ris. '94	Y	4
●	Chianti Classico Clemente VII '94	Y	5
●	Chianti Classico S. Angelo Vico l'Abate '91	Y	5

Fattoria Corzano e Paterno

Fraz. S. Pancrazio
Via Paterno, 8
50026 S. Casciano Val di Pesa (FI)
tel. 055/8248179 - 8249114

Located on the edge of the Chianti Classico zone, Sig. Wendelin Gelpke's estate, directed by the oenologist Aljoscha Goldschmidt has always made wines with a recognizable personality. Their style is closely bound to the terroir, which gives strong character, a bit hard at first, to the wines of Corzano, but also a lot of personality. And this is no small merit in an era of excellent but also rather similar wines. This year's star, as expected, is Il Corzano '95, a blend of sangiovese and cabernet sauvignon that easily picked up Two Glasses. This is a powerful wine that is still developing, very expressive, "Tuscan" in every fiber of its being, rather than varietal. Its intense aromas are still a bit dumb, but display mineral, vegetal and woody notes on a background of dark fruit. Its attack is bold and hot and it progresses apace, with dense but still untamed tannins. This is a wine to wait for as it ages in the bottle. The Chianti Riserva '95 also put in a good performance, with a color between ruby and garnet, an intense broad bouquet offering notes of oak, earth and tobacco, and a generously alcoholic impact in the mouth. The concentration is good, the tannins lively and sweet and the finish rather long, with oak in evidence. The chardonnay, Aglaia '97, was not at all bad, characterized by intense aromas of toasted hazelnuts, a fresh, well-balanced palate and a slightly simple but pleasing finish. The Chianti '96 is more than acceptable.

	Wine	Glasses	Price
●	Chianti Terre di Corzano Ris. '95	🍷🍷	4
●	Il Corzano '95	🍷🍷	5
○	Aglaia '97	🍷	4
●	Chianti '96	🍷	3
●	Chianti Terre di Corzano Ris. '90	🍷🍷	4
●	Il Corzano '88	🍷🍷	5
○	Vin Santo '90	🍷🍷	5
●	Chianti Terre di Corzano '90	🍷	3
●	Chianti Terre di Corzano '92	🍷	3
●	Chianti Terre di Corzano '93	🍷	3
●	Chianti Terre di Corzano '94	🍷	3
●	Chianti Terre di Corzano Ris. '88	🍷	4

S. CASCIANO VAL DI PESA (FI)

La Sala

Via Sorripa, 34
50026 S. Casciano Val di Pesa (FI)
tel. 055/828111

Hats off to Laura Baronti, the dedicated owner of La Sala, which has never before presented such a successful and interesting range of wines as it has this year. We'd like to begin our review with the wine that, in our opinion, marks the beginning of a new trend in their vinification style: the Chianti Classico '96, an absolutely delicious red. Its nose is exemplary, the fruity sangiovese distinctly perceptible, and the wood very well judged and almost perfectly blended in the bouquet. It is full in body and long in finish, with a light acid undertone: in short, a modern and well-made Chianti Classico. The top of the line, the star, is the Campo all'Albero '95, made from sangiovese grapes with some cabernet sauvignon. It has an intense and aristocratic balsamic bouquet, and displays a very elegant palate with good if not overwhelming body and dense, sweet tannins. Excellent. It needs only a little more depth, but this is San Casciano, where the wines are soft and the drinking is easy. It's hard to do any better. We close with the Chianti Classico Riserva '95, perhaps the least distinct of the three on the nose and the only one to confront us with some obvious acidic sharpness. All the same, it is a modern, well-made red wine.

	Wine	Glasses	Price
●	Campo all'Albero '95	🍷🍷	4*
●	Chianti Classico '96	🍷🍷	3*
●	Chianti Classico Ris. '95	🍷	4
●	Campo all'Albero '94	🍷🍷	4
●	Campo all'Albero '93	🍷	4
●	Chianti Classico '90	🍷	3*
●	Chianti Classico '91	🍷	3*
●	Chianti Classico '93	🍷	3
●	Chianti Classico '95	🍷	3
●	Chianti Classico Ris. '90	🍷	4*
●	Chianti Classico Ris. '93	🍷	4

Fattoria Le Corti - Corsini

Via San Piero di Sotto, 1
50026 S. Casciano Val di Pesa (FI)
tel. 055/820123

The selection of wines presented by the Fattoria Le Corti, owned by the princes of the Corsini line, is a sure indication that the improvements under way in the cellar and, in particular, the vineyards, have developed a momentum of their own. The advice supplied by Carlo Ferrini is doing wonders, and the young Duccio Corsini has taken over the management of the winery. So far the results are very good, but if things keep going at this rate, there could be even greater surprises in store. The wines tasted this year are all admirable in their respective categories. The most interesting is the Chianti Classico Don Tommaso '96, which easily wins Two Glasses once again. The elegance of its bouquet, the well-judged new wood and filigree of especially delicate tannins make this an excellent wine. The Chianti Classico Cortevecchia Riserva '95 is a little rustic, with harsher tannins and a nose that is a little more closed and less distinct. The agreeable non-Riserva Chianti Classico '96 has more body than formerly, but its fragrances are still too simple and burdened by a few vegetal hints.

Wine	Glasses	Price
● Chianti Cl. Cortevecchia Ris. '95	🍷🍷	5
● Chianti Classico Don Tommaso '96	🍷🍷	5
● Chianti Classico '96	🍷	4
● Chianti Classico '93	🍸🍸	4
● Chianti Classico Don Tommaso '94	🍸🍸	5
● Chianti Classico Don Tommaso '95	🍸🍸	5
● Chianti Classico Ris. '93	🍸🍸	4
● Chianti Cl. Cortevecchia Ris. '94	🍸	4
● Chianti Classico '90	🍸	4
● Chianti Classico '91	🍸	4
● Chianti Classico '92	🍸	4
● Chianti Classico '94	🍸	4
● Chianti Classico '95	🍸	4

S. CASCIANO VAL DI PESA (FI)

Antica Fattoria Machiavelli Serristori

Loc. S. Andrea in Percussina
50026 S. Casciano Val di Pesa (FI)
tel. 0577/989001

Another good showing by the wines from the two wineries Antica Fattoria Machiavelli and Conti Serristori, the two separate firms which the old and famous Serristori di Sant'Andrea in Percussina has spawned. Both are owned by the Gruppo Italiano Vini, which conceived of the former as a producer of excellent wines and the latter as a purveyor of affordable Chianti Classico of good quality. We are more interested in Machiavelli, particularly since no wines were presented to us by Conti Serristori. The most interesting newcomer is a pinot noir cru called Il Principe in honor of Niccolò Machiavelli's celebrated treatise. We tasted two vintages. The '94 is a well-made red wine with good structure, a touch too much acidity, and a bouquet that falls a little short on varietal notes. It seems more like an excellent Tuscan red than a pinot noir. But the '95 is splendid. It's powerful and soft, its fragrances are distinctly redolent of pinot noir grapes and the oak is well incorporated into the bouquet: a distinctly modern wine that resembles certain pinot noirs of the Willamette Valley in Oregon. Three Glasses for a wonderful new wine. The Chianti Classico Fontalle Riserva '95 is excellent with a slightly forward nose but a soft and balanced palate. The cabernet sauvignon, Ser Niccolò Solatio del Tani '94, is somewhat under par, more diluted than other vintages, and less successful on the palate, with a disappointing finish.

Wine	Glasses	Price
● Il Principe '95	🍷🍷🍷	4
● Chianti Classico Fontalle Ris. '95	🍷🍷	4*
● Il Principe '94	🍷🍷	4
● Ser Niccolò Solatio del Tani '94	🍷	5
● Ser Niccolò Solatio del Tani '88	🍸🍸🍸	4*
● Chianti Classico Fontalle Ris. '88	🍸🍸	4
● Chianti Classico Fontalle Ris. '90	🍸🍸	4
● Chianti Classico Fontalle Ris. '93	🍸🍸	4
● Chianti Classico Fontalle Ris. '94	🍸🍸	4
● Ser Niccolò Solatio dei Tani '87	🍸🍸	5
● Ser Niccolò Solatio del Tani '93	🍸🍸	5
● Chianti Classico Conti Serristori Ris. '94	🍸	3*

S. CASCIANO VAL DI PESA (FI)

FATTORIA POGGIOPIANO
VIA DI PISIGNANO, 26/30
50026 S. CASCIANO VAL DI PESA (FI)
TEL. 055/8229629

This is not a repeat performance, but it comes close. The Fattoria Poggiopiano made its debut in the Guide last year and hit the bull's-eye its first go, winning Three Glasses for its Rosso di Sera '95, a super-Tuscan made from sangiovese with a little colorino: an oenological gem devised by Alessandro Bartoli, the owner, and Luca D'Attoma, the young and promising Pisan oenologist. This year the '96 came awfully close but didn't make it. The difference is not great: the two wines are very similar. They both have intensely fruity bouquets, with notes of sour cherry and red currants, with vanilla in the background. Most notably they both have sweet tannins and a remarkable depth on the palate, thanks to a great concentration of extract. But the '96 is a miniature version: it doesn't last as long, and it has a slightly bitter aftertaste, which suggests that the polyphenols, particularly the tannins, are a little oxidated. It is an excellent wine, but it may not last as long. Hence its missing Glass. But we should point out that this estate shows an admirable consistency of quality and fully expresses the varying characteristics of different vintages. Nevertheless, while we have no serious criticism to offer about the Rosso di Sera, we were not altogether happy with the Chianti Classico. The '96 has a forward nose, there doesn't seem to be sufficient body and it comes to a rather hasty conclusion. We think they could do better.

	Wine	Glasses	Price
●	Rosso di Sera '96	🍷🍷	5
●	Chianti Classico '96	🍷	3
●	Rosso di Sera '95	YYY	5
●	Chianti Classico '95	Y	3

S. GIMIGNANO (SI)

BARONCINI
LOC. CASALE, 43
53037 S. GIMIGNANO (SI)
TEL. 0577/940600

How could you not reward such a good wine made just from trebbiano toscano? We refer, of course, to La Faina, made by Bruna and Stefano Baroncini, who, with the '96, have made another significant wine. Made from late-harvest grapes (not more than five thousand kilograms per hectare), La Faina is "white"-fermented and aged in the bottle for at least four months. The result is a deep straw-yellow wine with an aromatic bouquet of ripe fruit reminiscent of roses and vanilla. On the palate, a sweet tone and general balance prevail. In short, a singular and interesting wine. We found the Vernaccia Dometaia slightly less fascinating than in previous years, when it soared to remarkable heights. The '96 vintage was not propitious and the nose is muffled, but it is still a well-structured and full-bodied white wine, with some fruit on the palate. The Vernaccia Poggio ai Cannicci '97 also performs nicely, well-balanced and soft on the palate, with a rather pleasant bitter close. This year's news is the purchase of a farm in the Maremma, which has led to the production of an extremely interesting Morellino di Scansano, the Aia della Macina '97. It has a dark ruby hue and intense red fruit aromas with a characteristic vegetal note, and it displays lots of substance in the mouth, with alcoholic punch and tannins just as you want them. A fine debut. The interesting Spumante Brut wins One Glass.

	Wine	Glasses	Price
○	La Faina '97	🍷🍷	4
○	Baroncini Brut	🍷	3
●	Morellino di Scansano Aia della Macina '97	🍷	3
○	Vernaccia di S. Gimignano Poggio ai Cannicci '97	🍷	2*
○	Vernaccia di S. Gimignano Dometaia Ris. '96	🍷	3
○	Vernaccia di S. Gimignano Dometaia Ris. '93	YY	2*
○	Vernaccia di S. Gimignano Dometaia Ris. '94	YY	3
○	Vernaccia di S. Gimignano Dometaia Ris. '95	YY	3*
●	Cortegiano - Sovestro '95	Y	3

Casa alle Vacche

Loc. Lucignano, 73
53037 S. Gimignano (SI)
tel. 0577/955103

After three years in the Guide Fernando and Lorenzo Ciappi's Pancole estate has consolidated its position as a reliable producer of good wine. The estate consists of thirteen hectares under vine which face east by northeast in one of the best grape-growing areas in S. Gimignano, and has the benefit of the advice of the expert oenologist Luigino Casagrande, and benefits from the serious and correct approach of its owners: these are the preconditions for the four good wines that we tasted this year. The Vernaccia di San Gimignano '97 Crocus almost won Two Glasses, being made from a blend of the best grapes and fermented in barriques. Pale straw yellow in hue, it releases moderately intense floral scents that are followed by a concentrated and fairly long flavor. The finish is still a little disjointed, but we have to admit that our tasting of this and many other wines took place just a few days after their bottling. The Chianti Colli Senesi '97 Cinabro is also good this year, and judging from its cinnabar hue, it bears just the right name. Its nose unfolds in satisfying vegetal aromas that reveal the judicious use of wood and careful craftsmanship. It is round, albeit of medium length, in the mouth. The tannins are less aggressive than usual, in line with the '97 vintage, and we think that this aspect should be nurtured more to make this an even higher quality wine. After a rather flat '96 version, the Vernaccia '97 I Macchioni has recaptured our interest, with scents of almond and a medium body, good construction, and appeal. The Chianti Colli Senesi '97 is wholly typical and pleasant, it too in a softer version than normal.

	Wine	Glasses	Price
●	Chianti Colli Senesi '97	🍷	1*
●	Chianti Colli Senesi Cinabro '97	🍷	3
○	Vernaccia di S. Gimignano Crocus '97	🍷	3
○	Vernaccia di S. Gimignano I Macchioni '97	🍷	2
○	Vernaccia di S. Gimignano '97		2
●	Chianti Colli Senesi '95	🍷 (previous)	1*
●	Chianti Colli Senesi '96	🍷 (previous)	1*
●	Chianti Colli Senesi Cinabro '93	🍷 (previous)	3
●	Chianti Colli Senesi Cinabro '95	🍷 (previous)	3
○	Vernaccia di S. Gimignano '96	🍷 (previous)	2
○	Vernaccia di S. Gimignano Crocus '96	🍷 (previous)	3

S. GIMIGNANO (SI)

Vincenzo Cesani

Loc. Pancole, 82/d
53037 S. Gimignano (SI)
tel. 0577/955084

Here's a good motto for this winery: Not just Vernaccia! In fact, Vincenzo Cesani's obstinate intention to produce good wines is at least equal to our expectation of finding some great reds in the San Gimignano zone, which, in our opinion, has all the potential to produce them. So here's the best local red we tasted this year, which confirms our good impression of last year: Two overflowing Glasses for Vincenzo Cesani's red table wine, Luenzo '96. Anyone who thought the '96 would not do as well as the '95 was neglecting to take into account the scarcity of rain in the Pancole area that year. "For red wine, '96 was better than '95 in Pancole", Vincenzo Cesani kept telling us. Hence beautiful grapes, combined with the usual meticulous care in vineyard and cellar. Made from late-harvested sangiovese and colorino fermented in barriques and aged in the bottle, the wine is a deep ruby red. It has a broad, intense bouquet with attractive notes of vanilla that enhance the distinct aromas of red fruit and blackberry, all reflected on the palate to make an ample, soft, structured and warm wine. The Vernaccia Sanice '97 has come out well. Straw-yellow in color, it displays light fragrances with notes of mint, all well supported by excellent wood; on the palate, consistently with the trend for '97, it is soft and round with a certain overall elegance. The standard Vernaccia '97 is a well-made and quite quaffable wine.

	Wine	Glasses	Price
●	Luenzo '96	🍷🍷	4
○	Vernaccia di S. Gimignano '97	🍷	2
○	Vernaccia di S. Gimignano Sanice '97	🍷	4
●	Luenzo '95	🍷🍷 (previous)	4
●	Chianti Colli Senesi '93	🍷 (previous)	2
●	Chianti Colli Senesi '94	🍷 (previous)	2
○	Vernaccia di S. Gimignano '95	🍷 (previous)	2
○	Vernaccia di S. Gimignano '96	🍷 (previous)	2
○	Vernaccia di S. Gimignano Sanice '95	🍷 (previous)	3
○	Vernaccia di S. Gimignano Sanice '96	🍷 (previous)	4

S. GIMIGNANO (SI)

Guicciardini Strozzi

Fattoria di Cusona
53037 S. Gimignano (SI)
tel. 0577/950028

An estate of such size and historical tradition is virtually forced to produce great wines: "noblesse oblige ", one might almost say. Thus once again this year Roberto Guicciardini and Girolamo Strozzi, with the expert oenological assistance of Vittorio Fiore and Ivaldo Volpini, have offered us a vast range of very interesting wines produced from their 60 hectares of vineyards. Their second Millanni, vintage '95, reclaims the Two Glasses won with its debut vintage. Created to celebrate the thousandth anniversary of the Cusona estate, it is made from sangiovese and other grapes whose identity is a state secret. Vinification follows tradition, with an extremely long maceration and nine months in French oak barriques before further aging in the bottle. The color is dark ruby and the attack on the nose round, with hints of grass and notes of blackberry and wood. On the palate it is concentrated, with lively tannins and a long finish, while the overall quality of its fruit is superior to the '94's. The Vernaccia Perlato '97 has made a welcome return to Two Glasses. Of a brilliant pale straw yellow color, it has a floral nose and a straightforward but dense and balanced body with quite a long finish. The sangiovese table wine Sodole '96 is again very good. Intensely ruby-hued, it offers delicate aromas and a warm, structured palate. We found Cusona's first merlot (including 10% colorino), the Selvascura '96, successful and an easy One Glass winner. It is vinous and varietal on the nose and powerful in the mouth, but not very elegant in this version; we expect improvement.

	Wine	Glasses	Price
●	Millanni '95	🍷🍷	6
○	Vernaccia di S. Gimignano Perlato '97	🍷🍷	4
●	Selvascura '96	🍷	5
●	Sodole '96	🍷	5
○	Vernaccia di S. Gimignano S. Biagio '97	🍷	3
●	994 Millanni '94	🍷🍷 (previous)	6
●	Sodole '91	🍷🍷 (previous)	5
●	Sodole '93	🍷🍷 (previous)	5
○	Vernaccia di S. Gimignano Perlato '94	🍷🍷 (previous)	3
●	Sodole '95	🍷 (previous)	5
○	Vernaccia di S. Gimignano Perlato '96	🍷 (previous)	4

S. GIMIGNANO (SI)

Il Lebbio

Loc. S. Benedetto, 11/c
53037 S. Gimignano (SI)
tel. 0577/944725

Another newcomer to the Guide this year, Il Lebbio is situated in the San Benedetto district northeast of San Gimignano and covers about fifteen hectares, ten of which are under vine. It is owned by Dino Niccolini and his wife Emilia Aureli, who have lived here practically forever, but their sons Luciano and Roberto are the ones in charge of the vineyards and cellar.. They have been producing wine for several years, but it was only in 1991 that they started bottling, and in 1993 they renovated and re-equipped the cellar, which they plan to expand and bring further up to date next year. What we particularly liked from Il Lebbio was I Grottoni '97, which we had already noted last year in the final pages for the region. This is a red wine named after its vineyard and made from 40% montepulciano d'Abruzzo, 40% cabernet sauvignon and 20% merlot. It has a deep ruby hue and a bouquet of some intensity and finesse that features vinous aromas of black currant and raspberry with notes of grass. In the mouth it is full-bodied, tannic and distinctly fruity. It clearly earned its Two Glasses, but that's not all: this wine offers exceptional value for money. The Chianti '97 is good too and had no trouble winning One Glass. It is ruby in hue with fresh and pleasant vinous aromas. It makes the mouth pucker slightly, but is quite drinkable and typical of its kind. The Vernaccia Riserva '96 and the standard Vernaccia '97 are correctly made. A final bulletin: in the cellar there's a red wine maturing, made from ciliegiolo, colorino and sangiovese, and it seems very promising.

	Wine	Glasses	Price
●	I Grottoni '97	🍷🍷	2*
●	Chianti '97	🍷	2
○	Vernaccia di S. Gimignano '97		2
○	Vernaccia di S. Gimignano Ris. '96		3

S. GIMIGNANO (SI)

La Lastra

Loc. Santa Lucia
Via R. De Grada, 9
53037 S. Gimignano (SI)
tel. 0577/941781

"How hard it is to convince my harvesters to start picking the grapes at nine o 'clock in the morning instead of eight!" This remark, this concern that extends even to the percentage of excess moisture, is a fine example of the unwavering and painstaking determination of Nadia Betti and Renato Spanu to produce excellent wines. Nadia and Renato are northerners, she from the Trentino and he from Alto Adige, and both graduates of the Istituto Agrario di San Michele all'Adige who moved to Tuscany about twenty years ago. In its second appearance, the Vernaccia Riserva has again won Two Glasses. The '96 is a brilliant straw yellow color and offers light but elegant aromas of broom and mint with notes of vanilla. On the palate it is structured, round and stylish, a well-executed wine that is a modern but faithful interpretation of vernaccia. The Chianti Colli Senesi '97 is surprisingly rich in fruit. Of a lovely ruby hue, it has a fine bouquet of blackberry and cherry with a light vanilla undertone. Its attack on the palate is gentle but pleasant, with soft tannins and a sweet finish. It's one of the best in the area. The Vernaccia '97 is balanced and correct. "Let the Scirocco, Garbino or Rovaio blow ", intones the 13th-century poet Folgòre da San Gimignano in his "Sonnets for the Months of the Year ", in which Rovaio is the icy north wind. This northern air introduces their red table wine, Rovaio '96, a blend of sangiovese, merlot and cabernet, characterized by an overall equilibrium and tannic docility which differentiate it from almost all its cousins from San Gimignano and Tuscany in general. Of a dark ruby hue, ample and vinous on the nose, with notes of spice and blackberry on the palate, it is structured and soft, with round and light tannins. A somewhat different approach for a San Gimignano red, but most intriguing.

	Wine	Glasses	
○	Vernaccia di S. Gimignano Ris. '96	🍷🍷	3
●	Chianti Colli Senesi '97	🍷	4
●	Rovaio '96	🍷	5
○	Vernaccia di S. Gimignano '97	🍷	3
○	Vernaccia di S. Gimignano Ris. '95	🍸🍸	3
●	Chianti Colli Senesi '95	🍸	4
●	Chianti Colli Senesi '96	🍸	4
●	Rovaio '95	🍸	4
○	Vernaccia di S. Gimignano '96	🍸	3

S. GIMIGNANO (SI)

Tenuta Le Calcinaie

Loc. Monteoliveto, 36
53037 S. Gimignano (SI)
tel. 0577/943007

It was a good year for Tenuta Le Calcinaie, which Simone Santini has been running for several years now. Indeed although its production aims were well calculated (yields of 8 tons for Vernaccia and 4 tons for reds and a lot of care given to the vines), the cellar used to leave something to be desired. Now that this problem has been taken care of, here are four quite good wines, modern and clean in style. The Teodoro '96, a red table wine made from sangiovese and merlot with small amounts of malvasia nera and cabernet, has a deep ruby hue with violet highlights and red fruit aromas with vegetal notes. The tannins are in need of further smoothing, but good structure is apparent: an appealing red wine that should improve with aging. The Vernaccia '97 is a fresh clean wine with a light floral fragrance. It is crisp and balanced on the palate, well-made if not imposing in structure. In short, a Vernaccia that represents the '97 vintage quite faithfully. The Vernaccia '97 Vigna ai Sassi has a little more concentration: there's a hint of vanilla on the nose and a fairly rounded and balanced palate. The Chianti Colli Senesi '97 is interesting, the fruit of a vintage that produced rather soft wines, an unusual characteristic for this type of wine, which, around San Gimignano, tends to be lean, tannic and easy to drink. Le Calcinaie's '97, on the other hand, is rather soft and concentrated with good aromas of blackberry and an unusually vivid color.

	Wine	Glasses	
●	Chianti Colli Senesi '97	🍷	4
●	Teodoro '96	🍷	4
○	Vernaccia di S. Gimignano '97	🍷	3
○	Vernaccia di S. Gimignano Vigna ai Sassi '97	🍷	3
●	Chianti Colli Senesi Geminiano '94	🍸	4
●	Chianti Colli Senesi Geminiano '95	🍸	4
●	Teodoro '94	🍸	4
●	Teodoro '95	🍸	4
○	Vernaccia di S. Gimignano '96	🍸	3
○	Vernaccia di S. Gimignano Vigna ai Sassi '96	🍸	3

Mormoraia

Loc. S. Andrea
53037 S. Gimignano (SI)
tel. 0577/940096

There are certain sunsets viewed from the portico of La Mormoraia, with the Tuscan countryside rolling off towards a horizon punctuated by the towers of San Gimignano, that exemplify what foreign visitors have been in raptures about over the centuries. And the beauty of this landscape also inspired Giuseppe Passoni and Francesca Zago, who have admirably renovated the old buildings (formerly a convent), and imagined and then created wines that keep pace with all these wonders. Their policy is to produce very few wines, but good ones. Its second time out, the Ostrea '96 has retained the best qualities of the '95, placing itself among the best white wines in the region. The vernaccia and chardonnay grapes, fermented without their skins, blended and transferred to barriques, are perfectly fused in a delightful, elegant whole. Of a pale straw yellow, it has delicate fragrances of fruit and sweet wood. It is intense and lingering in the mouth with a vigorous attack and a solid and balanced structure. Franco Bernabei looked after this wine, and you can tell. The standard Vernaccia '97 is quite good and offers fairly intense aromas of ripe fruit and a perfect note of vanilla. The palate reflects the nose, revealing a medium body with a good balance between crispness and the sweetness of the wood (and the sweetness of the Vernaccias of this vintage in general): certainly one of the best '97s. The red Neitea '96, which made an excellent debut last year, wasn 't ready to appear at our tastings, held somewhat earlier, this time, so we 'll have to review it in our next edition.

	Wine	Glasses	
○	Ostrea '96	▼▼	4
○	Vernaccia di San Gimignano '97	▼	3
●	Neitea '95	▽▽	4
○	Ostrea '95	▽▽	4
○	Vernaccia di San Gimignano '96	▽	3

S. GIMIGNANO (SI)

Palagetto

Via Monteoliveto, 46
53037 S. Gimignano (SI)
tel. 0577/943090 - 942098

Luano Niccolai's Azienda Agricola Palagetto has been run since its founding by his son Simone, who has done wonders in the course of just a few years. It consists of a total of 17 hectares under vine divided into three separate properties, all near San Gimignano, and a modern and well-equipped cellar, and it enjoys the expert advice of the oenologist Paolo Salvi. At this year's tastings we found the Sottobosco '96 particularly interesting. It is a sangiovese, with just 5% cabernet sauvignon, aged for one year in barriques, and it vaunts a lovely dark ruby hue. Notes of bell pepper and spice and a hint of vanilla emerge on the nose. On the palate it is warm, structured and rich in alcohol (almost 14%), with a slightly bitter finish. It seems a well-made wine that should continue to develop in the bottle for another four or five years. The quite good Vernaccia '97 Santa Chiara, a pale straw yellow in the glass, offers a faint fresh floral fragrance, followed by a pleasing palate characterized by green almond essence. The '97 Vernaccia is good too, with its mild aromas of flowers and ripe fruit, medium body and restrained acidity.

	Wine	Glasses	
●	Sottobosco '96	▼	4
○	Vernaccia di S. Gimignano '97	▼	3
○	Vernaccia di S. Gimignano V. Santa Chiara '97	▼	3
●	Chianti Colli Senesi '95	▽	3
●	Palagetto Rosso '	▽	2
●	Sottobosco '94	▽	3
●	Sottobosco '95	▽	4
○	Vernaccia di S. Gimignano '96	▽	3
○	Vernaccia di S. Gimignano Ris. '95	▽	4
○	Vernaccia di S. Gimignano V. Santa Chiara '95	▽	3
○	Vernaccia di S. Gimignano V. Santa Chiara '96	▽	3

S. GIMIGNANO (SI)

GIOVANNI PANIZZI
LOC. RACCIANO
S. MARGHERITA
53037 S. GIMIGNANO (SI)
TEL. 0577/941576 - 02/90938796

Gianni Panizzi has got it right once again. His Vernaccia Riserva has now won Two very full Glasses five times since 1991. Vines near Santa Margherita, with fine exposure and lots of air, in tufaceous clayey soil, very low yields per hectare of 100% vernaccia grapes, handpicking and loading in crates, fermentation in Allier and Nevers barriques for 12 months, 13.3% alcohol content, 6.76% total acidity, 23.35% extracts: this is the résumé of the great wine made by Gianni Panizzi with the technical advice of Salvatore Maule. The '96 vintage shows a fine, vivid straw yellow hue. Intense and elegant aromas of ripe fruit with perfectly judged vanilla are followed by an intriguing, full-bodied, balanced and long-lingering palate. The Chianti Colli Senesi '96 is also in its best form ever, and earns One Glass. Of a deep ruby color tinged with violet, it has a headily fruity nose with an undertone of vanilla. It is quite soft and fruity in the mouth and fairly well-balanced. The Bianco di Gianni '96 is a newcomer, made from vernaccia and oak-aged chardonnay, after both are fermented without their skins. The result is a pale straw yellow wine with intense aromas including vegetal and fruity notes and a distinct accent of toasty oak. The palate is good and fairly persistent, but the wood is still a bit discordant. The Ceraso '97, half-way between a rosé and a red wine, is good. Rich in fruit and powerfully heady, it is nonetheless fresh and enchanting. The standard Vernaccia '97 also maintains standards.

	Wine	Glasses	Price
○	Vernaccia di S. Gimignano Ris. '96	🍷🍷	5
○	Bianco di Gianni '96	🍷	5
●	Ceraso '97	🍷	3
●	Chianti Colli Senesi '96	🍷	4
○	Vernaccia di S. Gimignano '97	🍷	4
○	Vernaccia di S. Gimignano Ris. '91	🍷🍷 (empty)	5
○	Vernaccia di S. Gimignano Ris. '92	🍷🍷 (empty)	5
○	Vernaccia di S. Gimignano Ris. '93	🍷🍷 (empty)	5
○	Vernaccia di S. Gimignano Ris. '94	🍷🍷 (empty)	5
○	Vernaccia di S. Gimignano Ris. '95	🍷🍷 (empty)	5

S. GIMIGNANO (SI)

FATTORIA PARADISO
LOC. STRADA, 21/A
53037 S. GIMIGNANO (SI)
TEL. 0577/941500

There 's no doubt about it: Graziella Cappelli and Vasco Cetti have a way with chardonnay. For three years now, with the help of the oenologist Paolo Caciornia, they have been presenting us with a wine of surprising depth, and this time it may well be the best ever. (Although we would not wish to slight the Paradiso Chardonnay, vintage '92, tasted again a few days ago and still in excellent form.) Lo Cha, as it is to be called henceforth, is a straw yellow wine lightly tinged with gold; the intensely fruity fragrances include notes of peach and vanilla. It has structure, body, length and well-judged wood. The Saxa Calida '95, a red table wine made from merlot and cabernet, is on an upward curve and just missed Two Glasses. It has remarkable concentration, a dark ruby hue and a vegetal attack on the fruity nose with notes of red currants and spice. It is full and dense in the mouth, but the tannins are still a bit rough and the finish a little bitter. It is a powerful wine that needs only to tame its own aggressiveness. The '95 vintage of their other thoroughbred red, the Paterno II, is very good. Named after its vineyard, it is made from late-harvested 100% sangiovese macerated for four weeks. It displays a lovely dark ruby hue and a bouquet of wild fruit and blackberry, with sweet wood and spice. It's succulent in the mouth and there are meaty tannins on the finish. It is definitely getting better. The Vernaccia Biscondola '97 is also good, but, although it scored well, it didn't get Two Glasses because the vintage didn't quite live up to expectations. Its aromas are appealing and it has structure. As usual, there 's a fine performance from their standard Vernaccia, and from the Chianti Colli Senesi and the Vernaccia Brut, which is the best in the zone.

	Wine	Glasses	Price
○	Lo Cha '96	🍷🍷	4
●	Chianti Colli Senesi '97	🍷	2
●	Paterno II '95	🍷	4
●	Saxa Calida '95	🍷	4
○	Vernaccia Brut	🍷	4
○	Vernaccia di S. Gimignano '97	🍷	3
○	Vernaccia di S. Gimignano Biscondola '96	🍷	4
○	Chardonnay '94	🍷🍷 (empty)	4
○	Chardonnay '95	🍷🍷 (empty)	4
○	Vernaccia di S. Gimignano Biscondola '95	🍷🍷 (empty)	4
●	Chianti Colli Senesi '96	🍷 (empty)	2
●	Paterno II '94	🍷 (empty)	4
●	Saxa Calida '94	🍷 (empty)	4

S. GIMIGNANO (SI)

FATTORIA PONTE A RONDOLINO
LOC. CASALE, 19
53037 S. GIMIGNANO (SI)
TEL. 0577/940143

There are estates and producers who pave the way that many others follow sooner or later. This is true of Enrico Teruzzi, to whom much of the credit is due for the renaissance of Vernaccia di San Gimignano in the mid-'80s. Hence we are watching with considerable interest the transformation of the Terre di Tufi into a table wine (however, the blend has remained virtually unchanged, as has the quality, which has improved if anything) and the attention that Enrico Teruzzi is newly focusing on the oenological challenges posed by the area. Not to mention newly acquired vineyards and vines new-planted in splendid positions, and also one of the best-equipped cellars in Italy. So hats off to the over 200 thousands bottles of Terre di Tufi that are excellent year after year. The '96 vintage has a brilliant straw yellow hue and soft, fruity and elegant aromas. It is crisp, well-balanced and full-bodied on the palate, with a pleasing undertone of vanilla and a long finish. It's a wine with something to it and a delight to drink. The Carmen '96, made from trebbiano, vermentino, vernaccia di San Gimignano, and sangiovese fermented without its skin, is of a straw yellow hue, and has a delicate nose with floral nuances of hawthorn blossom and vanilla. It has medium body, but is well-balanced. Unusual as ever, the Peperino '97 has a pale ruby color and a headily spicy nose with a distinct note of cherry. It is structured on the palate and well-balanced by acidity. The standard Vernaccia '97 and the Vigna a Rondolino are quite up to par.

	Wine	Glasses	Price
○	Carmen '96	▼▼	4
○	Terre di Tufi '96	▼▼	5
●	Peperino '97	▼	3
○	Vernaccia di S. Gimignano '97	▼	3
○	Vernaccia di S. Gimignano Vigna a Rondolino '97	▼	4
○	Carmen '94	▽▽	4
○	Carmen '95	▽▽	4
○	Terre di Tufi '92	▽▽	5
○	Terre di Tufi '93	▽▽	5
○	Terre di Tufi '94	▽▽	5
○	Terre di Tufi '95	▽▽	5
●	Peperino '95	▽	3
○	Vernaccia di S. Gimignano '96	▽	3

S. GIMIGNANO (SI)

FATTORIA SAN DONATO
LOC. S. DONATO, 6
53037 S. GIMIGNANO (SI)
TEL. 0577/941616

About four kilometers from San Gimignano, along the road that leads to Volterra, you can find the Fattoria di San Donato in the medieval village named after the same saint, its vineyards extending over 15 hectares of sunny, well-aired slopes about 300 meters above sea level. Estate methods have become more modern in the last few years, as we have had occasion to note. After a couple of years of good scores, the owner Umberto Fenzi and the young San Gimignano oenologist Paolo Salvi have given us a wine that breaks the Two Glass barrier: the Vernaccia '97 Selezione. Straw-colored, it has a good impact on the nose, with aromas of fruit and vanilla. On the palate it is concentrated and rich in alcohol, with well-judged wood. The least successful thing about this excellent wine is, in our opinion, the shape of the bottle. The Vernaccia Riserva '96 is again good, indeed one of the best of its vintage. It has a deep straw yellow color, floral aromas and hints of vanilla with a light note of toasty oak. It is structured and soft on the palate, with appropriate wood and a traditional almond finish. They round off the line with the quite acceptable Vernaccia '97, a deep straw yellow-hued wine with aromas of broom. It does not linger in the mouth, but it is fairly substantial and highly drinkable.

	Wine	Glasses	Price
○	Vernaccia di S. Gimignano Sel. '97	▼▼	4
○	Vernaccia di S. Gimignano '97	▼	3
○	Vernaccia di S. Gimignano Ris. '96	▼	4
●	Chianti Colli Senesi '95	▽	2
●	Chianti Colli Senesi '96	▽	2
○	Vernaccia di S. Gimignano '96	▽	3
○	Vernaccia di S. Gimignano Ris. '95	▽	4
○	Vernaccia di S. Gimignano Sel. '96	▽	4
○	Vin Santo	▽	5

Signano

Via di San Matteo, 101
53037 S. Gimignano (SI)
tel. 0577/940164

This was quite an interesting year for Manrico and Ascanio Biagini's estate, which has done very well with the Vernaccia '96 Riserva and the Selezione as well as with the Poggiarelli cru and the standard version, both '97s. Indeed, the Selezione '96 won Two Glasses and is the best yet produced by Signano. Made with the expert assistance of the oenologist Paolo Salvi from late-harvested vernaccia grapes fermented in Allier and Nevers barriques for a year, it is further aged in the bottle for six months. Its color is a straw yellow and it has an ample, aromatic nose with a light note of vanilla and delicate toasty nuances. Its attack on the palate is sweet, fleshy and very soft with well-judged wood and a good aromatic finish. The Vernaccia Riserva '96 maintains standards. It is redolent of ripe fruit and honey, fairly soft on the palate and typically almondy on the finish. The Vernaccia Poggiarelli '97 has kept its characteristic crispness, although coming from a vintage that did not especially favor this quality in white wines. Of a pale straw yellow hue, it offers delicate floral aromas and the crisp palate typical of the wine. The Chianti Colli Senesi '96 Poggiarelli, almost entirely sangiovese, is good. It has an attractive ruby color and a heady fragrance of red fruit; then it is soft in the mouth, and its finish is quite pleasing and long.

	Wine	Glasses	Price
○	Vernaccia di S. Gimignano Sel. '96	▼▼	4
●	Chianti Colli Senesi Poggiarelli '96	▼	4
○	Vernaccia di S. Gimignano Poggiarelli '97	▼	3
○	Vernaccia di S. Gimignano Ris. '96	▼	3
●	Chianti Colli Senesi Poggiarelli '93	▽	2
●	Chianti Colli Senesi Poggiarelli '94	▽	3
●	Chianti Colli Senesi Poggiarelli '95	▽	4
●	Chianti Colli Senesi Signano '94	▽	1*
○	Vernaccia di S. Gimignano Poggiarelli '96	▽	3
○	Vernaccia di S. Gimignano Sel. '95	▽	4

F.lli Vagnoni

Loc. Pancole, 82
53037 S. Gimignano (SI)
tel. 0577/955077

The Vernaccia Mocali '97, made from the best grapes grown at the vineyard called Il Mulino, has for some time been the top of the line at Gigi Vagnoni's dynamic winery, as well as being one of the best wines from San Gimignano. For a few years this estate has had all it takes to make good wines: excellent vineyards, a well-equipped cellar and the advice of the top-rank oenologist Salvatore Maule. The barrique-fermented Vernaccia Mocali '97 has a deep straw yellow color verging on gold; its nose offers intense ripe fruit and vanilla aromas with a distinct note of toasty oak (our tasting took place just a few days after the assemblage). On the palate it is full-bodied, structured, long-lasting and balanced. The standard Vernaccia '97 is one of the absolute best, displaying a pale straw hue and clean, distinct floral aromas. On the palate it is fairly concentrated, rich in glycerin, soft and balanced without losing its crispness. It's a good bottle in a year that tended to produce Vernaccias that were soft but not very fresh. The red I Sodi Lunghi, made from sangiovese, canaiolo and cabernet, is up to par. Ruby-hued, it has fairly intense red berry aromas and some structure on the palate, but its tannins are not yet very soft, perhaps because of their youth. This is something to work on in a wine that, in fact, leaves room for improvement. The '97 version of the Chianti Colli Senesi, on the other hand, is softer than usual: it is of a lovely purplish-red color with heady aromas and an inviting refreshing flavor. As usual, the Rosato is in a category of its own, like a red in structure, and a perfect accompaniment to local salamis.

	Wine	Glasses	Price
○	Vernaccia di S. Gimignano Mocali '97	▼▼	4
●	Chianti Colli Senesi '97	▼	3
●	I Sodi Lunghi '96	▼	4
○	Vernaccia di S. Gimignano '97	▼	3
⊙	Rosato di S. Gimignano '97		2
○	Vernaccia di S. Gimignano Mocali '94	▽▽	3
○	Vernaccia di S. Gimignano Mocali '95	▽▽	4
○	Vernaccia di S. Gimignano Mocali '96	▽▽	4
●	Chianti Colli Senesi '95	▽	3
●	I Sodi Lunghi '94	▽	4
●	I Sodi Lunghi '95	▽	4

S. PANCRAZIO (LU)

La Badiola
Via del Parco, 10
55100 S. Pancrazio (LU)
tel. 0583/30633

After several years ' absence La Badiola, one of the most interesting wine estates of the Colline Lucchesi, is happily back in the Guide. This is a winery to remember: it manages to produce excellent wines at unbeatable prices. Four wines were presented and each one is well made and got a good score. The best is the Vigna Flora '96, a cabernet and merlot blend that deserved its Two Glasses for its impeccable balance and the purity of its fruit. The aromas are distinct and intense, if perhaps a bit too vegetal. The palate however is soft, rounded, consistent and pleasing. The interesting white Stoppielle '97 offers agreeable straightforward aromas, with notes of white fruit and a delicate hint of wood; on the palate it is full-bodied, clean and balanced. The Colline Lucchesi Rosso '97 is quite successful; we particularly liked its direct, sound nose with notes of red fruit and pepper and vegetal hints. Its palate, although light, is well-balanced and corresponds to the nose. To conclude, the Colline Lucchesi Bianco is properly made and substantial.

●	Vigna Flora '96	🍷🍷	3*
○	Colline Lucchesi Bianco '97	🍷	2*
●	Colline Lucchesi Rosso '97	🍷	2*
○	Stoppielle '97	🍷	3
○	Vigna Flora '92	🍸🍸	3
●	Vigna Flora '93	🍸🍸	3
●	Colline Lucchesi Rosso '93	🍸	2

SCANSANO (GR)

Erik Banti
Loc. Fosso dei Mulini
58054 Scansano (GR)
tel. 0564/508006

We used to call him Erik the Viking, because he has certainly crossed the water, but never following in the wake of others or relying on propitious winds or the breezes from terra firma. Erik Banti has always preferred to sail upwind, beset by high waves and impending storms, because if you really believe in an idea, or way of life, then there is no obstacle you can 't overcome, no problem too great: if you want get there, you do. And he was the first one to get there and be able to say "Land ho! ", the first, at any rate, in the Maremma, where wine was very different fifteen years ago. He was the precursor who showed the way and shook the world of wine with bottles that have by now passed into the annals of history. On occasion we have scolded Erik for a use of new barriques that seemed excessive to us. For the last couple of years his wines, while retaining their marked terroir nature, have been more balanced and elegant, particularly in their incorporation of oak. This year we especially enjoyed the Aquilaia '96, a wine with exquisitely finished tannins and long-lasting flavor that fully deserves Two Glasses. Another good wine is the Ciabatta, with delectable notes of black cherry, and the Riserva '96, with its "sweet " tannins and perfect softness. At the moment, the Morellino '97 lags a bit behind.

●	Aquilaia '96	🍷🍷	4
●	Ciabatta '95	🍷	4
●	Morellino di Scansano '97	🍷	3
●	Morellino di Scansano Ris. '96	🍷	3
●	Aquilaia '90	🍸🍸	4*
●	Aquilaia '94	🍸🍸	4
●	Aquilaia '95	🍸🍸	4
●	Ciabatta '90	🍸🍸	4
●	Morellino di Scansano '94	🍸🍸	3
●	Aquilaia '89	🍸	4
●	Aquilaia '92	🍸	4
●	Ciabatta '92	🍸	4
●	Ciabatta '94	🍸	4
●	Morellino di Scansano '90	🍸	3
●	Morellino di Scansano '93	🍸	3

SINALUNGA (SI)

TENUTA FARNETA
LOC. FARNETA, 161
53048 SINALUNGA (SI)
TEL. 0577/631025

The bittersweet tradition of the Farneta estate, one of the most important in Tuscany, rolls on. Their best offerings are, once again, their two top wines, the Bongoverno and the Bentivoglio: well-made, clean and excellent red wines. The bitter side of the story involves, as usual, the second line, the Bianco, the Rosato and, to a lesser extent, the Chianti, correctly executed but, once again, not in keeping with the reputation of the estate. Let's start with the top of the bill. Bongoverno and Bentivoglio, both made exclusively from sangiovese, were presented this year in their '94 and '95 vintage versions respectively. The former obviously has greater weight and structure, more aromatic depth and richness of flavor. Nevertheless we can also say that it is less wonderful than its predecessors, partly due to the mediocre weather that year in Tuscany. Somewhat oak-dominated and substantial, if not extraordinarily so, it has a slightly vegetal nuance on the palate, not uncommon for wines of this vintage. The Bentivoglio is the supple and more easily drinkable counterpart. Fruity (with very simple primary notes of fruit) and not perfectly distinct on the nose, it has a pleasant, direct quaffability. As we suggested above, both the Farneta Bianco, grassy, dry and rough, and the Chianti are less convincing. The latter, although not very substantial, has in its favor lovely fruit and impeccable cleanness.

	Wine	Glasses	Price
●	Bongoverno '94	🍷🍷 (black)	6
●	Bentivoglio '95	🍷 (black)	2*
●	Chianti '97	🍷 (black)	2
○	Farneta Bianco '97		2
●	Bentivoglio '89	🍷🍷	6
●	Bentivoglio '91	🍷🍷	4
●	Bongoverno '85	🍷🍷	6
●	Bongoverno '86	🍷🍷	6
●	Bongoverno '88	🍷🍷	6
●	Bongoverno '90	🍷🍷	6
●	Bongoverno '91	🍷🍷	6
●	Bongoverno '92	🍷🍷	6
●	Bongoverno '93	🍷🍷	6
●	Bentivoglio '93	🍷	2
●	Bentivoglio '94	🍷	2*

SINALUNGA (SI)

CASTELLO DI FARNETELLA
FRAZ. FARNETELLA
RACCORDO AUTOSTRADALE
SIENA-BETTOLLE, KM 37
53040 SINALUNGA (SI)
TEL. 0577/663520

Born in the shadow of Felsina, one of the most celebrated estates in Tuscany, the Castello di Farnetella is carving out its own niche and acquiring ever more respect and renown. It has the same philosophy (Giuseppe Mazzocolin), the same expert guidance (Franco Bernabei) and the same passionate quest for quality. Last year the pick of the pack was the Sauvignon, which is similar in the '96 vintage presented this year, once again fragrant and flavorful, but with less extract. The Nero di Nubi '94, a pure pinot noir, offers elegance of bouquet, with a marked presence of oak (in a decidedly toasty note), but also a less focused nose and a somewhat anemic palate, compared with the structure of previous vintages. The Chianti Colli Senesi, on the other hand, was a pleasant surprise, a red wine that is usually a little lighter and made for easy drinking, but in good form in the '96: ruby in hue, it offers clear, fruity notes and delightful hints of spice. On the palate it is full-bodied, clean and soft: a really well-made red that also does justice to an occasionally neglected denomination. But this year the estate's best red is the Poggio Granoni '93, which walks off with Three Glasses for its debut performance. Predominantly sangiovese with some cabernet, merlot and syrah, bottled exclusively in one-and-a-half-liter magnums, it has an intense ruby hue. Its bouquet, of great finesse and complexity, offers sensual aromas of red fruit, while the palate displays a firm underlying structure with excellent balance and a fantastically long finish. We have witnessed the birth of a great red wine.

	Wine	Glasses	Price
●	Poggio Granoni '93	🍷🍷🍷 (black)	5
●	Chianti Colli Senesi '96	🍷🍷 (black)	3
●	Nero di Nubi '94	🍷 (black)	5
○	Sauvignon '96	🍷 (black)	4
○	Sauvignon '91	🍷🍷	4
○	Sauvignon '95	🍷🍷	4
●	Chianti Colli Senesi '91	🍷	3*
●	Nero di Nubi '92	🍷	5
●	Nero di Nubi '93	🍷	5
○	Sauvignon '92	🍷	4
○	Sauvignon '93	🍷	4
○	Sauvignon '94	🍷	4

SOIANA (PI)

ELYANE & BRUNO MOOS
VIA PIER CAPPONI, 98
56030 SOIANA (PI)
TEL. 0587/654180

Once again Bruno and Elyane Moos' wines are generally very good, although there is no outstanding champion. Their most promising offering, which came close to winning Two Glasses, is the sangiovese Fontestina '95. It has an intense color between garnet and ruby and a nose of some depth, with aromas of ripe dark fruit and sour cherry jam. Its impact on the palate is rich in alcohol, the acidity is contained and the tannins are mature; the finish is neither long nor short. The Soianello '95, mostly sangiovese with some other red grapes from the Moos vineyards, is similar in quality but slightly different in style. The color is of a lovely intensity, as is its bouquet, which displays aromas ranging from wild berries to earth and tobacco. On the palate it is dense, with evident tannins and a still somewhat hard finish. The Fontestina '94 also got One Glass, but a smaller one. It is quite good, if not very elegant, on the nose, with notes of dark fruit, preserves and vanilla; it reveals a certain character on the palate, but the roughness of the tannins reduces its balance and one's pleasure.

Wine	Glasses	Price
● Fontestina '94	🍷	4
● Fontestina '95	🍷	4
● Soianello '95	🍷	3
● Elige '94	🍷	4
● Fontestina '93	🍷	4
● Soianello '93	🍷	3
● Soianello '94	🍷	3
● Soianello '96	🍷	3
○ Soiano '94	🍷	2
○ Vio '94	🍷	2

SOVANA (GR)

SASSOTONDO
LOC. PIANI DI CONATI, 52
58010 SOVANA (GR)
TEL. 0546/614218

The policy of our Guide has always been to make space for quality, for those who labor dedicatedly in the vineyard and are consequently rewarded for their efforts, making a name for themselves. We tend to be on the lookout for new developments and are delighted when we make a discovery. But space is limited and we cannot write about everyone we'd like to mention, although we make a special effort for newcomers. This year, in the Maremma, we tasted the wines from a new estate, Sassotondo, which knows what it's about and produces eminently respectable wines. Sassotondo is run according to organic farming principles by Carla Benini and Edoardo Ventimiglia, assisted in the vineyards by Remigio Bordini and in the cellar by Paolo Caciorgna and the renowned Attilio Pagli. Of the 72 hectares they own, approximately eight are taken up by the vineyards. The cellar, carved out of the tufa, has been completely redone and provided with state-of-the-art equipment. The results are a Bianco di Pitigliano that is quite drinkable, crisp and pleasant, and, more notably, a red made from ciliegiolo and alicante, Sassotondo, still headily young but well-made and balanced, with delectable fruit. They have many plans for the future (sangiovese and merlot in particular) that sound very interesting. A final note of praise for a modern, professional and apt use of graphics on the label. Image counts, and how! Congratulations, Carla and Edoardo!

Wine	Glasses	Price
○ Bianco di Pitigliano '97	🍷	3
● Sassotondo Rosso '97	🍷	3

SUVERETO (LI)

GUALDO DEL RE
LOC. NOTRI, 77
57028 SUVERETO (LI)
TEL. 0565/829888 - 829361

This year's tastings were probably the most satisfying that Gualdo del Re has ever provided for us. The quality of the wines was consistently good, without lapses, and their leading wine, the Val di Cornia Riserva '95, advanced to Two Glasses. This promotion can be attributed to its concentration, both of bouquet, with notes of preserves and sweet tobacco, and of flavor, with rounded ripe tannins and a finish not wanting in style.. The Federico Primo '95, a cabernet, merlot and sangiovese blend, came very close to Two Glasses. This is a wine of moderate intensity but fine execution, with notes of dark fruit and roasting coffee on the nose, and soft, balanced and agreeable in the mouth. The Valentina '97, a monovarietal vermentino, has risen again to its rightful level, with a rounded structure and ripe fruitiness. The flavor of the Pinot Bianco '97 is expressive and well-defined, and it displays fullness of body and a touch more sinew than recent versions. We finish with the two Val di Cornias: the Rosso is admirable for its cleanness, good fruit and the sweetness of its tannins, and the Bianco for its overall correctness.

●	Val di Cornia Gualdo del Re Ris. '95	🍷🍷	5
●	Federico Primo '95	🍷	5
○	Pinot Bianco '97	🍷	3
●	Val di Cornia Rosso '97	🍷	2*
○	Vigna Valentina '97	🍷	3
○	Val di Cornia Bianco '97		2
●	Federico Primo '93	🍷🍷	5
○	Vigna Valentina '95	🍷🍷	2*
●	Federico Primo '94	🍷	4
○	Pinot Bianco '96	🍷	3
○	Val di Cornia Bianco '96	🍷	2
●	Val di Cornia Gualdo del Re '92	🍷	5
●	Val di Cornia Gualdo del Re '93	🍷	5
●	Val di Cornia Gualdo del Re '94	🍷	5

SUVERETO (LI)

MONTEPELOSO
LOC. MONTEPELOSO, 82
57028 SUVERETO (LI)
TEL. 0565/828180

In the course of just a few years, Montepeloso has achieved a level of success and a renown in the world of wine that no one could have imagined a short time ago. It's a little like the way you go about rediscovering old treasures buried among the odds and ends in the attic: all you need is someone to put everything in order. Thus, with increasing frequency in a variety of areas and individual estates, natural potential is being revealed with the happy result that excellent wines are created in unsuspected places. Montepeloso is a case in point, and Nardo has become its flagship. Astutely blending the strong sangiovese produced by the soil of Suvereto with a portion of cabernet sauvignon, they have realized this characterful red wine, a bit wayward at times, but genuinely expressive. Its encouraging appearance is dark and concentrated, so the intensity of the nose is not surprising, but the richness of aromas is: black fruit gives the note and is joined by vegetal, mineral (typical for this zone), animal and smoky tones; it's a rich but somewhat disorganized bouquet. On the other hand, its palate requires no interpretative effort: soft, powerful, continuous, with an excellent polyphenolic density. Their other wines, two Val di Cornias, are simple, well made, impeccably correct but rather less than what we had hoped.

●	Nardo '95	🍷🍷	5
○	Val di Cornia Bianco '97		3
●	Val di Cornia Rosso '96		3
●	Val di Cornia Rosso Montepeloso '95	🍷🍷	4
●	Nardo '94	🍷	5
●	Val di Cornia Rosso Montepeloso '94	🍷	4

SUVERETO (LI)

Tua Rita

Loc. Notri, 81
57028 Suvereto (LI)
tel. 0565/829237

The numerous admirers of this Suvereto winery can draw a sigh of relief: within a few years they will not have to resort to formal combat to win a precious bottle of Redigaffi or Giusto di Notri. The news from Tua Rita is that as soon as the newly planted vines bear appropriate fruit, the available bottles of the two winery gems may actually increase tenfold. Meanwhile the estate has walked off with its third consecutive Three Glasses, this time for the Redigaffi '96, a meaty and beautifully structured wine that shows how well the immigrant merlot has become integrated around Suvereto. The typically potent alcohol provided by this grape is in fact perfectly blended with the richness of the fruit and the tannic texture.
Consequently one has a sensation of great volume and, at the same time, of depth, for which both its color, dark and very intense, and its aromas, with abundant black fruit and roasting coffee, are a preparation. This time the Giusto di Notri '96 plays second fiddle. It is a blend of cabernet and merlot with a no less robust and concentrated palate, but a slightly unfocused nose featuring an excessively earthy tone. The very successful Sangiovese Perlato del Bosco '96 is sound and intense on the nose, with notes of blackberry, cocoa and spice, and then dense and well-balanced in the mouth. The Sileno '97 is not quite up to its usual high standards. The Perlato Bianco '97 is correct and straightforward.

●	Redigaffi '96	🍷🍷🍷	6
●	Giusto di Notri '96	🍷🍷	5
●	Perlato del Bosco Rosso '96	🍷🍷	4
○	Perlato del Bosco Bianco '97	🍷	3
○	Sileno '97		4
●	Giusto di Notri '94	🍸🍸🍸	5
●	Giusto di Notri '95	🍸🍸🍸	5
●	Giusto di Notri '92	🍸🍸	5
●	Giusto di Notri '93	🍸🍸	5
●	Redigaffi '95	🍸🍸	6
○	Sileno '95	🍸🍸	4
○	Sileno '96	🍸🍸	4
○	Perlato del Bosco Bianco '96	🍸	3
●	Perlato del Bosco Rosso '95	🍸	4
○	Val di Cornia Bianco '96	🍸	2

SUVERETO (LI)

Villa Monte Rico

Loc. Poggio al Cerro
57028 Suvereto (LI)
tel. 0565/829550

While sangiovese occasionally provokes controversy, this variety is and remains the undisputed prince of red grapes in Tuscany. Coastal areas, like the Val di Cornia, have witnessed the growing success of important international varietals such as cabernet and merlot in recent years, and the beginnings of a dismissive neglect of sangiovese. But some excellent results more recently produced with this native grape are gradually focusing attention on it again. At Monte Rico faith in the qualities of this typical Tuscan grape has never wavered. The estate now belongs to Signora Reichenberg, who continues with keen determination the work started about ten years ago by her late husband. This year we tasted two vintages, the '94 and '95, of the winery's leading wine, the Villa Monte Rico. This is a pure sangiovese that has produced uneven results, probably because of the varying characteristics of the two vintages. While the '94 clearly shows signs of precocious evolution, with very forward aromas, and dry tannins dominating the palate, the '95 is in splendid form and bodes well for the future. It has a lively ruby hue, intense and distinct aromas with black fruit, especially blackberry and plum, in evidence, enhanced by sweet accents of vanilla. Its entry on the palate is soft and dense, and a proper and elegant progression leads to a long convincing finish.

●	Villa Monte Rico '95	🍷🍷	5
●	Villa Monte Rico '94		4

TAVARNELLE VAL DI PESA (FI)

PODERE LA CAPPELLA

LOC. S. DONATO IN POGGIO
STRADA CERBAIA, 10/A
50028 TAVARNELLE VAL DI PESA (FI)
TEL. 055/8072727

A fine debut in the Guide for La Cappella, owned by the Rossinis, husband and wife. The splendid performance of the pure sangiovese Corbezzolo '96, also a debutant, is largely responsible. Their vineyards cover just under five hectares, planted mainly in sangiovese, with a small quantity of merlot (which gives rise to another wine, Cantico, not ready for this year's tastings) and a little vermentino. The distinguished oenologist Luca D 'Attoma is in charge of the technical side, and the aim of everyone involved is apparently to create excellent wines. The Corbezzolo went way over the minimum score required for Two Glasses, clearly suggesting the possibility of a yet more glorious future, perhaps even for the '97 vintage. It has an excellent, highly concentrated color, and a bouquet that reveals depth of fruit and a modern style, confirmed by the notes of mint and toasty oak. On the palate it displays confident power, softness, good structure and a fresh acidity that makes it particularly drinkable. The Chianti Classico Querciolo '96 did well too, getting very close to Two Glasses. On the nose oak-derived notes of vanilla have the upper hand at the moment, while it is lively, compact and dense in its progression on the palate, with sweet, soft tannins. The Vermentino '97 is less convincing, but we 're generally very pleased indeed with this first appearance of La Cappella.

●	Corbezzolo '96	🍷🍷	5
●	Chianti Classico Querciolo '96	🍷	4
○	Vermentino '97		3

TAVARNELLE VAL DI PESA (FI)

MONTECCHIO

VIA MONTECCHIO, 4
50020 TAVARNELLE VAL DI PESA (FI)
TEL. 055/8072907

Again this year there are many wineries that are back in the Guide after an absence or are appearing for the first time. One of these debutants is Montecchio, a vast estate in the San Donato zone. It has been owned for about the last 25 years by Ivo Nuti, who is very keen but mostly involved in a totally different endeavor; hence a few years ago he decided to entrust viticulture and wine-making to the expert direction of the oenologist Stefano Chioccioli. There are 26 hectares of vineyards, two-thirds of which are planted with old vines that have been reorganized and regrafted as well as possible, and include sangiovese and a little cabernet; the remaining third has a completely new look: it was planted this year with 7 thousand vines per hectare, divided equally between sangiovese and merlot. So the best is yet to come, but considering how tired the old vines are, we must confess that results are already quite good. They probably couldn 't be any better. The Chianti Classico Riserva '95 has a ruby hue of lovely intensity and a rather elegant and well-defined nose with notes of bell pepper, black fruit and noble wood. Its attack on the palate is a little "green ", acidity is perceptible and concentration medium, but it develops steadily to a long smooth finish. The Chianti Classico '96 is very similar, both on the nose, which also features vegetal notes, and on the palate, which is lean rather than broad. These two wines compensate for insufficient flesh, fat and ripe fruit with a harmonious, elegant and very pleasing palate.

●	Chianti Classico '96	🍷🍷	4
●	Chianti Classico Ris. '95	🍷🍷	4

TAVARNELLE VAL DI PESA (FI)

POGGIO AL SOLE
LOC. SAMBUCA VAL DI PESA
50028 TAVARNELLE VAL DI PESA (FI)
TEL. 055/8071504

There's no doubt about it: this is one of the finest wineries in the Chianti Classico zone. It just missed winning Three Glasses for at least two of its wines, and we feel sure that if they carry on with the care they 've been showing, great rewards will be theirs in the future. The vineyards are quite high up with, as the estate name suggests (it means Sunny Knoll), excellent exposure. The results are wines that are refractory at first, but characterful, with richly ripe fruit. The Riserva Casasilia '95 is a powerful, sunny, vigorous wine, modern in style, characterized by rich fruit; its great concentration is already evident on the nose, which offers notes of toasty oak, cocoa and blackberry jam and a hint of overripeness. The palate, after a generous entry, is broad and dense, and, although the finish is still a little rigid, the wine is very promising. The Syrah has a similar style, very substantial and eloquent, its noble grape clearly marked by the terroir. The third standard-bearer of Poggio al Sole, Seraselva '95, a cabernet and merlot blend, does not betray the house colors: its hue is intense, its deep bouquet offers notes of plum, blackberry and toasty oak, and its soft and very robust palate requires further taming that time, we feel confident, will provide. The Riserva '95 is not as powerful as the wines we 've just described but it is very good all the same, evincing intensity and smoothness. To conclude, the Chianti Classico '96 is more than satisfying, a simple wine that is lively and pleasant to drink.

●	Chianti Classico Casasilia Ris. '95	🍷🍷	5
●	Chianti Classico Ris. '95	🍷🍷	4
●	Seraselva '95	🍷🍷	5
●	Syrah '96	🍷🍷	5
●	Chianti Classico '96	🍷	3
●	Chianti Classico Casasilia '93	YY	5
●	Chianti Classico Casasilia '94	YY	5
●	Chianti Classico '95	YY	3*
●	Chianti Classico Ris. '91	YY	4
●	Seraselva '94	YY	5
●	Chianti Classico '93	Y	3
●	Chianti Classico '94	Y	3
●	Chianti Classico Ris. '94	Y	4

TERRICCIOLA (PI)

BADIA DI MORRONA
LOC. LA BADIA
56030 TERRICCIOLA (PI)
TEL. 0587/658505

At the Badia di Morrona work is proceeding confidently but without a lot of fuss. We tasted some very interesting wines in the cellar, and it is easy to predict an impending leap in quality that will surprise some, but not anyone who reads these notes with care. This year's tastings did not disappoint, and, as usual, N 'Antia was the pick of the crop. The '95 vintage is sangiovese with 40% cabernet sauvignon, but, starting with the '96, the wine will have a new design, orthodox Bordeaux in make-up, with the sangiovese being seconded to the Vigna Alta, which has not been released in a '95 version. The N 'Antia '95 is not particularly full-bodied, aiming instead at balance and elegance. Its nose reveals vegetal notes and accents of toasty oak on a background of black fruit. On the palate it is fresh, elegant and very well distributed, and the finish is long and satisfying. Of the other wines presented by the Counts Gaslini Alberti's estate, we have particular praise for the Chianti Sodi del Paretaio '97, which came very close to winning Two Glasses thanks to its delectable pure fruit and a concentration that is quite a surprise in a wine of this type, particularly in one sold at such a good price. One full Glass goes as well to the chardonnay La Suvera '97, distinguished by delightful notes of citrus fruit and vanilla. Final congratulations for the very correct execution of the San Torpè Felciaio '97.

●	N'Antia '95	🍷🍷	5
●	Chianti Sodi del Paretaio '97	🍷	2*
○	La Suvera '97	🍷	3
○	S. Torpè Felciaio '97	🍷	2
○	La Suvera '94	YY	3
●	N'Antia '91	YY	5
●	N'Antia '93	YY	5
●	N'Antia '94	YY	5
●	Vigna Alta '94	YY	5
●	Chianti '95	Y	1*
●	Chianti Ris. '93	Y	3
●	Chianti Sodi del Paretaio '94	Y	2
●	Chianti Sodi del Paretaio '96	Y	2
●	N'Antia '92	Y	5
○	Vin Santo '88	Y	4

VAGLIA (FI)

CAMPOSILIO
LOC. MONTORSOLI
VIA BASCIANO, 8
50030 VAGLIA (FI)
TEL. 055/696456

Try asking a Florentine if it's possible to make good wine near Vaglia: you 're sure to be told that there aren 't even any vines there. This gives you some idea of the kind of environment Alessandro Rustioni is working in. He is an impassioned winegrower who is lavishing time and money on the family estate in order to exalt an area not generally identified with the idea of viticultural excellence. Splendidly assisted by the oenologist Francesco Naldi, he has succeeded in creating a fine winery in an area still unknown to the general public. He has had on his side the excellent exposure of his vineyards and a wonderful native clone of sangiovese. We tasted two vintages of their only wine, Camposilio, a blend of sangiovese and cabernet sauvignon. The '94 has a beautifully limpid and brilliant ruby hue. The nose is redolent of ripe fruit, especially plum, that gives way to more developed aromas of leather, finishing with balsamic notes. Its attack on the palate is good but not forceful, and it is then quite engaging, with already softened tannins perfectly blended with the alcohol. The finish is a little short but pleasant. The '95, intensely ruby in color, offers a broad array of fruity aromas, red currant and blueberry in particular, of great elegance. The entry on the palate is decisive and well distributed; the substantial tannins are counterpoised by the other components of the flavor; the finish is long and fully satisfying.

●	Camposilio '95	🍷🍷	5
●	Camposilio '94	🍷	5

VINCI (FI)

CANTINE LEONARDO
BIVIO DI STREDA
VIA PROVINCIALE MERCATALE, 921
50059 VINCI (FI)
TEL. 0571/902444

The first appearance of the Cantine Leonardo in the Guide is one of the most important new developments in Tuscany recorded in this edition. This is a cooperative winery that uses the grapes supplied by its members, and no such structure, at least in Tuscany, would have dreamed of aiming at any sort of excellence in its wines until just a few years ago. But the people at Cantine Leonardo have perfectly understood that you cannot think only in terms of total volume produced: you must also work towards upmarket expansion. And so the number of vineyards owned by the cooperative itself is increasing, the technical side has been entrusted to the oenologist Riccardo Pucci with the valuable assistance of the consultant Alberto Antonini, and the results of this dynamism are already perceptible in tastings. The Sant 'Ippolito '96, an unusual blend of merlot and syrah, made an excellent impression, winning Two Glasses without any trouble. This is a muscular, highly concentrated wine, with layers of black fruit on the nose and soft tannins on the palate. It's powerful and compact and we can hardly wait to try the '97. Two Glasses were also collected by the SanZio '96, primarily sangiovese, with a lovely density on the palate and thickly knit tannins that are just a little bitter at the end. The Vin Santo Tegrino d'Anchiano '93 is fine, notwithstanding the tongue-twister of a name: it's a little vegetal on the nose but sweet, continuous and mouth-filling. In closing, we must mention the Chianti '97: more than a million absolutely acceptable bottles!

●	Sant'Ippolito '96	🍷🍷	4
●	SanZio '96	🍷🍷	4
●	Chianti '97	🍷	2*
○	Vin Santo Tegrino d'Anchiano '93	🍷	4

OTHER WINERIES

The following producers obtained good scores in our tastings with one or more of their wines:

PROVINCE OF AREZZO

Santa Vittoria
Foiano della Chiana, tel. 0575/66807,
Chardonnay '97,
Vin Santo '92

Fattoria di Rendola
Montevarchi, tel. 055/9707497,
Merlot '96

PROVINCE OF FIRENZE

Casa Sola
Barberino Val d'Elsa, tel. 055/8075028,
Chianti Classico '95,
Chianti Classico Ris. '94,
Montarsiccio '94

Il Vivaio
Barberino Val d'Elsa, tel. 055/8075185,
Semifonte '95

Il Poggiolo
Carmignano, tel. 055/8711242,
Carmignano '95

Fattoria di Piazzano
Empoli, tel. 0571/999044,
Piazzano '96

Villa Buonasera
Strada in Chianti, tel. 055/8547932,
Chianti Classico Casa Eri '96

Villa Calcinaia
Greve in Chianti, tel. 055/854008,
Chianti Classico Ris. '94

Vignano
Marcialla, tel. 0571/660041,
Vignano Rosso n.13 '96,
Vignano Rosso n.15 '95,
Vignano Rosso n.15 '96

Montagliari
Panzano in Chianti, tel. 055/852014,
Chianti Classico La Quercia '96

Fattoria Sant'Andrea
Panzano in Chianti, tel. 055/8549090,
Chianti Classico '96,
Chianti Classico Ris. '95

Travignoli
Pelago, tel. 055/8311031,
Chianti Rufina '97

Lavacchio
Pontassieve, tel. 055/8317395,
Chardonnay '97,
Cortigiano '96,
Oro del Cedro '96

Castello Il Palagio
S. Casciano Val di Pesa, tel. 055/8218157,
Campolese '94

Vitiano
S. Polo in Chianti, tel. 055/855037,
Chianti Classico '96,
Chianti Classico Ris. '95

Fattoria La Ripa
Tavarnelle Val di Pesa, tel. 055/8072948,
Chianti Classico Ris. '95,
Santa Brigida '95

PROVINCE OF GROSSETO

Montebelli
Caldana, tel. 0566/887100,
Fabula '97

Motta
Grosseto, tel. 0564/405105,
Merlot Massaio '95

San Giuseppe-Mantellassi
Magliano in Toscana,
tel. 0564/592037,
Morellino di Scansano Le Sentinelle Ris. '94,
Querciolaia '94

Eredi Danei
Orbetello, tel. 0564/863935,
Ansonica Costa dell'Argentario '97,
Morellino di Scansano '97

La Parrina, Orbetello, tel. 0564/862636,
Morellino di Scansano Ris. '95

Rascioni Cecconello
Orbetello, tel. 0564/885642,
Poggio Capitana '94,
Poggio Ciliegio '96

Cantina Cooperativa Morellino di Scansano
Scansano, tel. 0564/507288,
Morellino di Scansano '97,
Morellino di Scansano Vigna Benefizio '97

I Botri, Scansano, tel. 0564/507921,
Morellino di Scansano '96,
Morellino di Scansano Ris. '93

La Carletta
Scansano, tel. 0564/585045,
Morellino di Scansano '97

Macereto
Scansano, tel. 0564/507219,
Morellino di Scansano Antico Casale '96

Provveditore-Bargagli
Scansano, tel. 0564/599237,
Bianco di Pitigliano '97,
Morellino di Scansano Primo Ris. '95

PROVINCE OF LIVORNO

Jacopo Banti
Campiglia Marittima, tel. 0565/838802,
Val di Cornia Bianco Poggio Angelica '97

Graziani
Campiglia Marittima, tel. 0565/843043,
Val di Cornia Rosso Di Ciocco '97

Volpaiole
Campiglia Marittima, tel. 0565/843194,
Val di Cornia Rosso '96

Cecilia
Isola d'Elba, tel. 0565/977322,
Ansonica '97

Sapere, Isola d'Elba, tel. 0565/95033,
Aleatico '97

Podere San Luigi
Piombino, tel. 0565/220578,
San Luigi Rosso '95

Daniele Rocchi
Piombino, tel. 0565/35226,
Gli Astri Bianco '97

Ambrosini, Suvereto, tel. 0565/829301,
Riflesso Antico '95,
Subertum '95

Martelli Busdraghi
Suvereto, tel. 0565/829401,
Val di Cornia Rosso Incontri '96,
Vermentino '97

PROVINCE OF LUCCA

Camigliano
Capannori, tel. 0583/490420,
Colline Lucchesi Bianco '97,
Colline Lucchesi Vermentino '97

Fattoria di Fubbiano
Capannori, tel. 0583/978311,
Pampini '96

Fattoria Maionchi
Capannori, tel. 0583/978194,
Colline Lucchesi Bianco '97

Fattoria La Torre
Montecarlo, tel. 0583/22330,
Altair '97,
Montecarlo Bianco '97

Mazzini
Montecarlo, tel. 0583/22010,
Montecarlo Bianco La Salita '97

Michi
Montecarlo, tel. 0583/22011,
Montecarlo Bianco '97

Vigna del Greppo
Montecarlo, tel. 0583/22593,
Vermentino '97

PROVINCE OF PISA

Fattoria di Sassolo
San Miniato, tel. 0571/460001,
Fiorile '93,
Vin Santo '93

PROVINCE OF SIENA

Gagliole
Castellina in Chianti, tel. 0577/740369,
Gagliole Rosso '96

San Leonino
Castellina in Chianti, tel. 0577/743108,
Chianti Classico '96,
Chianti Classico Monsenese Ris. '95,
Salivolpe '93

Borgo Scopeto
Castelnuovo Berardenga, tel. 0577/356827,
Chianti Classico Ris. '94

Poggio Bonelli
Castelnuovo Berardenga, tel. 0577/355382,
Chianti Classico Ris. '94,
Tramonto d'Oca '93

Villa Arceno
Castelnuovo Berardenga, tel. 0577/359346,
Chianti Classico '95,
Chianti Classico Vigna La Porta '95

Colle Santa Mustiole
Chiusi, tel. 0578/63462,
Poggio ai Chiari '96

Podere Il Palazzino
Gaiole in Chianti, tel. 0577/747008,
Chianti Classico '96

Le Miccine
Gaiole in Chianti, tel. 0577/749526,
Chianti Classico '96

Rietine
Gaiole in Chianti, tel. 0577/731110,
Chianti Classico '96

Rocca di Castagnoli
Gaiole in Chianti, tel. 0577/731004,
Buriano '95,
Chianti Classico Poggio 'a Frati Ris. '95

Casanuova delle Cerbaie
Montalcino, tel. 0577/849284,
Brunello di Montalcino '93,
Rosso di Montalcino '96

Cerbaiona
Montalcino, tel. 0577/848660,
Brunello di Montalcino '93

Ciacci Piccolomini d'Aragona
Montalcino, tel. 0577/835616,
Brunello di Montalcino '93

Collemattoni
Montalcino, tel. 0577/864009,
Brunello di Montalcino '93

Il Poggiolo
Montalcino, tel. 0577/864057,
Brunello di Montalcino '93,
Brunello di Montalcino Il Beato '93

La Fornace
Montalcino, tel. 0577/848465,
Brunello di Montalcino '93

La Poderina
Montalcino, tel. 0577/835737,
Brunello di Montalcino '93

La Togata
Montalcino, tel. 0577/847107,
Brunello di Montalcino '93

Le Chiuse
Montalcino, tel. 055/597052,
Brunello di Montalcino '93,
Rosso di Montalcino '96

Poggio Antico
Montalcino, tel. 0577/848044,
Brunello di Montalcino '93

Poggio San Polo
Montalcino, tel. 0577/835522,
Brunello di Montalcino '93

Poggio di Sotto di Piero Palmucci
Montalcino, tel. 0577/835502,
Brunello di Montalcino '93

Solaria
Montalcino, tel. 0577/849426,
Brunello di Montalcino '93,
Rosso di Montalcino '96

Villa Le Prata
Montalcino, tel. 0577/848325,
Brunello di Montalcino '93

Ercolani
Montepulciano, tel. 0578/757811,
Rosso di Montepulciano '97,
Vino Nobile di Montepulciano '95

Ormanni
Poggibonsi, tel. 0577/937212,
Chianti Classico Ris. '94

Pruneto
Radda in Chianti, tel. 0577/738013,
Chianti Classico '95

Vignavecchia
Radda in Chianti, tel. 0577/738090,
Chianti Classico Ris. '95

Villa Buoninsegna
Rapolano Terme,
tel. 0577/724380,
Cabernet Sauvignon '95

Canneta
S. Gimignano, tel. 0577/941540,
Vernaccia di S. Gimignano
La Luna e le Torri '97

Casale-Falchini
S. Gimignano, tel. 0577/941305,
Campora '94

Fontaleoni
S. Gimignano, tel. 0577/950193,
Vernaccia di S. Gimignano '97

La Rampa di Fugnano
S. Gimignano, tel. 0577/941655,
Vernaccia di S. Gimignano Ballata '97

Montenidoli
S. Gimignano, tel. 0577941565,
Vernaccia di S. Gimignano Carato '96

Fattoria di Pietrafitta
S. Gimignano, tel. 0577/943200,
Vin Santo '89

San Quirico
S. Gimignano, tel. 0577/955007,
Vernaccia di S. Gimignano Ris. '96

MARCHE

The overall impression of our tastings in Marche this year once again confirmed the extraordinarily vigorous health of Verdicchio. The fact that quite a number of estates present a wide, well-differentiated range of Verdicchios for tasting has now become a matter of course. And lingering on our noses and palates we still sense such a wealth of tones and nuances (typical fresh vegetal notes plus ripe peaches, tobacco and hazelnut—slim elegance and opulence) that we are more and more convinced that this grape variety and this wine are among the top products of the Italian wine industry. Starting with the Verdicchios from Castelli di Jesi, the Gaiospino from the Fattoria Coroncino is absolutely astonishing; there are two vintages, the '96 (in a magic moment just now) and the '97, a truly great wine with a long future ahead of it. The latter fully deserves our Three Glasses. Its single-minded, individualistic producer has succeeded, step by step, in turning out one of the best white wines in Italy. The Verdicchio Podium '96 from Garofoli, an estate that presented a number of other prize-winning labels, wins the Three Glasses hands down. Although Umani Ronchi failed to reach the top score, it won high points with many of its wines, including Cùmaro (an exemplary Rosso Conero) and Pélago (a innovative blend of cabernet, montepulciano and merlot), both '95. We should also mention the good Rosso Conero produced by estates like Le Terrazze (Sassi Neri '96), Moroder (Dorico '95) and Garofoli (Grosso Agontano '95). Once again the Marche red first past the post was the Cabernet Sauvignon Akronte, a '95 vintage from the young Boccadigabbia estate: this magnificent wine is now sailing into the stratosphere and can stand comparisons which only a few years ago seemed unthinkable. The Verdicchio dei Castelli di San Michele '97 of Vallerosa Bonci repeats last year's success, confirming the importance of clonal selection. We had good results from the tiny (both in hectares and total production) appellation of the Lacrima di Morro d'Alba and the growth (still limited in respect to potential) in the southern part of the region with Rosso Piceno (also in the Superiore version). A few years ago Cocci Grifoni was more or less the patriarch of this appellation, but today names like Velenosi, Saladini Pilastri, Rio Maggio, De Angelis and even Villa Pigna are turning out more arresting wines, including whites. While on the subject of whites we should mention some praiseworthy wines and producers who have yet again achieved levels that are nothing short of excellent: La Monacesca with the cru of the same name as Verdicchio di Matelica, and with another white from chardonnay grapes, Ecclesia '97; Bucci with the Verdicchio dei Castelli di Jesi Villa Bucci '95 and Sartarelli with Tralivio '97.

ANCONA

LUCA E BEATRICE LANARI
VIA POZZO, 142
FRAZ. VARANO
60029 ANCONA
TEL. 071/2861343

Luca Lanari and his sister Beatrice, with the collaboration of wine expert Giancarlo Soverchia, have been managing this small rather homespun winery in a typical Rosso Conero area. They have only ten hectares under vines; another four (with 4,500 plants per hectare) are due to come into production in three to four years time; the grape varieties grown should guarantee the yield and the selections for production of a great red wine, and this is precisely the goal the estate is aiming for in the shortest possible time. Once achieved, they have every intention of maintaining it for many years to come. The Casino '97 derives from a chance mix of different sorts of grapes in the vineyard: trebbiano, malvasia and moscato. Produced in 2,500 bottles it has a light straw-yellow color; distinct and lasting scents of chlorophyll, green citrus fruit and sage; the wine is deliciously drinkable owing to a reasonable acidity that makes it crisp and zestful, while it displays a rather thin body in its overall softness. The basic Rosso Conero '97 has a good deep thick purple color, it is lively and stable on the nose with aromas of cherry, blackberry and blueberry against a vinous background; on the palate (soft, concentrated and well-structured) it displays sweet tannins; the creamy taste has an elegant finish. We shall discuss the Riserva in the next edition of the Guide: however early tastings indicate that this winery is on the right road to achieve its goal, the production of a great Rosso Conero.

●	Rosso Conero '97	🍷🍷	3*
○	Casino '97	🍷	2
●	Rosso Conero Fibbio '94	ΥΥ	4
●	Rosso Conero '96	Υ	2

ANCONA

MARCHETTI
VIA DI PONTELUNGO, 166
60100 ANCONA
TEL. 071/897386

In production since the 'Sixties, the Marchetti estate is mostly famous for its Rosso Conero, although in the last few years it has reached appreciable results with the Verdicchio dei Castelli di Jesi. This change has generally characterized almost all the Marche estates, but particularly this one. The red wines have become softer and still retain their ability to improve with time. The basic wine of the estate is the Rosso Conero '97; it displays a dark impenetrable purplish-red color. The fragrances are vinous with notes of cherry; on the palate it is powerful and densely concentrated. The wine still tastes young but it is obviously going to evolve in interesting ways. The Rosso Conero Riserva Villa Bonomi '96, with its elegant ruby color, displays clear cut scents of black cherry, vanilla and plum; on the palate it reveals good structure with admirable softness and overall balance. A clear cut finish with a good length indicates that the wine is ready, but still has ample room to evolve. Two '97 Verdicchios surprised us. The Classico is agreeable and ready for drinking, displaying proper freshness and structure with a nice balance of essential features. The Verdicchio Classico Superiore, with its straw-yellow color and green tints, has fragrances of white flowers, apple and apricot. On the palate it has a good balance of acidity, structure and body; there is a sensation of finesse and delicate softness conferred by a period of time in barrique.

●	Rosso Conero Villa Bonomi Ris. '96	🍷🍷	3
○	Verdicchio dei Castelli di Jesi Cl. Sup. Villa Bonomi '97	🍷🍷	2
●	Rosso Conero '97	🍷	2*
○	Verdicchio dei Castelli di Jesi Cl. '97	🍷	1

ANCONA

ALESSANDRO MORODER
FRAZ. MONTACUTO, 112
60029 ANCONA
TEL. 071/898232

The estate of Alessandro and Serenella Moroder boasts a spacious restaurant hall to receive tourists and a smaller one for snacks: obviously to provide an opportunity for tasting the products of the winery (wine, fruit and vegetables, and much more). This estate enjoys the collaboration of Franco Bernabei and has so far reaped a long list of awards for its excellent interpretation of Rosso Conero. Over the last ten years the Moroders have produced a Rosso Conero that has now become a model for everyone else. The '96 version is only partly affected by this troublesome vintage: the light ruby color is followed by a vinous aroma with toasted and spicy scents; the rather full structure is due to the fact that the unmarketed Dorico '96 (the winery claims that it is not up to the standards set by preceding vintages) has been used to blend the basic Rosso Conero. The Dorico '95 is decidedly better and displays a dense ruby color. The nose has a clear jammy aroma of blackberry and cherry amalgamated with sweet scents of violets and spices. The palate is full, with a large and opulent concentration and discernible, but soft and unobtrusive tannins. This wine possesses excellent balance and finesse. The Rosa di Montacuto '97, mostly made from montepulciano grapes, is easy to drink, thanks to a medium body that harmonizes well with its freshness. We will wind up with the Oro '95, from sun-dried trebbiano, moscato and malvasia grapes (which was previously the grape blend for Candiano, a white they no longer produce): it has a fine golden color and the right amount of sugar content, which makes it a very agreeable dessert wine.

	Wine	Glasses	Price
●	Rosso Conero Dorico '95	🍷🍷	4
○	L'Oro di Moroder '95	🍷	4
⊙	Rosa di Montacuto '97	🍷	2
●	Rosso Conero '96	🍷	2
●	Rosso Conero Dorico '90	YYY	4
●	Rosso Conero Dorico '93	YYY	4
●	Rosso Conero Dorico '92	YY	4

ASCOLI PICENO

ERCOLE VELENOSI
VIA DEI BIANCOSPINI, 11
63100 ASCOLI PICENO
TEL. 0736/341218

This Ascoli Piceno estate has chalked up yet another year of good results for all the different types of wine it produces. The main aim of the Velenosi, with the technical collaboration of Romeo Taraborelli, is to produce quality both in the local appellations (Rosso Piceno Superiore and Falerio dei Colli Ascolani, of which they produce two selections, the Roggio del Filare and the Vigna Solaria, as well as the well-established Brecciarolo line which also lists a Rosato) and in other wines from non-local grape varieties. Among the latter we should mention the Villa Angela '97, from chardonnay grapes, with its intense scents of tropical fruit and a rather fat but fresh palate. The Barricato Villa Angela '96 (again from chardonnay grapes, but made in small oak casks) displays a bouquet of vanilla well-amalgamated with ripe fruit. Among the whites we recall the excellent Falerio Vigna Solaria '97. It has generous elegant aromas (mineral and floral) echoed fragrantly and softly on the palate and is due for good evolution in the course of 1999. The basic Falerio '97 in the Brecciarolo line has surprising structure and character with deep aromas and a full taste. Well-deserving of mention are the whites, Linagre and Floreo, respectively from sauvignon and müller thurgau, and the tasty Rosato '97. One well deserved Glass also goes to the spumante obtained with traditional bottle fermentation. Moving on to the reds, the Rosso Piceno Superiore Brecciarolo '95 easily wins a Glass; it has fragrances of plum and licorice and good body; but a higher score must go to the Roggio del Filare of the same vintage; it expresses greater complexity, with balsamic notes and a mouth-filling palate.

	Wine	Glasses	Price
○	Falerio dei Colli Ascolani Vigna Solaria '97	🍷🍷	3*
○	Il Barricato di Villa Angela '96	🍷🍷	4
●	Rosso Piceno Sup. Roggio del Filare '95	🍷🍷	3*
○	Villa Angela Chardonnay '97	🍷🍷	3
○	Falerio dei Colli Ascolani Il Brecciarolo '97	🍷	1*
⊙	Rosato Il Brecciarolo '97	🍷	1*
●	Rosso Piceno Sup. Il Brecciarolo '95	🍷	2
○	Velenosi Brut Metodo Classico	🍷	4
○	Floreo di Villa Angela '96		2
○	Linagre Sauvignon di Villa Angela '97		3

BARBARA (AN)

SANTA BARBARA
BORGO MAZZINI, 35
60010 BARBARA (AN)
TEL. 071/9674249

Ten years after Stefano Antonucci set off in a new direction and completely renewed his winery, the present trend of his estate seems to be towards top-quality production, with a varied range of excellent products. Starting with the whites, the most outstanding are a basic Verdicchio and the Pignocco selection. The former has well expressed varietal characteristics and, in spite of being an easy-to-drink wine, it doesn't lack substance. It is, in fact, very much on the same level as the Verdicchio Pignocco, which confirms its usual true-to-type standard. Among the Verdicchio dei Castelli di Jesi selections, Le Vaglie '97 shows remarkable strength: its high alcoholic content makes it an impressive wine, and its staying power will permit an interesting evolution. The Riserva Stefano Antonucci '95, a Verdicchio with scintillating scents of assorted tropical fruit with notes of vanilla, is not aggressive on the palate and lends unexpected variety to the offerings. Among the reds we tasted the Pignocco '97, from an unusual blend of different varieties of grape (both local and not), very successful for its richness of aroma and good clean taste. The San Bartolo '96 confirms its characteristic softness and the fact that it is an easy drink, rather like a young Chianti. The new edition of the Riserva Stefano Antonucci Rosso, from classic bordeaux grapes, is a great success. The '95 vintage still has some aroma notes approaching green peppers, together with more complex and softer tones. On the palate this wine, with its substantial tannic strength, promises a splendid evolution. We may close with the ever true and consistent Moscatell made from moscato grapes.

	Wine	Glasses	Price
●	Pignocco Rosso '97	🍷🍷	3*
●	Rosso delle Marche Stefano Antonucci '95	🍷🍷	4
○	Verdicchio dei Castelli di Jesi Cl. Le Vaglie '97	🍷🍷	3
○	Verdicchio dei Castelli di Jesi Cl. Stefano Antonucci Ris. '95	🍷🍷	4
○	Moscatell '97	🍷	3
●	San Bartolo '96	🍷	3
○	Verdicchio dei Castelli di Jesi Cl. '97	🍷	1*
○	Verdicchio dei Castelli di Jesi Pignocco '97	🍷	2
●	Rosso delle Marche Stefano Antonucci '93	🍸🍸 (white glasses)	4

CASTEL DI LAMA (AP)

TENUTA DE ANGELIS
VIA S. FRANCESCO, 10
63030 CASTEL DI LAMA (AP)
TEL. 0736/87429

Among the wines presented this year we were favorably impressed by the Rosso Piceno '97. It still has purple nuances; the rich fruity sensations on the nose are reflected on the palate which has good length with the possibility of growth. The consistent Piceno Superiore '95 has a color tending to garnet. A little austere on the nose (with notes of black cherry and plum), its palate is distinctly rich in tannins. The interesting new Chardonnay Brut is to be praised for the intensity of its nose reminiscent of banana and apricot; the mousse, which is not particularly fine but long, adds to the pleasant taste and ease of drinking. Moving on to De Angelis' still white wines, we find the Falerio Colli Ascolani '97 middling in character, well-expressed in bouquet and with just the right flavors on the palate. The Prato Grande '97, from chardonnay grapes, is consciously sprightly; a drinkable wine with a floral and fruity character.

	Wine	Glasses	Price
●	Rosso Piceno '97	🍷🍷	1*
○	Falerio dei Colli Ascolani '97	🍷	1*
●	Rosso Piceno Sup. '95	🍷	3
○	Prato Grande '97		1
○	Chardonnay Brut		2
●	Rosso Piceno Sup. '94	🍸🍸 (white glasses)	3

CASTELPLANIO (AN)

Fazi Battaglia
Via Roma, 117
60032 Castelplanio (AN)
tel. 0731/813444

This is one of the colossals of the Marche wine industry as well as being an historic estate (the inauguration of its first premises at Cupramontana coincided with the launching of Verdicchio). Today the Fazi Battaglia vineyards cover 340 hectares, distributed over twelve different areas. The technical staff (including Dino Porfiri, the agronomists Mario Ghergo and Antonio Verdolini, and in recent years wine expert Franco Bernabei as consultant) have created a new wine from verdicchio grapes, named after its locality. This Arkezia Muffo di San Sisto '96 is characterized by its sugar concentration and the presence of noble rot, with an interesting nose and moderately sweet taste. The Verdicchio '97 Titulus has once more proved itself reliable and fresh; a very typical Verdicchio with vegetal scents, it is tasty on the palate, with a characteristic bitterish finish. The broader Le Moie '97 comes from a special clonal selection of verdicchio grapes experimented in some of the winery's vineyards: it is a fresh wine with other more complex characteristics and displays a harmonious taste with considerable length. The evolution of San Sisto '94 is also interesting since it uses small oak casks for fermentation and aging. The Spumante Brut, from verdicchio grapes, lives up to its customary standard of pleasantness, while the white Attimi '97 is an easy youthful drink. Moving on to the reds, the Rosso Conero '97, with its elegant balsamic notes and soft taste, and the Sangiovese Rutilus of the same vintage, another new wine from this estate, are both particularly well-made.

○ Verdicchio dei Castelli di Jesi Cl. Sup. Le Moie '97	🍷🍷	3*
○ Arkezia Muffo di San Sisto '96	🍷	5
● Rosso Conero '97	🍷	2
● Rutilus Sangiovese '97	🍷	1*
○ Verdicchio dei Castelli di Jesi Cl. Titulus '97	🍷	3
○ Verdicchio dei Castelli di Jesi Fazi Battaglia Brut	🍷	3
○ Attimi Bianco '97		1
○ Verdicchio dei Castelli di Jesi Cl. Sup. Le Moie '96	YY	3
○ Verdicchio dei Castelli di Jesi Cl. San Sisto '94	YY	4

CINGOLI (MC)

Vigneti Tavignano
Lucangeli Aymerich di Laconi
Loc. Tavignano
62011 Cingoli (MC)
tel. 0733/617303

The progress of the Verdicchio dei Castelli di Jesi has often resulted in the creation of new wineries which, having taken on the right sort of capital and technical assistance, come barging onto the wine market with first class products. Usually these companies are short-lived or improvised, but become consolidated over the years through well-aimed strategies and the constant quality of their products. Lucangeli, who has only recently entered the Guide, is certainly reliable thanks to his particularly favorable '97 vintage. The 40,000 bottles of good quality wine are all Verdicchio dei Castelli di Jesi. The Classico Vigneti di Tavignano '97 is exemplary in its category: a clear-cut nose of green apple, fresh fruit and acacia flowers is followed by a broad palate, backed by a fair structure plus crisp acidity to provide an agreeably pleasant drink with a clean almond finish. The Verdicchio Classico Selezione Misco '97 improves on the features of its younger brother: the color is straw-yellow with clear green nuances; a nose of ripe fruit (apricot and pineapple), a remarkable structure and general softness lead in to a satisfyingly opulent palate. We tasted a superselection from the tanks due for bottling very soon. Named for Sante Lancerio, a well-known and much-esteemed 16th-century writer on wine, this label will once again demonstrate the versatility of this excellent Marche grape.

○ Verdicchio dei Castelli di Jesi Cl. Selezione Misco '97	🍷🍷	3*
○ Verdicchio dei Castelli di Jesi Cl. Vigneti di Tavignano '97	🍷🍷	2*
○ Verdicchio dei Castelli di Jesi Cl. Vigneti di Tavignano '96	YY	2*
○ Verdicchio dei Castelli di Jesi Cl. Selezione Misco '96	YY	3

CIVITANOVA MARCHE (MC)

Boccadigabbia

C.da Castelletta, 56
62012 Civitanova Marche (MC)
tel. 0733/70728

In a little over ten years Elvio Alessandri, in consultation with wine experts and agronomists Fabrizio Ciufoli and Giovanni Basso, has brought his estate to a remarkable level. It is no stroke of luck that his Akronte '95, by now an established classic, has been awarded Three Glasses for the fourth consecutive time. This Cabernet Sauvignon has a beautiful rich color of eggplant purple tending to garnet; on the nose there are clear-cut scents of plum and cherry mingled with notes of balsam, spices and tobacco; and good correspondence with a palate that displays strong tannins, pulpiness and admirable length. Among the other red wines of this Civitanova Marche estate we should mention the good Rosso Piceno Saltapicchio '95 with its medium dense ruby color, bouquet of red berry jam and the right full-bodied and slightly balsamic taste. The Girone '95 is also a success; this is a pinot nero with considerable structure, a deep ruby red color with a nose of licorice and leather: scents that find a consistent follow-up on the palate. Among the whites the Aldonis '97 is definitely a good wine; it is a Chardonnay with an intense yellow color and a nose that is reminiscent of bread crust and ripe tropical fruit; backed by a good alcoholic level it is soft and balanced on the palate. The Castelletta '95 is, in fact, a Pinot Grigio with mineral and spicy scents whose evolution will be interesting to follow. As always the Rosso Piceno '96 and the Garbì '97 are true-to-type, while of the two wines produced by Villamagna (recently acquired by Elio Alessandri) the white Colli Maceratesi '97 proves the most satisfactory.

●	Akronte '95	🍷🍷🍷	4
○	Aldonis '97	🍷🍷	3
●	Girone '95	🍷🍷	3
●	Rosso Piceno Saltapicchio '95	🍷🍷	3*
○	Colli Maceratesi Bianco Villamagna '97	🍷	2
○	Garbì '97	🍷	3
○	La Castelletta Pinot Grigio '97	🍷	3
●	Rosso Piceno '96	🍷	2
●	Rosso Piceno Villamagna '96		2
●	Akronte '92	YYY	5
●	Akronte '93	YYY	5
●	Akronte '94	YYY	5
●	Girone '93	YY	3
●	Rosso Piceno Saltapicchio '93	YY	2

CIVITANOVA MARCHE (MC)

La Monacesca

Via D'Annunzio, 1
62012 Civitanova Marche (MC)
tel. 0733/812602

The factors accounting for the steady growth of the La Monacesca estate are vineyards at an altitude of 450 meters above sea level, careful selection of the grape varieties planted, late harvests, solid collaboration from wine expert Roberto Cipresso and the strong-minded policy set by Aldo Cifola for the production of excellent quality wines. Today the estate can count on eighteen hectares of vines under verdicchio, chardonnay and sauvignon, producing around 100,000 bottles, and another five hectares under sangiovese and merlot which, within next year, will go to make a red wine, whose name, for the time being, must remain a mystery. The '97 vintage has been exceptionally generous in the Matelica area and its impact is clearly apparent in Cifola's wines. The Verdicchio '97 La Monacesca is a deep bright straw-yellow color; the bouquet has a scent of acacia flowers, apple, slightly sun-dried fruit and hazelnut; the wine displays good acidity on the palate to sustain a considerable level of alcohol; the rich concentration and noticeable but pleasant saltiness lend ample length to the finish with its elegant notes of bitter almonds. All this is obtained without using oak casks. The Chardonnay Ecclesia '97 has a good straw-yellow color with golden tints; its aroma of yellow plum and quince is enriched by a faint scent of banana; on the palate it has a pleasing freshness and good balance among the various components; the finish is clean and long with notes of pineapple. Owing to the unfortunate vintage of 1996 the Mirum was not produced; we shall review the '97 edition next year.

○	Chardonnay delle Marche Ecclesia '97	🍷🍷	4
○	Verdicchio di Matelica La Monacesca '97	🍷🍷	3
○	Mirum '94	YYY	4
○	Mirus '91	YYY	4
○	Verdicchio di Matelica La Monacesca '94	YYY	3
○	Mirum '95	YY	4
○	Mirus '93	YY	4
○	Verdicchio di Matelica La Monacesca '96	YY	3

CUPRAMONTANA (AN)

VALLEROSA BONCI

VIA TORRE, 13
60034 CUPRAMONTANA (AN)
TEL. 0731/789129

The San Michele vineyards are famous for being among the finest in the entire production area of Verdicchio dei Castelli di Jesi. These are the vineyards that produce grapes with the same name as the cru of Verdicchio. Here in the last few years the Bonci have replanted and made clonal selections with scientific assistance from Leonardo Valenti (University of Milan) and consultation with wine expert Sergio Paolucci. The result is that once again their Verdicchio stands in the front rank and well deserves its Three Glasses. The wine has an intense fragrance (linden tree and peach) supported by a good alcoholic level that lends softness and elegance to the taste; the palate is remarkable for its fullness and the length of the finish. The other selection, Le Case '97, is only slightly inferior in quality; its spicy notes, which are enhanced by aging in large casks, do not dominate the spectrum of aromas, while the taste is rather full and satisfying. In its debut, the Barré, vintage '95, is unusually interesting; it expresses great balance between the contribution of the cask and the ripeness of the fruit; it is worth remembering as one of the best Marche whites aged in wood. The Verdicchio Passito Rojano '96 (another very promising new wine) has a good gold yellow color; the nose recalls dates and honey, followed by a sweet pulpy taste. We also wish to call attention to the lesser Verdicchio selection, the Focus: a more drinkable wine, but certainly true-to-type and coherent in nose and palate. The grapes for the Bronci Brut come from the vineyards of Carpeneto and Torre; the bright straw-yellow color, with a subtle mousse, is followed by varietal scents and a taste that is intense, lively and well-balanced.

	Wine	Glasses	Price
O	Verdicchio dei Castelli di Jesi Cl. Sup. San Michele '97	🍷🍷🍷	3*
O	Verdicchio dei Castelli di Jesi Cl. Barré Ris. '95	🍷🍷	4
O	Verdicchio dei Castelli di Jesi Cl. Sup. Le Case '97	🍷🍷	3*
O	Verdicchio Spumante Brut Bonci	🍷	3
O	Verdicchio dei Castelli di Jesi Cl. Focus '97	🍷	3
O	Verdicchio dei Castelli di Jesi Passito Rojano '96	🍷	4
O	Verdicchio dei Castelli di Jesi Cl. Sup. San Michele '96	♀♀♀	3

CUPRAMONTANA (AN)

COLONNARA VITICULTORI IN CUPRAMONTANA

VIA MANDRIOLE, 6
60034 CUPRAMONTANA (AN)
TEL. 0731/780273

On the fortieth anniversary of its foundation the Collonnara winery can toast the occasion with its best wine: the Cuprese, which combines freshness and strong varietal notes with maturity and complexity. Established in 1959, the Colonnara now includes around two hundred small wine growers. Organized to produce its own grapes for its own production the Collonnara relies on the experience of an agronomist for wine-making and an associated company, Cupravit, for the management of the vineyards; the entire wine-producing cycle is carried out without the use of sulphur dioxide, but through microbiological control of the musts. The selection of Verdicchio grapes from the vineyards high on the hill (between Cupramontana, Staffolo and Maiolato) produced by this cooperative has always been one of the most successful and reliable Marche whites for its unfailing quality. The '97 vintage is no exception: it was already soft at the time of tasting, with broad margins for growth. The scents are reminiscent of linden tree and hazelnut; the full almondy taste is fresh. The tastings of some of the previous years have confirmed the wine's great possibilities for evolution and a genuine complexity, rare for a wine intended for drinking young and marketed at an affordable price. The basic Verdicchio '97 is no disappointment, with its vegetal tones and the proper level of tastiness. The Verdicchio Collonnara Metodo Classico is a spumante with personality and substance. The red Tornamagno '94 (from sangiovese grosso, sangiovese montanino and montepulciano) aged in small French oak casks, is characterized by berry scents and a soft taste.

	Wine	Glasses	Price
O	Verdicchio dei Castelli di Jesi Cl. Sup. Cuprese '97	🍷🍷	3*
O	Colonnara Brut Metodo Classico Millesimato '90	🍷	4
O	Verdicchio dei Castelli di Jesi Cl. '97	🍷	1*
O	Verdicchio dei Castelli di Jesi Cl. Sup. Cuprese '94	♀♀	4
O	Verdicchio dei Castelli di Jesi Cl. Sup. Cuprese '95	♀♀	4
O	Verdicchio dei Castelli di Jesi Cl. Sup. Cuprese '96	♀♀	3
●	Tornamagno '94	♀	3

FABRIANO (AN)

Enzo Mecella
Via Dante, 112
60044 Fabriano (AN)
tel. 0732/21680

Enzo Mecella, wine expert and owner of this Fabriano estate, is a master when it comes to selecting grapes. This year he is presenting an admirable range of wines: for example the new edition of the Braccano '95, an important red from ciliegiolo grapes and a small percentage of merlot. The wine appears very concentrated with a nose of spice, balsamic and vanilla scents with red berries gradually coming through. The taste corresponds to the nose with good strength and tannins that tend to sweetness. This wine has the same finesse as Mecella's other champion, the selection of Rosso Conero '94 called Rubelliano, which we reviewed last year: it has a bouquet of well-amalgamated scents of camphor, vanilla and red fruit (especially black currants), while its impact on the palate is soft with an easy fluidity and a long finish with a distinct aftertaste of coffee. The Rosso Conero I Lavi is true-to-type in a less than memorable vintage; its aromas are typically plums and red fruit. While waiting for a new edition of the excellent Antico di Casa Fosca we tasted the Casa Fosca and the Pagliano, both Verdicchio di Matelica '97. Both wines had typically fresh fragrances and were flavorful on the palate. We return to the reds with a cabernet, the Longobardo '96, and the selection Rosso Piceno '95 Colle Malvano. The first is a medium-bodied wine with varietal scents; the second is garnet-colored, and appears to be somewhat mature. As always the Rosa Gentile is a success, with its onion-skin color followed by floral and fruity aromas; it is fruity and very agreeable on the palate.

	Wine	Glasses	Price
●	Braccano '95	▼▼	4
●	Longobardo '96	▼	4
⊙	Rosa Gentile '97	▼	2
●	Rosso Conero I Lavi '96	▼	1*
○	Verdicchio di Matelica Casa Fosca '97	▼	2
○	Verdicchio di Matelica Pagliano '97	▼	1*
●	Rosso Piceno Colle Malvano '95		3
●	Braccano '93	▽▽	4
●	Rosso Conero Rubelliano '93	▽▽	4
●	Rosso Conero Rubelliano '94	▽▽	4
○	Verdicchio di Matelica Antico di Casa Fosca '94	▽▽	3

FANO (PS)

Claudio Morelli
V.le Romagna, 47/b
61032 Fano (PS)
tel. 0721/823352

The grapes Morelli uses for the cru of Bianchello del Metauro La Vigna delle Terrazze come from the vineyards of Roncosambaccio, a beautiful terrace facing the Adriatic coast. The '97 edition of this wine has a yellow color with greenish tints; then come floral fragrances corresponding to a pleasantly soft palate with an almondy finish. Morelli is specialized in the appellation of the Pesaro area obtained from the biancame variety, of which he produces various versions. His Borgo Torre is also a success, with a consistency similar to the previous cru, as well as his San Cesareo which also has substance: the latter has a straw-yellow color with greenish tints, scents of ripe fruit and a palate already soft with a pleasantly almondy finish. Moving on to the reds, the Sangiovese Vigna le Terrazze is a pleasant, honest drink: light ruby-red in color, its aromas recall wild berries; there is an enjoyable strength about it but there is still a slight astringency on the palate. The other red presented for tasting was again a Colli Pesaresi appellation, a selection of Sangiovese Sant'Andrea in Villis '95: the wine is already mature, with fruity scents amalgamated with a boisé note and a palate revealing precocious evolution.

	Wine	Glasses	Price
○	Bianchello del Metauro La Vigna delle Terrazze '97	▼▼	2*
○	Bianchello del Metauro Borgo Torre '97	▼	2
●	Colli Pesaresi Sangiovese La Vigna delle Terrazze '97	▼	2
○	Bianchello del Metauro San Cesareo '97		1
●	Colli Pesaresi Sangiovese Sant'Andrea in Villis '95		3

JESI (AN)

MARIO E GIORGIO BRUNORI
V.LE DELLA VITTORIA, 103
60035 JESI (AN)
TEL. 0731/207213

For several years the winery of the Brunori brothers has been synonymous with reliability, in view of their commitment to a linear interpretation of the wines of the appellation. This classical area includes a series of townships which form part of the ancient Contado of Jesi. The Brunoris' Jesi address refers to their business premises, with a wine shop next door. The actual estate is in the commune of San Paolo di Jesi, in the contrada San Nicolò (hence the selection of Verdicchio dei Castelli di Jesi of the same name), at an altitude of 200 meters above sea level. Their own vineyards face south/south-west and produce yields varying between 80 and 90 quintals of grapes per hectare. In the '97 vintage the cru San Nicolò was made as usual by the technique of allowing no more than eighteen hours contact with the grape skins, resulting in a wide, complex array of aromas; there are varietal scents of linden trees and field grass, but also of ripe fruit. The basic version of the Verdicchio dei Castelli di Jesi '97, a noteworthy wine, displays a fine correspondence between palate and nose; the same may be said for the Lacrima di Morro d'Alba which, in a generally favorable vintage year for this type, offers alluring scents of violets and roses and an agreeably vinous taste.

	Wine	Glasses	Price
○	Verdicchio dei Castelli di Jesi Cl. San Nicolò '97	🍷🍷	3
●	Lacrima di Morro d'Alba '97	🍷	3
○	Verdicchio dei Castelli di Jesi Cl. '97	🍷	2

LORETO (AN)

GIOACCHINO GAROFOLI
VIA ARNO, 9
60025 LORETO (AN)
TEL. 071/7820163

The Podium '96 of the Garofoli estate has rated another Three Glasses award. Made from late-harvest verdicchio grapes, it has a deep yellow color, a nose of ripe apricot with scents of honey and sweet spices. It is persuasive and opulent on the palate, with a rich concentrated structure where saltiness and alcohol create perfect balance, elegance and softness. Positive results also for the Serra Fiorese '95: the vanilla scents from aging in wood are a pleasure for the nose, while the palate is powerful, variegated and very soft, with a suave elegant finish tasting of almonds. Macrina '97 displays a fine structure on the palate with a flavorful and alluring softness. The Rosso Piceno Colle Ambro '96 has a bright ruby color, vinous scents of ripe red fruit and a balanced soft palate. In spite of the unfortunate vintage year, the Rosso Conero Vigna Piancarda '96 has a bright limpid ruby red color and rich aromas with notes of blackberry and cherry; on the palate pronounced tannins by no means spoil a delightful drink. The Rosso Conero Riserva Grosso Agontano '95 has a darkish ruby color; the vinous scents offer toasty notes of ripe red berries; the palate is textured (a good presence of tannins) and concentrated. From the Comete selection, the Kres '94 made from cabernet sauvignon grapes is noteworthy: on the nose, the varietal aromas are well blended with toasty and sweet spices; the structure may not be particularly strong but it displays finesse. Also we should not forget the simple rosato, Komaros, and the easy-to-drink white Rondini, both of the '97 vintage.

	Wine	Glasses	Price
○	Verdicchio dei Castelli di Jesi Cl. Sup. Podium '96	🍷🍷🍷	3*
●	Rosso Conero Grosso Agontano Ris. '95	🍷🍷	4
○	Verdicchio dei Castelli di Jesi Cl. Serra Fiorese Ris. '95	🍷🍷	4
●	Kres '94	🍷	4
●	Rosso Conero Vigna Piancarda '96	🍷	3
○	Verdicchio dei Castelli di Jesi Cl. Sup. Macrina '97	🍷	2
⊙	Komaros '97		2
○	Rondini '97		2
○	Verdicchio dei Castelli di Jesi Cl. Sup. Podium '95	🍷🍷🍷 (outline)	3

MAIOLATI SPONTINI (AN)

La Vite
Via Vivaio
Fraz. Monte Schiavo
60030 Maiolati Spontini (AN)
tel. 0731/700385 - 700297

In the last few years, thanks to their acquisition by the Pieralisi Group (formerly the majority partner) the Monte Schiavo winery has shifted its status from cooperative to private company, changing their appellation from Monte Schiavo to La Vite. Today the company is working on lines proposed by their wine consultant, Pierluigi Lorenzetti, to go for improved quality while expanding and renovating the winery structures and projecting new wines. Among these we noted the first appearance of a red for which the company has great expectations: the Esio '95, made from a mix of montepulciano and cabernet sauvignon grapes. Its restrained but elegant aromas offer hints of berries and faint notes of spices. Although not broad, the palate is balanced and linear. The range of wines, produced from more than a hundred hectares of their own vineyards, always assigns a special space to the various crus of Verdicchio (Bando di San Settimo, Coste del Molino, Palio di San Floriano, Colle del Sole): each reflects a different vineyard location and even display differences in style. Among them the one that really hits the mark is Coste del Molino, a wine of abundant freshness together with good consistency. Likewise interesting are the Palio di San Floriano, which we enjoyed for its mineral content and softness, and the Bando di San Settimo, a wine whose evolution will be well worth following in time to come. The basic Verdicchio '97 has also proved true-to-type and an agreeable drink. Returning to the reds we should mention a Lacrima di Morro d'Alba that has turned out very well indeed, with a handsome glowing color and floral and fruity scents, the drinkable Rosso Conero Bottaccio and the Rosso Piceno Superiore '95 Sassaiolo.

	Wine	Glasses	Price
○	Verdicchio dei Castelli di Jesi Cl. Coste del Molino '97	🍷🍷	2*
●	Lacrima di Morro d'Alba '97	🍷	3
●	Rosso Conero Bottaccio '97	🍷	2
●	Esio '95	🍷	4
○	Verdicchio dei Castelli di Jesi Cl. Bando di S. Settimio '97	🍷	4
○	Verdicchio dei Castelli di Jesi Cl. Sup. Palio di S. Floriano '97	🍷	2
●	Rosso Piceno Sup. Sassaiolo '95		2
○	Verdicchio dei Castelli di Jesi '97		2

MATELICA (MC)

Belisario Cantina Sociale
di Matelica e Cerreto d'Esi
Via Merloni, 12
62024 Matelica (MC)
tel. 0737/787247

The Belisario, that dynamic Matelica winery which for years has been pursuing a project aimed at quality improvement, is now extending its range of wines. This year, together with its fine Verdicchio series (still the major share of their bottled output), a new red has appeared, the San Leopardo '94, which we have every reason to consider a "important" wine in embryo. Another red wine from Belisario is the Colferraio, a wine without pretensions that should be drunk immediately. However the most interesting section remains the Verdicchios, starting from the Ritratti '97; vegetal scents that are decidedly typical and alluring, followed by a tasty freshness. The Del Cerro '97 selection (destined to show surprisingly lasting qualities in the future) has more structure, with scents that are still very fresh but well-pronounced; it has substance on the palate with a typically bitter finish. The other selection, the Belisario '97, probably has more elegance; with a discernible alcoholic level, it has fewer vegetal scents and softer and more mouth-filling flavors. The third edition of the Cinque Annate al Duemila '96 (after the '94 and '95 vintages, already reviewed, the project envisages a series of five wines from the next vintages up to the Year 2000) suffers a little from the unfavorable 1996 season. The Cambrugiano '95 Riserva (a name chosen under the new order of Verdicchio production) which we reviewed last year, has shown interesting evolution after its promising appearance. Finally, the Ferrante, under the new Marche appellation of Esino deserves mention; a quaffable white that is fresh and just the thing for summer drinking.

	Wine	Glasses	Price
○	Verdicchio di Matelica Belisario '97	🍷🍷	3
○	Verdicchio di Matelica Del Cerro '97	🍷🍷	2*
○	Verdicchio di Matelica Cinque Annate al Duemila '96	🍷	3
○	Verdicchio di Matelica Ritratti '97	🍷	1*
●	Colferraio '97		1
○	Esino Bianco Ferrante '97		1
●	San Leopardo '94		3
○	Verdicchio di Matelica Cambrugiano Ris. '95	🍷🍷 (white glasses)	3

MATELICA (MC)

Castiglioni - F.lli Bisci
Via Fogliano, 120
62024 Matelica (MC)
tel. 0737/787490

This winery has always held its place in the Guide, which attests its solid structure and the reliable quality displayed in producing the tricky Verdicchio di Matelica. The vineyards (located in a valley parallel to the Apennines at altitudes varying between 250 and 450 meters) are exposed to patches of intense heat and high humidity. The wine requires long aging before it can lose the acidity and roughness typical of its youth. The property of the Bisci brothers covers an area of over a hundred hectares, distributed around the communes of Matelica (province of Macerata) and Cerreto d'Esi (province of Ancona); twenty-five of these are under specialized vineyards. The two Verdicchio di Matelica '97 possess quite different characteristics. The basic version has a delicate light straw-yellow color, an unobtrusive aroma of ripe apple and varietal characteristics sufficiently true-to-type; the palate has good fragrance (despite acidity) and a satisfactory structure, and is well balanced enough to make a pleasant, if not particularly vigorous, drink. The Verdicchio '97 selection Vigneto Fogliano rather surprised us because of characteristics (especially the aromas) that failed to correspond to the type of wine: the straw-yellow color is darker in respect to the other Verdicchios; the aroma (with notes of bitter almond and chlorophyll) are out of balance; on the palate it tastes acidic, still far from mature and there is an distinct lack of harmony between fragrance and alcoholic content. A rather rustic wine, but one which may still improve with time.

○	Verdicchio di Matelica '97	🍷	3
○	Verdicchio di Matelica Vigneto Fogliano '97	🍷	3

MONTECAROTTO (AN)

Terre Cortesi Moncaro
Via Piandole, 7/a
60036 Montecarotto (AN)
tel. 0731/89245

The Moncaro estate, one of the most productive Marche wine properties, was created in 1964: today this winery has more than seven hundred participating associates all concentrated in the Verdicchio dei Castelli di Jesi area, but also, through recent acquisitions, in the Rosso Conero zone. Since 1980 the Moncaro estate has been cultivating 30 hectares practicing organic agriculture. Technical assistance and weather monitoring for a cultivation with low environmental impact has been provided for all associates. We shall begin our overall view of the most recent wines with the biological Verdicchio '97: this is an important wine both for its type, and in its own right, in that it is capable of maintaining its integrity with the passing of time, as was demonstrated when the older vintages were given another tasting. We appreciated the Verde di Ca' Ruprae '97 with distinct varietal notes, and the Vigna Novali '96. The latter, a wine of depth and thickness is aged, for 20 percent, in barriques. Again among the Verdicchios, we should mention the cru Le Busche '97, already soft, with typical scents of linden trees and chamomile, and the Passito Tordiruta, presented for the first time. The basic Verdicchio and the Esino Bianco display their usual standards of correctness. The Le Vele '97, the other successful version of Verdicchio (in its third year of production), has intense attractive scents and a fresh taste, but it is also full and variegated. The Rosso Conero Riserva '95 deserves One full Glass; its production was not yet completely overseen by the present technical staff (including wine experts Giulio D'Ignazi and Alberto Mazzoni, with Marco Monchiero as consultant).

○	Verdicchio dei Castelli di Jesi Cl. Sup. Verde di Ca' Ruptae '97	🍷🍷	3*
○	Verdicchio dei Castelli di Jesi Cl. Sup. Vigna Novali '96	🍷🍷	4
●	Rosso Conero Ris. '95	🍷	3
○	Verdicchio dei Castelli di Jesi Cl. Biologico Tordiruta '97	🍷	3
○	Verdicchio dei Castelli di Jesi Cl. Le Busche '97	🍷	2
○	Verdicchio dei Castelli di Jesi Cl. Le Vele '97	🍷	3
○	Verdicchio dei Castelli di Jesi Cl. Passito Tordiruta '95	🍷	4
○	Esino Bianco '96		1

MONTEGRANARO (AP)

Rio Maggio

C.da Vallone, 41
63014 Montegranaro (AP)
tel. 0734/889587

The estate managed by the brothers Simone and Pierpaolo Santucci appears for the first time in the Guide. With consultation from wine expert Giancarlo Soverchia, the Rio Maggio has already taken giant steps to capture the attention of the public with a series of unquestionably interesting wines. The winery lies in the country near Montegranaro, a small town more noted for its shoe production than for wine, but the Santucci brothers had faith in the quality of the land and are now reaping the first accolades for their tenacity. Among their various wines we should mention the Falerio '97, straw-colored, with a delicate floral nose followed by a decidedly fragrant palate, and pleasantly drinkable owing to the softness of the fruit. The Telusiano is a selection of Falerio with a straw-yellow color and strongly developed scents of apple, honey and apricot. On the palate it displays a splendid balance between acidity and alcohol. The Chardonnay Artias '97, a light straw-yellow color, has barely perceptible scents of banana and dried fruit; on the palate it reveals good acidity not yet balanced with the rest of the components. The interesting Sauvignon Ombra '97 unites a straw-yellow color with green tints to clear-cut aromas of chlorophyll, peppermint and sage; the palate is well balanced with the acid content. The Santarosa '97 is a true-to-type rosato from sangiovese grapes that tastes vinous, fresh and soft; the Rosso Piceno '97 is a strong ruby color with purple tints, distinct vinous scents and a soft, adequately concentrated palate with sweet tannins.

○	Falerio dei Colli Ascolani Telusiano '97	🍷🍷	3*
○	Sauvignon Ombra '97	🍷🍷	3*
○	Chardonnay Artias '97	🍷	3
○	Falerio dei Colli Ascolani '97	🍷	1*
●	Rosso Piceno '97	🍷	2
⊙	Santarosa '97		1

MORRO D'ALBA (AN)

Stefano Mancinelli

Via Roma, 62
60030 Morro d'Alba (AN)
tel. 0731/63021

The decision Stefano Mancinelli made in the mid-eighties to concentrate on the Lacrima di Morro d'Alba grape and vinify this one variety on its own has been proven correct year after year: the quality of the wines presented is further confirmation. We begin our review with the Sensazioni di Frutto '97; this is a trendy wine with a good, densely-textured purple color. Its nose is decidedly fruity and spicy with good intensity, followed by a rich taste and long finish. Along the same lines he presented the Lacrima S. Maria del Fiore '97, always Stefano's sure thing, made with grapes picked from old vines. The wine is purplish with a scent of roses and spice followed by an already soft and full flavor. Also interesting are the Verdicchios dei Castelli di Jesi from the latest vintage, both the basic one and the cru S. Maria del Fiori: the first is characterized by its clean freshness and well-expressed varietal characteristics; the second, by its straw-yellow color with green tints, and aromas of almond and flowers. Here the taste is more consistent and savory and has an almondy finish. Before mentioning the last wine we ought not to forget that for a few vintages Mancinelli has been the only wine-maker in the region who has personally distilled the wine lees of his production, and with excellent results. The Rosso Piceno S. Michele '97 is an enjoyable drink, purple in color and with a moderate backbone.

●	Lacrima di Morro d'Alba S. Maria del Fiore '97	🍷🍷	3*
●	Lacrima di Morro d'Alba Sensazioni di Frutto '97	🍷🍷	3*
○	Verdicchio dei Castelli di Jesi Cl. S. Maria del Fiore '97	🍷🍷	2*
●	Rosso Piceno S. Michele '97	🍷	2
○	Verdicchio dei Castelli di Jesi Cl. '97	🍷	2
●	Lacrima di Morro d'Alba S. Maria del Fiore '95	🥂🥂	3
●	Lacrima di Morro d'Alba Sensazioni di Frutto '95	🥂🥂	3

NUMANA (AN)

CONTE LEOPARDI DITTAJUTI
VIA MARINA II, 26
60026 NUMANA (AN)
TEL. 071/7390116 - 7391479

Piervittorio Leopardi continues to present us with convincing proof of the quality of his wines. His estate in the Monte Conero area enjoys the technical services of Romeo Taraborelli in the winery; in accordance with the owners, Taraborelli has always aimed for continuing quality and is constantly presenting good wines, even in less favorable vintage years. The Vigna d'Oro '97 (60 percent trebbiano and the rest sauvignon) is the basic wine among the whites produced on the estate. It has delicate scents but, although it has a pleasantly fresh palate, it is a little thin. The Bianco del Coppo '97, made with pure sauvignon, has a deep straw-yellow color and the typical notes of the sauvignon grape, here particularly elegant and sweet. It is soft on the palate, with a full taste (owing to a rich, long structure) and there are interesting possibilities of evolution. Certainly this is the best Bianco del Coppo produced in the last few years, benefiting from a perfect vintage. The Calcare '97, a light straw-yellow color, has a faint subtle aroma with the barely perceptible grassy note of the sauvignon; on the palate it displays good concentration, the right degree of flavor and fragrance (with some room for improvement). The Rosso Conero '96 Vigneti del Coppo is a fine ruby color with purplish tints; the nose has a distinct but not prevalent herbaceous note (well mingled with the montepulciano grape) recalling black cherry; on the palate it is soft, with gentle tannins, broad structure and a clean finish.

	Wine	Glasses	Price
○	Bianco Calcare Sauvignon '97	🍷🍷	4
○	Bianco del Coppo Sauvignon '97	🍷🍷	3*
●	Rosso Conero Pigmento '94	🍷🍷	4
●	Rosso Conero Vigneti del Coppo '96	🍷	3
○	Vigna d'Oro '97		2
●	Rosso Conero Pigmento '93	YY	4
●	Rosso Conero Vigneti del Coppo '93	YY	3

NUMANA (AN)

FATTORIA LE TERRAZZE
VIA MUSONE, 4
60026 NUMANA (AN)
TEL. 071/7390352

The wines presented this year by the Numana estate show a new and substantial quickening of pace: the results will certainly be evident with more favorable vintages, as in the harvests of '95 and '96 when the estate showed it could produce wines well above the average. With the appearance of the reds from the '97 vintage we shall have appellation wines that will stand any comparison. The Terni family (owners of almost 150 hectares in the Conero area, only a few hundred meters from the sea) are reserving most of their production for the DOCs, on the advice of consultants Attilio Pagli and Leonardo Valente. The Sassi Neri '96, a good selection of Rosso Conero and top wine of the estate, is impressive for the complexity of its aromas which combine plum and black cherry with notes of balsam and leather, while the important palate lacks only a touch of roundness. Antonio and Giorgina Terni also propose a basic, very well made version of Rosso Conero, even though the '96 vintage now on sale is not exactly the best. A fairly dense color is followed by striking aromas of berries; these correspond to the taste which is rather soft with a pronounced vein of acidity. The Numana winery completes its mostly Rosso Conero line with the Le Cave '97, a very successful new Chardonnay. The wine has an elegant luminous yellow color and well expressed scents (tropical fruit, acacia and slight nuances of vanilla); there is a well judged balance of components on the palate. Finally, as always, the Donna Giulia, made from montepulciano grapes, is a successful sparkling wine made with the Metodo Classico.

	Wine	Glasses	Price
○	Le Cave '97	🍷🍷	2*
●	Rosso Conero Sassi Neri '96	🍷🍷	4
●	Rosso Conero '96	🍷	3
○	Spumante Donna Giulia	🍷	4
●	Rosso Conero '95	YY	2
●	Rosso Conero Sassi Neri '93	YY	4
●	Rosso Conero Sassi Neri '94	YY	4
●	Rosso Conero Sassi Neri '95	YY	4

OFFIDA (AP)

VILLA PIGNA
C.DA CIAFONE, 63
63035 OFFIDA (AP)
TEL. 0736/87525

In the territory where Rosso Piceno Superiore is produced, the Villa Pigna estate owned by the Rozzi family certainly possesses the largest production capacity (over 300 hectares of vineyards) and modern, updated winery structures. The technical side is in the hands of the young and determined wine expert Massimo Urriani. This year the best wine from the wide range the estate produces is the Cabernasco '97, a claret-colored cabernet sauvignon with a slight rim; the nose has assorted varietal scents and distinct berry aromas; on the palate this wine (whose growth we shall follow) is pulpy, with noticeable sweet tannins. Among the other wines, mention must be made of the Vellutato '95, from montepulciano grapes, with typical scents of plum, dark cherry and notes of licorice; the palate is coherent, if somewhat thin. The Rosso Piceno Superiore '94, characterized by sweet aromas of vanilla and spice, offers an elegant and rather concentrated palate; in spite of its elegance the Rozzano '96 suffers from the poor vintage year and consequently turns out less rich compared to previous editions. Moving on to the whites, there is a new wine, the Colle Malerbí, from chardonnay grapes; intense scents of acacia and white flowers correspond to a very fresh and clean palate. The Selezione di Falerio dei Colli Ascolani and the Rugiasco, both from chardonnay and riesling grapes, live up to their customary standards of quality. Very true-to-type, as always, the Spumante Extra Brut.

	Wine	Glasses	Price
●	Cabernasco '97	🍷🍷	4
●	Rozzano '96	🍷🍷	4
○	Colle Malerbì '97	🍷	3
○	Falerio dei Colli Ascolani Selezione '97	🍷	2*
●	Rosso Piceno Sup. '94	🍷	2*
○	Rugiasco '96	🍷	3
○	Spumante Riserva Extra Brut	🍷	4
●	Vellutato '95	🍷	2*
●	Rozzano '94	🍷🍷 (outline)	4
●	Cabernasco '95	🍷 (outline)	4

OSIMO (AN)

UMANI RONCHI
S.S. 16 KM. 310+400, 74
60028 OSIMO (AN)
TEL. 071/7108019

Year after year, while actively engaged in improving its structures, the status of this Osimo estate is boosted by its flattering successes at an international level. The technical staff (consisting of wine expert Umberto Trombelli with Luigi Piersanti and Carlo Modi in charge of the vineyards) can also count on the collaboration of Giacomo Tachis. Among the new wines, starting with the reds, the most outstanding is the Pélago '95, characterized by a complex nose (spices, licorice, plum and boisé) and made from cabernet sauvignon, montepulciano and merlot grapes; the taste is broad with room for evolution. The extraordinarily successful Rosso Conero Cùmaro, of the same vintage, has an inviting nose combining scents of red berries with well-balanced notes of balsam and vanilla; the palate displays sweet tannins. While we are on the subject of Rosso Coneros, the San Lorenzo '96 is well worth our attention for its fine expression of typical characteristics in a poor vintage year, and also the more drinkable, but structured and rich '97; we should also mention the very typical and clean Montepulciano d'Abruzzo Jorio '96. The most substantial white is the Verdicchio Plenio, presented for the first time in this '95 edition: the faint, well-absorbed wood helps to bring out its characteristic notes of hazelnut and ripe fruit. Scents of ripe fruit, particularly white peach, also combine in the structured Casal di Serra '97, which as always is more opulent than the equally sound and fresh Villa Bianchi (same vintage) and the Sauvignon Tajano. Finally Two Glasses go to the Maxim '94, which upholds its reputation of being the best after-dinner wine now being produced in the region.

	Wine	Glasses	Price
●	Pélago '95	🍷🍷	5
●	Rosso Conero Cùmaro '95	🍷🍷	4
○	Verdicchio dei Castelli di Jesi Cl. Sup. Casal di Serra '97	🍷🍷	3
○	Verdicchio dei Castelli di Jesi Cl. Plenio Ris. '95	🍷🍷	3
○	Maximo '94	🍷🍷	4
○	Le Busche '96	🍷	4
●	Montepulciano d'Abruzzo Jorio '96	🍷	3
●	Rosso Conero '97	🍷	3
●	Rosso Conero San Lorenzo '96	🍷	3
○	Tajano '97	🍷	3
○	Verdicchio dei Castelli di Jesi Cl. Villa Bianchi '97	🍷	2
●	Pélago '94	🍷🍷 (outline)	5

OSTRA VETERE (AN)

F.lli Bucci

Via Cona, 30
Fraz. Pongelli
60010 Ostra Vetere (AN)
tel. 071/964179 - 02/6570558

Yet another award for Ampelio Bucci this year and very well deserved. Those familiar with the wines of this estate (many quite rightly regard the Bucci label as a guarantee of high quality and hold that a Bucci wine is immediately recognizable) also know that Ampelio Bucci is in no hurry to put his extraordinarily long-lasting, full-flavored wines on the market. Hence the term Riserva (established by the new production regulations) that accompanies the Villa Bucci is no more than confirmation of an established practice. The estate has eighteen hectares under vineyards: fifteen growing verdicchio and the others producing red grapes (especially sangiovese and montepulciano). The verdicchio production comes from five vines, differentiated in regard to exposure and altitude (between 200 and 350 meters); the grapes are vinified separately and then assembled in cuvée. Beginning with the last to reach the wine shops, the basic '97, we found the scents vegetal, with distinct notes of hazelnut; already the taste is buttery with a sweet almondy flavor which will develop further along in time. The Villa Bucci '95 has complex aromas (articulated but still very fresh); the palate is rich in nuances and structure, though by no means aggressive. This chance to sample the various vintages of Villa Bucci was a little journey back in time, with new surprises all the way.

	Wine	Rating	Price
○	Verdicchio dei Castelli di Jesi Cl. '97	🍷🍷	3
○	Verdicchio dei Castelli di Jesi Cl. Villa Bucci Ris. '95	🍷🍷	4
○	Verdicchio dei Castelli di Jesi Cl. '96	🍷🍷	3
○	Verdicchio dei Castelli di Jesi Cl. Villa Bucci '90	🍷🍷	5
○	Verdicchio dei Castelli di Jesi Cl. Villa Bucci '92	🍷🍷	4
○	Verdicchio dei Castelli di Jesi Cl. Villa Bucci '94	🍷🍷	4
●	Rosso Piceno Tenuta Pongelli '94	🍷	3

PESARO

Fattoria Mancini

Strada dei Colli, 35
61100 Pesaro
tel. 0721/51828

Among the sub-appellations of the Colli Pesaresi DOC whose production regulations were altered a few years ago, we must mention this Roncaglia expertly produced in the Fattoria Mancini. The basic version of this white has a deep straw-yellow color with greenish tints and fruity and floral aromas in evolution. The palate is linear and soft and promises to be ageworthy. The selection of Roncaglia Bianco Vigna Valserpe is of the same vintage year: the vivid yellow color precedes aromas of ripe fruit with notes of hazelnut; the taste is fresh and full with good aromatic length and a pleasant almond finish. The winery covers more than thirty-five hectares of vineyards in the Pesaresi hills and produces the various types of wine established under the regulations; it therefore grows sangiovese and montepulciano grapes, as well as the local albanella and a little sauvignon and moscato. In fact the moscato is used for the Moscardino '97, a dry, fresh and scented white that makes an excellent apéritif. Our review of the reds begins with the Sangiovese '97, one of Fattoria Mancini's simplest and easiest-to-drink wines: its fairly light ruby color leads to a rather fruity nose that is coherent with its taste. The wine is an unpretentious but enjoyable drink. The red Focara, of the same vintage and same breadth of expression, has a moderately deep color, a fruity nose and palate, but this time there is a touch of bitterness at the finish. Finally, the Montebacchino '97, an interesting wine from montepulciano grapes, promises an interesting evolution.

	Wine	Rating	Price
○	Colli Pesaresi Bianco Roncaglia '97	🍷	2*
○	Colli Pesaresi Bianco Roncaglia Vigna Valserpe '97	🍷	2*
●	Montebacchino '97	🍷	2
○	Moscardino '97	🍷	2
●	Colli Pesaresi Rosso Focara '97		2
●	Colli Pesaresi Sangiovese '97		2

POGGIO S. MARCELLO (AN)

SARTARELLI
VIA COSTE DEL MULINO, 26
60030 POGGIO S. MARCELLO (AN)
TEL. 0731/89732 - 89571

This estate has produced convincing wines with elegant finesse from the '97 harvest, one of the best in recent years. Once again Patrizio Chiacchierini and his wife Donatella Sartarelli have succeeded in making the most of a magnificent vintage; while the winery has accustomed us to expect performances at this level ever since it entered the Guide. Year after year the owners have striven to realize the full potential of their vineyards (the Costa del Mulino facing south-west and the Contrada Balciana, facing north). The two vineyards produce wines that deserve and indeed win accolades. They are always characterized by a firm alcoholic content (at the levels of a great red) and a perfect balance between concentration (these whites have very high extract) and acidity. The Verdicchio di Jesi '97, the basic wine of the estate, is again very good; typical aromas (rather intense and fragrant) are followed in the mouth by well-balanced structure, fresh acidity and fair concentration. The selection Tralivio '97 is the usual Verdicchio with a straw-yellow color and luminous green tints; the range of ripe fruit, hazelnut, apple and apricot aromas is rather broad; on the palate it is vigorous, soft, elegant and concentrated, and there is a clear-cut bitter almond finish. The Contrada Balciana '97, which we tasted in a sample drawn from the tanks, made an excellent impression, but we shall have more to say about this one next year.

○	Verdicchio dei Castelli di Jesi Cl. Sup. Tralivio '97	▼▼	3*
○	Verdicchio dei Castelli di Jesi Cl. '97	▼▼	2*
○	Verdicchio dei Castelli di Jesi Cl. Sup. Contrada Balciana '94	▽▽▽	4
○	Verdicchio dei Castelli di Jesi Cl. Sup. Contrada Balciana '95	▽▽▽	4
○	Verdicchio dei Castelli di Jesi Cl. Sup. Tralivio '96	▽▽	3

RIPATRANSONE (AP)

TENUTA COCCI GRIFONI
C.DA MESSIERI, 12
FRAZ. S. SAVINO
63030 RIPATRANSONE (AP)
TEL. 0735/90143

The contrada Messieri winery lies among the most famous hills for the production of Rosso Piceno Superiore, a wine whose potential has still not been fully expressed. Guido Cocci Grifone is the winemaker who created the history of the Piceno appellation: the first vintage year of Rosso Piceno Superiore, '69, was a milestone for the area and continues to serve as an important reference point. So we shall begin our review of the wines tasted in '98 with Rosso Piceno Superiore '96 Vigna Messieri, the favorite of the whole estate. This wine cannot help suffering a little from an inferior vintage year; it is however true-to-type, has fruity notes on the nose and a harmonious taste, though the body is no more than average. The Rosso Piceno Superiore '95 with its ruby tending to garnet color compares well to the selected version: the nose has notes of ripe fruit, particularly raspberry; there is good correspondence on the palate which is soft and still has a note of acidity. The Falerio dei Colli Ascolani '97 displays floral scents and a fresh palate with a typical almondy finish. The selection of Falerio Vigneti San Basso, yellow with greenish tints in color, has floral and fruity scents, a palate with good length, an appreciable structure and closes with an almond finish. Best of the whites is once again the Podere Colle Vecchio, purely from local pecorino grapes. It has fairly broad floral and fruity scents and a substantial, well-balanced structure. Finally a mention should go to the Passerina Brut, which has been made with success for the last few years.

○	Podere Colle Vecchio '97	▼▼	3*
○	Falerio dei Colli Ascolani Vigneti S. Basso '97	▼	2
○	Passerina Brut '97	▼	3
●	Rosso Piceno Sup. Vigna Messieri '96	▼	3
●	Rosso Piceno Superiore '95	▼	2
○	Falerio dei Colli Ascolani '97		1
●	Rosso Piceno '97		1
●	Rosso Piceno Sup. Vigna Messieri '95	▽▽	3

RIPATRANSONE (AP)

LE CANIETTE
VIA CANALI, 23
63038 RIPATRANSONE (AP)
TEL. 0735/9200

Established for some time in the country near Piceno, this estate now enters the Guide for the first time. Among the wines presented by young Luigi and Giovanni Vagnoni, with the help of wine expert Giancarlo Soverchia, the selection of Falerio Lucrezia (in its first year of production) has proved a triumph. Its straw-yellow color is followed by a nose of ripe fruit combined with mineral notes; it is rich on the palate and possesses good length on the finish. The other Falerio produced in the '97 vintage, the Veronica, has more freshness and is easier to drink. Apart from these good results (obtained from a varietal that is fortunately regaining ground), the Vagnoni brothers should also be mentioned for reinstating an ancient traditional wine produced at Ripatransone (in the Marche), but also in Sant'Angelo in Vado: the Vin Santo, from local passerina grapes sun-dried on wicker panels. The Sibilla Cumana '94 (a good name for this fascinating after dinner wine) has a yellow to amber color; the aromas of honey and dried figs are slightly disturbed by not altogether convincing scents of biscuit; the taste is warm and full. The red wines the estate is counting on for the future to some extent suffer from the unfavorable vintage years: the Morellone '94 (tasted last year), a selection of Rosso Piceno from sangiovese and montepulciano grapes, has tones that are already evolved. The other Rosso Piceno, the Rosso Bello '96, aged for a brief period in barrique, is easier to drink, and is certainly a clean wine; its fruity aromas are followed by a coherent medium-bodied palate.

○	Falerio dei Colli Ascolani Lucrezia '97	🍷	1*
○	Falerio dei Colli Ascolani Veronica '97	🍷	1*
●	Rosso Piceno Rosso Bello '96	🍷	1
○	Sibilla Cumana '94	🍷	5

SERRA DE' CONTI (AN)

CASALFARNETO
VIA FARNETO, 16
60030 SERRA DE' CONTI (AN)
TEL. 0731/889001

This young winery, which has its own vineyards on the hills between Serra de' Conti and Montecarotto, enters the Guide thanks to a monovarietal but differentiated production. This year Danilo Solustri and Massimo Arcangeli, both passionate winemakers, have decided to dedicate themselves, with two partners, to a project for quality winegrowing and winemaking using eighteen hectares of vineyards (out of the fifty-two hectares of joint property) lying at 300 meters above sea level. Between the two selections of Verdicchio dei Castelli di Jesi Classico presented by the Casalfarneto in the '97 vintage (only the second year of the estate's production), the Fontevecchia displays the best characteristics of the varietal type. Straw-yellow in color with green tints, it has a fairly broad bouquet with scents reminiscent of linden trees, white flowers, field grass and summer fruit; these correspond to a palate where finesse combines with muscle. This is a wine we shall want to follow in the course of the next few months. The Gran Casale selection is made from overripe grapes, leaving part of the skins to macerate cold with the must; aging is partly done in stainless steel and to a lesser degree in small oak casks; the two parts are then assembled and bottled for a further period of aging. This wine promises an interesting evolution, with pronounced aromatic notes, scents of geranium and herbs blending with an emerging note of white peach which is also present on the palate.

○	Verdicchio dei Castelli di Jesi Cl. Gran Casale '97	🍷🍷	3
○	Verdicchio dei Castelli di Jesi Cl. Fontevecchia '97	🍷	2*

SERRAPETRONA (MC)

Massimo Serboni
Via Case Sparse, 6
62020 Serrapetrona (MC)
tel. 0733/904088

The Vernaccia di Serrapetrona is an off-beat wine, little known outside the strictly local community, but it deserves a much wider public. It has nothing to do with the other DOC Vernaccias (San Gimignano and Oristano) since it is red and mostly produced in a sparkling version; the only point they have in common is the name. The Latin 'vernaculum', when speaking of wine , refers to local products. The creation of Vernaccia di Serrapetrona is yet another example of making a virtue out of necessity: the considerable cold and high altitude of the vineyards forced winemakers to dream up a way of sustaining the sugar level of the wine. At that time it was thought that sun-drying part of the harvested grapes and, towards December, adding the accumulated must to the wine would spark off a second fermentation. A few months later the wine with its vinous and fruity scents of remarkable length and a pleasantly varietal taste, is ready for the drinking. Among the interpreters (not too many to tell the truth, as you can count them on the fingers of one hand) the winery of Massimo Serboni must also be mentioned because it offers agro-tourist hospitality. He makes two versions of this wine (Secco and Amabile). Both are clean, fairly concentrated and reveal the range of aromas of the grape. The violets and red fruit scents are present in both versions; to these the Secco adds a lively vinousness, while the Amabile finishes in sweetness, but avoids syrupy tones.

●	Vernaccia di Serrapetrona Secco '97	🍷	3
●	Vernaccia di Serrapetrona Amabile '97	🍷	3

SPINETOLI (AP)

Saladini Pilastri
Via Saladini, 5
63030 Spinetoli (AP)
tel. 0736/899534

With the wines presented this year, the Spinetoli estate (dating from the early 1970s, the period of the first local DOCs) shows that it has taken a decisive step towards the production of quality wines: the results are very convincing on the whole, especially for some wines which are now the best of their type. A good example is the Rosso Piceno selection Vigna Piediprato '97, the most important wine from the estate (which has revamped its wine growing practices to conform to European regulations on biological production). This extraordinarily interesting wine has a deep brownish color with seductive scents of black cherry and plum; on the palate it is fluid, concentrated and elegant. This wine is the result of the recent collaboration between wine expert Domenico D'Angelo and Roberto Cipresso. We were most impressed by the basic version of Rosso Piceno '97: not only is there outstanding strength but it is a good easy drink, with a far from negligible structure that wins it the Two Glasses award. The Pregio del Conte Rosso '95, from a mix of aglianico and montepulciano grapes, also came close to the same award: this wine has a considerably complex nose (with balsamic nuances), and is soft to the palate. The Pregio del Conte Bianco, using different grapes from the ones used for the Falerio (fiano and falanghina, among others), makes a more delineated and original impression compared to previous editions: the nose is fresh and the palate inviting. Finally, there are good results from the two Falerio dei Colli Ascolani '97 (basic and cru version of the Vigna Palazzi): the first is the more typical and has a fair consistency; the second comes closer to ripe fruit, and presents a soft and balanced palate.

●	Rosso Piceno '97	🍷🍷	2*
●	Rosso Piceno Vigna Piediprato '97	🍷🍷	3*
○	Falerio dei Colli Ascolani '97	🍷	1
○	Falerio dei Colli Ascolani Vigna Palazzi '97	🍷	2
○	Pregio del Conte Bianco '97	🍷	2
●	Pregio del Conte Rosso '95	🍷	3
●	Rosso Piceno Vigna Piediprato '95	🍷🍷 (white glasses)	3

STAFFOLO (AN)

Fattoria Coroncino
C.da Coroncino, 7
60039 Staffolo (AN)
tel. 0731/779494

Year after year, without any special publicity or retouching of their image, the Staffolo winery has continued to reveal its commitment to quality. This has been achieved through methodical perseverance and good hard work backed by a passion for winemaking. The Gaiospino, the estate's most important wine, was recently brought out in two vintages ('96 and '97) and both were an enormous success, setting an example for substance and power of expression. The '96 version is especially praiseworthy in view of the poor vintage year; now it has blossomed into a great wine rare for its type; we earnestly recommend our readers to try it. You will discover even greater merits, if that were possible, in regard to strength and sweetness in the Gaiospino '97, although it is still at a rather green stage of sun-warmed linden tree, but with a truly rosy future before it. Our award of Three Glasses went to this wine without a moment's hesitation. Lucio Canestrari 's wine list also includes a Verdicchio Coroncino that should not be underrated: although inferior to the Gaiospino it has a fairly long conservation capacity and distinct, expressive tones. The basic Verdicchio dei Castelli di Jesi (named for the figure of Bacchus on the label) is a more drinkable wine, although with the texture of a Staffolo Verdicchio. Finally the Le Lame '97, from verdicchio and trebbiano grapes (and marketed at an extremely reasonable price) displays similar qualities, with aromatic notes closer to field grasses, chamomile and hay.

	Wine	Glasses	Price
○	Verdicchio dei Castelli di Jesi Cl. Sup. Gaiospino '97	🍷🍷🍷	4
○	Verdicchio dei Castelli di Jesi Cl. Sup. Gaiospino '96	🍷🍷	4
○	Verdicchio dei Castelli di Jesi Cl. Sup. Il Coroncino '97	🍷🍷	3*
○	Le Lame '97	🍷	2*
○	Verdicchio dei Castelli di Jesi Cl. Sup. Bacco '97	🍷	2*
○	Verdicchio dei Castelli di Jesi Cl. Sup. Il Coroncino '96	🍷🍷 (white)	3

STAFFOLO (AN)

F.lli Zaccagnini & C.
Via Salmàgina, 9/10
60039 Staffolo (AN)
tel. 0731/779892

The commune of Staffolo, within the territory of the Castelli di Jesi, can be proud of one of the largest communities of quality winemakers in Italy. Among these the Zaccagnini family are at the forefront: young though their winery may be, it immediately opted for quality selection and cru production, such as the Salmámagina. This wine takes its name from the district where the winery is located, at an altitude of 450 meters. In 1997 this selection of Verdicchio, which expresses itself better year after vintage year, has proved a success thanks to its intense aromas (white flowers, linden tree, chlorophyll) and a tasty palate that is at once substantial and elegant. The good basic Verdicchio, intended to be an easily drinkable wine, has aromas reminiscent of field grass and fresh fruit. On the palate it is tasty and has a fresh finish. The Verdicchio Pier delle Vigne needs more attention given to its production: the '95 version now on sale has too much wood dominating the other aromas. The successful Cesolano '93, obtained from sun-drying verdicchio grapes, has a nose of dried figs, honey, candied citrus peel and toasted almonds, supported by good alcoholic content; on the palate this golden yellow wine has well-balanced sweetness. We shall wind up our review of the Verdicchios with the tried and true Spumanti, Zaccagnini Metodo Tradizionale and the Zaccagnini Brut, made according to the Metodo Charmat. Finally we should mention the red Vigna Vescovi '94 , from montepulciano, pinot nero and cabernet grapes: the color is a darkish red with a mauvish tinge; its nose of ripe fruit and leather lead into a palate of barely perceptible acidity.

	Wine	Glasses	Price
●	Vigna Vescovi '94	🍷🍷	3
○	Verdicchio dei Castelli di Jesi Cl. Salmàgina '97	🍷🍷	3
○	Verdicchio dei Castelli di Jesi Cl. '97	🍷	2
○	Verdicchio dei Castelli di Jesi Cl. Pier delle Vigne '95	🍷	4
○	Cesolano Passito '93	🍷	4
○	Zaccagnini Brut	🍷	3
○	Zaccagnini Metodo Tradizionale	🍷	4

OTHER WINERIES

The following producers obtained good scores in our tastings with one or more of their wines:

PROVINCE OF ANCONA

Angelo Accadia
Serra S. Quirico, tel. 0731/85172,
Verdicchio Castelli di Jesi Cl. Cantorì '97

Maurizio Benigni
S. Paolo di Jesi, tel. 0731/704042,
Verdicchio Castelli di Jesi Cl.
La Scappaia '97

Amato Ceci
S. Paolo di Jesi, tel. 0731/779052,
Verdicchio Castelli di Jesi Cl. Sup.
Vignamato '97

Medoro Cimarelli
Staffolo, tel. 0731/779307
Verdicchio Castelli di Jesi Cl.
Frà Moriale '97

Crognaletti, Montecarotto, tel. 0731/89656,
Verdicchio Castelli di Jesi Cl. San Lorenzo '97

Finocchi, Staffolo, tel. 0731/779573,
Verdicchio Castelli di Jesi Cl. '97

Luciano Landi
Belvedere Ostrense, tel. 0731/62353
Lacrima di Morro d'Alba '97

Mario Luchetti
Morro d'Alba, tel. 0731/63314,
Lacrima di Morro d'Alba '97

Poggio Montali
Monteroberto, tel. 0731/702825,
Verdicchio Castelli di Jesi
Cl. Sup. Deserto '97

Umberto Socci
Castelplanio, tel. 071/9160725,
Verdicchio Castelli di Jesi Cl. Cantorì '97

Anna Maria Strozzi
Castelplanio, tel. 0731/813006,
Verdicchio Castelli di Jesi Cl.
Tenuta dell'Ugolino '97

PROVINCE OF ASCOLI PICENO

Aurora, Offida, tel. 0736/810007,
Rosso Piceno '97

La Cantina dei Colli Ripani
Ripatransone, tel. 0735/99940,
Rosso Piceno Sup. Il Castellano '94

Cantina di Castignano
Castignano, tel. 0736/822216,
Bianco Castello '97

Romolo e Remo Dezi
Servigliano, tel. 0734/750408,
Rosso Piceno Regina del Bosco '95

San Giovanni
Offida, tel. 0736/889032,
Falerio dei Colli Ascolani Leo Guelfus '97

PROVINCE OF MACERATA

Antonio Canestrari
Apiro, tel. 0733/611315,
Verdicchio Castelli di Jesi Cl. Lapiro '97

Fattoria dei Cavalieri
Matelica, tel. 0737/84859,
Verdicchio di Matelica
Podere dei Cavalieri '97

Fattoria di Forano
Appignano, tel. 0733/57102,
Colli Maceratesi Bianco Villa Forano '97

Gino Gagliardi, Matelica, tel. 0737/85611,
Verdicchio di Matelica Maccagnano '97

Lanfranco Quacquarini
Serrapetrona, tel. 0733/908103,
Vernaccia di Serrapetrona Amabile

San Biagio
Matelica, tel. 0737/83997,
Verdicchio di Matelica '97

Saputi, Colmurano, tel. 0733/508137,
Colli Maceratesi Bianco Castru Vecchio '97

PROVINCE OF PESARO

Anzilotti Solazzi
Saltara, tel. 0721/895491
Bianchello del Metauro '97

Fattoria Villa Ligi
Pergola, tel. 0721/734351,
Grifoleto Vernaculum '97

Valentino Fiorini, Barchi, tel. 0721/97151,
Bianchello del Metauro Tenuta Campioli '97

UMBRIA

If we ranked the up-and-coming wine producing regions, Umbria would find itself promoted to first place. The era when enormous quantities of white and red wine were carelessly produced in bulk and then sold to Tuscan dealers at rock bottom prices, or else distributed only within the region, is now light years away. An unbelievable ferment is bubbling in "the green heart of Italy": new estates emerging, vineyards and wineries undergoing restructuring, international grape varieties being tried out, selections being made from the traditional ones. It is an encouraging scene. We find that some of the most expert winemakers in Italy are working as they never have before. It all began in the 1970s, when the Antinoris acquired the Castello della Sala, near Orvieto, and set up an experimental winery. It had a major impact on their production, and not only on theirs. After many years the continual success of this company (and this means the entire region) is embodied in a single della Sala wine; refined and elegant, it is one of the few labels capable of representing Italy on the international scene. With a splendid '96 (of all years!) the Cervaro takes a place for the eighth time (a near record) among the élite of Italian winemaking. The Orvieto area also has a wide variety of wines to offer, from simple ones to the more serious and interesting versions of DOCs, from the new innovative labels based on international grape varieties to the great classic reds. One of the biggest changes over the last years has been the discovery of the Orvieto region's ability to produce important reds. After Giovanni Dubini's award winning Armeleo '95 last year, we tried another excellent red, the Calanco '95 from the Tenuta Le Velette which also reaches very high all-round levels. It is a wine that acknowledges tradition (it is mostly from sangiovese grapes) but, through the use of cabernet and aging in new wood, has acquired a character and distinction that well deserves our Three Glasses. The blend of local with imported grapes, however, is not the only path to follow. The Caprai in Montefalco have scored their third consecutive Three Glasses with a wine solidly based on a typically local grape, the magnificent Sagrantino di Montefalco '95 Riserva Venticinque Anni. We can only add that this is a "revolutionary" red, in its grand structure, its concentration of polyphenols and the careful attention given to the use of new wood. This red need fear no comparison at a world level, and has contributed towards redefining winemaking in Umbria for the next century. The region has proven that it can rediscover its most ancient roots by adopting the most modern techniques. Many wineries have overhauled their production methods and it seriously looks as though others have decided to follow their example. For these and all the others, it is worth bearing in mind that no one can go on living on memories and laurels won in the past.

AMELIA (TR)

CANTINA SOCIALE DEI COLLI AMERINI
LOC. FORNOLE
STRADA AMERINA KM 7.100
05020 AMELIA (TR)
TEL. 0744/989721

By now we should have got used to the quality of the wines from the Cantina dei Colli Amerini, but even so the production standards of this cooperative surprise us again and again every year. With its 700 hectares of vineyards, plus technical consultation from oenologist Riccardo Cotarella, this winery has once more reaped numerous accolades in the present edition. Among the white wines, three have won Glasses awards: Orvieto Classico '97, with floral notes of broom and good body, the Grechetto dell'Umbria Il Vignolo '97, with subtle fruity scents, slightly acidic and elegant; then there is the Chardonnay dell'Umbria Amiro '97 with a richly floral bouquet, and a palate that has elegance and length. We need only mention the Malvasia dei Colli Amerini La Corte '97, which is less pristine than in previous versions. In the range of reds, the Colli Amerini Rosso Terre Arnolfe '97 holds its own. It has a ruby red color, fruity scents that are distinctly plummy and spicy, while the taste is acidic and slightly tannic. For the last few years, the best of all has been the Colli Amerini Rosso Superiore Carbio '96, with its impressive structure and character. Made from merlot, sangiovese, montepulciano and ciliegiolo grapes, it is a darkish ruby color, broad and ethereal on the nose with aromas of ripe red fruit and spices. It has a solid, intense, long taste, enriched with complex notes of spice. Lastly we come to two excellent sweet wines: the Moscato dell'Umbria Donna Olimpia '97, with its delicate, refined fragrance, and the Umbria Aleatico Bartolomeo '97, which has intense aromas recalling stewed plums and a richly harmonious body.

●	Colli Am. Rosso Sup. Carbio '96	🍷🍷	4
●	Aleatico Bartolomeo '96	🍷	3
○	Chardonnay Amiro '97	🍷	2*
●	Colli Am. Rosso Terre Arnolfe '97	🍷	2*
○	Grechetto dell'Umbria Il Vignolo '97	🍷	2*
○	Moscato Donna Olimpia '97	🍷	3
○	Orvieto Classico '97	🍷	2
○	Colli Am. Malvasia La Corte '97		2
●	Colli Am. Rosso Sup. Carbio '94	🍷🍷	4
●	Colli Am. Rosso Sup. Carbio '95	🍷🍷	4
●	Colli Am. Sangiovese Torraccio '95	🍷🍷	3*
○	Colli Am. Grechetto Villa Gioiosa '95	🍷	2*
●	Colli Am. Rosso Sup. Carbio '92	🍷	4
●	Colli Am. Rosso Terre Arnolfe '94	🍷	2
●	Colli Am. Rosso Terre Arnolfe '95	🍷	2*

BASCHI (TR)

BARBERANI - VALLESANTA
LOC. CERRETO
05023 BASCHI (TR)
TEL. 0744/950113

A few miles from Orvieto the Barberani-Vallesanta estate stretches for more than 70 hectares over the hills facing Lake Corbara, and follows the course of the Tiber. Barberani has around 40 hectares of specialized vineyards, with one of the finest parks in the country, from a viticultural point of view. Apart from typical grapes of the area it grows an extremely rich range of international grapes; chardonnay, sauvignon, sémillon, riesling renano, cabernet sauvignon and franc, and pinot nero, to list but a few. The winery employs very advanced technology, and for some years has enjoyed the consulting services of exceptional wine expert and technician Maurizio Castelli. The range of wines presented are good on the whole, but we feel obliged to repeat word for word what we wrote last year: they are "not yet the outstanding wines which would place the company among Italy's absolute élite". The only really new wine is the Moscato Passito Villa Monticelli '97. Made solely from white moscato grapes and aged five months in oak casks, it has a deep straw-yellow color, and a nose of pear and dried apricot. On the palate it is warm, elegant and long. The Orvieto Classico Superiore Calcaia'96, a sweet wine from botrytized grapes, is a little under tone with a nose and palate that are not particularly well expressed. The whites are good: the Umbria Grechetto '97, with pleasant scents of plum and white peach, and the fruity and vegetal Umbria Pomaio '97, mostly from sauvignon blanc. We might also mention the good Umbria Foresco '96, from sangiovese, cabernet sauvignon and franc grapes, but we are still expecting something more from this wine.

○	Moscato Passito Villa Monticelli '97	🍷🍷	6
●	Foresco '96	🍷	4
○	Grechetto '97	🍷	3
○	Orvieto Classico Sup. Calcaia '96	🍷	5
○	Pomaio '97	🍷	3
●	Foresco '93	🍷🍷	4
○	Orvieto Classico Calcaia '92	🍷🍷	5
○	Orvieto Classico Calcaia '93	🍷🍷	5
○	Orvieto Classico Calcaia '94	🍷🍷	5
○	Orvieto Classico Calcaia '95	🍷🍷	5
●	Foresco '94	🍷	4
●	Foresco '95	🍷	4
○	Orvieto Classico Castagnolo '96	🍷	3
○	Pomaio '96	🍷	3

BEVAGNA (PG)

FATTORIA MILZIADE ANTANO
LOC. COLLE ALLODOLE
06031 BEVAGNA (PG)
TEL. 0742/360371

The Fattoria of Milziade Antano is re-entering the Guide. Its last mention was quite a few years ago, in the 1994 edition. So it is a pleasure to find it listed once more in the pages on Umbria, owing to the very successful presentation of its wines this year. We particularly liked the well-produced wines made from red grapes, all very typical ones, starting with the good Rosso di Montefalco '94. The ruby red color with garnet tints has a nose of warm ripe fruit of good intensity. It has a broad, full-bodied taste with good overall balance. The Sagrantino di Montefalco '95 is also a really well-made wine: dark ruby red in color, it has an intense and powerful nose, with notes of fruit and oriental spices. The taste is ethereal, warm and spicy, with well-balanced and rather mature tannins. The Sagrantino di Montefalco Passito is excellent, and from our tastings we find it the best of the '94 vintage. It too has a darkish ruby color, with fruity notes reminiscent of plum jam. The taste is warm, complex, with a well-balanced sugar and tannin content. We need only mention the Rosso di Montefalco '96; it has a slightly closed nose and rather green tannins. We cannot conclude without expressing the hope that the seesaw results we have come to expect from the Antano winery over the years will finally come to a halt.

●	Sagrantino di Montefalco '95	🍷🍷	5
●	Sagrantino di Montefalco Passito '94	🍷🍷	5
●	Rosso di Montefalco '94	🍷	3
●	Rosso di Montefalco '96		3

CASTEL VISCARDO (TR)

VI.C.OR.
FRAZ. MONTERUBIAGLIO
LOC. LE PRESE, 22
05014 CASTEL VISCARDO (TR)
TEL. 0763/66064

The Vitivinicola Colli Orvietani, established in 1957, with a good 300 supplier-members, has always enjoyed the reputation of being one of the best cooperatives in the Orvieto area. A technologically very well-equipped winery, for some years it has had an exceptional consultant in wine expert Riccardo Cotarella. Its range of wines is well-articulated. The company produces three versions of Orvieto Classico. The Orvieto Classico Salceto '97 has rich fruity scents of golden apple and light balsamic notes; its taste is clean and full-bodied. The Orvieto Classico Roio '97 makes a good impact on the nose with fruity notes of white peach and plum, while the taste has a good level of acidity and intensity. The Orvieto Classico Superiore Fiorile '97 has a deep straw-yellow color, a fragrant nose with clear-cut scents of white fruit and slight vegetal tones of broom. The taste has good intensity and length. The Umbria Bianco Le Coste '97 is also good, with scents recalling hawthorn flowers, while the palate is perfectly linear and clean. This year's revelation, however, is the Rosso dell'Umbria L'Olmaia '96 which thoroughly deserves its Two Glasses. Made from merlot, pinot nero, cabernet sauvignon and franc grapes, fermented and aged in barriques, it shows splendid personality. A rather intense ruby red in color, it has richly fruity notes well blended with hints of wood and a wide, powerful, slightly tannic but well-balanced taste.

●	L'Olmaia '96	🍷🍷	4
○	Bianco Le Coste '97	🍷	1*
○	Orvieto Classico Roio '97	🍷	1*
○	Orvieto Classico Salceto '97	🍷	2*
○	Orvieto Classico Sup. Fiorile '97	🍷	3
○	Orvieto Classico Roio '93	🍸	1*
○	Orvieto Classico Salceto '93	🍸	2*

CASTIGLIONE DEL LAGO (PG)

Fanini

C.da Cucchi
Loc. Petrignano del Lago
06060 Castiglione del Lago (PG)
tel. 075/9528116

This is the first time in the Guide for the Fanini winery, and it enters in style. Lying on the hills of Lake Trasimeno, near the Tuscan border, this estate deserves our heartiest applause for the excellence performance of its wines. Two wines were presented for tasting this year; and both easily reached the Two Glasses level. The first is a Chardonnay dell'Umbria called Robbiano '96, aged for some months in French oak barriques. It has a mild straw-yellow color, with a broad and powerful nose of well-ripened fruit. The wood is well-dosed and well-integrated, with sweet tones and slightly toasty nuances. Its taste is broad and long, with a well expressed fruity component supported by zestful acidity. The second is a red wine, from sangiovese and canaiolo grapes, the Colli di Trasimeno Rosso Morello del Lago '95. Here too the wine is aged in barriques for a time, with decidedly convincing results: a ruby red color, with a long and intense nose displaying aromas of undergrowth and the right dose of sweet wood. The taste is deep with good power and notes of properly ripened red fruit. It is complex and spicy with an excellent tannin component while the finish has noteworthy length. One additional merit worth mentioning is its excellent quality/price ratio.

	Wine	Glasses	Price
○	Chardonnay Robbiano '96	🍷🍷	3*
●	Colli del Trasimeno Rosso Morello del Lago '95	🍷🍷	3*

CIVITELLA DEL LAGO (TR)

Tenuta di Salviano

Loc. Salviano
05020 Civitella del Lago (TR)
tel. 0744/950459

For centuries the property of the Corsini princes, the Tenuta di Salviano spreads along the shores of Lake Corbara for more than two thousand hectares (about 60 under vineyards) on both sides of the Tiber between Todi and Orvieto. The winemaking and aging premises, near the Castello di Salviano, are entirely excavated out of tufa and furnished with modern equipment. Under the able management of Sebastiano Rosa (also in charge of Tenuta di Argiano at Montalcino), Salviano wines have scored high in our tastings this year. Two wines are noteworthy. The Orvieto Classico Superiore '97, from typically local grapes plus minor additions of sauvignon blanc (15%), turns out to be one of the best of the vintage. A light straw-yellow color, it displays a broad nose with floral notes, clear-cut balsamic scents of sage closing in slightly mineral tones, while the taste has medium concentration but a good balance among the various components. Another good wine is the Lago di Corbara Rosso Turlò '97, from a blend of sangiovese (60%) and cabernet sauvignon (40%) grapes: darkish ruby in color with purplish tints, it has a broad nose with lively herbaceous scents. The taste is fruity, rather clean, with a tannic emphasis that perhaps goes a bit too far. A good wine, although still very young, it will present no problems as it evolves in the bottle.

	Wine	Glasses	Price
○	Orvieto Classico Salviano '97	🍷🍷	3*
●	Lago di Corbara Rosso Turlò '97	🍷	3
○	Orvieto Classico Salviano '95	🍷🍷 (previous)	3
○	Orvieto Classico Salviano '96	🍷🍷 (previous)	3*
○	Vin Santo	🍷🍷 (previous)	5
●	Lago di Corbara Rosso '95	🍷 (previous)	3

CORCIANO (PG)

Pieve del Vescovo
Via G. Leopardi, 82
06073 Corciano (PG)
tel. 075/6978874

Near the little medieval village of Corciano on Lake Trasimeno, the Pieve del Vescovo is considered the most interesting winery in the whole of the Colli del Trasimeno area. Dominated by the majestic castle of Pieve del Vescovo (from which the estate takes its name) the company is run by the dynamic Iolanda Tinarelli, with technical consultation from Riccardo Cotarella. This year the level of quality is once again as high as in the past. The four wines of the estate are all produced under the DOC Colli del Trasimeno. The jewel in the crown of the company's production is the Lucciaio '96. Made from canaiolo, gamay and sangiovese grapes and aged in barriques for nearly a year, it has a darkish, limpid, ruby red color. The nose is a little closed at first but then opens with distinct notes of black currants and black cherry. The taste is fruity, intense and long, with concentrated tannins and unobtrusive sweet notes of wood. Also excellent is the Colli del Trasimeno Rosso '97, which staunchly retains its Two Glasses. The color is ruby red. The nose has primary fruity scents of strawberry and cherry, with a fruity, intense and long palate. The two Pieve del Vescovo whites are also excellent. The selection Etesiaco '97, from grechetto, malvasia and trebbiano toscano grapes, is a clear straw-yellow, with vegetal scents of lemon grass and broom, and a good full-bodied palate. The Colli del Trasimeno Bianco '97 has aromas reminiscent of plum and white peach, while the taste is fresh and clean with a good long finish.

	Wine	Glasses	Price
●	Colli del Trasimeno Rosso '97	▼▼	2*
●	Colli del Trasimeno Rosso Lucciaio '96	▼▼	4
○	Colli del Trasimeno Bianco '97	▼	2*
○	Colli del Trasimeno Bianco Etesiaco '97	▼	3
●	Colli del Trasimeno Rosso Lucciaio '94	▽▽	4
●	Colli del Trasimeno Rosso Lucciaio '95	▽▽	4
●	Colli del Trasimeno Rosso '94	▽	1*
●	Colli del Trasimeno Rosso '95	▽	2*
●	Colli del Trasimeno Rosso '96	▽	2*
●	Colli del Trasimeno Rosso Lucciaio '93	▽	4

FICULLE (TR)

Castello della Sala
Loc. Sala
05016 Ficulle (TR)
tel. 0763/86051

The Castello della Sala, the huge estate in Umbria owned by the Antinoris, still remains one of the key, influential wineries in the region. To be sure, its wines are made from so-called international grapes. Chardonnay, sauvignon, pinot nero and gewürztraminer are still the basis of the estate's most important wines, but in our opinion this hardly diminishes their quality. If chardonnay grapes can give us a great white like the Cervaro '96, then being nationalistic about viticulture makes absolutely no sense at all. The fact is, this is one of the best Cervaros ever made. It may not quite reach the concentration and complexity of the '94, but we feel it is clearly superior to both to the '95 and the '93, to refer only to the most recent versions. The nose is complex, varietal and elegant, with intense aromas of pineapple, vanilla and peanut butter. The taste is full-bodied, fat, rich and stays on the palate for a long time, which is just as it should be in a great white based on chardonnay (by now the grechetto grape is no more than 10% of the blend). The same may be said of a Muffato '96, from sauvignon, gewürztraminer, riesling and grechetto with slightly aromatic botrytis scents and a sweet, full bodied, concentrated taste. The Pinot Nero '95 is varietal and clear-cut in taste and aromas. We also admired a magnificent Chardonnay '97, a white aged in small casks, and beginning to acquire a dignity all its own, rather than just being the younger brother of the more famous and noble Cervaro. Finally, there is the Sauvignon '97, the "baby" of the family. It has fairly varietal scents, but a body of only medium structure.

	Wine	Glasses	Price
○	Cervaro della Sala '96	▼▼▼	5
○	Chardonnay della Sala '97	▼▼	3*
○	Muffato della Sala '96	▼▼	5
●	Pinot Nero '95	▼▼	5
○	Sauvignon della Sala '97	▼	3
○	Cervaro della Sala '89	▽▽▽	5
○	Cervaro della Sala '90	▽▽▽	5
○	Cervaro della Sala '92	▽▽▽	5
○	Cervaro della Sala '93	▽▽▽	5
○	Cervaro della Sala '94	▽▽▽	5
○	Cervaro della Sala '95	▽▽▽	5
○	Muffato della Sala '93	▽▽▽	5
○	Muffato della Sala '94	▽▽	5
○	Muffato della Sala '95	▽▽	5
○	Chardonnay della Sala '96	▽	3*

GUALDO CATTANEO (PG)

Colpetrone

Fraz. Marcellano
Loc. Madonnuccia
Via della Collina, 4
06035 Gualdo Cattaneo (PG)
tel. 0578/767722

In the last few years the Saiagricola, owners of the Fattoria del Cerro di Montepulciano and the Poderina di Montalcino, have crossed the borders of Tuscany and set up in Umbria. The Colpetrone estate, in the commune of Gualdo Cattaneo, province of Perugia, is beyond question one of the most interesting Umbrian wineries. Last year we spoke of its "re-entry in the Guide", this year the word is "going full steam ahead". With five hectares under vineyards and another 13 hectares coming into production very soon, the constant improvement of quality in these wines through the last vintages has come as a surprise. With Lorenzo Landi, a young wine expert in great demand, firmly at the helm, Colpetrone has scored high in our annual tastings. Two wines were presented. To start with, an excellent Sagrantino di Montefalco '95 has pushed its way up from the One Glass award to the class above. It is certainly very well-produced; the darkish ruby color with tints of bright purple is broad and intense on the nose, with aromas of fruit and complex spicy tones. The taste is structured, broad and clean with notes of black cherry and ripe plum, with an excellent tannic content. There is a good Rosso di Montefalco '96, purplish ruby in color, a fruity nose with clear-cut scents of cherry and a taste of good concentration and length. Very interesting the Rosso di Montefalco '95 (tasted a year late), with its good darkish ruby color, aromas of red fruit and fine spices, and excellent concentration and intensity.in the mouth.

● Rosso di Montefalco '95	🍷🍷	3*
● Sagrantino di Montefalco '95	🍷🍷	4
● Rosso di Montefalco '96	🍷	3
● Rosso di Montefalco '93	🍷 (white)	3
● Sagrantino di Montefalco '93	🍷 (white)	4

MONTECASTRILLI (TR)

Fattoria Le Poggette

Loc. Le Poggette
05026 Montecastrilli (TR)
tel. 0744/940338

Excellent results for the Fattoria Le Poggette from its very first bottling. Thanks to the remarkable standard of the wines presented for tasting this year, it has every right to enter the Guide and win its Glasses. The Fattoria Le Poggette (twelve hectares of specialized vineyards) lies in the commune of Montecastrilli, province of Terni, and is yet another of the up-and-coming estates on the Umbrian scene. Under the technical guidance of wine expert Claudio Gori, the wines immediately turned out to be well-produced and with a certain character. We tried two reds, both very persuasive. The Montepulciano '95, from exclusively montepulciano d'Abruzzo grapes (the owner brought the vine from its region of origin) and aged for 18 months in oak cask, proved to be a thoroughbred. The darkish red ruby color is limpid. Broad and complex scents of fruit and fine spices are elegant and long; on the palate it is concentrated, elegant and soft, with a mature and integrated tannic component. Fattoria Le Poggette's second wine is Colli Amerini Rosso Superiore '96. Ruby red in color, the nose has fruity scents of cherry, plum and slightly spicy notes. Soft on the palate, full bodied, it possesses an excellent overall harmony. So, congratulations and. . . see you next vintage.

● Montepulciano '95	🍷🍷	5
● Colli Amerini Rosso Sup. '96	🍷	3

MONTEFALCO (PG)

Antonelli - San Marco

Loc. San Marco, 59
06036 Montefalco (PG)
tel. 0742/379158

Filippo Antonelli, owner of the estate, has always been an excellent interpreter of the natural resources that the Montefalco area offers to viticulture, and this year his wines have once again fulfilled expectations. With an estate of 140 hectares, 15 of which are vineyards, the Antonelli-San Marco winery again shows its preference for red grapes. Their wines have vigor and character, especially when one considers the levels of the other local producers (a level of honest simplicity with only very few above-average labels). But Filippo's wines are rich in personality, starting with the powerful Sagrantino di Montefalco '95. Darkish ruby in color, it has an intense, long nose of ripe red fruit and spices. The taste is broad and ethereal with notes of plum and ripe black cherry, and a clean, well-balanced finish. Another of the company's important labels is the Sagrantino di Montefalco Passito, whose '94 edition shows good character: it has a darkish ruby red color and a fruity nose. The palate is full-bodied with hints of stewed plums, well-supported by a sturdy tannin content. The elegant Rosso di Montefalco '95 has good concentration, but once again we find that the white wines have done less than brilliantly. They have simple aromas and are rather too thin in the mouth.

	Wine	Glasses	
●	Sagrantino di Montefalco '95	🍷🍷	4
●	Rosso di Montefalco '95	🍷	3
●	Sagrantino di Montefalco Passito '94	🍷	4
●	Sagrantino di Montefalco '94	🍸🍸	4*
●	Rosso di Montefalco '92	🍸	2*
●	Rosso di Montefalco '93	🍸	3
●	Rosso di Montefalco '94	🍸	3
●	Sagrantino di Montefalco '90	🍸	4
●	Sagrantino di Montefalco '91	🍸	4
●	Sagrantino di Montefalco '92	🍸	4
●	Sagrantino di Montefalco '93	🍸	4
●	Sagrantino di Montefalco Passito '90	🍸	4
●	Sagrantino di Montefalco Passito '91	🍸	4
●	Sagrantino di Montefalco Passito '93	🍸	4

MONTEFALCO (PG)

Arnaldo Caprai - Val di Maggio

Loc. Torre
06036 Montefalco (PG)
tel. 0742/378802 - 378523

The Caprai estate is an important presence in Montefalco wine production: the fact that it has won Three Glasses, our highest award, three years running is by no means a stroke of luck. The success is due above all to the undoubted abilities of the owner, Marco Caprai, as well as those of the well-known and highly esteemed wine expert, Attilio Pagli. Concentrated, powerful, broad, fat; these are the adjectives that spring to mind to describe the exceptional Sagrantino di Montefalco 25 Anni '95. This year too, its depth and balance have put many of the great Italian reds in their place. Its darkish red ruby color is intense and compact; the nose has powerful scents of ripe currants and blackberries, and there is complexity and elegance in its sweet oaky tones. The taste is fat and concentrated, almost overbearing in its wealth of extracts. A very great red wine indeed—powerful, but perhaps a jot too young at the moment; however looking ahead a few years it is sure to fulfill its entire potential. We move on to what is probably the best version ever presented of Sagrantino di Montefalco '95: powerful and concentrated like its elder brother, scented and juicy, it displays even better harmony and quaffability (at least for the moment). We found the Rosso di Montefalco Riserva '95 very good, with its purple tones and good structure; while the Rosso di Montefalco '95 was true to type and soft. The best of the whites, we thought, was the Colli Martani Grechetto Grecante Vigna Belvedere '96, with good, slightly dark, straw-yellow color. A nose of exotic fruit and complex tones of sweet wood led into a palate with good acidity and length. Finally, the Colli Martani Grechetto Grecante '97 is a pleasing drink.

	Wine	Glasses	
●	Sagrantino di Montefalco 25 Anni '95	🍷🍷🍷	6
●	Rosso di Montefalco Ris. '95	🍷🍷	5
●	Sagrantino di Montefalco '95	🍷🍷	6
○	Colli Martani Grechetto Grecante Vigna Belvedere '96	🍷	4
○	Colli Martani Grechetto Grecante '97	🍷	3
●	Rosso di Montefalco '95	🍷	3
●	Sagrantino di Montefalco 25 Anni '93	🍸🍸🍸	6
●	Sagrantino di Montefalco 25 Anni '94	🍸🍸🍸	6
●	Rosso di Montefalco Ris. '94	🍸🍸	5
●	Sagrantino di Montefalco '94	🍸🍸	6

MONTEFALCO (PG)

ROCCA DI FABBRI
LOC. FABBRI
06036 MONTEFALCO (PG)
TEL. 0742/399379

Thanks to the solid results at our tastings this year, the Rocca di Fabbri estate has earned every right to reappear in the Guide. Owned by the Vitali family, this winery is situated inside the 14th-century fortress of the same name. Before discussing the merits of their wines we thought it worth mentioning that the owners have undertaken a complete renovation of their equipment. Without wishing to detract from the merits of previous versions now on the market, there can be no doubt that this year's wines come much closer to the winery's real potential. So let us start out with the Grechetto dei Colli Martani '97: color, straw-yellow; then a fine and fruity, rich nose of plum and white peach. On the palate it demonstrates substantial extracts and a lengthy finish. The Trebbiano dei Colli Martani Gaio '97 has a light straw-yellow color, and is more floral than fruity on the nose, with hints of lemon grass; the taste is clean and elegant. As far as the reds are concerned, we found the Rosso di Montefalco '95 interesting, starting with its good bright ruby color. The nose is fruity, with scents of plum and black cherry, while the taste is intense and broad with a good body. The only exception to these excellent all-round results is the Sagrantino di Montefalco '94; while it does deserve mention for its wealth of aromas, the structure and character are just not at the level of the wines listed above.

○	Colli Martani Grechetto '97	🍷	3
○	Colli Martani Trebbiano Gaio '97	🍷	3
●	Rosso di Montefalco '95	🍷	3
●	Sagrantino di Montefalco '94		4
●	Pinot Nero dell'Umbria '90	YY	5
●	Cabernet Sauvignon '90	Y	3
●	Colli Martani Sangiovese Satiro '93	Y	2*
●	Sagrantino di Montefalco '90	Y	4

ORVIETO (TR)

BIGI
LOC. PONTE GIULIO, 3
05018 ORVIETO (TR)
TEL. 0763/316224 - 316391

With over 100 years of active production behind it, the Bigi company (founded in 1880) must without a doubt be considered the historical winery par excellence in the Orvieto area. Today it is owned by the Gruppo Italiano Vini who have 193 hectares of vineyards (188 leased and 5 of their own property) with a production capacity of around three million bottles a year; of these, about half are destined for international markets. For many years now the company has been run by Francesco Bardi, a widely experienced wine expert, with the help of Massimo Panattoni. The wines they presented for our tasting were, as usual, very well-made. The true-to-type Orvieto Classico '97 has subtle and pleasant floral notes of broom and lemon grass. Nothing diminishes the excellence of the Orvieto Classico Vigneto Torricella '97, with fresh fruity notes and a good, rather pronounced flavor. Very good too, is the Grechetto dell'Umbria '97, with scents of Golden apple and peach, and fine notes of fresh fruit on the palate. This may come as a surprise, but the wine that made the greatest impression on us this year was a red, a Sangiovese dell'Umbria, a very well-made wine indeed. It has a good purplish ruby color, and a nose of fresh fruit, strawberry and cherry. The taste is also fruity and fresh, with a good concentration of extracts. The Marrano '96 is slightly under tone; made from grechetto grapes and fermented in barrique, this year it shows a distinct evolution in aroma and taste.

●	Sangiovese dell'Umbria '97	🍷🍷	2*
○	Grechetto dell'Umbria '97	🍷	2*
○	Orvieto Classico Vigneto Torricella '97	🍷	2*
○	Marrano '96		4
○	Orvieto Classico '97		2
○	Marrano '93	YY	4
○	Marrano '94	YY	4
○	Grechetto dell'Umbria '96	Y	2
○	Marrano '95	Y	4
○	Orvieto Classico Vigneto Torricella '96	Y	2*

ORVIETO (TR)

Co.Vi.O.
Fraz. Sferracavallo
Loc. Cardeto, 18
05019 Orvieto (TR)
tel. 0763/343189 - 341286

Cooperative Vitivinicola per la zona di Orvieto: this is the full name of the largest production estate in the Orvieto territory. The facts speak for themselves: 400 supplier-members, 1,200 hectares under vines, a potential of around a million hectoliters of wine, up-to-the-minute winery technology, plus Riccardo Cotarella, the famous wine expert and technician. After concentrating on relaunching local production (60% white grapes) over the last years, the Co. Vi. O. has now put in new and extremely efficient winery equipment and, beyond any question, has become the most serious wine producer of the Orvieto area. It must be said that it fought and won its battle several years ago, when it achieved a range of high quality wines from this staggering mass of grapes. A long and varied line of wines was presented this year. First of all, in the Orvieto Classico line come the Cardeto '97 and the Febeo '97 selection, both noteworthy for their excellence as easy refreshing drinks. One step above these is, again this year, the Jazz '97 selection, clean and fresh with intense scents of white flowers and fresh fruit. Also among the One Glass wines we have the pleasant and true-to-type Umbria Matile Bianco '97, Umbria Grechetto '97 and Rosso dell'Umbria Cardeto '97. This year's revelations have turned out to be the excellent Orvieto Classico Dolce Vendemmia Tardiva Cardeto '96, with its elegant aromas of both tropical and citrus fruits, and good fullness and balance on the palate, as well as the Rosso dell'Umbria Fantasie del Cardeto. This last wine, a selection from local grapes aged in barriques, has displayed remarkable power and complexity. An intense, scented and harmonious wine, it has just the right length on the finish.

●	Fantasie del Cardeto '95	🍷🍷	3*
○	Orvieto Classico Dolce V. T. Cardeto '96	🍷🍷	4
●	Cardeto Rosso '97	🍷	1*
○	Grechetto Cardeto '97	🍷	1*
○	Matile Bianco '97	🍷	1*
○	Orvieto Classico Cardeto '97	🍷	1*
○	Orvieto Classico Febeo '97	🍷	2
○	Orvieto Classico Jazz '97	🍷	1*
○	Orvieto Classico Febeo '94	🍸🍸	2*
●	Cardeto Rosso '96	🍸	1*
●	Fantasie del Cardeto '94	🍸	3*
○	Orvieto Classico Cardeto '96	🍸	1*
○	Orvieto Classico Febeo '96	🍸	2*
○	Orvieto Classico Jazz '96	🍸	1*

ORVIETO (TR)

Decugnano dei Barbi
Loc. Fossatello di Corbara, 50
05019 Orvieto (TR)
tel. 0763/308255

The Decugnano dei Barbi, owned by Claudio and Marina Barbi since 1978, has always been one of the best estates in Umbria, and this year it has come well up to expectations. It possesses 25 hectares under vineyards and a production of around 100-120 thousand bottles a year, most of it Orvieto Classico. The two "IL" selections may be considered the top labels. The Orvieto Classico "IL" '97, from grechetto, procanico, verdello and drupeggio grapes, with additions of chardonnay, is a very good wine. Fermented and aged in wood, it has a straw-yellow color, a broad and complex nose of ripe fruit and slightly spicy notes of vanilla. The taste is elegant, savory and full-bodied. This year the Rosso dell'Umbria "IL" '95 is probably the best that Decugnano has ever released. Made from sangiovese, canaiolo and montepulciano d'Abruzzo grapes, aged 24 months in Nevers and Vosges barriques, it has a dark ruby red color, and an intense, long nose with clear cut scents of raspberry and juniper berries; the taste is clean, harmonious and well structured. The fresh and delicate Orvieto Classico Decugnano dei Barbi '97 fulfilled our expectations, while the Decugnano dei Barbi Rosso '96 struck us as elegant, with notes of violets and undergrowth. Excellent work has been done on the basics: the Orvieto Classico Barbi '97 and the red Lago di Corbara '95 easily win a Glass apiece for their admirable pleasantness. However we did expect something more in the way of structure from the agreeable Orvieto Classico Pourriture Noble '95. The Brut '93 remains one of the best metodo classico in Umbria.

●	"IL" '95	🍷🍷	5
○	Orvieto Classico "IL" '97	🍷🍷	4
○	Decugnano dei Barbi Brut M. Cl. '93	🍷	5
●	Decugnano dei Barbi Rosso '96	🍷	3
●	Lago di Corbara '95	🍷	3
○	Orvieto Classico Barbi '97	🍷	2*
○	Orvieto Classico Decugnano dei Barbi '97	🍷	3
○	Orvieto Classico Pourriture Noble '95	🍷	5
●	"IL" '92	🍸🍸	5
●	"IL" '93	🍸🍸	5
●	"IL" '94	🍸🍸	5
●	Decugnano dei Barbi Rosso '94	🍸🍸	3*
○	Orvieto Classico "IL" '96	🍸🍸	4

ORVIETO (TR)

La Carraia

Loc. Tordimonte, 56
05018 Orvieto (TR)
tel. 0763/304013

Now in the Guide for the second year running, this excellent Orvieto winery can no longer be considered a revelation, but a sure bet. All its wines have reached an even higher level of quality. The top wine, and we need hardly say that it is yet another brain child of Riccardo Cotarella, is the Rosso dell'Umbria Fobiano '96. Made from a mix of merlot (90%), and cabernet sauvignon (10%), it has been given almost a year of aging in Nevers oak barriques. A dark, ruby red color, it has a broad and complex nose with vegetal tones and scents of wild red berries. What is really outstanding in all respects is the element of wood that blends well with the fruity content. The taste shows excellent concentration and is intense and long, with subtle notes of spice and good tannins. It is a wine with an assured style, especially in its use of oak. Another Two Glasses for La Carraia's most recent product, a Sangiovese dell'Umbria '97 that really came as a surprise to us. A ruby red color with purplish tints, its rich intense nose has floral notes of violets and fruity aromas. The taste is broad and clean, with vegetal notes and spices. Also good is the Orvieto Classico Poggio Calvelli '97, from typical local grapes fermented and aged in barrique for two months. A light straw-yellow color, it is vegetal to the nose with scents of lemon grass, while the taste has substance and is slightly spicy. Lastly, we shall mention only the Orvieto Classico '97 with a nose of fragrant floral notes, but somewhat thin in structure on the palate.

	Wine	Glasses	Price
●	Fobiano '96	🍷🍷	4
●	Sangiovese dell'Umbria '97	🍷🍷	3*
○	Orvieto Classico Poggio Calvelli '97	🍷	3
○	Orvieto Classico '97		2
●	Fobiano '95	🍷🍷	4
○	Orvieto Classico Poggio Calvelli '96	🍷	3

ORVIETO (TR)

Tenuta Le Velette

Loc. Le Velette, 23
05019 Orvieto (TR)
tel. 0763/29090

With 95 hectares of vineyards near Orvieto, the Tenuta Le Velette can be regarded as this year's revelation in Umbria. The performance of its wines is truly exceptional. So we will begin with an exceptional wine, the Calanco '95, a red to which the Guide has awarded its maximum rating of Three Glasses. Made with sangiovese (65%) and cabernet sauvignon grapes (35%), and aged in barrique, it shows a good dark ruby color with purplish tints. The nose is fruity with vegetal notes; it is complex and has exceptional elegance and length. A broad warm taste displays sensual notes of red fruit and sweet spices, and an excellent tannin content. The Rosso di Spicca '97 is also good. A blend of sangiovese and canaiolo grapes, it has typical fruity aromas, while the palate has sufficient intensity and good structure. Made from the same blend of grapes, the Monaldesco '97 is Umbria's best rosato this year: it has a good onion skin color and a nose with notes of strawberry and cherry; the palate is fresh and has good length. The whites of this winery are good too; first comes the Traluce '97, a sauvignon with the typical pleasant scents of tomato leaf and slightly balsamic notes of sage, while the taste is varietal and clean. The Orvieto Classico wines are well made. The basic '97 has a straw-yellow color and a fruity nose with scents of white peach and plum. The taste is long and full-bodied. We might also mention the Classic '97, fermented in barrique; it has subtle floral scents, and a good intense, clean taste.

	Wine	Glasses	Price
●	Calanco '95	🍷🍷🍷	5
⊙	Monaldesco '97	🍷	2*
○	Orvieto Classico '97	🍷	2*
○	Orvieto Classico Lunato '97	🍷	3
●	Rosso di Spicca '97	🍷	2*
○	Traluce '97	🍷	4
●	Calanco '91	🍷🍷	5
○	Traluce '96	🍷🍷	3*
●	Calanco '92	🍷	5
●	Calanco '93	🍷	5
●	Calanco '94	🍷	5
○	Orvieto Classico '96	🍷	2*
○	Orvieto Classico Amabile '96	🍷	2*
○	Orvieto Classico Velico '96	🍷	3
●	Rosso di Spicca '94	🍷	2

ORVIETO (TR)

PALAZZONE
LOC. ROCCA RIPESENA, 68
05019 ORVIETO (TR)
TEL. 0763/344166

No Armaleo this year, alas. Giovanni Dubini, owner of the estate, decided not to release it. But luckily we have the consolation of knowing there are other wines from the Palazzone winery, and mostly all are well-made and worthwhile. All the versions of white wine are interesting, the pick being the Chardonnay and the Grechetto, both bearing the curious name of L'Ultima Spiaggia. The first has a nose of vegetal notes and fruity scents of plum, while the taste is clean and long; the second offers fruity aromas of apricot and white peach and a well-structured palate. The line up of Orvieto Classicos opens with the Terre Vineate '97; it has intense floral notes of lemon grass and broom, while the taste is full-bodied and clean. The Orvieto Classico Campo del Guardiano '96 strikes us as the best this firm has ever presented: a dark straw-yellow color, with a nose of fruity nuances, then notes of spices and hints of honey on the finish. The taste is long and clean, and there is good balance between fruit and wood. The Orvieto Classico Vendemmia Tardiva '97 (Giovanni only produces this one in the best vintage years) has pleasant scents of white flowers and fine spices, and a palate with notes of tropical and citrus fruits. The Muffa Nobile '97 is still among the best sweet wines of Umbria. Made from botrytized sauvignon grapes and fermented in casks, it is complex and intense on the nose, with subtle floral notes together with hints of candied fruit; the taste has good concentration and structure. Finally, the one red presented this year, the Rubbio '97: a good dark red color with youthful purplish tints and a fruity nose of plum and black cherry, it is harmonious on the palate with a good fullness of extracts.

○	Muffa Nobile '97	🍷🍷	4
○	Orvieto Cl. Campo del Guardiano '96	🍷🍷	3*
●	Rubbio '97	🍷🍷	3*
○	Chardonnay L'Ultima Spiaggia '97	🍷	3
○	Grechetto L'Ultima Spiaggia '97	🍷	3
○	Orvieto Cl. Terre Vineate '97	🍷	3
○	Orvieto Cl. Vendemmia Tardiva '97	🍷	3
●	Armaleo '95	YYY	4
●	Armaleo '92	YY	4
●	Armaleo '94	YY	4
○	Muffa Nobile '95	YY	4
○	Muffa Nobile '96	YY	4
○	Orvieto Cl. Terre Vineate '94	YY	3
○	Viognier L'Ultima Spiaggia '95	YY	4
○	Viognier L'Ultima Spiaggia '96	YY	3

PENNA IN TEVERINA (TR)

RIO GRANDE
LOC. MONTECCHIE
05028 PENNA IN TEVERINA (TR)
TEL. 0744/993102 - 06/66416440

The Rio Grande estate in the commune of Penna in Teverina, a short distance from the border of Lazio, is owned by the Pastore family. Acquired by Francesco Pastore in 1988, it covers about 52 hectares along the hills sloping down to the Tiber. Twelve hectares are under vineyards, with a planting of around 4,000 stock vines per hectare, and almost all of them are international grapes (chardonnay, cabernet sauvignon, merlot, pinot nero, but also grechetto). To complete the picture, for years Francesco has been successfully following the sound advice from that much sought-after wine expert, Riccardo Cotarella. Again this year we were impressed by two of the wines presented by Rio Grande. The Colle delle Montecchie '97; made from chardonnay (80%) and small quantities of grechetto grapes (20%), it has a pale straw-yellow color. There is a nose with good intensity and pleasant notes of fresh fruit and white flowers; the palate is full-bodied and flavorful with medium length on the finish. The Rosso dell'Umbria Casa Pastore '96, based on a blend of cabernet sauvignon (80%) and merlot (20%), is aged for 10-12 months in barriques. The color is ruby red with purplish tints, and there is a broad intense nose of undergrowth and elegant nuances of wood on the finish. The taste is refined and elegant, perhaps slightly less concentrated than in past years, but on the whole it has merit.

●	Casa Pastore Rosso '96	🍷	4
○	Chardonnay Colle delle Montecchie '97	🍷	3
●	Casa Pastore Rosso '95	YY	4
○	Chardonnay Colle delle Montecchie '94	YY	3
○	Chardonnay Colle delle Montecchie '95	YY	3
●	Casa Pastore Rosso '93	Y	4
●	Casa Pastore Rosso '94	Y	4
○	Chardonnay Colle delle Montecchie '96	Y	3

PERUGIA

Gisberto Goretti

Loc. Pila
Strada del Pino, 4
06070 Perugia
tel. 075/607316

As we have repeated again and again, the aim of this Guide is to trace the development of the wine producing estates of all the regions of Italy; the Goretti estate is a promising newcomer to the wineries of Umbria. Owned by the same family for generations, the estate lies only a few miles from Perugia, in the hamlet of Pila. Stefano and Gianluca Goretti, the managing directors, have presented some really interesting and well-made wines. Three of the labels are especially good. First of all two whites: a good Grechetto dell'Umbria '97, with a light straw-yellow color, a fruity refined nose and a fresh well-concentrated palate; then an excellent Chardonnay dell'Umbria '97, with a pale straw-yellow color, a fine and intense nose and good structure and length on the palate. But there can be no doubt about the wine that impressed us most. The Colli Perugini Rosso l'Arrigatore '95. Made from a rich assemblage of sangiovese, montepulciano, ciliegiolo and merlot grapes, it displays a darkish ruby color with lively highlights. It is intense and persistent on the nose and has fruity scents, especially plum and black cherry, and well-integrated hints of wood. The palate is broad and complex, with excellent aromatic intensity supported by proper acidity and solid tannin content. So these are delicious, flavorful wines, and especially good, considering the extraordinarily honest price they sell at.

	Wine	Glasses	Price
●	Colli Perugini Rosso L'Arringatore '95	🍷🍷	3*
○	Chardonnay dell'Umbria '97	🍷	2*
○	Grechetto dell'Umbria '97	🍷	2*

SPELLO (PG)

F.lli Sportoletti

Via Lombardia, 1
06038 Spello (PG)
tel. 0742/651461

Perhaps the wine producing area of the Assisi countryside is not the best known in Italy, but it does include firms with good standards of quality. The estate of the brothers Remo and Ernesto Sportoletti up in the hills between Spello and Assisi, has always been considered the area's best. Their vineyards cover around 20 hectares, yielding them about 200 thousand bottles a year. Most of the wines marketed by the Sportoletti company today falls under the DOC Assisi classification (in force since 1998). Both the Assisi Biancos are good. The '97 vintage is a light straw-yellow color, a panoply of fruity aromas with notes of ripe Golden apple; on the palate it has good all round harmony, a nice clean taste with no rough edges. The Assisi Bianco Villa Fidelia '97 is also interesting: deep straw-yellow in color, it possesses a fairly broad nose of ripe fruit with sweet tones of wood. The taste is warm and intense, well balanced and very clean. We need no more than mention the Assisi Rosato '97: it has a pleasing nose but is slightly thin when it comes to body. Among the reds, the Assisi Rosso Villa Fidelia '96 turn out to be very good; made from merlot and pinot nero grapes it gives off convincing and intense aromas of fruit and spices; the taste has good length and breadth with a presence of tannins that is, on the whole, fairly mature and well-balanced.

	Wine	Glasses	Price
○	Assisi Bianco '97	🍷	2*
○	Assisi Bianco Villa Fidelia '96	🍷	4
●	Assisi Rosso Villa Fidelia '96	🍷	4
⊙	Assisi Rosato '97		2
○	Villa Fidelia Bianco '95	🍷🍷 (prev.)	4
●	Villa Fidelia Rosso '91	🍷🍷 (prev.)	4*
○	Assisi Bianco '96	🍷 (prev.)	2
●	Assisi Rosso '96	🍷 (prev.)	1*
●	Villa Fidelia Rosso '94	🍷 (prev.)	4

STRONCONE (TR)

LA PALAZZOLA
LOC. VASCIGLIANO
05039 STRONCONE (TR)
TEL. 0744/607735 - 272357

Whom would you expect to find as the wine consultant for Stefano Grilli, owner of the La Palazzola estate? Why, Riccardo Cotarella of course. And consequently the entire range of wines presented this year is absolutely splendid, starting out with the Riesling Brut '93, a spumante made by someone who really knows his job. A pale straw-yellow color, it has finesse and complexity on the nose, with scents of bread crust. The taste reveals the right intensity and good length. There is a pleasant Umbria Verdello '97, pale straw-yellow, a nose with rich vegetal notes of broom. It has only a medium structure on the palate but is impeccably clean. Moving on to the reds, the Pinot Nero '96 seems interesting but there is still room for improvement; a light ruby color, it has faint scents of ripe red fruit and spices; on the palate it is medium alcoholic, with only a fair weight of extracts. The best however is certainly the Rubino '96, a really superb red that only misses our top award by a whisker. A darkish ruby red color with bright purplish tints; the nose is faintly herbaceous, backed by scents of wild berries, and then it is clean and complex. It has a broad, intense and well-balanced palate. As always amongst the best wines presented by La Palazzola, there is the Vendemmia Tardiva '96. With its good straw-yellow color and golden tints, it has elegant scents of tropical fruits (pineapple and mango), faint notes of balsam, and a long flavor with clear notes of apricot and citrus peel.

○	La Palazzola V. T. '96	🍷🍷	5
●	Rubino '96	🍷🍷	5
●	Pinot Nero '96	🍷	4
○	Riesling Brut M. Cl. '93	🍷	4
○	Verdello '97	🍷	3
○	La Palazzola V. T. '93	🍷🍷	5
○	La Palazzola V. T. '94	🍷🍷	5
●	Merlot '95	🍷🍷	4
○	Riesling Brut M. Cl. '94	🍷🍷	4
●	Rubino '93	🍷🍷	5
●	Rubino '94	🍷🍷	5
●	Rubino '95	🍷🍷	5
○	La Palazzola V. T. '94	🍷	5
●	Pinot Nero '94	🍷	4
●	Pinot Nero '95	🍷	4

TORGIANO (PG)

CANTINE LUNGAROTTI
VIA MARIO ANGELONI, 16
06089 TORGIANO (PG)
TEL. 075/9880348

There have been times when we criticized this important Umbrian winery to which the emergence of quality wine production in Umbria owes so much. The fact is that Lungarotti had been resting on the well-deserved laurels it won years ago, without making much of an effort towards substantial improvements. This year, however, we must revise our judgment to a considerable extent because some of the wines they have presented are among the best of all time. Obviously we are the first to celebrate. The best of all is the Cabernet Sauvignon '95, a rather modern red, varietal in bouquet and concentrated in taste; it indeed marks the turning point in a production outlook which has always been dedicated to the search for softness and evolution, particularly in the case of red wines. The two top labels of the estate are very good. They actually come from the '88 vintage, in line with the theory that it requires at least ten years aging in cask and bottle for the most full-bodied wines. The San Giorgio, from sauvignon, sangiovese and canaiolo grapes, has a grand structure and concentration, probably unequaled in the past. The bouquet is complex, with animal and fruit scents. The Torgiano Rosso Vigna Monticchio Riserva, still '88, has a complex and evolved bouquet, with scents of leather and black cherry jam, while the palate has no harshness, entirely abandoning itself to languid velvety sensations. The simpler wines are satisfactory: the Torgiano Rosso Rubesco '95, the Vessillo '94 ('93 was better), the Chardonnay '97 and the Torgiano Bianco Torre di Giano '97. It all adds up to a triumph in a minor key, but we have hopes that it will prove a prelude to even better wines to come.

●	Cabernet Sauvignon '95	🍷🍷	4
●	San Giorgio '88	🍷🍷	5
●	Torgiano Rosso Vigna Monticchio Ris. '88	🍷🍷	5
○	Chardonnay '97	🍷	3
●	Il Vessillo '94	🍷	4
○	Torgiano Bianco Torre di Giano '97	🍷	3
●	Torgiano Rosso Rubesco '95	🍷	3
●	Torgiano Rosso Vigna Monticchio Ris. '78	🍷🍷🍷	6
●	Il Vessillo '93	🍷🍷	4
●	San Giorgio '86	🍷🍷	5
●	Torgiano Rosso Vigna Monticchio Ris. '86	🍷🍷	5

OTHER WINERIES

The following producers obtained good scores in our tastings with one or more of their wines:

PROVINCE OF PERUGIA

Tili
Assisi, tel. 075/8064370,
Assisi Grechetto '97,
Muffa Reale '94

Eredi Benincasa
Bevagna, tel. 0742/361307,
Sagrantino di Montefalco '94

F.lli Adanti
Bevagna, tel. 0742/360295,
Rosso d'Arquata '94,
Sagrantino di Montefalco Arquata '94

Di Filippo
Cannara, tel. 0742/72310,
Colli Martani Sangiovese Properzio '96,
Rosso dell'Umbria Terre di S. Nicola '96

Cantina del Trasimeno
Castiglione del Lago, tel. 075/9652493,
Colli del Trasimeno
Duca della Corgna Baccio del Rosso '96,
Colli del Trasimeno
Duca della Corgna Gamay dell'Umbria '96

Villa Po' del Vento
Città della Pieve, tel. 0578/299950,
Colli del Trasimeno
Rosso del Duca '90

Terre dei Trinci
Foligno, tel. 0742/320165,
Rosso di Montefalco '95

Cantina Intercomunale del Trasimeno
Magione, tel. 075/840298,
Colli del Trasimeno Rosso Erceo '97

Ruggeri
Montefalco, tel. 0742/379294,
Sagrantino di Montefalco Passito '95

Scacciadiavoli
Montefalco, tel. 0742/378272,
Sagrantino di Montefalco Passito '94

Spoletoducale
Spoleto, tel. 0743/56224,
Sagrantino di Montefalco '93

Cantina Sociale Tudernum
Todi, tel. 075/8989403,
Colli Martani Grechetto di Todi '97,
Colli Martani Trebbiano '97

PROVINCE OF TERNI

Poggio del Lupo
Allerona Scalo, tel. 0763/68850,
Orvieto Abboccato '97,
Orvieto Secco '97

Petrangeli
Orvieto, tel. 0763/304189,
Orvieto Classico Dolce Cinèreo '97,
Rosso dell'Umbria Cannicello '93

LAZIO

A region on the rise. This briefly is the impression we get from a careful analysis of Lazio's wine production. It is not easy to assess an uneven vintage like '97, but from our privileged vantage point we saw energetic reform and renewal throughout the region from north to south. The results, alas, were not consistent. But let's get down to details. Yet again Falesco in Montefiascone has deservedly been awarded Three Glasses for its sumptuous Montiano '96. The wines of this estate, managed by the much-decorated Riccardo Cotarella, have made more progress than ever before. Now some other estates are beginning to approach the level of Falesco, undisputably the local leader. We note, for example, the success of Mottura in Civitella d'Agliano, which has shown what grechetto is capable of with its excellent Latour a Civitella and Poggio della Costa. Then there's Mazziotti, offering a powerful Canuleio, a white made of the typical Montefiascone grapes and aged in wood. On the other hand the Cantina di Cerveteri seems to be marking time and having trouble keeping up with its own standards of previous years. The Castelli Romani area also offers a wide variety of novelties. In Marino, Paola di Mauro has produced an excellent Marino Colle Picchioni '97, possibly the best yet. Adriana and Giulio Santarelli in Grottaferrata make their bid with Frascati Castel de Paolis '97 and the special selection Vigna Adriana '97, both wines which have achieved a balance and complexity previously unattained. The production of the local colossus Fontana Candida cannot be faulted: sometimes it is possible to find quality lying down with quantity. Piero Costantini's Villa Simone, without causing a stir, is clearly maintaining its position with a delicious Vigna dei Preti '97 and a very elegant Cannellino '97. Our compliments to Antonio Santarelli, the owner of Casale del Giglio, whose years of effort have at last been rewarded by a series of excellent wines. Some rather unusual names like Mater Matuta, Madre Selva and Antinoo are soon going to become household words to wine lovers. The winds of change have not bypassed two long-established Castelli wineries, Conte Zandotti and Casale Marchese, but have not yet, we feel, brought the desired results. We found a decline in bouquet, while freshness seems to have given way to less lively sensations, low on vibrancy. Are these wines that will evolve? We shall see. Southern Lazio is the stage on which Giovanni Palombo has this year made his debut with an excellent Bordeaux blend called Colle della Torre. It consistently scored very high in our tastings. Massimi Berucci has suffered the whims of the weather, however: his Cesanese Casal Cervino '97 has been transformed into a sort of semi-sweet dessert wine with an imposing structure.

ANAGNI (FR)

COLACICCHI
LOC. ROMAGNANO
03012 ANAGNI (FR)
TEL. 06/4469661

We're not able to go into full detail about Colacicchi's wines this year. When we went to press neither the Romagnano Bianco '97 nor the Romagnano Rosso '96 was available for tasting. As our readers know, this small estate in the Ciociaria has for some years been run by the Trimanis of Rome. Who knows what effort they have had to devote to replanting much of the vineyard, which had got into a deplorable state? Quite apart from the difficulty of vinifying with inadequate equipment! But the Trimanis do not easily give up, and this year their many fans are rewarded with an enchanting Torre Ercolana '91. The blend of grapes has changed slightly, their goal, which, by the way, they have achieved, being to produce a more elegant wine. Hence a higher percentage of cabernet and merlot and less cesanese. Although it can't be compared to the sumptuous '90, it is nevertheless satisfyingly complex in nose and mouth. There is still a considerable amount of substance on the palate, although it's inevitably not so richly concentrated. As usual there is a complex bouquet, ranging from berry fragrances to delicate herbal notes. An admirable wine which should mature slowly but surely over the next five or six years.

●	Torre Ercolana '91	🍷🍷	5
○	Romagnano Bianco '92	🍷🍷	4
○	Romagnano Bianco '93	🍷🍷	3
○	Romagnano Bianco '94	🍷🍷	4
●	Torre Ercolana '87	🍷🍷	5
●	Torre Ercolana '88	🍷🍷	6
●	Torre Ercolana '90	🍷🍷	5
○	Romagnano Bianco '96	🍷	4
●	Romagnano Rosso '91	🍷	4
●	Romagnano Rosso '93	🍷	4
●	Romagnano Rosso '95	🍷	4

ATINA (FR)

GIOVANNI PALOMBO
C.SO MUNANZIO PLANCO
03042 ATINA (FR)
TEL. 0776/610228 - 610639

Giovanni Palombo is a new name in the world of wine in Lazio. It would not be an exaggeration to say that his arrival was like a bombshell. We were greatly struck at our tastings by what this small estate in the Ciociaria had to offer. Giovanni and his two children, whose family has been making wine for generations, had decided to replant some grapes, such as cabernet, merlot, petit verdot and sémillon, to name but a few, known to have been in the area since 1860 at least. This was by no means an easy matter because their vineyards are scattered. The Palombos were already well-known for a pleasant Cabernet di Atina, a pure version of the grape, which they also produced in a barrique-aged form. But they really moved to a higher level with a new range of extremely interesting wines. The most impressive is Colle della Torre '97, a powerful red composed of merlot and cabernet matured in French oak casks. It is mouth-filling and substantial, with a long finish and great character. The nose is spicy and herby, with suggestions of berries and licorice. The Rosso delle Chiaie '97 is also very good: it's mostly merlot, with some cabernet, and is of a lovely brilliant ruby color. The nose has notes of berries and preserved fruits, and it's tasty and mouth-filling. The Bianco delle Chiaie '97, a blend of sémillon and sauvignon, is worthy of notice. It is pleasantly fruity and fresh, with a basic vivacity and a satisfying finish. Not at all bad for the first appearance of an estate that will have a lot more to say for itself in the future.

●	Colle della Torre '97	🍷🍷	4
●	Rosso delle Chiaie '97	🍷	3
○	Bianco delle Chiaie '97		2
●	Cabernet di Atina '96		3

BOLSENA (VT)

ITALO MAZZIOTTI
L.GO MAZZIOTTI, 5
01023 BOLSENA (VT)
TEL. 0761/799049

What a delightful surprise we had when we tasted the wine from this estate, which has been quietly but steadfastly pursuing its course for some time! It was Italo, the greatgrandson of Gerardo, the founder, who first started people talking about this winery, now run by the gracious Flaminia and her husband Alessandro. The real surprise was the latest version - vintage '94 - of the Canuleio. This used to be a pleasant enough white, however nothing special. But now! The excellent advice of Gaspare Buscemi has helped produce a wine that is altogether transformed. The grapes - the traditional Est Est Est blend - were carefully selected, and a few months in oak preceded two years' bottle aging. The resultant wine is of exceptional complexity and dense texture, with a rich bouquet including hints of ripe fruit, vanilla and spice. There's also a solid acid base, suggesting that it's a wine for keeping, at least for a while. Their traditional Est Est Est di Montefiascone '97 has graceful and delicate aromas that suggest ripe fruit; on the palate it's dry, with a vinous accent and an almondy finish.

	Wine	Rating	Price
○	Est Est Est di Montefiascone Canuleio '94	🍷🍷	4
○	Est Est Est di Montefiascone '97	🍷	2
○	Est Est Est di Montefiascone '96	🍸	2
○	Est Est Est di Montefiascone Canuleio '92	🍸	3

BORGO MONTELLO (LT)

CASALE DEL GIGLIO
STRADA CISTERNA-NETTUNO KM 13
04010 BORGO MONTELLO (LT)
TEL. 06/5742529 - 5746359

It has been a long struggle, or so one is tempted to describe the vicissitudes of Casale del Giglio, where for years Tony Santarelli and the admirable Paolo Tiefenthaler have devoted themselves to study and experimentation in vineyard and cellar in pursuit of a success it seemed they would never achieve. And all at once here it is! Casale del Giglio has presented a wide range of wines, all of remarkable quality. Consider, for example, the delicious Merlot '96: fermented partly in wood, it has structure and a finish which are hard to come by in a wine that doesn't empty your pockets. The Madreselva '94, a successful and attractive classic Bordeaux blend, is full-bodied and has a dense and intriguing bouquet. Their range of "standard" whites is excellent too: the Chardonnay '97, Sauvignon '97 and the classic Satrico '97 (trebbiano and chardonnay) are a trio of fresh, fruity and distinctly varietal wines. We tasted the Antinoo '95 and the Mater Matuta '94 again after they had been a while in the bottle, and we found them in fine shape. The former, a blend of chardonnay and viognier, is a good example of a wine whose varietal aroma has not been dominated by wood; the latter is a succulent mixture of syrah and petit verdot. We were pleased by the delicate rosé, Albiola '97, with its fragrant hint of cherries.

	Wine	Rating	Price
●	Madreselva '94	🍷🍷	3*
○	Chardonnay '97	🍷🍷	2*
●	Merlot '96	🍷🍷	3*
⊙	Albiola '97	🍷	2
○	Satrico '97	🍷	2
○	Sauvignon '97	🍷	2
○	Antinoo '95	🍸🍸	3
○	Chardonnay '96	🍸	2
●	Madreselva '92	🍸	3
●	Mater Matuta '94	🍸	3
○	Satrico '96	🍸	2
●	Shiraz '96	🍸	2*
●	Shiraz '95	🍸	2*

CERVETERI (RM)

CANTINA COOPERATIVA DI CERVETERI
VIA AURELIA KM 42.700
00052 CERVETERI (RM)
TEL. 06/9905677

What has caused the Cantina Cooperativa di Cerveteri to tread water this year? Various factors have contributed, in our opinion. In the white wines, the acid-sugar balance was tipped over to the sweet side by the most unusual weather. The expert remedial efforts of Riccardo Cotarella could do only so much. His extraordinary care in vinification did succeed in maintaining a certain freshness, but there was not much that even he could do to preserve the primary and varietal aromas. As a result Fontana Morella '97 is a rather neutral white, somewhat faint in bouquet, with quite a soft taste revealing only occasional hints of freshness. The winery seems to have concentrated its efforts on the special selection Vigna Grande '97, a blend of malvasia, trebbiano, tocai and some other grapes, which in fact has done well. The standard red Fontana Morella '97, made from montepulciano and sangiovese, suffered a fate similar to its white sister's: it's much thinner than usual, and although you do get an unexciting vinous taste, it doesn't last long, and there's a general weakness. It must be said, however, that all these wines cost very little for what they are. The Cerveteri Rosso Vigna Grande '96, fruit of a vintage that was not really favorable to red wine, is unfortunately below par. First of all, it lacks the dense texture and compactness that have characterized it in recent years. And although it is still very agreeable drinking, it doesn't have much persistence in nose or on the palate. We are not in the habit of expressing negative opinions without a thorough analysis of the situation, so we feel we can confidently state that Cotarella did everything in his power in a lopsided year to produce wines that are at least well made.

	Wine	Glasses	Price
○	Cerveteri Bianco Vigna Grande '97	▼	2
●	Cerveteri Rosso Vigna Grande '96	▼	3
○	Cerveteri Bianco Fontana Morella '97		1
●	Cerveteri Rosso Fontana Morella '97		1
●	Cerveteri Rosso Vigna Grande '95	▽▽	3*
○	Cerveteri Bianco Vigna Grande '96	▽	2
●	Cerveteri Rosso Vigna Grande '94	▽	3
○	Cerveteri Bianco Fontana Morella '96		1

CIVITELLA D'AGLIANO (VT)

TENUTA MOTTURA
LOC. RIO CHIARO, 1
01020 CIVITELLA D'AGLIANO (VT)
TEL. 0761/914533

We'd been watching this winery for so long that we had just about given up hope of seeing any improvement. But something has happened. Sergio Mottura, a native of Piedmont who has chosen to settle in Lazio, has, with the help of his delightful countryman Marco Monchiero, caused quite a stir by producing a really exciting range of wines. The most outstanding is the Latour a Civitella '96, made from grechetto grapes and matured in barriques from the celebrated French négociant Louis Latour. The nose has lovely varietal notes which are "dissolved" in the butter and vanilla of the oak. This is a silky and persistent wine. The Poggio della Costa '97 is remarkable as well. There's no oak, but lots of varietal aromas, which are reflected on the palate, forming a splendidly harmonious whole which fully deserves the Two Glasses that it too has received. The Orvieto Vigna Tragugnano '97 makes a good showing also. Its aromas are delicate and it has an attractive fresh drinkability. Special mention must be made of the sweet wine called Muffo '95. It is striking in its sumptuous structure, at once fat and sweet, and in its clearly displayed fig and apricot aromas. It's an opulent wine with a very long finish, and not at all hard to drink. With his taste for danger, Mottura has even come out with a classic spumante, 100% chardonnay. Not a bad try! Its yeasty, toasty nose is pleasantly distinct, its structure solid, freshness evident and finish long.

	Wine	Glasses	Price
○	Grechetto Latour a Civitella '96	▼▼	4
○	Grechetto Poggio della Costa '97	▼▼	3
○	Muffo '95	▼▼	4
○	Orvieto Vigna Tragugnano '97	▼	2
○	Spumante Mottura	▼	4
○	Grechetto Poggio della Costa '94	▽▽	3
○	Grechetto Poggio della Costa '95	▽▽	3
○	Muffo '94	▽	4
○	Orvieto Vigna Tragugnano '94	▽	2
○	Orvieto Vigna Tragugnano '95	▽	2
●	Rosso di Civitella Magone '93	▽	4
●	Rosso di Civitella Magone '94	▽	4

FRASCATI (RM)

Casale Marchese

Via di Vermicino, 34
00044 Frascati (RM)
tel. 06/9408932

A transformation is under way at Casale Marchese. The arrival of the fine oenologist Sandro Facca has brought about a significant change in the style of the wine produced by this lovely estate. First of all, they have decided on making a break with the past: no more easy wines for immediate consumption. The Frascati Superiore that Casale Marchese made in '97 is definitely more intense, very elegant and possessed of solid structure. So the change is readily perceptible. But this new "interpretation" has somehow undermined the array of aromas in a wine we have always admired, and the wine is the poorer for it. Since they are surrounded by 30 hectares of their own vineyards, they could, we feel, profitably do further research so as to be able to bring out the aromatic wealth of the Lazio malvasia, a grape which has already produced remarkably good results elsewhere. With just a little more effort this estate could move to the top ranks of regional wineries. On the other hand, Facco has given a touch of class to the montepulciano, merlot and cesanese blend, Rosso Casale Marchese '97. Its color is an attractive deep ruby, its intense and persistent nose reveals hints of sour cherry and red berries, giving way to a grassy fragrance, and it's mouth-filling, silky and soft. This is a wine you'll want to keep your eye on.

	Wine	Glasses	Price
●	Rosso di Casale Marchese '97	🍷🍷	3
○	Frascati Superiore '97	🍷	2
○	Cortesia di Casale Marchese '93	YY	3
○	Cortesia di Casale Marchese '94	YY	3
○	Cortesia di Casale Marchese '95	YY	3
○	Frascati Superiore '93	YY	2
○	Frascati Superiore '94	YY	2
○	Frascati Superiore '95	YY	2*
○	Frascati Superiore '96	Y	2

GROTTAFERRATA (RM)

Castel De Paolis

Via Val De Paolis, 41
00046 Grottaferrata (RM)
tel. 06/9413648 - 94316025

At last Giulio and Adriana Santarelli have done themselves proud. We have never spared our criticism of the wines produced on this splendid estate located in one of the corners of the Castelli Romani most suited to viticulture. Often these wines were too highbrow to be credible and too high-priced to be affordable. At least up to now. This year things seem to have taken a new direction. The Frascati Superiore '97 is very well-balanced, with a long finish in nose and palate enlivened by notes of delightful fresh fruit. The special selection Vigna Adriana '97 has a new depth and a more concentrated bouquet. On the palate there's a firm texture and considerable elegance, with a long finish. The red Quattro Mori '96 has also improved, its unusual blend of syrah, merlot, petit verdot and cabernet sauvignon having achieved more balance. Hints of spice, cocoa and tobacco take their place in an imposing structure. The Cannellino '97, made from a local grape, and the Muffa Nobile '97, in which the aristocratic sémillon makes its presence known, are both luscious and elegantly sweet wines. In this year's Rosathea, the '97, whose sweetness is balanced by a pleasing acid crispness, we found graceful hints of dried rose petals. The two less expensive wines of Castel de Paolis also make an excellent showing: the Frascati Superiore Campo Vecchio '97 reveals delicate notes of fruit balanced by an enchanting freshness, and the Campo Vecchio Rosso '96 is appealingly fruity. Its blend is that of its big brother, and it doesn't disgrace the family, since it's sustained by a solid and rather elegant structure.

	Wine	Glasses	Price
○	Frascati Sup. V. Adriana '97	🍷🍷	5
○	Muffa Nobile '97	🍷🍷	5
●	Quattro Mori '96	🍷🍷	5
●	Campo Vecchio Rosso '96	🍷	3
○	Frascati Sup. Campo Vecchio '97	🍷	4
○	Frascati Sup. Cannellino '97	🍷	5
○	Frascati Superiore '97	🍷	4
●	Rosathea '97	🍷	5
○	Frascati Sup. Cannellino '96	YY	4
○	Frascati Sup. V. Adriana '95	YY	5
○	Frascati Sup. V. Adriana '96	YY	5
○	Muffa Nobile '94	YY	5
●	Quattro Mori '93	YY	5
●	Quattro Mori '94	YY	5
●	Rosathea '95	YY	5

MARINO (RM)

Paola Di Mauro - Colle Picchioni

Via Colle Picchione di Marino, 46
00040 Marino (RM)
tel. 06/93546329

Armando and Paola Di Mauro have presented an excellent collection of wines this year. The red Vigna del Vassallo confirms the new direction this legendary Castelli Romani estate has taken. The vintage '95 version of the pride of the house, a cabernet and merlot blend, seems to have developed an extra dimension. It has a lovely dark ruby color and an intense and elegant nose with notes of spice and vanilla; on the palate it reveals great concentration and a long aromatic finish. In part this is thanks to a fine harvest, but also to the renewal of their fleet of barrels, which began in '95 and will produce more marked results in the next few years. The Marino Colle Picchioni Oro '97 is one of the most successful, captivating and well-balanced white wines produced this year in Lazio. Its color is a brilliant light straw yellow tinged with green, and its intense and well-defined bouquet is rich in fruity and floral tones, with a touch of vanilla from its time in the wood, a delectable combination. In the mouth it reveals its structure, with notes of white peaches and pears, and delicate vegetal hints leading to a soft vanilla echo in the finish. The Marino Etichetta Verde is up to its usual high standard, as fragrant, fresh, full-bodied and fruity as ever. Considering its price, it is one of the best buys in the region.

	Wine	Glasses	Price
○	Marino Colle Picchioni Oro '97	🍷🍷	4
●	Vigna del Vassallo '95	🍷🍷	5
○	Marino Etichetta Verde '97	🍷	3*
●	Vigna del Vassallo '85	🍷🍷🍷	5
●	Vigna del Vassallo '88	🍷🍷🍷	5
○	Le Vignole '91	🍷🍷	4
○	Le Vignole '92	🍷🍷	4
○	Le Vignole '93	🍷🍷	4
●	Vigna del Vassallo '89	🍷🍷	5
●	Vigna del Vassallo '90	🍷🍷	5
●	Vigna del Vassallo '92	🍷🍷	5
●	Vigna del Vassallo '93	🍷🍷	5
●	Colle Picchioni Rosso '93	🍷	3

MARINO (RM)

Gotto d'Oro

Fraz. Frattocchie
Via del Divino Amore, 115
00040 Marino (RM)
tel. 06/9302221

If you should happen to be dining out and find that you fancy a white wine that's fresh, fruity and appealing, a lively and crisp tipple with a light aromatic aftertaste, and if, furthermore, you don't want to ruin yourself paying for it, see whether the wine list features Gotto d'Oro's Marino Superiore, particularly one of those made for restaurants and wine shops, in Bordeaux bottles of transparent glass. This vast winery, whose annual production is now in the hundreds of thousands of bottles, continues to be one of the most trustworthy producers in the region. Apart from the classic Marino, with its full-bodied structure and attractive fruit, your wine shop may also have their fragrant and floral Frascati Superiore, another Castelli Romani classic. They have, by the way, named their fragrant, soft vintage '97 red, another wine with admirable structure, after this wine-making zone: Castelli Romani. Last of all, the interesting Malvasia del Lazio serves as proof that they're not just resting on their laurels at Gotto d'Oro, but are constantly seeking to perfect their wine-making technique, improve their vineyards and experiment with new possibilities.

	Wine	Glasses	Price
●	Castelli Romani '97	🍷	2*
○	Frascati Superiore '97	🍷	2*
○	Marino Superiore '97	🍷	2*
○	Malvasia del Lazio '97		2
○	Marino Superiore '96	🍷	2*

MONTECOMPATRI (RM)

Tenuta Le Quinte
Via delle Marmorelle, 71
00040 Montecompatri (RM)
tel. 06/9438756

Pineapple, mango, papaya and banana: no, not a fruit cocktail, but a combination of aromatic delights to be found in the Montecompatri Virtù Romane which Francesco Papi and his family produced in 1997. The overwhelming strength of these aromas, which are a little bit "showy", and a distinctly sweet finish both weigh heavily on the wine's freshness, almost obscuring it. But this is a very pleasing wine, a cut above his usual standard, and sold, furthermore, at a strikingly modest price. His Montecompatri Casale dei Papi '97 is also a very respectable effort. Even though decisions at harvest time tend to favor its big brother, it is aromatically harmonious and consistently fresh. The red Rasa di Marmorata '96 is a well-made wine, as usual. Its combination of cesanese, montepulciano and other red grapes gives it an interesting complexity, and though not yet an important wine it continues to improve. When we went to press their Dulcis Vitis '97 wasn't yet available, so we'll discuss it next year.

	Wine	Glasses	Price
○	Montecompatri Colonna Sup. Virtù Romane '97	🍷	2*
○	Montecompatri Colonna Sup. Casale dei Papi '97	🍷	1*
○	Rasa di Marmorata '96	🍷	2
○	Montecompatri Colonna Sup. Virtù Romane '94	🍷🍷	2*
○	Montecompatri Colonna Sup. Virtù Romane '95	🍷🍷	2
○	Montecompatri Colonna Sup. Virtù Romane '96	🍷🍷	2*
○	Dulcis Vitis '96	🍷	3
○	Montecompatri Colonna Sup. Casale dei Papi '96	🍷	1

MONTEFIASCONE (VT)

Falesco
S. S. Cassia Nord km 94.155
01027 Montefiascone (VT)
tel. 0761/827032

Falesco has hit the bull's-eye once again. For the third year running Montiano has received Three Glasses, our highest award. The '96 version of this great merlot seems even more intense, complex and dense than the '95. It is a fascinating wine, redolent of red berries, with touches of tobacco, oriental spices, chocolate and lead pencil; in addition, it is sold at a very fair price. It goes without saying that the mastermind behind this extraordinary result is Riccardo Cotarella. What further adjectives can we use to describe this small but well-equipped winery just outside of Montefiascone? Every year we wait impatiently for their wines to come out and every year Cotarella's wine-making ability manages to astonish us. Take for example their delicious bottom-of-the-line white, Est Est Est Falesco '97. Its freshness and pleasant drinkability make it an excellent accompaniment to a light fish luncheon. Or consider their special selection Poggio dei Gelsi '97: clearly the best white from the area, it offers aromatic richness followed by a big, fruity mouthful of great length and finesse. It is offered at an incredible price for a wine which wins two very full glasses. The '97 Grechetto has also made great progress. The hints of vanilla resulting from a brief period in contact with the noble oak do not overpower the characteristic fruitiness of its grape, but join forces to create a wine of great harmony and elegance. An easy Two Glasses for the enviable performance of the '97 Vitiano as well. Never before has this wine seemed so generous in its grassy bouquet and in its warm, engrossing intensity. The '97 Vitiano is unrivalled in its category.

	Wine	Glasses	Price
●	Montiano '96	🍷🍷🍷	5
○	Est Est Est di Montefiascone Poggio dei Gelsi '97	🍷🍷	3*
○	Grechetto '97	🍷🍷	3*
●	Vitiano '97	🍷🍷	2*
○	Est Est Est di Montefiascone Falesco '97	🍷	1
●	Montiano '94	🍷🍷🍷	5
○	Est Est Est di Montefiascone Vendemmia Tardiva '94	🍷🍷	4
○	Est Est Est di Montefiascone Vendemmia Tardiva '95	🍷🍷	4
●	Montiano '92	🍷🍷	5
●	Montiano '93	🍷🍷	5
●	Vitiano '96	🍷🍷	2

Fontana Candida

Via Fontana Candida, 11
00040 Monteporzio Catone (RM)
tel. 06/9420066

Would you be interested in trying one of Lazio's best whites? Come to Fontana Candida and ask for Frascati Superiore Santa Teresa '97. Franco Bardi and his staff have made more than 100,000 bottles of excellent wine from the Santa Teresa vineyard, not far from Fontana Candida headquarters. It's the nuanced elegance of this wine that first arrests your attention: there's the delectable aromatic quality of these grapes, lively freshness and a gentle persistence that winds up with a lovely note of almonds. And its price alone should win it an award. In their newer category, Terre dei Grifi, we find a very good Malvasia del Lazio '97, made completely from the local malvasia puntinata grape, a rare treat. Bardi has taken great care to make the most of its richness of perfume. The wine is straw yellow in color and yields hints of sage and bananas to both nose and mouth. The Frascati Superiore '97 from the same range is much more than satisfactory. A careful selection of the best local grapes is followed by a process of vinification that brings out all their aromatic qualities. (Indeed, when one compares this wine to the perfectly respectable Frascati Superiore Fontana Candida '97, the difference in variety and richness of perfume is abundantly clear.) The floral bouquet is enhanced by intense suggestions of fruit, and in the mouth it is full and tasty, with a very pleasing consistent freshness.

	Wine	Rating	Price
O	Frascati Sup. Santa Teresa '97	**YY**	2*
O	Malvasia del Lazio '97	**YY**	2*
O	Frascati Sup. Terre dei Grifi '97	**Y**	2
O	Frascati Superiore '97	**Y**	2
O	Frascati Sup. Santa Teresa '95	YY	2
O	Frascati Sup. Santa Teresa '96	YY	2*
O	Frascati Sup. Terre dei Grifi '95	YY	2*
O	Malvasia del Lazio '95	YY	2
O	Malvasia del Lazio '96	YY	2*

Villa Simone

Via Frascati Colonna, 29
00040 Monteporzio Catone (RM)
tel. 06/3213210 - 9449717

Villa Simone is the country retreat of Piero Costantini, the well-known Roman wine merchant. Our friend spends much of his time these days at his estate, which is situated on the gently rolling volcanic hills near Frascati with a view of the Eternal City. The wine cellar, carefully organized and very well-equipped, is hidden, in effect, under a hanging garden and surrounded by about thirty hectares of vineyards, some owned, some rented. Assisted by his nephew Lorenzo and by the oenologist Bisleti, Piero remains true to his ideals: no chemicals in the vineyards or cellar, and the greatest respect for the natural characteristics of his grapes and wines. As usual, yields have been kept low, and the results are excellent. The respectable Frascati Villa Simone '97, made from malvasia puntinata, trebbiano and bellone grapes, is perhaps a bit lightweight in structure but is nevertheless intriguing to the nose and palate. Once again we prefer the Frascati Vigna dei Preti: this '97 version presents a generous fruity nose of tart apples and bananas, and is light, fresh, tasty and well-balanced in the mouth. His prize wine, Frascati Filonardi '97, is a little off this year. Nonetheless this vineyard, once Sergio Zavoli's, has produced a wine in which aromas of peaches and wild flowers are elegantly balanced. On the other hand, his Cannellino '97 is in superb form. This frequently tricky wine, which Costantini offers us in a version both sweet and intense, is redolent of fruit and honey, and unctuous without being cloying. The finish goes on forever.

	Wine	Rating	Price
O	Frascati Sup. Cannellino '97	**YY**	5
O	Frascati Sup. V. dei Preti '97	**YY**	2
O	Frascati Sup. Vign. Filonardi '97	**YY**	3
O	Frascati Sup. Villa Simone '97	**Y**	2
O	Frascati Sup. Cannellino '91	YY	5
O	Frascati Sup. Cannellino '92	YY	5
O	Frascati Sup. V. dei Preti '94	YY	2
O	Frascati Sup. V. dei Preti '95	YY	2
O	Frascati Sup. Vign. Filonardi '93	YY	3
O	Frascati Sup. Vign. Filonardi '94	YY	3
O	Frascati Sup. Vign. Filonardi '95	YY	3
O	Frascati Sup. Villa Simone '93	YY	2
O	Frascati Sup. Villa Simone '95	YY	2
O	Frascati Sup. Cannellino '95	Y	5
O	Frascati Sup. Vign. Filonardi '96	Y	3

PIGLIO (FR)

Massimi Berucci
Via Prenestina km 42
03010 Piglio (FR)
tel. 0775/501303 - 06/68307004

The '97 vintage is a hard one to call. While in some parts of Italy they say it's a miraculously good year, here in the Ciociaria they're wondering what will happen to it with the passage of time. Little rain and punishing heat have indeed made for a high degree of sugar in the grapes, but have on the other hand created wines too low in the acidity that makes a wine fresh to the taste. Massimi Berucci's wines have also not been spared by these bizarre weather conditions. The overabundance of sugars in the red grapes which are the foundation of his Cesanese Casal Cervino blocked the fermentation process, leaving a distinct sweetish strain and residual carbon dioxide. For these reasons, our friend Berucci has followed the advice of Domenico Tagliente and decided to keep his eye on the Casal Cervino as it develops, and to release a Cesanese del Piglio '97, made of grapes selected from some of his other vineyards. A charming note of sweet, ripe, red fruits is what one first tastes in this wine, with an explosion in the mouth of a not inconsiderable alcoholic charge (indeed it's over 14%). While sweetness is less obvious here, it is still present, although blended with spices and licorice. The white, Passerina del Frusinate '97, seems untouched by these troubles, and is unusually fresh and fruity. Palates not accustomed to these wines may not immediately appreciate their naive touches, but we feel that they merit attention since they still represent the best of non-industrial wine-making in the area.

	Wine	Rating	Price
●	Cesanese del Piglio '97	🍷	3
○	Passerina del Frusinate '97	🍷	1
●	Cesanese del Piglio Casal Cervino '90	🍷🍷	3*
●	Cesanese del Piglio Casal Cervino '93	🍷🍷	3
●	Cesanese del Piglio Casal Cervino '94	🍷🍷	3
●	Cesanese del Piglio Casal Cervino '95	🍷	3
○	Passerina del Frusinate '95	🍷	1

ROMA

Conte Zandotti
Via Vigne Colle Mattia, 8
00132 Roma
tel. 06/20609000 - 6160335

Big news in the wind, and that's unusual at the Conte Zandotti winery, famous for its great caution in tampering with anything to do with its wine production. This year, however, there has been a real transformation in their approach to wine-making with the arrival of their new young oenologist, Marco Ciarla. Their Frascati Superiore '97 has changed. It is more subtle in its perfume, as elegant as ever and still fairly long in its finish, so it will probably last well. What pleases us less is the sense that there has been too much technology at work here, diminishing the structure and flavors of the wine. Their De Copa '97 version is more interesting. Made from the same classic mixture of grapes as the above, it is kept briefly in the wood before bottling, and the quiet notes of vanilla mix well with the fruity tones of the wine. But here too there are traces of the hand of the technician: one doesn't find the complexity that a wooded wine generally promises. The delicate Frascati Cannellino '97 is as good as ever, as is its oaked version, the De Copa '97; in both one finds graceful hints of honey and acacia flowers. These are lovely end-of-the-meal wines that go well with desserts made with fruit. It is a pity, though, that they both display a slight leanness which reduces their complexity both to the nose and in the mouth.

	Wine	Rating	Price
○	Frascati Cannellino '97	🍷	3
○	Frascati Cannellino De Copa '97	🍷	3
○	Frascati Superiore '97	🍷	2
○	Frascati Superiore De Copa '97	🍷	3
○	Frascati Cannellino '95	🍷🍷	3
○	Frascati Cannellino '96	🍷🍷	3
○	Frascati Superiore '94	🍷🍷	2
○	Frascati Superiore '95	🍷🍷	2
○	Frascati Cannellino '93	🍷	3*
○	Frascati Cannellino '94	🍷	3
○	Frascati Superiore '93	🍷	2
○	Frascati Superiore '96	🍷	2

OTHER WINERIES

The following producers obtained good scores in our tastings with one or more of their wines:

PROVINCE OF FROSINONE

Coletti Conti
Anagni, tel. 0775/728610,
Cesanese del Piglio Hernicus '97,
Passerina del Frusinate Hernicus '97

Giuseppe Iucci
Cassino, tel. 0776/311883,
Merlot di Atina Tenuta La Creta '96

La Selva
Paliano, tel. 0775/533125,
Cesanese del Piglio '97,
Passerina del Frusinate '97

Cantina Sociale Cesanese del Piglio
Piglio, tel. 0775/502355,
Cesanese del Piglio Etichetta Oro '96,
Cesanese del Piglio Etichetta Rossa '96

PROVINCE OF LATINA

Cantina Sociale Cincinnato
Cori, tel. 06/9679380,
Rosso dei Dioscuri '97

Pouchain
Ponza, tel. 06/30365644,
Vino di Bianca '97

PROVINCE OF ROMA

Casale Mattia
Frascati, tel. 06/9426249,
Frascati Superiore '97

Casale Vallechiesa
Frascati, tel. 06/9417270,
Frascati Superiore Vallechiesa '97

Femar Vini
Frascati, tel. 06/9419491
Frascati Sup. Poggio alle Volpi '97

L'Olivella
Frascati, tel. 06/9424527,
Frascati Sup. Racemo '97

Cantina San Marco
Frascati, tel. 06/9422689,
Frascati Sup. Selezione '97

Tenuta di Pietra Porzia
Frascati, tel. 06/9464392,
Frascati Sup. Regillo Etichetta Nera '97

Baldassarri
Genzano, tel. 06/9396106,
Colli Lanuvini Sup. '97

Cantina Sociale La Selva
Genzano, tel. 06/9396085,
Colli Lanuvini Sup. Fontanatorta '97

Cantina Sociale San Tommaso
Genzano, tel. 06/9375863,
Colli Lanuvini Sup. Castel S. Gennaro '97

Camponeschi
Lanuvio, tel. 06/9374390,
Colli Lanuvini Superiore '97

CO.PRO.VI
Velletri, tel. 06/8625305,
Velletri Bianco Villa Ginnetti '97,
Velletri Rosso Ris. '95

Cesare Loreti
Zagarolo, tel. 06/9575956,
Zagarolo Sup. Vigneti Loreti '97

PROVINCE OF VITERBO

Cantina Sociale di Gradoli
Gradoli, tel. 0761/456087,
Aleatico di Gradoli Ris. '94

Trappolini
Castiglione in Teverina, tel. 0761/948381,
Castiglione Rosso '97,
Grechetto dell'Umbria Brecceto '97

Vittorio Puri
Montefiascone, tel. 0761/799190,
Est Est Est di Montefiascone Villa Puri '97

Cantina Sociale Colli Cimini
Vignanello,
tel. 0761/754591,
Greco di Vignanello '97

ABRUZZO AND MOLISE

In recent years the Abruzzo has progressed by leaps and bounds, thanks to a variety of factors which have made it one of the top up-and-coming regions. Wine-producers today are more aware of the land's potential and are discovering that many microzones are capable of getting the best out of not only the local grapes montepulciano and trebbiano but also non-native ones, particularly cabernet sauvignon and chardonnay, (which some more adventurous winegrowers are experimenting with). More attention is being paid (though there is still room for improvement) to the care of the vine and to the choice of harvest times. Moreover, considerable investments have been made in new technological equipment and the renovation of the wineries themselves, including reception rooms for oeno-tourists following the Wine Routes. Last but not least, there is a greater number of competent young oenologists at work here, together with experts from outside the region who provide advice part-time. This year's tastings show a notable increase in quality and the Guide reflects this by including six more entries than two years ago. This time around, Montepulciano and Trebbiano d'Abruzzo are still the leading lights, and the fine '97 vintage will be remembered around these parts for having given us some of the best young white wines and Cerasuolo of the decade. The best results come, as usual, from the exciting 'poet of wine' Edoardo Valentini, with his Trebbiano d'Abruzzo, and from the enterprising Gianni Masciarelli, who earns his second consecutive Three Glass award with a formidable Montepulciano d'Abruzzo Villa Gemma. It should be borne in mind that at least five or six other wines from these and other producers did well enough to be admitted to the final round. There was an unprecedented number of Two Glass wines, many of them given to Montepulciano d'Abruzzo, long the object of high praise from wine critics, and also to interesting cabernets and chardonnays, all substantial and correctly executed, some given a classical stamp, others a modern touch: for example, Illuminati (with Lumen, Zanna and Nicò), Zaccagnini (with the two new Abbazia S. Clemente wines), Cataldi Madonna (Toni), Montori (Leneo Moro) and Nicodemi (Bacco); also the up-and-coming Orlandi Contucci Ponno (Liburnio and Colle Funaro), Marramiero (Inferi), Fattoria La Valentina, Barone Cornacchia (Poggio Varano), Pasetti (Tenuta di Testarossa) and even the Cantina Tollo, the queen of regional cooperatives, with their Cagiòlo. In Molise things are moving, as we foresaw last year: coming up behind the evergreen Di Majo Norante, who offers an interesting range of white wines and a few good reds, is the new Borgo di Colloredo run by the young Enrico di Giulio, who in his second year of bottling has already notably improved his two top-range wines.

BOLOGNANO (PE)

CICCIO ZACCAGNINI
C.DA POZZO
65020 BOLOGNANO (PE)
TEL. 085/8880195

Last year we toasted the return to the Guide of Marcello Zaccagnini, one of the best-known producers of the region. This year our tasting of the Capsico Rosso, long considered his leading wine, was done only from the barrel (there's no doubt it has great potential), since this wine will not be on the market until early '99. What else is new? First of all there are two new wines that show a modern touch in both grape selection and in the careful use of barriques, and reveal the expert hand of the oenologist Concezio Marulli. The Montepulciano d'Abruzzo Abbazia S. Clemente '96 is a clear, dark-colored wine with considerable density on both nose and palate, reminiscent of wild berries and licorice. The white of the same name is also excellent, made from chardonnay grapes fermented and aged in barriques: of a brilliant, intense color, it has notes of yellow flowers, ripe fruit and toasty oak. Two of the three rosés are worthy of note: the Ibisco Rosa '97 and especially the Myosotis '97 (briefly barrel-aged), which displays a notable structure and a good variety of aromas. The '95 Riserva of Montepulciano d'Abruzzo is in line with the house style; while not immediately convincing on the nose, it recoups in the mouth with the roundness of its tannins and the long-lasting fruity notes. The Bianco di Ciccio '97 (trebbiano d'Abruzzo and chardonnay) displays brilliant color and pleasant fruity nuances underpinned by good acidity. The rest of the second line is of fairly good quality, though there is room for improvement.

	Wine	Glasses	Price
○	Chardonnay Abbazia S. Clemente '97	▼▼	4
●	Montepulciano d'Abruzzo Abbazia S. Clemente '96	▼▼	4
○	Bianco di Ciccio '97	▼	2*
●	Montepulciano d'Abruzzo Ris. '95	▼	3
⊙	Myosotis Rosé '97	▼	3
○	Ibisco Bianco '97		3
⊙	Ibisco Rosa '97		2
●	Montepulciano d'Abruzzo '96		2
⊙	Montepulciano d'Abruzzo Cerasuolo '97		2
●	Capsico Rosso '93	▽	3
●	Montepulciano d'Abruzzo '90	▽	3
●	Montepulciano d'Abruzzo Ris. '93	▽	3

CAMPOMARINO (CB)

DI MAJO NORANTE
C.DA RAMITELLO, 4
86042 CAMPOMARINO (CB)
TEL. 0875/57208

Di Majo Norante is still the only producer in Molise who offers a substantial range of wines made from grapes that are thoroughly southern, with which he has been assiduously experimenting for some time now. Of the reds, we were favorably impressed by the Aglianico and, especially, the Ramitello. The structured Aglianico displays aromas of ripe blackberry, plum and leather; in the mouth, after an alcohol-rich entry, pleasant notes of candied peel emerge. The Ramitello (made from aglianico and montepulciano) offers a generous bouquet with intense aromas of red fruit and delicate balsamic notes. On the palate it is warm, full and richly fruity with tasty hints of licorice. The whites are all clean and well-made. The Falanghina is fairly good (fresh and lasting floral and citrus notes). The Fiano is good (a fresh, pungent nose). The Greco, Ramitello and Molì get One Glass each. The Biblos '96 is good too: a blend of falanghina and greco, less balanced than the previous vintage but nevertheless properly acidic with fruity aromas and a light hazelnut finish.

	Wine	Glasses	Price
●	Biferno Rosso Ramitello '96	▼▼	3*
●	Aglianico '96	▼	3
○	Biblos '96	▼	4
○	Biferno Molì Bianco '97	▼	1*
●	Biferno Molì Rosso '97	▼	1*
○	Falanghina '97	▼	3
○	Fiano '97	▼	3
○	Greco '97	▼	3
●	Prugnolo '96	▼	3
○	Ramitello Bianco '97	▼	3
○	Apianae '93	▽▽	4
○	Biblos '95	▽▽	4
○	Apianae '94	▽	4
●	Biferno Rosso Ramitello '93	▽	3

COLONNELLA (TE)

LEPORE
C.DA CIVITA
64010 COLONNELLA (TE)
TEL. 0861/70860 - 085/4222835

Things seem to be going well again for Lepore after his dramatic exit from the Guide a few years back and subsequent fallow period. He's back in full form, deservedly reinstated, having dropped his economy range to concentrate his efforts on his two leading wines and a range of three others, all quite correctly executed: the Cerasuolo, from montepulciano grapes, has just the right color and aromas (sour cherry) and a good balance of alcohol and acidity; the Trebbiano d'Abruzzo has a brilliant straw color and a light white flower fragrance, and is not very concentrated on the palate; thirdly, the Montepulciano d'Abruzzo is fruity, pleasantly mature and warm but just a little rough. We were not totally convinced by the Luigi Lepore Riserva '93: although it is better than the preceding vintage, the elegance of its bouquet is marred by excessive woodiness, which also masks the fruit on the palate. It's quite a different story with the white, made from the native passerina. We tasted this wine a few days after its bottling; it is now clear that, in the best vintages, this wine takes a few months longer to mature and acquire proper balance. We found it clear and brilliant, rich in aromas which have yet to come out altogether, with a decent structure and good acidity. The red Passito also deserves its One Glass for its evanescent but delicate aromas and its good balance on the palate.

	Wine	Glasses	Price
●	Montepulciano d'Abruzzo '96	🍷	3
⊙	Montepulciano d'Abruzzo Cerasuolo '97	🍷	3*
●	Montepulciano d'Abruzzo Luigi Lepore Ris. '93	🍷	5
○	Passera delle Vigne '97	🍷	3
●	Passito dei Lepore '95	🍷	5
○	Trebbiano d'Abruzzo '97		3

CONTROGUERRA (TE)

DINO ILLUMINATI
C.DA S. BIAGIO, 18
64010 CONTROGUERRA (TE)
TEL. 0861/808008

The success of the Lumen '94 should be sufficient to persuade the Illuminati family to continue aiming for excellence. This goes for their whole yearly output of around one million bottles. The Lumen is made from montepulciano with a touch of cabernet sauvignon. On the nose it is rich and round with ripe fruity and spicy notes; on the palate it is full-bodied with enticing tannins. The other red of merit, the Zanna, displays intense color and aromas of ripe red fruit and tar, and is fairly full-bodied and complex. Excellent results were obtained with the Nicò, thanks to an inspired blend of montepulciano, merlot and cabernet. On the nose it displays compound aromas and in the mouth a rounded taste of great depth and balance. Our review of the reds ends with the Montepulciano d'Abruzzo Riparosso '97, which seemed to us already round and harmonious. From the same grapes comes the Cerasuolo Campirosa, with a rich fruity fragrance and great quaffability. Among the whites we were very interested by the Ciafrè '97 (made from trebbiano, garganega, riesling and passerina). Though slow to open on the nose, it then offers aromatic length and lots of character. The Daniele '96 again failed to live up to expectations. The Cenalba Chardonnay displays a distinct varietal character, with pleasant nuances of banana.

	Wine	Glasses	Price
●	Montepulciano d'Abruzzo Lumen '94	🍷🍷	5
●	Montepulciano d'Abruzzo Zanna Vecchio '94	🍷🍷	4
●	Nicò '94	🍷🍷	5
○	Cenalba Chardonnay '97	🍷	2*
○	Ciafré '97	🍷	2*
⊙	Montepulciano d'Abruzzo Cerasuolo Campirosa '97	🍷	2*
●	Montepulciano d'Abruzzo Riparosso '97	🍷	2*
○	Trebbiano d'Abruzzo Daniele '96	🍷	4
●	Montepulciano d'Abruzzo Zanna Vecchio '93	🍷🍷 (outline)	4
●	Lumen '93	🍷 (outline)	5

CONTROGUERRA (TE)

CAMILLO MONTORI
PIANE TRONTO, 23
64010 CONTROGUERRA (TE)
TEL. 0861/809900

Camillo Montori's winery is one of the most reliable in the region. It was Montori who took the lead in promoting the Controguerra DOC, after having established the (alas underdeveloped) sub-zone of Colline Teramane. However, the Leneo Moro (made from montepulciano and cabernet sauvignon) will have to wait for the next vintage to have DOC on its label. It is a concentrated and harmonious wine with predominant fruit on both nose and palate, a vegetal nuance and appreciable tannins. Not far behind comes the Montepulciano d'Abruzzo Fonte Cupa '95, which has a rich ruby color, quite good balance and well-judged wood on the palate; it would be a perfect example of its type were it not diminished by a lack of definition on the nose. In the same range the Trebbiano d'Abruzzo, with its light but straightforward aromatic array and interesting structure, is back up to scratch. The Cerasuolo, well-balanced and fruity, is also up to the mark. The basic range is not so exciting, with the exception of the Montepulciano d'Abruzzo '97, which was still young when we tasted it but already distinctive in its vegetal components and decidedly promising. The white Leneo d'Oro was not offered us for tasting because Montori did not consider it up to his standards.

	Wine	Glasses	Price
●	Leneo Moro '95	🍷🍷	5
●	Montepulciano d'Abruzzo '97	🍷	2*
⊙	Montepulciano d'Abruzzo Cerasuolo Fonte Cupa '97	🍷	3*
●	Montepulciano d'Abruzzo Fonte Cupa '95	🍷	4
○	Trebbiano d'Abruzzo Fonte Cupa '97	🍷	3*
○	Fauno '97		2
⊙	Montepulciano d'Abruzzo Cerasuolo '97		2
○	Trebbiano d'Abruzzo '97		2
●	Leneo Moro '94	🍷🍷 (outline)	5
●	Montepulciano d'Abruzzo Fonte Cupa '94	🍷🍷 (outline)	4*

FRANCAVILLA A MARE (CH)

FRANCO PASETTI
C.DA PRETARO, 61
VIA S. PAOLO
66023 FRANCAVILLA A MARE (CH)
TEL. 085/61875

After a few years' absence, Mimmo Rocco Pasetti's winery returns to the Guide. Its return coincides with the completion of a period of growth and change: partial renovation of the cellar and doubling of the area under vine (now 40 hectares). So there's good news on the horizon: a new white in the offing! Meanwhile, both past and present confirm the Pasetti family's solid commitment to the production of traditional wines, eminently typical of their categories. Only large or medium-sized barrels are used for both versions of the Montepulciano d'Abruzzo. We tasted the last four vintages of the Tenuta di Testarossa, of which about 7 thousand bottles a year are made, and found the '94 admirably typical. Deep red in color with a slightly orange rim, it offers a rich bouquet of preserves and, on the palate, pleasant notes of tobacco and licorice. The Montepulciano Fattoria Pasetti '96 is, considering the vintage, slow to open on the nose, but it then offers light fruity nuances, although it has somewhat aggessive tannins. The fairly good Cerasuolo has a brilliant cherry color and captivating heady aromas of fresh fruit.

	Wine	Glasses	Price
⊙	Montepulciano d'Abruzzo Cerasuolo Fattoria Pasetti '97	🍷	2*
●	Montepulciano d'Abruzzo Fattoria Pasetti '96	🍷	2*
●	Montepulciano d'Abruzzo Tenuta di Testarossa '94	🍷	4
○	Trebbiano d'Abruzzo Fattoria Pasetti '97		2

LORETO APRUTINO (PE)

EDOARDO VALENTINI
VIA DEL BAIO, 2
65014 LORETO APRUTINO (PE)
TEL. 085/8291138

The countryside around the medieval town of Loreto Aprutino is among the most beautiful in Italy. With olive groves stretching as far as the eye can see, orchards and vineyards, it is a landscape straight out of a 19th century print. This is the realm of Edoardo Valentini, a prince among wine producers, a man profoundly attached to his land and the rhythms of the countryside. He has overseen 48 harvests, and this long experience is the only secret of his deep knowledge of vines and their cultivation, grape harvesting and wine-making. For almost half a century he has carefully observed the different vintages and has learnt the secrets of grape selection. At present he bottles only about ten to fifteen per cent of his production; the rest he hands over to a local cooperative winery of which he is a member. But the wines that bear his name must be exactly as he wants them, with no room for compromise. This year he was in doubt about whether to release the Trebbiano d'Abruzzo '94 which, according to him, fell short of expectations. We, however, found it excellent and encouraged him to bring it out. But his selection was merciless and he ended up producing only a third of the normal quantity. So he also released the Trebbiano d'Abruzzo '95, a very young wine according to him. This is a masterly white with the true Valentini touch, even more elegant and distinctive in aroma than usual. The Montepulciano d'Abruzzo '93 is already mature, almost ready to drink, it's so delightful. But it won't evolve like the '88, '90 and '92. The Cerasuolo '96, too, is a hairsbreadth inferior to the '95. But that white Trebbiano, made from a grape that used to be so rudely treated, really gives you food for thought! It has taken 50 vintages - a lifetime - to make it like that.

	Wine	Rating	Price
○	Trebbiano d'Abruzzo '95	🍷🍷🍷	5
●	Montepulciano d'Abruzzo '93	🍷🍷	6
⊙	Montepulciano d'Abruzzo Cerasuolo '96	🍷🍷	5
○	Trebbiano d'Abruzzo '94	🍷🍷	5
●	Montepulciano d'Abruzzo '77	🍷🍷🍷 (white)	6
●	Montepulciano d'Abruzzo '85	🍷🍷🍷 (white)	6
●	Montepulciano d'Abruzzo '88	🍷🍷🍷 (white)	6
●	Montepulciano d'Abruzzo '90	🍷🍷🍷 (white)	6
●	Montepulciano d'Abruzzo '92	🍷🍷🍷 (white)	6
○	Trebbiano d'Abruzzo '88	🍷🍷🍷 (white)	5
○	Trebbiano d'Abruzzo '92	🍷🍷🍷 (white)	5
●	Montepulciano d'Abruzzo '87	🍷🍷 (white)	6
○	Trebbiano d'Abruzzo '90	🍷🍷 (white)	6
○	Trebbiano d'Abruzzo '93	🍷🍷 (white)	5

NOTARESCO (TE)

BRUNO NICODEMI
C.DA VENIGLIO, 8
S. P. 19
64024 NOTARESCO (TE)
TEL. 085/895493 - 895135

This is one of the most reliable and best-equipped wineries in the region, consistently producing well-made, clean wines. It can only be said to lack a truly outstanding wine, one decidedly above the average quality of the range. The Montepulciano d'Abruzzo Bacco '94 is an excellent wine: a deep intense red in color, fruity with a predominant aroma of sour cherry and pleasant hints of roasted coffee. In the same range, the Trebbiano d'Abruzzo is, as always, interesting for its bright straw color and bouquet of white flowers, Golden Delicious apple and grapefruit, which is underpinned in the mouth by well-balanced acidity. Other good wines are the Trebbiano Colli Venia (a well-made wine, pleasantly quaffable, with mild but distinct aromas) and the Cerasuolo, which has never been so pleasant and well-defined in recent years as this. It is a fresh, appealing, cherry-colored wine, rich in fruity notes both on the nose and on the palate. We are not able to speak so highly of the 'basic' Montepulciano d'Abruzzo which has the defects of its vintage. But we are sure it will regain its customary quality with the '97, soon to be bottled.

	Wine	Rating	Price
●	Montepulciano d'Abruzzo Bacco '94	🍷🍷	5
⊙	Montepulciano d'Abruzzo Cerasuolo Colli Venia '97	🍷	2*
○	Trebbiano d'Abruzzo Bacco '97	🍷	3
○	Trebbiano d'Abruzzo Colli Venia '97	🍷	2*
●	Montepulciano d'Abruzzo Colli Venia '96		2
●	Montepulciano d'Abruzzo Bacco '93	🍷🍷 (white)	5
●	Montepulciano d'Abruzzo Colli Venia '95	🍷 (white)	2*

OFENA (AQ)

TENUTA CATALDI MADONNA
LOC. PIANA, 1
67025 OFENA (AQ)
TEL. 0862/954252 - 085/4911680

Luigi Cataldi Madonna is a brave man. He has had the strength of character to change production techniques and market image just when his winery had reached a good level of quality and had begun to experiment a little. As supervisor he called in Giovanni Ballo, a promising Piedmontese oenologist, whose influence should be perceptible starting next year. In the meantime we can say that their top wine, the Montepulciano d'Abruzzo Toni '93, only just bottled, is already displaying great complexity and elegance, good extract and aromas ranging from ripe fig to coffee and caramel. The two versions of Cerasuolo are worthy of note: the classic one, cherry-colored with intense aromas of red fruit, was, as always, among the most admired, but the novelty is the Pié delle Vigne, obtained by the procedure called "svacata": during the gentle pressing to produce the must and during fermentation, some unpressed montepulciano grapes (called "vachi" in the local dialect) are added, giving a more intense color and a denser texture on both the nose and the palate. The Montepulciano d'Abruzzo '96, ruby-colored with ripe fruity notes on the nose and fairly full on the palate, and the deep and structured Pecorino are both good. The Vigna Cona Rosso, from cabernet sauvignon, is getting better: it is dark in color with grassy, vegetal notes on the nose, and fairly full-bodied.

	Wine	Glasses	Price
●	Montepulciano d'Abruzzo Tonì '93	🍷🍷	5
●	Montepulciano d'Abruzzo '96	🍷	3*
⊙	Montepulciano d'Abruzzo Cerasuolo '97	🍷	2*
⊙	Montepulciano d'Abruzzo Cerasuolo Pié delle Vigne '97	🍷	3
○	Pecorino '97	🍷	3
●	Vigna Cona Rosso '95	🍷	4
○	Trebbiano d'Abruzzo '97		2
○	Vigna Cona Bianco '97		3
●	Montepulciano d'Abruzzo Tonì '91	🍷🍷 (prev.)	4*
●	Montepulciano d'Abruzzo '95	🍷 (prev.)	2
●	Montepulciano d'Abruzzo Rubino '94	🍷 (prev.)	2
●	Montepulciano d'Abruzzo Tonì '90	🍷 (prev.)	3

POPOLI (PE)

LORENZO FILOMUSI GUELFI
VIA MARCONI, 28
65026 POPOLI (PE)
TEL. 085/98353

The centuries-old Pescara winery of Lorenzo Filomusi Guelfi, after an absence of a couple of years due only to his wines' not being ready in time for our tastings, is back in the Guide. There are three wines (and a red aged for a long time is on the horizon), all well-made and eminently quaffable. Only the white (made from sauvignon, malvasia and chardonnay from one of their ten hectares under vine) is not up to its usual standard, owing to an excessive and pungent acidity. Another wine not quite up to scratch is the Montepulciano d'Abruzzo, created by the oenologist Romano D'Amarico in the good old style using large barrels: it has an intense ruby color, good structure, tannins that are just a little rough and a licorice finish. Not a bad result, though, considering this red is from a mediocre vintage, and it proves that this estate is faithful to its plan of always going for a low yield, producing not more than 20 thousand bottles. The Cerasuolo '97, from montepulciano, is also good: cherry-colored with lingering heady and fruity aromas, and well-balanced generally, with a short, characteristically bitterish finish.

	Wine	Glasses	Price
⊙	Montepulciano d'Abruzzo Cerasuolo '97	🍷	2*
○	Le Scuderie del Cielo '97		3
●	Montepulciano d'Abruzzo '96		3

ROSCIANO (PE)

Marramiero
C.da S. Andrea, 1
65010 Rosciano (PE)
tel. 085/8505766

This winery, on its fourth year of bottling and recently renovated, is doing very well thanks to young Enrico Marramiero's decision to engage one of the region's most enterprising oenologists, Romeo Taraborrelli. The tastings highlighted the Montepulciano d'Abruzzo Inferi '94. It has an intense red color and on the concentrated nose, together with notes of ripe fruit, a more moderate use of wood is immediately apparent (and appreciated). On the palate good balance and smooth tannins accompany notes of tobacco, roasted coffee and licorice. One Glass goes to the Trebbiano d'Abruzzo Altare '96, with its intense straw color and aromas of vanilla and yellow flowers well blended with the wood. On the palate it is soft and well-balanced but lacking in depth. You can see just from looking at it that the Chardonnay Punta di Colle '97 is a fairly substantial wine. It opens on the nose with intense floral notes, while on the mouth it is of medium density and soft, with a slightly bitter finish. Of the wines in the Dama range, we found only the Cerasuolo truly interesting. It has a fine light, bright cherry color, and good acidity which enriches the fresh fruit, fills the mouth and enhances the almond finish. The Trebbiano Anima '97 does not reach this standard. It has faint aromas and a slight alcohol imbalance.

	Wine	Glasses	Price
●	Montepulciano d'Abruzzo Inferi '94	🍷🍷	4
○	Chardonnay Punta di Colle '97	🍷	3
⊙	Montepulciano d'Abruzzo Cerasuolo Dama '97	🍷	2*
○	Trebbiano d'Abruzzo Altare '96	🍷	4
●	Montepulciano d'Abruzzo Dama '96		3
○	Trebbiano d'Abruzzo Anima '97		3
○	Trebbiano d'Abruzzo Dama '97		2
●	Montepulciano d'Abruzzo Inferi '93	🍸🍸	4

ROSETO DEGLI ABRUZZI (TE)

Orlandi Contucci Ponno
C.da Voltarrosto
Via Piana degli Ulivi, 1
64026 Roseto degli Abruzzi (TE)
tel. 085/8944049

It shouldn't seem strange that many wineries have obtained their best results from non-native grapes. As those working this land well know, in Abruzzo the terroir is ideal for growing many noble varietals. People just had to recognize the fact, and to entrust part of the work to the new generation of wine technicians, as Marina Orlandi Contucci has done at her old family estate in the Roseto hills. Four years ago she started bottling wines, with the advice of the oenologist Donato Lanati. Among the various bottles, the Liburnio '93 is outstanding, a well-balanced blend (already interesting in the '92 version) of lots of cabernet sauvignon with merlot, malbec and sangiovese, all perfectly assembled to create a concentrated red with enticing aromas of blackberry jam, blueberry and sour cherry, well-integrated with the wood. On the palate it is dense, ample and wonderfully full-bodied. The Cabernet Colle Funaro '95 is also a substantial wine, displaying clear notes of wild berries and hints of toasty oak and tar. The Montepulciano d 'Abruzzo Podere La Regia Specula '96 is good: a sour cherry jam fragrance is joined by grassy notes and hints of vanilla. Of the whites, the best of the vintage is the Sauvignon Ghiaiolo '97 which, despite a disturbing excess of carbon dioxide, displays good structure and a wealth of subtle aromas. One Glass goes to the Pinot for its floral and composite notes and also to the Cerasuolo Vermiglio, a crisp, pleasantly fruity and grassy wine.

	Wine	Glasses	Price
●	Cabernet Sauvignon Colle Funaro '95	🍷🍷	3
●	Liburnio '93	🍷🍷	5
⊙	Montepulciano d'Abruzzo Cerasuolo Vermiglio '97	🍷	2*
●	Montepulciano d'Abruzzo La Regia Specula '96	🍷	3*
○	Sauvignon Ghiaiolo '97	🍷	3
○	Pinot Adrio '97	🍷	3
●	Cabernet Sauvignon Colle Funaro '94	🍸	3
●	Montepulciano d'Abruzzo La Regia Specula '95	🍸	2

S. MARTINO SULLA MARRUCINA (CH)

GIANNI MASCIARELLI
VIA GAMBERALE, 1
66010 S. MARTINO
SULLA MARRUCINA (CH)
TEL. 0871/85241

Once again Gianni Masciarelli has unveiled some great wines of which the whole region has reason to be proud. This is the result of excellent work performed in one of the most propitious zones ("but the whole of Abruzzo is one big terroir, " Gianni insists) in Abruzzo, situated 50 kilometers from the sea on the slopes of the Majella. Rigorous selection during the harvest and considerable investment in the renovated and re-equipped cellar and the new vineyard have proved the strong suits of Gianni Masciarelli and his wife Marina Cvetic. This year we tasted four wines of a modern stamp. Despite the poor vintage, the Trebbiano '96 still has something to offer with its light aromas of yellow flowers and ripe fruit, fair body and appealing range of tastes from honey to tobacco to a delicate smokiness. The magnificent Montepulciano d 'Abruzzo Villa Gemma '93, at once powerful and extremely elegant, displays a full and complex bouquet with notes of ripe fruit and spice which in the mouth become amazingly deep ginger, tar and licorice. The masterful Chardonnay Marina Cvetic '96 shows a fine intense color and aromas reminiscent of yellow flowers, candied peel and acacia honey which carry through onto the palate. The Cabernet Sauvignon is just as good, with concentration in color and the bouquet, which offers notes of berries (red currant and blueberry) that get on well with the wood; on the palate it is even more powerful yet well-balanced. The other wines are simpler but irreproachable. The Bianco (cryomacerated trebbiano and cococciola) is soundly flowery and fairly structured, the Cerasuolo Villa Gemma is better than ever in color and aromas, and the standard Montepulciano d 'Abruzzo is ruby-colored and has good structure.

●	Montepulciano d'Abruzzo Villa Gemma '93	🍷🍷🍷	5
●	Cabernet Sauvignon Marina Cvetic '93	🍷🍷	5
○	Chardonnay Marina Cvetic '96	🍷🍷	4
○	Trebbiano d'Abruzzo Marina Cvetic '96	🍷🍷	4
○	Bianco Villa Gemma '97	🍷	3*
●	Montepulciano d'Abruzzo '96	🍷	2*
⊙	Montepulciano d'Abruzzo Cerasuolo Villa Gemma '97	🍷	3
⊙	Rosé '97		1
○	Trebbiano d'Abruzzo '97		1
●	Montepulciano d'Abruzzo Villa Gemma '92	🍸🍸🍸	5

SPOLTORE (PE)

FATTORIA LA VALENTINA
VIA COLLE CESI, 10
65010 SPOLTORE (PE)
TEL. 085/4478158

Encouraging results yet again from Sabatino Di Properzio 's winery, started in 1990 and already in a position to widen its commercial scope. The Fattoria La Valentina is turning out wines that are good value for money and is perhaps now ready to aim for excellence. For the time being we still prefer the Montepulciano d 'Abruzzo (both the Riserva and the standard version). The Riserva is excellent, thanks to the meticulous care of the oenologist Anselmo Paternoster. It has an intense ruby color tinged with garnet and pungent aromas of ripe fruit and spice. In the mouth it is soft with smooth tannins. Its younger brother the non-Riserva '96 is perhaps more rustic, but has an admirable density on the palate. There are also two versions of the Trebbiano d 'Abruzzo. In our opinion changes should be made to the Vigneto Spilla, not so much to the basic idea as to its realization. It has a deep yellow color, aromas of broom and peach with good acidity but a little forward. The classic Trebbiano offers less captivating aromas, but is crisp and pleasantly quaffable. A final wine worthy of mention is the Lusinga, a pleasant semi-sweet red.

●	Montepulciano d'Abruzzo Ris. '93	🍷🍷	3
●	Montepulciano d'Abruzzo '96	🍷	2*
●	Lusinga		3
⊙	Montepulciano d'Abruzzo Cerasuolo '97		2
○	Trebbiano d'Abruzzo '97		2
○	Trebbiano d'Abruzzo Vigneto Spilla '97		2
●	Montepulciano d'Abruzzo '95	🍸	2*
●	Montepulciano d'Abruzzo Ris. '92	🍸	3

TOLLO (CH)

CANTINA TOLLO
VIA GARIBALDI
66010 TOLLO (CH)
TEL. 0871/961726

What more can be said about the Cantina Tollo, the most up-to-date of the 40 or more cooperatives in the region? It manages admirably to keep prices down while maintaining or even improving quality. Not satisfied with this achievement, the oenologist Goffredo Agostini and his colleagues are trying out new techniques in the cellars. For the moment things couldn 't be going better. The Cagiòlo '94 easily qualifies for Two Glasses with its solid structure, fruity and slightly toasty aroma and elegant palate which gradually reveals notes of blackberry, leather and licorice. The two Montepulciano d 'Abruzzo Colle Secco '96s are not far behind. The Rubino is more elegant with its soft and delicate notes of fruit preserves. The other is more rustic but equally full-bodied and well-balanced. The Cerasuolo Valle d 'Oro '97, with its characteristic nose and palate, is accustomed to receiving One Glass. It is cherry-colored and fruity, and its good structure implies no loss of freshness or quaffability. The Trebbiano d 'Abruzzo Colle Secco '97 is very good. It has a bright straw color, white flowers and apple on the nose and a crisp palate. The other two wines in the Valle d 'Oro range are worth a mention. But the Cagiòlo Bianco, made from barrique-fermented chardonnay and on its maiden voyage, needs working on.

	Wine	Glasses	Price
●	Montepulciano d'Abruzzo Cagiòlo '94	🍷🍷	3*
●	Montepulciano d'Abruzzo Colle Secco Rubino '96	🍷🍷	2*
⊙	Montepulciano d'Abruzzo Cerasuolo Valle d'Oro '97	🍷	1*
●	Montepulciano d'Abruzzo Colle Secco '96	🍷	2*
○	Trebbiano d'Abruzzo Colle Secco '97	🍷	2
○	Cagiòlo Bianco '96		3
●	Montepulciano d'Abruzzo Valle d'Oro '96		1
○	Trebbiano d'Abruzzo Valle d'Oro '97		1

TORANO NUOVO (TE)

BARONE CORNACCHIA
C.DA TORRI
64010 TORANO NUOVO (TE)
TEL. 0861/887412

The well-kept vineyards of the Tenuta Barone Cornacchia are located in some of the most beautiful countryside of the region. From an oenological point of view as well Pietro Cornacchia deserves attention, thanks to his wines, particularly those made from montepulciano grapes. (They are all excellent value for money, by the way.) His best wines for some time have been the Poggio Varano and the Vigna Le Coste, and the '96s are surprisingly complex and dense, considering that '96 was by no means a good vintage in these parts. Poggio Varano is a mature, concentrated red, rich in aromatic nuances of cherry and sour cherry preserved in spirits, full-bodied and rounded. The equally mature Vigna Le Coste has a less imposing structure, but is nevertheless full-bodied and soft, with a deep licorice finish. Not far behind is the latest vintage of the standard Montepulciano d'Abruzzo, still young and somewhat closed on the nose, and marked by a little roughness but essentially well-made.

	Wine	Glasses	Price
●	Montepulciano d'Abruzzo Poggio Varano '96	🍷🍷	3*
●	Montepulciano d'Abruzzo '97	🍷	2
●	Montepulciano d'Abruzzo Vigna Le Coste '96	🍷	3
○	Chardonnay Villa Torri '97		1
⊙	Montepulciano d'Abruzzo Cerasuolo '97		1
○	Trebbiano d'Abruzzo '97		1

OTHER WINERIES

The following producers obtained good scores in our tastings with one or more of their wines: .

PROVINCE OF CAMPOBASSO

Borgo di Colloredo
Campomarino, tel. 0875/57453,
Gironia Bianco '97,
Gironia Rosso '95

PROVINCE OF CHIETI

Cooperativa Casalbordino
Casalbordino, tel. 0873/918107,
Montepulciano d'Abruzzo
Contea di Bordino Ris. '94

Santoleri
Guardiagrele, tel. 0871/82250 - 893301,
Montepulciano d'Abruzzo '95,
Montepulciano d'Abruzzo Crognaleto Ris. '93

Cooperativa Citra
Ortona, tel. 085/9031342,
Montepulciano d'Abruzzo
Caroso Ris. '93

Sarchese Dora
Ortona, tel. 085/9031249,
Montepulciano d'Abruzzo '96,
Montepulciano d'Abruzzo
Rosso di Macchia Ris. '94

Tenuta di Valletta - Mezzanotte
Ripa Teatina,
tel. 0871/390152,
Laus Deo Muffato '94,
Montepulciano d'Abruzzo
Cenacolo della Mezzanotte '95

Buccicatino
Vacri,
tel. 0871/720273,
Cabernet Sauvignon '96,
Montepulciano d'Abruzzo '96

PROVINCE OF PESCARA

Bosco Nestore
Nocciano,
tel. 085/847345,
Il Grappolo Rosso '97,
Montepulciano d'Abruzzo Ris. '94

Roxan Casa Vinicola
Rosciano,
tel. 085/8505683,
Montepulciano d'Abruzzo Galelle '97

PROVINCE OF TERAMO

Faraone
Giulianova,
tel. 085/8071804,
Brut Metodo Classico '95,
Trebbiano d'Abruzzo Le Vigne '97

CAMPANIA

For some years now Campania has been making rapid strides, at least in terms of wine production. On the brink of a new millennium we are witnessing a curious world-wide phenomenon: the ever more decided southward shift of the oenological center of gravity. This is particularly true of contemporary Italy. In such regions as Campania, Sicily, Puglia and Sardinia, to name but a few, constant progress is the order of the day. And in Campania the rate of progress is astonishing. From Massico in its northernmost reaches to Cilento on the Basilicata border there is an increasing number of wineries that have set about restructuring both cellar and vineyards. After years of relative lethargy the wine-makers of Campania are accomplishing in the space of a couple of vintages what took a decade in other regions. Paradoxically, the easy-going wait-and-see attitude that we have so energetically condemned in the past has enabled local wine-makers to learn a great deal from the experience (and mistakes) of others. So it's not just a matter of chance that some of the most distinguished oenologists in Italy are employed in this region and that they are reviving and improving native varietals. These are, after all, yet another of the great natural resources of Campania. There are not many areas in Italy that can boast of such a variety of both red and white wine grapes. And very few indeed have so lovingly preserved this part of their ancient heritage. This doesn't mean that you can't find cabernet sauvignon, merlot or chardonnay in the vineyards down here, but rather that they tend to take their place in blends with traditional grapes like aglianico, piedirosso, fiano and greco. Such is the case with the superlative Montevetrano, in which cabernet predominates but is joined by merlot and aglianico, and which is once again absolutely first-class, and with the excellent Terra di Lavoro, in which cabernet and merlot play second fiddle to piedirosso and aglianico. One of the best Italian red wines made from native grapes that we've tasted in recent years is the great Taurasi '94 produced by Feudi di San Gregorio, a young winery that has been making some of the finest reds and whites in the region, mostly from local varietals, as in their Greco and their Falanghina, but also including some recent innovations, like Serpico and Campanaro, where barriques and international grape types hold sway. But these are isolated cases. Wine production in Campania is solidly based on such white wines as Biancolella from Ischia and Greco and Fiano from Irpinia and Sannio, and on reds made from per' 'e palummo, piedirosso and aglianico, among others. And from Massico to Cilento, from the vineyards along the enchanting coastline and on the inland slopes and plains, we expect to have greater and greater wines. Many of them are probably already in the barrel.

ATRIPALDA (AV)

ANTONIO, CARLO E PIETRO
MASTROBERARDINO
VIA MANFREDI, 75/81
83042 ATRIPALDA (AV)
TEL. 0825/626123

This is a winery that has taught us to expect high quality, and this year once again we were not disappointed. Perhaps the most interesting news is that they've released their first Fiano di Avellino More Maiorum, vintage '95, a result of their desire to experiment with whites that can stand moderate aging. Obviously we're happy about it: for some time we've been singing the praises of Fiano di Avellino wines that have had the chance to spend a few years in the bottle. Their real star, however, is, as usual, the Taurasi Radici, which has become a local classic. The '94 version of this aglianico wine is rich in elegantly structured aromas of red berries, plums and undeniable licorice. On the palate it's well-defined and fairly complex, both concentrated and persistent. The Greco di Tufo Vignadangelo '97, which came very close to getting Two Glasses, has a well-developed and significant floral and vegetal nose, and is fresh and full-bodied in the mouth. The rest of their range is well-made and attractive, from the Mastro d'Irpinia Rosso to their two Lacryma Christis.

	Wine	Glasses	Price
●	Taurasi Radici '94	🍷🍷	5
○	Fiano di Avellino More Maiorum '95	🍷	5
○	Fiano di Avellino Radici '97	🍷	4
○	Fiano di Avellino Vignadora '97	🍷	4
○	Greco di Tufo Vignadangelo '97	🍷	3
●	Lacryma Christi Rosso '97	🍷	3
●	Mastro d'Irpinia Rosso '97	🍷	2
○	Lacryma Christi Bianco '97		3
●	Taurasi Radici '90	🍸🍸🍸	6
○	Fiano di Avellino Radici '95	🍸🍸	4
○	Fiano di Avellino Vignadora '95	🍸🍸	4
●	Taurasi Radici '93	🍸🍸	5
○	Fiano di Avellino Radici '96	🍸	4
●	Lacryma Christi Rosso '96	🍸	3

CASTELLABATE (SA)

SAN GIOVANNI
PUNTA TRESINO
84123 CASTELLABATE (SA)
TEL. 089/237331 - 224896

There is no mistaking the enthusiasm and dedication of Mario Corrado, the young director of this new Cilento winery. And his firm desire to produce excellent wine is just as evident. Once again San Giovanni's good Fiano, vintage '97 this time, has earned them a place in the Guide. The grapes come from four hectares of vineyards in the midst of the Parco Nazionale del Cilento, on a magnificent terrace overlooking the Mediterranean. This is again an agreeable wine, if not quite up to last year's version, but at this year's tasting the wine was probably suffering from insufficient bottle aging. It is, however, still an attractive blend of at least 85% fiano, with greco and trebbiano. It has a brilliant straw-yellow color, a fair amount of body, and ripe fruit aromas, with clear hints of citrus. Concentration on the palate is moderate, and there's a proper amount of acidity and a long aromatic finish.

	Wine	Glasses	Price
○	Fiano '97	🍷	3
○	Fiano '96	🍸🍸	3*

CELLOLE (CE)

Villa Matilde

S. S. Domitiana km. 4,700
81030 Cellole (CE)
tel. 0823/932088 - 932134

Ever since the first edition of this Guide, Maria Ida and Salvatore Avallone's estate has been an important reference point on the Campania wine map. A passionate desire to make excellent wine that reflects the identity of the land it comes from has informed their choices from the start. Hence it is no surprise that, as of last year, they have enlisted the help of the expert oenologist, Riccardo Cotarella. Their Falerno del Massico Vigna Caracci '97, its characteristic acidity softened by a brief and partial stay in new Allier barriques, has an elegantly fruity and balsamic bouquet and is unctuous and persistent on the palate. The Vigna Camarato '92 is a "table wine" made from the aglianico grape, produced only in very good years and aged, traditionally, in the barrel. The '92 reveals all the nobility of its vigorous and pleasing tannins. Its volatile and subtle nose presents a rich and complex array of aromas in which spices and preserved cherries stand out. The Falerno del Massico Rosso '96, a blend of aglianico and piedirosso, is agreeably vegetal and grassy, with hints of ripe red fruit, black currants and blackberries. In the mouth it is soft and tannic, well-balanced and long-lasting. The Falerno del Massico Bianco, made completely from falanghina cryomacerated to emphasize its aromatic qualities, is a cleanly made, pleasant wine, both fruity and balsamic. The Falanghina, the Aglianico and the Piedirosso di Roccamonfina are correct, well-made wines. The rosato Terre Cerase, as attractive as ever, is also worthy of mention..

	Wine	Rating	Price
○	Falerno del Massico Bianco Vigna Caracci '97	🍷🍷	4
●	Vigna Camarato '92	🍷🍷	4
●	Aglianico di Roccamonfina '97	🍷	3
○	Falanghina di Roccamonfina '97	🍷	3
○	Falerno del Massico Bianco '97	🍷	3
●	Falerno del Massico Rosso '96	🍷	3
●	Piedirosso di Roccamonfina '96	🍷	2
⊙	Terre Cerase Rosato '97	🍷	3
○	Falerno del Massico Bianco Vigna Caracci '96	🍷🍷 (white)	4
●	Falerno del Massico Rosso '96	🍷🍷 (white)	3
●	Falerno del Massico Rosso '93	🍷 (white)	3
●	Vigna Camarato '90	🍷 (white)	4

FORIO (NA)

Cantine di Pietratorcia

Loc. Forio
Via Provinciale Panza, 267
80075 Forio (NA)
tel. 081/908206 - 997406

If one remembers the situation on the island of Ischia twenty or thirty years ago, when an unbridled construction industry seemed to guarantee that viticulture would become a thing of the past, it is all the more wonderful to come upon a new winery like the Cantine di Pietratorcia, very young still but full of promise. The owners want to produce first-class wine in keeping with the island's predisposition for viticulture. Established in Forio, on the western slopes of Ischia, the estate has seven hectares replanted with native vines, including biancolella and forastera for their whites and per' 'e palummo and guarnaccia for the reds. The wines go down very easily and have an elegant aromatic structure. We especially liked the white Vigne del Cuotto '97, a fruity, vegetal and slightly mineral wine with pleasing citrus notes, crisp and fairly persistent. The Vigne di Chignole '97, another white, reveals a faint fragrance of vanilla and fruit; in the mouth it is rich in extract with complex notes of minerals and agreeably soft citrus fruits. The Tifeo Rosso, made from both piedirosso and guarnaccia grapes, is easy and fun to drink. The Pietratorcia Gran Riserva '96 is also pleasurable. Aged in oak barrels, it is made completely from biancolella grapes. The small barrels lend it an elegant aromatic quality, and the resultant wine expresses the clear desire of this nascent winery to preserve their local varietals and to improve the wine that is made from them.

	Wine	Rating	Price
○	Pietratorcia Gran Ris. '96	🍷🍷	5
○	Ischia Bianco Vigne del Cuotto '97	🍷	4
○	Ischia Bianco Vigne di Chignole '97	🍷	4
●	Tifeo Rosso '97		3

FORIO (NA)

D'Ambra Vini d'Ischia
Loc. Panza
S. S. 270
Via Mario D'Ambra
80075 Forio (NA)
tel. 081/907210 - 907246

Casa d'Ambra is the oenological beacon of the island of Ischia. The unfailing commitment of the cousins Corrado and Andrea d'Ambra has encouraged others to believe that it is still possible, despite the encroachments of a construction industry geared to quick gain, to make a go of agriculture. This year some of their classic wines are appearing for the first time with the Epomeo Igt denomination. The Epomeo Tenuta Frassitelli '97 is, as usual, an extremely pleasant wine. Made from the biancolella grape, it is elegantly aromatic with fresh and balanced vegetal notes, and is concentrated and long-lasting on the palate. Their Epomeo Vigne di Piellero '97 is also made from biancolella but from different vineyards; it is pleasingly fruity and structured on the nose, and intense and long-lasting on the palate. The Epomeo Vigna Cimentorosso'97, from forastera grapes, is, as we expected, a wine of structure, rich in fruit, soft and intriguing on the palate. The rest of their wines don't let the side down: the Biancolella '97 is agreeably clean and structured, the Forastera '97 has light varietal aromas, and the Per' 'e Palummo '97, the typical Ischian red, vaunts an elegant, intense and delightful aromatic structure. A yet nobler structure is to be found in the special selection Tenuta Montecorvo '97, which has all the pleasing characteristics of this grape, most notably an elegant note of violets. The lovely Kalimera Brut, a well-made "metodo classico" bubbly, is the result of experimentation on the part of Andrea D'Ambra, who brilliantly performs as the estate oenologist.

	Wine	Glasses	Price
○	Cimentorosso '97	▼▼	3
○	Tenuta Frassitelli '97	▼▼	4
○	Vigne di Piellero '97	▼▼	3
○	Ischia Biancolella '97	▼	3
○	Ischia Forastera '97	▼	2
●	Ischia Per' 'e Palummo '97	▼	2
●	Ischia Per' 'e Palummo Tenuta Montecorvo '97	▼	4
○	Kalimera Brut dell'Isola d'Ischia '97	▼	5
○	Biancolella Tenuta Frassitelli '90	▽▽▽	2
○	Biancolella Tenuta Frassitelli '96	▽▽	4
○	Biancolella Vigne di Piellero '96	▽▽	3
○	Ischia Forastera '96	▽▽	2*
●	Ischia Per' 'e Palummo Tenuta Montecorvo '94	▽▽	4

FURORE (SA)

Cuomo
Via G. B. Lama, 14
84010 Furore (SA)
tel. 089/830348 - 0336/610544

Furore is a small village overlooking the splendid sea off the Amalfi coast, and it has lent its name, for several years now, to one of the most interesting wines in the rich and lively Campania wine scene. Andrea Ferraioli and his wife Marisa Cuomo make their Bianco, Rosso and Riserva wines from grapes grown there, and also from the not very distant Ravello, the other sub-zone of the Costa d'Amalfi DOC. Their cellar is small but technologically up-to-the-minute, and it is used by Andrea with the wisdom of those born on the land. As he is thoroughly convinced that the quality of a wine depends upon the quality of the grapes from which it is made, he is very careful to select only the very best at harvest time from vines that cling to terraces between 300 and 500 meters above the sea. This year's tasting, as usual, confirms the attractiveness of these wines. The whites, the Furore Bianco '97 and the Ravello Bianco '97 are very pleasant to drink. To the nose they are somewhat complex, elegant and flowery. In the mouth they are soft, but balanced by their acidity, more decisively so in the case of the Ravello which also has greater complexity. At our tastings we found the Furore Rosso '97, from piedirosso and aglianico grapes, quite impressive in its character and balance. But the real surprises were the Ravello and Furore '95 Riservas, which both clearly earned their Two Glasses: they are harmonious, clean, judiciously woody, well-balanced, and softly delicious.

	Wine	Glasses	Price
●	Costa d'Amalfi Furore Rosso Ris. '95	▼▼	4
●	Costa d'Amalfi Ravello Rosso Ris. '95	▼▼	4
○	Costa d'Amalfi Furore Bianco '97	▼	3
●	Costa d'Amalfi Furore Rosso '97	▼	3
○	Costa d'Amalfi Ravello Bianco '97	▼	3
○	Costa d'Amalfi Furore Bianco '95	▽▽	3*
○	Costa d'Amalfi Furore Bianco '96	▽	3
●	Costa d'Amalfi Furore Rosso '95	▽	3
●	Costa d'Amalfi Furore Rosso '96	▽	3
○	Costa d'Amalfi Ravello Bianco '96	▽	3

GROTTOLELLA (AV)

MARIANNA
VIA FILANDE, 6
83030 GROTTOLELLA (AV)
TEL. 0825/627252

This producer, who first appeared in the Guide last year, has again offered correctly made and well-balanced wines which bear witness to his intelligent quest for a personal style in wine-making. His two standard-bearers, the Fiano di Avellino '97 and the Greco di Tufo '97, are particularly worthy of searching out. The first of these, of a brilliant straw color, has pleasing and delicate scents of flowers and almonds and reasonable length on the palate. The Greco di Tufo '97 has aromas of yeasts and tropical fruits with hints of minerals mixed in, while in the mouth it is fairly harmonious even if a little too acidulous, a fault that will in all likelihood pass off with some more time in the bottle. The Irpinia Bianco '97, from coda di volpe, fiano, and greco grapes, and the Irpinia Rosso '97, from aglianico, piedirosso and sciascinoso, are simple, correct, well-structured and easy to drink. The entire range of his wines proves the worth of the labors passionately and competently performed by Ciriaco Coscia, the owner of the estate, and convinces us that, in the not too distant future, Marianna will come yet closer to realizing its potential.

	Wine	Glasses	Price
○	Fiano di Avellino '97	🍷	4
○	Greco di Tufo '97	🍷	3
○	Irpinia Bianco '97		3
●	Irpinia Rosso Plinio il Giovane '97		3
○	Fiano di Avellino '96	YY	4
○	Greco di Tufo '96	Y	3
●	Irpinia Rosso Plinio il Giovane '95	Y	3

GUARDIA SANFRAMONDI (BN)

DE LUCIA
C.DA STARZE
82034 GUARDIA SANFRAMONDI (BN)
TEL. 0824/817705

In previous editions of the Guide we have stated that this young winery run by the congenial De Lucia cousins, Enrico, Cosimo and, once again, Enrico was destined for success because of both the good judgment of the owners and their obvious desire to make excellent wines. So it is a source of pleasure for us to present three of their '97 wines which have fully merited Two Glasses. The three wines are all from the new Campania DOC, Sannio. The Sannio Aglianico '97 offers hints of berries, currants and spice to the nose, while in the mouth it is full, complex and rich in soft tannins. The Falanghina '97 is pleasingly fruity, clean and distinctly reminiscent of both sweet and tart apples. It is blessed with good structure and a long aromatic finish. The Sannio Greco '97 has excellent balance with pleasingly intense perfumes of white flowers, green apples and apricots. It is fat and long-lasting in the mouth. In fact it's a wine that gives much pleasure, and also fully expresses the style of this new Sannio estate with its clean, agreeable and very reasonably priced wines. Their line is completed by the Sannio Coda di Volpe '97, the Solopaca Bianco '97 and the Solopaca Rosso Vassallo '97: clean, well-made wines to remake the reputation of this historic Campania denomination too often dragged in the mud by overly "commercial" wine-making decisions. And in closing, we'll mention their Ginestraio '97, made from different types of local grapes, which, although simple, is a correct, and definitely interesting wine.

	Wine	Glasses	Price
●	Sannio Aglianico '97	🍷🍷	3
○	Sannio Falanghina '97	🍷🍷	3
○	Sannio Greco '97	🍷🍷	3
○	Ginestraio '97	🍷	3
●	Solopaca Rosso Vassallo '97	🍷	2
○	Sannio Coda di Volpe '97		3
○	Solopaca Bianco '97		2
●	Aglianico del Sannio Beneventano '96	Y	3
○	Greco del Sannio Beneventano '96	Y	3
○	Solopaca Bianco '96	Y	2*
○	Solopaca Falanghina '96	Y	3
●	Solopaca Rosso '95	Y	2*
●	Solopaca Rosso '96	Y	2*

LAPIO (AV)

Colli di Lapio
Fraz. Arianiello
83030 Lapio (AV)
tel. 0825/982191 - 982184

The land around Lapio has a natural affinity for the fiano grape, out of which this craftsmanlike producer has again made a very good wine. The '97 Fiano di Avellino has a pale straw color with green tints when the light catches it, and a pleasingly balanced and evident varietal character with a typical note of honey. Although it is not quite up to last year's version it is definitely an agreeable wine and we are prepared to wager that it will get a lot better in the bottle. On the other hand, we are well aware that to hold wines back for aging before putting them on the market is a ticklish business for a small producer. Nor is it an easy matter to wait for wines to reach their optimum development when there is such a big market for white wines that are fresh and young. We should add that this is a wine that really benefits from a moderately long period of aging. Indeed when we tasted the earlier vintages again, we found them softer and better balanced. At the moment, however, the Romanos, proprietors of Colli di Lapio, are virtually obliged to continue with their current marketing policy and must just hope that their wine will find its way to a patient wine merchant or a wise restaurateur.

	Wine	Rating	Price
○	Fiano di Avellino '97	🍷🍷	4
○	Fiano di Avellino '95	🍸🍸	4
○	Fiano di Avellino '96	🍸🍸	4

MANOCALZATI (AV)

Vega - D'Antiche Terre
C.da Lo Piano
S. S. 7 bis
83030 Manocalzati (AV)
tel. 0825/675358

The Vega estate has become an important landmark on the Irpinia wine map, constantly doing more and getting better. Our tastings revealed a quite acceptable general level, as well as a new-comer, the Taurasi '94, made from grapes culled some 500 meters above sea level. It has a concentrated ruby color, aromas of cherries with a light vegetal tone and, in the mouth, freshness, lovely fruit, fine and well-integrated tannins and a fairly long finish. The other wines on their list are all reliable, starting with the Coriliano '96, an Irpinia Rosso made from aglianico, piedirosso and sciascinoso grapes briefly matured in the barrel, which calms the adolescent exuberance of their tannins. It has a brilliant ruby color and berry-like aromas, which are repeated on the palate and into the finish. The Fiano di Avellino '97 and the Eliseo di Serra '97, while not unpleasing, are not up to last year's level. The former has a faint straw color and delicate aromas of Golden Delicious apple and chamomile, while in the mouth it is soft and suggestive of fresh almonds. The latter, made from fiano and coda di volpe grapes, has a vegetal nose with hints of citrus fruit, and some finesse and persistence in the mouth.

	Wine	Rating	Price
●	Irpinia Rosso Coriliano '96	🍷	2
●	Taurasi '94	🍷	4
○	Eliseo di Serra '97		3
○	Fiano di Avellino '97		4
○	Fiano di Avellino '96	🍸🍸	4
●	Coriliano '96	🍸	2
○	Eliseo di Serra '95	🍸	3
○	Eliseo di Serra '96	🍸	3
○	Fiano di Avellino '95	🍸	4
○	Greco di Tufo '95	🍸	3
○	Greco di Tufo '96	🍸	3

MONTEFREDANE (AV)

Vadiaperti

Fraz. Arcella
C.da Vadiaperti
83030 Montefredane (AV)
tel. 0825/36263 - 607270

Campania's wine community has lost one of its leading members. Antonio Troisi, winegrower in Montefredane, was the heart and soul of the Vadiaperti estate. His friends held him in high esteem, especially for the passion and courage of which he was emblematic, and will not forget him. Professor Troisi was a man of great dignity who had an unusually vivid, and in the end contagious, sense of belonging to the land he came from. He was a pioneer in Irpinia in the '80s with his Fiano di Avellino, whose capacity for improvement with several years of bottle aging he had foreseen. The wines have all kept a clearly expressed personality, beginning with the two special selections from '96, the Greco di Tufo Federico II, and the Fiano di Avellino Arechi. They both have an intense and well-developed aromatic structure and a warm, full-bodied and seductive palate, while each expresses the characteristics of its grape. The Fiano di Avellino is interesting too. It has a clearly defined fragrance and is well-balanced and pleasingly easy to drink. The Greco di Tufo and the Coda di Volpe, both reliable and properly made wines, complete their list. To Raffaele, who for some years had been devotedly assisting his father at Vadiaperti, we offer our best wishes and the hope that he may have the strength to follow in Antonio's footsteps.

○	Fiano di Avellino '97	▼	4
○	Fiano di Avellino Arechi '96	▼	4
○	Greco di Tufo Federico II '96	▼	4
○	Coda di Volpe '97		2
○	Greco di Tufo '97		3
○	Coda di Volpe '96	▽▽	3*
○	Fiano di Avellino '93	▽▽	4
○	Fiano di Avellino '94	▽▽	4
○	Fiano di Avellino '95	▽▽	4
○	Fiano di Avellino '96	▽▽	4
○	Greco di Tufo Vigna del Principato '94	▽▽	4
○	Greco di Tufo '96	▽	3
○	Greco di Tufo Federico II '95	▽	4

MONTEFUSCO (AV)

Terre Dora di Paolo

Via Serra
83030 Montefusco (AV)
tel. 0825/968215 - 963022

Terre Dora di Paolo is the new name of the estate that belongs to Walter Mastroberardino and his children. They have 120 hectares of vines planted to produce a restricted yield, their cellar is all that high technology can offer and, besides their notable experience in marketing, they are devoted to their land and have an ardent desire to produce the best possible wine on it. Their Taurasi Fatica Contadina '94 received very high marks, but their whole line has done extremely well. Only the Rosaenovae '97 and the Irpinia Rosso '97 seemed hardly above average. (But don't be confused: the Irpinia Rosso Il Principio '96 is a lovely wine.) The Taurasi has a harmoniously complex bouquet of ripe red fruit, indicating its stay in new barrels, with vegetal hints and laurel. In the mouth it is long-lasting and full, with soft tannins and distinct suggestions of leather, tobacco and licorice. Their Fiano di Avellino wines are both likeable, with the nod going to the Terre di Dora '97, with its flowery finesse, and its length and rich intensity. All three versions of Greco di Tufo: the Terra degli Angeli, the Loggia della Serra and their standard version, are elegantly structured and extremely well made. The Terra degli Angeli '97 seemed perhaps most strikingly complex and harmonious, but all three are excellent. The Falanghina d'Irpinia '97 is notably varietal, rich in aromatic evocations of Mediterranean underbrush, and possessed of finesse and moderate persistence.

○	Fiano di Avellino '97	▼▼	4
○	Fiano di Avellino Terre di Dora '97	▼▼	4
○	Greco di Tufo '97	▼▼	3
○	Greco di Tufo Loggia della Serra '97	▼▼	3
○	Greco di Tufo Terra degli Angeli '97	▼▼	3
○	Irpinia Bianco Falanghina '97	▼▼	3
●	Irpinia Rosso Il Principio '96	▼▼	4
●	Taurasi Fatica Contadina '94	▼▼	5
⊙	Irpinia Rosato Rosaenovae '97	▼	3
●	Irpinia Rosso Aglianico '97	▼	3

MONTEMARANO (AV)

SALVATORE MOLLETTIERI
VIA MUSANNI, 19/B
83040 MONTEMARANO (AV)
TEL. 0827/63424

At Montemarano, in the heart of Taurasi territory, Campania's only DOCG wine, a new interpreter of the venerable wine-making tradition of this part of the south has begun to attract attention. Salvatore is the present owner of the Mollettieri vineyards which his family has worked for many generations, and he is determined to make the best wine he can there. He uses only grapes grown, for low yield, on his own seven hectares, and this year, his first in the Guide, his wines have made a very favorable impression. His interesting Taurasi Vigna Cinque Querce '94 reveals berries, licorice and light vegetal touches on the nose. On the palate red currants emerge with warm structure and dense, well-balanced tannins, followed by a long, full and opulent finish. The Irpinia Cinque Querce '96 is also pleasing, with its fruity aromas featuring plums and its full-bodied, fat, softly tannic, crisp palate that offers agreeable notes of spice. His white, the Irpinia Bianco Cinque Querce '97, principally from coda di volpe, has a characteristically intense straw-yellow color, an interesting, freshly varietal, harmonious bouquet, and a clean and well-developed palate. Salvatore has made an excellent debut, which promises great things to come.

●	Cinque Querce '96	🍷🍷	3
●	Taurasi Vigna Cinque Querce '94	🍷🍷	4
○	Cinque Querce '97	🍷	3

PONTE (BN)

OCONE
VIA DEL MONTE, 56
82030 PONTE (BN)
TEL. 0824/874040 - 874328

Domenico Ocone is one of the most energetic and able wine-makers in Campania. He was also among the first to understand, back in the '80s, that people were getting interested in better wine. His beautiful vines, nearly 5,000 per hectare, surround his modern and well-appointed winery in Madonnella. At our tastings his reds were much more popular than his whites, a sign that something could, indeed should, be done to improve the latter. The most interesting of the newcomers is his Alglianico del Taburno Diomede '96, a wine which has spent about six months in barrique. To the nose it reveals intense notes of berries with vegetal nuances and vanilla. It is full-bodied and structured in the mouth, with abundant sweet tannins. The Aglianico del Taburno '95 and the Piedirosso '97 are both good. The first is quite delicate, offering berries in a fresh and well-balanced body with agreeable tannins, and the second is fuller and more substantial and also pleasing to the palate. The whites, including the Falanghina, seem correctly made, but are not altogether convincing.

●	Aglianico del Taburno Diomede '96	🍷🍷	4
●	Aglianico del Taburno '95	🍷	4
●	Piedirosso del Taburno '97	🍷	3
○	Falanghina del Taburno '97		3
●	Aglianico del Sannio Vigna Pezza la Corte '91	🍷🍷 (prev.)	4
●	Aglianico del Sannio Vigna Pezza la Corte '93	🍷🍷 (prev.)	4
●	Aglianico Taburno '94	🍷🍷 (prev.)	4
○	Falanghina del Taburno '96	🍷 (prev.)	3
○	Greco del Taburno '96	🍷 (prev.)	3

PRIGNANO CILENTO (SA)

ALESSANDRO DE CONCILIIS E FIGLI
LOC. QUERCE, 1
84060 PRIGNANO CILENTO (SA)
TEL. 0974/831090

Another new addition to the Campania section of the Guide: Bruno De Conciliis, son of the owner of the estate, together with his sister Paola and his brother Luigi, has in a very few years succeeded in producing wines of remarkable quality. Expert oenological advice, intelligent use of cellar technology and careful grape selection have once again proven themselves the stepping stones to success. The Temparubra '97, aglianico with 40% sangiovese, has a lovely dense red hue. Its aromas of red berries, sour cherries and spice are exactly reflected on the palate. And its price is decidedly modest. The white Tempadoro '97, made from equal parts of trebbiano, coda di volpe and malvasia with 10% of fiano, offers vegetal and fruity perfumes, sweet and vanilla-laden, while a comforting softness greets the palate. A particular fiano grape from Cilento called Santa Sofia is what goes into their Vigna Perella '97, which has a delicate and pleasing fragrance of acacia honey and rennet apples, with a fairly substantial and intriguing palate and a long finish. The Donna Luna '97 is the only wine produced by this admirable estate that sports a DOC label. This Cilento white reveals an interesting nose, a subtle and harmonious blend of fruit and white flowers, while on the palate it is fat, substantial and long-lasting: a clean and agreeable wine.

●	Temparubra '97	🍷🍷	2*
○	Donna Luna '97	🍷	3
○	Tempadoro '97	🍷	2
○	Vigna Perella '97	🍷	3

QUARTO (NA)

CANTINE GROTTA DEL SOLE
VIA SPINELLI, 2
80010 QUARTO (NA)
TEL. 081/8762566

The winery Cantine Grotta del Sole has once again earned a place in the Guide with its wide range of simple, clean and agreeable wines covering many of the DOC categories of Campania. Their state-of-the-art cellar is in the Flegrean Fields, one of the most evocative parts of the province around Naples. The wines that the Martusciello family started by producing, in what was virtually an effort of oenological archeology, were wines that typified this area: Piedirosso, of which they also produce a Passito version (from almost dried grapes), and Falanghina. The vines are among the very few not grafted to American root stock. This zone, in fact, thanks to the volcanic origin of its soil, was unaffected by the plague of phylloxera that ravaged the vineyards of Europe last century. Gennaro Martusciello, family oenologist, has also succeeded in adding promising versions of two typical wines of the Sorrento Peninsula: Lettere and Gragnano. The estate's richly varied offerings end with two Irpinia wines, Greco di Tufo and Fiano di Avellino. The Greco di Tufo '97 in particular is nicely structured and characteristic of its grape, and has a nose redolent of exotic fruit and rennet apples, shot through with delicate floral tones. On the palate it reveals personality and fine balance, fully justifying the Glass we awarded it.

●	Campi Flegrei Piedirosso '97	🍷	3
○	Greco di Tufo '97	🍷	3
●	Lacryma Christi Rosso '97	🍷	3
○	Campi Flegrei Falanghina '97		3
●	Campi Flegrei Piedirosso Passito '94		5
○	Fiano di Avellino '97		4
●	Gragnano '97		3
●	Lettere '97		3
○	Asprinio d'Aversa '96	🍸	3
○	Asprinio d'Aversa Brut	🍸	3
○	Campi Flegrei Falanghina '96	🍸	3
○	Grotta del Sole Extra Brut '91	🍸	4

RAVELLO (SA)

ETTORE SAMMARCO
VIA CIVITA, 9
84010 RAVELLO (SA)
TEL. 089/872774

This winery, which is very well-known on the Amalfi coast and sells bottles throughout Italy and abroad, is making its debut in the Guide this year. The cellar, dug out of a cliff overlooking the Mediterranean, produces about 25 thousand bottles of DOC wine, Costa d'Amalfi Ravello. The winery is perhaps better known for the 700 thousand bottles of much less exalted 'table wine' it turns out annually. But the owner, Ettore Sammarco, is proud of his two Costa d'Amalfi wines, one white and one red. The Bianco '97 is made from falanghina and biancolella grapes, locally known as bianca zita and bianca tenera. It's a wine with pleasing fruity and floral aromas, and on the palate it shows good structure, balance and a finish of medium length. The Costa d'Amalfi Ravello Rosso '96, a blend of per' 'e palummo and aglianico aged in oak barrels, has a nose of almost ripe red berries, with a spicy and grassy note that blends in fairly harmoniously.

○	Costa d'Amalfi Ravello Bianco '97	🍷	3
●	Costa d'Amalfi Ravello Rosso '96	🍷	3

S. AGATA DEI GOTI (BN)

MUSTILLI
VIA DEI FIORI, 20
82019 S. AGATA DEI GOTI (BN)
TEL. 0823/717433

With the '97 vintage the wines of this important Campania wine producer are getting better again after a few worrying years in which they were not themselves. The Falanghina Sant'Agata dei Goti '97 is pleasantly full-bodied and, after offering grassy and bitter almond notes to the nose, is fruity and of moderate length in the mouth. Their Sant'Agata dei Goti Greco '97 is a quite interesting wine and very nearly received Two Glasses. The aromas are pleasant and clean, with an intense fruitiness and hints of white blossoms and vanilla. In the mouth it is full, soft and balanced, with a touch of almonds at the end. The Greco Primicerio '97 has a sweet, clean, vegetal nose with lovely hints of white flowers and crusty bread. In the mouth it is long, full and harmonious. The Mustilli reds are mostly made from aglianico and piedirosso. From a combination of these two comes their Conte Artus. It has a ruby color and a rich bouquet of berries and is well-balanced and pleasant enough, but it's worthy of mention only.

○	S. Agata dei Goti Greco di Primicerio '97	🍷🍷	4
○	S. Agata dei Goti Falanghina '97	🍷	3
○	S. Agata dei Goti Greco '97	🍷	3
●	S. Agata dei Goti Rosso Conte Artus '94		3
●	Vigna Cesco di Nece '91	🍷🍷 (previous edition)	3
○	Greco di S. Agata dei Goti '95	🍷 (previous edition)	2
○	Greco di S. Agata dei Goti Vigna Fontanella '95	🍷 (previous edition)	3
○	S. Agata dei Goti Greco di Primicerio '96	🍷 (previous edition)	4
●	S. Agata dei Goti Piedirosso '95	🍷 (previous edition)	3
●	S. Agata dei Goti Rosso Conte Artus '95	🍷 (previous edition)	4

S. CIPRIANO PICENTINO (SA)

MONTEVETRANO
VIA MONTEVETRANO
84099 S. CIPRIANO PICENTINO (SA)
TEL. 089/882285

In a country with Italy's ancient wine-making tradition, a really peerless wine tends to come into being in one of two ways: either it bears the illustrious name of some eminent wine-making family that has been engaged in this endeavor for scores of years if not centuries, or else it is the child of the intuitive intelligence of a lone visionary. Such is the case with Silvia Imparato and her Montevetrano. Created virtually out of nothing, wine-historically speaking, in the countryside near San Cipriano Picentino, this wine has, in its very few years of existence, risen to the top ranks of the great wines of the world with a lightning ascent that is the envy of many. The first vintages, '91, '92 and '93, after rave reviews on both sides of the Atlantic, have become the object of frenzied pursuit on the part of collectors and have climbed to prices worthy of a Bordeaux Premier Cru. You have a better chance of finding the more recent vintages, but single-minded dedication and sangfroid may be necessary for bagging them. The '96, a blend, as always, of cabernet sauvignon, merlot and aglianico, does not disappoint. In fact, it has an even more distinct personal style, thanks, of course, to Silvia's steadfast determination, but also to the extraordinary ability of the oenologist Riccardo Cotarella, whose praises we have been singing for some time. Its color is a deep, noble ruby, and in its bouquet one can distinguish blackberry and red currant jam, enhanced by a judiciously balanced note of oak. In the mouth the harmony of all its parts is perhaps its master-stroke: not a single one of its components, from alcohol to tannins, from acidity to the spicy tones lent it by the barrique, dominates the others. There is no question about whether it has earned its Three Glasses.

	Wine	Glasses	Price
●	Montevetrano '96	🍷🍷🍷	5
●	Montevetrano '95	🍷🍷🍷 (white)	5
●	Montevetrano '93	🍷🍷🍷 (white)	5
●	Montevetrano '94	🍷🍷 (white)	5

S. MARCO DI CASTELLABATE (SA)

LUIGI MAFFINI
LOC. CENITO
84071 S. MARCO
DI CASTELLABATE (SA)
TEL. 0974/966345

We'd like to introduce Luigi Maffini, from the up-and-coming Cilento area, a wine-maker of whom one at first heard little, but who has goals that are anything but modest. He has taken over the care of the vineyards planted by his father, an agronomist like himself, and he has succeeded in producing from them wines of a very high level indeed. We tasted two reds and a white which are all, by his choice, "table wines". The white, Kràtos '97, is made exclusively from the fiano grape. It is well-balanced, rich in ripe fruits, delicate and vegetal on the nose, and it offers lots of body, round full flavor and a long finish in the mouth. This is a wine that fully merits its Two Glasses. The Klèos '97, another Two Glass winner, is a red made from piedirosso and aglianico and matured in steel. It is harmoniously complex and fruity, with fine vegetal notes, on the elegant nose; in the mouth, where a distinct flavor of cherries emerges, it displays good balance, proper acidity and soft tannins. It is, in short, an extremely pleasant and elegant wine. Perhaps the greatest surprise from this small and very promising producer is his Cenito (which is where the winery is). He made so few bottles that it seems almost like a whim, but it gives you some idea of the enormous potential of this estate. The wine has a dense ruby color, and reveals aromas of red fruit, black and red currants and spices with notes of sage. Perhaps it is somewhat less elegant in the mouth, but it certainly has impact, and is pleasingly soft and seductive.

	Wine	Glasses	Price
●	Cenito '97	🍷🍷	5
●	Klèos '97	🍷🍷	2*
○	Kràtos '97	🍷🍷	2*

SESSA AURUNCA (CE)

FONTANA GALARDI
FRAZ. SAN CARLO
VIA PROVINCIALE
81030 SESSA AURUNCA (CE)
TEL. 06/4741190 - 0823/708034

Last year this winery was a revelation, and the good work seems to be continuing. Run by an enthusiastic group of dedicated cousins, Roberto and Maria Luisa Selvaggi, Arturo and Dora Celentano and Francesco Catello, it is firmly committed to making wine of the highest quality, and has reaffirmed this commitment by hiring the distinguished oenologist Riccardo Cotarella. They have, so far, presented three different vintages: '94, '95 and '96, but only a few thousand bottles each time from their three hectares planted in aglianico, piedirosso and merlot. (This number will soon be increased to twelve, however.) We wrote about the excellent '94 last year, and further tastings in the course of this year give us the measure of a wine which is extremely youthful and still far from the structure and complexity which will come in its maturity. The '95, tasted this year, seems an even more fascinating wine, with its intriguing scents of blackberries and ripe plums, tobacco and spice, all elegantly fused with the toastiness of the oak. In the mouth it is warm and full-bodied, showing the elegance and finesse of the great southern reds. It misses getting Three Glasses, perhaps because of "inexperience", only by a hair. The '96 has great power and concentration, but is doesn't begin to have the balance of the '95. Its aromas, particularly, are closed and not altogether well-defined. It is not a clear-cut vintage, but that's all right. The '97 currently aging in barrique shows promise of a power and richness that we are willing to bet on. A lot.

Wine	Glasses	Price
● Terra di Lavoro '95	▼▼	5
● Terra di Lavoro '96	▼	5
● Terra di Lavoro '94	▽▽	5

SORBO SERPICO (AV)

FEUDI DI SAN GREGORIO
LOC. CERZA GROSSA
83050 SORBO SERPICO (AV)
TEL. 0825/986266 - 986230

With the Taurasi '94, Feudi di San Gregorio has advanced to Three Glasses, but in fact their whole range is excellent. The magnificent Taurasi has a complex and harmonious nose, full of red fruit, blackberries and plums, spice, leather and licorice. In the mouth one finds all that was promised by the nose now enhanced in a densely woven, ample, persistent and seductive texture with elegant tannins still in the process of integration. One finds, in other words, all the characteristics of a wine with a long life ahead of it, and certainly one that represents these excellent wine-makers at the height of their powers. Their Serpico '96, made from aglianico, piedirosso and sangiovese, has a complex and harmonious bouquet and an ample, opulent and clean palate with elegant, rich tannins. Next comes the Rubrato '96, a pleasantly elegant Irpinia Rosso made from aglianico, piedirosso and primitivo. It offers a complex aromatic structure in which vanilla, spice, and attractive vegetal tones emerge, while in the mouth it seems soft and broad with well-balanced tannins and a long finish. A newcomer among the whites is the Campanaro '96, made principally from wood-aged fiano, and elegantly balanced and pleasing. Among the others the Greco di Tufo Cutizzi '96 stands out, rich in vegetal aromas and hints of white flowers, with a broad and still very young palate. We also liked the Falanghina '97, suggestive of honey and dried fruits on the nose, and rich and substantial in the mouth.

Wine	Glasses	Price
● Taurasi '94	▼▼▼	5
○ Campanaro '96	▼▼	4
○ Falanghina '97	▼▼	3
○ Greco di Tufo Cutizzi '96	▼▼	4
● Rubrato '96	▼▼	3
● Serpico '96	▼▼	6
○ Fiano di Avellino '96	▽▽	4
○ Fiano di Avellino Pian delle Vigne '96	▽▽	4
○ Fiano di Avellino Pietracalda '96	▽▽	4
○ Greco di Tufo Camigliano '96	▽▽	4
● Serpico '95	▽▽	6
● Taurasi '91	▽▽	5
● Taurasi '92	▽▽	5

TAURASI (AV)

ANTONIO CAGGIANO
C.DA SALA
84030 TAURASI (AV)
TEL. 0827/74043

Last year Antonio Caggiano appeared in the Guide for the first time, and his latest range of powerful wines, elegant and well-structured, easily earns him a place this year. Started almost by chance, this winery has quickly become one of the best new producers in Campania. This time he has presented his eagerly awaited Taurasi Vigna Macchia dei Goti '94, a red with warm oak-derived vanilla tones and pleasing lightly caramelized red fruit on the nose; in the mouth it is concentrated, deep and long-lasting. The Saledomini '96 is even better. At our tastings we were all won over by this "table wine" from aglianico grapes, with its full and complex bouquet of red fruit of a delightful freshness, with notes of vanilla and a well-balanced medley of spice, leather, tobacco, pepper and chocolate. On the palate it is clean, opulent, full and velvety, with elegant tannins and a remarkably long finish. It's an excellent wine, and it gives some idea of the potential of this winery. The Taurì '97, made from aglianico with a little piedirosso and fiano, has intense and attractive aromas of red fruit with hints of sage and laurel. The palate is fat and broad, with good if slightly rough tannins. The Fiagrè '97 is made from fiano with 30% greco barrique-fermented and matured in new wood barrels. The nose is reminiscent of fruit jam, with vegetal and mineral notes in its elegant aromatic structure; the palate is solid, straightforward and clean, and the finish is fairly long.

●	Saledomini '96	🍷🍷	5
●	Taurasi Vigna Macchia dei Goti '94	🍷🍷	5
●	Taurì '96	🍷🍷	3
○	Fiagrè '97	🍷	3
○	Fiagrè '96	🍸🍸	3
●	Taurì '95	🍸🍸	3*
●	Saledomini '95	🍸	5

TORRECUSO (BN)

ORAZIO RILLO
C.DA FONTANAVECCHIA
82030 TORRECUSO (BN)
TEL. 0824/876275

The Rillo estate comprises eight hectares of hilly land near Torrecuso in the province of Benevento. Here, in a craftsman-like fashion, they produce wines of notable quality. The Aglianico Riserva Vigna Cataratte '94 wins Two Glasses, but everything they make is good. The Vigna Cataratte, pure aglianico, has eight months in barrique and another eight in bottle. Very alcoholic and richly concentrated in extracts, it is an imposing wine. The nose is pleasingly reminiscent of red fruit, especially red currants and sour cherries, while in the mouth the tannins display a certain finesse and elegance, and the finish is long and intense. The Aglianico del Taburno '95 offers subtle red fruit aromas, complex and harmonious, and fine tannins contribute to full body on the palate. The pleasing Aglianico del Taburno Rosato '97, a rosé of a brilliant cherry color, displays a bouquet as well as flavors of ripe peaches and sour cherries. The straw-yellow Falanghina '97 is worthy of mention. It smells lingeringly of apple, and is warm and full on the palate.

●	Aglianico Vigna Cataratte Ris. '94	🍷🍷	5
●	Aglianico del Taburno '95	🍷	3
⊙	Aglianico del Taburno Rosato '97	🍷	2
○	Falanghina '97		3

VENTICANO (AV)

GIOVANNI STRUZZIERO
VIA L. CADORNA, 214/216
83030 VENTICANO (AV)
TEL. 0825/965065

This well-established Irpine wine cellar, which dates back to 1928, is run with artisanal passion by Giovanni Struzziero and his son, Mario. Their Fiano di Avellino '97, which received Two Glasses, has a lovely straw color, a nose rich in fruits and flowers and of good finesse, and in the mouth is clean, balanced and of decent length. The Greco di Tufo '97 has been made in various versions. The best one, it seems to us, is the Villa Giulia '97, which hints at asparagus, and reveals tropical fruits balanced by a sufficient level of acidity. The "normal" Greco di Tufo is quite similar to the nose, but has less harmony and finesse in the mouth. Their Vigna delle Brecce, on the other hand, is a little disappointing. It seems a bit weak and not altogether attractive. The Falanghina '97 has good finesse and pleasant hints of ripe fruit, and in the mouth has good balance and a nice tang. We had hoped for more from the Taurasi Campoceraso '93, which got a high grade last year. It does offer berries and cherries in a certain abundance to the nose, but in the mouth, though it has some persistence, it seems quite ordinary. The Riserva '90 is more interesting. Garnet colored, a nose of spices and tobacco, it offers in the mouth the warm body and notes of minerals to be found in the wines of the older tradition.

	Wine	Glasses	Price
○	Fiano di Avellino '97	🍷🍷	4
○	Falanghina '97	🍷	3
○	Greco di Tufo '97	🍷	3
○	Greco di Tufo Villa Giulia '97	🍷	3
●	Taurasi Campoceraso '93	🍷	4
●	Taurasi Ris. '90	🍷	5
○	Greco di Tufo Villa Giulia '96	YY	3
●	Taurasi Campoceraso '92	YY	4
○	Fiano di Avellino '96	Y	4

VITULAZIO (CE)

VILLA SAN MICHELE
VIA APPIA KM. 198
81050 VITULAZIO (CE)
TEL. 0823/963775 - 081/666773

Villa San Michele, which is making its second appearance in the Guide, is impeccably run by Giulio Iannini, who is getting to be a significant figure in the wine world of Campania. His wines are all Indicazione Geografica Tipica (Igt) Terre del Volturno. The Greco '97 has a lovely intense varietal nose, and is pleasantly full and spicy in the mouth. The Falanghina '97 has characteristic scents of flowers and fruit, including notes of grapefruit, while it is fairly balanced and dry on the palate, with a typically acidulous finish. Among the reds, we particularly liked the Aglianico '96 for its intense aromas of red fruit, reminiscent of plum jam, with hints of leather and vanilla. In the mouth it is well-balanced and has a moderately long finish. This winery has long produced "metodo classico" sparkling wines and this year again they seem well-made and reliable. The Don Carlos Brut, made from pinot bianco, chardonnay and greco (25%), and revealing attractive and typical hints of toasted bread, came close to winning Two Glasses. The perlage is fine and persistent and the taste is very pleasant and long-lasting. The Demi-Sec version is good too.

	Wine	Glasses	Price
○	Don Carlos Brut	🍷	4
○	Don Carlos Démi-Sec	🍷	4
●	Aglianico '96	🍷	2
○	Falanghina '97	🍷	2
○	Greco '97	🍷	2
○	Don Carlos Brut	Y	4
○	Don Carlos Démi-Sec	Y	4
○	Falanghina '96	Y	2*
●	Piedirosso '96		2

OTHER WINERIES

The following producers obtained good scores in our tastings with one or more of their wines:

PROVINCE OF AVELLINO

Bonaventura
Aiello del Sabato, tel. 0825/666020,
Fiano di Avellino '97

Nicola Romano
Lapio, tel. 0825/982189,
Fiano di Avellino '97

Montesole - Colli Irpini
Montemileto, tel. 0825/963972,
Fiano di Avellino '97,
Greco di Tufo '97,
Irpinia Bianco Fiano '97,
Irpinia Rosso Aglianico '96

Giulia
Prata di Principato Ultra,
tel. 0825/961219,
Fiano di Avellino '97,
Greco di Tufo '97,
Irpinia Rosso '97

Casa dell'Orco
Pratola Serra,
tel. 0825/967038,
Fiano di Avellino '97,
Greco di Tufo '97

Di Meo
Salza Irpinia, tel. 0825/981419,
Taurasi '94

Guido Marsella
Summonte,
tel. 0825/691446,
Fiano di Avellino '96

Di Marzo
Tufo, tel. 0825/998022,
Greco di Tufo '97,
Irpinia Rosso '96

PROVINCE OF BENEVENTO

Antica Masseria Venditti
Castelvenere,
tel. 0824/940306,
Sannio Barbera Vandari '97,
Sannio Falanghina Vandari '97,
Sannio Rosso '97,
Solopaca Bianco Vigna Bacalàt '97

Fattoria Ciabrelli
Castelvenere,
tel. 0824/940565,
Benevento Bianco Falanghina '97,
Benevento Rosso '97,
Solopaca Bianco Vigna Castelvenere '97,
Solopaca Rosso Vigna Castelvenere '97

Fattoria Torre Gaia
Dugenta,
tel. 0824/978172,
Asprinio di Aversa '97,
Sannio Aglianico Beneventano '96,
Sannio Falanghina '97

Cantina del Taburno
Foglianise,
tel. 0824/871338,
Taburno Falanghina '97,
Taburno Greco '97,
Taburno Rosso '95

Cantina Soc. di Solopaca
Solopaca, tel. 0824/977921,
Falanghina Beneventano '97,
Solopaca Bianco '97,
Solopaca Falanghina '97,
Solopaca Rosso Sup. '94

PROVINCE OF CASERTA

I Borboni
Lusciano, tel. 081/8141386,
Asprinio d'Aversa '97,
Asprinio d'Aversa Brut

Cantine Caputo
Teverola, tel. 081/5033955,
Lacryma Christi del Vesuvio Bianco '97,
Lacryma Christi del Vesuvio Rosso '96,
Sannio Aglianico Beneventano '96

PROVINCE OF NAPOLI

Sorrentino
Boscotrecase,
tel. 081/8584194,
Lacryma Christi del Vesuvio Bianco '97,
Lacryma Christi del Vesuvio Rosato '97,
Lacryma Christi del Vesuvio Rosso '97,
Passito Fior di Ginestra '97

La Caprense
Capri, tel. 081/8376835,
Capri Bianco Bordo '97,
Capri Bianco Punta Vivara '97,
Capri Rosso Solaro '97

De Falco
S. Sebastiano al Vesuvio, tel. 081/5745510,
Greco di Tufo '97,
Lacryma Christi del Vesuvio Rosso '97,
Penisola Sorrentina Gragnano '97,
Sannio Aglianico Beneventano '95

De Angelis
Sorrento, tel. 081/8781648,
Lacryma Christi del Vesuvio Bianco '97,
Lacryma Christi del Vesuvio Rosso '96,
Penisola Sorrentina Gragnano '97

PROVINCE OF SALERNO

Episcopio
Ravello, tel. 089/857244,
Costa d'Amalfi Ravello Bianco '97

Ianniello-Scorziello
Roccadaspide,
tel. 089/756037,
Castel San Lorenzo Barbera Bios '97

Francesco Rotolo
Rutino,
tel. 0974/830050,
Cilento Aglianico '96,
Cilento Bianco '97

Giuseppe Apicella
Tramonti,
tel. 089/876075,
Costa d'Amalfi
Tramonti Bianco S. Maria '97,
Costa d'Amalfi Tramonti Rosato '97,
Costa d'Amalfi Tramonti Rosso '96

BASILICATA

Given its climate and geographical characteristics, Basilicata is one of southern Italy's greatest potential wine-growing regions. It has the capacity to achieve much, but although there are some positive signs of change, local wine-making is still closely bound to tradition and the aglianico grape. The quality-led approach to production is attracting newcomers among both privately owned estates and cooperative wineries. The Rionero, Barile and Venosa wineries are praiseworthy examples of the part played by the cooperatives, and alone are responsible for two-thirds of the total output of Aglianico on the market. A welcome novelty in the extremely limited group of independent producers is Pisani, an entirely organically-farmed estate in the Val d'Agri which this year has its own profile in the Guide. With 20 hectares under vine, this recently established winery produces many non-regional varietals, and although this does not automatically guarantee first-class wines, it does at least represent an innovative attitude in an area generally unresponsive to new ideas. Among the older established wineries, producers such as D'Angelo, Paternoster, Martino and Sasso can be relied on for a steady focus on quality in the range they offer. Sasso has undertaken a complete reorganization and has therefore decided to halt production for a year. Among the most exciting wines we tasted for the '99 edition of the Guide, we particularly praise D'Angelo's Vigna dei Pini, a white with a fine aromatic structure which earned particularly high marks. Two Aglianico del Vulture wines, Paternoster's Don Anselmo and the Carpe Diem from the Consorzio Vitcoltori Associati, likewise stood out for their excellent performance. These indications of a move in the right direction are encouraging, but it is too soon to speak of a general trend. There is a lack of concerted effort on the part of the producers and they have yet to prove that they can express to the full the intrinsic value of this region.

BARILE (PZ)

Consorzio Viticoltori Associati del Vulture

S. S. 93
85022 Barile (PZ)
tel. 0972/770386

This consortium is a major group incorporating five separate cooperative wineries, with a vast area of land covered by its member growers. Established at the end of the 1970s, it is equipped to handle 80 thousand hectoliters of wine, of which five thousand are destined for varying periods of maturation in oak. With such a potential it is not surprising that this year yet again some excellent results have been achieved. The deep ruby red Aglianico del Vulture '96 offers attractive vegetal, balsamic aromas mingling with typical ripe red fruits on the nose, enriched by nuances of leather, tobacco and pencil lead. The palate is broad, rich and structured, with a good long finish. The equally satisfying Aglianico del Vulture Carpe Diem is a red whose name refers to the two thousandth anniversary, a few years ago, of the death of the poet Horace. Deep in color, it has fruity notes of plum and raisins with very ripe overtones, followed by a warm, alcohol-rich palate with good body and tannins as yet unassimilated. Two traditional sparkling wines deserve a mention, the Ellenico and the Moscato. The first, a sparkling aglianico, has typical slightly sweet notes and is lively, fruity and fresh ready drinking. The bubbly Moscato has intense, varietal aromas and a medium-sweet, aromatic palate with adequate length.

	Wine	Rating	Price
●	Aglianico del Vulture '96	ΨΨ (black)	2*
●	Aglianico del Vulture Carpe Diem '95	ΨΨ (black)	3
●	Aglianico Spumante Ellenico		2
○	Moscato Spumante		2
●	Aglianico del Vulture Carpe Diem '93	ΨΨ	3*
●	Aglianico del Vulture '94	Ψ	2*

BARILE (PZ)

Paternoster

Via Nazionale, 23
85022 Barile (PZ)
tel. 0972/770224 - 770658

Thanks to meticulously cared-for vineyards, lying at an altitude of 450 to 600 meters, and the technical expertise of the Paternoster brothers Vito, Sergio and Anselmo, it is no surprise that this estate is one of the leaders of the small group of wineries dedicated to the pursuit of quality in this magnificent but somewhat neglected wine-making area of the south. The flag-bearer wine this year is the Aglianico del Vulture Don Anselmo, a wine made only in the best vintages. The '93 version is a wonderful deep ruby in color, with inviting aromas of berries mingling with balsamic, spicy notes, leading into a soft, structured palate with elegant tannins. The normal Aglianico is also a highly reliable wine. The '95 vintage displays distinct, refined varietal character, with its fruity aromas of red currant and plum and rich concentration of flavor. The impact on the palate is good and it has exceptional overall harmony. The Barigliott, a typical, lightly sparkling red, is freshly flavored, while the Antico, a bubbly wine from aglianico grapes, is traditionally medium-sweet. The Bianco della Corte, a lightly oaked monovarietal white from fiano grapes, is correctly made but shows room for improvement. Finally, the Clivius, a pleasant sparkling Moscato, deserves a mention.

	Wine	Rating	Price
●	Aglianico del Vulture '95	ΨΨ (black)	3
●	Aglianico del Vulture Don Anselmo Ris. '93	ΨΨ (black)	5
●	Antico Spumante Aglianico '97		3
○	Bianco della Corte '96		3
○	Moscato Clivius '97		2
●	Aglianico del Vulture '94	ΨΨ	3*
●	Aglianico del Vulture Don Anselmo Ris. '88	ΨΨ	5
●	Aglianico del Vulture Don Anselmo Ris. '90	Ψ	5
●	Aglianico del Vulture Don Anselmo Ris. '92	Ψ	5

 RIONERO IN VULTURE (PZ)

D'Angelo

Via Provinciale, 8
85028 Rionero in Vulture (PZ)
tel. 0972/721517

Established in 1930, the D'Angelo winery has for decades been one of the leading producers in the Vulture district. Although deeply rooted in tradition and never losing their sense of their inheritance from the past, they have unhesitatingly kept up with market trends. The cornerstone of the production line is of course the aglianico grape. The normal Aglianico '95, of a deep, intense ruby color, easily earned Two Glasses, offering elegant aromas of quince, violet and tobacco, followed by a clean, long palate with good concentration. Surprisingly, we found the Aglianico del Vulture Riserva Vigna Caselle '93 less convincing, although a reliable wine. Leather, tobacco and red fruit emerge on the nose, while the palate is balanced and correct but reveals peculiar notes of carob which detract from its appeal. The Canneto '95, the estate's pioneer wine (it is barrique-aged) and the third premium-quality Aglianico label, was released too late for us to taste. However the most startling success was achieved by a white, the Vigna dei Pini, a blend of chardonnay and pinot blanc with 20% of incrocio Manzoni. A density of 5 thousand vines per hectare, very high for this area, combined with low yields, resulted in exceptionally concentrated grapes. The wine has a brilliant yellow color, with ripe fruit aromas of pear, peach and melon mingling with flowery notes, leading into a full, soft palate underpinned by a good acidity. An altogether elegant, well-made white wine.

	Wine	Glasses	Price
●	Aglianico del Vulture '95	▼▼	3
○	Vigna dei Pini '97	▼▼	3*
●	Aglianico del Vulture Vigna Caselle Ris. '93	▼	4
●	Canneto '91	▽▽	5
●	Canneto '93	▽▽	5
●	Canneto '94	▽▽	5
○	Vigna dei Pini '94	▽▽	3
●	Aglianico del Vulture '93	▽	3
●	Aglianico del Vulture '94	▽	3
●	Aglianico del Vulture Vigna Caselle Ris. '90	▽	4
●	Aglianico del Vulture Vigna Caselle Ris. '91	▽	4
○	Vigna dei Pini '95	▽	3

Armando Martino

Via Luigi La Vista, 2/a
85028 Rionero in Vulture (PZ)
tel. 0972/721422

Armando Martino can be considered a staunch upholder of Vulture tradition. Every year he presents a range in the typical style of this area, without paying too much attention to more modern vineyard and wine-making techniques. Whatever the pros and cons of this production policy, the wines we tasted this year performed at more or less their usual standard. The Aglianico del Vulture '96, a wine very much in the traditional style and not without its followers, has clean aromas, good concentration and a well-evolved fruit with notes of cherries in spirit and plums. The simple, correctly made Rosato Donna Lidia, from aglianico and malvasia bianca, is a lively wine with good overall balance, while the Carolin, a monovarietal aglianico, has lots of sparkle and a light flavor. Finally, the Moscato Spumante deserves our mention.

	Wine	Glasses	Price
⊙	Aglianico Rosato Donna Lidia '97	▼	3
●	Aglianico del Vulture '96		3
●	Carolin '97		3
○	Moscato Spumante		2
●	Aglianico del Vulture '93	▽	3
●	Aglianico del Vulture '94	▽	3
●	Aglianico del Vulture '95	▽	3*
●	Carolin '93	▽	2*
●	Carolin '95	▽	2*
●	Aglianico del Vulture '90		2

VENOSA (PZ)

CANTINA RIFORMA FONDIARIA
DI VENOSA
C.DA VIGNALE SAN FELICE
85029 VENOSA (PZ)
TEL. 0972/35891

The Cantina Riforma Fondiaria di Venosa, which last year made its first, highly-merited appearance in the Guide with an excellent Aglianico del Vulture of the '94 vintage, is back again with slightly less exciting but reliable wines. An offshoot of the former Ente di Riforma Fondiaria of Puglia, Lucania and Molise, this cooperative was established in 1957, and with over 500 member growers and a capacity for handling around 60 thousand quintals of grapes, its potential output is considerable. The Aglianico '96 has a good, clear color and faintly overripe aromas of red fruit preserves, plums and sour cherries. The palate is full, round and alcoholic, with a satisfyingly long finish, but the overall structure of the wine is not comparable to the '94 version. It should be added that due to the Guide's publishing deadline we were not in time to taste the estate's flag-bearer, the Aglianico del Vulture Carato, which we will review next year. To end with, the Rosato Boreano is a correctly-made wine worthy of mention.

●	Aglianico del Vulture '96	🍷	3
⊙	Rosato Boreano		2
●	Aglianico del Vulture '94	🍷🍷	3

VIGGIANO (PZ)

PISANI
C.DA SAN LORENZO
85059 VIGGIANO (PZ)
TEL. 0975/352603

This estate is making its debut in the Guide this year. It has an average annual output of around 270 thousand bottles and is for various reasons an exception in Basilicata. The novelty is the fact that the 20 hectares belonging to the estate, which is situated in the Val d'Agri in a hilly area typical of the Apennines, with the highest parts of the property lying at an altitude of 650 meters, are entirely organically farmed. Another unusual factor is the number of varieties grown, including freisa, cortese, ciliegiolo, merlot, cabernet, malvasia and chardonnay. From this highly assorted range some attractive wines are produced. Our favorite was the Basilicata Rosso '97, with fresh, inviting, perhaps not fully evolved vegetal aromas, followed by a clean, enjoyable palate with adequate body and powerful tannins. The Basilicata Bianco of the same vintage is worthy of mention, although a little too light and characterless.

●	Basilicata Rosso '97	🍷	2
○	Basilicata Bianco '97		2

PUGLIA

With an average annual output of around 10 million hectoliters, Puglia ranks as Italy's top wine-producing region from the standpoint of quantity offered on the market. And the quality is improving. The Two Glasses awarded to several Salento rosés and those assigned to wines made from such local grapes as negroamaro, primitivo, montepulciano and uva di Troia highlight the exceptional quality of the '97 vintage in this region. An outstanding year, as witnessed also by the high scores given to some white wines obtained from international varietals. The year was less noteworthy, however, for native white grapes (verdeca, bianco d'Alessano, greco, bombino bianco, pampanuto), with quality varying from one growing area to another. Nevertheless, our tastings confirmed that things are looking up in Puglia. There has been improvement almost everywhere, although the Salentine Peninsula, Castel del Monte and the land of Primitivo are a clear step ahead of the pack. Much of what we describe here is of excellent quality, whether it be from Taurino, Candido, Vallone, Rosa del Golfo, Masseria Monaci, the Cantina Cooperativa di Copertino, Calò or Zecca. As for individual wines, the cream of the crop consisted of Taurino's Patriglione, the Graticciaia produced by the Sorelle Vallone, the Duca D'Aragona made by the Fratelli Candido, and Felline's Primitivo di Manduria. The star of this season is the Salice Salentino Donna Lisa made by Leone de Castris, which is Puglia's Three Glass wine. We hasten to add that this red has achieved this recognition not just for its obvious excellence, but also because, in our opinion, it combines the best elements of tradition with modern and painstaking wine-making technique, a combination we can heartily recommend to various other wineries in the region. Moving from the Salentine zone to the north of the region, we pass through Primitivo di Manduria territory, which this year yielded wines (mainly from the '96 vintage) that are full-bodied, pleasantly fruity and exceptionally warm and velvety. Castel del Monte also achieved good results, particularly in the case of its red Riservas: indeed all three producers won Two Glasses. The other strong point that Puglia should emphasize to attract more serious attention amongst wine lovers is the excellent value for money it offers. This advantage, combined with the potential of its native grapes and its adaptability to international ones, such as chardonnay, sauvignon and cabernet, is gradually convincing many entrepreneurs of Central and Northern Italy to look to Puglia both as a potential investment and as a supplier of excellent wine grapes.

ALEZIO (LE)

ROSA DEL GOLFO
VIA GARIBALDI, 56
73011 ALEZIO (LE)
TEL. 0833/281045

Technology by itself is not sufficient to achieve excellence: you also need passion to make wine. From this standpoint Mino Calò could take on all comers. We said as much some years ago in these pages, and found it confirmed again by last autumn's vintage, when Mino, although ailing (he died in the spring, having just had time to taste the fruit of his last efforts), insisted on following in person every stage of the harvest and vinification of the negroamaro, malvaisa nera, verdeca and chardonnay grapes used to produce his range of wines. Working alongside him was his son, Damiano, still in his twenties, imbibing the spirit, commitment and passion needed to continue his father's work – the production of excellent wines. And the Rosa del Golfo is a real thoroughbred: the '97, blessed with a fragrant bouquet rich in aromas of berries, is well-structured on the palate, which is lingeringly fruity. Even its color is lovely, a brilliant and intense rose with coral highlights. The Bolina, a blend of selected verdeca and chardonnay grapes from the Martina Franca zone, also reveals good structure and fresh, delicate and pleasantly fruity aromas with clear notes of apple and subtle herbal hints; on the palate it is elegant, balanced and pleasingly acidic. The reds, Portulano and Quarantale, are still maturing in the cellar. It will be up to Damiano to offer these in due time to the friends of Mino Calò.

	Wine	Glasses	Price
○	Salento Bianco Bolina '97	🍷🍷 (black)	3
⊙	Salento Rosato Rosa del Golfo '97	🍷🍷 (black)	3
○	Salento Bianco Bolina '95	🍷🍷 (white)	2*
○	Salento Bianco Bolina '96	🍷🍷 (white)	3
⊙	Salento Rosato Rosa del Golfo '95	🍷🍷 (white)	2*
⊙	Salento Rosato Rosa del Golfo '96	🍷🍷 (white)	3
●	Salento Rosso Portulano '93	🍷🍷 (white)	2*
●	Portulano '90	🍷 (white)	4
●	Quarantale '88	🍷 (white)	5
⊙	Salento Rosato Rosa del Golfo '94	🍷 (white)	3

ANDRIA (BA)

RIVERA
C.DA RIVERA
S. S. 98, KM 19.800
70031 ANDRIA (BA)
TEL. 0883/569501 - 569510

A tray full of Two Glass awards this year for one of the historic houses of Puglia, with its Falcone, a Riserva of Castel del Monte, leading the pack. This is a red obtained from selected uva di Troia and montepulciano grapes harvested in the oldest vineyards of the Corato family holdings. The '95 has a ruby color, an intense, fresh bouquet of red fruit, and a warm, round, harmonious and lasting palate. But amongst the great Rivera wines offered for this year's tasting are some made from grapes that have only recently been introduced into Puglia, like chardonnay and aglianico. Indeed two Castel del Montes of the Terre al Monte line easily won Two Glasses, and some others came very close. The two were Preludio n.1, a fragrant, soft chardonnay, which this year was better than ever, and the Aglianico, with proper tannins and concentration. Two Glasses also went to the Moscato di Trani which, starting with this '96, is no longer a fortified dessert wine, but naturally sweet; it boasts a brilliant golden yellow color, a balanced bouquet of lavender and rose and a delightful taste of freshly gathered honey and is one of the finest sweet wines of the region. The classic Castel del Monte wines, though certainly interesting and correct, are not as impressive as the monovarietals. The best is the red Rupicolo '96, a robust wine that is excellent with pastas and meat dishes.

	Wine	Glasses	Price
●	Castel del Monte Aglianico Terre al Monte '96	🍷🍷 (black)	3
○	Castel del Monte Terre al Monte Preludio n. 1 '97	🍷🍷 (black)	3*
●	Castel del Monte Rosso Il Falcone Ris. '95	🍷🍷 (black)	4
○	Moscato di Trani Piani di Tufara '96	🍷🍷 (black)	4
●	Castel del Monte Rosso di Rivera '97	🍷 (black)	2*
●	Castel del Monte Rosso Rupicolo di Rivera '96	🍷 (black)	2*
○	Castel del Monte Sauvignon Terre al Monte '97	🍷 (black)	3

COPERTINO (LE)

CANTINA SOCIALE COPERTINO
VIA MARTIRI DEL RISORGIMENTO, 6
73043 COPERTINO (LE)
TEL. 0832/947031

Rosé is not central to the production of this major Salentino wine cooperative. It is made only in very generous years, when the grape supply is more than sufficient to produce the renowned Copertino and its Riservas. Nonetheless, the Rosato del Salento Cigliano we tasted this year (the '97) received high marks for its brilliant salmon color and its flowery, fruity bouquet, which is, however, still slightly covered by alcohol. In the mouth it reveals a rich and pleasing fruitiness, although it is generally a bit forward. It is still a structured rosé that goes particularly well with fish, pasta dishes and grilled chicken or lighter meats. But the most interesting of the Cigliano line is the monovarietal chardonnay. The '97 vintage will be remembered as the finest of the last thirty years in Puglia, but for chardonnay it was truly exceptional: the Cigliano that Severino Garofano, the manager of the Cantina Sociale, produced this year has all the characteristics and fragrance of the best Italian Chardonnays (and not just the Italian!): crispness, intense aromas reminiscent, curiously enough, of sauvignon, succulence and body. The Copertino, however, we found to be slightly disappointing, even in its Riserva version, and this is the first time it failed to earn Two Glasses. On the other hand, the '96 vintage was not one of the best in the micro-area where this famed DOC wine is produced. We shall just have to wait for the excellent '97 which is even now maturing in the cellar. Meanwhile we should point out the excellent value for money of all the wines from this cooperative.

○	Salento Chardonnay Cigliano '97	▼▼	2*
●	Copertino '96	▼	2*
●	Copertino Ris. '96	▼	2*
⊙	Salento Rosato Cigliano '97	▼	2*
●	Copertino '94	▽▽	2*
●	Copertino Ris. '89	▽▽	2*
●	Copertino Ris. '91	▽▽	2*
●	Copertino Ris. '94	▽▽	2*
●	Copertino '95	▽	2
●	Copertino Ris. '92	▽	2
○	Salento Chardonnay Cigliano '95	▽	2*
○	Salento Chardonnay Cigliano '96	▽	2*

COPERTINO (LE)

MASSERIA MONACI
TENUTA MONACI
73043 COPERTINO (LE)
TEL. 0832/947512

There has been a great fuss in Puglia over the so-called international style which, many say, should characterize the wines of the region. Tasting the Simposia, from a blend of negroamaro and montepulciano, one grasps immediately that it is not so much a standardized style that the Pugliese wine-makers should seek, as a different production technique. Make modern, clean, correct wines which, as in the case of the Simposia, still maintain the typical characteristics of the local terroir, and you will have wines that will sell well anywhere. In fact, the combination of aromas, spicy tastes and the balanced structure that indicates you can keep this wine for several years makes Simposia one of the best reds produced in Puglia. But Severino Garofano, the driving force behind Masseria Monaci, also offers us another great example of Salentine wine-making: the Primitivo I Censi. We tasted the '95 and '96 vintages, and both ranked among the finest Primitivos we have had the opportunity to taste in recent years. They have the vermilion hue typical of this grape (which is finally coming into its own), an intense, heady bouquet with pleasing notes of ripe plum, red fruit in spirit and balsamic and spicy hints, and good structure (more substantial in the case of the '96). The Copertino Eloquenzia, on the other hand, was less impressive than its debut version, which won Two Glasses. A product of the '96 vintage, which was not very favorable in this zone, it will have to be content with One Glass. Nevertheless it is a warm wine of fair body and good overall quality.

●	Salento Rosso Simposia '95	▼▼	3
●	Salento Primitivo I Censi '95	▼▼	2*
●	Salento Primitivo I Censi '96	▼▼	2*
●	Copertino Rosso Eloquenzia '96	▼	2*
●	Copertino Rosso Eloquenzia '94	▽▽	2*
●	Salento Rosso Simposia '94	▽▽	3
●	Copertino Rosso '92	▽	1*
○	Le Vicarie '96	▽	2*
⊙	Santa Brigida Rosato '96	▽	2*

CORATO (BA)

SANTA LUCIA
STRADA COMUNALE SAN VITTORE, 1
70033 CORATO (BA)
TEL. 080/8721168

The Perrone Capano family has long owned this lovely winery in rural Corato, an operation which combines a craftsmanlike approach with an almost industrial volume: the Santa Lucia winery produces more than 100 thousand bottles of wine per year. For Giuseppe and Roberto, father and son, and noted Neapolitan professionals, this winery is a hobby, an excuse to get away from Naples on the weekend. Their ambition, however, is to make important wines. And, with the '95 Castel del Monte Rosso Riserva, one begins to see the results of the efforts they have lavished here. It is obtained exclusively from uva di Troia, aged for two years in Slavonian oak barrels and then for more than six months in the bottle. It shows a garnet color with orange highlights, a broad, heady and spicy bouquet, and a well-structured, elegant, balanced, warm, soft and properly tannic palate. The Castel del Monte Rosso, Rosato and Bianco all seemed good. The Rosso Vigna del Pozzo, 70% uva di Troia and the remainder montepulciano, is aged in barrels for ten months and in the bottle for six. It is a warm, velvety wine with good structure and tannins of some finesse. The Rosato Lama di Carro is a monovarietal bombino nero with a brilliant pink color, a very intense, fruity fragrance and a dry, fresh and balanced palate. Pampanuto and bombino bianco are the grapes used for the Castel del Monte Bianco Vigna Tufaroli, a dry, crisp, fruity wine with a finesse that puts it at the head of its class. Last of all, the '96 Rosso della Murgia is correct, warm and agreeably quaffable .

	Wine	Glasses	Price
●	Castel del Monte Rosso Ris. '95	▼▼	3
○	Castel del Monte Bianco Vigna Tufaroli '97	▼	2*
⊙	Castel del Monte Rosato Vigna Lama di Carro '97	▼	2*
●	Castel del Monte Rosso Vigna del Pozzo '95	▼	2*
●	Murgia Rosso '96	▼	2*
○	Castel del Monte Bianco '96	▽	2*
●	Castel del Monte Rosso '94	▽	2
●	Castel del Monte Rosso '95	▽	2*
●	Castel del Monte Rosso '96	▽	2*
●	Castel del Monte Rosso Ris. '92	▽	3
○	Quarati '96	▽	2*

CORATO (BA)

TORREVENTO
LOC. CASTEL DEL MONTE
S. S. 170, KM 28
70033 CORATO (BA)
TEL. 080/8980973 - 8980929

Gaetano and Francesco Liantonio are by now well launched on the road to quality. And to be even more certain of offering top-notch wines, they have combined state-of-the-art equipment with the charms of the 17th century winery located just below Castel del Monte. Currently, their oenologist, Lino Carparelli, who also produces wines under his own label, I Pastini, but markets them through Torrevento, seems to be specializing in reds, to judge from the high scores they all have rated. The '96 Vigna Pedale, a Castel del Monte Riserva, presents an intense heady fragrance, and a well-structured, warm, balanced and rounded palate with soft tannins and attractive spicy notes. The Rosso della Murgia '96 I Pastini is a modern, well-made wine with good structure and the characteristic aromas of its cabernet franc and montepulciano grapes. From the same line, the vermilion-hued Primitivo del Tarantino '96 offers a pleasantly spicy fragrance with aromas of fruit in spirit. The '97 Castel del Monte Rosso has a dark ruby red color, a good nose, softness and fair concentration. Among the whites, the '96 Moscato di Trani Dulcis in Fundo, a fortified sweet dessert wine, with its well-balanced aromas of fresh rose and lavender and its pleasing honey taste, was very near capturing Two Glasses.

	Wine	Glasses	Price
●	Castel del Monte Rosso '97	▼▼	1*
●	Castel del Monte Rosso V. Pedale Ris. '96	▼▼	2*
●	Murgia Rosso I Pastini '96	▼▼	2*
●	Primitivo del Tarantino I Pastini '96	▼▼	2*
○	Castel del Monte Bianco '97	▼	1*
⊙	Castel del Monte Rosato '97	▼	1*
○	Locorotondo I Pastini '97	▼	2
○	Moscato di Trani Dulcis in Fundo '96	▼	3
⊙	Castel del Monte Rosato '95	▽▽	1*
●	Castel del Monte Rosso V. Pedale Ris. '94	▽▽	2*
●	Castel del Monte Rosso '96	▽	1*

FASANO (BR)

BORGO CANALE
LOC. SELVA
V.LE CANALE DI PIRRO, 23
72015 FASANO (BR)
TEL. 080/4331351

Borgo Canale, a fine winery which in the past specialized in the production of white wines, such as Locorotondo and Martina, and the semi-sparkling Agorà, is back in the Guide. For some time now things have been hopping here, following a restructuring of shareholdings, and the winery has taken a new turn, of which the arrival of the new manager, Lino Carparelli, an oenologist of proven experience, is emblematic. The number of labels has been cut down and the accent is on quality. Proof of this is their Maestro, a full-bodied red, mainly montepulciano with 30% uva di Troia grapes from the excellent '97 vintage. It is a wine rich in fruity aromas with subtle floral and balsamic notes; on the palate it is dry, warm, harmonious and fruity, with hints of ripe berries, plum and spice: an easy Two Glasses. The other Borgo Canale wines are interesting as well, especially the fragrant Locorotondo, a blend of verdeca and bianco d'Alessano with a small percentage of fiano, which got One Glass, and also the Rosa di Selva and the semi-sparkling Agorà, both worthy of mention.

	Wine	Glasses	Price
●	Maestro '97	🍷🍷	3
○	Locorotondo '97	🍷	2*
⊙	Rosa di Selva '97		2
○	Valle d'Itria Agorà '97		2
○	Chardonnay del Salento Robur '94	🍷 (outline)	4
○	Divo '93	🍷 (outline)	4
○	Divo '94	🍷 (outline)	4

GRAVINA IN PUGLIA (BA)

CANTINA COOPERATIVA BOTROMAGNO
VIA F.LLI CERVI, 12
70024 GRAVINA IN PUGLIA (BA)
TEL. 080/3265865

The Gravina '97, although it is still the best Pugliese white made from native grapes (local clones of greco and malvasia), does not have the same nose, those floral and fruity aromas that made it so successful in recent years. But we don't want to be misunderstood: it easily wins One Glass, with its good balance and structure and a pleasant touch of acidity, characteristics which make it well-suited to seafood dishes, light soups and fresh cheeses. On the other hand, we found distinct improvement in the quality of the Botromagno red, the Pier delle Vigne, made from a blend of montepulciano and aglianico. It boasts a delicate bouquet of red fruit, vanilla, and toasty notes of oak, and is warm, velvety and balanced on the palate, with the smooth tannins of a wine of breeding that can age well for several years. Two vintages were released in close succession, i.e. the '93, which is a little more forward, as its orange-garnet tinges show, and has a solid tannic structure, and the '94, which displays a fresher fruitiness, softness and good length. The interesting Silvium rosé, made exclusively from montepulciano, has a good nose and a substantial body and goes down fairly easily.

	Wine	Glasses	Price
●	Pier delle Vigne '93	🍷🍷	2*
●	Pier delle Vigne '94	🍷🍷	2*
○	Gravina '97	🍷	2*
⊙	Silvium '97		2
○	Gravina '95	🍷🍷 (outline)	2*
○	Gravina '96	🍷🍷 (outline)	2*
○	Gravesano '92	🍷 (outline)	4
○	Gravina '93	🍷 (outline)	2*
○	Gravina '94	🍷 (outline)	2*
●	Pier delle Vigne '91	🍷 (outline)	2*
●	Pier delle Vigne '92	🍷 (outline)	2*

GUAGNANO (LE)

Cosimo Taurino

S. S. 605 Salice-Sandonaci
73010 Guagnano (LE)
tel. 0832/706490

This year the assortment is complete. They are all there, from the greatest to the least important, reds and whites, even a rosé. The Cosimo Taurino – Severino Garofano duo, respectively the owner and the oenologist of this winery, have got the best out of the fine vintages of '93, with their Patriglione and Nortapanaro, and of '97, with their Chardonnay and Scaloti. The Patriglione, no longer a Brindisi DOC, is up to its finest vintages of the past. It shows great breeding, with its intense ruby red color, excellent structure and great complexity on both nose and palate. Indeed, it reveals a composite, heady, very ample bouquet, and in the mouth it is clean, dry, warm and velvety, although a slightly overripe and evolved tone diminishes its definition. It is nonetheless a wine surpassed by few in expressing the intimate ties which link a territory with its native grapes, in this instance the negroamaro and the malvasia nera harvested when almost raisins. Great sinew and substance are the hallmarks of the Notarpanaro, the other red offered by Taurino. Its bouquet is full and elegant, and on the palate it is dry, concentrated and rich in hints of red fruit and ripe plum preserves, with an elegant, slightly bitter undertone. The Chardonnay, fermented and aged in barriques, is equally good. It presents an intense fragrance of wildflowers and, on the palate, good structure, fruity succulence and pleasing toasty overtones of new oak and vanilla. The Salice Salentino Rosso '95 is good, if not particularly exciting, the Rosato Scaloti is fruity and powerful, and the Chardonnay del Salento Stria is agreeably crisp.

	Wine	Glasses	Price
●	Patriglione '93	▼▼	5
○	Salento Chardonnay '97	▼▼	3
●	Salento Rosso Notarpanaro '93	▼▼	4
⊙	Salento Rosato Scaloti '97	▼	3
●	Salice Salentino Rosso '95	▼	3
○	Salento Chardonnay Stria '97		3
●	Patriglione '85	▽▽▽	5
●	Patriglione '88	▽▽▽	5
●	Salento Rosso Notarpanaro '86	▽▽	3*
●	Salento Rosso Notarpanaro '88	▽▽	3*
●	Salento Rosso Notarpanaro '90	▽▽	3*
●	Salice Salentino Rosso Ris. '88	▽▽	3
●	Salice Salentino Rosso Ris. '90	▽▽	3*
●	Salice Salentino Rosso Ris. '93	▽▽	3
●	Salice Salentino Rosso Ris. '94	▽▽	3*

LECCE

Cantele

Zona Industriale, b. 12
73100 Lecce
tel. 0832/307018

We had lost track of Augusto Cantele. The last news we had was that he was involved in producing large quantities of wine in response to the market demand in the English-speaking world, a growth area for marketing Italian wines. This year he returns to the Guide with three good wines which only just missed Two Glasses. We found his Salice Salentino Riserva Cenobio '94 excellent, a well-structured wine with a complex, heady and fruity bouquet, and a warm, harmonious and velvety palate, richly spicy with overtones of fruit and ripe plum preserves. The '96 Rosso del Salento Cerbinare is a complex, balanced, warm and rounded wine rich in fruity aromas that evolve in the mouth toward hints of cherry preserves, vanilla and toasty oak, and a pleasant though somewhat brief bitterish finish. The '96 Primitivo del Salento is well-structured, complex and characterized by vanilla and intense fragrances of wild berries and white pepper. The Chardonnay '97 did not seem on a level with the reds; its nose was barely more than acceptable, but it's still a white wine worthy of mention.

	Wine	Glasses	Price
●	Salento Primitivo '96	▼	2*
●	Salento Rosso Cerbinare '96	▼	3
●	Salice Salentino Rosso Cenobio Ris. '94	▼	2*
○	Salento Chardonnay '97		3
●	Salento Rosso Cerbinare '92	▽	2
⊙	Salice Salentino Rosato Cenobio '94	▽	2
●	Salice Salentino Rosso Cenobio '92	▽	2*

LECCE

AGRICOLE VALLONE

VIA XXV LUGLIO, 7
73100 LECCE
TEL. 0832/308041

This year once again the Graticciaia produced by Maria Teresa and Vittoria Vallone won unanimous praise at our tastings, confirming its ranking as one of southern Italy's finest red wines for both structure and balance. The '93 is made from negroamaro and malvasia nera grapes harvested late and left to dry on racks (graticci) prior to pressing, whence its name. Its bouquet is complex, offering enchanting notes of ripe berries, tobacco and cherries in alcohol; on the palate it is well-structured, warm, elegant and suggestive of fruit preserves, licorice, vanilla and dried fruit. But Donato Lazzari, the manager of the winery, and Severino Garofano, the oenologist, are rigorous in their grape selection and consequently offer a choice range of wines, all Two Glass winners. We were very interested in the Brindisi Rosso della Vigna Flaminio, produced also in a rosé version, made from negroamaro and malvasia nera grapes from the vineyard of the same name, and the Salice Salentino Vereto, both '95s. The '97 Corte Valesio, a sauvignon, has varietal aromas, good structure and some length. Lastly, the Passo delle Viscarde '93 is a delicious sweet white produced from semi-dried sauvignon and malvasia bianca and named after its vineyard of origin near Brindisi. It is aged for a year in Allier and Nevers oak and thereafter for a good long while in the bottle. It is fat, balanced, rich in aromas of candied peel, aromatic and long-lasting.

	Wine	Rating	Price
⊙	Brindisi Rosato Vigna Flaminio '97	🍷🍷	1*
●	Brindisi Rosso Vigna Flaminio '95	🍷🍷	2*
●	Graticciaia '93	🍷🍷	5
○	Passo delle Viscarde '93	🍷🍷	4
●	Salice Salentino Vereto '95	🍷🍷	2*
○	Sauvignon del Salento Corte Valesio '97	🍷🍷	2*
●	Brindisi Rosso Vigna Flaminio '94	🍸🍸	2*
●	Graticciaia '90	🍸🍸	5
●	Graticciaia '92	🍸🍸	5
●	Salice Salentino Rosso '93	🍸🍸	2*
●	Salice Salentino Rosso '94	🍸🍸	2*
●	Brindisi Rosso Vigna Flaminio '93	🍸	2*

LEVERANO (LE)

CONTI ZECCA

VIA CESAREA
73045 LEVERANO (LE)
TEL. 0832/922606 - 925613

The Zecca family vineyards are the largest and most modern in Puglia. In the cellar new technology is constantly introduced and there is continuous experimentation with new wines. One result of this innovative program is a Leverano white from late-harvested malvasia grapes. It's an elegant wine, with a complex nose offering clear floral notes; the palate is well-structured, modern, dry and characteristically aromatic. Ten thousand bottles were produced and nearly that many have been sold abroad. Of the Leverano DOC wines, leaving aside the Rosso '96 which has not yet been released, we tasted the good Bianco '97, which proved fresh, fruity and pleasant. The excellent Donna Marzia '96, a blend of negroamaro (60%), malvasia nera (20%), sangiovese and montepulciano, has a bright ruby red color tinged with orange, an ample and lasting bouquet and a palate of exceptional freshness, with an elegant, slightly bitter, warm and velvety finish. The very good Salice Salentino Rosso Cantalupi '95 has a dark ruby color and intense aromas of stewed ripe red fruit; in the mouth it has body, softness and finesse and is somewhat forward. The Salice Salentino Bianco, made from a blend of chardonnay (90%) and pinot blanc, has a fruity fragrance and a dry, crisp and richly fruity palate. Rounding off the range is a lively and pleasantly drinkable semi-sparkling Pinot-Chardonnay, to be drunk very cold with fish-based dishes.

	Wine	Rating	Price
○	Leverano Malvasia V. del Saraceno '96	🍷🍷	2*
●	Salento Rosso Donna Marzia '96	🍷🍷	2*
○	Leverano Bianco V. del Saraceno '97	🍷	2*
⊙	Leverano Rosato V. del Saraceno '97	🍷	2*
○	Salento Bianco Donna Marzia '97	🍷	2*
○	Salento Pinot-Chardonnay '97	🍷	2*
⊙	Salento Rosato Donna Marzia '97	🍷	1*
○	Salice Salentino Bianco Cantalupi '97	🍷	2*
●	Salice Salentino Rosso Cantalupi '95	🍷	2*

LOCOROTONDO (BA)

CANTINA SOCIALE
COOPERATIVA DI LOCOROTONDO
VIA MADONNA DELLA CATENA, 99
70010 LOCOROTONDO (BA)
TEL. 080/4311644

Once again, this time with the '97, the cru In Tallinajo confirms that it is one of the most interesting wines of the Locorotondo zone. It is a well-made white with a fresh fragrance, dry and soft but hardly complex in the mouth, where delicious notes of apple are however perceptible. This is a fine Locorotondo, modern in style, rewarding the efforts which this important cooperative has devoted to it for some years now. The classic Locorotondo has also improved, although it's not up to the In Tallinajo. The grape blend is traditional: verdeca, bianco d'Alessano and fiano. It has a brilliant straw-yellow-pale green color, faintly fruity aromas and a dry, soft taste with barely noticeable aromatic hints. The good Case Bianche rosé, made from vertically trained pinot noir, displays a light pink color, intensely fruity aromas, and a fresh, dry palate with overtones of ripe red fruit and a delicate acidity. The red of the Case Bianche line is a blend of typical southern grapes (aglianico and uva di Troia) and an international varietal (cabernet sauvignon). But the wine lacks the structure which these grapes generally provide: it is somewhat fleeting, and in any case suited to immediate consumption. The attractive Olimpia, made from moscato bianco, is a richly aromatic sweet wine. And the '96 Rosso Casale San Giorgio is quite pleasing.

	Wine	Glasses	Price
○	Locorotondo in Tallinajo '97	🍷	2
○	Olimpia '97	🍷	3
⊙	Case Bianche '97	🍷	3
●	Casale San Giorgio '96	🍷	2*
○	Locorotondo '97		1
●	Case Bianche '95		3
○	Locorotondo in Tallinajo '95	🍸	2
○	Locorotondo in Tallinajo '96	🍸	2
○	Locorotondo Riserva del Presidente '93	🍸	3

LOCOROTONDO (BA)

CARDONE
VIA MARTIRI DELLA LIBERTÀ, 28
70010 LOCOROTONDO (BA)
TEL. 080/4311624

The first time the Cardone winery appeared in the Guide it was because of their splendid Locorotondo. Over the subsequent years this wine has never been a disappointment, although we have always found it a bit too pricey. This time, however, Franco Cardone wins a place in the Guide for his reds, and especially the excellent '94 Gioia del Colle Primitivo Riserva, a wine from the very zone where this grape, brought to Puglia by the Benedictine monks centuries ago, was first planted. Cardone's Primitivo has a lovely intense ruby color tinged with garnet and intense varietal aromas; in the mouth it is full, warm and velvety, with pleasant hints of spice, especially cinnamon. It's a wine to be drunk with red meats and strong cheeses, but it's also a wine for sipping on its own, thanks to its pleasingly soft, almost sweet character. The very good Primitivo di Murgia, two years younger than the foregoing and made from a blend of primitivo di Gioia del Colle and primitivo di Manduria, offers interesting complexity to both nose and palate, a fairly substantial body and dry, warm and velvety sensations in the mouth. You can drink it straight through dinner. In the company of reds like these the Locorotondo, the key wine of this winery, although it is amongst the best of its kind, is rather overshadowed.

	Wine	Glasses	Price
●	Gioia del Colle Primitivo Ris. '94	🍷🍷	3
○	Locorotondo '97	🍷	2
●	Primitivo della Murgia '96	🍷	2
○	Chardonnay di Puglia Placeo '95	🍸	2
○	Chardonnay di Puglia Placeo '96	🍸	2
○	Locorotondo '94	🍸	2
○	Locorotondo '95	🍸	2
○	Locorotondo '96	🍸	2
●	Primaio Rosso '95	🍸	2

MANDURIA (TA)

FELLINE

VIA N. DONADIO, 20
74024 MANDURIA (TA)
TEL. 099/9711660

The oenological future of Puglia is probably to be found in the primitivo grape. The Perrucci family believes as much, and their oenologist, Roberto Cipresso, one of the most renowned in Italy, has adopted this creed body and soul. In consequence, the Primitivo di Manduria '97 has exceeded all the expectations aroused by last year's version. It is a modern, clean wine, perfectly harmonious in all its components, dark dense ruby in color, offering a complexity of aromas ranging from vanilla to toasty oak, ripe red fruit and india ink. On the palate it displays impressive depth and concentration, and is warm, velvety, of perfect structure and great balance. It is quite simply a great red wine, the fruit of patient labor and research which led to the recovery of vineyards over forty years old, mostly gobelet-trained and all very low-yielding. In the cellar up-to the-minute vinification techniques and the finest woods for aging are the only choice. A further confirmation that they're getting it right comes from the Alberello, a blend of equal parts of primitivo and negroamaro. This wine, too, has great structure, and is dark red, with intense aromas of red fruit and elegant notes of spice. In the mouth, it is dry, warm, velvety and reminiscent of ripe red plum and wild berries. Finally, we should note that the Vigna del Feudo red, made from montepulciano (50%), primitivo (40%), cabernet sauvignon and merlot, is still aging, so we withhold our judgment until the next edition. These wines are really extraordinary bargains.

	Wine	Glasses	
●	Primitivo di Manduria '97	🍷🍷 (black)	4
●	Salento Rosso Alberello '97	🍷🍷 (black)	3*
●	Primitivo di Manduria '96	🍷🍷 (white)	4

MANDURIA (TA)

PERVINI

VIA SANTO STASI PRIMO - Z. I.
C.DA ACUTI
74024 MANDURIA (TA)
TEL. 099/9711660

The three young Perrucci siblings, Gregory, Fabrizio and Alessia, are beating every speed record on the road to quality. And not only with their Primitivo (as Gregory says, why shouldn't we produce in Manduria a wine as good as the California Zinfandel?): the other Pervini wines are also highly appreciated in Italy and abroad. For example, the Bizantino Rosso, a blend of negroamaro and malvasia nera, when presented at tastings in London and New York, was snatched up almost entirely by importers who serve those markets. It is a wine of considerable structure, with fruity aromas and undertones of tobacco and spice, warm and velvety in the mouth, with a complexity of tastes ranging from blueberry jam and raspberry to pencil lead. Indeed, it proved to be one of the most interesting Salentine reds. Another good performer is the '96 Primitivo, with its vermilion color. It has very intense heady aromas, and a warm, harmonious, velvety palate, rich in spicy overtones - consequently, another Two Glass wine. Then there is the '96 Primitivo del Tarantino I Monili, which needs only a slightly improved structure to move up a full step. The Rosato and the Chardonnay of the Bizantino line are both good, and easily picked up One Glass each.

	Wine	Glasses	
●	Primitivo di Manduria '96	🍷🍷 (black)	2*
●	Salento Rosso Bizantino '96	🍷🍷 (black)	2*
●	Primitivo del Tarantino I Monili '96	🍷 (black)	2*
○	Salento Chardonnay Bizantino '97	🍷 (black)	2*
⊙	Salento Rosato Bizantino '97	🍷 (black)	2*
●	Primitivo di Manduria '92	🍷 (white)	2
●	Primitivo di Manduria '93	🍷 (white)	2*
●	Primitivo di Manduria '94	🍷 (white)	2
○	Salento Chardonnay Bizantino '96	🍷 (white)	2
⊙	Salento Rosato Bizantino '96	🍷 (white)	2
●	Salento Rosso Bizantino '94	🍷 (white)	2
●	Salento Rosso Bizantino '95	🍷 (white)	2*

SALICE SALENTINO (LE)

Leone de Castris

Via Senatore de Castris, 50
73015 Salice Salentino (LE)
tel. 0832/731112

The Counts Leone de Castris own the oldest winery in Puglia. Piero, the father of the current owner, Salvatore, is credited with having invented not only Five Roses, and hence Salento rosé, but also the Salice Salentino, thanks to the innovations he introduced in both vineyard and cellar half a century ago. With the '93 Donna Lisa, a Salice Salentino Riserva that the oenologist Dino Pinto ages in barriques for 6-8 months, the Leone de Castris have hit the jackpot. It has an intense ruby hue with a thin rim of orange, and a great complexity of aromas in which the fruit is integrated perfectly with the toasty and spicy notes of the new wood. Once in the mouth it is structured, harmonious, warm and velvety, with suggestions of cherry and preserved fruit, but also of vanilla, tobacco and spice. It goes beautifully with grilled red meats, rich poultry and game. The excellent (Two Glasses) Salice Salentino Bianco Imago, a monovarietal chardonnay, embodies the best characteristics of this grape: fruity aromas, charm, body and freshness. Another enjoyable and pleasingly structured wine is the historic Five Roses, the first Pugliese rosé to acquire a worldwide market. To round off the line, the Salice Salentino Riserva seemed a bit forward, the Copertino is perfectly acceptable and the Primitivo del Salento La Rena is well made.

	Wine	Glasses	Price
●	Salice Salentino Rosso Donna Lisa Ris. '93	3 (black)	4
⊙	Salento Rosato Five Roses '97	2 (black)	3
●	Copertino '97	1 (black)	2
●	Salento Primitivo La Rena '97	1 (black)	3
○	Salice Salentino Bianco Imago '97	1 (black)	3
●	Salice Salentino Rosso Ris. '95	1 (black)	3
○	Salento Sauvignon Vigna Case Alte '97		3
○	Salento Verdeca Messapia '97		3
●	Salice Salentino Rosso Ris. '94	2 (white)	3
●	Salice Salentino Rosso Donna Lisa Ris. '92	2 (white)	4
●	Salento Primitivo La Rena '96	1 (white)	3
●	Salice Salentino Rosso Maiana '95	1 (white)	2*

SAN SEVERO (FG)

Giovanni D'Alfonso del Sordo

C.da Sant'Antonino
S. S. 89 km 5
71016 San Severo (FG)
tel. 0882/221444

The '95 Casteldrione is without doubt the best wine submitted this year for our tasting by Gianfelice d'Alfonso del Sordo. Made from a blend of sangiovese and montepulciano (40% each) with uva di Troia, it is aged in oak barrels for six months. The wine is of an attractive ruby-garnet color with a bouquet of fair complexity ranging from red fruit to toasty and balsamic overtones; the taste is dry, warm and harmonious, with hints of ripe wild berries which blend very well with the smooth tannins and a pleasant note of vanilla. Another good wine is the San Severo Rosso which, starting with the '96 vintage, is called Montero. It is made from selected montepulciano grapes from the Coppanetta vineyard. It displays a brilliant ruby color, a fairly broad and heady bouquet and a full-bodied, dry, harmonious and velvety palate. The '94 Contrada del Santo, on the other hand, is made from uva di Troia and montepulciano, aged for a year in 30-hectoliter oak barrels and refined at length in the bottle. Its characteristics are a very intense ruby red color, slightly heady aromas and a full-bodied, warm, dry and harmonious palate. Another quite interesting wine is the Catapanus white, made from bombino grapes: it is crisp and fragrant, redolent of apple and fruity on the palate. The S. Severo '95 reviewed last time seems to be developing very well.

	Wine	Glasses	Price
●	Casteldrione '95	2 (black)	2*
●	Contrada del Santo '94	1 (black)	3
○	Bombino Bianco Catapanus '97	1 (black)	2
●	San Severo Rosso Montero '96	1 (black)	2*
○	San Severo Bianco '97		2
⊙	San Severo Rosato '97		2
○	Bombino '95	1 (white)	1*
○	Bombino Bianco Catapanus '96	1 (white)	1*
●	Casteldrione Ris. '92	1 (white)	2*
●	Contrada del Santo '92	1 (white)	3
●	San Severo Rosso '95	1 (white)	2

SANDONACI (BR)

Francesco Candido
Via A. Diaz, 46
72025 Sandonaci (BR)
tel. 0831/635674

Excellence has by now become a constant feature of the Candido brothers' wines. This year once again the excellent Duca d'Aragona is one of the most interesting reds in the region. Severino Garofano, who has been the oenologist of this fine winery since the very beginning, has done a splendid job with this '92, a wine of an international style, rounded and well-balanced, with an intense fruity bouquet, and great complexity on the palate, with toasty notes, hints of vanilla and a balsamic finish rich in ripe red fruit. The other classics of this winery, the '95 Cappello di Prete and the '94 Salice Salentino Rosso Riserva, are equally good. They are both blends of negroamaro and malvasia nera, but the vineyards and the vinification and aging techniques are different. The Cappello di Prete spends some time in barriques, which adds elegant vanilla and toasty notes to the good structure and general charm of the wine. The Paule Calle is an elegant sweet wine made from malvasia grapes left to dry on racks. It has a lovely golden yellow color and admirably complex aromas of honey, aromatic herbs and marmalade, as well as a delectable taste. The Vigna Vinera is a barrique-aged sauvignon. It has a fine straw color tinged with green, intense varietal aromas with nuances of vanilla and toasty oak, and, on the palate, it is fat, structured and satisfyingly long. The Salice Le Pozzelle is one of the best rosés we tasted this year; it is full, fat and rich in aromas of red fruit. The good Salice Salentino Bianco '97 is correct and well-balanced.

	Wine	Glasses	Price
●	Cappello di Prete '95	▼▼	3*
●	Duca d'Aragona '92	▼▼	5
○	Paule Calle '97	▼▼	4
○	Salento Bianco Vigna Vinera '97	▼▼	2*
●	Salice Salentino Rosso Ris. '94	▼▼	2*
○	Salice Salentino Bianco '97	▼	2*
⊙	Salice Salentino Rosato Le Pozzelle '97	▼	2*
●	Cappello di Prete '90	▽▽	3
●	Cappello di Prete '92	▽▽	3
●	Cappello di Prete '93	▽▽	3
●	Cappello di Prete '94	▽▽	3*
●	Duca d'Aragona '89	▽▽	5
●	Duca d'Aragona '90	▽▽	5
●	Duca d'Aragona '91	▽▽	5

TUGLIE (LE)

Michele Calò & Figli
Via Masseria Vecchia, 1
73058 Tuglie (LE)
tel. 0833/596242

That the Mjere red should be ranked among the best wines of Puglia is an important milestone for the Calò family, even though they seem to be more interested in the production of rosés, which they consider their staple. At every tasting, however, it is the reds which garner the highest praise, as in the case of the excellent Vigna Spano, of which just a few thousand bottles are produced, and only in very good years, and which was, in fact, not presented this year. We consoled ourselves by drinking the Mjere Rosso '96, a blend of negroamaro and malvasia nera, which revealed a fruity bouquet and a dry, warm, velvety palate with full tones of wild berries and ripe plum. It has the balance of a wine you could drink right now, but it would stand up to being laid down for a few years too. Another wine that performed well was the Alezio Rosato which, thanks to the good '97 vintage, earns Two Glasses. It has intense aromas of fresh fruit and an equally fruity taste with distinct notes of cherry and a delicately bitter finish, and is an excellent accompaniment to fish dishes, white meats and medium-cured cheeses. The Mjere Bianco, verdeca with a small percentage of chardonnay, is interesting if not altogether convincing. It has a greenish straw color and pleasant fresh fruit aromas and is succulent and pleasantly fruity in the mouth, with hints of rennet apple and pineapple.

	Wine	Glasses	Price
⊙	Alezio Rosato Mjere '97	▼▼	3
●	Alezio Rosso Mjere '96	▼▼	3
○	Salento Bianco Mjere '97	▼	3
⊙	Alezio Rosato Mjere '95	▽▽	2*
●	Alezio Rosso Mjere '90	▽▽	3*
●	Alezio Rosso Mjere '92	▽▽	3
●	Alezio Rosso Mjere '94	▽▽	3
●	Alezio Rosso Mjere '95	▽▽	3
○	Salento Bianco Mjere '95	▽▽	2*
●	Vigna Spano '90	▽▽	4
●	Vigna Spano '93	▽▽	4
●	Alezio Rosso Mjere '91	▽	3*

OTHER WINERIES

The following producers obtained good scores in our tastings with one or more of their wines:

PROVINCE OF BARI

Masseria Fatalone
Gioia del Colle, tel. 080/848037,
Gioia del Colle Primitivo '97,
Gioia del Colle Primitivo Ris. '95

Cooperativa della Riforma Agraria
Ruvo di Puglia, tel. 080/9501611,
Castel del Monte Grifo Ris. '96,
Le Carrare '96

Nugnes
Trani, tel. 0883/586837,
Moscato di Trani Dolce Naturale '96

Coppi, Turi, tel. 080/8915049,
Gioia del Colle Primitivo Peucetico '96,
Gioia del Colle Primitivo Vanitoso Ris. '91,
Gioia del Colle Primitivo Siniscalco '93,
Gioia del Colle Rosso Terre al Sole '96

PROVINCE OF BRINDISI

Due Palme
Cellino San Marco, tel. 0831/619728,
Brindisi Rosso '97,
Salento Primitivo '97,
Salento Rosso Canonico '97,
Squinzano Rosso '97

Tenuta La Mea
Cellino San Marco, tel. 0831/617689,
Brindisi Rosso Sire '96,
Salento Primitivo Fra Diavolo '97,
Squinzano Rosso '96

Lomazzi & Sarli
Latiano, tel. 0831/725898,
Brindisi Rosato Solise '97,
Brindisi Rosso Solise '96

Antica Masseria Torre Mozza
Mesagne, tel. 0338/9152333,
Salento Rosso Finibusterre '94,
Salice Salentino Rosso '95

Santa Barbara
San Pietro Vernotico, tel. 0831/652749,
Brindisi Rosato '97,
Brindisi Rosso '95,
Squinzano Rosato '97,
Squinzano Rosso '95

PROVINCE OF FOGGIA

Antica Enotria
Cerignola, tel. 0885/424688,
Aglianico '96,
Montepulciano '97,
Sangiovese '97

Cooperativa Svevo
Lucera, tel. 0881/542301,
Cacc'e Mmitte di Lucera Feudo '96

D'Araprì
San Severo,
tel. 0882/333927,
Brut Metodo Classico,
Brut Rosé Metodo Classico,
Pas Dosé Metodo Classico

PROVINCE OF LECCE

Coppola
Alezio, tel. 0833/281014,
Alezio Rosato Li Cuti '97,
Alezio Rosso Li Cuti '96

Valle dell'Asso
Galatina, tel. 0836/561470,
Galatina Bianco '97,
Galatina Rosato '97

Duca Guarini di Poggiardo
Scorrano,
tel. 0836/460288,
Salento Negramaro Tenuta Piutri '97,
Salento Primitivo Vigne Vecchie '97

PROVINCE OF TARANTO

Consorzio Produttori Vino
Manduria,
tel. 099/97305332,
Primitivo di Manduria 14° '96,
Primitivo di Manduria Dolce Naturale Il Madrigale '96

Miali
Martina Franca, tel. 080/4303222,
Martina Franca '97

Vinicola Savese
Sava,
tel. 099/9726232,
Primitivo del Tarantino Desiderium '95,
Primitivo del Tarantino Le Petrose '96,
Primitivo del Tarantino Vermiglio '97,
Primitivo di Manduria Terrarossa '96

CALABRIA

For all practical purposes, Calabrian viticulture is dominated by two local varietals: gaglioppo, a red grape, and greco, a white. But there are certain facts which prompt reflection. One is the excellent level achieved by Librandi, the first winery in the region to win Three Glasses, which we awarded to a great red, the Gravello, fruit of a blend of gaglioppo and cabernet sauvignon, a wine which in '93 experienced one of its best years. And how could one fail to take account of the performance of the whites and reds produced by Odoardi, which has scored high with wines obtained from blends of traditional local grapes and international varietals? What this shows is that the region offers an excellent habitat, not just for its traditional grapes, but also for cabernet sauvignon and merlot, and even chardonnay, riesling, sauvignon and pinot blanc, to name just a few. These innovative blends cannot replace wines made from local grapes, but they certainly offer a stimulus to the producers of the region. After all, gaglioppo, which is the basis for Cirò Rosso, represents 80% of the Calabrian output. And it is from this grape that Calabria makes some of its finest reds, such as the Librandi Duca di Sanfelice and the Donna Madda of the Fattoria San Francesco. These too are wines from wineries which have understood how to reinterpret the great traditional wines with a modern technique and style, wines from exceptional vineyards, with gobelet-trained vines, a naturally low yield and grapes that ripen perfectly. But there is also another type of wine for which Calabria could be excellently suited (it has had thousands of years of experience): sweet wines, the great sipping wines made from semi-dried grapes. We would have liked to write more reviews, but the labels of note are relatively few, apart from the Odoardi Valeo and the Librandi Le Passule. Where are such wines as Mantonico, Greco di Gerace, the Frascineto and Saracena Moscatos, not to mention Balbino from Altomonte, Catanzaro Malvasia and the Briatico Zibibbo?
Except for some very small producers of Greco di Bianco whose wines one can find only on the spot, on the Ionian coast near Reggio Calabria, it is extremely difficult to taste those golden wines, with their orange blossom and lotus bouquet and taste of orange blossom honey and candied peel. It's a great shame, but also a fascinating suggestion for some Calabrian producers.

CIRÒ (KR)

FATTORIA SAN FRANCESCO
LOC. QUATTROMANI
88071 CIRÒ (KR)
TEL. 0962/32228

Francesco Siciliani now has a winery all his own, and is thus in a position to exploit to the full the potential of the traditional Calabrian grapes, gaglioppo and greco. Proof of this is his Donna Madda, a '95 vintage Cirò Classico Superiore, made exclusively from selected gaglioppo grapes from the Cirò vineyards, and which now has the honor of raising this winery back to the Two Glass level. It is a wine subjected to a full year's aging in barrique (not necessarily a brand-new one), which has a ruby red color tinged with garnet, and a full, intense and enduring bouquet. On the palate it is warm, soft and tannic, of good structure, stylish and fruity, with suggestions of black cherry, but also spice and tobacco, all of which linger a good while. It is altogether an excellent wine, that goes well with red meats, game and aged, sharp cheeses. We also liked the '96 Cirò Rosso, characterized by a deep ruby color, an ample bouquet, and a warm, velvety, medium-bodied palate with hints of red fruit. It is a vigorous wine you can drink straight through the meal, but you'd better open it a good hour before starting. The gaglioppo grape is also used to produce the '97 Rosato, an onion-skin-colored wine with a floral and fruity bouquet, and a dry, soft taste with overtones of mature cherry. The '97 Bianco, made entirely from greco, has good aromas and a dry, savory taste, but rates only a mention.

	Wine	Glasses	Price
●	Cirò Rosso Classico Sup. Donna Madda '95	▼▼	4
⊙	Cirò Rosato '97	▼	2
●	Cirò Rosso Classico '96	▼	2*
○	Cirò Bianco '97		2
●	Cirò Rosso Classico Ronco dei Quattro Venti '92	▽▽	4
●	Cirò Rosso Classico Sup. '91	▽▽	3*
●	Cirò Rosso Classico Sup. Donna Madda '92	▽▽	3
●	Cirò Rosso Classico Sup. Donna Madda '93	▽▽	4
●	Cirò Rosso Classico '94	▽	2
●	Cirò Rosso Classico Sup. Donna Madda '94	▽	4

CIRÒ MARINA (KR)

CAPARRA & SICILIANI
BIVIO S. S. 106
88072 CIRÒ MARINA (KR)
TEL. 0962/371435

There is something going on in this well-known winery controlled by the Caparra and Siciliani families. Luigi Siciliani, president of and connecting link between the various members of the co-operative, is in fact implementing a new production policy at Caparra & Siciliani, introducing all new equipment in the cellar, replanting the vineyards and experimenting with new varietals. Already next season a new Chardonnay may be ready, which will be followed by other new wines, probably made from blends of local and international grapes. The first result of the new production program is evident in the Cirò Bianco called Curiale, a monovarietal greco. It has a straw yellow color with golden highlights, a flowery and fruity bouquet of medium intensity, and a dry, fresh, savory and balanced taste, delicately fruity with hints of rennet apple and pineapple. Then there is the Volvito, a Cirò Rosso Classico Superiore obtained from vintage '94 gaglioppo. It is a wine which follows the Cirò tradition, but is rather modern and carefully made. Aged in small barrels of Allier oak, it offers fair fruity tones to the nose, and in the mouth is warm, velvety and somewhat concentrated, with suggestions of spice and vanilla. The Rosso and the Rosato, both '97s, are a step down.

	Wine	Glasses	Price
○	Cirò Bianco Curiale '97	▼	2*
●	Cirò Rosso Cl. Sup. Volvito '94	▼	3
⊙	Cirò Rosato '97		2
●	Cirò Rosso Cl. '97		2
●	Cirò Rosso Cl. '90	▽	2*
●	Cirò Rosso Cl. '91	▽	2*
●	Cirò Rosso Cl. '92	▽	2*
●	Cirò Rosso Cl. '93	▽	2
●	Cirò Rosso Cl. '94	▽	2
●	Cirò Rosso Cl. Sup. '92	▽	2
●	Cirò Rosso Cl. Sup. Volvito '89	▽	3
●	Cirò Rosso Cl. Sup. Volvito '91	▽	3
●	Cirò Rosso Cl. Sup. Volvito '92	▽	3

ENOTRIA
C.DA S. GENNERO
S. S. 106
88072 CIRÒ MARINA (KR)
TEL. 0962/371181

As far as the production plant is concerned, the Enotria winery is one of the most modern in Calabria. The complex extends over 12 thousand square meters, of which 4 thousand are indoors. It is furnished with advanced equipment for vinifying the grapes of the 23 member growers, who cultivate a total of 120 hectares under vine, all devoted to the typical local grapes gaglioppo and greco bianco. The Enotria production is thus concentrated on Cirò. At the head of the line is the Rosso Classico of the excellent '97 vintage, which offers a good ruby red color tinged with orange, and a rather complex bouquet with a heady fragrance; in the mouth it is dry, well-structured and alcohol-rich, with a certain finesse, good tannins and notes of vanilla and spice. It is a wine well suited to savory first courses, roasted meats and medium-cured cheeses. The Cirò Rosato '97 was equally good, while the Cirò Bianco of the same year seemed a bit more modest. The former, made exclusively from galioppo, has a faint bouquet, but in the mouth it is harmonious, fruity, balanced and properly acidic. The Bianco, a greco, is a delicately floral and fruity wine with a dry, crisp, savory taste, but light in structure and not particularly persistent.

⊙	Cirò Rosato '97	🍷	2*
●	Cirò Rosso Classico '97	🍷	2*
○	Cirò Bianco '97		2
●	Cirò Rosso Classico '95	🍸	2
●	Cirò Rosso Classico Superiore Ris. '91	🍸	3

CIRÒ MARINA (KR)

LIBRANDI
C.DA S. GENNARO
S. S. 106
88072 CIRÒ MARINA (KR)
TEL. 0962/31518 - 31519

After a hiatus in '91, the '93 Gravello returns to its traditional splendor. So once again Nicodemo Librandi, the owner, and Severino Garofano, the consultant oenologist of this fine winery, have succeeded in offering us a great wine, a highly successful blend of gaglioppo, a grape emblematic of Calabrian tradition, and cabernet sauvignon, international grape par excellence. It is a concentrated wine of impressive structure, richly complex as only great wines manage to be. It has a dark, impenetrable ruby color and a captivating nose, with a wealth of notes of ripe red fruit and spicy tones of new wood and balsamic overtones, all perfectly integrated. In the mouth it is full-bodied and fat, with lots of substance and tannins; it opens with great elegance, young as it is, and closes with great length on notes of blackberry, ripe plum and vanilla, with delicate grassy overtones. Another excellent wine is the Cirò Riserva Duca di Sanfelice '93, which has a lovely dark ruby color with a slightly orange rim. It is rich in spicy fragrances, and in the mouth shows remarkable structure and body. The admirable Critone '97 is a white born of a successful mating of two grapes hardly traditional to the region, sauvignon and chardonnay. It has an attractive brilliant straw color, and an intense and elegant varietal nose, displaying aromas of rennet apple, apricot and ripe exotic fruit. The rest of the Librandi line is also noteworthy for quality, from the Rosato Terre Lontane to the various versions of Cirò.

●	Gravello '93	🍷🍷🍷	5
●	Cirò Rosso Duca Sanfelice Ris. '93	🍷🍷	3
○	Critone '97	🍷🍷	2*
○	Cirò Bianco '97	🍷	2*
⊙	Cirò Rosato '97	🍷	2*
●	Cirò Rosso Classico '96	🍷	2*
⊙	Terre Lontane '97	🍷	2
●	Gravello '89	🍸🍸🍸	5
●	Gravello '90	🍸🍸🍸	5
●	Cirò Rosso Duca Sanfelice Ris. '91	🍸🍸	3*
●	Gravello '88	🍸🍸	5
●	Gravello '91	🍸🍸	5

COSENZA

GIOVAN BATTISTA ODOARDI

V.LE DELLA REPUBBLICA, 143
87100 COSENZA
TEL. 0984/29961

From Giambattista, his father, Gregorio Odoardi inherited, first, a lovely vineyard, overlooking the Mediterranean at an altitude ranging from 150 to 500 meters, between Nocera Terinese and Falerna, second, the medical profession, and third, a great passion for wine. And such is his enthusiasm and desire to produce fine wines that he has entrusted the technical management of his winery to the young Tuscan oenologist Luca D'Attoma. His goal, which he has reached, is to produce modern wines of great lineage, which can tell the world of the wine-making potential of the toe of the boot of Italy. This is the case with the excellent Scavigna Vigna Garrone '96 (a blend of aglianico, merlot, cabernet franc and sauvignon), a wine with an intense and lasting fruity bouquet. On the palate it is structured, velvety and harmonious, pleasingly balsamic and spicy, with overtones of vanilla and red fruit preserves. We thought Odoardi's other red, the Savuto Vigna Mortilla '95, was excellent too. This is a complex blend of gaglioppo, sangiovese, magliocco canino, malvasia, pecorino, nerello cappuccio and greco nero, all of which are to be found in his old seven-hectare vineyard. It is aged in Slavonian oak barrels and Tronçais barriques and displays an intense bouquet and a warm, mouth-filling taste, rich in notes of spice and vanilla. Elegant aromas and a fruity palate (pineapple, apple and apricot) are the marks of the Scavigna Pian della Corte '97, obtained from chardonnay, pinot blanc and riesling italico. The '97 Valeo, finally, is a delicate sweet wine made from semi-dried zibibbo grapes, and only 1,200 half-bottles are produced.

●	Savuto Sup. Vigna Mortilla '95	🍷🍷	4
○	Scavigna Pian della Corte '97	🍷🍷	4
●	Scavigna Vigna Garrone '96	🍷🍷	4
○	Valeo '97	🍷🍷	5
○	Scavigna Bianco '97	🍷	3*
⊙	Scavigna Rosato '97	🍷	3
●	Savuto Sup. Vigna Mortilla '93	🍸🍸	4
○	Valeo '95	🍸🍸	5
●	Savuto '95	🍸	2*
○	Scavigna '96	🍸	2*
○	Scavigna Pian della Corte '96	🍸	4
○	Scavigna Pian della Corte Etichetta Blu '96	🍸	4

MARINA DI STRONGOLI (KR)

DATTILO

C.DA DATTILO
88078 MARINA DI STRONGOLI (KR)
TEL. 0962/865613

Dattilo is the name of Roberto Ceraudo's organic farm, mainly devoted to olive-growing, but including an artisanal winery. This sort of set-up, at least in the wine-making world, while it guarantees the maximum purity, does not always result in modern wines of an impeccable style. Certainly there is little doubt as to the purity of the Ceraudo production, whether of wine or oil, since he makes use of no chemical fertilizers, much less pesticides. The flagship wine of the firm, the Amineo, takes its name from an inscription referring to wine, which was found in nearby Petelia in the course of an archaeological dig. The wine is obtained from a blend of gaglioppo with 20% cabernet sauvignon and aglianico, aged for several months in barriques. It has a ruby red color, broad and enticing aromas, and a full, savory, harmonious taste with quite distinct notes of ripe cherry. It is of medium structure and certainly not suited to long aging. The best thing is to drink it up within its first two years. The '97 Donnasusi white is obtained from a blend of greco and verdicchio, and offers a pleasing fragrance of broom and wildflowers; finally, the Donnamaria '97 is made from chardonnay, which lends it perceptible floral and fruity characteristics.

●	Amineo '97	🍷	3
○	Donnamaria '97		3
○	Donnasusi '97		3
●	Amineo '95	🍸	3

SICILY

Never before has Sicily done as well in our Guide as it has this year. Five wines have been awarded Three Glasses, and the wineries included for detailed consideration have gone from 20 to 28. It's a triumph. But it also confirms that making really good wine is actually easier in these parts than elsewhere, and that you need only be conscientious, keep your eye on the goal you have set yourself and act accordingly. Of course oceans of wine are still sold in bulk and used to blend with the weak wines of the north (even with some from over the border). They are traded for very few liras a liter and serve to improve neither the image nor the financial situation of their place of origin. And this occurs when it's now as clear as day that the vines and the soil of this region are the new frontier in serious Italian viticulture. There are thousands of hectares of vineyards generating enormous quantities of wine, excellent native grape varieties and perfect climatic conditions for producing first-class results. It's as good as or better than in California, the best regions of Australia and almost all the wine-growing areas of Europe. One has only to believe in it and carry on logically from there. If there is a problem it's with local entrepreneurs and their ability to understand how to make the most of a region which has long been uniquely well-endowed for viticulture. There is a real danger that Sicily will become a sort of grab-bag of exploitable colonies for big conglomerates, both Italian and foreign. Not very long from now, in a few years at most, the problem of privatizing the big winery Corvo, which currently belongs to the Region of Sicily, will have to be resolved, and a sort of feverish unofficial auction has already started up. A few big and important Tuscan and Veneto firms are negotiating for and acquiring vineyards, particularly in the southeastern part of the island and inland from Palermo. And side by side with these great commotions, there begin to emerge tiny wineries that produce exceptional wines, just as in the best viticultural areas of the world. This year four examples stand out: Palari near Messina, Melìa in Alcamo and Salvo Murana and D'Ancona in Pantelleria. They are pioneers in what will, we fully believe, grow exponentially in the next few years more or less all over. And meanwhile important wineries of moderate size but great ambition are getting themselves properly organized, i.e. Planeta, COS, Benanti, Valle dell'Acate and Abbazia di Santa Anastasia, and pulling up alongside of Corvo and Regaleali there are large and well-regarded wineries such as Donnafugata and, to some extent, Torrevecchia and Rapitalà. Clearly there's a situation of great ferment here, and although we can't yet say where it will all lead, it seems to promise some fantastic surprises for the near future.

ACATE (RG)

CANTINA VALLE DELL'ACATE
C.DA BIDINI
97011 ACATE (RG)
TEL. 0932/874166

This vast winery (with more than 150 hectares of vineyards), located in one of the southernmost viticultural areas of Italy, has again done very well: without doubt this is thanks to their young and capable wine manager Gaetana Jacono, one of the most able and dynamic women of wine in all of Italy. This year there is a particularly interesting range, with wines that are indeed technically well made, but that are also starting to have a certain depth of nose and palate. The Frappato '97 is a real surprise: a red with an intensely fruity nose, including the suggestions of morello and sour cherries that this grape can provide. But, most significantly, it is a soft, sunny, elegant and properly concentrated wine. It's a minor masterpiece that gives us a notion of the intentions of a winery that has by now established a place for itself in the top ranks of Sicilian wine-making. The Cerasuolo di Vittoria '96 is very interesting as well, although '96 was not such a successful vintage as the following one, and we should have a better idea of what this wine can offer next year when the '97 is released. To complete their range they offer Inzolia '97, a well-made typical local white, and Milaro '97, which, until recently, was perhaps their best-known wine, but now can't keep pace with the two Cerasuolos.

	Wine	Rating	Price
●	Frappato '97	🍷🍷	2*
●	Cerasuolo di Vittoria '96	🍷	3
○	Inzolia '97	🍷	2
●	Milaro '97	🍷	3
○	Bidis '95	♀	2*
○	Bidis '96	♀	2*
●	Cerasuolo di Vittoria '94	♀	2*
●	Cerasuolo di Vittoria '95	♀	2*
●	Cerasuolo di Vittoria Frappato '95	♀	2*
●	Cerasuolo di Vittoria Frappato '96	♀	2*

ALCAMO (TP)

ANTONINO MELIA
VIA ENEA, 18
91011 ALCAMO (TP)
TEL. 0924/507860

The adventurous and rather romantic side of viticulture sometimes seems most interesting, particularly for those of our readers who are wine lovers rather than wine professionals. And there certainly is enough and to spare of a pioneering sort of adventure in the history of this tiny estate, the property of Antonino Melia, a farmer, who is assisted by his two brothers, Giuseppe, an oenologist, and Vincenzo, an agronomist (and the director of experimentation in viticulture and viniculture at the Istituto Regionale della Vite e del Vino). Of course it's true that the three brothers are professionals in their respective fields. But it must be emphasized that wine-making is, as it were, a hobby for them. At the moment they have at their disposal a "full" two hectares of vines, from which they produce no fewer than 13 thousand bottles of a red wine that struck us as outstanding. It's called Ceuso and is a vintage '96. It's a "Sicilian-Bordeaux" blend of nero d'Avola, merlot and cabernet sauvignon. Vinification took place in their garage (but now they have acquired a nineteenth-century vessel which has been transformed into a modern winery) and the wine was aged for slightly over a year in Allier oak barriques. The result is an enormous success. Ceuso '96 has a concentrated ruby color, intense aromas of berries, especially blackberry and raspberry, and of vanilla, and it's soft and harmonious on the palate, with a satisfying thickness. The tannins are decidedly sweet - not at all agressive, and the only trouble is that there's so little of it. Vincenzo Melia, the agronomist brother, swears by the '97, which is still in the barrel. He says it will be even better. We shall see.

	Wine	Rating	Price
●	Ceuso '96	🍷🍷	5

CASTELBUONO (PA)

Abbazia Sant'Anastasia
C.da Santa Anastasia
90013 Castelbuono (PA)
tel. 0921/671959

We were sure that great wines could flow from the vineyards of Sant'Anastasia which dominate the coast at the point where the provinces of Messina and Palermo meet. These are lands where the exposure is perfect, the sun constant and the light enchanting, particularly when, as often, there is a dramatic sunset on the sea. We never imagined, however, that it could happen so soon. Hence when we discovered that the cabernet sauvignon that had held the field in blind tastings, receiving higher grades than Italy's greatest stars, was none other than Sant'Anastasia's Litra '96, we ourselves were stunned. It is a great Mediterranean red, rich and soft, with intense, ample, and enticing aromas, quite free of vegetal nuances. Its attack is majestic and the finish of exceptional length. The tannins are completely integrated in a velvety texture. The languid roundness of its body could not but inspire passion. More than a wine, this is a dream. The other wines on their list are also among the best in the region. The Passomaggio '96 made from nero d'Avola and merlot, the Baccante '97 from chardonnay and the Santa Anastasia Rosso '96, from nero d'Avola, are all exceptional. And the Zurrica '97 and the Cinquegrani '96, which is delicately sweet, are both good too. This rising star has become a brilliant presence in the Sicilian wine firmament.

	Wine	Glasses	Price
●	Litra '96	▼▼▼	5
○	Baccante '97	▼▼	5
●	Passomaggio '96	▼▼	4
●	Santa Anastasia Rosso '96	▼▼	3
○	Zurrica '97	▼▼	3
○	Cinquegrani '96	▼	4
●	Passomaggio '95	▽▽	4
●	Santa Anastasia Rosso '95	▽	3

CASTELDACCIA (PA)

Duca di Salaparuta - Vini Corvo
Via Nazionale, S. S. 113
90014 Casteldaccia (PA)
tel. 091/945111 - 02/77399211

Corvo, to wine aficionados all over the world, means Sicilian wine. This is true not only because this famous winery is owned by the Region of Sicily itself, but also because in its many years of activity it has become as well-known as any other Italian producer. At the moment, Corvo is going through a period of transition. The new management, although it does include some people with experience at the highest levels at Corvo, is just settling in. And in these situations it takes a year or two before everything runs perfectly smoothly again. All this serves to explain why this year, for the first time, the Duca Enrico '93, their great red made from nero d'Avola, has not received Three Glasses. It is a little less concentrated, a little more forward than usual. This is not to say that it isn't an excellent wine. It is just not the great champion we are used to. We are sure that this is merely a brief interlude, not least because their red Terre d'Agala '94, made from the frappato grape, is better than ever. It is intensely fruity to the nose, and wonderfully balanced in the mouth. The good Colomba Platino '97 is fragrant and easy to drink. The workhorses of the firm, the Corvo Bianco '97, the Glicine '97 and the Rosso '96, are well-made and reliable. No Bianca di Valguarnera, on the other hand, at least at present. The '95 was not yet available when we went to press.

	Wine	Glasses	Price
○	Corvo Colomba Platino '97	▼▼	3
●	Duca Enrico '93	▼▼	6
●	Terre d'Agala '94	▼▼	3
○	Corvo Bianco '97	▼	2*
○	Corvo Glicine '97	▼	2*
●	Corvo Rosso '96	▼	2*
●	Duca Enrico '84	▽▽▽	6
●	Duca Enrico '85	▽▽▽	6
●	Duca Enrico '86	▽▽▽	6
●	Duca Enrico '87	▽▽▽	6
●	Duca Enrico '88	▽▽▽	6
●	Duca Enrico '90	▽▽▽	6
●	Duca Enrico '92	▽▽▽	6
○	Bianca di Valguarnera '94	▽▽	4

CATANIA

BARONE SCAMMACCA DEL MURGO
P.ZZA SCAMMACCA, 1
95131 CATANIA
TEL. 095/7130090

The '95 version of Tenuta San Michele is one the best, if not "the" best version ever made, and seems almost to celebrate the presence of this lovely and important Etna estate in the Guide. It matters very little that the wine is made from cabernet sauvignon and not from local varieties. The wine itself is sufficient to silence any grumbling on this point. The Tenuta San Michele '95 has complex, slightly mature and intensely seductive aromas with light vegetal nuances. It tastes well-balanced, elegant and forthright, with its body well sustained by its unaggressive tannins. This is a very good wine indeed. The two Etnas have less character. The Bianco '97 seems somewhat less concentrated and aromatic than the '96 and especially the '95, which was its best vintage so far. The Rosso '96, suffering perhaps as a result of the infelicitous year, is, nonetheless, honest and correct, although we feel we ought to say that we expect more from this winery. We'll have to wait for the Rosso '97, to be released next year, to see what their intentions are. That is, are they going to make a fit companion for their excellent Tenuta San Michele, or are they going to opt for a lighter and easily drinkable Etna Rosso?

	Wine	Rating	Price
●	Tenuta San Michele '95	🍷🍷	4
○	Etna Bianco '97	🍷	2
●	Etna Rosso '96	🍷	3
○	Etna Bianco '95	🍸🍸	2*
●	Tenuta San Michele '92	🍸🍸	4
●	Tenuta San Michele '94	🍸🍸	4
○	Etna Bianco '96	🍸	2*
●	Etna Rosso '93	🍸	3
●	Etna Rosso '94	🍸	3
●	Etna Rosso '91	🍸	3
●	Tenuta San Michele '91	🍸	4
●	Tenuta San Michele '93	🍸	4

COMISO (RG)

VITIVINICOLA AVIDE
C.DA MENDOLILLA
S. P. 7 KM 1.5
97013 COMISO (RG)
TEL. 0932/967456

This winery, situated near Ragusa in the deep south of the island, is back in the Guide after a year's absence. And it makes its return with a list of good wines, perhaps the best selection they've ever presented. As usual, their most interesting wine is the Vigne d'Oro, a chardonnay aged in small barrels. The '96 has delicate scents of vanilla and a soft and concentrated taste, much as one would expect of a chardonnay from these parts. Furthermore, it is sold at a very reasonable price. Their flagship wine, however, is still the Cerasuolo di Vittoria Etichetta Nera '96. It is an enticing wine, with clearly presented fruity tones, and, in its uncomplicated fashion, pleasantly easy to drink. The white Dalle Terre di Herea Bianco, vintage '97, continues to be a decent wine, but the Cerasuolo di Vittoria Barocco '94, like its predecessors, leaves something to be desired. It seems to have gone too far in ripeness, and to be less immediate and elegant than the normal version.

	Wine	Rating	Price
○	Vigne d'Oro '96	🍷🍷	3*
●	Cerasuolo di Vittoria Barocco '94	🍷	4
●	Cerasuolo di Vittoria Etichetta Nera '96	🍷	2*
○	Dalle Terre di Herea Bianco '97	🍷	2*
●	Cerasuolo di Vittoria Barocco '91	🍸	4
●	Cerasuolo di Vittoria Barocco '92	🍸	4
●	Cerasuolo di Vittoria Barocco '93	🍸	4
●	Cerasuolo di Vittoria Etichetta Nera '95	🍸	2
○	Vigne d'Oro '94	🍸	2*

LICATA (AG)

Barone La Lumia

Fraz. Pozzillo
92027 Licata (AG)
tel. 0922/891709

Our impressions from last year have been confirmed. This is certainly one of the most traditional wineries on the island, and its wines are like the products of another era. The Signorio Rosso '94 has the characteristics that the greatest Sicilian wines of the 19th century were meant to have. Its aromas are somewhat forward but still intense and enticing, and it is full-bodied but a bit harsh, as nero d'Avola wines tend to be. It is generously alcoholic and long-lasting, but is not perfectly balanced, and its acidity is not well integrated. Nevertheless, we are reluctant to be excessively critical because of its territorial fidelity and loyal adherence to local traditions, which make it seem like a precious relic from Noah's Ark. The Signorio Bianco '97 is also decent, offering ripe fruity aromas, and then good body with a final touch of bitterness in the mouth. There are two new wines. One is the red Stemma '97 which is pleasantly easy to drink, and surprisingly modern when one considers where it was made. The other, their Cadetto '95, also a red, is much less satisfactory. It has the faults but not the virtues of the Signorio, and definitely seems a lesser wine. All of their wines are still excellent value for money.

	Wine	Rating	Price
○	Signorio Bianco '97	🍷	2
●	Signorio Rosso '94	🍷	3
●	Stemma '97	🍷	2*
●	Cadetto '95		2
○	Signorio Bianco '95	🍸	2
●	Signorio Rosso '93	🍸	3

MARSALA (TP)

Alvis - Rallo

Via Vincenzo Florio, 2
91025 Marsala (TP)
tel. 0923/721633 - 721635

Alvis of Marsala last year bought both the brand name and the historic reserves of marsala from Rallo, one of the most prestigious local producers. So this year, in addition to the wines in their Vesco line, they have presented some excellent marsalas. The best one, it seems to us, is the Marsala Superiore Ambra Semisecco which should do much to renew the good name of the legendary Rallo. Our hopes and good wishes are, obviously, that the new owners will know how to relaunch this winery, and the first signs are encouraging. The two wines of the Vesco line, not marsalas, are both good and have been technically well made. The Bianco '97 is lightly fruity in its aroma and offers a bit of carbon dioxide in the mouth. We preferred the Vesco Rosso '96 which is correctly executed and has a certain amount of body and reasonable length. The Arete '97, made from müller thurgau, is light, drinkable, and unpretentious.

	Wine	Rating	Price
○	Marsala Sup. Ambra Semisecco	🍷	3*
○	Vesco Bianco '97	🍷	3
●	Vesco Rosso '96	🍷	4
○	Areté '97		1

MARSALA (TP)

MARCO DE BARTOLI
C.DA FORNARA, 292
91025 MARSALA (TP)
TEL. 0923/962093 - 918344

Marco De Bartoli is a perfect romantic hero. He puts himself at risk, courageously says exactly what he thinks, and pays the consequences out of his own pocket. One of which is that he doesn't make a lot of friends. He is going through a difficult moment now, since a mistake in paperwork drew the attention of the tax collectors, and the situation doesn't seem to have been as easily resolved as we had hoped. It is strange, certainly, that the partial shut-down of his winery governmentally ordered three years ago has not yet been rescinded, and that all Marco's efforts to resolve matters have up to now been vain. We certainly hope that the difficulties are only bureaucratic, and not a legal vendetta. Despite all his troubles, Marco continues to produce wine, especially at Pantelleria, and he seems, this year, to have returned to being a leading figure in the local world of wine. The Vecchio Samperi Riserva 30 Anni is extraordinary, although there are not many half bottles available of this star among Italian solera-method wines. His Pietranera '97, a dry white made from zibbibo, is very good. We found it particularly striking for its aromas of lemon grass and ginger, and its elegantly well-balanced taste. The always delightful Moscato Passito di Pantelleria Bukkuram is sweet and concentrated, and we also fully approve of the standard version of the Vecchio Samperi, and, perhaps especially, of the Vigna La Miccia, now that it is no longer a "light" version of a marsala, but a splendidly strong and dry wine that goes extremely well with Italy's best cheeses.

	Wine	Rating	Price
○	Moscato Passito di Pantelleria Bukkuram	▼▼	4
○	Pietranera '97	▼▼	4
○	Vecchio Samperi	▼▼	4
○	Vecchio Samperi Ris. 30 Anni Solera	▼▼	6
○	Vigna La Miccia	▼▼	4
○	Marsala Sup. Oro Vigna La Miccia '90	▽▽	4
○	Marsala Sup. Oro Vigna La Miccia '91	▽▽	4
○	Marsala Superiore	▽▽	4
○	Moscato Passito di Pantelleria '91	▽▽	5
○	Vecchio Samperi Ris. 20 Anni Solera	▽▽	5

MARSALA (TP)

TENUTA DI DONNAFUGATA
VIA SEBASTIANO LIPARI, 18
91025 MARSALA (TP)
TEL. 0923/999555

We can't review the best wine from this estate because it won't be released until the second half of next year. It is a splendid vintage '95 red made from nero d'Avola and cabernet sauvignon and bearing the suggestive name Mille e una Notte (a thousand and one nights). It is one of the best Sicilian wines ever made, in our opinion, but it still is a bit rough. With a few more months in the bottle it will be a little gem. But all the wines made this year at Donnafugata are better than they have ever been before. The Tancredi '96, another nero d'Avola and cabernet sauvignon blend, is excellent, and more harmonious and concentrated than in previous versions. The very successful Passito di Pantelleria Ben Ryé '97 is redolent of india ink and apricot, and is particularly elegant and not at all cloying in the mouth, although it is not quite as concentrated as we might have hoped. The Chiarandà del Merlo '96, a chardonnay that has spent some time in barrique, doesn't have the body of the '95, but it is elegant and not overcome by its acquired scents of vanilla. The acceptable Chardonnay La Fuga and Vigna di Gabri are both Contessa Entellina DOCs and vintage '97s. They are a bit more forward than the '96s, but they also have more body. The Lighea '97 is a less ambitious and lighter wine, but certainly correctly made.

	Wine	Rating	Price
○	Chiarandà del Merlo '96	▼▼	4
○	Passito di Pantelleria Ben Ryé '97	▼▼	5
●	Tancredi '96	▼▼	5
○	Contessa Entellina Chardonnay La Fuga '97	▼	4
○	Contessa Entellina Vigna di Gabri '97	▼	3
○	Moscato di Pantelleria '97	▼	3
○	Lighea '97		2
○	Chiarandà del Merlo '93	▽▽	4
○	Chiarandà del Merlo '94	▽▽	4
○	Chiarandà del Merlo '95	▽▽	4
○	Contessa Entellina Vigna di Gabri '96	▽▽	3

MARSALA (TP)

Vinicola Italiana Florio
Via Vincenzo Florio, 1
91025 Marsala (TP)
tel. 0923/781111

There are very few wine-makers whose names are indissolubly linked to the wines they produce. A prime example is Florio and its marsala. This historic and splendid winery is one of the very last still working to preserve and improve the great tradition of marsala wines, a tradition which has been threatening to go under in recent years as a result of the ultimately self-defeating policies of many of its producers. As a result, marsala has been reduced, for many people, to being a "cooking wine". Fortunately there are still some who aim to make great classic marsalas, like Florio's prestigious Vergine Oro Baglio Florio first of all, but also their Vergine Terre Arse and Superiore Targa. And they produce a fine and inexpensive standard marsala, Marsala Superiore Vecchioflorio. These are the best made and most reliable wines in this area, and they stand comparison with their great counterparts from other lands, like sherry, white port and madeira. The sweet Morsi di Luce '95 is worthy of special attention. It is well-balanced, not at all cloying and very interesting. We found it among the very best wines made from overripe or sun-dried muscat grapes.

	Wine	Rating	Price
○	Marsala Sup. Targa Ris. '89	🍷🍷	4
○	Marsala Vergine Terre Arse '87	🍷🍷	4
○	Morsi di Luce '95	🍷🍷	4
○	Marsala Sup. Vecchioflorio '94	🍷	3*
○	Marsala Soleras Oro Baglio Florio '79	ΥΥ	6
○	Marsala Sup. Targa Ris. '88	ΥΥ	4
○	Marsala Vergine Baglio Florio '85	ΥΥ	5
○	Marsala Vergine Baglio Florio '86	ΥΥ	5
○	Marsala Vergine Terre Arse '86	ΥΥ	4

MARSALA (TP)

Carlo Pellegrino
Via del Fante, 37/39
91025 Marsala (TP)
tel. 0923/951177

By far the most interesting wine this year from this producer is the Gorgo Tondo Rosso '96, a blend of cabernet sauvignon and various other red grapes. It has fairly complex aromas with hints of grass and wild berries, and a well-supported full body with an acidity that doesn't disturb the balance. The Cent'Are Bianco '97, a white made from grecanico, and the Cent'Are Rosso '95, made from various local red grapes, are both pleasant and well-made, if not particularly complex. The Alcamo Fiorile '97 is not as interesting as usual. Like most other Sicilian whites this year, it has developed too quickly and seems somewhat heavy. Their Marsala Vergine Soleras della Pellegrino is reliable as always and quite a bargain. Everything this winery offers, as a matter of fact, tends to be very good value for money.

	Wine	Rating	Price
●	Gorgo Tondo Rosso '96	🍷🍷	3*
○	Cent'Are Bianco '97	🍷	3
●	Cent'Are Rosso '95	🍷	3
○	Marsala Vergine Soleras	🍷	3
○	Alcamo Fiorile '97		2
○	Marsala Vergine Vintage '62	ΥΥ	5
○	Alcamo Duca di Castelmonte '95	Υ	2*
●	Cent'Are '92	Υ	3
●	Etna Rosso Duca di Castelmonte '92	Υ	2
●	Etna Rosso Ulysse '94	Υ	3
○	Fiorile Bianco '96	Υ	2*
●	Fiorile Rosso '95	Υ	2*
○	Marsala Superiore	Υ	3
○	Moscato di Pantelleria '94	Υ	3

MENFI (AG)

Settesoli
S. S. 115
92013 Menfi (AG)
tel. 0925/75255

The best news about what this important Sicilian wine cooperative has presented this year is that Il Feudo dei Fiori '97 has easily bagged Two Glasses. Made from chardonnay and inzolia, it is a delicious white wine, soft and fruity, and easy to drink but full of character. It could well become the flagship of this excellently run winery. This result is particularly encouraging because it was not an easy year for making white wines in Sicily. Hence the signs of progress at Settesoli that we noticed last year are abundantly confirmed. The good Bonera '94, their leading red, is made from nero d'Avola and cabernet sauvignon. Tasted again this year, it again displayed good structure and a certain complexity, but perhaps also a little too much wood. The acceptable Porto Palo Bianco '97 , made from equal parts of inzolia and catarratto, is a lighter and simpler wine than the Feudo dei Fiori, and has some aromas of fermentation. In conclusion, we would like to underline what a wonderful bargain all their wines are.

○	Feudo dei Fiori '97	🍷🍷	2*
○	Porto Palo Bianco '97	🍷	2*
●	Bonera '94	🍷🍷	3*
○	Feudo dei Fiori '96	🍷	2*
○	Porto Palo '96	🍷	2
●	Soltero Rosso '95	🍷	2*

MESSINA

Palari
Loc. S. Stefano Briga
98123 Messina
tel. 090/694281

Have you heard of the man who restored his family's 17th century villa only to turn it into a winery? Who has put the fermentation vats in what was once the drawing-room and stores the wine in the former rooms for guests? Well, it's Salvatore Geraci, an architect from Messina who is also (need we say it?) a passionate winegrower. He conscripted his younger brother, Piero, as his expert cellar master, and enlisted the Piedmontese wine guru, Donato Lanati, as consultant oenologist, and with their help he has made a DOC wine, Faro di Messina, which almost no one knows and which was in danger of extinction. His version is called Faro Palari and the '96 has walked off with Three Glasses. He only makes a few thousand bottles a year, and they are extraordinary. Made from nerello mascalese, nerello cappuccio and calabrese, it has an intense and seductive bouquet with hints of sour cherries and raspberries and faint vanilla notes in the background. It is soft and velvety, innocent of harshness, and generously round and rich in extract, with a harmony well underpinned by its gentle tannins. And then it's a wine that expresses its "terroir", a true child of the vineyards of Santo Stefano Briga, between Messina and Taormina on the foothills of the Pelorian mountains, dominating the sea and looking across the Straits of Messina to Aspromonte. Second fiddle to this great Mediterranean red is the Rosso del Soprano '96. It comes from the same grapes and vines, but is aged in barriques discarded by Geraci and Lanati. It is a little less concentrated, but otherwise very hard to tell from its older brother.

●	Faro Palari '96	🍷🍷🍷	5
●	Rosso del Soprano '96	🍷🍷	4
●	Faro Palari '94	🍷🍷	5
●	Faro Palari '95	🍷🍷	5
●	Rosso del Soprano '95	🍷🍷	4

MONREALE (PA)

I.VI.COR.

C.DA MALVELLO
90046 MONREALE (PA)
TEL. 091/8462922

I.VI.COR presented four wines for our tasting, and each one received One Glass. This cellar, already quite well known in Sicily has been quite successful commercially with its Principe di Corleone line. Of the wines we tasted, the best one we found to be their Pinot Bianco '97. It is fruity and varietal to the nose, and pleasant and easy to drink. Almost as good, and the best Alcamo of the year, is their Alcamo Principe di Corleone '97. It is very well made, has clean, fruity aromas, and is light-bodied but not at all prickly or rustic. We can say almost the same thing about the Chardonnay Vigna di Corte '97, but had hoped that it would have had more complexity since it seems to be a special selection. It's pleasantly fruity but doesn't have any body to speak of. The Cabernet Sauvignon '96 seems a bit old and sour to the nose, but is softer and quite drinkable in the mouth. Taken all together, this is a quite satisfactory effort, particularly in the way the fermentation and aging were done. What we hope for, though, are wines with more depth and body.

	Wine	Glass	Price
○	Alcamo Principe di Corleone '97	🍷	2*
●	Cabernet Sauvignon Principe di Corleone '96	🍷	3
○	Chardonnay V. di Corte Principe di Corleone '97	🍷	2
○	Pinot Bianco Principe di Corleone '97	🍷	2*
○	Alcamo Principe di Corleone '94	🍷 (empty)	2

PALERMO

M.I.D.

VIA AMMIRAGLIO
SALVATORE DENTI DI PIRAINO, 7
90142 PALERMO
TEL. 091/6396111

M.I.D. stands for Miceli Ignazio Distribuzione. For those who know nothing about Ignazio Miceli, who died last September, it is perhaps sufficient to say that he not only contributed decisively to the success of Count Tasca d'Almerita's wines, particularly Regaleali Bianco and Rosso, on the world market, but, in effect, invented the marketing of wines of high quality in Sicily. Thus he was a key figure in the Sicilian wine world, and he also founded a very up-to-date winery in Palermo, putting paid once and for all to the idea that such a thing couldn't be done in the backward south. For some years M.I.D has not been limiting itself to distributing Regaleali wines throughout Italy and selling many other great Italian wines in Sicily, but has also been producing wines of its own, almost all Sicilia IGTs, which are great value for money. With a series of these well-made and reliable wines, M.I.D. has earned its place in the Guide. We find their Garighe '97 particularly noteworthy. Made from a filtered and partially fermented must obtained from the zibibbo grape, it contains only 3% alcohol and is aromatic, sweet and delicious. By law it can't be called wine, because it isn't strong enough, but it's the law that seems defective here and not this delectable liquid. The Moscato Passito di Pantelleria Tanit is a label which had been abandoned and which Miceli successfully revived. Last of all, the light and fruity Bianco d'Alcamo '97 is decidedly acceptable.

	Wine	Glass	Price
○	Bianco d'Alcamo '97	🍷	1*
○	Garighe Zibibbo '97	🍷	2*
○	Grecanico '97	🍷	1*
○	Moscato Passito di Pantelleria Tanit	🍷	3
○	Inzolia '97		1
●	Nero d'Avola '96		2

PALERMO

RAPITALÀ ADELKAM
VIA SEGESTA, 9
90141 PALERMO
TEL. 091/332088

We can essentially confirm the good review we gave last year to Rapitalà, one of the largest and most famous wineries in Sicily. The only real difference is that their Alcamo Rapitalà Grand Cru '96 is not quite as successful as the '95. It seems a bit forward to the nose, and is a bit shorter on the palate. But this is, of course, not worrying, since vintages vary, as we all know. The acceptable Alcamo Rapitalà '97 is not very concentrated, but is well-made, delicately fruity and medium-bodied. The Rapitalà Rosso '97, which we found better than the '96, is light, easy to drink, fragrant and finely fruity. It is, as it were, a Sicilian Beaujolais-Villages. The Chardonnay '97 is a quaffable white that seems to have no particular ambitions, except to be a good example of a properly made light wine.

○	Alcamo Rapitalà '97	▼	3
○	Alcamo Rapitalà Grand Cru '96	▼	4
●	Rapitalà Rosso '96	▼	3
○	Chardonnay '97		3
○	Alcamo Rapitalà Grand Cru '95	YY	4
○	Alcamo Rapitalà '96	Y	3
●	Rapitalà Rosso '95	Y	3

PALERMO

SPADAFORA
VIA A. DE GASPERI, 58
90146 PALERMO
TEL. 091/514952 - 518544

This was a very difficult year for Sicilian whites, or so it seemed from our tastings, which inspired us to write positive reviews of exceedingly few of them. Spadafora was not immune to the vagaries of the vintage, so we have decided not to discuss their whites this year, but to put our faith in the future, consoling ourselves meanwhile with the umpty-umpth excellent version of their Don Pietro Rosso, the '96. Made from nero d'Avola, cabernet sauvignon and merlot, it evinces its customary breeding. Intense aromas that include lightly balsamic notes and vanilla, and a good full flavor, lots of body and vegetal notes on the finish characterize this wine that, after a string of successes, seems to be a sure thing. The classic young and light Vigna Virzì '97 is less concentrated and persistent, but then it only aspires to easy drinkability. Some news, to close: starting with the '98 vintage, Spadafora will have the assistance of the very promising young Tuscan oenologist Luca D'Attoma.

●	Don Pietro Rosso '96	▼▼	3*
●	Vigna Virzì Rosso '97		2
●	Don Pietro Rosso '95	YY	3*
○	Alcamo '96	Y	1*
○	Alcamo Vigna Virzì '95	Y	1*
○	Alcamo Vigna Virzì '96	Y	2*
○	Don Pietro Bianco '94	Y	2
○	Don Pietro Bianco '96	Y	2*
●	Don Pietro Rosso '94	Y	3
●	Vigna Virzì Rosso '95	Y	2*

PALERMO

CANTINE TORREVECCHIA
VIA LUDOVICO ARIOSTO, 10/A
90144 PALERMO
TEL. 091/342208

Torrevecchia, which is getting better and better, has clearly become established as one of the best wineries in the region. The most impressive of their excellent wines is, as usual, the Casale dei Biscari '95. Made solely from nero d'Avola, a grape that is at its best in southeastern Sicily, it has intensely concentrated aromas with hints of spice and notes of sour cherry and ripe plum. Its taste is full and persistent, with a slight residual acidic bite well balanced by plenty of extract. This is a very good red which should just get better with age. Their admirable Bianco Biscari '96, made mostly from chardonnay and matured in small barrels, has excellent body, and exemplifies the softness and concentrated richness that this grape can offer in a Mediterranean environment. The Pietra di Zoe '97, made from frappato, another typical local grape, has interestingly complex aromas, including notes of ripe red fruit, and is fairly substantial and balanced in the mouth. Further whites, the Inzolia '97 and the Chardonnay '97, both Sicilia IGTs, are quite good, completing a really attractive range of wines, which are also notable for being excellent value for money.

	Wine	Glasses	Price
○	Bianco Biscari '96	▼▼	3*
●	Casale dei Biscari '95	▼▼	3*
○	Chardonnay '97	▼	2*
○	Inzolia '97	▼	2*
●	Pietra di Zoe '97	▼	2*
●	Casale dei Biscari '93	▽▽	3*
●	Casale dei Biscari '94	▽▽	3*
●	Cerasuolo di Vittoria '94	▽	2*
●	Cerasuolo di Vittoria '92	▽	2
●	Pietra di Zoe '96	▽	2*

PANTELLERIA (TP)

SALVATORE MURANA
C.DA KHAMMA, 276
91017 PANTELLERIA (TP)
TEL. 0923/915231

Salvatore Murana, Pantelleria fireman and prince of local winegrowers, has given us another unforgettable wine, the vintage '94 of his Moscato Passito from his Martingana vineyard. It is a dream captured in the bottle, and one of the greatest sweet wines of the world. What does one ask of a great sweet wine? It should have structure and not be cloying, it should offer, together with a concentrated sweetness, a complex bouquet with aromas given it by its "noble rot", and it should age well. This Martingana excels in all these ways. Its perfumes of dried apricots and dates, its opulent and sweet palate of exceptional fullness and length place it among the world's greatest wines, and, it goes without saying, earn it our Three Glasses. Murana's other "cru", the Khamma '94, is very nearly as good, and answers the complexity of the Martingana with a more aromatic bouquet and a leaner body. His Mueggen '97, an aromatic triumph, is a Moscato too, but made from the grapes when ripe but not dried. It is simpler and, of course, less concentrated. The Moscato di Pantelleria Turbè '97, the lightest and most up-front of all, and the Gadì '97, an aromatic only just semi-sweet white, made from zibibbo (as are all Moscato di Pantelleria wines, if it comes to that), complete this list of superlative wines.

	Wine	Glasses	Price
○	Moscato Passito di Pantelleria Martingana '94	▼▼▼	6
○	Moscato Passito di Pantelleria Khamma '94	▼▼	6
○	Moscato Passito di Pantelleria Martingana '89	▼▼	6
○	Moscato Passito di Pantelleria Mueggen '97	▼▼	5
○	Gadì '97	▼	3
○	Moscato di Pantelleria Turbè '97	▼	4
○	Moscato Passito di Pantelleria Martingana '93	▽▽▽	6
○	Moscato Passito di Pantelleria Khamma '93	▽▽	6

PANTELLERIA (TP)

D'Ancona

C.da Cimilia
91017 Pantelleria (TP)
tel. 0923/918350

If there should ever be a movement to save traditional wines, those that are still produced in the traditional ways, as they were centuries ago, Giacomo and Solidea D'Ancona's Moscato Passito di Pantelleria will have absolutely to be among those chosen. Their wine constitutes one of those extremely rare cases in which an old-fashioned craftsmanlike approach to the wine-making process and an extraordinarily high quality of wines produced go hand in hand. At this year's tastings we found their wines even better than those we described in the last edition of the Guide. The Moscato Passito di Pantelleria in particular seemed yet richer and more concentrated, superior even to their special selection, the Solidea '95. This latter wine is a bit too forward, and is forced to face the world in an appallingly hyper-modern bottle altogether out of keeping with the style of this excellent tiny winery with an annual production of 9 thousand bottles. The Moscato di Pantelleria made of undried grapes is excellent, and the Bianco Sciuvaki '97, a very slightly sweet white made from zibibbo, which offers elegant aromas and lots of body, is a very pleasant surprise.

	Wine	Rating	Price
○	Bianco Scuvaki '97	🍷🍷	3*
○	Moscato di Pantelleria	🍷🍷	3*
○	Moscato Passito di Pantelleria	🍷🍷	3
○	Moscato Passito di Pantelleria Solidea '95	🍷🍷	5
○	Moscato Passito di Pantelleria Solidea '93	♀♀	5
○	Scirocco '96	♀♀	2*
○	Bianco Sciuvaki '96	♀	3

ROSOLINI (SR)

Cooperativa Interprovinciale Elorina

Via Bellini, 17
96019 Rosolini (SR)
tel. 0931/857068

The vineyards of nero d'avola, gobelet-trained and planted with at least 6 thousand vines per hectare, are a characteristic of the landscape for those who take the main road from Noto to Pachino and on to Portopalo and Capo Passero. Vines have grown here since time immemorial, or at least as long as the olive and the prickly pear, but we have seldom had the opportunity to taste a red from these parts that was not just a strong wine to be used for blending. However, for the last few years the admirable Elorina wine cooperative has quietly been producing wines from vineyards between Syracuse and Ragusa that are of notable quality. The most surprising of these is a red wine impenetrable to the eye and blessed with aromas of sour cherry jam and oriental spices. Mouth-filling and perhaps a bit rustic, it has great depth and exceptional concentration. This Pachino red, their Eloro Pachino '96, is literally astounding. If a bit more attention were paid to its vinification and maturation this wine would be comparable to Penfolds Grange or Guigal's Côte-Rotie La Turque. It's not just chance that these are two great examples of syrah wines, and they would seem to confirm the hypothesis that the name of the grape comes, not from the Persian city Shiraz, but from the ancient local city, Siracusa. And also that nero d'Avola is not very different from that highly prized and world-famous grape. Their other wine, the Eloro Rosso '96, is simpler and less concentrated, and is a blend of nero d'Avola, frappato and perricone.

	Wine	Rating	Price
●	Eloro Rosso Pachino '96	🍷🍷	4
●	Eloro Rosso '96	🍷	3
●	Eloro Rosso Pachino '95	♀	4

S. CIPIRELLO (PA)

CALATRASI - TERRE DI GINESTRA
C.DA PIANO PIRAINO
90040 S. CIPIRELLO (PA)
TEL. 091/8576767 - 8578080

Terre di Ginestra has acquired a partner, Calatrasi, and is back in the Guide in great style. They offer, of course, a number of decently made wines at exceptionally good prices. Their sangiovese and nero d'Avola blend, Terre di Ginestra Rosso '96, is perfectly acceptable, as usual. But what really struck us this year was their new line, which they call "D'Istinto". The Bianco '97 made from catarratto is simple but correct. Then the Catarratto/Chardonnay '97 is more intense in aroma and has more weight in the mouth. The Nero d'Avola/Nerello Mascalese '97 is immediately pleasing, and the other red, the Sangiovese/Merlot '97 is far more concentrated and muscular. Let's get back to the Terre di Ginestra range, to what we consider their best wine this year, the Pelavet Rosso '95, a blend of nero d'Avola, cabernet and syrah. It is rich and elegant on the nose, and has an especially intense and concentrated palate. But apart from the individual wines of this winery and their particular qualities, what is most encouraging to us is the strategy apparently underlying all their activity. It involves a search for innovative techniques, better and more up-to-date styles both in the varietals chosen and in the vinification and aging processes. The success of their wines on the international market, particularly in America, has had positive effects on their way of thinking. This is a fact that is worthy of further reflection.

	Wine	Glasses	Price
●	Pelavet Rosso '95	🍷🍷	4
○	D'Istinto Bianco '97	🍷	3
○	D'Istinto Catarratto/Chardonnay '97	🍷	3
●	D'Istinto Nero d'Avola Nerello Mascalese '97	🍷	3
●	D'Istinto Sangiovese/Merlot '97	🍷	3
●	Terre di Ginestra Rosso '96	🍷	2*
○	Terra di Ginestra Bianco '94	🍸	2
●	Terre di Ginestra Rosso '93	🍸	2

SALINA (ME)

HAUNER
FRAZ. LINGUA DI SALINA
98050 SALINA (ME)
TEL. 090/9843141

We are very happy to welcome back into the Guide this small but famous winery on the island of Salina. Several years after the death of its founder, the unforgettable Carlo Hauner, his heirs are continuing in his footsteps and have succeeded in creating a Malvasia delle Lipari Passita '96 that went all the way to the finals for Three Glasses. Although it didn't make it in the end, the fact of its getting that far is, we feel, an important sign of the quality of a winery that many people had stopped taking seriously. Instead, here they are again, those scents of dried apricot, those balsamic notes and that sweet and aromatic taste which have always characterized the Hauner Malvasia delle Lipari in its best years. It was like coming upon a dear old friend we hadn't seen for years: a great pleasure. And then the Malvasia '96 was not their only good wine this year. For the first time the Salina Bianco '97, from catarratto grapes, and the Salina Rosso '96, a blend of various nerellos, seemed quite good. These are well-made wines, free of any signs of the oxidation and overripeness which got in the way of our pleasure in the recent past. We hope the Hauner heirs continue confidently along this path.

	Wine	Glasses	Price
○	Malvasia delle Lipari Passita '96	🍷🍷	5
○	Salina Bianco '97	🍷	3
●	Salina Rosso '96	🍷	3
○	Malvasia delle Lipari Passita '95	🍸🍸	5
○	Malvasia delle Lipari Naturale '95	🍸	4

SAMBUCA DI SICILIA (AG)

PLANETA

C.DA ULMO E MARACCOLI
92017 SAMBUCA DI SICILIA (AG)
TEL. 0925/80009

Bingo! Planeta has set Three Glasses to ringing with an "awesome" Chardonnay '96. The aromas are intense and engaging, with well-integrated oak and a touch of ripe fruit (pineapple, banana and white plum) reminiscent of California's great whites, Steve Kistler's, for example, or the Marcassin wines presided over by Helen Turley. Most strikingly, the taste is soft and explosive, persistent, rich and not at all harsh. And then it goes right down, which you might not have expected. It is a masterpiece created by young Chiara, Francesca and Alessio Planeta, with the magic touch of the oenologist Carlo Corino together with Mother Nature herself. But that's not all. The Alastro '96, made from grecanico and catarratto grapes, is greatly superior to last year's version, and the ripe and evolved bouquet is much more elegant. To finish, their two standard wines, La Segreta Rosso '97, from nero d'Avola and merlot, and La Segreta Bianco '97, a blend of grecanico, catarratto and chardonnay, are better than ever. The first is winy and fragrant and has a surprisingly full taste, and the second is soft on the palate and offers delicately fruity aromas. There is no Merlot or Cabernet '96. They have made the difficult and admirable decision not to produce a vintage '96 because they considered the grapes below par. Italy's wine world has just witnessed the birth of a new star.

○	Chardonnay '96	▼▼▼	5
○	Alastro '96	▼▼	4
○	La Segreta Bianco '97	▼▼	3
●	La Segreta Rosso '97	▼▼	3*
●	Cabernet Sauvignon '95	▽▽	5
○	Chardonnay '95	▽▽	5
○	La Segreta Bianco '96	▽▽	3
●	La Segreta Rosso '95	▽▽	3
●	Merlot '95	▽▽	5
○	Alastro '95	▽	5

VALLELUNGA PRATAMENO (CL)

TASCA D'ALMERITA

C.DA REGALEALI
90029 VALLELUNGA PRATAMENO (CL)
TEL. 0921/544011 - 542522

Unfortunately the most important news about this glorious estate right in the center of Sicily is that we have lost its founder and guiding light. Count Giuseppe Tasca d'Almerita died last spring, and with his departure an entire era has come to a close. The winery is now in the hands of his son Lucio, who has inherited a sort of two-edged sword, since his father, a man of great character and extraordinary wine-making ability, is a hard act to follow. This brings us to the wine. This year Three Glasses go to the Cabernet Sauvignon '95, a great red of international style which has become a Regaleali classic. It's a wine with a nose of extraordinary concentration, and it has succeeded in combining the ripe and enticing qualities of a Mediterranean cabernet with the classic grip and elegance of the best Pauillacs. The Chardonnay '96, an excellent wine, is not at the same exalted level. This time the aromas seemed less stylish and the palate less well-balanced than the '95 or, even more, the exceptional '94. The Nozze d'Oro '96, on the other hand, is sensational and reminds us of the glory of the first of its line, the magical '85, which is still perfectly drinkable today. Made from a grape they call sauvignon Tasca at the estate, the new vintage is wonderfully full-bodied and displays delicate, slightly mineral aromas. The Regaleali Bianco '97 is very good, maybe even the best it has been in recent years. As always, the Regaleali Rosso '96 and the Villa Tasca '97, an agreeable light white with a very fair price, are dependable. To conclude, the Regaleali Rosato '97 is the best of its type in Sicily, and one of the best rosés in the country.

●	Cabernet Sauvignon '95	▼▼▼	6
○	Chardonnay '96	▼▼	6
○	Nozze d'Oro '96	▼▼	4
○	Regaleali Bianco '97	▼▼	2*
⊙	Regaleali Rosato '97	▼▼	2*
●	Regaleali Rosso '96	▼	3
○	Villa Tasca '97	▼	2*
●	Cabernet Sauvignon '89	▽▽▽	6
●	Cabernet Sauvignon '90	▽▽▽	6
●	Cabernet Sauvignon '92	▽▽▽	6
○	Chardonnay '92	▽▽▽	6
○	Chardonnay '93	▽▽▽	6
○	Chardonnay '94	▽▽▽	6
○	Chardonnay '95	▽▽▽	6
●	Cabernet Sauvignon '94	▽▽	6

VIAGRANDE (CT)

BENANTI

VIA G. GARIBALDI, 475
95029 VIAGRANDE (CT)
TEL. 095/7893533

Lamoremio '95, a blend of cabernet sauvignon, nero d'Avola and nerello mascalese in very nearly equal parts, is the top of the line this year at Benanti. It's an excellent red with a concentrated and elegant bouquet, intense and particularly well-balanced on the palate thanks to its velvety tannins and well-judged underlying alcohol: an aristocratic wine to complete the ever more interesting range of one of the best wine-makers in the south of Italy. Their very good Etna Rosso Rovittello '95 is less concentrated than the Lamoremio but just as stylish, particularly on the nose. As usual the Etna Bianco Superiore Pietramarina '95 is splendid, and offers noble mineral aromas worthy of a great riesling, even though it is made from the less well-known carricante, widely planted in the Etna area. On the palate it seems to have regained the freshness and elegance whose absence we lamented last year. The littler siblings, the Etna Rosso Rosso di Verzella '95, and the Etna Bianco Bianco di Casselle '96, both DOCs, are no embarrassment to the rest of the family. They are pleasingly well made, without, of course, having the complexity and stature of their older brothers.

○	Etna Bianco Sup. Pietramarina '95	▼▼	4
●	Etna Rosso Rovittello '95	▼▼	5
●	Lamoremio '95	▼▼	5
○	Etna Bianco Bianco di Caselle '96	▼	3
●	Etna Rosso Rosso di Verzella '95	▼	3
○	Etna Bianco Sup. Pietramarina '93	▽▽	4
●	Etna Rosso Rovittello '93	▽▽	5
●	Etna Rosso Rovittello '94	▽▽	5
○	Etna Bianco Sup. Pietramarina '94	▽	4
●	Etna Rosso Rosso di Verzella '94	▽	3
●	Etna Rosso Rosso di Verzella '92	▽	3

VITTORIA (RG)

COS

P.ZZA DEL POPOLO, 34
97019 VITTORIA (RG)
TEL. 0932/864042

Even though 1996 wasn't a wonderful year for Sicilian reds, here at Cos in Vittoria, one of the southernmost points of the island, there are a number of very satisfactory wines. They may not have all the concentration and richness of the '95s, but it is in lesser years like this that one can really see the technical expertise and general reliability of a winery. Once again, in our opinion, their Cerasuolo di Vittoria Sciri '96 is the best in its category. It has good structure and the usual enticing perfumes, just a touch forward, with hints of ripe fruits and sour cherry jam. In the mouth its smooth softness is only slightly disturbed by a vein of acidity which is necessary to balance the alcohol. It's only a short step down to their normal Cerasuolo di Vittoria '96. It is less complicated and concentrated than the Sciri, but extremely well made, and offered at an extremely reasonable price. Their Ramingallo Bianco '97 is decidedly convincing. Made from inzolia or anzonica (they are used synonymously down here), it is perhaps the best one they have ever produced. It does not have those overripe nuances too often found in white wines in these parts. It does, however, have a fresh, clean, fruity nose and a well-balanced pleasant taste, although it would not be harmed by more concentration. Their chardonnay aged in small barrels, Le Vigne di Cos Bianco '96, seemed too flat and forward to us, but not without personality. We refrain from passing judgment on the '97, because its extreme youth makes it impossible to evaluate fairly.

●	Cerasuolo di Vittoria '96	▼▼	3*
●	Cerasuolo di Vittoria Sciri '96	▼▼	4
○	Ramingallo '97	▼▼	3
○	Le Vigne di Cos Bianco '96	▼	4
●	Cerasuolo di Vittoria '94	▽▽	3
●	Cerasuolo di Vittoria '95	▽▽	3*
●	Cerasuolo di Vittoria Sciri '95	▽▽	4
●	Cerasuolo di Vittoria V. di Bastonaca '95	▽▽	4
○	Le Vigne di Cos Bianco '95	▽▽	4
●	Le Vigne di Cos Rosso '93	▽▽	4
●	Le Vigne di Cos Rosso '94	▽▽	4
●	Le Vigne di Cos Rosso '95	▽▽	4

OTHER WINERIES

The following producers obtained good scores in our tastings with one or more of their wines:

PROVINCE OF CATANIA

Barone di Villagrande
Milo,
tel. 095/7082175,
Etna Bianco Sup. '97

PROVINCE OF MESSINA

Caravaglio
Malfa Salina,
tel. 090/9844368,
Salina Bianco '96

Colosi
Messina, tel. 090/53852,
Malvasia delle Lipari Naturale '96,
Malvasia delle Lipari Passita '96

Grasso
Milazzo, tel. 090/9281082,
Moscato Passito di Pantelleria Ergo '93

Paone
Scala Torregrotta, tel. 090/9981101,
Funnari Rosso '96

PROVINCE OF TRAPANI

Firriato, Paceco, tel. 0923/882755,
Altavilla della Corte Bianco '97

SARDEGNA

The data regarding the amount of land under vine in Sardegna are worrying when compared with the figures of eight to ten years ago. The over 80 thousand hectares of that time have fallen to less than 20 thousand today. The reasons are well known: a decline in consumption, children electing not to pursue traditional family occupations and the abandonment of vineyards as unprofitable. Many growers delivering to local cooperative wineries still have to wait for several years to be paid for their grapes. But it is equally true that the quality of Sardinian wines continues to improve. Indeed, there has been a leap in quality which has brought Sardinian wines due recognition, both in Italy and abroad. Last season, defined by many as the "vintage of the century", there were, in fact, no significant upswings. The good producers continued to propose interesting wines, while the others continued at their customary pace. The market is rather diversified, and the most flourishing segment is that of low-cost but correct wines. The great wineries, including those privately owned (whatever their size), such as Sella & Mosca, Ariolas, Contini and Capichera, and the emerging ones, such as Gabbas and Naìtana, solidified their positions. Then there are those co-operatives that have done a great deal to restore faith in this kind of winery. There are others, however, that have been chugging along to no good effect for too many years, thanks to public financing. The admirable ones include Santadi in Sulcis, Tempio Pausania in Gallura, Trexenta in the zone of the same name, S. Maria La Palma near Alghero and Monti in Gallura. And some other wineries, both co-op and private, are not just standing on the sidelines, but are working, with professional skill, to develop new wines of particular interest, and doubtless we shall hear more about them in the future. It is comforting to know that one can find true oenological "gems", even among the wines offered by the small producers. The new Arcone winery offers a very respectable red, whereas Gabbas, with its Dule and Cannonau di Sardegna Lillovè, has become the new ambassador of Cannonau. The important reds that are maintaining their reputation include Marchese di Villamarina and Tanca Farrà produced by Sella & Mosca, Turriga by Argiolas, Terre Brune, Rocca Rubia and Baia Rosse from Santadi, and Dolmen from Tempio Pausania. Standouts among the whites included various Vermentinos: Gallura Canayli and Gallura Piras from Tempio Pausania, Capichera's, Mancini's Cucaione, and the Aghiloia from Monti. Further excellent whites are Argiolas' Argiolas, Vermentino di Sardegna Costamolino and Nuragus di Cagliari S'Elegas, Sella & Mosca's Le Arenarie and Vermentino di Sardegna la Cala, and the Villa di Chiesa and Cala Silente from Santadi. As far as dessert wines are concerned, there has been a rediscovery of old traditional wines such as Meloni's Girò di Cagliari Donna Jolanda and the Nasco di Cagliari by Picciau and from Dolianova. Wines which maintained their excellent level include the Angialis by Argiolas, the Planargia Murapiscados, a malvasia, by Naìtana, and the Vernaccia di Oristano by Contini and that of the Cantina Sociale, a wine which continues to suffer from the limited market demand today for wines of this type, a problem compounded by the identity crisis from which it has suffered for several years now.

ALGHERO (SS)

CANTINA SOCIALE SANTA MARIA LA PALMA

LOC. SANTA MARIA LA PALMA
07041 ALGHERO (SS)
TEL. 079/999008

For years now we have followed with interest the development of this cooperative winery. From frequent tastings we have noted that their wines have levelled off: most are correct, but nothing has stood out. Certainly, producing a range of some 15 wines is no easy task, especially when the grapes are essentially the same. This year the Cantina has managed to add a couple of Glasses, but we are sure that many of the wines mentioned could be better. We encountered another problem in the corking of the Alghero Rosato Cantavigna: two out of three bottles were corked. This raises again the question of using cork at all, which has never really been thoroughly resolved, especially for wines not meant for laying down. The '97 Vermentino di Sardegna Aragosta is good, and rich in clean, fresh notes, both to the nose and in the mouth. The very good Alghero Bianco Vigne del Mare '97 is harmonious and balanced on both nose and palate, with agreeable fruity overtones. The delicate and pleasing Alghero Punta Rosa '97 has won its first Glass. Among the reds, the Cannonau di Sardegna Le Bombarde '96 is particularly intense on the nose, with vegetal overtones, and soft, moderately long and reasonably balanced in the mouth. The Alghero Vigne del Mare Rosso '96 has an added dimension; fruity and heady aromas precede a full, warm and velvety palate. Finally, mention should be made of the Vermentino di Sardegna I Papiri and the two bubbly wines, the Brut di Vermentino and the sweet Briccone Spumante Dolce.

	Wine	Glasses	Price
○	Alghero Bianco Vigne del Mare '97	🍷	2*
⊙	Alghero Punta Rosa '97	🍷	2*
●	Alghero Rosso Vigne del Mare '96	🍷	2*
○	Vermentino di Sardegna Aragosta '97	🍷	2
●	Briccone Spumante Dolce		3
○	Brut di Vermentino		3
●	Cannonau di Sardegna Le Bombarde '96		2
○	Vermentino di Sardegna I Papiri '97		3
●	Cannonau di Sardegna Le Bombarde '93	YY	2*
●	Alghero Rosso Vigne del Mare '95	Y	1*

ALGHERO (SS)

TENUTE SELLA & MOSCA

LOC. I PIANI
07041 ALGHERO (SS)
TEL. 079/997700

It can happen that tasting a wine reveals the personality of its producer. The name Sella & Mosca immediately makes one think of a great winery, well organized in every detail, from the vineyard all the way to merchandising. But in the wines one senses the passion of a small producer whose first aim is quality. A great winery and great wines. Our tastings confirmed the excellence of the Marchese di Villamarina '93, which has become the standard-bearer of this winery, winning Three Glasses for the third time in row. Rich and intense to the nose, with well-blended vanilla and herbaceous nuances, it is full-bodied, balanced and long-lasting on the palate. The '94 vintage was certainly one of the best in this decade for this winery's reds. The Cannonau di Sardegna Riserva is good, but the Tanca Farrà, made from cannonau and cabernet sauvignon, in which intense and forward aromas enrich an already rich bouquet, is even better. The smooth tannins create a sensation of pleasing roundness and harmony on the palate. The Oleandro rosé is agreeably fruity and offers aromas of bell pepper and faint grassy hints, and, in the mouth, freshness and balance. The whites have simply marked time. There have been no leaps forward, but also no falling behind. The pleasant and crisp Vermentino di Sardegna La Cala is excellent value for money. Two Glasses to the Sauvignon Le Arenarie for its fragrance and full body. One full Glass goes to the Terre Bianche for its freshness of taste. We had another taste of the '87 Anghelu Ruju Riserva, reviewed last year, and found it further improved, particularly on the palate.

	Wine	Glasses	Price
●	Alghero Marchese di Villamarina '93	🍷🍷🍷	6
○	Alghero Le Arenarie '97	🍷🍷	3
●	Alghero Tanca Farrà '94	🍷🍷	3
○	Vermentino di Sardegna La Cala '97	🍷🍷	3
⊙	Alghero Oleandro '97	🍷	2
○	Alghero Torbato Terre Bianche '97	🍷	3
●	Cannonau di Sardegna Ris. '94	🍷	3
●	Alghero Marchese di Villamarina '90	YYY	5
●	Alghero Marchese di Villamarina '92	YYY	6
●	Alghero Anghelu Ruju Ris. '87	YY	4
●	Alghero Marchese di Villamarina '89	YY	6
●	Tanca Farrà '89	YY	3
●	Tanca Farrà '90	YY	3
●	Tanca Farrà '92	YY	3

ARZACHENA (SS)

Tenute Capichera
Loc. Capichera
07021 Arzachena (SS)
tel. 0789/80612

We have followed this little winery with great curiosity and interest, for it has always done something different from the others. It is also true that many wineries come up with new ideas which really have absolutely nothing to do with their wine, just so that people will talk about them. People have always talked about the Ragnedda brothers, sometimes critically: we've done it ourselves. They were the first to propose the "fiaschetta" (little round-bodied bottle), with the thousand problems it presents for serving the wine cool, and at a higher cost than was normal. For some years the Ragneddas have been making an excellent Vermentino Vendemmia Tardiva, first called a Riserva. Now they have expanded the line with the Assajè Rosso. Perhaps the name sounds a bit pretentious ("assai è" or "quite a lot"), but this was not the intention of the Ragneddas, who wanted to make a wine that was young, immediate and, above all, pleasing. The results have once again proven them right. Produced from carignano grapes grown in the distant Sulcis zone, and not aged at all in wood, it is notable for its delightfully fruity nose and properly crisp taste. The very good Vermentino di Gallura Vendemmia Tardiva is, in part, vinified in oak barrels. The aromas are amply fruity and elegant, while in the mouth the acidity is well balanced by a softness which makes it mouth-filling and harmonious. Somewhat thinner, the Capichera and the Vigna'ngena are still well-made and agreeable; the latter is simpler and goes down very easily.

○	Vermentino di Gallura Vendemmia Tardiva '97	🍷🍷	5
●	Assajè Rosso '97	🍷	4
○	Vermentino di Gallura Capichera '97	🍷	5
○	Vermentino di Gallura Vigna 'Ngena '97	🍷	4
○	Capichera '95	ΥΥ	5
○	Vermentino di Gallura Vendemmia Tardiva '96	ΥΥ	5
○	Vigna 'Ngena '94	ΥΥ	4
○	Vermentino di Gallura Capichera '96	Υ	5
○	Vermentino di Gallura Vigna 'Ngena '96	Υ	4

CABRAS (OR)

Attilio Contini
Via Genova, 48/50
09072 Cabras (OR)
tel. 0783/290806

Unfortunately one sees no signs of commercial recovery for the Vernaccia di Oristano, a wine which is passing through a profound crisis of both identity and market. Nevertheless this winery continues to produce it with the enthusiasm of a century ago. The winery was in fact established in 1898, and ever since then Vernaccia di Oristano has been its keystone. For the past few years, however, Contini has been concentrating on wines of a different style, geared to respond better to consumer needs. The range is quite diversified and includes wines common to other zones. The Karmis, a very interesting white made from vernaccia vinified with modern techniques that emphasize its fruitiness, is reminiscent of almond and peach blossoms. The Nieddera red, typical of this zone, is better yet. It is aged partly in oak barrels and partly in barriques for around ten months. One still senses a slight imbalance between the acidity and the tannins, but it has such structure that time will have a chance to work its softening effect. Starting this year, the range has been expanded to include Pontis, made from moscato grapes grown in Gallura. It is delicately fruity and pleasing on the nose, and there is a good balance between sugars and acidity on the palate. Of the various Vernaccias we tasted, we particularly admired the '80. It offers broad, intense aromas of toasted almond and hazelnut, and a warm and enticing palate with a long finish; it has all the characteristics of an exceptional wine. We hope that it develops well in the bottle.

○	Vernaccia di Oristano Ris. '80	🍷🍷	3
○	Karmis '97	🍷	2
●	Nieddera Rosso '95	🍷	3
○	Pontis '97	🍷	3
○	Vernaccia di Oristano Ris. '71	ΥΥΥ	5
○	Antico Gregori	ΥΥ	6
○	Elibaria '93	ΥΥ	2
○	Karmis '96	ΥΥ	2
●	Nieddera Rosso '91	ΥΥ	3
○	Vernaccia di Oristano '88	ΥΥ	3

CARDEDU (NU)

Alessandro Loi & Figli

S. S. Orientale Sarda km. 124,200
08040 Cardedu (NU)
tel. 0782/75807

Work and transformation continue apace at the Loi winery. At the moment they have about 30 hectares under vine, which for the most part surround the Cardedu winery. The old vineyards continue to be guyot-trained, whereas the newly planted vines have low vertical training and relatively limited yields per hectare. In addition to the traditional cannonau, the Lois have planted varietals which are now to be found throughout Italy, such as merlot, cabernet, sangiovese, montepulciano, etc. As far as the cellar is concerned, they have introduced high tech equipment and large, temperature-controlled, stainless steel tanks into the vinification section. Aging takes place farther down, and barriques have been installed in some of the chambers. The other change has to do with the new design of the labels, which in our opinion could be improved. But the changes which we found most satisfying were those encountered in our tastings. The wines have acquired a new dimension. The reds are cleaner, more balanced and, above all, younger. The '96 Sa Mola Rubia offers heady and moderately intense aromas; better balance and a succulent freshness make the palate more successful. The '93 Riserva, which they have dedicated to their father, Alberto, is a red with body, good structure and the significant presence of smooth and well-integrated tannins. On the nose it reveals faint hints of vanilla, notes of ripe red fruit and a light touch of licorice.

	Wine	Glasses	Price
●	Cannonau di Sardegna Alberto Loi Ris. '93	🍷🍷	4
●	Cannonau di Sardegna Sa Mola Rubia Ris. '96	🍷	3
●	Cannonau di Sardegna Cardedo '95	🍸	3

DOLIANOVA (CA)

Cantina Sociale di Dolianova

Loc. Sant'Esu
S. S. 387 km. 17,150
09041 Dolianova (CA)
tel. 070/740643

We understand perfectly that to satisfy market demand it is appropriate to diversify production. This winery actually has five different ranges of wines, but only two of them are interesting to us. What we find difficult to understand is how a Chardonnay and a Sauvignon came to be included in the Vigne Sarde line. Maybe it's a question of price, since they are the most expensive, although we found several very good wines in the Dolia range as well. But putting aside these commercial considerations, which could be confusing to the consumer, we tasted a number of good wines. The best, a Two Glass winner, was the Falconaro red, the fruit of an interesting blend of cannonau, pascale, carignano, barbera and some other local grapes. It has a very intense nose, with complex aromas of red fruit and a hint of ink. In the mouth it is warm and full, still developing but quite well-balanced, although it does not reveal great depth. The traditional whites were not particularly exciting. The Vermentino di Sardegna is admirable for the delicacy and cleanness of its bouquet; in the mouth it is fresh, with a lightly acidic vein and a moderately long finish. The fresh and lightly fruity Sibiola is a good rosé that wins One Glass. We were less struck by the Dolicante Sauvignon and the Capidiana Chardonnay. The Nuragus di Cagliari failed to match the level of last year's version. We end our review with two good sparkling wines: the Caralis Brut, made from chardonnay, and the Scaleri Demi-Sec, a malvasia.

	Wine	Glasses	Price
●	Falconaro '96	🍷🍷	3*
○	Caralis Brut	🍷	3
○	Scaleri Démi-Sec	🍷	3
⊙	Sibiola Rosato '97	🍷	2
○	Vermentino di Sardegna '97	🍷	2
○	Capidiana Chardonnay '97		4
○	Dolicante '97		3
○	Nuragus di Cagliari '97		2
○	Dolicante '96	🍸🍸	3
○	Caralis Brut	🍸	3
●	Falconaro '95	🍸	3
●	Monica di Sardegna '96	🍸	2
○	Nuragus di Cagliari '96	🍸	2
○	Vermentino di Sardegna '96	🍸	2

DORGALI (NU)

CANTINA SOCIALE DI DORGALI
VIA PIEMONTE, 11
08022 DORGALI (NU)
TEL. 0784/96143

One of the problems plaguing many Sardinian wineries is their reluctance to change. Among these is the Dorgali wine cooperative, which for many years has focussed on correct, standard wines destined for the mass market. But something is changing here, thanks in part to the considerable amount of land under vine at their disposal. In addition to the traditional guyot-trained vineyards surrounding the village, many hectares of new vineyards have been planted in the Isalle valley, along the road that leads from Nuoro to Siniscola. There are already more than 700 hectares here, spread over a vast area. Thanks to this enormous viticultural potential, it has been possible to identify micro-zones particularly adapted to the production of excellent wines. The technology employed in the winery is up-to-date, and the oenologist Nicola Pignatelli is already planning a different type of red, which will be more important and something of a new departure. Having had a taste here and there, we're in a position to reveal that the next few years should offer some pleasant surprises. Of the wines we tasted for this edition, the Filieri Rosso was the best. It has a rich, enchanting nose, with fruity notes and vegetal nuances, especially bell pepper; in the mouth it is charmingly fresh and not very demanding; you can drink it straight through dinner. The clean and quite correct Filieri Rosato slips down with no trouble at all. The Cannonau di Sardegna '97 is less interesting, especially on the short and not very intense palate. The nose does better, with nuances of fresh fruit, particularly strawberry and raspberry.

●	Filieri Rosso '97	🍷	2
●	Cannonau di Sardegna '97		3
⊙	Filieri Rosato '96		2
●	Cannonau di Sardegna '94	🍸	3
●	Cannonau di Sardegna Filieri '95	🍸	2
●	Filieri Rosso '96	🍸	2

FLORINAS (SS)

TENUTE SOLETTA
VIA SASSARI, 77
07030 FLORINAS (SS)
TEL. 079/438160

Here is another winery which, although it has been marketing wines for several years, shows a certain inconsistency in quality. Perhaps the young owners are still seeking a style of their own. They are lively and active, especially Pina, who looks after the sales, whereas Umberto and Francesco devote themselves to production. Their range continues to grow, and the winery now offers all sorts of wines. Great importance has been given to naming them, with somewhat pretentious results, such as Firmadu (which means "signed") and Prestizu ("prestige"). Leaving aside these commercial considerations, we tasted an excellent Cannonau di Sardegna '96 Firmadu. The nose is very interesting, with distinct aromas of blackberry and raspberry, vegetal hints and notes of green peppercorn. On the palate the tannins are somewhat noticeable, but should be smoothed by the passage of time; fruit is in evidence, however, mouth-filling and distinct. The tasty Moscato Passito Dolce Valle is redolent of very ripe fruit. In the mouth it's fat but not cloying, full and lingering. Finally, we should mention the pleasant Rosato Petalo, clean, correct and moderately intense on the nose, fresh and unpretentious on the palate.

●	Cannonau di Sardegna Firmadu '96	🍷	3
○	Moscato Passito Dolce Valle '96	🍷	4
⊙	Petalo Rosato '97		2
●	Cannonau di Sardegna '92	🍸	3
●	Cannonau di Sardegna Firmadu '91	🍸	3

JERZU (NU)

Cantina Sociale di Jerzu
Via Umberto I, 1
08044 Jerzu (NU)
tel. 0782/70028

Once again this year the Cantina Sociale di Jerzu offered us its '93 Cannonau Riserva for tasting. It did not seem very different from last year: in our opinion, the wine has peaked. We can console ourselves with the '96, with aromas that are still heady, fresh and pleasurable. In the mouth it is soft, with only just perceptible tannins; the acidity is good, as are the finish on the palate and the persistence on the nose. We also tasted the Pardu, a sweet red made from cannonau, and happily assigned it One Glass for its delightful aromas, with mature fruit and walnut skin to the fore. On the palate it is warm, sweet but not cloying, with moderate intensity and length. It is ideal with aged, sharp cheeses rather than with dessert. This winery has done little to pinpoint particular vineyards in its territory, despite the fact that the Ogliastra zone is one of the most traditional and suitable areas for Cannonau. A recently established Cannonau Consortium and Cannonau District have not yet contributed substantially to improving the image of this famous wine. And as the years pass, people are ever less likely to associate Jerzu with Cannonau.

	Wine	Glasses	Price
●	Cannonau di Sardegna '96	🍷	2
●	Pardu Dolce '91	🍷	3
●	Cannonau di Sardegna Ris. '91	🍷🍷	3
●	Cannonau di Jerzu Dolce Pardu '90	🍷	3
●	Cannonau di Sardegna '92	🍷	2
●	Cannonau di Sardegna '93	🍷	2
●	Cannonau di Sardegna '95	🍷	2

MAGOMADAS (NU)

Gianvittorio Naitana
Via Roma, 2
08010 Magomadas (NU)
tel. 0785/35333

Gianvittorio Naìtana is the youngest producer of Malvasia della Planargia, but he is also the one who has focussed most on saving Malvasia in its young, semi-sweet or sweet form, which is most admired and sought after. The denomination regulations require aging for a minimum of two years, but the wine offered by other wineries is the dry type, which tends with time to resemble Vernaccia di Oristano. Clearly, there is room for both types, but up to now very little has been done to include the younger version in the regulations. Naìtana has chosen the more difficult route, but in our opinion the right one. He names his wines after their vineyards of origin, all of them being small "crus" located in the best spots of the zone. These are small plots worked with care and devotion and producing only a few hundred kilos per hectare. Starting with the '98 vintage he has taken over the management of some other small vineyards that would have been abandoned in the course of a few years. He is not a missionary, just a simple winegrower devoted to the land he comes from, who hopes that restoring the vineyards, and also the olive groves, will mean the economic salvation of the entire area. The '97 Planargia Murapiscados has acquired an extra dimension in this year's version; it easily deserves its Two Glasses for the finesse and elegance of its aromas of peach and apricot, which create a dense and captivating bouquet. On the palate you can rediscover the mouth-filling elegance that sugars and glycerine, in perfect harmony with acidity, are capable of bestowing.

	Wine	Glasses	Price
○	Planargia Murapiscados '97	🍷🍷	4
○	Planargia Murapiscados '96	🍷🍷	4

MONTI (SS)

CANTINA SOCIALE DEL VERMENTINO
VIA S. PAOLO, 1
07020 MONTI (SS)
TEL. 0789/44012

The people at the cooperative in Monti know very well just how versatile Vermentino can be. They produce it in all its possible versions, from the lightly fizzy one to the sparkling Brut and Demi-Sec, and from the still, young version to the "passito". Evidently, their intention is to produce an entire line of wines that will represent the past and future of this zone that straddles the Bassa Gallura and the Logudoro. Apart from the light, fizzy Balari and the Rosato Thaora (made from native red grapes), we tasted a good '97 Vermentino di Gallura Funtanaliras. On the nose it displays interesting exotic fruit aromas, but it is disappointingly short in the mouth; nevertheless it's a crisp and pleasing wine. We awarded a Glass also to the Vermentino di Gallura Superiore Aghiloia, although it isn't up to last year's; it has a fainter nose, but it's full, warm and well-structured on the palate. The Vermentino di Gallura S'Eleme, which has long been the flagship of this winery, is more successful. It is notably fresh and quaffable. The Vermentino di Sardegna Soliana is less convincing, with its forward aromas and lack of length in the mouth. We were quite favorably impressed by the sweet version of the Aldiola: it is a curious wine, with few pretensions, except that of being a boon companion to slightly strong and savory cheeses. It has a delicate fragrance with notes of dried fruit, and a warm, full taste. The red Abbaìa, pleasant to the nose, fresh and undemanding on the palate, is worthy of mention.

	Wine	Glasses	
●	Abbaìa '97	🍷	1*
○	Aldiola '95	🍷	3
○	Vermentino di Gallura Funtanaliras '97	🍷	3
○	Vermentino di Gallura S'Eleme '97	🍷	2*
○	Vermentino di Gallura Sup. Aghiloia '97	🍷	2*
○	Vermentino di Sardegna Soliana '97		3
○	Vermentino di Gallura Sup. Aghiloia '94	YY	2
○	Vermentino di Gallura Sup. Aghiloia '96	YY	2*
●	Abbaìa '96	Y	1*
○	Aldiola '94	Y	3

NUORO

GIUSEPPE GABBAS
VIA TRIESTE, 65
08100 NUORO
TEL. 0784/31351 - 33745

The name of Giuseppe Gabbas is increasingly linked to that of Cannonau, or better, to the new generation of Cannonau. Born and raised among the vineyards of Barbagia, he knows all the typical reds drunk in the wine cellars and bars of this zone. Doubtless this played its part in inspiring him to go about wine-making differently, in order to do justice to this noble grape. In his beautiful vineyard, up in the hills between Orgosolo and Oliena, he cultivates cannonau, but also other native and imported varietals. Pascale, bovale and muristella happily rub shoulders with sangiovese, montepulciano, merlot, nebbiolo and cabernet. The excellent exposure of the vineyards, and even more the attentive care lavished on the vines, mean that the grapes ripen here in perfect health. For technical support, Gabbas relies on the advice of a young Tuscan oenologist, Claudio Gori. This year's wines are more successful; unquestionably the longer maceration period (over 20 days) has helped make them richer in color and fuller-bodied. The Cannonau di Sardegna Lillovè '97, to which is added small percentages of local grapes, is a step up from last year. The very rich bouquet is dominated by an intense fruitiness with notes of cherry and black cherry. In the mouth it is soft, and offers an imposing structure and a long finish. The Dule '97 is also richer this time, displaying a heady and engrossing bouquet, with fruity notes of red currant, plum and hints of vanilla. On the palate it is mouth-filling, with notable structure and lots of body, but its youth concedes a still obvious presence of tannins and acidity. However, it has all the characteristics of a wine that should improve as it ages for many years to come.

	Wine	Glasses	
●	Cannonau di Sardegna Lillovè '97	🍷🍷	3
●	Dule '97	🍷🍷	4
●	Cannonau di Sardegna Lillovè '96	YY	3
●	Dule '94	YY	4
●	Dule '95	YY	4
●	Dule '96	YY	4
●	Cannonau di Sardegna Lillovè '93	Y	2
●	Cannonau di Sardegna Lillovè '94	Y	2
●	Cannonau di Sardegna Lillovè '95	Y	2

OLBIA (SS)

PIERO MANCINI
LOC. CALA SACCAIA
08026 OLBIA (SS)
TEL. 0789/50717

The Mancini brothers, under the watchful eye of their father Piero, are showing great skill in managing this winery. Well aware of the changes occurring in the wine world, they are always on the lookout for new possibilities, but without neglecting tradition. Their range of wines is subject to change, with the inclusion of new wines, but also with certain exclusions. This year we tasted three good wines, two reds and a white. The Saccaia (which no longer indicates the year on the label) is the one we liked most. A blend of cabernet sauvignon, cannonau and merlot, it seems to have a new dimension, compared to last year's. The interesting, intense and lingering nose is fresh and clean, with vegetal notes and a touch of chocolate. On the palate it is balanced, soft, heady and lively. The Cannonau di Sardegna was also surprisingly long-lasting on the nose, where aromas of flowers and ripe fruit emerge. It is dry and warm on the palate, but not particularly rich in structure; alcohol, fresh acidity and substantial tannins are all still evident, but as a whole it is balanced and harmonious. The Vermentino di Gallura Cucaione has a fruity fragrance, especially apple and pear, with fainter exotic notes of banana and pineapple. This symphony of aromas is reflected on the crisp and lively palate, underpinned by a good acidity. Finally, we should also mention the pleasant Chardonnay Colli del Limbara, a bit light but quite quaffable.

	Wine	Glasses	Price
●	Saccaia	🍷🍷	3*
●	Cannonau di Sardegna '96	🍷	3
○	Vermentino di Gallura Cucaione '97	🍷	3
○	Chardonnay dei Colli del Limbara '96		2
●	Saccaia '94	🍸🍸	3
○	Chardonnay dei Colli del Limbara '95	🍸	2
○	Pinot Chardonnay Brut '95	🍸	3
●	Saccaia '92	🍸	3
●	Saccaia '93	🍸	3
○	Vermentino di Gallura Cucaione '96	🍸	3

SANT'ANTIOCO (CA)

CANTINA SOCIALE DI SANT'ANTIOCO
VIA RINASCITA, 46
09017 SANT'ANTIOCO (CA)
TEL. 0781/83055

After many years of relative obscurity, this cooperative winery has succeeded in bottling wines of good quality, thus accepting the challenge of an ever more demanding market. Some of their vineyards are on the island of Sant'Antioco and others are in Sulcis, home of carignano, a grape of considerable potential that is being watched with great interest by producers both in Sardegna and on the mainland. The winery has all the elements needed to produce better wines, but they need to be supported by appropriate promotion and perhaps also by more attractive labels. This year, however, was not quite as good as last year, especially for the whites, such as the '97 Vermentino di Sardegna. This is a fragile wine, with a relatively shallow nose that seems to lack the fresh aromas characteristic of young wines; in the mouth it's a bit short, slightly unbalanced, and does not correspond much to the nose. The reds do better, although we mention the Monica di Sardegna '97 mainly because of its intense and pleasing fruity and vegetal aromas; it too is a bit short in the mouth. The Carignano del Sulcis Rosato '97 is admirable for its cleanness and correctness; it's an undemanding wine for easy drinking. The Rosso version of it we were given to taste had already been reviewed last year. One Glass was awarded to the Sardus Pater Rosso: it has a nose of remarkable immediacy, with pleasingly concentrated berry aromas. On the palate it is dry, succulent, moderate in length and harmonious.

	Wine	Glasses	Price
●	Sardus Pater Rosso	🍷	1*
⊙	Carignano del Sulcis Rosato '97		1
●	Monica di Sardegna '97		2
○	Vermentino di Sardegna '97		2
●	Carignano del Sulcis Rosso '95	🍸	1*
●	Monica di Sardegna '95	🍸	2
●	Sardus Pater Rosso	🍸	1*

SANTADI (CA)

CANTINA SOCIALE DI SANTADI
VIA SU PRANU, 12
09010 SANTADI (CA)
TEL. 0781/950012 - 950127

Last year's fine results were not just a flash in the pan for this great wine cooperative. Few wineries in Italy today can claim such a fine range of wines combined with such a high level of quality. And we cannot fail to give due recognition. We begin with the Three Glass winner, the '94 Terre Brune, a great red wine with a dark ruby color, concentrated and intense even in its bouquet, with aromas of ripe fruit joined by spicy and toasty notes of great finesse. On the palate it is warm, full-flavored, concentrated, mouth-filling and powerful, with a very long aromatic finish. You shouldn't miss it. Just a step behind is another red, produced together with the nearby cooperative of Calasetta, the '95 Carignano del Sulcis Baie Rosse. It has intense and persistent aromas, and in the mouth it is fat and rich in notes of ripe red fruit. The Araja had to work a little harder than last year to get its Two Glasses; distinct juicy aromas of fresh plum emerge on the nose, and it's full-bodied and ripe on the palate. The other reds are very good too: the '94 Carignano del Sulcis Rocca Rubia, the '95 Carignano del Sulcis Grotta Rossa and the '96 Monica di Sardegna Antigua. Honorable mention is due to the pleasing and quaffable Carignano Rosato Tre Torri. Their range of whites is interesting as well. At the top is the '96 Villa di Chiesa, delicate, elegant and concentrated, but this was a re-tasting. We are eager to see how the '97 will be. The Villa Solais has made a leap forward, winning Two Glasses for its excellent length, supported by a good acidity; it offers delightful nuances of grapefruit and sage. The Vermentino di Sardegna Cala Silente is maintaining its high standard: it is concentrated on the nose, and soft and substantial in the mouth. The Nuragus di Cagliari Pedraia is also on its way up.

●	Terre Brune '94	▼▼▼	6
●	Araja '95	▼▼	3
●	Carignano del Sulcis Baie Rosse '95	▼▼	4
○	Vermentino di Sardegna Cala Silente '97	▼▼	3
○	Villa Solais '97	▼▼	2
●	Carignano del Sulcis Rocca Rubia Ris. '94	▼	3
●	Monica di Sardegna Antigua '94	▼	2*
○	Nuragus di Cagliari Pedraia '97	▼	2
●	Terre Brune '93	▽▽▽	6
●	Carignano del Sulcis Rocca Rubia Ris. '93	▽▽	3
○	Villa di Chiesa '96	▽▽	4

SASSARI

ARCONE
V.LE ITALIA, 3
07100 SASSARI
TEL. 079/233721

This is a debut appearance in the Guide for Arcone, the only winery near Sassari. Situated along the Alghero road in the village of Montepedrosu, it is about ten kilometers from the city. The estate consists of over 70 hectares of gently rolling slopes, including nine under vine and some olive groves, the rest being Mediterranean scrub. There are already plans to extend the vineyards, to cultivate clonal selections of native varietals, flanked by some of the more common international ones. At the moment they grow mainly vermentino and sangiovese, with small percentages of local grapes such as bovale, cagnulari and pascale. The winery is in the center of the property, dominating it, and it too is being modernized. The manager and wine technician is Gabriele Palmas, son of the owners. He is young and full of enthusiasm and has proven that he knows what he is about, especially with red wines. The Arcone, which has Isola dei Nuraghi as its geographic indication, is a red wine thoroughly worthy of respect. The blend consists of almost 80% sangiovese with various local red grapes. Maceration lasted for about ten days, and the wine was then aged in the bottle for 5-6 months. It has a Mediterranean bouquet with evident balsamic notes and hints of rosemary; in the mouth it reveals traditional body and structure and is soft, warm and succulent, mirroring the nose quite nicely. The Montepedrosu white, a vermentino, is still sharp and in need of improvement.

●	Arcone '96	▼▼	3
○	Montepedrosu '97		2

SENORBÌ (CA)

CANTINA SOCIALE DELLA TREXENTA

V.LE PIEMONTE, 28
09040 SENORBÌ (CA)
TEL. 070/9808863 - 9809378

A more convincing showing this year than last for this cooperative, but still not up to its potential. Its vineyard sites are considered particularly well-suited to viticulture, and most of the grapes cultivated are typical local varieties: monica, pascale, cannonau, bovale, nuragus and vermentino. It is also an ideal area for producing dessert wines, Moscato and Malvasia. In accordance with the newly evolved strategy of this winery, some viticultural innovations are planned, and new vines are already producing chardonnay, sauvignon, cabernet, merlot, sangiovese and montepulciano, among others. Their aim is to produce more modern wines that correspond to international tastes. This decision is the result of extensive contact with foreign markets, to which the firm has devoted considerable attention. Presenting new types of wines side-by-side with the traditional ones could provide a stimulus to many who, especially in this part of Sardinia, would otherwise give up wine-making. In our most recent tastings we discovered a good Nuragus di Cagliari: not very structured, and a bit short on body, but correct, clean and fresh. We also mention the Vermentino di Sardegna, with a deep color and a pleasing floral fragrance, but somewhat lacking in structure on the palate. Two Glasses, on the other hand, go to the '97 Monica di Sardegna: a captivating bouquet of red fruit, a bit of cherry and red currant, and harmonious on the palate, thanks to its balanced acidity, which adds to its succulence. Among the other reds, we should mention the '94 version of the Cannonau di Sardegna, which is correct and clean, but not as full-bodied as it has been.

●	Monica di Sardegna '97	🍷🍷	1*
○	Nuragus di Cagliari '97	🍷	1*
●	Cannonau di Sardegna '94		4
○	Vermentino di Sardegna '97		1
●	Cannonau di Sardegna '93	🍸	4
●	Cannonau di Sardegna La Venere '94	🍸	2
●	Monica di Sardegna '93	🍸	1*
●	Monica di Sardegna '94	🍸	1*
●	Monica di Sardegna '96	🍸	1*
●	Segolai Rosso '95	🍸	1*
○	Simieri Moscato Liquoroso	🍸	4
●	Tanca Su Conti '93	🍸	5
○	Vermentino di Sardegna '95	🍸	1*
○	Vermentino di Sardegna '96	🍸	1*

SERDIANA (CA)

ANTONIO ARGIOLAS

VIA ROMA, 56/58
09040 SERDIANA (CA)
TEL. 070/740606

Yet another triumph for the Argiolas brothers, Franco and Pepetto, and yet another Three Glasses for their Turriga. But this year the Angialis, their dessert wine, made mostly from nasco grapes, just missed receiving the top prize this Guide has to offer. In fact, the '95 Angialis is an excellent example of finesse, elegance, balance and harmony on both nose and palate. The Turriga '93 is robust, but none the less elegant for that. This great red offers a fantastic intensity to the nose, where the barrique-derived vanilla is well integrated in the dense and captivating bouquet, reminiscent of ripe red fruit, tobacco and Mediterranean undergrowth. It shows some signs of youth on the palate, with smooth but still evident tannins which, once they have evolved over time, should offer a wealth of pleasant surprises. Two Glasses to the '97 Argiolas for its intense and clean aromas, with notes of fresh fruit, particularly peach; in the mouth it shows powerful yet balanced structure. And the '97 Vermentino di Sardegna Costamolino has scored a few more points, just enough to push it over the border into Two Glass territory. It has aromas of ripe fruit and white flowers, linden and acacia blossom primarily, and is soft and lingering in the mouth. Captivating is the word for the fragrance of the Nuragus di Cagliari S'Elegas, especially for its nuances of exotic fruit and melon. On the palate it is crisp, clean and quite intense. The Cannonau di Sardegna Costera is also very good, but does not have quite the fullness of previous years. The Rosato Serralori is pleasing to both the nose and the palate: indeed, it is among the best rosés we tasted this year, while the '96 Monica di Sardegna Perdera is a little under par. All in all, this is a range of wines of an excellence equaled by very few Italian wineries.

●	Turriga '93	🍷🍷🍷	6
○	Angialis '95	🍷🍷	5
○	Argiolas '97	🍷🍷	3
○	Vermentino di Sardegna Costamolino '97	🍷🍷	2*
●	Cannonau di Sardegna Costera '96	🍷	3
○	Nuragus di Cagliari S'Elegas '97	🍷	2
⊙	Serralori Rosato '97	🍷	2
●	Monica di Sardegna Perdera '96		2
●	Turriga '90	🍸🍸🍸	6
●	Turriga '91	🍸🍸🍸	6
●	Turriga '92	🍸🍸🍸	6
●	Turriga '88	🍸🍸	6
●	Turriga '89	🍸🍸	6

TEMPIO PAUSANIA (SS)

Cantina Sociale Gallura
Via Val di Cossu, 9
07029 Tempio Pausania (SS)
tel. 079/631241

The results that Dino Addis, manager and oenologist of this cooperative winery, has achieved are truly surprising. Ten years ago, not very many people would have bet on wines produced by the co-ops. But it must be stressed that quite a number of cooperatives continue to survive thanks to people like Addis, who contribute to the professional growth of the member growers themselves. The '97 Vermentino di Gallura Superiore Canayli offers rich fruity aromas of apple with exotic overtones, and in the mouth it is powerful, harmonious, intense and lasting, confirming its position as one of the best Italian whites made from native varietals. Their other great white, the '97 Vermentino di Gallura Piras, is also very good, with its remarkably intense fragrance, and crisp and clean taste with a delightful floral and fruited finish. The Vermentino di Gallura Mavriana, the simplest of the whites we've described, also came very close to getting Two Glasses, with its excellent correspondence between nose and palate and perfect balance on both. The surprising Campos Rosato del Limbara offers fresh cherry aromas, and a succulent balance in the mouth. Passing to the reds, we're no longer surprised by the Karana, made from nebbiolo: it is simple and immediate, with delicately fruity aromas, and is, as usual, a great bargain. The excellent Dolmen '95 is made from nebbiolo grapes that have been specially selected to produce a wine that can be laid down for a while. It is first aged in barriques and then further aged in the bottle for about a year. The bouquet opens with an array of aromas ranging from tar to blackberry and plum, but including clear spicy and balsamic notes. On the palate it displays the body of a great red wine, and is warm, soft and mouth-filling. The sparkling Moscato di Tempio is also very good.

	Wine	Glasses	
●	Dolmen '95	🍷🍷	4
●	Karana Nebbiolo dei Colli del Limbara '97	🍷🍷	1*
○	Vermentino di Gallura Piras '97	🍷🍷	2
○	Vermentino di Gallura Sup. Canayli '97	🍷🍷	2*
⊙	Campos Rosato del Limbara '97	🍷	1*
○	Moscato di Tempio Pausania	🍷	4
○	Vermentino di Gallura Mavriana '97	🍷	1*
●	Dolmen '94	🍷🍷 (1998)	4
●	Karana Nebbiolo di Sardegna '94	🍷🍷 (1998)	1*
○	Vermentino di Gallura Piras '95	🍷🍷 (1998)	2
○	Vermentino di Gallura Sup. Canayli '96	🍷🍷 (1998)	2*

USINI (SS)

Giovanni Cherchi
Via Ossi, 18/20
07049 Usini (SS)
tel. 079/380273

Further surprises from this winery, which for several years now has been presenting strangely inconsistent wines. We eagerly await Cherchi's "awakening" so that we can taste his great whites once again. Our tastings, we repeat, so as to avoid misunderstanding, are conducted blind, and oftentimes we are a bit disappointed when we unveil the bottles. Last year, the wine that scored highest was the Billìa, perhaps the white considered least important by the winery. This year it scored lowest. In fact, given its rather faded and unbalanced aromas and pronounced acidity, we give it no more than a mention. The '97 Vermentino di Sardegna is good: it offers broad and intense aromas, with notes of apple and banana as well as vegetal hints, and the intense fruitiness carries through onto the palate, with well-balanced acidity. The Vermentino di Sardegna Tuvaoes, for many years their flagship wine, is, in its '97 version, worthy of mention. It shows middling intensity and persistence on the nose, and is fair on the palate, but a bit short and not very concentrated. The interesting Alghero Cagnulari '97 is clean, pleasing and immediate, with intense, fresh aromas of red fruit. Although it lacks great body, the palate nicely reflects the nose.

	Wine	Glasses	
○	Vermentino di Sardegna '97	🍷	2
○	Billìa		1
●	Alghero Cagnulari di Sardegna '97		2
○	Vermentino di Sardegna Tuvaoes '97		4
○	Billìa	🍷 (1998)	1*
●	Cagnulari di Sardegna '94	🍷 (1998)	2
●	Luzzana '91	🍷 (1998)	4
●	Luzzana '93	🍷 (1998)	4
●	Luzzana '94	🍷 (1998)	4
●	Luzzana '96	🍷 (1998)	4
○	Vermentino di Sardegna '94	🍷 (1998)	2
○	Vermentino di Sardegna '95	🍷 (1998)	2
○	Vermentino di Sardegna Tuvaoes '96	🍷 (1998)	4

OTHER WINERIES

The following producers obtained good scores in our tastings with one or more of their wines:

PROVINCE OF CAGLIARI

Gigi Picciau
Pirri, tel. 070/560224,
Vermentino di Sardegna '97

Villa di Quartu
Quartu Sant'Elena,
tel. 070/826997,
Malvasia di Cagliari '97

Fattoria Mauritania
Santadi,
tel. 070/401465,
Barrua '95

Meloni Vini
Selargius,
tel. 070/852822,
Cannonau di Sardegna Le Ghiaie '93,
Moscato di Cagliari Donna Jolanda '93

PROVINCE OF NUORO

Zarelli - Sanna
Magomadas,
tel. 0785/35311,
Malvasia della Planargia Brut

Arcadu
Oliena, tel. 0784/288417,
Cannonau di Sardegna Nepente '97,
Cantico '97

Cantina Sociale di Sorgono
Sorgono, tel. 0784/60113,
Mandrolisai Rosso '97

PROVINCE OF ORISTANO

Cantina Sociale Marrubiu
Marrubiu, tel. 0783/859213,
Arborea Sangiovese '97,
Campidano di Terralba
Bovale Madrigal '96

Cantina Sociale Il Nuraghe
Mogoro, tel. 0783/990285,
Vermentino di Sardegna Don Giovanni '97

Cantina Sociale Terralba
Terralba, tel. 0783/81824,
Terralba Bovale '97,
Vermentino di Sardegna
Marchese Darchi '97

PROVINCE OF SASSARI

F.lli Tamponi
Calangianus, tel. 079/660945,
Tamponi Brut Metodo Classico

INDEX OF WINES

INDEX OF PRODUCERS